Special Edition for Siena College

SOURCES OF TWENTIETH-CENTURY GLOBAL HISTORY

James H. Overfield
University of Vermont

and

SOURCES IN THE HISTORY OF THE MODERN MIDDLE EAST

Akram Fouad Khater
North Carolina State University

Houghton Mifflin Harcourt Publishing Company
Boston   New York

SOURCES OF TWENTIETH-CENTURY GLOBAL HISTORY
by James H. Overfield
Copyright © 2002 by Houghton Mifflin Harcourt Publishing Company. All rights reserved.

Editor-in-Chief: Jean Woy
Sponsoring Editor: Nancy Blaine
Associate Editor: Julie Dunn
Senior Project Editor: Bob Greiner
Senior Production Coordinator: Jodi O'Rourke
Senior Manufacturing Coordinator: Marie Barnes
Senior Marketing Manager: Sandra McGuire

Source and photo credits appear on pages 453-456, which constitute an extension of the copyright page.

SOURCES IN THE HISTORY OF THE MODERN MIDDLE EAST
by Akram Fouad Khater
Copyright © 2004 by Houghton Mifflin Harcourt Publishing Company. All rights reserved.

Vice President and Publisher: Charles Hartford
Editor-in-Chief: Jean Woy
Senior Associate Editor: Fran Gay
Associate Project Editor: Lindsay Frost
Editorial Assistant: Teresa Huang
Production/Design Assistant: Bethany Schlegel
Manufacturing Manager: Florence Cadran
Senior Marketing Manager: Sandra McGuire

Custom Publishing Editor: Melissa Barcomb
Custom Publishing Production Manager: Christina Battista
Project Coordinator: Elise Gross
Cover Designer: Kyle Kabel
Cover Image: Stock.xchng

This book contains select works from existing Houghton Mifflin Harcourt Publishing Company resources and was produced by Houghton Mifflin Harcourt Custom Publishing for collegiate use. As such, those adopting and/or contributing to this work are responsible for editorial content, accuracy, continuity and completeness.

Printed in the United States of America.

ISBN-13: 978-0-547-22297-4
ISBN-10: 0-547-22297-1
1061766

1 2 3 4 5 6 7 8 9 – WP – 10 09 08

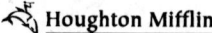 **Houghton Mifflin**
Custom Publishing

222 Berkeley Street • Boston, MA 02116

Address all correspondence and order information to the above address.

Contents

Preface

Several goals and principles have guided the writing of *Sources of Twentieth Century Global History*. Primary among them is the conviction that students of history at any level need to meet the challenge of analyzing primary sources, thereby becoming active inquirers into the past. Involvement with primary-source evidence accomplishes what is beyond the capacity of even the best textbooks and the most stirring lectures: It reveals to students that historical scholarship is more than memorizing facts and someone else's conclusions; it is an intellectual process of drawing inferences and discovering patterns from clues — primary sources — yielded by the past.

Structure and Themes

At a time when this project was just getting started, an outside reviewer of a very preliminary outline of the proposed book stated that the author would undoubtedly find it an "interesting" challenge to choose just one hundred or so sources that would capture the richness and complexity of twentieth century global history. Several years and many outlines later, I can state unequivocally that this outside reviewer was correct. Choosing what sources should comprise *Sources of Twentieth Century Global History* has been interesting . . . and frequently frustrating, humbling, and at times overwhelming.

From start to finish, however, my decisions were guided by a number of considerations:

- First, I wanted to produce a book that was truly global in scope. Without an understanding and appreciation of the experiences of *all* the world's major regions and peoples, no true understanding of the twentieth century is possible.

- Second, I wanted the book to cover the whole twentieth century, not just the "short twentieth century" from 1914 to 1991.

- Third, I wished to show the book's student readers that history is more than the study of past wars, politics, and diplomacy. Although these topics are amply covered in *Sources of Twentieth-Century Global History,* the arts, popular culture, social change, intellectual developments, economics, technology, and the environment also are represented. Special efforts were made to include sources pertaining to the experiences of women in the twentieth century.

- Fourth, I was interested in introducing students to a variety of sources, both written and nonwritten. The collection contains speeches, private letters, treaties, poems, memoirs, advertisements, magazine illustrations, government documents, newspaper accounts, and diplomatic correspondence.

- Fifth, I never lost sight of the fact that the book's ultimate test would be its class-room effectiveness. I have tried to include sources that will capture and hold students' interests, while at the same time providing instructors with material that can be woven into lectures and can serve as the basis for class discussions and a variety of written assignments.

The result is a book of more than one hundred sources, divided into four parts.

Part I, which consists of two chapters, takes the story of the twentieth century back to its roots in the late nineteenth century and ends in 1914. Chapter 1 focuses on the growing interaction among the world's peoples and the extent and effect of the West's economic and political power throughout the world. Chapter 2 concentrates on forces of change in the years before World War I — political revolution, feminism, and new intellectual currents.

Part II, the longest section in the book, begins with a chapter on World War I. This is followed by four chapters on the Western world and the Soviet Union (Chapter 4), Latin America (Chapter 5), Africa (Chapter 6), and Asia (Chapter 7) in the 1920s and 1930s.

Part III covers the period from World War II to the early 1970s. Chapter 8, on World War II and the origins of the Cold War, is followed by chapters on the industrialized, capitalistic West (Chapter 9), the Soviet bloc and Communist China (Chapter 10), and Latin America, Africa, and those parts of Asia emerging from colonialism (Chapter 11). In other words, this section is organized around the concept of the "three worlds," first, second, and third, a way of viewing the world that originated and gained wide currency in the 1950s, 1960s, and 1970s.

Part IV deals with the period from the 1970s through the 1990s. It consists of two chapters, both of which are global in scope. This final section of the book reflects the degree to which by century's end globalization had broken down the world's traditional ideological and geo-political divisions.

I have chosen and organized the sources so that each one of them is connected thematically with others in the book. No source exists in isolation. Each chapter is divided into several smaller sections in which two or three sources that center on a common theme are grouped together. In some cases the sources in these sections complement one another, and in other cases they present different perspectives on the same phenomenon. Many sources, especially those dealing with key topics such as nationalism, colonialism, gender relations, race, war and peace, and migration, are linked with sources in other chapters. Such linkages give students a sense of change and development, and provide opportunities to make cross-cultural comparisons.

Learning Aids

Analysis of primary sources can be a daunting challenge for any student. With this in mind, every effort has been made to make these sources as accessible as possible by providing the student-reader with a variety of aids.

- The *Prologue* defines primary sources, discusses their importance, and provides guidelines for their analysis.

- Extensive *part, chapter, section, and individual source introductions* help the reader place each selection in historical context and understand the source's historical significance.

- Suggested *Questions for Analysis* precede each source. Their purpose is to help students make sense of each piece of evidence and wrest from it as much insight as possible. They are also intended to resemble the historian's approach to source analysis and to help students make historical and cross-cultural comparisons. Some questions are quite specific and are intended to assist the reader in picking out important pieces of information. Questions of this type require the student to address two issues: What does the document or artifact say, and what meaningful facts can I garner from it? Addressing concrete questions of this sort prepares the student for the next, more important level of analysis: drawing inferences. Questions that require inferential conclusions follow the fact-oriented questions. Finally, whenever possible, we have included questions that require students to make comparisons between two or more sources.

- Many of the sources have *extensive footnotes*. These explain words and allusions that most college students cannot reasonably be expected to know.

In summary, the goal of *Sources of Twentieth-Century Global History* has been to prepare the student-reader for success — success being defined as comfort with historical analysis, proficiency in critical thinking, greater understanding of twentieth century global history, and a greater awareness of the rich varieties, as well as shared characteristics, of the world's peoples.

Feedback

If you have questions or comments about the book, please address them to James.Overfield@uvm.edu.

Acknowledgments

I am in debt to many individuals who provided help, assistance, and encouragement during the preparation of *Sources of Twentieth-Century Global History*. They include editors at Houghton Mifflin, especially Julie Dunn and Nancy Blaine; many reference and circulation librarians at the University of Vermont; and scholars and colleagues at the University of Vermont including Abbas Alnasrawi, Robert V. Daniels, Denise J. Youngblood, Sean Stilwell, Peter Seybolt, Walter Hawthorn, and Mark Stoler. I owe a special debt to my colleague, co-author, and friend, Alfred J. Andrea, who provided much of the inspiration for the Prologue to *Sources of Twentieth Century Global History*.

I would also like to thank the following historians who read and commented on the book at various stages in its development: Tyra Benoit, *Butte Community College;* Donald N. Clark, *Trinity University;* Joel S. Cleland, *Lander University;* Kenneth P. Czech, *St. Cloud State University;* Hal M. Friedman, *Henry Ford Community College;* Robert

Irwin, *University of Alaska, Fairbanks;* Thomas W. Judd, *SUNY Oswego;* John F. Lyons, *Joliet Junior College;* Nicholas C. J. Pappas, *Sam Houston State University;* David Prochaska, *University of Illinois, Urbana-Champaign;* Kenneth Pomeranz, *University of California at Irvine;* Barbara Reinfeld, *N.Y. Institute of Technology;* James C. Riley, *Indiana University;* Arthur Schmidt, *Temple University;* Jutta K. Scott, *South Carolina State University;* John Snetsinger, *Cal Poly San Luis Obispo;* and Bruce B. Solnick, *SUNY Albany.*

Thanks, finally, to Susan, for her constant support on this project and much else.

James H. Overfield
Essex Center, Vermont
June, 2001

PROLOGUE

Primary Sources and How to Read Them

Imagine a course in organic chemistry in which students never set foot in a laboratory; or a literature course in which they read commentaries on Shakespeare's plays but none of the plays themselves; or a course on the history of jazz in which they never listen to a note of music. Most students would consider such courses both strange and deficient, and many would soon be beating a path to the door of their academic advisor or college dean with complaints about flawed teaching methods and wasted tuition payments. One simply cannot understand chemistry without doing experiments. Nor can one understand literature without reading plays, poetry, and fiction; or music without listening to performances.

In much the same way, one cannot truly understand history without reading and analyzing *primary sources*. Primary sources are historical records produced at a time that is contemporary with the event or period that is being studied. They are distinct from *secondary sources* — books, articles, television documentaries, and even historical films — that were produced after the events they describe have already occurred. Secondary sources — "histories" in the conventional sense of the term — organize the jumble of past events into understandable narratives; provide interpretations; make comparisons; and discuss questions of motive and causation. When well done, they provide pleasure and insight to their readers. But such works are still *secondary,* in that they are written after the fact and, more importantly, derive their evidence and information from primary sources.

History is an ambitious discipline that deals with all aspects of past human activity and belief. This means that the primary sources historians use to recreate the past are equally wide-ranging and diverse. Most of the primary sources they use are written sources — government records, law codes, private correspondence, literary works, religious texts, merchants' account books, memoirs, and an almost endless list of others. So important are written records to the study of history that past societies with no alphabet or system of writing are called "prehistoric" — not because they lacked a history but because there is no way of retrieving their history due to the lack of records. Nonwritten records can also be primary sources for historians. Important insights about the past have been derived from humble objects that are part of everyday life — fabrics, tools, kitchen implements, weapons, farm equipment, jewelry, pieces of furniture — as well as from paintings, buildings, sculpture, musical compositions, photographs, and film.

To be a historian is to work with primary sources. But to do so effectively is not easy. Each source provides only one glimpse of reality, and no single source by itself gives us the whole picture of past events and developments. Many sources are difficult to understand, and can be interpreted accurately only after the precise meaning of their words have been deciphered and their backgrounds thoroughly investigated. Many sources contain distortions and errors that can be discovered only by rigorous internal analysis and comparison with evidence from other sources. Only after all these source-related difficulties have been overcome can a historian hope to achieve a coherent and accurate understanding of the past.

To illustrate some of the challenges of working with primary sources, let us imagine a time in the mid-twenty-first century when a historian decides to write a history of your college class in connection with its fiftieth reunion. Since no previous books or articles about your class have been written, our historian has no secondary sources to consult, and must rely entirely on primary sources. What primary sources might he or she use? The list would be a long one: the school catalogue, class lists, academic transcripts, yearbooks, college rules and regulations, and similar official documents; lecture notes, syllabi, examinations, term papers, and textbooks; diaries and private letters; articles from the campus newspaper and programs for sporting events, concerts, and plays; posters and handbills; and recollections written down or otherwise recorded by some of your classmates long after they graduated. With a bit of thought you could add other items to the list, among them some unwritten sources, such as recordings of music popular at the time and photographs and videotapes of student life and activity.

Even with this imposing list of sources our future historian will only have an incomplete record of the events that made up your class's experiences. Many of these events — telephone conversations, discussions between students and professors, and gossip exchanged at the student union — never made it into any written records. Also, consider the fact that those sources that will be available to our future historian in the mid twentieth century will be fortunate survivors. They will represent only a small percentage of the vast amount of material generated by you, your classmates, professors, and administrators over a two- or four-year period. Wastebaskets and recycling bins will have claimed much written material; the "delete key" and inevitable changes in computer technology may make it impossible to retrieve basic sources such as your university's website, email, and a vast amount of other online materials. It is also probable that it will be difficult to find information about certain groups within your class. Fewer records might have been generated and preserved regarding the experiences of part-time students, non-traditional students, and commuters.

For all these reasons, the evidence available to our future historian will be fragmentary at best. This is always the case when doing historical research. The records of the past cannot be retained in their totality, not even those pertaining to the recent past.

How will our future historian utilize the many individual pieces of surviving documentary evidence about your class? As he or she reviews the list, it will quickly become apparent that no single primary source provides a complete or unbiased picture. Each source has its perspective, value, and limitations. Imagine that the personal essays submitted by applicants for admission were a historian's only sources of information about the student body. On reading them, would it not be reasonable for this researcher to conclude that your school attracted only the most gifted, talented, interesting, and intellectually committed students imaginable?

Despite their flaws, however, essays composed by applicants for admission can still be important pieces of historical evidence. They certainly reflect the would-be students' perceptions of the school's cultural values and the types of people it hopes to attract, and usually the applicants are right on the mark because they have read the school's catalogue and the brochures prepared for prospective students by the admissions office. Admissions office materials and, to a degree, even the catalogue, are forms of creative advertizing, and both present an idealized picture of campus life. But such publications have value for the careful researcher because they reflect the values of the faculty and administrators who composed them. The catalogue also provides useful information regarding rules and regulations, courses, instructors, school organizations, and similar items. Such factual information, however, is the raw material of history, not history itself, and certainly it does not reflect anything close to the full historical reality of your class's collective experience.

What is true of the catalogue is equally true of the student newspaper and every other piece of evidence pertinent to your class. Each primary source is a part of a larger whole, but as we have already seen, we do not have all the pieces. Think of historical evidence in terms of a jigsaw puzzle. Many of the pieces are missing, but it is possible to put most, though probably not all, of the remaining pieces together in a fashion to form a fairly accurate and coherent picture. The picture that emerges will not be complete, but it is useful and valid. The keys to fitting these pieces together are hard work and imagination. Each is absolutely necessary.

Examining Primary Sources

Hard work speaks for itself, but students are often unaware that historians also need imagination to reconstruct the past. After all, many students ask, doesn't history consist of strictly defined and irrefutable dates, names, and facts? Where does imagination enter into the process of learning these facts? Again, let us consider your class's history and its documentary sources. Many of those documents provide factual data — dates, names, grades, statistics. While these data are important, individually and collectively they have no historical meaning until they have been *interpreted*. Your college class is more than a collection of statistics and facts. It is a group of individuals who, despite their differences, share and help mold a collective experience. It is a community evolving within a particular time and place. Any valid or useful history must reach beyond dates, names, and facts and interpret the historical characteristics and role of your class. What were its values? How did it change and why? What impact did it have? These are some of the important questions a historian asks of the evidence.

To arrive at answers, the historian must examine each and every piece of relevant evidence in its full context and wring from that evidence as many *inferences* as possible. *An inference is a logical conclusion drawn from evidence, and it is the heart and soul of historical inquiry.* Facts are the raw materials of history, but inferences are its finished products.

By the time you complete your course on twentieth-century global history you will have learned many historical facts: for example, that on June 28, 1914, Gavrilo Princip assassinated the archduke and archduchess of Austria-Hungary in the Bosnian city of Sarajevo; that on March 6, 1957, the former British colony of the Gold Coast became the independent state of Ghana; and that in 1962 and 1963 Rachel Carson's book about insecticides, *Silent Spring,* topped the bestseller charts in the United States. Knowing these facts will be of little value, however, unless it contributes to your understanding of twentieth-century global history. What motivated Princip, and why did his murder of the archduke and archduchess bring about World War I? What caused Ghanian independence and what was its significance in African history? Why did Carson's book become a bestseller, and what was its role in inspiring the environmental movement in the United States? Finding answers to questions such as these are the historian's ultimate goal, and these answers can be found in primary sources.

One noted historian, Robin Winks, has written a book entitled *The Historian as Detective,* and the image is appropriate although inexact. Like a detective, the historian examines evidence to reconstruct events. Like a detective, the historian is interested in discovering what happened, who did it and why. Like a detective interrogating witnesses, *the historian also must carefully examine the testimony of sources.*

First and foremost, the historian must evaluate the *validity* of the source. Is it what it purports to be? Artful forgeries have misled many historians. Even authentic sources still can be misleading if the author lied or deliberately misrepresented reality. In addition, the historian can easily be led astray by not fully understanding the *perspective* reflected in the document. As is soon learned by any detective who has examined eyewitnesses to an event, witnesses' accounts often differ widely. The detective has the opportunity to reexamine witnesses and offer them the opportunity to change their testimony in the light of new evidence and deeper reflection. The historian is not so fortunate. Even when the historian compares a piece of documentary evidence with other evidence in order to uncover its flaws, there is no way to cross-examine its author. Given this fact, it is absolutely necessary for the historian to understand as fully as possible the source's perspective. Thus, the historian must ask several key questions — all of which share the letter W.

- *What* kind of document is this?

- *Who* wrote it?

- For *whom* and *why*?

- *Where* was it composed and *when*?

What is important because understanding the nature of a source will give the historian an idea of what kind of information he or she can expect to find in it. Many sources simply do not address the questions a historian would like to ask of them, and knowing this can save a great deal of frustration. Your class's historian would be foolish to try to learn much about the academic quality of your school's courses from a study of the registrar's class lists and grade sheets. Student and faculty class notes, copies of syllabi, examinations, student papers, and textbooks would be far more useful.

Who, for whom, and *why* are equally important questions. The school catalogue and publicity materials prepared by the admissions office undoubtedly address some issues pertaining to student social life. But should documents like these — designed to attract potential students and to place the school in the best possible light — be read and accepted uncritically? Obviously not. They must be tested against student testimony, which is discovered in such sources as private letters, memoirs, posters, the student newspaper, and the yearbook.

Where and *when* are also important questions to ask of any primary source. As a rule, distance from an event in space and time colors perceptions and can diminish the reliability of a source's testimony. Recollections of a person celebrating a twenty-fifth class reunion could be an insightful and valuable source of information for your class's historian. Conceivably this graduate would have a perspective and information that he or she lacked a quarter of a century earlier. Just as conceivably, however, that person's memory of what college was like might have faded to the point where his recollections have little value.

You and the Sources

This book will actively involve you in the work of historical inquiry by asking you to draw inferences based on your analysis of primary source evidence. This may prove difficult at first, but it is well within your capability.

You will analyze two types of evidence: documents and artifacts. Each source will be authentic, so you do not have to worry about validating it. Editorial material in this book also supplies you with the information necessary to place each piece of evidence into its proper context and will suggest questions you legitimately can and should ask of each source.

It is important to keep in mind that historians approach each source they consider with questions, even though they might be vaguely formulated. Like detectives, historians want to discover some particular truth or shed light on a particular issue. This requires asking specific questions of the witnesses or, in the historian's case, of the evidence. These questions should not be prejudgments. One of the worst errors a historian can make is setting out to prove a point or to defend an ideological position. Questions are simply starting points, nothing else, but they are essential. Therefore, as you approach a source, have your question or questions fixed in your mind and constantly remind yourself as you work your way through a source what issue or issues you are investigating. Each source in this anthology is preceded by a number of suggested Questions for Analysis. You or your professor may want to ask other questions. Whatever the case, keep focused on your questions and issues, and take notes as you read a source. Never rely on unaided memory; it will almost inevitably lead you astray.

Above all else, you must be honest and thorough as you study a source. Read each explanatory footnote carefully to avoid misunderstanding a word or allusion. Try to understand exactly what the source is saying and what its author's perspective is. Be careful not to wrench items, words, or ideas out of context, thereby distorting them. Above all, read the entire source so that you understand as fully as possible what it says and does not say.

This is not as difficult as it sounds. But it does take concentration and work. And do not let the word "work" mislead you. True, primary source analysis demands attention to detail and some hard thought, but it is also rewarding. There is great satisfaction in developing a deeper and truer understanding of the past based on a careful exploration of the evidence.

Good luck, and have fun!

Sources of
Twentieth-Century
Global History

PART ONE

The World in an Era of Transformation and Western Dominance, 1880–1914

To gain a sense of the direction of late-nineteenth- and early-twentieth-century history, one needs only to consider the following events:

- In 1881 the sultan of the Ottoman Empire, Abdul Hamid II, agreed to the formation of the Ottoman Public Debt Administration, whose seven-member board assumed oversight over tax collection, budget planning, and expenditures for the sultan's government and control of the empire's overall economic development, including railroad construction. Only two board members were to be Ottoman subjects, one chosen by the sultan and one nominated by the European-controlled Ottoman bank. The rest were European financiers representing European banks and bondholders.

- In November 1884 representatives of fourteen European nations and the United States met in Berlin to decide a number of questions relating to Africa. After several months of discussions, they accepted freedom of trade and navigation on the Congo and Niger Rivers and gave control of the territory in the Congo Basin to the International Association of the Congo, a self-styled philanthropic organization founded by King Leopold II of Belgium. They also established certain rules that European nations would have to follow when annexing African territory. No one thought it strange that no Africans attended the conference and that no effort was made to solicit their opinions.

- In 1901, a year after a mostly European-U.S. force of forty-five thousand troops quelled an antiforeign uprising in China known as the Boxer Rebellion, the victors forced the Chinese to accept the Boxer Protocol, which required them to execute ten high government officials and imprison hundreds more, destroy forts, allow foreign troops to guard railway stations, and pay an indemnity of $333,990,000.

- In 1898 British and British-trained Indian troops invaded Sudan from Egypt to make good Great Britain's claim to Sudanese territory. They met a Sudanese army at the Battle of Omdurman, which resulted in approximately eleven thousand casualties for the Sudanese and a mere forty dead for the British and Indians.

After the battle, English troops dug up the grave of the Sudanese charismatic religious leader known as the Mahdi, who had died in 1885, and used his skull for a soccer game. Sudan became Anglo-Egyptian Sudan, a British colony.

- In 1903, with the aid of the U.S. Navy and the U.S. State Department, Panamanian rebels won their independence from Colombia and established an independent Panamanian state on the thin link of land connecting North and South America. Within two weeks the new government agreed to the Hay-Bunau-Varilla Treaty, in which in return for $10,000,000 it granted the United States authority over the land where it planned to build a canal linking the Atlantic and Pacific Oceans. Here, in the Canal Zone, the U.S. government established its own postal service, custom houses, and commissaries. In Panama itself, the United States disbanded the local army, stationed Marines throughout the country, and established a virtual protectorate over the newly "independent" state. The Panama Canal opened in 1914.

All of these episodes reveal the gap that by 1900 had opened up between "the West" — essentially the states of Europe and a small group of European offshoots such as the United States — and the people of Africa, Asia, and Latin America. Better armed, more efficiently governed, immeasurably wealthier, and confident of their moral and technological superiority, Europeans conquered and colonized Africa and much of Asia, manipulated the foreign policy and finances of dozens of "sovereign" Asian and Latin American states, and turned the world into a market for their manufactures, a supplier of their food, and a source of raw materials for their factories. Throughout the world they built railroads and telegraph systems, used steam-driven machinery to dig harbors and canals, introduced new political and economic concepts, and undermined centuries-old customs and values. At an ever-accelerating rate, the people and governments of the West were transforming the globe.

Such an outcome would have surprised an observer of world affairs as late as the eighteenth century, even though Europe's importance had been growing for some two hundred years. In the 1500s and 1600s Europeans used their maritime skills and gunpowder weapons to take control of the Americas and establish a commercial presence in Africa and Asia. Even after two centuries of economic growth, however, in the mid-eighteenth-century Europeans were on average no wealthier than the people in China, Japan, and parts of India, and still paid for coveted Asian silks and porcelain with silver because their own products were of little interest to sophisticated Asian buyers. Aside from the Philippines and some islands in the East Indies, they had established their political authority only in the Americas; even here the descendants of European settlers were about to throw off European rule in a series of anticolonial revolts between the 1770s and 1810s.

By 1900, however, Europeans held sway over much of the world. This dramatic development resulted from two revolutions, one economic and one political, that began in the late eighteenth century. Europe's economic transformation, known as the industrial revolution, resulted from the application of new machines and energy sources to the tasks of manufacturing, transportation, and communications. It began in the 1760s in England, where the manufacture of cotton textiles was transformed by the use of new spinning, carding, and weaving machines that were driven first by water power and from the 1780s onward by coal-burning steam engines. In the 1800s industrialization spread to the European continent and the United States, and at the end of the century entered a new phase of innovation and growth. In this so-called second industrial revolution, new industries based on discoveries in chemistry and the utilization of electricity were created, and steel production boomed. Utilizing steamships, railroads, and the telegraph, and drawing on its vast financial resources, Europe became the center of an international trade network through which industrialized nations exported textiles, chemicals, tools, weapons, machines, ceramics, and hardware to every corner of the globe. In return they imported beef, wheat, and bananas from Latin America; diamonds, gold, and palm oil from Africa; cotton from India and Egypt; tin from Malaya; and countless other agricultural products and raw materials from around the world.

Far-reaching political changes accompanied Europe's economic transformation. Beginning in the late eighteenth century with the American (1776–1783) and French (1789–1799) Revolutions, Americans and Europeans rejected the principles of absolutism, divine right monarchy, and aristocratic privilege and sought to establish popularly elected governments based on the rule of law, individual freedom, and legal equality. By 1900, after a century of experimentation and upheaval, most European states were still monarchies, but they were now constitutional monarchies, in which popularly elected parliaments made laws, approved budgets, held ministers accountable for their actions, and exerted at least some influence on foreign policy. Citizens of these states closely identified their own interests with those of their governments, prided themselves on their nations' traditions and accomplishments, and developed a strong emotional attachment to their compatriots. Nationalism had become a potent political force.

The people of Asia, Africa, and Latin America had little choice but to acquiesce to Western dominance. Those who lived in European colonies had no meaningful say in their affairs whatsoever. Leaders of states that still had a measure of sovereignty drew up plans for economic modernization and military reform but faced formidable obstacles in carrying them out. In the opening years of the twentieth century, there was every reason to believe that the West's domination of the world would continue indefinitely.

In retrospect, however, the foundations of Western dominance were being undermined in those very years when they seemed so secure. Beginning in 1868, Japan transformed itself from a preindustrial society, vulnerable to Western aggression, into a modern industrial state with a formidable army and navy. In 1905 the world took notice when Japan defeated Russia, one of the "great powers" of Europe, in the Russo-Japanese War. In 1885 Indian professionals and civil servants, most with European-style educations and some with degrees from Oxford or Cambridge, founded the Indian National Congress, dedicated to expanding Indian participation in political decision-making and the Indianization of the Indian Civil Service. This organization spearheaded the drive for Indian independence in the first half of the twentieth century. In the early 1900s several states — Persia in 1905, the Ottoman Empire in 1908, China and Mexico in 1911 — experienced political revolutions. In the short run none of them was successful; all led to further turmoil and, in the case of China, complete political collapse. Even in their failure, however, they indicated that non-Western peoples were breaking with their pasts and moving along paths previously followed only by Europeans.

Meanwhile nationalism intensified and diplomatic tensions grew in Europe. Newly united Germany maintained Europe's most powerful army, built a formidable navy, sought colonies in Africa and Asia, and aggressively competed with Great Britain for control of world markets. France brooded over its defeat by Germany in the Franco-Prussian War (1870–1871), and, while waiting for revenge, sought to bolster its status as a great power by building an overseas empire second in size only to that of Great Britain. Great Britain resented Germany's economic success, military power, and diplomatic bluster, but until the early 1900s also competed with Russia and France for territories in Africa and Asia. Statesmen worried about Russian expansion into the Balkans and Asia Minor, should the Hapsburg Empire of Austria-Hungary disintegrate or should Ottoman military power continue to decline.

As tensions grew, statesmen sought security through alliance systems, and politicians approved huge military budgets to pay for new weapons and ever-expanding armies and navies. Generals developed strategies and drew up timetables to fight the major war that everyone expected. In 1914 that war — World War I — finally came, setting in motion events that dramatically altered the course of twentieth-century history.

CHAPTER I

Global Interaction in an Era of Imperialism and Migration

The level of global interaction among the world's peoples began to increase in the fifteenth and sixteenth centuries after European mariners sailed around Africa to reach Asia and, more importantly, crossed the Atlantic and discovered the Americas. These voyages inaugurated a new era in world commerce in which Europeans traded directly with India, Southeast Asia, and China, and turned the Atlantic into a thoroughfare of international exchange linking Europe, Africa, and the Americas. The European discoveries also led to the increased movement of people. Between the fifteenth and eighteenth centuries, millions of Africans, who went as slaves, and millions of Europeans, who went voluntarily, migrated to the Americas, where they repopulated a hemisphere whose native inhabitants had been ravaged by the introduction of Old World diseases. The Old World pathogens that caused the American epidemics are just one example of the many biological exchanges that took place from the fifteenth century onward. Cattle, horses, swine, fruit trees, and grain crops were introduced to the Americas, while New World crops such as maize, tobacco, and the potato spread to Africa and Eurasia.

These developments set the stage for the rapid acceleration of global integration that took place in the nineteenth century. The amount of international trade, for example, tripled between 1780 and 1840, quadrupled between 1840 and 1870, and doubled again between 1870 and 1910. The types of goods traded also changed. No longer was international commerce dominated by luxuries such as silks and porcelains from China and nonessentials such as sugar, cocoa, tobacco from the Americas. Increasingly, world trade shifted to necessities. By 1900 Europe could not have fed itself without importing Canadian wheat and Argentinean beef; nor would Canadian farmers and Argentinean ranchers have had a market for their products without European buyers.

In addition, in the nineteenth century Europe's industries became dependent on raw materials imported from around the world: rubber from the Congo and Amazon River Basins; palm oil from Africa; cotton from the United States, India, and Egypt; jute from India and Africa; tin from the Malay Peninsula; copper from Chile, Peru, and Central Africa; and gutta-percha, a plastic derived from tree sap and used to coat undersea telegraph cables, from Malaya. During the century, Asians and Africans stopped making many of the articles needed for daily living and bought them from industrialized nations. India, the world's leading exporter of cotton textiles in the eighteenth century, imported most of its cotton cloth from Great Britain by the end of the 1800s.

These changes in world trade would not have occurred without revolutionary developments in transportation. The first commercial railroad began hauling coal to the English North Sea port of Stockton in 1820. By 1900 close to 300,000 miles of track had been laid around the world, on which more than one hundred thousand steam locomotives pulled almost a million freight and passenger cars that carried unprecedented quantities of goods and people. Steam engines also revolutionized ocean travel. The first oceangoing steamship, the *Savannah,* had a wooden hull and side-wheels powered by a steam engine so inefficient that it relied on sails for twenty-three of the twenty-seven days it took to reach England from the United States in 1819. By 1900 steamships had steel hulls, efficient compound engines that drove propellers, rather than side-wheels, and refrigerators if they carried perishable foodstuffs. After 1869, when making the passage between Asia and Europe, navigators reduced the length of their voyage almost 50 percent by using the Suez Canal rather than making the long voyage around Africa.

Changing trends in international trade, along with advances in steamship and railroad technology, contributed to another dimension of increasing global interchange in the nineteenth century — namely, the rising tide of migration. From the mid 1800s to the early twentieth century, approximately a million Indians left the Asian subcontinent to seek economic opportunities in South America, the Caribbean, Malaya, and Africa, and large numbers of Chinese immigrated to Pacific islands, Malaya, Singapore, Peru, Canada, and the United States. As large as it was, the number of Asian immigrants was dwarfed by the swarm of Europeans who migrated to the United States, Canada, Argentina, Australia, and New Zealand. In the 1830s and 1840s between 300,000 and 400,000 emigrants left Europe every year; by the early twentieth century, between 1,000,000 and 1,400,000 European immigrants arrived each year in the United States alone.

While railroads and steamships revolutionized travel, the electric telegraph revolutionized international communications. Introduced in England in 1837 and the United States in 1844, the telegraph was useful only on land until the 1860s when the placement of effective, durable telegraph wires at the bottom of the world's oceans became possible. Soon several hundred thousand miles of cables undersea and on land linked every continent in a communication network that carried millions of messages a year. In 1800 it might have taken a letter ten months to two years to reach England from China. By 1900 a telegram from China to England arrived in a matter of minutes.

Trade, technology, and migration all played a role in integrating the world's peoples and regions in the 1800s, but so too did military conquest. The late nineteenth century was an age of imperialism, in which a small number of states, predominantly European, used their superior weaponry — repeating rifles, light machine guns, and dum-dum bullets that exploded on contact — to conquer or simply annex all of Africa except Liberia and Ethiopia, much of Southeast Asia, and hundreds of Pacific islands. Surpassing the conquests of legendary figures such as Alexander the Great and Ghengis Khan, imperialism was a monument to the West's political, economic, and military ascendancy and a powerful expression of the world's growing integration.

◆

Imperialism: Western Justifications

In the late nineteenth and early twentieth centuries — the era of imperialism — the long history of Western expansion culminated in a land-grab unprecedented in human history. The amount of territory and the numbers of human beings added to European empires between 1871 and 1900 are astounding: Great Britain, 4.25 million square miles and 66 million people; France, 3.5 million square miles and 26 million people; Germany, 1 million square miles and 13 million people; Belgium, 900,000 square miles and 13 million people; Italy, 900,000 square miles and just under a million people. Portugal expanded its holdings in Africa, and Spain, although it lost Cuba and the Philippines, annexed Morocco and some sparsely populated lands in the Western Sahara. The only non-European imperialist nations were the United States, which took over Cuba, the Philippines, and a few Pacific islands, and Japan, which acquired Korea and Taiwan.

Late-nineteenth-century imperialism was made possible by a number of key technological developments. The replacement of sailing vessels by steel-hulled steamships reduced two-month ocean voyages to two weeks; undersea telegraph lines enabled government officials and business owners to communicate in seconds, not weeks or months; medical advances and new drugs protected Europeans from tropical diseases such as malaria; rapid-fire rifles and machine guns gave Western troops an insurmountable advantage over Africans or Asians who offered resistance.

But technological capability alone cannot explain the expansionist fever that swept through the West in the late 1800s. As the sources in this section reveal, anticipated economic gains, national rivalries, missionary fervor, a strong sense of racial superiority, and faith in the West's civilizing mission all contributed to the psychological and political atmosphere that led to this final chapter of Western expansion.

A Defense of French Imperialism

1 ◆ Jules Ferry, SPEECH BEFORE THE FRENCH CHAMBER OF DEPUTIES, 1883

Jules Ferry (1832–1893) was a French politician who twice served as premier during the Third Republic, the name of the French government from 1871 until 1940. Ferry was an ardent imperialist, and during his premierships France annexed Tunisia and parts of Indochina and began exploring Africa. He frequently defended his policies in debates in the French Chamber of Deputies against both socialist and conservative critics, who for different reasons were anti-imperialist. The following selection from his speech on July 28, 1883, summarizes Ferry's reasons for supporting French expansionism and also sheds light on his opponents' views.

QUESTIONS FOR ANALYSIS

1. According to Ferry, what recent developments in world trade have made it urgent for France to have colonies?
2. What ideological arguments against imperialism have been raised by Ferry's critics? How does Ferry counter them?
3. Aside from providing markets for French goods, what other economic advantages do colonies offer, according to Ferry?
4. What noneconomic arguments does Ferry offer in favor of patriotism?

M. Jules Ferry. . . . It is as strenuous for me as for you, but I believe that there is some benefit in summarizing and condensing, in the form of arguments, the principles, the motives, and the various interests by which a policy of colonial expansion may be justified; it goes without saying that I will try to remain reasonable, moderate, and never lose sight of the major continental interests which are the primary concern of this country. What I wish to say . . . is that . . . the policy of colonial expansion is a political and economic system; I wish to say that one can relate this system to three orders of ideas: economic ideas, ideas of civilization in its highest sense, and ideas of politics and patriotism.

In the area of economics, I will allow myself to place before you, with the support of some figures, the considerations which justify a policy of colonial expansion from the point of view of that need, felt more and more strongly by the industrial populations of Europe and particularly those of our own rich and hard working country: the need for export markets. . . . I will formulate only in a general way what each of you, in the different parts of France, is in a position to confirm. Yes, what is lacking for our great industry, drawn irrevocably on to the path of exportation by the . . . treaties of 1860,[1] what it lacks more and more is export markets. Why? Because next door to us Germany is surrounded by barriers, because beyond the ocean, the United States of America has become protectionist, protectionist in the most extreme sense, because not only have these great markets, I will not say closed but shrunk, and thus become more difficult of access for our industrial products, but also these great states are beginning to pour products not seen heretofore onto our own markets. . . . It is not necessary to pursue this demonstration any farther. . . .

. . . Gentlemen, there is a second point, a second order of ideas to which I have to give equal attention, but as quickly as possible, believe me; it is the humanitarian and civilizing side of the question. On this point the honorable M. Camille Pelletan[2] has jeered in his own refined and clever manner; he jeers, he condemns, and he says "What is this civilization which you impose with cannon-balls? What is it but another form of barbarism? Don't these populations, these inferior races, have the same rights as you? Aren't they masters of their own houses? Have they called upon you? You come to them against their will, you offer them violence, but not civilization." There, gentlemen, is the thesis; I do not hesitate to say that this is not politics, nor is it history: it is political metaphysics. ("Ah, Ah" *on far left.*)[3]

. . . Gentlemen, I must speak from a higher and more truthful plane. It must be stated openly that, in effect, superior races have rights over inferior races. (*Movement on many benches of the far left.*)

M. Jules Maigne.[4] Oh! You dare to say this in the country which has proclaimed the rights of man!

M. de Guilloutet. This is a justification of slavery and the slave trade!

M. Jules Ferry. If M. Maigne is right, if the declaration of the rights of man was written for the blacks of equatorial Africa, then by what right do you impose regular commerce upon them? They have not called upon you.

M. Raoul Duval. We do not want to impose anything upon them. It is you who wish to do so! . . .

M. Jules Ferry. I repeat that superior races have a right, because they have a duty. They have the duty to civilize inferior races. . . .

That is what I have to answer M. Pelletan in regard to the second point upon which he touched.

He then touched upon a third point, more delicate, more serious, and upon which I ask your permission to express myself quite frankly. It is the political side of the question. . . .

"It is a system," he says, "which consists of seeking out compensations in the Orient with a circumspect and peaceful seclusion which is actually imposed upon us in Europe."

I would like to explain myself in regard to this. I do not like this word "compensation," and, in effect, not here but elsewhere it has often been used in a treacherous way. If what is being said or insinuated is that a republican minister could possibly believe that there are in any part of the world compensations for the disasters which we have experienced,[5] an injury is being inflicted . . . and an injury undeserved by that government. (*Applause at the center and*

---

[1]These agreements with Great Britain lowered tariffs between the two nations.
[2]Pelletan (1815–1846) was a radical republican politician and an ardent patriot.
[3]Going back to a tradition begun in the legislative assemblies of the French Revolution, democrats sat on the left,

moderates in the center, and conservatives and monarchists on the right. By the 1880s, the "left" also included socialists.
[4]Maigne and the speakers who follow, Guilloutet and Duval, were members of the Chamber of Deputies.
[5]The reference is to France's defeat by Prussia and other German states in the Franco-Prussian War of 1870–1871.

eft.) I will ward off this injury with all the orce of my patriotism! (*New applause and bravos rom the same benches.*)

Gentlemen, there are certain considerations vhich merit the attention of all patriots. The onditions of naval warfare have been prooundly altered. ("Very true! Very true!")

At this time, as you know, a warship cannot arry more than fourteen days' worth of coal, no natter how perfectly it is organized, and a ship vhich is out of coal is a derelict on the surface of the sea, abandoned to the first person who comes along. Thence the necessity of having on he oceans provision stations, shelters, ports for defense and revictualing. (*Applause at the center and left. Various interruptions.*) And it is for this hat we needed Tunisia, for this that we needed Saigon and the Mekong Delta, for this that we need Madagascar, that we are at Diégo-Suarez and Vohemar[6] and will never leave them! (*Applause from a great number of benches.*) Gentlemen, in Europe as it is today, in this competition of so

many rivals which we see growing around us, some by perfecting their military or maritime forces, others by the prodigious development of an ever growing population; in a Europe, or rather in a universe of this sort, a policy of peaceful seclusion or abstention is simply the highway to decadence! Nations are great in our times only by means of the activities which they develop; it is not simply "by the peaceful shining forth of institutions" that they are great at this hour. . . .

The Republican Party has shown that it is quite aware that one cannot impose upon France a political ideal conforming to that of nations like independent Belgium and the Swiss Republic; that something else is needed for France: that she cannot be merely a free country, that she must also be a great country, exercising all of her rightful influence over the destiny of Europe, that she ought to propagate this influence throughout the world and carry everywhere that she can her language, her customs, her flag, her arms, and her genius. (*Applause at center and left.*)

---

[5]Madagascar port cities.

Imperialism and the Life of Manly Courage

❖

2 ◆ *Theodore Roosevelt, THE STRENUOUS LIFE*

The expanding role of the United States in world affairs is one of the twentieth century's momentous developments. As late as the 1890s, the United States was on no one's list of "great powers" despite its growing population, resources, and industrial expansion. It had no colonies, a tiny army, a "washtub" navy, and a diplomatic corps notorious for its unprofessionalism. The United States had played a key role in opening Japan to foreign trade in the 1850s and 1860s, and although it intervened frequently in Latin American affairs, the U.S. government and the American people showed little interest in the affairs of Europe or Asia.

This changed in the late 1890s. Motivated by nationalism, anticipated economic gains, a sense of national mission, and fears that European imperialism might spill over into the Caribbean and Latin American, the United States built up its navy, annexed Hawaii in 1898, assumed a more aggressive role in China, and, after the Spanish American War (1898), became an imperialist power when it took over Cuba, the Philippines, Guam, and Puerto Rico.

Among the advocates of an expanded international role for the United States, none was more enthusiastic and vociferous than Theodore Roosevelt. Born in 1858 in New York and a graduate of Harvard, Roosevelt was an author, rancher, state assemblyman, New York City police commissioner, and undersecretary of the navy before being elected vice-president on the Republican ticket in 1900. He became president in 1901 after the assassination of President McKinley, and was reelected in 1904. As president, Roosevelt directed the construction of the Panama Canal, helped broker an end to the Russo-Japanese War in 1905, sent the Navy on a world cruise to "show the flag," and announced the "Roosevelt Corollary" to the Monroe Doctrine, by which the United States proclaimed the right to intervene in the political affairs of Latin American states.

Roosevelt delivered the following speech in early 1899 during the heated national debate following the U.S. victory over Spain in the Spanish American War. According to the armistice agreement of August 12, 1898, Spain ceded to the United States Puerto Rico, Cuba, and Guam. In December the two sides negotiated the Treaty of Paris, by which the United States would receive the Philippines in return for twenty million dollars. Senate ratification of the treaty was bitterly opposed by most Democrats and members of the Anti-Imperialism League, who believed that annexing the Philippines clashed with the nation's commitment to liberty and freedom. In his Chicago speech, "The Strenuous Life," and in many other statements, Roosevelt vigorously opposed the anti-imperialists' arguments. He and other supporters of the new U.S. imperial role won the day when the Senate narrowly approved the Treaty of Paris in February 1899.

QUESTIONS FOR ANALYSIS

1. According to Roosevelt, what lessons does the example of China offer for the United States?
2. In Roosevelt's view, what is the ultimate purpose of colonialism?
3. Roosevelt often refers to "duty" in his speech. What does he mean by the term?
4. What are Roosevelt's views of the people of Cuba and the Philippines? How do these views resemble his views of Native Americans?
5. How does Roosevelt characterize the opponents to increased U.S. military spending and expansion?

We of this generation do not have to face a task such as that our fathers faced, but we have our tasks, and woe to us if we fail to perform them! We cannot, if we would, play the part of China, and be content to rot by inches in ignoble ease within our borders, taking no interest in what goes on beyond them, sunk in a scrambling commercialism; heedless of the higher life, the life of aspiration, of toil and risk, busying ourselves only with the wants of our bodies for the day, until suddenly we should find, beyond a shadow of question, what China has already found, that in this world the nation that has trained itself to a career of unwarlike and isolated ease is bound, in the end, to go down before other nations which have not lost the manly and adventurous qualities. If we are to be a really great people, we must strive in good faith to play a great part in the world. We cannot avoid meeting great issues. All that we can determine for ourselves is whether we shall meet them well or ill. In 1898 we could not help being brought face to face with the problem of war with Spain. All we could decide was whether we should shrink like cowards from the contest, or enter into it as beseemed a brave and high-spirited people; and, once in, whether failure or success should crown our banners. So it is now. We cannot avoid the responsibilities that confront us in Hawaii,[1] Cuba, [Puerto] Rico, and the Philippines. All we can decide is whether we shall meet them in a way that will redound to the national credit, or whether we shall make of our dealings with these new problems a dark and shameful page in our history. . . .

. . . The timid man, the lazy man, the man who distrusts his country, the over-civilized man, who has lost the great fighting, masterful virtues, the ignorant man, and the man of dull mind, whose soul is incapable of feeling the mighty lift that thrills "stern men with empires in their brains" — all these, of course, shrink from seeing the nation undertake its new duties; shrink from seeing us build a navy and an army adequate to our needs; shrink from seeing us do our share of the world's work, by bringing order out of chaos in the great, fair tropic islands from which the valor of our soldiers and sailors has driven the Spanish flag. . . .

. . . The guns that thundered off Manila and Santiago[2] left us echoes of glory, but they also left us a legacy of duty. If we drove out a medieval tyranny[3] only to make room for savage anarchy, we had better not have begun the task at all. It is worse than idle to say that we have no duty to perform, and can leave to their fates the islands we have conquered. Such a course

would be the course of infamy. It would be followed at once by utter chaos in the wretched islands themselves. Some stronger, manlier power would have to step in and do the work, and we would have shown ourselves weaklings, unable to carry to successful completion the labors that great and high-spirited nations are eager to undertake. . . .

The problems are different for the different islands. [Puerto] Rico is not large enough to stand alone. We must govern it wisely and well, primarily in the interest of its own people. Cuba is, in my judgment, entitled ultimately to settle for itself whether it shall be an independent state or an integral portion of the mightiest of republics. But until order and stable liberty are secured, we must remain in the island to insure them, and infinite tact, judgment, moderation, and courage must be shown by our keeping the island pacified, in relentlessly stamping out brigandage, in protecting all alike, and yet in showing proper recognition to the men who have fought for Cuban liberty. The Philippines offer a yet graver problem. Their population includes half-caste and native Christians, warlike Moslems, and wild pagans. Many of their people are utterly unfit for self-government, and show no signs of becoming fit. Others may in time become fit but at least can only take part in self-government under a wise supervision, at once firm and beneficent. We have driven Spanish tyranny from the island. If we now let it be replaced by savage anarchy, our work has been for harm and not for good. I have scant patience with those who fear to undertake the task of governing the Philippines, . . . or that they shrink from it because of the expense and trouble; but I have even scanter patience with those who make a pretense of humanitarianism to hide and cover their timidity, and who cant about "liberty" and the "consent of the governed," in order to excuse

---

[1]The United States annexed Hawaii in 1898 after almost a century of economic penetration and missionary activity.
[2]The naval battles of Manila Bay, in the Philippines, and

Santiago, in Cuba, were major U.S. victories in the Spanish American War.
[3]This is a disparaging reference to Spain.

themselves for their unwillingness to play the part of men. Their doctrines, if carried out, would make it incumbent upon us to leave the Apaches of Arizona to work out their own salvation, and to decline to interfere in a single Indian reservation. Their doctrines condemn your forefathers and mine for ever having settled in these United States. . . .

I preach to you, then, my countrymen, that our country calls not for the life of ease but for the life of strenuous endeavor. The twentieth century looms before us big with the fate of many nations. If we stand idly by, if we seek merely swollen, slothful ease and ignoble peace, if we shrink from the hard contests where men must win at hazard of their lives and at the risk of all they hold dear, then the bolder and stronger peoples will pass us by, and will win for themselves the domination of the world. Let us therefore boldly face the life of strife, resolute to do our duty well and manfully; resolute to uphold righteousness by deed and by word; resolute to be both honest and brave, to serve high ideals, yet to use practical methods. Above all, let us shrink from no strife, moral or physical, within or without the nation, provided we are certain that the strife is justified, for it is only through strife, through hard and dangerous endeavor, that we shall ultimately win the goal of true national greatness.

◆

The Economics of Imperialism

Throughout history, imperialism has meant not just political subordination but also economic exploitation in the form of land confiscation, plunder of wealth and resources, new taxes, and forced labor. Western imperialism before World War I had its share of outright plunder, but its economic ramifications went well beyond simple exploitation. In Africa and Asia, the imperialists built railroads, deepened harbors, strung telegraph lines, brought in machines to extract minerals and metals from deep in the earth, and mandated the cultivation of crops they needed to feed their people and supply their factories. They transformed isolated agrarian economies into component parts of a single world economy driven by Western industrialization and capitalism.

Furthermore, late nineteenth-century imperialism involved more than newly drawn boundaries and direct political control by colonial administrators. For many states that remained theoretically sovereign, imperialism meant economic, not political, subordination. Latin America became a vast area of U.S. and European investment, with a country such as Nicaragua becoming almost a private fiefdom of the United Fruit Company, the Boston-based corporation that supplied Europe and North America with bananas. The Ottoman Empire and Persia acquiesced to extensive foreign control of their finances and economic development. China by 1900 was divided into "spheres of influence," in which Britain, Germany, France, Japan, Russia, and to a degree the United States enjoyed exclusive trading rights and favorable tariffs, leased large tracts of land, and held concessions to build railroads, exploit mines, and establish banks. Such examples of Western economic penetration are just as much a part of the history of imperialism as the political takeover of Africa and Asia.

Cotton Growing and Rebellion in German East Africa

❖

3 ◆ RECORDS OF THE MAJI-MAJI UPRISING

The Germans were latecomers to imperialism, but after they gained control of territories in Africa and Oceania, they were quick to adopt the view that colonies exist to serve the economic interests of the colonial master. This was their philosophy in German East Africa, a large and politically diverse region on Africa's east coast, surrounded by Kenya to the north, the Belgian Congo to the west, and Northern Rhodesia and Mozambique to the south.

German economic policy lacked direction in the 1880s and 1890s as the Germans struggled to overcome resistance and experimented with various plans to coerce Africans into growing crops such as cotton that the Germans needed for their home industries. In 1902 the Germans implemented a plan to cultivate cotton in the coastal and southern sections of the colony according to which each village was compelled to provide workers to grow cotton a certain number of days a year on government estates, settler plantations, and especially village fields. To force Africans to accept these low-paying jobs, the Germans instituted a head tax payable only in cash.

Opposition to the German plan led to rebellion in 1905. Encouraged by religious leaders who supplied the rebels with *maji,* a supposedly magic water that would protect warriors from bullets, the rebellion spread throughout the colony's central and southern regions. The Germans fought back with maxim guns, mass executions, and the burning of villages. The rebellion ended in 1907, at a cost of seventy-five thousand African deaths, many caused by famine.

The following testimony concerning the Maji-Maji revolt was gathered and published in 1967 in a book by two Tanzanian historians, G. C. K. Gwassa and John Iffle. Most of the information deals with the experiences of the Matumbi, highlanders who lived in the southeastern part of the colony.

QUESTIONS FOR ANALYSIS

1. What do these records and testimonies reveal about the German approach to administering its colony?
2. Why did the Africans object so strongly to German agricultural policy?
3. What other aspects of German rule did the Africans find objectionable?
4. What does the source reveal about German views of Africans and of their African colonies?
5. What information does the source provide about the role of women in the African village?

[RECOLLECTION OF AMBROSE NGOMBALE MWIRU CONCERNING THE ARRIVAL OF A GERMAN AGENT IN 1897]

Then when that European arrived he asked, "Why did you not answer the call by drum to pay tax?" And they said, "We do not owe you anything. We have no debt to you. If you as a stranger want to stay in this country, then you will have to ask us. Then we will ask of you an offering to propitiate the gods. You will offer something and we will propitiate the gods on your behalf; we will give you land and you will get a place to stay in. But it is not for us as hosts to give you the offering. That is quite impossible."

[RECOLLECTIONS OF NDUNDULE MANGAYA]

The cultivation of cotton was done by turns. Every village was allotted days on which to cultivate at Samanga Ndumbo[1] and at the Jumbe's[2] plantation. One person came from each homestead, unless there were very many people. Thus you might be told to work for five or ten days at Samanga. So a person would go. Then after half the number of days another man came from home to relieve him. If the new man did not feel pity for him, the same person would stay on until he finished. It was also like this at the Jumbe's. If you returned from Samanga then your turn at the Jumbe's remained, or if you began at the Jumbe's you waited for the turn at Samanga after you had finished. No woman went unless her husband ran away; then they would say she had hidden him. Then the woman would go. When in a village a former clan head was seized to go to cultivate he would

offer his slave in his stead. Then after arriving there you all suffered very greatly. Your back and your buttocks were whipped, and there was no rising up once you stooped to dig. The good thing about the Germans was that all people were the same before the whip. If a jumbe or akida[3] made a mistake he received the whip as well. Thus there were people whose job was to clear the land of trees and undergrowth; others tilled the land; others would smooth the field and plant; another group would do the weeding and yet another the picking; and lastly others carried the bales of cotton to the coast . . . for shipping. Thus we did not know where it was taken. Then if that European gave out some bakshishi[4] to the akida or jumbe they kept it. We did not get anything. In addition, people suffered much from the cotton, which took three months to ripen and was picked in the fourth. Now digging and planting were in the months of Ntandatu and Nchimbi, and this was the time of very many wild pigs in this country.[5] If you left the chasing of the pigs to the women she could not manage well at night. In addition, the pigs are very stubborn at that period and will not move even if you go within very close range. Only very few women can assist their husbands at night and these are the ones with very strong hearts. There were just as many birds, and if you did not have children it was necessary to help your wife drive away the birds, while at the same time you cleared a piece of land for the second maize crop, because your wife would not have time. And during this very period they still wanted you to leave your home and go to Samanga or to work on the jumbe's plantation. This was why people became furious and angry. The work was astonishingly hard and full of grave suffering, but its wages were the whip on one's back and buttocks. And yet he [the

---

[1] A coastal town.

[2] A chief or headman given low-level administrative responsibilities by the Germans.

[3] An official appointed by the Germans with functions

similar to those of jumbes; akidas, however, were recruited from coastal towns and were usually Muslims.

[4] A bribe or, in this case, a payment.

[5] A threat to cultivated crops.

German] still wanted us to pay him the tax. Were we not human beings? And Wamatumbi . . . since the days of old, did not want to be troubled or ruled by any person. They were really fierce, ah! Given such grave suffering they thought it better for a man to die rather than live in such torment.

Thus they hated the rule which was too cruel. It was not because of agriculture, not at all. If it had been good agriculture which had meaning and profit, who would have given himself up to die? Earlier they had made troubles as well, but when he began to cause us to cultivate cotton for him and to dig roads and so on, then people said, "This [man] has now become an absolute ruler. Destroy him."

[RECOLLECTION OF NDULI NJIMBWI CONCERNING WORK ON A PLANTATION OWNED BY A GERMAN SETTLER NAMED STEINHAGEN].

During the cultivation there was much suffering. We, the labor conscripts, stayed in the front line cultivating. Then behind us was an overseer whose work it was to whip us. Behind the overseer there was a jumbe, and every jumbe stood behind his fifty men. Behind the line of jumbes stood Bwana Kinoo[6] himself. . . . The overseer had a whip, and he was extremely cruel. His work was to whip the conscripts if they rose up or tried to rest, or if they left a trail of their footprints behind them.[7] Ah, brothers, God is great — that we have lived like this is God's Providence! And on the other side Bwana Kinoo had a bamboo stick. If the men of a certain jumbe left their footprints behind them, that jumbe would be boxed on the ears and Kinoo would beat him with the bamboo stick using both hands, while at the same time the overseer lashed out at us laborers.

[EXCERPTS FROM AN INTERVIEW WITH A GERMAN OFFICIAL VON GEIBLER CONCERNING THE COMMUNAL PLOTS]

Village plots were set up in each akida's and headman's area early in 1902 (September–October). Bushland was mainly chosen. The people were consulted in choosing the post. Each headman made a plot for his area in the neighborhood of his headquarters. The principle was that every 30–50 men were to cultivate 2½ acres. . . . Where possible, the advice of the natives was obtained as to the crop to be grown. So far as possible, one crop was to be grown on each plot, according to the type of soil. Some 2,000 acres were cleared and cultivated. The size varied from 2½ to 35 acres; the average was about 12½ acres.

In 1903–04 it was ordered that each village plot should be extended by at least a quarter. The total area in that year came to 3,215 acres. Maize, millet, simsim,[8] groundnuts, rice, and coconut palms were grown during 1902–03. Cotton was added in 1903–04.

No extension took place in 1904–05, but the cultivation of other crops was abandoned in favor of cotton.

What was the labor situation and the supervision?

. . . According to returns by the headmen, the number of able-bodied men amounted to:

1902–03	c. 25,000 men
1903–04	c. 26,000 men
1904–05	c. 25,000 men

During the last year, women and children had to be brought in to help, since the men frequently refused to work.

In Herr von Geibler's opinion, two days' work a week, as proposed by the District Office

---

[6]The Matumbi's name for Steinhagen.
[7]Such a trail would mean that the person had walked away from his or her assigned work.

[8]Sesame.

order, was insufficient from the start; 50–100 per cent more had to be worked from the first. When cotton became a main crop, continuous work was sometimes necessary. . . .

The akidas were relied upon to report on the condition of the plots, and they were also responsible for punishing those whom the headmen reported as refractory workers. There was no European control of this — who among the natives worked, and for how many days — although agricultural students (some of them children) were sent out, each with a note-book, to judge the condition of the plots and the work performed, and to report to the District Officer. Only once a year did a European visit the plots, to measure them out and select the land. No lists of workers were kept anywhere; the profits were distributed only according to the total numbers.

Work on most of the plots was *flatly* refused during 1904–05. The headmen complained that they no longer had the people in hand. The officials of the Commune believed at the time that they could detect a state of ferment.

Were refractory workers punished, and by whom?

Last year (1904–05), following reports from the akidas and from Sergeant Holzhausen, who was sent to inspect the headmen, numerous headmen were punished by the District Office with imprisonment in chains or solitary confinement for totally neglecting their village plots as a result of the natives' refusal to work. The last, in June, was headman Kibasila, who got one month in chains.

Indian Railroads and the People's Welfare

4 ◆ G. V. Joshi,
THE ECONOMIC RESULTS OF FREE TRADE AND RAILWAY EXTENSION

An enduring monument to British imperialism in India is the railway system, which at the time of independence in 1947 was the fourth largest in the world in terms of track mileage, following only that of the United States, Canada, and the Soviet Union. The first railway was built in India in 1850, and by 1915 India had over forty thousand miles of track and approximately one hundred million railroad passengers per year. Railway construction was supported by several powerful groups: British cotton manufacturers, for whom railways were a cheap and efficient way to get cotton to the coast for shipment to England; British manufacturers, who supplied India with most of its rails, locomotives, moving stock, and equipment; colonial officials, who saw railroads as a means of quickly moving troops to trouble spots and as an essential part of the Indian postal system; and millions of Indians, who took to rail travel with great enthusiasm.

But was India's new railway system a good investment? Did it contribute to India's overall economic development? Did it justify its enormous costs? Among those who answered "no" to these questions, few were as eloquent or persistent in their criticisms of British economic policy as G. V. Joshi (1851–1911), a teacher and schoolmaster who also was one of India's leading economic writers. His essay on public works and free trade was published in 1884.

QUESTIONS FOR ANALYSIS

1. What benefits for the Indian people does Joshi see in the program of railroad construction?
2. Why is it wrong in Joshi's view to base Indian economic policy on the model of the United States?
3. According to Joshi, what were Lord Dalhousie's motives for building India's railway system?
4. What long-term effects has India's railway system had on India's economic situation, according to Joshi?
5. If Joshi had been given an opportunity to draw a blueprint for India's economic development, what would it have looked like?

ECONOMIC REALITIES

In this country, which is economically in such a primitive and backward condition, a too exclusive policy of pushing on Railways at American speed, beyond the resources of Indian finance, will, unless accompanied by other economic measures of far greater importance, only end in national impoverishment. We are not opposed to the growth of Railways *per se.* They are good in their own way as providing cheap transit, and promoting national solidarity, and facilitating trade-movements, but when their extension is made the ultimate goal of State action on its economic side, their tendency to prevent, in a country like India, a healthy material advance on *normal lines* must be duly taken into account; for, unless they are accompanied by other and more important measures conducive to a better organisation of national industries, they do not add to the intensive strength of the country, which alone furnishes a firm foundation to its expansive greatness. . . .

Every consideration, therefore, of prudence and justice alike dictate that the action of

Government,[1] in such circumstances, shall be thoroughly national in its aims, purposes, and principles of execution. It might employ foreign talent for the prosecution of such works; it might borrow foreign capital for the purpose. But it is on no grounds justified in bringing the foreigner with his talent and capital into the country, and suffering him to appropriate permanently the national field of improvement, to the exclusion of the native element, and forming the nucleus of a domineering foreign aristocracy in the land with purposes and interests adverse to those of the nation — a result which cannot but be regarded as at once a serious political danger, and a great economic evil. . . .

THE EFFECTS OF FREE TRADE

The Public Works policy of the Government of India was first formulated by Lord Dalhousie,[2] under whose administration the proposal of a separate Department for the promotion of Public Works undertaken on Government account, or with Government guarantee,[3] was carried out.

---

[1] The "Government," or the "Government of India," consisted of a British governor-general, his six-man Executive Council, and a Legislative Council consisting of the Executive Council and six to twelve additional members. All these various Councils were dominated by the British.
[2] The Marquis of Dalhousie had been head of the Railway Department of the English Board of Trade before serving as governor-general of India between 1848 and 1856. He was a strong advocate of India's economic modernization

and sponsored a host of public works projects, including railroads, canals, roads, and irrigation systems. He created the Department of Public Works to oversee the many new undertakings.
[3] The "guarantee" was a policy by which railroad companies were guaranteed a 5 percent profit on their investment and were reimbursed by the government if profits fell below that percentage.

. . . It was Lord Dalhousie's dream to strengthen the domination not only of English rule, but of English trade and commerce in India, and the permanent interests of this country were subordinated to this all-engrossing ambition. The contemporaneous rise of the school of Free Trade[4] in England, and the great reputation which its apostles enjoyed, furnished the metaphysical ground-work for this essentially selfish and grasping policy. The value of India to the British nation was measured by the quantity of raw material which the resources of Indian agriculture enabled it to export for the feeding and maintenance of the Lancashire manufactures.[5] India was to devote all its energies to raise the raw exports; and canals, Railroads and improved communications were to be pushed on at any cost to facilitate the export of raw articles and the import of English manufactures. India's own industrial needs were of comparatively no consequence. . . . So far as this result was inevitably due to natural conditions, we have no fault to find with Government. But surely it was not a legitimate exercise of the State's parental functions to help with Indian resources the one country which needed no such help, at the cost of paralyzing its great unfortunate dependency, whose salvation from its depression of ages depends upon its industrial growth in all directions. . . .

The extent of the mischief that has been worked already is admitted by the more keen-sighted of English statesmen, and is witnessed to by the ghastly spectacle so recently witnessed of a condition of things when six millions of people died during a single year of scanty rainfall, . . . and one-third of the population lives from hand to mouth on a single meal a day. And yet Government professes itself to be powerless to raise its little finger to stop the drain,[6] or divert it into less exhaustive channels. It cannot

undertake to subsidize native industrial growth, or stimulate local manufactures without exposing itself to the fire of Free-Trade fanatics, and the opposition of the vested foreign interests which it has created. . . . The abolition of these duties [on imports to India] has worked mischief in that it has exposed to the unrestricted competition of the world the rude and undeveloped industries of the country. These duties were not, as in England, levied upon raw products, but upon finished articles such as cotton, silk and woollen manufactured goods, and wrought metal. These imported articles were all of them machine-made, and necessarily displaced the hand-made products of native skill. This displacement was to a certain extent inevitable, but Government, as the protector of national Indian interests, should not have gone out of its way to stimulate this process of the violent disintegration of important industries in this country. . . . People point out with pride to the fact that, in the course of fifty years, the imports have risen from six to sixty crores of Rupees.[7] To enable our readers to understand the true character of these figures, we append below a table showing the growth in the import of manufactured goods during the last 25 years.

Articles	1859–60	1870–71	1881–82
	£	£	£
Woollen goods	358,557	582,330	1,276,263
Cotton goods	11,698,928	19,044,869	24,000,237
Metal	454,457	850,319	2,772,178
Sugar	220,270	555,801	1,243,758
Umbrellas	136,670	Not available	209,572

These figures show what displacement has occurred in the consumption of the chief manufactured goods of home production. It cannot be maintained for one moment that India did not

---

[4]Advocates of free trade espoused the teachings of Adam Smith in the *Wealth of Nations* (1776). They called for the abolition of all tariffs on imports and exports. In England such doctrines were popular among industrialists who believed the lowering or end of tariffs would ensure markets for British manufactured goods and keep down the price of imported foodstuffs.

[5]The region of England where cotton manufacturing was concentrated.

[6]A term used by critics of British colonialism to describe the loss of Indian wealth to Britain through taxes and trade.

[7]The rupee was the basic coin in the Indian currency system; one crore equaled ten million rupees.

clothe itself in cotton or other fabrics in times past. As a matter of fact, India did not only clothe itself, but even so late as the first quarter of this century, it exported its fine muslims[8] to Europe in large quantities, and even to this day the raw material of cotton and wool is exported in larger quantities than the imported goods. . . .

NATIVE VERSUS FOREIGN MANAGEMENT

. . . Even where native capitalists have embarked their capital in such [manufacturing] enterprises, they are not able to command native skill of management, but find it necessary to import foreign talent and skill. With a partial exception in Bombay, these new industries are all managed throughout by European skill, thus giving the foreigners a monopoly of the advantages reaped, over and above their natural monopoly as shippers, and carriers and insurers. Even in those departments of money dealings where the native has a natural claim to succeed, European enterprise has driven out native talent. We refer here to the banking enterprise of the country. As many as 323 banking companies have been established in this country since 1861, and 140 of these establishments are in active operation to this day. All these are managed by Europeans, though their dealings are for the most part with native customers, and their funds are derived to a large extent from native depositors.

RAILWAYS AND TECHNICAL TRAINING

Notwithstanding this financially burdensome and economically ruinous policy of the Government . . . the people of India would have had good reason to welcome this diversion of public funds by the State, if the vast expenditure incurred for railway construction had the effect of training the nation by suitable arrangements for their technical education, and liberal association in the management, to take up in course of time in their own hands the new sphere of industrial activity represented by railway enterprise. . . . The people of India needed above all things a technical training in mechanical arts and manufacturing processes, and pecuniary aid in the shape of State subsidies in starting new enterprises. Above all, they had to be protected from the predominance of a foreign plutocracy, with vested interests opposed to those of the Native producer. None of these considerations have attracted the attention of Government as they deserved. The system of public education, . . . is mainly intended to qualify native youths for inferior service in the State departments. The scientific branches of the service are all but sealed to the natives by reason of their education not fitting them to take their natural place in mechanical and engineering enterprises. . . . The result is that, after 25 years of continuous State direction, the natives of the country are as unfitted to take up this work of railway construction or management, as ever they were when Lord Dalhousie first sanctioned the proposal of covering India with a network of railway lines. The railway establishments in all the higher grades are a close[d] preserve for the foreigner and even the lower duties of collecting or clipping tickets are entrusted to other hands than those of the natives of the country. A few native guards and drivers and fitters are all that the companies can show in the way of training natives for higher work, and the position and status of these people are anything but comfortable. . . . Everything for the people, and nothing by the people, this was the maxim of the great Napoleon, and in no country in the world has it been more vigorously carried out than in India, where the foreigner does everything for the people, who look upon all that is done with rustic amazement.

---

[8]A term for a number of types of plain, finely woven cotton textiles.

Responses to Western Domination

Africans who saw their communal lands turned into European-owned plantations; Indians offended by the racism of British colonial officials; Chinese humiliated by their empire's military impotence; Persians who saw their country partitioned between Great Britain and Russia in 1907; Filipinos who in 1898 shed one colonial master, Spain, only to be claimed by a new one, the United States; and countless others in Asia, Africa, and Latin America — all faced the same question in the years around 1900: How should we respond to the economic strength, military power, and ever-increasing political ascendancy of the West?

For many Asians and Africans whose independence was under attack, the first response to this question was often "Fight back!" Africans fiercely resisted the European takeover of their continent, and European troops had to engage in hundreds of battles and skirmishes before securing their rule. It took the Germans twenty-five years of fighting before they finally pacified their colony, German East Africa, in 1907. In Asia the Burmese, Filipinos, and Vietnamese fought against the British, Americans, and French, respectively, before they succumbed to colonial rule.

By the early twentieth century, however, it was clear that fighting back was futile. Only Ethiopia, whose King Menelik had equipped his soldiers with modern weapons in the 1890s, successfully repulsed the European imperialists when its army defeated Italy, the least great of the great powers, at the Battle of Aduwa in 1896. Once armed resistance ended and colonial administrations were in place, asking how to respond to the West became a meaningless exercise for the colonized. "Natives" might have low-echelon jobs as clerks, policemen, or soldiers, but they had no voice in making policy. Acquiescence, at least for the time, was the only reasonable option for people under direct European rule.

India was an exception. Having been under British rule for better than a century and with a sizable number of educated Indians who had studied in British-sponsored schools, India experienced the first stirrings of nationalism in the late nineteenth century. A key step was taken in 1885 with the founding of the Indian National Congress, an organization dedicated to improving the prospects of Indians in the colonial administration and ultimately to winning Indian independence.

Debates about how to respond to the West were most intense and meaningful in those states in which Western imperialism fell short of outright political control. In China and the Ottoman Empire, for example, there were ardent Westernizers, who believed that progress and survival depended on making a clean break with the past and embracing Western values, practices, and institutions. At the opposite extreme were those who hated Western values and sought to preserve their society's unique traditions. Between these two extremes were those who represented every form of compromise between unbending traditionalism and single-minded zeal for Westernization.

China and the Foreign Devils

❖

5 ❖ TWO PROCLAMATIONS OF THE BOXER REBELLION

No country was more deeply humiliated by its inability to prevent Western aggression in the nineteenth century than China. Despite its great size, long imperial tradition, and centuries of achievement in the arts, scholarship, and technology, China experienced military defeat, punitive treaties, territorial losses, foreign political interference, and an influx of missionaries and traders from nations the Chinese had always viewed as barbaric and inferior.

The Boxer Rebellion of 1898 was partly an expression of Chinese rage over almost a century of foreign exploitation. It was also the culmination of a decades-long struggle within the imperial administration between reformers and conservatives. Reformers were convinced that only radical changes could rescue China from its domestic morass and prevent its dismemberment by foreigners. They rejected much of China's Confucian heritage, and called for the introduction of Western-style military training, industrialization, and educational reforms. Conservatives affirmed China's inherent superiority to the West, and sought to preserve the emperor's power, Confucianism's intellectual ascendancy, and China's traditional agrarian economy.

The deadlock ended in 1898 when Emperor Guangxu (r. 1875–1908) initiated the Hundred Days' Reform. With the guidance of reform-minded advisors, he issued dozens of decrees to weed out corrupt officials, streamline the government, stimulate education, reform the military, and introduce Chinese-owned banks, railroads, and newspapers. Opposition coalesced around the emperor's aunt, Empress Dowager Cixi, who in September 1898, with the help of generals and threatened officeholders, placed the emperor under house arrest and annulled his reforms. To further their conservative, antiforeign agenda, in 1899 Cixi and her supporters encouraged the popular movement led by a Chinese secret society known as the "Righteous and Harmonious Fists." The result was the Boxer Rebellion, another sad chapter in the history of Chinese-Western relations.

The Society of Righteous and Harmonious Fists, known to Westerners as Boxers because their formal exercises resembled boxing, was one of many secret societies that flourished in late imperial China. The Boxers believed that foreigners, especially foreign missionaries, were the cause of China's problems. In 1899 they launched a murder campaign against foreign missionaries and business owners, many of whom fled to Beijing for protection in the foreign legation quarter. The Boxers pursued them and, encouraged by Cixi and her followers, placed the legation quarter under siege. A force of European, Japanese, and U.S. troops easily lifted the siege, and in 1901 China was forced to sign another humiliating treaty, the Boxer Protocol, which among other things required an indemnity payment of $333,900,000.

As the Boxer movement gathered strength in 1900, the Boxers posted and distributed thousands of proclamations in the hope of gaining followers. The two following selections are representative samples.

QUESTIONS FOR ANALYSIS

1. What do these proclamations reveal about the Boxers' vision of China's future?
2. What is the Boxer attitude toward Western technology?
3. According to the Boxers, what evils have resulted from the foreign presence in China?
4. Why were the Boxers confident of their ultimate victory?

The Gods assist the Boxers,
The Patriotic Harmonious corps,
It is because the "Foreign Devils" disturb the "Middle Kingdom."
Urging the people to join their religion,
To turn their backs on Heaven,
Venerate not the Gods and forget the ancestors.

Men violate the human obligations,
Women commit adultery,
"Foreign Devils" are not produced by mankind,
If you do not believe,
Look at them carefully.

The eyes of all the "Foreign Devils" are bluish,
No rain falls,
The earth is getting dry,
This is because the churches stop Heaven,
The Gods are angry;
The Genii[1] are vexed;
Both come down from the mountain to deliver the doctrine.

This is no hearsay,

The practices of boxing will not be in vain;

Reciting incantations and pronouncing magic words,
Burn up yellow written prayers,
Light incense sticks
To invite the Gods and Genii of all the grottoes.

The Gods come out from grottoes,
The Genii come down from mountains,
Support the human bodies to practice the boxing.

When all the military accomplishments or tactics
Are fully learned,
It will not be difficult to exterminate the "Foreign Devils" then.

Push aside the railway tracks,
Pull out the telegraph poles,
Immediately after this destroy the steamers.

The great France
Will grow cold and downhearted.
The English and Russians will certainly disperse.

Let the various "Foreign Devils" all be killed.
May the whole Elegant Empire of the Great Qing Dynasty be ever prosperous!

---

[1]Minor spirits.

Attention: all people in markets and villages of all provinces in China — now, owing to the fact that Catholics and Protestants have vilified our gods and sages, have deceived our emperors and ministers above, and oppressed the Chinese people below, both our gods and our people are angry at them, yet we have to keep silent. This forces us to practise the Yike[2] magic boxing so as to protect our country, expel the foreign bandits and kill Christian converts, in order to save our people from miserable suffering. After this notice is issued to instruct you villagers, no matter which village you are living in, if there are Christian converts, you ought to get rid of them quickly. The churches which belong to them should be unreservedly burned down. Everyone who intends to spare someone, or to disobey our order by concealing Christian converts, will be punished according to the regulation when we come to his place, and he will be burned to death to prevent his impeding our program. We especially do not want to punish anyone by death without warning him first. We cannot bear to see you suffer innocently. Don't disobey this special notice!

---

[2]Yike means "United in Righteousness." It identifies the type of martial arts (yikequan) practiced by the boxers.

"Freedom Is My Birthright"

❖

6 ❖ *Bal Gangadhar Tilak,* SPEECH TO THE INDIAN NATIONAL CONGRESS, 1907

Living in a country that had seen many conquerors, most Indians greeted the increase of British authority on the subcontinent from the 1770s onward with indifference. Some, who anticipated benefits from Western science and law, even greeted it with approval. By the end of the nineteenth century, however, disillusionment with the British and opposition to colonialism were growing. Such feelings were strongest among middle-class Hindus, especially those who had been educated in British-sponsored schools and held posts in the Indian Civil Service. They resented the colonial administration's economic policies and its failure to give Indians anything but menial government jobs. In 1885 dissatisfied Indians formed the Indian National Congress, a moderate group dedicated to achieving a greater Indian voice in government and ultimately independence.

In 1906, however, the annual meeting of the Congress was rocked by a bitter conflict precipitated by a split between the Moderates, who endorsed the Congress's policy of cooperation with the British and gradual reform, and the Extremists, who sought the immediate expulsion of the British — if necessary, through violence. Frustration with British rule had earlier reached a flash point when in 1905 the British announced the partition of the province of Bengal, with one part to be predominantly Hindu and the other predominantly Muslim. The British claimed that administrative efficiency dictated the change, but the Indians considered it another example of British high-handedness and an effort to weaken Indian nationalism by encouraging religious antagonism. Support grew for the Extremists, who formed a new organization within the Congress called the New Party.

The leading spokesman of the New Party was Bal Gangadhar Tilak (1856–1920), a scholar and religious philosopher who, as the editor of a widely read Marathi-language newspaper, thundered against the evils of British rule and defended Hindu traditions. His mottos — "Militancy not Mendicancy" and "Freedom Is My Birthright, and I Shall Have It" — spread throughout India. The British considered him a rabble-rouser and imprisoned him in 1897 and 1908 for sedition. He delivered the following speech to the 1906 meeting of the Indian National Congress at which the Moderate-Extremist split surfaced. In it he outlines the New Party's beliefs and expresses his support for the newly organized boycott movement.

QUESTIONS FOR ANALYSIS

1. According to Tilak, what are the major differences between the Moderates and the Extremists?
2. In Tilak's view, why were many Indians at first convinced that British rule was a good thing?
3. Why, according to Tilak, have most Indians become disillusioned with British rule?
4. What does Tilak mean by "boycott?" Does it mean an economic boycott only?
5. What is Tilak's ultimate goal for India?

. . . One thing is granted, namely, that this government does not suit us. As has been said by an eminent statesman — the government of one country by another can never be a successful, and therefore, a permanent government. There is no difference of opinion about this fundamental proposition between the old and new schools. One fact is that this alien government has ruined the country. In the beginning, all of us were taken by surprise. We were almost dazed. We thought that everything that the rulers did was for our good and that this English government has descended from the clouds to save us from the invasions of Tamerlane and Genghis Khan,[1] and, as they say, not only from foreign invasions but from internecine warfare, or the internal or external invasions, as they call it. We felt happy for a time, but it soon came to light that the peace which

was established in this country did this . . . — that we were prevented from going at each other's throats, so that a foreigner might go at the throat of us all. *Pax Britannica* has been established in this country in order that a foreign government may exploit the country. That this is the effect of this *Pax Britannica* is being gradually realized in these days. It was an unhappy circumstance that it was not realized sooner. We believed in the benevolent intentions of the government, but in politics there is no benevolence. Benevolence is used to sugar-coat the declarations of self-interest and we were in those days deceived by the apparent benevolent intentions under which rampant self-interest was concealed. That was our state then. But soon a change came over us. English education, growing poverty, and better familiarity with our rulers, opened our eyes and our

[1]Genghis (also Chingis or Jenghis) Khan (ca. 1167–1277) was the Mongol conqueror who founded the largest land empire in history. By the time of his death he ruled an area that stretched from the Pacific to the Black Sea and from Siberia to Southeast Asia. Tamerlane, or Timur the Lame (1336–1405), of Turco-Mongol descent, was another famous conqueror who invaded India and took Delhi in 1398.

leaders'; especially, the venerable leader[2] who presided over the recent Congress was the first to tell us that the drain from the country was ruining it, and if the drain was to continue, there was some great disaster awaiting us. So terribly convinced was he of this that he went over from here to England and spent twenty-five years of his life in trying to convince the English people of the injustice that is being done to us. He worked very hard. He had conversations and interviews with secretaries of state, with members of Parliament — and with what result?

He has come here at the age of eighty-two to tell us that he is bitterly disappointed. . . .

You can now understand the difference between the old and the new parties. Appeals to the bureaucracy are hopeless. On this point both the new and old parties are agreed. The old party believes in appealing to the British nation and we do not. That being our position, it logically follows we must have some other method. There is another alternative. We are not going to sit down quiet. We shall have some other method by which to achieve what we want. We are not disappointed, we are not pessimists. It is the hope of achieving the goal by our own efforts that has brought into existence this new party. . . .

We have come forward with a scheme which if you accept [it], shall better enable you to remedy this state of things than the scheme of the old school. Your industries are ruined utterly, ruined by foreign rule; your wealth is going out of the country and you are reduced to the lowest level which no human being can occupy. In this state of things, is there any other remedy by which you can help yourself? The remedy is not petitioning but boycott. We say prepare your forces, organize your power, and then go to work so that they cannot refuse you what you

demand. . . . We are not armed, and there is no necessity for arms either. We have a stronger weapon, a political weapon, in boycott. We have perceived one fact, that the whole of this administration, which is carried on by a handful of Englishmen, is carried on with our assistance. We are all in subordinate service. This whole government is carried on with our assistance and they try to keep us in ignorance of our power of cooperation between ourselves by which that which is in our own hands at present can be claimed by us and administrated by us. The point is to have the entire control in our hands. I want to have the key of my house, and not merely one stranger turned out of it. Self-government is our goal; we want a control over our administrative machinery. We don't want to become clerks and remain clerks. At present, we are clerks and willing instruments of our own oppression in the hands of an alien government, and that government is ruling over us not by its innate strength but by keeping us in ignorance and blindness to the perception of this fact. . . . What the new party wants you to do is to realize the fact that your future rests entirely in your own hands. If you mean to be free, you can be free; if you do not mean to be free, you will fall and be for ever fallen. So many of you need not like arms; but if you have not the power of active resistance, have you not the power of self-denial and self-abstinence in such a way as not to assist this foreign government to rule over you? This is boycott and this is what is meant when we say, boycott is a political weapon. We shall not give them assistance to collect revenue and keep peace. We shall not assist them in fighting beyond the frontiers or outside India with Indian blood and money. We shall not assist them in carrying on the administration of justice. We shall have our own courts, and when time comes we shall not pay taxes. Can

[2]A reference to Dadabhai Naoroji (1825–1917), founder and, at the time of Tilak's speech, president of the Indian National Congress. Born into a prominent Hindu family, Naoroji abandoned a career as a mathematician to live in England, where he tried to convince the government to improve conditions in India. While in England he was elected to Parliament in 1892. Naoroji formulated the concept of the "drain," the process by which Britain systematically depleted Indian wealth and resources.

you do that by your united efforts? If you can, you are free from tomorrow. . . . This is a lesson of progress, a lesson of helping yourself as much as possible, and if you really perceive the force of it, if you are convinced by these arguments, then and then only is it possible for you to effect your salvation from the alien rule under which you labor at this moment.

There are many other points but it is impossible to exhaust them all in an hour's speech. If you carry any wrong impression come and get your doubts solved. We are prepared to answer every objection, solve every doubt, and prove every statement. We want your cooperation; without your help we cannot do anything singlehanded. We beg of you, we appeal to you, to think over the question, to see the situation, and realize it, and after realizing it to come to our assistance, and by our joint assistance to help in the salvation of the country.

A Blueprint for Japanese Military Modernization

❖

7 ◆ Yamagata Aritomo, OPINION ON MILITARY AFFAIRS AND CONSCRIPTION

Japan's response to the West had no parallels anywhere else in the world. Under the government of the Tokugawa shoguns, who took power in the early 1600s, Japan had pursued a policy of commercial and cultural isolation until Commodore Perry arrived on behalf of the U.S. government in 1853 and forced Japan to open its ports to foreign trade. Dreading the prospect of foreign domination and disillusioned with the ineffectual response of the Tokugawa government, in 1868 aristocrats led by the Satsuma and Chosu clans seized power and reinstated the emperor, until then a figurehead living in seclusion in Kyoto, as head of the Japanese state. The emperor took Meiji as his reign name, and hence the events of 1868 are known as the Meiji Restoration.

During the Meiji Era (1878–1912), a small group of aristocratic reformers, claiming to act on behalf of the emperor, embarked upon a vigorous program of Westernization in keeping with their motto "Enrich the Nation, Strengthen the Army." In short order, they abolished the shogunate, stripped the feudal aristocrats, or samurai, of their privileges, and plunged headlong into modernizing the economy. Railroads, steamships, factories, the telegraph, and silk mills along with Western dress and even baseball became part of Japanese life. The ultimate goal, however, was to build a strong army and navy to keep the Westerners at bay and make Japan a power to be reckoned with in Asia. The Meiji reformers were spectacularly successful, as victories over China in 1895 and Russia in 1905 amply proved.

Few individuals played a more important role in the history of Meiji Japan than did Yamagata Aritomo (1838–1922), best known as the architect of the Japanese army, but also a statesman who influenced economic policy, education, and the writing of Japan's constitution. Born into a low-ranking samurai family, he committed himself to the antiforeign, antishogun movements of the 1860s and was a supporter of the imperial restoration. The new regime immediately assigned him its most pressing task, the modernization of Japan's military. After an eighteen-month trip to Europe to observe military practices, he submitted the following memorandum to Japan's leaders on the nation's military needs. One year later, in 1873, he framed the imperial decree that established Japan's conscript army.

QUESTIONS FOR ANALYSIS

1. According to Yamagata, why is it necessary for Japan to strengthen its army and navy?
2. What are some of the lessons Yamagata learned from his observations of Western military practices?
3. In his view, what lessons should Japan learn specifically from the example of Belgium and the Netherlands?
4. What can you infer from this document about the arguments being made by opponents to a military build-up?
5. On the basis of Yamagata's proposals, what might you conclude about the ways Japan's new military affected Japanese society as a whole?

. . . The status of our armed forces today is as follows: We have the so-called Imperial Guards whose functions are nothing more than to protect the sacred person of His Majesty and to guard the Imperial Palace. We have altogether more than twenty battalions manning the four military garrisons who are deployed to maintain domestic tranquility, and are not equipped to fight against any foreign threat. As to our navy, we have a few battleships yet to be completed. How can they be sufficient to counteract foreign threats? . . .

The first concern of the Ministry of Military Affairs is to set up a system to defend our homeland. For this purpose two categories of soldiers are required: a standing army and those on the reserve list. The number of troops differ from country to country. Of the major countries, Russia maintains the largest number of troops and the United States the smallest. The reason for this discrepancy comes from the fact that the governmental system differs from one country to another. Consequently the regulations governing each of the countries also differ. The Netherlands and Belgium are among the smallest countries, but they are located between large countries, and in order to avoid contempt and scorn from their neighbors, they diligently go about the business of defending their countries. Even though one of these countries has a total area not exceeding one-third of the area of our country, it maintains a standing army numbering not less than forty to fifty thousand. If we apply the existing standards prevailing in our country to judge these two countries, they may appear to be concerned only with military affairs to the neglect of other matters. However, they do attend to hundreds of other affairs of state and do not abandon them. This is possible because their national goals are already set, and they can act accordingly to implement them.

At a time like this it is very clear where the priority of this country must lie. We must now have a well-trained standing army supplemented by a large number of reservists. We must build warships and construct batteries. We must train officers and soldiers. We must manufacture and store weapons and ammunitions. The nation may consider that it cannot bear the expenses. However, even if we wish to ignore it, this important matter cannot disappear from us. . . .

Therefore the creation of a standing army for our country is a task which cannot be delayed. It is recommended that a certain number of strong and courageous young men be selected from each of the prefectures in accordance with the size of the prefectures, and that such young men be trained in the Western-type military science and placed under rigorous drills, so that they may by deployed as occasion demands. . . . All of the countries in Europe have reservists, and amongst them Prussia has most of them. There is not a single able-bodied man in Prussia who is not trained in military affairs. Recently Prussia and France fought each other and the former won handily.[1] This is due in large measure to the strength of its reservists.

It is recommended that our country adopt a system under which any able-bodied man twenty years of age be drafted into military service, unless his absence from home will create undue hardship for his family. There shall be no distinction made between the common man and those who are of the samurai class. They shall all be formed into ranks, and after completion of a period of service, they shall be returned to their homes.[2] In this way every man will become a soldier, and not a single region in the country will be without defense. Thus our defense will become complete.

The second concern of the Ministry is coastal defense. This includes building of warships and constructing coastal batteries. . . . Our country has thousands of miles of coastline, and any mobile corner of our country can become the advance post of our enemy. However, since it is not possible to construct batteries along the coastline everywhere, it is imperative to expand our navy and construct the largest warships. . . .

The third concern of the Military is to create resources for the navy and the army. There are three items under consideration, namely military academics, a bureau of military supplies, and a bureau of munitions depots. It is not difficult to have one million soldiers in a short time but it is difficult to gain one good officer during the same span of time. Military academies are intended to train officers for these two services. If we pay little attention to this need today, we shall not be able to have the services of capable officers for another day. Therefore, without delay military academies must be created and be allowed to prosper. Students shall be adequately trained by the faculty consisting of experts from several countries. . . . The bureau of military supplies shall be in charge of procuring military provisions and manufacturing weapons of war for the two services. The bureau of munitions depots shall store such provisions and munitions. If we lack military provisions and weapons and our munitions depots are empty, what good will the million soldiers in the army or thousands of warships do? Therefore, well-qualified craftsmen from various countries must be hired to make necessary machines and build strong storage houses. We must make our own weapons and store them, and must become self-sufficient without relying on foreign countries. The goal is to create a sufficient amount and if there is any surplus it may be sold to other countries.

Some people may argue that while they are aware of the urgency in the need for the Ministry of Military Affairs, they cannot permit the entire national resources to be committed to the need of one ministry alone. . . . This argument fails to discern the fundamental issues. The recommendations herein presented by the Ministry of Military Affairs in no way asks for the stoppage of all governmental activities or for the monopolization of all government revenues. But in a national emergency, a new set of priorities must be established. Those of us who are given the task of governing must learn from the past, discern the present, and weigh all matters carefully.

---

[1] A reference to the Franco-Prussian War (1870–1871), in which the German states under the leadership of Prussia defeated the French.

[2] This means they will become reservists.

In the past there was Emperor Peter[3] who was determined to make his country a great nation. He went overseas and studied naval sciences. After his return he built many battleships and constructed St. Petersburg. He created a standing army numbering several million, and was able to engage in the art of international politics against five or six of the strongest nations. . . . It is to him that the credit is due for making Russia a great nation.

Those of us who govern must first of all discern the conditions prevailing in the world, set up priorities and take appropriate measures. In our opinion Russia has been acting very arrogantly. Previously, contrary to the provisions of the Treaty of Sevastopol[4] she placed her warships in the Black Sea. Southward, she has shown her aggressive intent toward Muslim countries and toward India. Westward, she has crossed the borders of Manchuria and has been navigating the Amur River. Her intents being thus, it is inevitable that she will move eastward sooner or later by sending troops to Hokkaido,[5] and then taking advantage of the seasonal wind move to the warmer areas.

---

[3]A reference to Peter the Great, tsar of Russia from 1689 to 1725, famous for his efforts to Westernize Russia. Much of what Yamagata claims about Peter is exaggerated, either because he received false information or because he intentionally distorted the facts. His statements that Peter constructed "many battleships," recruited an army of "several million," and fought "five or six" strong nations are inaccurate.

[4]Yamagata seems to be referring to the 1858 Treaty of Paris, which ended the Crimean War; it denied the defeated Russians access to the Black Sea. Sevastopol is a city on the Black Sea.
[5]A Japanese island north of Honshu.

◆

Migrants and Their Experiences

Migration — over land and water, by laborers and conquerors, hunters and herdsmen, farmers and traders — has always been a part of human history. In the years around 1900, however, people were on the move in unprecedented numbers. Southern blacks were moving to northern cities in the United States; rural Europeans were moving to new industrial centers; Indians left for Southeast Asia, the Caribbean, Africa, and South America; Chinese were moving to Malaya, Singapore, and the Americas. Most dramatically of all, millions of Europeans were migrating to the United States, Argentina, Australia, New Zealand, and Canada.

As in the past, population pressure was an incentive to move. China's population increased from approximately 142 million in the mid eighteenth century to 432 million around 1850, and to better than 450 million in 1900. India's population increased from approximately 150 million in 1850 to 250 million in 1881, while the population of Europe grew from 187 million in 1800 to 266 million by midcentury, and 435 million by 1914. This demographic surge ruined the economic prospects of many peasants and agricultural workers, who faced land shortages at a time when rural unemployment was growing as a result of the commercialization and mechanization of agriculture.

Economic necessity drove millions of Europeans and smaller numbers of Asians to seek new lives in Australia, New Zealand, and especially the Americas. Steamships made long-distance travel across the world's oceans cheaper, more reliable, and quicker than in the age of sailing ships. By the end of the nineteenth century, crossing the Atlantic was so inexpensive that it made economic sense for Italian workers known as "swallows" to travel to Argentina every year to harvest the wheat crop, then return home.

How were immigrants greeted in their new homelands? What experiences did they have? The documents in this section provide some answers to these questions.

Indian Merchants in South Africa and Their Problems

◆

8 ◆ *Abdool Rehman,*
MEMORANDUM TO LORD SELBORNE, HIGH COMMISSIONER OF TRANSVAAL, OCTOBER 1905

Although Indians had traded on the east African coast for centuries, only in the nineteenth century did they begin to settle in Africa's interior. In the 1880s and 1890s approximately thirty-two thousand indentured Indian laborers worked on the construction of the East Africa Railway, which on its completion stretched from the Kenyan port of Mombasa all the way to Lake Victoria in Uganda. Elsewhere in Africa most Indian immigrants were indentured farm laborers, imported to work five-year stints on European-owned plantations. Approximately a quarter of these laborers remained in Africa after their five years of required service, and they were joined by increasing numbers of "passenger Indians" who paid their own way. Among these was Mohandas Gandhi, later the leader of the Indian independence movement, who practiced law in South Africa between 1893 and 1914.

By 1900 approximately one hundred thousand Indians lived in Natal, a British territory on the east coast of South Africa. Smaller numbers lived in Transvaal, a republic to the north of Natal that for several decades had been a source of conflict between the British, who had annexed the territory in 1877, and the Dutch-speaking Boers, who had rebelled against British rule in 1880–1881 and won back their independence. After the defeat of the Boers in the Boer, or South African, War (1899–1902), Transvaal again came under British rule. In Natal and Transvaal Indians were laborers, small farmers, cooks, waiters, clerks, masons, and carpenters, but most were merchants who sold their wares in small shops, on street corners as hawkers, or door-to-door. Indian merchants encountered intense opposition from white competitors, who successfully pressured officials in Natal and Transvaal to withhold licenses from Indian merchants or charge them prohibitive licensing fees. The Indians responded by hiring lawyers, forming political organizations, and deluging government officials with letters and petitions.

The following letter was written by Abdool Rehman, an Indian merchant who was secretary of the Indian Association in the Transvaal town of Potchefstroom.

He sent the letter to the highest-ranking British official in South Africa, High Commissioner Lord Selborne, to answer criticisms of Indian merchants made by a white merchants' association, the Anti-Asiatic Vigilance Society.

QUESTIONS FOR ANALYSIS

1. What allegations against the Indian merchant community have been made by the Anti-Asiatic Vigilance Society?
2. How would you characterize Rehman's response to these allegations?
3. What can be learned about the characteristics of Indian trade in Transvaal from Rehman's letter?
4. Aside from the difficulties experienced by the merchants, what other forms of discrimination were encountered by Indians in Transvaal?
5. What does the source reveal about general attitudes toward Indians on the part of Transvaal's white population?

Did we not know that what has been called the Anti-Asiatic Vigilance Society is to make representations to Your Excellency with reference to the British Indians, so far as regards Potchefstroom, we would not have given any trouble whatsoever to Your Excellency, especially as we are aware that Your Excellency is to meet very shortly a deputation of the British Indian Association at Johannesburg.[1]

Mr. Loveday it was who stated that Potchefstroom was being inundated with indentured Indians from Natal. To this we beg to give an emphatic contradiction. Some of us know the Natal laws, and we know that [it] is next to impossible for an indentured Indian to escape. In any case not a single instance has been brought forward to prove the statement above referred to.

Another statement was made by the mayor of Johannesburg when he was here. He is reported to have said that, whereas there were nineteen licences issued to Asiatics before the war,[2] now there were ninety-six traders' licences and thirty-seven hawkers'[3] licences. This statement, so far as

traders are concerned, is not true. We supplied before the war a list of British Indian traders in the town of Potchefstroom to the British Agent, and there were twenty-two British Indian stores in the town of Potchefstroom, as distinguished from the district. We have a true copy of the list that was sent to the British Agent, and we are today in a position, not only to give the names, but to locate each of the store-keepers. Seeing that Mr. Goch[4] mentions ninety-six traders' licences in connection with the nineteen before the war, we take it that he refers to ninety-six traders' licences for the town of Potchefstroom. If so, this is grossly untrue. There are only twenty-four British Indian stores in this town at the present day. We state this with a full sense of responsibility and knowledge, and we challenge our detractors to prove the contrary.

A third statement that has been made against us in Potchefstroom is with reference to the so-called insanitary condition of our dwellings and shops. These, indeed, speak for themselves, but when the charge was made, we took the

---

[1] Apparently a member of the Anti-Asiatic Vigilance Society.
[2] The South African War (1899–1902), also known as the Boer War, resulted in a hard-fought British victory over South Africans of Dutch descent who sought independence from British rule.
[3] Street vendors.
[4] The mayor of Johannesburg.

opportunity of showing our places to the district surgeon of Potchefstroom, and the following is the report that [he] gave:

In going through the various premises, I am pleased to say I was greatly impressed with the general condition of each place I visited, both internally as well as externally. Taking all things into consideration, the backyards are all perfectly clean and sanitary. I saw no accumulation of rubbish, this I understand being carried away daily by the contractor. The bucket system is enforced as in other parts of the town, which is also attended to by the Sanitary Department, and I can find no fault from what I saw. There appears to me to be no overcrowding as regards sleeping accommodation. At the back of each business premise, in addition, I noticed a kind of mess room capable of seating about five to eight persons, and each has its own kitchen; these are also well kept.

We mention these things to show under what disadvantages, we have to labour, and what misrepresentations are made against us. We have no hesitation in saying that the whole of the anti-Asiatic agitation is due to trade jealousy. Nothing can be further from our wish than to enter into an unfair competition with the white store-keepers.

Much has been said against our mode of life. We are proud to think that we are sober and simple in our habits, and if thereby we have an advantage over the rival white traders, we hardly think that it should be brought up against us in order to traduce and degrade us. It is totally forgotten, in this connection, by those who denounce us, that the white traders have other advantages which we cannot dream of having, namely their European connection, their knowledge of the English language, and their better organising powers. Moreover, we are able to carry on our trade only because of the goodwill of the poor whites, and our ability to please the poorest class of customers; also, we have the support of wholesale European houses.

It has been said that our competition resulted in many European shops being closed. We deny this. In the first instance, some of the shops that have been closed were not shops with which we could possibly enter into competition, for instance hairdressers and others. Some general goods stores have undoubtedly closed, but to connect their closing with Asiatic competition would be [as] unfair as to connect the closing of several Asiatic shops with European competition in this town. There is trade depression all over South Africa, and it has only resulted in getting rid of overtrading that was indulged in soon after the war, based, as it was, on high expectations which have never been fulfilled.

May we also, in this connection, state that much of the agitation against us is kept up not by bona-fide British subjects but by aliens who can have very little indeed to complain of against us. The policy adopted to drive us out of the township is a policy of irritation and insults which, though petty in themselves, are galling enough to be very much felt by us.

Without the slightest occasion, we are now served at special counters in the Post Office. We are debarred from having a breath of fresh air in a park which is called a 'public' park, and which is kept up from rates which we are called upon to pay in common with other citizens. We mention these instances to draw Your Excellency's attention to the awkward position in which we are placed without any fault of ours. No opportunity is missed of degrading us and humiliating us. We do not wish to burden Your Excellency with such other instances. We have a right, we submit, to expect the British Government to protect us from such humiliation, and insure for us that freedom to which, as loyal British subjects, we are entitled wherever the Union Jack flies.

We beg to thank Your Excellency for giving us a patient hearing, and in conclusion hope that, as a result of Your Excellency's visit to this township, there will be an amelioration in our condition.

"The Gates Should No Longer Be Left Unguarded"

◈

9 ◆ *Henry Cabot Lodge,*
SPEECH TO THE UNITED STATES SENATE,
MARCH 16, 1896

In the decades following the Civil War, immigration to the United States reached new heights, with more than twenty million new arrivals between 1870 and 1910. Although these millions included appreciable numbers of Japanese and Chinese, close to 98 percent of them came from Europe. Unlike previous European migrants, who mostly had come from England, Germany, and, beginning in the 1840s, Ireland, migrants of the late nineteenth century mainly were from Italy, the Austro-Hungarian Empire, Russia, and Poland (which was mostly under Russian rule). Most were Roman Catholics or, in the case of many of the emigrants from Poland and Russia, Jews.

Anti-immigrant sentiment, or nativism, which had flared up in the 1840s and 1850s in response to the influx of the Irish, again became a powerful force in American life. Workers and small business owners worried about competition from the new immigrants; many Protestants were troubled by the growing numbers of Catholics and Jews; and Americans in general wondered if the republic could survive if the country was overrun by people unfamiliar with democracy and constitutional government. Anti-immigrant prejudice was given a "scientific" justification by contemporary racial theories, which ranked the world's races in a hierarchy with northern Europeans (except the Irish) at the top. Although there was some disagreement about other peoples' exact "ranking," most experts agreed that among Europeans, Italians, Slavs, and Jews were at the bottom, but at least were superior to Asians and Africans.

Anti-immigrant groups had some legislative success. In 1870 Congress passed the Naturalization Act, which barred the Chinese from citizenship. This was followed in 1882 by the Chinese Exclusion Act, which barred Chinese immigration altogether. Then in the 1890s the Immigration Restriction League (IRL), founded in 1894, proposed legislation to require new immigrants to pass a literacy test, which, IRL members hoped, the least desirable would fail.

A leader in the fight for immigration restriction was Henry Cabot Lodge, a member of a distinguished Boston family who served in the House of Representatives from 1887 to 1893 and the Senate from 1893 until his death in 1924. He presented the following remarks to the Senate in support of anti-immigration legislation under consideration in 1896. The bill failed to pass, and millions of immigrants continued to pour into the United States until Congress passed a series of restrictive laws in the 1920s.

QUESTIONS FOR ANALYSIS

1. What, according to Lodge, distinguishes "desirable" and "undesirable" immigrants?
2. What fears does Lodge entertain about the future of the United States unless immigration is restricted?
3. What are Lodge's views of race, and how do they affect his attitude toward immigration? According to Lodge, what are the qualities of the various "races" he discusses?
4. The bill Lodge supported was defeated in the Senate. What arguments against immigration restriction do you think were made by the bill's opponents?

. . . The question before the committee was . . . by what method the largest number of undesirable immigrants and the smallest possible number of desirable immigrants could be shut out. Three methods of obtaining this further restriction have been widely discussed of late years and in various forms have been brought to the attention of Congress. The first was the imposition of a capitation tax on all immigrants. . . .

The second scheme was to restrict immigration by requiring consular certification of immigrants. . . .[1]

The third method was to exclude all immigrants who could neither read nor write, and this is the plan which was adopted by the committee and which is embodied in this bill. . . . It is found, in the first place, that the illiteracy test will bear most heavily upon the Italians, Russians, Poles, Hungarians, Greeks, and Asiatics, and very lightly, or not at all, upon English-speaking emigrants or Germans, Scandinavians, and French. In other words, the races most affected by the illiteracy test are those whose emigration to this country has begun within the last twenty years and swelled rapidly to enormous proportions, races with which the English-speaking people have never hitherto assimilated, and who are most alien to the great body of the people of the United States.

On the other hand, immigrants from the United Kingdom and of those races which are most closely related to the English-speaking people, and who with the English-speaking people themselves founded the American colonies and built up the United States, are affected but little by the proposed test. . . . These kindred races also are those who alone go to the Western and Southern states, where immigrants are desired, and take up our unoccupied lands. The races which would suffer most seriously . . . furnish the immigrants who do not go to the West or South, where immigration is needed, but who remain on the Atlantic seaboard, where immigration is not needed and where their presence is most injurious and undesirable. . . .

It now remains for me to discuss the second and larger question, as to the advisability of restricting immigration at all. . . . It has two sides, the economic and the social. As to the former, but few words are necessary. There is no one thing which does so much to bring about a reduction of wages and to injure the American wage earner as the unlimited introduction of cheap foreign labor through unrestricted immigration. Statistics show that the change in the race character of our immigration has been accompanied by a corresponding decline in its

---

[1]U.S. consuls in overseas cities would judge immigration eligibility.

quality. The number of skilled mechanics and of persons trained to some occupation or pursuit has fallen off, while the number of those without occupation or training, that is, who are totally unskilled, has risen in our recent immigration to enormous proportions. This low, unskilled labor is the most deadly enemy of the American wage earner, and does more than anything else toward lowering his wages and forcing down his standard of living. . . .

. . . There is no danger, at present at all events, to our workingmen from the coming of skilled mechanics or of trained and educated men with a settled occupation or pursuit, for immigrants of this class will never seek to lower the American standard of life and wages. On the contrary, they desire the same standard for themselves. . . .

I now come to the aspect of this question which is greater and more serious than any other. . . . That which it concerns us to know and that which is more vital to us as a people than all possible questions of tariff or currency is whether the quality of our citizenship is endangered by the present course and character of immigration to the United States. To determine this question intelligently we must look into the history of our race. . . .

The English-speaking race . . . has been made slowly during the centuries. Nothing has happened thus far to radically change it here. In the United States, after allowing for the variations produced by new climatic influences and changed conditions of life and of political institutions, it is still in the great essentials fundamentally the same race. . . . Analysis shows that the actual mixture of blood in the English-speaking race is very small, and that while the English-speaking people are derived through different channels, no doubt, there is among them nonetheless an overwhelming preponderance of the same race stock, that of the great Germanic tribes who reached from Norway to the Alps. They have been welded together by more than a thousand years of wars, conquests, migrations, and struggles, both at home and abroad, and in so doing they have attained a fixity and definiteness of national character unknown to any other people. . . .

When we speak of a race, then, we do not mean its expressions in art or in language, or its achievements in knowledge. We mean the moral and intellectual characters, which in their association make the soul of a race and which represent the product of all its past, the inheritance of all its ancestors, and the motives of all its conduct. The men of each race possess an indestructible stock of ideas, traditions, sentiments, modes of thought, an unconscious inheritance from their ancestors, upon which argument has no effect. . . . These are the qualities which determine their social efficiency as a people, which make one race rise and another fall. . . .

Those qualities are moral far more than intellectual, and its is on the moral qualities of the English-speaking race that our history, our victories, and all our future rest. There is only one way in which you can lower those qualities or weaken those characteristics and that is by breeding them out. If a lower race mixes with a higher in sufficient numbers, history teaches us that the lower race will prevail. The lower race will absorb the higher, not the higher the lower, when the two strains approach equality in numbers. In other words, there is a limit to the capacity of any race for assimilating and elevating an inferior race, and when you begin to pour in unlimited numbers people of alien or lower races of less social efficiency and less moral force, you are running the most frightful risk that any people can run. The lowering of a great race means not only its own decline but that of human civilization. . . .

The time has certainly come, if not to stop at least to check, to sift, and to restrict those immigrants. In careless strength, with generous hand, we have kept our gates wide open to all the world. If we do not close them, we should at least place sentinels beside them to challenge those who would pass through. The gates which admit men to United States and to citizenship in the great republic should no longer be left unguarded.

CHAPTER 2

Seeds of Change: Politics, Society, and Culture

It is a truism that every historical era carries within it the seeds of future change. This was never more the case than in the forty years that preceded the outbreak of World War I in 1914. Those living through these decades experienced remarkable changes themselves — the colonization of Africa and Asia; the ongoing shrinkage of time and space through railroads, steamships, and the telegraph; industrial growth and rapid urbanization; and in Western nations, the steady advance of democracy and liberalism accompanied by the broad acceptance of middle-class values and culture. Those of the prewar generation who lived into the 1920s and 1930s were stunned by how much of their pre-1914 world was swept away in the onrush of postwar revolution, cultural change, and social conflict, and by their realization of the extent to which these upheavals had been anticipated by events and developments before the war.

This was especially true in Europe and the rest of the Western world. The years before World War I had seen the triumph of the railroad, steamship, and telegraph, but also inventions that would relegate them to secondary importance — the telephone in 1876, the automobile in the 1890s, and the airplane in 1903. The prewar years had seen the almost universal acceptance of liberal, parliamentary governments, but also the emergence of antidemocratic philosophies that in the 1920s and 1930s brought many liberal democracies to ruin. The years before World War I had seen the ascendancy of middle-class, "Victorian" values of patriarchy, religion, and morality, but also the appearance of militant feminism and the emergence of a cultural and artistic avant-garde committed to the demolition of bourgeois taste and sensibilities. The late nineteenth and early twentieth centuries had been years of peace, but also of growing nationalist fervor and militarism, the two prime causes of World War I.

Seeds of future change were also apparent in the non-Western world before World War I. The founding of the moderate Indian National Congress in 1885 and the emergence just twenty years later of an aggressive "Extremist" faction within it were indications of nationalism's explosive power among the victims of colonialism. Japan's successful modernization and subsequent aggression in East Asia revealed that neither industrialization nor imperialist expansion would remain Western monopolies. More fundamentally, revolutions in the Ottoman Empire, Iran, and China revealed that some Asian societies were discarding centuries-old traditions that had rendered their early response to the West so ineffectual. There also were signs — primarily the Mexican Revolution of 1911 — that some Latin Americans were prepared to seek broader and more sweeping solutions to their problems of poverty, dictatorship, and inequality. In all these ways, the decades before World War I prepared the way for the momentous transformations that were to follow.

◆

Revolutionaries and Revolutions in the Early 1900s

Because revolutions occur in societies already undergoing intellectual, economic, and social transformations, until the twentieth century they took place mainly in Western Europe and the Americas, where economic and intellectual changes undermined traditional notions of aristocratic privilege, ecclesiastical power, and authoritarian government. England's seventeenth-century revolutions blocked royal absolutism, preserved and expanded the powers of Parliament, and strengthened the principle of constitutionalism. Revolutions in Britain's Thirteen Colonies and in Latin America between the 1770s and the 1810s affirmed the principle of freedom from colonial domination and, in the case of the United States, created a new type of government based on personal liberty and limited democracy.

Of all the West's revolutions, the French Revolution (1789–1799) was by far the most significant. It involved more social groups, was more violent and more democratic in its outcome, and inspired Europe's first nationalist movements. Its memory helped spark revolutionary movements across Europe in 1820, 1830, and 1848, and convinced the founder of communism, Karl Marx, that an earthshaking, apocalyptic revolution pitting the proletariat against the bourgeoisie would destroy capitalism and usher in a classless society.

After the bloody suppression of the Paris Commune in 1871, however, for the next several decades revolutions ceased in Western and Central Europe, and revolutionary activity shifted to Russia (1905), Persia (1905), the Ottoman Empire (1908), Mexico (1910), and China (1911). All of these revolutions were directed against governments and leaders that were corrupt, incompetent, out of touch with their subjects, and out of their depth in dealing with their country's momentous problems. Since the 1890s China had been ruled indirectly by Empress Dowager Cixi, who had scuttled the reforms of her nephew, Emperor Guangxu, in 1898, had encouraged the disastrous Boxer Rebellion in 1900, and had used funds for the navy to build a handsome marble boat that sat in a lake on the grounds of the imperial summer palace and was a fine place for picnics. Iran's shahs since the 1880s eagerly turned over much of their country's economy to foreigners in return for large personal bribes and modest payments to the treasury. Bored and overwhelmed by the perplexities of politics and finance, they escaped whenever possible to Europe's spas and capitals. Russia's Tsar Nicholas II was well-meaning but indecisive; the Ottoman sultan Abdul Hamid II was inflexible in his conservatism; and Mexico's aging dictator Porfirio Díaz showed utter indifference to his people's poverty while enriching himself and his cronies.

When intellectuals, politicians, despairing ministers, and dedicated revolutionaries considered alternatives to such regimes, they drew inspiration from both their own past and from Western models. Most reformers sought at minimum to establish Western-style liberal governments with elected parliaments, protection of individuals' rights, and constitutions. In Russia, China, and Mexico, revolutionaries had more ambitious dreams of redistributing land, helping impoverished factory workers, and ending the privileges of the rich. Marxists and anarchists dreamed of getting rid of the rich altogether. In ever-greater numbers, those who were dissatisfied saw revolution as their best hope for achieving their goals. This too was something they had learned from the political experience of the West.

A Revolutionary Formula for China's Revival

❖

10 ◆ Sun Yat-sen, THE THREE PEOPLE'S PRINCIPLES AND THE FUTURE OF THE CHINESE PEOPLE

By 1900 the prognosis for China's imperial regime had deteriorated from poor to critical. Plagued throughout the nineteenth century by peasant revolts, military defeats, foreign exploitation, and failed reforms, China in the 1890s and early 1900s reached a low point. Its humiliating defeat in 1895 by Japan in the Sino-Japanese War set off a struggle between conservatives and reformers, with conservatives ascendant after the suppression of the One Hundred Days reform movement by Empress Dowager Cixi in 1898. Reformers regained the upper hand after the failure of the Boxer Rebellion in 1900. Their New Policy Reforms encouraged Chinese youths to study abroad; introduced science, mathematics, and foreign languages to schools; established military academies; sought to foster Chinese-owned businesses; and changed the system of recruiting government officials when the ancient civil service examinations were abolished in 1905. The reforms backfired. They burdened the peasantry with higher taxes; alienated large landowners; and failed to satisfy the generals, business people, and intellectuals who were convinced that China's only hope lay in ousting the Qing Dynasty and rebuilding China from its foundations.

China's leading revolutionary was Sun Yat-sen (1866–1925), a man far different from previous Chinese reformers. Born to a poor rural family from the Guangzhou region and educated in Hawaii and missionary schools in China, he developed a worldview more Western than Confucian. Galled by China's military impotence and Qing ineptitude, in 1894 he founded the secret Revive China Society, which in 1895 made plans to overthrow the Guangzhou provincial government. The plot was uncovered, and Sun was forced into exile. After sixteen years of traveling, planning, writing, and organizing, his hopes were realized when revolution broke out in 1911 and ended the Qing Era in 1912.

On his return to China from the United States (he had read about the revolution in a Denver newspaper while on a train to Kansas City), he was elected provisional president of the United Provinces of China on December 30, 1911. Sun's moment of glory, however, was short-lived. Without an army or organized political party to back him up, he resigned as president in 1912 in favor of the military strongman Yuan Shikai, who in 1913 exiled Sun as part of his plan to establish a dictatorship. Sun returned to Guangzhou in 1917 and attempted to establish a parliamentary government, but by then China had begun to descend into the chaos of warlord rule. When Sun died in 1925, the prospects of national unity and orderly government for China were still dim, but for his efforts Sun was viewed even then as the "father of modern China."

In the following selection Sun presents an early formulation of his "three people's principles," which served as the ideology of the United League, an organization he founded in 1905 in Tokyo that combined secret societies from China, overseas Chinese groups, and Chinese students in Japan. When the United League joined several other groups to form the Guomindang, or Nationalist, Party in 1912, Sun's three principles provided its platform. Sun presented the following analysis of his three principles in a speech to the United League in Tokyo in 1906 to help celebrate the first anniversary of the League's publication, *Min Pao* (the People's Journal).

QUESTIONS FOR ANALYSIS

1. What is meant by Sun's principle of nationalism? Against whom is nationalism directed?
2. What does he mean by the principle of democracy, and why does he consider it so important to the future of China?
3. What, according to Sun, have been the good and bad effects of the "advances of civilization"? Why have the benefits of these advances been so poorly distributed?
4. Briefly describe Sun's "land valuation procedure" and its relation to the principle of livelihood. What are its strengths and flaws?
5. What is Sun's attitude toward the West? How and in what ways will the future government and society of China be superior to those of the West?
6. To what extent are Sun's ideas inspired by Western ideologies and to what extent do they draw on Chinese thought and practice?

Let us pause to consider for a moment: Where is the nation? Where is the political power? Actually, we are already a people without a nation! The population of the globe is only one billion, several hundred million; we Han,[1] being 400 million, comprise one-fourth of that population.

Our nation is the most populous, most ancient, and most civilized in the world, yet today we are a lost nation. Isn't that enormously bizarre? The African nation of the Transvaal has a population of only 200,000, yet when Britain tried to destroy it, the fighting lasted three years.[2] The Philippines have a population of only several million, but when America tried to subdue it, hostilities persisted for several years.[3] Is it possible that the Han will gladly be a lost nation?

We Han are now swiftly being caught up in a tidal wave of nationalist revolution, yet the Manchus continue to discriminate against the Han. They boast that their forefathers conquered the Han because of their superior unity and military strength and that they intend to retain these qualities so as to dominate the Han forever. . . . Certainly, once we Han unite, our power will be thousands of times greater than theirs, and the success of the nationalist revolution will be assured.

As for the Principle of Democracy, it is the foundation of the political revolution. . . . For several thousand years China has been a monarchical autocracy, a type of political system intolerable to those living in freedom and equality. A nationalist revolution is not itself sufficient to get rid of such a system. Think for a moment: When the founder of the Ming dynasty expelled the Mongols and restored Chinese rule, the nationalist revolution triumphed, but his political system was only too similar to those of the Han, Tang, and Song dynasties.[4] Consequently, after another three hundred years, foreigners again began to invade China. This is the result of the inadequacy of the political system, so that a political revolution is an absolute necessity. . . . The aim of the political revolution is to create a constitutional, democratic political system. . . .

◆ ◆

Now, let me begin by discussing the origins of the Principle of the People's Livelihood, a principle that began to flourish only in the latter part of the nineteenth century. . . . As civilization advanced, people relied less on physical labor and more on natural forces, since electricity and steam could accomplish things a thousand times faster than human physical strength. For example, in antiquity a single man tilling the land could harvest at best enough grain to feed a few people, notwithstanding his toil and trouble. Now, however, as a result of the development of scientific agriculture, one man can grow more than enough to feed a thousand people because he can use machinery instead of his limbs, with a consequent increase in efficiency. . . .

In view of this, everyone in Europe and America should be living in a state of plenty and happiness undreamed of in antiquity. If we look around, however, we see that conditions in those countries are precisely the opposite. Statistically, Britain's wealth has increased more than several thousandfold over the previous generation, yet poverty of the people has also increased several thousandfold over the previous generation. Moreover, the rich are extremely few, and the poor extremely numerous. This is because the power of human labor is no match for the power

---

[1]*Han* in the Chinese language means "the Chinese people." Essentially it applies to those who speak Chinese and share a common Chinese culture and history.

[2]A reference to the South African War, or Boer War (1899–1902), fought between Great Britain and the two Afrikaner, or Boer, states in south Africa – Transvaal and the Orange Free State. Cultural friction and political conflict between the British settlers and administrators in the region and the Dutch residents of the two states caused the war.

[3]Between 1899 and 1901, Filipinos under the leadership of Emilio Aguinalado fought against their new colonial master, the United States, after the United States took over the Philippines from Spain at the conclusion of the Spanish American War.

[4]The Ming Dynasty ruled from 1368 to 1644 C.E. The Han (202 B.C.E.–220 C.E.), Tang (618–906 C.E.), and Song (960–1279 C.E.) were Chinese dynasties.

of capital. In antiquity, agriculture and industry depended completely on human labor; but now, with the development of natural forces that human labor cannot match, agriculture and industry have fallen completely into the hands of capitalists. The greater the amount of capital, the more abundant the resources that can be utilized. Unable to compete, the poor have naturally been reduced to destitution. . . .

Indeed, this constitutes a lesson for China. . . . Civilization yields both good and bad fruits, and we should embrace the good and reject the bad. In the countries of Europe and America, the rich monopolize the good fruits of civilization, while the poor suffer from its evil fruits. . . . Our current revolution will create a nation that not only belongs to the citizenry but is socially responsible. Certainly, there will be nothing comparable to it in Europe or America.

Why have Europe and America failed to solve their social problems? Because they have not solved their land problem. Generally speaking, wherever civilization is advanced, the price of land increases with each passing day. . . . In China capitalists have not yet emerged, so that for several thousand years there has been no increase in land prices. . . . After the revolution, however, conditions in China will be different. For example, land prices in Hong Kong and Shanghai are currently as much as several hundred times higher than those in the interior. This increment is the result of the advance of civilization and the development of communications. It is inevitable that, as the entire nation advances, land prices everywhere will rise accordingly. . . . Fifty years ago, land along the banks of the Huangpu River in Shanghai was worth up to a million dollars a *mou*.[5] This is evidence of the clearest sort, from which we can see that in the future the rich will get richer every day, and the poor poorer. . . . Consequently, we must come up with a solution now. . . .

With respect to a solution, although the socialists have different opinions, the procedure I most favor is land valuation. For example, if a landlord has land worth 1,000 dollars, its price can be set at 1,000 or even 2,000 dollars. Perhaps in the future, after communications have been developed, the value of his land will rise to 10,000 dollars; the owner should receive 2,000, which entails a profit and no loss, and the 8,000 increment will go to the state. Such an arrangement will greatly benefit both the state and the people's livelihood. Naturally, it will also eliminate the shortcomings that have permitted a few rich people to monopolize wealth. This is the simplest, most convenient, and most feasible method. . . .

Once we adopt this method, the more civilization advances, the greater the wealth of the nation, and then we can be sure our financial problems will not become difficult to handle. After the excessive taxes of the present have been abolished, the price of consumer goods will gradually fall and the people will become increasingly prosperous. We will forever abolish the vicious taxation policies that have prevailed for several thousand years. . . . After China's social revolution is accomplished, private individuals will never again have to pay taxes. The collection of land revenues alone will make China the richest nation on earth. . . .

Obviously, . . . it is necessary to give considerable attention to what the constitution of the Republic of China should be. . . . The British constitution embodies the so-called separation of powers into executive, legislative, and judicial, all mutually independent. . . . The Frenchman [Montesquieu][6] later embraced the British system and melded it with his own ideals to create his own school of thought. The American constitution was based on Montesquieu's theories

---

[5]A *mou* equals 1.5 acres.
[6]Montesquieu (1689–1755) was a French political philosopher, best known for his *The Spirit of the Laws* (1748), in which he argues that individual freedom is safest in a state in which the three powers of government, the judicial, executive, and legislative, are kept separate.

but went further in clearly demarcating the separation of powers. . . . As to the future constitution of the Republic of China, I propose that we introduce a new principle, that of the "five separate powers."

Under this system, there will be two other powers in addition to the three powers just discussed. One is the examination power. . . . American officials are either elected or appointed. . . .

With respect to elections, those endowed with eloquence ingratiated themselves with the public and won elections, while those who had learning and ideals but lacked eloquence were ignored. Consequently, members of America's House of Representatives have often been foolish and ignorant people who have made its history quite ridiculous. As for appointees, they all come and go with the president. The Democratic and Republican parties have consistently taken turns holding power, and whenever a president is replaced, cabinet members and other officials, comprising no fewer than 60,000–70,000 people, including the postmaster general, are also replaced. As a result, the corruption and laxity of American politics are unparalleled among the nations of the world. . . . Therefore, the future constitution of the Republic of China must provide for an independent branch expressly responsible for civil service examinations. Furthermore, all officials, however high their rank, must undergo examinations in order to determine their qualifications. Whether elected or appointed, officials must pass those examinations before assuming office. This procedure will eliminate such evils as blind obedience, electoral abuses, and favoritism. . . .

The other power is the supervisory power, responsible for monitoring matters involving impeachment. For reasons that should be evident to all, such a branch is indispensable to any nation. The future constitution of the Republic of China must provide for an independent branch. Since ancient times, China had a supervisory organization, the Censorate,[7] to monitor the traditional social order. Inasmuch as it was merely a servant of the monarchy, however, it was ineffectual. . . .

With this added to the four powers already discussed, there will be five separate powers. That constitution will form the basis of the sound government of a nation that belongs to its own race, to its own citizens, and to its own society. This will be the greatest good fortune for our 400 million Han people. I presume that you gentlemen are willing to undertake and complete this task. It is my greatest hope.

---

[7]The Censorate, or Board of Censors, was a unique feature of Chinese government during the Ming and Qing Eras. Members of the board were responsible for reviewing the conduct of officials and reporting to the emperor when they discovered dereliction of duty. They were considered the "eyes and ears" of the emperors.

A Marxist Blueprint for Russia

❖

11 ◆ *PLATFORM OF THE RUSSIAN SOCIAL DEMOCRATIC PARTY, 1903*

Russia was full of discontent around 1900. Its two hundred million peasants, having been emancipated by Tsar Alexander II in 1861, were no longer serfs, but they were still bound to the land, abysmally poor, illiterate, and taxed to their capacity and beyond. Its urban working class, a product of Russia's recent and ongoing industrialization, experienced poverty and squalor in the slums of St. Petersburg and Moscow that rivaled the poverty and squalor in the peasant villages from which most workers had come. Its intellectuals, students, professionals, business owners, and some members of the landed gentry were disgusted with their inefficient and arbitrary government and troubled by the enormous gap between rich and poor. For decades these alienated Russians espoused political causes ranging from anarchism to constitutional monarchy. With the fervor of religious zealots, they argued, organized, hatched plots, planned revolutions, assassinated government officials, and tried, not always successfully, to stay a step ahead of the secret police.

By 1921, after the dust had settled on years of war, revolution, and civil war, one group of revolutionaries, a faction of the Social Democratic Party known as the Bolsheviks, gained power. They changed the course of Russian and global history by establishing the world's first Marxist government.

When the Social Democratic Party was founded in 1898 in the city of Minsk, it joined numerous other parties and organizations dedicated to overthrowing the tsarist autocracy. In the 1890s the two most prominent of these organizations were the Constitutional Democrats, moderates who sought to turn Russia into a constitutional monarchy, and the Social Revolutionaries, who sought a rural-based insurrection that would end the inequalities in Russian society. The Social Democrats also sought a revolution, but, as followers of Karl Marx, they believed it would be a revolution of the urban working class, or proletariat, which would eliminate capitalism and class exploitation.

In 1903 the Social Democrats, with most of their leaders in exile, split into two factions during their second party congress in London and Brussels. The Mensheviks, following orthodox Marxist doctrine, believed Russia was not ready for a communist revolution. It first had to fully industrialize and eliminate tsarist autocracy. The Bolsheviks, led by Lenin (Vladimir Ilyich Ulyanov, 1870–1924), believed that revolution was possible immediately if planned and organized by a small core of dedicated party members.

Despite the split, the two factions managed to agree on a platform in 1903, excerpts from which follow. The first part summarizes Marxist views of the class struggle, capitalism, and revolution. The second part outlines the party's short-term goals for Russia before the achievement of true communism.

QUESTIONS FOR ANALYSIS

1. What views of capitalism are expressed in the first part of the party platform? What implications does capitalism have for class relationships?
2. The document speaks of "contradictions in bourgeois society." What are these contradictions, and how will they affect capitalism's future?
3. To what extent does the state envisioned by the Social Democrats embrace the liberal principles of freedom and representative government?
4. To what extent does the statement show particular concern on the part of the Social Democrats for women and peasants?
5. What does the document reveal about the condition of the Russian working class?

Considering itself one of the detachments of the universal army of the proletariat, Russian social democracy is pursuing the same ultimate goal, as that for which the social democrats in other countries are striving. This ultimate goal is determined by the nature of contemporary bourgeois society and by the course of its development. The main characteristic of such a society is production for the market on the basis of capitalist production relations, whereby the largest and most important part of the means of production and exchange of commodities belongs to a numerically small class of people, while the overwhelming majority of the population consists of proletarians and semi-proletarians who, by their economic conditions, are forced either continuously or periodically to sell their labor power; that is, to hire themselves out to the capitalists, and by their toil to create the incomes of the upper classes of society.

The expansion of the capitalist system of production runs parallel to technical progress, which, by increasing the economic importance of large enterprises, tends to eliminate the small independent producers, to convert some of them into proletarians, to reduce the socio-economic role of others and, in some localities, to place them in more or less complete, more or less open, more or less onerous dependence on capital.

Moreover, the same technical progress enables the entrepreneurs to utilize to an ever greater extent woman and child labor in the process of production and exchange commodities. And since, on the other hand, technical improvements lead to a decrease in the entrepreneur's demand for human labor power, the demand for labor power necessarily lags behind the supply, and there is in consequence greater dependence of hired labor upon capital, and increased exploitation of the former by the latter.

Such a state of affairs in the bourgeois countries, as well as the ever growing competition among those countries on the world market, render the sale of goods which are produced in greater and greater quantities ever more difficult. Overproduction, which manifests itself in more or less acute industrial crises . . . is the inevitable consequence of the development of the productive forces in bourgeois society. Crises and periods of industrial stagnation, in their turn, tend to impoverish still further the small producers, to increase still further the dependence of hired labor upon capital and to accelerate still further the . . . deterioration of the condition of the working class.

Thus, technical progress, signifying increased productivity of labor and the growth of social wealth, becomes in bourgeois society the cause of increased social inequalities, of wider gulfs between the wealthy and the poor, of greater insecurity of existence, of unemployment, and of numerous privations for ever larger and larger masses of toilers.

But together with the growth and development of all these contradictions inherent in bourgeois society, there grows simultaneously dissatisfaction with the present order among the toiling and exploited masses; the number and solidarity of the proletarians increases, and their struggle against the exploiters sharpens. At the same time, technical progress . . . creates more and more rapidly the material possibility for replacing capitalist production relations by socialist ones; that is, the possibility for social revolution, which is the ultimate aim of all the activities of international social democracy as the class-conscious expression of the proletarian movement.

By replacing private with public ownership of the means of production and exchange, . . . the social revolution of the proletariat will abolish the division of society into classes and thus emancipate all oppressed humanity, and will terminate all forms of exploitation of one part of society by another. . . .

In Russia, where capitalism has already become the dominant mode of production, there are still preserved numerous vestiges of the old pre-capitalist order, when the toiling masses were serfs of the landowners, the state, or the sovereign. . . .

The most outstanding among these relics of the past, the mightiest bulwark of all this barbarism, is the tsarist autocracy. By its very name it is bound to be hostile to any social movement, and cannot but be bitterly opposed to all the aspirations of the proletariat toward freedom.

By reason of the above, the first and immediate task put before itself by the Russian Social Democratic Workers' Party is to overthrow the tsarist authority and to replace it with a democratic republic whose constitution would guarantee the following:

1. The sovereignty of the people; that is, the concentration of all supreme state power in the hands of a legislative assembly. . . .
2. Universal, equal, and direct suffrage for all male and female citizens, twenty years old or over, at all elections . . .; biennial parliaments; salaries to be paid to the people's representatives.
3. Broad local self-government. . . .
5. Unlimited freedom of religion, speech, press, assembly, strikes, and unions.
6. Freedom of movement and occupation.
7. Abolition of classes; equal rights for all citizens, irrespective of sex, religion, race, or nationality.
8. The right of any people to receive instruction in its own language, to be secured by creating schools at the expense of the state and the local organs of self-government. . . .
12. Replacement of the standing army by a general armament of the people. . . .
14. Free and compulsory general and professional education for all children of both sexes up to the age of sixteen; provision by the state of food, clothing, and school supplies for poor children. . . .

In order to *safeguard the working class* against physical and moral degeneration, as well as to insure the development of its power to carry on the struggle for freedom, the party demands the following:

1. Eight-hour working day for all hired labor.
2. A law providing a weekly uninterrupted forty-two-hour respite for all hired labor, of both sexes, in all branches of the national economy.
3. Complete prohibition of overtime work.
4. Prohibition of night work (from 9 p.m. to 6 a.m.) in all branches of the national economy, with the exception of those in which this is absolutely necessary because of technical considerations approved by labor organizations.
5. Prohibition of the employment of children of school age (up to sixteen) and restriction of the working day of minors (from sixteen to eighteen) to six hours.
6. Prohibition of female labor in those branches of industry which are injurious to women's health; relief from work four weeks before and six weeks after childbirth, with regular wages paid during all this period.
7. Establishment of nurseries for infants and children in all shops, factories, and other enterprises that employ women; permission for freedom of at least a half-hour's duration to be granted at three-hour intervals to all nursing mothers.
8. Old-age state insurance, and insurance against total or partial disability. . . .
11. Appointment of an adequate number of factory inspectors in all branches of the national economy . . .; participation of representatives, elected by the workers and paid by the state, in supervising the enforcement of the factory laws, the fixing of wage scales, and in accepting or rejecting the finished products and other results of labor.
12. Control by organs of local self-government, together with representatives elected by the workers, over sanitation in the dwellings assigned to the workers by the employers, as well as over internal arrangements in those dwellings and the renting conditions. . . .
13. Establishment of properly organized sanitary control over all establishments employing hired labor . . .; in times of illness, free medical aid to be rendered to the

workers at the expense of the employers, with the workers retaining their wages. . . .

In order to *remove the vestiges of serfdom* that fall directly and heavily upon the peasants, and to encourage the free development of the class struggle in the *village,* the party demands above all:

1. Abolition of redemption payments and quit rents as well as all obligations which presently fall on the peasantry, the tax-paying class.[1]
2. Repeal of all laws which restrict the peasant in disposing of his land.
3. Return to peasants of money collected from them in the form of redemption payments and quit rents; confiscation of monastery

and church properties as well as property belonging to princes, government agencies, and members of the royal family. . . .

To attain its immediate goals, the Russian Social Democratic Workers' Party will support every opposition and revolutionary movement directed against the existing social and political system in Russia. . . .

On its own part, the Russian Social Democratic Workers' Party is firmly convinced that a full, consistent, and thorough realization of the indicated political and social changes can only be attained by the overthrow of autocracy and by the convocation of a Constituent Assembly freely elected by the entire people.

---

[1]After serfdom was ended in 1861, emancipated peasants still had to pay redemption fees to reimburse the gentry for lands they had lost. They also paid landowners special fees and quitrents for the use of woodlands and pastureland.

Agrarian Reform and Revolution in Mexico

❖

12 ◆ *THE PLAN OF AYALA*

When Porfirio Díaz was elected president in 1876, Mexico had no railroads, factories, or significant foreign investment; it had a capital, Mexico City, notorious for floods and epidemics, an outdated silver industry, farms without modern equipment or fertilizers, and a desperately poor population that was 85 percent illiterate. When he left office in 1911, Mexico had an oil industry; fifteen thousand miles of railroads; improved harbors; factories making cement, textiles, furniture, brick, and glass; a modernized silver industry; and a capital, Mexico City, that had a drainage system, electric trams, a new municipal palace, and a splendid national theater. It still had a desperately poor population that was 85 percent illiterate.

Díaz's almost total disregard for the Mexican people's poverty was one reason why a small but articulate group of Mexicans turned against him in the opening years of the twentieth century. Another reason was his flouting of the 1857 constitution through censorship, manipulation of elections, and the packing of the judiciary and provincial administration with favorites. Around 1900 Díaz's opponents, some of whom were in exile, began to demand an end to the dictatorship and its replacement with a constitutional government dedicated to social reform. Their expectations were heightened in 1908 when Díaz announced he would not stand for reelection as president, then dashed in 1910 when he reversed himself and decided to run. In June 1910, with his main rival Francisco I. Madero and thousands of his opponents in jail, Díaz was reelected. Madero called on the Mexican people to rise up against Díaz, and even named a date, November 20, 1910, when it should happen. On cue, rebellions erupted throughout the country, and when federal troops were unable to quell them, Díaz resigned, paving the way for Madero's election as president in October 1911.

By this time, however, divisions had appeared among the revolutionaries. No less than six rebellions against the Madero presidency took place within a year, and turmoil plagued Mexico until 1920. The first faction to break from Madero was led by Emiliano Zapata (1879–1919), a small landowner, muleteer, horse trainer, and stable master who had led a small rebel army against pro-Díaz troops in 1911 in his native state of Morelos, just to the south of Mexico City. His followers were mainly poor villagers, many of whom had lost their land to wealthy hacienda owners during the Díaz regime. In late 1911 Zapata turned against Madero after he became convinced that the new president was not committed to social reform.

In November 1911 Zapata and his followers officially broke from the president by issuing their Plan of Ayala. Although its exact authorship is uncertain, its importance in Mexican history is indisputable. It served as a bible for Zapata's followers during the civil war of the 1910s and remained a symbol of the Mexican Revolution's commitment to rural social reform long after Zapata was murdered by federal troops in 1919.

QUESTIONS FOR ANALYSIS

1. According to the document, what caused Zapata and his followers to break from Madero?
2. According to Zapata's followers, aside from Madero, what individuals and groups in Mexico are responsible for holding back the revolution?
3. What solutions does the document propose to the problem of Mexico's rural poverty?
4. What is there about the Plan of Ayala that accounts for its popularity?

Taking into consideration that the Mexican people led by Don Francisco I. Madero went to shed their blood to reconquer liberties and recover their rights which had been trampled on, and not for a man to take possession of power, violating the sacred principles which he took an oath to defend . . . taking into consideration that that man to whom we refer is Don Francisco I. Madero, . . . who . . . having no in-

tentions other than satisfying his personal ambitions, his boundless instincts as a tyrant, and his profound disrespect for the fulfillment of the preexisting laws emanating from the immortal code of '57, written with the revolutionary blood of Ayutla;[1]

Taking into account that the so-called Chief of the Liberating Revolution of Mexico, Don Francisco I. Madero, through lack of integrity

---

[1]The Revolution of Ayutla, which took place in 1855, deposed General Santa Anna and led to the Constitution of

1857, which placed authority in a unicameral legislature and included extensive protections of individual freedoms.

and the highest weakness, did not carry to a happy end the revolution which gloriously he initiated with the help of God and the people, since he left standing most of the governing powers and corrupted elements of oppression of the dictatorial government of Porfirio Díaz . . . ; taking also into account that the aforementioned Sr. Francisco I. Madero, present President of the Republic, tries to avoid the fulfillment of the promises which he made to the Nation . . . by means of false promises and numerous intrigues against the Nation nullifying, pursuing, jailing, or killing revolutionary elements who helped him to occupy the high post of President of the Republic;

Taking into consideration that the so-often-repeated Francisco I. Madero has tried with the brute force of bayonets to shut up and to drown in blood the pueblos[2] who ask, solicit, or demand from him the fulfillment of the promises of the revolution, calling them bandits and rebels, condemning them to a war of extermination without conceding or granting a single one of the guarantees which reason, justice, and the law prescribe; taking equally into consideration that the President of the Republic Francisco I. Madero has made of Effective Suffrage a bloody trick on the people, . . . entering into scandalous cooperation with the científico[3] party, feudal landlords, and oppressive bosses, enemies of the revolution proclaimed by him, so as to forge new chains and follow the pattern of a new dictatorship more shameful and more terrible than that of Porfirio Díaz. . . .

For these considerations we declare the aforementioned Francisco I. Madero inept at realizing the promises of the revolution of which he was

the author, because he has betrayed the principles with which he tricked the will of the people and was able to get into power: incapable of governing, because he has no respect for the law and justice of the pueblos, and a traitor to the fatherland, because he is humiliating in blood and fire Mexicans who want liberties, so as to please the científicos, landlords, and bosses who enslave us, and from today on we begin to continue the revolution begun by him, until we achieve the overthrow of the dictatorial powers which exist. . . .

The Revolutionary Junta of the State of Morelos manifests to the Nation under formal oath: that it makes its own the plan of San Luis Potosí,[4] with the additions which are expressed below in benefit of the oppressed pueblos, and it will make itself the defender of the principles it defends until victory or death. . . .

As an additional part of the plan we invoke, we give notice: that [regarding] the fields, timber, and water which the landlords, científicos, or bosses have usurped, the pueblos or citizens who have the titles corresponding to those properties will immediately enter into possession of that real estate of which they have been despoiled by the bad faith of our oppressors, maintaining at any cost with arms in hand the mentioned possession. . . .

In virtue of the fact that the immense majority of Mexican pueblos and citizens are owners of no more than the land they walk on, suffering the horrors of poverty without being able to improve their social condition in any way or to dedicate themselves to Industry or Agriculture, because lands, timber, and water are monopolized in a few hands, for this cause there will be expropriated the third part of those monopolies

---

[2]*Pueblo* in Spanish means "village"; in this context *pueblos* refers to villagers as collective owners of property.

[3]*Científico* means "scientific." *Científicos* were advisors and confidants of Díaz who prided themselves on being pragmatic and scientific in their approach to Mexico's economic and social problems. The term was used broadly to refer to the Díaz political establishment.

[4]Madero's Plan of San Luis Potosí was written in San Antonio, Texas, in the middle of October 1910. In order to

avoid complications with the U.S. government, however, Madero dated it October 5, the last day he spent in prison in San Luis Potosí, Mexico, after his arrest by federal police. It was an appeal to the Mexican people to overthrow Díaz and establish a constitutional state, but contained only a few references to social reform.

from the powerful proprietors of them, with prior indemnization, in order that the pueblos and citizens of Mexico may obtain . . . foundations for pueblos or fields for sowing or laboring, and the Mexicans' lack of prosperity and well-being may improve in all and for all.

Regarding the landlords, científicos, or bosses who oppose the present plan directly or indirectly, their goods will be nationalized and the two third parts which [otherwise would] belong to them will go for indemnizations of war pensions for widows and orphans of the victims who succumb in the struggle for the present plan.

In order to execute the procedures regarding the properties aforementioned, the laws of dis-amortization[5] and nationalization will be applied as they fit, for serving us as norm and example can be those laws put in force by the immortal Juárez on ecclesiastical properties,[6] which punished the despots and conservatives who in every time have tried to impose on us the ignominious yoke of oppression and backwardness. . . .

Once triumphant the revolution which we carry into the path of reality, a Junta of the principal revolutionary chiefs from the different States will name or designate an interim President of the Republic, who will convoke elections for the organization of the federal powers. . . .

Mexicans: consider that the cunning and bad faith of one man is shedding blood in a scandalous manner, because he is incapable of governing; consider that his system of government is choking the fatherland and trampling with the brute force of bayonets on our institutions; and thus, as we raised up our weapons to elevate him to power, we again raise them up against him for defaulting on his promises to the Mexican people and for having betrayed the revolution initiated by him, we are not personalists, we are partisans of principles and not of men!

Mexican People, support this plan with arms in hand and you will make the prosperity and well-being of the fatherland.

Ayala, November 25, 1911

---

[5]In this context this means the return of lands that had been confiscated from the pueblos.
[6]Benito Juárez, secretary of justice following the Revolution of Ayutla, sponsored laws that limited Catholic clerics'

immunity from trial in nonecclesiastical courts. Later, the government passed laws forbidding the Church to own property other than churches, monasteries, and seminaries.

◆

The New Voice of Women in the Early Twentieth Century

At the start of the twentieth century, feminism was already an important force in Western societies. Drawing on the natural rights philosophy of the eighteenth-century Enlightenment and the democratic principles of the French Revolution, nineteenth-century women had campaigned to achieve political and legal rights, greater vocational opportunities, and equal access to education. By century's end these feminists had made modest gains. In Europe, the United States, Canada, Australia, and New Zealand, girls had access to primary and secondary education, and small numbers of women were able to attend universities and enter professions such as medicine and journalism. As a result of industrialization, urbanization, and the growth of government and private businesses, more women also were entering the paid work force as teachers, white-collar workers, factory workers, and nurses. Legal changes gave married women greater control of their property and easier access to divorce.

Nowhere, however, could women vote in national elections. To change this, women around 1900, especially in England and the United States, campaigned energetically to win the vote. When World War I began in 1914, feminists had achieved their goal in only Norway, Finland, and a few western states in the United States. But feminism had emerged as a powerful political and social force in Western societies.

Women's lives and expectations were also changing in non-Western societies around 1900, in many cases as a result of contacts with the West. Colonialism, for example, had brought an end to the practice of *sati* in India after British administrators banned this custom of ritual suicide expected of widows of certain castes. Colonialism had also altered the legal status of women in Algeria, Tunisia, and Libya, where European legal systems superseded Islamic law, including family law.

Both in colonies and semicolonial areas such as China and the Ottoman Empire, foreign missionary schools created new opportunities for female education. They made primary and secondary schooling available to girls on a more or less equal footing with boys, and introduced students of both genders to Western concepts of equality and individualism. In Egypt, India, and Southeast Asia, increasing numbers of upper-class city dwellers hired tutors to teach their daughters European languages and culture as part of their efforts to emulate Europeans. Around 1900 the growing number of women authors and many of their readers were products of these new educational experiences.

In addition to colonialism, nationalism in non-Western lands encouraged an interest in women's issues. Nationalist reformers in Ottoman Turkey, Arab lands, India, China, and Japan came to see the oppression and abuse of women as an impediment to modernization and a source of national embarrassment. They supported greater freedom, education, and vocational opportunities for women, and sought to end perceived symbols of their society's backwardness such as foot-binding in China and the veiling and seclusion of women in Islamic lands.

Advocates of women's rights outside the West faced formidable obstacles. Their audience was small, and their views were bitterly opposed by conservatives who considered their demands subversive to religion and morals. Patriarchal values remained strong despite the mounting feminist critique. Even in Meiji Japan, which sought universal literacy for boys and girls alike through a system of state-supported elementary schools, girls were barred from advanced academic high schools, technical schools, and universities. But new issues had been raised, positions staked out, and agendas clarified. As much as in Europe and the United States, the efforts of Arab, Chinese, Indian, and Japanese feminists before World War I prepared the way for the profound changes in women's status and opportunities that occurred during the rest of the twentieth century.

An Early Voice of Arab Feminism

❖

13 ◆ *Bahithat al-Badiya,* A LECTURE IN THE CLUB OF THE UMMA PARTY, 1909

Malak Hifni Nasif, better known by her pen name, Bahithat al-Badiya (Arabic for "Seeker in the Desert"), was an early Egyptian feminist. Born into a prosperous Cairo family, she was educated at home and then at the Saniyya School in Cairo, a school for women. On graduating she became a teacher at the school, and a regular contributor of essays and poems to Cairo literary journals. Her life abruptly changed in 1911 when at the age of twenty-four she moved to an oasis west of Cairo following an arranged marriage to a Bedouin chief. To her chagrin she discovered that the chief already had a wife and a daughter, whom she was expected to tutor. Despite disappointment and anger, she remained with her husband until she died of influenza in 1918.

In her writings and speeches, which were published in 1910 under the title *Al-Nisaiyat* (Feminist Pieces), Bahithat addressed a wide range of issues pertaining to Egyptian women, including education, paid work, and especially proper public attire. The following remarks were delivered in 1909 as part of a weekly lecture series that catered to well-to-do Cairo women. It was held in the hall of the Umma Party, a moderate Egyptian nationalist party founded in 1906.

QUESTIONS FOR ANALYSIS

1. What does the source tell us about the arguments being made by opponents of women entering the paid work force? How does the author counter these arguments?
2. What does the source reveal about relations between males and females in Egypt in the early 1900s?
3. What are the shortcomings of upper-class Egyptian women, according to Bahithat?
4. How does she view European women? Why does she consider them poor role models for Egyptian women?
5. How much of what the author says relates to the experiences of lower- and middle-class Egyptian women?
6. If the provisions of the author's program had been carried out, how would Egyptian women's lives have changed?

Men say when we become educated we shall push them out of work and abandon the role for which God has created us. But, isn't it rather men who have pushed women out of work? Before, women used to spin and to weave cloth for clothes for themselves and their children, but men invented machines for spinning and weaving and put women out of work. In the past, women sewed clothes for themselves and their households but men invented the sewing machine. . . . Then men took up the profession of tailoring and began to make clothes for our men and children. Before women winnowed the wheat and ground flour on grinding stones for the bread they used to make with their own hands, sifting flour and kneading dough. Then men established bakeries employing men. They gave us rest but at the same time pushed us out of work. . . .

The question of monopolizing the workplace comes down to individual freedom. One man wishes to become a doctor, another a merchant. Is it right to tell a doctor he must quit his profession and become a merchant or vice versa? No. Each has the freedom to do as he wishes. . . . Work at home now does not occupy more than half the day. We must pursue an education in order to occupy the other half of the day but that is what men wish to prevent us from doing under the pretext of taking their jobs away. . . .

The division of labor is merely a human creation. We still witness people like the Nubians[1] whose men sew clothes for themselves and the household while the women work in the fields. Some women even climb palm trees to harvest the dates. Women in villages in both Upper and Lower Egypt help their men till the land and plant crops. Some women do the fertilizing, haul crops, lead animals, draw water for irrigation, and other chores. You may have observed that women in the villages work as hard as the strongest men and we see that their children are strong and healthy.

Specialised work for each sex is a matter of convention. It is not mandatory. We women are now unable to do hard work because we have not been accustomed to it. . . . After long centuries of enslavement by men, our minds rusted and our bodies weakened. Is it right that they accuse us of being created weaker than them in mind and body?

Men criticize the way we dress in the street. They have a point because we have exceeded the bounds of custom and propriety. We claim we are veiling but we are neither properly covered nor unveiled. I do not advocate a return to the veils of our grandmother because it can rightly be called being buried alive, not *hijab*,[2] correct covering. The woman used to spend her whole life within the walls of her house not going out into the street except when she was carried to her grave. I do not, on the other hand, advocate unveiling, like Europeans, and mixing with men, because they can be harmful to us. . . .

If we had been raised from childhood to go unveiled and if our men were ready for it I would approve of unveiling for those who want it. But the nation is not ready for it now. Some of our prudent women do not fear to mix with men, but we have to place limits on those who are less prudent because we are quick to imitate and seldom find our authenticity in the veil. . . .

If the change that some women have made in the *izar*[3] is in order to shed it when they go out that would be all right if these women would only uncover their faces but keep their hair and figures concealed. I think the most appropriate way to dress outside is to cover the head and wear a coat with long sleeves which touches the ground the way the European women do. I am told this is the way women in Istanbul[4] dress when they go out shopping. . . .

On the subject of customs and veiling I would like to remind you of something that causes us

---

[1]A Negroid people who inhabit the region in southern Egypt and northern Sudan between the Nile and the Red Sea.
[2]*Hijab* in Arabic literally means "veil" or "partition"; it also means adherence to certain standards of modest dress for women.

[3]A loose-fitting shawl, usually made of white calico.
[4]The largest city in Turkey and the seat of Ottoman government.

great unhappiness — the question of engagement and marriage. Most sensible people in Egypt believe it is necessary for fiancés to meet and speak with each other before their marriage. It is wise and the Prophet[5] himself, peace be upon him and his followers, did not do otherwise. . . .

By not allowing men to see their prospective wives following their engagement we cause Egyptian men to seek European women in marriage. They marry European servants and working class women thinking they would be happy with them rather than daughters of pashas and beys[6] hidden away in 'a box of chance'. If we do not solve this problem we shall become subject to occupation by women of the West. We shall suffer double occupation, one by men and the other by women. The second will be worse than the first because the first occurred against our will but we shall have invited the second by our own actions. . . . Most Egyptian men who have married European women suffer from the foreign habits and extravagance of their wives. The European woman thinks she is of a superior race to the Egyptian and bosses her husband around after marriage. When the European woman marries an Egyptian she becomes a spend-thrift while she would be thrifty if she were married to a westerner. . . .

◆ ◆

Our beliefs and actions have been a great cause of the lesser respect that men accord us. How can a sensible man respect a woman who believes in magic, superstition, and the blessing of the dead and who allows women peddlars and washerwomen, or even devils, to have authority over her? Can he respect a woman who speaks only about the clothes of her neighbor and the jewellery of her friend and the furniture of a bride? This is added to the notion imprinted in a man's mind that woman is weaker and less intelligent than he is. . . .

We shall advance when we give up idleness. The work of most of us at home is lounging on cushions all day or going out to visit other women. . . . Being given over to idleness or luxury has given us weak constitutions and pale complexions. We have to find work to do at home. At a first glance one can see that the working classes have better health and more energy and more intelligent children. The children of the middle and lower classes are, almost all of them, in good health and have a strong constitution, while most of the children of the elite are sick or frail and prone to illness despite the care lavished on them by their parents. . . .

Now I shall turn to the path we should follow. If I had the right to legislate I would decree:

1. Teaching girls the Quran and the correct Sunna.[7]
2. Primary and secondary school education for girls, and compulsory prepatory school education for all.
3. Instruction for girls on the theory and practice of home economics, health, first aid, and childcare.
4. Setting a quota for females in medicine and education so they can serve the women of Egypt.
5. Allowing women to study any other advanced subjects they wish without restriction.
6. Upbringing for girls from infancy stressing patience, honesty, work and other virtues.
7. Adhering to the *Sharia*[8] concerning betrothal and marriage, and not permitting any woman and man to marry without first meeting each other in the presence of the father or male relative of the bride.
8. Adopting the veil and outdoor dress of the Turkish women of Istanbul.

---

[5]Islam's greatest prophet and founder, Muhammad lived from 570 to 632 C.E. God's revelations to him comprise Islam's most holy book, the Quran, or Koran.
[6]Courtesy titles for Egyptian gentlemen of high rank.

[7]*Sunna* refers to the customs and traditions of the Islamic community.
[8]Literally, the "right path," or Islamic law.

9. Maintaining the best interests of the country and dispensing with foreign goods and people as much as possible.

10. Make it encumbent upon our brothers, the men of Egypt, to implement this program.

"Race Decadence" and the U.S. Women's Movement

❖

14 ◆ *Anna Howard Shaw,*
PRESIDENTIAL ADDRESSES AT THE CONVENTIONS OF NATIONAL AMERICAN WOMAN SUFFRAGE ASSOCIATION, 1905, 1906

For many opponents of feminism in Europe and the United States, its most disturbing figure was not Elizabeth Cady Stanton, a founder of the U.S. women's rights movement who insisted that "obey" be left out of her marriage vows; it was not Margaret Sanger, who pioneered the birth control movement in the United States; it was not even Emmeline Pankhurst and her daughters, E. Sylvia and Christabel, who led the militant fight for women's suffrage in England. It was not a real woman at all. It was Nora, the fictional heroine of the Norwegian playwright Henrik Ibsen's *A Doll's House,* which was performed throughout Europe and the United States after its premiere in 1880. Having endured a childhood dominated by a stifling father and eight years of an empty marriage, Nora abandons her husband and three children to begin a quest for self-enlightenment and fulfillment.

To opponents of women's rights, Nora's rejection of domesticity epitomized the unhealthy individualism and egotism that underlay women's search for equality, meaningful work, and independence. Such egotism, they feared, threatened to consign woman's traditional role as wife and mother to oblivion. Anxieties over the incompatibility of motherhood and female emancipation were deepened in the 1880s by declining birth rates in industrialized nations, especially for the middle class. This troubled European nationalists, who feared manpower shortages for the military. It also worried many Americans of northern European stock, who feared inundation by the millions of new immigrants from southern and eastern Europe.

Never one to skirt such issues, U.S. President Theodore Roosevelt (1858–1919) discussed women's true calling and duties in a speech to the National Congress of Mothers in Washington, D.C., in 1905. Although a supporter of women's suffrage and equal rights, Roosevelt was an advocate of "equality in difference." In his view, men should run the government, manage businesses, and earn a living; women should marry, become mothers, and raise children. In his speech he expressed contempt for women who out of "viciousness, coldness, shallow-heartedness, or self-indulgence" neglected their duty to raise families. He further stated that "the existence of women of this type was one of the most unpleasant and unwholesome features of modern life."

The president's remarks gained a quick response from Anna Howard Shaw (1847–1919), president of the National American Woman Suffrage Association from 1904 to 1915. Born in England and raised in Michigan, she obtained degrees in divinity and medicine from Boston University. She chose a life of political action, however, first through the Women's Christian Temperance Union, and then on behalf of women's suffrage. She remained single to better accomplish her life's work.

The following excerpts come from her presidential addresses to the annual meetings of the National American Woman Suffrage Association in 1905 and 1906. In both excerpts she discusses women's work and its relationship to motherhood and the family.

QUESTIONS FOR ANALYSIS

1. What evidence is there that Shaw accepts Roosevelt's premise that "race decadence" is a problem in the United States? How does her view of its causes differ from that of the president?
2. What ulterior motives does she ascribe to those who blame women for "race-suicide"? What are the flaws in their arguments?
3. How does Shaw link the problems she describes in U.S. society to women's lack of political rights?
4. What similarities, if any, do you see between the points made in Shaw's speech and those made by Bahithat al-Badiya in her 1909 lecture in the club of the Umma Party?

[1905]

When the cry of race-suicide is heard, and men arraign women for race decadence, it would be well for them to examine conditions and causes, and base their attacks upon firmer foundations of fact. Instead of attacking women for their interest in public affairs and relegating them to their children, their kitchen, and their church, they will learn that the kitchen is in politics; that the children's physical, intellectual, and moral well-being is controlled and regulated by law; that the real cause of race decadence is not the fact that fewer children are born, but to the more fearful fact that, of those born, so few live, not primarily because of the neglect of the mother, but because men themselves neglect their duty as citizens and public officials. If men honestly desire to prevent the causes of race decadence, let them examine the accounts of food adulteration, and learn that from the effect of impure milk alone, in one city 5,600 babies died in a single year. Let them examine the water supply, so impregnated with disease that in some cities there is continual epidemic of typhoid fever. Let them gaze upon the filthy streets, from which perpetually arises contagion of scarlet fever and diphtheria. Let them examine the plots of our great cities, and find city after city with no play places for children, except the streets, alleys, and lanes. Let them examine the school buildings, many of them badly lighted, unsanitary, and without yards. Let them turn to the same cities, and learn that from five to a score or thousand children secure only half-day tuition because there are not adequate schoolhouse facilities. Let them watch these half-day children playing in the streets and alleys and viler places, until they have learned the lessons which take them to ever-growing numbers of reformatories, whose inmates are increasing four times as rapidly as the population. Let them follow the children who survive all these ills of early childhood, until they enter the sweat-shops and factories, and behold there the maimed, dwarfed, and blighted little ones, 500,000 of whom under 14 years of age are employed in these pestilential places. Let them behold the legalized saloons and the dens of iniquity where so many of the voting population spend the money that should be used in feeding, housing, and caring for their children. Then, if these mentors of women's clubs and mothers' meetings do not find sufficient cause for race degeneracy where they have power to control conditions, let them turn to lecturing women. . . . That which is desirable is not that the greatest possible number of children should be born into the world; the need is for more intelligent motherhood and fatherhood, and for better born and better educated children. . . .

The great fear that the participation of women in public affairs will impair the quality and character of home service is irrational and contrary to the tests of experience. Does an intelligent interest in the education of a child render a woman less a mother? Does the housekeeping instinct of woman, manifested in a desire for clean streets, pure water, and unadulterated food, destroy her efficiency as a home-maker? Does a desire for an environment of moral and civic purity show neglect of the highest good of the family? It is the "men must fight and women must weep" theory of life which makes men fear that the larger service of women will impair the high ideal of home. The newer ideal, that men must cease fighting and thus remove one prolific cause for women's weeping, and that they shall together build up a more perfect home and a more ideal government, is infinitely more sane and desirable. . . .

[1906]

. . . To draw sweeping and universal conclusions in regard to a matter upon which there is an "almost complete dearth of data" is never wise. While it is true that marriage and the birth-rate have decreased within recent years, before the results are charged to the participation of women in industry, one must answer many questions.

Is it true that there is more "domestic infelicity" to-day than in times past? Is it true that there is greater "domestic infelicity" in homes where women are engaged in gainful pursuits than in those homes in which the strength of women is never taxed by toil, even to the extent of self-service? Is it true that there is a lower birth-rate among working women than among those of the wealthy class? Are not the effects of over-work and long hours in the household as great as are those of the factory or of the office?

. . . Is the birth-rate less among women who are engaged in the new pursuits or occupations unknown to women of the past? Or is the decline alike marked among those who are pursuing the ancient occupations which women have followed from time immemorial, but under different conditions? . . .

Woman as an industrial factor and wage-earner is not new. But woman as an industrial competitor and wage-collector with man is new, not because of woman's revolt against her own industrial slavery, but because changed economic conditions through inventive genius and industrial centralization have laid their hands upon the isolated labors and products of woman's toil, and brought them forth from the tent, the cottage, and the farm house, to the shop, the factory, and the marketplace.

If conditions surrounding their employment are such as to make it a "social question of the first importance" it is unfortunate the President had not seen that women, the most deeply interested factor in the problem, should constitute at least a part of any commission authorized to investigate it. No body of men, unaided by women, can be qualified to do so "in a sane and scientific spirit." . . .

But if the required investigations were made, even with women upon the committee, what power would the five millions of disfranchised women possess to enact beneficent laws or enforce needed reform?

One can not but wish that with his recognized desire for "fair play" and his policy of "a square deal," it had occurred to the President that, if five millions of American women are employed in gainful occupations, every principle of justice known to a Republic would demand that these five millions of toiling women should be enfranchised to enable them to secure enforced legislation for their own protection.

An Attack on Foot-binding in China

◆

15 ◆ Qiu Jin,
AN ADDRESS TO TWO HUNDRED MILLION FELLOW COUNTRYWOMEN

Beginning in the late ninth and tenth centuries C.E., and continuing until the twentieth century, millions of Chinese girls between the ages of five and nine had their feet tightly wrapped and gradually bent until the arch was broken and all the toes except the big toe, were turned under. With feet growing to only half their normal size, these girls were condemned to lives as semicripples. Originally, foot-binding was limited to wealthy families who wanted to demonstrate that their women did not have to work. Gradually, however, the practice spread to all levels of society, and small feet began to have a strong erotic attraction for Chinese males. Girls with "big feet" were considered unmarriageable.

Although foot-binding always had its opponents, only at the end of the nineteenth century did the practice come under widespread criticism. Many reformers and intellectuals considered foot-binding, along with opium smoking, one of the social customs that underlay the country's backwardness. Protestant missionaries, many of them women, also denounced the practice, and one of their number, Mrs. Archibald Little, founded the Natural Foot Society in 1895. Also in the 1890s, anti-foot-binding societies, whose members agreed to arrange marriages for their daughters with unbound feet, were founded in major cities. In 1902 Empress Dowager Cixi outlawed foot-binding, but it took decades for the practice to die out completely.

Among the Chinese women writers who attacked foot-binding, the most outspoken was Qiu Jin (1875–1907), who devoted her life to women's liberation and the overthrow of the Qing Dynasty. Raised in a moderately wealthy family and well-educated, Qiu was married to an older man at age twenty-one, but left him in 1903 to study in Japan. On her return in 1906 she founded a women's magazine and became principal of a girls' school. In 1907 she and her cousin were arrested and beheaded for revolutionary activity. In the following speech, delivered probably in 1906, she denounces foot-binding and other examples of women's oppression in China.

QUESTIONS FOR ANALYSIS

1. As described by Qiu, what kind of relationship did most Chinese girls have with their parents?

2. What can be learned from the source concerning Chinese marriage customs and the relationship between husbands and wives?
3. What were the motives, according to Qiu, for subjecting women to foot-binding and preventing them from learning how to read?
4. In Qiu's view, what share of the blame for their oppression must be assumed by women themselves?
5. What are Qiu's solutions for China's problems?
6. What similarities do you see between the views of Qiu Jin and those of Bahithat al-Badiya?

Alas! The greatest injustice in this world must be the injustice suffered by our female population of two hundred million. If a girl is lucky enough to have a good father, then her childhood is at least tolerable. But if by chance her father is an ill-tempered and unreasonable man, he may curse her birth: "What rotten luck: another useless thing." Some men go as far as killing baby girls while most hold the opinion that "girls are eventually someone else's property" and treat them with coldness and disdain. In a few years, without thinking about whether it is right or wrong, he[1] forcibly binds his daughter's soft, white feet with white cloth so that even in her sleep she cannot find comfort and relief until the flesh becomes rotten and the bones broken. What is all this misery for? Is it just so that on the girl's wedding day friends and neighbors will compliment him, saying, "Your daughter's feet are really small"? Is that what the pain is for?

But that is not the worst of it. When the time for marriage comes, a girl's future life is placed in the hands of a couple of shameless matchmakers and a family seeking rich and powerful in-laws. A match can be made without anyone ever inquiring whether the prospective bridegroom is honest, kind, or educated. On the day of the marriage the girl is forced into a red and green bridal sedan chair, and all this time she is not allowed to breathe one word about her future. After her marriage, if the man doesn't do her any harm, she is told that she should thank Heaven for her good fortune. But if the man is bad or he ill-treats her, she is told that her marriage is retribution for some sin committed in her previous existence. If she complains at all or tries to reason with her husband, he may get angry and beat her. When other people find out they will criticize, saying, "That woman is bad; she doesn't know how to behave like a wife." What can she do? When a man dies, his wife must mourn him for three years and never remarry. But if the woman dies, her husband only needs to tie his queue[2] with blue thread. Some men consider this to be ugly and don't even do it. In some cases, three days after his wife's death, a man will go out for some "entertainment." Sometimes, before seven weeks have passed, a new bride has already arrived at the door. . . . Why is there no justice for women? We constantly hear men say, "The human mind is just and we must treat people with fairness and equality." Then why do they greet women like black slaves from Africa? How did inequality and injustice reach this state?

Dear sisters, you must know that you'll get nothing if you rely upon others. You must go out and get things for yourselves. In ancient times when decadent scholars came out with such nonsense as "men are exalted, women are lowly," "a virtuous woman is one without talent," and

---

[1] Despite Qiu's use of the male pronoun, the actual work of binding feet was performed by female members of the girls' families, usually mothers.

[2] The braid of hair worn at the back of the head by Chinese men.

"the husband guides the wife," ambitious and spirited women should have organized and opposed them. . . . Men feared that if women were educated they would become superior to men, so they did not allow us to be educated. Couldn't the women have challenged the men and refused to submit? It seems clear now that it was we women who abandoned our responsibilities to ourselves and felt content to let men do everything for us. As long as we could live in comfort and leisure, we let men make all the decisions for us. When men said we were useless, we became useless; when they said we were incapable, we stopped questioning them even when our entire female sex had reached slave status. At the same time we were insecure in our good fortune and our physical comfort, so we did everything to please men. When we heard that men liked small feet, we immediately bound them just to please them, just to keep our free meal tickets. As for their forbidding us to read and write, well, that was only too good to be true. We readily agreed. . . . It was only natural that men, with their knowledge, wisdom, and hard work, received the right to freedom while we became their slaves. And as slaves, how can we escape repression? Whom

can we blame but ourselves since we have brought this on ourselves? . . .

. . . Let us all put aside our former selves and be resurrected as complete human beings. Those of you who are old, do not call yourselves old and useless. If your husbands want to open schools, don't stop them; if your good sons want to study abroad, don't hold them back. Those among us who are middle-aged, don't hold back your husbands lest they lose their ambition and spirit and fail in their work. After your sons are born, send them to schools. You must do the same for your daughters and, whatever you do, don't bind their feet. As for you young girls among us, go to school if you can. If not, read and study at home. Those of you who are rich, persuade your husbands to open schools, build factories, and contribute to charitable organizations. Those of you who are poor, work hard and help your husbands. . . . You must know that when a country is near destruction, women cannot rely on the men any more because they aren't even able to protect themselves. If we don't take heart now and shape up, it will be too late when China is destroyed.

Sisters, we must follow through on these ideas!

New Trends in Western Culture and Thought

Beginning in earnest during the era of imperialism, and continuing even after the dissolution of Europe's empires following World War II, Western science, literature, political ideologies, educational theories, art, and architecture have affected non-Western thought and expression profoundly and, in doing so, have created a culture more truly global than at any time in human history. Paradoxically, this export of Western ideas and artistic taste began at time when many of the age-old certainties of Western thought and culture were being challenged and discarded.

The fundamentals of European thought had taken shape between the Renaissance of the fourteenth and fifteenth centuries and the Enlightenment of the eighteenth century. Its basic premise was that nature was orderly, reasonable, and operated according to universal physical laws. Human beings, creatures of reason and capable of moral improvement through education, could understand this natural order through scientific inquiry and could improve the human condition through increased understanding of nature and society. Furthermore, being rational, human beings were capable of governing themselves and could do so most effectively when their freedom of self-expression was protected. Such beliefs were the foundation for the nineteenth century's faith in liberalism and parliamentary government. Western views of art, music, and literature also embodied many of these assumptions about nature and humanity. Since the Late Middle Ages and Renaissance, naturalism — the effort to accurately represent nature in paintings and sculpture — had been the central feature of Western art, and the achievement of harmony and beauty was the goal of composers.

Every one of these beliefs was being challenged around 1900. Scientists discarded old assumptions about motion, light, matter, and the universe. Atoms were not tiny, solid spheres of matter, as had been imagined, but complexes of electrically charged particles; light and other forms of radiant energy were emitted not in a steady stream, but in discrete units, or quanta; mathematics had a realm in which theories capable of rational proof contradicted what the senses apprehended in the "real" world. Most disturbing of all were the theories of Albert Einstein (1879–1955), who in papers published between 1905 and 1916 proposed that matter and energy were a single entity, and that absolute time and distance did not exist but were dependent on the speed and position of the observer.

Although the implications of this "second scientific revolution" were at first only dimly perceived by the European and American publics, changes in philosophy, psychology, and the arts were more conspicuous. Painters, composers, and writers provided one shock after another. Considering themselves to be in the forefront of artistic creativity (like the small group of soldiers trained to attack in front of the main body of troops — an avant-garde), these artists, writers, and composers defied convention and seemed bent on upsetting and insulting their audiences. Painters filled their canvases with barely recognizable images often painted in bright, unnatural colors, with little attention to detail or traditional drawing; architects rejected the classical and Gothic styles for a severe "modern" idiom more attuned to the Machine Age; poets filled their works with arcane symbols and abstruse meanings but rarely with rhymes or, in some cases, even punctuation; composers wrote atonal music and abandoned traditional rhythms; choreographers produced ballets that horrified devotees of the classical repertoire.

Fundamentally disturbing questions were also being raised by philosophers, psychologists, and anthropologists. What if the West's ethical values were enslaving and debilitating humanity? What if the West's moral teachings were no better than those of the "primitive" peoples of Africa and the Pacific islands? What if all human behavior could be reduced to a series of physical responses, thus calling into question the concepts of mind and consciousness? What if, as the Viennese psychiatrist Sigmund Freud suggested, human behavior was not controlled by reason but was instead driven by deep unconscious drives, most of them sexual, that were barely perceptible to the individual?

These were just a few of the questions confronting Westerners as the optimism and confidence of the nineteenth century gave way to the uncertainties and anxieties of the twentieth century.

"God Is Dead . . . We Have Killed Him"

◈

16 ◆ *Friedrich Nietzsche,* *THE GAY SCIENCE and ON THE GENEALOGY OF MORALS*

Among the philosophers of the late nineteenth century, none offered a more trenchant and piercing rejection of rationalism, democracy, Christianity, and traditional Western morality than the German philosopher Friedrich Nietzsche (1844–1900). Born into the family of a Lutheran minister, Nietzsche studied the Greek and Roman classics at the universities of Bonn and Leipzig, and then accepted a professorship at the University of Basel, Switzerland, in 1872. Forced to resign for reasons of health in 1879, he spent the last two decades of his life in Switzerland, Italy, and Germany seeking a cure for his deteriorating mental and emotional state. Before he lapsed into insanity in 1889, he published a series of provocative treatises in which he denounced Judaism, Christianity, and democratic egalitarianism as obstacles to the evolutionary development of a new race of superior human beings who would rule through the "will to power." His ideas influenced countless twentieth-century thinkers and movements, including existentialism and Nazism.

The first excerpt is taken from *The Gay Science* (sometimes translated as *The Joyful Wisdom*), a collection of aphorisms on diverse topics written in 1882 after Nietzsche had recovered from a period of illness. The second excerpt is taken from *On the Genealogy of Morals*, published in 1887.

QUESTIONS FOR ANALYSIS

1. What does Nietzsche mean by the "death of God" and his assertion that "we have killed him"?
2. Is the death of God good or bad for humanity, according to Nietzsche?
3. What distinctions does Nietzsche draw between "slave morality" and "noble morality"? How does the "pioneer" called for in the passage from *The Gay Science* embody the ideal of "noble morality"?
4. What implications do Nietzsche's ideas on morality have for democratic theory?
5. Overall, would you characterize Nietzsche's philosophy as optimistic or pessimistic?

[THE GAY SCIENCE]

The Madman — Have you ever heard of the madman who on a bright morning lighted a lantern and ran to the market-place calling out unceasingly: "I seek God! I seek God!" — As there were many people standing about who did not believe in God, he caused a great deal of amusement. Why! is he lost? said one. Has he strayed away like a child? said another. Or does he keep himself hidden? Is he afraid of us? Has he taken a sea-voyage? Has he emigrated? — the people cried out laughingly, all in a hubbub. The insane man jumped into their midst and transfixed them with his glances. "Where is God gone?" he called out. "I mean to tell you! *We have killed him,* — you and I! We are all his murderers! But how have we done it? How were we able to drink up the sea? Who gave us the sponge to wipe away the whole horizon? What did we do when we loosened this earth from its sun? Whither does it now move? Whither do we move? Away from all suns? Do we not dash on unceasingly? Backwards, sideways, forewards, in all directions? Is there still an above and below? Do we not stray, as through infinite nothingness? Does not empty space breathe upon us? Has it not become colder? Does not night come on continually, darker and darker? Shall we not have to light lanterns in the morning? Do we not hear the noise of the grave-diggers who are burying God? Do we not smell the divine putrefaction? — for even Gods putrefy! God is dead! God remains dead! And we have killed him! How shall we console ourselves, the most murderous of all murderers? The holiest and the mightiest that the world has hitherto possessed, has bled to death under our knife, — who will wipe the blood from us? . . . There never was a greater event, — and on account of it, all who are born after us belong to a higher history than any history hitherto!" — Here the madman was silent and looked again at his hearers; they also were silent and looked at him in surprise. At last he threw his lantern on the ground, so that it broke in pieces and was extinguished. . . . It is further stated that the madman made his way into different churches on the same day, and there intoned his *Requiem aeternam deo.*[1] When led out and called to account, he always gave the reply: "What are these churches now, if they are not the tombs and monuments of God?" —

Pioneers. — I greet all the signs indicating that a more manly and warlike age is commencing, which will, above all, bring heroism again into honour! For it has to prepare the way for a yet higher age, and gather the force which the latter will one day require, — the age which will carry heroism into knowledge, and *wage war* for the sake of ideas and their consequences. For that end many brave pioneers are now needed, who, however, cannot originate out of nothing, — and just a little out of the sand and slime of present-day civilisation and the culture of great cities: men silent, solitary and resolute, who know how to be content and persistent in invisible activity: men who with innate disposition seek in all things that which is *to be overcome* in them: men to whom cheerfulness, patience, simplicity, and contempt of the great vanities belong just as much as do magnanimity in victory and indulgence to the trivial vanities of all the vanquished: . . . men with their own holidays, their own work-days, and their own periods of mourning; accustomed to command with perfect assurance, and equally ready, if need be, to obey, proud in the one case as in the other, equally serving their own interests: men more imperiled, more productive, more happy! For believe me! — the secret of realising the largest productivity and the greatest enjoyment of existence is *to live in danger!* Build your cities on the slope of Vesuvius![2] Send your ships into unexplored seas! Live in war with your equals and with yourselves! Be robbers and spoilers, ye knowing ones, as long as ye cannot be rulers and possessors! The time will soon pass when you can be satisfied to live like timorous deer concealed in the forests. . . .

[ON THE GENEALOGY OF MORALS]

— "But what is all this talk about nobler values? Let us face facts: the people have triumphed — or the slaves, the mob, the herd, whatever you wish to call them — and if the Jews brought it

---

[1] Latin meaning requiem (a solemn chant for the dead) to the eternal god.

[2] A volcano in southern Italy.

about, then no nation ever had a more universal mission on this earth. The lords are a thing of the past, and the ethics of the common man is completely triumphant. . . . The 'redemption' of the human race (from the lords, that is) is well under way; everything is rapidly becoming Judaized, or Christianized, or mob-ized — the word makes no difference. The progress of this poison throughout the body of mankind cannot be stayed; . . .

The slave revolt in morals begins by rancor turning creative and giving birth to values — the rancor of beings who, deprived of the direct outlet of action, compensate by an imaginary vengeance. All truly noble morality grows out of triumphant self-affirmation. Slave ethics, on the other hand, begins by saying *no* to an "outside," and "other," a non-self, and that *no* is its creative act. . . . Slave ethics requires for its inception a sphere different from and hostile to its own. Physiologically speaking, it requires an outside stimulus in order to act at all; all its action is reaction. The opposite is true of aristocratic valuations: such values grow and act spontaneously, seeking out their contraries only in order to affirm themselves even more gratefully and delightedly. Here the negative concepts, *humble, base, bad,* are late, pallid counterparts of the positive, intense and passionate credo, "We noble, good, beautiful, happy ones." . . .

All this stands in utter contrast to what is called happiness among the impotent and oppressed, who are full of bottled-up aggressions. Their happiness is purely passive and takes the form of drugged tranquility, stretching and yawning, peace, "sabbath," emotional slackness. Whereas the noble lives before his own conscience with confidence and frankness. . . . Among the noble, mental acuteness always tends slightly to suggest luxury and overrefinement. The fact is that with them it is much less

important than is the perfect functioning of the ruling, unconscious instincts or even a certain temerity to follow sudden impulses, court danger, or indulge spurts of violent rage, love, worship, gratitude, or vengeance. . . .

Here I want to give vent to a sigh and a last hope. Exactly what is it that I, especially, find intolerable; that I am unable to cope with; that asphyxiates me? A bad smell. The smell of failure, of a soul that has gone stale. God knows it is possible to endure all kinds of misery — vile weather, sickness, trouble, isolation. All this can be coped with, if one is born to a life of anonymity and battle. There will always be moments of re-emergence into the light, when one tastes the golden hour of victory and once again stands foursquare, unshakable, ready to face even harder things, like a bowstring drawn taut against new perils. But, you divine patronesses — if there are any such in the realm beyond good and evil — grant me now and again the sight of something perfect, wholly achieved, happy, magnificently triumphant, something still capable of inspiring fear! Of a man who will justify the existence of mankind, for whose sake one may continue to believe in mankind! . . . The leveling and diminution of European man is our greatest danger; because the sight of him makes us despond. . . . We no longer see anything these days that aspires to grow greater; instead, we have a suspicion that things will continue to go downhill, becoming ever thinner, more placid, smarter, cosier, more ordinary, more indifferent, more Chinese, more Christian — without doubt man is getting "better" all the time. . . . This is Europe's true predicament: together with the fear of man we have also lost the love of man, reverence for man, confidence in man, indeed the *will to man.* Now the sight of man makes us despond.

Aesthetics for the Machine Age

◆

17 ◆ *EXCERPTS FROM FUTURIST MANIFESTOS, 1909–1914*

The late nineteenth and early twentieth centuries witnessed an eruption of new artistic movements, all seeking liberation from the dead hand of the past. *Impressionists* left exact copying to photographers and sought to depict momentary sense impressions before they could be fully apprehended and studied by the brain; *pointillists* painted canvases in which color was broken down into thousands of tiny individual dots of pigment; *postimpressionists,* or *expressionists,* were less interested in depicting what they saw than in revealing the inner worlds of their imagination and feelings; *les fauves* ("wild beasts," a name given them by a shocked Parisian critic in 1905) painted pictures made up of color, line, and form, but no real objects; *cubists* dismantled objects and figures and reassembled them in sharp, flat, distorted geometrical patterns. Within a few decades, perspective, realistic color, detail, and narrative all had been abandoned for an art that was abstract, personal — and modern.

Futurism, which burst on the scene in 1909, was the last new artistic movement in prewar Europe and in many ways the most outrageous and iconoclastic. It proposed new standards not just for painting and sculpture but for poetry, music, architecture, and even fashion. Carried away by the cult of youth, the power and dynamism of the airplane and automobile, the wild energies of urban life, and the heroic possibilities of warfare, futurists called for an unequivocal break with the past and a new aesthetic consonant with the age of machines.

The movement began in February 1909 when Tomasso Marinetti published his "futurist manifesto" in the Parisian newspaper, *Le Figaro.* Italian painters and sculptors Gino Severini, Umberto Boccioni, Giacomo Balla, Luigi Russolo, and Carlo Carra identified themselves with the movement and sought in their works to capture the speed, energy, and dynamism of modern life through a style reminiscent of cubism. A number of other young Italians with interests in music, literature, and fashion also adopted the futurist label. They, like futurist painters and sculptors, were quick to issue manifestos that proclaimed their views.

Futurism ended abruptly during World War I when most of its adherents volunteered to fight in Italy's army. In its brief life, however, it was a prime example of the restlessness, unfocused energy, and appetite for innovation that affected many Europeans as they moved fully into the Machine Age and ever closer to the dark abyss of World War I.

The following excerpts are taken from three manifestos issued by futurists between 1909 and 1913. They begin with Marinetti's 1909 manifesto from *Le Figaro,* and continue with later manifestos on painting (issued by Boccioni, Carra, Russolo, Balla, and Severini in 1910), and music (issued by Russolo in 1913).

QUESTIONS FOR ANALYSIS

1. What symbolic attraction do modern machines have for the futurists? How do the characteristics of machines affect the futurists' views?
2. What are the weaknesses and flaws of past artistic styles, according to the futurists?
3. How do you explain the futurists' self-proclaimed veneration of warfare?
4. What might explain the futurists' stated opposition to feminism (see article 9 in Marinetti's manifesto)?
5. What common features or views can be seen in all three futurist manifestos?
6. What similarities, if any, do you see between the views of the futurists and those of Nietzsche?

MANIFESTO OF FUTURISM (1909)

1. We intend to sing the love of danger, the habit of energy and fearlessness.
2. Courage, audacity, and revolt will be essential elements of our poetry.
3. Up to now literature has exalted a pensive immobility, ecstasy, and sleep. We intend to exalt aggressive action, a feverish insomnia, the racer's stride, the mortal leap, the punch and the slap.
4. We affirm that the world's magnificence has been enriched by a new beauty: the beauty of speed. A racing car whose hood is adorned with great pipes, like serpents of explosive breath — a roaring car that seems to ride on grapeshot is more beautiful than the *Victory of Samothrace.*
5. We want to hymn the man at the wheel, who hurls the lance of his spirit across the Earth, along the circle of its orbit.
6. The poet must spend himself with ardour, splendour, and generosity, to swell the enthusiastic fervour of the primordial elements.
7. Except in struggle, there is no more beauty. No work without an aggressive character can be a masterpiece. Poetry must be conceived as a violent attack on unknown forces, to reduce and prostrate them before man.

8. We stand on the last promontory of the centuries! . . . Why should we look back, when what we want is to break down the mysterious doors of the Impossible? Time and Space died yesterday. We already live in the absolute, becaue we have created eternal, omnipresent speed.
9. We will glorify war — the world's only hygiene — militarism, patriotism, the destructive gesture of freedom-bringers, beautiful ideas worth dying for, and scorn for woman.
10. We will destroy the museums, libraries, academies of every kind, will fight moralism, feminism, every opportunistic or utilitarian cowardice.
11. We will sing of great crowds excited by work, by pleasure, and by riot; we will sing of the multicoloured, polyphonic tides of revolution in the modern capitals; we will sing of the vibrant nightly fervour of arsenals and shipyards blazing with violent electric moons; greedy railway stations that devour smoke-plumed serpents; factories hung on clouds by the crooked lines of their smoke; bridges that stride the rivers like giant gymnasts, flashing in the sun with a glitter of knives; adventurous steamers that sniff the horizon; deep-chested locomotives whose wheels paw the tracks like the hooves of enormous steel horses bridled

by tubing; and the sleek flight of planes whose propellers chatter in the wind like banners and seem to cheer like an enthusiastic crowd.

It is from Italy that we launch through the world this violently upsetting incendiary manifesto of ours. With it, today, we establish *Futurism,* because we want to free this land from its smelly gangrene of professors, archaeologists, *ciceroni* and antiquarians. For too long has Italy been a dealer in second-hand clothes. We mean to free her from the numberless museums that cover her like so many graveyards.

MANIFESTO OF THE FUTURIST PAINTERS 1910

TO THE YOUNG ARTISTS OF ITALY!

The cry of rebellion which we utter associates our ideals with those of the Futurist poets. These ideals were not invented by some aesthetic clique. They are the expression of a violent desire which boils in the veins of every creative artist today.

We will fight with all our might the fanatical, senseless and snobbish religion of the past, a religion encouraged by the vicious existence of museums. We rebel against that spineless worshipping of old canvases, old statues and old bric-a-brac, against everything which is filthy and worm-ridden and corroded by time. We consider the habitual contempt for everything which is young, new and burning with life to be unjust and even criminal. . . .

These are our final CONCLUSIONS:

With our enthusiastic adherence to Futurism, we will:

1. Destroy the cult of the past, the obsession with the ancients, pedantry and academic formalism.
2. Totally invalidate all kinds of imitation.
3. Elevate all attempts at originality, however daring, however violent.

4. Bear bravely and proudly the smear of 'madness' with which they try to gag all innovators.
5. Regard art critics as useless and dangerous.
6. Rebel against the tyranny of words: 'Harmony' and 'good taste' and other loose expressions which can be used to destroy the works of Rembrandt, Goya, Rodin. . . .
7. Sweep the whole field of art clean of all themes and subjects which have been used in the past.
8. Support and glory in our day-to-day world, a world which is going to be continually and splendidly transformed by victorious Science.

THE ART OF NOISES (EXTRACTS) 1913

We cannot see that enormous apparatus of force that the modern orchestra represents without feeling the most profound and total disillusion at the paltry acoustic results. Do you know of any sight more ridiculous than that of twenty men furiously bent on redoubling the mewing of a violin? All this will naturally make the music-lovers scream, and will perhaps enliven the sleepy atmosphere of concert halls. Let us now, as Futurists, enter one of these hospitals for anaemic sounds. There: the first bar brings the boredom of familiarity to your ear and anticipates the boredom of the bar to follow. Let us relish, from bar to bar, two or three varieties of genuine boredom, waiting all the while for the extraordinary sensation that never comes.

Meanwhile a repugnant mixture is concocted from monotonous sensations and the idiotic religious emotion of listeners buddhistically drunk with repeating for the nth time their more or less snobbish or second-hand ecstasy.

Away! Let us break out since we cannot much longer restrain our desire to create finally a new musical reality, with a generous distribution of resonant slaps in the face, discarding violins, pianos, double-basses and plaintive organs. Let us break out! . . .

Let us cross a great modern capital with our ears more alert than our eyes, and we will get enjoyment from distinguishing the eddying of water, air and gas in metal pipes, the grumbling of noises that breathe and pulse with indisputable animality, the palpitation of valves, the coming and going of pistons, the howl of mechanical saws, the jolting of a tram on its rails, the cracking of whips, the flapping of curtains and flags. We enjoy creating mental orchestrations of the crashing down of metal shop blinds, slamming doors, the hubbub and shuffling of crowds, the variety of din, from stations, railways, iron foundries, spinning mills, printing works, electric power stations and underground railways. . . .

Here are the 6 *families of noises* of the Futurist orchestra which we will soon set in motion mechanically:

1	2	3
Rumbles	Whistles	Whispers
Roars	Hisses	Murmurs
Explosions	Snorts	Mumbles
Crashes		Grumbles
Splashes		Gurgles
Booms		

4	5	6
Screeches	Noises	Voices of
Creaks	obtained	animals
Rustles	by	and men:
Buzzes	percussion	Shouts
Crackles	on metal,	Screams
Scrapes	wood,	Groans
	skin,	Shrieks
	stone,	Howls
	terracotta,	Laughs
	etc.	Wheezes
		Sobs

PART TWO

Decades of War, Economic Upheaval, and Revolution, 1914–1939

In early August 1914, to the sounds of cheering crowds and military bands, the European-dominated world of the nineteenth and early twentieth centuries began to unravel. On June 28, bullets fired by a Serbian nationalist had killed the future emperor and empress of Austria-Hungary in Sarajevo, setting off a diplomatic crisis that soon escalated beyond the crises that European statesmen had managed to settle peacefully in the previous decade and a half. This time diplomacy failed, and in August what came to be known at first as the Great War, and later as World War I, began.

Many welcomed the conflict. Politicians hoped it would provide a respite from strikes, class antagonisms, socialist agitation, and suffragist demands. Nationalists dreamed of winning glorious victories and settling old scores. Young men with humdrum jobs in shops or offices envisioned excitement, heroism, and being part of a great cause. Not a few philosophers and poets maintained that the war would rouse men from apathy, ennoble them, and inspire them to acts of self-sacrifice and courage; it would weed out the unfit, ensure a place for the strong, and thus contribute to human progress.

Those who hoped for war got their wish, but as they soon learned, it was not what they wanted at all. The short war promised by leaders became an unendurable four-year struggle in which the cheers, rousing marches, resplendent uniforms, and gleaming weapons of the first few weeks gave way to a reality of rat-infested trenches, land mines, shell shock, poison gas, barbed wire, suicide charges against machine-gun nests, massive battles that changed nothing, and unbearably long casualty lists. By the end of 1914, German and French forces had combined casualties of 300,000 dead and 600,000 wounded, and this was only a foretaste of the war's final toll: 65 to 75 million men mobilized; approximately 9 million killed; 22 million wounded, of whom 7 million were permanently disabled. Costs were immense. In the 1920s the Carnegie Endowment for International Peace put the war's cost, including government expenditure, property damage, and the value of lives lost, at \$338 billion, a figure so high that errors of plus or minus several billions of dollars are insignificant.

Such sacrifice might have been bearable if the war had settled anything, if it had "made the world safe for democracy," or at least had enabled the belligerents to return to prewar "normalcy" once it was over. Instead, it was the first act of a two-decade tragedy that ended with the onset of another, even more terrible catastrophe, World War II.

The post–World War I treaties, dictated by the winners at the Paris Peace Conference, were censured for being too harsh or too lenient, too idealistic or too hardheaded. In any case, they failed. They fed old grievances, created new probelms, and within fifteen years generally were being ignored. Economic disaster struck winners and losers alike. War debts and reparations entangled international finance; inflation ruined much of the middle class in Germany and Austria; sagging prices plagued farmers; unemployment remained high, even during the "Roaring Twenties." Then the Great Depression struck in 1929, and with international trade halved and unemployment at all-time highs, capitalism's demise seemed imminent. The future of democracy and liberalism looked no brighter. Dictators replaced parliaments in much of Europe, and surviving democracies seemed flabby and weak compared to the dynamic new fascist and totalitarian regimes. Such was the sorry record of a civilization that only a few years earlier regarded its institutions and values as the pinnacle of human achievement and expected a future of continuing progress.

While the industrialized nations lurched from one crisis to another, Asians, Africans, and Latin Americans continued to struggle with problems of colonialism, economic dependency, and political instability. World War I and its aftermath redefined these problems and encouraged new perspectives. The war itself had a wide-ranging impact. It spurred industrialization in Japan, India, and South America when European factories could no longer supply overseas markets. Its senseless slaughter weakened colonialism by undermining the West's claim of moral superiority. The postwar treaties redrew the map of the Middle East by demolishing the Ottoman Empire, and angered Africans, Arabs, and especially Indians by ignoring their interests despite wartime contributions as soldiers and taxpayers.

The Great Depression was a calamity for the nonindustrialized world. As factories closed in Europe and the United States, demand for raw materials plummeted. By 1932 cotton was selling at one-third, and raw rubber at one-fourth, their pre-1929 prices. Prices for Malayan tin, Chilean copper, Japanese silk, and South African diamonds all plunged. Agricultural prices, which had been falling worldwide before 1929, also were hard hit. The price of basic grains sank to historic lows, with Burmese rice farmers and Argentinean wheat growers suffering alike. The price of Brazilian coffee slumped from 22.5 cents per pound in 1929 to 8 cents in 1931, at which point coffee growers began burning coffee beans to keep up prices. With their export-based economies in tatters, unemployment grew, poverty deepened, and demand for European manufactured goods slumped, accelerating the downward cycle of an imploding world economy.

Reaction to the Great Depression varied in the non-Western world. In Japan economic catastrophe strengthened hard-line nationalists, who trumpeted the benefits of imperialist expansion. In Latin America it elicited a variety of political responses, mostly authoritarian, and inspired efforts to end the region's dependency on foreign manufactures. Throughout colonial Africa and Asia, it strengthened nationalism. It unified educated elites, peasants, and factory workers in opposition to colonial regimes that had created the system of export dependency and did nothing to fix it when it collapsed between 1929 and 1933. From the East Indies to Africa, strikes, mass demonstrations, the emergence of popular nationalist leaders, and even revolutions were signs of increasingly restive colonial populations.

Many nationalist leaders, especially in Asia, were now also communists. This link between anticolonialism and Marxism in Latin America, Asia, and even parts of Africa is another example of how events in Europe — in this case the Russian Revolution of 1917 — influenced non-Western politics. Impressed by a revolution that had taken place in a backward agrarian society and by the success of Soviet economic development strategies in the 1930s, increasing numbers of Africans, Asians, and Latin Americans saw Marxism/Leninism as a two-edged weapon to end capitalism and colonialism alike. The strongest communist movement was in China, where in the 1930s the Communist Party under Mao Zedong battled Chiang Kai-shek's Nationalists in China's civil war.

The communists ultimately won the civil war in China, and nationalists throughout Asia and Africa won the struggle for freedom and independence. In each case, World War II played a key role. But without World War I and the tumultuous events of the 1920s and 1930, neither victory would have been possible.

CHAPTER 3

World War I and Its Global Significance

What if the Serb nationalist Gavrilo Princip had failed to assassinate Archduke Ferdinand of Austria-Hungary on June 28, 1914, in Sarajevo? What if German diplomats had discouraged their ally Austria-Hungary from its plan to invade Serbia for its alleged part in the crime? What if the Austro-Hungarians had abandoned their war plans when the Serbs accepted almost all the terms of the Austro-Hungarian ultimatum on July 25? What if Great Britain had made its proposal for a Great Power conference to mediate the crisis early in July, and not on July 26, when chances of success were minimal? What if European statesman had better understood what modern war was like and had worked harder to prevent it?

What if World War I had never happened?

Definitive answers to such questions are impossible, but one thing is certain. Without World War I, twentieth-century history would have been different, profoundly so. World War I has been described as a turning point, a watershed, and a great divide between two eras. All of these descriptions are true. Between 1914 and 1918 the war killed or wounded almost thirty million human beings. After the killing stopped, it continued to put its stamp on all that followed.

In Europe World War I was a prelude to political disaster. In the short run, it triggered the Russian Revolution of 1917, which in turn raised the specter of communism in the rest of Europe and played into the hands of right-wing dictators who promised to smash the "red menace." In the long run, it raised doubts about the wisdom of elected officials, eroded support for parliamentary governments, and thus contributed to the demise of liberalism and democracy in much of Europe in the 1920s and 1930s. The war fostered regimentation, encouraged the use of propaganda, made demands for total obedience and total commitment for soldiers and civilians alike, and transformed politics into a moral crusade. It created new grievances and resentments, and stirred unresolved hatreds that played into the hands of demagogues with seductive and simplistic solutions to their nations' problems. In all these ways it prepared the ground for fascism and totalitarianism.

World War I also contributed to the economic catastrophes of the 1920s and 1930s. Without the massive borrowing by governments to pay for the war, the inflation of the early 1920s might have been avoided. Without reparations and war debts, international financial markets might have avoided the unhealthy dependence on U.S. loans and capital in the 1920s, a situation that spelled disaster after the U.S. stock market crash of 1929. Without the expansion of agricultural production outside of Europe during the war, the surpluses of the 1920s might have been avoided, and with them the slump in farm incomes.

The war's impact stretched well beyond Europe. It encouraged colonized peoples to question the superiority and invulnerability of their European masters. It also planted seeds of doubt among Europeans about their capacity to rule. The war aroused nationalism by drafting colonial subjects from Africa and Asia into the fighting and then, due to the provisions of the postwar treaties, by dashing their hopes for greater self-rule.

But Gavrilo Princip did assassinate Archduke Ferdinand; Germany offered Austria-Hungary a "blank check," not words of restraint; Austria-Hungary disregarded Serbia's response to its ultimatum; Great Britain's proposal for a Great Powers conference came too late. Statesmen could not prevent the Sarajevo crisis from becoming a war. The world was forever changed.

◆

The Trauma of the Trenches

Wars by their very nature are unpredictable, but rarely was the gap between expectations and reality greater than in World War I. Generals and politicians alike promised a short war. A few quick campaigns and a few decisive victories would "bring the boys home by Christmas," perhaps even by the fall. These victories would be won by tactics still inspired by the French commander Napoléon Bonaparte (1769–1821), whose legendary victories had taught that rapid troop movement, surprise, massive artillery fire, and huge infantry and cavalry charges were the keys to battlefield success. Elan and spirit would conquer all obstacles.

This was the war that soldiers anticipated as they marched off to what they imagined would be glorious adventure — an opportunity to fight for the flag or kaiser or queen, to wear colorful uniforms, and to win glory in battles that would decided by spirit and bravery. The war they fought was nothing like the war they envisioned. After the Germans had almost taken Paris early in the fighting, the Western front became the scene of a stalemate that lasted until the armistice on November 11, 1918. Along a four-hundred-mile line stretching from the English Channel through Belgium and France to the Swiss border, defense — a combination of trenches, barbed wire, land mines, poison gas, and machine guns — proved superior to offense — massive artillery barrages followed by charges of troops across no man's land to overrun enemy lines. Such attacks resulted in numbingly long casualty lists, but gains of territory that were measured in yards not miles.

There are many reasons why Europeans found World War I so demoralizing, so unsettling, and so devoid of any aspect or outcome that might have justified its costs. The disparity between expectations and reality — the theme of the sources in this section — is one of them.

The Romance of War

❖

18 ◆ *POPULAR ART AND POSTER ART FROM GERMANY, ENGLAND, AUSTRALIA, AND FRANCE*

By December 1914, the muddy reality of stalemate had replaced bright dreams of quick victory, and as casualties mounted, shock replaced enthusiasm. Governments no longer could rely on that early burst of patriotic fervor to ensure that men would volunteer, soldiers would reenlist, and citizens would buy war bonds and stoically endure food and fuel shortages. All sides therefore tried to prop up morale through censorship and propaganda. Press reports distorted casualty statistics, misrepresented troop morale, downplayed the hardships of trench warfare, and even described nonexistent victories in which troops overran enemy lines while brandishing swords. Ministries of propaganda churned out broadsheets and circulars describing the enemy's unreasonable war aims and atrocities. They also covered walls with thousands of posters, which with their bright colors, catchy designs, and positive messages encouraged citizens to enlist, buy bonds, save fuel, start vegetable plots, and donate money to care for wounded veterans. Casualty lists and stories from soldiers on leave belied the messages of the broadsheets and posters, and as people came to recognize them for what they were — government-sponsored lies — cynicism about the war deepened.

The four illustrations in this section portray the positive attitudes toward the war that all belligerents shared at the outset and which governments sought to perpetuate as the war dragged on. The first, entitled *The Departure,* shows a German troop train departing for the front. Printed originally in the German periodical *Simplicissimus* in August 1914, it is the work of B. Hennerberg, a Swedish artist and a regular contributor to the magazine. That *Simplicissimus* published such an illustration shows the strength of nationalism at the war's start. Noted before the war for its irreverent satire and criticism of German militarism, *Simplicissimus,* on a decision by its editors, abandoned its antiestablishment stance and lent full support to the war effort.

The second illustration is from a series of cards included by the Mitchell Tobacco Company in its packs of Golden Dawn cigarettes early in the war. It shows a sergeant offering smokes to his soldiers before battle. Tobacco advertising with military themes reached a saturation point in England during the war.

The third illustration is an Australian recruitment poster issued in 1915. Although Australia controlled its domestic affairs, its foreign policy was still managed by Great Britain, and hence when Great Britain went to war, so did Australia. The Australian parliament refused to approve conscription, however, so the government had to work hard to encourage volunteers. This poster appeared in 1915, when Australian troops were heavily involved in the Gallipoli campaign, the Allied effort to knock the Ottoman Empire out of the war. Appealing to members of sports clubs, it promised young men the opportunity to enlist in a battalion made up entirely of fellow sportsmen.

The fourth illustration, a poster from France, was designed to encourage the purchase of war bonds, which were sold by all major belligerents to finance the war. It appeared in 1916 during the German offensive at Verdun, which lasted from February to November and resulted in more than five hundred thousand French casualties. The French soldier shouts, "On les aura!" or "We'll get them!" — words ascribed to General Henri-Philippe Pétain, who was in charge of the Verdun defense until he was given command of all French armies in the field in the summer of 1916.

QUESTIONS FOR ANALYSIS

1. What messages about the war does each of the four illustrations communicate?
2. In what specific ways does each of them romanticize war and the life of a soldier?
3. What impressions of combat do the English tobacco card and the French war bond poster communicate?
4. What does Hennerberg's painting suggest about women's anticipated role in the war?

Advertisement card from Golden Dawn cigarettes

B. Hennerberg, The Departure

Australian recruitment poster (1915)

French poster encouraging purchase of war bonds (1916)

The Reality of War in Verse

◈

19 ◆ *Wilfred Owen,*
DULCE ET DECORUM EST and DISABLED

So great was the carnage of World War I that no historian has captured its horror as vividly as have the poets and novelists who experienced it. Every major belligerent nation had writers who evoked the desolation and inhumanity of trench warfare. Among the most powerful was the British poet Wilfred Owen (1893–1918), who enlisted in the British army in 1915 at the age of 22. Wounded in 1917, he was hospitalized, released, and sent back to the trenches, where he was killed on November 4, 1918, one week before the armistice. His poem, "Dulce et Decorum Est," written in 1915, takes its title from a line by the ancient Roman poet Horace: "It is sweet and fitting to die for one's country." Its subject is a poison gas attack. The Germans launched the first large-scale gas attack in April 1915 when they released chlorine gas from cylinders and let the wind carry it toward French and Canadian troops in the vicinity of Ypres. Subsequently, both sides used poison gas, with phosgene and mustard gas being delivered by artillery shells by 1918. "Disabled," also written in 1915, describes a badly mutilated Scottish soldier who enlisted before he was eighteen, and now sits in a wheelchair in an institution where he survives, but barely.

QUESTIONS FOR ANALYSIS

1. How in "Dulce et Decorum Est" does Owen describe the mental and physical condition of the foot soldiers?
2. What imagery does he apply to the body of the gas victim?
3. Why does Owen find the plight of the young Scottish soldier so compelling?
4. In what specific ways do Owen's poems attempt to dispel the illusions about war represented in the art in the previous section?

DULCE ET DECORUM EST

Bent double, like old beggars under sacks,
Knock-kneed, coughing like hags, we cursed
   through sludge,
Till on the haunting flares we turned our backs
And towards our distant rest began the trudge.
Men marched asleep. Many had lost their boots
But limped on, blood-shod. All went lame; all
   blind;

Drunk with fatigue; deaf even to the hoots
Of tired, outstripped Five-Nines[1] that dropped
   behind.

Gas! GAS! Quick, boys! — An ecstasy of
   fumbling,
Fitting the clumsy helmets just in time;
But someone still was yelling out and
   stumbling,
And flound'ring like a man in fire or lime . . .

---

[1] Slang for artillery shells used by the Germans.

Dim, through the misty panes and thick green
    light,
As under a green sea, I saw him drowning.
In all my dreams, before my helpless sight,
He plunges at me, guttering, choking,
    drowning.

If in some smothering dreams you too could
    pace
Behind the wagon that we flung him in,
And watch the white eyes writhing in his face,
His hanging face, like a devil's sick of sin;
If you could hear, at every jolt, the blood
Come gargling from the froth-corrupted lungs,
Obscene as cancer, bitter as the cud
Of vile, incurable sores on innocent tongues, —
My friend, you would not tell with such high
    zest,
To children ardent for some desperate glory,
The old Lie: Dulce et decorum est
Pro patria mori.

DISABLED

He sat in a wheeled chair, waiting for dark,
And shivered in his ghastly suit of grey,
Legless, sewn short at elbow. Through the park
Voices of boys rang saddening like a hymn,
Voices of play and pleasure after day,
Till gathering sleep had mothered them from
    him.

About this time Town used to swing so gay
When glow-lamps budded in the light blue
    trees,
And girls glanced lovelier as the air grew
    dim, —
In the old times, before he threw away his
    knees.
Now he will never feel again how slim
Girls' waists are, or how warm their subtle
    hands.
All of them touch him like some queer
    disease.

There was an artist silly for his face,
For it was younger than his youth, last year.
Now, he is old; his back will never brace;
He's lost his colour very far from here,
Poured it down shell-holes till the veins ran
    dry,
And half his lifetime lapsed in the hot race
And leap of purple spurted from his thigh.

One time he liked a bloodsmear down his leg,
After the matches, carried shoulder-high.
It was after football, when he'd drunk a peg,
He thought he'd better join. — He wonders
    why.
Someone had said he'd look a god in kilts.
That's why; and maybe, too, to please his Meg,
Aye, that was it, to please the giddy jilts[2]
He asked to join. He didn't have to beg;
Smiling they wrote his lie; aged nineteen
    years.
Germans he scarcely thought of; all their guilt
And Austria's, did not move him. And no fears
Of Fear came yet. He thought of jewelled hilts
For daggers in plaid socks; of smart salutes;
And care of arms; and leave, and pay arrears;
Esprit de corps; and hints for young recruits.
And soon, he was drafted out with drums and
    cheers.

Some cheered him home, but not as crowds
    cheer Goal.
Only a solemn man who brought him fruits
Thanked him; and then inquired about his
    soul.

Now, he will spend a few sick years in insti-
    tutes,
And do what things the rules consider wise,
And take whatever pity they may dole.
Tonight he noticed how the women's eyes
Passed from him to the strong men that were
    whole.
How cold and late it is! Why don't they come
And put him to bed? Why don't they come?

---

[2]Scottish slang for young girls.

The Reality of War in Art

◆

20 ◆ *Christopher Nevinson, THE HARVEST OF BATTLE*
and
Otto Dix, STORM TROOP ADVANCING UNDER GAS

Many European artists fought in World War I or were sent to the front to serve as official painters. During the war itself, their subject matter was carefully monitored by their governments. In England, for example, it was illegal to display a painting that portrayed a dead English soldier. Thus most of the paintings that expressed disillusionment with the war appeared only after hostilities ended. Such was the case with the two works in this section.

The first painting, *The Harvest of Battle,* was completed by the English painter Christopher Nevinson in 1919. Born is 1889, Nevinson was an art student in France when the war started. He served in the Red Cross and the Royal Army Medical Corps before rheumatic fever forced him out of active service in 1916. He returned to the war zone as an official painter in late 1917. On his return to England in early 1918, he exhibited large numbers of war-related paintings and drawings that expressed his deep emotions about the war's human costs. He found little demand for his war-related paintings in the 1920s, and the rest of his career was devoted to townscapes and flower pictures. While serving as a war artist in World War II, he suffered a stroke and died in 1946.

Otto Dix (1891–1969), who created the etching *Storm Troop Advancing Under Gas,* was one of Germany's most important twentieth-century artists. He was on active duty throughout the war, serving as machine gunner, artilleryman, and aerial observer on both the Eastern and Western fronts. Deeply disillusioned with postwar society and its failure to appreciate the sacrifices of veterans, Dix became an ardent pacifist, whose powerful antiwar drawings and paintings contributed to his condemnation and arrest by the Nazis. Only in the desperate closing days of World War II was he drafted into the army.

Storm Troop Advancing Under Gas is one of a series of fifty etchings Dix produced in 1923 and 1924, collectively entitled *War.* Storm troops were highly trained soldiers armed with machine guns, mortars, and flamethrowers whose job was to attack rear areas and artillery positions before direct, large-scale infantry assaults were launched on enemy trenches.

QUESTIONS FOR ANALYSIS

1. What statements about war is each artist attempting to make in his work?
2. What specific details help the artist put his message across?
3. Why do you suppose Nevinson chose the title *The Harvest of Battle* for his work?

C. R. W. Nevinson, The Harvest of Battle

Otto Dix, Storm Troop Advancing Under Gas Attack

The Century's First Genocide

"A coordinated plan of different actions aiming at the destruction of the essential foundations of the life of national groups, with the aim of annihilating the groups themselves." This was the chilling definition of a new word coined in 1944 by the American jurist Raphael Lemkin. The new word was *genocide,* and Lemkin used it to describe the Nazis' systematic extermination of Gypsies, Poles, Russians, and especially Jews during World War II. Sadly, Lemkin's new word applies equally well to dozens of other episodes in the twentieth century, most recently to ethnic cleansing in Bosnia and the mass murder of Tutsis by the Hutus of Rwanda.

The century's first genocide took place in eastern Turkey in 1915, three decades before Lemkin coined a word to describe it. Its victims, numbering from six hundred thousand to one million, were Armenians, a people who since the seventh century B.C.E. had lived in the region south of the Caucasus Mountains and between the Black and Caspian Seas. They became Christians around 300 C.E., and over time developed a distinctive Armenian Apostolic Church close to the Eastern Orthodox Church in most respects. The Armenian heartland was captured by the Ottoman Turks in the sixteenth century and, except for a portion conquered by Persia and taken over by Russia in 1828, remained under Ottoman rule until the empire's demise after World War I. Numbering slightly more than two million, the Armenians, like Jews and other Christian minorities in the Ottoman Empire, were allowed to practice their religion and maintain their distinctive culture. However, they paid special taxes, could not own weapons, and were excluded from government positions.

During the nineteenth century, tensions worsened between the Armenians and Ottoman officials on the one hand and the general Muslim population on the other. Many Muslims were deeply resentful that the Armenian community was experiencing a cultural and economic renaissance while the Ottoman Empire itself was falling apart. Dozens of Armenian schools were founded during the nineteenth century, many by missionaries from the United States and Europe, and increasing numbers of Armenians went abroad to study at Russian or European universities. New Armenian-language newspapers were founded, and Armenian literature flourished. Although most Armenians remained small farmers, many became successful in trade, industry, and banking. Muslim-Armenian relations deteriorated even further when Armenian leaders began to call for greater autonomy and fairer treatment within the empire, although not for total independence.

Against this background, attacks on Armenians grew in the late 1800s, culminating in the massacre of as many as one hundred thousand Armenians by Ottoman troops between 1894 and 1896. The sultan who ordered these massacres (or, according to some interpretations, stood by idly while they occurred), Abdul Hamid II, was overthrown in the Revolution of 1908, which brought to power the Young Turks, or the Committee of Union and Progress. The party controlled Turkey during World War I and was responsible for the genocide of

1915. To jealousy, religious antagonism, and political fears, the Young Turks added another deadly ingredient to the anti-Armenian mix — nationalism. Rejecting the ethnic and religious pluralism of the Ottoman Empire, they favored an exclusively Turkish state. Some even dreamed of extending Turkey's borders to the east to include other Turkic peoples in Russian Central Asia. In neither scenario was there a place for two million Armenians.

World War I, in which Turkey was allied with Germany, offered the Young Turks a pretext and opportunity to deal with the "Armenian problem." By early 1915 the Turkish offensive against Russia in the Caucasus had failed, and the Allies had begun their campaign to take the Dardanelles. Young Turk extremists, specifically Minister of Internal Affairs Talaat Pasha and Minister of War Enver Pasha, sought to make the Armenians scapegoats for military defeats and settle the Armenian issue once and for all. On the night of April 23–24, 1915, scores of Armenian churchmen, intellectuals, educators, and businessmen were arrested in Istanbul, sent to the countryside, and executed. The century's first genocide had begun.

Caravans of Death

21 ◆ *Mary L. Graffam,*
LETTER FROM TURKEY, SUMMER 1915

Like the Nazi effort to exterminate Europe's Jews, the Turkish attempt to obliterate the Armenians took place under the cover of a world war, thus minimizing the chance of outside intervention. In the case of the Nazis, the outside world was unable to grasp the enormity of their crimes until the closing stages of the war. This was not the case in Turkey. With the United States still neutral in 1915, thousands of American missionaries, diplomats, and businessmen resided in Turkey, and as a result, newspaper accounts, reports to the U.S. ambassador, Henry Morgenthau, and hundreds of personal letters detailed the massacres. Germans and visitors from other neutral nations also provided testimony.

Witnesses described how in the weeks following the arrests of April 23–24, Armenians serving in the Turkish army were disarmed, placed in labor battalions, or simply shot. The general Armenian population faced deportation. Forced from their homes, men were executed by Turkish troops, police, or local Turks and Kurds, while women, children, and old men were driven for weeks over mountains and deserts in caravans that were preyed upon by bandits and local people. Those who reached the Syrian Desert or the swampy regions of the upper Euphrates River were left to die from heat, starvation, or disease. Further atrocities against the Armenians were perpetrated at the war's close when the Turkish army reoccupied portions of eastern Anatolia that had been abandoned by the Russians.

The following is typical of the many letters written by foreign eyewitnesses and later published in newspapers, missionary journals, or Armenian-language publications outside of Turkey. The author is Mary L. Graffam, a Protestant missionary from Massachusetts who was principal of a girls' school in Sivas, a city in north-central Turkey. It reveals the confusion and disbelief that attended the early deportations. Although the letter is undated, the events it describes took place in July 1915.

QUESTIONS FOR ANALYSIS

1. What can be learned from Graffam's letter about the motives of those who attacked the Armenians?
2. What evidence does the letter provide about the ways different groups of Armenians were treated?
3. The author is uncertain about the government's responsibility for ordering the massacres. What experiences did she have that help explain her uncertainty?
4. What do you make of the efforts of government officials to separate Graffam from the Armenian deportees? How does your answer relate to the issue raised in question 3?

When we were ready to leave Sivas, the Government gave forty-five ox-carts for the Protestant townspeople and eighty horses, but none at all for our pupils and teachers; so we bought ten ox-carts, two horse arabas [wagons], and five or six donkeys, and started out. In the company were all our teachers in the college, about twenty boys from the college and about thirty of the girls'-school. It was as a special favour to the Sivas people, who had not done anything revolutionary, that the Vali[1] allowed the men who were not yet in prison to go with their families.

The first night we were so tired that we just ate a piece of bread and slept on the ground wherever we could find a place to spread a yorgan [blanket]. It was after dark when we stopped, anyway. We were so near Sivas that the gendarmes[2] protected us, and no special harm was done; but the second night we began to see what was before us. The gendarmes would go ahead and have long conversations with the villagers, and then stand back and let

them rob and trouble the people until we all began to scream, and then they would come and drive them away. Yorgans [Blankets] and rugs, and all such things, disappeared by the dozen, and donkeys were sure to be lost. Many had brought cows; but from the first day those were carried off, one by one, until not a single one remained.

We got accustomed to being robbed, but the third day a new fear took possession of us, and that was that the men were to be separated from us at Kangal. . . . Our teacher from Mandjaluk was there, with his mother and sisters. They had left the village with the rest of the women and children, and when they saw that the men were being taken off to be killed the teacher fled to another village, four hours away, where he was found by the police and brought safely with his family to Kangal, because the tchaoush [officer] who had taken them from Mandjaluk wanted his sister. I found them confined in one room. I went to the Kaimakam[3] and got an order for them all to come with us.

---

[1] A provincial governor.
[2] Armed rural police representing the Ottoman government.

[3] A district official.

At Kangal some Armenians had become Mohammedans, and had not left the village, but the others were all gone. . . . They said that a valley near there was full of corpses. At Kangal we also began to see exiles from Tokat. The sight was one to strike horror to any heart; they were a company of old women, who had been robbed of absolutely everything. At Tokat the Government had first imprisoned the men, and from the prison had taken them on the road. . . . After the men had gone, they arrested the old women and the older brides, perhaps about thirty or thirty-five years old. There were very few young women or children. All the younger women and children were left in Tokat. . . .

When we looked at them we could not imagine that even the sprinkling of men that were with us would be allowed to remain. We did not long remain in doubt; the next day we . . . had come to Hassan Tehelebi . . . and it was with terror in our hearts that we passed through that village about noon. But we encamped and ate our supper in peace, and even began to think that perhaps it was not so, when the Mudir [the official in charge] came round with gendarmes and began to collect the men. . . .

The night passed, and only one man came back to tell the story of how every man was compelled to give up all his money, and all were taken to prison. The next morning they collected the men who had escaped the night before and extorted forty-five liras from our company, on the promise that they would give us gendarmes to protect us. One " company" is supposed to be from 1,000 to 3,000 persons. Ours was perhaps 2,000, and the greatest number of gendarmes would be five or six. In addition to these they sewed a red rag on the arm of a Kurdish villager[4] and gave him a gun, and he had the right to rob and bully us all he pleased.

Broken-hearted, the women continued their journey. . . .

As soon as the men left us, the Turkish drivers began to rob the women, saying: "You are all going to be thrown into the Tokma Su,[5] so you might as well give your things to us, and then we will stay by you and try to protect you." Every Turkish woman that we met said the same thing. The worst were the gendarmes, who really did more or less bad things. One of our schoolgirls was carried off by the Kurds twice, but her companions made so much fuss that she was brought back. . . .

As we approached the bridge over the Tokma Su, it was certainly a fearful sight. As far as the eye could see over the plain was this slow-moving line of ox-carts. For hours there was not a drop of water on the road, and the sun poured down its very hottest. As we went on we began to see the dead from yesterday's company, and the weak began to fall by the way. The Kurds working in the fields made attacks continually, and we were half-distracted. I piled as many as I could on our wagons, and our pupils, both boys and girls, worked like heroes. One girl took a baby from its dead mother and carried it until evening. Another carried a dying woman until she died. We bought water from the Kurds, not minding the beating that the boys were sure to get with it. I counted forty-nine deaths, but there must have been many more. One naked body of a woman was covered with bruises. I saw the Kurds robbing the bodies of those not yet entirely dead. . . .

The hills on each side were white with Kurds, who were throwing stones on the Armenians, who were slowly wending their way to the bridge. I ran ahead and stood on the bridge in the midst of a crowd of Kurds, until I was used up [exhausted]. I did not see anyone thrown into the water, but they said, and I believe it, that a certain Elmas, who has done handwork for me for years, was thrown over the bridge by a Kurd. Our Badvelli's wife was

---

[4]Kurds were a Sunni Muslim people who lived in territory that today makes up parts of southeastern Turkey, northwest Iraq, and northeast Syria; the "red rag" was an arm band that gave the Kurds special status.

[5]A local river.

riding on a horse with a baby in her arms, and a Kurd took hold of her to throw her over, when another Kurd said: "She has a baby in her arms," and they let her go. . . .

The police for the first time began to interfere with me here, and it was evident that something was decided about me. The next morning after we arrived at this bridge, they wanted me to go to Malatia; but I insisted that I had permission to stay with the Armenians. During the day, however, they said that [I had been ordered] to come to Malatia, and that the others were going to Kiakhta. Soon after we heard that they were going to Ourfa, there to build villages and cities, &c.

In Malatia I went at once to the commandant, a captain who they say has made a fortune out of these exiles. I told him how I had gone to Erzeroum last winter, and how we pitied these women and children and wished to help them, and finally he sent me to the Mutessarif.[6] The latter is a Kurd, apparently anxious to do the right thing; but he has been sick most of the time since he came, and the "beys"[7] here have had things more or less

their own way, and certainly horrors have been committed. . . .

My friends here are very glad to have me with them, for they have a very difficult problem on their hands and are nearly crazy with the horrors they have been through here. The Mutessarif and other officials here and at Sivas have read me orders from Constantinople[8] again and again to the effect that the lives of these exiles are to be protected, and from their actions I should judge that they must have received such orders; but they certainly have murdered a great many in every city. Here there were great trenches dug by the soldiers for drilling purposes. Now these trenches are all filled up, and our friends saw carts going back from the city by night. A man I know told me that when he was out to inspect some work he was having done, he saw a dead body which had evidently been pulled out of one of these trenches, probably by dogs. . . . The Beledia Reis [village chief] here says that every male over ten years old is being murdered, that not one is to live, and no woman over fifteen. The truth seems to be somewhere between these two extremes. . . .

---

[6]A district official.
[7]Kurdish chiefs.
[8]Founded in 660 B.C.E. as Byzantium, the city was renamed Constantinople in 330 C.E. by Constantine the Great, and

served as the seat of the Ottoman government from the thirteenth century until after World War I. In 1930 Istanbul became the city's official name.

An Official Version of the Deportations

❖

22 ◆ Talaat Pasha, *POSTHUMOUS MEMOIRS*

At the conclusion of the war, foreign diplomats and officials of the Ottoman government and Great Britain declared their intention to punish the perpetrators of the Armenian genocide. Ottoman courts ordered the execution of two minor officials and one police officer, but other guilty parties were given prison sentences or convicted in absentia. Judicial proceedings were halted and all prisoners released when the Ottoman government was replaced by a new Turkish government under Mustafa Kemal in 1921. In that same year British efforts to try Turkish officials in British military courts, already bogged down by legal and political difficulties, also were abandoned. Throughout the process, efforts to punish those responsible were weakened by the fact that in November 1918 Turkey's wartime leaders fled the country with German help and hence could not be tried in person.

Among those who fled was Talaat Pasha (1874–1921), the Ottoman minister of the interior during the war. A former postal clerk and telegraph operator, he had risen rapidly in the Ottoman administration after the Young Turk Revolution of 1908. Although the precise lines of authority in the Ottoman government are murky, there is little question that Talaat Pahsa along with Enver Pasha (minister of war) and Kemal Pasha (navy minister and military governor of Syria) were the three key figures in the wartime administration. There is also little doubt that Talaat and Enver were mainly responsible for the government's Armenian policy. After he fled Turkey in 1918, Talaat lived in Europe until he was assassinated by an Armenian student in a Berlin suburb in 1921. The assassin was acquitted when a German court ruled that his act was justifiable homicide in view of Talaat's role in the 1915 massacres.

Before his death, Talaat had written a memoir that was unpublished at the time of his assassination. After his assassin's acquittal, Talaat's wife released the memoir to a Turkish newspaper. It was published in 1921 with the enigmatic opening words, "I do not tell all the truth, but all I tell is truth." In the following section he gives his perspective on the Armenian Question.

QUESTIONS FOR ANALYSIS

1. In what ways were the Armenians responsible for their deportation, according to Talaat Pasha?
2. How credible do you find Talaat's arguments about the Armenians' responsibility for their fate?
3. How would you characterize Talaat's portrayal of his role in the massacres? Does he admit any personal responsibility for the massacres?
4. Why in Talaat's view have the numbers of victims been exaggerated?
5. How and in what ways are Talaat's assertions confirmed or refuted by evidence provided in Graffam's letter?

The deportation of the Armenians, in some localities of the Greeks, and in Syria of some of the Arabs, was used inside and outside the empire as a source of attack on the Turkish Government. First of all, I wish to inform the public that the rumors of deportation and assassination were exceedingly exaggerated. The Greeks and the Armenians, taking advantage of the ignorance of the American and European public of the Near Eastern situation and of the character of the Turks, used the deportation as a means for propaganda, and painted it as best suited their

aim. In saying this, I do not mean to deny the facts. I desire only to eliminate the exaggerations and to relate the facts as they occurred.

I admit that we deported many Armenians from our eastern provinces, but we never acted in this matter upon a previously prepared scheme. The responsibility for these acts falls first of all upon the deported people themselves. Russia, in order to lay hand on our eastern provinces, had armed and equipped the Armenian inhabitants of this district, and had organized strong Armenian bandit forces in the said area. When we entered the great war, these bandits began their destructive activities in the rear of the Turkish Army on the Caucasus front, blowing up the bridges, setting fire to the Turkish towns and villages and killing the innocent Mohammedan[1] inhabitants, regardless of age and sex. They spread death and terror all over the eastern provinces, and endangered the Turkish Army's line of retreat. All these Armenian bandits were helped by the native Armenians. When they were pursued by the Turkish gendarmes, the Armenian villages were a refuge for them. When they needed help, the Armenian peasants around them, taking their arms hidden in their churches, ran to their aid. Every Armenian church, it was later discovered, was a depot of ammunition. In this disloyal way they killed more than 300,000 Mohammedans, and destroyed the communication of the Turkish Army with its bases.[2]

The information that we were receiving from the administrators of these provinces and from the commander of the Caucasian Army gave us details of the most revolting and barbarous activities of the Armenian bandits. It was impossible to shut our eyes to the treacherous acts of the Armenians, at a time when we were engaged in a war which would determine the fate of our country. Even if these actrocities had occurred in a time of peace, our Government would have been obliged to quell such outbreaks. The Porte,[3] acting under the same obligation, and wishing to secure the safety of its army and its citizens, took energetic measures to check these uprisings. The deportation of the Armenians was one of these preventive measures.

I admit also that the deportation was not carried out lawfully everywhere. In some places unlawful acts were committed. The already existing hatred among the Armenians and Mohammedans, intensified by the barbarous activities of the former, had created many tragic consequences. Some of the officials abused their authority, and in many places people took preventive measures into their own hands and innocent people were molested. I confess it. I confess, also, that the duty of the Government was to prevent these abuses and atrocities, or at least to hunt down and punish their perpetrators severely. In many places, where the property and goods of the deported people were looted, and the Armenians molested, we did arrest those who were responsible and punished them according to the law. I confess, however, that we ought to have acted more sternly, opened up a general investigation for the purpose of finding out all the promoters and looters and punished them severely. . . .

But we could not do that. Although we punished many of the guilty, most of them were untouched. These people, whom we might call outlaws, because of their unlawful attitude in disregarding the order of the Central Government, were divided into two classes. Some of them were acting under personal hatred, or for individual profit. Those who looted the goods of the deported Armenians were easily punishable and we punished them. But there was another group, who sincerely believed that the general interest of the community necessitated the punishment alike of those Armenians who massacred the guiltless Mohammedans and those who helped the Armenian bandits to endanger our national life. The Turkish elements here referred to were short-sighted, fanatic, and yet sincere in their belief. The public encouraged them, and they had the general approval behind them. They were numerous and strong. Their

---

[1]Muslim.

[2]That Armenians served in the Russian army is hardly remarkable because many Armenians were Russian subjects. Although it is true some Armenians sympathized with the Allies and hoped for Turkey's defeat, many thousands of Armenians fought in the Ottoman army. It is also true that many Armenians were armed, but this was mainly before the war and for self-defense. Blaming the Armenians for the death of three hundred thousand Turks is a wild exaggeration.

[3]The Porte, or Sublime Porte, is a term for the Ottoman government. It refers to the building that housed the high officials of the Ottoman state.

open and immediate punishment would have aroused great discontent among the people, who favored their acts. An endeavor to arrest and to punish all these promoters would have created anarchy in Anatolia at a time when we greatly needed unity. It would have been dangerous to divide the nation into two camps, when we needed strength to fight outside enemies. We did all that we could, but we preferred to post-pone the solution of our internal difficulties until after the defeat of our external enemies. . . .

These preventive measures were taken in every country during the war, but, while the regrettable results were passed over in silence in the other countries, the echo of our acts was heard the world over, because everybody's eyes were upon us.

The Russian Revolution and the Beginnings of the Soviet State

Among the results of World War I, the downfall of Russia's tsarist regime and its replacement by a Marxist-inspired Bolshevik dictatorship is one of the most important. Tsar Nicholas II (r. 1894–1917), facing military defeat, defections within the army, and rioting in Petrograd, abdicated in March 1917, and the tsarist autocracy was replaced by a provisional government that would govern Russia until a constituent assembly could meet and devise a new constitution. Seven months later, the Bolsheviks wrested power from the Provisional Government and, after three years of civil war, established the world's first communist state.

Discontent had plagued Tsar Nicholas's reign from the start, but it intensified after 1905 when Russia's defeat in the Russo-Japanese War sparked a wave of strikes, rural violence, and demands for constitutional reform. The tsar responded with his October Manifesto, in which he promised a democratically elected parliament, or duma, and freedom of the press. Russians soon realized, however, that the tsar had no intention of abandoning control of such crucial areas as finance, defense, and ministerial appointment. Nor did he have any interest in working with recalcitrant parliaments. He dissolved the first two dumas and then changed the election rules in 1907 to disenfranchise workers, peasants, and his non-Russian subjects. His chief minister Peter Stolypin sought to hold things together by cracking down on dissidents and implementing modest reforms. Meanwhile Constitutional Democrats, Social Revolutionaries, Mensheviks, and Bolsheviks, although deeply divided on tactics and goals, plotted to achieve their one common purpose — the overthrow of the tsar's government.

It was a weak and tottering tsarist Russia that entered World War I in August 1914. Less than three years later it became the war's most significant political casualty.

Lenin's Call for Revolution

❖

23 ◆ *Lenin, APRIL THESES*

After Tsar Nicholas II's abdication on March 2, 1917 (according to the Russian calendar, which was thirteen days behind the Western calendar), an awkward political situation developed in which power was divided between the Provisional Government, backed mainly by Constitutional Democrats, and the Petrograd Soviet of Workers' Deputies, a council representing the Petrograd workers and soldiers. With its membership divided among Mensheviks, Social Revolutionaries, and a few Bolsheviks, the Petrograd Soviet exercised no political authority as such, but its broad support among workers meant that the Provisional Government could take no significant action without its support. With one agency of government, the Soviet, unwilling to rule, and the other, the Provisional Government, unable to, a *"dual power"* resulted in which effective government was impossible.

This was just the type of situation in which an intense, persuasive, ruthless, and single-minded revolutionary might be able to take control of events and achieve an outcome that matched his personal vision. Such a man was Vladimir Ilyich Ulyanov (1870–1924), better known by his adopted revolutionary name, Lenin. The son of a government official and a law school graduate, Lenin dedicated himself to revolution at an early age and was exiled to Siberia with other Marxists in 1895. After his release he left Russia and became a member of the Russian Social Democratic Labor Party. In 1903 he became the leader of the "majority men," or Bolsheviks, who, in opposition to the "minority men," or Mensheviks, demanded highly centralized party leadership, noncooperation with bourgeois liberals, and single-minded devotion to revolution.

Having spent World War I in exile in Switzerland, Lenin returned to Russia on April 3, 1917, with the help of the German army. He immediately sought to convince his fellow Bolsheviks to reject compromise with the Provisional Government and press forward toward a true socialist revolution. His rationale and goals were outlined in two Bolshevik Party meetings on April 4, and then printed on April 7 in the Bolshevik newspaper, *Pravda*. Officially titled "On the Tasks of the Proletariat in the Present Revolution," his proposals are better known as the "April Theses."

Although viewed as unrealistic by many Bolsheviks, Lenin's proposals were soon adopted by the Party. Seven months later Lenin achieved his goal when the Bolsheviks took power in late October and created the world's first Marxist state.

QUESTION FOR ANALYSIS

1. What is Lenin's attitude toward World War I? Under what circumstances would it be possible for him to support Russia's continuing involvement?
2. What unique circumstances exist in Russia, according to Lenin, that make it possible to envision a successful Bolshevik revolution?

3. What does Lenin see as the alternative to the Provisional Government?
4. How does Lenin hope to win over the peasants and greater numbers of workers to the Bolshevik side? What role will the Party play in this process?

1. In our attitude towards the war, which under the new government of Lvov[1] and Co. unquestionably remains on Russia's part a predatory imperialist war owing to the capitalist nature of that government, not the slightest concession to " revolutionary defencism"[2] is permissible. . . .

In view of the undoubted honesty of those broad sections of the mass believers in revolutionary defencism who accept the war only as a necessity, and not as a means of conquest, in view of the fact that they are being deceived by the bourgeoisie, it is necessary with particular thoroughness, persistence and patience to explain their error to them, to explain the inseparable connection existing between capital and the imperialist war, and to prove that without overthrowing capital *it is impossible* to end the war by a truly democratic peace, a peace not imposed by violence. . . .

The most widespread campaign for this view must be organised in the army at the front. . . .

2. The specific feature of the present situation in Russia is that the country is *passing* from the first stage of the revolution — which, owing to the insufficient class-consciousness and organization of the proletariat, placed power in the hands of the bourgeoisie — to its *second* stage which must place power in the hands of the proletariat and the poorest sections of the peasants. . . .

This peculiar situation demands of us an ability to adapt ourselves to the *special* conditions of Party work among unprecedentedly large masses of proletarians who have just awakened to political life.

3. No support for the Provisional Government; the utter falsity of all its promises should be made clear, particularly of those relating to the renunciation of annexations.[3] Exposure in place of the impermissible, illusion-breeding "demand" that *this* government, a government of capitalists, should *cease* to be an imperialist government. . . .

4. . . . The masses must be made to see that the Soviets of Workers' Deputies are the *only possible* form of revolutionary government, and that therefore our task is, as long as *this* government yields to the influence of the bourgeoisie, to present a patient, systematic, and persistent *explanation* of the errors of their tactics, an explanation especially adapted to the practical needs of the masses.

As long as we[4] are in the minority we carry on the work of criticizing and exposing errors and at the same time we preach the necessity of transferring the entire state power to the Soviets of Workers' Deputies, so that the people may overcome their mistakes by experience.

5. Not a parliamentary republic . . . — but a republic of Soviets of Workers', Agricultural Laborers' and Peasants' Deputies throughout the country, from top to bottom.

Abolition of the police, the army and the bureaucracy.

The salaries of all officials, all of whom are elective and displaceable at any time, not to exceed the average wage of a competent worker.

6. The weight of emphasis in the agrarian program to be shifted to the Soviets of Agricultural Laborers' Deputies.

Confiscation of all landed estates.

---

[1]Prince Georg Lvov (1861–1925) was a liberal aristocrat who served as prime minister of the Provisional Government until July 1917, when he was succeeded by Alexandr Kerensky.

[2]Lenin's phrase to describe the position of revolutionaries who supported Russia's involvement in the war.
[3]Territories conquered by Russia during World War I.
[4]The Bolsheviks.

Nationalization of *all* lands in the country, the land to be disposed of by the local Soviets of Agricultural Laborers' and Peasants' Deputies. The organization of separate Soviets of Deputies of Poor Peasants. The setting up of a model farm on each of the large estates . . . under the control of the Soviets of Agricultural Laborers' Deputies and for the public account.

7. The immediate amalgamation of all banks in the country into a single national bank, and the institution of control over it by the Soviet of Workers' Deputies.

8. It is not our *immediate* task to "introduce" socialism, but only to bring social production and the distribution of products at once under the *control* of the Soviets of Workers' Deputies.

9. Party tasks:
    a) Immediate convocation of a Party congress;
    b) Alteration of the Party Program, mainly:
        1) On the question of imperialism and the imperialist war;
        2) On our attitude towards the state and *our* demand for a "commune state";[5]
        3) Amendment of our out-of-date minimum program.[6]
    c) Change of the Party's name.[7]
10. A new International.[8]

We must take the initiative in creating a revolutionary International, an International against the *social-chauvinists* and against the "Centre." . . .

---

[5]In the wake of France's defeat in the Franco-Prussian War (1870–1871), a coalition of republicans, anarchists, socialists, and anticlericals proclaimed Paris a commune in March following national elections that returned a large majority of conservatives and monarchists to the French National Assembly. Government troops crushed the Commune in May, killing approximately twenty-five thousand. To Lenin the Commune was a precursor of proletarian revolution.

[6]A "minimum statement" that set forth the Party's short-term goals.

[7]Lenin believed that the name *Social Democrat* had been besmirched by the European Social Democratic parties that

had supported the war. His proposal that the Bolshevik Social Democrats should call themselves Communists was accepted in 1918.

[8]The International Workingmen's Association, or First International, was an organization founded in 1864 dedicated to the spread of socialism among workers' organizations. The Second International Workingmen's Association, founded in Paris in 1889, was a loose association of national socialist groups. Its annual meetings ceased when war broke out in 1914.

Forging the Soviet State

❖

24 ◆ COMMUNIST DECREES AND LEGISLATION, 1917–1918

On October 25, 1917, with the Bolsheviks in control of public buildings and other key points in Petrograd, Lenin confidently opened the Second Congress of Soviets with the words, "We shall now proceed to construct the Socialist order." As Lenin soon found out, building that new socialist order proved difficult. For one thing, while the Bolsheviks had a broad set of revolutionary aspirations for Russia, they had no blueprint for how to govern the country or how to restructure Russian society. Furthermore, the Bolsheviks were a minority party, as shown by the results of the elections for the Constituent Assembly in November 1917, which gave the Bolsheviks only 29 percent of the vote, as opposed to 58 percent for the

Social Revolutionaries. Finally, they faced formidable problems — a ruined economy, continuing involvement in World War I until March 1918, and civil war from 1918 to 1921.

Despite these challenges, the Bolsheviks had no choice but to plunge ahead. In their first year in power they issued hundreds of decrees that touched every aspect of Russian life and government, and initiated programs and policies that in some cases lasted until the Soviet Union's demise in 1991.

The following is a sample of the decrees issued by the Bolsheviks in 1917 and 1918. The *Decree on Land,* issued on October 26 by the Second Congress of Soviets only hours after the Bolsheviks seized power, recognized land seizures that peasants had already carried out.

The *Decree on Suppression of Hostile Newspapers* and the *Decree Dissolving the Constituent Assembly* were two important steps toward one-party dictatorship. The Bolsheviks, both before and after seizing power, had supported convening a popularly elected Constituent Assembly. But the election of November 1917 resulted in only 168 Bolshevik deputies out of 703 and a clear Social Revolutionary majority. The Assembly convened on January 5, 1918, only to be dissolved by the Bolsheviks on January 7. It was the Soviet Union's last democratically elected parliament until 1989.

The *Edict on Child Welfare,* issued in January 1918, was the brainchild of Alexandra Kollontai (1873–1952), a leading Social Democrat who fled Russia in 1908 to escape arrest and, like Lenin, returned to Petrograd after the downfall of the tsar's government. She became a member of the executive committee of the Petrograd Soviet and played a leading role in the events leading up to the Bolshevik coup. As commissioner of social welfare under the Bolsheviks, she was responsible for laws that legalized abortion, liberalized marriage and divorce, and granted women equal standing with men.

The *Decree on Nationalization of Large-Scale Industries* was issued in June 1918 after the beginning of the civil war. Until then, industry had remained under private ownership, supposedly subject to "workers' control." Now it was nationalized without compensation to the owners.

QUESTION FOR ANALYSIS

1. What rationale is provided in these documents for the "undemocratic" steps taken by the Bolsheviks to dissolve the Constituent Assembly and close down hostile newspapers?
2. What are the economic ramifications of the decrees on land use and nationalization of industry? Who benefits and who is hurt?
3. How will these decrees change essential features of Russian society and social relationships?
4. How do the policies outlined in these decrees compare to the platform adopted by the Russian Social Democrats in 1903 (see "A Marxist Blueprint for Russia" on page 43)?
5. In what specific ways do these decrees increase the role of the state? What implications might this have for the Soviet Union's future?

DECREE ON LAND, OCTOBER 26, 1917

"1) *Private ownership of land shall be abolished forever* . . .

All land . . . *shall be alienated without compensation* and become the property of the whole people, and pass into the use of all those who cultivate it. . . .

2) All mineral wealth, e.g., ore, oil, coal, salt, etc., as well as all forests and waters of state importance, shall pass into the exclusive use of the state. All the small streams, lakes, woods, etc., shall pass into the use of the communities, to be administered by the local self-government bodies.

3) Lands on which *high-level scientific* farming is practised, e.g., orchards, plantations, seed plots, nurseries, hot-houses, etc. *shall not be divided up, but shall be converted into model farms,* to be turned over for exclusive use *to the state or to the communities,* depending on the size and importance of such lands. . . .

6) The right to use the land shall be accorded to all citizens of the Russian state (without distinction of sex) desiring to cultivate it by their own labor, with the help of their families, or in partnership, but only as long as they are able to cultivate it. . . .

DECREE ON SUPPRESSION OF HOSTILE NEWSPAPERS, OCTOBER 27, 1917

Everyone knows that the bourgeois press is one of the most powerful weapons of the bourgeoisie. Especially in this critical moment when the new authority, that of the workers and peasants, is in process of consolidation, it was impossible to leave this weapon in the hands of the enemy at a time when it is not less dangerous than bombs and machine guns. This is why temporary and extraordinary measures have been adopted for the purpose of cutting off the stream of mire and calumny in which the . . . press would be glad to drown the young victory of the people.

As soon as the new order will be consolidated, all administrative measures against the press will be suspended; full liberty will be given it within the limits of responsibility before the laws, in accordance with the broadest and most progressive regulations in this respect. . . .

DECREE DISSOLVING THE CONSTITUENT ASSEMBLY, JANUARY 7, 1918

The October Revolution, by giving the power to the Soviets, and through the Soviets to the toiling and exploited classes, aroused the desperate resistance of the exploiters, and in the crushing of this resistance it fully revealed itself as the beginning of the socialist revolution. The toiling classes learnt by experience that the old bourgeois parliamentarism had outlived its purpose and was absolutely incompatible with the aim of achieving Socialism, and that not national institutions, but only class institutions (such as the soviets), were capable of overcoming the resistance of the propertied classes and of laying the foundations of a socialist society. To relinquish the sovereign power of the soviets, to relinquish the Soviet republic won by the people, for the sake of bourgeois parliamentarism and the Constituent Assembly, would now be a retrograde step and cause the collapse of the October workers' and peasants' revolution. . . .

The Right Socialist Revolutionary and Menshevik parties are in fact waging outside the walls of the Constituent Assembly a most desperate struggle against the Soviet power, calling openly in their press for its overthrow and characterizing as arbitrary and unlawful the crushing by force of the resistance of the exploiters by the toiling classes, which is essential in the interests of emancipation from exploitation. They are defending the saboteurs, the servitors of capital, and are going to the length of undisguised calls to terrorism, which certain "unidentified groups" have already begun to practice. It is obvious that under such circumstances the remaining part of the Constituent Assembly could only serve as a screen for the struggle of the counterrevolutionaries to overthrow the Soviet power.

Accordingly, the Central Executive Committee resolves: The Constituent Assembly is hereby dissolved.

EDICT ON CHILD WELFARE, JANUARY 1918

After a search that has lasted centuries, human thought has at last discovered the radiant epoch where the working class, with its own hands, can freely construct that form of maternity protection which will preserve the child for the mother and the mother for the child. . . .

The new Soviet Russia calls all you working women, you working mothers with your sensitive hearts, you bold builders of a new social life, you teachers of the new attitudes, you children's doctors and midwives, to devote your minds and emotions to building the great edifice that will provide social protection for future generations. From the date of publication of this decree, all large and small institutions under the commissariat of social welfare that serve the child, from the children's home in the capital to the modest village creche,[1] shall be merged into one government organization and placed under the department for the protection of maternity and childhood. As an integral part of the total number of institutions connected with pregnancy and maternity, they shall continue to fulfil the single common task of creating citizens who are strong both mentally and physically. . . .

For the rapid elaboration and introduction of the reforms necessary for the protection of childhood in Russia, commissions are being organized under the auspices of the departments of maternity and childhood. . . . The commissions must base their work on the following main principles:

1. The preservation of the mother for the child: milk from the mother's breast is invaluable for the child.
2. The child must be brought up in the enlightened and understanding atmosphere provided by the socialist family.
3. Conditions must be created which permit the development of the child's physical and mental powers and the child's keen comprehension of life.

DECREE ON NATIONALIZATION OF LARGE-SCALE INDUSTRIES, JUNE 28, 1918

For the purpose of combating decisively the economic disorganization and the breakdown of the food supply, and of establishing more firmly the dictatorship of the working class and the village poor, the Soviet of People's Commissars has resolved:

1. To declare all of the following industrial and commercial enterprises which are located in the Soviet Republic, with all their capital and property, whatever they may consist of, the property of the Russian Socialist Federated Soviet Republic. [A long list of mines, mills, and factories follows.]
2. The administration of the nationalized industries shall be organized . . . by the different departments of the Supreme Council of National Economy. . . .
4. Beginning with the promulgation of this decree, the members of the administration, the directors, and other responsible officers of the nationalized industries will be held responsible to the Soviet Republic both for the intactness and upkeep of the business and for its proper functioning. . . .
5. The entire personnel of every enterprise — technicians, workers, members of the board of directors, and foremen — shall be considered employees of the Russian Socialist

---

[1] A day nursery.

Federated Soviet Republic; their wages shall be fixed in accordance with the scales existing at the time of nationalization and shall be paid out of the funds of the respective enterprises. . . .

6. All private capital belonging to members of the boards of directors, stockholders, and owners of the nationalized enterprises will be attached pending the determination of the relation of such capital to the turnover capital and resources of the enterprises in question. . . .

◆

The Peace That Failed

On January 19, 1919, thousands of diplomats, ministers, journalist, and observers gathered in Paris for the first session of the peace conference that was to reorder the world after World War I. Participants included delegates from the thirty-two nations that had been on the winning side, observers from the defeated Central Powers, and spokespersons of numerous religious and ethnic groups — Arabs, Egyptians, Kurds, Irish, Zionists, Persians, Indians, Vietnamese, Africans, African-Americans, and Armenians. Women's organizations and even supporters of the tsarist cause in Russia also were represented.

By May the Paris Peace Conference had completed the treaty dealing with Germany, the Treaty of Versailles, which the Germans grudgingly signed on June 28, 1919. The Conference also produced broad outlines of treaties to be completed later for Austria, Hungary, Bulgaria, and Ottoman Turkey. No one was entirely happy, and many were deeply angry, with the results. Negative feelings intensified in the 1920s and 1930s as the world stumbled toward another, more terrible world war, the prevention of which had been one of the treaty writers' major goals.

The postwar treaties were largely the work of just three leaders: Prime Minister Georges Clemenceau of France, Lloyd George of Great Britain, and President Woodrow Wilson of the United States. A year earlier, in January 1918, Wilson had issued his famous Fourteen Points, a document that many assumed would be the basis of the postwar treaties. Wilson called for open diplomacy, free trade, reduced armies, and national self-determination in Europe. Although Germany would be required to return Alsace-Lorraine to France and abandon conquered territories in Russia and Belgium, there was no talk of harshly punishing Germany or blocking "in any way her legitimate influence and power." Colonial claims were to be "readjusted," in a process in which "the interests of the populations concerned must have equal weight with the equitable claims of the government whose title is being determined." Finally, Wilson called for the founding of a "general association of nations" whose purpose was to preserve peace and guarantee the political integrity of great and small nations alike.

Lloyd George and especially Clemenceau had different agendas. Clemenceau wanted to protect French security by weakening and punishing Germany. Lloyd George was more flexible, but whatever moderate inclinations he might have had were outweighed by his recent election promises to "hang the emperor" and "squeeze the German lemon until the pips squeak." Neither leader was interested in considering the opinions of Africans and Asians in "readjusting colonial claims."

Divided by personal and philosophical conflicts, saddled by conflicting claims and promises, and subject to intense political pressures, the peacemakers faced issues of daunting complexity. In just a few months they were expected to solve political problems around the globe, which had they been addressed one by one without undue pressure still would have taxed fully their wisdom and foresight. Mistakes and blunders were made, and it is easy to understand why. Understanding them makes them no less tragic.

The Allies' "Last Horrible Triumph"

25 ◆ *COMMENTS OF THE GERMAN DELEGATION TO THE PARIS PEACE CONFERENCE ON THE CONDITIONS OF PEACE, OCTOBER 1919*

The Germans had expected to win the Great War but had lost. In defeat they had expected to be treated with justice and moderation, and again they were bitterly disappointed. The new democratic German government was excluded from the Paris Peace Conference, and when it received a draft of the treaty in late April, 1919, it responded with a list of complaints and counterproposals. All but a few of them were rejected. Germany's chancellor Philip Scheidemann resigned, saying, "What hand would not wither when it signed such a treaty?" The German National Assembly voted in June to accept the treaty but with two reservations: It rejected the claim that Germany was solely responsible for the war and the provision that the kaiser and other high officials were to be tried as war criminals. The Allies dismissed their complaints, and demanded a positive reply in twenty-four hours. Threatened with invasion, the assembly accepted the treaty as written. It was signed on June 28, 1919, and German humiliation was complete.

Germany lost all of its colonies, 13 percent of its land, and 10 percent of its population. Alsace and Lorraine, won from France in 1871, were returned to France. Northern Schleswig went to Denmark, parts of Posen and West Prussia went to Poland, while smaller bits of territory went to Belgium and Czechoslovakia. The coal mines of the Saar Basin were given to France for fifteen years, at which time the German government could buy them back; the Saar region itself was to be administered by the League of Nations. East Prussia was cut off from the rest of Germany by territory ceded to Poland, and the largely German port of Danzig on the Baltic Sea came under Polish economic control. The Germans were permitted to have no air force, a navy of approximately two dozen ships, and a volunteer army of no more than one hundred thousand officers and men. Article 231, the "war-guilt" clause, held Germany and its allies responsible for causing the war. On the basis of this claim, Germany was held accountable for all Allied losses and damages, and would be required to pay reparations. In 1921 the sum was set at $33 billion.

On the day the treaty was signed, the nationalist newspaper *Deutsche Zeitung* published the following statement on its front page:

> Vengeance! German nation! Today in the Hall of Mirrors the disgraceful treaty is being signed. Do not forget it! . . . The German people will with un-ceasing labor, press forward to reconquer the place among nations to which it is entitled. Then will come vengeance for the shame of 1919!

Few Germans did not harbor such sentiments somewhere in their hearts dur-ing the 1920s. Nationalist and antidemocratic politicians learned how to play on these resentments, and in so doing undermined the democratic government that had signed the treaty. Of those politicians, the most successful was Adolf Hitler, whose Nazis took power in 1933 and immediately set out to destroy the Versailles settlement.

The reasons for German resentment are spelled out in the following com-ments and observations. They were submitted in October 1919 by the German delegation to the Paris Peace Conference, which continued to meet after the signing of the Versailles Treaty until January 21, 1920.

QUESTIONS FOR ANALYSIS

1. In Germany's view, how would the country have been treated differently if the principles they attribute to President Wilson had been applied?
2. What does the document reveal about the difficulty of applying the principle of ethnic self-determination in Europe?
3. To what higher "fundamental" laws does the document appeal to in order to strengthen German assertions?
4. What view of colonialism is expressed in the document? Why do the authors claim that Germany has a right to its colonies?
5. According to the authors of the German complaint, how will various provi-sions of the treaty hurt Germany's economy?
6. Do you agree with the authors of the document that Germany was being poorly treated? What response to their complaints might defenders of the treaty have made?

Although President Wilson, in his speech of October 20th, 1916, has acknowledged that "no single fact caused the war, but that in the last analysis the whole European system is in a deeper sense responsible for the war, with its combina-tion of alliances and understandings, a compli-cated texture of intrigues and espionage that unfailingly caught the whole family of nations in its meshes," . . . Germany is to acknowledge that Germany and her allies are responsible for all damages which the enemy Governments or their subjects have incurred by her and her allies' aggression. . . . Apart from the consideration that there is no incontestable legal foundation for the obligation for reparation imposed upon Germany, the amount of such compensation is to be determined by a commission nominated solely by Germany's enemies, Germany taking no part. . . . The commission is plainly to have power to administer Germany like the estate of a bankrupt.[1]

As there are innate rights of man, so there are innate rights of nations. The inalienable fundamental right of every state is the right of self-preservation and self-determination. With this fundamental right the demand here made upon Germany is incompatible. Germany must promise to pay an indemnity, the amount of which at present is not even stated. The German rivers are to be placed under the control of an international body upon which Germany's delegates are always to be but the smallest minority. Canals and railroads are to be built on German territory at the discretion of foreign authorities.

These few instances show that that is not the just peace we were promised, not the peace "the very principle of which," according to a word of President Wilson, "is equality and the common participation in a common benefit. . . ."

In such a peace the solidarity of human interests, which was to find its expression in a League of Nations, would have been respected. How often Germany has been given the promise that this League of Nations would unite the belligerents, conquerors as well as conquered, in a permanent system of common rights! . . .

. . . But in contradiction to them, the Covenant of the League of Nations has been framed without the cooperation of Germany. Nay, still more. Germany does not even stand on the list of those States that have been invited to join the League of Nations. . . . What the treaty of peace proposes to establish, is rather a continuance of the present hostile coalition which does not deserve the name of "League of Nations." . . . The old political system based on force and with its tricks and rivalries will thus continue to thrive!

Again and again the enemies of Germany have assured the whole world that they did not aim at the destruction of Germany. . . .

In contradiction to this, the peace document shows that Germany's position as a world power is to be utterly destroyed. The Germans abroad are deprived of the possibility of keeping up their old relations in foreign countries and of regaining for Germany a share in world commerce, while their property, which has up to the present been confiscated and liquidated, is being used for reparation instead of being restored to them. . . .

In this war, a new fundamental law has arisen which the statesmen of all belligerent peoples have again and again acknowledged to be their aim: the right of self-determination. To make it possible for all nations to put this privilege into practice was intended to be one achievement of the war. . . .

Neither the treatment described above of the inhabitants of the Saar[2] region as accessories to the [coal] pits nor the public form of consulting the population in the districts of Eupen, Malmédy and Prussian Moresnet[3] — which, moreover, shall not take place before they have been put under Belgian sovereignty — comply in the least with such a solemn recognition of the right of self-determination.

The same is also true with regard to Alsace-Lorraine. If Germany has pledged herself "to right the wrong of 1871," this does not mean any renunciation of the right of self-determination of the inhabitants of Alsace-Lorraine. A cession of the country without consulting the population

---

[1] A Reparations Commission appointed by the Peace Conference set the final sum at $33 billion in 1921. In the meantime Germany was required to make an interim payment of $5 billion.

[2] After fifteen years, the people of the Saar would have a plebiscite to decide if they would remain under the administration of a League of Nations commission or become part of France or Germany. In 1935 they voted to become part of Germany.

[3] Moresnet, an area of some fourteen hundred acres and the site of a valuable zinc mine, was annexed outright by Belgium. In Eupen and Malmédy, those who objected to the transfer of the areas to Belgium could sign their names in a public registry. On the basis of this "plebiscite," both areas became Belgian.

would be a new wrong, if for no other reason, because it would be inconsistent with a recognized principle of peace.

On the other hand, it is incompatible with the idea of national self-determination for two and one-half million Germans to be torn away from their native land against their own will. By the proposed demarcation of the boundary, unmistakably German territories are disposed of in favor of their Polish neighbors. Thus, from the Central Silesian districts of Guhrau and Militsch certain portions are to be wrenched away, in which, beside 44,900 Germans, reside at the utmost 3,700 Poles. . . .

This disrespect of the right of self-determination is shown most grossly in the fact that Danzig[4] is to be separated from the German Empire and made a free state. Neither historical rights nor the present ethnographical conditions of ownership of the Polish people can have any weight as compared with the German past and the German character of that city. . . . Likewise the cession of the commercial town of Memel, which is to be exacted from Germany, is in no way consistent with the right of self-determination. The same may be said with reference to the fact that millions of Germans in German-Austria are to be denied the union with Germany which they desire and that, further, millions of Germans dwelling along our frontiers are to be forced to remain part of the newly created Czecho-Slovakian State.

Even as regards that part of the national territory that is to be left to Germany, the promised right of self-determination is not observed. A Commission for the execution of the indemnity[5] shall be the highest instance for the whole State. Our enemies claim to have fought for the great aim of the democratization of Germany. To be sure, the outcome of the war has delivered us from our former authorities, but instead of them we shall have in exchange a foreign, dictatorial power whose aim can and must be only to exploit the working power of the German people for the benefit of the creditor states. . . .

The fact that this is an age in which economic relations are on a world scale, requires the political organization of the civilized world. The German Government agrees with the Governments of the Allied and Associated Powers in the conviction that the horrible devastation caused by this war requires the establishment of a new world order, an order which shall insure the "effective authority of the principles of international law," and "just and honorable relations between the nations." . . .

There is no evidence of these principles in the peace document which has been laid before us. Expiring world theories, emanating from imperialistic and capitalistic tendencies, celebrate in it their last horrible triumph. As opposed to these views, which have brought unspeakable disaster upon the world, we appeal to the innate sense of right of men and nations, under whose token the English State developed, the Dutch People freed itself, the North American nation established its independence, France shook off absolutism. The bearers of such hallowed traditions cannot deny this right to the German people, that now for the first time has acquired in its internal politics the possibility of living in harmony with its free will based on law.

---

[4]Danzig was administered by the League of Nations, but its economy would be controlled by Poland.
[5]This concern was well-founded. After the Germans fell behind in their payments in 1923, the French-controlled Reparations Commission ordered French, Belgian, and Italian technicians into Germany's Ruhr region to collect coal and transport it to the border under military protection.

The Betrayal of Arab Nationalism

❖

26 ❖ *GENERAL SYRIAN CONGRESS OF DAMASCUS, RESOLUTION OF JULY 2, 1919*

Lured by Great Britain's promises of an independent Arab state, Arabs under Sharif Husayn (1856–1931), the ruler of the western lands of the Arabian Peninsula, revolted against the Ottomans in 1916. In 1918, with the end of the war and the defeat of Ottoman Empire, the Arabs looked forward to self-rule.

At the Paris Peace Conference, however, it became apparent that the British and French had no interest in "adjusting colonial claims" or honoring wartime promises to the Arabs. Instead, they planned to divide the Arab Middle East between them, as they had agreed to do during the war. This troubled Woodrow Wilson, who proposed in March 1919 that a commission of inquiry composed of U.S., British, French, and Italian representatives visit the Middle East to gather information so that a settlement could be achieved on the "most scientific basis." The French, British, and Italians refused to cooperate, however, so the commission became a U.S. undertaking, led by educator Henry C. King and industrialist and diplomat Charles R. Crane.

By the time the commission began its inquiry in the summer of 1919, the fate of the region had been sealed by Article 22 of the League of Nations Covenant, which was part of the Versailles Treaty. Article 22 decreed that Germany's former colonies and the Arab regions of the defunct Ottoman Empire were to become League of Nations mandates administered by Great Britain, France, Japan, Australia, and South Africa. The whole system was correctly viewed as a thinly disguised version of old-style colonialism.

Faced with the prospect of French or British rule and in anticipation of the King-Crane Commission's visit, Syrian nationalists called a congress, also attended by Palestinian and Lebanese delegates, and adopted the following resolution on July 2, 1919. The King-Crane Commission included the resolution in its report, but Britain and France ignored it and proceeded with their plans to establish mandates. In March 1920, a second Syrian congress proclaimed Syrian independence, but the new state, which included Palestine and Lebanon, lasted only four months. In July 1920, the French easily crushed the Syrian army, whose ammunition ran out after only a few hours of fighting. On July 25, 1920, the French entered Damascus, ushering in two decades of turbulent French rule.

QUESTIONS FOR ANALYSIS

1. In what ways and for what reasons does the resolution reject the premises of Article 22 of the League of Nations Covenant?
2. How do the delegates envision the mandate system, if forced to accept it?
3. How does the resolution distinguish between Zionists and Jews already residing in Palestine?

4. Why did the delegates prefer the United States as the nation to offer Syria economic and technical aid?

5. All of the resolutions except resolution 5 were accepted unanimously at the congress. Why do you think it was the exception?

We the undersigned members of the General Syrian Congress, meeting in Damascus on Wednesday, July 2nd, 1919 . . . provided with credentials and authorizations by the inhabitants of our various districts, Muslims, Christians, and Jews, have agreed upon the following statement of the desires of the people of the country who have elected us to present them to the American Section of the International Commission; the fifth article was passed by a very large majority; all the other articles were accepted unanimously.

1. We asked absolutely complete political independence for Syria within these boundaries. The Taurus System on the North; Rafah and a line running from Al Jauf to the south of the Syrian and the Hejazian line to Akaba on the south; the Euprates and Khabur Rivers and a line extending east of Abu Kamal to the east of Al Jauf on the east; and the Mediterranean of the west.[1]

2. We ask that the Government of this Syrian country should be a democratic civil constitutional Monarchy on broad decentralization principles, safeguarding the rights of minorities, and that the King be the Emir Feisal, who carried on a glorious struggle in the cause of our liberation and merited our full confidence and entire reliance.[2]

3. Considering the fact that the Arabs inhabiting the Syrian area are not naturally less [capable] than other more advanced races and that they are by no means less developed than the Bulgarians, Serbians, Greeks, and Romanians at the beginning of their independence, we protest against Article 22 of the Covenant

of the League of Nations, placing us among the nations in their middle stage of development which stand in need of a mandatory power.

4. In the event of the rejection by the Peace Conference of this just protest for certain considerations that we may not understand, we, relying on the declarations of President Wilson that his object in waging war was to put an end to the ambition of conquest and colonization, can only regard the mandate mentioned in the Covenant of the League of Nations as equivalent to the rendering of economical and technical assistance that does not prejudice our complete independence. And desiring that our country should not fall a prey to colonization and believing that the American Nation is farthest from any thought of colonization and has no political ambition in our country, we will seek the technical and economical assistance from the United States of America, provided that such assistance does not exceed 20 years.

5. In the event of America not finding herself in a position to accept our desire for assistance, we will seek this assistance from Great Britain, also provided that such assistance does not infringe the complete independence and unity of our country and that the duration of such assistance does not exceed that mentioned in the previous article.

6. We do not acknowledge any right claimed by the French Government in any part whatever of our Syrian country and refuse that she should assist us or have a hand in our country under any circumstances and in any place.

7. We oppose the pretentions of the Zionists to create a Jewish commonwealth in the

---

[1]The region described includes today's states of Syria, Lebanon, Israel, and Jordan.
[2]Prince Feisal (also spelled *Feysel* and *Faysal*), the son of

Sharif Husayn, was an Arab military hero in the Anglo-Arab struggle against the Turks. After the French drove him from Syria in 1920, the British installed him as king of Iraq.

southern part of Syria, known as Palestine, and oppose Zionist migration to any part of our country; for we do not acknowledge their title but consider them a grave peril to our people from the national, economical, and political points of view. Our Jewish compatriots shall enjoy our common rights and assume the common responsibilities.

8. We ask that there should be no separation of the southern part of Syria, known as Palestine, nor of the littoral western zone, which includes Lebanon, from the Syrian country. We desire that the unity of the country should be guaranteed against partition under whatever circumstances.

9. We ask complete independence for emancipated Mesopotamia[3] and that there should be no economic barriers between the two countries.

10. The fundamental principles laid down by President Wilson in condemnation of secret treaties impel us to protest most emphatically against any treaty that stipulates the partition of our Syrian country and against any private engagement aiming at the estab-

lishment of Zionism in the southern part of Syria; therefore we ask the complete annulment of these conventions and agreements.[4]

The noble principles enunciated by President Wilson[5] strengthen our confidence that our desires emanating from the depths of our hearts, shall be the decisive factor in determining our future; and that President Wilson and the free American people will be our supporters for the realization of our hopes, thereby proving their sincerity and noble sympathy with the aspiration of the weaker nations in general and our Arab people in particular.

We also have the fullest confidence that the Peace Conference will realize that we would not have risen against the Turks, with whom we had participated in all civil, political, and representative privileges, but for their violation of our national rights, and so will grant us our desires in full in order that our political rights may not be less after the war than they were before, since we have shed so much blood in the cause of our liberty and independence.

---

[3]The region of modern Iraq.
[4]The passage refers to the Balfour Declaration of 1916, in which Great Britain pledged its support for a Jewish state in Palestine, and the Sykes-Picot Agreement of 1916, in

which Great Britain and France agreed to divide former Ottoman territories between them.
[5]Wilson's Fourteen Points.

The Chinese May Fourth Movement and the Versailles Treaty

<>

27 ◆ *Deng Yingchao, MEMOIRS*

By the mid-1910s, the dreams of Chinese revolutionaries who had toppled the Qing Dynasty and founded a republic in 1911 and 1912 had turned to dust. Sun Yat-sen, the intellectual father of the revolution, resigned his presidency in 1912 after serving only one month. His successor, General Yuan Shikai, undermined the deliberations of the parliament elected to write a constitution, outlawed Sun Yat-sen's political party, the Guomindang, and by late 1915 was preparing to have himself elevated to the position of emperor. With the central government bankrupt and the country falling under the control of local warlords, the Japanese seized German concessions in Shandong province at the beginning of World War I, and in 1915 presented China with the Twenty-One Demands. They demanded that China recognize their political and economic ascendancy in Shandong, Manchuria, and Inner Mongolia; grant a number of economic concessions; and accept Japanese advisors in its ministries of police, the military, and finance. Militarily impotent and dependent on Japanese loans, the government successfully resisted Japanese demands to place advisors in its ministries, but otherwise acquiesced.

Although it had no army or navy capable of fighting, China entered World War I in August 1917 on the Allied side, mainly to gain an advantage in the post-war peace negotiations. In the following months, some one hundred thousand Chinese arrived in Europe after crossing the Pacific to Canada, traveling across Canada by train, and finally shipping across the Atlantic. In France and Belgium they built roads and docks, dug trenches, and worked in factories and munitions dumps. Two thousand Chinese perished in Europe, and another 543 died when their ship was sunk in transit.

When the Chinese delegation left for the Paris Peace Conference, the Chinese had high hopes that China would regain control of Shandong province and perhaps win other concessions. But the treaty writers rejected every Chinese claim and plea. When the news reached China, it sparked the May Fourth Movement, an outburst of public anger, nationalism, and reforming zeal that opened new possibilities for Chinese culture and politics in the 1920s and 1930s.

The following memoir describes the events of May 4, 1919 and their background and their influence on subsequent political and cultural movements. It was written by Deng Yinchao (1904–1992), who at the time was a student in Tianjin, a city in Hebei province some seventy-five miles east of Beijing. She soon joined the Communist Party, married Zhou Enlai, later foreign minister of the Peoples' Republic of China, and remained active in Party affairs until her death in 1992.

QUESTIONS FOR ANALYSIS

1. The students originally demonstrated over the Versailles Treaty, but quickly moved on to other issues. What were these other issues and how were they connected with the treaty?
2. What attitude did the participants in the May Fourth Movement have toward the West?
3. What methods did the students utilize to spread their ideas among the people? How effective were they?
4. What effect did the May Fourth Movement have on Chinese feminism?

On May 4, 1919, the students in Beijing staged a massive demonstration, demanding the punishment of traitors and the rejection of the Versailles Peace Treaty. In a moment of extreme anger, they burned down [a residential building] and beat up many traitors. The news of this demonstration reached Tianjin the next day, shaking the façade of complacency to its very foundation. Students gathered in groups to discuss the Beijing demonstration, and it was decided that we should not hesitate for a moment in rallying behind our Beijing compatriots in this patriotic movement. On May 7 the Tianjin students staged a demonstration of their own, and shortly afterwards such organizations as the Association of Tianjin Students and the Association of Patriotic Women in Tianjin came into existence. Most members of the latter organization were actually women students. . . . Simple and uncomplicated, we relied heavily on our selfless patriotism for our strength. Besides the two slogans previously mentioned, we also called for the abolition of the Twenty-One Demands, the return of Qingdao,[1] the boycott of Japanese goods, the use of Chinese goods only, and, most important of all, "We are determined that we shall not be slaves to any foreigners in our own country."

At that time the government was in the hands of the Peiyang warlords who responded to the students' patriotic movement with suppression and employed such methods as secret informers, bayonets, bullets, high-pressured water hoses, clubs, and massive arrests to carry out their policy of oppression. Like a piece of steel, we were tempered with fire during this period of struggle and gradually raised our own level of political consciousness. Keep in mind that the May Fourth Movement occurred at the end of World War I when new cultures and new ideas rushed into old China like a roaring torrent. These new cultures and new ideas, plus the knowledge of the successful October Revolution in Russia made a deep impression on every youth of China. Not surprisingly, young people played a most important and most progressive role in the May Fourth Movement; it was they who pushed the movement ahead and enabled it to continue to advance. . . .

. . . Nevertheless, our own intuition told us that a patriotic movement, to be effective, had to be more than just a students' movement and that we had to awaken all of our brethren for the attainment of a common goal. We therefore stressed the importance of propaganda work. Many oratorical teams were organized, and I was elected captain of speakers for the Association of Patriotic Women as well as head of the oratorical division for the Association of Tianjin Students. My duty was to provide speakers in different areas on a regular basis.

At the beginning we, as female students, did not enjoy the same freedom of movement as our male counterparts, insofar as our speaking tours were concerned. According to the feudal custom of China, women were not supposed to make speeches in the street; we, therefore, had to do our work indoors. We gave speeches in such places as libraries and participated in scheduled debates, all inside a hall or room. The audience was large and responsive in each of these meeting, as we emphasized the duty of everyone to save our country and the necessity of punishing those who sold out our country to the enemy. Many speakers broke down when they spoke of the sufferings of the Koreans under the Japanese rule, the beatings of the Beijing students by the secret police, and our inherent right to assembly for patriotic purposes. Needless to say, the audience was greatly moved by speakers of this kind.

Besides making speeches, we also conducted house-to-house visits which often took us to more remote areas of the city and also to the slums. Some of the families we visited received us warmly, while others slammed their doors in our faces before we could utter a single word. In the latter case we simply moved on to the next house instead of being discouraged. . . .

In addition to speaking tours and house-to-house visits, we also paid great attention to the use of written words as a means of spreading the patriotic sentiments. The Association of Tianjin Students published a journal which started as a half-weekly but became a daily shortly afterwards. . . .

On October 10, 1919, the various patriotic organizations in Tianjin sponsored an all-citizen congress, in which the participants would demand the punishment of [officials who were traitors], the boycott of Japanese goods, and the

---

[1] A port city in the German concession in Shandong province occupied by the Japanese early in World War I.

exercise of such inalienable rights as those of free speech and demonstrations. Before the congress was called into session, we received information that Yang Yide (nicknamed Gangster Yang), the police commissioner of Tianjin, was ready to use force to dissolve the congress if it were held and to disperse any crowd gathered for the purpose of staging a demonstration. . . .

As had been expected, the police, with fixed bayonets, quickly moved in to surround us as soon as the meeting began. . . . Not until the meeting was over and the march began did they clash with us. Steadily they closed in, as our vanguards proceeded to march forward. . . .

We shouted loudly, trying desperately to convert brutal police into compassionate patriots. But the police refused to be converted as they hit us with rifle butts and systematically broke the eyeglasses of many students. In retaliation we hit them with bamboo placards and knocked hats from their heads. When they bent down to pick up their hats, we pushed forward so as to continue our march.

. . . We marched through the city streets until we finally arrived at police headquarters. We demanded to see commissioner Yang and protested against his brutality toward the students. Not until dawn the next day did we finally disperse and proceed home.

Angered by the October Tenth Incident as described above, we female students in Tianjin decided that no longer did we wish to honor the feudal custom of China and that we, female students in Tianjin, had as much right to speak in the street as our male counterparts. The very next day we began to make speeches in the street. From street to street and before one audience after another, we condemned commissioner Yang for having committed brutality against the students.

In the wake of the May Fourth Movement came the feminist movement which was in fact one of its democratic extensions. Among the demands we raised at that time were sexual equality, abolition of arranged marriage, social activities open to women students, freedom of romantic love and marriage, universities open to women students, and employment of women in government institutions. The first step we took toward sexual equality was to merge the associations of male and female students in Tianjin to form a new organization which students of both sexes could join. . . .

As pioneers in the feminist movement who had had the rare opportunity to work side by side with men, we female students in the merged association were conscious of the example we had to set so that no man in the future could deny women the opportunity to work on the ground of alleged incompetence. In short, we worked doubly hard. Fortunately for us, the male students in the association, having been imbued with the new thought of the West, were ready to accept us as equals and judged us according to our performance rather than our sex. . . .

CHAPTER 4

Decades of Crisis in the Western World and the Soviet Union

In May 1920, Warren G. Harding, senator from Ohio and soon to be twenty-ninth president of the United States, told an audience in Boston, "America's present need is not heroics, but healing; not nostrums, but normalcy; not revolution, but restoration, . . . not surgery, but serenity." The term *normalcy* caught the public's attention, and "return to normalcy" became a phrase that expressed the aspirations of millions on both sides of the Atlantic after years of war and postwar conflict. Normalcy had no precise definition, but to most it conjured up vague and not very accurate images of the way things were before 1914 — a time of moral certitudes and political calm, when men and women could lead lives free of turmoil and conflict.

Dreams of normalcy never came close to being realized in the 1920s and 1930s. The war's wounds were too deep, its political and economic consequences too profound, and its psychological impact too devastating. There would be no going back to "normal times," but rather a stumbling forward into a world whose contours were being continually redrawn by political conflict, economic catastrophe, new trends in mass culture, and the transformation of daily life by urbanization, the automobile, and radio. Crisis and conflict were "normal" in the 1920s and 1930s, not the tranquility Harding and so many others yearned for.

For Europe and the rest of the industrialized world, the interwar years fall into three distinct periods. From 1918 through 1923, winners and losers alike faced a host of postwar political and economic problems. The Bolshevik Revolution of 1917 spawned civil war in Russia, inspired communist revolts in Germany and Hungary, and raised fears of revolution throughout Europe and the United States. Border disputes and ethnic conflict embroiled the newly created states of Eastern and Central Europe. Demobilization, the closing of wartime industries, and inflation caused economic hardship and sparked dozens of major strikes in Western Europe and the United States. In 1923 the postwar settlement itself almost collapsed when the Germans defaulted on their reparations payments, and in response, the Belgians and French dispatched one hundred thousand soldiers to the Ruhr region to make sure that they would continue to receive their allocations of German coal. German miners responded with slowdown strikes and sabotage, and the German mark collapsed, its value sinking to 4.2 billion marks to the dollar by the end of 1923.

In another year, however, the Ruhr crisis ended, and the West entered a brief period of economic revival and political calm. A German coalition government under Gustav Stresemann called in the worthless marks and introduced a gold-based currency, and an international commission restructured Germany's reparations payments and helped devise a plan for Germany's economic recovery. The resolution of the 1923 crisis was just one of several hopeful signs between 1923 and 1929. Street fighting and insurrections gave way to political stability, albeit at the expense of democratic institutions in several states. The Locarno Treaty of 1925 was hailed as the first step toward international cooperation and harmony. In it Germany renounced claims to Alsace-Lorraine and its right to remilitarize unilaterally, in return for League of Nations membership and French promises to accelerate troop withdrawals from the Rhineland. Three years later in 1928 almost every country in the world, including all the Great Powers, signed the Kellogg-Briand Pact, in which war was renounced as an instrument of national policy. After 1923 Western economies leaped forward, and as "good times" returned, many hoped that the Roaring Twenties were the start of a better era for a crisis-ridden world.

Such hopes came crashing to the ground with the collapse of the U.S. stock market in October 1929. The ensuing financial crisis laid bare the weaknesses of the brief economic recovery, and soon the world was engulfed in an economic slump of unprecedented severity. Bank failures, boarded-up factories, and unemployment rates as high as 40 percent spelled misery for millions of people in Europe and the United States, and accelerated the collapse of liberal, democratic governments in Europe. To the list of six parliamentary governments that had given way to some form of authoritarianism in the 1920s, nine were added in the 1930s. The most significant failure was the Weimar Republic in Germany, which was crushed into dust by Hitler and the Nazis. As Hitler rearmed Germany and embarked on his plan to overturn the Versailles settlement, one diplomatic crisis followed another until in the fall of 1939, Europe again was at war.

Underlying the ebb and flow of economic shifts and political events were broader, more fundamental changes in Western life and culture. Politics no longer was the exclusive domain of aristocrats and wealthy bourgeoisie. Mass politics was the order of the day, not only in democracies, but also in dictatorships such as Nazi

Germany and Fascist Italy, where propaganda campaigns and political spectacles were carefully orchestrated to ensure popular support. This was also an era of mass culture. Radio programming, popular tabloid newspapers, and the cinema all were geared to mass audiences, as were advertising campaigns to encourage consumption of automobiles, household appliances, golf clubs, phonographs, canned goods, beauty aids, and hundreds of other products. Some intellectuals and social commentators welcomed these changes as positive and liberating; others deplored the debasement of taste and the erosion of standards. All could agree, however, that culture and society were changing in fundamental ways.

Modernism and Mass Culture Between the Wars

Western cultural life between the world wars was intense, spirited, and distinctively "modern," but not particularly innovative. It is difficult to find anything in the music, art, and literature of the 1920s and 1930s that did not have antecedents before World War I. Yet a palpable change in the cultural landscape did take place in the 1920s. Tradition was now in full retreat, and modernism reigned. Before the war, iconoclastic poets, composers, architects, and choreographers were outsiders, an avant-garde of self-conscious rebels issuing manifestos in Paris, St. Petersburg, or Milan on behalf of ideas and movements with a handful of disciples. Elite culture in the 1920s was unabashedly and unequivocally modernistic; the rejection of convention itself became conventional.

The term *modernism* is used to describe the art, music and literature that emerged in Europe and the United States in the 1920s and continued to set the tone for Western culture until the 1950s and beyond. It is difficult to define. If one examines modern literature, modern painting, modern architecture, modern sculpture, modern music, and modern dance to see what characteristics they share in common, modernism is reduced to something broad and general: a rejection of tradition; an abandonment of inherited rules, forms, and themes; and a commitment to experimentation.

The triumph of modernism after World War I can be explained in part by demographics. The prewar avant-garde consisted mainly of young men who, if they survived combat, reached maturity and gained followings after the war. The composer Igor Stravinsky was thirty-two when the war began and lived until 1971; the painter Pablo Picasso founded the cubist movement around 1907 and lived until 1973; the poet T. S. Eliot wrote his first important poems between 1909 and 1911 and lived until 1967. But it was the war itself that consigned the old order to oblivion and affirmed modernism's triumph. It confirmed the bankruptcy of traditional values and the need to create a new culture in keeping with the modern age.

Along with modernism, mass culture was another feature of the 1920s and 1930s. It too had prewar roots. Before 1914, the appearance of mass circulation newspapers, increasing sales of light novels and inexpensive magazines, the popularity of music hall entertainment, and the size of crowds flocking to baseball parks and soccer stadiums all indicated that the "masses" — factory workers, shopkeepers, clerks, stenographers, servants, and laborers — were becoming an important cultural force. They became an even greater force in the 1920s and 1930s.

Mass culture between the wars was a culmination of a century-long process in which urban workers and the lower middle class gradually acquired greater literacy, income, and leisure. By the 1920s the eight-hour workday, paid vacations, and workless weekends had become standard, and incomes had risen to the point that people below the ranks of the bourgeoisie could afford their own entertainment and recreation. The emergence of mass culture also had much to do with three prewar inventions that in the 1920s and 1930s were refined, commercialized, and made affordable to the general public: the radio, the phonograph, and the cinema.

The radio, developed by the Italian Guglielmo Marconi in the 1890s and used on the limited basis by armies during World War I, became fully commercialized in the 1920s. Radios became commonplace in American and European households, and by the end of the decade millions of listeners could gather around their sets and hear the programs transmitted by the BBC or NBC. The phonograph, invented by Edison in 1878, reached a level of quality and affordability in the 1920s that made it a major part of the evolving mass culture. In the United States alone manufacturers turned out more than two million phonographs and one hundred million records annually. The film industry, which in 1908 was already attracting an estimated ten million customers a year in the United States, moved into an era of full-length films, better quality, sound, and sumptuously decorated movie palaces seating as many as five thousand patrons. By the 1930s trips to the movies became routine on both sides of the Atlantic, and Hollywood became synonymous with glamour, adventure, and escape from the drabness of the Great Depression. The age of the masses had arrived, and for better or worse, the soap opera, matinee idol, Hollywood epic, tabloid newspaper, sports hero, and jitterbug were now all part of Western culture.

The Look of Modernity

❖

28 ◆ Walter Gropius,
DESSAU BAUHAUS — PRINCIPLES OF
BAUHAUS CONSTRUCTION
and EXAMPLES OF BAUHAUS DESIGN

Much of modern art, music, and literature has been geared toward a small, sophisticated audience of individuals who can appreciate and understand its complexities, obscurities, and frequently disturbing messages. Even in the heyday of modernism, only a tiny minority could say honestly that their lives had been much affected by dadaist painting, atonal music, or stream-of-consciousness literature. This is not the case, however, in regard to modern architecture and design. In these two areas, modernism has given a distinctive twentieth-century look to man-made objects that are part of people's daily lives around the world: the buildings where they work, live, and study; the furniture in their homes; the clothes and jewelry they wear; the utensils, plates, and appliances they use in their kitchens; and much else. For this, a German school of art and design that lasted only fourteen years, the Bauhaus, can be given much of the credit.

The Bauhaus — German for House of Construction, or Building School — was the creation of the architect Walter Gropius. Born in 1883 in Berlin and trained in Berlin and Munich, Gropius achieved continentwide prominence for the factories and office buildings he designed before World War I. After the war, he became director of two state-supported schools — one for art and one for crafts — in Weimar. He merged these in 1919 to form the Bauhaus. With some of Central and Eastern Europe's most brilliant architects, painters, and sculptors on its faculty, the Bauhaus integrated crafts and aesthetic training. Its objective was to develop every area of design (architecture, painting, sculpture, furniture, fabrics, jewelry, ceramics, stagecraft, and costume) in ways appropriate to modern industrial society. Forced to move to Dessau in 1925 after the German state of Thuringia cut off funds, and then to Berlin when Nazis took over the Dessau city council, the school was shut down for good after Hitler took power in 1933. The Bauhaus, claimed the Nazis, represented Jewish-Marxist art. Gropius, who had resigned as director of the school in 1927, emigrated to the United States, where as head of Harvard's architecture department he helped train a generation of U.S. architects. He died in 1969.

This section illustrates through writings and examples some of the basic principles of Bauhaus and, by extension, modern design. It begins with a brief statement by Gropius from a pamphlet published in 1927 entitled "Dessau Bauhaus — Principles of Bauhaus Construction." Four examples of Bauhaus design follow: (a) the main Bauhaus building in Dessau, designed by Gropius; (b) a master's (faculty member's) house from the Dessau complex, also designed by Gropius; (c) a chair designed in 1927 by Marcel Breuer (an alumnus of the school who fled Germany and later joined Gropius at Harvard) made of steel tubing and steel thread; and (d) a brass and ebony teapot made in 1924 from a design by Marianne Brandt (a member of the Bauhaus faculty).

QUESTIONS FOR ANALYSIS

1. Why, in Gropius's view, have recent developments dictated the need for a new approach to housing and furnishings design?
2. According to Gropius, what characteristics will a modern dwelling and its furnishings have to put them "in harmony" with the modern world?
3. What views of the modern world are implied or stated by Gropius?
4. What have been the differences between craft production and industrial production in the view of Gropius? What changes in their relationship does he anticipate?

5. What characteristics do Gropius's Dessau buildings, Breuer's tubular chair, and Brandt's teapot have in common?
6. In what ways do these buildings and objects exemplify Gropius's ideals?

The Bauhaus intends to contribute to the development of housing — from the simplest appliance to the complete dwelling — in a way which is in harmony with the spirit of the age. . . .

Convinced that household appliances and furnishings must relate to each other rationally, the Bauhaus seeks — by means of systematic theoretical and practical research into formal, technical and economic fields — to derive the form of an object from its natural functions and limitations.

Modern man, who wears modern not historical dress, also requires a modern dwelling which is in harmony with himself and with the times in which he lives, and is equipped with all the modern objects in daily use.

The nature of an object is determined by what it does. Before a container, a chair or a house can function properly its nature must first be studied, for it must perfectly serve its purpose; in other words it must function practically, must be cheap, durable and 'beautiful'. Research into the nature of objects leads one to conclude that forms emerge from a determined consideration of all the modern methods of production and construction and of modern materials. These forms diverge from existing models and often seem unfamiliar and surprising. . . .

Only by constant contact with advanced technology, with the diversity of new materials and with new methods of construction, is the creative individual able to bring objects into a vital relationship with the past, and to develop from that a new attitude to design, namely:

Determined acceptance of the living environment of machines and vehicles.

Organic design of objects in terms of their own laws and determined by their contemporaniety, without Romantic beautification and whimsy.

Exclusive use of primary forms and colors comprehensible to everyone.

Simplicity in multiplicity, economical use of space, material, time and money.

The creation of standard types for all objects in daily use is a social necessity.

For most people the necessities of life are the same. The home, its furnishings and equipment are required by everybody, and their design is more a matter of reason than of passion. The machine, which creates standard types, is an effective means of liberating the individual from physical labor through mechanical aids — steam and electricity — and giving him mass-produced products cheaper and better than those made by hand. . . .

The Bauhaus workshops are essentially laboratories in which prototypes suitable for mass production and typical of their time are developed with care and constantly improved. . . .

The Bauhaus believes that the difference between industry and the crafts consists less in the tools each uses than in the division of labor in industry and the unity of labor in the crafts. But the crafts and industry are constantly moving closer. Traditional crafts have changed: the crafts of the future will have a unity of labor in which they will be the medium of experimental work for industrial production. . . .

Bauhaus production is therefore not in competition with industry and craftsmen; it rather provides them with new opportunities for growth. . . .

Dessau Bauhaus Building (1925–1926), Walter Gropius, architect

Master's (faculty member's) House (1926) from the Dessau complex, Walter Gropius, architect

Marcel Breuer, Tubular Steel Chair (1925)

Marianne Brandt, Small Tea-Essence Pot (1924)

Perils of Mass Culture: The Threat to Morality

◈

29 ◆ *Senator Henry L. Myers,*
U.S. SENATE SPEECH, JUNE 29, 1922

Is mass culture dangerous to morals? So it would seem from the persistent out-
cries directed toward many of its twentieth-century manifestations: jazz music,
rock and roll, pulp fiction, rap lyrics, television violence, dance styles too numerous to count, and more than anything else, films. Early filmmakers knew that
sex, violence, and sensationalism sold tickets, and hence produced more than
their share of films featuring bawdy comedy, lurid murder scenes, and, by the
standards of the day, torrid romance. In 1908, citing moral dangers, the mayor of
New York City, George B. McClellan, threatened to close all of the city's cinemas,
and during the 1910s state and local censorship boards proliferated. In response,
filmmakers in 1909 founded their own self-regulating body, the National Board
of Censorship (later named the National Board of Review), which they hoped
would head off federal censorship.

The industry's problems with censorship peaked in 1921 and 1922. In their
efforts to fill seats in thousands of new theaters built after the war, producers
released a spate of films with titles such as *The Blushing Bride, Forbidden Fruit,
The Plaything of Broadway, Luring Lips, The Restless Sex,* and *Passion's Playground.* In 1920 scandal rocked Hollywood when one of its biggest stars, Roscoe
"Fatty" Arbuckle, was accused (and later acquitted) of raping and murdering a
young actress at a wild San Francisco party; a Hollywood producer, William
Desmond Taylor, was found dead in a drug-related murder; and a number of
prominent actors and actresses, including Rudolph Valentino, became involved in
highly publicized divorces.

Against this background several congressmen reintroduced legislation to set
up a national board of film censorship. One of its supporters was Senator Henry
Myers (1861–1929) of Montana, who presented his observations on the film industry in a Senate speech in June 1922.

The efforts of Myers and other like-minded congressmen failed. Bills calling for
federal regulation of films were voted down, in no small part because of the
lobbying efforts of Will Hays, recently hired by the film industry to serve as a
front man for a new organization, the Motion Picture Producers and Distributors
of America. However, Hays did ban Arbuckle, a convenient scapegoat for the
industry's problems, from the screen, thereby showing his seriousness of purpose.

QUESTIONS FOR ANALYSIS

1. What is Myer's rationale for involving the federal government in censoring
   the film industry?
2. What signs of moral deterioration does Myers detect in the United States of
   his day? To what degree does he believe the film industry can be blamed for
   this deterioration?

3. Why does Myers believe that industry efforts to regulate itself will fail?
4. What type of regulation of the film industry does he foresee?

The motion picture is a great invention, and it has become a powerful factor for good or bad in our civilization. . . .

Through motion pictures the young and the old may see depicted every good motive, laudable ambition, commendable characteristic, ennobling trait of humanity. They may be taught that honesty is the best policy; that virtue and worth are rewarded; that industry leads to success. . . .

However, from all accounts, the business has been conducted, generally speaking, upon a low plane and in a decidedly sordid manner. Those who own and control the industry seem to have been of the opinion that the sensual, the sordid, the prurient, the phases of fast life, the ways of extravagance, the risqué, the paths of shady life, drew the greatest attendance and coined for them the most money, and apparently they have been out to get the coin, no matter what the effect upon the public, young or old; and when thoughtful people have suggested or advocated official censorship, in the interest of good citizenship and wholesome morals, the owners of the industry have resented it and, in effect, declared that it was nobody's business other than theirs and concerned nobody other than them what kind of shows they produced; that if people did not like their shows they could stay away from them; that it was their business, and they would conduct it as they might please. . . .

In that they are mistaken. The State has an interest in citizenship and a concern in the education of the young. The State has an interest in good morals. It regulates in many ways all of those things. The motion-picture industry vitally concerns all of those things — citizenship, education, morals — and is therefore subject to regulation by the State. It has become a public utility, and is therefore the legitimate subject of State regulation. . . .

The industry has gone so far in defying public sentiment, and has been so flagrant in its abuse of its privileges that a public sentiment for censorship has been aroused which will not be brooked. It may be temporarily checked; it may be temporarily lulled by fair promises, but it is bound to grow, because censorship is needed and would be a good thing. . . .

I believe that a great deal of the extravagance of the day, a great deal of the disposition to live beyond one's means, yea, a great deal of the crime of the day comes from moving pictures. Through them young people gain ideas of fast life, shady ways, laxity of living, loose morals. Crime is freely depicted in alluring colors. Lax morals are held up lightly before them. The sensual is strongly appealed to. Many of the pictures are certainly not elevating; some, at least, are not fit to be seen.

About 18 months ago, in this city, there occurred a foul and most shocking murder. . . . Four youths of this city, in age from 15 to 20 years, as I recollect, stole an automobile, and in it followed an honest, peaceable, industrious barber as he was going to his loving family and quiet home after a day's work, and overtaking him, one of the youths jumped out of the automobile, in a residential section of the city, and murdered him by firing a pistol at him at close range. The victim dropped dead. The youths became panic-stricken on account of close-at-hand pedestrians and fled in the stolen machine. . . .

I have no doubt those young criminals got their ideas of the romance of crime from moving pictures. I believe moving pictures are doing as much harm to-day as saloons did in the days of the open saloon — especially to the young. They are running day and night, Sunday and every other day, the year round, and in most jurisdictions without any regulation by censorship. I would not abolish them. . . . I would close them on Sunday and regulate them week days by judicious censorship. . . .

When we look to the source of the moving pictures, the material for them, the personnel of those who pose for them, we need not wonder that many of the pictures are pernicious. . . .

At Hollywood, Calif., is a colony of these people, where debauchery, riotous living, drunkenness, ribaldry, dissipation, free love, seem to be conspicuous. Many of these "stars," it is reported, were formerly bartenders, butcher boys, sopers, swampers,[1] variety actors and actresses, who may have earned $10 or $20 a week, and some of whom are now paid, it is said, salaries of something like $5,000 a month or more, and they do not know what to do with their wealth, extracted from poor people, in large part, in 25 or 50 cent admission fees, except to spend it in riotous living, dissipation, and "high rolling."

There are some of the characters from whom the young people of to-day are deriving a large part of their education, views of life, and character-forming habits. From these sources our young people gain much of their views of life, inspirations, and education. Rather a poor source, is it not? Looks like there is some need for censorship, does it not? . . .

There was recently some reference in Washington papers to a suggested effort by the Washington Chamber of Commerce or Board of Trade, one or the other, I do not recall which, to induce the Hollywood motion-picture colony to move to this community and establish itself at Great Falls, near this city. I hope it may not be done. From all accounts the Washington Chamber of Commerce or Board of Trade would better invite here a colony of lepers or an institution for the propagation and dissemination of smallpox. . . .

---

[1]In American slang, *butcher boys* were street vendors; *sopers* were drug addicts; *swampers* were truck drivers.

◆

The Impact of the Great Depression

For a few glorious years from 1924 to 1929, people in the industrialized world could believe that postwar economic problems had been solved. Fueled by investments and loans from a booming United States, Europe's economy revived. Inflation seemed under control. Industrialized nations experienced higher employment, increased output, and expanded foreign trade. Despite lagging agricultural prices and pockets of high unemployment, optimism reigned, and the price of stocks, especially on the New York Stock Exchange, skyrocketed. In the summer of 1929, an article in a U.S. magazine touted stock market investing as a sure way to wealth. It was entitled "Everyone Ought to be Rich."

Optimism evaporated in October 1929, when prices on the Exchange began a decline that soon laid bare all the underlying weaknesses of the international economy. As personal fortunes disappeared, banks began to fail by the thousands, investment plummeted, prices and wages fell, and unemployment lines and soup kitchens became features of the urban landscape. The stock market crash caused U.S. bankers to call in short-term loans from European creditors, and in the spring of 1931, major banks in Austria and Germany failed. Worse, the crash stopped the flow of investment dollars to Europe, where the number of boarded-up factories, unemployed workers, and ruined farmers soon reached frightening levels.

More than anything else, the Great Depression was a human tragedy for millions of men and women who lost jobs, farms, investments, homes, savings, personal possessions, health, dignity, and hope. But it also had important political ramifications. In the short run, it undermined parliamentary governments in Germany, Austria, and other Central and Eastern European states, and nearly ended parliamentary governments in Belgium and France. It heightened social tensions and encouraged many of its victims to believe that economic hardship was the fault of Jews, communists, capitalists, or some other convenient scapegoat. International cooperation declined as politicians immersed themselves in domestic issues, raised tariffs, and convinced themselves and their compatriots that their economic problems could be blamed on foreigners or perhaps solved by rearmament or foreign conquests.

The Great Depression also prompted new thinking about the role and purposes of government. It soon became apparent that time-honored governmental responses to recessions — encouraging private charity, slashing government spending, raising tariffs, or just waiting passively for the business cycle to turn upward — were inadequate and perhaps even counterproductive. A new vision of governmental activism, exemplified by Franklin D. Roosevelt's "New Deal" in the United States, emerged. It viewed the state as responsible for society's economic well-being and its citizens' social welfare from "cradle to grave." It utilized economic planning, regulation, and deficit spending to stimulate demand and maintain high employment. It viewed tax policy as a means of redistributing wealth from the rich to the poor. And it envisioned and ultimately created a host of new programs and entitlements to protect people from poverty and ensure decent housing, adequate health care, and "social security" in old age. The trend toward big government and the welfare state was of necessity strengthened and accelerated as a result of the economic catastrophe of the 1930s.

The Victims of the Depression in Germany

❖

30 ◆ H. Hessel Tiltman,
SLUMP! A STUDY OF STRICKEN EUROPE TODAY

H. Hessel Tiltman (1897–1977) was a British author-journalist best known for his coverage of East Asia during the 1930s and 1940s. During 1931 and 1932 as European correspondent for the *Manchester Guardian,* he traveled across Europe to observe the effects of the Great Depression. On his return he recorded his impressions in a widely read book, *Slump! A Study of Stricken Europe Today.* In the following selection he describes the economic and emotional effects of the Depression on three families from Berlin.

QUESTIONS FOR ANALYSIS

1. How has the Great Depression affected the economic situations of the German families?
2. How does the situation of the laborer's family differ from those of the former baker and the former salesman?

3. What does Tiltman's account have to say about the emotional and psychological damage of unemployment?
4. What connection does Tiltman make between Germany's economic woes and the appeal of Nazism?

In the course of those two days beneath the surface of Berlin life I saw overcrowding, because those living on relief can rarely afford more than one room, however large the family. . . . I saw hunger, because, as I have said, these victims cannot escape that horror. I saw rags, because the welfare centers can no longer supply anyone with even secondhand shoes until *both* the soles of the existing pair have been worn to nothing. The mass need is now so great that it has swamped every channel along which relief trickles. . . .

But more painful than any of these things, I saw utter despair. Some of the wives could still hold up their heads and be interested in the life about them, but most of the men were shattered in spirit and breaking in health. They had fought despair for one year, two years, maybe even three years. But it got them in the end. . . .

The first house I entered was still supported by the second category "dole,"[1] the husband, a baker, having been out of work only seven months.

The family comprised husband, wife, and four children, and the total income amounted to 94/-[2] a month, made up of 82/- unemployment benefit, and 12/- a month orphans' pension received for one of the children.

For one room and a kitchen in a large tenement building, with a wall blocking out both view and light, they paid 20/- a month rent, leaving a balance of 74/-.

Electric light and gas cost about 7/- a month, soap 6d. a month, and a burial insurance policy for the family another 1/6 a month. Payments on this policy were being discontinued on the week that I called.

The rest of the income, amounting to 15/- a week, went to buy food for six people, a task made easier by the fact that three of the children were supplied with a midday meal — and a good meal — at the school they attended.

The weekly menus in this home consisted of oatmeal, potato soup, herrings and bread. Only in the case of the husband was there any sign of physical strain, and he was well below the standard of fitness enforced in the German Army in which he had served in what, tragically enough, he spoke of as "happier days." . . .

In another home a family of seven — man, wife, and five children — were living in two rooms. The man, workless since the beginning of 1931, had formerly been employed, first as a clerk, and later as a salesman in a store, his wage in the latter occupation being 42/- a week.

The total income of the family, from the "second category" dole, had amounted to about 30/- a week, but this sum was subject to a cut of 20 percent on June 27, 1932. On the same date the rent of 10/- a week was raised to 12/6, or nearly half their total income, by the reimposition of a rent tax formerly waived in the case of the workless. Thus the relentless march of the crisis forces the living standards of its victims down and down.

Sitting on the only sound chair in that home, in which a sewing machine was the sole article of furniture which would have sold for more than a few pence, I listened while the wife, a woman of twenty-five whose face bore clear marks of strain, explained to me how they managed to feed seven people on 15/- a week.

A loaf of bread a day cast 6d. A pound of dripping[3] a week cost the same sum. They bought

---

[1] The English term for government payments to the unemployed.
[2] Tiltman expresses income and expenditures in units of British money. The number left of the slash represents shillings, twenty of which make up a pound; the number on the right of the slash represents pence, twelve of which make up a shilling. The symbol of pence is "*d.*"
[3] Animal fat.

one liter . . . of milk a day for the two youngest children, and 1/4 lb. of butter a week for the youngest child. Three lbs. of sugar a week, two tins of condensed milk for the baby, aged nine months, and five cigarettes a day for the man, costing one penny a packet, completed the list of "luxuries." For the rest, they had 8 lbs. of potatoes a day and, twice a week, 3 lbs. of cabbage costing 3d., boiled into a soup to which, on Sundays, was added a penny-worth of bones. Occasionally — not more frequently than once a month — they bought half a pound of pork at the specially reduced prices charged, under government supervision, to those in receipt of "doles." . . .

From that home I went to another near by — two rooms occupied by a builders' laborer, unemployed for over two years. The rooms were in a cellar below the level of the street, and approached through quarters occupied by another family. The income for a family of three was 16/- a week, "a little higher than the average," as the man explained to me. The rent, including the new tax, was 6/- a month. The wife produced the rent book, showing that they owed two months' rent, and in view of the new law, already mentioned, which rendered them liable to eviction at any time upon twelve hours' notice, it worried them. If that happened, they explained, there would be no alternative to a shed somewhere on the outskirts of the city, which would mean living like pigs, and necessitate a long walk for the man every time he had to report to the relief officer.

The husband had just drawn 32/-, two weeks' relief payment, and I went out with the wife to spend it.

The first 9/- went to pay a debt at the grocer's. A cwt.[4] of coal cost another 1/6½; 12/- went to pay the fortnight's rent; 2/6 liquidated a debt for potatoes eaten during the previous week. Seven shillings were left, and the wife spent this on eggs, dripping, bread, potatoes and cabbage — which may be described as the universal diet of the German workless. On that menu, they had to exist for another week at least.

When we returned, the husband was sitting on a box, his head in his hands — gazing fixedly into space. Looking for what? As a trade unionist, he had been a member of the Social Democratic Party[5] the bulwark of the German Republic. Now he was nothing — too broken in spirit to care. Sitting there, a picture of dejection, he might have been looking back to the pre-war days, when the Junkers[6] thundered forth claims to a "place in the sun," and at least found work for their people. If he was, who will blame him? It is one of the misfortunes of these years that troubles have crowded in upon Germany under the republican regime.

A moment later two young men, clad in leather jackets, burst into that cellar-room with a stamp of feet, to provide another glimpse of the curses which afflict Germany today. This time the curse, not of poverty, but of Hitlerism.

It could not truthfully be said that the visitors entered that room. Their domineering manners and assertive attitude somehow preceded them though the door, which they slammed after entering. Compared with the Socialist worker, wearied by waiting for the turn of the tide, these two members of the Nazi "S.A."[7] . . . represented another world — a Germany which has lost its patience and demands the impossible under threat of instant reprisals. . . .

Those two young workless men were walking evidence, seen beside that Socialist, of the fact that whatever else Adolf Hitler has, or has not, done, he has enabled a large number of Germans to keep up their spirits — the great demagogue would himself call it "saving the soul of Germany" — at a time when Germany's spirits were in danger of sinking to zero.

---

[4]Abbreviation for a hundredweight, a unit of weight in the British Imperial System equal to 112 pounds.
[5]The Social Democrats were Marxist, but sought to achieve socialism through legislation, not revolution. The Social Democratic Party was a major supporter of the Weimar Republic.

[6]Aristocrats from the German state of Prussia, who for centuries dominated the Prussian and, after German unification in 1871, the army's officer corps.
[7]Abbreviation for Sturmabteilung, a Nazi paramilitary organization noted for its violence and antisemitism, also known in English as the "Brown Shirts" or "Storm Troopers."

Government Promises a "New Deal"

❖

31 ◆ *Franklin D. Roosevelt,*
ANNUAL ADDRESS TO CONGRESS,
JANUARY 4, 1935

Herbert Hoover, who was just finishing his first year as president when the stock market crashed, was deeply concerned about the human costs of the Depression, but his commitment to volunteerism and a balanced budget doomed to failure his efforts to mitigate its effects. His refusal to commit the federal government to relief or recovery programs infuriated Americans who came to believe he was indifferent to their suffering and interested mainly in protecting business. In 1932 the voters overwhelmingly supported the Democrat Franklin D. Roosevelt, who in the campaign had promised them a new deal.

Franklin D. Roosevelt was born into a wealthy upstate New York family in 1882. A Harvard graduate and a lawyer, he had served as a New York state legislator, assistant secretary of the navy under Wilson, the Democratic vice-presidential candidate in 1920, and governor of New York between 1928 and 1932. Taking office when the Depression was at its worst and promising "bold and persistent experimentation," the new president pushed forward an unprecedented program to resolve the crises of a collapsing banking system, crippling unemployment, and agricultural and industrial breakdown. Two years later, in 1935, with the Depression far from over, Roosevelt shifted his priorities, in what is sometimes called the "Second New Deal," from relief and recovery to basic social and economic reforms.

In the following message to Congress, delivered in January 1935, Roosevelt outlines some of his ideas about the role of government and the nation's economic well-being.

QUESTIONS FOR ANALYSIS

1. How does Roosevelt perceive the "state of the nation" in 1935? What has been accomplished and what still needs to be done by his administration?
2. What evidence does Roosevelt' speech provide that his administration's interests were shifting from relief and recovery to more basic reforms? What groups and regions in U.S. society were most likely to benefit from his proposals?
3. How would you describe Roosevelt's long-term goals for American society?
4. Taken as a whole, how would his proposals result in an expansion of the federal government?

Throughout the world change is the order of the day. In every nation economic problems, long in the making, have brought crises of many kinds for which the masters of old practice and theory were unprepared. In most nations, social justice, no longer a distant ideal, has become a definite goal, and ancient governments are beginning to heed the call. . . .

We find our population suffering from old inequalities, little changed by past sporadic remedies. In spite of our efforts and in spite of our talk, we have not weeded out the overprivileged and we have not effectively lifted up the underprivileged. Both of these manifestations of injustice have retarded happiness. No wise man has any intention of destroying what is known as the "profit motive," because by the profit motive we mean the right by work to earn a decent livelihood for ourselves and for our families.

We have, however, a clear mandate from the people, that Americans must forswear that conception of the acquisition of wealth which, through excessive profits, creates undue private power over private affairs and, to our misfortune, over public affairs as well. In building toward this end we do not destroy ambition, nor do we seek to divide our wealth into equal shares on stated occasions. We continue to recognize the greater ability of some to earn more than others. But we do assert that the ambition of the individual to obtain for him and his a proper security, a reasonable leisure, and a decent living throughout life is an ambition to be preferred to the appetite for great wealth and great power. . . .

In defining immediate factors which enter into our quest, I have spoken to the Congress and the people of three great divisions: first, the security of a livelihood through the better use of the national resources of the land in which we live; second, the security against the major hazards and vicissitudes of life; third, the security of decent homes.

I am now ready to submit to the Congress a broad program designed ultimately to establish all three of these factors of security — a program which because of many lost years will take many future years to fulfill.

A study of our national resources, . . . shows the vast amount of necessary and practicable work which needs to be done for the development and preservation of our national wealth for the enjoyment and advantage of our people

in generations to come. The sound use of land and water is far more comprehensive than the mere planting of trees, building of dams, distributing of electricity, or retirement of submarginal land. It recognizes that stranded populations, either in the country or the city, cannot have security under the conditions that now surround them.

To this end we are ready to begin to meet this problem — the intelligent care of population throughout our nation in accordance with an intelligent distribution of the means of livelihood for that population. A definite program for putting people to work, of which I shall speak in a moment, is a component part of this greater program of security of livelihood through the better use of our national resources.

Closely related to the broad problem of livelihood is that of security against the major hazards of life. Here also a comprehensive survey of what has been attempted or accomplished in many nations and in many states proves to me that the time has come for action by the national government. I shall send to you, in a few days, definite recommendations based on these studies. These recommendations will cover the broad subjects of unemployment insurance and old-age insurance, of benefits for children, for mothers, for the handicapped, for maternity care, and for other aspects of dependency and illness where a beginning can now be made.

The third factor — better homes for our people — has also been the subject of experimentation and study. Here, too, the first practical steps can be made through the proposals which I shall suggest in relation to giving work to the unemployed. . . .

The first objectives of emergency legislation of 1933 were to relieve destitution, to make it possible for industry to operate in a more rational and orderly fashion, and to put behind industrial recovery the impulse of large expenditures in government undertakings. The purpose of the National Industrial Recovery

Act[1] to provide work for more people succeeded in a substantial manner within the first few months of its life, and the act has continued to maintain employment gains and greatly improved working conditions in industry. . . .

But the stark fact before us is that great numbers still remain unemployed. A large proportion of these unemployed and their dependents have been forced on the relief rolls. . . . The lessons of history, confirmed by the evidence immediately before me, show conclusively that continued dependence upon relief induces a spiritual and moral disintegration fundamentally destructive to the national fiber. To dole out relief in this way is to administer a narcotic, a subtle destroyer of the human spirit. . . . Work must be found for able-bodied but destitute workers. . . .

I am not willing that the vitality of our people be further sapped by the giving of cash, of market baskets, of a few hours of weekly work cutting grass, raking leaves, or picking up papers in the public parks. We must preserve not only the bodies of the unemployed from destitution but also their self-respect, their self-reliance, and courage and determination. This decision brings me to the problem of what the government should do with approximately 5 million unemployed now on the relief rolls.

About 1.5 million of these belong to the group which in the past was dependent upon local welfare efforts. Most of them are unable, for one reason or another, to maintain themselves independently — for the most part, through no fault of their own. Such people, in the days before the great depression, were cared for by local efforts — by states, by counties, by towns, by cities, by churches, and by private welfare agencies. . . .

There are, however, an additional 3.5 million employable people who are on relief. With them the problem is different and the responsibility is different. This group was the victim of a nationwide depression caused by conditions which were not local but national. The federal government is the only governmental agency with sufficient power and credit to meet this situation. . . . It is a duty dictated by every intelligent consideration of national policy to ask you to make it possible for the United States to give employment to all of these 3.5 million employable people now on relief, pending their absorption in a rising tide of private employment. . . .

It is my thought that, with the exception of certain of the normal public-building operations of the government, all emergency public works shall be united in a single new and greatly enlarged plan. With the establishment of this new system, we can supersede the Federal Emergency Relief Administration[2] with a coordinated authority which will be charged with the orderly liquidation of our present relief activities and the substitution of a national chart for the giving of work. . . .

The work itself will cover a wide field, including clearance of slums, which for adequate reasons cannot be undertaken by private capital; in rural housing of several kinds, where, again, private capital is unable to function; in rural electrification; in the reforestation of the great watersheds of the nation; in an intensified program to prevent soil erosion and to reclaim blighted areas; in improving existing road systems and in constructing national highways designed to handle modern traffic; in the elimination of grade crossings; in the extension and enlargement of the successful work of the Civilian Conservation Corps;[3] in nonfederal work,

---

[1]The National Industrial Recovery Act established the National Recovery Administration (NRA), which sought to revive U.S. industry by allowing industrial and trade associations to draft codes setting production levels, wages, price policies, and working conditions.
[2]The Federal Emergency Relief Administration (FERA)

furnished funds to state and local agencies for relief. It spent close to $3 billion before it was replaced in 1935 by programs that provided work rather than cash payments.
[3]The Civil Conservation Corps (CCC) employed 2.5 million young men to work on reforestation and flood control projects.

mostly self-liquidating and highly useful to local divisions of government; and on many other projects which the nation needs and cannot afford to neglect. . . .

The ledger of the past year shows many more gains than losses. Let us not forget that, in addition to saving millions from utter destitution, child labor has been for the moment outlawed, thousands of homes saved to their owners, and, most important of all, the morale of the nation has been restored. Viewing the year 1934 as a whole, you and I can agree that we have a generous measure of reasons for giving thanks.

◆

Nazism in Theory and Practice

The Nazi movement was born on January 5, 1919, when seven men gathered in a Munich tavern to form the German Workers' Party, renamed a year later the National Socialist German Workers' Party. It died on April 30, 1945, in a bunker beneath the streets of a ravaged and burning Berlin when Adolf Hitler put a gun to his head and committed suicide. The Nazi movement existed for slightly more than twenty-six years, and its leader, Hitler, was Germany's dictator for only thirteen of them, from 1933 to 1945. Yet in this brief time so heinous were the Nazis' deeds, and so great their transgressions, that as long as even the slightest moral sense remains among human beings, Nazism will be remembered as an archsymbol of human depravity and viciousness.

During the 1920s the National Socialists espoused a program of nationalism, anticommunism, opposition to the Weimar Republic, antisemitism, repudiation of the Versailles Treaty, remilitarization, and a return to the old German values of home, hearth, family, and land. Despite the appeal of such ideas to many Germans and Hitler's unquestioned skill as an agitator and orator, the party made little progress in the 1920s. In 1928 it had fewer than one hundred thousand members and won only 2.8 percent of the vote in the national elections held that year. The Nazis' fortunes improved dramatically in 1929 and 1930 as the economy slowed and then crashed, and the Weimar government limped from one crisis to another. In the elections of September 1930, the Nazis won 107 seats in the Reichstag, making them the second largest party after the Social Democrats. They became the largest party in November 1932 when they won 196 seats and approximately one-third of the popular vote. With coalition governments dissolving almost as soon as they were formed and Germany close to political collapse, in January 1933 President von Hindenburg offered Hitler the chancellorship in the hope that as the leader of Germany's largest party Hitler could end the parliamentary crisis. In a way he did just that. On March 23, 1933, with nearly one hundred communist and socialist deputies in jail or in hiding from the secret police, and with Hitler's supporters surrounding the Reichstag and screaming threats against anyone who voted against Hitler, Germany's postwar experiment with democracy ended. Two-thirds of the deputies to the Reichstag voted for the Enabling Act, which gave Hitler dictatorial powers and an opportunity to implement his cruel, fantastic dreams.

The Dreams of the Führer

❧

32 ◆ Adolf Hitler, MEIN KAMPF

Born the son of an Austrian customs official and his German wife in 1889, Adolf Hitler moved to Vienna at the age of nineteen to pursue a career as an artist and architect. He failed, however, and lived at the bottom of Viennese society, drifting from one low-paying job to another. In 1912 he moved to Munich, where his life fell into the same purposeless pattern. Enlistment in the German army in World War I gave Hitler comradeship, a sense of direction, and an opportunity to escape his meaningless existence. After the war, a shattered Hitler returned to Munich where he joined the German Workers' Party, which in 1920 changed its name to the National Socialist German Workers' Party, or the Nazi Party.

After becoming leader of the National Socialists, Hitler staged an abortive coup d'état, or putsch, against the government of the German state of Bavaria in 1923. For this he was sentenced to a five-year prison term (serving only nine months), during which he wrote the first volume of his major political work, *Mein Kampf* (My Struggle). To a remarkable degree, this work, completed in 1925, provided the ideas that inspired his millions of followers and guided the National Socialists until their destruction in 1945.

QUESTIONS FOR ANALYSIS

1. What broad purpose does Hitler see in human existence?
2. What, in Hitler's view, are the basic dissimilarities between Aryans and Jews?
3. What is Hitler's view of political leadership?
4. What role do parliaments play in a "folkish" state, according to Hitler?
5. How does Hitler plan to reorient German foreign policy? What goals does he set for Germany, and how are they to be achieved?
6. In what ways are Hitler's ideas reminiscent of those of Nietzsche (see source 16 on p. 62)?
7. Based on these excerpts, what can you guess about Hitler's attitude toward the ideologies of democracy, liberalism, and socialism?

NATION AND RACE

There are some truths that are so plain and obvious that for this very reason the everyday world does not see them or at least does not apprehend them. . . .

So humans invariably wander about the garden of nature, convinced that they know and understand everything, yet with few exceptions are blind to one of the fundamental principles Nature uses in her work: the intrinsic segregation of the species of every living thing on the earth. . . . Each beast mates with only one of its own species: the titmouse with titmouse, finch with finch, stork with stork, field mouse with field mouse, house mouse with house mouse, wolf with wolf. . . . This is only natural.

Any cross-breeding between two not completely equal beings will result in a product that is in between the level of the two parents.

That means that the offspring will be superior to the parent who is at a biologically lower level of being but inferior to the parent at a higher level. This means the offspring will be overcome in the struggle for existence against those at the higher level. Such matings go against the will of Nature for the higher breeding of life.

A precondition for this lies not in the blending of beings of a higher and lower order, but rather the absolute victory of the stronger. The stronger must dominate and must not blend with the weaker orders and sacrifice their powers. Only born weaklings can find this cruel, but after all, they are only weaker and more narrow-minded types of men; unless this law dominated, then any conceivable higher evolution of living organisms would be unthinkable. . . .

Nature looks on this calmly and approvingly. The struggle for daily bread allows all those who are weak, sick, and indecisive to be defeated, while the struggle of the males for females gives to the strongest alone the right or at least the possibility to reproduce. Always this struggle is a means of advancing the health and power of resistance of the species, and thus a means to its higher evolution.

As little as nature approves the mating of higher and lower individuals, she approves even less the blending of higher races with lower ones; for indeed otherwise her previous work toward higher development perhaps over hundreds of thousands of years might be rendered useless with one blow. If this were not the case, progressive development would stop and even deterioration might set in. . . .

All the great civilization of the past died out because contamination of their blood caused them to become decadent. . . . In other words, in order to protect a certain culture, the type of human who created the culture must be preserved. But such preservation is tied to the inalterable law of the necessity and the right of victory of the best and the strongest.

Whoever would live must fight. Whoever will not fight in this world of endless competition does not deserve to live. Whoever ignores or despises these laws of race kills the good fortune that he believes he can attain. He interferes with the victory path of the best race and with it, the precondition for all human progress. . . .

It is an idle undertaking to argue about which race or races were the original standard-bearers of human culture and were therefore the true founders of everything we conceive by the word humanity. It is much simpler to deal with the question as it pertains to the present, and here the answer is simple and clear. What we see before us today as human culture, all the yields of art, science, and technology, are almost exclusively the creative product of the Aryans.[1] Indeed this fact alone leads to the not unfounded conclusion that the Aryan alone is the founder of the higher type of humanity, and further that he represents the prototype of what we understand by the word: MAN. He is the Prometheus[2] from whose brow the bright spark of genius has forever burst forth, time and again rekindling the fire, which as knowledge has illuminated the night full of silent mysteries, and has permitted humans to ascend the path of mastery over the other beings of the earth. Eliminate him — and

---

[1]*Aryan* strictly speaking, is a linguistic term referring to a branch of the Indo-European family of languages known as Indo-Iranian. It is also used to refer to a people who around 2000 B.C.E. began to migrate from their homeland in the steppes of western Asia to Iran, India, Mesopotamia, Asia Minor, and Europe. Their related family of languages, based on an even older language know as *Proto-Indo-European,* is believed to be the ancestor of all Indo-European languages, including Greek, Latin, Celtic, Persian, Sanskrit, and Balto-Slavonic, as well as their derivatives. In the nineteenth century, Aryan was used to refer to the *racial group* that

spoke these languages. According to Hitler and the Nazis, the Aryans provided Europe's original racial stock and stood in contrast to other peoples such as the Jews, who spoke *Semitic* languages.

[2]In Greek mythology Prometheus was the titan (titans were offspring of Uranus, heaven, and Gaiea, earth) who stole fire from the gods and gave it to humans, along with all other arts and civilization. He was also variously regarded as the creator of man (from clay), the first mortal man (along with his brother Epimetheus), and humanity's preserver when Zeus threatened to kill all human beings.

deep darkness will again descend on the earth after a few thousand years; human civilization will die out and the earth will become a desert.

If we were to divide mankind into three categories — the founders of culture, the bearers of culture, and the destroyers of culture, only the Aryans can be considered to be in the first category. From them are built the foundations and walls of all human creations, and only the outward form and colors of these are to be attributed to varying characteristics of the other individual peoples. He provides the mightiest building stones and designs for all human progress. . . .

The Jew provides the greatest contrast to the Aryan. With no other people of the world has the instinct for self-preservation been so developed as by the so-called chosen race.[3] The best proof of this statement rests in the fact that this race still exists. Where can another people be found in the past 2,000 years that has undergone so few changes in its inner qualities, character, etc. as the Jews? What people has undergone upheavals as great as this one — and nonetheless has emerged unchanged from the greatest catastrophes of humanity? What an infinitely tenacious will to live and to preserve one's kind is revealed in this fact. . . .

Since the Jew . . . never had a civilization of his own, others have always provided the foundations of his intellectual labors. His intellect has always developed by the use of those cultural achievements he has found ready at hand around him. Never has it happened the other way around.

For though their drive for self-preservation is not smaller, but larger than that of other people and though their mental capabilities may easily give the impression that their intellectual powers are equal to those of other races, the Jews lack the most basic characteristic of a truly cultured people, namely an idealistic spirit.

It is a remarkable fact that the herd instinct brings people together for mutual protection only so long as there is a common danger that makes mutual assistance necessary or unavoidable. The same pack of wolves that for an instant are combined to overcome their prey will soon after satisfying their hunger again become individual beasts . . . It goes the same way with the Jews. His sense of self sacrifice is only apparent. It lasts only so long as it is strictly necessary. As soon as the common enemy departs, however, as soon as the danger is gone and the booty secured, the superficial harmony among the Jews ends, and original conditions return. Jews act together only when a common danger threatens them or a common prey attracts them. When these two things are lacking, then their characteristic of the crassest egoism returns as a force, and out of this once unified people emerges in a flash a swarm of rats fighting bloodily against one another.

If the Jews existed in the world by themselves, they would wallow in their filth and disasters; they would try to get the best of the other in a hate-filled struggle, and even exterminate one another, that is, if their absolute lack of a sense of self-sacrifice, which is expressed in their venality, did not turn this drama into comedy also. . . .

That is why the Jewish state — which should be the living organism for the maintenance and improvement of the race — has absolutely no borders. For the territorial definition of a state always demands a certain idealism of spirit on the part of the race which forms the state and especially an acceptance of the idea of work. . . . If this attitude is lacking then the prerequisite for civilization is lacking.

◆ Hitler describes the process by which Jews in concert with communists have come close to subverting and controlling the peoples and nations in Europe.

Here he stops at nothing, and his vileness becomes so monstrous that no one should be surprised if among our people the hateful figure of

---

[3] A reference to the Jewish conviction developed in the Hebrew scriptures that God had chosen the Jews to enter into a special relationship or covenant in which God promised to be the God of the Hebrews and favor them in return for true worship and obedience.

the Jew is taken as the personification of the devil and the symbol of evil. . . .

How close they see their approaching victory can be seen in the frightful way that their dealings with members of other races develop.

The black-haired Jewish youth, with satanic joy on his face, lurks in wait for hours for the innocent girls he plans to defile with his blood, and steal the young girl from her people. With every means at hand he seeks to undermine the racial foundations of the people they would subjugate . . . For a people which is racially pure and is conscious of its blood will never be able to be subjugated by the Jews. The Jew in this world will forever only be the masters of bastardized people. . . .

Around those nations which have offered sturdy resistance to their internal attacks, they surround them with a web of enemies; thanks to their international influence, they incite them to war, and when necessary, will plant the flag of revolution, even on the battlefield.

In economics he shakes the foundations of the state long enough so that unprofitable business enterprises are shut down and come under his financial control. In politics he denies the state its means of self-preservation, destroys its means of self-maintenance and defense, annihilates faith in state leadership, insults its history and traditions, and drags everything that is truly great into the gutter.

Culturally, he pollutes art, literature and theater, make a mockery of natural sensibilities, destroys every concept of beauty and nobility, the worthy and the good, and instead drags other men down to the sphere of its own lowly type of existence.

Religion is made an object of mockery, morality and ethics are described as old-fashioned, until finally the last props of a people for maintaining their existence in this world are destroyed.

PERSONALITY AND THE IDEAL OF THE FOLKISH[4] STATE

The folkish world view differs from the Marxist world view fundamentally in that it not only recognizes the value of race, but also that of the individual, and makes these the pillars of its very structure. These are the sustaining factors in its view of the world.

The folkish state must care for the well-being of its citizens by recognizing in everything the worth of the person, and by doing so direct it to the highest level of its productive capability, thus guaranteeing for each the highest level of participation.

Accordingly, the folkish state must free the entire leadership, especially those in political leadership, from the parliamentary principle of majority rule by the multitude, so that the right of personality is guaranteed without any limitation. From this is derived the following realization. *The best state constitution and form is that which with unquestioned certainty raises the best minds from the national community to positions of leading authority and influence. . . .*

There are no majority decisions, rather only responsible individuals, and the word "advice" will once again have its original meaning. Each man will have advisers at his side, *but the decision will be made by one man.*

The principle that made the Prussian army in its time the most splendid instrument of the German people will have to become someday the foundation for the construction of our completed state: *authority of every leader downward and responsibility upward. . . .*

This principle of binding absolute responsibility with absolute authority will gradually bring forth an elite group of leaders which today in an era of irresponsible parliamentarianism is hardly thinkable.

---

[4]The word Hitler uses, *völkisch,* is an adjective derived from *Volk,* meaning "people" or "nation," which Hitler defined in a racial sense; thus a "folkish" state is one that expresses the characteristics of and furthers the interests of a particular race, in this case, the Aryans.

THE DIRECTION AND POLITICS OF EASTERN EUROPE

The foreign policy of the folkish state has as its purpose to guarantee the existence on this planet of the race that it gathers within its borders. With this in mind it must create a natural and healthy ratio between the number and growth of the population and the extent and quality of the land and soil. The balance must be such that it accords with the vital needs of the people. What I call a healthy ratio is one in which the support of the people is assured by its own land and soil. Any other condition, even if it lasts centuries or a thousand years, is nevertheless an unhealthy one and will lead sooner or later to damage, if not the total destruction of the affected people. Only a sufficiently large space on the earth can assure the independent existence of a people. . . .

If the National Socialist Movement really is to be consecrated in history as fulfilling a great mission for the people, it must, spurred by knowledge and filled with pain over its true situation on this earth, boldly and with a clear sense of direction, take up the battle against the aimlessness and incompetence of our foreign policy. It must, without consideration of "traditions" or preconceived notions, find the courage to gather our people and their forces and advance them on the path from their present restricted living space to new land and soil. This will free the people from the dangers of disappearing from the earth altogether or becoming a slave people in the service of another.

The National Socialist movement must seek to eliminate the disproportion between our people's population and our territory — viewing this as a source of food as well as a basis for national power — and between our historical past and our present hopeless impotence. While doing so it must remain conscious of the fact that we as protectors of the highest humanity on earth are bound also by the highest duty that will be fulfilled only if we inspire the German people with the racial ideal, so that they will occupy themselves not just with the breeding of good dogs, horses, and cats but also show concern about the purity of *their own* blood.

Against everything else we National Socialists must hold unflinchingly to our goal of foreign policy, namely, *to secure for the German people the land on this earth to which they are entitled. . . .*

State boundaries are made by man and can be changed by man.

The fact that a nation has acquired a large amount of land is no mandate that this should be recognized forever. This only goes to prove the strength of the conqueror and the weakness of the conquered. And only in force lies the right of possession. If today the German people are imprisoned within an impossible territorial area and for that reason are face to face with a miserable future, this is not the commandment of fate, any more than a revolt against such a situation would be a violation of the laws of fate; . . . the soil on which we now live was not bestowed upon our ancestors by Heaven; rather, they had to conquer it by risking their lives. So with us, in the future we will win soil and with it the means of existence of the people not through some sort of folkish grace but only through the power of the triumphant sword.

But we National Socialists must go further: *The right to land and soil will become an obligation if without further territorial expansion a great people is threatened with its destruction.* And that is particularly true when the people in question is not some little nigger people, but the German mother of life, which has given cultural shape to the modern world. *Germany will either become a world power or will no longer exist.* To achieve world power an expansion in size is needed, which will give the state meaning in today's world and will give life to its citizens. . . .

And so we National Socialists consciously draw a line below the direction of our foreign policy before the war. We take up where we broke off six hundred years ago. We put a stop to the eternal pull of the Germans toward the south and western Europe and turn our gaze to the lands of the east. We put an end to the colonial and commercial policy of the prewar period and shift to the land-oriented policy of the future.

When today we speak of new territory and soil in Europe, we think primarily of *Russia* and her subservient border states.

Motherhood, Duty, and the Nazi Ideal

◆

33 ◆ *Gertrud Scholtz-Klink,*
SPEECH TO THE NATIONAL SOCIALIST
WOMEN'S ASSOCIATION, SEPTEMBER, 1935

Along with Judaism and Bolshevism, feminism, according to Hitler, was one of
the great afflictions of modern Germany. While all of Weimar Germany's mainline political parties, even the conservative Nationalist Party and People's Party,
endorsed women's equality and actively sought women's votes, the Nazis made
no secret of their belief that women had no place in their party, politics, or government. Nor did they believe that women belonged in the work force. They
should stay at home, bearing children, accepting their husbands' authority, and
overseeing their families' happiness and health. Their role in creating a strong
Germany was important, but it was distinct from the public lives of men.

Once in power, the Nazis dissolved communist and socialist women's organizations and sought to bring the hundreds of remaining organizations under the
umbrella of the National Socialist Women's Association (National Sozialistische
Frauenschaft, or NSF). They also created the Frauenwerk (Women's Bureau), an
agency to oversee government programs relating to women, In 1934, Gertrud
Scholtz-Klink, a thirty-two-year-old widowed mother of four (her husband had
died of a heart attack during the excitement of a Nazi Party rally) was appointed
National Women's Leader, with the responsibility to oversee all party and state
matters relating to women. Despite her imposing title, Scholtz-Klink had no
independent power and until the war's end was content to carry out tasks dictated by the all-male party leadership.

In the following speech, delivered at the 1935 Nazi Party Congress in Nuremberg to members of the NSF, Scholtz-Klink outlines some of her strategies for
helping women to combine work and motherhood, while encouraging them to
become enthusiastic disciples of National Socialism.

QUESTIONS FOR ANALYSIS

1. What is Scholtz-Klink's vision of women's role in the Nazi state?
2. What special tasks do women who are Nazi Party members have in rebuilding Germany?
3. What characteristics and values should the ideal German woman have,
   according to Scholtz-Klink?
4. What, according to the speaker, are the special problems of working-class
   women? How is the Party attempting to deal with these problems?
5. What are the reasons, stated and unstated, for the effort to recruit female
   university students for the Reich Labor Service?
6. On the basis of Scholtz-Klink's speech, what can you conclude about the
   success of the Nazis in achieving their goal of having women devote their
   lives to motherhood and family?

A year has passed since the day we met here for the first time as a unified group of German women, to demonstrate our willingness to cooperate in our Führer's work of reconstruction.

This year has been inspired by the desire to mark our times with our best efforts so that our descendants will be able to forget our nation's fourteen years of weakness and sickness. We women knew, quite as well as German men, that we had to teach a people, partially sunk in self-despair, attitudes requiring those very qualities that had been deliberately suppressed in our nation. In order to carry out our intentions to unite and to march shoulder to shoulder, we demanded honor and loyalty, strength and sincerity, humility and respect — such virtues appeal to the soul of a people. In matters of the soul, however, it is no longer the majority who decide, but the strength and inner freedom of upright individuals. Therefore, we could only fulfill our task if it enabled us to penetrate the soul of the individual. . . .

When we came to the point of recognizing that the human eye reflected a nation's soul, we had to reach the women of our nation, once and for all, through our labor on women's behalf. Because as mothers our women have carried the heavy burden of the past fourteen years — and the ruins of the war and post-war period — in their hearts; and as future mothers other women must presently develop an understanding of the demands of our times — to both of these groups we dedicated the first important path that we built to the hearts of German women: our Reichs-Maternity Service.

Urged on by the tired eyes of many over-burdened mothers and the responsibility for the coming generation of mothers, we joined together under the leadership of the National Socialist Women's Association . . . and appealed to the German women especially trained for this work. When I tell you today that, between the 1st of October 1934 and the 1st of April 1935, we enrolled more than 201,700 women in 7,653 maternity school courses in about 2,000 locations

throughout the German Reich, it may not seem much at first glance. But we must not forget that we had no funds and met with much opposition, and that we had no patronage since we were quite unknown. But we did have absolute and unshakable faith. None of our traveling teachers asked: How much will I earn? Or, What are my pension rights? We have done this work out of a sense of duty to our nation — and our nation has responded. On Mothers' Day this year we were presented with 3.5 million marks for this work of maternity training. Moreover, on this day of honor for the mothers of Germany, when we all collected money in the streets, we found that our humblest fellow-countrymen were the most generous. This was surely the most wonderful reward for all of us, but it also gave practical evidence of where our major efforts must be directed. And when, only one or two months from now, we open our Reichs-Maternity School in Wedding, formerly one of the most solidly "red"[1] quarters of Berlin, we will be able to congratulate ourselves on having prepared a place, on behalf of our Party and our State, that will reveal to all of you how we are solving our problems.

In this place, mothers of all ages and classes discuss their problems and their needs. Here they will become acquainted with the aims of a National Socialist state and will receive inspiration to pass them on from woman to woman, and thus to recover our national faith in ourselves. If by means of the Reichs-Maternity Service we gradually succeed in brightening the eyes of our mothers and in bringing some joy into their often difficult lives, perhaps even a song to their lips, we may consider that we have accomplished our task, because happy mothers will raise happy children. But our Reichs-Maternity Service must also make a point of teaching our young and future mothers those things that a liberal era did not teach them — for the omission of which our nation has had to pay dearly — namely, that though marriage we consciously become mothers of the nation; that is, we understand and share every national requirement laid upon German

---

[1]Communist.

men, and that, therefore, as wives we must unconditionally become the companions of our men — not merely in personal terms, but in all national requirements.

First we pursued our task by appealing to the mothers of the nation, and then to that generation closest to the mothers, the girls between eighteen and twenty-five years of age. We called upon them to join voluntarily in the chain of helping hands and to create a relationship of unbreakable trust among German women. And they came, our girls of the German Women's Labor Service.[2]

You, my girls, who have now spent two years with me in the struggle for the autonomy of the German people, have learned to carry every responsibility and have become the inspiration of our mothers. No matter whether our girls are cheerfully helping German settlers on the moors in their difficult work of creating new homes; or whether they are working in Rhön, Spessart, or in eastern Bavaria, hand in hand with the National Socialist Welfare Organization in giving help to careworn adults and joyless children, in reawakening a taste for beauty and a belief in themselves; or whether they are helping German peasant women harvest from dawn to dusk — one thing unites them all, for they know: We are needed, we are of some use, and we are playing our parts in the rebirth of our nation. . . .

Since at present we cannot satisfy all these demands [for compulsory labor service], owing to financial and organizational difficulties, we have begun by making only those demands that professional and university women can take the lead in supporting. . . . At one time, it was considered the height of achievement in Germany to know everything and thereby to lose the simplemindedness of childhood. We wish to impress on our women at the universities that, as university students, they must place the intellectual abilities entrusted to them at the disposal of their na-

tion with the same humility as that with which women workers and mothers fulfill their duties. . . . This summer our women students began to live in this manner and thereby joined the chain of helping hands we have created among ourselves. They went to German factories and replaced working women and mothers, enabling them to have a real vacation in order to regain strength for their hard day-to-day existence. For it is these women, these mothers of families, who are hardest hit by the short working hours or unemployment of their husbands, because at home their children sap their strength. . . .

This brings us to the point where we must consider the millions of German women who perform heavy labor in factories day in and day out. If we consider the human eye as the measure of people's soul, it is here that we find the deepest imprints of that fourteen-year-long attempt to strangle our national soul. We know that a great deal of industrial work must always be done by women, but it is essential that the woman at the machine should feel that she, in her position, represents her nation, in common with all other women. That is to say, we awaken her consciousness so that she will say to herself: "This is my responsibility, my attitude determines the attitude of the nation." . . .

I must deal briefly with a question that is constantly brought to our attention, that is, how our present attitude toward life differs from that of the previous women's movement. First, in principle we permit only Germans to be leaders of German women and to concern themselves with matters of importance to Germans. Second, as a matter of principle we never have demanded, nor shall we ever demand, equal rights for women with the men of our nation. Instead we shall always make women's special interests dependent upon the needs of our entire nation. All further considerations will follow from this unconditional intertwining of the collective fate of the nation.

---

[2]The Reich Labor Service (Reichsarbeitdienst, or RAD) grew out of various government-sponsored programs begun in the Weimar period in which unemployed young men worked on agricultural and construction projects. Under the Nazis, labor service was mandatory for young men between the ages of eighteen and twenty-five, and was brought under Party control. The Women's Labor Service was smaller, and participation was not mandatory until 1939.

The Stalin Revolution in the Soviet Union

After Lenin suffered a debilitating stroke in 1922 and died in January 1924, the Communist Party of the Soviet Union was racked by controversy over its future leadership and direction. Factions led by Leon Trotsky, Lev Kamenev, Gregory Zinoviev, and Nikolai Bukharin fought for Party offices and engaged in highly intellectualized debates about industrial policy, the peasant question, the meaning of socialism, international communism, and party governance. The winner in the power struggle, however, was Joseph Stalin, a man noted more for his political and organizational skills than his intellect. As general secretary of the Party, his control of patronage and his ability to dispense favors to local officials meant that he was able to steadily increase the number of his supporters in party congresses and ultimately the politburo, the Party's central executive committee. One by one, his opponents were voted down, removed from office, expelled from the Party, and frequently exiled to Siberia. When the Fifteenth Party Congress in December 1927 condemned "all deviations from the party line" (then largely decided by Stalin himself), Stalin's control was complete. The stage was set for a new round of earthshaking economic and political changes for the Soviet people.

Joseph Stalin (1879–1953), born Joseph Dzhugashvili, was the son of a shoe-maker from the province of Georgia. He was a candidate for the priesthood before he abandoned Christianity for Marxism and joined the Bolshevik wing of the Social Democratic Party in 1903. His position in the party rose steadily, and between periods of exile he attended party congresses in Stockholm and London. Exiled to Siberia, he returned to Petrograd in 1917 after the fall of the tsar and sat on the twelve-member Central Committee that organized the October Revolution. In 1922 he was named general secretary of the Bolshevik Party and, a few years later, commissar of nationalities. Having crushed his opponents in the struggles following Lenin's death, Stalin launched a bold restructuring of the Soviet economy in 1928, setting the Soviet Union on a political and cultural path it would follow in certain respects until the mid-1980s.

The Soviet Model of Economic Planning

34 ◆ Joseph Stalin,
THE RESULTS OF THE FIRST FIVE-YEAR PLAN

In 1928, the New Economic Policy (NEP), which Lenin had adopted in 1921, still guided Soviet economic life. Through the NEP, Lenin had sought to restore agriculture and industry after seven years of war, revolution, and civil strife. Although the state maintained control of banks, foreign trade, and heavy industry, peasants could sell their goods on the open market, and small business owners could hire laborers, operate small factories, and keep their profits. The NEP saved the USSR from economic collapse, but its acceptance of private profit and economic competition troubled Marxist purists and did little to foster large-scale industrialization. Thus in 1928 Stalin abandoned the NEP and replaced it with the first Five-Year Plan, which established a centralized planned economy in which Moscow bureaucrats regulated agriculture, manufacturing, finance, and transportation. In agriculture, the Plan abolished individual peasant holdings and combined them into large collective and state farms. This meant the obliteration of the class of prosperous and successful peasant farmers known as kulaks. In manufacturing, the Plan concentrated on heavy industry and the production of goods such as tractors, trucks, and machinery. Second and third Five-Year Plans were launched in 1933 and 1938.

In the following report, delivered to the Central Committee of the Communist Party of the Soviet Union in January 1933, Stalin outlines the goals and achievements of the first Five-Year Plan.

QUESTIONS FOR ANALYSIS

1. According to Stalin, was socialist theory or the defense of the Soviet Union the more important reason for launching the Five-Year Plans?
2. Why did heavy industry play such an important role in the Five-Year Plans?
3. Why, in Stalin's view, was the collectivization of agriculture such a key component of the Five-Year Plan?
4. What, according to Stalin, were the main obstacles to the success of the Five-Year Plan?
5. In Stalin's view, how have the people of the Soviet Union benefited from the Five-Year Plan? What sacrifices have they been asked to make?
6. How, according to Stalin, does the success of the Five-Year Plan prove communism's superiority to capitalism?

The fundamental task of the Five-Year Plan was to convert the U.S.S.R. from an agrarian and weak country, dependent upon the caprices of the capitalist countries, into an industrial and powerful country, fully self-reliant and independent of the caprices of world capitalism.

The fundamental task of the Five-Year Plan was, in converting the U.S.S.R. into an industrial country, fully to eliminate the capitalist elements, to widen the front of the socialist forms of economy, and to create the economic base for the abolition of classes in the U.S.S.R., for the construction of socialist society.

The fundamental task of the Five-Year Plan was to create such an industry in our country as would be able to re-equip and reorganize, not only the whole of industry, but also transport and agriculture — on the basis of socialism.

The fundamental task of the Five-Year Plan was to transfer small and scattered agriculture onto the lines of large-scale collective farming, so as the ensure the economic base for socialism in the rural districts and thus to eliminate the possibility of the restoration of capitalism in the U.S.S.R.

Finally, the task of the Five-Year Plan was to create in the country all the necessary technical and economic prerequisites for increasing to the utmost the defensive capacity of the country, to enable it to organize determined resistance to any and every attempt at military intervention from outside. . . .

The main link in the Five-Year Plan was heavy industry, with machine building at its core. For only heavy industry is capable of reconstructing industry as a whole, as well as the transport system and agriculture, and of putting them on their feet. . . . Hence, the restoration of heavy industry had to be made on the basis of the fulfillment of the Five-Year Plan. . . .

But the restoration and development of heavy industry, particularly in such a backward and poor country as our country was at the beginning of the Five-Year Plan period, is an extremely difficult task; for, as is well known, heavy industry calls for enormous financial expenditures and the availability of a certain minimum of experienced technical forces, without which, speaking generally, the restoration of heavy industry is impossible. Did the party know this, and did it take this into consideration? Yes, it did. . . . The party declared frankly that this would call for serious sacrifices, and that we must openly and consciously make these sacrifices if we wanted to achieve our goal. . . .

◆ ◆

What are the results of the Five-Year Plan in four years in the sphere of *industry*? . . .

We did not have an iron and steel industry, the foundation for the industrialization of the country. Now we have this industry.

We did not have a tractor industry. Now we have one.

We did not have an automobile industry. Now we have one.

We did not have a machine-tool industry. Now we have one.

We did not have a big and up-to-date chemical industry. Now we have one.

We did not have a real and big industry for the production of modern agricultural machinery. Now we have one.

We did not have an aircraft industry. Now we have one.

In output of electric power we were last on the list. Now we rank among the first.

In the output of oil products and coal we were last on the list. Now we rank among the first. . . .

And as a result of all this the capitalist elements have been completely and [irrevocably] eliminated from industry, and socialist industry has become the sole form of industry in the U.S.S.R.

And as a result of all this our country has been converted from an agrarian into an industrial country; for the proportion of industrial output, as compared with agricultural output, has risen from 48 per cent of the total in the beginning of the Five-Year Plan period (1928) to 70 per cent at the end of the fourth year of the Five-Year Plan period (1932). . . .

Finally, as a result of all this the Soviet Union has been converted from a weak country, unprepared for defense, into a country mighty in defense, a country prepared for every contingency, a country capable of producing on a mass scale all modern weapons of defense and of equipping its army with them in the event of an attack from without. . . .

We are told: This is all very well; but it would have been far better to have abandoned the policy of industrialization, . . . and to have produced more cotton, cloth, shoes, clothing, and other articles of general use. . . .

. . . Of course, out of the 1,500,000,000 rubles in foreign currency that we spent on purchasing equipment for our heavy industries, we could have set apart a half for the purpose of importing raw cotton, hides, wool, rubber, etc. Then we would now have more cotton cloth, shoes and clothing. But we would not have a tractor industry or an automobile industry; we would not have anything like a big iron and steel industry; we would not have metal for the manufacture of machinery — and we would be unarmed, while we are surrounded by capitalist countries which are armed with modern technique. . . . Our position would be more or less analogous to the present position of China, which has no heavy industry and no war industry of her own and which is pecked at by everybody who cares to do so. . . .

◆ ◆

The Five-Year Plan in the sphere of agriculture was a Five-Year Plan of collectivization. What did the party proceed from in carrying out collectivization?

The party proceeded from the fact that in order to consolidate the dictatorship of the proletariat and to build up socialist society it was necessary, in addition to industrialization, to pass from small, individual peasant farming to large-scale collective agriculture equipped with tractors and modern agricultural machinery, as the only firm basis for the Soviet power in the rural districts.

The party proceeded from the fact that without collectivization it would be impossible to lead our country onto the highroad of building the economic foundations of socialism, impossible to free the vast masses of the laboring peasantry from poverty and ignorance. . . .

The party has succeeded, in a matter of three years, in organizing more than 200,000 collective farms and about 5,000 state farms specializing mainly in grain growing and livestock raising, and at the same time it has succeeded, in the course of four years, in enlarging the crop area by 21,000,000 hectares.[1]

The party has succeeded in getting more than 60 per cent of the peasant farms, which account for more than 70 per cent of the land cultivated by peasants to unite into collective farms, which means that we have *fulfilled* the Five-Year Plan *threefold.*

The party has succeeded in creating the possibility of obtaining, not 500,000,000 to 600,000,000 poods[2] of marketable grain, which was the amount purchased in the period when individual peasant farming predominated, but 1,200,000,000 to 1,400,000,000 poods of grain annually.

The party has succeeded in routing the kulaks as a class, although they have not yet been dealt the final blow; the laboring peasants have been emancipated from kulak bondage and exploitation, and a firm economic basis for the Soviet government, the basis of collective farming, has been established in the countryside.

The party has succeeded in converting the U.S.S.R. from a land of small peasant farming into a land where agriculture is run on the largest scale in the world. . . .

Do not all these facts testify to the superiority of the Soviet system of agriculture over the capitalist system? Do not these facts go to show that the collective farms are a more virile form of farming than individual capitalist farms? . . .

. . . Was the party right in pursuing the policy of an accelerated tempo of collectivization? Yes, it was absolutely right, even though certain excesses were committed in the process.[3] In pursuing the policy of eliminating the kulaks as a class, and in destroying the kulak nests, the party could not stop half way. It was necessary to carry this work to completion. . . .

◆ ◆

What are the results of these successes as regards the improvement of the material conditions of the workers and peasants? . . .

In our country, in the U.S.S.R., the workers have long forgotten unemployment. Some three years ago we had about one and a half million unemployed. It is already two years now since unemployment has been completely abolished. . . . Look at the capitalist countries: what horrors are taking place there as a result of unemployment! There are now no less than thirty to forty million unemployed in those countries. . . .

---

[1] In the metric system a hectare is slightly less than 2.5 acres.
[2] A Russian measure of weight equal to about thirty-six pounds.
[3] Stalin is understating the case more than a little. It is estimated that as many as fifteen million peasants were deported to labor camps, exiled to Siberia, or sent to work in factories in the late 1920s and early 1930s; of these 15 to 20 percent died or were executed.

Every day they try to get work, seek work, are prepared to accept almost any conditions of work but they are not given work, because they are "superfluous." And this is taking place at a time when vast quantities of goods and products are wasted to satisfy the caprices of the darlings of fate, the scions of capitalists and landlords. The unemployed are refused food because they have no money to pay for the food; they are refused shelter because they have no money to pay rent. How and where do they live? They live on the miserable crumbs from the rich man's table; by raking [searching through] refuse cans, where they find decayed scraps of food; they live in the slums of big cities, and more often in hovels outside of the towns, hastily put up by the unemployed out of packing cases and the bark of trees. . . .

One of the principal achievements of the Five-Year Plan in four years is that we have abolished unemployment and have relieved the workers of the U.S.S.R. of its horrors.

The same thing must be said in regard to the peasants. They, too, have forgotten about the differentiation of the peasants into kulaks and poor peasants, about the exploitation of the poor peasants by the kulaks, about the ruin which, every year, caused hundreds of thousands and millions of poor peasants to go begging. . . .

[The Five-Year Plan] has undermined and smashed the kulaks as a class, thus liberating the poor peasants and a good half of the middle peasants from bondage to the kulaks. . . . It has thus eliminated the possibility of the differentiation of the peasantry into exploiters — kulaks — and exploited — poor peasants. It has raised the poor peasants and the lower stratum of the middle peasants to a position of security in the collective farms, and has thereby put a stop to the process of ruination and impoverishment of the peasantry. . . .

Now there are no more cases of hundreds of thousands and millions of peasants being ruined and forced to hang around the gates of factories and mills. That is what used to happen; but that was long ago. Now the peasant is in a position of security; he is a member of a collective farm which has at its disposal tractors, agricultural machinery, a seed fund, a reserve fund, etc., etc.

Such are the main results of the realization of the Five-Year Plan in industry and agriculture; in the improvement of the conditions of life of the working people and the development of the exchange of goods; in the consolidation of the Soviet power and the development of the class struggle against the remnants and survival of the dying classes.

The Abortion Debate Under Stalin

❖

35 ❖ *LETTERS TO* IZVESTIYA *ON THE ABORTION ISSUE, MAY–JUNE 1936*

On taking power in Russia in 1917, the Bolsheviks, true to the heritage of European socialism, immediately took steps to liberate women from the shackles of religion, ignorance, and male dominance. In its first few months of existence, the Bolshevik government declared marriage a civil, not religious, union, and made divorce more or less available on demand. In 1920 it legalized abortion. After the civil war, women were encouraged to work, and the Ministry of Social Welfare established a system of nationwide day-care centers for children of working mothers. Government schools taught girls how to read and write, and party functionaries from the Zhenotdel, or women's bureau, went into cities, villages, and remote provinces to inform women of their rights, teach literacy, fight prostitution, and explain communism. In 1926 the party reaffirmed its commitment to female equality and women's rights in the revised Family Code adopted by the All Union Council of Soviets.

In the 1930s, however, the Soviet government under Stalin became more authoritarian, and its policies less libertarian and egalitarian. Nationalism, social conservatism, industrialization, and the collectivization of agriculture became its focus. Like many other European leaders, Stalin was disturbed by the Soviet Union's declining birth rate, which fell 50 percent between 1930 and 1935. In response, the government launched a campaign to glorify motherhood and the family, and couples were urged to have larger families. A key step was taken in 1936 when the government proposed legislation to make divorce more difficult and to outlaw abortions except to protect the health of the mother. These issues were never debated in a political forum, but newspapers such as *Pravda* and *Izvestia* were permitted to publish readers' opinions in the form of letters to the editor.

The following excerpts from letters to *Izvestia* provide a sampling of the arguments for and against changing the abortion law. Not surprisingly, despite strong public support for keeping abortion legal, Stalin's government went ahead with its plans. On June 27, 1936, abortion became illegal in the Soviet Union.

QUESTIONS FOR ANALYSIS

1. What arguments for and against abortion are offered by the letter writers?
2. What do the letters reveal about living conditions in the Soviet Union during the 1930s?
3. What views of motherhood are revealed in the letters?
4. What reasons might the government have had for allowing readers' letters to be published?

Letter from a Student [K. B.]

I have read in the press the draft law on the prohibition of abortion, aid to expectant mothers, etc., and cannot remain silent on this matter.

There are thousands of women in the same position as myself. I am a student reading the first course of the second Moscow Medical Institute. My husband is also a student reading the same course at our Institute. Our scholarships amount jointly to 205 rubles. Neither he nor I have a room of our own. Next year we intend to apply for admission to a hostel, but I do not know whether our application will be granted. I love children and shall probably have some in four or five years' time. But can I

have a child now? Having a child now would mean leaving the Institute, lagging behind my husband, forgetting everything I have learnt and probably leaving Moscow because there is nowhere to live.

There is another married couple in our Institute, Mitya and Galya, who live in a hostel. Yesterday Galya said to me: "If I become pregnant I shall have to leave the Institute; one cannot live in a hostel with children."

I consider that the projected law is premature because the housing problem in our towns is a painful one. Very often it is the lack of living quarters that is the reason behind an abortion. If the draft included an article assuring married couples, who are expecting a baby, of a room — that would be a different matter.

In five years' time when I am a doctor and have a job and a room I shall have children. But at present I do not want and cannot undertake such a responsibility. . . .

Letter from an Engineer [E.T.]

. . . I am non-party, married, with a 5-year-old son. I work as an engineer and have been and still am in a responsible position. I regard myself as a good citizen of the U.S.S.R.

I cannot agree with the prohibition of abortions. And I am very glad that this law has not entered into force but has been submitted to the workers for discussion.

The prohibition of abortion means the compulsory birth of a child to a woman who does not want children. The birth of a child ties married people to each other. Not everyone will readily abandon a child, for alimony is not all that children need. Where the parents produce a child of their own free will, all is well. But where a child comes into the family against the will of the parents, a grim personal drama will be enacted which will undoubtedly lower the social value of the parents and leave its mark on the child.

A categorical prohibition of abortion will confront young people with a dilemma: either complete sexual abstinence or the risk of jeopardizing their studies and disrupting their life. To my mind any prohibition of abortion is bound to mutilate many a young life. Apart from this, the result of such a prohibition might be an increase in the death-rate from abortions because they will then be performed illegally.

Answer to the Student K. B. . . .

Your paper recently published a letter from a student, K. B., in which she raised objections to the prohibition of abortions. I think the author of the letter . . . has not grasped the full

significance of the projected law. The difficulties about which K. B. writes and which, according to her, justify abortion are, she thinks, the difficulties of to-day which will have disappeared to-morrow. The writer of that letter completely ignored the fact that the government, by widening the network of child-welfare institutions, is easing the mother's task in looking after the child. The main mistake K. B. makes is, in my view, that she approaches the problem of childbearing as though it were a private matter. This would explain why she writes: "I shall have them (children) in four or five years' time." She hopes by that time to have completed her studies, obtained a medical diploma and found both a job and a room. But one must be logical! If during these years, K. B. intends to have recourse to abortions, who can vouch that by the time when she desires to have children she will still be able to do so? And for a normal woman to be deprived of the possibility of having children is as great a misfortune as the loss of a dear one.

I used to study in a factory and received a very small allowance while bringing up my small son whom I had to bring up on my own. (His father was dead.) It was a hard time. I had to go and unload trains or look for similar work that would bring in some money . . . that was in 1923. Now my son is a good, rough Komsomol[1] and a Red Army soldier in the Far East. How great are my joy and pride that I did not shun the difficulties and that I managed to bring up such a son.

Letter from Professor K. Bogorekov, Leningrad

Abortions are harmful. One cannot disagree with that. But situations in life do exist when this harmful remedy will allow a woman to preserve normal conditions of life.

If a single child already ties a woman down, two, three or four children leave her no possibility

---

[1] A member of the Communist Youth Organization; one could stay in the organization until the age of twenty-five.

at all of participating in social life and having a job. A man suffers less. He gives the family his salary irrespective of the number of children — and the whole burden falls upon the mother.

Sometimes abortion is an extreme but decisive means of averting the disruption of a young woman's life. It may become imperative, through the accident of an unlucky liaison for a young girl-student without means for whom a child would be a heavy penalty, or through bad heredity of the parents or a number of other contingencies which play an important part in life and can often lead to its mutilation. All this must be taken into account.

It must not be thought that the majority of abortions are the result of irresponsible behavior. Experience shows that a woman resorts to abortion as a last resource when other methods of safeguard against pregnancy have failed and the birth of a child threatens to make her life more difficult.

Simple statistics show that in spite of this the birth-rate of our country is increasing rapidly.[2] And what is needed is not pressure, but a stimulation of the birth-rate by means of financial assistance, improved housing conditions, legal action against those who fail to pay alimony, etc. . . .

. . . Abortions will become obsolete by themselves when knowledge of human anatomy spreads, methods of birth-control are more widely used and — last but not least — when housing conditions are improved. . . .

Letter from Professor M. Malinovsky

Performing an abortion is an operation undoubtedly involving great risks. There are few operations so dangerous as the cleaning out of the womb during pregnancy. Under the best of conditions and in the hands of the most experienced specialist this operation still has a "normal" percentage of fatal cases. It is true that the percentage is not very high. Our surgeons have brought the technique of performing abortions to perfection. The foreign doctors who have watched operations in our gynæcological hospitals have unanimously testified that their technique is irreproachable. And yet . . . here are still cases in which it is fatal. This is understandable. The operation is performed in the dark and with instruments which, so far as their effect on so tender an organ as the womb is concerned, remind one of a crowbar. And even the most gifted surgeons, virtuosi at their job, occasionally cause great and serious injuries for which the woman often pays with her life. . . .

The slave-like conditions of hired labor, together with unemployment and poverty, deprive women in capitalist countries of the impulse for childbearing. Their "will to motherhood" is paralyzed. In our country all the conditions for giving birth to and bringing up a healthy generation exist. The "fear of motherhood", the fear of the morrow, the anxiety over the child's future are gone.

The lighthearted attitude towards the family, the feeling of irresponsibility which is still quite strong in men and women, the disgusting disrespect for women and children — all these must come before our guns. Every baseness towards women and every form of profligacy must be considered as serious antisocial acts. . . .

---

[2]From what is known, a false statement.

CHAPTER 5

Latin America in an Era of Economic Challenge and Political Change

A popular slogan among Latin America's politicians and land-owners in the late nineteenth and early twentieth centuries was "order and progress," and to an extent that was exceptional in the region's history, they achieved both. Around 1870 Latin America's economy entered a period of export-driven expansion that continued until the 1920s. In an updated version of colonial-era economic relationships, the region became a major supplier of wheat, beef, mutton, coffee, raw rubber, nitrates, copper, tin, and a host of other primary products to Europe and a major market for European manufactured goods. Land prices soared, and English and U.S. capital flowed into Latin America to finance railroads, banks, and food-processing facilities and to lend governments money for the construction of roads, bridges, and public buildings. The defects of this neocolonial economic order soon would be revealed; in the short run, however, it brought riches to the landowners and modernization to the cities.

Latin America's economic boom took place in a climate of relative political stability. In Argentina, Chile, and Brazil this stability was achieved under republican governments controlled by an oligarchy of landowning families, sometimes in alliance with merchants in the import-export trade; in Mexico, Peru, Ecuador, and Venezuela, it resulted from rule by a strong man or dictator (*caudillo*). Dictators and oligarchs alike sought economic growth by maintaining law and order and by encouraging foreign investment, free trade, and land confiscations from the Roman Catholic Church and Native Americans. They faced little opposition. The rural masses were politically apathetic; an urban working class hardly existed; and the small middle class accepted its limited political role as long as prosperity continued.

By the 1930s, however, oligarchic rule and the neocolonial economic order on which it had been based were both in shambles. The turning point was the Great Depression of the 1930s, which exposed the dangers of dependency on industrialized nations for markets, manufactured goods, and capital. Demand for Latin

America's food products and raw materials collapsed, depriving the region of the foreign exchange needed to buy manufactured goods. The collapse of the international financial system shut off the flow of loans and investments from Europe and the United States. Governments faced insolvency, and capital shortages impeded plans to end the economic slump through industrialization. Latin Americans came to resent European and especially U.S. ownership of tin and copper mines, oil fields, railroads, banks, processing plants, and prime agricultural land. Once welcomed as a means of attracting capital and encouraging growth, foreign ownership in the 1930s more frequently was condemned as imperialist plunder.

The oligarchical political order had already begun to disintegrate by the time the Great Depression struck. Economic expansion had generated social changes that undermined the region's two-class system — an elite of wealthy and powerful landowners and a mass of illiterate and impoverished peasants and laborers. Urbanization, fueled by European immigration, modest industrialization, and an influx of people from the countryside, made society more complex and diversified. In Mexico City, Rio de Janeiro, Buenos Aires, and other cities, a factory-based working class emerged, and a middle class made up of professionals, office workers, teachers, writers, and small business owners grew steadily. These groups rejected the oligarchy's economic priorities, and their growing assertiveness undermined the political monopoly of the landowning elite. Their strength was revealed in Argentina in 1912 when the government extended the right to vote to all adult males, and in Mexico in 1910 when middle-class reformers in alliance with rural rebels overthrew the dictatorship of Porfirio Díaz.

Political and social conflict in the 1920s and 1930s was accompanied by the breakdown of the intellectual and cultural assumptions of the era of "order and progress." These assumptions included a faith in science and liberalism, a belief in white racial superiority, and a conviction that things European equaled progress, while things American, or Indian, represented backwardness. The liberalism of the white ruling class faced opposition not only from conservative Catholics, but also from nationalists, communists, anarchists, trade unionists, and fascists who in various contexts and at different times spoke on behalf of the middle class, the proletariat, the military, and the Indians, blacks, and mixed bloods. Modernist artists and writers, like their counterparts in Europe, rejected liberalism, questioned reason and science, and sought to articulate the components of a new cultural identity and of a new society. By the 1920s this quest for self-definition led many intellectuals to discover popular traditions and ethnic, especially Indian, lore, which they regarded as the touchstones of cultural identity.

This current of nativism, or *indigenismo,* strengthened cultural nationalism in states such as Mexico and Peru and prepared the way for the economic nationalism of the Depression years.

Out of this ideological and cultural ferment, no new consensus emerged. In Chile, Uruguay, and Venezuela, oligarchic rule gave way to dominance by new middle-class groups who frequently disagreed about fundamental issues. Mexico became a one-party state controlled by the National Revolutionary Party, which, despite its name, until the mid-1930s was more interested in capitalist development than social reform. A new kind of populist, quasi-fascist leader emerged in the persons of Getúlio Vargas in Brazil and Juan Perón in Argentina. Strong-arm dictators, essentially old-style *caudillos,* held sway in Cuba, the Dominican Republic, El Salvador, Haiti, Honduras, Nicaragua, Paraguay, and Guatemala.

As a result of all these factors, Latin America in the 1920s and 1930s faced a crisis of political legitimacy, as well as deepening fragmentation, instability, and conflict. Old views and institutions were discredited, but no one could agree on what should replace them. A democratic government might come to power briefly, only to be overthrown by the army; populist politicians might institute reforms, only to be replaced by a conservative government that canceled them. There were threats from the left, counterstrikes from the right, divisions in the center — and repeated clashes among them all. A few countries — Mexico, Chile, Uruguay for a time, Costa Rica, Venezuela, and perhaps Colombia — had some success dealing with these competing cross-currents, but in the rest, the conflicts were so deep and the gaps between regions and classes so vast that no government could govern effectively or even hope to survive for long.

◆

New Social and Political Currents: Feminism and *Indigenismo*

Among the issues that confronted Latin American politicians, intellectuals, and civic-minded citizens in the early 1900s, none was more fundamental than the perceived lack of nationhood throughout the region. Their states, many Latin Americans came to believe, lacked not just political consensus but, more fundamentally, any sense of unity or common purpose among their people. Latin American nations were loose amalgams of groups and subgroups differing in speech, ethnic background, economic expectations, and perspectives. Issues were seen through the prisms of class, region, race, gender, and economic self-interest, not the general good. Many became convinced they needed a new type of state with governments committed to serving the interests of all its component groups and drawing on all their energies. This meant breaking the political monopoly of the great landowners and opening up politics to groups who had largely been ignored during the era of oligarchical rule — the bourgeoisie, urban workers, immigrants, and two groups that are the subjects of the documents in this section, women and Native Americans.

The drive for women's rights in Latin America began in the 1870s in the most urbanized and economically advanced states — Argentina, Chile, Uruguay, and Brazil. In all four, liberal governments in the late 1800s established secular schools for girls as part of an effort to end the Roman Catholic Church's monopoly on education. This led to the founding of teacher-training schools for women and the emergence of teaching as an important female profession.

Schoolteachers, along with small numbers of professional women, recent arrivals from Europe, and socialists, provided leadership and energy for Latin American feminism in the early 1900s. They edited journals, attended conferences, and formed societies for the purposes of self-improvement and publicity. Most feminists supported better education for women, access to the professions, improved health care, and greater equality between husbands and wives. There were disagreements, however, on issues of divorce and women's suffrage. Moderates feared liberalized divorce laws would weaken marriage, while socialists and liberals feared that if devout Catholic women were given the right to vote, they would tilt the balance in favor of conservative clerical parties.

Feminists made some gains in the 1920s and 1930s. In 1929 Ecuador, whose conservative leaders hoped women's votes would favor them over their liberal and socialist rivals, was the first Latin American state to grant women the right to vote. In the 1930s women won the right to vote in national elections in Brazil, Uruguay, and Cuba, and in provincial and municipal elections in Mexico, Peru, and Argentina. Progress also was made in education. In Cuba females gained equal access to public schools in 1901, and in several states increasing numbers of women were admitted to universities. In Chile in the 1920s, women received 25 percent of all degrees. Few gains were made in the area of married women's rights; by the late 1930s, only Mexico, Argentina, Chile, and Uruguay had revised their civil codes to limit husbands' authority.

Along with *feminismo, indigenismo* was another word added to Latin America's vocabulary in the early twentieth century. Sometimes translated into English as "Indianism," *indigenismo* became an important movement in states with large Indian populations such as Mexico, Bolivia, Peru, Guatemala, and Ecuador. A term with cultural and political connotations, *indigenismo* meant both an affirmation of the intrinsic value of the Indians' culture and a commitment to improving their economic and social condition. It was part of the general reaction against the assumptions and policies of the late-nineteenth- and early-twentieth-century oligarchies, whose leaders had disdained the Indians' culture and condoned the landowning elite's exploitation of the native population. It also was a result of greater awareness of Indian problems that grew out of Indian revolts in Peru and the demands of Emiliano Zapata and his followers for land reform during the Mexican Revolution.

In the 1920s and 1930s increasing numbers of Latin American writers explored the theme of Indian exploitation, and many intellectuals asserted that Indian culture and values could become a source of national regeneration. Politicians also showed greater interest in Indian problems. The Mexican Constitution of 1917 committed the government to land reform, and during the 1920s and 1930s, millions of acres of land were returned to peasant communities. No one solved the "Indian problem," however, and in Mexico and the Andean states, Indians today remain at the bottom of the economic and social order.

Costs and Benefits of Latin American Feminism

36 ◆ Amanda Labarca, *WHERE IS WOMAN GOING?*

Amanda Labarca was born in 1886 into the family of a successful Chilean merchant in Santiago. Educated in private girls' schools, she attended the University of Chile, where she received a degree in education. After her marriage to Guillermo Hubertson, the couple pursued graduate studies at both Columbia University and the Sorbonne in Paris, and traveled extensively in the United States and Europe. By the time Labarca returned to Chile in 1918, she was a feminist. She became the director of a girls' school in Santiago and in 1919 helped found the National Council of Women of Chile, an organization dedicated to improving women's legal, civil, and educational status. In 1922 she became a professor of education at the University of Chile, and in 1931 was appointed director of secondary education for the entire nation. A well-known figure in international feminist circles, she traveled extensively and published more than twenty books of fiction and social commentary.

The following excerpt is take from an article, "¿Adónde va la mujer?" (Where Is Woman Going?), which first appeared in the 1920s and was republished in an anthology by the same name in 1934. In it she discusses the positive and negative effects of feminism on the region's middle-class women.

QUESTIONS FOR ANALYSIS

1. On the basis of Labarca's essay, how can one characterize views of women and the status of women in Latin American societies before the rise of feminism?
2. In Labarca's view, how have twentieth-century developments eroded traditional views? What were the underlying causes of these developments?
3. According to Labarca, what "losses" have middle-class Latin American women experienced as a result of women's changing social role? Who is largely to blame for these losses?
4. How does Labarca view the essential characteristics of men and women?
5. Is Labarca optimistic about women's future in Latin America? Why or why not?

Has feminism brought gains or losses to the Latin-American middle-class girl of today?

Gains. First of all, the consciousness of her own worth in the totality of human progress. Today's girl knows that there are no insurmountable obstacles to the flight of her intelligence; that the question of whether her entire sex is intelligent will not be raised before she is permitted to engage in any intellectual activity; that in the eyes of the majority her womanhood does not mark her with the stigma of irremediable inferiority, and that if she has talent she will be allowed to display it.

The law codes have returned to her, in large part, control over her life and property. She has well-founded hopes of seeing abolished within her lifetime the laws that still relegate her, in certain aspects, to the position of a second-class citizen, and that accord her unequal legal treatment.

She has made progress in economic liberty, [the] basis of all independence, whether it be a question of a simple individual or one of nations. Today she is gaining admission into fields of labor forbidden to her mother.

Before her extends an unbounded horizon of opportunities. Hopes! She can live her years of illusions imagining — like every adolescent male — that the whole world awaits her, and that only her own limitations can prevent her from ascending the highest peaks of this world.

She has won liberty, including — it may seem ridiculous to mention it — the liberty of going about without papa or the classic brother at her side. . . .

She has lost, in the first place, the respect of the male majority. One might say that formerly consideration for women formed part of good breeding, and it was denied only to one who by her conduct showed that she did not merit it. Today it is the other way around. In general, woman receives no tribute, and she must prove convincingly that she is a distinguished personage before receiving the homage that once was common.

Which has diminished — the respect or the quality of respectability? . . .

Men used to expect of woman a stainless virtue, perfect submission — after God, thy husband, orders the epistle of St. Paul[1] — and a life-long devotion to the orbit in which her man revolved. A saint in the vaulted niche of her home, saint to the world, mistress of her four walls, and slave to her man. In exchange for this — respect and devotion. True, the father or husband sometimes played the role of sacristan[2] to the saint. They allowed no one to fail to reverence her, but they themselves took liberties and even mistreated her — conduct that the saint had to bear with resignation . . . she had no recourse. . . .

It is unnecessary to refer again to the upheavals that the invention of machinery brought to the world, the sharp rise in the cost of living, and the pauperization of the household, which from producer was reduced to being a simple consumer. It became impossible for a man of average means to satisfy the needs of all his womenfolk, and women had to enter offices, the professions, and other remunerative employment that had been men's traditional source of income. Woman has gone out into the world, and although this fact in itself is an economic imperative and does not essentially imply the abandonment of any virtue, the ordinary man has denied her his respect. . . .

. . . For the ordinary man, woman's freedom is license; her equality, the right to treat her without courtesy.

She has lost in opportunities for marriage, for establishing a household, and for satisfying that yearning for maternity that is her fundamental instinct. The more cultured a woman, the more difficult for her to find a husband, because it is normal for her to seek refuge, understanding,

---

[1] The apostle Paul in I Corinthians 7:39 and other places in his epistles speaks of the need for wives to be obedient to their husbands.

[2] A sacristan is a church official in charge of caring for the vestments and sacred utensils used in religious services, and, in some cases, the entire church building.

and guidance in a person superior to herself. And the latter do not always prefer cultured women. They imagine that knowledge makes them unfeeling — an absurd notion — that it makes them domineering — which concerns not acquired knowledge but character — or that it makes them insufferably pedantic. . . . For their wives men prefer the "old-fashioned" girl.

That is the pathos of the tragedy of middle-class women in the Latin countries. Evolution has taken place in opposition to the fundamental convictions of men, who only tolerate it — in the case of their daughters, for example — because imperious necessity dictates it, and only with profound chagrin. Men — I repeat that I speak of the majority — continue to judge women from the viewpoint of fifty years ago, and if they retain some respect and esteem in their inner beings, they tender it to the woman who remained faithful to the classic type — the woman who has progressed they place very close to those for whom they have no respect.

Men cannot understand that external conditions — culture, profession, liberty — have not radically transformed the classic femininity, the maternal instincts, the impulses of the sweet Samaritan,[3] the yearnings of a noble spirituality. The cases of this kind that he knows about do not convince him; he imagines that they constitute exceptions.

Not are men of more advanced ideas free from this attitude. And it would be amusing — if it did not have tragic implications — to observe what a socialist, a radical, a communist, proclaims on the public platform and what he praises in the intimacy of his home.

Man and woman. Feared and beloved master; slave, sweetly, or tyrannically subjugated; wall and ivy. Today divergent and almost hostile, but not comrades. Woman and man cannot yet be comrades, save in an infinitely small number of cases. The relationship of comrades implies equality, confidence, and the same criteria for judging each other.

"But if she acknowledges her bitter lot, why not turn back?" more than one naive soul asks. Impossible. Time does not turn back. . . . New social theories will solve these problems and create new ones on the way to an inscrutable future that human faith — a flame that wavers but that only death can extinguish — imagines must be a better one.

Meanwhile, sisters, let us not preach feminism to women; let us win over the men, in the hope that our daughters may pay less dearly for their cup of happiness.

---

[3] In the parable of the Good Samaritan (Luke 10:30–37), Jesus tells the story of the Samaritan woman who helped an injured man who had been ignored by others. A samaritan thus came to mean a compassionate person, one willing to help the distressed.

The Indian in Peru: A Marxist Perspective

❖

37 ◆ José Carlos Mariátegui,
THE PROBLEM OF THE INDIAN AND THE PROBLEM OF THE LAND

Beginning in the 1870s, the economic situation of Peru's Indians, already one of extreme poverty, deteriorated even further. With worldwide demand for Peruvian agricultural products increasing and land prices soaring, wealthy creole landowners (*hacendados*), with the help of lawyers, local officials, and favorable laws passed by the central government, acquired increasing amounts of Indian communal lands. As a result, by the early 1900s Peru's Indians, more than 50 percent of the population, overwhelmingly were landless peasants providing cheap labor for white hacienda owners and bound to the land either through long-term labor contracts or because of debts owed to the landowner. Apathy, illiteracy, and alcoholism marked their lives.

The deterioration of Peruvian Indian life was accompanied by increasing concern for their welfare on the part of some Peruvians. Intellectuals at the University of San Marcos in Lima sought to dispel the notion that Indians were inherently inferior to whites. Some went further to suggest that Indian culture and values could serve as a source for national revival. Educators and clergy recommended programs of education and moral instruction to teach Indians sobriety and good work habits. The radical writer Manuel Gonzalez Prada (1848–1918) went further; he urged the Indians to arm themselves and rebel.

José Carlos Maríategui (1895–1930) was not, therefore, the first Peruvian to speak out on Indian issues. Nor was he Peru's first Marxist. In the 1920s the Peruvian exile Raúl Haya de la Torre founded the Alianza Popular Revolucionaria Americana (APRA), a party with a strong Marxist component, and the author Luís E. Valcarel hailed peasant revolts in the highlands as the first rumblings of a revolution that would usher in true egalitarianism. Maríategui's accomplishment was to provide an analysis of Peruvian society by bringing together a passionate concern for the Indians' welfare and the scientific socialism of Marx.

Maríategui, born in 1895 and raised in poverty by his mother, a seamstress, had only a few years of schooling. At age fourteen he became a printer's apprentice for a newspaper in Lima, Peru's largest city, and continued his self-education. By the age of twenty-one he was writing news stories, poetry, and reviews for his newspaper and other Lima periodicals, and had written a full-length drama performed in a Lima theater. A harsh critic of Peru's politicians for their neglect of the poor, especially the Indians, Maríategui was exiled to Europe in 1919. Returning to Peru in 1923 as a Marxist, he worked to strengthen the labor movement, wrote hundreds of articles, and helped found the Socialist Party of Peru in 1928. His *Seven Interpretative Essays on Peruvian Reality*, his most popular work, appeared in 1928. Before he died at age thirty-five, he participated in discussions leading to the formation of the Peruvian Communist Party, formally organized a month after his death in 1930.

The following selection is made up of excerpts from two essays in *Seven Interpretive Essays on Peruvian Reality*, "The Problem of the Indian," and "The Problem of Land."

QUESTIONS FOR ANALYSIS

1. According to Maríategui, what is at the root of the problems of Indian poverty in Peru?
2. Maríategui rejects previous "solutions" to the problem of Indian poverty. What were they, and why, in his opinion, did they fail?
3. What in Maríategui's view is the only viable solution to the "problem of the Indian"?
4. Does Maríategui indicate how he hopes to accomplish his goals?

[THE PROBLEM OF THE INDIAN]

Any treatment of the problem of the Indian . . . that fails or refuses to recognize it as a socio-economic problem is but a sterile, theoretical exercise destined to be completely discredited. . . . The socialist critic exposes and defines the problem because he looks for its causes in the country's economy and not in its administrative, legal, or ecclesiastic machinery, its racial dualism or pluralism, or its cultural or moral conditions. The problem of the Indian is rooted in the land tenure system of our economy. Any attempt to solve it with administrative . . . measures, through education or by a road building program, is superficial and secondary as long as the feudalism of the *gamonales* [great landowners] continues to exist.

Gamonalismo[1] necessarily invalidates any law or regulation for the protection of the Indian. The hacienda owner, the *latifundista*[2] is a feudal lord. The written law is powerless against his authority, which is supported by custom and habit. Unpaid labor is illegal, yet unpaid and even forced labor survive in the latifundium. The judge, the subprefect, the commissary, the teacher, the tax collector, all are in bondage to the landed estate. The law cannot prevail against the *gamonales*. Any official who insisted on applying it would be abandoned and sacrificed by the central government. . . .

The oldest and most obvious mistake is, unquestionably, that of reducing the protection of the Indian to an ordinary administrative matter. From the days of Spanish colonial legislation, wise and detailed ordinances, worked out after conscientious study, have been quite useless. The republic,[3] since independence, has been prodigal in its decrees, laws, and provisions intended to protect the Indian against exaction and abuse. The *gamonal* of today, . . . however,

has little to fear from administrative theory; he knows that its practice is altogether different.

The individualistic character of the republic's legislation has favored the absorption of Indian property by the latifundium system. . . . The appropriation of most communal and individual Indian property is an accomplished fact. . . .

The assumption that the Indian problem is ethnic is sustained by the most outmoded repertory of imperialist ideas. The concept of inferior races was useful to the white man's West for purposes of expansion and conquest. To expect that the Indian will be emancipated through a steady crossing of the aboriginal race with white immigrants is an anti-sociological naiveté that could only occur to the primitive mentality of an importer of merino sheep. The people of Asia, who are in no way superior to the Indians, have not needed any transfusion of European blood in order to assimilate the most dynamic and creative aspects of Western culture. The degeneration of the Peruvian Indian is a cheap invention of sophists who serve feudal interests. . . .

The tendency to consider the Indian problem as a moral one embodies a liberal, humanitarian, enlightened nineteenth-century attitude. . . . The anti-slavery conferences and societies in Europe that have denounced more or less futilely the crimes of the colonizing nations are born of this tendency, which always has trusted too much in its appeals to the conscience of civilization. . . .

Humanitarian teachings have not halted or hampered European imperialism, nor have they reformed its methods. The struggle against imperialism now relies only on the solidarity and strength of the liberation movement of the colonial masses. . . .

On a moral and intellectual plane, the church took a more energetic or at least a more authoritative stand centuries ago. This crusade, however, achieved only very wise laws and provisions. The

---

[1]A term for the social and political domination of rural Peru by wealthy landowners; sometimes translated as "feudalism."

[2]The owner of a *latifundio*, a large landed estate worked by farm laborers in a state of partial serfdom.

[3]The period after Peruvian independence in 1824.

lot of the Indian remained substantially the same. . . . To wipe out abuses, it would have been necessary to abolish land appropriation and forced labor, in brief, to change the entire colonial regime. Without the toil of the American Indian, the coffers of the Spanish treasury would have been emptied.

But today a religious solution is unquestionably the most outdated and antihistoric of all. . . . If the church could not accomplish its task in a medieval era, when its spiritual and intellectual capacity could be measured by friars like Las Casas,[4] how can it succeed with the elements in commands today? . . . The belief that the Indian problem is one of education does not seem to be supported by even a strictly and independently pedagogical criterion. . . . School and teacher are doomed to be debased under the pressure of the feudal regime, which cannot be reconciled with the most elementary concept of progress and evolution. When this truth becomes partially understood, the saving formula is thought to be discovered in boarding schools for Indians. But the glaring inadequacy of this formula is self-evident in view of the tiny percentage of the indigenous school population that can be boarded in these schools.

The pedagogical solution, advocated by many in good faith, has been discarded officially. . . .

The new approach locates the problem of the Indian in the land tenure system.

[THE PROBLEM OF LAND]

Those of us who approach and define the Indian problem from a Socialist point of view must start out by declaring the complete obsolescence of the humanitarian and philanthropic points of view. . . . We shall try to establish the basically economic character of the problem. First, we protest against the instinctive attempt of the criollo or mestizo[5] to reduce it to an exclusively administrative, pedagogical, ethnic, or moral problem in order to avoid at all cost recognizing its economic aspect. . . . We are not satisfied to assert the Indian's right to education, culture, progress, love, and heaven. We begin by categorically asserting his right to land. . . .

The agrarian problem is first and foremost the problem of eliminating feudalism in Peru, which should have been done by the democratic-bourgeois regime that followed the War of Independence. But in its one hundred years as a republic, Peru has not had a genuine bourgeois class, a true capitalist class. The old feudal class — camouflaged or disguised as a republican bourgeoisie — has kept its position. . . . During a century of Republican rule, great agricultural property actually has grown stronger and expanded, despite the theoretical liberalism of our constitution and the practical necessities of the development of our capitalist economy. There are two expressions of feudalism that survive: the latifundium and servitude. Inseparable and of the same substance, their analysis leads us to the conclusion that the servitude oppressing the indigenous race cannot be abolished unless the latifundium is abolished. . . .

Everyone knows that the liberal solution for this problem, in conformity with individualist ideology, would be to break up the latifundio in order to create small landed properties. . . .

In conformity with my ideological position, I think that in Peru the hour for trying the liberal method, the individualist formula, has already passed. Leaving doctrinal reasons aside, I regard as fundamental an indisputable and concrete factor that gives a peculiar stamp to our agrarian problem: the survival of the Indian community and of elements of practical socialism in Indian life and agriculture.

In Peru, communal property does not represent a primitive economy that has gradually been replaced by a progressive economy founded on

---

[4]Bartolomé de Las Casas (1474–1566) was a Spanish friar who denounced the exploitation of Amerindians by the Spanish.

[5]A criollo is a Peruvian of European descent; a mestizo is a person of European-Indian descent.

individual property. No; the "communities" have been despoiled of their land for the benefit of the feudal or semi-feudal latifundium, which is constitutionally incapable of technical progress.

The latifundium compares unfavorably with the "community" as an enterprise for agricultural production. . . . Large property seems to be justified by the interests of production, which are identified, at least in theory, with the interests of society. But this is not the case of the latifundium and, therefore, it does not meet an economic need. Except for sugar-cane plantations — which produce *aguardiente* [liquor] to

intoxicate and stupefy the Indian peasant — the latifundium of the sierra generally grows the same crops as the "community," and it produces no more. . . .

The "community," on the one hand, is a system of production that keeps alive in the Indian the moral incentives that stimulate him to do his best work. . . .

By dissolving or abandoning the "community," the system of the feudal latifundium has attacked not only an economic institution but also, and more important, a social institution, one that defends the indigenous tradition [and] maintains the function of the rural family. . . .

◆

Political Responses to the Great Depression

As the Great Depression spread economic misery across Latin America, one government after another fell in an epidemic of election swings, revolts, coups, and countercoups. The military seized power in Argentina and Peru in 1930, and Uruguay's constitutional government collapsed in 1933 when the elected president, Gabriel Terra, established a dictatorship. Dictators also seized power in El Salvador, Guatemala, and Honduras, and, with the help of the U.S. government, in Nicaragua and the Dominican Republic. In Chile, however, the onset of the Depression led in 1931 to the fall of a dictator, Carlos Ibáñez. This was followed by a brief constitutional interlude and more military coups before the establishment of a center-right government under Arturo Alessandri. In Cuba, the dictator Gerardo Machado was forced into exile in 1933, but another dictator, Fulgencio Batista, took his place in 1934. Ecuador had no fewer than fourteen presidents between 1931 and 1940, and Paraguay, four different dictators. Only a few states such as Colombia managed to maintain a measure of political stability.

While most of these regimes had little lasting impact, political changes in Mexico and Brazil had long-term consequences for the two nations themselves and for Latin America as a whole. In Mexico, these changes took place during the presidency of Lázaro Cárdenas, who between 1934 and 1940 revitalized Mexico's revolutionary tradition through educational reform, land redistribution, and nationalization of foreign-owned businesses. In Brazil, they were connected with the career of Getúlio Vargas, who seized power in 1930 and dominated Brazilian politics until 1945 and again from 1951 to 1954. By the end of the 1930s his *Estado Novo* (New State), a mixture of dictatorship, repression, anti-colonialism, economic planning, nationalism, industrialization, and government-sponsored programs for housing, improved wages, and medical care, provided Latin America with an authoritarian model for entry into the era of mass politics.

Economic Nationalism in Mexico

❖

38 ◆ *Lázaro Cárdenas, SPEECH TO THE NATION*

During the 1920s and early 1930s, Mexico's revolution had stalled. Its 1917 constitution called for land reform, granted extensive rights to labor, and proclaimed
the state's right to control foreign-owned businesses. But the two dominant
politicians of the 1920s and early 1930s, Alvaro Obregón and Plutarco Elías Calles,
had little enthusiasm for social reform despite their revolutionary rhetoric. Their
rule mainly benefited generals, businessmen, and landowners, and their modest
gestures in the direction of land redistribution were meant to head off rural rebellion. When in 1929 Calles organized Mexico's only national political party, the
National Revolutionary Party (PNR), out of dozens of local political machines, his
and his henchmen's political domination appeared secure.

Six years later, however, Calles was in exile in the United States, and progressives had taken control of the PNR. The reasons were twofold: the Great Depression and the emergence of a new leader, Lázaro Cárdenas. Born in 1895 to a poor
family and with little formal education, Cárdenas achieved prominence in the
1910s as an officer in the revolutionary armies fighting the dictator Victoriano
Huerta. In 1920 he was named governor of the state of Michoacan in west central
Mexico, where he earned a reputation as a progressive and honest administrator;
between 1931 and 1934 he served as Mexico's minister of the interior and of war.
In December 1933, Cárdenas, the candidate of the PNR's progressive wing, was
nominated for president, and in 1934 he was duly elected. Immediately embark-
ing on a program of land and labor reform, Cárdenas was opposed by Calles, who
in 1935 was implicated in a plot to overthrow the new president. Calles was
arrested and deported to the United States, while Cárdenas proceeded with his
sweeping program of economic and social reform.

Cárdenas confiscated millions of acres of land from large estates for redistribution to peasants, introduced free and compulsory primary education, and sponsored legislation to provide medical and unemployment insurance. His most
audacious step, however, was the nationalization of Mexico's oil industry. In 1936
a labor dispute erupted into a strike against U.S.- and British-owned petroleum
companies, and in the ensuing legal battle, seventeen oil companies rejected both
the prounion ruling of an arbitration board appointed by Cárdenas and the decision of the Mexican Supreme Court, which upheld the board's ruling. In response,
in 1938 Cárdenas expropriated the property of the oil companies.

Cárdenas announced this decision in a radio address to the Mexican people on
March 18, 1938. In the following excerpt, Cárdenas, after recounting the events
of the labor dispute, comments on the oil companies' role in Mexico's economic
and social development.

QUESTIONS FOR ANALYSIS

1. In Cárdenas's account, which actions by the foreign oil companies forced him to nationalize their property?
2. According to Cárdenas, what truth is there in the oil companies' claims that their presence has been beneficial to Mexico?
3. Who, according to Cárdenas, is ultimately responsible for the actions of the oil companies?
4. Which political activities of the oil companies does Cárdenas condemn?
5. What hardship does Cárdenas foresee for the Mexican people as a result of nationalization?
6. In what ways does Cárdenas appeal to Mexican nationalism in his speech?

In each and every one of the various attempts of the Executive to arrive at a final solution of the conflict within conciliatory limits . . . the intransigence of the companies was clearly demonstrated.

Their attitude was therefore premeditated and their position deliberately taken, so that the Government, in defense of its own dignity, had to resort to application of the Expropriation Act, as there were no means less drastic or decision less severe that might bring about a solution of the problem.

For additional justification of the measure herein announced, let us trace briefly the history of the oil companies' growth in Mexico and of the resources with which they have developed their activities.

It has been repeated *ad nauseam* that the oil industry has brought additional capital for the development and progress of the country. This assertion is an exaggeration. For many years throughout the major period of their existence, the oil companies have enjoyed great privileges for development and expansion, including customs and tax exemptions and innumerable prerogatives; it is these factors of special privilege, together with the prodigious productivity of the oil deposits granted them by the Nation often against public will and law, that represent almost the total amount of this so-called capital.

Potential wealth of the Nation; miserably underpaid native labor; tax exemptions; economic privileges; governmental tolerance — these are the factors of the boom of the Mexican oil industry.

Let us now examine the social contributions of the companies. In how many of the villages bordering on the oil fields is there a hospital, or school or social center, or a sanitary water supply, or an athletic field, or even an electric plant fed by the millions of cubic meters of natural gas allowed to go to waste?

What center of oil production, on the other hand, does not have its company police force for the protection of private, selfish, and often illegal interests? These organizations, whether authorized by the Government or not, are charged with innumerable outrages, abuses, and murders, always on behalf of the companies that employ them.

Who is not aware of the irritating discrimination governing construction of the company camps? Comfort for the foreign personnel; misery, drabness, and insalubrity for the Mexicans. Refrigeration and protection against tropical insects for the former; indifference and neglect, medical service and supplies always grudgingly provided, for the latter; lower wages and harder more exhausting labor for our people.

The tolerance which the companies have abused was born, it is true, in the shadow of the ignorance, betrayals, and weakness of the country's rulers; but the mechanism was set in motion by investors lacking in the necessary moral resources to give something in exchange for the wealth they have been exploiting.

Another inevitable consequence of the presence of the oil companies, strongly characterized by their anti-social tendencies, and even more harmful than all those already mentioned, has been their persistent and improper intervention in national affairs.

The oil companies' support to strong rebel factions against the constituted government in the Huasteca region of Veracruz and in the Isthmus of Tehuantepec during the years 1917 to 1920 is no longer a matter for discussion by anyone. Nor is anyone ignorant of the fact that in later periods and even at the present time, the oil companies have almost openly encouraged the ambitions of elements discontented with the country's government, every time their interests were affected either by taxation or by the modification of their privileges or the withdrawal of the customary tolerance. They have had money, arms, and munitions for rebellion, money for the anti-patriotic press which defends them, money with which to enrich their unconditional defenders. But for the progress of the country, for establishing an economic equilibrium with their workers through a just compensation of labor, for maintaining hygienic conditions in the districts where they themselves operate, or for conserving the vast riches of the natural petroleum gases from destruction, they have neither money, nor financial possibilities, nor the desire to subtract the necessary funds from the volume of their profits.

Nor is there money with which to meet a responsibility imposed upon them by judicial verdict, for they rely on their pride and their economic power to shield them from the dignity and sovereignty of a Nation which has generously placed in their hands its vast natural resources and now finds itself unable to obtain the satisfaction of the most elementary obligations by ordinary legal means.

As a logical consequence of this brief analysis, it was therefore necessary to adopt a definite and legal measure to end this permanent state of affairs in which the country sees its industrial progress held back by those who hold in their hands the power to erect obstacles as well as the motive power of all activity and who, instead of using it to high and worthy purposes, abuse their economic strength to the point of jeopardizing the very life of a Nation endeavoring to bring about the elevation of its people through its own laws, its own resources, and the free management of its own destinies.

With the only solution to this problem thus placed before it, I ask the entire Nation for moral and material support sufficient to carry out so justified, important, and indispensable a decision.

The Government has already taken suitable steps to maintain the constructive activities now going forward throughout the Republic, and for that purpose it asks the people only for its full confidence and backing in whatever dispositions the Government may be obliged to adopt.

Nevertheless, we shall, if necessary, sacrifice all the constructive projects on which the Nation has embarked during the term of this Administration in order to cope with the financial obligations imposed upon us by the application of the Expropriation Act to such vast interests; and although the subsoil of the country will give us considerable economic resources with which to meet the obligation of indemnization which we have contracted, we must be prepared for the possibility of our individual economy also suffering the indispensable readjustments, even to the point, should the Bank of Mexico deem it necessary, or modifying the present exchange rate of our currency, so that the whole country may be able to count on sufficient currency and resources with which to consolidate this act of profound and essential economic liberation of Mexico.

It is necessary that all groups of the population be imbued with a full optimism and that each citizen, whether in agricultural, industrial, commercial, transportation, or other pursuits, develop a greater activity from this moment on, in order to create new resources which will reveal that the spirit of our people is capable of saving the nation's economy by the efforts of its own citizens.

And, finally, as the fear may arise among the interests now in bitter conflict in the field of international affairs[1] that a deviation of raw materials fundamentally necessary to the struggle in which the most powerful nations are engaged might result from the consummation of this act of national sovereignty and dignity, we wish to state that our petroleum operations will not depart a single inch from the moral solidarity maintained by Mexico with the democratic nations, whom we wish to assure that the expropriation now decreed has as its only purpose the elimination of obstacles erected by groups who do not understand the evolutionary needs of all peoples and who would themselves have no compunction in selling Mexican oil to the highest bidder, without taking into account the consequences of such action to the popular masses and the nations in conflict.

---

[1]World War II in Europe was still more than a year away, but the Japanese invasion of China was in full swing, Spain was in the midst of its civil war, and Nazi Germany had just annexed Austria.

Brazilian Mass Politics and the *Estado Novo*

❖

39 ◆ Getúlio Vargas,
EXCERPTS FROM SPEECHES AND
INTERVIEWS, 1937–1940

Not without growing opposition from the middle class and the military, wealthy coffee growers from the states of São Paulo and Minas Gerais maintained their grip on Brazilian politics during the "Old Republic" from 1889 to 1930. In 1930, however, with coffee prices in free fall, a disputed election led to the military overthrow of the government and the installation as president of Getúlio Vargas. The era of the coffee oligarchy was over, and Brazilian politics embarked on a new path.

Born in 1883 into a politically active family of landowners from the state of Rio Grande do Sol, Vargas served in the army, studied law, and was elected as Rio Grande do Sol's congressman and governor before joining the national government as finance minister in 1926 and 1927. In 1930 he ran for president as the candidate of the Liberal Alliance, a coalition of the urban bourgeoisie, intellectuals, some landowners, and reform-minded army officers. He lost the fraud-filled election, and in its wake, his opponents refused to allow his supporters to take their seats in the congress; in all probability these same opponents were behind the murder of his vice-presidential running mate. At this point Vargas's supporters in the army deposed the president, and named Vargas as head of a provisional government.

Having come to power in 1930 with the support of a diverse coalition, Vargas proceeded cautiously at first. He raised tariffs, encouraged industrialization, and sought to prop up the price of coffee. In 1932 he reduced the voting age to eighteen and granted working women the right to vote. In 1934 a new constitution strengthened the executive, gave the government greater control of the economy, and called for the gradual nationalization of foreign-owned businesses.

In 1935 Vargas began to move toward one-man rule. First the communist and fascist Integralist parties were banned, and then in 1937 he canceled elections, promulgated a new constitution, and assumed dictatorial powers. Brazil, he announced, had entered the era of the *Estado Novo,* the New State.

In the following excerpts from interviews and speeches given between 1937 and 1940, Vargas outlines the general philosophy and goals of his New State.

QUESTIONS FOR ANALYSIS

1. According to Vargas, what were the major flaws of Brazilian politics before he took power?
2. What steps did Vargas take or does he plan to take in order to rid Brazil of these flaws?
3. Vargas claims his New State is democratic. Do his comments in his various speeches and interviews support such a claim?
4. Some commentators have discerned elements of fascism in Vargas's political philosophy and policies. Do you agree with such as assessment?
5. What specific policies does Vargas propose in order to appeal to the urban bourgeoisie and working class?

[INTERVIEW, APRIL 1938]

The movement of November 10th[1] was, without doubt, brought about by the national will. We had need of order and security in order to carry on; conspiring against that was the critical state of political decomposition to which we had arrived. Slowly our public life had been transformed into an arena of sterile struggles where plots, clashing interests of the oligarchy, personal competitions, and differences in personal interests were decided. Men of character without ambition to govern drew away from it nauseated, leaving the field open to political professionals and to demagogic and audacious adventurers. It was thus that communism succeeded in infiltrating and came to be at one time a national danger.[2] Defeated in its violent attempt to seize power, it continued, nevertheless, its work of undermining authority by utilizing as its weapons the other evils that make the situation of the nation so unstable and chaotic: the weakness of political parties, regional jealousies, and dictatorial flights of fancy. Those three evils are in the final analysis simply the result of a single general cause, well formed and known: the sterility and [depletion] of the sources from which the agents of stimulation and renovation of public life ought to come. The political parties had abdicated their social function. . . . Foresight of the danger in which we found ourselves and which was felt by all caused us decisively to favor the political unification of the nation which is precisely why the regime was established on November 10th. The Estado Novo embodies, therefore, the will and ideas which oppose and work against all the factors tending to weaken and dissolve the fatherland — extremism sabotage, and compromise. It is ready to fight

[1]On November 10, 1937, Vargas announced in a radio message to the nation that he had canceled the upcoming presidential elections, dissolved the legislature, and assumed dictatorial powers under a new constitution.

[2]In 1937 a wing of the Communist Party took part in an anti-Vargas revolt that was crushed by the government. Later in the year, the government circulated a forged document that supposedly outlined a communist plan to seize power.

against those evils. It will mobilize all the best that we possess in order to make our nation strong, dignified, and happy.

[SPEECH, JULY 1938]

As Chief of Government, I systematically seek to hear those who are informed, to appreciate the word of the technicians, to study and to boldly face the reality of facts. It was thus that, feeling the profound sentiment of the Brazilian people, I did all possible in order to save them from the dangers of extremism, both — from the right as well as from the left — contrary to our sentiments of understanding and Christian tolerance.

I can affirm to you with certainty that the hours of greatest apprehension now have passed. . . .

Through the spirit of good sense and through the persistent intention of conciliating the peace of the people with national dignity, we have given an appreciable example to the world. Thus we proceed . . . trying to assure . . . to all and to each a greater share of well-being and tranquility within the just equilibrium between the duties and prerogatives of the citizen.

[INTERVIEW, MARCH 1938]

Among the profound changes brought about by the new regime are: the [limitation] of direct, universal suffrage, applicable only to specific questions that pertain to all citizens . . . , the municipality as the nuclear base of the political system; the substitution of the principle of the independence of powers[3] by the supremacy of the Executive; the strengthening of the power of the Union; the effective and efficient participation of the economy, through its own organizations, in the constructive and integrating work of the government.

The new system consecrates a government of authority by instituting as law the legislative decree, by giving to the President of the Republic powers to expedite law-decrees when congress is not in session, by attributing to him the [prerogative to] dissolve it in special cases, and by taking from the Judiciary the privilege of supreme interpretation of the constitutionality or unconstitutionality of the laws which involve public interests of great importance. These new powers, placed under the guard of the government, always overcome private interests.

Profoundly nationalistic, the regime insures and consolidates national unity and formally restricts the autonomy of the states[4] by suppressing regional symbols, extending intervention, establishing the supremacy of federal over local laws in the case of concurrent legislation by attributing to the central government the power to requisition at any time the state militias, etc.

The professions are represented in their own and independent chamber with consultative functions in all the projects concerning the national economy, and eventually it will have legislative functions.[5]

Truly we have instituted an essentially democratic regime because it does not base its representation on a system of indications and artificialities but rather on the direct collaboration of the people through their economic forces and their organizations of production and labor. Only thus can our present political structure make known the effective representation of Brazil. . . .

[SPEECH, JULY 1938]

If you would ask me what is the program of the Estado Novo, I would tell you that its program is to crisscross the nation with railroads, highways, and airlines; to increase production; to provide for the laborer and to encourage agricultural

[3]The separation of the executive, legislative, and judicial powers within government.
[4]In the Old Republic the states of Brazil had exercised extensive political powers, and politicians from two states, São Paulo and Minas Gerais, dominated the federal government.
[5]Economic and professional groups would be represented in addition to districts, provinces, etc.

credit; to expand exports; to prepare the armed forces so that they are always ready to face any eventuality; to organize public opinion so that there is, body and soul, one Brazilian thought.

[SPEECH, JANUARY, 1939]

By examining the government's activities, anyone can verify with his own eyes that the basic problems of Brazilian life, without regional distinctions or political preferences, were resolutely attacked: the increase and expansion of industrial and agrarian [nuclei]; the creation of new sources of wealth and the improvement of the processes of exportation . . . ; the measures taken to raise the standard of living of the masses; financial support to the producing classes; economic assistance to the worker by means of social security, . . . a just salary, a good home, and the guarantee of his rights; the increase in the number of centers of technical, physical, and intellectual training; care for public hygiene and rural sanitation by making possible the remunerative utilization of large areas of soil abandoned or sacrificed because of climactic disturbances; the systematic repudiation of extremist ideologies and their . . . followers; the combating of all agents of dissolution or weakening of the national energies by the reinforcement of Brazilian traditions and sentiments and the prohibition from functioning in this country of any organization with anti-national activities or linked to foreign political interests; finally the preparation of internal and external defense by the rearmament of our brave armed forces and the simultaneous education of the new generations inculcating in them the spirit and love of the fatherland, faith in its destinies and the desire to make it strong and respected.

◆

The Mexican Muralists and the Revolution in Mexican Art

After the fall of the dictator Porfirio Díaz in 1910, nationalism intensified in revolutionary Mexico, and *indigenismo* was its most outstanding expression. In 1917 President Alvaro Obregón established a government office of anthropology to study and preserve Indian art, artifacts, and customs, and during the 1920s Mexican anthropology made impressive strides. Obregón also appointed as secretary of education José Vasconcelos (1882–1959), a visionary and enthusiast who foresaw a new race, "a cosmic race," taking root in Spanish America as a result of the blending of Indian and Spanish blood. In his view, the values and cultures of the Indians were not to be scorned and dismissed as they had been under the European-oriented dictator Díaz; instead, they would become a source of national pride and regeneration.

In addition to sponsoring schools and health clinics in thousands of Indian villages, Vasconcelos encouraged composers, choreographers, writers, and artists to explore Mexico's Indian past and incorporate revolutionary themes into their work. In Mexico City he made available to painters walls of public buildings, and in the 1920s they were covered with murals that brought international fame to artists such as Diego Rivera, José Clemente Orozco, and David Alfaro Siqueiros. In bright colors and bold compositions they portrayed the historical experiences of Mexicans and other Latin American peoples as part of the universal human striving to overcome injustice and exploitation.

The Beginnings of the Mexican Muralist Movement

❖

40 ◆ *José Clemente Orozco, AUTOBIOGRAPHY*

José Clemente Orozco (1883–1949) originally intended to become an architect, but at age twenty-six began training as a painter in the Mexican Academy of Fine Arts. As a Marxist and supporter of the Mexican Revolution, he sought to use his artistic talents in the service of the Mexican people. This meant breaking from the style of the officially approved European masters and introducing themes and topics dealing with the struggles of Mexico's Indian and mestizo population. In the following excerpt from his autobiography, first published in the early 1940s, Orozco recalls how in the 1910s and early 1920s he and other painters in Mexico City developed a new vision of Mexican art.

QUESTIONS FOR ANALYSIS

1. According to Orozco, what were the deficiencies of Mexican art before the beginnings of the muralist movement?
2. How did the new school of Mexican art attempt to overcome these deficiencies?
3. What in Orozco's view is the social function of art and the artist?

[In the past, the] Mexican had been a poor colonial servant, incapable of creating or thinking for himself; everything had to be imported ready-made from European centers, for we were an inferior and degenerate race. They let us paint, but we had to paint the way they did in Paris, and it was the Parisian critic who would pass upon the result and pronounce the final verdict.

Architecture was refried chalets and French chateaux. The marbles and carvings in public and private buildings came from Italy.

It was inconceivable that a wretched Mexican should dream of vying with the world abroad, and so he went to that world abroad to "dedicate himself" to art, and if he ever afterward gave a thought to the backward country in which he was born it was only to beg for help in time of need, momentarily swallowing his proud "dedication," which in any case had never protected him from the suspicion of being a vulgar millionaire from the tropics.

Academic criteria held sway: "The ancients long ago reached perfection, they did everything that could be done, and nothing is left for us except to copy them and humbly imitate them. Florentine drawing with Venetian coloring. And if any painter wishes to be a modernist, let him be off to Montparnasse and there take orders."

In the nightly sessions in the Academy . . . , we began to suspect that the whole colonial situation was nothing but a swindle foisted upon us by international traders. We too had a character, which was quite the equal of any other. We would learn what the ancients and the foreigners could teach us, but we could do as much as they, or more. It was not pride but self-confidence that moved us to this belief, a sense of our own being and our destiny.

Now for the first time the painters took stock of the country they lived in. . . .

I set out to explore the wretchedest barrios in the city. On every canvas there began to appear, bit by bit, like a dawn, the Mexican landscape, and familiar forms and the colors. It was only a first and still timid step toward liberation from foreign tyranny, but behind it there was thorough preparation and a rigorous training.

Why must we be eternally on our knees before the Kants and the Hugos? All praise to the masters indeed, but we too could produce a Kant or a Hugo.[1] We too could wrest iron from the bowels of the earth and fashion it into ships and machines. We could raise prodigious cities, and create nations, and explore the universe. Was it not from a mixture of two races that the Titans[2] sprang? . . .

We can summarize Mexican thought about art in the year 1920. . . .

Many people held that pre-Cortesian[3] Art was our true tradition and they even talked of a "renaissance of indigenous art."

Excitement over the [handicrafts] of the contemporary indigenes was at its height. This was the moment when Mexico was first inundated with articles of woven straw, stewpots, huaraches [sandals], dancing figures . . . , serapes, and rebozos,[4] and when the wholesale export of all this began. It was the apogee of the tourist trade in Cuernavaca and Taxco.[5]

There was popular art in all its forms in painting, in sculpture, in the theater, in music, and in literature.

Extreme nationalism put in an appearance. Mexican artists considered themselves the equals or the superiors of foreigners. Their themes had necessarily to be Mexican.

The cult of the Worker was more sharply defined: "Art at the service of the Worker." It was believed that art must be essentially an offensive weapon in the Conflict of the Classes. . . .

Artists were passionately preoccupied with sociology and history. . . .

Later, some of them came to cherish the theme of the painting with such passion that they completely abandoned the field of art and gave themselves over to [revolutionary] activities no longer bearing any relation to their profession.

Mural painting began under good auspices. Even the errors it committed were useful. It broke with the routine into which painting had fallen. It disposed of many prejudices and served to reveal social problems from a new point of view. It liquidated a whole epoch of brutalizing Bohemianism,[6] of frauds who lived the life of a drone in their ivory towers — their fetid dens — where, drunkenly strumming on their guitars, they kept up a pretense of absurd idealism, beggars in a society that was already rotten and close to extinction.

The painters and sculptors of the coming time would be men of action, strong, sound, well trained; ready like a good laborer to work eight or ten hours a day. They found their way into shops, universities, barracks, and schools, eager to learn and understand everything, and as soon as possible to do their part in creating a new world. They wore overalls and mounted the scaffoldings.

---

[1]Immanuel Kant (1724–1804) was a German philosopher; Victor Hugo (1802–1885) was a French novelist, poet, and playwright.
[2]In Greek mythology, the Titans were giants born of Uranus (heaven) and Gaiea (earth).
[3]Cortés was the Spanish adventurer who conquered the Aztecs between 1519 and 1521.

[4]A serape (sarape) is a wool blanket worn as a shawl; a rebozo is a scarf.
[5]Taxco, in southern Mexico, and Cuernavaca, in south central Mexico, were both resort cities.
[6]A Bohemian was a writer or artist who adopted an individualistic, or eccentric, lifestyle with little regard for social conventions.

Political Visions of the Mexican Muralists

❖

41 ◆ *José Clemente Orozco, HISPANIC-AMERICAN SOCIETY, and Diego Rivera, IMPERIALISM*

After completing murals at the National Preparatory School and several other buildings inside and outside of Mexico City, between 1927 and 1934 José Clemente Orozco resided in the United States, where he painted murals at Pomona College in California, the New School for Social Research in New York City, and Dartmouth College in New Hampshire. His theme for the Dartmouth murals was the history of the Americas from the Preconquest Era to the Modern Age. The section from the Dartmouth murals shown on page 164, entitled *Hispano-American Society,* shows an armed Mexican peasant standing against a background filled with crumbling churches, an abandoned factory, politicians, soldiers, and capitalists.

Another great Mexican muralist, Diego Rivera (1886–1957) also was working in the United States when Orozco was painting his Dartmouth murals. Trained in Mexico and Europe, Rivera, like Orozco, painted murals in the 1920s for the National Preparatory School and other public buildings in Mexico City. A visit to the Soviet Union in 1927 reinforced his Marxist views. In 1931 he traveled to the United States to paint murals for the San Francisco Stock Exchange, the Detroit Institute of Art, and Rockefeller Center in New York. The latter work was destroyed by its sponsors because it included a portrait of Lenin.

In 1933, directly after the controversy surrounding the Rockefeller Center murals, Rivera completed a series of twenty-one paintings depicting U.S. history, collectively known as his *Portrait of America.* The paintings covered the walls of the New Workers School, a lecture hall and study center of the Communist Party Opposition, an anti-Stalinist organization that broke with the Communist Party U.S.A. in 1929. The thirteenth painting, *Imperialism,* shown on page 165, is dominated by the guns of U.S. tanks and warships, which emerge from around the portal of the New York Stock Exchange. In the forefront is a mass of Latin American rebels, in whose midst are seen a murdered Caribbean black and a Cuban revolutionary. In the upper right, Augusto Sandino, the Nicaraguan revolutionary executed by the Nicaraguan government in 1934, looks down on the operations of Standard Oil and United Fruit, two U.S. corporations heavily involved in Central and South America.

QUESTIONS FOR ANALYSIS

1. In Orozco's painting, what message is the painter communicating by the crumbling churches, the abandoned factories, the business owners, and the military officers?

2. What message does Orozco convey about the character and qualities of the main central figure, the Mexican peasant?

3. What does Rivera's painting imply about the character, motives, and impact of U.S. imperialism in Latin America?
4. In what specific ways do the paintings reveal the Marxist sympathies of the two Mexican painters?
5. What is the overall message of the two paintings? Is it optimistic about Latin America's prospects?

José Clemente Orozco, Hispano-American Society

Diego Rivera, Imperialism

CHAPTER 6

Africa Under Colonial Rule

By 1920 the preliminaries of European colonialism in Africa were over. Disputes among the colonial powers had been settled, African resistance crushed, and the deck of colonialists reshuffled when Germany lost its "place in the sun" after World War I and had its colonies taken over as League of Nations mandates by France, Britain, Belgium, and South Africa. Africa after World War I consisted of some fifty European-controlled colonies and three independent states. The three independent states were Liberia, with an economy almost completely controlled by a U.S. corporation, the Firestone Rubber Company; Ethiopia, whose independence ended in 1935 and 1936 when it was conquered and turned into a colony by Italy; and South Africa, where whites, who made up slightly less than 20 percent of the population, ruled the 80 percent who were black, Asian, or "colored."

During the 1920s and 1930s Europeans focused on creating an Africa in which they could exploit the continent's mineral wealth and agricultural products in efficiently run colonies populated by submissive, taxpaying natives. Europeans would, so they promised, educate some Africans, teach them moral principles, and gradually give them enough government experience so that someday they could rule themselves. No one had a timetable for independence, but all agreed it would take place far in the future. Some Europeans believed colonialism in Africa would last for centuries, not just for decades.

Although Africa's European masters each had somewhat different philosophies about their role in Africa, colonial administrations were all essentially alike. Authority in each colony was exercised by a governor, who in theory took orders from London, Paris, Brussels, or Lisbon, but in practice decided many matters on the spot. Under the governor was a hierarchy of subgovernors and regional, provincial, and district officers, in addition to officials responsible for education, public works, and public health. The number of European administrators was small. In Nigeria in 1938, approximately forty million Nigerians were governed by fewer than fifteen hundred British officials, whose decisions and policies were carried out by African chiefs, clerks, policemen, and soldiers under the command of British officers. Nowhere did Africans hold positions of responsibility or have a meaningful voice in advisory or legislative councils.

Economic policies of the colonial powers were also broadly similar. All focused on a single goal: to extract maximum wealth and profit from Africa at minimum cost. How this was to be achieved in any given colony depended on climate, mineral deposits, agricultural potential, access to the coast, and the size of the European population. In colonies with good farmland and valuable minerals, white rule meant large-scale land confiscations. In Kenya, Rhodesia, South Africa, Mozambique, Angola, Uganda, and the Belgian Congo, millions of acres of mineral-rich lands and productive farmland were appropriated and sold cheaply or given to Europeans. In 1913, for example, the government of South Africa passed a law that allocated 90 percent of the country's land to whites, who made up under 20 percent of the population. In the 1920s approximately one thousand English settlers controlled almost five million acres of the best farmland in Kenya. In British West Africa and most of French West Africa, where few whites settled, African farmers held on to their land and grew cocoa, peanuts, palm kernels, cotton, and coffee for export. When marketing their products, however, their only option was to sell to European exporters, who offered them prices well below the world market.

To make their economic plans work, Europeans needed African labor. Few Africans, however, had any interest in accepting the Europeans' job offers, since most craftsmen and farmers had no use for European money and could provide adequately for their families by working for themselves. One European solution to this problem was force. Relying on loyal chiefs or colonial police to enforce their mandates, Europeans coerced men to go to work building roads and offices, clearing fields, constructing railroads, carrying goods from place to place, and harvesting crops. Such systems of forced labor continued in the French colonies until 1946 and in Portuguese colonies until the 1960s. Another less blatantly coercive method to pressure African men to accept wage-paying work was government-imposed taxation. Required to pay taxes in cash only, Africans were forced to take wage-paying jobs in mines and fields to earn what they needed to pay the government. Colonial administrations used the taxes to pay their own costs, maintain infrastructure, and, if anything was left, to build schools and medical clinics.

The colonialists' assumption that Africans would endure the injustices of colonial rule for decades or even centuries was a glaring miscalculation. It is true that some Africans — chiefs, petty traders, farmers who grew export crops, and the small number of Africans who had opportunities to study in Europe — welcomed European rule. Most, however, found colonialism oppressive and repugnant. For some, opposition to European rule meant joining new African Christian churches that were run by blacks and preached that God did not want white people to rule over Africans. For others, mainly educated city-dwellers, it meant supporting the Pan-African movement, whose meetings in the interwar years demanded fairness for black people and urged recognition of Africa's achievements and potential. For still others, it meant joining organizations such as the African National Congress, which sought to hold back the racist tide in South Africa, or the National Congress of British West Africa, which sought a greater voice for Africans in colonial administrations. In the 1930s, economic hardship resulting from the Great Depression and outrage over the Italian conquest of Ethiopia in 1935 and 1936 deepened African alienation. African nationalism had taken root, and within fifteen years after World War II, its dreams of freedom and independence would be realized.

◆

European Perspectives on Africa's Future

Having completed the "scramble for Africa" in a scant two decades, Europeans had only sketchy knowledge of African society and culture when they became the continent's colonial masters in the early twentieth century. They also lacked ready answers to many questions about their role in Africa's future. How should Africa be governed? How much should Europeans intervene in colonial affairs? Should they assume responsibility for Africa's economic development or leave it to private capitalists? What part should Africans play in colonial administration? How could the goals and ambitions of missionaries, business interests, and administrators be reconciled? What efforts should be made to introduce Africans to European technology, philosophy, and culture? Should efforts be made to preserve African customs? How long would the colonial order last, and what should Africa look like when it ended?

Answers to these questions differed over time and according to the nationality and interests of the persons providing them, but, broadly speaking, from the late nineteenth century onward, they fell into two general categories. Some Europeans, probably a minority, considered colonialism a form of trusteeship. Such a view inspired nineteenth-century humanitarians who went to Africa to abolish slavery and the slave trade and missionaries who provided schooling and medical care for Africans in addition to instruction in Christianity. After World War I, the ideal of trusteeship found expression in Article 22 of the League of Nations Covenant. In transferring control of Africans in former German colonies to Britain, France, Belgium, and South Africa, it stated that "the well-being and development of such peoples form a sacred trust of civilization." The advanced nations should maintain law and order, guarantee freedom of religion, prohibit abuses such as the slave and liquor trades, and, most importantly, prepare Africans for self-rule.

The competing view saw colonialism as an opportunity to generate wealth for the colonizers. Its proponents had no interest in the Africans except to the degree that they served as miners, farm workers, porters, and minor agents of colonial government. Such a view was represented in the 1890s by men such as Cecil Rhodes, who dreamed of turning Africa into a continent of white settlement, and King Leopold II of Belgium, the professed humanitarian whose agents in the Congo forced thousands of Africans into the rain forest to collect raw rubber, cutting off their hands or feet or shooting them if they failed to meet their quotas. Leopold's atrocious (and short-lived) Congolese regime was an extreme case, but as late as the 1920s, the French forced more than 127,000 Africans to work on constructing a 150-mile railroad line from Pointe Noire, on the Atlantic coast of French Equatorial Africa, to Brazzaville. More than ten thousand Africans died of hunger or disease while working on the project.

For those intent on exploitation, racism provided a convenient rationale for their actions. Was it not the Africans' indolence and backwardness that prevented them from utilizing their continent's riches? Were not Europeans contributing to the good of humanity by making Africa's products and resources available to the world? Nor was racism lacking among the well-meaning Europeans who wanted to improve the Africans' lives. Missionaries taught that all human beings were spiritually equal before God, but this did not mean that black converts could be considered responsible Christians on the European model. The major denominations all excluded blacks from positions as church leaders and administrators. It was a rare European who thought Africans capable of managing their own affairs effectively; rarer still was the European who looked upon an African as his or her equal.

Of the following two sources, one represents the position that Africa's destiny was white settlement, and the other, that Europeans were in Africa to improve the Africans' lot and prepare them for independence. Together, they provide a fair sampling of the opinions and beliefs that shaped European policies in Africa.

Blacks in a White Man's Africa

◈

42 ◆ Jan Smuts, *RHODES MEMORIAL LECTURES*

Jan Smuts, a leading South African statesman, general, and philosopher, was born in 1870. Educated in South Africa and England, where he studied law, Smuts became state attorney for Transvaal in 1898 and fought on the side of the Boers against the British in the South African War (1899–1902). After the war he played a significant role in the founding of the Union of South Africa as a self-governing British dominion in 1910. He served as minister of defense between

1910 and 1919, and during World War I was commander of Allied forces fighting Germany in East Africa. After the war, he represented South Africa at the Paris Peace Conference, and helped plan and organize the League of Nations. As leader of the South Africa Party and later the Union Party, he served as South Africa's prime minister between 1919 and 1924 and between 1939 and 1948. An advocate of racial segregation throughout his life, he nevertheless opposed the extreme Afrikaner nationalists who gained power in 1948 and went on to implement South Africa's apartheid policy.

The following remarks reveal Smuts's views of African affairs in the late 1920s. They are taken from two speeches, "The African and African Settlement" and "Native Policy in Africa," which he delivered as part of the Rhodes Memorial Lectures in November 1929 at Oxford University. A year later they were published in his book, *Africa and Some World Problems.* The selection begins with Smuts's discussion of African employment by whites.

QUESTIONS FOR ANALYSIS

1. What is Smuts's view of the African character and personality? What factors in the Africans' experience have shaped these characteristics?
2. According to Smuts, how does the European personality differ from that of the Africans?
3. How does Smuts view Africa's future? What roles will whites and blacks play in it?
4. What advantages does Smuts see in the practice of maintaining the power of local chiefs?
5. What are the advantages of racial segregation, according to Smuts?

[THE AFRICAN AND AFRICAN SETTLEMENT]

It takes the raw native some time to acquire the habit of going out to work for the white employer. But as his economic needs develop, and they develop rapidly, and as he learns the value of ready money, it soon becomes habitual for him to spend part of his time in white employment. . . .

No inducement is necessary beyond their ordinary growing economic needs. Employment in European industries or with European settlers soon becomes the regular routine, and the natives are quite satisfied and happy to fall into this routine of part-time employment. By temperament they have not much initiative, and if left to themselves and their own tribal routine

they do not respond very well to the stimulus for progress. They are naturally happy-go-lucky, and are not oppressed with the stirrings of that divine discontent which have made the European the most unhappy but the most progressive of all humans. They are easily satisfied and a very little goes a long way with them. As workers they are slow, unintelligent, and essentially imitative. They have little foresight and display little forethought. But these very characteristics make them take readily to a routine which is settled for them by a white employer. And if they are well treated they respond with that good temper and that slow honest toil which makes them so easy to work with and so acceptable to the white employer. For thousands of years they have been accustomed to domination by their chiefs, and therefore they readily accept the firm handling, the lead, and the mastery of the white employer. It fits in with their character and their age-long training. . . .

From all this it follows that the easiest, most natural and obvious way to civilize the African native is to give him decent white employment. White employment is his best school; the gospel of labour is the most salutary gospel for him. The civilization of the African continent will be a vain dream apart from white employment, without the leading hand of the settler and the employer, away from the continuous living contact with the actual example and the actual practice of European industry and agriculture. The civilization of Africa therefore calls for a definite policy, the policy of European settlement, the establishment of a white community inside Africa which will form the steel framework of the whole ambitious structure of African civilization. . . .

. . . It is certainly a very significant fact that in that part of Africa where a great white community exists alongside the natives they have shown the greatest economic progress, the largest increase, and the greatest advance in education and civilization.[1] The fact gives additional force to my argument that the existence of a white community, so far from being contrary to native interests, is indeed a stimulus and guarantee of native progress. . . . [T]he white man's rule in South Africa has on the whole been of immense benefit to the natives, and the economic conditions of the natives in South Africa are far in advance of anything existing anywhere among African natives. . . .

[NATIVE POLICY IN AFRICA]

. . . The negro and the negroid Bantu[2] form a distinct human type which the world would be poorer without. . . . This type has some wonderful characteristics. It has largely remained a child type, with a child psychology and outlook. A child-like human cannot be a bad human, for are we not in spiritual matters bidden to be like unto the little children? Perhaps as a direct result of this temperament the African is the only happy human I have come across. No other race is so easily satisfied, so good-tempered, so care-free. . . . This happy-go-lucky disposition is a great asset, but it has also its drawbacks. There is no inward incentive to improvement, there is no persistent effort in construction, and there is complete absorption in the present, its joys and sorrows. . . . No indigenous religion has been evolved, no literature, no art. . . . These children of nature have not the inner toughness and persistence of the European, nor those social and moral incentives to progress which have built up European civilization in a comparatively short period. But they have a temperament which suits mother Africa, and which brings out the simple joys of life and deadens its pain, such as no other race possesses. . . .

. . . In the interests of the native as well as those of the European administrations responsible for their welfare, we are called upon to retrace our steps, to take all proper measures which are still possible to restore or preserve the authority of the chiefs, and to maintain the bonds of solidarity and discipline which have supported the tribal organization of the natives in the past. This authority or discipline need not be exercised in a barbarous way, and should be shorn of all old-time cruelty and other undesirable features. But in essence it should be maintained, and under the general supervision and check of the European magistrate it should continue to be exercised. . . .

The white administration remains responsible for the larger functions of government, such as the combating of human and animal diseases, the organization of education, the improvement of agriculture, and the construction of public

---

[1] The reference is to South Africa.

[2] The dominant native African group in South Africa.

works, and maintains a staff for these and similar purposes. But all the purely tribal concerns are left to the chief and his counsellors whose actions are supervised by the white officer only in certain cases intended to prevent abuses. . . .

Another important consequence will follow from this system of native institutions. Wherever Europeans and natives live in the same country, it will mean separate parallel institutions for the two. The old practice mixed up black with white in the same institutions; and nothing else was possible, after the native institutions and traditions had been carelessly or deliberately destroyed. But in the new plan these will be what is called in South Africa 'segregation' — separate institutions for the two elements of the population, living in their own separate areas. . . . Institutional segregation carries with it territorial segregation. The new policy therefore gives the native his own traditional institutions on land which is set aside for his exclusive occupation. For agricultural and pastoral natives, living their tribal life, large areas or reserves are set aside, adequate for their present and future needs. . . . For urbanized natives, on the other hand, who live, not under tribal conditions but as domestic servants or industrial workers in white areas, there are set aside native villages or locations, adjoining to the European towns. . . . Such is the practice now in vogue in South Africa and it is likely to develop still further, and to spread all over Africa where white and black live and work together in the same countries. . . . This separation is imperative, not only in the interests of a native culture, and to prevent native traditions and institutions from being swamped by the more powerful organization of the whites, but also for other important purposes, such as public health, racial purity, and public good order. . . .

Colonialism as Trusteeship

◈

43 ◆ *Sir Frederick Gordon Guggisberg,* THE KEYSTONE

Sir Frederick Gordon Guggisberg (1879–1930) was unusual among Africa's colonial governors in that his background was engineering rather than government administration. Born in Toronto, Canada, he joined the British army, and was named director of surveys in Southern Nigeria in 1910 and acting surveyor general for all of Nigeria in 1913. After serving in World War I, he was named governor of the Gold Coast in 1919, a post he held until 1927. On becoming governor, the idealistic and energetic Guggisberg announced his Ten-Year Plan, a program to bring the Gold Coast new roads and railroads, hospitals, improved harbors, and especially better schools. Improved education, he believed, would encourage the Africanization of the colonial administration, which Guggisberg favored for reasons of economy and justice. With loans and grants from the British government and income from the Gold Coast's healthy cocoa exports, Guggisberg accomplished much of his plan before he was named governor of British Guyana in 1927. Poor health prevented him from taking his new post, and he died in 1930.

In the following excerpt, taken from his book *The Keystone* (1924), Guggisberg sets forth his ideas about education, development, and Africa's future.

QUESTIONS FOR ANALYSIS

1. What is Guggisberg's case for improving and increasing educational opportunities for Africans?
2. What do you suppose Guggisberg means by "character-training," and why
does he consider it so necessary?
3. What are Guggisberg's views of the Africans? How do his views differ from
those of Smuts?
4. Describe Guggisberg's vision of Africa's future. How does it differ from that
of Smuts?

Wherever one turns in the Gold Coast one meets the same demand — a better education for Africans than our present schools are capable of providing. Apart from the fact that the people themselves are clamouring for a better education, the future of the country demands it. In the Government Service alone the need is urgent; the development of the country is progressing so rapidly that we can no longer afford the proportionately larger number of Europeans required to deal with the work, for their long leave, their steamer-passages, and the higher rates of salary due to their employment in what can never be a "White Man's Country" are prohibitive. Government has definitely adopted the policy of employing Africans in appointments hitherto held by Europeans provided that the former are equally qualified in education, ability, *and character*, but progress in carrying out this policy is slow owing to the scarcity of suitably qualified Africans. When, besides the need of Government, that of the Europeans firms — mercantile, banking, and professional — is considered, it is apparent that there is a great field for the employment of well-educated Africans throughout the country.

More important still is the demand of the educated African of the existing literate classes for an education and training that will fit him to take a greater share in the development of his own land. We have not to look far for the reason. To begin with, the southern portions of the Gold Coast have been in closer contact with European civilization for a far longer period than any other of Britain's West African colonies. In the second place, our great agricultural wealth and trade are far greater in proportion to our size and population than those of almost any other tropical unit of the British Empire. . . . The annual increase of trade has naturally been accompanied by a steady increase of wealth until to-day we are far richer per head of the population than any of our neighbours. Now, prosperity brings a desire for the better things of life, and when this desire is heightened by the knowledge brought by the steady development of elementary education it is not surprising that there is to-day a rapidly increasing demand for better conditions of living, better sanitation, good water supplies, hospitals and dispensaries, and all the other benefits of modern civilization.

To comply with all these demands, to cope with rapidly changing conditions, Government acting by itself will make insufficient progress; its efforts must be supplemented by African enterprise. Government's duty at present is to lay the foundations of development in every direction, to organise the departmental machinery necessary for dealing with each system, and to provide such European staff as the revenue permits; while at the same time it must prepare, organise, and bring into being a system of schools where Africans can obtain the better and higher education that will fit them to enter the various trades and professions, both in the public service and in private enterprise. . . .

Higher education by itself will not solve the problem of the country. It must be accompanied by a better system of training in handicrafts, agriculture, and all those trades that go to provide for the necessities of a community; for although higher education may be the brain of a country, its productive capacity is its heart. Of what use is the brain if the heart ceases to beat? The education of the brain and the training of the hand, *each accompanied by the moulding of the mind*, must proceed together if success is to be sure. . . .

I am well aware of the belief held by some critics — and who has not heard it enunciated? — that the African is not capable of exercising those qualities that will be conferred on him by higher education.

Now, whatever may be my own belief . . . there are two sides to every question, so I am going to examine the contention of these critics dispassionately and ask them four questions.

Firstly, have the critics ever considered that character-training — the essential factor in every branch of education but the all-essential factor in higher education — had hitherto been omitted from the African's curriculum, at any rate in Africa? . . . If they persist in their belief, then they deny that a human being can rise from a lower to a higher plane of development and it does not appear to me that they receive the support of history.

Secondly, are they aware that the African races, in spite of the lack of educational facilities, of character-training, have produced men who have distinguished themselves in various walks of life, many intellectually, a number morally? America, where they have long studied the question of African education, has furnished many examples. . . . Our own African and West Indian colonies furnish others, sufficiently numerous to warrant the belief that, had character-training been in their school curriculum, success would have been wider and more complete.

Thirdly, are the critics aware of the immense field in Africa for the employment of Africans, and if so are they deliberately going to turn men who have an earnest desire for intellectual advancement — and some of whom have shown that they can benefit by it — into a race

of malcontents by confining them to the subordinate work of trades and professions?

And lastly, do the critics honestly believe that we have the right to deny the African the chance of proving that his race is capable of doing what other races have done in the past? If so, they have forgotten that Britain stands where she does to-day by giving her peoples and her opponents alike a "sporting chance." . . .

Other critics have it that, in advocating the provision of a higher education locally for Africans, we are deliberately inviting political troubles in the Gold Coast. Surely the absolute contrary is the case. If politics are to come — and come they must if history is of any value as a guide — surely the safeguards *against* trouble is the local education of the many, accompanied by character-training, rather than the education in Europe of a few, an education that invariably lacks character-training and that more often than not results in bad European habits replacing good African characteristics? If secondary education is not introduced to fill the gap between the English University-trained African and the semi-literate product of our primary schools, we shall be continuing our present system of providing the easy prey of the demagogue. . . .

Another criticism is, that in educating Africans to fill higher appointments in the Government service we shall be deliberately interfering with European employment in the Gold Coast. This is a short-sighted view. I have already pointed out that the development of the country necessitates an annual increase in staff. No Government in the world could afford proportionately the immense financial burden . . . if this increase was to consist of Europeans only. Apart from that, the married European with children has not and never will have a real home life in West Africa, whereas there is a great field of employment for him in the good climates of the Dominions. It will be many long years before Africans are fit to fill the higher appointments in the Government service; in the meantime there is ample room for both. . . .

It has been said that we must go slow, that we must not force education on the people. With regard to the last point there is no question of forcing; one has only to see the crowd of applicants for admission surrounding the primary schools of this country at the beginning of every term. As for going slow, we are going too slow. Although it is perfectly true that the races of the Gold Coast are now in a phase through which every other race has had to pass since time immemorial, yet every century sees a quicker rate of advance made by the primitive peoples of the world. Therefore, although we may draw lessons from the past experience of other nations, it is essential that we should move faster, quicker even than the educational authorities did in the days of our youth. . . .

◆

African Society and Identity Under Colonial Rule

Colonialism in Africa involved more than authoritarian government and economic exploitation. Despite its relative brevity, it profoundly affected every aspect of African life. It fostered population growth, encouraged urbanization, undermined African religions, altered gender relationships, introduced new sports and pastimes, changed how people dressed and what language they spoke, and created new African perspectives on themselves and their place in the world. In the process, much of old Africa — traditional names, music, art, marriage customs, and systems of inheritance — was lost. Africans in the twenty-first century continue to debate whether such changes in the colonial era benefited or harmed Africa in the long run. Unquestionably, however, for most Africans who lived through them in the 1920s and 1930s, these changes were both unsettling and dispiriting.

The Africans' experiences were dispiriting because so much of what took place under colonialism was predicated on the assumption of black inferiority. Colonialism's message, stated or unstated, was that Africans were incapable of governing themselves, or at least incapable of governing themselves effectively; nor were they capable of managing a modern economy or of creating a viable culture and social order. For all these tasks they needed Europeans, who justified their authority by asserting their moral and intellectual superiority. Furthermore, Africans were told that to improve themselves as individuals — to become clerks or civil servants in the colonial administration or to become "assimilated" (for example, to become an *évolué,* or "evolved one" in French Africa) — they would have to shed their Africanness and adopt the ideas, views, work habits, dress, and customs of Europeans. This was the price Africans needed to pay to overcome their backwardness.

Some Africans came to accept their supposed inferiority as a reality, causing them to discard their traditions in the pursuit of "civilization." As the following sources show, however, others resisted colonialism's message. They sought ways to preserve Africa's traditions and strengthen the African's self-respect.

Eagles into Chickens

❖

44 ◆ *James Aggrey, PARABLE OF THE EAGLE*

James Aggrey, an educator and clergyman who was among the most prominent Africans of his day, was born in 1875 in the Gold Coast, a British colony. Educated in a Protestant mission school and a convert to Christianity, at age twenty-three he traveled to the United States to study for the ministry. He remained in the United States for twenty years, studying economics and agriculture, speaking out against racial prejudice, and working among the poor blacks of South Carolina. He returned to Africa in 1918 and died in 1927. His "Parable of the Eagle" was written in the early 1920s.

QUESTIONS FOR ANALYSIS

1. According to the lesson of Aggrey's parable, what psychological damage results from colonialism?
2. What possible implications does the parable have for colonial policies?

A certain man went through a forest seeking any bird of interest he might find. He caught a young eagle, brought it home and put it among his fowls and ducks and turkey, and gave it chickens' food to eat even though it was an eagle, the king of birds.

Five years later a naturalist came to see him and, after passing through his garden, said: "That bird is an eagle, not a chicken."

"Yes," said its owner, "but I have trained it to be a chicken. It is no longer an eagle, it is a chicken, even though it measures fifteen feet from tip to tip of its wings."

"No," said the naturalist, "it is an eagle still; it has the heart of an eagle, and I will make it soar high up to the heavens."

"No," said the owner, "it is a chicken, and it will never fly."

They agreed to test it. The naturalist picked up the eagle, held it up, and said with great intensity: "Eagle, thou art an eagle; thou dost belong to the sky and not to this earth; stretch forth thy wings and fly."

The eagle turned this way and that, and then, looking down, saw the chickens eating their food, and down he jumped.

The owner said: "I told you it was a chicken."

"No," said the naturalist, "it is an eagle. Give it another chance tomorrow."

So the next day he took it to the top of the house and said: "Eagle, thou art an eagle; stretch forth thy wings and fly." But again the eagle, seeing the chickens feeding, jumped down and fed with them.

Then the owner said: "I told you it was a chicken."

"No," asserted the naturalist, "it is an eagle, and it still has the heart of an eagle; only give it one more chance, and I will make it fly tomorrow."

The next morning he rose early and took the eagle outside the city, away from the houses, to the foot of a high mountain. The sun was just rising, gilding the top of the mountain with gold, and every crag was glistening in the joy of that beautiful morning.

He picked up the eagle and said to it: "Eagle, thou art an eagle; thou dost belong to the sky and not to this earth; stretch thy wings and fly!"

The eagle looked around and trembled as if new life were coming to it; but did not fly.

The naturalist then made it look straight at the sun. Suddenly it stretched out its wings and, with the screech of an eagle, it mounted higher and higher and never returned. It was an eagle, though it had been kept and tamed as a chicken!

My people of Africa, we were created in the image of God, but men have made us think that we are chickens, and we still think we are; but we are eagles. Stretch forth your wings and fly! Don't be content with the food of chickens!

The Value of African Religion

❖

45 ◆ Kabaka Daudi Chwa, EDUCATION, CIVILIZATION, AND "FOREIGNIZATION" IN BUGANDA

The Great Lakes region of east central Africa, dominated by the kingdom of Buganda, was one of the earliest areas of European missionary activity in the nineteenth century. British Protestant missionaries arrived in the region in 1877, and were followed by French Catholic missionaries in 1879. With the traditional Baganda religion already weakened by conversions to Islam, the missionaries made numerous converts, especially among young courtiers in the entourage of the hereditary Baganda ruler, known as the *kabaka*. In the 1880s, Protestant-Catholic rivalries among the chiefs led to civil war, the weakening of the *kabaka*'s power, and the establishment of a British protectorate in 1894. In 1900 British authorities and the Baganda chiefs signed the Buganda Agreement, which recognized Baganda dominance over other peoples in the Uganda protectorate and maintained the chiefs' traditional powers as a means of carrying out British policy. Uganda itself was divided into twenty chieftaincies, of which ten were Protestant, eight were Catholic, and two were Muslim.

Daudi Chwa (1897–1939) as a two-year-old was named *kabaka* of Buganda after his father was deposed and exiled for leading a campaign against the British. A convert to Christianity, Chwa was a figurehead ruler, since the British more or less gave his chiefs a free hand to administer the colony. He did play an active and successful role in opposing the plan to consolidate Uganda, Kenya, and Tanganyika in the 1930s. Toward the end of his life he became disillusioned about the effects of colonial rule, especially on African culture and religion. In 1935 he published his views in a pamphlet, "Education, Civilization, and 'Foreignization' in Buganda." In it, he deplored Christianity's impact on African beliefs and practices.

QUESTIONS FOR ANALYSIS

1. How would you characterize the traditional system of justice of the Baganda? By what means did it try to deter behavior that ran counter to the people's rules and customs?

2. According to the *kabaka*, how and in what ways do traditional Baganda moral values resemble those of Christianity?

3. What have the Baganda gained and lost as a result of European colonialism, according to Chwa?
4. What sort of thinking about the "backwardness" of the Baganda does the *kabaka* try to counter in his letter?
5. In Chwa's view, what should be the proper balance between traditional and European beliefs and practices?

Every one knows that education and civilization were started simultaneously in this country in their respective rudimentary forms by the kind efforts of the members of the various Missionary Societies and have now been enhanced largely due to the assistance rendered by the Protectorate Government.

Naturally education and civilization gained tremendous favour among the Baganda,[1] and as a consequence there are numerous Schools in remote villages in Buganda Kingdom for the education of the young generation; while every facility and luxury which are the outcome of civilization are today being extended to all the Baganda, who can afford to avail themselves of the same, throughout the country.

Now my fears are that instead of the Baganda acquiring proper and legitimate education and civilization there is a possible danger that they may be drifting to 'foreignisation.' . . . To be more explicit, what I mean by the word 'foreignisation' is that instead of the Baganda acquiring proper education at the various Schools and of availing themselves of the legitimate amenities of civilization, I am very much afraid the young generation of this country is merely drifting wholesale towards 'foreignization' of their natural instincts and is discarding its native and traditional customs, habits and good breedings. What is at present popularly termed as education and civilization of a Muganda[2] may be nothing more nor less than mere affectation of the foreign customs and habits of the Western Countries which in some instances are only injurious to our own inherent morals and ideals of native life.

I am well aware that it has been said more than once that the Baganda have neither morals nor public opinion, but I . . . have always been very strongly opposed to this . . . false accusation brought against the Baganda as a nation. There has always been and shall always be "black sheep" among all nations and tribes throughout the World and naturally I do not wish to be considered in this article to uphold the Baganda as a Nation of Angels — But what I do maintain is that prior to the advent of the Europeans the Baganda had a very strict moral code of their own which was always enforced by a constant and genuine fear of some evil or incurable or even fatal disease being suffered invariably by the breaker of this moral code. In fact I maintain the Baganda observed most strictly the doctrine of the Ten Commandments in spite of the fact that Christianity and the so-called Christian morals were absolutely unknown to the Baganda. For instance there was a very strong public opinion against the following offenses, which are the fundamental principles of the doctrine of the Ten Commandments:

(a) Theft was always punished very severely, invariably by the loss of the right hand of the offender, so as to render him incapable of committing the same offence again.
(b) Adultery was almost unknown among the Baganda and any man found guilty of such offence was always ostracised from Society.

---

[1] The Baganda are the people of the kingdom of Buganda.
[2] *Muganda* is the word (singular) for an individual living in the kingdom of Buganda.

(c) Murder was invariably followed by a very severe vendetta between the members of the family or clan of the victim and those of the offender.

(d) Filial obedience was most honoured among the Baganda and disobedience or disrespect of one's parents was always supposed to be punished by some higher power by the infliction of some horrible or incurable disease upon the offender.

(e) False evidence was looked upon with contempt. The person who bore false evidence and the person against whom it was given were both subjected to a very severe test by forcing them to drink a certain kind of strong drug known as 'Madudu', which was supposed to result in making one of the parties who was in the wrong unconscious.

In this connection I should like to point out that although polygamy was universally recognized among the Baganda and was never considered as immoral yet prostitution was absolutely unheard of. Civilization, education and freedom are the direct causes of the appalling state of affairs as regards prostitution and promiscuous relationships between the Baganda men and women. . . . As [an] illustration of the strictness of the old moral code of the Baganda I should like to point out here one of the most important native custom[s] of looking after the daughters in a Muganda's home. It was one of the worst filial offence[s] for a daughter to become pregnant while living with her parents. As soon as she was discovered in that condition she was at once expelled from her parents' house, and was absolutely cut off from them. She could not eat with them nor would her parents touch her until the child was born and some rites had been gone through which necessitated a great deal of hardship and shame on the part of the girl and her seducer. This custom was intended to stimulate morality among the Baganda girls, since any girl who went astray before she was given in marriage suffered this indignity and

was always looked upon with contempt by all her relatives and friends. Furthermore any girl who was given in marriage and was found not to be virgin merited unspeakable disfavour in the eyes of her parents, relations and friends. All this, however, is of course, no longer the case. The present so-called education and civilization prevailing in this country has completely destroyed this moral code by removing the constant fear just referred to above from the minds of the young generation of the Baganda by the freedom and liberty which are the natural consequences of the present World civilization.

I think it would not be out of place to state here definitely that it is my firm belief that prior to the introduction of Christianity in this country the Baganda could not be classified as the worst type of a heathen tribe of Africa since they never indulged in any of the worst heathen customs or rites such as human sacrifice or torture which are found in other parts of Africa. Whilst on the other hand apart from their ignorance of Christianity and their practice of polygamy I am strongly of [the] opinion that most of the traditional customs and etiquette of the Baganda . . . were quite [consistent] with the principles of Christianity. In support of this argument it is only necessary to mention a few customs of the Baganda to show that they unconsciously possessed a sense of modern Christian morality:

(a) It was one of the most important [behaviors] among the Baganda for one's neighbour to be considered as his own relative and to share with him in his happiness or unhappiness. For instance a Muganda would always invite his neighbour if he killed a chicken or goat to share it with him, whilst in case of any danger or misfortune it was always the duty of the nearest neighbour to render every assistance to the party in danger or distress.

(b) It was the recognized etiquette for a Muganda to salute every one that he met on the road, whether he knew him or not.

(c) When a Muganda was taking his meal and any one passed by, it was always the custom to invite him to share it with him.

(d) It was always the duty of every one who hears an alarm at any time of day or night or a cry for help to go at once and render assistance to the party in distress or danger. . . .

(e) It was the duty of every Muganda, when requested, to assist any traveller in directing him to his destination, or to give him food or water, and even to give him shelter from rain or for the night. . . .

My intention therefore in this article is to emphasize the fact that while boasting of having acquired Western education and civilization in an amazingly short period, we have entirely and completely ignored our native traditional customs. In other words we have 'foreignised' our native existence by acquiring the worst foreign habits and customs of the Western people. I am only too well aware that this is inevitable in all countries where Western civilization has reached, so I have considered it my duty in this article to warn very strongly all members of the young generation of the Baganda that while they are legitimately entitled to strive to acquire education and civilization they should also take a very great care that acquisition of Western education and civilization does not automatically destroy their best inherent traditions and customs which, in my own opinion, are quite as good as those found among the Western Civilized countries but which only require developing and remodelling where necessary on the lines and ideas of western civilization. . . .

White Rule, African Families

❖

46 ◆ *Charlotte Maxeke,*
SOCIAL CONDITIONS AMONG BANTU WOMEN AND GIRLS

Few groups in Africa were affected more by colonialism than were women. In the precolonial African village, a division of labor between men and women had existed in which women were responsible for planting, weeding, harvesting, food preparation, and child care, while men cleared the land, built houses, herded cattle, and sometimes helped with fieldwork. Such arrangements broke down in West Africa when cash-crop agriculture was introduced. Men took over the farming of cotton or cocoa, leaving responsibility for growing food for domestic consumption exclusively to women. Worse disruption took place in southern and eastern Africa where men left their villages for wage-paying jobs in mines or the cities. This meant long absences of husbands from their families, greater work and domestic responsibilities for women, and frequently the breakdown of family life altogether.

All these issues concerned the South African woman Charlotte Maxeke, the founder of the African National Congress Women's League and a social worker, teacher, and leader in the African Methodist Episcopal Church. Born Charlotte Makgomo in 1874, she received her primary and secondary education in South Africa. While in her early twenties, she toured England, Canada, and the United states with an African choir. She remained in the United States to study at Wilberforce College in Ohio, where she received her bachelor of science degree and met and married another South African, Reverend Marshall Maxeke. On her return to South Africa, she cofounded a secondary school with her husband and remained active in the African National Congress and church affairs until her death in 1939.

In 1930 she presented her views on the plight of black South African women and families in a speech delivered to a rally attended by white and black Christian youth.

QUESTIONS FOR ANALYSIS

1. What, according to Maxeke, are the reasons for the Bantu exodus from the countryside to cities?
2. What special challenges and difficulties confront newly arrived blacks in urban areas?
3. How do the problems of men and women in such circumstances differ?
4. What seems to have been the effect of the changes Maxeke describes on children and young people?
5. What solutions to the problems confronting African women and their families does Maxeke propose? If implemented, are her suggestions likely to be successful?

There are many problems pressing in upon us Bantu,[1] to disturb the peaceful working of our homes. One of the chief is perhaps the stream of Native life into the towns. Men leave their homes, and go into big towns like Johannesburg, where they get a glimpse of a life such as they had never dreamed existed. At the end of their term of employment they receive the wages for which they have worked hard, and which should be used for the sustenance of their families, but the attractive luxuries of civilisation are in many instances too much for them, they waste their hard earned wages, and seem to forget completely the crying need of their family out in the veld.[2]

The wife finds that her husband has apparently forgotten her existence, and she therefore makes her hard and weary way to the town in search of him. When she gets there, and starts looking round for a house of some sort in which to accommodate herself and her children, she meets with the first rebuff. The Location Superintendent[3] informs her that she cannot rent accommodation unless she has a husband. Thus she is driven to the first step on the downward path, for if she would have a roof to cover her children's heads a husband must be found, and so we get these poor women forced by circumstances to consort with men in order to provide shelter for their families. Thus we see that the authorities in enforcing the restrictions in regard to accommodation are often doing Bantu society a grievous harm, for they are forcing its womanhood, its wedded womanhood, to the first step on the downward path of sin and crime.

---

[1] In this context, blacks of South Africa who spoke languages in the Bantu family and who traditionally had been farmers and herders.

[2] Afrikaans (the Dutch-based language spoken by South Africans of Dutch descent) for the grasslands of southern and eastern Africa.

[3] A white official in charge of a black township. Adjacent to white towns or cities, these townships were areas where blacks were by law compelled to live.

Many Bantu women live in the cities at a great price, the price of their children; for these women, even when they live with their husbands, are forced in most cases to go out and work, to bring sufficient [food] into the homes and to keep their children alive. The children of these unfortunate people therefore run wild, and as there are not sufficient schools to house them, it is easy for them to live an aimless existence, learning crime of all sorts. . . .

If these circumstances obtain when husband and wife live together in the towns, imagine the case of the woman, whose husband has gone to town and left her, forgetting apparently all his responsibilities. Here we get young women, the flower of the youth of the Bantu, going up to towns in search of their husbands, and as I have already stated, living as the reputed wives of other men, because of the location requirements, or becoming housekeepers to men in the locations and towns, and eventually their nominal wives.

. . . Thus we see that the European is by his treatment of the Native in these ways which I have mentioned, only pushing him further and further down in the social scale, forgetting that it was he and his kind who brought these conditions about in South Africa, forgetting his responsibilities to those who labour for him and to whom he introduced the benefits, and evils, of civilisation. . . .

Then we come to the *Land Question*. This is very acute in South Africa, especially from the Bantu point of view. South Africa in terms of available land is shrinking daily owing to increased population, and to many other economic and climatic causes. Cattle diseases have crept into the country, ruining many a stock farmer, and thus Bantu wealth is gradually decaying. As a result there are more and more workers making their way to the towns and cities such as Johannesburg to earn a living. And what a living! The majority earn about £3 10s. per month, out of which they must pay 25s. for rent, and 10s. for tram fares, so I leave you to imagine what sort of existence they lead on the remainder.

Here again we come back to the same old problem . . . that of the woman of the home being obliged to find work in order to supplement her husband's wages, with the children growing up undisciplined and uncared for, and the natural following rapid decay of morality among the people. We find that in this state of affairs, the woman in despair very often decides that she cannot leave her children thus uncared for, and she therefore throws up her employment in order to care for them, but is naturally forced into some form of home industry, which, as there is very little choice for her in this direction, more often than not takes the form of the brewing and selling of Skokiaan.[4] Thus the woman starts on a career of crime for herself and her children, a career which often takes her and her children right down the depths of immorality and misery. The woman, poor unfortunate victim of circumstances, goes to prison, and the children are left even more desolate than when their mother left them to earn her living. . . . The children thus become decadent, never having had a chance in life. About ten years ago, there was talk of Industrial schools being started for such unfortunate children, but it was only talk, and we are to-day in the same position, aggravated by the increased numbers steadily streaming in from the rural areas, all undergoing very similar experiences to those I have just outlined. . . .

Many of the Bantu feel and rightly too that the laws of the land are not made for Black and White alike. Take the question of permits for the right to look for work.[5] To look for work, mark you! The poor unfortunate Native, fresh

---

[4]Skokiaan is Afrikaans for Bantu beer, an alcoholic beverage brewed from sorghum.

[5]To prevent too many unemployed blacks from living in towns, the South African government required every black to carry a pass, which showed the name of his or her employer. Those looking for work were required to have temporary passes. Without a valid pass, blacks could be fined, arrested, deported to a rural reserve, or forced to accept a low-paying job for a white employer.

from the country does not know of these rules and regulations, naturally breaks them and is thrown into prison; or if he does happen to know the regulations and obtains a pass for six days, and is obliged to renew it several times, as is of course very often the case, he will find that when he turns up for the third or fourth time for the renewal of his permit, he is put into prison, because he has been unsuccessful in obtaining work. And not only do the Bantu feel that the law for the White and the Black is not similar, but we even find some of them convinced that there are two Gods, one for the White and one for the Black. I had an instance of this in an old Native woman who had suffered much, and could not be convinced that the same God watched over and cared for us all, but felt that the God who gave the Europeans their life of comparative comfort and ease, could not possibly be the same God who allowed his poor Bantu to suffer so. As another instance of the inequalities existing in our social scheme, we have the fact of Natives not being allowed to travel on buses and trams in many towns, except those specially designed for them.

In connection with the difficulty experienced through men being employed almost exclusively in domestic work in the cities, I would mention that this is of course one of the chief reasons for young women, who should rightly be doing that work, going rapidly down in the social life of the community; and it is here that joint service councils of Bantu and White women would be able to do so much for the good of the community. The solution to the problem seems to me to be to get women into service, and to give them proper accommodation, where they know they are safe. Provide hostels, and club-rooms, and rest rooms for these domestic servants, where they may spend their leisure hours, and I think you will find the problem of the employment of female domestic servants will solve itself, and that a better and happier condition of life will come into being for the Bantu.

. . . What we want is more co-operation and friendship between the two races, and more definite display of real Christianity to help us in the solving of these riddles. Let us try to make our Christianity practical.

Nationalism, Pan-Africanism, and Anticolonialism

Although it was clear by the 1920s that efforts to block the European takeover of their continent had failed, Africans in the interwar years did not abandon the fight against colonial rule and its injustices. Not a year passed in which a colonial government somewhere did not use police or troops to quell a tax rebellion, halt demonstrations against forced labor, or forcefully remove individuals from land confiscated by the government. Africans also found legal, nonviolent ways to defend their traditions and resist European rule. They organized political associations, edited journals, wrote books and newspaper editorials, joined independent African Christian churches, attended international meetings, and sent representatives to European capitals to state their grievances.

The short- and long-term goals of African opponents to colonialism varied widely. The Pan-African movement, in which blacks from the United States and the West Indies played important roles, sponsored international meetings to publicize the abuses of colonialism and draw attention to black people's accomplishments; in the 1930s some Pan-Africans concluded that Africans should seek immediate independence from colonial rule. Africans also joined political organizations to protect their rights and advance their interests within colonies and the white-ruled state of South Africa. These organizations included the African National Congress, founded in South Africa in 1912; the National Congress of British West Africa, founded in 1920 by representatives from Nigeria, the Gold Coast, the Gambia, and Sierra Leone; and the Kikuyu Association and the East African Association, founded in Kenya in 1920 and 1921. African workers joined labor unions and went on strike to improve wages and working conditions. Others joined sports and literary associations, singing groups, youth organizations, dance clubs, and African Christian churches that had broken away from mainline European dominations. Although not overtly political, such organizations gave Africans opportunities to express dissatisfaction with European rule in ways not likely to attract the attention of colonial officials. They also enabled Africans to preserve elements of their culture that otherwise might have been eradicated by Europeanization.

African anticolonial movements faced many obstacles in the 1920s and 1930s: the indifference of chiefs, farmers, and petty traders who benefited from European rule; the paucity of Africans with advanced education and political experience; the gap between educated city dwellers and the illiterate villagers; and rivalries between different linguistic and ethnic groups. They also faced active opposition from the colonial governments they sought to change. Despite these barriers, new leaders emerged, political movements multiplied, and critics of colonialism gained followers. After World War II, Africans were ready to demand their independence.

Colonialism and West Africa's Educated Elite

❖

47 ◆ RESOLUTIONS OF THE NATIONAL CONGRESS OF BRITISH WEST AFRICA, 1920

Under the leadership of Casely Hayford, a barrister from the Gold Coast, fifty-two delegates from four British West African colonies — the Gambia, Sierra Leone, Nigeria, and the Gold Coast — met in Accra in 1920 to discuss the role of blacks in colonial and municipal government. This was the beginning of the National Congress of British West Africa, an organization that held subsequent meetings at Freetown in 1923, Bathurst in 1925 and 1926, and Lagos in 1929 and 1930. On each occasion the delegates issued demands similar in tone and themes to those of the resolutions adopted in their first meeting in 1920.

The fact that the Congress issued more or less similar demands at each of its meetings is an indication of its failure to achieve most of its goals. Although the Congress took some credit for the decision of British officials in the Gold Coast to institute elections among Africans for positions on the Legislative Council, on the whole the British ignored the Congress's demands, and many rural-based chiefs actively opposed them. The chiefs feared that the authority delegated to them by the British would be undermined if the demands of educated Congress members were met. The National Congress lost direction and leadership after the death of Casely Hayford in 1930, and disbanded in 1933.

Although the Congress achieved few concrete results, it played an important role in the evolution of African nationalism. Its meetings and petitions to London were closely followed in the West African press. It was also one of the first groups to support the idea that colonies could make progress toward independence by turning into nations, and furthermore that these new nations should adopt the British system of government, not the systems formed in Africa's own history.

QUESTIONS FOR ANALYSIS

1. What specific changes in the colonial administration do the resolutions demand? Who would benefit from these proposed changes?
2. How do the resolutions reflect British political and educational views?
3. To what extent are the authors of the resolutions concerned with the preservation of traditional African culture?
4, What demands, if any, in the resolutions would have benefited the colonies' rural population on being implemented?

LEGISLATIVE (INCLUDING MUNICIPAL) REFORMS AND THE GRANTING OF THE FRANCHISE AND ADMINISTRATIVE REFORMS WITH PARTICULAR REFERENCE TO EQUAL RIGHTS AND OPPORTUNITIES

Resolutions
1. That ... the time has arrived for a change in the Constitutions of the several British West African Colonies, so as to give the people an effective voice in their affairs both in the Legislative and Municipal Governments. . . .
2. That this Conference recommends a Constitution on the following lines: (1) An Executive Council[1] as at present composed.

(2) A Legislative Council[2] composed of representatives of whom one-half shall be nominated by the Crown and the other half elected by the people, to deal with Legislation generally. (3) A House of Assembly, composed of the members of the Legislative Council together with six other financial representatives elected by the people, who shall have the power of imposing all taxes and of discussing freely and without reserve the items on the Annual Estimates of Revenue and Expenditure prepared by the Governor in the Executive Council and approving of them.
3. That each British West African Community[3] shall have the power of electing members to both the Legislative Council and the House of Assembly through such local

---

[1]The Executive Council, an advisory body to the governor, consisted of a small number of British officials named by the governor.
[2]The Legislative Councils in British West African colonies were made up of approximately two dozen individuals

named by the governor. They included representatives of the British business community and some Africans, most of whom were chiefs. The councils met annually and were purely advisory.
[3]The peoples who made up the various colonies.

groups as may be found most convenient and expedient, and that where indigenous institutions do not provide a ready means of ascertaining the will of the people, other qualifying methods for voting, such as a property or an Educational standard, shall be resorted to. . . .

5. That this Conference desires to place on record its disapprobation of the invidious distinctions made in the present West African Civil Service by reason of colour, and is of the opinion that all future entries should be based on merit by competitive examinations. . . .

6. That Municipal Corporations[4] with full powers of local self-government be established in each principal town of the British West African Colonies, and that of the members of such Municipal Corporations four-fifths shall be elected by the rate-payers and one-fifth nominated by the Crown, and that such elected and nominated members have the power of electing the Mayor of the Corporation, who however must be an elected member.

EDUCATION WITH PARTICULAR REFERENCE TO A WEST AFRICAN UNIVERSITY

Resolutions

1. That this Conference is of the opinion that the system of Education best suited to the needs and conditions of the various British West African peoples under British influence is one which, whilst enabling the students to attain the highest possible proficiency in the many departments of learning, will least interfere with the development by the student of a proper spirit of reverence for indigenous institutions and modes of life not opposed to equity and good conscience.

2. That in the opinion of this Conference the time has come to found a British West

African University on such lines as would preserve in the students a sense of African Nationality, and therefore recommends that all existing Secondary Schools throughout West Africa, or those about to be formed, should promote a course of training that shall best attain the end in view. . . .

5. That compulsory Education throughout the British West African Colonies be introduced by law, and that the standard of both the Primary and the Secondary Schools be uniformly raised to meet the Standard of the University. . . .

COMMERCIAL ENTERPRISE

Resolutions

1. That this Conference . . . is strongly of the opinion that the natural resources of the British West African Dependencies are not for the exploitation of the Concessionaires[5] under State control. . . .

3. That this Conference, being strongly convinced that the time has come for the co-operation of the peoples of the British West African Dependencies in promoting their economical development, recommends the consideration by the various Committees of the formation of a Corporation, to be known as the British West African Co-operative Association . . . with powers . . . to found Banks, promote shipping facilities, establish Co-operative Stores, and produce buying centres, in such wise as to inspire and maintain a British West African National Economical development.

JUDICIAL REFORMS . . .

Resolutions . . .

3. That the time has come to open definitely to African practitioners of experience all Judicial appointments. . . .

[4]Town and city governments.
[5]Businessmen who have received exclusive rights in some economic or commercial activity.

5. That this Conference deplores the gradual modification in successive Ordinances throughout British West Africa of the right of citizens to trial by Jury in Criminal cases, and recommends that the right should be regulated in accordance with English Common and Statute Laws. . . .

12. That this Conference wholly condemns the barbarous practice of flogging African women for any offence whatsoever. . . .

WEST AFRICAN PRESS UNION

Resolutions . . .

3. That this Conference is strongly of the opinion that the liberty of the Press is the birthright of every Community within the British Empire, and deprecates any Legislation that threatens such a right. . . .

THE POLICY OF THE GOVERNMENT IN RELATION TO THE LAND QUESTION

Resolutions

1. That in the opinion of this Conference the principle of Trusteeship with respect of the lands of the people of British West Africa by Government has been overdone, and that it is proper to declare that the average British West African is quite capable of controlling and looking after his own interests in the land. . . .

THE RIGHT OF THE PEOPLE TO SELF-DETERMINATION

Resolutions

1. That the Conference views with alarm the right assumed by the European powers of exchanging or partitioning Countries between them, without reference to, or regard for, the wishes of the people, and records the opinion that such a course is tantamount to a species of slavery. . . .

4. That this Conference desires to place on record the attachment of the peoples of British West African to the British connection and their unfeigned loyalty and devotion to the throne and person of His Majesty the King-Emperor, and directs that copies of these Resolutions be forwarded in due course to His Majesty's Principal Secretary of State for the Colonies and to each of the Governors of the several Dependencies.

A Plea to the World for Racial Equality

❖

48 ◆ *1921 PAN-AFRICAN CONGRESS, LONDON MANIFESTO*

Pan-Africanism, a movement that played a key role in African liberation and in postcolonial politics, was originally inspired by black leaders from the United States and the West Indies in the early 1900s. With the partition of Africa in full swing, color barriers increasing in the West Indies, and lynchings and racial violence growing in the United States, a West Indian lawyer, Henry Sylvester Williams, organized a Pan-African conference in London in 1900. Although most of the thirty-two delegates came from the United States and the West Indies, it caught the attention of Africans. A Nigerian newspaper, *The Lagos Standard,* called the meeting "an event in the history of race movements which for its importance and probable results is perhaps without parallel."

Pan-Africanism was revived in 1919 when the prominent American black W. E. B. Du Bois organized what is recognized as the First Pan-African Conference in Paris to coincide with the Paris Peace Conference. He hoped to demonstrate the solidarity of black people and publicize their needs to the diplomats writing the postwar treaties. In 1921 Du Bois organized a second conference that met sequentially in London, Brussels, and Paris. At the beginning of the 1921 meeting, the 113 delegates from Africa, the United States, England, and the West Indies adopted the following document, known as the London Manifesto. Its demands for racial justice and fair treatment of blacks were widely publicized in Africa, especially in the British colonies of West Africa.

Two more Pan-African conferences were held in the 1920s, but the meeting scheduled for late 1929 had to be canceled as a result of the U.S. stock market crash. Riddled by internal disagreements, the Pan-African movement weakened in the 1930s, but at the Fifth Pan-African Conference at Manchester, England, in 1945, it came alive with a new sense of purpose. With its call for African unity and independence, it was the first step in the post–World War II era toward the realization of African independence.

QUESTIONS FOR ANALYSIS

1. On what grounds does the London Manifesto reject the idea of inequality among the world's races?
2. According to the Manifesto, what is the main obstacle to African advancement in the modern world?
3. What attitude is expressed in the Manifesto toward whites?
4. According to the Manifesto, why should "advanced" people aid Africans?
5. Do the authors of the Manifesto believe Africa is ready for independence? Why or why not?

The absolute equality of races, physical, political and social, is the founding stone of World Peace and human advancement. No one denies great differences of gift, capacity and attainment among individuals of all races, but the voice of Science, Religion and practical Politics is one in denying the God-appointed existence of super races or of races naturally and inevitably and eternally inferior.

That in the vast range of time, one group should in its industrial technique or social organisation or spiritual vision lag a few hundred years behind another or forge fitfully ahead or come to differ decidedly in thought, deed and ideal is proof of the essential richness and variety of human nature, rather than proof of the co-existence of demi-gods and apes in human form. The doctrine of racial equality does not interfere with individual liberty, — rather fulfills it.

And of all the various criteria by which masses of men have in the past been judged and classified that of the color of the skin and texture of the hair is surely the most adventitious [accidental] and idiotic. . . .

The insidious and dishonourable propaganda for which selfish ends so distorts and denies facts as to represent the advancement and development of certain races as impossible and undesirable should be met with wide-spread dissemination of the truth; the experiment of making the Negro slave a free citizen in the

United States is not a failure; the attempts at autonomous government in Haiti and Liberia are not proofs of the impossibility of self-government among black men; the experience of Spanish America does not prove that mulatto democracy will not eventually succeed there; the aspirations of Egypt and India are not successfully to be met by sneers at the capacity of darker races. . . .

If it be proven that absolute world segregation by group, colour or historic affinity is the best thing for the future world, let the white race leave the dark world and the dark races will gladly leave the white. But the proposition is absurd. This is a world of men, — of men whose likenesses far outweigh their differences; who mutually need each other in labour and thought and dream, but who can successfully have each other only on terms of equality, justice and mutual respect. They are the real and only peace-makers who work sincerely and peacefully to this end.

The beginning of Wisdom in inter-racial contact is the establishment of political institutions among suppressed Peoples. The habit of democracy must be made to encircle the earth. Despite the attempt to prove that its practice is the secret and divine Gift of the Few, no habit is more natural and more widely spread among primitive peoples or more easily capable of development among wide masses. Local self-government with a minimum of help and oversight can be established tomorrow in Asia, Africa, America and the Isles of the Sea [the Pacific Islands]. It will in many instances need general control and guidance but it will fail only when that guidance seeks ignorantly and consciously its own selfish ends and not the people's liberty and good.

Surely in the 20th century of the Prince of Peace [Jesus], in the millennium of Buddha and Mahmoud [Muhammad], and in the mightiest era of Human Reason there can be found in the civilised world enough of human altruism, learning and benevolence to develop native institutions for the native's good rather than continuing to allow the majority of mankind to be brutalised and enslaved by ignorant and selfish agents of commercial institutions whose one aim is profit and power for the few.

And this brings us to the crux of the matter; it is to the shame of the world that to-day the relations between the main groups of mankind and their mutual [estimation] and respect is determined chiefly by the degree in which one can subject the other to its service, — enslaving labour, making ignorance compulsory, uprooting ruthlessly religion and custom and destroying government so that the favoured few may luxuriate in the toil of the tortured many. . . .

The day of such world organisation is past and whatever excuse may be made for it in other ages, the 20th century must come to judge men as men and not as merely material and labour. . . .

If we are coming to recognise that the great modern problem is to correct maladjustment in the distribution of wealth, it must be remembered that the basic maladjustment is in the outrageously unjust distribution of the world income between the dominant and suppressed peoples, — in the rape of land and raw material, the monopoly of technique and culture. . . .

What, then, do those demand who see these evils of the colour line and racial discrimination, and who believe in the divine right of Suppressed and Backward Peoples to learn and aspire and be free?

The Suppressed Races through their thinking leaders are demanding:

1. The recognition of civilised men as civilised despite their race and colour.
2. Local self-government for backward groups, deliberately rising as experience and knowledge grow to complete self-government under the limitations of a self-governed world.

3. Education in self-knowledge, in scientific truth and in industrial technique, undivorced from the art of beauty.
4. Freedom in their own religion and customs and with the right to be non-conformist and different.
5. Co-operation with the rest of the world in government, industry and art on the basis of Justice, Freedom and Peace.
6. The ancient common ownership of the Land and its natural fruits and defence against the unrestrained greed of invested capital.

The world must face two eventualities; either the complete assimilation of Africa with two or three of the great world states, with political, civil and social power and privileges absolutely equal for its black and white citizens, or the rise of a great black African State, founded in Peace and Good Will, based on popular education, natural art and industry and freedom of trade, autonomous and sovereign in its internal policy, but from its beginning a part of a great society of peoples in which it takes its place with others as co-rulers of the world. . . .

African Militancy in the 1930s

49 ◆ Gilbert Coka,
THE AFRICAN LIBERATOR, OUR MESSAGE

African nationalism and Pan-Africanism in the 1920s were minority movements, supported mainly by educated city dwellers who sought reforms in the colonial system rather than independence. Because they made moderate demands and had little mass following, colonial officials could afford to ignore them. During the 1930s, however, several developments intensified African opposition to white rule. The calamitous decline in prices for African agricultural products caused economic misery among many black Africans, and forced colonial administrators to cut back on social, educational, and development programs. In South Africa, the removal of blacks from the Cape Province's common voters' roles in 1936 was one of many laws passed in the 1930s to further restrict blacks' rights and freedoms. In 1935 and 1936 African anger exploded when the world stood by and allowed Mussolini's Italian army and air force to conquer Ethiopia, Africa's last remaining truly independent state.

For all these reasons, African nationalists in the 1930s became more defiant, more intent on independence, more willing to use force and economic coercion, and more open to enlisting mass support. The 1930s saw the emergence of new youth movements such as the Gold Coast Youth Conference (1930), the Nigerian Youth Movement (1933), and the West African Youth League (1935). Although all were led by educated city dwellers, they took their message of the need for independence to rural villages. In 1937 cocoa growers in the Gold Coast withheld their cocoa from the market, forcing the British to pay more for their crops. The number of strikes increased in Nigeria, Kenya, and especially South Africa.

In South Africa in 1935, Africans from all parts of the country and all shades of the political spectrum — members of the African National Conference, communists, union leaders, clergy, prominent women, and professionals — met in Bloemfontein at the All-African Convention to denounce recent government actions. The delegates issued the usual list of grievances but also approved a proposal to organize mass meetings to pressure the government. They refused, however, to approve economic boycott as an antigovernment weapon. As a result, when the representatives of the convention met with government officials in 1936, they received a polite reception but no action on their demands.

The lack of response was disappointing to South African militants such as Gilbert Coka. Born in 1910 to the family of a sharecropper in Natal province, Coka attended secondary school, but left in 1927 to work for the black workers' Industrial and Commercial Workers' Union (ICU). Disillusioned with the union's weaknesses and divisions, in the early 1930s he joined the Communist Party of South Africa and went to work for its party newspaper. In 1935 he left the Party and founded his own newspaper, *The African Liberator.* He wrote the following editorial for the newspaper's first issue, which appeared shortly after the Italian invasion of Ethiopia and just weeks before the meeting of the All-African Convention. In it he called on Africans to use their economic strength to break the grip of white racism. After World War II, Coka became active in the African National Congress and died in the 1960s.

QUESTIONS FOR ANALYSIS

1. Why does Coka believe that a new era of African history is about to dawn?
2. What, according to Coka, has held back the liberation of the African people?
3. What strategy does Coka recommend to bring an end to African oppression?
4. What similarities and differences do you see between Coka's editorial and the manifestos of the Pan-African Congress and the National Congress of British West Africa?

War is on. Fascism has let loose the hounds of hell. Greed and envy have their little hour. International conventions and treaties have been treated like a scrap of paper. Wars and rumours of war, are in the air. But the divinity that shapes our ends, has also brought forward the opportunity of liberty to the captive, freedom to the oppressed and opportunity to those who struggle. . . . Africa is opening another era in human history. As she started the era of knowledge, culture, education, civilisation and worship, so today she commences a new era of goodwill, magnanimity and triumph.

The hour of African freedom has struck. That for which Toussaint L'Ouverture[1] suffered and died, that for which Frederick Douglass and Booker [T.] Washington lived and died,[2] that for which Menelik, Shaka, Makana, Lewanika,

---

[1]Toussaint L'Ouverture (1743–1803) led the black rebellion against French rule in Haiti, thus creating the first independent nation in Latin America.

[2]Frederick Douglass (1817–1895), born a slave in Maryland, was a leading spokesman for abolition and, after the U.S. Civil War, for black political rights. Booker T. Washington (1856–1915), a leading American educator, was the first president of the Tuskegee Institute in Alabama.

Lobengula, Langalibalele and other great sons of Africa, lived, suffered and died. . . .[3] The complete liberty of Africans to shape their own destiny in their own way, has come. . . . Justice will have her way. Africans must be ready to take their great opportunity towards freedom. They must be prepared to act the part of men. The dreams and prophecies of Marcus Garvey,[4] the solidarity of Africans throughout the world, is becoming a fact. And but for a few traitors, Africans had reached the land of Promise — liberty, equality, opportunity and justice.

But this good time coming, will not come of its own volition. It will be brought by Africans themselves when they purge themselves free of envy, jealousies and other manifestations of the inferiority complex which debar them from unity and solidarity. . . . However, the unfortunate thing about us is that we take the monkey apings of our so-called distinguished men for progress. There is no progress in Africans aping Europeans and telling us that they represent the best in the race, for any ordinarily well trained monkey would do the same. The slave mentality still holds our people in chains and they firmly believe that they can only exist through the good graces of their "Masters". Before doing anything worthwhile, they must have the stamp of approval, from some European, otherwise they have no confidence in their work, thoughts and ideas. . . . But in the bottom of their hearts, Europeans as well as other men respect Africans who work out their salvation, [more] than . . . they could ever respect the groups of helpless apes and beggars who make a monopoly of undermining themselves and their people by being "Good Boys" instead of able men. But such spineless creatures who live by deceit will not forever remain deceiving Africans and therefore cannot permanently impede African progress towards unity, liberty, justice and freedom.

The present war is destroying the Old Africa, which has been undermined for over three centuries. The new Africa is being born. The pangs of suffering attendant upon new birth will follow the bringing forth of a New Africa. But where there is courage there will be a way. Africans must unite and co-operate in their enterprises. They must spend their money where they will get fair returns. As long as they are buyers they will remain despised and powerless, but when they become sellers they will be respected. It is therefore time that Africans reorganized their economic life in order to enter into the new era. They must face the realities of life which are that Nothing can be obtained for nothing and that Money at present is the ruling power of the world. Consequently as workers, they must struggle and obtain higher wages. As buyers they must spend it for tangible returns and that can only be best done by organising consumers cooperatives in every locality. The time has come for Africans to supply themselves with the necessities of life. Our reply to War, oppressive legislation, discrimination, injustice, pauperisation, unemployment and oppression, must be "Let all African money circulate through African friends". An economic boycott against unjust and tyrannical employers, coupled with a persistent struggle for more wages and shorter working conditions [hours], as a part of a national consumers league, supplying all African

---

[3]King Menelik II (1844–1913) led the successful Ethiopian resistance against the attempted Italian takeover in 1896. Shaka (1788–1828) was the Zulu king whose soldiers conquered large parts of southeastern Africa in the early 1800s. Makana was an early-nineteenth-century prophet among the Xhosa people of South Africa whose writings inspired Xhosa resistance to whites from the 1860s through the 1880s. Lewanika was an Ngwato king who converted to Christianity, but was successful for a time in resisting dispossession of his people's lands by Boer settlers. Lobengula (ca. 1828–1894) was king of the Ndebele people during their rebellion against the British in 1893. Langalibalele (1818–1889) was a chieftain of the AmaHlabi people in Natal who was sentenced to lifetime imprisonment on Robbens Island after three whites were killed in a skirmish with his people over the registration of firearms; on appeal, an English court reversed the sentence, and Langalibalele was released.

[4]Marcus Garvey (1887–1940), born in Jamaica, was a charismatic leader whose pan-Africanism and anticolonialism won him a wide following among Africans.

buyers with the necessities of life, a national liberation movement for equal democratic rights for all South Africans irrespective of colour, creed or race and an independent National newspaper of Africans for Africans by Africans to tell [the] truth about our conditions in the Union, will be worth tons of pious hopes.

Africans! rescue yourselves from degradation, poverty and oppression. . . . African workers unite into your Trade Unions and fight for your rights. African buyers, buy from African traders, put up your cooperatives and get your biggest returns from your monies. Kill envy. Work together. Unite for the greater common good of a free African. . . . But, fellow Africans! Put your house in order. Sink petty selfish jealousies. Organise your consumers cooperatives, Organise your Trades Unions, demand your "Citizen rights," cooperate with all lovers of justice and fair play and make of Africa a land fit for the dwelling of the brave, the just, the humane, the loving, the rich, the powerful, the free and the honest as it was in ancient [times]. Smother internal jealousies, prejudice, injustice and exploitation. To be fit for a new Africa, Unite and cooperate, think and act, struggle and win.

CHAPTER 7

Asia in an Era of Nationalism and Revolution

Asia is the world's largest continent and, in terms of human history, arguably its most important. Asia's river valleys — the Tigris-Euphrates in modern Iran and Iraq, the Indus and Ganges in India, the Yangzi and Hoang He in China — gave rise to humankind's first civilizations some six thousand years ago. Asian sages, prophets, mystics, and teachers developed many of the world's great religions and philosophical traditions — Confucianism, Hinduism, Buddhism, Judaism, Islam, and Christianity. Asian peoples created large and successful states; invented printing, gunpowder, the compass, writing, and metallurgy; made important discoveries in mathematics and astronomy; and had the world's wealthiest and most sophisticated economies during much of human history.

Yet by the 1920s virtually all of Asia consisted of Western colonies, dependencies, or, in the case of Siberia, Central Asia, and Transcaucasia, component parts of a European-based state, the Soviet Union. The beginnings of Asia's subservience to the West can be traced back to the sixteenth century when in their search for trade and converts to Christianity, the Spaniards took over the Philippines and the Portuguese established a line of fortified trading posts stretching from the Red Sea and the Persian Gulf to China and Japan. In the seventeenth century the Dutch, after forcing out the Portuguese, established a commercial and political empire in Sumatra, Java, Borneo, and the Malay Peninsula. More significantly, in the eighteenth century the British East India Company gained control of Bengal in northeast India; from this base the British extended their authority over the whole Indian subcontinent in the nineteenth century.

The British takeover of India was just one example of Western expansion in Asia during the nineteenth and early twentieth centuries. Great Britain and France turned most of Southeast Asia into colonies, the Dutch extended their authority in the East Indies, and the United States replaced Spain as colonial master of the Philippines. In addition, the Western powers established spheres of influence up and down the coast of China, forcefully opened Japan to trade, and took over government finances and much of the economy of the Ottoman Empire and Persia. Except for Japan, which successfully industrialized in the late nineteenth century, Asia became dependent on the West as a market for its raw materials, a supplier of manufactured goods, and a source of capital and technology. Finally, after World War I, Lebanon, Syria, Palestine, Iraq, and Jordan became colonies in all but name when the French and British took them over as parts of League of Nations mandates. In the 1920s only three major Asian states — Turkey, Thailand, and Japan — stood outside the sphere of Western colonialism.

The high point of Western imperialism in Asia, reached after World War I, was followed by its rapid demise after World War II. Of the many factors that contributed to this sudden turnabout, nationalism was the most important. Nationalism in the region first took root in the early twentieth century as Asians came to resent the economic exploitation and political oppression that accompanied colonialism. It gathered strength from the examples of Japan and China. Japan's transformation into a Great Power, exemplified by its victory in the Russo-Japanese War of 1904–1905, awakened Asians to the possibility that they, not just Europeans, were capable of industrialization and military modernization. In addition, China's break with its imperial, Confucian past in the Revolution of 1911 inspired hopes that meaningful political changes also could occur elsewhere in the region.

Events outside of Asia also strengthened nationalist movements. The slaughter of World War I, the failure of the Allies to honor wartime promises to the Arabs and Indians, and the hypocrisy of the League of Nations mandate system undermined the Europeans' claims of moral superiority and further embittered Asians against their colonial masters. The Russian Revolution and its communist ideology also encouraged nationalism, especially in Southeast Asia and China. The new leaders of the Soviet Union denounced colonialism in all its forms and pledged support for political movements and parties working to end the political and economic exploitation of Asia by the capitalist West.

Asian nationalism between the wars meant more than anti-colonialism. It also had social, economic, and cultural implications. Painfully aware of their own societies' shortcomings, nationalist leaders understood that political independence would be meaningless if poverty, illiteracy, and economic underdevelopment continued. Thus with the exception of Gandhi, who venerated manual labor and India's village-based agrarian economy, nationalists were committed to programs of economic and political modernization, and some, such as Mao Zedong in China and Ho Chi Minh in Vietnam, sought revolutionary social changes. As a result, many nationalists found themselves in a dual struggle — against rule by foreigners and also against the social and political conservatism of some of their compatriots.

Nationalists faced other problems as well. With their urban backgrounds and Western educations, many had difficulty drawing the illiterate rural masses into their movements. They also struggled with the concept of nationhood itself. Opposition to Dutch, French, or English rule might bring people together in the short run, but after independence, how would peoples divided by ethnic background, language, and religion stay united?

Despite nationalism's growing strength, only a few colonies — Iraq in 1932 and Egypt in 1936 — became independent between the wars. Elsewhere, the Western powers tenaciously held on to their colonies, and attempted to reassert or maintain their control during and after World War II. This proved beyond their will and capacity, however, and beginning with the independence of Lebanon (1943), Syria (1945), Jordan and the Philippines (1946), and India and Pakistan (1947), colonialism in Asia began to unravel.

◆

Political and Religious Currents in the Middle East

The aftermath of World War I spelled political disaster for the people of the Middle East. The Turks, a defeated ally of Germany, in 1920 were forced to accept the humiliating Treaty of Sèvres, which stripped Turkey of its Arab territories; limited the Turkish army to fifty thousand men; gave France, Britain, and Italy control of its finances; and proposed to cede parts of Turkey itself to Italy, Greece, and the new states of Kurdistan and Armenia. The Arabs, who in 1916 had rebelled against their Turkish overlords in the hope that France and Great Britain would recognize an independent Arab state, soon learned that the British and French had agreed in 1916 to divide the Arab portions of the Ottoman Empire between themselves. This is exactly what happened when, in keeping with Article 22 of the League of Nations Covenant, Iraq, Syria, Palestine, Lebanon, and Jordan became British or French mandates. Farther east, another major Islamic state, Persia, under the decrepit rule of the Qajar Dynasty, was threatened by British plans to turn it into a protectorate.

Efforts to reverse the region's bleak postwar prospects had mixed results. Under the leadership of Mustafa Kemal, between 1919 and 1922 the Turks rallied to drive out Italian and Greek invaders and smash the nascent Armenian state. As a result, in 1923 the European powers agreed to replace the Treaty of Sèvres with the Treaty of Lausanne, which recognized Turkey's integrity and independence. In Iran, another strong military leader, Reza Khan (1878–1944), after engineering an anti-Qajar coup in 1921, reorganized the army and established a government strong enough to discourage the British from pursuing their plan to establish a protectorate.

Arab efforts to attain independence and prevent Jewish immigration to Palestine were less successful. Of the twenty Arab states that stretched from Morocco in the west to Iraq in the east, only relatively backward Saudi Arabia and Yemen were truly independent in the interwar years. Egypt and Iraq attained a measure of self-rule, but continuing British control of foreign policy and military affairs caused resentment in both countries. The drive for independence was even more frustrating in French-controlled Lebanon and Syria. Despite promises to the contrary, the French maintained control of Lebanon until 1943 and Syria until 1945. Arabs also were angered by the British tolerance of Jewish migration to Palestine, which rose dramatically in the 1930s as a result of the Nazi takeover in Germany and immigration restrictions in the United States.

While confronting these immediate postwar problems, the peoples and leaders of the region faced other more fundamental issues. Was the final goal of Arab nationalism the explusion of the British and French and the stifling of Jewish immigration to Palestine? Or was it the attainment of a single united Arab state? What was the best solution to the problem of the region's poverty and illiteracy? How could the teachings and expectations of Islam be reconciled with the realities and demands of modernization? Was modernization itself desirable, and if so, how was it to be achieved? Questions such as these were not new. But in the face of the rapid changes that swept through the region in the first half of the twentieth century, finding answers to them became more urgent and difficult.

Secularism and Nationalism in Republican Turkey

❧

50 ◆ Mustafa Kemal, *SPEECH TO THE CONGRESS OF THE PEOPLE'S REPUBLICAN PARTY*

The archsymbol of aggressive secularism and nationalism in the Muslim world in the interwar years was Mustafa Kemal (1881–1938), who first achieved prominence as a Turkish military hero during World War I and went on to serve as first president of the Republic of Turkey. Disgusted by the Ottoman sultan's acquiescence to the punitive Treaty of Sèvres and the Greek occupation of the Turkish port of Smyrna in 1919, Kemal assumed leadership of a resistance movement against both the sultan's government and the Allies. He led his supporters to victory over the Greeks and forced the annulment of the Sèvres treaty in 1923.

One year earlier, in 1922, Kemal had convened a National Assembly, which deposed the sultan and set the stage for a decade and a half of revolutionary change. Exercising his broad powers as president, he sought to transform Turkey into a modern secular nation-state. To accomplish this, he broke the power of the Islamic establishment over education and the legal system, encouraged industrialization, accorded women full legal rights, mandated the use of a new Turkish alphabet, and ordered Turks to assume Western-style dress. Directing all Turks to adopt hereditary family names, he took for himself the name Ataturk, or "Great Turk."

Having consolidated his authority, in 1927 Kemal decided to review his accomplishments and impress upon his subjects the need for continued support. He chose as the occasion the meeting of the People's Republican Party, founded by Ataturk and Turkey's only legal political party. Here he delivered an extraordinary speech. Having worked on it for three months (in the process exhausting dozens of secretaries), he delivered it over a period of six days.

In these excerpts, Kemal discusses Turkey's past and future; explains his reasons for abolishing the caliphate, the ancient office by virtue of which Turkish sultans had been the theoretical rulers of all Muslims; and justifies his suppression of the Progressive Republican Party, which despite its name was a party of conservatives who opposed Kemal's plans to modernize Turkey.

QUESTIONS FOR ANALYSIS

1. What, according to Kemal, were the "erroneous ideas" that had guided the Ottoman state in the past?
2. Why does Kemal argue that nation-states, not empires, are the most desirable form of political organization?
3. What is Kemal's view of the West?
4. What are his views of Islam?
5. What arguments does Kemal offer against the continuation of the caliphate?
6. How does Kemal justify his suppression of the Progressive Republicans? What, in his view, were the positive results of this step?

[NATIONALISM AND EMPIRE]

We turn our minds to the times when the Ottoman state in Istanbul . . . was master of the crown and the throne of the East-Roman [Byzantine] Empire. Among the Ottoman rulers there were some who endeavored to form a gigantic empire by seizing Germany and West-Rome [Western Europe]. One of these rulers hoped to unite the whole Islamic world in one body, to lead it and govern it. For this purpose he obtained control of Syria and Egypt and assumed the title of Caliph.[1] Another Sultan pursued the twofold aim, on the one hand of gaining the mastery over Europe, and on the other of subjecting the Islamic world to his authority and government.

The continuous counterattacks from the West, the discontent and insurrections in the Muslim world, as well as the dissensions between the various elements which this policy had artificially brought together within certain limits, had the ultimate result of burying the Ottoman Empire, in the same way as many others, under the pall of history. . . .

To unite different nations under one common name, to give these different elements equal rights, subject them to the same conditions and thus to found a mighty State is a brilliant and attractive political ideal; but it is a misleading one. It is an unrealizable aim to attempt to unite in one tribe the various races existing on the earth, thereby abolishing all boundaries.

---

[1]The reference is to Selim I, who conquered Egypt and Syria in 1515 and 1516; it is doubtful that he actually considered himself caliph.

Herein lies a truth which the centuries that have gone by and the men who have lived during these centuries have clearly shown in dark and sanguinary events.

There is nothing in history to show how the policy of Panislamism[2] could have succeeded or how it could have found a basis for its realization on this earth. As regards the result of the ambition to organize a State which should be governed by the idea of world-supremacy and include the whole of humanity without distinction of race, history does not afford examples of this. For us, there can be no question of the lust of conquest. . . .

The political system which we regard as clear and fully realizable is national policy. . . . This is borne out in history and is the expression of science, reason, and common sense.

In order that our nation should be able [to] live a happy, strenuous, and permanent life, it is necessary that the State should pursue an exclusively national policy and that this policy should be in perfect agreement with our internal organization and be based on it. When I speak of national policy, I mean it in this sense: To work within our national boundaries for the real happiness and welfare of the nation and the country by, above all, relying on our own strength in order to retain our existence. But not to lead the people to follow fictitious aims, of whatever nature, which could only bring them misfortune, and expect from the civilized world civilized human treatment, [and] friendship based on mutuality. . . .

[THE ISSUE OF THE CALIPHATE]

I must call attention to the fact that Hodja Shukri,[3] as well as the politicians who pushed forward his person and signature, had intended to substitute the sovereign bearing the title of Sultan or Padishah by a monarch with the title of Caliph. The only difference was that, instead of speaking of a monarch of this or that country or nation, they now spoke of a monarch whose authority extended over a population of three hundred million souls belonging to manifold nations and dwelling in different continents of the world. Into the hands of this great monarch, whose authority was to extend over the whole of Islam, they placed as the only power that of the Turkish people, that is to say, only from 10 to 15 millions of these three hundred million subjects. The monarch designated under the title of Caliph was to guide the affairs of these Muslim peoples and to secure the execution of the religious prescriptions which would best correspond to their worldly interests. He was to defend the rights of all Muslims and concentrate all the affairs of the Muslim world in his hands with effective authority. . . .

If the Caliph and Caliphate, as they maintained, were to be invested with a dignity embracing the whole of Islam, ought they not to have realized in all justice that a crushing burden would be imposed on Turkey, on her existence; her entire resources and all her forces would be placed at the disposal of the Caliph?

According to their declarations, the Caliph-Monarch would have the right of jurisdiction over all Muslims and all Muslim countries, that is to say, over China, India, Afghanistan, Persia, Iraq, Syria, Palestine, Hijaz,[4] Yemen, Assyria, Egypt, Libya, Tunis, Algeria, Morocco, the Sudan. It is well known that this Utopia has never been realized. . . .

I made statements everywhere, that were necessary to dispel the uncertainty and anxiety of the people concerning this question of the Caliphate. . . . I gave the people to understand

---

[2]The program of uniting all Muslims under one government or ruler.
[3]The events took place in January 1923. After Sultan Mehmed V was deposed as sultan on November 1, 1922, his cousin, Abdul Mejid, was designated caliph. Shukri was

a *hodja* (or *hojja*), a Turkish religious leader; he hoped that the new Turkish state would continue to support the caliphate even after the sultanate was abolished. In 1924, however, Kemal abolished the caliphate.
[4]Western Arabia.

that neither Turkey nor the handful of men she possesses could be placed at the disposal of the Caliph so that he might fulfill the mission attributed to him, namely, to found a State comprising the whole of Islam. The Turkish nation is incapable of undertaking such an irrational mission.

For centuries our nation was guided under the influence of these erroneous ideas. But what has been the result of it? Everywhere they have lost millions of men. "Do you know," I asked, "how many sons of Anatolia have perished in the scorching deserts of the Yemen? Do you know the losses we have suffered in holding Syria and Iraq and Egypt and in maintaining our position in Africa? And do you see what has come out of it? Do you know? "New Turkey, the people of New Turkey, have no reason to think of anything else but their own existence and their own welfare. She has nothing more to give away to others." . . .

[THE SUPPRESSION OF THE PROGRESSIVE REPUBLICANS]

. . . As you know, it was at the time that the members of the opposition had founded a party under the name of "Republican Progressive Party" and published its program. . . .

Could seriousness and sincerity be attributed to the deeds and attitude of people who avoided pronouncing even the word Republic and who tried to suppress the Republic from the very beginning, but who called the party Republican and even Republican Progressive? . . .

Did those who appeared under the same flag, but who wanted to be regarded as progressive Republicans, not follow the deep design of provoking the religious fanaticism of the nation, putting them thus completely against the Republic, progress and reform?

Under the mask of respect for religious ideas and dogmas the new Party addressed itself to the people in the following words:

"We want the re-establishment of the Caliphate; we do not want new laws; we are satisfied with the . . . religious laws . . . ; we shall protect the Medressas, the Tekkes, the pious institutions, the Softahs, the Sheikhs,[5] and their disciples. Be on our side; the party of Mustapha Kemal, having abolished the Caliphate, is breaking Islam into ruins; they will make you into unbelievers. . . ."

Read these sentences, Gentlemen, from a letter written by one of the adherents of this program . . . : "They are attacking the very principles which perpetuate the existence of the Mohamedan [Muslim] world. . . . The assimilation with the Occident means the destruction of our history, our civilisation. . . ."

Gentlemen, facts and events have proved that the program of the Republican Progressive Party has been the work emanating from the brain of traitors. This Party became the refuge and the point of support for reactionary and rebellious elements. . . .

. . . The Government and the Committee found themselves forced to take extraordinary measures. They caused the law regarding the restoration of order to be proclaimed, and the Independence Courts to take action. For a considerable time they kept eight or nine divisions of the army at war strength . . . for the suppression of disorders, and put an end to the injurious organisation which bore the name "Republican Progressive Party."

The result was, of course, the success of the Republic. . . .

There were persons who disseminated and sought to gain credence to the thought that we were making use of the law for Restoration of Order and the Courts of Independence as tools of dictatorship or despotism. . . .

---

[5] A *medressa* is an advanced school of Islamic learning. A *tekke* is a small teaching mosque usually built over the tomb of a saint. A *softah* is a student in an Islamic school. A sheikh, or *shaykh,* is a master of a religious order of Sufis, Muslims who adopted a mystical approach to their religion.

Can anyone be of the opinion that this decision of the High Assembly was intended to hand over to us the means for the carrying on of a dictatorship?

Gentlemen, it was necessary to abolish the fez,[6] which sat on our heads as a sign of ignorance, of fanaticism, of hatred to progress and civilization, and to adopt in its place that hat, the customary headdress of the whole civilised world, thus showing, among other things, that no difference existed in the manner of thought between the Turkish nation and the whole family of civilized mankind. We did that while the law for the Restoration of Order was still in force. If it had not been in force we should have done so all the same; but one can say with complete truth that the existence of this law made the thing much easier for us. As a matter of fact the application of the law for the Restoration of Order prevented the morale of the nation being poisoned to a great extent by reactionaries. . . .

Gentlemen, while the law regarding the Restoration of Order was in force there took place also the closing of the Tekkes, of the convents, and of the mausoleums, as well as the abolition of all sects[7] and all kinds of titles such as Sheikh, Dervish . . . , Occultist, Magician, Mausoleum Guard, etc.[8]

One will be able to imagine how necessary the carrying through of these measures was, in order to prove that our nation as a whole was no primitive nation, filled with superstitions and prejudices.

Could a civilized nation tolerate a mass of people who let themselves be led by the nose by a herd of Sheikhs, Dedes, Seids, Tschelebis, Babas and Emirs;[9] who entrusted their destiny and their lives to chiromancers,[10] magicians, dice-throwers and amulet sellers? Ought one to conserve in the Turkish State, in the Turkish Republic, elements and institutions such as those which had for centuries given the nation the appearance of being other than it really was? Would one not therewith have committed the greatest, most irreparable error to the cause of progress and reawakening?

If we made use of the law for the Restoration of Order in this manner, it was in order to avoid such a historic error; to show the nation's brow pure and luminous, as it is; to prove that our people think neither in a fanatical nor a reactionary manner.

Gentlemen, at the same time the new laws were worked out and decreed which promise the most fruitful results for the nation on the social and economic plane, and in general in all the forms of the expression of human activity . . . the Citizens' Legal Code which ensures the liberty of women and stabilizes the existence of the family.

Accordingly we made use of all circumstances only from one point of view, which consisted therein: to raise the nation on to that step on which it is justified in standing in the civilized world, to stabilize the Turkish Republic more and more on steadfast foundations . . . and in addition to destroy the spirit of despotism for ever.

---

[6]The fez was a brimless hat popular among Turkish men during the nineteenth century. Its lack of a brim allowed the wearer to touch his forehead to the ground while kneeling during prayer without removing the hat.

[7]Islamic religious orders.

[8]A dervish, or *darvish,* was a member of an Islamic sect famous for its whirling dances that symbolized the movement of the heavenly spheres. An Occultist was a Sufi who

achieved a state of withdrawal from the world. A mausoleum guard guarded the tomb of a saint or holy person.

[9]A *dede* was the head of a Sufi order. *Seids,* or *sayyids,* were descendants of the prophet Muhammad through his daughter Fatima. *Baba* was a popular surname among Sufi preachers. In this context, emir is an honorary Turkish title.

[10]People who told the future by reading palms.

The Meaning of Zionism

◆

51 ◆ *Hayyim Nahman Bialik,*
SPEECH AT THE INAUGURATION OF THE
HEBREW UNIVERSITY OF JERUSALEM

After their exile from Palestine by Roman authorities in 70 C.E., Jews resettled in other parts of the Middle East, North Africa, Europe, and years later the Americas. Wherever they went, they were a tiny minority in predominantly Muslim or Christian societies and were often victims of persecution. In all these years, they retained a strong attachment to the "Land of Canaan" in Palestine, which, according to their scriptures, God had given them as their promised land after they had become God's "chosen people." Only in the late nineteenth century, however, in the face of mounting antisemitism in Europe, especially in Russia, where a majority of Europe's Jews lived, did some Jewish intellectuals and religious leaders conclude that Jews could escape persecution and preserve their traditions only if they had their own homeland in Palestine. This Jewish nationalist movement came to be known as Zionism, derived from Mount Zion, one of the two major hills overlooking Jerusalem, the capital of the ancient Jewish kingdom and the site of the temple destroyed by the Romans in 70 C.E.

Although the first advocates of Jewish resettlement in Palestine were Russian Jews reacting to anti-Jewish pogroms in the 1880s, political Zionism, which specifically advocates the foundation of a Jewish state, dates from 1896, when the Vienna-based journalist Theodor Herzl published his book *Der Judenstaat* (The Jewish State), and 1897, when he convened the first international Zionist Congress in Basel, Switzerland. Despite the indifference and outright opposition to Zionism on the part of many assimilated Jews in Western Europe, and despite bitter disputes among Zionists themselves over their visions of a future Jewish state, on the eve of World War I approximately ninety thousand Jews lived in Palestine, almost half of whom were recent immigrants from Europe.

Prospects for Jewish migration to Palestine improved when the British took control of Palestine as a League of Nations mandate after World War I. During the war, Britain's foreign minister, Arthur Balfour, in what came to be known as the Balfour Declaration, committed his government to facilitating "the establishment in Palestine of a national home for the Jewish people." This was a wartime promise the British kept. Under the British mandate, the number of Jews in Palestine increased, especially after the Nazis took control of Germany in 1933. Between 1919 and 1939, the percentage of Jews in Palestine's population grew from slightly under 10 percent to slightly more than 30 percent. These Jews purchased land, established industries, and provided a basis for the growth of Jewish culture in the area through the founding of the Hebrew University of Jerusalem and a technical institute in Haifa in 1925. Despite the opposition of Palestinian Arabs, the Zionists' dreams were becoming a reality. In 1947 the independent state of Israel was born.

The Zionists' hopes and expectations are captured in the following speech delivered by Hayyim Nahman Bialik at the opening of the Hebrew University of Jerusalem in 1925. Born in 1873 in Ukraine, Bialik, after receiving a traditional Jewish education and working briefly as a businessman and as a Hebrew language teacher, became one of the most prominent modern poets and short story writers in Hebrew and Yiddish. In his work he explores the tensions between the Jews' historical experience, especially their persecution, and the modern world. A strong supporter of Zionism, he received permission to leave the Soviet Union in 1921 and settled in Palestine in 1924. He died in 1934 in Vienna, where he had gone for medical treatment, and was buried in Tel Aviv.

In his 1925 speech he describes the Jewish resettlement of Palestine as a historic turning point — not just for the Jews but potentially for all humanity.

QUESTIONS FOR ANALYSIS

1. According to Bialik, why have education and study played such an important role in Jewish history?
2. Why does Bialik feel so strongly about the need of the Jews to have their own state?
3. What in particular does he deplore about the Jews' experience during the diaspora?
4. How does Bialik view the Jews' historic contributions to human culture?
5. What kind of vision does Bialik have for an independent Jewish state? Is his vision shaped primarily by religious or secular concerns?

The solemnity and exaltation of this moment can only be desecrated by any sort of exaggeration. . . . I am sure that the eyes of tens of thousands of Israel that are lifted from all parts of the Diaspora to this hill are shining with hope and comfort; their hearts and their flesh are singing a blessing of thanksgiving unto the Living God Who hath preserved us and sustained us and let us live to see this hour. They all realize that at this moment Israel has kindled . . . the first candle of the renaissance of her intellectual life. . . .

For let people say what they may: This peculiar people called Israel has, despite all the vicissitudes which for two thousand years have daily, yea hourly, attempted to expel it from its own milieu and uproot it from its spiritual climate — this people, I assert, has accepted upon its body and soul the burden of eternal allegiance to the Kingdom of the Spirit. Within that Kingdom it recognizes itself as a creative citizen and in that eternal soil it has planted its feet with all its might for all time. All the sordidness of the accursed Galut[1] and all the pain of our people's poverty did not disfigure its fundamental nature. . . . Within the boundaries of the realm of the Spirit the Jewish nation fashioned the bases of its national heritage and its principal national institutions. These preserved it through millennia of wandering, safeguarded its inner freedom amid outward bondage and have led up to this joyful event. . . . The

---

[1] Hebrew for exile.

national school in all its forms — the *heder,* the *yeshivah,* the *betmidrash*[2] — these have been our securest strongholds throughout our long, hard struggle for existence, and for the right to exist, in the world as a separate and distinct people among the peoples. In times of tempest and wrath we took refuge within the walls of these fortresses, where we polished the only weapon we had left — the Jewish mind — lest it become rusty. . . .

Ladies and Gentlemen! You all know what has become of our old spiritual strongholds in the Diaspora in recent times and I need not dwell upon this theme now. For all their inner strength, and for all the energy the nation had expended upon creating and preserving these centers, they stood not firm on the day of wrath; by the decree of history they are crumbled and razed to the foundations and our people is left standing empty-handed upon their ruins.[3] This is the very curse of the Galut, that our undertakings do not, indeed cannot, prosper. In every land and in every age we have been sowing a bushel and reaping less than a peck. The winds and hurricanes of history always begin by attacking the creating of Israel and, in a moment, uproot and utterly destroy that which hands and minds have produced over a period of generations. Through cruel and bitter trials and tribulations, through blasted hopes and despair of the soul, through innumerable humiliations, we have slowly arrived at the realization that without a tangible homeland, without private national premises that are entirely ours, we can have no sort of a life, either material or spiritual. Without Eretz Israel — Eretz means land, literally land — there is no hope for the rehabilitation of Israel anywhere, ever. . . .

We have come to the conclusion that a people that aspires to a dignified existence must create a culture; it is not enough merely to make use of a culture — a people must create its own, with its own hands and its own implements and materials, and impress it with its own seal. Of course our people in its "diasporas" is creating culture. . . . But as whatever the Jew creates in the Diaspora is always absorbed in the culture of others, it loses its identity and is never accounted to the credit of the Jew. . . . The Jewish people is therefore in a painfully false position: Whereas its true function culturally is that of a proletariat — i.e., it produces with the materials and implements of others for others — it is regarded by others, and at times even by itself, as a cultural parasite, possessing nothing of its own. A self-respecting people will never become reconciled to such a lot; it is bound to arise one day and resolve: No more. Better a little that is undisputedly my own than much that is not definitely either mine or somebody else's. Better a dry crust in my own home and on my own table than a stall-fed ox in the home of others and on the table of others. Better one little university but entirely my own, entirely my handiwork from foundations to coping stones,[4] than thousands of temples of learning from which I derive benefit but in which I have no recognized share. Let my food be little and bitter as the olive, if I may but taste in it the delicious flavor of a gift from myself.

It was in this frame of mind that we took refuge in this land. We are not come here to seek wealth, or dominion, or greatness. How much of these can this poor little country give us? We wish to find here only a domain of our own for our physical and intellectual labor. . . . Already at this early hour we experience cultural needs that cannot be postponed and must be satisfied at once. Besides, we are burdened with heavy cares for the cultural fate of our people in

---

[2]These are schools in the traditional Jewish educational system. *Heder* is an elementary school; *yeshiva* is a higher academy of religious studies; *betmidrash* is a house of learning in which advanced students can pursue studies of sacred literature.

[3]The reference is to the destruction of Jewish schools during pogroms.
[4]Stones having special shapes for use in capping the exposed top of a wall.

the Diaspora. Nations born only yesterday foolishly imagine that through intellectual parching,[5] by means of a *numerus clausus*,[6] they can do to death an old nation with a past of four thousand years of Torah.[7] We must therefore hasten to light here the first lamp of learning and science and of every sort of intellectual activity in Israel, ere the last lamp grows dark for us in foreign lands. . . .

Ladies and Gentlemen! Thousands of our youth, obeying the call of their hearts, are streaming from the four corners of the earth to this land for the purpose of redeeming it from desolation and ruin. They are prepared to pour all their aspirations and longings and to empty all the strength of their youth into the bosom of this wasteland in order to revive it. They are plowing rocks, draining swamps, and building roads amid singing and rejoicing. These young people know how to raise simple and crude labor — physical labor — to the level of highest sanctity, to the level of religion. . . . Let those youths build the Earthly Jerusalem with fire and let them who work within these walls build the Heavenly Jerusalem with fire, and between them let them build and establish our House of Life.

Four thousand years ago there gathered in this land . . . some groups of wandering shepherds divided into a number of tribes. They became in time, in consequence of events of apparently no great importance, a people small and poor in its day — the people Israel. Few and unhappy were the days of this people on its land as "a people dwelling apart, not counted among the nations." But this people produced men . . . like their brethren — who carried the tempest of the spirit of God in their hearts and His earthquakes and thunders in their mouths. Those men . . . dared to turn to eternity, to the Heavens and to the Earth. And it was they who in the end provided the foundation for the religious and moral culture of the world. . . . After the proclamation of Cyrus,[8] some tens of thousands of exiles rallied again to this poor, waste country and again formed a poor small community, even poorer and smaller than the first. After only some three hundred years, there arose again in this land a man of Israel, the son of an Israelite carpenter,[9] who conveyed the gospel of salvation to the pagan world and cleared the way for the days of the Messiah. Since then two thousand years have elapsed, and we are all witnesses this day that idols have not yet disappeared from the face of the earth; the place of the old has been taken by new ones, no better than the former. And then came the Balfour Declaration. Israel is assembling in Eretz Israel for a third time. Why should not the miracle be repeated again this time? . . .

Who knows but that the task in which great nations have failed amid the tumult of wealth may be achieved by a poor people in its small country? Who knows but in the end of days this doctrine of responsibility for the fate of humanity may go forth from its house of learning and spread to all the people? Surely not for nothing has the hand of God led this people for four thousand years through the pangs of hell and now brought it back unto its land for the third time.

The Books of Chronicles,[10] the last of the Scriptures, are not the last in this history of Israel. To its two small parts there will be added a third, perhaps more important than the first two. And . . . the third will undoubtedly begin with the Proclamation of Balfour and end with a new gospel, the gospel of redemption to the whole of humanity.

---

[5]*Parch* means "to dry up or shrivel."

[6]The reference is to the quota system adopted by universities in Europe to limit Jewish enrollment.

[7]The body of wisdom and law contained in Jewish Scripture, other sacred literature, and oral tradition.

[8]Cyrus the Great, king of Persia (599–530 B.C.E.), after conquering Babylonia in 539 B.C.E., freed the Jewish captives in Babylonia and allowed them to return to Jerusalem. He also approved the rebuilding of the Jewish temple.

[9]A reference to Jesus.

[10]The two Books of Chronicles, part of the Jewish Bible, recount history from Adam to the time of Cyrus the Great.

A Call for Islamic Social and Political Action

❖

52 ◆ *The Muslim Brotherhood, TOWARD THE LIGHT*

Although the commitment to modernization advocated by Mustafa Kemal had many supporters throughout the Middle East, it also had staunch opponents. Many Muslims — from all classes of society and across all educational levels — were troubled by the prospect of a secularized, Westernized future and sought instead to establish a true Islamic society guided by the Quran and Islamic law. In the interwar years their hopes were best represented by the Muslim Brotherhood, an organization founded in 1929 by an Egyptian schoolteacher, Hasan al-Banna (1906–1949).

Born in a small town in the Nile Delta, Hasan al-Banna as a student in Cairo after World War I was troubled by the factionalism, social conflict, poverty, and religious indifference he observed in Egypt. He concluded that British colonialism and the widespread acceptance of Western values had caused these ills and that a return to fundamental Islamic teachings would cure them. In 1927 he became a schoolteacher in the Sinai town of Ismailia, where he organized religious study groups and committed himself to Islamic renewal. In 1929 he founded the Muslim Brotherhood, an organization dedicated to the realization of Islamic states in Egypt and other Muslim lands.

In the 1930s the Brotherhood grew into a tightly knit, disciplined organization with approximately a million members. It built mosques, schools, and small hospitals; sponsored youth programs, social clubs, and handicraft industries; and promoted its religious message through preaching, books, and pamphlets. In the 1940s, the organization's increasing political activism led to clashes with British authorities and the Egyptian government itself. Linked to the assassination of several officials, the Brotherhood was outlawed by the Egyptian government in 1949, the same year Hasan al-Banna was assassinated by Egyptian agents.

The Brotherhood was legalized in Egypt in 1950, and since then it has continued to be an important religious and political force in the Arab world. It has branches in Sudan, Syria, and other Arab states; vast financial resources; and an estimated membership of two million. It has accomplished this despite attempts by the Egyptian government to suppress the organization on two occasions in the 1950s and 1960s after members of the Brotherhood were implicated in attempted assassinations and antigovernment conspiracies. The organization also faced internal divisions between militants and moderates. In Egypt, the Brotherhood officially rejected violence in the 1980s and sought to advance its program by winning elected offices and increasing its commitment to social service activities. This official endorsement of moderation caused defections to more militant groups. Islamic Jihad and Hamas, organizations committed to Palestinian liberation and opposed to any compromise with Israel, are both offshoots of the Muslim Brotherhood.

The following excerpt is drawn from a pamphlet issued by the Brotherhood in 1936 and directed to King Faruq of Egypt and other Arab leaders. It summarizes the major goals of the Brotherhood in its first decade of existence.

QUESTIONS FOR ANALYSIS

1. How would you characterize the views of the Brotherhood concerning the purpose and goals of government?
2. According to this document, what is the Brotherhood's conception of the ideal government official?
3. What does the document reveal about the attitude of the Brotherhood toward the West? Are there aspects of Western culture the Brotherhood finds acceptable?
4. What role does the Brotherhood envision for women in Islamic society?
5. According to the Brotherhood, what should be the content and goals of education?
6. What policies does the Brotherhood support to help the poor?
7. What is there in the statement that helps account for the widespread support of the Brotherhood within Middle Eastern Islamic societies?

After having studied the ideals which ought to inspire a renascent nation on the spiritual level, we wish to offer, in conclusion, some practical suggestions. We will list here only the chapter headings because we know very well that each suggestion will require profound study as well as the special attention of experts; we know also that the needs of the nation are enormous; we do not believe that the fulfilling of the needs and the aspirations of the country will be an easy thing; what is more, we do not think that these goals can be reached in one journey or two. We realize the obstacles which these problems must overcome. The task will require a great deal of patience, a great deal of ability, and a willing tenacity.

But one thing is certain: resolve will lead to success. A dedicated nation, working to accomplish the right, will certainly reach, with God's help, the goals toward which it strives.

The following are the chapter headings for a reform based upon the true spirit of Islam:

I. In the political, judicial, and administrative fields:

1st. To prohibit political parties and to direct the forces of the nation toward the formation of a united front;

2nd. To reform the law in such a way that it will be entirely in accordance with Islamic legal practice;

3rd. To build up the army, to increase the number of youth groups; to instill in youth the spirit of holy struggle, faith, and self-sacrifice;

4th. To strengthen the ties among Islamic countries and more particularly among Arab countries which is a necessary step toward serious examination of the question of the defunct Caliphate,[1]

5th. To propagate an Islamic spirit within the civil administration so that all officials will understand the need for applying the teachings of Islam;

6th. To supervise the personal conduct of officials because the private life and the administrative life of these officials forms an indivisible whole;

7th. To advance the hours of work in summer and in winter so that the accomplishment of religious obligations will be eased and to prevent all useless staying up late at night;

8th. To condemn corruption and influence peddling; to reward only competence and merit;

---

[1] The office of caliph, the successor of Muhammad and head of the Muslim community, had been held by the Ottoman sultans but was abolished by Mustafa Kemal in 1924.

9th.   Government will act in conformity to the law and to Islamic principles; the carrying out of ceremonies, receptions, and official meetings, as well as the administration of prisons and hospitals should not be contrary to Islamic teachings. The scheduling of government services ought to take account of the hours set aside for prayer.

10th.   To train and to use Azharis, that is to say, the graduates of Al-Azhar University,[2] for military and civil roles;

II.   In the fields of social and everyday practical life:

1st.   The people should respect public mores: this ought to be the object of special attention — to strongly condemn attacks upon public mores and morality;

2nd.   To find a solution for the problems of women, a solution that will allow her to progress and which will protect her while conforming to Islamic principles. This very important social question should not be ignored because it has become the subject of polemics and of more or less unsupported and exaggerated opinion;

3rd.   To root out clandestine or public prostitution and to consider fornication as a reprehensible crime the authors of which should be punished;

4th.   To prohibit all games of chance (gaming, lotteries, races, golf);

5th.   To stop the use of alcohol and intoxicants — these obliterate the painful consequences of people's evil deeds;

6th.   To stop attacks on modesty, to educate women, to provide quality education for female teachers, school pupils, students, and doctors;

7th.   To prepare instructional programs for girls; to develop an educational program for girls different than the one for boys;

8th.   Male students should not be mixed with female students — any relationship between unmarried men and women is considered to be wrong until it is approved;

9th.   To encourage marriage and procreation — to develop legislation to safeguard the family and to solve marriage problems;

10th.   To close dance halls; to forbid dancing;

11th.   To censor theater productions and films; to be severe in approving films;

12th.   To supervise and approve music;

13th.   To approve programs, songs, and subjects before they are released, to use radio to encourage national education;

14th.   To confiscate malicious articles and books as well as magazines displaying a grotesque character or spreading frivolity;

15th.   To carefully organize vacation centers;

16th.   To change the hours when public cafes are opened or closed, to watch the activities of those who habituate them — to direct these people towards wholesome pursuits, to prevent people from spending too much time in these cafes;

17th.   To use the cafes as centers to teach reading and writing to illiterates, to seek help in this task from primary school teachers and students;

18th.   To combat the bad practices which are prejudicial to the economy and to the morale of the nation, to direct the people toward good customs and

---

[2]An educational institution in Cairo specializing in Islamic studies.

praiseworthy projects such as marriage, orphanages, births, and festivals; the government should provide the example for this;

19th. To bring to trial those who break the laws of Islam, who do not fast, who do not pray, and who insult religion;

20th. To transfer village primary schools to the mosque and to carry on all beneficial activities there (selecting officers, matters of health, interested support for young children learning their religious duties, introducing the old to science);

21st. Religious teaching should constitute the essential subject matter to be taught in all educational establishments and faculties;

22nd. To memorize the Quran in state schools — this condition will be essential in order to obtain diplomas with a religious or philosophical specialty — in every school students should learn part of the Quran;

23rd. To develop a policy designed to raise the level of teaching, to unify the different teaching specialties, to bring together the different branches of culture — emphasis should be put upon teaching morality and physics;

24th. Interested support for teaching the Arabic language in all grades — absolute priority to be given to Arabic over foreign languages (primary teaching);

25th. To study the history of Islam, the nation, and Muslim civilization;

26th. To study the best way to allow people to dress progressively and in an identical manner;

27th. To combat foreign customs (in the realm of vocabulary, customs, dress,

nursing) and to Egyptianize all of these (one finds these customs among the well-to-do members of society);

28th. To orient journalism toward wholesome things, to encourage writers and authors, who should study specifically Muslim and Oriental[3] subjects;

29th. To safeguard public health through every kind of publicity — increasing the number of hospitals, doctors, and out-patient clinics;

30th. To call particular attention to the problems of village life (administration, hygiene, water supply, education, recreation, morality).

III. The economic field:

1st. Organization of the zakat tax[4] according to Islamic precepts, using zakat proceeds for welfare projects such as aiding the indigent, the poor, orphans; the zakat should also be used to strengthen the army;

2nd. To prevent the practice of usury, to direct banks to implement this policy; the government should provide an example by giving up the interest fixed by banks for servicing a personal loan or an industrial loan, etc.;

3rd. To facilitate and to increase the number of economic enterprises and to employ the jobless there, to employ for the nation's benefit the skills possessed by the foreigners in these enterprises;

4th. To protect workers against monopoly companies, to require these companies to obey the law, the public should share in all profits;

5th. Aid for low-ranking employees and enlargement of their pay, lowering the income of high-ranking employees; . . .

---

[3] As opposed to Western studies.
[4] A fixed share of income or property that all Muslims must pay as a tax or as charity for the welfare of the needy.

7th. To encourage agricultural and industrial works, to improve the situation
of the peasants and industrial workers;

8th. To give special attention to the technical and social needs of the workers,
to raise their level of life and aid
their class;

9th. Utilization of certain natural resources (unworked land, neglected
mines; etc.);

10th. To give priority to projects whose
accomplishment is vital to the
country.

◆

Anticolonialism in India and Southeast Asia

During the late nineteenth century, at a time when many Indians were already debating their colonial relationship with Great Britain and some were demanding independence, Southeast Asians were just beginning to experience the full effects of direct European rule. Nevertheless, developments in both areas between the two world wars showed some marked similarities. In India and Southeast Asia alike, nationalism became a potent force, shaking the foundations of Europe's colonial empires.

Indian nationalism in the 1920s and 1930s under the leadership of Mohandas Gandhi was transformed from an ideology of the educated elite into a mass movement. Despite differences in religion, education, and caste status, millions of Indians marched, demonstrated, boycotted British goods, and refused to obey British-imposed laws in an effort to force the British to "quit India" and to achieve Indian self-rule. The British responded with minor concessions but mostly with delaying tactics and armed repression.

Nationalist movements also intensified in Southeast Asia between the wars, but their strength, priorities, and tactics varied widely across a region marked by many ethnic, cultural, and political differences and by dissimilar styles of Western rule. Nationalism was weakest in areas such as the British-controlled Malay States and the French protectorates in Laos and Cambodia, where traditional rulers were retained and little economic modernization or urbanization occurred. National-ism was strongest in the Dutch East Indies, Burma, and Vietnam, where Western economic penetration and direct rule disrupted traditional economic, political, and social relationships.

Drawing strength and inspiration from both Western ideologies and their own religious and cultural traditions, nationalist leaders formed political parties and attempted to broaden nationalism's appeal by using newspapers, magazines, and the radio. Without exception, however, armed rebellions failed. Communist-inspired uprisings in Indonesia in 1926 and 1927 were crushed by the Dutch; so too was the anti-French mutiny led by the Vietnamese Nationalist Party in 1930.

These failures resulted in part from the colonial powers' superior military strength and in part from divisions within the nationalist movements. Western-educated intellectuals and politicians argued among themselves over political doc-trine, and founded a plethora of political parties to represent different ideologies.

Conflicting regional loyalties and disagreements between secularized, European-ized leaders and those with traditional religious views also weakened nationalist movements. Even Gandhi was unable to prevent the splintering of Indian nation-alism into antagonistic Muslim and Hindu camps on the eve of World War II.

Interwar nationalist movements in India and Southeast Asia prepared the groundwork for independence after World War II. They also foretold the conflicts and divisions that would plague the new states of the region once independence had been achieved.

Gandhi's Hopes for India

❖

53 ◆ Mohandas Gandhi, *INDIAN HOME RULE*

Mohandas Gandhi, the outstanding figure in modern Indian history, was born in 1869 in a village north of Bombay on the Arabian Sea. His father was a prominent government official who presided over an extended family devoted to strict Hindu practices. Gandhi studied law in England and, after failing to establish a law practice in Bombay, moved to South Africa in 1893 to serve the Indian population.

In South Africa he became incensed over discriminatory laws against Indian settlers, most of whom were indentured servants, laborers, or small merchants. In his efforts to improve the lot of South Africa's Indians, Gandhi developed his doc-trine of *satyagraha,* usually translated as "soul force." *Satyagraha* sought social justice not through violence but through love, noncompliance to unjust laws, a willingness to suffer, and conversion of the oppressor. Central to its strategy was nonviolent resistance: Gandhi's followers disobeyed unjust laws and accepted the consequences — even beatings and imprisonment — to reach the hearts of the British and change their thinking.

In 1915 Gandhi at the age of forty-five returned to India, where he spent his remaining thirty-three years. By 1920, he was the dominant figure in the Congress Party, which under his leadership launched a noncooperation campaign against British rule between 1920 and 1922. When in 1922 villagers attacked and killed twenty-one policemen and rural watchmen, Gandhi called off the noncooperation campaign, but he continued the tactic of civil disobedience, organizing boycotts of British goods and leading protest marches against unpopular British measures such as the salt tax in 1930. Living a life of self-imposed chastity and poverty, he wrote letters, pamphlets, and books and delivered speeches in every corner of India denouncing British rule and urging Indians to address their own society's ills, especially the treatment of women and untouchables. During the 1930s and the war years, his attacks on British rule intensified, and along with other Con-gress leaders he spent months in jail. As independence approached, he struggled to preserve Hindu-Muslim cooperation and prevent the partition of the nation into a predominantly Muslim Pakistan and a predominantly Hindu India. On Jan-uary 30, 1948, just over four months after Indian and Pakistani independence,

Gandhi was shot and killed by a Hindu zealot who resented Gandhi's commitment to Hindu-Muslim harmony.

The following selection is taken from *Hind Swaraj* (Indian Home Rule), a pamphlet Gandhi wrote in 1908 after meeting with a group of Indian nationalists in England who urged the use of force to oust the British from India. Although written early in his political career and well before he emerged as India's inspirational leader, it contains ideas and principles that guided Gandhi throughout his life. Composed in the form of a dialogue between a reader and an editor (Gandhi), *Indian Home Rule* appeared in hundreds of editions and remains his most widely read work.

QUESTIONS FOR ANALYSIS

1. What does Gandhi see as the major deficiencies of modern civilization?
2. How, according to Gandhi, has modern civilization affected women?
3. What is the basis for Gandhi's faith that Hindus and Muslims will be able to live together in peace in India?
4. What, according to Gandhi, is true civilization, and what is India's role in preserving it?
5. What leads Gandhi to conclude that love is stronger than force?
6. In your view, why did Gandhi's attack on civilization win him support among India's masses?

CIVILIZATION

READER: Now you will have to explain what you mean by civilization. . . .

EDITOR: Let us first consider what state of things is described by the word "civilization." Its true test lies in the fact that people living in it make bodily welfare the object of life. We will take some examples: The people of Europe today live in better-built houses than they did a hundred years ago. This is considered an emblem of civilization, and this is also a matter to promote bodily happiness. Formerly, they wore skins, and used as their weapons spears. Now, they wear long trousers, and for embellishing their bodies they wear a variety of clothing, and, instead of spears, they carry with them revolvers containing five or more chambers. If people of a certain country, who have hitherto not been in the habit of wearing much clothing, boots, etc., adopt European clothing, they are supposed to have become civilized out of savagery. Formerly, in Europe, people plowed their lands mainly by manual labor. Now, one man can plow a vast tract by means of steam-engines, and can thus amass great wealth. This is called a sign of civilization. Formerly, the fewest men wrote books, that were most valuable. Now, anybody writes and prints anything he likes and poisons people's minds. Formerly, men traveled in wagons; now they fly through the air, in trains at the rate of four hundred and more miles per day. This is considered the height of civilization. It has been stated that, as men progress, they shall be able to travel in airships and reach any part of the world in a few hours. Men will not need the use of their hands and feet. They will press a button, and they will have their clothing by their side. They will press another button, and they will have their newspaper. A third, and a motor-car will be in waiting for them. They will have a variety of delicately dished up food. Everything will be done by machinery. Formerly, when people wanted to fight with one another, they measured between them their bodily strength; now it is possible to take away thousands of lives by one man working behind a gun from a hill. This is civilization. Formerly, men worked in the open air only so much as they liked. Now, thousands of workmen meet together and for the sake of maintenance work in factories or mines. Their condition is worse than that of beasts. They are obliged to work, at the risk of their lives, at most dangerous occupations, for the sake of millionaires. Formerly, men were made slaves under physical compulsion, now they are enslaved by temptation of money and of the luxuries that money can buy. There are now diseases of which people never dreamed before, and an army of doctors is engaged in finding out their cures, and so hospitals have increased. This is a test of civilization. Formerly, special messengers were required and much expense was incurred in order to send letters; today, anyone can abuse his fellow by means of a letter for one penny. True, at the same cost, one can send one's thanks also. Formerly, people had two or three meals consisting of homemade bread and vegetables; now, they require something to eat every two hours, so that they have hardly leisure for anything else. What more need I say? . . .

This civilization is irreligion, and it has taken such a hold on the people in Europe that those who are in it appear to be half mad. They lack real physical strength or courage. They keep up their energy by intoxication. They can hardly be happy in solitude. Women, who should be the queens of households, wander in the streets, or they slave away in factories. For the sake of a pittance, half a million women in England alone are laboring under trying circumstances in factories or similar institutions. This awful fact is one of the causes of the daily growing suffragette movement.

This civilization is such that one has only to be patient and it will be destroyed.

THE CONDITION OF INDIA (CONTINUED)

The Hindus and the Muslims

READER: But I am impatient to hear your answer to my question. Has the introduction of Islam not unmade the nation?

EDITOR: India cannot cease to be one nation because people belonging to different religions live in it. The introduction of foreigners does not necessarily destroy the nation, they merge in it. A country is one nation only when such a condition obtains in it. That country must have a faculty for assimilation. India has ever been such a country. In reality, there are as many religions as there are individuals, but those who are conscious of the spirit of nationality do not interfere with one another's religion. If they do, they are not fit to be considered a nation. If the Hindus believe that India should be peopled only by Hindus, they are living in dreamland. The Hindus, the Muslims, the Parsees[1] and the Christians who have made India their country are fellow-countrymen, and they will have to live in unity if only for their own interest. In no part of the world are one nationality and one religion synonymous terms; nor has it ever been so in India.

READER: But what about the inborn enmity between Hindus and Muslims?

EDITOR: That phrase has been invented by our mutual enemy.[2] When the Hindus and Muslims fought against one another, they certainly spoke in that strain. They have long since ceased to fight. How, then, can there be any inborn enmity? Pray remember this too, that we did not cease to fight only after British occupation. The Hindus flourished under Muslim sovereigns and Muslims under the Hindu. Each party recognized that mutual fighting was suicidal, and

[1]Disciples of the Zoroastrian religion in India who descended from Persian refugees of the seventh and eighth centuries.

[2]The British.

that neither party would abandon its religion by force of arms. Both parties, therefore, decided to live in peace. With the English advent the quarrels recommenced. . . .

Hindus and Muslims own the same ancestors, and the same blood runs through their veins. Do people become enemies because they change their religion? Is the God of the Muslim different from the God of the Hindu? Religions are different roads converging to the same point. What does it matter that we take different roads, so long as we reach the same goal? . . .

WHAT IS TRUE CIVILIZATION?

READER: You have denounced railways, lawyers and doctors. I can see that you will discard all machinery. What, then, is civilization?

EDITOR: The answer to that question is not difficult. I believe that the civilization India has evolved is not to be beaten in the world. Nothing can equal the seeds sown by our ancestors. Rome went, Greece shared the same fate, the might of the Pharaohs was broken, Japan has become westernized, of China nothing can be said, but India is still, somehow or other, sound at the foundation. . . . India remains immovable, and that is her glory. It is a charge against India that her people are so uncivilized, ignorant, and stolid, that it is not possible to induce them to adopt any changes. It is a charge really against our merit. What we have tested and found true on the anvil of experience, we dare not change. . . .

Civilization is that mode of conduct which points out to man the path of duty. Performance of duty and observance of morality are convertible terms. To observe morality is to attain mastery over our mind and our passions. So doing, we know ourselves. The Gujarati[3] equivalent for civilization means "good conduct."

If this definition be correct, then India, as so many writers have shown, has nothing to learn from anybody else, and this is as it should be.

PASSIVE RESISTANCE

READER: Is there any historical evidence as to the success of what you have called soul-force or truth-force? No instance seems to have happened of any nation having risen through soul-force. I still think that the evil-doers will not cease doing evil without physical punishment.

EDITOR: . . . The force of love is the same as the force of the soul or truth. We have evidence of its working at every step. The universe would disappear without the existence of that force. . . .

Thousands, indeed, tens of thousands, depend for their existence on a very active working of this force. Little quarrels of millions of families in their daily lives disappear before the exercise of this force. Hundreds of nations live in peace. History does not and cannot take note of this fact. History is really a record of every interruption of the even working of the force of love or of the soul. . . . Soul-force, being natural, is not noted in history.

READER: According to what you say, it is plain that instances of the kind of passive resistance are not to be found in history. It is necessary to understand this passive resistance more fully. It will be better, therefore, if you enlarge upon it.

EDITOR: Passive resistance is a method of securing rights by personal suffering; it is the reverse of resistance by arms. When I refuse to do a thing that is repugnant to my conscience, I use soul-force. For instance, the government of the day has passed a law which is applicable to me: I do not like it; if, by using violence, I force the government to repeal the law, I am employing what may be termed body-force. If I do not obey the law and accept the penalty for its breach, I use soul-force. It involves sacrifice of self.

Everybody admits that sacrifice of self is infinitely superior to sacrifice of others. Moreover, if this kind of force is used in a cause that is unjust, only the person using it suffers. He does not make others suffer for his mistakes. . . .

---

[3]An Indian dialect spoken in Gujarat, in northwest India.

READER: From what you say, I deduce that passive resistance is a splendid weapon of the weak but that, when they are strong, they may take up arms.

EDITOR: This is gross ignorance. Passive resistance, that is, soul-force, is matchless. It is superior to the force of arms. How, then, can it be considered only a weapon of the weak? Physical-force men are strangers to the courage that is requisite in a passive resister. . . .

What do you think? Wherein is courage required — in blowing others to pieces from behind a cannon or with a smiling face to approach a cannon and to be blown to pieces? Who is the true warrior — he who keeps death always as a bosom-friend or he who controls the death of others? Believe me that a man devoid of courage and manhood can never be a passive resister.

This, however, I will admit: that even a man, weak in body, is capable of offering this resistance. One man can offer it just as well as millions. Both men and women can indulge in it. It does not require the training of an army; it needs no Jiu-jitsu. Control over the mind is alone necessary, and, when that is attained, man is free like the king of the forest, and his very glance withers the enemy.

Passive resistance is an all-sided sword; it can be used anyhow; it blesses him who uses it and him against whom it is used. Without drawing a drop of blood, it produces far-reaching results.

A Muslim's View of India's Future

❖

54 ◆ Muhammad Ali Jinnah, *SPEECH TO THE MUSLIM LEAGUE, 1940*

Muhammad Ali Jinnah (1876–1948), the leader of India's Muslims between the wars and the founder of the state of Pakistan, was raised in Lahore in modern Pakistan, where his father was a successful businessman. A brilliant and prosperous lawyer who had studied in London and dressed like an English gentleman, Jinnah joined the Indian National Congress in 1906 and the Muslim League in 1913. For several years he served as a liaison between the two organizations, but in 1920 he resigned from the Congress because of his opposition to Gandhi's civil disobedience campaign and Gandhi's refusal to support the concept of weighted voting rights for India's Muslim minority. Nonetheless, during the 1920s and early 1930s Jinnah continued to work for cooperation between Hindus and Muslims to further the cause of Indian independence.

In the late 1930s, however, chronic disagreements between Hindus and Muslims and mounting communal violence convinced Jinnah that Muslims had no future in an independent India. He lent his support to the founding of an independent Muslim state, Pakistan, meaning "land of the pure." In 1947 his efforts were rewarded when, with the end of British rule in South Asia, not one new state, but two, India and Pakistan, were born. Jinnah served as Pakistan's first governor-general, a post he held for only a year before his death in 1948.

The following selection is from one of this most famous speeches, delivered to a meeting of the Muslim League in Lahore in 1940. On this occasion Jinnah expressed his support for the establishment of independent states in the northwestern and eastern parts of India where Muslims were the majority of the population.

QUESTIONS FOR ANALYSIS

1. What is the basis of Jinnah's objection to the statement he quotes from the London *Times*?
2. Why does Jinnah have so little hope that Hindus and Muslims will ever be able to live together peacefully in a united India?
3. What is the basis of Jinnah's assertion that Islam and Hinduism are "not religions in the strict sense of the word"?
4. How do Jinnah's views of Hindu-Muslim relations differ from those of Gandhi?
5. What is the basis of Jinnah's assertion that Muslims in India are "a nation according to any definition of a nation"?

A leading journal like the London *Times,* commenting on the Government of India Act of 1935, wrote: "Undoubtedly the differences between the Hindus and Muslims are not of religion in the strict sense of the word but also a law and culture, that they may be said, indeed, to represent two entirely distinct and separate civilizations. However, in the course of time, the superstition will die out and India will be molded into a single nation." So, according to the London *Times,* the only difficulties are superstitions. . . . But surely it is a flagrant disregard of the past history of the subcontinent of India as well as the fundamental Islamic conception of society vis-à-vis that of Hinduism to characterize them as mere "superstitions." Notwithstanding a thousand years of close contact, nationalities, which are as divergent today as ever, cannot at any time be expected to transform themselves into one nation merely by means of subjecting them to a democratic constitution and holding them forcibly together by unnatural and artificial methods of British parliamentary statute. What the unitary government of India for one hundred fifty years had failed to achieve cannot be realized by the imposition of a central federal government. . . .

. . . If the British government are really in earnest and sincere to secure [the] peace and happiness of the people of this subcontinent, the only course open to us all is to allow the major nations separate homelands by dividing India into "autonomous national states." There is no reason why these states should be antagonistic to each other. On the other hand, the rivalry and the natural desire and efforts on the part of one to dominate the social order and establish political supremacy over the other in the government of the country will disappear. It will lead more towards natural good will by international pacts between them, and they can live in complete harmony with their neighbors. . . .

It is extremely difficult to appreciate why our Hindu friends fail to understand the real nature of Islam and Hinduism. They are not religions in the strict sense of the word, but are, in fact, different and distinct social orders, and it is a dream that the Hindus and Muslims can ever evolve a common nationality, and this misconception of one Indian nation has gone far beyond the limits and is the cause of most of [our] troubles and will lead India to destruction if we fail to revise our notions in time. The Hindus and Muslims belong to two different religious philosophies, social customs, literatures. They neither intermarry nor interdine together and, indeed, they belong to two different civilizations which are based mainly on conflicting ideas and conceptions. . . . To yoke together two such nations under a single state, one as a numerical minority and the other as a majority, must lead to growing discontent and final destruction of any fabric that may be so built up for the government of such a state.

. . . History has also shown us many geographical tracts, much smaller than the subcontinent of India, which otherwise might have been called one country, but which have been divided into as many states as there are nations inhabiting them. [The] Balkan Peninsula comprises as many as seven or eight sovereign states. Likewise, the Portuguese and the Spanish stand divided in the Iberian Peninsula. Whereas under the plea of the unity of India and one nation, which does not exist, it is sought to pursue here the line of one central government, we know that the history of the last twelve hundred years has failed to achieve unity and has witnessed, during the ages, India always divided into Hindu India and Muslim India. The present artificial unity of India dates back only to the British conquest and is maintained by the British bayonet, but termination of the British regime, which is implicit in the recent declaration of His Majesty's government, will be the herald of the entire break-up with worse disaster than has ever taken place during the last one thousand years under Muslims. . . .

Muslim India cannot accept any constitution which must necessarily result in a Hindu majority government. Hindus and Muslims brought together under a democratic system forced upon the minorities can only mean Hindu rāj [rule]. Democracy of the kind with which the Congress

High Command is enamored would mean the complete destruction of what is most precious in Islam. We have had ample experience of the working of the provincial constitutions during the last two and a half years and any repetition of such a government must lead to civil war and raising of private armies. . . .

Mussalmans [Muslims] are a nation according to any definition of a nation, and they must have their homelands, their territory, and their state. We wish to live in peace and harmony with our neighbors as a free and independent people. We wish our people to develop to the fullest our spiritual, cultural, economic, social, and political life in a way that we think best and in consonance with our own ideals and according to the genius of our people. Honesty demands and the vital interests of millions of our people impose a sacred duty upon us to find an honorable and peaceful solution, which would be just and fair to all. But at the same time we cannot be moved or diverted from our purpose and objective by threats or intimidations. We must be prepared to face all difficulties and consequences, make all the sacrifices that may be required of us to achieve the goal we have set in front of us.

Revolution and Oppression in Vietnam

❖

55 ◆ Nguyen Thai Hoc, *LETTER TO THE FRENCH CHAMBER OF DEPUTIES, 1930*

Having seized Vietnam's three southernmost provinces, the region known as Cochin China, in 1862, the French extended their authority over Tongking (northern Vietnam) and Annam (central Vietnam) in the 1880s. Convinced of their civilizing mission, they sought to undermine Vietnam's Confucian culture by creating a French-trained Vietnamese elite willing to cooperate with the colonial regime. Although some members of Vietnam's upper class resisted French rule (including the young emperor Duy-tan, whose plot to overthrow the French was uncovered in 1916), most at first sought some sort of compromise between Western and Vietnamese culture and accepted French rule.

Accommodation and compromise gave way to revolutionary nationalism in the 1920s as a result of Vietnamese anger over continued economic exploitation and political oppression, despite the ninety thousand Vietnamese troops and laborers who had served in Europe during World War I. The leading nationalist organization was the Viet Nam Qoc Dan Dang (Vietnamese Nationalist Party, or VNQDD), founded in 1927 by Nguyen Thai Hoc, a teacher from Hanoi. At first he had moderate goals of more economic and educational opportunities for the Vietnamese, but he soon became disillusioned with French rule and turned to revolution. The VNQDD was modeled on Sun Yat-sen's Chinese Nationalist Party, or Guomindang, and was dedicated to achieving an independent and democratic-socialist Vietnam. In 1929, with its membership at about fifteen hundred and its leaders convinced that the general populace was ready for revolution, the VNQDD plotted an anti-French insurrection. The revolt, known as the Yen Bay uprising, was crushed by the French in 1930, and the VNQDD leaders were arrested and executed.

While awaiting execution, Nguyen Thai Hoc wrote the following letter to France's parliament, the Chamber of Deputies. A defense of his actions and a denunciation of French colonialism, the letter was also released to the Vietnamese public.

QUESTIONS FOR ANALYSIS

1. In Nguyen Thai Hoc's view, what are French intentions in Vietnam and what has been the effect of French occupation?
2. How and why did Nguyen Thai Hoc evolve from a moderate reformer to a revolutionary?
3. If they had been implemented, how would his suggestions to Governor General Varenne have improved the lot of the Vietnamese people?
4. What does the French response to the Yen Bay uprising reveal about the nature of French colonial rule?
5. What do you suppose Nguyen Thai Hoc hoped to accomplish by writing this letter?

Gentlemen: . . .

According to the tenets of justice, everyone has the right to defend his own country when it is invaded by foreigners, and according to the principles of humanity, everyone has the duty to save his compatriots when they are in difficulty or in danger. As for myself, I have assessed the fact that my country has been annexed by you French for more than sixty years. I realize that under your dictatorial yoke, my compatriots have experienced a very hard life, and my people

will without doubt be completely annihilated, by the naked principle of natural selection. Therefore, my right and my duty have compelled me to seek every way to defend my country which has been invaded and occupied, and to save my people who are in great danger.

At the beginning, I had thought to cooperate with the French in Indochina in order to serve my compatriots, my country and my people, particularly in the areas of cultural and economic development. As regards economic development, in 1925 I sent a memorandum to

Governor General Varenne,[1] describing to him all our aspirations concerning the protection of local industry and commerce in Indochina. I urged strongly in the same letter the creation of a Superior School of Industrial Development in Tongking. In 1926 I again addressed another letter to the then Governor General of Indochina in which I included some explicit suggestions to relieve the hardships of our poor people. In 1927, for a third time, I sent a letter to the Résident Supérieur[2] in Tongking, requesting permission to publish a weekly magazine with the aim of safeguarding and encouraging local industry and commerce. With regard to the cultural domain, I sent a letter to the Governor General in 1927, requesting (1) the privilege of opening tuition-free schools for the children of the lower classes, particularly children of workers and peasants; (2) freedom to open popular publishing houses and libraries in industrial centers.

It is absolutely ridiculous that every suggestion has been rejected. My letters were without answer; my plans have not been considered; my requests have been ignored; even the articles that I sent to newspapers have been censored and rejected. From the experience of these rejections, I have come to the conclusion that the French have no sincere intention of helping my country or my people. I also concluded that we have to expel France. For this reason, in 1927, I began to organize a revolutionary party, which I named the Vietnamese Nationalist Party, with the aim of overthrowing the dictatorial and oppressive administration in our country. We aspire to create a Republic of Vietnam, composed of persons sincerely concerned with the happiness of the people. My party is a clandestine organization, and in February 1929, it was uncovered by the security police. Among the members of my party, a great number have been arrested. Fifty-two persons have been condemned to forced labor ranging from two to twenty years. Although many have been detained and many others unjustly condemned, my party has not ceased its activity. Under my guidance, the Party continues to operate and progress towards its aim.

During the Yen Bay uprising someone succeeded in killing some French officers. The authorities accused my party of having organized and perpetrated this revolt. They have accused me of having given the orders for the massacre. In truth, I have never given such orders, and I have presented before the Penal Court of Yen Bay all the evidence showing the inanity of this accusation. Even so, some of the members of my party completely ignorant of that event have been accused of participating in it. The French Indochinese government burned and destroyed their houses. They sent French troops to occupy their villages and stole their rice to divide it among the soldiers. Not just members of my party have been suffering from this injustice — we should rather call this cruelty than injustice — but also many simple peasants, interested only in their daily work in the rice fields, living miserable lives like buffaloes and horses, have been compromised in this reprisal. At the present time, in various areas there are tens of thousands of men, women, and children, persons of all ages, who have been massacred.[3] They died either of hunger or exposure because the French Indochinese government burned their homes. I therefore beseech you in tears to redress this injustice which otherwise will annihilate my people, which will stain French honor, and which will belittle all human values.

I have the honor to inform you that I am responsible for all events happening in my country under the leadership of my party from 1927 until the present. You only need to execute me. I beg your indulgence for all the others who at the

---

[1] Alexandre Varenne was governor-general of Indochina from 1925 to 1929.
[2] In the French colonial hierarchy, the *résident-supérieur* of Tongking was the chief administrator of northern Vietnam.

[3] A substantial number of civilian deaths did occur as a result of French actions following the revolt, but Nguyen Thai Hoc's estimate of tens of thousand of deaths is an exaggeration.

present time are imprisoned in various jails. I am the only culprit, all the others are innocent. They are innocent because most of them are indeed members of my party, and have joined it only because I have succeeded in convincing them of their duties as citizens of this country, and of the humiliations of a slave with a lost country. Some of them are not even party members. . . . I have the honor to repeat once again that you need execute only me. If you are not satisfied with killing one man, I advise you to kill also the members of my family, but I strongly beg your indulgence towards those who are innocent.

Finally, I would like to declare in conclusion: if France wants to stay in peace in Indochina, if France does not want to have increasing troubles with revolutionary movements, she should immediately modify the cruel and inhuman policy now practiced in Indochina. The French should behave like friends to the Vietnamese, instead of being cruel and oppressive masters. They should be attentive to the intellectual and material sufferings of the Vietnamese people, instead of being harsh and tough.

Please, Gentlemen, receive my gratitude.

◆

Intellectual Ferment and Revolution in China

The overthrow of the Qing Dynasty in 1911 resulted not in China's long-awaited national revival, but instead in four decades of invasion, civil war, and immense suffering for the Chinese people. In the aftermath of the revolution, Sun Yat-sen and his dreams of a democratic China were pushed aside by General Yuan Shikai, who ruled the Chinese "republic" as a dictator between 1912 and 1916, and was planning to have himself declared emperor when he died in 1916. After his death, China was carved up by dozens of generally unscrupulous and irresponsible warlords, military men whose local authority was based on their control of private armies and whose grip on China was not completely broken until the Communists took power in 1949. With a weak national government, the Chinese endured continuing Western domination of their coastal cities, and offered only feeble resistance when the Japanese conquered Manchuria in 1931 and invaded China itself in 1937. Massive flooding of the Yellow River and widespread famine in north China in the 1920s compounded the people's misery.

The chaos of the 1920s and 1930s prompted an intense debate about China's future. The 1920s in particular were years of intellectual experimentation and inquiry, in which journalists, poets, writers of fiction, academics, and university students scrutinized what it meant to be Chinese and debated what would save China from catastrophe. Most of these intellectuals rejected traditional Chinese values, customs, and philosophical traditions, arguing that only a radical break from the past would allow China to become an equal of Japan and the West. Most turned to the West for inspiration, although they disagreed about what aspects of Western thought and values should be borrowed.

In politics, Chinese who grieved over warlord depredation, Western imperialism, and Japanese aggression had two options. Two revolutionary parties, — the

Nationalist Party, or Guomindang (GMD), and the Chinese Communist Party (CCP) — emerged, each of which sought to unify and govern China. The Guomindang, founded in 1912 by Sun Yat-sen, was theoretically dedicated to Sun's "three principles of the people" — democracy, nationalism, and livelihood — and came to be identified with the educated, Western-oriented bourgeoisie of China's coastal cities. In practice, under General Chiang Kai-shek (1887–1975) the Guomindang showed little enthusiasm for either social reform or democracy and concentrated mainly on fighting the warlords in the 1920s and the Communists in the 1930s. The Chinese Communist Party, founded in 1921, was dedicated to Marxism-Leninism, with its leadership provided by intellectuals and its major support eventually coming from the rural masses.

Aided by agents of the Soviet Union, the Guomindang and Communists formed a coalition in 1923 to rid China of its warlords. With their forces combined into the National Revolutionary Army, the Guomindang and their less numerous Communist allies launched the Northern Expedition against the warlords in 1926. The alliance lasted only until 1927, when Chiang Kai-shek, buoyed by early victories and generous financial support from Chinese businessmen, purged the Communists from the alliance and ordered his troops to kill Communist leaders who were gathered in Shanghai. Communist troops and their commanders fled to the countryside, where under the leadership of Mao Zedong (1893–1975), they rebuilt the party into a formidable military and political force. After a long struggle against the Guomindang and the Japanese, the Communists gained control of China in 1949.

The New Culture Movement and the West

❖

56 ◆ Hu Shi,
OUR ATTITUDE TOWARD MODERN CIVILIZATION OF THE WEST

The New Culture Movement, an outburst of literary activity and intellectual inquiry into China's past and future in the 1920s, is traditionally dated from May 4, 1919, when students from thirteen area colleges and universities met in Beijing and demonstrated against provisions of the Paris peace settlement that granted the former German concession in Shandong province to Japan. The events of May 4, however, only served to intensify and accelerate intellectual and literary developments that had begun several years earlier at Beijing University, where a number of young professors had begun to explore new intellectual and cultural paths for China after it jettisoned its Confucian past.

All intellectuals connected with the New Culture Movement looked to the West for guidance and inspiration, but none more so than Hu Shi (1891–1962), a professor of philosophy at Beijing University and one of the movement's leading figures. Born in Shanghai and raised by his mother in poverty after his father, a government official, died when he was four, Hu had an education that included the Confucian classics, English, and Western science. At the age of nineteen he received a scholarship to study at Cornell University, where he earned a bachelor's degree in philosophy, and later at Columbia University, where he worked toward his doctorate. On his return to China in 1917, he joined the Beijing University faculty. In his writings on philosophy, literature, and politics, he espoused Western pragmatism and science, and called on intellectuals to use vernacular Chinese rather than classical Chinese as a written language. After serving as ambassador to the United States between 1938 and 1943, he returned to China in 1946 to serve as chancellor of Beijing University. He fled China after the Communist victory in 1949, and lived in semiretirement in New York City until his death in 1962.

The following excerpt is taken from an essay written in 1926. In it, Hu answers his critics who had argued that traditional Chinese values were more humane and less materialistic than those of the West, and hence more beneficial to humankind's spiritual development.

QUESTIONS FOR ANALYSIS

1. How does Hu explain the attraction of condemning Western civilization for its materialism while praising Eastern civilization for its "spirituality"?
2. On what basis does Hu reject this argument?
3. What does Hu see as the major accomplishments of Western civilization?
4. What does Hu mean when he refers to the "new religion" developing in Western civilization?
5. In what ways do Hu's attitudes toward the West differ from those of Gandhi? How might one explain these differences?

[THE "MATERIALISM" OF WESTERN SOCIETIES]

One of the most baseless, most harmful statements has to do with the condemnation of Western civilization as "materialistic" and the praise of Oriental civilization as "spiritual." . . . In the past it was used to provide some kind of psychological lift, or self-congratulatory consolation, when we, the Oriental people, were cruelly oppressed and badly humiliated by the Occidentals. During the past few years when the Westerners themselves, in reaction to the disastrous World War I, became increasingly disillusioned with a modern civilization based upon the advance of science and technology, we have often heard from their scholars the praise of the so-called spiritual civilization of the East. Though this praise results from an abnormal,

though understandable, mentality of a temporary nature, it is more than welcome to the culturally chauvinistic Orientals. It strengthens the bias about the alleged superiority of Oriental civilization. . . .

. . . While a man in an ocean liner should not look down upon another man sailing a junk, it is ridiculous for the latter to brag about his spiritual superiority simply because his junk is more primitive and less convenient than the ocean liner. Technological backwardness is not synonymous with spiritual advancement. . . .

. . . Throughout history the greatest tragedy has always been man's inability to ward off hunger and cold despite his hard labor. How can we in good conscience lecture a man about to be starved to death on the virtue of contentment, fate, and self-satisfaction? A man who condemns material comfort for no other reason than its unavailability to him can be compared to the fox in a Western fable who announces proudly that it does not like sour grapes when the grapes, ripe and sweet, are too high for it to reach. Poverty is not something to be proud of: those who state otherwise are either indulging in self-deception or too lazy to do something about it. More pathetic still are those who fast, mutilate their bodies, or commit suicide by fire, all in the name of "spiritual civilization." All these people — the self-congratulators, the self-deceivers, the self-mutilators, and the suicides — are mentally ill, really, since their attitude toward life is that of a dying man. . . .

Unlike its Oriental counterpart, the modern civilization of the West takes into full consideration the importance of material enjoyment. It has as its foundation two basic concepts. First, the purpose of life is the pursuit of happiness. Second, poverty is a sin; so is physical weakness or illness. The second concept, logically, is a derivative of the first. The goal of this civilization is, in short, the enrichment of life. As poverty is a sin, the Westerners devote their energy to the opening up of natural resources, the promotion of industry, the improvement of manufactured products, and the expansion of commerce. As physical weakness or illness is also a sin, they spare no effort in the study and improvement of medical care, the promotion of sanitation, hygiene, physical fitness and sports, the prevention of contagious disease, and the improvement of heredity. Since the pursuit of happiness is the purpose of life, they busy themselves with the enhancement of comfort in their living quarters, the improvement of transportation and communication, the beautification of their cities, the promotion of the arts, the assurance of safety in their streets, and finally, the security of incorruptibility in government and among government officials. To be sure, Western civilization contains in it certain elements that sometimes prompt its adherents to commit aggression, pillage, or even mass murder, which has to be condemned, of course. Neither can it be denied that it has brought benefit to those who embrace it.

THE NEW RELIGION

Though modern civilization of the West has not yet dissociated itself from the religion of the past [Christianity], one nevertheless senses that a new religion has been slowly developing. . . . Not surprisingly, the first characteristic of the new religion is its logic and rationality. As modern science enables man to discover new knowledge, to conquer nature for his own benefit, and to do a multitude of things that historically have been regarded as unattainable or even inconceivable, man's confidence in himself has increased enormously, and he believes, for the first time, that he can shape the future in accordance with his own wishes. Not surprisingly, the second characteristic of the new religion is its humanism. The acquisition of more and more knowledge not only enhances man's ability to cope with his environment but also broadens his social perspective, thus increasing his empathy with his fellow men. Not surprisingly, the third characteristic of the new religion is its social ethics.

. . . All the old religions stress salvation on an individual basis, and all the old ethics centers on the civilization of moral worth, again of a personal nature. The adherents of old religions do occasionally speak of the necessity of "saving" others, but they are more than satisfied if they can somehow save themselves. Forever looking inward and, as a result, becoming more and more involved with no one except themselves, they lose contact with the outside world. They do not understand worldly problems, let alone resolve them. . . . What is the use of this so-called self-cultivation of virtues if the net result is a mummy-like parasite, totally ignorant of practical matters and insensitive to the suffering of others? . . .

OCCIDENTAL AND ORIENTAL CIVILIZATIONS COMPARED

As "discontent" characterizes the modern civilization of the West, "content" characterizes the traditional civilization of the East. Being content, we Orientals do not strive for the improvement of our living standard, do not pay much attention to new discoveries and new inventions, and do not, even remotely, contemplate upon such "strange" ideas as the conquest of nature. We relish our ignorance, find satisfaction with the status quo, however unpleasant, and speak resignedly about our "fate." We are not even reformers, let alone revolutionaries. We are, in fact, the obedient servants of our rulers, whomever they happen to be.

Basic Tenets of Chinese Communism

❖

57 ◆ Mao Zedong,
REPORT ON AN INVESTIGATION OF THE PEASANT MOVEMENT IN HUNAN and STRATEGIC PROBLEMS OF CHINA'S REVOLUTIONARY WAR

Mao Zedong (1893–1975) was born into a well-to-do peasant family in Hunan province and as a university student participated in the anti-Qing revolution of 1911. During the next several years, while serving as a library assistant at Beijing University, he embraced Marxism and helped organize the Chinese Communist Party, which was officially founded in 1921. Originally given the task of working with urban labor unions, Mao gradually came to believe that peasants, whose capacity for class revolution was discounted by orthodox Marxist-Leninists, would lead China to socialism.

After the break with the Guomindang in 1927, the Communists took their small army to the remote and hilly region on the Hunan-Jiangxi border, where in 1931 they proclaimed the Chinese Soviet Republic. In 1934 Chiang Kai-shek's troops surrounded the Communists' forces, but as they moved in for the kill, more than one hundred thousand Communist troops and officials escaped and embarked on what came to be known as the Long March. This legendary trek lasted more than a year and covered more that six thousand miles before the survivors found safety in the remote mountains around Yan'an in Shaanxi province. Mao, now the party's recognized leader, rebuilt his army and readied himself and his followers for what would be fourteen more years of struggle against the Japanese and Guomindang.

Mao was a prolific writer who from the 1920s until his death in 1976 produced many hundreds of treatises, essays, and even works of poetry. The following excerpts are from two of his most important writings. The first, his *Report on an Investigation of the Peasant Movement in Hunan,* was written in 1927 after he visited Hunan province to study the activities of peasant associations, groups of peasants who with the help of Communist organizers had seized land, humiliated and killed landlords, and taken control of their villages. In it Mao expresses his faith in the poor peasantry as the source of revolution in China. The second excerpt is taken from his *Strategic Problems of China's Revolutionary War,* which was based on a series of lectures presented to the Red Army College in late 1936. In it Mao assesses China's military situation and outlines his strategy for victory through guerrilla warfare.

QUESTIONS FOR ANALYSIS

1. What specific developments in Hunan reinforced Mao's convictions about the peasantry's potential as a revolutionary force?
2. What criticisms have been made of the Hunan peasant movement, and how does Mao attempt to counter these criticisms?
3. What can be learned from these two writings about Mao's view of the role of the Communist Party in China's revolutionary struggle?
4. According to Mao, what have been the sources of oppression for the Chinese people? Once these sources of oppression have been removed, what will China be like?
5. What, according to Mao, are the four unique characteristics of China's revolutionary war, and how do they affect his military strategy?
6. What are the characteristics of Mao's "active defense" as opposed to "passive defense"?

REPORT ON AN INVESTIGATION OF THE PEASANT MOVEMENT IN HUNAN

. . . All talk directed against the peasant movement must be speedily set right. All the wrong measures taken by the revolutionary authorities concerning the peasant movement must be speedily changed. Only thus can the future of the revolution be benefited. For the present upsurge of the peasant movement is a colossal event. In a very short time, in China's central, southern and northern provinces, several hundred million peasants will rise like a mighty storm, like a hurricane, a force so swift and violent that no power, however great, will be able to hold it back. They will smash all the trammels that bind them and rush forward along the road to liberation. They will sweep all the imperialists, warlords, corrupt officials, local tyrants and evil gentry into their graves. Every revolutionary party and every revolutionary comrade will be put to the test, to be accepted or rejected as they decide. There are three alternatives. To march at their head and lead them? To trail behind them, gesticulating and

criticizing? Or to stand in their way and oppose them? Every Chinese is free to choose, but events will force you to make the choice quickly. . . .

"Yes, peasant associations are necessary, but they are going rather too far." This is the opinion of the middle-of-the-roaders. But what is the actual situation? True, the peasants are in a sense "unruly" in the countryside. Supreme in authority, the peasant association allows the landlord no say and sweeps away his prestige. This amounts to striking the landlord down to the dust and keeping him there. . . . People swarm into the houses of local tyrants and evil gentry who are against the peasant association, slaughtering their pigs and consuming their grain. They even loll for a minute or two on the ivory-inlaid beds belonging to the young ladies in the households of the local tyrants and evil gentry. At the slightest provocation they make arrests, crown the arrested with tall paper-hats, and parade them through the villages, saying, "You dirty landlords, now you know who we are!" . . . This is what some people call "going too far," or "exceeding the proper limits in righting a wrong," or "really too much." Such talk may seem plausible, but in fact it is wrong. First, the local tyrants, evil gentry and lawless landlords have themselves driven the peasants to this. For ages they have used their power to tyrannize over the peasants and trample them underfoot; that is why the peasants have reacted so strongly. . . . Secondly, a revolution is not a dinner party, or writing an essay, or painting a picture, or doing embroidery; it cannot be so refined, so leisurely and gentle, so temperate, kind, courteous, restrained and magnanimous. A revolution is an insurrection, an act of violence by which one class overthrows another. A rural revolution is a revolution by which the peasantry overthrows the power of the feudal landlord class. Without using the greatest force, the peasants cannot possibly overthrow the deep-rooted authority of the landlords which has lasted for thousands of years. . . . To put it bluntly, it is necessary to create terror for a while in every rural area, or otherwise it would be impossible to suppress the activities of the counter-revolutionaries in the countryside or overthrow the authority of the gentry.

A man in China is usually subjected to the domination of three systems of authority: (1) the state system, . . . ranging from the national, provincial and county government down to that of the township; (2) the clan system, . . . ranging from the central ancestral temple and its branch temples down to the head of the household; and (3) the supernatural system (religious authority), ranging from the King of Hell down to the town and village gods belonging to the nether world, and from the Emperor of Heaven down to all the various gods and spirits belonging to the celestial world. As for women, in addition to being dominated by these three systems of authority, they are also dominated by the men (the authority of the husband). These four authorities — political, clan, religious and masculine — are the embodiment of the whole feudal-patriarchal system and ideology, and are the four thick ropes binding the Chinese people, particularly the peasants. . . .

The political authority of the landlords is the backbone of all the other systems of authority.

With that overturned, the clan authority, the religious authority and the authority of the husband all begin to totter. . . . In many places the peasant associations have taken over the temples of the gods as their offices. Everywhere they advocate the appropriation of temple property in order to start peasant schools and to defray the expenses of the associations, calling it "public revenue from superstition." In Liling County, prohibiting superstitious practices and smashing idols have become quite the vogue. . . .

In places where the power of the peasants is predominant, only the older peasants and the women still believe in the gods, the younger peasants no longer doing so. Since the latter control the associations, the overthrow of religious authority and the eradication of superstition are going on everywhere. As to the authority of the husband, this has always been weaker among the poor peasants because, out of economic necessity, their womenfolk have to do more manual labor than the women of the richer classes and therefore have more say and greater power of decision in family matters. With the increasing bankruptcy of the rural economy in recent years, the basis for men's domination over women has already been weakened. With the rise of the peasant movement, the women in many places have now begun to organize rural women's associations; the opportunity has come for them to lift up their heads, and the authority of the husband is getting shakier every day. In a word, the whole feudal-patriarchal system and ideology is tottering with the growth of the peasants' power.

STRATEGIC PROBLEMS OF CHINA'S REVOLUTIONARY WAR

What then are the characteristics of China's revolutionary war?

I think there are four.

The first is that China is a vast semi-colonial country which is unevenly developed both politically and economically. . . .

The unevenness of political and economic development in China — the coexistence of a frail capitalist economy and a preponderant semi-feudal economy; the coexistence of a few modern industrial and commercial cities and the boundless expanses of stagnant rural districts; the coexistence of several millions of industrial workers on the one hand and, on the other, hundreds of millions of peasants and handicraftsmen under the old regime; the coexistence of big warlords controlling the Central government and small warlords controlling the provinces; the coexistence of two kinds of reactionary armies, i.e., the so-called Central army under Chiang Kai-shek and the troops of miscellaneous brands under the warlords in the provinces; and the coexistence of a few railway and steamship lines and motor roads on the one hand and, on the other, the vast number of wheel-barrow paths and trails for pedestrians only, many of which are even difficult for them to negotiate. . . .

The second characteristic is the great strength of the enemy.

What is the situation of the Guomindang, the enemy of the Red Army? It is a party that has seized political power and has relatively stabilized it. It has gained the support of the principal counter-revolutionary countries in the world. It has remodeled its army, which has thus become different from any other army in Chinese history and on the whole similar to the armies of the modern states in the world; its army is supplied much more abundantly with arms and other equipment than the Red Army, and is greater in numerical strength than any army in Chinese history, even than the standing army of any country in the world. . . .

The third characteristic is that the Red Army is weak and small. . . .

Our political power is dispersed and isolated in mountainous or remote regions, and is deprived of any outside help. In economic and cultural conditions the revolutionary base areas are more backward than the Guomindang areas. The revolutionary bases embrace only rural districts and small towns. . . .

The fourth characteristic is the Communist Party's leadership and the agrarian revolution.

This characteristic is the inevitable result of the first one. It gives rise to the following two features. On the one hand, China's revolutionary war, though taking place in a period of reaction in China and throughout the capitalist world, can yet be victorious because it is led by the Communist Party and supported by the peasantry. Because we have secured the support of the peasantry, our base areas, though small, possess great political power and stand firmly opposed to the political power of the Guomindang which encompasses a vast area; in a military sense this creates colossal difficulties for the attacking Guomindang troops. The Red Army, though small, has great fighting capacity, because its men under the leadership of the Communist Party have sprung from the agrarian revolution and are fighting for their own interests, and because officers and men are politically united.

On the other hand, our situation contrasts sharply with that of the Guomindang. Opposed to the agrarian revolution, the Guomindang is deprived of the support of the peasantry. Despite the great size of its army it cannot arouse the bulk of the soldiers or many of the lower-rank officers, who used to be small producers, to risk their lives voluntarily for its sake. Officers and men are politically disunited and this reduces its fighting capacity. . . .

Military experts of new and rapidly developing imperialist countries like Germany and Japan positively boast of the advantages of strategic offensive and condemn strategic defensive. Such an idea is fundamentally unsuitable for China's revolutionary war. Such military experts point out that the great shortcoming of defense lies in the fact that, instead of gingering up {enlivening} the people, it demoralizes them. . . . Our case is different. Under the slogan of safeguarding the revolutionary base areas and safeguarding China, we can rally the greatest majority of the people to fight single-mindedly, because we are the victims of oppression and aggression. . . .

In military terms, our warfare consists in the alternate adoption of the defensive and the offensive. It makes no difference to us whether our offensive is regarded as following the defensive or preceding it, because the turning-point comes when we smash the campaigns of "encirclement and annihilation." It remains a defensive until a campaign of "encirclement and annihilation" is smashed, and then it immediately begins as an offensive; they are but two phases of the same thing, as one campaign of "encirclement and annihilation" of the enemy is closely followed by another. Of the two phases, the defensive phase is more complicated and more important than the offensive phase. It involves numerous problems of how to smash the campaign of "encirclement and annihilation." The basic principle is for active defense and against passive defense.

In the civil war, when the Red Army surpasses the enemy in strength, there will no longer be any use for strategic defensive in general. Then our only directive will be strategic offensive. Such a change depends on an overall change in the relative strength of the enemy and ourselves.

◆

Nationalism and Militarism in Japan

As the experience of modern Japan reveals, nationalism can inspire great achievements, but it can also cause great disasters. In the late nineteenth and early twentieth centuries, cultural pride and a stubborn refusal to succumb to the West united the Japanese behind the Meiji reformers. A national effort that included peasants, business leaders, aristocrats, government officials, soldiers, and workers transformed Japan from an isolated, feudal society into a major industrial and military power within decades. In the 1920s and 1930s nationalism continued to be a major force in Japan. This time, however, it led to a crushing military defeat in World War II.

Japanese nationalism between the wars became increasingly xenophobic, militaristic, and authoritarian. It appealed to generals, right-wing politicians, and millions of peasants who were dissatisfied with parliamentary government, socialism, the Westernization of Japanese culture, and the influence of the *zaibatsu,* or large business conglomerates, on Japanese politics. Nationalists praised Japanese virtues of duty and harmony, sought absolute obedience to the emperor, and idealized warrior values. They demanded military expansion, claiming that only a Japanese empire in Asia would prevent the nation's economic ruin. Nationalists supported the conquest of Manchuria in 1931, the invasion of China in 1937, and the bombing of the U.S. fleet at Pearl Harbor in 1941. They set Japan on a course that ended in August 1945 with nuclear attacks on Hiroshima and Nagasaki, total defeat, and unconditional surrender.

In the 1920s the political balance had shifted from the armed forces and bureaucracy, both subject only to the emperor, to the political parties, whose power base was the elected Diet and whose leaders had close ties with big business. This shift translated into solid gains for democracy, liberalism, social reform, and a foreign policy of international cooperation. But party government lost its appeal once the Great Depression struck Japan in the 1930s. Japanese exports dropped in value by 50 percent between 1929 and 1931, workers' incomes fell, and unemployment reached three million. As a result of the rice crop failure in 1931 in northern Japan, families were reduced to begging, eating bark and roots, and selling daughters to brothel keepers.

The economic crisis broadened support for Japanese ultranationalism, and persuaded its advocates in the military to take bold steps. In 1931 army officers arranged an explosion on the tracks of a Japanese-controlled railroad in Manchuria and, without the approval of the civilian government, used this as an excuse to capture the important cities in the region and establish the puppet state of Manchukuo. In Japan itself, right-wing extremists assassinated business and political leaders, and plotted to overthrow the government. In February 1936 officers and troops of the First Division attacked and briefly occupied government offices in downtown Tokyo. The government suppressed the rebellion and executed its leaders, but to many Japanese the rebels were heroes, not traitors. Constitutional government survived on paper, but when Japanese and Chinese troops clashed outside Beijing in the summer of 1937, the ensuing war between China and Japan put political authority firmly in the hands of militarists and nationalists.

Nationalism continued to inspire the Japanese during World War II. Citizens accepted privation, soldiers fought with fanatical determination, and young pilots sacrificed their lives by crashing their planes into U.S. warships. But this time nationalism was not enough, and defeat came in August 1945.

The Agenda of Ultranationalism

58 ◆ The Black Dragon Society, *ANNIVERSARY STATEMENT, 1930*

In 1881, a group of former samurai (warrior-aristocrats) founded the Genyosha, a secret society dedicated to Japanese expansion in Asia, the preservation of traditional Japanese culture, and absolute dedication to the emperor. In 1901, several of its members broke away and founded the Black Dragon Society, which promoted war with Russia as a means of expanding Japan's influence on the Asian mainland. In the early twentieth century, the Society continued to advocate an aggressive foreign policy to enable Japan to become the dominant force in Asia. It also denounced democracy, capitalism, Americanization, socialism, party politics, and big business, all of which it viewed as threats to Japanese culture or to their plans for Japanese expansionism. Although the membership of the Black Dragon Society and similar organizations was small, their self-promotion, assassinations, and strong-arm tactics kept alive their brand of extreme nationalism, allowing it to flourish in the troubled atmosphere of the 1930s.

In 1930 the Black Dragon Society published the two-volume *Secret History of the Annexation of Korea,* in which it claimed a key role in inspiring early Japanese expansionism. The second volume concluded with the following statement.

QUESTIONS FOR ANALYSIS

1. What is there in the Black Dragon Society's philosophy that explains its interventions in Korea, China, and the Philippines?
2. In what ways, according to the authors of the document, has Japanese foreign policy been thwarted in the years since World War I?
3. According to the Society, how has Japan's domestic situation deteriorated?
4. According to the Society, what is the root of Japan's problems, and what solutions does it offer?
5. What might explain the appeal of such ideas to the Japanese populace?

From the first, we members of the Amur [Black Dragon] Society have worked in accordance with the imperial mission for overseas expansion to solve our overpopulation; at the same time, we have sought to give support and encouragement to the peoples of East Asia. Thus we have sought the spread of humanity and righteousness throughout the world by having the imperial purpose extend to neighboring nations.

Earlier, in order to achieve these principles, we organized the Heavenly Blessing Heroes in Korea in 1894 and helped the Tong Hak rebellion there in order to speed the settlement of the dispute between Japan and China.[1] In 1899 we helped Aguinaldo in his struggle for independence for the Philippines.[2] In 1900 we worked with other comrades in helping Sun Yat-sen start the fires of revolution in South China. In 1901 we organized this Society and became exponents of the punishment of Russia, and thereafter we devoted ourselves to the annexation of Korea while continuing to support the revolutionary movement of China. . . .

During this period we have seen the fulfillment of our national power in the decisive victories in the two major wars against China and Russia,[3] in the annexation of Korea, the acquisition of Formosa [Taiwan] and Sakhalin, and the expulsion of Germany from the Shandong peninsula.[4] Japan's status among the empires of the world has risen until today she ranks as one of the three great powers, and from this eminence she can support other Asiatic nations. . . .

However, in viewing recent international affairs it would seem that the foundation established by the great Meiji emperor is undergoing rapid deterioration. The disposition of the gains of the war with Germany was left to foreign powers, and the government, disregarding the needs of national defense, submitted to unfair demands to limit our naval power.[5] Moreover, the failure of our China policy[6] made the Chinese more and more contemptuous of us, so

---

[1]The Tonghak, or Eastern Learning, movement was a late-nineteenth-century religious movement that drew on Daoist (Taoist), Buddhist, Confucian, and Catholic traditions. In 1894 members of the movement rebelled against the China-oriented government of Korea because of its corruption and indifference to the plight of the poor. Japanese and Chinese troops intervened, leading to the Sino-Japanese War of 1894–1895. The result was the recognition of Korea's independence by China.

[2]Emilio Aguinaldo (1869–1964) led an insurrection against the Spaniards in 1898 and established the Philippine Republic in January 1899. Following the Spanish American War, he resisted the U.S. takeover, but was defeated and retired from politics.

[3]Victory over China in the Sino-Japanese War and over Russia in the Russo-Japanese War (1904–1905).

[4]Japan received Taiwan (Formosa) after the Sino-Japanese War. Its authority over Korea and its claim to the southern half of Sakhalin Island were recognized after the Russo-Japanese War. Japan was granted former German concessions in China's Shandong province after World War I.

[5]The Washington Conference of 1921 set Japan's naval strength at 60 percent of that of the United States and that of Great Britain.

[6]The Twenty-One Demands, submitted by Japan to China in 1915, would have established extensive Japanese influence over the Chinese government. These demands were successfully resisted by China.

much so that they have been brought to demand the surrender of our essential defense lines in Manchuria and Mongolia. Furthermore, in countries like the United States and Australia our immigrants have been deprived of rights which were acquired only after long years of struggle, and we now face a highhanded anti-Japanese expulsion movement which knows no bounds.[7] Men of purpose and of humanity who are at all concerned for their country cannot fail to be upset by the situation.

When we turn our attention to domestic affairs, we feel more than deep concern. There is a great slackening of discipline and order. Men's hearts are becoming corrupt. Look about you! Are not the various government measures and establishments a conglomeration of all sorts of evils and abuses? The laws are confusing, and evil grows apace. The people are overwhelmed by heavy taxes, the confusion in the business world complicates the livelihood of the people, the growth of dangerous thought threatens social order, and our national polity, which has endured for three thousand years, is in danger. This is a critical time for our national destiny; was there ever a more crucial day? What else can we call this time if it is not termed decisive?

And yet, in spite of this our government, instead of pursuing a farsighted policy, casts about for temporary measures. The opposition party simply struggles for political power without any notion of saving our country from this crisis. And even the press, which should devote itself to its duty of guiding and leading society, is the same. For the most part it swims with the current, bows to vulgar opinions, and is chiefly engrossed in money making. Alas! Our empire moves ever closer to rocks which lie before us. . . .

. . . Therefore we of the Amur Society have determined to widen the scope of our activity. Hereafter, besides our interest in foreign affairs,

we will give unselfish criticism of internal politics and of social problems, and we will seek to guide public opinion into proper channels. . . . We . . . are resolved to reform the moral corruption of the people, restore social discipline, and ease the insecurity of the people's livelihood by relieving the crises in the financial world, restore national confidence, and increase the national strength, in order to carry out the imperial mission to awaken the countries of Asia. In order to clarify these principles, we here set forth our platform to all our fellow patriots:

Platform

1. Developing the great plan of the founders of the country, we will widen the great Way [Dao] of Eastern culture, work out a harmony of Eastern and Western cultures, and take the lead among Asian peoples.

2. We will bring to an end many evils, such as formalistic legalism; it restricts the freedom of the people, hampers common sense solutions, prevents efficiency in public and private affairs, and destroys the true meaning of constitutional government. Thereby we will show forth again the essence of the imperial principles.

3. We shall rebuild the present administrative systems. We will develop overseas expansion through the activation of our diplomacy, further the prosperity of the people by reforms in internal government, and solve problems of labor and management by the establishment of new social policies. Thereby we will strengthen the foundations of the empire.

4. We shall carry out the spirit of the Imperial Rescript[8] to Soldiers and Sailors and stimulate a martial spirit by working toward the goal of a nation in arms. Thereby we look toward the perfection of national defense.

5. We plan a fundamental reform of the present educational system, which is copied

---

[7]Both Australia and the United States severely restricted Japanese (and Chinese) immigration in the 1920s.
[8]Issued by the emperor in 1882, the rescript stated that

supreme command of the armed forces rested in the hands of the emperor alone, thus strengthening the military's independence from civilian control.

from those of Europe and America; we shall set up a basic study of a national education originating in our national polity. Thereby we anticipate the further development and heightening of the wisdom and virtue of the Yamato race.[9]

---

[9]According to tradition, Japan's imperial line can be traced back to the state founded by a descendant of the sun goddess on the Yamato plain around 660 B.C.E.

Foreign Policy Priorities on the Eve of the China War

❖

59 ◆ FUNDAMENTAL PRINCIPLES OF NATIONAL POLICY, 1936

Despite the failure of the takeover of central Tokyo by nationalist soldiers and officers of the First Division in early 1936, the military retained a strong voice in government. Many politicians bent over backward in support of the military and its right-wing agenda in order to prevent renewed violence. The cabinet of Hirota Koti, in power from March 1936 to February 1937, increased military spending and passed stricter laws against communists and socialists.

In August 1936 the Hirota cabinet approved the following policy statement on foreign and domestic policy. It is an effort to strike a balance between the army's traditional focus on north China and Manchuria as a means of countering the Soviet Union's strength and the navy's new southward policy and its concerns with U.S. naval strength. It also shows the degree to which militarism and expansionism had become the bedrock of Japanese politics on the eve of the war with China.

QUESTIONS FOR ANALYSIS

1. What view of Japan's role in Asian affairs is expressed in this statement?
2. What views of the Soviet Union and the Western powers does the document express?
3. According to the authors of the document, what steps must be taken to prepare Japan for the foreign policy challenges it will meet?
4. What specific statements in the document reveal the militarist priorities of the Hirota government?
5. How do the ideas expressed in this document compare to those of the Black Dragon Society's 1930 anniversary statement?

(1) Japan must strive to eradicate the aggressive policies of the great powers, and share with East Asia the joy which is based on the true principle of co-existence and co-prosperity. This is the realization of the spirit of the Imperial Way which must be accepted as the consistent guiding principle in Japan's policy of foreign expansion.

(2) Japan must complete her national defense and armament to protect her national security

and development. In this way, the position of the Empire as the stabilizing force in East Asia can be secured both in name and in fact.

(3) The policy toward the continent must be based on the following factors: in order to promote Manchukuo's[1] healthy development and to stabilize Japan-Manchukuo national defense, the threat from the north, the Soviet Union, must be eliminated;[2] in order to promote our economic development, we must prepare against Great Britain and the United States and bring about close collaboration between Japan, Manchukuo, and China. In the execution of this policy, Japan must pay due attention to friendly relations with other powers.

(4) Japan plans to promote her racial and economic development in the South Seas, especially in the outerlying South Seas[3] areas. She plans to extend her strength by moderate and peaceful means and without rousing other powers. In this way, concurrently with the firm establishment of Manchukuo, Japan may expect full development and strengthening of her national power.

B. Utilizing the above fundamental principles as the axis, we must unify and coordinate our foreign and domestic policies, and reform our administration thoroughly to reflect the current conditions. The following are the basic outlines.

(1) Japan's national defense and armament must be completed in the following manner:

a. The Army's arms preparations must have as their goal, the ability to withstand the forces which can be deployed by the Soviet Union in the Far East. The Army must expand its Kwantung[4] and Chōsen (Korean) forces to the extent that they can deliver the first decisive blow against the Soviet Far Eastern Army at the outbreak of war.

b. The Navy's arms preparations must have as their goal, creation of forces sufficient to withstand an attack from the U.S. Navy to secure the control of the Western Pacific for Japan.

(2) Our foreign policy must be based on the principle of the smooth execution of the fundamental national policies. It must therefore be coordinated and reformed. In order to facilitate the smooth functioning of activities of diplomatic bureaus, the military must endeavor to give behind-the-scenes assistance, and must avoid overt activities.

(3) In order to conform to the above basic national policies, in effecting reform and improvement in political and administrative organizations, in establishing financial and economic policies, and in administering other agencies, appropriate actions must be taken on the following matters:

a. The domestic public opinion must be led and unified, so as to strengthen the nation's resolve in coping with the present national emergency.

b. Appropriate reforms in administrative agencies and economic organizations must be effected to bring about improvement in industries and important foreign trade necessary for executing national policies.

c. Appropriate measures must be taken to ensure stabilization of national life, strengthening of physical fitness, and development of sound national thought.

d. Appropriate plans must be undertaken to promote rapid growth in aviation and maritime transportation industries.

e. We must promote the establishment of a policy of self-sufficiency with regard to important natural resources and materials required for national defense and industries.

f. Concurrently with the reform of diplomatic bureaus, information and propaganda organizations must be well established to enhance vigorously diplomatic functions and cultural activities overseas.

---

[1]The southern Pacific.
[2]The Japanese name for the puppet government of Manchuria established after the 1931 conquest.
[3]In the mid-1930s the Soviet Union had approximately

240,000 troops in its far eastern provinces, compared to 160,000 Japanese troops in Manchuria.
[4]The Kwantung forces were Japan's army in Manchuria; the Chōsen army was in Korea.

PART THREE

From World War II to the Early 1970s: Decades of Conflict, Decolonization, and Economic Recovery

Inexorably, like blind men without memories approaching an abyss with no one to stop them, the world's Great Powers in the 1930s marched and stumbled into the century's second world war. With the global economy in tatters and no effective response from the League of Nations or individual states, authoritarian, militarist regimes in Italy, Germany, and Japan committed one act of aggression after another: Japan invaded Manchuria in 1931 and China in 1937; Italy conquered Ethiopia in 1935; Nazi Germany, having begun to rearm in 1935, reoccupied the Rhineland in 1936, annexed Austria in 1938, and destroyed Czechoslovakia in March 1939. Then just before dawn on September 1, 1939, assured that its new ally, the Soviet Union, would do nothing, Germany unleashed its troops, tanks, and planes on Poland. Two days later Great Britain and France declared war on Germany, and for the second time in just over two decades, Europe was at war.

In 1941 the European war and the Sino-Japanese War, which had begun in 1937, became parts of a truly global struggle, fully deserving the title World War II. In June 1941 Germany invaded the Soviet Union, and in December Japan attacked the Philippines, the Dutch East Indies, and the British colony of Malaya. Most importantly, Japan bombed the U.S. naval base at Pearl Harbor in Hawaii, thus bringing the United States into the war. For three and a half more years, humanity's most costly and deadly war was fought on and under the world's oceans, on tiny South Pacific islands, in North Africa, and across Eurasia. Only in 1945, with the unconditional surrender of Germany in May and of Japan in August, did the fighting stop.

Unlike the mood following World War I, when victors and vanquished alike failed to comprehend how many things the war had changed and dreamed of a "return to normalcy," the atmosphere after World War II was pervaded by a sense that human affairs had changed irrevocably. When the war ended, much of Europe, the Soviet Union, and Japan had been reduced to rubble; forty, fifty, or sixty million human beings had been killed; and the obliteration of Hiroshima and Nagasaki by atomic bombs in August 1945 presaged a new and even more terrible chapter in the history of warfare. Of the early twentieth century's Great Powers, Germany, Japan, and Italy had been crushed, Great Britain was economically exhausted, and France was haunted by its capitulation to the Germans in 1940 after only six weeks of fighting. World affairs were now dominated by two superpowers, the United States and the

Soviet Union, whose ideological differences, mutual distrust, and clashes over the future of Europe made a third world war seem likely.

In the immediate postwar years, Asia and Africa also seemed on the brink of momentous and unsettling changes. China erupted into civil war, and in dozens of colonies nationalists prepared to renew their struggle for independence. France sent troops to Vietnam to reestablish its authority after the Vietnamese declaration of independence in 1945, and the Dutch did the same in the East Indies after the colony announced its independence in 1945. An era of colonial war seemed imminent. Great Britain, it is true, peacefully granted independence to India and Pakistan in 1947 and to Burma in 1948, but religious and ethnic strife in all three new states did not bode well for their futures.

Soviet-U.S. conflict, the threat of atomic war, daunting economic problems, the full disclosure of Nazi war crimes, the advance of communism in China and Eastern Europe, potential upheaval in colonial Africa and Asia — there were many reasons for pessimism in the late 1940s. Instead, it should have been a time for optimism. The next twenty-five years witnessed unparalleled economic expansion and impressive strides in medicine and public health. The Cold War remained cold, and, despite profound social changes, the political climate in most of the world remained moderate and generally calm. Although vast economic disparities still existed between the world's developed and nondeveloped regions, most human beings in these years were more prosperous and better fed, experienced more material comfort, had more education, and lived longer and healthier lives. After decades of war and economic upheaval, it was possible once more to be hopeful about humanity's prospects.

Although Cold War rhetoric remained shrill and pugnacious, Soviet and U.S. leaders exercised restraint. Confrontations over Berlin (1948 and 1958), Soviet intervention in Hungary (1956) and Czechoslovakia (1968), Egyptian nationalization of the Suez Canal (1956), and the Cuban missile crisis (1962) were all resolved without warfare, and the one hot war between communist and noncommunist forces, in Korea (1950–1953), remained localized. Furthermore, colonialism ended in Asia and Africa in the 1950s and 1960s without the bloody struggles many had anticipated. Of the approximately sixty colonies that became independent between 1947 and 1975, most did so peacefully. Those that did not included Vietnam and the East Indies, where the French and Dutch, respectively, unsuccessfully used force in the late 1940s to prevent independence, and Algeria, Kenya, and Rhodesia, where relatively large European settler populations blocked or complicated independence movements.

The postwar era's most impressive achievement was economic growth. World War I had been followed by currency devaluations, slumping agricultural prices, an international financial crisis caused by war debt and reparation payments, the U.S. stock market crash, and ultimately the Great Depression. World War II, in contrast, was followed by a few years of economic hardship and readjustment and then twenty-five years of expansion. World output of manufactured goods quadrupled between the early 1950s and the 1970s, and world trade in manufactured products increased tenfold. Most of this manufacturing still took place in the capitalist countries of Western Europe, Japan, the United States, Canada, and Australia, where increased rates of automobile and home ownership and a surge in the purchase of televisions, refrigerators, washers and dryers, and a host of new electronic gadgets all indicated a rise in overall prosperity.

The economic boom was not limited to the capitalist West and Japan, however. Economic growth in the Soviet Union and its satellites was even more rapid than in the West, lending substance to Soviet Premier Nikita Khrushchev's boast in 1959 that the Soviet Union would economically "bury" the United States. Even Africans and Asian, who remained poor by Western standards, benefited from strong demand for their nations' minerals and agricultural exports. A dramatic increase in worldwide food production essentially made famines nonexistent in the 1950s and 1960s, except in China during the Great Leap Forward of 1958 to 1960, when government policies led to mass starvation.

By the late 1960s, however, signs of economic decline and political discontent were apparent. Grassroots rebellions in Poland and Czechoslovakia challenged Soviet domination of Eastern Europe. Western Europe experienced turmoil as students and workers rioted in Germany and Italy, protested Francisco Franco's authoritarian government in Spain, and attacked the university system and the DeGaulle regime in France. In the United States, radicalized students protested the Vietnam War, social injustice, and university policies through strikes and demonstrations, and urban black ghettos erupted into violence. Against this backdrop of political turmoil, the revival of feminism and the emergence of a powerful environmental movement added to the atmosphere of protest and disenchantment.

Conflict was not limited to the Western democracies and Eastern Europe. The mid to late 1960s saw a drift toward military rule in much of Africa, civil war in Nigeria, and clashes between right-wing military governments and radical leftist groups in Latin America. Chaos gripped China after Mao Zedong launched the Great Proletarian Cultural Revolution in 1965.

The economic boom was also slowing down. In the West, rates of industrial production began to fall, and inflation and labor-management conflict increased. The delicate balance of international finance was threatened by ballooning government deficits in the United States. In the Soviet bloc, agricultural and industrial output also began to slump despite rosy government reports to the contrary. Then in the wake of the October War between Egypt and Israel in 1973, Arab oil-producing countries embargoed oil shipments to the United States, and in 1974 the Organization of Petroleum Exporting Countries quadrupled the price of oil. Decline and retrenchment struck oil-dependent industrialized states and commodity-producing Third World economies alike. The twentieth century's closest approximation of a golden age was coming to an end.

CHAPTER 8

World War II and Its Aftermath

Whether World War II is dated from July 7, 1937, when Japan declared war on China, or from September 1, 1939, when Germany invaded Poland, by the time it ended in August 1945, it had become the most murderous and costly war in history. It involved no fewer than sixty belligerent states, which together mobilized over ninety million men and women to fight in their armed forces. Costs were enormous. One estimate places the expenditures for World War II at $1,150,000,000,000. Battles were fought by armies of unprecedented size. Hitler attacked the Soviet Union in June 1941 with the largest invasion force in history; it included ten thousand to fifteen thousand tanks, eight thousand planes, and 2.9 million troops, 1.3 million of whom were dead or wounded within a year. Three years later, in June 1944 the Allies launched their cross-Channel invasion of Nazi-held northern Europe, the largest amphibian military operation in history. It involved fifty thousand tanks, armored cars, and trucks; eleven thousand aircraft; and three million troops.

Inevitably, casualties in World War II were enormous. As many as sixty million men, women, and children died, six times more than in World War I, which for a mere twenty-five years had held the distinction of being history's deadliest war. The United States lost three hundred thousand soldiers and civilians; Great Britain, four hundred thousand; Japan, two million; Germany, over four million; Poland, six million; China, fifteen million; and the Soviet Union, between twenty and twenty-five million.

The human losses in World War II were unique in other ways. Over half the victims were civilians. According to the doctrine of "total war" embraced by all belligerents, obliterating the enemies' industries and infrastructure and killing or crushing the spirit of civilians were as important as winning battles. Bombing raids by Japan on Shanghai in 1937 and by Germany on Warsaw in 1939 and on London, Coventry, and Rotterdam in 1940 set a precedent for aerial attacks on enemy population centers throughout the war. In 1942 the British and Americans began bombing major German cities. Among their deadliest raids were the firebombing of Hamburg in 1943, which killed fifty thousand civilians, and the

bombing of Dresden only eight weeks before Germany's surrender, which also killed fifty thousand. Allied bombing raids on Germany resulted in Anglo-American losses of fifty thousand pilots,
gunners, and navigators, but they killed approximately six hundred
thousand German civilians and undoubtedly weakened Germany's
capacity to produce armaments. Japan became the target of massive American bombing raids in 1944 and 1945. The firebombing of
Tokyo in March 1945, which killed 125,000, was a only a prelude
to the dropping of atomic bombs on Hiroshima and Nagasaki in
August 1945, which killed two hundred thousand human beings
but ended the war.

The brutalization of warfare took other grotesque and atrocious forms. Examples include the Japanese "rape of Nanjing" in
October 1937, in which approximately one hundred thousand
Chinese were massacred and thousands of Chinese women were
raped; the Soviet murder of close to twenty thousand Poles considered unfriendly to the Soviet Union; German treatment of
Russian prisoners of war, which led to three million deaths
through famine and exposure; the use of slave labor in munitions
plants and construction projects by the Japanese and Germans;
and the German murders of hostages in response to assassinations and acts of sabotage. Most appalling was the Nazis'
war against Europe's Jews. Directed by the German government,
tens of thousands of Germans and other European antisemites
gassed, shot, tortured, starved to death, worked to death, killed
in medical experiments, or murdered in acts of individual cruelty
six million Jews, approximately half of the twelve million the Nazis
had hoped to exterminate.

Such enormous suffering was not entirely in vain. The war's
perpetrators — Italy, Germany, and Japan — were crushed, and
the ideologies that had inspired them — radical nationalism,
racism, and militarism — were discredited. The war came to sym-
bolize the triumph of good over evil, and fueled hope that human
beings might still be capable of creating and living in a just, peaceful, and humane society. At war's end, those who had such hopes
put their faith in the newly created United Nations, which in
December 1948 approved the Universal Declaration of Human
Rights. It condemned tyranny and oppression, and proclaimed as
humanity's highest goal the recognition of the inherent dignity of
all human beings and their right to peace, justice, and freedom.

How far the human community has fallen short of these goals is
clear to anyone familiar with recent history. World War II left behind not only a legacy of achievement and hope but also a host of
new and intractable problems, not the least of which was the conflict between the world's two new superpowers, the United States
and the Soviet Union. Tensions that first surfaced in the closing

months of the fighting soon blossomed into a full-fledged ideological conflict, with the stakes nothing less than the world's political and economic future. This legacy of World War II — the Cold War — would dominate international politics for the next fifty years, until it, like every other war in human history, came to an end.

◆

Appeasement and the Origins of World War II in Europe

On taking power in January 1933, Hitler immediately set out to overturn the Treaty of Versailles, the hated "dictated treaty" forced upon Germany after World War I. He took Germany out of the League of Nations, ordered German rearmament, reoccupied the Rhineland, and annexed Austria. Then in 1938 Hitler turned his attention to Czechoslovakia, a nation created just twenty years earlier by the Treaty of Versailles. He demanded the Sudetenland, a swath of territory on Czechoslovakia's western border that contained some three million ethnic Germans and much of the nation's industry. The Czechs stood firm, and in mid September Hitler announced that he would risk world war to unite the Sudeten Germans with the fatherland. Frantic efforts to preserve peace came to a climax in late September with the Munich conference, attended by Hitler, the Italian dictator Benito Mussolini, and the prime ministers of France and Great Britain, Edouard Daladier and Neville Chamberlain. Czechoslovakia was not represented.

Daladier and Chamberlain agreed to the immediate German occupation of the Sudetenland, Polish annexation of Czechoslovakia's coal-rich area of Teschen, and the transfer of parts of the eastern province of Slovakia to Hungary. Hitler agreed to "personally guarantee" the boundaries of the shrunken Czechoslovak state. War was avoided.

With the world breathing a sigh of relief, Chamberlain, the architect of the Munich agreement, returned home to cheering crowds. For a few months he was a hero, the savior of the peace, the statesman who had ensured "peace in our time." History has been less kind to Neville Chamberlain and the Munich agreement he masterminded. "Munich" is remembered not as a triumph but as a symbol of cowardice, betrayal, capitulation to aggression, and the failure of the policy of appeasement. In March 1939 Hitler sent troops into Czechoslovakia and occupied Prague; in September 1939 he invaded Poland. War, as it turned out, had not been avoided for long.

The Munich agreement was the climax of an appeasement policy pursued throughout the 1930s by Great Britain and, to a degree, France in their dealings with Germany, Italy, and Japan, three states that sought to overturn the Versailles settlement. To its advocates, appeasement was a policy based on realism and pragmatism; it strove to avoid war over peripheral issues while seeking an overall settlement of diplomatic problems in Europe, the Mediterranean, and

East Asia. This meant a willingness to jettison some aspects of the Versailles Treaty and to tolerate acts of aggression in Manchuria, China, Ethiopia, and Central Europe as long as vital Anglo-French interests were not threatened. Such a policy aimed to placate the dissatisfied nations that threatened the peace, and make them respectable, cooperative members of the international community.

Was appeasement a reasonable and morally justifiable policy to prevent the great powers from stumbling into wars over nonvital issues? Or was it an admission of weakness and an invitation to further aggression? As the following documents show, the merits and limitations of appeasement were topics of intense debate in prewar Britain. They have continued to be so to the present day.

The Search for "Peace in Our Time"

❖

60 ◆ *Neville Chamberlain,*
EXCERPTS FROM CORRESPONDENCE, DIARY, AND SPEECHES

Neville Chamberlain, the son of the prominent politician Joseph Chamberlain, was born in 1869 in Birmingham, a city where he had a successful business and political career before entering national politics on being elected to Parliament as a Conservative in 1918. Having been chancellor of the exchequer and minister of health in the 1920s, he again served as chancellor of the exchequer during the darkest times of the Great Depression between 1931 and 1937. He succeeded Stanley Baldwin in 1937 as prime minister, an office he held until May 1940, when, in the wake of Britain's failed attempt to take back Norway from the Germans, he was forced to turn over the premiership to Winston Churchill. He served in Churchill's war cabinet until he was struck down with cancer. He died in November 1940.

The following excerpts from Chamberlain's writings and speeches provide insights into his thinking about war and peace, the interests of the British Empire, and the best means of dealing with Hitler. The first excerpt is taken from a letter he wrote to his sister Ida in March 1938. It was written directly after the Anschluss (unification) of Germany and Austria and at a time when the Spanish Civil War was turning in favor of Francisco Franco and the Nationalists, who, with the help of Germany and Italy, were overcoming the republican Loyalists. The second excerpt is from a speech Chamberlain delivered to Parliament on July 26, 1938, when Hitler was pressing his demands for the Sudetenland. The third excerpt is from a diary entry written on September 11, 1938, when the threat of war over the Sudetenland seemed imminent. Four days later, a week of intense diplomacy commenced when Chamberlain flew to Berchtesgaden to meet with Hitler. On September 22 he returned to Germany, informing Hitler in Godesberg that the Sudetenland was his as long as he would guarantee Czechoslovakia's new borders. Believing the crisis had passed, Chamberlain was shocked to learn on September 27 that Hitler was threatening to occupy the

Sudetenland immediately and demanding that Czechoslovakia give up other territories to Poland and Hungary. This new demand provided the background for the fourth excerpt, Chamberlain's radio address to the nation on September 28.

On September 29 Chamberlain flew to Munich, and there with Daladier acquiesced to all of Hitler's demands. For his part, Hitler promised to make no further territorial demands on Czechoslovakia.

QUESTIONS FOR ANALYSIS

1. What views does Chamberlain express about Hitler and the strength of Germany? Is he consistent in his views?
2. Why is Chamberlain convinced that Great Britain can do nothing militarily to help the Czechs in their conflict over the Sudetenland?
3. How would you characterize Chamberlain's attitude toward Czechoslovakia?
4. Were there any circumstances under which Chamberlain would have been willing to take Britain to war in 1938?
5. What role does public opinion seem to play in Chamberlain's foreign policy decisions?
6. Aside from his short-term goal of preventing war over the Sudetenland issue, what was Chamberlain's long-term diplomatic goal?

[LETTER TO HIS SISTER, MARCH 1938]

With Franco in Spain by the aid of German guns and Italian planes, with a French government in which one cannot have the slightest confidence and which I suspect to be in closish [close] touch with our Opposition,[1] with the Russians stealthily and cunningly pulling all the strings behind the scenes to get us involved in war with Germany . . . and finally with a Germany flushed with triumph, and all too conscious of her power, the prospect looked bleak indeed. In face of such problems, to be badgered and pressed to come out and give a clear, decided, bold, and unmistakable lead, show "ordinary courage", and all the rest of the twaddle, is calculated to vex the man who has to take responsibility for the consequences. As a matter of fact, the plan of the "Grand Alliance", as Winston calls it, had occurred to me long before he mentioned it.[2] . . . It is a very attractive idea; indeed, there is almost everything to be said for it until you come to examine its practicability. From that moment its attraction vanishes. You have only to look at the map to see that nothing that France or we could do could possibly save Czechoslovakia from being overrun by the Germans, if they wanted to do it. The Austrian frontier is practically open; the great Skoda[3] munition works are within easy bombing distance of the German aerodromes, the railways all pass through German territory, Russia is 100 miles away. Therefore we could not help Czechoslovakia — she would simply be a pretext for going to war with Germany. That we could not think of unless we had a reasonable prospect of being able to beat her to her

---

[1]The Labour Party, the main rival to Chamberlain's party, the Conservatives.

[2]Winston Churchill had been demanding a common front among Britain, the Soviet Union, and France against Hitler.

[3]Located in Pilzen, the Skoda works, founded by Emil von Skoda (1839–1900), were a major weapons producer.

knees in a reasonable time, and of that I see no sign. I have therefore abandoned any idea of giving guarantees to Czechoslovakia, or the French in connection with her obligations to that country.

[SPEECH TO PARLIAMENT, JULY 26, 1938]

If only we could find some peaceful solution of this Czechoslovakian question, I should myself feel that the way was open again for a further effort for a general appeasement — an appeasement which cannot be obtained until we can be satisfied that no major cause of difference or dispute remains unsettled. We have already demonstrated the possibility of a complete agreement between a democratic and a totalitarian state, and I do not myself see why that experience should not be repeated. When Herr Hitler made his offer of a naval treaty[4] under which the German fleet was to be restricted to an agreed level bearing a fixed ratio to the size of the British fleet, he made a notable gesture of a most practical kind in the direction of peace, the value of which it seems to me has not ever been fully appreciated as tending toward this general appeasement. . . . Since agreement has already been reached on that point, I do not think that we ought to find it impossible to continue our efforts at understanding, which, if they were successful, would do so much to bring back confidence. . . .

[DIARY ENTRY, SEPTEMBER 11, 1938]

I fully realise that, if eventually things go wrong and the aggression takes place, there will be many, including Winston, who will say that the British government must bear the responsibility, and that if only they had had the courage to tell Hitler now that, if he used force, we should at once declare war, that would have stopped him. By that time it will be impossible to prove the contrary, but I am satisfied that we should be wrong to allow the most vital decision that any country could take, the decision as to peace or war, to pass out of our hands into those of the ruler of another country, and a lunatic at that. I have been fortified in this view by reading a very interesting book on the foreign policy of Canning.[5] . . . Over and over again Canning lays it down that you should never menace unless you are in a position to carry out your threats, and although, if we have to fight I should hope we should be able to give a good account of ourselves, we are certainly not in a position in which our military advisers would feel happy in undertaking to begin hostilities if we were not forced to do so.

[RADIO SPEECH TO THE NATION, SEPTEMBER 28, 1938]

First of all I must say something to those who have written to my wife or myself in these last weeks to tell us of their gratitude for my efforts and to assure us of their prayers for my success. Most of these letters have come from women — mothers or sisters of our own countrymen. But there are countless others besides — from France, from Belgium, from Italy, even from Germany, and it has been heart-breaking to read of the growing anxiety they reveal and their intense relief when they thought, too soon, that the danger of war was past.

If I felt my responsibility heavy before, to read such letters has made it seem almost overwhelming. How horrible, fantastic, incredible it is that we should be digging trenches and trying on gas-masks here because of a quarrel in

---

[4]The Anglo-German Naval Agreement of 1935, by which Great Britain agreed to allow Germany to build a navy 35 percent as large as Britain's.
[5]George Canning (1770–1827) was foreign secretary between 1822 and 1827, and served briefly as prime minister in

1827. The book referred to is probably Harold Temperle, *The Foreign Policy of Canning, 1822–1827* (London: 1925).

a far-away country between people of whom we know nothing. . . .

You know already that I have done all that one man can do to compose this quarrel. After my visits to Germany I have realized vividly how Herr Hitler feels that he must champion other Germans, and his indignation that grievances have not been met before this. He told me privately, and last night he repeated publicly, that after this Sudeten German question is settled, that is the end of Germany's territorial claims in Europe. . . .

However much we may sympathize with a small nation confronted by a big and powerful neighbor, we cannot in all circumstances undertake to involve the whole British Empire in war simply on her account. If we have to fight it must be on larger issues than that. I am myself a man of peace to the depths of my soul. Armed conflict between nations is a nightmare to me; but if I were convinced that any nation had made up its mind to dominate the world by fear of its force, I should feel that it must be resisted. Under such a domination life for people who believe in liberty would not be worth living; but war is a fearful thing, and we must be very clear, before we embark on it, that it is really the great issues that are at stake, and that the call to risk everything in their defense, when all the consequences are weighed, is irresistible.

"A Disaster of the First Magnitude"

◆

61 ◆ *Winston Churchill,*
SPEECH TO PARLIAMENT, OCTOBER 5, 1938

Sir Winston Churchill, one of the twentieth century's most outstanding statesmen, was born in 1874 at Blenheim Palace, outside of Oxford, the son of Lord Randolph Churchill and his American wife, Jennie Jerome. An undistinguished student at Harlow School, he attended the Royal Military College at Sandhurst and, after receiving his commission, served in Cuba, the Sudan, and India. While covering the Boer, or South African, War (1899–1902) as a correspondent for the *Morning Post,* his daring escape from captivity made him a celebrity.

In 1900 he was elected to Parliament as a Conservative. He served in Parliament for the next fifty years, in which time he held almost all the high offices of state, including two terms as prime minister. Out of office from 1929 to 1939, he became a vocal critic of Prime Minister Stanley Baldwin's India policy, which seemed to point to independence, and a strong voice in favor of British rearmament and a tough line against Hitler. When war was declared, Churchill was invited to become First Lord of the Admiralty by Chamberlain, whom he succeeded as prime minister in May 1940.

In the following speech — one of his most famous — Churchill denounced the Munich settlement on October 5, 1938. At a time when Chamberlain had overwhelming approval, Churchill's views were unpopular but uncannily prescient.

QUESTIONS FOR ANALYSIS

1. In what specific ways does Churchill view the Munich agreement as a "total and unmitigated defeat"?

2. What, according to Churchill, were the specific mistakes of British diplomacy in their dealings with Hitler?
3. How do Churchill's and Chamberlain's views of Germany differ? How do these views affect their ideas on foreign policy?
4. What, according to Churchill, will be the consequences of appeasement?
5. If given the opportunity, how might Chamberlain have responded to Churchill's speech?

If I do not begin this afternoon by paying the usual, and indeed almost invariable, tributes to the prime minister for his handling of this crisis, it is certainly not from lack of any personal regard. We have always, over a great many years, had very pleasant relations, and I have deeply understood from personal experiences of my own in a similar crisis the stress and strain he has had to bear; but I am sure it is much better to say exactly what we think about public affairs, and this is certainly not the time when it is worth anyone's while to court political popularity. . . .

I will, therefore, begin by saying the most unpopular and most unwelcome thing. I will begin by saying what everybody would like to ignore or forget but which must nevertheless be stated, namely, that we have sustained a total and unmitigated defeat, and that France has suffered even more than we have. . . .

. . . The utmost my right honourable Friend, the prime minister, has been able to secure by all his immense exertions, by all the great efforts and mobilization which took place in this country, and by all the anguish and strain through which we have passed in this country, the utmost he has been able to gain [*Hon. Members: "Is Peace"*]. I thought I might be allowed to make that point in its due place, and I propose to deal with it. The utmost he has been able to gain for Czechoslovakia and in the matters which were in dispute has been that the German dictator, instead of snatching his victuals from the table has been content to have them served to him course by course. . . .

◆ ◆

All is over. Silent, mournful, abandoned, broken, Czechoslovakia recedes into the darkness. She has suffered in every respect by her association with the Western democracies and with the League of Nations, of which she has always been an obedient servant. . . .

I venture to think that in the future the Czechoslovak state cannot be maintained as an independent entity. You will find that in a period of time which may be measured by years, but may be measured only by months, Czechoslovakia will be engulfed in the Nazi regime. . . . It is the most grievous consequence which we have yet experienced of what we have done and of what we have left undone in the last five years: five years of futile good intention, five years of eager search for the line of least resistance, five years of uninterrupted retreat of British power, five years of neglect of our air defenses. . . .

When I think of the fair hopes of a long peace which still lay before Europe at the beginning of 1933 when Herr Hitler first obtained power, and of all the opportunities of arresting the growth of the Nazi power which have been thrown away, when I think of the immense combinations and resources which have been neglected or squandered, I cannot believe that a parallel exists in the whole course of history. So far as this country is concerned the responsibility must rest with those who have the undisputed control of our political affairs. They neither prevented Germany from rearming, nor did they rearm ourselves in time. They quarrelled with Italy without saving Ethiopia. They exploited and discredited the vast institution of the League of Nations and they neglected to make alliances and combinations which might have repaired previous errors, and thus they left us in the hour of trial without adequate national defense or effective international security. . . .

We are in the presence of a disaster of the first magnitude which has befallen Great Britain and France. Do not let us blind ourselves to that. It must now be accepted that all countries of Central and Eastern Europe will make the best terms they can with the triumphant Nazi power. . . . The road down the Danube Valley to the Black Sea, the resources of corn and oil, the road which leads as far as Turkey, has been opened. In fact, if not in form, it seems to me that all those countries of middle Europe, all those Danubian countries, will, one after another, be drawn into this vast system of power politics (not only power military politics but power economic politics) radiating from Berlin, and I believe this can be achieved quite smoothly and swiftly and will not necessarily entail the firing of a single shot. . . . We are talking about countries which are a long way off and of which, as the prime minister might say, we know nothing. (*Interruption*) . . .

. . . What will be the position, I want to know, of France and England this year and the year afterward? What will be the position of that Western Front of which we are in full authority the guarantors? . . . Relieved from all anxiety in the East, and having secured resources which will greatly diminish, if not entirely remove, the deterrent of a naval blockade, the rulers of Nazi Germany will have a free choice open to them in what direction they will turn their eyes. If the Nazi dictator should choose to look westward, as he may, bitterly will France and England regret the loss of that fine army of ancient Bohemia[1] which was estimated last week to require not fewer than thirty German divisions for its destruction. . . . Many people,

no doubt, honestly believe that they are only giving away the interests of Czechoslovakia, whereas I fear we shall find that we have deeply compromised, and perhaps fatally endangered, the safety and even the independence of Great Britain and France. . . . You have to consider the character of the Nazi movement and the rule which it implies. The prime minister desires to see cordial relations between this country and Germany. There is no difficulty at all in having cordial relations with the German people. Our hearts go out to them. But they have no power. You must have diplomatic and correct relations, but there can never be friendship between the British democracy and the Nazi power, that power which spurns Christian ethics, which cheers its onward course by a barbarous paganism, which vaunts the spirit of aggression and conquest, which derives strength and perverted pleasure from persecution, and uses, as we have seen, with pitiless brutality, the threat of murderous force. That power cannot ever be the trusted friend of the British democracy. . . .

We have passed an awful milestone in our history, when the whole equilibrium of Europe has been deranged, and that the terrible words have for the time being been pronounced against the Western democracies:

"Thou art weighed in the balance and found wanting."

And do not suppose that this is the end. This is only the beginning of the reckoning. This is only the first sip, the foretaste of a bitter cup which will be proffered to us year by year unless by a supreme recovery of moral health and martial vigor, we arise again and take our stand for freedom as in the olden times.

---

[1]A centuries-old kingdom of central Europe with its capital in Prague, Bohemia was the major western province of Czechoslovakia.

The Final Solution: Perpetrators and Victims

Antisemitism was not a Nazi invention. In Europe's Middle Ages, Jews were victims of mob violence, forced to live in restricted neighborhoods, or ghettos, subjected to special taxes, and excluded from most professions. By 1500 persecution and expulsions had driven most Jews out of Western Europe to the East, where intolerance, ghettoization, and sporadic massacres continued. In the nineteenth century, anti-Jewish laws were abolished in most Western European states, and Jews were free to attend universities and participate fully in their country's economic, political, and cultural life. But old prejudices persisted, and in an era of social change, nationalism, and new racial doctrines emerging from Charles Darwin's theories of evolution, antisemitism intensified. The Jews fared worst in Russia and the Russian-governed areas of Poland, Ukraine, and Lithuania. In these areas, where millions of Jews lived, Russia's tsarist government enforced and extended anti-Jewish laws and encouraged mob attacks (pogroms) on Jewish communities to deflect attention from its own failures.

As evidenced in *Mein Kampf* (see Chapter 4, source no. 16), Hitler made virulent antisemitism a cornerstone of National Socialism. Millions of Germans were attracted to his racial theories and comforted by his claim that a Jewish-communist conspiracy had caused Germany's defeat in World War I. Their votes carried the Nazis to power in January 1933.

Once in authority, the Nazis began to implement the anti-Jewish policies Hitler had promised. Jewish shops were plundered while police looked the other way; Jewish physicians were excluded from hospitals; Jewish judges lost their posts; Jewish students were denied admission to universities; and Jewish veterans were stripped of their benefits. In 1935 the Nazis promulgated the Nuremberg Laws, which deprived Jews of citizenship and outlawed marriage between Jews and non-Jews. On the night of November 9 to 10, 1938, the Nazis organized nationwide violence against Jewish synagogues and shops in what came to be known as *Kristallnacht,* night of the broken glass.

After the war began, conquests in Eastern Europe provided the Nazis new opportunities to deal with the "Jewish problem." In early 1941, they began to deport Jews from Germany and conquered territories to Poland and Czechoslovakia, where they were used as slave laborers or placed in concentration camps. In June 1941 special units known as *Einsatzgruppe* (special action forces) were organized to exterminate Jews in conquered territories on the Eastern front. In eighteen months, they gunned down over one million Jews. In January 1942 at the Wannsee conference outside Berlin, the Nazi leadership approved the Final Solution to the Jewish problem. Their goal was the extermination of European Jewry, and to reach it they constructed special death camps where their murderous work could be carried out efficiently and quickly.

When World War II ended, the Nazis had not achieved their goal of annihilating all of Europe's Jews. They did, however, slaughter close to six million, thus earning themselves a permanent place in the long history of humankind's inhumanity.

"Führer, You Order, We Obey"

❖

62 ❖ *Rudolf Höss, MEMOIRS*

Born in 1900, Rudolf Höss abandoned plans to become a priest after serving in World War I, and became active in a number of right-wing political movements, including the Nazi Party, which he joined in 1922. After serving a jail sentence for participating in the murder of a teacher suspected of "treason," he became a farmer and then in 1934, on the urging of Heinrich Himmler, a member of the Nazi SS, or *Schutzstaffel* (guard detachment). Under Himmler the SS grew from a small security force whose principal role was to guard Hitler and other high-ranking Nazis into a powerful organization involved in police work, state security, intelligence gathering, administration of conquered territories, and management of the concentration camps. After postings at the Dachau and Sachsenhausen camps, Höss was appointed commandant of Auschwitz, which began as a camp for Polish political prisoners but became a huge, sprawling complex where over a million Jews were gassed or shot and tens of thousands of prisoners served as slave laborers in nearby factories. In 1943 Höss become overseer of all the Third Reich's concentration camps, but he returned to Auschwitz in 1944 to oversee the murder of four hundred thousand Hungarian Jews. After his capture in 1946, Höss was tried and convicted for crimes against humanity. He was hanged on April 16, 1947, within sight of the villa where he and his family had lived while he served at Auschwitz.

While awaiting trial, Höss was encouraged by prosecutors to compose his memoirs to sharpen his recollection of his experiences. In the following passage he discusses his views of the Jews and his reaction to the mass killings he planned and witnessed.

QUESTIONS FOR ANALYSIS

1. According to Höss, what was his attitude toward the Jews and the Final Solution?
2. How do his statements about the Jews fit in with his assertion that he was a "fanatic National Socialist"?
3. How does Höss characterize his role in the mass extermination of the Jews?
4. How did his involvement in the Holocaust affect him personally? How, according to Höss, did it affect other German participants?
5. What would you describe as the key components of Höss's personality? To what extent was his personality shaped by the Nazi philosophy to which he was dedicated?
6. How can one balance Höss's role as a commandant of a killing center and his comments about his family life?
7. What insights does this excerpt provide about the extent to which the German people knew of and participated in the Holocaust?

Since I was a fanatic National Socialist, I was firmly convinced that our idea would take hold in all countries, modified by the various local customs, and would gradually become dominant. This would then break the dominance of international Jewry. Anti-Semitism was nothing new throughout the whole world. It always made its strongest appearance when the Jews had pushed themselves into positions of power and when their evil actions became known to the general public. . . . I believed that because our ideas were better and stronger, we would prevail in the long run. . . .

I want to emphasize here that I personally never hated the Jews. I considered them to be the enemy of our nation. However, that was precisely the reason to treat them the same way as the other prisoners. I never made a distinction concerning this. Besides, the feeling of hatred is not in me, but I know what hate is, and how it manifests itself. I have seen it and I have felt it.

This original order of 1941 to annihilate all the Jews stated, "All Jews without exception are to be destroyed." . . .

When [Himmler] gave me the order personally in the summer of 1941 to prepare a place for mass killings and then carry it out, I could never have imagined the scale, or what the consequences would be. Of course, this order was something extraordinary, something monstrous. However, the reasoning behind the order of this mass annihilation seemed correct to me. At the time I wasted no thoughts about it. I had received an order; I had to carry it out. I could not allow myself to form an opinion as to whether this mass extermination of the Jews was necessary or not. At the time it was beyond my frame of mind. Since the Führer himself had ordered "The Final Solution of the Jewish Question," there was no second guessing for an old National Socialist, much less an SS officer. "Führer,

you order. We obey" was not just a phrase or a slogan. It was meant to be taken seriously.[1]

Since my arrest I have been told repeatedly that I could have refused to obey this order, and even that I could have shot Himmler dead. I do not believe that among the thousands of SS officers there was even one who would have had even a glimmer of such a thought. . . . Of course, many SS officers moaned and groaned about the many harsh orders. Even then, they carried out every order. . . . As leaders of the SS, Himmler's person was sacred. His fundamental orders in the name of the Führer were holy. There was no reflection, no interpretation, no explanation about these orders. They were carried out ruthlessly, regardless of the final consequences, even if it meant giving your life for them. Quite a few did that during the war.

It was not in vain that the leadership training of the SS officers held up the Japanese as shining examples of those willing to sacrifice their lives for the state and for the emperor, who was also their god. SS education was not just a series of useless high school lectures. It went far deeper, and Himmler knew very well what he could demand of his SS.

Outsiders cannot possibly understand that there was not a single SS officer who would refuse to obey orders from Himmler, or perhaps even try to kill him because of a severely harsh order. Whatever the Führer or Himmler ordered was always right. Even democratic England has its saying, "My country, right or wrong," and every patriotic Englishman follows it.

Before the mass destruction of the Jews began, all the Russian politruks[2] and political commissars were killed in almost every camp during 1941 and 1942. According to the secret order given by Hitler, the Einsatzgruppe searched for

---

[1]All SS members swore the following oath: "I swear to you Adolf Hitler, as Führer and Chancellor of the Reich, loyalty and bravery. I vow to you and to the authorities appointed by you obedience unto death, so help me God."

[2]Communist Party members.

and picked up the Russian politruks and commissars from all the POW camps. They transferred all they found to the nearest concentration camp for liquidation. . . . The first small transports were shot by firing squads of SS soldiers.

While I was on an official trip, my second in command, Camp Commander Fritzsch, experimented with gas for killings. He used a gas called Cyclon B, prussic acid,[3] which was often used as an insecticide in the camp to exterminate lice and vermin. There was always a supply on hand. When I returned Fritzsch reported to me about how he had used the gas. We used it again to kill the next transport.

The gassing was carried out in the basement of Block 11. I viewed the killings wearing a gas mask for protection. Death occurred in the crammed-full cells immediately after the gas was thrown in. Only a brief choking outcry and it was all over. . . .

At the time I really didn't waste any thoughts about the killing of the Russian POWs. It was ordered; I had to carry it out. But I must admit openly that the gassings had a calming effect on me, since in the near future the mass annihilation of the Jews was to begin. Up to this point it was not clear to me . . . how the killing of the expected masses was to be done. Perhaps by gas? But how, and what kind of gas? Now we had discovered the gas and the procedure. I was always horrified of death by firing squads, especially when I thought of the huge numbers of women and children who would have to be killed. I had had enough of hostage executions,

and the mass killings by firing squad order by Himmler and Heydrich.[4]

Now I was at ease. We were all saved from these bloodbaths, and the victims would be spared until the last moment. That is what I worried about the most when I thought of Eichmann's[5] accounts of the mowing down of the Jews with machine guns and pistols by the Einsatzgruppe. Horrible scenes were supposed to have occurred: people running away even after being shot, the killing of those who were only wounded, especially the women and children. Another thing on my mind was the many suicides among the ranks of the SS Special Action Squads who could no longer mentally endure wading in the bloodbaths. Some of them went mad. Most of the members of the Special Action Squads drank a great deal to help get through this horrible work. According to [Captain] Höffle's accounts, the men of Globocnik's[6] extermination section drank tremendous quantities of alcohol.

In the spring of 1942 the first transports of Jews arrived from Upper Silesia. All of them were to be exterminated. They were led from the ramp across the meadow, later named section B-II of Birkenau,[7] to the farmhouse called Bunker I. Aumeier, Palitzsch, and a few other block leaders led them and spoke to them as one would in casual conversation, asking them about their occupations and their schooling in order to fool them. After arriving at the farmhouse they were told to undress. At first they went very quietly into the rooms where they were

---

[3]Cyclon (or Zyclon) B is a blue crystalline substance whose active ingredient, hydrocyanic acid, sublimates into a gas when exposed to air. It causes death by combining with the red blood cells and preventing them from carrying oxygen to the body.

[4]Reinhard Heydrich (1904–1942) was Himmler's chief lieutenant in the SS. He organized the execution of Jews in Eastern Europe in 1941.

[5]Adolf Eichmann (1906–1962) was a Nazi bureaucrat originally involved with Jewish emigration. After the Wannsee conference he was given responsibility for organizing the deportation of approximately three million Jews to death camps. He fled to Argentina in 1946, but was captured by

Israeli agents who took him to Israel, where he was tried and executed in 1962.

[6]Odilio Globocnik (1904–1945) was the officer responsible for organizing and training SS units in Poland for the purpose of carrying out the Final Solution. In 1943 he was transferred to Trieste, where he oversaw the annihilation of two thousand Italian Jews in the San Saba death camp. Captured by British troops at the end of the war, he committed suicide in May 1945.

[7]Birkenau was the German name for the town where a large addition to the Auschwitz complex was built in late 1941 and early 1942.

supposed to be disinfected. At that point some of them became suspicious and started talking about suffocation and extermination. Immediately a panic started. Those still standing outside were quickly driven into the chambers, and the doors were bolted shut. In the next transport those who were nervous or upset were identified and watched closely at all times. As soon as unrest was noticed these troublemakers were inconspicuously led behind the farmhouse and killed with a small-caliber pistol, which could not be heard by the others. . . .

I also watched how some women who suspected or knew what was happening, even with the fear of death all over their faces, still managed enough strength to play with their children and to talk to them lovingly. Once a woman with four children, all holding each other by the hand to help the smallest ones over the rough ground, passed by me very slowly. She stepped very close to me and whispered, pointing to her four children, "How can you murder these beautiful, darling children? Don't you have any heart?" . . .

Occasionally some women would suddenly start screaming in a terrible way while undressing. They pulled out their hair and acted as if they had gone crazy. Quickly they were led behind the farmhouse and killed by a bullet in the back of the neck from a small-caliber pistol. . . . As the doors were being shut, I saw a woman trying to shove her children out the chamber, crying out, "Why don't you at least let my precious children live?" There were many heartbreaking scenes like this which affected all who were present. . . .

The mass annihilation with all the accompanying circumstances did not fail to affect those who had to carry it out. They just did not watch what was happening. With very few exceptions all who performed this monstrous

"work" had been ordered to this detail. All of us, including myself, were given enough to think about which left a deep impression. Many of the men often approached me during my inspection trips through the killing areas and poured out their depression and anxieties to me, hoping that I could give them some reassurance. During these conversations the question arose again and again, "Is what we have to do here necessary? Is it necessary that hundreds of thousands of women and children have to be annihilated?" And I, who countless times deep inside myself had asked the same question, had to put them off by reminding them that it was Hitler's order. I had to tell them that it was necessary to destroy all the Jews in order to forever free Germany and the future generations from our toughest enemy.

It goes without saying that the Hitler order was a firm fact for all of us, and also that it was the duty of the SS to carry it out. However, secret doubts tormented all of us. Under no circumstances could I reveal my secret doubts to anyone. I had to convince myself to be like a rock when faced with the necessity of carrying out this horrible severe order, and I had to show this in every way, in order to force all those under me to hang on mentally and emotionally. . . .

Hour upon hour I had to witness all that happened. I had to watch day and night, whether it was the dragging and burning of the bodies, the teeth being ripped out, the cutting of the hair,[8] I had to watch all this horror. For hours I had to stand in the horrible, haunting stench while the mass graves were dug open, and the bodies were dragged out and burned. I also had to watch the procession of death itself through the peephole of the gas chamber because the doctors called my attention to it. I had to do all this because I was the one to whom everyone looked, and because I had to

---

[8]Teeth extracted from the corpses were soaked in muriatic acid to remove muscle and bone before the gold fillings were extracted. Some of the gold was distributed to dentists who used it in fillings for SS men and their families; the rest was deposited in the Reichsbank. Hair was used to make felt and thread.

show everybody that I was not only the one who gave the orders and issued the directives, but that I was also willing to be present at whatever task I ordered my men to perform. . . .

And yet, everyone in Auschwitz believed the Kommandant really had a good life. Yes, my family had it good in Auschwitz, every wish that my wife or my children had was fulfilled. The children could live free and easy. My wife had her flower paradise. . . . By the same token no former prisoner can say that he was treated poorly in any way in our house. My wife would have loved to give a present to every prisoner who performed a service for us. The children constantly begged me for cigarettes for the prisoners. The children especially loved the gardeners. In our entire family there was a deep love for farming and especially for animals. Every Sunday I had to drive with them across all the fields, walk them through the stables, and we could never skip visiting the dog kennels.

Their greatest love was for our two horses and our colt. The prisoners who worked in the household were always dragging in some animal the children kept in the garden. Turtles, martens, cats, or lizards; there was always something new and interesting in the garden. The children splashed around in the summertime in the small pool in the garden or the Sola River. Their greatest pleasure was when daddy went into the water with them. But he had only a little time to share all the joys of childhood.

Today I deeply regret that I didn't spend more time with my family. I always believed that I had to be constantly on duty. Through this exaggerated sense of duty I always had made my life more difficult than it actually was. My wife often urged me, "Don't always think of your duty, think of your family too." But what did my wife know about the things that depressed me? She never found out.[9]

---

[9]In an interview with a court-appointed psychiatrist during the Nuremberg trials in 1946, Höss stated that his wife actually did learn of his involvement in the mass executions at the camp, and that afterward they became estranged and ceased having sexual relations.

Evil

63 ◆ "B.F.," RECOLLECTIONS

B.F. was a Jew born in Warsaw, Poland, in 1925. In 1935 he and his family moved to Lodz, also in Poland, where he resided at the time of the Nazi conquest in 1939. Sent to the Warsaw ghetto, he escaped, was recaptured, and was finally sent to Sobibor, a Nazi extermination camp at which approximately 250,000 Jews were executed in 1942 and 1943. In the fall of 1943, just before the camp closed, B.F. participated in a breakout in which several hundred Jewish prisoners turned on their captors and escaped. Having survived the war, he recounted his experiences in an interview recorded in 1945.

QUESTIONS FOR ANALYSIS

Readers are encouraged to formulate their own questions about the events described in this source.

After our train moved in, the doors were thrown open and armed Germans and Ukrainians, cracking whips, drove us out of the wagons. We had bloody welts all over our bodies. The day we came to Sobibor was May fifth in the year '42. We were led through a second tower to an assembly point which was ringed by barbed-wire fences, with posts on the wire perimeters capped by some sort of metal hoods. They split us up here — men to one side and women and children to the other. Soon, SS squads came in and led the women with the children away. Where they were being taken to we didn't know, but off in the distance we heard screams of people being beaten and stripped and then we heard the rumblings of motors being started. It was the women and children being killed. We could sense in the air that, locked up like this between the wires, we'd be slaughtered right here. Night fell and we fell into a panic. We'd been told that in Belzec, people were burned alive in pits. We wouldn't believe this while we were in the ghetto, but here, when we saw a fire in the distance, we were sure they were burning people. We were overcome with fear and started saying our *viduyim*.[1]

It was a nightmare. The Ukrainians beat us and wouldn't let us out to relieve ourselves. People evacuated on the spot. . . .

There were thirty men in our group. They divided us up right away. Some were used to sort our belongings. . . . I was taken into the second group and set to work digging a latrine. I never held a shovel in my life and a German who guarded us at work noticed my "skill" and let fly such a blow over my head that he nearly split my skull. That was when I learned how to work.

We worked from daybreak till nine, then they gave us breakfast. Bread and fingerbowls of fat was all we got and afterwards, they put us to work till late evening. As night fell, we were all lined up and an SS man informed us nothing would happen to us if we behaved well. If we

didn't — they'd "make us a gift" of a bullet to the head. . . . Then, simply because he had the urge, he picked two men out — one who had stomach pains and the other who just wasn't to his liking — and led them off into the woods where he shot them. Most of the time, the men returned from work beaten, bloodied, and injured all over the body. . . .

This is what the system of going into the "bath" was like: As soon as a train with a transport of people arrived, everyone was either pulled off violently or made to jump. They were all forced to march into that sealed area. Later, the people were led off in groups of thousands, sometimes groups of hundreds. An SS man addressed them, saying since there was a war on, everyone had to work and they were about to be transported somewhere else for labor. They'd be well taken care of. Children and the old wouldn't have to work, but wouldn't lack food either. So great attention must be paid to cleanliness and we had to take a bath first. Those from the West would always applaud at this point. Later, when the Polish Jews arrived, they knew all this ended in death and screamed and made an uproar. So he said to them: "*Ruhe*,[2] I know you long for death already, but you won't be obliged so easily. First, you must work." And he kept punishing them and demoralizing them like this.

Inside the first barrack, they had their coats, jackets, and pants taken off and in the second barrack, had to strip down completely nude. They were told in that first speech that they wouldn't need any towel or soap — they'd find all that in the bath. All this led to them being brought naked into the third barrack near the bath. There was a special cell there where they were kept on arranged benches, guarded by Germans. Not a sound was permitted. Twenty barbers cut off the women's hair. When the women came in naked and saw the men there, they pulled back, but the Germans dragged them and beat them forward. They had to sit

---

[1]A prayer of confession said by Jews before their death.

[2]German, meaning "Be calm."

naked. I was one of the barbers. To shave some-one's head lasted half a minute. We held the long hair out from the head and snipped it off all along the scalp so that "stairs" were left — tufts of hair sticking out from the scalp. The foreign Jews[3] didn't suspect anything, they were just sorry about losing their hair. The Germans said it didn't matter — in half a year, the hair'd grow back. But on the other side, the Polish Jews screamed and wouldn't let us cut their hair, and they were beaten, and tortured. From there, they went straight through a corridor into a chamber. . . .

◆ ◆

I was in the camp eighteen months already. The next day, a transport of Czech Jews was brought to the camp. They came at three in the morning and we were chased out of the bunks in the dead of night. We hauled the bundles off the train, running between two rows of Ukrainians who did nothing but beat us savagely. . . .

That evening, SS man Paul harangued us as usual. He says he has to have five men for the *Lazarett.* What's a *Lazarett?* Well, a *Lazarett* is a place you don't have to work, you can sleep without interruption and don't have to bear any more burdens. But the real *Lazarett,* which means field hospital, was a small structure with a cross and icon of Jesus inside — probably from before the war — and there was a pit there where he'd lower people down and shoot them. This was his own *Lazarett.* . . . Every day, that monster had to have from three to five Jews in his *Lazarett* and he'd pick them out himself or just ask, "*Ja,* well, who's sick today? Who doesn't want to work anymore?" Or he just grabbed them at random. If he hated someone, he simply pointed his finger at them and said, "*Komm, komm,*[4] you look like you don't want to work anymore," and then led them away. There were times when some Jews had heard before what the *Lazarett* meant, and they came forward

to die voluntarily, because this life had driven them mad with despair. Victims succumbed like this every day. . . . Death came in many ways: sometimes by shooting, sometimes being bludgeoned to death with clubs. Some committed suicide. There were times we got up in the barrack in the morning, and before our eyes, saw several Jews hanging from the rafters.

The most cruel death was at the jaws of Paul's dog, "Bari." Paul would yell at him: "Bari! Be my deputy!" and the dog tore people into pieces and devoured them. As soon as he got his jaws on you, there was no way out. He snapped you around, whirling you and tearing at you so long, till there was nothing left for his jaw to clamp down on. . . .

In the year '43, our group kept growing till it reached 600 people — 120 women and 480 men.

Paul the murderer fell bewitched of a Czech Jewish girl. She cleaned up in his barrack and his attitude to us now became less sadistic. The other Germans realized this. One time, they waited till he left for the day, then came and shot the girl. When he got back, they teased him: "Well, Paul, where's your Jewish girl now?" He was so enraged, he persecuted us even more than before. He'd stand by the barrack door through which we hauled the packs, with a hatchet in his hand, and whenever the urge took him, he just swung away till he hacked someone down in a pool of blood. When the new latrines were dug and he came upon some impurity, he threatened all of us with execution. Once, he walked into the latrine area and saw two Jews stooping over the ditch, but there was a pile nearby so he dragged the two Jews over and made them eat it. They fell into a swoon, begging to be shot instead. But he wouldn't call back his order. They had to keep eating and then heaved up for the rest of the day. . . .

Sometimes, naked women hid out under the garbage, under rags. One time, I was about to

---

[3] Jews from outside of Poland.

[4] German for "Come, come."

sort through the rags when I take a look and see a woman lying among them. What do I do? I can't pull the rags away because a German will spot her immediately, so I went off to another pile of rages, but it didn't work — she was found out. She was led off and clubbed to death.

Another time, after one of the disinfections,[5] we found a child, one and a half years old, among the rags. But a Ukrainian immediately ordered me to take the child to the garbage pit, where he said: "*Ach,* a waste of a bullet!" and took a garbage shovel and split open the baby into pieces. The child hardly let out a whipper.

Often, mothers bore children during the night. Whenever found, the babies were thrown straight into the garbage pits or were torn apart down the middle by their legs, or just flung up and shot in the air or wherever they landed.

They made no fuss over children. Finally, the women rebelled. While stripping, they would scream out and attack the Germans, clawing at them and yelling. "You've lost the war anyway! Your death will be a lot crueller than ours! We're defenseless, we have to go to our death — but your women and children will be burned alive!!!" And they screeched and wailed. . . .

While we cut their hair, we stole some conversation with the women — as long as no German was watching, of course. . . .

They asked us how we were still able to work for "them" while everyone else was dead. We answered, "You have it better. You're going to die soon — but we have to keep working, getting beaten all the time, till we're finally exterminated too."

---

[5]Disinfection of clothes.

◆

The Dawn of the Atomic Age

The chain of events and decisions that led to the dropping of atomic bombs on Hiroshima and Nagasaki on August 6 and August 9, 1945, began with a letter to President Franklin D. Roosevelt written in 1939 by Leo Szilard and Albert Einstein, both of whom were distinguished European-born physicists who had immigrated to the United States to escape the scourge of Nazi antisemitism. The letter, signed only by Einstein because of his worldwide fame and because Szilard was considered a security risk, warned that German scientists were pursuing research on nuclear chain reactions with the goal of producing weapons of enormous power. The letter recommended that the U.S. government fund and coordinate similar research. Encouraged by his scientific advisors and by reports on the progress of nuclear research in England, in the early summer of 1941 the president ordered an all-out effort to produce an atomic weapon. A year later the project was placed under the control of the Army and code-named the Manhattan Project.

Under the direction of Brigadier General Leslie Groves, the Manhattan Project became a huge, desperate enterprise, costing approximately two billion dollars and employing over one hundred thousand persons, who worked under the direction of the country's leading nuclear physicists and engineers at thirty-seven installations and a dozen university laboratories. Success was achieved on July 16, 1945, when the first atomic bomb, equal in force to twenty thousand tons of TNT and two thousand times more powerful than the largest conventional bomb, was exploded in the New Mexico desert. In less than a month, atomic bombs reduced Hiroshima and Nagasaki to ashes, and World War II was over.

The Atomic Age had begun, accompanied by an intense debate over the decision to use the bomb. Had it been morally and militarily justified? Had there been ways to have demonstrated the power of the bomb without using it against Japanese cities? Had the bombs been dropped to gain a diplomatic advantage over the Soviet Union in the anticipated postwar competition for power? Had racism played a role in the decision to bomb Japan? Had the military use of atomic bombs made it more difficult to control the postwar development of nuclear weapons? These are just a few of the questions to consider as you read the following sources.

Scientists' Warnings

64 ◆ THE FRANCK REPORT

When it became clear in the spring of 1945 that the testing of the first atomic bomb was near at hand, hard questions were raised about how and where the weapon should be used, if at all. Some scientists, whose primary incentive had been to beat the Nazis in the race to develop nuclear weapons, had misgivings about its military use after Germany had been defeated and ultimate victory over Japan was assured. Beginning in April, several prominent physicists, most of whom had worked at the Chicago Metallurgical Laboratory, sent personal letters and petitions to President Roosevelt and, after his death, to President Truman asking them to refrain from using the bomb militarily. Several, including Leo Szilard, made in-person appeals to presidential advisors and military officials.

Scientific opposition to the military use of the atomic bomb was crystallized in the so-called Franck Report, drawn up in June 1945 by scientists at the Chicago Metallurgical Laboratory who had formed the Committee on the Social and Political Implications of Atomic Energy. Its chairperson was codirector of the laboratory James Franck, a German-born chemist and Nobel laureate (1925) for his work on the bombardment of atoms by electrons. The Committee's recommendations, which were challenged by other leading scientists, were sent to Washington, but ultimately were rejected by the Interim Committee, appointed by President Truman to advise him on the use of atomic weapons.

QUESTIONS FOR ANALYSIS

1. Why, according to the authors of the report, had Germany's defeat changed their thinking about the use of nuclear weapons?
2. According to the report, how would nuclear weapons best be limited and controlled in the postwar era?
3. In the scientists' opinions, would the military use of nuclear weapons undermine any postwar agreement on their control and limitation?

4. What is meant when the report states that "only lack of *trust*" can stand in the way of effective control of nuclear weapons?
5. What kind of future does the report envision in the absence of an agreement to limit nuclear weapons?

Scientists have often before been accused of providing new weapons for the mutual destruction of nations, instead of improving their well-being. It is undoubtedly true that the discovery of flying, for example, has so far brought much more misery than enjoyment and profit to humanity. However, in the past, scientists could disclaim direct responsibility for the use to which mankind had put their disinterested discoveries. We feel compelled to take a more active stand now because the success which we have achieved in the development of nuclear power is fraught with infinitely greater dangers than were all the inventions of the past. All of us, familiar with the present state of nucleonics, live with the vision before our eyes of sudden destruction visited on our own country, of a Pearl Harbor disaster repeated in thousand-fold magnification in every one of our major cities. . . .

. . . The consequences of nuclear warfare, and the type of measures which would have to be taken to protect a country from total destruction by nuclear bombing, must be as abhorrent to other nations as to the United States. England, France, and the smaller nations of the European continent, with their congeries of people and industries, would be in a particularly desperate situation in the face of such a threat. Russia and China are the only great nations at present which could survive a nuclear attack. However, even though these countries may value human life less than the peoples of Western Europe and America, and even though Russia, in particular, has an immense space over which its vital industries could be dispersed and a government which can order this dispersion the day it is convinced that such a measure is necessary — there is no doubt that Russia will shudder at the possibility of a sudden disintegration of

Moscow and Leningrad and of its new industrial cities in the Urals and Siberia. Therefore, only lack of mutual *trust,* and not lack of *desire* for agreement, can stand in the path of an efficient agreement for the preventing of nuclear warfare. The achievement of such an agreement will thus essentially depend on the integrity of intentions and readiness to sacrifice the necessary fraction of one's own sovereignty, by all the parties to the agreement.

From this point of view, the way in which the nuclear weapons now being secretly developed in this country are first revealed to the world appears to be of great, perhaps fateful importance. . . . Although important tactical results undoubtedly can be achieved by a sudden introduction of nuclear weapons, we nevertheless think that the question of the use of the very first available atomic bombs in the Japanese war should be weighed very carefully, not only by military authorities, but by the highest political leadership of this country. If we consider international agreement on total prevention of nuclear warfare as the paramount objective, and believe that it can be achieved, this kind of introduction of atomic weapons to the world may easily destroy all our chances of success. Russia, and even allied countries which bear less mistrust of our ways and intentions, as well as neutral countries may be deeply shocked. It may be very difficult to persuade the world that a nation which was capable of secretly preparing and suddenly releasing a weapon as indiscriminate as the rocket bomb and a million times more destructive is to be trusted in its proclaimed desire of having such weapons abolished by international agreement. . . .

Thus, from the "optimistic" point of view — looking forward to an international agreement on the prevention of nuclear warfare — the military advantages and the saving of American lives achieved by the sudden use of atomic bombs against Japan may be outweighed by the ensuing loss of confidence and by a wave of horror and repulsion sweeping over the rest of the world and perhaps even dividing public opinion at home.

From this point of view, a demonstration of the new weapon might best be made, before the eyes of representatives of all the United Nations, on the desert or a barren island. The best possible atmosphere for the achievement of an international agreement could be achieved if America could say to the world, "You see what sort of a weapon we had but did not use. We are ready to renounce its use in the future if other nations join us in this renunciation and agree to the establishment of an efficient international control."

After such a demonstration the weapon might perhaps be used against Japan if the sanction of the United Nations (and of public opinion at home) were obtained, perhaps after a preliminary ultimatum to Japan to surrender or at least to evacuate certain regions as an alternative to their total destruction. This may sound fantastic, but in nuclear weapons we have something entirely new in order of magnitude of destructive power, and if we want to capitalize fully on the advantage their possession gives us, we must use new and imaginative methods.

It must be stressed that if one takes the pessimistic point of view and discounts the possibility of an effective international control over nuclear weapons at the present time, then the advisability of an early use of nuclear bombs against Japan becomes even more doubtful — quite independently of any humanitarian considerations. If an international agreement is not concluded immediately after the first demonstration, this will mean a flying start toward an unlimited armaments race. If this race is inevitable, we have every reason to delay its beginning as long as possible in order to increase our head start still further. . . .

. . . Thus it is to our interest to delay the beginning of the armaments race. . . . The benefit to the nation, and the saving of American lives in the future, achieved by renouncing an early demonstration of nuclear bombs and letting the other nations come into the race only reluctantly, on the basis of guesswork and without definite knowledge that the "thing does work," may far outweigh the advantages to be gained by the immediate use of the first and comparatively inefficient bombs in the war against Japan. . . .

Another argument which could be quoted in favor of using atomic bombs as soon as they are available is that so much taxpayers' money has been invested in these Projects that the Congress and the American public will demand a return for their money. The attitude of American public opinion, . . . in the matter of the use of poison gas against Japan, shows that one can expect the American public to understand that it is sometimes desirable to keep a weapon in readiness for use only in extreme emergency; and as soon as the potentialities of nuclear weapons are revealed to the American people, one can be sure that they will support all attempts to make the use of such weapons impossible.

Once this is achieved, the large installations and the accumulation of explosive material at present earmarked for potential military use will become available for important peace time developments, including power production, large engineering undertakings, and mass production of radioactive materials. In this way, the money spent on wartime development of nucleonics may become a boon for the peace time development of [the] national economy.

"The Face of War Is the Face of Death"

◈

65 ◆ *Henry L. Stimson,*
THE DECISION TO USE THE ATOMIC BOMB

President Truman, who did not even know about the Manhattan Project as a senator from Missouri and as vice-president under Roosevelt, learned of the new weapon in a meeting with Secretary of War Henry L. Stimson on April 25, two weeks after President Roosevelt's death. Truman's first response was to appoint a small committee, known as the Interim Committee, to advise him on the use of atomic weapons during and after the war. Its members included Stimson and seven others: George Harrison, an insurance executive who was a special assistant to Stimson; James Byrnes, a presidential advisor and soon secretary of state; Ralph Bard, undersecretary of the navy; William Clayton, assistant secretary of state; Vannevar Bush, president of the Carnegie Institution in Washington; Karl Compton, president of the Massachusetts Institute of Technology; and James Conant, president of Harvard University. They were advised by the Scientific Panel made up of four persons who had played leading roles in the Manhattan Project: Enrico Fermi, of Columbia University; Arthur H. Compton, of the University of Chicago; Ernest Lawrence, of the University of California at Berkeley; and Robert Oppenheimer, director of the atomic energy research project at Los Alamos, New Mexico.

The chair of the Interim Committee, and the author of the following excerpt, was Stimson. Born in 1867 in New York City, and a graduate of Harvard University and Yale Law School, Stimson had a distinguished career as a lawyer and public servant. Having served as secretary of war under President Taft and secretary of state under President Hoover, he was named secretary of war by Roosevelt in 1940, even though he was a Republican. In 1947, after his retirement from public service and less than three years before his death in 1950, he published the article "The Decision to Use the Atomic Bomb" in *Harper's Magazine.* It focused on the work of the Interim Committee and the reasons why Stimson advised President Truman to drop atomic bombs on Japan without warning. Excerpts from the article follow.

QUESTIONS FOR ANALYSIS

1. How did the background and specific purposes of the Manhattan Project affect decision-making in 1945?
2. For those who supported the immediate use of the bombs, what specific goals did they hope to achieve?
3. How was the choice of Hiroshima and Nagasaki as targets related to these goals?
4. How seriously does it appear that the views expressed in the Franck Report were considered by the Intermin Committee and Stimson? Why did they ultimately reject the Report's proposals?

5. What were Stimson's views of the nature of war? How did his views affect his decision to support the immediate use of atomic bombs?

GOALS OF THE MANHATTAN PROJECT

The original experimental achievement of atomic fission had occurred in Germany in 1938, and it was known that the Germans had continued their experiments. In 1941 and 1942 they were believed to be ahead of us, and it was vital that they should not be the first to bring atomic weapons into the field of battle. Furthermore, if we should be the first to develop the weapon, we should have a great new instrument for shortening the war and minimizing destruction. At no time, from 1941 to 1945, did I ever hear it suggested by the President, or by any other responsible member of the government, that atomic energy should not be used in the war. All of us of course understood the terrible responsibility involved in our attempt to unlock the doors to such a devastating weapon; President Roosevelt particularly spoke to me many times of his own awareness of the catastrophic potentialities of our work. But we were at war, and the work must be done. . . .

RECOMMENDATION OF THE INTERIM COMMITTEE AND THE SECRETARY OF WAR

The discussions of the committee ranged over the whole field of atomic energy, in its political, military, and scientific aspects. . . . The committee's work included the drafting of the statements which were published immediately after the first bombs were dropped, the drafting of a bill for the domestic control of atomic energy, and recommendations looking toward the international control of atomic energy. . . .

On June 1, after its discussions with the Scientific Panel, the Intermin Committee unanimously adopted the following recommendations:

(1) The bomb should be used against Japan as soon as possible.
(2) It should be used on a dual target — that is, a military installation or war plant surrounded by or adjacent to houses and other buildings most susceptible to damage, and
(3) It should be used without prior warning [of the nature of the weapon]. One member of the committee, Mr. Bard,[1] later changed his view and dissented from recommendation. . . .

In reaching these conclusions the Interim Committee carefully considered such alternatives as a detailed advance warning or a demonstration in some uninhabited area. Both of these suggestions were discarded as impractical. They were not regarded as likely to be effective in compelling a surrender of Japan, and both of them involved serious risks. Even the New Mexico test would not give final proof that any given bomb was certain to explode when dropped from an airplane. Quite apart from the generally unfamiliar nature of atomic explosives, there was the whole problem of exploding a bomb at a predetermined height in the air by a complicated mechanism which could not be tested in the static test of New Mexico. Nothing would have been more damaging to our effort to obtain surrender than a warning or a demonstration followed by a dud — and this was a real possibility. Furthermore, we had no bombs to waste. It was vital that a sufficient effect be quickly obtained with the few we had. . . .

---

[1]Undersecretary of the navy and a member of the Interim Committee. He was the only member of the Committee to oppose its recommendations. In protest, he resigned.

. . . The committee's function was, of course, entirely advisory. The ultimate responsibility for the recommendation to the President rested upon me, and I have no desire to veil it. The conclusions of the committee were similar to my own, although I reached mine independently. I felt that to extract a genuine surrender from the Emperor and his military advisers, they must be administered a tremendous shock which would carry convincing proof of our power to destroy the Empire. Such an effective shock would save many times the number of lives, both American and Japanese, that it would cost.

The facts upon which my reasoning was based and steps taken to carry it out now follow.

The principal political, social, and military objective of the United States in the summer of 1945 was the prompt and complete surrender of Japan. Only the complete destruction of her military power could open the way to lasting peace. . . .

As we understood it in July, there was a very strong possibility that the Japanese government might determine upon resistance to the end, in all the areas of the Far East under its control. In such an event the Allies would be faced with the enormous task of destroying an armed force of five million men and five thousand suicide aircraft, belonging to a race which had already amply demonstrated its ability to fight literally to the death.

The strategic plans of our armed forces for the defeat of Japan, as they stood in July, had been prepared without reliance upon the atomic bomb, which had not yet been tested in New Mexico. We were planning an intensified sea and air blockade, and greatly intensified strategic air bombing, through the summer and early fall, to be followed on November 1 by an invasion of the southern island of Kyushu. This would be followed in turn by an invasion of the main island of Honshu in the spring of 1946. The total U.S. military and naval force involved in this grand design was of the order of 5,000,000 men; if all those indirectly concerned are included, it was larger still.

We estimated that if we should be forced to carry this plan to its conclusion, the major fighting would not end until the latter part of 1946, at the earliest. I was informed that such operations might be expected to cost over a million casualties to American forces alone. Additional large losses might be expected among our allies, and, of course, if our campaign were successful and if we could judge by previous experience, enemy casualties would be much larger than our own. . . .

◆ After Japan on July 28 rejected the Postdam ultimatum, which gave their leaders the choice of immediate surrender or the "utter destruction of the Japanese homeland," plans went forward for using the atomic bombs.

Because of the importance of the atomic mission against Japan, the detailed plans were brought to me by the military staff for approval. With President Truman's warm support I struck off the list of suggested targets the city of Kyoto. Although it was a target of considerable military importance, it had been the ancient capital of Japan and was a shrine of Japanese art and culture. We determined that it should be spared. I approved four other targets including the cities of Hiroshima and Nagasaki.

Hiroshima was bombed on August 6, and Nagasaki on August 9. These two cities were active working parts of the Japanese war effort. One was an army center; the other was naval and industrial. Hiroshima was the headquarters of the Japanese Army defending southern Japan and was a major military storage and assembly point. Nagasaki was a major seaport and it contained several large industrial plants of great wartime importance. We believed that our attacks had struck cities which must certainly be important to the Japanese military leaders, both Army and Navy, and we waited for a result. We waited one day.

FINAL REFLECTIONS

. . . As I look back over the five years of my service as Secretary of War, I see too many stern and heartrending decisions to be willing to pretend that war is anything else than what it is. The face of war is the face of death; death is an inevitable part of every order that a wartime leader gives. The decision to use the atomic bomb was a decision that brought death to over a hundred thousand Japanese. No explanation can change that fact and I do not wish to gloss it over. But this deliberate, premeditated destruction was our least abhorrent choice. The destruction of Hiroshima and Nagasaki put an end to the Japanese war. It stopped the fire raids and the strangling blockade; it ended the ghastly specter of a clash of great land armies.

August 6, 1945

◆

66 ◆ *Iwao Nakamura and Atsuko Tsujioka,* *RECOLLECTIONS*

In 1951 Dr. Arata Osada, a professor of education at the University of Hiroshima, sponsored a project in which Japanese students from primary grades through the university level were asked to write down their memories of the August 6 bombing and its aftermath. Moved by their recollections, he arranged to have published a sample of their compositions in 1951. His stated purpose was to reveal the horrors of nuclear war and thereby encourage nuclear disarmament. An English translation appeared in 1980.

QUESTIONS FOR ANALYSIS

Readers are encouraged to formulate their own questions about the events and experiences described in these sources.

IWAO NAKAMURA

11th Grade Boy (5th Grade at the Time)
Today, as I begin to write an account of my experiences after five years and several months have passed, the wretched scenes of that time float up before my eyes like phantoms. And as these phantoms appear, I can actually hear the pathetic groans, the screams.

In an instant it became dark as night, Hiroshima on that day. Flames shooting up from wrecked houses as if to illuminate this darkness. Amidst this, children aimlessly wandering about, groaning with pain, their burned faces twitching and bloated like balloons. An old man, skin flaking off like the skin of a potato, trying to get away on weak, unsteady legs, praying as

he went. A man frantically calling out the names of his wife and children, both hands to his forehand from which blood trickled down. Just the memory of it makes my blood run cold. This is the real face of war. . . .

I, who cannot forget, was in the fifth year of primary school when it happened. To escape the frequent air raids, I and my sisters had been evacuated to the home of our relatives in the country, but on August 2 returned to my home at Naka Kakomachi (near the former Prefectural Office) during the summer vacation, to recover from the effects of a summer illness that had left me very weak. . . .

It was after eight on August 6 and the midsummer sun was beginning to scorch down on Hiroshima. An all-clear signal had sounded and with relief we sat down for breakfast a little later than usual. Usually by this time, my father had left the house for the office and I would be at the hospital for treatment.

I was just starting on my second bowl of rice. At that moment, a bluish-white ray of light like a magnesium flare hit me in the face, a terrific roar tore at my eardrums and it became so dark I could not see anything. I stood up, dropping my rice bowl and chopsticks. I do not know what happened next or how long I was unconscious. When I came to, I found myself trapped under what seemed like a heavy rock, but my head was free. It was still dark but I finally discovered that I was under a collapsed wall. It was all so sudden that I kept wondering if I was dreaming. I tried very hard to crawl free, but the heavy wall would not budge. A suffocating stench flooded the area and began to choke me. My breathing became short, my ears began to ring, and my heart was pounding as if it were about to burst. "I can't last much longer," I said to myself, and then a draft of cold air flowed past me and some light appeared. The taste of that fresh air is something I shall never forget. I breathed it in with all my might. This fresh air and the brighter surroundings gave me renewed vigor and I somehow managed to struggle out from under the wall. . . .

Nothing was left of the Hiroshima of a few minutes ago. The houses and buildings had been destroyed and the streets transformed into a black desert, with only the flames from burning buildings giving a lurid illumination to the dark sky over Hiroshima. Flames were already shooting out of the wreckage of the house next door. We couldn't see my two brothers. My mother was in tears as she called their names. My father went frantic as he dug among the collapsed walls and scattered tiles. It must have been by the mercy of God that we were able to rescue my brothers from under the wreckage before the flames reached them. They were not hurt, either. The five of us left our burning home and hurried toward Koi. Around us was a sea of flames. The street was filled with flames and

smoke from the burning wreckage of houses and burning power poles which had toppled down blocked our way time after time, almost sending us into the depths of despair. It seems that everyone in the area had already made their escape, for we saw no one but sometimes we heard moans, a sound like a wild beast. . . . As we passed Nakajima Primary School area and approached Sumiyoshi Bridge, I saw a damaged water tank in which a number of people had their heads down, drinking. I was so thirsty and attracted by the sight of people that I left my parents' side without thinking, and approached the tank. But when I got near and was able to see into the tank, I gave an involuntary cry and backed away. What I saw reflected in the blood-stained water were the faces of monsters. They had leaned over the side of the tank and died in that position. From the burned shreds of their sailor uniforms, I knew they were schoolgirls, but they had no hair left and their burned faces were crimson with blood; they no longer appeared human. After we came out on the main road and crossed Sumiyoshi Bridge, we finally came across some living human beings — but maybe it would be more correct to say that we met some people from Hell. They were naked and their skin, burned and bloody, was like red rust and their bodies were bloated up like balloons. . . . The houses on both sides of this street, which was several dozen yards wide, were in flames so that we could only move along a strip in the center about three or four yards wide. This narrow passage was covered with seriously burned and injured people, unable to walk, and with dead bodies, leaving hardly any space for us to get through. At places, we were forced to step over them callously, but we apologized in our hearts as we did this. Among them were old people pleading for water, tiny children seeking help, students unconsciously calling for their parents, brothers, and sisters, and there was a mother prostrate on the ground, moaning with pain but with one arm still tightly embracing her dead baby. But how could we help them when we ourselves did not know our own fate?

When we reached the Koi First Aid Station, we learned that we were among the last to escape from the Sumiyoshi Bridge area. After my father had received some medical treatment, we hurried over Koi Hill to our relatives at Tomo Village in Asa County. When we were crossing the hill late that evening, we could see Hiroshima lying far below, now a mere smoldering desert. After offering a silent prayer for the victims, we descended the hill toward Tomo.

ATSUKO TSUJIOKA

Student, Hiroshima Women's Junior College

It happened instantaneously. I felt as if my back had been struck with a big hammer, and then as if I had been thrown into boiling oil. I was unconscious for a while. When I regained my senses, the whole area was covered with black smoke. . . . I lay on the ground with my arms pressed against my chest, and called for help, again and again: "Mother! Mother! Father!"

But, of course, neither Mother nor Father answered me. . . . I could hear the other girls shouting for their mothers in the hellish darkness, and I sensed that they were getting away. I got up and just ran after them desperately. Near Tsurumi Bridge, a red hot electric wire got wrapped around my ankles. I pulled free of it somehow, without thinking, and ran to the foot of the Tsurumi Bridge. By that time, there was white smoke everywhere. I had been working in a place called Tanaka-cho, about 600 yards from the blast center. I seemed to have been blown quite a bit north and had to take a completely different route to the bridge, which would have been straight ahead of me if I was where I should have been.

There was a large cistern at the foot of the bridge. In the tank were some mothers, one holding her naked, burned baby above her head, and another crying and trying to give her baby milk from her burned breast. Also in the tank were schoolchildren, with only their heads, and their hands clasped in prayer, above the surface of the water. They were sobbing for their parents, but everyone had been hurt, so there was no one to help them. People's hair was white with dust, and scorched; they did not look human. "Surely not me," I thought, and I looked down at my hands. They were bloody and what looked like rags hung from my arms, and inside was freshlooking flesh, all red, white and black. I was shocked and reached for the handkerchief I carried in the pocket of my trousers, but there was no handkerchief or pocket. The lower part of the trousers had been burned away. I could feel my face swelling up, but there was nothing I could do about it. I and some friends decided to try to get back to our houses in the suburbs. Houses were blazing on both sides of the street as we walked along, and my back started hurting worse.

We heard people calling for help inside wrecked buildings, and then saw the same buildings go up in flames. A boy of about six, covered in blood, was jumping up and down in front of one of the burning houses, holding a cooking pot in is hands and yelling something we could not understand. . . . I wonder what happened to those people? And the ones trapped in the buildings. In our rush to get home quickly, the four of us were proceeding toward the center of the atomic explosion, in the opposite direction from everyone else. However, when we reached Inari-machi, we could not go any further because the bridge had been destroyed, so we headed for Futaba Hill, instead. My legs gave out near Futaba, and I almost crawled the last part of the way to the foot of the hill, saying, "Wait for me! Please wait for me!"

Luckily for us, we met some kind soldiers in white coats there, who took us to a place we could lie down and rest, and treated our wounds. They dug around and told me that they had removed pieces of tile from the back of my head. They bandaged my head for me and tried to console us by saying, "Rest here now. Your teacher is bound to come and get you soon." . . .

That first night ended. There were cries for water from early morning. I was terribly thirsty.

There was a puddle in the middle of the barracks. I realized that the water was filthy, but I scooped up some of it with my shoe and drank it. It looked like coffee with milk. . . . I found out that there was a river just behind the barracks and went out with my shoes and drank to my heart's content. After that, I went back and forth many times to get water for those lying near me, and for the injured soldiers. . . . Mercurochrome had been painted on my burns once, and they got black and sticky. I tried to dry them out in the sun. My friends and the other people were no longer able to move. The skin had peeled off of their burned arms, legs and backs. I wanted to move them, but there was no place on their bodies that I could touch. Some people came around noon on the second day and gave us some rice balls. Our faces were burned and swollen so badly that we could hardly open our mouths, so we got very little of the rice into them. My eyes had swollen up by the third day, and I could not move around. I lay down in the barracks with my friends. I remember being in a kind of dream world, talking on and on with my delirious friends. . . .

Another time, I must have been dreaming: I thought that my father and sister were coming up the hill to get me. I was so glad that I forced my eyes open with my fingers to see, but it was dark and I could not see anything. People who came to the barracks would call out the names and addresses of the people they were looking for. My father and four or five of our neighbors had been searching for me since the bombing. They found me in a corner of the barracks at the foot of Futaba Hill, on the evening of the third day. They were able to find me because the wooden name tag my father had written for me was on my chest. The writing on the tag had been burned all the way through it, as if it had been etched.

"Atsuko! This is your father!"

I was so happy I couldn't speak. I only nodded my head. My eyes were swollen closed. I could not see my father, but I was saved.

I still have the scars from that day; on my head, face, arms, legs and chest. There are reddish black scars on my arms and the face that I see in the mirror does not look as if it belongs to me. It always saddens me to think that I will never look the way I used to. I lost all hope at first. I was obsessed with the idea that I had become a freak and did not want to be seen by anyone. I cried constantly for my good friends and kind teachers who had died in such terrible way.

My way of thinking became warped and pessimistic. Even my beautiful voice, that my friends had envied, had turned weak and hoarse. When I think of the way it was then, I feel as if I were being strangled. But I have been able to take comfort in the thought that physical beauty is not everything, that a beautiful spirit can do away with physical ugliness. This has given me new hope for the future. I am going to study hard and develop my mind and body, to become someone with culture and inner beauty.

◆

From World War II to the Cold War

In April 1945, the Allies, led by Great Britain, the United States, and the Soviet Union, defeated Hitler and were planning their final victory over Japan. Less than a year later, however, in March 1946, the British wartime leader Winston Churchill warned that an "iron curtain" was descending across Soviet-dominated Eastern Europe, and called for an Anglo-American alliance to halt further Soviet expansion. One year after that, in March 1947, President Harry Truman in an address to Congress denounced the Soviet Union as a menace to world peace and committed the United States to support "free peoples who are resisting attempted subjugation by armed minorities or by outside pressures." Truman's aide, Clark Clifford, described the speech as "the opening gun in a campaign to bring the people up to the realization that the war isn't over by any means." In April 1947 another presidential aide, Bernard Baruch, gave the war a name. It was a "cold war," a war that would dominate international politics until the last decade of the twentieth century.

Historians have minutely explored the causes of the Cold War, and have written a great deal about which side — the Soviet Union or the United States — was to blame for bringing it about. One thing is certain, however: 1946 was a pivotal year in Soviet-U.S. relations. Until then, despite wartime disagreements and postwar conflicts over Iran and Turkey, there were still those on both sides who sought cooperation, not confrontation, between the two emerging super-powers. In 1946, however, attitudes hardened, and moderates such as U.S. Secretary of Commerce Henry Wallace and the Soviet career diplomat Maxim Litinov resigned or were removed from office. When negotiations over nuclear arms control failed in June and the Paris foreign ministers' conference over Eastern Europe ended acrimoniously in August, Soviet-U.S. conflict seemed inevitable.

Two documents written in 1946 illustrate this bleak assessment of U.S.-Soviet relations, and in no small measure contributed to it. The first, composed in February 1946 by the Moscow-based career diplomat George Kennan and known as the Long Telegram, profoundly affected U.S. policy toward the Soviet Union throughout the Cold War. It analyzed the historical and ideological roots of Soviet foreign policy and recommended a policy of "containment" to prevent Soviet expansion. The second document, a telegram written in October 1946 by the Soviet ambassador to the United States, Nikolai Novikov, warned Soviet leaders that the U.S. government was bent on crippling the Soviet Union and achieving world dominance. Although Novikov's cable seems to have had less impact on policy than Kennan's telegram, it nevertheless is a revealing example of Soviet perceptions during these early stages of the Cold War.

The Sources of Soviet Conduct

❖

67 ◆ George Kennan, THE LONG TELEGRAM

Born in Milwaukee in 1904 and raised in a strict Protestant household, George Kennan entered the U.S. Foreign Service directly after his graduation from Princeton in 1925. Having mastered the Russian language through studies at the University of Berlin, he had postings in Moscow, Berlin, and Prague before returning to Moscow in 1944 as special advisor to the U.S. ambassador to the Soviet Union, Averill Harriman. In early February 1946 he received a directive from the State Department to analyze the implications of a recent Stalin speech that Washington viewed as confrontational and hostile. Kennan, an advocate of a hard line against the Soviet Union, used the opportunity to write what is arguably the best-known such dispatch in the history of U.S. diplomacy. It was avidly read by State Department officials, cabled to U.S. embassies around the world, and made required reading for hundreds of military officers. In 1947 an edited version of the telegram was published as an article written by "X" in the journal *Foreign Affairs*. Kennan's telegram gave direction and purpose to U.S. foreign policy. Its recommendation to undertake long-term "containment" of Russia's expansionist tendencies through the application of counterforce became the foundation of U.S. Cold War strategy.

In 1947 Kennan was appointed head of the State Department's newly created policy planning staff and given responsibility for long-range planning. His opposition to the formation of the North Atlantic Treaty Organization (NATO), to increased military spending, and to U.S. involvement in the Korean War led to his resignation in 1951. Since then, with the exception of brief ambassadorships to the Soviet Union in 1952 and to Yugoslavia between 1961 and 1963, Kennan has devoted himself to research, writing, and university teaching on foreign policy and Soviet affairs.

QUESTIONS FOR ANALYSIS

1. What views of capitalism and socialism are presented, according to Kennan, in official Soviet propaganda?
2. What does Kennan consider to be the outstanding characteristics of Russia's past?
3. How, according to Kennan, has this past affected the policies and views of the Soviet government since 1917?
4. In Kennan's view, what role does communist ideology play in shaping the policies of the Soviet government?
5. According to Kennan's analysis, what strengths and weaknesses does the Soviet Union bring to the anticipated conflict with the United States?
6. What, in Kennan's view, are the implications of his analysis for U.S. foreign and domestic policy? What must be done to counter the inevitable Soviet threat?

PART 1: BASIC FEATURES OF POSTWAR SOVIET OUTLOOK, AS PUT FORWARD BY OFFICIAL PROPAGANDA MACHINE, ARE AS FOLLOWS

(a) USSR still lives in antagonistic "capitalist encirclement" with which in the long run there can be no permanent peaceful coexistence. . . .
(b) Capitalist world is beset with internal conflicts, inherent in nature of capitalist society. . . . Greatest of them is that between England and US.
(c) Internal conflicts of capitalism inevitably generate wars. Wars thus generated may be of two kinds: intra-capitalist wars between two capitalist states and wars of intervention against socialist world. Smart capitalists, vainly seeking escape from inner conflicts of capitalism, incline toward latter. . . .

PART 2: BACKGROUND OF OUTLOOK

. . . At bottom of Kremlin's neurotic view of world affairs is traditional and instinctive Russian sense of insecurity. Originally, this was insecurity of a peaceful agricultural people trying to live on vast exposed plain in neighborhood of fierce nomadic peoples. To this was added, as Russia came into contact with economically advanced West, fear of more competent, more powerful, more highly organized societies in that area. But this latter type of insecurity was one which afflicted Russian rulers rather than Russian people; for Russian rulers have invariably sensed that their rule was relatively archaic in form, fragile and artificial in its psychological foundations, unable to stand comparison or contact with political systems of Western countries. For this reason they have always feared foreign penetration, feared direct contact between Western world and their own, feared what would happen if Russians learned truth about world without or if foreigners learned truth about world within. And they have learned to seek security only in patient but deadly struggle for total destruction of rival power, never in compacts and compromises with it.

It was no coincidence that Marxism, which had smouldered ineffectively for half a century in Western Europe, caught hold and blazed for the first time in Russia. Only in this land which had never known a friendly neighbor or indeed any tolerant equilibrium of separate powers, either internal or international, could a doctrine thrive which viewed economic conflicts of society as insoluble by peaceful means. After establishment of Bolshevist regime, Marxist dogma, rendered even more truculent and intolerant by Lenin's interpretation, became a perfect vehicle for sense of insecurity with which Bolsheviks, even more than previous Russian rulers, were afflicted. In this dogma, with its basic altruism of purpose, they found justification for their instinctive fear of outside world, for the dictatorship without which they did not know how to rule, for cruelties they did not dare to inflict, for sacrifices they felt bound to demand. In the name of Marxism they sacrificed every single ethical value in their methods and tactics. Today they cannot dispense with it. It is fig leaf of their moral and intellectual respectability. Without it

they would stand before history, at best, as only the last of that long succession of cruel and wasteful Russian rulers who have relentlessly forced country on to ever new heights of military power in order to guarantee external security of their internally weak regimes. . . . Thus Soviet leaders are driven [by] necessities of their own past and present position to put forward a dogma which [apparent omission] outside world as evil, hostile and menacing, but as bearing within itself germs of creeping disease and destined to be wracked with growing internal convulsions until it is given final coup de grace by rising power of socialism and yields to new and better world. . . .

PART 3: PROJECTION OF SOVIET OUTLOOK IN PRACTICAL POLICY ON OFFICIAL LEVEL

We have now seen nature and background of Soviet program. What may we expect by way of its practical implementation? . . .

On official plane we must look for following:

(a) Internal policy devoted to increasing in every way strength and prestige of Soviet state: intensive military-industrialization; maximum development of armed forces; great displays to impress outsiders; continued secretiveness about internal matters, designed to conceal weaknesses and to keep opponents in the dark.

(b) Wherever it is considered timely and promising, efforts will be made to advance official limits of Soviet power. . . .

(c) Russians will participate officially in international organizations where they see opportunity of extending Soviet power or of inhibiting or diluting power of others. . . .

(d) Toward colonial areas and backward or dependent peoples, Soviet policy . . . will be directed toward weakening of power and influence and contacts of advanced Western nations, on theory that insofar as this policy is successful, there will be created a vacuum which will favor Communist-Soviet penetration. . . .

(e) Russians will strive energetically to develop Soviet representation in, and official ties with, countries in which they sense strong possibilities of opposition to Western centers of power. This applies to such widely separated points as Germany, Argentina, Middle Eastern countries, etc.

(f) In international economic matters, Soviet policy will really be dominated by pursuit of autarchy[1] for Soviet Union and Soviet-dominated adjacent areas taken together. . . .

power. Thus, persons who are financially independent — such as individual businessmen, estate owners, successful farmers, artisans — and all those who exercise local leadership or have local prestige — such as popular local clergymen or political figures — are anathema. . . .

(e) Everything possible will be done to set major Western Powers against each other. Anti-British talk will be plugged among Americans, anti-American talk among British. Continentals, including Germans, will be taught to abhor both Anglo-Saxon powers.[2] . . .

PART 4: FOLLOWING MAY BE SAID AS TO WHAT WE MAY EXPECT BY WAY OF IMPLEMENTATION OF BASIC SOVIET POLICIES ON UNOFFICIAL, OR SUBTERRANEAN PLANE . . .

(a) To undermine general political and strategic potential of major Western Powers. Efforts will be made in such countries to disrupt national self-confidence, to hamstring measures of national defense, to increase social and industrial unrest, to stimulate all forms of disunity. All persons with grievances, whether economic or racial, will be urged to seek redress not in mediation and compromise, but in defiant, violent struggle for destruction of other elements of society. Here poor will be set against rich, black against white, young against old, newcomers against established residents, etc. . . .

(d) In foreign countries Communists will, as a rule, work toward destruction of all forms of personal independence — economic, political or moral. Their system can handle only individuals who have been brought into complete dependence on higher

PART 5: PRACTICAL DEDUCTIONS FROM STANDPOINT OF US POLICY

In summary, we have here a political force committed fanatically to the belief that with US there can be no permanent modus vivendi,[3] that it is desirable and necessary that the internal harmony of our society be disrupted, our traditional way of life be destroyed, the international authority of our state be broken, if Soviet power is to be secure. . . . In addition, it has an elaborate and far-flung apparatus for exertion of its influence in other countries, an apparatus of amazing flexibility and versatility, managed by people whose experience and skill in underground methods are presumably without parallel in history. Finally, it is seemingly inaccessible to considerations of reality in its basic reactions. . . . This is admittedly not a pleasant picture. Problem of how to cope with this force [is] undoubtedly greatest task our diplomacy has ever faced and probably greatest it will ever have to face. . . . But I would like to record my conviction that problem is within our power to solve — and that without recourse to any general military conflict. And in support of this conviction

---

[1]Economic self-sufficiency as a national policy; getting along without goods from other countries.
[2]England and the United States.

[3]Latin for manner of living; hence, a temporary agreement in a dispute pending final settlement.

there are certain observations of a more encouraging nature I should like to make:

(1) Soviet power, unlike that of Hitlerite Germany, is neither schematic[4] nor adventuristic. It does not work by fixed plans. It does not take unnecessary risks. Impervious to logic of reason, and it is highly sensitive to logic of force. For this reason it can easily withdraw — and usually does — when strong resistance is encountered at any point. Thus, if the adversary has sufficient force and makes clear his readiness to use it, he rarely has to do so. . . .

(2) Gauged against Western world as a whole, Soviets are still by far the weaker force. Thus, their success will really depend on degree of cohesion, firmness and vigor which Western world can muster. . . .

(3) Success of Soviet system, as form of internal power, is not yet finally proven. . . .

(4) All Soviet propaganda beyond Soviet security sphere is basically negative and destructive. It should therefore be relatively easy to combat it by any intelligent and really constructive program.

For these reasons I think we may approach calmly and with good heart problem of how to deal with Russia. As to how this approach should be made, I only wish to advance, by way of conclusion, following comments:

(1) Our first step must be to apprehend, and recognize for what it is, the nature of the movement with which we are dealing. We must study it with same courage, detachment, objectivity, and same determination not to be emotionally provoked or unseated by it, with which doctor studies unruly and unreasonable individual.

(2) We must see that our public is educated to realities of Russian situation. . . .

(3) Much depends on health and vigor of our own society. World communism is like malignant parasite which feeds only on diseased tissue. This is point at which domestic and foreign policies meet. Every courageous and incisive measure to solve internal problems of our own society, to improve self-confidence, discipline, morale and community spirit of our own people, is a diplomatic victory over Moscow worth a thousand diplomatic notes and joint communiqués. . . .

(4) We must formulate and put forward for other nations a much more positive and constructive picture of sort of world we would like to see than we have put forward in past. . . .

(5) Finally we must have courage and self-confidence to cling to our own methods and conceptions of human society. After all, the greatest danger that can befall us in coping with this problem of Soviet communism is that we shall allow ourselves to become like those with whom we are coping.

---

[4]In this context, having a definite outline or plan to follow.

The U.S. Drive for World Supremacy

◆

68 ◆ *Nikolai Novikov, TELEGRAM, SEPTEMBER 27, 1947*

According to some scholars there is a Soviet version of Kennan's Long Telegram: a cable sent to Moscow from Washington in September 1946 by the recently appointed Soviet ambassador to the United States, Nikolai Novikov. Trained in the early 1930s at Leningrad University in Middle Eastern economies and languages, Novikov hoped to pursue an academic career, but instead was drafted into the foreign service. He was named ambassador to Egypt in 1941 and also served as liaison to the Yugoslav and Greek governments in exile, both of which were located in Cairo. Early in 1945 he was posted to Washington, D.C., where he was named deputy chief of the Soviet mission; in April he became Soviet ambassador to the United States. He resigned from the foreign service in 1947 and returned to the Soviet Union, where he lived in obscurity. He published a memoir of his foreign service career in 1989.

We have little information about the background of Novikov's telegram, which was unknown to scholars until it was distributed by a Soviet official to a group of Soviet and U.S. historians attending a meeting on the origins of the Cold War in Washington in 1990. According to Novikov's memoir, he was requested to write an analysis of U.S. foreign policy goals at the Paris foreign ministers' conference in late summer 1946 by the Soviet foreign minister Viacheslav Molotov (1890–1986). Also according to Novikov, Molotov examined an early outline of the document in Paris and made several suggestions on how it might be improved. This information lends credence to the theory that Molotov, who favored a hard line against the West, wanted Novikov's report to present a dark and perhaps exaggerated picture of U.S. foreign policy goals to strengthen his hand against moderates.

We know that Molotov read Novikov's completed cable. The passages underlined in the following excerpt were passages that Molotov himself underlined on the original document. What happened next is unclear. Did Molotov show the telegram to Stalin and other high-ranking officials? Did the telegram contribute to the atmosphere of confrontation building in 1946? The answer to both questions is probably "yes," but until historians gain complete access to Soviet archives, no one knows exactly what role Novikov's telegram played in the Cold War's murky beginnings.

QUESTIONS FOR ANALYSIS

1. What specific evidence does Novikov cite to prove his assertion that the ultimate goal of U.S. foreign policy is world domination?
2. In Novikov's view, how is the goal to be achieved?
3. What is Novikov's evaluation of U.S. strengths and weaknesses?
4. What point of view does he express concerning Anglo-American cooperation? Is this something the Soviet Union should fear? Why or why not?
5. How does Novikov's analysis compare with Kennan's description in the Long Telegram of the "Basic Features of Postwar Soviet Outlook, as Put Forward by Official Propaganda Machine"? What do your conclusions reveal about the reasons Novikov's memorandum was written?
6. How does Novikov's assessment of U.S. foreign policy compare with Kennan's assessment of Soviet foreign policy goals?

The foreign policy of the United States, which reflects the imperialist tendencies of American monopolistic capital, is characterized in the post-war period by a striving *for world supremacy*. . . . All the forces of American diplomacy — the army, the air force, the navy, industry, and science

— are enlisted in the service of this foreign policy. For this purpose broad plans for expansion have been developed and are being implemented through diplomacy and the establishment of a system of naval and air bases stretching far beyond the boundaries of the United States, through the arms race, and through the creation of ever newer types of weapons.

. . . The foreign policy of the United States is conducted now *in a situation that differs greatly* from the one that existed in the prewar period. This situation does not fully conform to the calculations of those reactionary circles which hoped that during the Second World War they would succeed in avoiding, at least for a long time, the main battles in Europe and Asia. . . .

In this regard, it was thought that the main competitors of the United States would be crushed or greatly weakened in the war, and the United States by virtue of this circumstance would assume *the role of the most powerful factor* in resolving the fundamental questions of the postwar world. These calculations were also based on the assumption . . . that the Soviet Union, which had been subjected to the attack of German Fascism in June 1941, would also be exhausted or even completely destroyed as a result of the war.

Reality did not bear out the calculations of the American imperialists. . . .

In actuality, despite all of the economic difficulties of the postwar period connected with the enormous losses inflicted by the war and the German fascist occupation, the Soviet Union continues to remain economically independent of the outside world and is rebuilding its national economy with its own forces. . . .

The enormous relative weight of the USSR in international affairs in general and in the European countries in particular, the independence of its foreign policy, and the economic and political assistance that it provides to neighboring countries, both allies and former enemies, has

led to the growth of the political influence of the Soviet Union in these countries and to the further strengthening of democratic tendencies in them.

Such a situation in Eastern and Southeastern Europe cannot help but be regarded by the American imperialists as an obstacle in the path of the expansionist policy of the United States. . . .

. . . One of the stages in the achievement of dominance over the world by the United States is its *understanding with England concerning the partial division of the world on the basis of mutual concessions.* The basic lines of the secret agreement between the United States and England regarding the division of the world consist, as shown by facts, in their agreement on the inclusion of Japan and China in the sphere of influence of the United States in the Far East, while the United States, for its part, has agreed not to hinder England either in resolving the Indian problem or in strengthening its influence in Siam[1] and Indonesia. . . .

The American policy *in China* is striving for the complete economic and political submission of China to the control of American monopolistic capital. Following this policy, the American government does not shrink even from interference in the internal affairs of China. At the present time in China, there are more than 50,000 American soldiers. . . .

China is gradually being transformed into a bridgehead for the American armed forces. American air bases are located all over its territory. . . . The measures carried out in northern China by the American army show that it intends to stay there for a long time.

In Japan, despite the presence there of only a small contingent of American troops, control is in the hands of the Americans. . . .

Measures taken by the American occupational authorities in the area of domestic policy and intended to support reactionary classes and groups, which the United States plans to use in the struggle against the Soviet Union, also

---

[1]Thailand.

meet with a sympathetic attitude on the part of England. . . .

◆ ◆

Obvious indications of the U.S. effort to establish world dominance are also to be found in the increase in military potential in peacetime and in the establishment of a large number of naval and air bases both in the United States and beyond its borders.

In the summer of 1946, for the first time in the history of the country, Congress passed a law *on the establishment of a peacetime army, not on a volunteer basis but on the basis of universal military service.* The size of the army, which is supposed to amount to about one million persons as of July 1, 1947, was also increased significantly. The size of the navy at the conclusion of the war decreased quite insignificantly in comparison with wartime. At the present time, the American navy occupies first place in the world, leaving England's navy far behind, to say nothing of those of other countries.

Expenditures on the army and navy have risen colossally, amounting to 13 billion dollars according to the budget for 1946–47 (about 40 percent of the total budget of 36 billion dollars). This is more than ten times greater than corresponding expenditures in the budget for 1938, which did not amount to even one billion dollars. . . .

The establishment of American bases on islands that are often 10,000 to 12,000 kilometers from the territory of the United States and are on the other side of the Atlantic and Pacific oceans clearly indicates *the offensive nature of the strategic concepts* of the commands of the U.S. army and navy. This interpretation is also confirmed by the fact that the American navy is intensively studying the naval approaches to the boundaries of Europe. For this purpose, American naval vessels in the course of 1946 visited the ports of Norway, Denmark, Sweden,

Turkey, and Greece. In addition, the American navy is constantly operating in the Mediterranean Sea.

All of these facts show clearly that a decisive role in the realization of plans for world dominance by the United States is played by its armed forces.

◆ ◆

. . . In recent years American capital has penetrated very intensively into the economy of the *Near Eastern* countries, in particular into the oil industry. At present there are American oil concessions in all of the Near Eastern countries that have oil deposits (Iraq, Bahrain, Kuwait, Egypt, and Saudi Arabia). American capital, which made its first appearance in the oil industry of the Near East only in 1927, now controls about 42 percent of all proven reserves in the Near East, excluding Iran. . . .

. . . The strengthening of U.S. positions in the Near East and the establishment of conditions for basing the American navy at one or more points on the Mediterranean Sea . . . will therefore signify the emergence of a new threat to the security of the southern regions of the Soviet Union.

. . . The ruling circles of the United States obviously have a sympathetic attitude toward *the idea of a military alliance with England,* but at the present time the matter has not yet culminated in an official alliance. Churchill's speech in Fulton[2] calling for the conclusion of an Anglo-American military alliance for the purpose of establishing joint domination over the world was therefore not supported officially by Truman or Byrnes,[3] although Truman by his presence [during the "Iron Curtain" speech] did indirectly sanction Churchill's appeal.

Even if the United States does not go so far as to conclude a military alliance with England just now, in practice they still maintain very close contact on military questions. The combined

---

[2]A reference to Churchill's Iron Curtain Speech, delivered at Westminster College in Fulton, Missouri, in March 1946.

[3]James Byrnes (1879–1972), secretary of state from 1945 to 1947.

Anglo-American headquarters in Washington continues to exist, despite the fact that over a year has passed since the end of the war. . . .

◆ ◆

. . . One of the most important elements in the general policy of the United States, which is directed toward limiting the international role of the USSR in the postwar world, is the *policy with regard to Germany.* In Germany, the United States is taking measures to strengthen reactionary forces for the purpose of opposing democratic reconstruction. Furthermore, it displays special insistence on accompanying this policy with completely inadequate measures for the demilitarization of Germany. . . .

. . . Instead, the United States is considering the possibility *of terminating the Allied occupation* of German territory before the main tasks of the occupation — the demilitarization and democratization of Germany — have been implemented. This would create the prerequisites for the revival of an imperialist Germany, which the United States plans to use in a future war on its side. One cannot help seeing that such a policy has a clearly outlined *anti-Soviet edge* and constitutes a serious danger to the cause of peace.

. . . The numerous and extremely hostile statements by American government, political, and military figures with regard to the Soviet Union and its foreign policy are very characteristic of the current relationship between the ruling circles of the United States and the USSR. These statements are echoed in an even more unrestrained tone by the overwhelming majority of the American press organs. *Talk about a "third war,"* meaning a war against the Soviet Union, and even a direct call for this war — with the threat of using the atomic bomb — such is the content of the statements on relations with the Soviet Union by reactionaries at public meetings and in the press. . . .

The basic goal of this anti-Soviet campaign of American "public opinion" is to exert political pressure on the Soviet Union and compel it to make concessions. Another, no less important goal of the campaign is the attempt *to create an atmosphere of war psychosis* among the masses, who are weary of war, thus making it easier for the U.S. government to carry out measures for the maintenance of high military potential. . . .

. . . Of course, all of these measures for maintaining a high military potential are not goals in themselves. They are only intended *to prepare the conditions for winning world supremacy* in a new war, the date for which, to be sure, cannot be determined now by anyone, but which is contemplated by the most bellicose circles of American imperialism.

Careful note should be taken of the fact that the preparation by the United States for a future war is being conducted with the prospect of *war against the Soviet Union,* which in the eyes of American imperialists is the main obstacle in the path of the United States to world domination.

CHAPTER 9

The Industrialized West in an Era of Economic Growth and Social Change

In the three decades after World War II, the people and nations of the industrialized West experienced swift and profound changes. Ideologies that before the war had commanded passionate devotion from millions either died, as did fascism, or showed signs of weakening, as did communism. Except for Spain and Portugal, where dictatorships persisted into the 1970s, democratic governments committed to guaranteeing their citizens' well-being through unemployment insurance, state-supported pension systems, public housing, and economic planning gave Western Europe and the United States almost two decades of political tranquility.

Diplomatic relationships were also transformed. European states accepted a diminished role in world affairs, while the United States took its place alongside the Soviet Union as one of the world's superpowers. Such role reversals were difficult for Europeans, who for more than a century had considered it their God-given right to manage world affairs, and Americans, many of whom were uncomfortable with political and military commitments outside the Western hemisphere.

European states lost something else after World War II: their colonies. Between 1947, when India and Pakistan gained their independence from Great Britain, and the early 1970s, by which time some seventy former colonies in Africa and Asia had become sovereign states, the era of European imperialism ended. For the former colonial powers, Asian and African independence was another sign of their dwindling importance in world affairs. For the United States, these regions were a vast new arena in which its ideological and political struggle with the Soviet Union could be played out.

Western economies were also transformed in the postwar era. The 1950s and 1960s were "golden years" of economic expansion, a time when economists, politicians, and journalists routinely used the word *miracle* to describe the transition from wartime devastation to postwar affluence. Between 1950 and 1973, the economies of Great Britain and the United States expanded at an annual rate of 3 percent. In Germany, the growth rate averaged 6 percent a year, and labor shortages required the importation of more than a million and a half workers from Italy, Greece, Turkey, and elsewhere. French and Italian economic growth matched that of Germany. The French gross national product more than doubled in the 1950s and tripled in the 1960s, while in Italy industrial production rose 70% between 1958 and 1963. Europe's smaller nations also participated in the postwar boom. By the 1970s the people of Switzerland and Scandinavia had the highest standards of living in the world.

Social change was the inevitable consequence of economic growth. Urbanization accelerated as million of small farmers, unable to survive economically in an era of mechanized, scientific agriculture, moved to cities. Before World War II, agriculture, fishing, and forestry still employed around 20 percent of the population in Great Britain and Belgium, 25 percent of the population in the United States, and between 35 and 40 percent in France, Austria, and the Scandinavian countries. In the 1950s and 1960s, these percentages decreased by half, and by the 1980s less than 5 percent of the U.S., British, and German populations were farmers.

The makeup of urban populations was also changing. The old middle class, mainly business people and professionals, expanded to include office managers, technicians, teachers, and government officials. Even many factory workers now had enough income and leisure to support the claim that they had entered the ranks of the middle class. Across the socioeconomic spectrum Europeans, Americans, Canadians, and Australians created a new consumer society. They filled their apartments and new suburban homes with refrigerators, televisions, stereos, electric toasters, washing machines, and telephones, products no longer viewed as luxuries but as necessities of modern life. The greatest symbol of postwar affluence was the automobile. In the United States, new car sales jumped from 69,500 in 1945 to 5.1 million in 1949, and to 7.9 million in 1955. In Europe, where car ownership was still rare before World War II, the number of cars on the road increased from 5 million in 1948 to 44 million in 1965.

In politics, liberal democracy triumphed throughout the West. After France granted voting rights to women in 1946, all adult citizens in what came to be known as the "Western democracies" could vote in national elections. These voters mainly supported parties of the moderate right or moderate left, resulting in centrist governments committed to capitalism but supportive of state economic planning and a wide range of state-supported social programs to protect their citizens from misfortunes connected with unemployment, poor health, and old age.

The postwar years were not without conflict. The United States was plagued by racial tensions and bitter divisions over the war in Vietnam. In the late 1950s, France came close to civil war over the issue of Algerian independence. Politicians everywhere continued to argue over taxes, social legislation, and foreign policy. But the wrenching divisions of previous decades — democracy or dictatorship, capitalism or socialism — no longer stirred passionate debate.

This changed in the late 1960s when a wave of protests, demonstrations, and radical movements, driven by young people and inspired mainly by events in the United States, swept across the West from Berlin to Berkeley. The first radical protests took place in the United States in the mid 1960s: Militant blacks challenged moderates such as Martin Luther King, Jr., for leadership of the civil rights movement; student sit-ins and demonstrations connected with the "free-speech movement" convulsed the University of California at Berkeley; and the first protests against U.S. participation in the Vietnam War took place. In 1968 university campuses across Europe and the United States experienced strikes, sit-ins, riots, and demonstrations in which students sought goals that ranged from changing examination policies to ending capitalism. The late 1960s also saw the emergence of movements for women's liberation, homosexual rights, justice for Chicanos and American Indians, and a wide spectrum of environmental causes. More broadly, the youth counterculture rejected old standards of decorum and behavior and replaced them with an ethos of liberation summed up by the motto "If it feels good, do it."

These were heady times, and some radicals excitedly talked of revolution. No revolutions occurred, however, and the political institutions of postwar Western societies remained intact. But the culture and values of the West were indelibly transformed by the ferment of ideas and movements that emerged in the late 1960s and early 1970s.

◆

The End of Empires

In 1939, when World War II began in Europe, a handful of nations — the United States, Belgium, Italy, the Netherlands, Portugal, and especially Great Britain and France — controlled territories in Africa, Asia, Oceania, and Caribbean that contained approximately one-third of the world's population and area. Although the United States, never fully comfortable as an imperialist power, had granted the Philippines self-rule in 1935 with the promise of complete independence ten years later, the other colonial powers during and after World War II were intent on maintaining their colonies. In 1943 British cabinet officials spoke of "many generations" before its colonial subjects were ready for full self-government. And at the Brazzaville Conference on the future of the French empire in Africa, held in 1944 in French Equatorial Africa, the forty French officials who attended declined to even discuss independence for the

African colonies since it was so far in the future. As late as 1948, even after Great Britain had granted independence to India and Pakistan, the British foreign secretary Ernest Bevins recommended that Britain should keep its colonies in Africa to counterbalance the growing world power of the Soviet Union and United States.

Despite such ambitions, by the mid 1970s most African and Asian colonies had become independent states. Although this sweeping change is often referred to by a single word, *decolonization,* it was a complex and variegated process that defies easy generalizations. What caused it, how it unfolded, and what it left behind depended on many variables, including the strength of indigenous nationalist movements, the effects of World War II, the extent of European settlement, differences in colonial policy, and the nature of the colonial societies themselves. Decolonization in India, in which a broadly based, well-organized nationalist movement had existed since the late nineteenth century, was different from decolonization in Africa, where nationalism was just taking root at the time of independence. Decolonization in Africa differed in French, British, Belgian, and Portuguese colonies, and it differed in British colonies such as Rhodesia, where two hundred fifty thousand whites had settled, and the Gold Coast, where essentially the only British residents were administrators.

It is easier to generalize about the broad significance of decolonization. It was, first of all, another symptom of Europe's declining political influence after World War II. It was, in addition, the beginning of a new stage in the Cold War. Having begun as a conflict over the political future of postwar Europe, the Cold War in the 1950s and 1960s expanded to include the new states of Asia and Africa. To win their support, the Soviet Union and the United States extended economic and military aid, sponsored cultural exchanges, and worked behind the scenes to prop up favored politicians. In the case of Vietnam, a former French colony, great power involvement went much further. From the late 1950s until 1973, the United States sent two million troops to Southeast Asia and spent billions of dollars to prevent the unification of Vietnam under communism. The United States failed and, in doing so, learned painful lessons about the limits of power and the strength of nationalism in the postcolonial era.

Great Britain Lets Go of India

69 ◆ DEBATE IN THE HOUSE OF COMMONS, MARCH 1947

A turning point in decolonization was the withdrawal of Great Britain from India and the creation of the new states of India and Pakistan in August 1947. After the world's leading imperial power released its hold on its largest colony — the "jewel in the crown" of its empire — nationalist leaders throughout Asia and Africa demanded equal treatment, and European politicians found it more difficult to justify their colonial rule.

British and Indian leaders had debated the timing and framework of Indian independence for decades, but World War II brought the issue to a head. Many Indians, embittered by the meager benefits they had received in return for their sacrifices in World War I, showed little enthusiasm for the British cause in World War II, especially after the British viceroy announced that India was at war with Germany in September 1939 without even consulting Indian leaders. In 1942, after Japan's lightning conquest of Southeast Asia, the British government sent Sir Stafford Cripps to Delhi to offer India full dominion status after the war in return for India's support in the war effort. Negotiations broke down, however, leading Gandhi to launch the "Quit India" movement, his last nationwide passive resistance campaign against British rule. Anti-British feeling intensified in 1943 when a disastrous famine took between one million and three million lives and the pro-Japanese Indian National Army organized by Subhas Bose declared war on Great Britain.

A shift in postwar British politics also affected India's future. Elections in 1945 initiated six years of rule by the Labour Party, which was less committed than the Conservatives to maintaining the empire. In the face of mounting restiveness in India, Prime Minister C. Clement Attlee dispatched a three-person cabinet mission to India in early 1946 charged with preserving Indian unity in the face of Hindu-Muslim enmity and arranging for India's independence as soon as possible. Although Hindus and Muslims could not reconcile their differences, on February 20, 1947, the Labour government went ahead and announced that British rule would end in India no later than June 1948.

This led to an emotional two-day debate in Parliament in which Conservatives and some Liberals argued that independence should be delayed. Labour had a strong majority, however, and in March 1947 Parliament approved its plan. At midnight on August 14 and 15, 1947, predominantly Hindu India and predominantly Muslim Pakistan became independent states.

The following excerpts are from the debates in Parliament on March 4 and 5, 1947. All speakers are in opposition to a proposal of Sir John Anderson, a Liberal from Scotland, that Great Britain should promise independence by June 1948 but withdraw the offer and require further negotiations if a suitable Hindu-Muslim agreement could not be achieved.

QUESTIONS FOR ANALYSIS

1. What disagreement is revealed among the speakers on the subject of the benefits and harm of British colonial rule in India?
2. Several speakers who believed that British rule had benefited India still support independence. Why?
3. The critics of British rule in India also supported immediate independence. What was their line of argument?
4. What view of India and its leaders do the speakers express?
5. According to the speakers, what military and economic realities make it impractical to continue British rule in India?
6. How do the speakers view developments in India as part of broader historical trends?

7. **Most of the speakers were members of the Labour Party and thus sympathetic to socialism. What examples of a socialist perspective can you find in their speeches?**

MR. CLEMENT DAVIES[1] (MONTGOMERY) It is an old adage now, that "the order changeth; yielding place to new," but there has been a more rapid change from the old to the new in our time than ever before. We have witnessed great changes in each one of the five Continents, and for many of those changes this country and its people have been directly or indirectly responsible. . . . In all the lands where the British flag flies, we have taught the peoples the rule of law and the value of justice impartially administered. We have extended knowledge, and tried to inculcate understanding and toleration.

Our declared objects were twofold — first, the betterment of the conditions of the people and the improvement of their standard of life; and, second, to teach them the ways of good administration and gradually train them to undertake responsibility so that one day we could hand over to them the full burden of their own self-government. Our teachings and our methods have had widespread effect, and we should rejoice that so many peoples in the world today are awake, and aware of their own individualities, and have a desire to express their own personalities and their traditions, and to live their own mode of life. . . . Our association with India during two centuries has been, on the whole — with mistakes, as we will admit — an honorable one. So far as we were able we brought peace to this great sub-continent; we have introduced not only a system of law and order, but also a system of administration of justice, fair and impartial, which has won their respect. . . . We have tried to inculcate into them the feeling that although they are composed of different races, with different languages,

customs, and religions, they are really part of one great people of India.

The standard of life, pathetically low as it is, has improved so that during the last 30 years there has been an increase in the population of 100 million and they now number 400 million people. We have brought to them schools, universities, and teachers, and we have not only introduced the Indians into the Civil Service but have gradually handed over to them, in the Provinces and even in the Central Government, the administration and government of their own land and their own people. . . . Then in 1946, there was the offer of complete independence, with the right again, if they so chose, of contracting in and coming back within the British Commonwealth of Nations.[2]

I agree that these offers were made subject to the condition that the Indian peoples themselves would co-operate to form a Central Government and draw up not only their own Constitution, but the method of framing it. Unfortunately, the leaders of the two main parties in India have failed to agree upon the formation of even a Constituent Assembly, and have failed, therefore, to agree upon a form of Constitution. . . .

What are the possible courses that could be pursued? . . . The first of the courses would be to restore power into our own hands so that we might not only have a responsibility but the full means of exercising that responsibility. I believe that that is not only impossible but unthinkable at this present stage. . . . Secondly, can we continue, as we do at present, to wait until an agreement is reached for the formation of a Central Government with a full Constitution, capable of acting on behalf of the whole of

---

[1] A London lawyer (1884–1962) who was a Liberal member of Parliament from 1929 until the time of his death.
[2] The British Commonwealth of Nations was founded by Parliament in 1931 through the Statute of Westminster. It is a free association of nations comprised of Great Britain

and a number of its former dependencies which have chosen to maintain ties of friendship and practical cooperation and acknowledge the British monarch as symbolic head of their association. Since 1946 it has been known as the Commonwealth of Nations.

India? The present state of affairs there and the deterioration which has already set in — and which has worsened — have shown us that we cannot long continue on that course.

The third course is the step taken by His Majesty's Government — the declaration made by the Government that we cannot and do not intend in the slightest degree to go back upon our word, that we do not intend to damp the hopes of the Indian peoples but rather to raise them, and that we cannot possibly go on indefinitely as we have been going on during these past months; that not only shall they have the power they now really possess but after June 1948, the full responsibility for government of their own peoples in India. . . .

MR. SORENSEN[3] (LEYTON, WEST) I have considerable sympathy with the hon. and gallant Member for Ayr Burghs (Sir T. Moore),[4] because, politically, he has been dead for some time and does not know it. His ideas were extraordinarily reminiscent of 50 years ago, and I do not propose, therefore, to deal with so unpleasant and decadent a subject. When he drew attention to the service we have rendered to India — and we have undoubtedly rendered service — he overlooked the fact that India has had an existence extending for some thousands of years before the British occupation, and that during that period she managed to run schools, establish a chain of rest houses, preserve an economy, and reach a high level of civilization, when the inhabitants of these islands were in a condition of barbarism and savagery. One has only to discuss such matters with a few representative Indians to realize that they can draw up a fairly powerful indictment of the evil we have taken to India as well as the good. . . .

Whatever may have been the origin of the various problems in India, or the degree of culpability which may be attached to this or that party or person, a situation now confronts us

which demands a decision. . . . That is why, in my estimation, the Government is perfectly right to fix a date for the transference of power. . . . Responsibility is ultimately an Indian matter. Acute problems have existed in India for centuries, and they have not been solved under our domination. Untouchability, the appalling subjugation of women, the division of the castes, the incipient or actual conflict between Muslim and Hindu — all those and many others exist.

I do not forget what is to me the most terrible of all India's problems, the appalling poverty. It has not been solved by us, although we have had our opportunity. On the contrary, in some respects we have increased that problem, because, despite the contributions that we have made to India's welfare, we have taken a great deal of wealth from India in order that we ourselves might enjoy a relatively higher standard of life. Can it be denied that we have benefited in the past substantially by the ignorant, sweated labor of the Indian people? We have not solved those social problems. The Indians may not solve them either. There are many problems that the Western world cannot solve, but at least, those problems are India's responsibility. Indians are more likely, because they are intimate with their own problems, to know how to find their way through those labyrinths than we, who are, to the Indian but aliens and foreigners.

Here I submit a point which surely will receive the endorsement of most hon. Members of this House. It is that even a benevolent autocracy can be no substitute for democracy and liberty. . . .

I would therefore put two points to the House tonight. Are we really asked by hon. Members on the other side to engage in a gamble, first by continuing as we are and trying to control India indefinitely, with the probability that we should not succeed and that all over India there would be rebellion, chaos, and breakdown? Secondly,

---

[3]Richard Sorensen (b. 1884–1971) was a clergyman who served in Parliament as a member of the Labour Party from 1929 to 1931 and from 1939 to 1954.

[4]Lieutenant-Colonel Thomas Moore (1888–1971) was a Conservative member of Parliament from 1929 to 1962. He had just spoken against the government's plan.

are we to try to reconquer India and in doing so, to impose upon ourselves an economic burden which we could not possibly afford? How many men would be required to keep India quiet if the great majority of the Indians were determined to defy our power? I guarantee that the number would not be fewer than a million men, with all the necessary resources and munitions of war. Are we to do this at a time when we are crying out for manpower in this country, when in the mines, the textile industry, and elsewhere we want every man we can possibly secure? There are already 1,500,000 men under arms. To talk about facing the possibility of governing and policing India and keeping India under proper supervision out of our own resources is not only nonsense, but would provide the last straw that breaks the camel's back. . . .

FLIGHT-LIEUTENANT CRAWLEY [5] (BUCKINGHAM) Right hon. and hon. Members opposite, who envisage our staying in India, must have some idea of what type of rule we should maintain. A fact about the Indian Services which they seem to ignore is that they are largely Indianized. Can they really expect the Services, Indianized to the extent of 80 or 90 percent, to carry out their policy any longer? Is it not true that in any situation that is likely to arise in India now, if the British remain without a definite date being given for withdrawal, every single Indian member of the Services, will, in the mind of all politically conscious Indians become a political collaborator? We have seen that in Palestine where Arab hates Arab and Jew hates Jew if they think they are collaborating with the British.[6] How could we get the Indianized part of the Service to carry out a policy which, in the view of all political Indians, is anti-Indian? The only conceivable way in which

we could stay even for seven years in India would be by instituting a type of rule which we in this country abhor more than any other — a purely dictatorial rule based upon all the things we detest most, such as an informative police, not for an emergency measure, but for a long period and imprisonment without trial. . . .

MR. HAROLD DAVIES[7] (LEEK) I believe that India is the pivot of the Pacific Ocean area. All the peoples of Asia are on the move. Can we in this House, by wishful thinking, sweep aside this natural desire for independence, freedom, and nationalism that has grown in Asia from Karachi to Peking, [8] from Karachi to Indonesia and Indo-China? That is all part of that movement, and we must recognize it. I am not a Utopian. I know that the changeover will not be easy. But there is no hon. Member opposite who has given any concrete, practical alternative to the decision, which has been made by my right hon. Friends. What alternative can we give?

This little old country is tottering and wounded as a result of the wars inherent in the capitalist system. Can we, today, carry out vast commitments from one end of the world to another? Is it not time that we said to those for whom we have spoken so long, "The time has come when you shall have your independence. That time has come; the moment is here"? I should like to recall what Macaulay[9] said:

> Many politicians of our times are in the habit of laying it down as a self-evident proposition, that no people ought to be free until they are fit to use their freedom. This maxim is worthy of the fool in the old story who resolved not to go into the water until he had learned to swim.

India must learn now to build up democracy.

---

[5] Aidan Crawley (1908–1992) was an educator and journalist who served in the Royal Air Force during World War II. He was a Labor member of Parliament from 1945 to 1951.
[6] The British were attempting to extricate themselves from Palestine, which they had received as a mandate after World War I and was the scene of bitter Arab-Jewish rivalry.
[7] Harold Davies (1904–1984) was an author and educator

who served in Parliament as a member of the Labor Party from 1959 to 1964.
[8] Karachi, a port city on the Arabian Sea, was soon to become Pakistan's first capital city. *Peking* is a variant spelling of Beijing.
[9] Thomas B. Macaulay (1800–1859) was an English essayist, historian, and statesman.

France Lets Go of Algeria

◈

70 ◆ *Charles de Gaulle,*
COMMENTS ON ALGERIA, APRIL 11, 1961

No other episode in the history of decolonization was as bloody and divisive as Algeria's tortuous path to independence from France in the 1950s and 1960s. A French colony since the 1830s and 1840s, Algeria after World War II had a population of approximately ten million, of which just over one million were French citizens. Known as *pieds noirs* (black feet) after the black boots worn by French soldiers, the Algerian French controlled administrative posts, owned the best land, dominated the economy, and elected representatives to the French National Assembly. Ruled directly by the French Department of the Interior, French Algeria was perceived not as a colony but as an integral part of France. The French who lived in Algeria and those who lived in France itself, regardless of their political views, agreed with the prime minister of the early 1950s, Pierre Mendes-France, when he said, "France without Algeria would not be France."

After World War II, French governments made only token concessions to the demands of moderate Algerian nationalists, and even these were bitterly opposed by the *pieds noirs,* who counted on their own power and that of the French army to maintain the status quo. Inevitably, French intransigence radicalized the Algerian nationalists, and in 1954 the Front de Libération Nationale (FLN), dedicated to achieving complete independence from France, rebelled. French authorities answered with repression, to which the FLN responded with assassinations and indiscriminate terrorism. More French troops were dispatched, and atrocities committed by both sides escalated. By 1958, many French politicians and much of the French public were sickened by the war in Algeria and were prepared to negotiate its end. But this was opposed by the Algerian French and the French generals, who, after defeats in World War II and Vietnam, considered victory in Algeria as the army's last chance to regain its honor. In the spring of 1958, the political deadlock over Algeria led to a constitutional crisis when army units in Algeria revolted against the Paris government and launched a coup d'état.

Civil war was averted by the return to power of General Charles de Gaulle (1890–1970), the hero of the French resistance in World War II and the first president of France's Fourth Republic. The rebellious generals halted their insurrection when de Gaulle agreed to rule for six months with emergency powers while forging a new constitution for France. The generals and the Algerian French were convinced that de Gaulle, a nationalist with an almost mystical sense of France's world mission, would support their struggle against the FLN and Algerian independence.

De Gaulle disappointed and enraged them. Once in power, he gradually came to the conclusion that continuing the struggle in Algeria would irreparably harm his efforts to revive France politically and economically. While the killing and torture continued, de Gaulle vacillated between making concessions to the FLN and the renewed use of force. Then in April 1961 he made what proved to be a definitive statement on Algeria. A referendum would be scheduled, and if, as anticipated, the Algerians voted for independence, France would not stand in their way. De Gaulle had abandoned French Algeria, and in 1962, after the Algerians overwhelmingly voted to sever ties with France, the independent state of Algeria was born.

The following excerpt is from de Gaulle's press conference on April 11, 1961, in which he announced that France would not stand in the way of an independent Algeria.

QUESTIONS FOR ANALYSIS

1. What solution does de Gaulle propose for ending the war in Algeria?
2. What considerations have led de Gaulle to the conclusion that Algerians must determine their own political fate?
3. What, according to de Gaulle, had been the motives of French imperialism in the nineteenth century?
4. How, in de Gaulle's view, does contemporary France's position in regard to colonies differ from that of nineteenth-century France?
5. What views of the Algerians does de Gaulle express in his remarks?
6. De Gaulle claims to have been a long-term advocate of decolonization. Do the content and tone of his remarks confirm this claim?

I should like it to be well understood that in France's policy toward Algeria, the following essential idea must be faced squarely: in the world of today and in the times in which we live, France has no interest whatsoever in maintaining under her jurisdiction and under her dependence an Algeria which would choose another destiny, and it would not be in France's interest to be responsible for the population of an Algeria which would have become master of its own fate and would have nothing to offer in exchange for what it would ask. The fact is that, to say the least, Algeria costs us much more than it is worth to us. Whether in the matter of administrative expenses, economic investments, social welfare, cultural development or the many obligations with regard to the maintenance of law and order — what we furnished to it in effort, money and human ability has no counterpart that anywhere nearly approaches it.

It must in the same way be realized that France's present responsibilities in Algeria constitute heavy military and diplomatic burdens for her. And that is why France would consider today with the greatest calm a solution whereby Algeria would cease to be a part of France — a solution which in former times might have seemed disastrous for us but which, I say it again, we consider with a perfectly calm mind. . . .

. . . There are people who will say: "But it is the rebellion which leads you to think in this way.". . . It is not this that makes me speak as I do; I do not deny that the events which have occurred, which are occurring in Algeria have confirmed what I have thought and demonstrated for more than twenty years, without any joy of course — and you can well understand why — but with the certainty of serving France well.

Since Brazzaville,[1] I have not ceased to affirm that the populations dependent on us should have the right to self-determination. In 1941, I granted independence to the mandated States of Syria and Lebanon. In 1945, I gave all Africans, including Algerian Moslems, the right to vote. In 1947, I approved the Statute of Algeria which, if it had been applied, would probably have led to the progressive institution of an Algerian State Associated with France.[2] . . . I agreed that the protectorate treaties concerning Tunisia and Morocco should be approved. . . . In 1958, having resumed leadership, I, along with my Government, created the Community[3] and later recognized and aided the independence of the young States in Black Africa and Madagascar. Not having returned to power in time to prevent the Algerian insurrection, immediately upon my return I proposed to its leader to conclude the peace of the brave and to open political talks. . . . and I and my government have not ceased to act in order to promote a Moslem leadership in Algeria and to put the Moslems in a position to take local affairs into their own hands, until such time as they are able to take over on the government level. . . .

In conclusion what does this add up to: to decolonization. But if I have undertaken and pursued this task for a long time, it is not only because we could foresee and later because we witnessed the vast movement toward freedom which the world war and its aftermath

unleashed in every corner of the globe, and which the rival bids of the Soviet Union and America did not fail to emphasize. I have done it also, and especially, because it seemed to me contrary to France's present interests and new ambition to remain bound by obligations and burdens which are no longer in keeping with the requirements of her strength and influence.

. . . Moreover, this is true for others as well. It must be recognized that in the great transformation which is taking place from one end of the universe to the other, the itching for independence of erstwhile dominated peoples and also the incitements thrown out by all the demagogues of the world are not the only motivating forces. There is another which is not always very clearly perceived. . . . We French built our empire at a time when our internal activities had reached a sort of ceiling — an industry which was not breaking any new ground, an agriculture which was not making any changes, trade channels which were fixed, salaries and wages unchanged, practically stereotyped budgets, gold currency, interest rates at 3%, etc. On the other hand, our old ambitions of European hegemony and natural frontiers were countered by the treaties of 1815 and, after 1870,[4] by the unity and strength of a threatening Germany. Then we sought in distant extensions a new role for the surplus of our enterprising abilities, a complement to our prestige and soldiers for our defense.

---

[1] The Brazzaville Conference, sponsored by the Free French government and held in French West Africa in 1944, was attended by de Gaulle and some forty colonial administrators. No Africans participated. The conference proposed a number of reforms in the French African colonies, including the abolition of forced labor, increased educational opportunities for Africans, a special form of French citizenship for Africans, and greater African control of African affairs. Independence was not considered as an option.

[2] True, Algerians were given the right to vote for members of the three assemblies that met in 1946 to determine the constitutional framework of postwar Algeria. Voting was weighted in such a way, however, to guarantee French dominance of the assemblies.

[3] The French Community was a plan proposed by de Gaulle in 1958, according to which French colonies, primarily in

Africa, would continue to receive French economic and technical aid and would gain control of their internal affairs; they would still be tied to France diplomatically and politically, however. Although all West African colonies except Guinea approved joining the French Community in 1958, within months they reversed themselves and chose complete independence.

[4] Following the defeat of Napoleon, the treaty approved at the Congress of Vienna (1815) essentially returned France to its borders before the beginning of the French Revolution in 1789. The Treaty of Paris (1870), which followed the French defeat by the Germans in the Franco-Prussian War, resulted in the French loss of the border region of Alsace and most of Lorraine.

France does not have to be at all sorry for what she has achieved overseas in this capacity and in this form. I have said it often and I repeat: it constitutes a great human accomplishment which — notwithstanding certain abuses and errors and despite all the endless spouting of all sorts of worthless demagogues — will forever be a credit to France. But how many things have changed today.

Now our great national ambition is our own national progress, constituting a real source of power and influence. Now the modern era permits us, compels us, to undertake a vast development. Now for this development to succeed we must first of all employ the means and resources at our disposal on our own behalf, in our own country. All the more so as we need these means and resources to ensure our own defense and that of our neighbors against the greatest imperialism that the world has ever known — the imperialism of the Soviet Union. We also need these means to win out in the tremendous economic, technical and social struggle now under way between the forces of humanity and the forces of slavery.[5]

It is a fact: our interest, and consequently our policy, lies in decolonization. Why should we continue to cling to costly, bloody and fruitless domination when our country has to undergo complete renovation, when all the underdeveloped countries, beginning with those which yesterday were our dependencies and which today are our favorite friends, ask for our aid and our assistance? But this aid and this assistance — why should we extend them if it is not worthwhile, if there is no cooperation, if what we give finds no return? Yes, it is a matter of exchange, because of what is due us, but also because of the dignity of those with whom we are dealing. . . .

Some people say, "What would happen to these territories if France withdrew? They would straightaway fall into misery and chaos, until Communism took over." That is, no doubt, what would happen to them; but then we would no longer have any duty toward them other than to pity them.

Some people say also, "Either the Soviet Union or the United States — or both at once — would try to take France's place in the territories from which she withdrew." My answer is: I wish both of them a lot of fun.

But it is also possible that the Algerian populations — through self-determination, while deciding on the institution of a sovereign State — will express their desire to see the new Algeria associated with the new France. In such an event, it would have to be known on both sides what this actually meant. That is why a solution should be submitted to the vote of the Algerian people — pending ratification by the French people — a solution agreed upon beforehand by the Government and the different political elements in Algeria, the rebels in particular. France would undoubtedly be willing to lend her economic, administrative, financial, cultural, military and technical aid to the young Mediterranean State, provided the organic cooperation between the Algerian communities, preferential conditions for economic and cultural exchange, and finally the bases and facilities necessary for our defense, are assured and guaranteed. . . .

Naturally we are anxious that, once peace has been re-established and civil liberties restored, the populations may sincerely choose their destiny. After which, if it is not in vain, France will undoubtedly be led, by her heart and her reason, to give her aid and friendship.

That is what I wanted to say about Algeria.

---

[5] The reference is to the Cold War.

Discontent in the Midst of Prosperity: The United States in the 1950s and Early 1960s

For most white, middle-class Americans, the 1950s and much of the 1960s were the best years in the nation's history. Americans had survived the Great Depression, won World War II, and made the difficult transition from all-out war to peacetime. Confident of their power, secure in their beliefs and values, and trusting of their leaders, Americans were content to enjoy their homes, their automobiles, their television sets, and other consumer goods. In 1954 the General Electric Company launched an advertising campaign with the motto "Progress Is Our Most Important Product." The phrase captured the mood of an optimistic era before assassinations, urban riots, the Vietnam War, oil spills, energy shortages, youth rebellion, and "stagflation" generated the conflict and self-doubt of the late 1960s and 1970s.

For most Americans of the 1950s and early 1960s, progress meant economic progress. Buoyed by cheap energy, large-scale government spending on defense and road-building, little foreign competition, and easy credit, the United States experienced high employment, low inflation, and growing prosperity. With only 6 percent of the world's population, the United States in the mid 1950s produced almost half of the world's manufactured goods and contained within its borders 75 percent of the world's automobiles, 60 percent of its telephones, and 30 percent of its radios and televisions. By 1960 more cars were owned in Los Angeles County than in the whole of Asia or South America. Between 1950 and 1963, the U.S. gross national product (GNP) nearly doubled, and despite the inflation that took place during the Korean War (1951–1953), real wages rose better than 30 percent. In the 1950s and early 1960s, the number of millionaires increased from twenty-seven thousand to almost eighty thousand. Never, so it seemed, had so many Americans had it so good, and never did so many expect it to get even better.

The postwar era was not, however, entirely a time of "happy days," as the popular television show of the same name in the 1970s saw it. Between 1950 and 1953, slightly more than fifty-four thousand U.S. troops died in the Korean War. Although after Korea the Cold War remained cold, Americans practiced civil defense drills and built bomb shelters in their backyards to calm their fears of nuclear attack. Unemployment hovered between 5 and 6 percent even in the midst of the 1950s boom, and reached 7.5 percent in 1958, a year of recession. Old inequalities remained. The wealthiest 5 percent of the population held 33 percent of the national wealth, while the bottom 20 percent held only 5 percent. More than half of all Americans had no savings, and 96 percent owned no corporate stocks. With poverty defined as having an annual income of $3,000 for a family of four and $4,000 for a family of six, 20 to 25 percent of the population lived in poverty and another 10 percent lived on the poverty line. This was a decrease from the dark days of the 1930s, but it still meant that forty million to fifty million Americans lived in poverty or close to it.

Those forty or fifty million poor Americans included people from every region and every ethnic category, but the largest single group within the poor was made up of African-Americans. Almost a century after the end of slavery and only a few years after fighting a war to defeat the Nazi's racist regime, the United States remained a racist society. In the early 1950s, Southern segregation laws required separate but rarely equal facilities for blacks and whites in public transportation, schools, swimming pools, drinking fountains, parking lots, and even cemeteries. Fewer than 5 percent of eligible blacks could vote. Conditions were only marginally better for the many blacks who had migrated to northern cities before and during World War II in search of factory jobs. Incomes were high in comparison to what they had earned in the South, but housing was in short supply, schools were underfunded, and employment opportunities were limited to unskilled, dead-end jobs.

As the United States moved into the 1960s under the presidency of John F. Kennedy, change was in the air. The new president, a young man in his forties, held out the promise of political change and social justice. American businesses were beginning to lose markets to Japanese and German competitors. Civil rights groups and the courts had already launched a full-scale assault on segregation. Women were beginning to question their prescribed roles as wives and mothers. The American public was becoming aware of the dangers of environmental pollution. By 1963, sixteen thousand U.S. troops were in Vietnam to prop up the regime of Ngo Dinh Diem in its struggle against communist insurgency. Then in November 1963 President Kennedy was assassinated in Dallas. His vice-president, Lyndon Baines Johnson, somberly assumed the presidency of a nation on the brink of enormous change.

"The Problem That Has No Name"

71 ◆ Betty Friedan, *THE FEMININE MYSTIQUE*

During World War II, economic need and the call of patriotism caused millions of women to take office and factory jobs vacated by men inducted into the military. By 1944, 19.4 million women (37 percent of the adult female population) held paying jobs outside the home, including three hundred fifty thousand women who served in the armed forces. After 1954, however, the family-centered ethos of the postwar era consigned women to a domestic role, in which their primary functions were cooking, cleaning, caring for husbands, and raising children. Young women faced strong pressure to marry rather than pursue careers. Popular television comedies of the 1950s and early 1960s, *Leave It to Beaver, The Adventures of Ozzie and Harriet,* and *Father Knows Best,* all centered on "ideal" American families made up of working fathers, stay-at-home mothers, and well-scrubbed children who lived in all-white suburbs in uncluttered homes.

That such a life was financially impossible for many U.S. women is confirmed by the large numbers of women who continued to hold paying jobs in the 1950s.

That such a life was emotionally and intellectually unfulfilling for millions of middle-class women is confirmed by the enormous popularity of a book published in 1963, Betty Friedan's *The Feminine Mystique*.

In the mid 1950s, Betty Friedan, a 1942 graduate of Smith College, was a housewife in a New York City suburb, a mother of three, and a writer for the popular women's magazines, *McCall's, Redbook,* and *Ladies' Home Journal.* By the standards of the day she was successful, yet she was troubled by a "nameless, aching dissatisfaction," and became convinced that "there was something very wrong about the way American women were trying to lead their lives." After five years of research and self-analysis, in 1963 she published *The Feminine Mystique,* in which she rejected the reigning belief that women's lives should revolve around home, husband, and family. The book caused millions of men and women on both sides of the Atlantic to reconsider the place of women in society and was a major inspiration for the emerging "women's liberation" movement. In 1966 Friedan cofounded the National Organization for Women (NOW) and served as its first president.

QUESTIONS FOR ANALYSIS

1. What is the social and educational background of the women whose lives Friedan discusses in *The Feminine Mystique*?
2. What is the problem facing these women, and why does it have no name?
3. Based on her description of the troubles facing women in American society, what solutions do you think Friedan would propose for solving them?

The problem lay buried, unspoken, for many years in the minds of American women. It was a strange stirring, a sense of dissatisfaction, a yearning that women suffered in the middle of the twentieth century in the United States. Each suburban wife struggled with it alone. As she made the beds, shopped for groceries, matched slipcover material, ate peanut butter sandwiches with her children, chauffeured Cub Scouts and Brownies, lay beside her husband at night — she was afraid to ask even of herself the silent question — "Is this all?"

For over fifteen years there was no word of this yearning in the millions of words written about women, for women, in all the columns, books and articles by experts telling women their role was to seek fulfillment as wives and mothers. . . . Experts told them how to catch a man and keep him, how to breastfeed children and handle their toilet training, how to cope with sibling rivalry and adolescent rebellion; how to buy a dishwasher, bake bread, cook gourmet snails, and build a swimming pool with their own hands; how to dress, look, and act more feminine and make marriage more exciting; how to keep their husbands from dying young and their sons from growing into delinquents. They were taught to pity the neurotic, unfeminine, unhappy women who wanted to be poets or physicists or presidents. They learned that truly feminine women do not want careers, higher education, political rights — the independence and the opportunities that the old-fashioned feminists fought for. Some women, in their forties and fifties, still remembered painfully giving up those dreams, but most of the younger women no longer even thought about them. A thousand expert voices applauded their femininity, their adjustment, their new maturity. All they had to do was devote their lives from earliest girlhood to finding a husband and bearing children. . . .

In the fifteen years after World War II, this mystique of feminine fulfillment became the cherished and self-perpetuating core of contemporary American culture. Millions of women lived their lives in the image of those pretty pictures of the American suburban housewife, kissing their husbands goodbye in front of the picture window, depositing their station-wagonsful of children at school, and smiling as they ran the new electric waxer over the spotless kitchen floor. . . . They had no thought for the unfeminine problems of the world outside the home; they wanted the men to make the major decisions. They gloried in their role as women, and wrote proudly on the census blank: "Occupation: housewife." . . .

If a woman had a problem in the 1950's and the 1960's, she knew that something must be wrong with her marriage, or with herself. Other women were satisfied with their lives, she thought. What kind of a woman was she if she did not feel this mysterious fulfillment waxing the kitchen floor? She was so ashamed to admit her dissatisfaction that she never knew how many other women shared it. . . . For over fifteen years women in America found it harder to talk about this problem than about sex. Even the psychoanalysts had no name for it. When a woman went to a psychiatrist for help, as many women did, she would say, "I'm so ashamed," or "I must be hopelessly neurotic." "I don't know what's wrong with women today," a suburban psychiatrist said uneasily. "I only know something is wrong because most of my patients happen to be women. And their problem isn't sexual.". . .

Gradually I came to realize that the problem that has no name was shared by countless women in America. . . . I saw the same signs in suburban ranch houses and split-levels on Long Island and in New Jersey and Westchester County; in colonial houses in a small Massachusetts town; on patios in Memphis; in suburban and city apartments; in living rooms in the Midwest. Sometimes I sensed the problem, not as a reporter, but as a suburban housewife, for during this time I was also bringing up my own three children in Rockland County, New York. I heard echoes of the problem in college dormitories and semi-private maternity wards, at PTA meetings and luncheons of the League of Women Voters, at suburban cocktail parties, in station wagons waiting for trains, and in snatches of conversation overheard at Schrafft's. The groping words I heard from other women, on quiet afternoons when children were at school or on quiet evenings when husbands worked late, I think I understood first as a woman long before I understood their larger social and psychological implications.

Just what was this problem that has no name? . . . Sometimes a woman would say "I feel empty somehow . . . incomplete." Or she would say, "I feel as if I don't exist." Sometimes she blotted out the feeling with a tranquilizer. Sometimes she thought the problem was with her husband, or her children, or that what she really needed was to redecorate her house, or move to a better neighborhood, or have an affair, or another baby. . . .

Most men, and some women, still did not know that this problem was real. But those who had faced it honestly knew that all the superficial remedies, the sympathetic advice, the scolding words and the cheering words were somehow drowning the problem in unreality. A bitter laugh was beginning to be heard from American women. They were admired, envied, pitied, theorized over until they were sick of it, offered drastic solutions or silly choices that no one could take seriously. They got all kinds of advice from the growing armies of marriage and child-guidance counselors, psychotherapists, and arm-chair psychologists, on how to adjust to their role as housewives. No other road to fulfillment was offered to American women in the middle of the twentieth century. Most adjusted to their role and suffered or ignored the problem that has no name. It can be less painful for a woman, not to hear the strange, dissatisfied voice stirring within her.

It is no longer possible to ignore that voice, to dismiss the desperation of so many American women. This is not what being a woman means, no matter what experts say. . . . The women who suffer this problem have a hunger that food cannot fill. It persists in women whose husbands are struggling interns and law clerks, or prosperous doctors and lawyers; in wives of workers and executives who make $5,000 a year or $50,000. It is not caused by lack of material advantages; it may not even be felt by women preoccupied with desperate problems of hunger, poverty or illness. And women who think it will be solved by more money, a bigger house, a second car, moving to a better suburb, often discover it gets worse. . . .

If I am right, the problem that has no name stirring in the minds of so many American women today is not a matter of loss of femininity or too much education, or the demands of domesticity. It is far more important than anyone recognizes. It is the key to these other new and old problems which have been torturing women and their husbands and children, and puzzling their doctors and educators for years. It may well be the key to our future as a nation and a culture. We can no longer ignore that voice within women that says: "I want something more than my husband and my children and my home."

A Cry for Racial Justice

❖

72 ◆ Martin Luther King, Jr., *LETTER FROM BIRMINGHAM JAIL*

On December 1, 1955, in Montgomery, Alabama, Mrs. Rosa Parks, a Negro seamstress who was sitting in the back of a bus in the "colored section," refused to give up her seat to a white man who had to stand. She was arrested and fined, and in response, a young pastor at the Dexter Avenue Baptist Church organized a citywide boycott by blacks of Montgomery's bus system. The United States civil rights movement had begun in earnest, and with it, the young pastor, Martin Luther King, Jr., achieved national and international fame as its leader. Until his assassination 1968, King's bravery, moral vision, and moving words inspired millions of followers and forced the nation to confront the implications of its long history of racial prejudice and suppression.

Martin Luther King, Jr., was born in Atlanta on January 15, 1929, the son of the Reverend Martin Luther King and Mrs. Alberta Williams King. Educated at Morehouse College, Crozier Theological Seminary, and Boston University, where he received a doctorate in philosophy, King served as pastor in Montgomery and then became copastor with his father of the Ebenezer Baptist Church in Atlanta. After the Montgomery bus boycott he became president of the Southern Christian Leadership Council and organized voter registration drives in Georgia, Alabama, and Virginia. His "I Have a Dream" speech at the March on Washington, D.C., in 1963 provided the civil rights movement with one of its most memorable moments. In the mid 1960s King extended his activities to northern cities and spoke out against the Vietnam War. In 1968 he traveled to Memphis, Tennessee, to support a strike by sanitation workers. There he was assassinated, a crime for which

James Earl Ray, a small-town thief and an escaped prisoner from the Missouri State Prison, was tried and convicted.

King's essay, "Letter from Birmingham Jail," was composed in 1963 while he was serving a jail sentence for participating in civil rights demonstrations in Birmingham, Alabama. It was a response to eight prominent Alabama clergymen who had criticized his leadership in the civil rights movement.

QUESTIONS FOR ANALYSIS

1. What specific criticisms have been leveled against King's campaign in Birmingham? What alternatives do King's critics recommend?
2. In what specific ways does King respond to these criticisms?
3. King describes his method as "nonviolent direct action." What does he mean by this?
4. According to King, what are the main obstacles preventing blacks from achieving their goals in the civil rights movement?
5. King identifies the U.S. civil rights movement with the efforts of Asians and Africans to throw off the bonds of imperialism. Is his analogy valid? Why or why not?

MY DEAR FELLOW CLERGYMEN,

While confined here in the Birmingham city jail, I came across your recent statement calling our present activities "unwise and untimely." Seldom, if ever, do I pause to answer criticism of my work and ideas. If I sought to answer all of the criticisms that cross my desk, my secretaries would be engaged in little else in the course of the day, and I would have no time for constructive work. But since I feel that you are men of genuine good will and your criticisms are sincerely set forth, I would like to answer your statement in what I hope will be patient and reasonable terms. . . .

You may well ask, "Why direct action? Why sit-ins, marches, etc.? Isn't negotiation a better path?" You are exactly right in your call for negotiation. Indeed this is the purpose of direct action. Nonviolent direct action seeks to create such a crisis and establish such creative tension that a community that has constantly refused to negotiate is forced to confront the issue. It seeks so to dramatize the issue that it can no longer be ignored. . . . Just as Socrates felt that it was necessary to create a tension in the mind so that individuals could rise from the bondage of myths and half-truths to the unfettered realm of creative analysis and objective appraisal, we must see the need of having nonviolent gadflies[1] to create the kind of tension in society that will help men to rise from the dark depths of prejudice and racism to the majestic heights of understanding and brotherhood. . . . Too long has our beloved Southland been bogged down in the tragic attempt to live in monologue rather than dialogue. . . .

We have waited for more than 340 years for our constitutional and God-given rights. The nations of Asia and Africa are moving with jet-like speed toward the goal of political independence, and we still creep at horse and buggy pace toward the gaining of a cup of coffee at a lunch counter. I guess it is easy for those who have

---

[1]A purposely annoying person who stimulates analysis and debate about ideas and behavior through persistent criticism.

never felt the stinging darts of segregation to say, "Wait." But when you have seen vicious mobs lynch your mothers and fathers at will and drown your sisters and brothers at whim; when you have seen hate-filled policemen curse, kick, brutalize and even kill your black brothers and sisters with impunity; when you see the vast majority of your twenty million Negro brothers smothering in an airtight cage of poverty in the midst of an affluent society; when you suddenly find your tongue twisted and your speech stammering as you seek to explain to your six-year-old daughter why she can't go to the public amusement park that has just been advertised on television, and see tears welling up in her little eyes when she is told that Funtown is closed to colored children, and see the depressing clouds of inferiority begin to form in her little mental sky, and see her begin to distort her little personality by unconsciously developing a bitterness toward white people; when you have to concoct an answer for a five-year-old son asking in agonizing pathos: "Daddy, why do white people treat colored people so mean?"; when you take a cross-country drive and find it necessary to sleep night after night in the uncomfortable corners of your automobile because no motel will accept you; when you are humiliated day in and day out by nagging signs reading "white" and "colored"; when your first name becomes "nigger" and your middle name becomes "boy" (however old you are) and your last name becomes "John," and when your wife and mother are never given the respected title "Mrs."; when you are harried by day and haunted by night by the fact that you are a Negro, living constantly at tiptoe stance never quite knowing what to expect next, and plagued with inner fears and outer resentments; when you are forever fighting a degenerating sense of "nobodiness," then you

will understand why we find it difficult to wait. . . . I hope, sirs, you can understand our legitimate and unavoidable impatience.

You express a great deal of anxiety over our willingness to break laws. This is certainly a legitimate concern. Since we so diligently urge people to obey the Supreme Court's decision of 1954[2] outlawing segregation in the public schools, it is rather strange and paradoxical to find us consciously breaking laws. One may well ask, "How can you advocate breaking some laws and obeying others?" The answer if found in the fact that there are two types of laws: there are *just* and there are *unjust* laws. I would agree with Saint Augustine[3] that "Any unjust law is no law at all."

Let me give an explanation. An unjust law is a code inflicted upon a minority which that minority had no part in enacting or creating because they did not have the unhampered right to vote. Who can say that the legislature of Alabama which set up the segregation laws was democratically elected? Throughout the state of Alabama all types of conniving methods are used to prevent Negroes from becoming registered voters and there are some counties without a single Negro registered to vote despite the fact that the Negro constitutes a majority of the population. Can any law set up in such a state be considered democratically structured?. . . .

You spoke of our activity in Birmingham as extreme. At first I was rather disappointed that fellow clergymen would see my nonviolent efforts as those of the extremist. I started thinking about the fact that I stand in the middle of two opposing forces in the Negro community. One is a force of complacency made up of Negroes who, as a result of long years of oppression, have been so completely drained of self-respect and a sense of "somebodiness" that they have adjusted to

---

[2]*Brown vs. Board of Education* is a famous Supreme Court decision which grew out of a suit filed in Kansas by Oliver Brown against the Topeka Board of Education when his daughter was denied permission to attend an all-white school in her neighborhood. The court ruled that segregation at all levels of public schooling is illegal.

[3]St. Augustine of Hippo (354–430 C.E.), a north African bishop and theologian, was a seminal figure in the history of Christian thought.

segregation, and, of a few Negroes in the middle class who, because of a degree of academic and economic security, and because at points they profit by segregation, have unconsciously become insensitive to the problems of the masses. The other force is one of bitterness and hatred, and comes perilously close to advocating violence. It is expressed in the various black nationalist groups that are springing up over the nation, the largest and best known being Elijah Muhammad's Muslim movement.[4] This movement is nourished by the contemporary frustration over the continued existence of racial discrimination. It is made up of people who have lost faith in America, who have absolutely repudiated Christianity, and who have concluded that the white man is an incurable "devil." I have tried to stand between these two forces, saying that we need not follow the "do-nothingism" of the complacent or the hatred and despair of the black nationalist. There is the more excellent way of love and nonviolent protest. I'm grateful to God that, through the Negro church, the dimension of nonviolence entered our struggle. If this philosophy had not emerged, I am convinced that by now many streets of the South would be flowing with floods of blood. . . .

I have no fear about the outcome of our struggle in Birmingham, even if our motives are presently misunderstood. We will reach the goal of freedom in Birmingham and all over the nation, because the goal of America is freedom. Abused and scorned though we may be, our destiny is tied up with the destiny of America. Before the Pilgrims landed at Plymouth we were here. Before the pen of Jefferson etched across the pages of history the majestic words of the Declaration of Independence, we were here. For more than two centuries our foreparents labored in this country without wages; they made cotton king; and they built the homes of their masters in the midst of brutal injustice and shameful humiliation — and yet out of a bottomless vitality they continued to thrive and develop. If the inexpressible cruelties of slavery could not stop us, the opposition we now face will surely fail. We will win our freedom because the sacred heritage of our nation and the eternal will of God are embodied in our echoing demands. . . .

Yours for the cause of Peace and Brotherhood,

MARTIN LUTHER KING, JR.

---

[4]Founded in Detroit in the early 1930s, the Black Muslims in 1934 came under the leadership of Elijah Muhammad, a Georgian originally named Elijah Poole. He moved the organization's headquarters to Chicago, where he preached black self-reliance and separatism from white society. At the time of his death in 1975, Black Muslims numbered between one hundred fifty thousand and two hundred thousand.

The Beginnings of Modern Environmentalism

73 ◆ *Rachel Carson, SILENT SPRING*

American environmentalism can be traced back to the 1890s, when rapid urbanization and the closing of the frontier gave rise to the conservation movement. Its leading advocates were Gifford Pinchot (1865–1946), who sought to protect the nation's forests, rivers, minerals, and grazing lands through scientific planning and regulation, and John Muir (1838–1914), who advocated preserving land as permanent wilderness. Conservation was a priority for President Theodore Roosevelt (1901–1908), who tripled the size of the forest reserves to 150 million acres and established dozens of wildlife refuges. New programs followed in the 1920s and 1930s. Among them was the Civil Conservation Corps, the Depression-era brainchild of President Franklin D. Roosevelt that in 1933 began to provide jobs for millions of young men who worked on reforestation and flood-control projects, built roads and bridges in national forests and parks, and fought forest fires.

For most of the twentieth century, however, environmental issues in the United States truly mattered to only small numbers of government officials and private citizens. This changed dramatically in the 1960s, when millions of Americans became deeply apprehensive about environmental degradation and committed themselves to a wide spectrum of environmental causes. It was easy for Americans to sense that things had gone drastically wrong when they could no longer swim or fish in dying lakes and rivers, listened to daily smog reports on the radio, and watched mountains of garbage pile up in their landfills. To a remarkable degree, however, this new environmental consciousness also resulted from the impact of a single book, *Silent Spring,* whose publication in 1963 can be said to mark the beginning of the modern environmental movement in the United States.

The author of *Silent Spring,* Rachel Carson, was a gifted writer and scientist from Pennsylvania who graduated from the Pennsylvania College for Women in Pittsburgh in 1925 and received further education at the Woods Hole Marine Biology Laboratory in Massachusetts and at Johns Hopkins University. She combined careers as a writer and as an official in the U.S. Fish and Wildlife Service until the royalties from her bestseller *The Sea Around Us* allowed her to devote herself completely to research and writing in 1952. Another bestseller, *The Edge of the Sea,* followed in 1955. Then in 1963 she published *Silent Spring* on a topic suggested to her by a friend who was convinced that a spraying program to exterminate mosquitoes around her hometown of Duxbury, Massachusetts, was also killing birds. Carson's main target in *Silent Spring* was DDT (dichlorodiphenyl trichlorothane), one of the many synthetic hydrocarbon pesticides that was widely used in the 1950s. Although her book was attacked by the scientific establishment and the chemical industry, its solid research and passionate concern for nature struck a responsive chord among the American people. The book challenged scientists, politicians, and corporations to confront the environmental implications of their actions and galvanized citizens to take steps to stem the tide of pollution. Just seven years after the appearance of Carson's book and six years after her death in 1964, on Earth Day in April 1970 nearly every community in the nation and thousands of schools and universities sponsored some type of activity emphasizing the need for action to improve environmental quality.

QUESTIONS FOR ANALYSIS

1. In Carson's assessment, how severe are the environmental problems facing society? What is the basis of her assessment?
2. According to Carson, who is to blame for environmental problems in the United States?
3. How would you describe Carson's attitude toward nature?

4. In Carson's view, what ethical issues are involved in the use of herbicides and insecticides?
5. According to Carson, what fundamental ways of thinking about nature will need to be changed to avert further environmental catastrophe?
6. What are the qualities of Carson's book that account for its popularity and influence?

THE OBLIGATION TO ENDURE

The history of life on earth has been a history of interaction between living things and their surroundings. To a large extent, the physical form and the habits of the earth's vegetation and its animal life have been molded by the environment. Considering the whole span of earthly time, the opposite effect, in which life actually modifies its surroundings, has been relatively slight. Only within the moment of time represented by the present century has one species — man — acquired significant power to alter the nature of his world.

During the past quarter century this power has not only increased to one of disturbing magnitude but it has changed in character. The most alarming of all man's assaults upon the environment is the contamination of air, earth, rivers, and sea with dangerous and even lethal materials. This pollution is for the most part irrecoverable; the chain of evil it initiates not only in the world that must support life but in living tissues is for the most part irreversible. In this now universal contamination of the environment, chemicals are the sinister and little-recognized partners of radiation in changing the very nature of the world — the very nature of its life. . . .

The rapidity of change and the speed with which new situations are created follow the impetuous and heedless pace of man rather than the deliberate pace of nature. Radiation is no longer merely the background radiation of rocks, the bombardment of cosmic rays, the ultraviolet of the sun that have existed before there was any life on earth; radiation is now the unnatural creation of man's tampering with the atom. The chemicals to which life is asked to make its adjustment are no longer merely the calcium and silica and copper and all the rest of the minerals washed out of the rocks and carried in rivers to the sea; they are the synthetic creations of man's inventive mind, brewed in his laboratories, and having no counterparts in nature. . . .

These sprays, dusts, and aerosols are now applied almost universally to farms, gardens, forest, and homes — nonselective chemicals that have the power to kill every insect, the "good" and the "bad," to still the song of birds and the leaping of fish in the streams, to coat the leaves with a deadly film, and to linger on in the soil — all this though the intended target may be only a few weeds or insects. Can anyone believe it is possible to lay down such a barrage of poisons on the surface of the earth without making it unfit for all life? They should not be called "insecticides," but "biocides.". . .

Along with the possibility of the extinction of mankind by nuclear war, the central problem of our age has therefore become the contamination of man's total environment with such substances of incredible potential for harm — substances that accumulate in the tissues of plants and animals and even penetrate the germ cells to shatter or alter the very material of heredity upon which the shape of the future depends. . . .

All this has been risked — for what? Future historians may well be amazed by our distorted sense of proportion. How could intelligent beings seek to control a few unwanted species by a method that contaminated the entire environment and brought the threat of disease and death even to their own kind?

Yet this is precisely what we have done. . . .

EARTH'S GREEN MANTLE

. . . The earth's vegetation is part of a web of life in which there are intimate and essential relations between plants and the earth, between plants and other plants, between plants and animals. Sometimes we have no choice but to disturb these relationships, but we should do so thoughtfully, with full awareness that what we do may have consequences remote in time and place. But no such humility marks the booming "weed killer" business of the present day, in which soaring sales and expanding uses mark the production of plant-killing chemicals. . . .

The chemical weed killers are a bright new toy. They work in a spectacular way; they give a giddy sense of power over nature to those who wield them, and as for the long-range and less obvious effects — these are easily brushed aside as the baseless imaginings of pessimists. . . .

I know well a stretch of road where nature's own landscaping has provided a border of alder, viburnum, sweet fern, and juniper with seasonally changing accents of bright flowers, or of fruits hanging in jeweled clusters in the fall. . . . But the sprayers took over and the miles along that road became something to be traversed quickly, a sight to be endured with one's mind closed to thoughts of the sterile and hideous world we are letting our technicians make. But here and there authority had somehow faltered and by an unaccountable oversight there were oases of beauty in the midst of austere and regimented control — oases that made the desecration of the greater part of the road the more unbearable. In such places my spirit lifted to the sight of the drifts of white clover or the clouds of purple vetch with here and there the flaming cup of a wood lily.

Such plants are "weeds" only to those who make a business of selling and applying chemi-

cals. In a volume of *Proceedings* of one of the weed-control conferences that are now regular institutions, I once read an extraordinary statement of a weed killer's philosophy. The author defended the killing of good plants "simply because they are in bad company." Those who complain about killing wildflowers along roadsides reminded him, he said, of antivivisectionists "to whom, if one were to judge by their actions, the life of a stray dog is more sacred than the lives of children." . . .

NEEDLESS HAVOC

[*Chapter 7 of* Silent Spring *describes the effects of spraying campaigns in Illinois and Michigan to eradicate Japanese beetles.*]

Perhaps no community has suffered more for the sake of a beetleless world than Sheldon, in eastern Illinois, and adjacent areas in Iroquois County. . . . The first "eradication" took place . . . when dieldrin[1] was applied to 1400 acres by air. Another 2600 acres were treated similarly in 1955, and the task was presumably considered complete. But more and more chemical treatments were called for, and by the end of 1961 some 131,000 acres had been covered. Even in the first years of the program it was apparent that heavy losses were occurring among wildlife and domestic animals. The chemical treatments were continued, nevertheless, without consultation with either the United States Fish and Wildlife Service or the Illinois Game Management Division. . . .

Conditions were made to order for poisoning insect-eating birds, both in the poisons used and in the events set in motion by their application. In the early programs at Sheldon, dieldrin was applied at the rate of 3 pounds to the acre. To understand its effect on birds one need only remember that in laboratory experiments on

---

[1]Dieldrin is an insecticide used in the 1950s and 1960s for mothproofing, termite control, and the extermination of mosquitoes, Japanese beetles, and tsetse flies. It was banned by the U.S. Environmental Protection Agency in 1974 except for use against termites.

quail dieldrin has proved to be about 50 times as poisonous as DDT. . . .

As the chemical penetrated the soil, poisoned beetle grubs crawled out on the surface of the ground, where they remained for some time before they died, attractive to insect-eating birds. Dead and dying insects of various species were conspicuous for about two weeks after the treatment. The effect on the bird populations could easily have been foretold. Brown thrashers, starlings, meadowlarks, grackles, and pheasants were virtually wiped out. Robins were "almost annihilated," according to the biologists' report. . . .

Incidents like the eastern Illinois spraying raise a question that is not only scientific but moral. The question is whether any civilization can wage relentless war on life without destroying itself, and without losing the right to be called civilized.

These insecticides are not selective poisons; they do not single out the one species of which we desire to be rid. Each of them is used for the simple reason that it is a deadly poison. It therefore poisons all life with which it comes in contact: the cat beloved of some family, the farmer's cattle, the rabbit in the field, and the horned lark out of the sky. These creatures are innocent of any harm to man. Indeed, by their very existence they and their fellows make his life more pleasant. Yet he rewards them with a death that is not only sudden but horrible. Scientific observers at Sheldon described the symptoms of a meadowlark found near death: "Although it lacked muscular coordination and could not fly or stand, it continued to beat its wings and clutch with its toes while lying on its side. Its beak was held open and breathing was labored." Even more pitiful was the mute testimony of the dead ground squirrels, which "exhibited a characteristic attitude in death. The back was bowed, and the forelegs with the toes of the feet tightly clenched were drawn close to the thorax . . . The head and neck were outstretched and the mouth often contained dirt, suggesting that the dying animal had been biting at the ground."

By acquiescing in an act that can cause such suffering to a living creature, who among us is not diminished as human being?

AND NO BIRDS SING

[*This is the concluding paragraph from Chapter 8, which describes the effects of insecticides on birds.*]

In each of these situations, one turns away to ponder the question: Who has made the decision that sets in motion these chains of poisonings, this ever-widening wave of death that spreads out, like ripples when a pebble is dropped into a still pond? Who has placed in one pan of the scales the leaves that might have been eaten by the beetles and in the other the pitiful heaps of many-hued feathers, the lifeless remains of the birds that fell before the unselective bludgeon of insecticidal poisons? Who has decided — who has the *right* to decide — for the countless legions of people who were not consulted that the supreme value is a world without insects, even though it be also a sterile world ungraced by the curving wing of a bird in flight? The decision is that of the authoritarian temporarily entrusted with power; he has made it during a moment of inattention by millions to whom beauty and the ordered world of nature still have a meaning that is deep and imperative.

THE OTHER ROAD

[*In the book's final Chapter, Carson makes a plea for the development and use of biological controls for insects populations. The book ends with the following words.*]

. . . As crude a weapon as the cave man's club, the chemical barrage has been hurled against the fabric of life — a fabric on the one hand delicate and destructible, on the other miraculously tough and resilient, and capable of striking back in unexpected ways. These extraordinary capacities of life have been ignored by the practitioners of chemical control who have brought to their task no "high-minded orientation," no humility before the vast forces with which they tamper.

The "control of nature" is a phrase conceived in arrogance, born of the Neanderthal age of biology and philosophy, when it was supposed that nature exists for the convenience of man. The concepts and practices of applied entomology for the most part date from the Stone Age of science. It is our alarming misfortune that so primitive a science has armed itself with the most modern and terrible weapons, and that in turning them against the insects it has also turned them against the earth.

◆

The Late 1960s: Years of Protest and Polarization

In 1960 the Student League for Industrial Democracy had chapters on three campuses — Michigan, Columbia, and Yale — and fewer than one hundred members. In that same year, however, with a new name — Students for Democratic Society (SDS) — and an increasingly radical agenda, the organization began to grow. By 1962 it had one thousand members, by 1964, twenty-five hundred members, and by 1968, more than one hundred thousand members on some three hundred campuses. In 1968 and 1969 the SDS played a key role in organizing demonstrations, sit-ins, teach-ins, student strikes, and building takeovers at Columbia, Harvard, Cornell, Berkeley, and other campuses across the country. With its radical critique of American higher education, its denunciations of corporate and bureaucratic power, and its opposition to the war in Vietnam, the SDS became a symbol of youthful political rebellion and a leading representative of the New Left.

The meteoric rise of the SDS from a fringe organization to a major, though ephemeral, force in American politics is just one example of the swift and bewildering changes that took place in the United States and Europe in the late 1960s and the early 1970s. Large numbers of previously apathetic young people, galvanized by their opposition to the war in Vietnam, rejected the values of consumerism, capitalism, imperialism, and the Cold War; rebelled against the authority of parents, teachers, politicians, corporations, and university administrators; and sought to "change the system" through campus activism and antiwar demonstrations. In 1968 student strikes and building takeovers took place at dozens of universities in Europe and the United States; militants viewed these actions as the first steps toward the destruction of capitalism and the end of bureaucratic oppression.

While many thousands of young people were drawn to radical politics, others rebelled against traditional values by becoming part of the counterculture. For a small minority this meant joining a rural commune or moving to a neighborhood such as Haight-Ashbury in San Francisco, where "hippies" embraced an alternative lifestyle based on sharing, free love, peace, and the copious use of marijuana and psychedelic drugs. Those not ready to "drop out," stayed in school or kept their jobs, joined the youth rebellion by wearing long hair and tie-dyed shirts, listening to acid rock, smoking pot, denouncing war, and ridiculing the values of their parents' generation.

Feminism also underwent far-reaching changes in the late 1960s. The moderate feminism that had grown in Europe and the United States after the publication of Simone de Beauvoir's *The Second Sex* in 1949 and Betty Friedan's *The Feminine Mystique* in 1963 gave way to the women's liberation movement. Many feminists became radical and confrontational, with an agenda that went beyond better pay, easier divorces, legalized abortions, and equal opportunities in jobs, schools, and athletics. Radical feminists questioned marriage, saw men as the enemy, and sought nothing less than the complete liberation of women from the weight of sexual taboos, archaic stereotypes, and male authority.

The struggle for civil rights in the United States also became more radical and confrontational. Beginning with the Watts riots in Los Angeles in 1965 and continuing for three more "long, hot summers," blacks in the nation's inner cities expressed their rage through a series of destructive riots. Leadership in the civil rights movement shifted from moderate organizations such as the National Association for the Advancement of Colored People (NAACP) and the Southern Christian Leadership Council (SCLC) to groups that rejected white members, appealed to black pride, and repudiated Martin Luther King, Jr.'s gospel of nonviolence. They included the Congress for Racial Equality (CORE), the Black Muslims, the Black Panthers, and the Student Nonviolent Coordinating Committee (SNCC). The Black Panthers donned menacing paramilitary outfits and carried rifles, while H. Rap Brown of SNCC announced that "if America don't come around, we're going to burn it down."

The storm of youthful protest and rebellion in the late 1960s was intense but brief. In Europe, the university strikes of May and June 1968 were never repeated. In the United States, campus demonstrations continued for a time, with the largest protests taking place in May 1970 after the shooting by National Guard troops of four Kent State University students who were protesting the U.S. invasion of Cambodia. Within two years after the Kent State protests, however, the SDS had broken apart; Haight-Ashbury had become a neighborhood of hard drugs, crime, and derelicts; "Black Power" was a forgotten motto; and radical feminism had lost much of its appeal.

Despite the brevity of the youth rebellion, neither Europe nor the United States would ever be the same after the assault of the 1960s on hierarchy, privilege, and tradition. Black violence and militancy forced white Americans to confront their racist past and made them appreciate the depth of black anger. Similarly, radical feminism alerted the European and American public to the full range of women's grievances, leading to expanded opportunities for women in schools, professions, marriage, and athletics. The counterculture did not inspire widespread acceptance of free love, but it did help dissolve the repressive sexual atmosphere of the 1950s. Campus protests helped end American involvement in Vietnam, brought about important changes in higher education, and created a culture of campus activism whose idealism and spirit were later redirected to causes such as environmentalism. Although no governments were toppled and no new utopias were achieved, the radical protests of the late 1960s had a permanent, perhaps even revolutionary impact on Western culture, values, and politics.

From Civil Rights to Black Power
❖

74 ❖ *Student Nonviolent Coordinating Committee,*
WE WANT BLACK POWER

By the mid 1960s the civil rights movement in the United States had made impressive gains. Legal segregation in the South had been eliminated through Supreme Court decisions and legislation such as the Civil Rights Act of 1964 and the Voting Rights Act of 1965. But legal and legislative victories did not translate into jobs, higher standards of living, or the end of de facto segregation and prejudice. Millions of blacks, both those in the South and those who had migrated to northern cities, lived in poverty, a fact highlighted by the efforts of the Johnson administration in 1964 and 1965 to eliminate poverty through its War on Poverty and Great Society programs. Rising expectations frustrated by poverty and prejudice stoked African-American anger, an anger that changed the nature of the civil rights movement and translated into riots in more than three hundred cities between 1964 and 1968.

The radicalization of the civil rights movement is epitomized by the history of the Student Nonviolent Coordinating Committee (SNCC), an organization mainly of college students founded in 1960 as a spinoff of Martin Luther King, Jr.'s Southern Christian Leadership Council. SNCC members led the fight for the integration of stores and restaurants in the South through sit-ins, and in 1964 organized a Freedom Summer in Mississippi to register black voters and teach literacy and black history in Freedom Schools. Nearly sixty thousand black Mississippians were registered to vote, but at great cost. Thirty buildings were bombed, hundreds of SNCC members were beaten and arrested, and seven members were murdered.

In 1966 a militant faction won control of the organization when it elected as chairman Stokely Carmichael, a recent graduate of Howard University in Washington, D.C. In 1966 Carmichael first began the chant "Black Power! Black Power!" in a speech during a civil rights march from Memphis, Tennessee, to Jackson, Mississippi. Soon "Black Power" replaced "We Shall Overcome" and "Freedom Now" as the slogan for the civil rights movement.

The Black Power movement had antecedents in Marcus Garvey's back-to-Africa crusade of the 1920s and organizations such as the Nation of Islam, founded in the 1930s, which called for a separate black nation. In the late 1960s Black Power became a rallying cry for black militancy and was embraced by the Congress for Racial Equality (CORE), the Black Panthers, and SNCC. A nebulous term, Black Power could mean black pride, black control of black communities, and resistance to assimilation into a totally integrated society. To some, however, it also meant hatred and an endorsement of violence, as is clear from the following pamphlet issued by SNCC in 1967, the year in which urban violence in the United States peaked.

QUESTIONS FOR ANALYSIS

1. What goals are defined in this document for the Black Power movement?
2. Why do the authors of the pamphlet believe that creating a black culture is so important to their goals?
3. According to the leaflet, why are ghetto blacks most suited to leading the Black Power movement?
4. What views of whites are contained in the pamphlet?
5. In what specific ways do the ideas expressed in this leaflet differ from those of Martin Luther King, Jr., in his Letter from Birmingham Jail (source 72)?

The black man in America is in a perpetual state of slavery no matter what the white man's propaganda tells us.

The black man in America is exploited and oppressed the same as his black brothers are all over the face of the earth by the same white man. We will never be free until we are all free and that means all black oppressed people all over the earth.

We are not alone in this fight, we are a part of the struggle for self-determination of all black men everywhere. We here in America must unite ourselves to be ready to help our brothers elsewhere.

We must first gain BLACK POWER here in America. Living inside the camp of the leaders of the enemy forces, it is our duty to our Brothers to revolt against the system and create our own system so that we can live as MEN.

We must take over the political and economic systems where we are in the majority in the heart of every major city in this country as well as in the rural areas. We must create our own black culture to erase the lies the white man has fed our minds from the day we were born. . . .

The black Brother in the ghetto will lead the Black Power Movement and make changes that are necessary for its success.

The black man in the ghetto has one big advantage that the bourgeois Negro does not have despite his "superior" education. He is already living outside the value system white society imposes on all black Americans.

He has to look at things from another direction in order to survive. He is ready. He received his training in the streets, in the jails, from the ADC[1] check his mother did not receive in time and the head-beatings he got from the cop on the corner. . . .

Once he makes that first important discovery about the great pride you feel inside as a BLACK MAN and the great heritage of the mother country, Africa, there is no stopping him from dedicating himself to fight the white man's system. . . .

The bourgeois Negro has been force-fed the white man's propaganda and has lived too long in the half-world between white and phony black bourgeois society. He cannot think for himself because he is a shell of a man full of

---

[1]ADC stands for Aid to Dependent Children, a form of welfare payment.

contradictions he cannot resolve. He is not to be trusted under any circumstances until he has proved himself to be "cured." There are a minute handful of these "cured" bourgeois Negroes in the Black Power Movement and they are most valuable but they must not be allowed to take control. . . .

We have to all learn to become leaders for ourselves and remove all white values from our minds. When we see a Brother using a white value through error, it is our duty to the Movement to point it out to him. We must thank our Brothers who show us our own errors. . . .

As a part of our education, we must travel to other cities and make contacts with the Brothers in all the ghettos in America so that when the time is right we can unite as one under the banner of BLACK POWER. . . .

We have to learn that black is so much better than belonging to the white race with the blood of millions dripping from their hands that it goes far beyond any prejudice or resentment. We must fill ourselves with hate for all white things. This is not vengeance or trying to take the white oppressors' place to become new black oppressors but is a oneness with a worldwide black brotherhood.

We must regain respect for the lost religion of our fathers, the spirits of the black earth of Africa. The white man has so poisoned our minds that if a Brother told you he practiced Voodoo, you would roll around on the floor laughing at how stupid and superstitious he was.

We have to learn to roll around on the floor laughing at the black man who says he worships the white Jesus. He is truly sick. . . .

We must infiltrate all government agencies. This will not be hard because black clerks work in all agencies in poor-paying jobs and have a natural resentment of the white men who run these jobs.

People must be assigned to seek out these dissatisfied black men and women and put pressure on them to give us the information we need. Any man in overalls, carrying a tool box, can enter a building if he looks like he knows what he is doing.

Modern America depends on many complex systems such as electricity, water, gas, sewerage, and transportation, and all are vulnerable. Much of the government is run by computers that must operate in air conditioning. Cut off the air conditioning and they cannot function.

We must begin to investigate and learn all these things so that we can use them if it becomes necessary. We cannot train an army in the local park, but we can be ready for the final confrontation with the white man's system.

Remember your Brothers in South Africa and do not delude yourselves that it could not happen here. . . .

We must stop fighting a "fair game." We must do whatever is necessary to win BLACK POWER. We must have to hate and disrupt and destroy and blackmail and lie and steal and become blood-brothers like the Mau-Mau.[2]

We must eliminate or render ineffective all traitors. We must make them fear to stand up like puppets for the white men, and we must make the world understand that these so-called men do not represent us or even belong to the same black race because they sold out their birthright for a mess of white society pottage.[3] Let them choke on it. . . .

The political system, economic system, military system, educational system, religious system, and anything else you name is used to

---

[2]Mau-Mau refers to a militant nationalist movement directed against British rule that originated among the Kikuyu people of Kenya in the 1950s. In 1952 the British government launched a military operation against the Mau-Mau movement that lasted until 1956 and cost tens of thousands of lives.

[3]Genesis 25 and 27 tell the story of how Esau, the other son of the patriarch Isaac, sold his birthright to his younger brother, Jacob, for a "mess of pottage" is a moment of hunger.

preserve the status quo of white America getting fatter and fatter while the black man gets more and more hungry.

We must spend our time telling our Brothers the truth.

We must tell them that any black woman who wears a diamond on her finger is wearing the blood of her Brothers and Sisters in slavery in South Africa, where one out of every three black babies dies before the age of one, from starvation, to make the white man rich.

We must stop wearing the symbols of slavery on our fingers.

We must stop going to other countries to exterminate our Brothers and Sisters for the white man's greed.

We must ask our Brothers which side they are on.

Once you know the truth for yourself, it is your duty to dedicate your life to recruiting your Brothers and to counteract the white man's propaganda.

We must disrupt the white man's system to create our own. We must publish newspapers and get radio stations. Black Unity is strength — let's use it now to get BLACK POWER.

The Emergence of Militant Feminism

❖

75 ❖ FEMINIST MANIFESTOES FROM THE LATE 1960S

After having won the right to vote in most Western democracies by the 1920s, the powerful feminist movements of the nineteenth and early twentieth centuries lost momentum. In the 1930s and 1940s women diverted their energies to surviving the Great Depression and winning World War II. In the immediate postwar years, with a return of prosperity, women in the United States and Europe were content to accept the domestic role prescribed for them by the family-centered ethos of the postwar era.

Beginning in the 1960s, feminism reemerged as a powerful force, with its impetus and energy derived from ideas and movements originating in the United States. The revival of feminism began in the early 1960s with the appointment of President Kennedy of the Presidential Commission on the Status of Women in 1961, the publication of Betty Friedan's *The Feminine Mystique* in 1963, and the inclusion of gender as one of the categories protected by the Civil Rights Act of 1964. The National Organization for Women (NOW), which concentrated on redressing gender-based vocational and educational inequalities, seemed ready after its founding in 1966 to assume leadership of a new feminist movement that was moderate and liberal.

Within only a few years, however, calls for legal equality gave way to angry demands for women's liberation, as the feminist movement, like the civil rights movement, became increasingly radical and militant. Radical feminists of the late 1960s were young, and, like the black militants, were angered by the huge disparity between American rhetoric about equality and the reality of their lives. Beginning in 1967 and 1968 the first radical feminist groups formed in Chicago, New York, and San Francisco, and the first radical feminist journals began to appear. In 1968 the New York Radical Women pioneered the technique of consciousness-raising, in which women met to participate in open-ended discussions of how societal oppression affected their personal lives.

Then in September 1968 an event took place that catapulted radical feminism into the headlines and made "women's liberation" a household phrase. On September 7, several hundred women, organized by the New York Radical Feminists, converged on Atlantic City, New Jersey, to protest the Miss America Pageant. Convinced that the Pageant epitomized the evils of gender stereotyping, the women picketed, tossed symbols of female enslavement and torture (high heels, girdles, bras, and kitchen detergents) into a trash can, briefly interrupted the nationally televised closing ceremony, and crowned a sheep as Miss America. While picketing, they handed out the ten-point manifesto included below.

Lavishly covered by the media, the Atlantic City demonstration brought the new feminist agenda into the limelight and was a catalyst for a half-decade of intense activity on behalf of women's liberation. Women demanded legalized abortion, denounced sexism in language and advertising, produced a huge quantity of feminist literature and scholarships, and founded hundreds of feminist organizations. Among them was the Westchester Radical Feminists, organized by suburban New York women in 1972. Their manifesto, printed below, offers an opportunity to compare their views with those of another suburban New York woman, Betty Friedan, whose *The Feminine Mystique* had appeared just nine years earlier.

QUESTIONS FOR ANALYSIS

1. According to the Atlantic City protesters, what qualities are rewarded in the Miss America Pageant? How is this a disservice to American women in general?
2. What does the document reveal about links between the Miss America Pageant protest and other protest movements of the late 1960s?
3. According to the Atlantic City protesters, what flaws in American life other than sexism does the Miss America Pageant reveal?
4. According to the Westchester manifesto, what is the underlying cause of female oppression?
5. What, according to the Westchester feminists, must be changed in U.S. society to achieve "women's liberation"?
6. How do the issues and tone of these two manifestoes differ from those of Friedan's *The Feminine Mystique*?

NO MORE MISS AMERICA

On September 7th in Atlantic City, the Annual Miss America Pageant will again crown "your ideal." But this year, reality will liberate the contest auction-block in the guise of "genyooine" de-plasticized, breathing women. Women's Liberation Groups, black women, high-school and college women, women's peace groups, women's welfare and social-work groups, women's job-equality groups, pro-birth control and pro-abortion groups — women of every political persuasion — all are invited to join us in a day-long boardwalk-theater event, starting at 1:00 p.m. on the boardwalk in front of Atlantic City's Convention Hall. . . .

Male reporters will be refused interviews. We reject patronizing reportage. *Only newswomen will be recognized.*

The Ten Points
We Protest:

1. The *Degrading Mindless-Boob-Girlie Symbol.* The Pageant contestants epitomize the roles we are all forced to play as women. The parade down the runway blares the metaphor of the 4-H Club county fair, where the nervous animals are judged for teeth, fleece, etc., and where the best "specimen" gets the blue ribbon. So are women in our society forced daily to compete for male approval, enslaved by ludicrous "beauty" standards we ourselves are conditioned to take seriously.

2. *Racism with Roses.* Since its inception in 1921, the Pageant has not had one Black finalist, and this has not been for a lack of test-case contestants. There has never been a Puerto Rican, Alaskan, Hawaiian, or Mexican-American winner. Nor has there ever been a *true* Miss America — an American Indian.

3. *Miss America as Military Death Mascot.* The highlight of her reign each year is a cheerleader-tour of American troops abroad — last year she went to Vietnam to pep-talk our husbands, fathers, sons and boyfriends into dying and killing with a better spirit. She personifies the "unstained patriotic American womanhood our boys are fighting for." The Living Bra and the Dead Soldier. We refuse to be used as Mascots for Murder.

4. *The Consumer Con-Game.* Miss America is a walking commercial for the Pageant's sponsors. Wind her up and she plugs your product on promotion tours and TV — all in an "honest, objective" endorsement. What a shill.

5. *Competition Rigged and Unrigged.* We deplore the encouragement of an American myth that oppresses men as well as women: the win-or-you're-worthless competitive disease. The "beauty contest" creates only one winner to be "used" and forty-nine losers who are "useless."

6. *The Woman As Pop Culture Obsolescent Theme.* Spindle, mutilate, and then discard tomorrow. What is so ignored as last year's Miss America? This only reflects the gospel of our society, according to Saint Male: women must be young, juicy, malleable — hence age discrimination and the cult of youth. And we women are brainwashed into believing this ourselves!

7. *The Unbeatable Madonna-Whore Combination.* Miss America and Playboy's centerfold are sisters over the skin. To win approval, we must be both sexy and wholesome, delicate but able to cope, demure yet titillatingly bitchy. Deviation of any sort brings, we are told, disaster: "You won't get a man!!"

8. *The Irrelevant Crown on the Throne of Mediocrity.* Miss America represents what women are supposed to be: unoffensive, bland, apolitical. If you are tall, short, over or under what weight The Man prescribes you should be, forget it. Personality, articulateness, intelligence, commitment — unwise. Conformity is the key to the crown — and, by extension, to success in our society.

9. *Miss America as Dream Equivalent To — ?* In this reputedly democratic society, where every little boy supposedly can grow up to be President, what can every little girl hope to grow up to be? Miss America. That's where it's at. Real power to control our own lives is restricted to men, while women get patronizing pseudopower, an ermine cloak and a bunch of flowers; men are judged by their actions, women by their appearance.

10. *Miss America as Big Sister Watching You.* The Pageant exercises Thought Control, attempts to sear the Image onto our minds,

to further make women oppressed and men oppressors; to enslave us all the more in high-heeled, low-status roles; to inculate false values in young girls; to use women as beasts of buying; to seduce us to prostitute ourselves before our own oppression.

WESTCHESTER RADICAL FEMINISTS' MANIFESTO

Suburban women, in common with all women, have lived in intimacy with and dependence on our oppressor. In isolation and tightly bound to our families, we have viewed the world and our condition from the level of patriarchal ideas of money and power. We now recognize that these patriarchal concepts have and still do dominate and control our lives, but our thinking, hopes and aspirations are changing. . . .

As suburban women, we recognize that many of us live in more economic and material comfort than our urban sisters, but we have come to realize through the woman's movement, feminist ideas and consciousness raising, that this comfort only hides our essential powerlessness and oppression. . . . Like dogs on a leash, our own status and power will reach as far as our husbands and their income and prestige will allow. As human beings, as individuals, we, in fact, own very little and should our husbands leave us or us them, we will find ourselves with the care and responsibility of children and without money, jobs, credit or power. For this questionable condition, we have paid the price of isolation and exploitation by the institutions of marriage, motherhood, psychiatry and consumerism. Although our life styles may appear materially better, we are, as all women, dominated by men at home, in bed and on the job; emotionally, sexually, domestically and financially. . . .

We believe that:

1. The notion of fixed sex roles is arbitrary and unjust.

2. That suburbia is a wasteland; a human ghetto for women minimizing their opportunity for growth.

3. That diverse forms of sexual relationships based on mutual consent are a matter of individual choice and right.

4. The institution of marriage presumes and establishes the lifelong servitude of women.

5. All economic institutions subject and deprive the suburban women, as well as all women, of economic power; even her power as a consumer is a myth since she spends and buys no more than her husband will allow.

6. Women are no more inherently suited to child rearing than men and men must be held responsible also for the emotional, educational and physical development of children.

7. The mutual dependence of mothers and children is in essence an act of tyranny which serves to thwart, retard and immobilize both mother and children.

8. The adjustment theories adhered to by most psychologists and psychiatrists and their institutions perpetuate destructive attitudes towards women, undermine their self value and self esteem and are generally harmful to the wholesome development and welfare of women.

9. The fact that we live with and even support some of these institutions which are sexist does not in any way alter our basic beliefs. We presently live the way we do because there are no good alternatives.

10. Women's liberation is not human liberation and we place the cause of women above all other causes.

11. We are committed to the understanding of our condition as women so that we may create and invent new ways to live and to find both collective and individual realization and strength.

Campus Outrage

❖

76 ◆ *THREE STUDENT PAMPHLETS FROM THE UNIVERSITY OF PARIS*

During the 1960s, the number of students enrolled in universities in Europe and the United States had never been higher. In prewar Germany, Great Britain, and France, with a combined population of 150,000,000, only 150,000 attended universities — approximately one-tenth of 1 percent of the total population. Between 1960 and 1970, however, the number of French university students increased more than threefold, from 211,000 to 651,000, while in Great Britain, West Germany, and Italy, the student population doubled. In the United States, which had pioneered mass college education, the 1960s began with 3,789,000 university students and ended with 7,850,000. For the first time in the history of the United States, or of any nation, there were more university students than farmers.

As the numbers of university students grew, so did their political activism. In 1964 the Berkeley campus of the University of California was disrupted by student strikes, demonstrations, and clashes with police when the Free Speech Movement challenged the university's decision to ban political and civil rights groups from using a strip of land at the edge of the campus. In 1965 the first teach-in protesting the Vietnam War took place at the University of Michigan, and by 1967 student-led campaigns against draft boards, ROTC programs, university research for the Defense Department, and campus recruitment by corporations such as the Dow Chemical Company (the maker of napalm) made college campuses the core of the antiwar movement. In Europe in the mid 1960s, the Socialist German Student League organized demonstrations against the Vietnam War, imperialism, and right-wing politicians, and Italian students occupied buildings and clashed with police to show their disgust with university policies and practices.

None of this prepared the world for the eruptions on European and American campuses in 1968, however. With a fury no one could have predicted, hundreds of thousands of students across Europe and the United States violently challenged the established order in campus takeovers, riots, and street clashes. Although opposition to U.S. involvement in Vietnam was a common theme — indeed, the dominant theme in the United States — no single cause or issue was at stake in the youth rebellion. In Berlin, student ire focused on the Springer Press, a chain of right-wing newspapers and publishing outlets that students blamed for inspiring the attempted assassination of the student radical Rudi Dutschke. In Italy, the issue was an authoritarian and impersonal university system characterized by decaying buildings and indifferent professors. At Nanterre, a branch campus of the University of Paris, it was sexual segregation in the dormitories. At Columbia, it was the university's plan to build a new gymnasium on land that included a neighborhood playground.

Although student rebellions shocked the public and unsettled authorities in the United States, Germany, and Italy, in France they came close to launching a revolution. The student rebellion began at the Nanterre campus, a new branch of the University of Paris built in the midst of one of France's worst slums. Agitation over teaching issues, examinations, and the right of males to visit females in their dormitories caused the dean to suspend classes on May 2. Nanterre student leaders then joined forces with radicals at the University of Paris, where demonstrations involving tens of thousands of students led to arrests, further demonstrations, and bloody clashes with riot police. In mid May, industrial workers, who were concerned with rising unemployment and stagnant wages, threw in their lot with the students and joined them in a march through Paris with six hundred fifty thousand to seven hundred thousand participants. In the following days, students reoccupied the university district, the Sorbonne, and approximately ten million workers, about 60 percent of the work force, went on strike. Revolution seemed imminent.

In late May and early June, however, the movement lost momentum in the face of a tough speech by President de Gaulle, a promised wage increase for workers, counterdemonstrations organized by the government, and ideological fissures among the students. After a final clash between police and students on June 12, 1968, students abandoned control of the Sorbonne, and workers ended their general strike. In parliamentary elections held in late June, de Gaulle's party, the Union for the Defense of the Republic, won a resounding victory. The student revolution in Paris was over, leaving a legacy of modest reforms in the French university system and the memory of idealistic young people who thought they could change the world.

The weeks of protest in France produced a mountain of pamphlets, manifestoes, editorials, speeches, and proclamations. The following three selections provide a sample of the profusion of ideas that was generated. The first, "How to Train a Stuffed Goose," is from a pamphlet, *Stuffed Geese,* circulated in February or March 1968 on the Nanterre campus. The second, "Why We Are Fighting," is an editorial printed on May 7 in *Action,* a pro-student newspaper. The third, "Your Struggle Is Our Struggle," is a proclamation issued on May 24 by the Movement of March 22, a student organization that had originated at Nanterre.

QUESTIONS FOR ANALYSIS

1. What image of French student life is portrayed in the pamphlet *Stuffed Geese?*
2. How do the views of the remaining two selections resemble and differ from those expressed in *Stuffed Geese?*
3. What do the three selections reveal about students' concerns and worries about their futures?
4. What are the students' views of the role that universities have played in French society? How do the students want to change that role?
5. Why, according to the last selection, is the students' struggle similar to that of the workers?
6. If the students had been given the opportunity of completely reshaping the French universities according to their ideas, what would these universities have looked like?

"HOW TO TRAIN A STUFFED GOOSE"

Lethargy, disappointment, and disgust compose the daily atmosphere of all lecture halls, nor is this peculiar to the first year. Collapse of any real vocation, dearth of professional openings and esteem, a specialty that boils down to making children count red balls and blue balls, these are the ultimate results for psychologists and sociologists of years of "study," during which all real value, all intellectual dynamism has been nibbled away. . . . Actually what the [faculty] offers us, when what we are looking for are possibilities of extending our mental horizons, is a crude paternalism which, by promoting the breeding of "stuffed geese". . . maintains us in a state of intellectual sterility. . . .

Teaching Methods

Existing To begin with, this type of teaching bores us even before we become disgusted by its mechanical, deadly aspects, as also by the banality and extremely insipid way it is presented. The student, being unconcerned by its insipidness, and maintained in a state of mental passivity, becomes a mere scribe who copies the teacher's lifeless words; later, these copies will be useful to him, since he will reproduce them, without omitting a comma, on his examination paper, as he is required to do by the teacher.

Demanded . . . We demand the introduction of genuine dialogue, of real student-professor cooperation. We demand that the insipidness and lethargy of the lecture halls be replaced by an atmosphere of life, enthusiasm, research, and real work in common. We demand that the courses . . . contain an incitement to original thought and research in the form of bibliographical information that corresponds to precise problems. Then the students will be able to work intelligently on real problems, analyze bibliographic relationships, and discuss among themselves, during their "work group" meetings, all the results of their individual research. In this way they will be glad to attend classes, since these classes will finally be discussion meetings in which a dialogue will be set up between the professor and the students. . . .

Examinations

Existing Copying: obviously, any eighth grader would exult in such tests as these, which would recall his easiest written interrogations. He would excel in these exams because he would lend himself perfectly to these checkups merely of the student's faculty of memory. . . . He would act in this way just as lots of us have acted because they had understood how to meet the requirements of an examination and how to get the approval of the teaching body, or at least of the assistants. Because quite evidently, for the latter, who give the validity of correction as alibi, the "value" of an answer is proportionate to the degree of perfection with which the lecture is copied, harking back to methods formerly used by primary school teachers for correcting their famous *"copy books."*

Demanded Open books, justice: we demand that examinations be held with our books open, and should take into consideration, above all, the student's capacity for intellectual initiative and his powers of analysis and in-depth reflection and not, as now, merely the sterile feat of memory.

Doubtless this genuine examination by its very nature would challenge the competence of certain assistants today who, in their hasty, superficial correcting, are too accustomed not to see this capacity for intellectual initiative, and only understand the premise through the exactness of the copy. . . .

These basic demands are vital of us, and must be presented immediately to the faculty members.

"WHY WE ARE FIGHTING"

For years students have been protesting the authoritarian methods that the government wanted to force upon them. . . . For years, calmly, but also in an atmosphere of general indifference, the government ignored their protests just as it ignored the workers' protests. For years these protests remained vain and without response.

Today, the students are resisting.

Their only crime is to reject a University the sole goal of which is to train future bosses and docile tools for the economy. Their only crime is to reject an authoritarian and hierarchical social system which rejects any radical opposition; this means refusing to be the servants of this system.

For this crime alone, they are being rewarded by blackjacks and prison sentences. . . . In Paris and in Nanterre they are not fighting alone; they are not fighting only for themselves. In Germany, on May first, tens of thousands of students and workers were *together,* on the initiative of the SDS,[1] in the first anti-capitalist demonstration that has taken place in Berlin since [Nazism]. The "handful of agitators" became a mass movement. Those who are combating the capitalist University stood shoulder to shoulder with those who are combating capitalist exploitation.

In France we also know that our fight has only begun; we know that youth is sensitive to the capitalist crisis and to the crisis of imperialism oppressing people in Vietnam, in Latin America, everywhere in the Third World. In Redon, in Caen,[2] young workers are revolting violently, more violently than we are. . . . In spite of the government, in spite of the silence and the manipulations of its servile press, our struggle and theirs will converge.

Today students are becoming aware of what they are being trained for: to be managers for the existing economic system, paid to make it function in the best possible way. Their fight concerns all workers because it is also the workers' fight: they refuse to become professors in the service of an educational system which chooses the sons of the bourgeoisie and eliminates the others; sociologists who manufacture slogans for governmental election campaigns; psychologists responsible for making "worker teams function"

in the best interest of the employers; managers responsible for applying against the workers a system to which they themselves are subjected.

Young people in the high schools, universities, and from the working class reject the future offered them by today's society; they reject unemployment, which is becoming a growing threat; they reject today's University, which gives them only worthless, ultra-specialized training and which, under the pretext of "selection," reserves know-how for sons of the bourgeoisie, and is but a tool for repression of all non-conformist ideas in the interest of the ruling class.

"YOUR STRUGGLE IS OUR STRUGGLE"

We are occupying the [colleges]; you are occupying the factories. Are we both fighting for the same thing?

Ten percent of the students in higher education are sons of workers. Are we fighting so that there will be a higher percentage, for a democratic reform of the University? It would be better, but it is not the most important thing. These sons of workers will become students like any others. That a son of a worker might become a director is not in our program. We want to do away with the separation between workers, laborers, and managers. . . .

We refuse to be scholars cut off from social reality. We refuse to be used for the benefit of the ruling class. We want to do away with the separation between carrying out work and planning and organizing it. We want to construct a classless society; the goal of your struggle is the same.

You demand a minimum salary of 1,000 francs . . . in the Paris area, retirement at 60, and a 40-hour week at the same salary now paid for a 48-hour week.

---

[1]Sozialistische Deutsche Studentenbund, a Marxist student organization active in Germany during the 1960s. Not to be confused with the American Students for a Democratic Society.

[2]Caen and Redon were two of several cities in which wildcat strikes and workers' demonstrations led to violence in March and April 1968.

These demands are fair and they are not new. Nevertheless, they seem to have no connection with our goals. But in fact, you are occupying the factories, you are taking the employers as hostages, you are striking without previous notice. . . .

These struggles are more radical than your legitimate demands because they do not only seek the betterment of the workers' lot within the capitalist system, they imply the destruction of this system. They are political in the true sense of the word; you are not fighting to have the Prime Minister replaced, but so the employer will no longer be in power, either in the factory or in society. The form of your struggle presents us, students, with a model of truly socialist action: appropriation of the means of production and the power of decision by the workers.

Your fight and our fight are convergent. All that separates one from the other must be destroyed.

CHAPTER 10

Worlds Apart: The USSR, the Soviet Bloc, and China

For three decades after the Russian Revolution of 1917, the Union of Soviet Socialist Republics (USSR) stood alone as the world's only Marxist state. Then in the decade following World War II, it was joined by twelve others. In Europe, Albania, Yugoslavia, Poland, Hungary, Bulgaria, Romania, Czechoslovakia, and East Germany became communist states between 1945 and 1948, while in Asia, communist regimes were established in North Korea in 1945, China and Mongolia in 1949, and North Vietnam in 1954. Although a handful of states, most notably Cuba in 1959, later became communist, they were small and relatively insignificant. In large measure, the era of communist expansion was over by the mid 1950s. By then, approximately one-third of the world's people lived under communist rule.

Until the closing years of the twentieth century, these states existed in a largely self-contained universe separated economically and culturally from the rest of the world. This separation began in the 1920s and 1930s when most nations refused to have dealings with the Soviet Union and Stalin concentrated on building "socialism in one country." It widened after World War II when the mutual fears and hostilities generated by the Cold War created innumerable figurative and real barriers to trade, tourism, and cultural exchange.

During the 1950s and 1960s, self-contained development, not foreign trade, was the goal of communist economies, and what little foreign trade did take place was largely among the communist states themselves. Currencies of communist countries, such as the Soviet ruble and Chinese yuan, were not traded on international markets, and communist states did not participate in the International Monetary Fund or the General Agreement on Tariffs and Trade. Tourism between communist and noncommunist states was discouraged, and when journalists or scholars from one bloc visited a nation in the other ideological camp, their activities were closely monitored by police and intelligence officials. Government censorship guaranteed that people under communism had little accurate information about the outside world, while propaganda in capitalist states created distorted images of life under communism. The most powerful symbol of the division between the communist and noncommunist worlds was the Berlin Wall, a twenty-five mile barrier through Berlin constructed in 1961 on order of the East German government to stop the flight of its citizens to the West.

The world's communist states shared a number of common characteristics. Most, out of choice or coercion, at first modeled their political systems and economies on those of Stalin's Soviet Union. This meant control of the government by the Communist Party, and control of the Party by a dictator or a small handful of officials. It also meant abolition of rival political parties; eradication of opponents; the suppression of civil liberties; censorship; state control of newspapers, radio, and television; and the lavish use of propaganda. These states' economic policies also followed the Stalinist model of central planning, nationalization of major industries and businesses, and the collectivization of agriculture. The goal was rapid industrialization, with an emphasis on iron and steel, heavy machinery, and power generation rather than consumer goods. Most communist regimes were aggressively secular and sought to undermine established religions.

The communist states' allegiance to Marxist socialism and their shared hostility to the United States and its allies encouraged diplomatic and economic collaboration. In 1949 the Soviet Union and its European satellites formed the Council of Mutual Economic Assistance (COMECON) to coordinate economic planning, and in 1955 they ratified the Warsaw Pact, by which they pledged to come to one another's defense if attacked. The Soviet Union and China signed a pact of friendship and cooperation in 1950, and during the 1950s the Soviet Union provided China with financial and technical aid for economic development.

But there were fissures within the socialist camp from the start, and they widened with time. Yugoslavia's Marshal Tito gradually broke with Stalin in 1947 and 1948, and later refused to join COMECON or the Warsaw Pact. Albania at first aligned itself with the Soviet Union, then switched to China, and in the early 1970s embarked on an independent course. China and the Soviet Union became bitter antagonists in the 1960s, and in the 1970s many world leaders anticipated a full-scale war between the two communist powers.

Furthermore, many communist states sought to develop their own variety of socialism distinct from the Soviet model. China under Mao Zedong abandoned central planning during the Great Leap Forward between 1958 and 1960; Tito's Yugoslavia fashioned a mixed economy in the 1950s, as did Hungary on a lesser scale in the 1960s. Poland resisted both agricultural collectivization and suppression of the Roman Catholic Church. East Germany in 1953, Hungary in 1956, and Czechoslovakia in 1968 all experienced broad-based movements for democratization only to have them crushed by military force. Even the Soviet Union itself experimented with liberalization and economic reform after Stalin's death in 1953.

The new socialist family of nations was neither static nor lacking in disagreements. It was composed of states that struggled with issues of economic development, dissent, and the exercise of state power, and sought their own paths toward socialism within the constraints of Marxist /Leninist ideology. Given their unique histories, distinct cultures, and differing needs, this could hardly have been otherwise.

◆

Dissent and Repression in the Soviet Union

The issue of whether political dissent should be tolerated in the Soviet Union was settled in 1921 when the Tenth Communist Party Conference banned all opposing political parties and outlawed factions within the Bolshevik Party itself. The issue of how much freedom of expression should be accorded to writers and artists was decided some years later. Under the tightening screws of Stalin's dictatorship, Soviet thought and culture were brought under control of the state in the 1930s, and scientists, writers, and artists were all required to serve Stalin and the Communist Party unequivocally. In 1934, 590 delegates to the First All-Union Congress of Soviet Writers approve the doctrine of "socialist realism," which required that all literature must promote the Party's goals and strengthen the masses' allegiance to socialism. During Stalin's purges between 1936 and 1938, writers who failed to pass the Party's test of ideological conformity were branded "enemies of the people." Hundreds disappeared without a trace. Temporarily relaxed during World Was II, rigid controls were revived after 1945.

Following Stalin's death in 1953, socialist realism continued to be the guiding principle of art and literature; but the dictator's demise ushered in a series of thaws and freezes in Soviet cultural and intellectual life that continued until the glasnost era of the mid 1980s. Nikita Khrushchev, Party secretary after Stalin's death and head of state after 1957, at first seemed sympathetic to greater artistic and intellectual freedom. As a member of the ruling collective that took power in 1953, he tolerated the outburst of literary creativity that followed Stalin's death. In 1956 he launched a campaign of destalinization after denouncing Stalin in a "secret speech" to the Twentieth Party Congress as a cruel, irrational tyrant. But destalinization under Khrushchev had its limits. Tugged and pulled between intellectuals who wanted more freedom and unrepentant Stalinists who yearned for the old controls, Khrushchev zigged and zagged between thaws and freezes. Before he fell from power in October 1964, he was tilting toward repression.

Tight controls and censorship continued under Khrushchev's cautious successors, Leonid Brezhnev and Alexis Kosygin. Nonconforming writers continued to produce literary works in great quantities, but with no publishing opportunities in the Soviet Union, they circulated them in handwritten, typed, or mimeographed version or had them published abroad. In 1966, however, the government sought to intimidate writers by bringing to trial and sentencing to hard labor two authors, Andrei Siniavsky and Juli Daniel, who had arranged to have their works smuggled into the Soviet Union after publication in the West. When outraged intellectuals campaigned to overturn the sentences, the government arrested four of their spokesmen in 1967, and gave them harsher punishments than those imposed on Siniavsky and Daniel.

The government's crackdown had unexpected results. Rather than silencing the intellectuals, it galvanized many of them to fight harder for their basic freedoms. In 1970 the physicist Andrei Sakharov organized the Human Rights Movement, and between 1968 and 1972, the underground journal *The Chronicle of Current Events* regularly published reports on human rights abuses. Other intellectuals were even bolder, addressing high government officials with demands for democratic reforms and criticism of policies such as the invasion of Czechoslovakia in 1968. The government responded by sending some of its more outspoken critics into exile or to psychiatric hospitals to cure their "insanity." But sensitivity to world opinion prevented harsher measures, and by the early 1970s, the Soviet secret police estimated that there were approximately three hundred thousand dissidents in the USSR, compared to just a few dozen a decade earlier. The tense standoff continued between intellectuals and their government as the Soviet Union drifted deeper into stagnation during the 1970s and early 1980s.

A Plea for Democratic Reform

❖

77 ❖ Andrei Sakharov, Roy Medvedev, and Valentin Turchin, *LETTER TO COMRADES BREZHNEV, KOSYGIN, AND PODGORNY*

By the late 1960s dissidents were no longer content to circulate their views in foreign publications or among themselves in "self-published' versions. They now addressed their leaders directly. One of the most important such appeals was a letter sent in 1970 to the three most powerful men in the Soviet government: Leonid Brezhnev, the Party secretary; Alexis Kosygin, premier; and Nicholas Podgorny, first secretary of the politburo. It was drafted by Andrei Sakharov, an internationally known thermonuclear physicist and three-time recipient of the Hero of Socialist Labor medal. In the late 1960s he became a critic of Soviet nuclear weapons testing and an advocate of civil liberties. He was awarded the Nobel Peace Prize in 1975 for his crusades advocating disarmament and democratization in the Soviet Union. The government refused him permission to leave the Soviet Union to receive the award, and in 1980 sent him into internal exile in the city of Gorky. Sakharov was released in 1986 and died three years later.

Sakharov's 1970 letter was sent to the Soviet leaders after it had been revised in minor ways and signed by two other dissidents, Roy Medvedev, a historian, and Valentin Turchin, a physicist. Although their call for the democratization of the Soviet Union was radical, they recommended a gradualist approach that would be implemented from above by the Party.

QUESTION FOR ANALYSIS

1. How would you characterize the three authors' attitude toward socialism and Marxism?
2. What, according to the authors, are the main problems facing the Soviet Union, and what has caused these problems?
3. How do the authors view the West?
4. What do the authors seem to mean by the term *democracy*?
5. How, in the authors' opinion, will democratic reforms help solve the Soviet Union's economic and political problems?

RESPECTED COMRADES:

Over the past decade, menacing signs of breakdown and stagnation have begun to show themselves in the economy of our country, the roots of which go back to an earlier period and are very deep-seated. . . . A great mass of data is available showing mistakes in the determination of technical and economic policy in industry and agriculture and an intolerable procrastination about finding solutions to urgent problems. Defects in the system of planning, accounting, and incentives often cause contradictions between local and departmental interests and those of the state and nation. As a result, new means of developing production potential are not being discovered or properly put to use, and technical progress has slowed down abruptly. For these very reasons, the natural wealth of the country is often destroyed with impunity and without any supervision or controls: forests are leveled, reservoirs polluted, valuable agricultural land flooded, soil eroded or salinized, and so on. The chronically difficult situation in agriculture, particularly in regard to livestock, is well known. The population's real income in recent years has hardly grown at all; food supply and medical and consumer services are improving very slowly, and with unevenness between regions. The number of goods in short supply continues to grow. There are clear signs of inflation.

Of particular concern regarding our country's future is the lag in the development of education: our total expenditures for education in all forms are three times below what they are in the United States, and are rising at a slower rate. Alcoholism is growing in a tragic way, and drug addiction is beginning to surface. In many regions of the country, the crime rate is climbing systematically. Signs of corruption are becoming more and more noticeable in a number of places. In the work of scientific and scientific-technical organizations, bureaucratism, departmentalism, a formal attitude toward one's tasks, and lack of initiative are becoming more and more pronounced. . . .

In comparing our economy with that of the United States, we see that ours lags behind not only in quantitative but also — most regrettable of all — in qualitative terms. . . . We outstrip America in coal production, but we lag behind in the output of oil, gas, and electric power; we lag behind tenfold in the field of chemistry, and we are infinitely outstripped in computer technology. The latter is especially crucial, because the introduction of electronic computers into the economy is a phenomenon of decisive importance that radically changes the outlines of the production system and of the entire culture. . . . Nevertheless, our stock of computers is *1 percent* of that of the United States. . . . We simply live in another age.

Things are no better in the sphere of scientific and technological breakthroughs. Our role in this area has not advanced either. Rather, the contrary has been true. . . .

The source of our difficulties does not lie in the socialist system; on the contrary, it lies in those peculiarities and conditions of our life that run counter to socialism and are hostile to it. The source lies in the antidemocratic traditions and norms of public life established in the Stalin era, which have not been decisively eliminated to this day.

Noneconomic coercion, limitations on the exchange of information, restrictions on intellectual freedom, and other examples of the antidemocratic distortion of socialism that took place under Stalin were accepted in our country as an overhead expense of the industrialization process. . . . But there is no doubt that since the beginning of the second industrial revolution these phenomena have become a decisive economic factor; they have become the main brake on the development of the productive forces in this country. As a consequence of the increased size and complexity of economic systems, the problems of management and organization have moved to the forefront. . . . These problems demand the creative participation of millions of people on all levels of the economic system. They demand the broad exchange of information and ideas. . . .

However, we encounter certain insurmountable obstacles on the road toward the free exchange of ideas and information. Truthful information about our shortcomings and negative manifestations is hushed up on the grounds that it "may be used by enemy propaganda." Exchange of information with foreign countries is restricted for fear of "penetration by an enemy ideology." Theoretical generalizations and practical proposals,

if they seem too bold to some individuals, are nipped in the bud without any discussion, because of the fear that they might "undermine our foundations." . . . Under such circumstances, the conditions are created for the advancement up the rungs of the official ladder not of those who distinguish themselves by their professional qualities and commitment to principles but of those who verbally proclaim their devotion to the Party but in practice are only concerned with their own narrow personal interests or are passive timeservers. . . .

The overwhelming majority of the intelligentsia and the youth recognize the need for democratization, and the need for it to be cautious and gradual, but they cannot understand or condone measures of a patently antidemocratic nature. And, indeed, how can one justify the confinement in prisons, camps, and insane asylums of people who hold oppositionist views but whose opposition stands on legal ground, in the area of ideas and convictions? In many instances, no opposition was involved, but only a striving for information, or simply a courageous and unprejudiced discussion of important social questions. . . .

. . . Democratization, with its fullness of information and clash of ideas, must restore to our ideological life its dynamism and creativity — in the social sciences, arts, and propaganda — and eliminate the bureaucratic, ritualistic, dogmatic, openly hypocritical, and mediocre style that reigns in these areas today. . . .

What is in store for our nation if it does not take the course toward democratization? The fate of lagging behind the capitalist countries and gradually becoming a second-rate provincial power . . .; the growth of economic difficulties; increasingly tense relations between the Party and government apparatus, on the one hand, and the intelligentsia, on the other; the danger of ill-considered moves to the left or right; exacerbation of national problems, because the movement for democratization emanating from below in the national republics inevitably assumes a nationalistic character. . . .

Respected comrades! There is no way out of the difficulties now facing our country except a course toward democratization, carried out by the Soviet Communist Party in accordance with a carefully worked-out plan. A turn to the right — that is, a victory for the forces that advocate a stronger administration, a "tightening of the screws" — would not only fail to solve any of the problems but, on the contrary, aggravate them to an extreme point and lead our country into a tragic impasse. The tactic of waiting passively would ultimately have the same result. Today, we still have the chance to take the right road and to carry out the necessary reforms. In a few years, it may be too late.

The Dissidents' Adversary

78 ◆ *SECRET KGB REPORT, DECEMBER 21, 1970*

With responsibility for domestic and foreign security, the KGB (*Komitét Gosudárstvennoĭ Bezopásnosti*), or the Committee on State Security, was both the Federal Bureau of Investigation and Central Intelligence Agency of the Soviet Union. Under Yuri Andropov, who was named director in 1967, the KGB established in 1969 a special division, the Fifth Main Directorate, to combat political opposition and to tighten control over the general population in the face of the emerging dissident movement. Dominated by hard-liners, the KGB submitted the following report on the dissident movement to Soviet leaders in December 1970.

QUESTION FOR ANALYSIS

1. According to the KGB report, what are the presuppositions of the democratic socialist movement concerning the Soviet Union's future?
2. What are the short-term goals of the democratic socialists, according to the KGB?
3. What does the report suggest about the strength of the democratic socialist movement?

TOP SECRET

Among the scientific, technical and part of the creative intelligentsia documents are being passed around in which various forms of 'democratic socialism' are being propounded. According to one of these schemes of 'democratic socialism', whose author is Academician Sakharov, the evolutionary path of internal political development of the USSR will inevitably lead to the creation in the country of a 'truly democratic system'. As part of this, mathematicians and economists should in good time develop its model so that it could be a synthesis of what is positive in existing socio-political systems.

In a number of projects for the 'democratization' of the USSR the 'restriction or liquidation of the monopoly power of the CPSU[1] and the national development of an opposition loyal to socialism' is envisaged. Their authors and

---

[1]Communist Party of the Soviet Union.

distributors consider that the current level of development of socialist democracy should allow opposition views to exist, and demand legal opportunities to express views that disagree with the official course to be made available. From this perspective they declare that criminal legislation that prosecutes anti-Soviet agitation and propaganda or the distribution of obviously false fabrications, smearing the Soviet state and its social system, it unconstitutional.

On the basis of the preparation and distribution of 'samizdat'[2] literature there is taking place a noticeable consolidation of like-minded persons, and there are marked indications of attempts to create something like an opposition.

Approximately towards the end of 1968–early 1969 there emerged out of oppositionally minded elements a political core, called the 'democratic movement', which in their view has the three characteristics of an opposition: they 'have leaders, activists and are based on a significant number of sympathizers, not taking on the clear shape of an organisation, but set themselves clear aims and choose a suitable tactic, to gain legality'.

The main aims of the 'movement', as formulated in the thirteenth issue of *The Chronicle of Current Events* issued by the Moscow group of the 'democratic movement' headed by Yakir,[3] is 'the democratization of the country by developing in people democratic and scientific convictions, resistance to Stalinism, self-defence from repression, the struggle against extremism of whatever sort'.

---

[2]Literally, "self-publication." The term refers to the hand-copied, typed, or mimeographed writings circulated by dissidents whose work was denied publication by the government.
[3]Peter Yakir (1923–1986) was a historian imprisoned between 1937 and 1954 for being the son of Iona Yakir, a general who had been executed as an enemy of the people during Stalin's purges. On his release, he studied at the Moscow State Historical Archive Institute, where he collected material on the abuse of psychiatry for political ends. After joining the dissident movement in 1966, he was arrested in 1972 and suffered a breakdown under interrogation. Freed in 1974, he lived in isolation in Moscow until his death.

◆

Unrest in Eastern Europe and Soviet Response

In February 1948, with communist trade unionists organized into armed "action units" and the Soviet army mobilized on his nation's borders, the president of Czechoslovakia, Eduard Beneš, agreed to an all-communist administration, and the Soviet Empire in Eastern Europe was complete. East Germany, Poland, Romania, Bulgaria, Hungary, and now Czechoslovakia were all one-party communist states that had been installed with the help of the Soviet army and were controlled by men willing to follow Moscow's line and turn their countries into small-scale replicas of the USSR. This meant the collectivization of agriculture, the nationalization of major industries, central planning, and an emphasis on heavy industry rather than consumer goods. It also meant the suppression of political opposition, the surveillance of intellectuals, attacks on the churches, censorship, show trials, and the imprisonment or execution of dissidents.

Despite strict state controls, protest and rebellion marked the forty-year history of the Soviet Empire. Soviet troops had to intervene in East Germany in

1953, when after Stalin's death, strikes in Berlin sparked nationwide demonstrations for better pay and free elections. Peace was restored, but several thousand civilians were killed and twenty thousand were arrested.

Serious disturbances took place in Poland and Hungary in 1956 after expectations for change were heightened by Khrushchev's destalinization campaign and his efforts to patch up differences with Yugoslavia, a communist state that had pursued an independent path toward socialism outside of the Soviet orbit. In Poland, nationwide demonstrations and strikes calling for economic reform, protection of the Catholic Church, and the removal of Soviet troops ended in a compromise between Khrushchev and Poland's new leader, Wladyslaw Gomulka: Poland would remain a one-party communist state and a member of the Warsaw Pact, but it would have more control over its domestic affairs.

In Hungary, protesters had a more ambitious agenda. They demanded free elections, the reinstatement of banned political parties, and Hungary's withdrawal from the Warsaw Pact. They also provoked a harsher Soviet response. In November, with the Hungarian security police disbanded, noncommunist political parties reorganizing, and free elections planned, Soviet leaders sent in troops. They crushed the revolt at the cost of three thousand Hungarians killed and thirteen thousand injured. In the crackdown that followed, two thousand to twenty-five hundred insurgents were executed, twenty thousand imprisoned, and thousands more were sent to Soviet prison camps.

History repeated itself in 1968 in Czechoslovakia, where moderate economic reforms in the mid 1960s raised hopes for political liberalization. The premier, Antonin Novotny, resisted further change, however, and in the face of demonstrations in Prague and mounting criticism from intellectuals, he resigned in favor of Alexander Dubček in January 1968. Dubček presided over the so-called Prague Spring, in which censorship was loosened, restrictions on travel were lifted, and a reduction of Party control over all aspects of society was promised. By summer, Soviet leaders were convinced that Czechoslovakia was about to become another Hungary. In August they ordered an invasion by a force of mainly Soviet troops, which faced only passive resistance and easily snuffed out the reform movement. Dubček was removed from office, and all communists who had supported reform — about one-third of the membership — were expelled or given menial jobs. For the next twenty years Czechoslovakia had the Soviet bloc's most oppressive regime.

Although the suppression of the Czechoslovakian reform movement resulted in only a few casualties, it had a greater psychological and political impact on Eastern Europe than the Soviet invasion of Hungary in 1956. Unlike the Hungarians, the Czechs had not sought the end of communist rule or withdrawal from the Warsaw Pact. Theirs was a program of moderate reform with broad support from Party members. Its destruction by military force crushed hopes for the liberalization of Eastern Europe's communist regimes, which now were revealed as lacking both political legitimacy and a capacity to change.

Socialism with a Human Face

❖

79 ◆ *Ludvik Vaculík,*
TWO THOUSAND WORDS TO WORKERS,
FARMERS, SCIENTISTS, ARTISTS,
AND EVERYONE

The climax of the Prague Spring came in April 1968, when after months of debate, the Czechoslovakian Communist Party issued its Action Program. A plan for achieving a less oppressive form of socialism, "socialism with a human face," it called for a reduction in state power, more freedom for farmers and factory managers, strengthening of the courts and parliament, and the recognition of civil liberties. The Communist Party would retain power, but it would be more responsive to the needs of farmers, consumers, students, workers, and other interest groups.

While Party leaders debated how to implement their program, and progressives called for more rapid and thoroughgoing reforms, pressure on Czechoslovakia from the Soviet Union and other Warsaw Pact countries intensified. In May the Soviet Union ordered twenty-five thousand troops to the Czech-Polish border and announced that military exercises would be held in Czechoslovakia in June. State-controlled newspapers throughout the Soviet bloc denounced the reform movement, especially after Dubček angered Moscow by welcoming to Prague Yugoslavia's Marshal Tito, who symbolized national independence within the communist movement.

Then on June 27, with special party elections about to begin, there appeared in four Prague newspapers an essay, "Two Thousand Words," written by Ludvik Vaculík, (pronounced Vaht-*soo*-leek), a prominent novelist and journalist. The essay, signed by many public figures, denounced the Communist Party and called on the people to maintain pressure on their leaders to press on with reform. It warned that unless the democratic movement kept moving forward, conservatives would reassert their authority and roll back the reforms.

Vaculík's essay elicited a strong positive response within the general population. Thousands of supporting letters, resolutions, and telegrams were sent to members of the National Assembly and leaders of the Czechoslovakian Communist Party. Vaculík's essay also elicited a response in Moscow and other Warsaw Pact capitals. By giving the impression that the Czech reform movement was about to spin out of control, it strengthened the hand of politicians who favored military intervention.

Intervention came on the night of August 20 to 21 1968, when Warsaw Pact troops invaded Czechoslovakia and occupied its major cities. Within weeks political conditions were "normalized," and strict Party rule was reimposed. Vaculík lost his job with the Writers' Union and, as an unemployed author, remained under police scrutiny until the collapse of Czechoslovakian communism in 1989.

QUESTIONS FOR ANALYSIS

1. What are Vačulík's views of the failings of the Czechoslovakian Communist Party? What role, if any, should the Party play in the process of reforming Czechoslovakian society?
2. According to Vačulík, what have been the results of communist rule of Czechoslovakian politics and society?
3. What strategy does Vačulík envision for saving the Czechoslovakian reform movement and pushing it forward?
4. If the reform movement had succeeded as Vačulík had hoped, what would Czechoslovakian government and society have looked like?
5. How do Vačulík's views compare to those expressed two years later by Sakharov, Medvedev, and Turchin in their letter to the Soviet leadership (source 77)?

After the war people had great confidence in the Communist party, but it gradually preferred to have official positions instead of the people's trust, until it had only official positions and nothing else. . . . The incorrect line of the leadership turned the party from a political party and ideological grouping into a power organization which became very attractive to power-hungry egotists, reproachful cowards, and people with bad consciences. When they came into the party, its character and behavior began to be affected. Its internal organization was such that good people, who might have maintained its development for it to have fitted into the modern world, could not wield any influence at all without shameful incidents occurring. Many communists opposed this decline, but not in one single case did they have any success in preventing what happened.

The conditions in the Communist party were the model for and the cause of an identical situation in the state. . . . There was no criticism of the activity of the state and economic organizations. Parliament forgot how to debate: The government forgot how to govern and the directors how to direct. Elections had no significance, and the laws lost their weight. We could not trust representatives on any committee, and even if we did, we could not ask them to do anything, because they could accomplish nothing. What was still worse was that we could hardly trust each other anymore. There was a decline of individual and communal honor. You didn't get anywhere by being honest, and it was useless expecting ability to be appreciated. Most people, therefore, lost interest in public affairs; they worried only about themselves and about their money. . . . To sum up, the country reached a point where its spiritual health and character were both threatened. . . .

In the future, we shall have to display personal initiative and determination of our own.

Above all, we shall have to oppose the view, should it arise, that it is possible to conduct some sort of a democratic revival without the communists or possibly against them. This would be both unjust and unreasonable. The communists have well-constructed organizations, and we should support the progressive wing within them. They have experienced officials, and last but not least, they also have in their hands the decisive levers and buttons. Their Action Program has been presented to the public. It is a program for the initial adjustment of the greatest inequalities, and no one else has any similarly concrete program. We must demand that local Action Programs be submitted to the public in each district and each community. By doing so, we shall have suddenly taken very ordinary and long-expected steps in the right direction. . . .

The practical quality of the future democracy depends on what becomes of the [factories] and what will happen in them. . . . We have to find good managers and back them up. It is true that, in comparison with the developed countries, we are all badly paid, and some are worse off than others.

We can demand more money — but although it can be printed, it will be worth less. We should instead demand that directors and chairmen explain to us the nature and extent of the capital they want for production, to whom they want to sell their products and for how much, what profit they can expect to make, and the percentage of this profit that is to be invested in the modernization of production and the percentage to be shared out.

Under quite superficially boring headlines, a very fierce struggle is going on in the press about democracy and who leads the country. Workers can intervene in this struggle by means of the people they elect to [factory] administrations and councils.[1] As employees, they can do what is best for themselves by electing as their representatives on trade union organs their natural leaders, capable and honest people no matter what their party affiliation is.

If at the moment we cannot expect any more from the central political organs, we must achieve more in the districts and smaller communities. We should demand the resignation of people who have misused their power, who have damaged public property, or who have acted in a dishonest or brutal way. We have to find ways and means to persuade them to resign, through public criticism, for instance, through resolutions, demonstrations, demonstration work brigades, collections for retirement gifts for them, strikes, and picketing their houses. . . . And let us set up special citizens' committees and commissions to deal with subjects that nobody is yet interested in. It's quite simple, a few people get together, elect a chairman, keep regular minutes, publish their findings, demand a solution, and do not allow themselves to be intimidated.

We must turn the district and local press, which has degenerated into a mouthpiece for official views, into a platform for all the positive political forces. . . . Let us establish committees for the defence of the freedom of the press. Let us organize our own monitoring services at meetings. If we hear strange news, let's check on it ourselves, and let's send delegations to the people concerned and, if need be, publish their replies . . .

This spring, as after the war, we have been given a great chance. We have once again the opportunity to take a firm grip on a common cause, which has the working title of socialism, and to give it a form which will much better suit the once good reputation that we had and the relatively good opinion that we once had of ourselves. The spring has now come to an end, and it will never return. By winter we will know everything.

---

[1]In the late spring, workers at many factories had formed councils to protect their interests during the anticipated process of economic reform.

The Brezhnev Doctrine

❖

80 ◆ *Leonid Brezhnev,*
SPEECH TO THE FIFTH CONGRESS OF THE POLISH UNITED WORKERS' PARTY

After the invasion of Czechoslovakia, the Soviet leader Leonid Brezhnev sought to justify what many perceived to have been an overreaction to a program of moderate reform that sought neither the end of communism nor independence form the Soviet bloc. In what became known as the Brezhnev Doctrine, Brezhnev claimed that socialist states have the right to intervene in the domestic affairs of another socialist state if communism is threatened. Such is his theme in the following selection, taken from a speech delivered to a Polish Communist Party congress in November 1968.

Although Soviet leaders denied that a Brezhnev Doctrine ever was official Soviet policy, the Soviet leader Mikhail Gorbachev formally repudiated it in 1989. The Brezhnev Doctrine, he said, was to be replaced by the "Sinatra Doctrine." Just as the American singer proudly proclaimed in his popular song that "I did things my way," the European satellites would not be allowed to do things "their way" in ordering their affairs.

QUESTION FOR ANALYSIS

1. What, or whom, does Brezhnev blame for the increased activity of forces hostile to socialism in Czechoslovakia?
2. What, according to Brezhnev, are the "common natural laws of socialist construction" that justify outside intervention in the affairs of socialist states?
3. How, according to Brezhnev, do socialist and "imperialist" nations view the issue of nations' "sovereign rights" differently?
4. Reduced to its basics, what is the definition of the Brezhnev Doctrine as spelled out in this speech?

The might of the socialist camp today is such that the imperialists fear military defeat in the event of a direct clash with the chief forces of socialism. . . . However, it is a fact that in the new conditions the imperialists are making increasingly frequent use of different and more insidious tactics. They are seeking out the weak links in the socialist front, pursuing a course of subversive ideological work inside the socialist countries, trying to influence the economic development of these countries, attempting to sow dissension, drive wedges between them and encourage and inflame nationalist feelings and tendencies, and are seeking to isolate individual socialist states so that they can then seize them by the throat one by one. In short, imperialism is trying to undermine socialism's solidarity precisely as a world system. . . .

Socialist states stand for strict respect for the sovereignty of all countries. We resolutely oppose interference in the affairs of any states and the violation of their sovereignty.

At the same time, affirmation and defense of the sovereignty of states that have taken the path of socialist construction are of special significance to us communists. The forces of imperialism and reaction are seeking to deprive the people first in one, then another socialist country of the sovereign right they have earned to ensure prosperity for their country and well-being and happiness for the broad working masses by building a society free from all oppression and exploitation. And when encroachments on this right receive a joint rebuff from the socialist camp, the bourgeois propagandists raise the cry of "defense of sovereignty" and "noninterference." It is clear that this is the sheerest deceit and demagoguery on their part. In reality these loudmouths are concerned not about preserving socialist sovereignty but about destroying it.

It is common knowledge that the Soviet Union has really done a good deal to strengthen the sovereignty and autonomy of the socialist countries. . . . But it is well known, comrades, that there are common natural laws of socialist construction, deviation from which could lead to deviation from socialism as such. And when external and internal forces hostile to socialism try to turn the development of a given socialist country in the direction of restoration of the capitalist system, when a threat arises to the cause of socialism in that country — a threat to the security of the socialist commonwealth as a whole — this is no longer merely a problem for that country's people, but a common problem, the concern of all socialist countries. *(Applause.)*

It is quite clear that an action such as military assistance to a fraternal country to end a threat to the socialist system is an extraordinary measure, dictated by necessity; it can be called forth only by the overt actions of enemies of socialism within the country and beyond its boundaries, actions that create a threat to the common interests of the socialist camp.

Experience bears witness that in present conditions the triumph of the socialist system in a country can be regarded as final, but the restoration of capitalism can be considered ruled out only if the Communist party, as the leading force in society, steadfastly pursues a Marxist–Leninist policy in the development of all spheres of society's life; only if the party indefatigably strengthens the country's defense and the protection of its revolutionary gains, and if it itself is vigilant and instills in the people vigilance with respect to the class enemy and implacability toward bourgeois ideology; only if the principle of socialist internationalism is held sacred, and unity and fraternal solidarity with the other socialist countries are strengthened. *(Prolonged applause.)*

Utopian Dreams in Mao's China

On October 1, 1949, with the armies of Chiang Kai-shek in full retreat in the south, Mao Zedong, the leader of the Chinese Communist Party, stood above the Gate of Heavenly Peace in Beijing and proclaimed the People's Republic of China. China's civil war had ended, and the fate of 540 million Chinese lay in the hands of Mao Zedong and a small number of followers who for twenty-five years had struggled to unify China under communist rule.

China's new leaders had ambitious, even grandiose, plans for their country. They envisioned a strong, independent China, no longer vulnerable to imperialism and its attendant humiliations. They envisioned a China in which poverty would be eradicated through agricultural modernization, industrialization, and a program of road-building, railroad construction, and energy development. They envisioned a China in which ancient inequalities — between men and women, landlords and peasants, the learned and the illiterate, bureaucrats and subjects — would no longer exist.

But was it possible to achieve rapid economic development in a truly egalitarian society? Finding an answer to this question became the great challenge for China's policymakers. Mao, whose opinion mattered most, believed that both goals could be achieved simultaneously by tapping the potential of the Chinese people, who, under the guidance of the Party, would dedicate themselves to achieving a modernized, communist China, not self-enrichment. Their energy and willpower, not the planning of bureaucrats, the research of scientists, or the know-how of engineers, would create a prosperous and egalitarian China.

Mao never realized his dreams. His economic and political experiments proved disastrous, and after his death in 1976, China's leaders abandoned revolutionary egalitarianism in favor of a development strategy based on a principle that Mao had despised — that the interests of society were best served when individuals were free to pursue their own personal gain.

Industrial Heroism in the Great Leap Forward

81 ◆ Tan Manni, *LUSHAN'S PIG-IRON "SPUTNIK"*

In its first decade, communist China experienced profound changes. Between 1949 and 1953, large-scale businesses were nationalized, and land was seized from rich landowners and redistributed to peasants. In 1953, in imitation of Stalin's Soviet Union, China instituted its first Five-Year Plan. Its key components were centralized economic planning, the collectivization of agriculture, and rapid industrialization, with emphasis on steel, industrial equipment, chemicals, and electric power.

Despite an average annual growth rate of 18 percent in the 1950s, Mao was unhappy with the Soviet model of economic development. Farm output registered only minor gains, and what increases had occurred largely came from privately owned plots rather than common lands. The Soviet model, he believed, had other dangers. Central planning meant larger and more powerful bureaucracies, while rapid industrialization brought disproportionate wealth and status to elite managers and engineers. Thus by late 1957, Mao was prepared to take China into a new stage of its socialist development — the Great Leap Forward.

The Great Leap Forward shifted the focus of China's economic development from cities to the countryside, where millions of peasants, in the selfless pursuit of socialism, would dedicate themselves to road construction, farming, stock-raising, iron-making, and other enterprises to transform China into a modern socialist society in just a few years. It began in late 1957 when million of peasants were put to work on hundreds of water control and irrigation projects that supposedly opened up eight hundred million acres to cultivation in a few months. It was thought that equally impressive gains could be achieved by consolidating China's 740,000 cooperative farms into giant communes. By the end of 1958, 120 million households, or 99 percent of the rural population, had joined 26,000 communes, which Party officials ran according to strict egalitarian principles: private plots were abolished; commune members all received the same pay and food ration irrespective of their work; families were organized collectively, with meals and child care provided by the commune. Commune members did more than farm. They also joined militias, built and operated backyard iron foundries and factories, worked on construction projects, and prospected for uranium. Those with talent were encouraged to write inspirational poetry and songs.

The Great Leap Forward had its share of achievements, but overall it was a disaster. People were worked to exhaustion; the backyard iron foundries produced millions of iron pots and tools, but most were unusable; worst of all, farm output failed to reach unrealistically high production targets, and as the communes' grain, vegetables, and meat were handed over to the state to feed city dwellers, famine swept through rural China. It claimed twenty million lives between 1959 and 1962.

Why did the Great Leap Forward fail? Some answers are provided by the following article, even though the author, Tan Manni, wrote it to impress his readers with its great achievements. In the article, which appeared in the journal *China Reconstructs* in 1959, Tan describes how a commune in Lushan county, a region in Jianxi Province, reached a "sputnik" in iron production. *Sputnik* was the name of the first man-made satellite sent into orbit by the USSR in 1957. During the Great Leap Forward, the term was used for high production goals in agriculture and manufacturing.

QUESTIONS FOR ANALYSIS

1. What does the selection reveal about the level of economic and technological development in Lushan county at the time of the Great Leap Forward?
2. According to the author, how do the workers view their labors? What methods have been used to motivate them?
3. What does the article reveal about the reason for the poor quality of pig iron produced in the Lushan county foundries?
4. How does the article help explain the reasons for the fall in agricultural production during the Great Leap Forward?
5. What changes in social and family relationships accompanied the Great Leap Forward? Why were they necessary?

Furnace fields are everywhere . . . plots of hundreds of small earthen furnaces were "growing," in late autumn when I was there, alongside fields of sweet potatoes and tobacco. . . .

Small red flags fly overhead indicating the sections belonging to the various companies and squads of farmer-steelworkers, who are organized like militia units. . . .

At one of the ten-foot-high furnaces, a man climbs a wooden ladder to dump coke and firewood through the top. After a few minutes beside the 1,000-degree heat, he descends and another worker goes up to tamp the fuel down with his rake. A third man follows to pull the hot rake away from the blast of the fire. Beside the furnace another crew is pushing the handle of the huge homemade wooden bellows. With all his might one of them pulls the handle, half as tall as himself, and pushes it back with the weight of his body. Three other men standing by to take their turns jokingly cheer him on. . . .

The river a few miles away from the county town is another scene of activity. Undaunted by cold north wind, 25,000 students, women, and local government workers are ankle-deep in the water, washing for the iron-bearing sand that has been carried down from the nearby mountains. On the banks, groups of students off their working shift hold classes, and a crew of older women minds the children for the mothers beside the temporary living quarters made for workers from distant parts of the county. . . .

The office of the county Communist Party committee where I stayed in the county town of Lushan is like the headquarters of an army, for the party had undertaken direct leadership of the iron campaign. Any time of the day or night, one can hear someone shouting into the telephone, "Long distance . . . urgent . . . coal . . . tons."

This is the verve which enabled Lushan, the small mountainous county which six months ago possessed neither a blast furnace nor an engineer, or even an automobile, to startle the entire country by proving it could turn out 1,000 tons of iron a day. That record on last August 28 opened a new page in the nation-wide campaign for iron and steel, for it did away with the belief that smelting by local methods does not add up to much.

Lushan's achievement was called a "sputnik," and within the next month it inspired seventy-three more counties to reach that level. Now the record has been surpassed hundreds of times, but the county's 430,000 people are still seized by the iron and steel fever. Each day 100,000 of them work directly in its production, and many thousands more "at the rear" help transport ore after a day's work in the fields.

The people of Lushan began making small amounts of iron early in the summer, in line with the country's policy of developing small local industry as well as large plants, and to meet their own needs in making labor-saving farm machinery. . . . In Lushan, local materials and simple homemade tools were used to cut down initial investment and half of the funds were contributed by the people themselves. A dozen blacksmiths who at the beginning did not know how to smelt ore, led by the party vice-secretary, studied and experimented until they found a suitable process, and then passed the technique on to 600 other farmer-steelworkers. . . .

. . . The farming had to be done with as few people as possible so as to free as many workers as possible to build and operate more furnaces, and mine and transport ore and coal. . . .

As the work could not go ahead without full mass support and understanding, the meetings to discuss the proposal [to set higher production goals] became hot debates — a struggle of ideas. It was through this that the farmers came to realize their real power to produce. Party leaders put the need for iron in terms of the county's own needs — it could bring hydroelectric power

stations on every one of the 600 reservoirs the people had built in the spring, better farm tools and machines, multi-storied buildings. They also pointed out that more iron for national construction would mean more tractors, rail lines and other improvements for all.

The way [to proceed], most people agreed, was large-scale organization. Lushan's mountains had ore but few people to do the mining. On the plains, on the other hand, there was manpower to spare. So their coops[1] decided that only by merging could they better deploy the working force. This later formed the basis for the people's commune which now embraces all of Lushan county.

Suggestions for nurseries and canteens to release more women were also adopted. In one large village alone, these measures freed 2,100 women for productive work. . . .

When the time came to sign up for iron work, 95 percent of the county's able-bodied persons applied, and 65,000 were soon actually making iron. Shock teams were organized to man the furnaces, mine the ore, mold crucibles, and repair roads to facilitate transport. They built 500 new furnaces, and methods were developed to make the older ones yield twenty times as much iron per heat.

In the fortnight which preceded the target date of August 28, few people got a full night's sleep. It was just in those weeks that news came of the aggressive military build-up by the United States in the Taiwan Straits area and of provocations against the mainland.[2] Determination became even greater. On August 27, just as the furnaces were being lit, word arrived about the nation-wide call to raise the 1958 national production of steel to 10.7 million tons, twice as much as the year before. On August 28, Lushan's furnaces yielded 1,068 tons of pig iron. The "sputnik" had succeeded and Lushan had set a new standard for local iron production.

---

[1]Cooperative farms.
[2]In August 1958 China demanded the withdrawal of U.S. forces from Taiwan after Chinese forces began bombing raids against Quemoy, an offshore island near the port of Amoy controlled by the Nationalist government of Taiwan. A standoff ensued. China continued the bombardment until December but made no attacks on the supply ships sent to Quemoy under U.S. navy escort.

Soon the daily average was far surpassing this one-time figure. In the autumn, 40,000 more workers came from neighboring counties. By early November 150,000 tons were being produced in one day — as much as had been planned for the whole year.

Creating a New China in the Great Proletarian Cultural Revolution

<hr>

82 ◆ ONE HUNDRED ITEMS FOR DESTROYING THE OLD AND ESTABLISHING THE NEW

By mid 1959, it was clear to millions of Chinese that the Great Leap Forward had failed. It was no less clear to members of the Central Committee of the Communist Party, who removed Mao from the day-to-day control of the Party and shifted power to Deng Xiaoping and Liu Shaoqi, who sought to revive China's economy by dismantling Mao's experiment. Communes were reduced in size, and hundreds of thousands of failed rural industrial enterprises were scrapped. Peasants once more were allowed to farm private plots and sell their products for profit. Central planning was reinstated, and material incentives for successful managers and productive workers were revived. As a result, between 1960 and 1965 industrial production grew by 11 percent a year, and grain production grew from 195 million tons in 1961 to 240 million tons in 1965.

Despite China's recovery, the Party leadership remained bitterly divided. On one side were the moderate supporters of Deng and Liu, who believed that China's most pressing need was economic development and that this goal could best be achieved through central planning; reliance on the contributions of university-trained engineers, managers, and scientists; and acceptance of incentives as a means of boosting production. On the other side were Chairman Mao and his disciples, who wanted economic development, but not at the expense of social equality, ongoing revolution, and ideological purity.

During the early 1960s, Mao gained support within the army and from a small but influential group of radical intellectuals. By late spring of 1966, Mao felt strong enough to launch what came to be known as the Great Proletarian Cultural Revolution. He and his supporters purged opponents from the Ministry of Culture and encouraged demonstrations by high school and university students against administrators and moderate Party members. Given red arm bands and copies of the "little red book," *Quotations from Chairman Mao*, students throughout China were released from classes to crusade against the "four olds" of Chinese society — old customs, old habits, old culture, and old thinking. These vague guidelines, along with Mao's directive to "destroy the old and construct the new," gave the student Red Guards many potential targets — as is demonstrated by the following document.

This list of demands was drawn up by Red Guards between the ages of fifteen and eighteen from the Maoism School, formerly known as Beijing Middle School Number 26. The students' list, compiled in August 1966, offers insights into the goals, opinions, and motives of the Red Guards, who, along with radicalized workers, kept China in an extraordinary state of turmoil between 1966 and 1969.

QUESTIONS FOR ANALYSIS

1. What view of Mao Zedong is presented in the students' list of proposals?
2. How do the authors of the manifesto characterize the bourgeoisie? What concrete steps are proposed to limit the wealth and status of the bourgeoisie?
3. What economic proposals are contained in the students' list? In what ways will their proposed changes benefit the peasants and workers?
4. According to the manifesto, what changes are necessary in Chinese family life and education in order to bring them into conformity with Mao Zedong thought?
5. The authors of the manifesto express an interest in ridding China of gambling, swearing, "decadent" music, drinking, smoking, and "weird" clothing. What may explain the students' strong views on these matters?

The onrushing tide of the Great Proletarian Cultural Revolution is just now crashing down on the remnant strength of the bourgeoisie with the might of a thunderbolt, washing the old ideology, the old culture, the old customs, and the old habits of the bourgeoisie down the stream. Chairman Mao tell us: "In the last analysis, all the truths of Marxism can be summed up in one sentence. 'To rebel is justified.'" The present Great Proletarian Cultural Revolution must overthrow the old ideology, the old culture, the old customs, and the old habits; to rebel all out against the bourgeoisie is to completely smash the bourgeoisie, to establish the proletariat on a grand scale, to make the radiance of great Mao Zedong Thought illuminate the entire capital, the entire nation, the entire world. Armed with great Mao Zedong Thought we are the most militant troops, the mortal enemy of the "four olds"; we are the destroyers of the old world; we are the creators of the new world. . . . We must thoroughly clear the books of the utterly illogical capitalist system. . . .

◆ ◆

. . . Under the charge of residential committees, every street must set up a quotation plaque;

every household must have on its walls a picture of the Chairman plus quotations by Chairman Mao.

. . . More quotations by Chairman Mao must be put up in the parks. Ticket takers on buses and conductors on trains should make the propagation of Mao Zedong Thought and the reading of Chairman Mao's quotations their primary task. . . .

. . . Printing companies must print quotations by the Chairman in large numbers; they must be sold in every bookstore until there is a copy of the *Quotations from Chairman Mao* in the hands of everyone in the whole country.

. . . With a copy of the *Quotations from Chairman Mao* in the hands of everyone, each must carry it with him, constantly study it, and do everything in accord with it. . . .

. . . Neighborhood work must put Mao Zedong Thought in first place, must set up small groups for the study of Chairman Mao's works, and must revolutionize housewives. . . .

. . . Broadcasting units must be set up in every park and at every major intersection, and, under the organizational responsibility of such organs as the Red Guards, propagate Mao Zedong Thought and current international and national events. . . .

. . . Letters and stamps must never have bourgeois things printed on them (such as cats, dogs, or other artistic things). Politics must be predominant. A quotation by Chairman Mao or a militant utterance by a hero must be printed on every envelope. . . .

. . . Shop windows cannot be dominated by displays of scents and perfumes. They must be decorated with simplicity and dignity and must put Mao Zedong Thought first.

. . . Theaters must have a strong political atmosphere. Before the movie starts, quotations from Chairman Mao must be shown. Don't let the bourgeoisie rule our stages. Cut the superfluous hooligan scenes, and reduce the price of tickets on behalf of the workers, peasants, and soldiers.

. . . Literary and art workers must energetically model in clay heroic images of workers, peasants and soldiers engaged in living study and living application of chairman Mao's works. Their works must be pervaded by the one red line of Mao Zedong Thought. . . .

. . . In a proletarian society, private enterprise cannot be allowed to exist. We propose to take all firms using joint state and private management and change them to state management and change joint state and private management enterprises into state-owned enterprises.

. . . Our socialist society absolutely cannot allow any hoodlums or juvenile delinquents to exist. We order you right this minute to get rid of your blue jeans, shave off your slick hairdos, take off your rocket shoes, and quit your black[1] organizations. Beijing is the heart of world revolution. . . . We warn you: You are not allowed to go on recklessly doing your evil deeds — if you do, you will be responsible for the consequences.

. . . All who are in service trades are not permitted to serve the bourgeoisie. Clothing stores are firmly prohibited from making tight pants, Hong Kong–style suits, weird women's outfits, and grotesque men's suits. . . .

. . . All daily necessities (perfume, snowflake cream,[2] etc.) that do not serve the broad worker, peasant, and soldier masses must be prohibited from sale right away. . . .

. . . All the landlords, rich-peasants, counter-revolutionaries, hooligans, Rightists, and other members of the bourgeois class are not permitted to collect pornographic books and decadent records. Whoever violates this rule will, when discovered, be treated as guilty of attempting to restore the old order, and his collections will be destroyed.

. . . Children must sing revolutionary songs. Those rotten tunes of the cat and dog variety must never again waft in the air of our socialist state. In this great socialist state of ours, absolutely no one is allowed to play games of chance.

. . . The bastards of the bourgeoisie are not allowed to hire governesses. Whoever dares to violate or resist this rule and thus continues to ride on the heads of the laboring people will be severely punished. . . .

. . . Every industrial enterprise must abolish the bourgeois bonus award system. In this great socialist nation of ours, the broad worker, peasant, soldier masses, armed with the great Mao Zedong Thought, have no need for material incentives.

. . . Heads of families are not allowed to educate their children with bourgeois ideology. The feudal family-head system[3] will be abolished.

. . . You old bastards of the bourgeoisie who receive high salaries, listen well: Before Liberation you rode on the heads of the people, sometimes severe, sometimes lenient. Now you still receive salaries many times more than ten times higher than those of the workers. You are thus drinking the blood of the people — you are

---

[1]Black was associated with reactionary politics.
[2]Facial cream.
[3]In the traditional Chinese family the father was the center of authority. In theory, he controlled the family's property and arranged marriages for his children and grandchildren. In en-

couraging young people to reject the values of their parents and elders — indeed, to denounce them to authorities for erroneous thinking — the Cultural Revolution rejected the age-old doctrine of filial piety, according to which children owed their parents unquestioned reverence and obedience.

guilty. Starting in September, you are ordered to lower your high salaries to the level of those of the workers. . . .

. . . Landlords, rich-peasants, counter-revolutionaries, hooligans, Rightists, and capitalists, when they go out, must wear plaques as monsters and freaks under the supervision of the masses. . . .

. . . All circus and theater programs must be changed. They must put on meaningful things. Actors are not allowed to dress up in strange fashions, because we don't need those filthy things. . . .

. . . Nobody may address letters to 'Sir" so and so. The whole range of feudal practices must be abolished and new customs advocated. . . .

. . . All those athletic activities that don't correspond with practical significance will be appropriately reduced. Physical education for national defense, such as swimming, mountain climbing, shooting, etc., will be greatly developed so that gradually every youth or adult over fifteen years of age will have a range of enemy-killing abilities. All the people are soldiers, always prepared to annihilate the invading enemy. . . .

. . . We order those under thirty-five to quit drinking and smoking immediately. Bad habits of this sort absolutely may not be cultivated.

. . . Telling jokes, uttering profanities, and doing vulgar things are strictly forbidden. . . .

. . . The responsible organizations must do their best to find ways to establish public toilets in the various alleys so as to reduce the heavy work of the sanitation workers. . . .

. . . From now on, all universities, high schools, and vocational schools will be run as communist schools with part-time work and part-time study and part-time farming and part-time study.

. . . We students must respond to Chairman Mao's appeal. Students must also learn from the workers, the peasants, and the soldiers, and each year during their vacations they must go to factories, farms, and military camps to train themselves. . . .

. . . Schools must use Mao's works as textbooks and educate the youth in Mao Zedong Thought. . . .

. . . Schools must destroy the feudal teacher-student etiquette and establish an equal relationship between teacher and student.

Visualizing the New China

❖

83 ◆ *POSTER ART FROM THE CULTURAL REVOLUTION*

At a conference of artists and writers held in 1942, Mao Zedong spelled out the principles of socialist art and literature. Art and literature existed for one purpose only — to advance the revolution by bringing the Party's message to workers, peasants, and soldiers. This was never more the case than during the Cultural Revolution, when graphic designers, artists, and printers, under close supervision from Party officials, produced literally millions of political posters. Pasted or tacked to public buildings, doors, bridges, buses, trucks, and the walls of schools, government offices, factories, army barracks, and private homes, these posters were the preferred method of publicizing the goals of the Cultural Revolution, glorifying Mao, and demonizing the regime's enemies.

Three representative posters follow. The first, from 1966, shows a crowd of people in Beijing's Tiananmen Square holding up Mao's "little red book," and proclaiming their wish that Mao might live many "ten thousands" of years.

The second, "Fully Criticize the Stinking Chinese Khrushchev," probably dates from 1967. It shows the obliteration of Liu Shaoqi, one of the earliest and most prominent victims of the Cultural Revolution. He is being painted over by a group of Mao's supporters. A long-time associate of Mao, head of state, and Mao's heir apparent, Liu, along with Deng Xiaoping, had dominated the Party after the failure of the Great Leap Forward. He was stripped of his office in 1966 and sent to prison, where he died in 1969 of probable neglect and abuse. The Soviet leader Khrushchev, out of power since 1964, was still considered a villain by the Chinese for his supposed perversion of Marxism-Leninism and his criticisms of the Great Leap Forward.

The third poster, from 1969, shows a struggle session in progress. A struggle session was an emotion-charged assembly in which "enemies of the people" were questioned, accused, and badgered until they confessed their crimes. The setting of this particular session is a Shanghai ink-manufacturing plant, where pictures of the individual being denounce and lists of his crimes are posted on the wall.

QUESTIONS FOR ANALYSIS

1. What different groups in Chinese society are featured in the posters? What generalizations can be made about their ages?
2. What generalizations can you make about the emotions of the most prominent figures and their physical appearance?
3. What do the posters reveal about attitudes toward Mao that inspired the Great Proletarian Cultural Revolution?
4. Compare the visual message of the three posters with the list of demands made by the students at the Maoism School (see source 82). To what extent do they present similar messages and themes?
5. What is your assessment of the strengths and weaknesses of these posters as a source for understanding the Cultural Revolution?

Chairman Mao Ten Thousand Years! Ten Thousand! Ten Thousand Years!

Fully Criticize the Stinking Chinese Khrushchev from a Political, Ideological, and Theoretical Perspective

Firmly Grasp Large-Scale Revolutionary Criticism

CHAPTER 11

The Emergence of a Third World

In an article titled "Three Worlds, One Planet," published in the French magazine *L'Observateur* in 1952, the demographer Alfred Sauvy coined the phrase *Third World* to describe the regions of Africa, Asia, and Latin America that were just beginning to emerge from colonialism after World War II. He sought to draw a distinction between these areas and the First World, made up of the Western capitalist states, and the Second World, made up of the Soviet Union and its Eastern European satellites. He also wanted to draw an analogy between the role of the *Third World* in the era of decolonization and that of the *Third Estate* in the French Revolution of the 1790s. Just as in France the oppressed Third Estate, made up of the bourgeoisie and peasants, had wrested power from the privileged first two estates, the clergy and nobility, the people of the Third World, "ignored, exploited, and despised," were seeking equality and justice in the postcolonial era.

Although the concept of three worlds is firmly entrenched in common usage and in the vocabulary of journalists, historians, and politicians, it continues to have many critics. These critics, who consider the concept imprecise and politically incorrect, have proposed a number of alternatives. The United Nations and the World Bank have opted for cold, analytical terms such as "developed countries" versus "developing countries," "less developed countries," or "countries of low human development." Others have suggested neutral geographical terminology of "North" versus "South" or the notion of "core" nations versus the "periphery." Still others have abandoned the search for appropriate descriptive terminology altogether. Why not avoid controversy and simply refer to the regions of Africa, Latin America, Asia, and the Caribbean as . . . the regions of Africa, Latin America, Asia, and the Caribbean? Each of these suggestions has its shortcomings, however, and none has come close to replacing the Third World as a term of description and analysis.

What then is meant by the Third World? As Sauvy emphasized in his article, all Third World societies (except Thailand and perhaps Iran) had once been colonies. In Africa and Asia this had meant the loss of political independence and the subordination of both regions' economic interests to those of the colonizers. In Latin America, where political independence from Spain and Portugal had been won in the early 1800s, it had meant foreign control of banks, railroads, mines, large-scale agricultural operations, and the petroleum industry and sporadic foreign intervention in domestic politics. It had also meant dependency on the United States and Europe as a source of capital, as a market for exports, and as the region's principal supplier of machinery and manufactured products.

General poverty was another characteristic of Third World societies in the postcolonial era. Poverty, in turn, was a result of their lack of industrialization, reliance on agriculture, rudimentary communications and transportation systems, and inadequate schools. In the optimistic atmosphere following the end of colonialism, it was an article of faith that Third World poverty would disappear once Asia, Africa, and Latin America experienced economic development and modernization. Development meant industrialization, accompanied ideally by the formation of stable, democratic governments, while modernization meant the transition from traditional customs and attitudes to the scientific and secular values of developed nations, primarily those in the West.

For a time, such optimism seemed well grounded. In the 1950s and 1960s, food production increased in Africa, Asia, and Latin America, and the worldwide economic boom ensured healthy prices for these regions' agricultural and mineral exports. Governments embarked on ambitious economic development plans, and in the 1960s, despite population increases, real per capita income grew. Only in the 1970s, with its spiraling oil prices and worldwide economic downturn, did Third World economic prospects darken.

Another characteristic of the emerging Third World was nonalignment, that is, neutrality in the Cold War between capitalism and communism. The concept of nonalignment first gained attention as a result of the African-Asian Conference held in the Indonesian city Bandung in 1955. Hosted by Indonesia's Premier Sukarno and attended by representatives of twenty-nine African and Asian countries, the Conference denounced colonialism, condemned runaway military spending by the superpowers, and called for increased economic aid from rich to poor nations. As the Cold War continued, many Asian and African countries found it expedient or necessary to abandon nonalignment, but during the 1950s and 1960s their commitment to an independent diplomatic course strengthened the idea that there really was a Third World with interests and ambitions different from those of the First and Second Worlds.

Since the 1970s the Third World has undergone many changes. South Korea, Taiwan, Singapore, and Hong Kong became industrial and financial powers and ceased being considered part of the Third World. Saudi Arabia, Kuwait, Bahrain, and other Middle Eastern oil producers became fabulously rich as a result of the spike in oil prices during the 1970s, and they too have been moved out of the Third World category or placed in a subcategory of their own. Post-Soviet Russia, on the other hand, with its collapsing economy, decaying infrastructure, and demoralized population, has, according to some, moved from the Second World to the Third.

The greatest change in our thinking about the Third World has been the loss of optimism. Economic development has proved infinitely more difficult than imagined, and for every success like South Korea there have been dozens of failures. Fifty years after Sauvy introduced the concept, the Third World still exists, but dreams of orderly government and economic progress have given way to nightmare visions of political breakdown, environmental catastrophe, and deepening human misery.

◆

New Sources of Conflict in the Middle East

For thousands of years geography ordained that the Middle East would play a central role in human affairs. As the western terminus of overland trade routes from East Asia and as the link between the Mediterranean Sea and the Indian Ocean via the Red Sea and the Persian Gulf, it was a center of international trade. At the juncture of Asia, Africa, and Europe, it was a place that attracted recurring waves of invaders and migrants who intermingled, competed, and shared ideas with one another. This explains in part why human beings made some of their greatest achievements in the Middle East. Here they developed agriculture, the alphabet, and metallurgy; established some of their most important religions — Judaism, Christianity, and Islam; and built some of their most impressive cities — Cairo, Baghdad, Damascus, and Isfahan.

After World War II, the Middle East continued to play a central role in human affairs, but for reasons more geological than geographical. Millions of years earlier, enormous quantities of one-celled marine plants and animals fell to the floor of the ocean that covered the region and, finding the right temperatures and rock formations, were slowly transformed into huge fields of oil and natural gas. These fields, which were discovered in Iran in 1908, Iraq in 1927, and Kuwait and Saudi Arabia in 1938, contain high-quality oil that is close to the surface and easy to extract. European and American companies soon were pumping millions of barrels of oil a day out of the earth, transporting it through pipelines to refineries, and supplying the world with fuel oil, heating oil, and gasoline. By the early 1970s Middle Eastern oil had become the life-blood of the world's economy, and maintaining political stability in the region became a priority of world leaders.

Achieving stability proved difficult, in part because all of the states in the region were new. Republican Turkey had emerged from the ruins of the Ottoman Empire in 1922 to 1923; Egypt gained control of its domestic affairs from Britain only in 1936; Iran, though technically independent, rid itself of Soviet and British occupying troops only after World War II; Saudi Arabia was created in the 1920s. Iraq, Transjordan (renamed Jordan in 1948), Syria, and Lebanon became fully independent when the British and French mandates ended after World War II.

Politics in the region was complicated further by ethnic rivalries, religious divisions, and fundamental political disagreements. Maronite Christians, Sunni Muslims, and Shiite Muslims shared power in Lebanon; Kurds made up a substantial minority in Turkey, Iran, and Iraq; Shiite Muslims and smaller sects such the Druze and the Aalawites (whom the orthodox do not even consider to be Muslim) lived in largely Sunni Syria; Shiites made up 20 percent of the population in Iraq. On political issues, nationalists, liberals, socialists, communists, and supporters of traditional monarchy competed for power and public support, as did secularists, who admired the West, and Muslim fundamentalists, who considered the West satanic.

By far the greatest destabilizing force in the region was the existence of Israel. The founding of Israel in 1948 was the culmination of events that go back to the 1890s, when European Zionists proclaimed as their goal the creation of a national Jewish homeland in Palestine, a region on the eastern Mediterranean which then was part of the Ottoman Empire. Jewish migration to the region, which became a British mandate after World War I, accelerated after the Nazis seized power in Germany in 1933, and resulted in a postwar Palestine populated by six hundred thousand Jews and 1.8 million Muslim Arabs. Both groups wanted an end to the British mandate, but the Arabs demanded a unified state ruled by the Arab majority, while the Jews demanded the partition of Palestine and their own Jewish state. With compromise impossible and violence mounting, the British handed over the Palestinian issue to the United Nations, which in November 1947 voted in favor of separate Jewish and Arab states. On May 14, 1948, Jewish leaders formally established the state of Israel, and on the same day Egypt, Iraq, Syria, and Jordan declared war on the new state, vowing its destruction.

Palestine as an Arab Homeland

84 ◆ *THE PALESTINE NATIONAL CHARTER*

Arab armies were defeated in the Arab-Israel War of 1948 to 1949, but the real losers were Palestinian Arabs. Approximately one hundred fifty thousand Palestinians remained in Israel during and after the war and became Israeli citizens, who, though subject to numerous restrictions, had political rights, economic benefits, and educational opportunities. Some four hundred thousand Palestinians who lived in the West Bank, a region of Palestine not conquered by Israel, became subjects of the king of Jordan, who annexed the territory in 1949.

Anywhere from five hundred thousand to eight hundred thousand Palestinians who had fled their homes in Israel during the war became refugees in squalid camps on the borders of Israel in the Gaza region, the West Bank, Syria, and Lebanon. In 1967, after the third Arab-Israeli war, the Six-Day War, the number of Palestinian refugees swelled by another two hundred thousand when the West Bank was conquered by the Israelis and incorporated into Israel.

During the 1950s, numerous welfare agencies, social organizations, and paramilitary groups were founded to serve the needs of refugees and keep alive the goal of Palestinian statehood. At a summit meeting in 1964, Arab leaders approved the founding of the Palestine Liberation Organization (PLO), with responsibility for overseeing and coordinating all these Palestinian organizations. Later in the year representatives of the organizations met in Jerusalem and formed a PLO executive board, laid plans for the formation of a Palestinian army, and began work on a national charter. The Palestine National Charter, after several revisions, was approved at a meeting of the Fourth Palestine National Council in 1968.

Excerpts from this document follow.

QUESTIONS FOR ANALYSIS

1. How does the Charter define a Palestinian?
2. Why does the Charter equate Zionism with imperialism? Why does it equate Zionism with racism?
3. How valid are these comparisons in your view?
4. On what grounds does the Charter reject the validity of the UN decision to partition Palestine in 1947?
5. How do the authors of the Charter propose to achieve liberation from Israel?

1. Palestine, the homeland of the Palestinian Arab people, is an inseparable part of the greater Arab homeland, and the Palestinian people are a part of the Arab Nation.

2. Palestine, within the frontiers that existed under the British Mandate, is an indivisible territorial unit.

3. The Palestinian Arab people alone have legitimate rights to their homeland, and shall exercise the right of self-determination after the liberation of their homeland, in keeping with their wishes and entirely of their own accord.

4. The Palestinian identity is an authentic, intrinsic and indissoluble quality that is transmitted from father to son. Neither the Zionist occupation nor the dispersal of the Palestinian Arab people as a result of the afflictions they have suffered can efface this Palestinian identity.

5. Palestinians are Arab citizens who were normally resident in Palestine until 1947. This includes both those who were forced to leave or who stayed in Palestine. Anyone born to a Palestinian father after that date, whether inside or outside Palestine, is a Palestinian.

6. Jews who were normally resident in Palestine up to the beginning of the Zionist invasion are Palestinians.

7. Palestinian identity, and material, spiritual and historical links with Palestine are immutable realities. It is a national obligation to provide every Palestinian with a revolutionary Arab upbringing, and to instill in him a

profound spiritual and material familiarity with his homeland and a readiness for armed struggle and for the sacrifice of his material possessions and his life, for the recovery of his homeland. . . .

8. The Palestinian people is at the stage of national struggle for the liberation of its homeland. For that reason, differences between Palestinian national forces must give way to the fundamental difference that exists between Zionism and imperialism on the one hand and the Palestinian Arab people on the other. On that basis, the Palestinian masses, both as organizations and as individuals, whether in the homeland or in such places as they now live as refugees, constitute a single national front working for the recovery and liberation of Palestine through armed struggle.

9. The Palestinian Arab people hereby affirm their unwavering determination to carry on the armed struggle and to press on towards popular revolution for the liberation of and return to their homeland. They also affirm their right to a normal life in their homeland, to the exercise of their right of self-determination therein and to sovereignty over it.

10. Commando action[1] constitutes the nucleus of the Palestinian popular war of liberation. This requires that commando action should be escalated, expanded and protected, and that all the resources of the Palestinian masses and all scientific potentials available to them should be mobilized and organized to play their part in the armed Palestinian revolution. . . .

12. The Palestinian Arab people believe in Arab unity. To fulfill their role in the achievement of that objective, they must, at the present stage in their national struggle, retain their Palestinian identity and all that it involves, work for increased awareness of it and oppose all measures liable to weaken or dissolve it. . . .

14. The destiny of the Arab nation, indeed the continued existence of the Arabs, depends on the fate of the Palestinian cause. This interrelationship is the point of departure of the Arab endeavor to liberate Palestine. The Palestinian people are the vanguard of the movement to achieve this sacred national objective.

15. The liberation of Palestine is a national obligation for the Arabs. It is their duty to repel the Zionist and imperialist invasion of the greater Arab homeland and to liquidate the Zionist presence in Palestine. . . .

16. On the spiritual plane, the liberation of Palestine will establish in the Holy Land an atmosphere of peace and tranquility in which all religious institutions will be safeguarded and freedom of worship and the right of visit guaranteed to all without discrimination or distinction of race, color, language or creed. For this reason the people of Palestine look to all spiritual forces in the world for support.

17. On the human plane, the liberation of Palestine will restore to the Palestinians their dignity, integrity and freedom. For this reason, the Palestinian Arab people look at all those who believe in the dignity and freedom of man for support. . . .

19. The partition of Palestine, which took place in 1947, and the establishment of Israel, are fundamentally invalid, however long they last, for they contravene the will of the people of Palestine and their natural right to their homeland and contradict the principles of the United Nations Charter, foremost among which is the right of self-determination.

20. The Balfour Declaration, the Mandate Instrument, and all their consequences, are hereby declared null and void.[2] The claim of historical or spiritual links between the Jews and Palestine is neither in conformity with historical fact nor does it satisfy the requirements for statehood. Judaism is a revealed religion; it is not a separate nationality, nor are the Jews a single people with a separate identity; they are citizens of their respective countries. . . .

---

[1]Commandos are highly trained soldiers who operate in small units usually inside enemy territory.

[2]The Balfour Declaration of 1917 pledged Great Britain to support the establishment of a Jewish state in Palestine.

22. Zionism is a political movement that is organically linked with world imperialism and is opposed to all liberation movements or movements for progress in the world. The Zionist movement is essentially fanatical and racialist; its objectives involve aggression, expansion and the establishment of colonial settlements, and its methods are those of the Fascists and the Nazis. Israel acts as cat's paw[3] for the Zionist movement, a geographic and manpower base for world imperialism and a springboard for its thrust into the Arab homeland to frustrate the aspirations of the Arab nation to liberation, unity and progress. Israel is a constant threat to peace in the Middle East and the whole world. Inasmuch as the liberation of Palestine will eliminate the Zionist and imperialist presence in that country and bring peace to the Middle East, the Palestinian people look for support to all liberals and to all forces of good, peace and progress in the world, and call on them, whatever their political convictions, for all possible aid and support in their just and legitimate struggle to liberate their homeland.

---

[3]Someone or something used by another as a tool.

Palestine as a Jewish Homeland

❖

85 ◆ *Chaim Herzog,*
SPEECH TO THE UNITED NATIONS GENERAL ASSEMBLY

In the mid 1970s the Palestine Liberation Organization, with the support of most Arab states, began a campaign to discredit Israel in international forums. In the summer of 1975, at the urging of the PLO, the Organization of African Unity and the Conference of Non-aligned Nations both condemned Zionism as racist and imperialist and grouped Israel with the white racist regimes of Rhodesia and South Africa. Several months later an anti-Israel resolution was proposed in the General Assembly of the United Nations.

Chaim Herzog, Israeli ambassador to the UN, denounced the resolution in the following speech delivered on November 10, 1975. Just hours later a coalition of Muslim, Arab, Third World, and Soviet-bloc nations approved the resolution which states that "Zionism is a form of racism and racial discrimination."

QUESTIONS FOR ANALYSIS

1. What does Herzog mean when he says, "Zionism is to the Jewish people what the liberation movements of Africa and Asia have been to their own people"?
2. How does Herzog's historical perspective on Palestine differ from that of the 1968 Palestine National Charter?
3. What is at stake in the debate on the resolution, other than the existence of Israel?

It is symbolic that this debate, which may well prove to be a turning point in the fortunes of the United Nations and a decisive factor in the possible continued existence of this organization, should take place on November 10. Tonight, thirty-seven years ago, has gone down in history as Kristallnacht, the Night of the Crystals. This was the night in 1938 when Hitler's Nazi storm-troopers launched a coordinated attack on the Jewish community in Germany, burned the synagogues in all its cities and made bonfires in the streets of the Holy Books and the Scrolls of the Holy Law and Bible. It was the night when Jewish homes were attacked and heads of families taken away, many of them never to return. It was the night when the windows of all Jewish businesses and stores were smashed, covering the streets in the cities of Germany with a film of broken glass which dissolved into the millions of crystals which gave the night its name. It was the night which led eventually to the crematoria and the gas chambers, Auschwitz, Birkenau, Dachau, Buchenwald, Teresienstadt and others. It was the night which led to the most terrifying holocaust in the history of man.

It is indeed befitting, Mr. President, that this debate, conceived in the desire to deflect the Middle East from its moves towards peace and born of a deep pervading feeling of anti-Semitism, should take place on the anniversary of this day. It is indeed befitting, Mr. President, that the United Nations, which began its life as an anti-Nazi alliance, should thirty years later find itself on its way to becoming the world center of anti-Semitism. Hitler would have felt at home on a number of occasions during the past year, listening to the proceedings in this forum, and above all to the proceedings during the debate on Zionism.

It is sobering to consider to what level this body has been dragged down if we are obliged today to contemplate an attack on Zionism. For this attack constitutes not only an anti-Israeli attack of the foulest type, but also an assault in the United Nations on Judaism — one of the oldest established religions in the world, a religion which has given the world the human values of the Bible, and from which two other great religions, Christianity and Islam, sprang. Is it not tragic to consider that we here at this meeting in the year 1975 are contemplating what is a scurrilous attack on a great and established religion which has given to the world the Bible with its Ten Commandments, the great prophets of old, Moses, Isaiah, Amos; the great thinkers of history, Maimonides, Spinoza, Marx, Einstein,[1] many of the masters of the arts and as high a percentage of Nobel Prize–winners in the world, in sciences, in the arts and in the humanities as has been achieved by any people on earth? . . .

I do not come to this rostrum to defend the moral and historical values of the Jewish people. They do not need to be defended. They speak for themselves. They have given to mankind much of what is great and eternal. They have done for the spirit of man more than can readily be appreciated by a forum such as this one.

I come here to denounce the two great evils which menace society in general and a society of nations in particular. These two evils are hatred and ignorance. These two evils are the motivating force behind the proponents of this resolution and their supporters. These two evils characterize those who would drag this world organization, the ideals of which were first conceived by the prophets of Israel, to the depths to which it has been dragged today.

The key to understanding Zionism is in its name. The eastern-most of the two hills of ancient Jerusalem during the tenth century B.C. was called Zion. In fact, the name Zion, referring to Jerusalem, appears 152 times in the Old Testament. The name is overwhelmingly a poetic and prophetic designation. The religious

---

[1]Maimonides (1135–1204) and Baruch Spinoza (1632–1677) were prominent philosophers. Einstein (1879–1955) was of course a giant of modern physics. There is some irony in Herzog's mention of Karl Marx; every communist state in the UN voted for the anti-Zionist resolution.

and emotional qualities of the name arise from the importance of Jerusalem as the Royal City and the City of the Temple. "Mount Zion" is the place where God dwells. Jerusalem, or Zion, is a place where the Lord is King, and where He has installed His King, David.

King David made Jerusalem the capital of Israel almost three thousand years ago, and Jerusalem has remained the capital ever since. During the centuries the term "Zion" grew and expanded to mean the whole of Israel. The Israelites in exile could not forget Zion. The Hebrew Psalmist sat by the waters of Babylon and swore: "If I forget thee, O Jerusalem, let my right hand forget her cunning." This oath has been repeated for thousands of years by Jews throughout the world. It is an oath which was made over seven hundred years before the advent of Christianity and over twelve hundred years before the advent of Islam, and Zion came to mean the Jewish homeland, symbolic of Judaism, of Jewish national aspirations.

While praying to his God every Jew, wherever he is in the world, faces towards Jerusalem. For over two thousand years of exile these prayers have expressed the yearning of the Jewish people to return to their ancient homeland, Israel. . . .

Zionism is the name of the national movement of the Jewish people and is the modern expression of the ancient Jewish heritage. The Zionist ideal, as set out in the Bible, has been, and is, an integral part of the Jewish religion.

Zionism is to the Jewish people what the liberation movements of Africa and Asia have been to their own people. . . .

In modern times, in the late nineteenth century, spurred by the twin forces of anti-Semitic persecution and of nationalism, the Jewish people organized the Zionist movement in order to transform their dream into reality. Zionism as a political movement was the revolt of an oppressed nation against the depredation and wicked discrimination and oppression of the countries in which anti-Semitism flourished. It is no coincidence that the co-sponsors and supporters of this resolution include countries who are guilty of the horrible crimes of anti-Semitism and discrimination to this very day.

Support for the aim of Zionism was written into the League of Nations Mandate for Palestine and was again endorsed by the United Nations in 1947, when the General Assembly voted by overwhelming majority for the restoration of Jewish independence in our ancient land.

The re-establishment of Jewish independence in Israel, after centuries of struggle to overcome foreign conquest and exile, is a vindication of the fundamental concepts of the equality of nations and of self-determination. To question the Jewish people's right to national existence and freedom is not only to deny to the Jewish people the right accorded to every other people on this globe, but it is also to deny the central precepts of the United Nations.

Revolution and Reaction in Latin America

In August 1961 delegates to a meeting of the Organization of America States in Punta del Este, Uruguay, approved a set of goals for the Alliance for Progress, a new program proposed by U.S. President John F. Kennedy to foster Latin American economic development and social reform with the help of billions of American dollars. Their list of goals, known as the Charter of Punta del Este, was ambitious. Within a decade participants hope to achieve economic growth of 2.5 percent per year, more equitable distribution of national income, greater industrialization, agrarian reform, elimination of adult illiteracy, price stability, improved health care, reduced infant mortality, increased life expectancy by at least five years, and much more. The result would be "maximum levels of well-being, with equal opportunities for all, in democratic societies adapted to their own needs and desires."

Viewed against the record of Latin American states in the 1960s and 1970s, the Punta del Este Charter makes depressing reading. The Alliance for Progress poured billions of dollars into hastily conceived programs that did little to advance economic development or democracy. Latin America floundered politically and economically; if anything, the problems the Alliance for Progress sought to eradicate in ten years became worse, not better.

By the early 1970s Latin America was experiencing widening trade deficits, weakened commodity prices, and double- and even triple-digit inflation. Some states, such as Brazil, had achieved growth in manufacturing, but this mainly benefited foreign corporations, mostly from the United States. With the aid of tax breaks and other government favors, these corporations swallowed up or bankrupted smaller national firms, and took approximately three dollars out of the region for each dollar invested. Most governments ignored the problem of mass poverty, which worsened as a result of population growth, depressed wages, and urbanization. Serious programs for social reform, adopted in Guatemala and Bolivia in the early 1950s, Peru in 1968, and Chile in the early 1970s, either languished or were quashed by right-wing coups.

One state that experienced major social reforms was Fidel Castro's Cuba. After the overthrow of the dictator Batista in 1959, Castro's socialist revolution carried out land reform, nationalized industries, provided universal health care and education, and succeeded in raising standards of living. Paradoxically, it also dimmed the prospects for social reform in the rest of the region. Although it raised hopes among the poor and inspired dozens of revolutionary movements, Castro's Cuba frightened Latin America's elites, who rallied behind military dictatorships that promised to halt the spread of communism.

Such military regimes were supported by the U.S. government, whose political involvement in Latin America reached new heights with the onset of the Cold War and after the Cuban Revolution. The Eisenhower administration sought to limit social and economic reform in Bolivia after a revolution in 1952; cooperated with Great Britain to overthrow a left-leaning administration in British Guiana; and trained and outfitted rebels who overthrew Guatemala's democratically elected government in 1954 after its plans for land reform threatened the Boston-based banana conglomerate, the United Fruit Company.

Similar efforts to overthrow Castro failed. Assassination plots came to nothing, and the CIA-planned invasion of Cuba by anti-Castro exiles was crushed in April 1961. The United States also attempted to counter communism with the Alliance for Progress, the program of social reform and economic development that failed, and support for right-wing governments, a program that in the short run succeeded. During the 1970s, repressive authoritarian regimes proliferated in Central and South America. They used death squads, assassins, torturers, and U.S.-equipped armies against leftist politicians, social reformers, and Marxist revolutionaries. Communism was contained, but rural poverty, inflation, foreign debt, and rampant urbanization became worse than ever.

"Create Two, Three, or Many Vietnams"

◈

86 ◆ *Ernesto "Che" Guevara,* MESSAGE TO THE TRICONTINENTAL CONFERENCE

Ernesto Guevara (nicknamed "Che" by Cubans after the colloquial Argentinean term for mate) was born into a well-to-do Argentinean family in 1928 and was trained as a doctor. After traveling through much of Latin America, including a stop in Guatemala where he fought against the CIA-sponsored invasion in 1954, he was introduced to Fidel Castro, a young Cuban, in Mexico City in 1955. Castro, who had been fighting to overthrow the Cuban dictator Fulgencio Batista since 1953, convinced Guevara to join the band of fighters he was organizing to land in Cuba and renew the struggle. After the expeditionary force reached Cuba in 1956, Guevara proved his mastery of guerrilla warfare and became Castro's second in command. He led the troops that took Havana in January 1959.

Once Castro was in power, Guevara served as head of the national bank and minister of industry. But he dedicated most of his efforts to the cause of Third World revolution, something he believed could be achieved by following the Cuban model of rural insurrection and guerrilla warfare. In 1966 he helped organize the first Tricontinental Conference in Havana, attended by Castro supporters from Asia, Africa, and Latin America. In 1967 his message to this conference was published in the journal *Tricontinental.*

By the time the article appeared, Guevara had left Cuba for Bolivia, where he sought to organize guerrillas fighting against the right-wing generals who had seized power in 1964. Hunted down and captured by government troops, he was executed by a firing squad in October 1967. Che lived on, however, as a revolutionary hero for student radicals around the world, who chanted "Che lives!" and carried posters with his image as they marched and demonstrated in the late 1960s.

QUESTIONS FOR ANALYSIS

1. According to Guevara, how is U.S. imperialism manifested in Latin America?
2. What factors, according to Guevara, make Latin America a promising area for revolutionary activity?
3. How does Guevara view the future of the revolutionary movement in Latin America?
4. What does Guevara specifically mean when he envisions "two, three, or many Viet Nams"?
5. What are Guevara's hopes for the future of Latin America and the world?

U.S. imperialism is guilty of aggression — its crimes are enormous and cover the whole world. We already know all that, gentlemen! . . . But imperialism is bogging down in Viet Nam, is unable to find a way out and desperately seeks one that will overcome with dignity this dangerous situation in which it now finds itself. . . .

What role shall we, the exploited people of the world, play? The peoples of the three continents focus their attention on Viet Nam and learn their lesson. Since imperialists blackmail humanity by threatening it with war, the wise reaction is not to fear war. The general tactics of the people should be to launch a constant and a firm attack on all fronts where the confrontation is taking place.

In those places where the meager peace we have has been violated, what is our duty? To liberate ourselves at any price. . . .

The fundamental field of imperialist exploitation comprises the three underdeveloped continents: America, Asia, and Africa. Every country has its own characteristics, but each continent, as a whole, also presents its own characteristics. America constitutes a group of more or less homogeneous countries and in most parts of its territory U.S. monopoly capital maintains an absolute supremacy. Puppet governments or, in the best of cases, weak and fearful local rulers, are incapable of contradicting orders from their Yankee master. . . . Its policy is to maintain that which has already been conquered. The line of action, at the present time, is limited to the brutal use of force with the purpose of thwarting the liberation movements, no matter of what type they might happen to be.

The slogan "we will not allow another Cuba" hides the possibility of perpetrating aggressions without fear of reprisal, such as the one carried out against the Dominican Republic, or before that, the massacre in Panama[1] — and the clear warning stating that Yankee troops are ready to intervene anywhere in America where the established order may be altered, thus endangering their interests. . . . But almost every country of this continent is ripe for a type of struggle that, in order to achieve victory, cannot be content with anything less than establishing a government of a socialist nature. . . .

. . . There is also such a great similarity among the classes of the different countries, that an identification exists among them, as an "international American" type, much more complete than that of other continents. Language, customs, religion, a common foreign master, unite them. The degree and forms of exploitation are similar in their effects for both the exploiters and the exploited in many of the countries of our America. And rebellion is ripening swiftly here.

We may ask ourselves: how will this rebellion come to fruition? What type will it be? We have maintained for quite some time now that, owing to the similarity of characteristics, the struggle in America will achieve, in due course, continental proportions. It will be the scene of many great battles fought for the liberation of humanity. . . . But if the foci of war are developed with sufficient political and military wisdom, they will become practically invincible, obliging the Yankees to send reinforcements. . . . Little by little, the obsolete weapons which are sufficient for the repression of small armed bands will be exchanged for modern armaments and the U.S. military "advisers" will be replaced by U.S. soldiers until, at a given moment, they will be forced to send increasingly greater numbers of regular troops to ensure the relative stability of a government whose national puppet army is disintegrating before the attacks of the guerrillas. It is the road of Viet Nam; it is the road that should be followed by the peoples; it is the road that will be followed in America. . . .

America, forgotten continent in the world's more recent liberation struggles, now beginning to make itself heard through the Tricontinental in the voice of the vanguard of its peoples, the

---

[1]In 1965 President Lyndon Johnson dispatched Marines to the Dominican Republic to suppress a rebellion against the military dictatorship that had taken power by a coup d'état two years earlier. In 1959 one hundred would-be revolutionaries who landed in Panama were trapped and annihilated by Panamanian and U.S. troops.

Cuban Revolution, will have a task of much greater relevance: to create a Second or a Third Viet Nam, or the Second and Third Viet Nam of the world. . . .

. . . The struggle will be long, harsh, and its battle fronts will be the guerrilla's refuge, the cities, the homes of the fighters — where the repressive forces will go seeking easy victims among their families — among the massacred rural population, in the villages or cities destroyed by the bombardments of the enemy. . . . The great lesson of the invincibility of the guerrillas will take root in the dispossessed masses. The galvanizing of national spirit, preparation for harder tasks, for resisting even more violent repressions. Hatred as an element of struggle; relentless hatred of the enemy that impels us over and beyond the natural limitations of man and transforms us into effective, violent, selective and cold killing machines. Our soldiers must be thus; a people without hatred cannot vanquish a brutal enemy.

We must carry the war as far as the enemy carries it: to his home, to his centers of entertainment, make it a total war. It is necessary to prevent him from having a moment of peace, a quiet moment outside his barracks or even inside; we must attack him wherever he may be, make him feel like a cornered beast wherever he may move. Then his morale will begin to fall. . . .

What a luminous, near future would be visible to us if two, three or many Viet Nams flourished throughout the world with their share of death and their immense tragedies, their everyday heroism and their repeated blows against imperialism obliging it to disperse its forces under the attack of the increasing hatred of all the peoples of the earth!

And if we were all capable of uniting to make our blows more solid and more infallible so that the effectiveness of every kind of support given to the struggling peoples were increased — how great and how near that future would be!

. . . Our very action is a battle cry against imperialism, and a call for the peoples' unity against the great enemy of mankind: the United States of America. Wherever death may surprise us, it will be welcome, provided that this, our battle cry, has reached a receptive ear and that another hand be extended to take up our weapons, and that other men come forward to intone the funeral dirge with the staccato of machine guns and new cries of battle and victory.

The Fall of Allende and the CIA

❖

87 ◆ *CHURCH COMMITTEE REPORT ON COVERT ACTIONS IN CHILE, 1963–1973*

Established by the National Security Act of 1947, the Central Intelligence Agency was in the vanguard of the U.S. campaign against international communism for the next forty years. CIA experts, researchers, and agents advised U.S. presidents on international developments; provided information on political and economic conditions in other countries; carried on counterintelligence activities; monitored foreign broadcasts, newspapers, and government communiqués; and engaged in more direct forms of espionage. As the following selection reveals, the goals of espionage included weakening or removing from power politicians perceived as threats to U.S. interests.

Chile, a country with a long democratic tradition and rich copper deposits, was the scene of intense CIA activity in the 1960s and early 1970s. In the 1964 presidential elections, the CIA helped undermine the candidacy of Salvador Allende, the physician turned politician who led a socialist-communist coalition on a platform of anti-imperialism, anticapitalism, land reform, and the nationalization of industry. Allende received 39 percent of the vote, but was handily defeated by Eduardo Frei, the leader of the centrist Christian Democrats. By the next presidential election in 1970, the political situation had changed. Frei's Christian Democrats had run out of ideas, inflation was surging, and, most importantly, the rightist parties were running their own candidate rather than backing the Christian Democrats. Allende received 36 percent of the vote — less than in 1964, but enough to win a plurality. In October 1970, after a military coup failed to overturn the election, Allende became president.

Despite his narrow victory, Allende boldly proceeded with his socialist program. The government froze prices and raised wages, nationalized the copper industry and dozens of other sectors of the economy, and liquidated large estates as part of its land reform program. But Allende faced formidable obstacles. Radicals in his coalition demanded faster change, while conservatives and moderates remained inalterably opposed to his policies. Furthermore, the cessation of U.S. aid and the halt in loans and foreign investments crippled a Chilean economy already weakened by the transition from private to government ownership. In September 1973 Allende's opponents within the military mounted a coup d'état that resulted in the death of Allende and five thousand other Chileans and the end of Chile's socialist experiment. It also resulted in the beginning of military rule under General Augusto Pinochet, who remained Chile's dictator until 1990.

Historians still debate the reasons for Allende's fall, but all agree his chances of survival were weakened by the campaign to destabilize his government orchestrated by the CIA and other U.S. government agencies. The full extent of this campaign was revealed in a report issued in 1975 by the Select Committee to Study Governmental Operations in Respect to Intelligence Activities. Better known as the Church Committee, after its chair, Senator Frank Church of Idaho, it had been charged by the Senate to investigate "illegal, improper, or unethical" operations by the CIA. The committee's findings, along with those of a House of Representatives committee, led to executive orders under Presidents Ford and Carter to increase presidential control over the CIA's covert operations and the passing by Congress of the Intelligence Oversight Act in 1980.

QUESTIONS FOR ANALYSIS

1. What does the Church Committee report reveal about U.S. Cold War attitudes and goals?
2. How much did the CIA destabilization efforts described in this document depend on the cooperation of Chileans?
3. What does the document reveal about the control and oversight of CIA operations by the executive branch?
4. The Church Committee was charged with judging whether CIA activities in Chile were "improper and immoral." What is your own judgment on this issue?

[THE 1964 ELECTION]

The United States was involved on a massive scale in the 1964 presidential election in Chile. . . . A total of nearly four million dollars was spent on some fifteen covert action projects, ranging from organizing slum dwellers to passing funds to political parties.

The goal, broadly, was to prevent or minimize the influence of Chilean Communists or Marxists in the government that would emerge from the 1964 election. Consequently, the U.S. sought the most effective way of opposing FRAP[1] (Popular Action Front), an alliance of Chilean Socialists, Communists, and several miniscule non-Marxist parties of the left which backed the candidacy of Salvador Allende. Specifically, the policy called for support of the Christian Democratic Party, the Democratic Front (a coalition of rightist parties), and a variety of anti-communist propaganda and organizing activities. . . .

Covert action during the 1964 campaign was composed of two major elements. One was direct financial support of the Christian Democratic campaign. The CIA underwrote slightly more than half of the total cost of that campaign. After debate, the Special Group[2] decided not to inform the Christian Democratic candidate, Eduardo Frei, of American covert support of his campaign. A number of intermediaries were therefore mobilized to pass the money to the Christian Democrats. . . .

In addition to support for political parties, the CIA mounted a massive anti-communist propaganda campaign. Extensive use was made of the press, radio, films, pamphlets, posters, leaflets, direct mailings, paper streamers, and wall painting. It was a "scare campaign," which relied heavily on images of Soviet tanks and Cuban firing squads and was directed especially to women. Hundreds of thousands of copies of the anti-communist pastoral letter of Pope Pius XI[3] were distributed by Christian Democratic organizations. They carried the designation, "printed privately by citizens without political affiliation, in order more broadly to disseminate its content." "Disinformation" and — "black propaganda" — material which purported to originate from another source, such as the Chilean Communist Party — were used as well.

The propaganda campaign was enormous. During the first week of intensive propaganda activity . . ., a CIA-funded propaganda group produced twenty radio spots per day in Santiago and on 44 provincial stations; twelve-minute news broadcasts five times daily on three Santiago stations and 24 provincial outlets; thousands of cartoons, and much paid press advertising. By the end of June, the group produced 24 daily newscasts in Santiago and the provinces, 26 weekly "commentary" programs, and distributed 3,000 posters daily. . . .

[COVERT ACTION: 1964–1969]

Covert action efforts were conducted during this period to influence the political development of various sectors of Chilean society. One project, conducted prior to the 1964 elections to strengthen Christian Democratic support among peasants and slum dwellers, continued to help train and organize "anti-communists" in these and other sectors until public exposure of CIA funding in 1967 forced its termination. A project to compete organizationally with the Marxists among the urban poor of Santiago was initiated shortly after the 1964 election, and was terminated in mid-1969 because the principal agent was unwilling to prejudice the independent posture of the organization by using it on a large scale to deliver votes in the 1969 and 1970 presidential elections. In the mid-1960s, the CIA

---

[1]FRAP stands for Frente de Action Popular, a coalition of leftist parties that competed in elections in the 1950s and 1960s.

[2]The CIA operatives responsible for activities relating to the election.

[3]Pius XI was pope from 1922 until 1939. A staunch anti-Marxist, in 1931 he issued the encyclical *Quadragesimo anno,* in which he stressed the need for Christian social action to deal with poverty.

supported an anti-communist women's group active in Chilean political and intellectual life. . . .

[THE 1970 ELECTION]

. . . In March 1970, the 40 Committee[4] decided that the United States should not support any single candidate in the election but should instead wage "spoiling" operations against the Popular Unity[5] coalition which supported the Marxist candidate, Salvador Allende. In all, the CIA spent from $800,000 to $1,000,000 on convert action to affect the outcome of the 1970 Presidential election. . . .

There was a wide variety of propaganda products: a newsletter mailed to approximately two thousand journalists, academicians, politicians, and other opinion makers; a booklet showing what life would be like if Allende won the presidential election; translation and distribution of chronicles of opposition to the Soviet regime; poster distribution and sign-painting teams. The sign-painting teams had instructions to paint the slogan "*su paredón*" (your wall) on 2,000 walls, evoking an image of communist firing squads. The "scare campaign" . . . exploited the violence of the invasion of Czechoslovakia[6] with large photographs of Prague and of tanks in downtown Santiago. Other posters, resembling those used in 1964, portrayed Cuban political prisoners before the firing squad, and warned that an Allende victory would mean the end of religion and family life in Chile. . . .

[BETWEEN SEPTEMBER 4 AND OCTOBER 24, 1970]

On September 4, 1970, Allende won a plurality in Chile's presidential election. Since no candidate had received a majority of the popular vote,

the Chilean Constitution required that a joint session of its Congress decide between the first- and second-place finishers. The date set for the congressional session was October 24, 1970.

The reaction in Washington to Allende's plurality victory was immediate. The 40 Committee met on September 8 and 14 to discuss what action should be taken prior to the October 24 congressional vote. On September 15, President Nixon informed CIA Director Richard Helms that an Allende regime in Chile would not be acceptable to the United States and instructed the CIA to play a direct role in organizing a military *coup d'etat* in Chile to prevent Allende's accession to the Presidency. . . .

. . . U.S. Government efforts to prevent Allende from assuming office proceeded on two tracks. Track I comprised all covert activities approved by the 40 Committee, including political, economic and propaganda activities. . . . Track II activities in Chile were undertaken in response to President Nixon's September 15 order and were directed toward actively promoting and encouraging the Chilean military to move against Allende. . . .

On October 24, 1970, Salvador Allende was confirmed as President by Chilean Congress. On November 3, he was inaugurated. U.S. efforts, both overt and covert, to prevent his assumption of office had failed.

[COVERT ACTION DURING THE ALLENDE YEARS, 1970–1973]

United States foreign economic policy toward Allende's government was articulated at the highest levels of the U.S. government, and coordinated by interagency task forces. . . . Richard Helms'[7] notes from his September 15, 1970, meeting with President Nixon, the meeting

---

[4]The 40 Committee was a subcabinet-level body of the executive branch with a mandate to review and approve major covert actions by the CIA. It was chaired by the president's assistant for national security affairs, and included the undersecretary of state for political affairs, the deputy secretary of defense, the chairman of the joint chiefs of staff, and the CIA director.

[5]Popular Unity (Unidad Popular) replaced FRAP as the coalition of the left in the 1970 election.
[6]A reference to the Soviet invasion of Czechoslovakia in 1968 to halt the reform movement in the Czechoslovakian Communist Party (see Chapter 10, source 79).
[7]Director of the CIA from 1965 to 1973.

which initiated Track II, contain the indication: "Make the economy scream." A week later Ambassador Korry[8] reported telling Frei, through his Defense Minister, that "not a nut or bolt would be allowed to reach Chile under Allende." . . .

The policy of economic pressure . . . was to be implemented through several means. All new bilateral foreign assistance was to be stopped. . . . The U.S. would use its predominant position in international financial institutions to dry up the flow of new multilateral credit or other financial assistance. To the extent possible, financial assistance or guarantees to U.S. private investment in Chile would be ended, and U.S. businesses would be made aware of the government's concern and its restrictive policies. . . .

After the failure of Track II, the CIA rebuilt its network of contacts and remained close to Chilean military officers in order to monitor developments within the armed forces. For their part, Chilean officers who were aware that the United States once had sought a coup to prevent Allende from becoming president must have been sensitive to indications of continuing U.S. support for a coup.

By September 1971 a new network of agents was in place and the Station was receiving almost daily reports of new coup plotting. The Station and Headquarters[9] began to explore ways to use this network. At the same time, and in parallel, the Station and Headquarters discussed a "deception operation" designed to alert Chilean officers to real or purported Cuban involvement in the Chilean army. . . .

The CIA's information-gathering efforts with regard to the Chilean military included activity which went beyond the mere collection of information. More generally, those efforts must be viewed in the context of United States opposition, overt and covert, to the Allende government. They put the United States Government in contact with those Chileans who sought a military alternative to the Allende presidency. . . .

[AFTER THE COUP D'ÉTAT]

Following the September 11, 1973, coup, the military Junta, led by General Augusto Pinochet, moved quickly to consolidate its newly acquired power. Political parties were banned, Congress was put in indefinite recess, press censorship was instituted, supporters of Allende and others deemed opponents of the new regime were jailed, and elections were put off indefinitely. . . .

In addition, charges concerning the violation of human rights in Chile continue to be directed to the Junta. Most recently, a United Nations report on Chile charged that "torture centers" are being operated in Santiago and other parts of the country. The lengthy document, issued October 14, 1975, listed 11 centers where it says prisoners are being questioned "by methods amounting to torture." . . .

The goal of covert action immediately following the coup was to assist the Junta in gaining a more positive image, both at home and abroad, and to maintain access to the command levels of the Chilean government. Another goal, achieved in part through work done at the opposition research organization before the coup, was to help the new government organize and implement new policies. Project files record that CIA collaborators were involved in preparing an initial overall economic plan which has served as the basis for the Junta's most important economic decisions.

[8]Edward Korry, U.S. ambassador to Chile.
[9]*Station* refers to the headquarters of agents in place in Chile; *Headquarters* refers to CIA headquarters in Langley, Virginia.

Racism and Ethnic Conflict in Independent Africa

Once the scramble for Africa began in the late nineteenth century, it took the European powers only two decades to impose their authority on the continent. After World War II, it took them even less time to leave. In the late 1940s European colonial administrators viewed African independence as an event so far off in the future that to discuss even the vaguest of timetables was premature. Actual events were far different from expectations. After the Gold Coast gained independence from Great Britain in 1957 and became Ghana, decolonization proceeded in a rush. Between 1957 and 1975 forty-six former African colonies became sovereign states. Zimbabwe (formerly Rhodesia) became independent in 1980 as did Namibia (occupied by South Africa since the 1920s) in 1990. The last vestige of white political rule in Africa ended when South Africa abandoned apartheid in 1994 and granted blacks full political rights.

At first the new African states made progress toward reaching one of their primary goals, improving their people's standard of living. Through the 1960s annual growth rates were between 3 percent and 4 percent, and inflation was kept to reasonable levels. Between 1960 and 1972, the number of African students attending schools at the primary, secondary, and university levels increased from 17.8 million to 37.6 million. Such accomplishments were short-lived, however. In a catastrophe no one could have anticipated in the 1960s, a host of problems, including rapid population growth, drought, falling commodity prices, increased energy costs, mismanagement, and government corruption soon sent the African economy into free fall.

Another goal of the new states, stable government, proved difficult from the start. Africa's new leaders were soon overwhelmed by a host of intractable problems: poor communications, low literacy levels, resistance of peasant societies to taxation by distant governments, widespread poverty, arbitrarily drawn national boundaries, foreign interference, and the persistence of local and ethnic loyalties. Some new states began to fall apart at the moment of independence. In the Congo Republic, the former Belgian Congo and now the Democratic Republic of Congo, civil war broke out in June 1960, within hours after Belgian rule ended. Nigeria, which became independent in 1960, also fell victim to civil war when its eastern province rebelled and declared itself the independent state of Biafra in 1967.

Most African states held together but quickly abandoned parliamentary government. The experience of Ghana, which won its independence in 1957, was not untypical. Kwame Nkrumah, the leader of the independence movement and Ghana's first prime minister, soon scuttled the Ghanian constitution, had political opponents jailed without trial, and abolished competing political parties. Even his own party, the Convention People's Party, withered away, having been made superfluous by Nkrumah's dictatorship. While the economy suffered from plummeting cocoa prices, Nkrumah shifted from capitalism to socialism and sponsored massive public works projects, one of which was turning his ancestral hut into a national shrine. In 1966 while visiting China, he was overthrown by the military, whose seizure of power set a pattern of military coups interspersed by periods of civilian government. An exile, Nkrumah died in a Romanian sanatorium in 1973.

Blacks in South Africa faced a different kind of political challenge. Ever since South Africa had gained its independence from Great Britain in 1910, blacks, along with Indians and coloreds (people of mixed blood), had steadily lost ground politically and economically as a result of discriminatory laws imposed by the white minority. In the 1950s and early 1960s, a barrage of legislation sponsored by the Nationalist Party turned South African discrimination policies into something much harsher, the apartheid system. Nonwhites lost their remaining political rights; mixed marriages and interracial sex were outlawed; racial segregation was decreed for schools, technical colleges, universities, public transportation, restaurants, theaters, and sports facilities. Apartheid also demanded residential segregation, requiring blacks to live in urban townships or rural homelands known as bantustans. Unlike European colonialism, which melted away at the first sign of black nationalism, apartheid persisted despite black resistance and pressure from the international community. It ended only in 1994 when blacks received the right to vote for members of a parliament that would serve for five years and write a new constitution. The era of white rule in sub-Saharan Africa was finally over.

The Onset of Military Rule in Uganda

❖

88 ◆ STATEMENTS FROM GENERAL IDI AMIN AND THE UGANDAN ARMY

While cultural and ethnic divisions led to civil wars in newly independent Zaire and Nigeria, in Uganda they led to a military coup engineered by generals who promised order and constructive change but whose legacy was ineptitude, brutality, and deepening chaos. Like other former colonies, ethnic and religious divisions made colonial Uganda an unpromising candidate for nationhood. Northerners were mainly Muslims, while southerners were mostly Christians — some Catholics and some Protestants. In addition, under British rule a special arrangement had been struck between colonial authorities and the Bagandans (residents of Buganda), an ethnic group from the south who in return for their cooperation received preferential treatment in education, commerce, and the colonial administration.

Such differences were papered over by British authorities and Ugandan nationalists, and in 1962 Uganda became independent. The first prime minister was Milton Obote, a member of the northern Langi tribe and head of the Uganda People's Congress; the president was Mutesa II, Kabaka (hereditary ruler) of Buganda, which enjoyed a special and separate position within the republic.

Obote sought to overcome Uganda's divisions through authoritarian rule and reliance on the army. In 1966 he proclaimed a new constitution under the slogan "one country, one parliament, one government, one people," and then drove the Kabaka out of the country when Bagandans resisted their loss of privileges. In 1969 he issued "The Common Man's Charter," which outlined his plans for a socialist Uganda. After an attempt on Obote's life, his opponents were jailed, and all political parties were banned except his own. In 1971 he ordered the arrest and execution of his enemies in the army, but before the command could be carried out, army leaders under Idi Amin executed a successful coup d'état while Obote was attending a meeting of British Commonwealth leaders in Singapore.

Uganda's new leader, Idi Amin, was a northerner and a self-described Muslim. Having risen through the ranks of the army under the British, he became Uganda's commander-in-chief after independence. Despite promises of free elections, on seizing power he suspended all political activity and introduced detention without trial. Before he was overthrown in 1978, Uganda experienced both a reign of terror, in which as many as three hundred thousand Ugandans were murdered or disappeared, and economic catastrophe, caused in part by Amin's expulsion of Uganda's seven thousand Asian residents. He fell from power in 1978 when Tanzanian troops conquered most of Uganda after Amin had invaded Tanzania over a border dispute.

In the following selection, Amin himself and a spokesperson for the Ugandan army explain their reasons for overthrowing Obote in January 1971. The first part is from a press statement issued by Amin two days after the insurrection; the second part is from a manifesto issued by the army a short time later.

QUESTIONS FOR ANALYSIS

1. According to Amin, what were Obote's major deficiencies as a ruler?
2. According to Amin, how had Obote kept himself in power?
3. How does the emphasis of the army's manifesto differ from that of Amin's statement?
4. How prominently do matters of political principle, as opposed to self-interest, figure in the two anti-Obote statements?

[COMMANDER IDI AMIN'S PRESS STATEMENT]

What can be said without any doubt whatsoever is that Obote's regime was one of great hypocrites. Obote himself always claimed that he was a great socialist and yet there were very many things that he did that showed that he way anything but a socialist.

Obote had two palaces in Entebbe, three in Kampala, one in Jinja (fifty miles away), one in Tororo, one in Mbale (twenty eight miles from Tororo), one in Lira and elsewhere. All these palaces had to be furnished and maintained at great public expense, and yet all but one remained idle and unused almost all the time! It is no wonder that the people in Jinja, in their great joy attacked and damaged the so-called President's Palace at Jinja, total destruction of the place only being prevented by the Army.

Obote's mode of living was also anything but socialist. He heavily indulged in drink, smoking and women, and carried a big retinue (including bodyguards) wherever he went. This idle living was maintained at public expense and was also indulged in by Obote's Ministers and close advisers. . . .

Obote talked lofty words and wrote high-sounding pamphlets about socialism and yet his actions never matched his words. The endless taxes and high prices of basic commodities also showed that socialist Obote never cared anything about the people. As an example, the price of sugar, salt, rice, meat and many other foods doubled when Uganda changed over from the imperial to the metric systems of weights and measures, and yet Obote never enquired why this was so.

Corruption in Obote's regime was so widespread that it was almost being taken for granted. Ministers, Chairmen of parastatal bodies[1] and top public servants owned fleets of cars, buses, scores of houses for renting, bars, petrol stations etc. and Obote never in one single instance questioned any of his men as to the way they had acquired this wealth. . . . The worst aspect of the financial greed of Obote's men was that most of them ran the very businesses that ought to have been left to the common people, e.g. the taxi business and butcheries.

When it came to proposals for National Service it was obvious that Obote did not have the interest of the Common Man[1] at heart. Obote proposed that 'all able bodied persons' should spend at least two years in a National Service Camp, far away from their home districts, digging and learning all about agriculture. The people were not to be paid for their work on the National Service Camps. In making his National Service proposals, 'socialist' Obote totally ignored the social problems that would inevitably arise if his proposals were put into effect, especially those relating to the split family. . . .

Regardless of public feeling and popular opinion, Obote was determined to stay in power, together with his whole bunch of corrupt Ministers. The last elections were held in Uganda in 1962, and Parliament was given a five year mandate expiring in 1967. . . .

In 1970 Obote solemnly declared that elections would be held in Uganda by April 1971, and he appointed an Electoral Commission to demarcate the electoral boundaries. He declared that candidates, all of whom would be nominated by the President's Election Commission, would have to stand in 4 widely scattered Constituencies.

This 4-Constituency idea was a trick by Obote to keep his henchmen in power since it obviously favoured the well known, and those who had funds to campaign in 4 scattered parts of the country. Obote's men obviously had funds, and moreover they all had embarked on intensive campaigns everywhere on Government expenses (under the guise of official tours) long before any official campaign period had been announced. . . .

Despite the fact that these confused electoral proposals were hedged around with safeguards and safety valves for Obote and his bunch of corrupt henchmen, Obote could never bring himself to announcing the date for a General Election. With most of the heavy pre-election programme not even started on by January 1971 . . . it was obvious to everybody that Obote's elections would not be held by April 1971 as he had solemnly promised. In fact he had already decided to 'postpone' the elections until October 1971, and no doubt . . . when that date arrived he would happily have 'postponed' the elections to some other date. . . .

Obote's actions in recent times showed that he hated and distrusted the Army which had kept him in power right from the day of Independence in 1962. He also greatly distrusted the people he ruled. For that reason Obote amassed hordes of weapons . . . and they have already been shown to the local and international press.

---

[1]Organizations that take on some roles of government through which the government operates indirectly.

[2]A sarcastic reference to Obote's "Common Man's Charter."

[MANIFESTO OF THE UGANDAN ARMY]

- Economic policies have left many people unemployed and even more insecure and lacking in the basic needs of life like food, clothing, medicine and shelter.
- High taxes have left the common man of this country poorer than ever before. Here are some of the taxes which the common man has to bear: Development Tax, Graduated Tax, Sales Tax, Social Security Fund Tax. The big men can always escape these taxes or pass them on to the common man.
- The prices which the common man gets for his crops like cotton and coffee have not gone up and sometimes they have gone down, whereas the cost of food, education, etc., has always gone up. . . .
- The creation of a wealthy class of leaders who are always talking of socialism while they grow richer and the common man poorer. . . .
- The Cabinet Office, by training large numbers of people (largely from the Akokoro County in Lango District where Obote and Akena Adoko, the Chief General Service Officer, came from) in armed warfare, has turned into a second army. Uganda therefore has had two armies, one in the Cabinet, the other Regular.
- The Lango development master plan written in 1967 decided that all key positions in

Uganda's political, commercial, army and industrial life have to be occupied and controlled by people from Akokoro County, Lango District. Emphasis was put on development of Akokoro County in Lango District at the expense of other areas of Uganda.

- Obote . . . has sought to divide the Uganda Armed Forces and the rest of Uganda by picking out his own tribesmen and putting them in key positions in the Army and elsewhere. Examples: the Chief General Service Office, the Export and Import Corporation, Uganda Meat Packers, the Public Service Commission, Nyanza Textiles and a Russian textile factory to be situated in Lango.
- From the time Obote took over power in 1962 his greatest and most loyal supporter has been the Army. The Army has always tried to be an example to the whole of Africa by not taking over the Government and we have always followed that principle. It is, therefore, now a shock to us to see that Obote wants to divide and downgrade the Army by turning the Cabinet Office into another army. In doing this, Obote and Akena Adoko have bribed and used some senior officers who have turned against their fellow soldiers.

We all want only unity in Uganda and we do not want bloodshed. Everybody in Uganda knows that. The matters mentioned above appear to us to lead to bloodshed only.

Apartheid's Bitter Fruits

❖

89 ❖ *Nelson Mandela,*
THE RIVONIA TRIAL SPEECH TO THE COURT

In 1912, two years after South Africa had been granted independence from Great Britain, blacks formed the African National Congress (ANC) to foster black unity and win political rights. At first the ANC sought to reach its goals through petitions and appeals to white politicians, but following the implementation of apartheid after World War II, it sponsored campaigns of passive resistance and supported strikes by black labor unions. The result was more government repression.

Predictably, some blacks abandoned moderation for sabotage and terrorism. Among them was Nelson Mandela (b. 1918), the son of a tribal chieftain, who became a lawyer and an ANC activist in the 1940s. After the ANC was outlawed in 1960, and after he organized a three-day stay-at-home protest in 1961, Mandela went into hiding. While avoiding a nationwide manhunt, he helped found Umkonto we Sizwe (Spear of the Nation), a branch of the ANC that carried out bombings in several cities. Arrested in 1963, he was convicted of treason and sent to the notorious prison on Robben Island, forty miles off South Africa's southern coast. He remained a prisoner until 1990, when he was released by President F. W. de Klerk as one of the first steps toward the abolition of the apartheid system.

The following excerpt comes from a speech delivered by Nelson Mandela on April 20, 1964, in which he opened his defense against charges of treason before an all-white court.

QUESTIONS FOR ANALYSIS

1. Why did Mandela decide that the ANC must resort to violence to achieve its goals?
2. What distinction does Mandela draw between sabotage and terrorism?
3. What attractions did Mandela and other ANC leaders see in communism?
4. What aspects of apartheid does Mandela find most degrading?
5. According to Mandela, how does apartheid affect the daily lives of the blacks?
6. How does Mandela's description of life in the black townships compare with Charlotte Maxeke's description of South African urban life in the 1930s (see Chapter 6, source 46)?

In my youth . . . I listened to the elders of my tribe telling stories of the old days. Amongst the tales they related to me were those of wars fought by our ancestors in defense of the fatherland. . . . I hoped then that life might offer me the opportunity to serve my people and make my own humble contribution to their freedom struggle. This is what has motivated me in all that I have done in relation to the charges made against me in this case. . . .

I have already mentioned that I was one of the persons who helped to form Umkonto. I, and the others who started the organization, did so for two reasons. Firstly, we believed that as a result of Government policy, violence by the African people had become inevitable, and that unless responsible leadership was given to canalize and control the feelings of our people, there would be outbreaks of terrorism which would produce an intensity of bitterness and hostility between the various races of this country which is not produced even by war. Secondly, we felt that without violence there would be no way open to the African people to succeed in their struggle against the principle of White supremacy. All lawful modes of expressing opposition to this principle had been closed by legislation, and we were placed in a position in which we had either to accept a permanent state of inferiority, or to defy the Government. . . .

But the violence which we chose to adopt was not terrorism. We who formed Umkonto were all members of the African National Congress, and had behind us the ANC tradition of non-violence and negotiation as a means of solving political disputes. We believed that South Africa belonged to all the people who lived in it, and not to one group, be it Black or White. We did not want an interracial war, and tried to avoid it to the last minute. . . .

The African National Congress was formed in 1912 to defend the rights of the African people. . . . For thirty-seven years — that is until 1949 — it adhered strictly to a constitutional struggle. It put forward demands and resolutions; it sent delegations to the Government in the belief that African grievances could be settled through peaceful discussion and that Africans could advance gradually to full political rights. But White Governments remained unmoved, and the rights of Africans became less instead of becoming greater. . . .

Even after 1949, the ANC remained determined to avoid violence. At this time, however, there was a change from the strictly constitutional means of protest which had been employed in the past. The change was embodied in a decision which was taken to protest against apartheid legislation by peaceful, but unlawful, demonstrations against certain laws. Pursuant to this policy the ANC launched the Defiance Campaign, in which I was placed in charge of volunteers. This campaign was based on the principles of passive resistance. More than 8,500 people defied apartheid laws and went to jail. Yet there was not a single instance of violence in the course of this campaign on the part of any defier. . . .

In 1960 there was the shooting at Sharpeville,[1] which resulted in the proclamation of a state of emergency and the declaration of the ANC as an unlawful organization. My colleagues and I, after careful consideration, decided that we would not obey this decree. The African people were not part of the Government and did not make the laws by which they were governed. We believed in the words of the Universal Declaration of Human Rights,[2] that "the will of the people shall be the basis of authority of the Government," and for us to accept the banning was equivalent to accepting the silencing of the Africans for all time. The ANC refused to dissolve, but instead went underground. . . .

. . . Each disturbance pointed clearly to the inevitable growth among Africans of the belief that violence was the only way out — it showed that a Government which uses force to maintain its rule teaches the oppressed to use force to oppose it. . . .

The avoidance of civil war had dominated our thinking for many years, but when we decided to adopt violence as part of our policy, we realized that we might one day have to face the prospect of such a war. . . . We did not want to be committed to civil war, but we wanted to be ready if it became inevitable.

Four forms of violence were possible. There is sabotage, there is guerrilla warfare, there is terrorism, and there is open revolution. We chose to adopt the first method and to exhaust it before taking any other decision.

In the light of our political background the choice was a logical one. Sabotage did not involve loss of life, and it offered the best hope for future race relations. Bitterness would be kept to a minimum and, if the policy bore fruit, democratic government could become a reality. . . .

Attacks on the economic life lines of the country were to be linked with sabotage on Government buildings and other symbols of apartheid. These attacks would serve as a source of inspiration to our people. In addition, they would provide an outlet for those people who were urging the adoption of violent methods and would enable us to give concrete proof to our followers that we had adopted a stronger line and were fighting back against Government violence. . . .

---

[1]The Sharpeville Massacre took place in 1960 when police killed 69 and wounded 178 anti-apartheid demonstrators.

[2]The Universal Declaration of Human Rights was adopted by the United Nations on December 10, 1948.

Another of the allegations made by the State is that the aims and objects of the ANC and the Communist Party are the same. . . .

It is true that there has often been close cooperation between the ANC and the Communist Party. But cooperation is merely proof of a common goal — in this case the removal of White supremacy — and is not proof of a complete community of interests. . . .

It is perhaps difficult for White South Africans, with an ingrained prejudice against communism, to understand why experienced African politicians so readily accept communists as their friends. But to us the reason is obvious. Theoretical differences amongst those fighting against oppression is a luxury we cannot afford at this stage. What is more, for many decades communists were the only political group in South Africa who were prepared to treat Africans as human beings and their equals; who were prepared to eat with us, talk with us, live with us, and work with us. They were the only political group which was prepared to work with the Africans for the attainment of political rights and a stake in society. Because of this, there are many Africans who, today, tend to equate freedom with communism. . . .

Our fight is against real, and not imaginary, hardships or, to use the language of the State prosecutor, "so-called hardships." Basically, we fight against two features which are the hallmarks of African life in South Africa and which are entrenched by legislation which we seek to have repealed. These features are poverty and lack of human dignity. . . .

South Africa is the richest country in Africa, and could be one of the richest countries in the world. But it is a land of extremes and remarkable contrasts. The Whites enjoy what may well be the highest standard of living in the world, whilst Africans live in poverty and misery. Forty percent of the Africans live in hopelessly overcrowded and, in some cases, drought-stricken Reserves, where soil erosion and the overworking of the soil make it impossible for them to live properly off the land. Thirty percent are laborers, labor tenants, and squatters on White farms and work and live under conditions similar to those of the serfs of the Middle Ages. The other 30 percent live in towns where they have developed economic and social habits which bring them closer in many respects to White standards. Yet most Africans, even in this group, are impoverished by low incomes and [the] high cost of living. . . .

The lack of human dignity experienced by Africans is the direct result of the policy of White supremacy. White supremacy implies Black inferiority. Legislation designed to preserve White supremacy entrenches this notion. Menial tasks in South Africa are invariably performed by Africans. When anything has to be carried or cleaned the White man will look around for an African to do it for him, whether the African is employed by him or not. Because of this sort of attitude, Whites tend to regard Africans as a separate breed. They do not look upon them as people with families of their own; they do not realize that they have emotions — that they fall in love like White people do; that they want to be with their wives and children like White people want to be with theirs; that they want to earn enough money to support their families properly, to feed and clothe them and send them to school. And what "house-boy" or "garden-boy" or laborer can ever hope to do this? . . .

Poverty and the breakdown of family life have secondary effects. Children wander about the streets of the townships because they have no schools to go to, or no money to enable them to go to school, or no parents at home to see that they go to school, because both parents (if there be two) have to work to keep the family alive. This leads to a breakdown in moral standards, to an alarming rise in illegitimacy, and to growing violence which erupts, not only politically, but everywhere. Life in the townships is dangerous. There is not a day that goes by without somebody being stabbed or assaulted. And violence is carried out of the townships in the White living areas. People are afraid to walk alone in the streets after dark. House-breakings and robberies are increasing, despite the fact that the death sentence can now be imposed for such offenses. Death sentences cannot cure the festering sore. . . .

During my lifetime I have dedicated myself to this struggle of the African people. I have fought against White domination, and I have fought against Black domination. I have cherished the ideal of a democratic and free society in which all persons live together in harmony and with equal opportunities. It is an ideal which I hope to live for and to achieve. But if needs be, it is an ideal for which I am prepared to die.

◆

South and Southeast Asia After Colonialism

In the two decades after World War II, the peoples of South and Southeast Asia achieved independence from foreign rule, though how they achieved it varied widely. In the Philippines, it was the culmination of a long-standing U.S. plan to prepare the Filipinos for self-government. In India, it was the result of a protracted struggle on the part of the Indian people against British rule. In the Dutch East Indies, French Indochina, and British-controlled Burma, Singapore, and Malaya, Western imperialism effectively ended with the Japanese conquests of 1942, but in the case of Indochina and the East Indies, it took several years of fighting after World War II before the Dutch and French realized this and relinquished control of their colonies.

After achieving independence, the new nations of South and Southeast Asia faced many similar problems. All had high levels of poverty, widespread illiteracy, and little industry. All but a few had populations divided by race, language, and ethnic background. India was predominantly Hindu, but had large Sikh and Muslim minorities; so great was its linguistic diversity that its parliament approved no less than fourteen official languages in the 1950s. Burma had a population in which approximately one-third of its people practiced different religions and spoke different languages from those of the Buddhist majority. In Malaysia, the Malays, mainly farmers, and the Chinese, mainly businesspeople, viewed each other with distrust, as did the Tamils and Sinhalese in Ceylon (Sri Lanka) and the Muslims and Catholics in the Philippines. Pakistan was divided into two sections, two thousand miles apart, in which the people of West Pakistan spoke Urdu, grew wheat, and worried about drought while those in East Pakistan spoke Hindi, grew rice, and worried about floods. Indonesia was a nation of seventy-six million people who spoke two hundred fifty different languages and lived on thousands of islands that stretched across a distance equal to that between Boston and Ireland.

The region's new states all faced formidable political challenges. Although most started out as parliamentary democracies, democracy soon gave way to authoritarian regimes installed by the military in Burma, Pakistan, Thailand, and Indonesia. Vietnam, which was divided into a communist north and a noncommunist south after the French departed in 1954, became the scene of major U.S. military intervention to prevent the unification of the country under communist rule. The number of U.S. troops fighting in Vietnam grew slowly under Presidents Eisenhower and Kennedy, peaked at over five hundred thousand under President Johnson, and then rapidly declined under President Nixon, whose policy of Vietnamization resulted in U.S. troop withdrawals but continued support for the army of South Vietnam. Laos and Cambodia were also drawn into the struggle. The Ho Chi Minh Trail, by which North Vietnam sent troops and supplies to the south, ran through both countries, and this led to U.S. bombings, intervention to prop up anticommunist rulers, and the invasion of Cambodia by U.S. and South Vietnamese troops in 1970.

The U.S. mission in Southeast Asia failed on all fronts. Although the United States lost fifty-eight thousand troops, dropped more bombs on North Vietnam than it had dropped in all of World War II, and spent billions of dollars, in April 1975 South Vietnamese resistance collapsed, and Vietnam was united under communist rule. Later in 1975 communist regimes also gained control of Cambodia and Laos.

For Cambodians, the horror was not quite over. During the rule of the communist dictator Pol Pot, forced labor, starvation, systematic torture, and massacres of intellectuals, political opponents, and resident Vietnamese resulted in an estimated 1.7 million deaths. Only the invasion and occupation of Cambodia by North Vietnam in 1979 brought this chapter in the history of Southeast Asia to a close.

Nehru's Blueprint for India

◆

90 ◆ *Jawaharlal Nehru,*
SPEECHES AND WRITINGS, 1952–1955

Born into a prestigious upper-class family in 1889, Jawaharlal Nehru was educated in England at Harrow School and at Cambridge University before studying law in London. On his return to India in 1912, he joined the Congress Party, which since 1885 had worked for increased Indian participation in the colonial administration and ultimately Indian independence. In 1919 Nehru decided to devote himself completely to the cause of Indian independence, after troops, on orders from a British officer, fired into a crowd of unarmed demonstrators in Amritsar, killing several hundred. He was elected president of the Congress Party in 1929. Repeatedly arrested by the British for participation in civil disobedience strikes and other political actions, he spent half of his next eighteen years in prison. After World War II, he took part in the negotiations that led to the creation of the separate states in India and Pakistan; after independece he helped craft India's constitution.

After Indian independence in 1947, Nehru served as head of the Congress Party and prime minister until his death in 1964. More so than any other individual, he shaped India's economic and political development. In the following excerpts from speeches and writings of the 1950s, he discusses his basic ideas.

QUESTIONS FOR ANALYSIS

1. What kind of society does Nehru envision for India, and how is it to be achieved? What role will capitalism play in India's future?
2. What does Nehru mean by "planning"?
3. Does Nehru seem to anticipate any difficulties that would prevent Indian planning from achieving its goals? What timetable does Nehru seem to have for achieving his economic goals for India?
4. What role should religion and the caste system play in modern India, according to Nehru?

[PLANNING AND THE WELFARE STATE]

As you all know, planning is essential, and without it there would be anarchy in our economic development. About five years ago, planning was not acceptable to many people in high places but today it has come to be recognized as essential even by the man in the street. . . .

. . . We cannot have a welfare state in India with all the socialism or even communism in the world unless our national income goes up greatly. Socialism or communism might help you to divide your existing wealth, if you like, but in India, there is no existing wealth for you to divide; there is only poverty to divide. It is not a question of distributing the wealth of the few rich men here and there. That is not going to make any difference in our national income. . . . We must produce wealth, and then divide it equitably. How can we have a welfare state without wealth? Wealth need not mean gold and silver but wealth in goods and services. Our economic policy must therefore aim at plenty. . . .

. . . The conception of planning today is not to think of the money we have and then to divide it up in the various schemes but to measure the physical needs, that is to say, how much of food the people want, how much of clothes they want, how much of housing they want, how much of education they want, how much of health services they want, how much of work

and employment they want, and so on. We calculate all these and then decide what everyone in India should have of these things. Once we do that, we can set about increasing production and fulfilling these needs. It is not a simple matter because in calculating the needs of the people, we have to calculate on the basis not only of an increasing population but of increasing needs. . . . Therefore, in making calculations, we have to keep in mind that the extra money that goes into circulation because of the higher salaries and wages, affects consumption. So we find out what in five years' time will be the needs of our people, including even items needed by our Defence Services. Then we decide how to produce those things in India. In order to meet a particular variety of needs we have now to put up a factory which will produce the goods that we need five years hence. Thus, planning is a much more complicated process than merely drawing up some schemes and fixing a system of priorities. . . .

But production is not all. . . . Mass production inevitably involves mass consumption, which in turn involves many other factors, chiefly the purchasing power of the consumer. Therefore planning must take note of the need to provide more purchasing power by way of wages, salaries and so on. Enough money should be thrown in to provide this purchasing power and to complete the circle of production and consumption. You will then produce more and consume more, and as a result your standard of living will go up. . . .

[SOCIALISM VS. CAPITALISM]

The whole of the capitalist structure is based on some kind of an acquisitive society. It may be that, to some extent, the tendency to acquisitiveness is inherent in us. A socialist society must try to get rid of this tendency to acquisitiveness and replace it by co-operation. You cannot bring about this change by a sudden law. There have to be long processes of training the people; without this you cannot wholly succeed. Even from the very limited point of view of changing your economic structure, apart from your minds and hearts, it takes time to build a socialist society. The countries that have gone fastest have also taken time. I would like you to consider that the Soviet Union, which has gone fast in industrialization, has taken thirty-five years or more over it. Chairman Mao of the People's Republic of China — which is more or less a communist state — said, about three or four years ago, that it would take China twenty years to achieve some kind of socialism. Mind you, this [is] in spite of the fact that theirs is an authoritarian state, and the people are exceedingly disciplined and industrious. Chairman Mao was speaking as a practical idealist. We must realize that the process of bringing socialism to India, especially in the way we are doing it, that is, the democratic way, will inevitably take time. . . .

[A SECULAR STATE]

Where the great majority of the people in a state belong to one religion, this fact alone may colour, to some extent, the cultural climate of that state. But nevertheless the state, as a state, can remain independent of any particular religion.

In a sense, this is a more or less modern conception. India has a long history of religious tolerance. That is one aspect of a secular state, but it is not the whole of it. In a country like India, which has many faiths and religions, no real nationalism can be built up except on the basis of secularity. Any narrower approach must necessarily exclude a section of the population, and then nationalism itself will have a much more restricted meaning than it should possess. In India we would have then to consider Hindu nationalism, Muslim nationalism, Sikh nationalism or Christian nationalism and not Indian nationalism.

As a matter of fact, these narrow religious nationalisms are relics of a past age and are no longer relevant today. They represent a backward and out-of-date society. In the measure we have even today so-called communal troubles, we display our backwardness as social groups. . . .

. . . The word 'secular' perhaps is not a very happy one. And yet, for want of a better word, we have used it. What exactly does it mean? It does not obviously mean a state where religion as such is discouraged. It means freedom of religion and conscience, including freedom for those who may have no religion. . . .

The word 'secular', however, conveys something much more to me, although that might not be its dictionary meaning. It conveys the idea of social and political equality. Thus, a caste-ridden society[1] is not properly secular. I have no desire to interfere with any person's belief, but when those beliefs become petrified in caste divisions, undoubtedly they affect the social structure of the state. They prevent us from realizing the idea of equality which we claim to place before ourselves. They interfere in political matters, just as communalism interferes.

---

[1]The Indian caste system, which dates from 1000–800 B.C.E., is a rigid form of social differentiation in which groups, traditionally linked to occupational specialties, are ranked on a hierarchical scale. Each caste has its own code of appropriate behavior, and marriage is generally restricted to members of the same caste.

Two Perspectives on the War in Vietnam

◈

91 ◆ *HO CHI MINH–JOHNSON CORRESPONDENCE, FEBRUARY 1967*

By early 1967 it was clear that there would be no quick American victory in Vietnam. Despite the commitment of approximately four hundred thousand U.S. troops and devastating bombing attacks on North Vietnam, the war had become a deadly stalemate and had bitterly divided the American people. Faced with these realities, President Johnson and his advisors renewed their efforts to end the war through negotiation. In February 1967 Johnson wrote directly to the North Vietnamese leader, Ho Chi Minh, spelling out the U.S. negotiating stance. Ho rejected Johnson's proposal, and formal negotiations between the two sides did not begin until May 1968. By then another one hundred thousand U.S. troops had been committed to Vietnam.

It is not surprising that Ho Chi Minh, an ardent nationalist and communist, was reluctant to negotiate an agreement that fell short of his goal of a united, communist Vietnam. Born in 1890, Ho, then known as Nguyen Sinh Cung, left French Indochina at the age of twenty-one to work on a French oceangoing ship and then at a hotel in London. Toward the end of World War I he moved to France, where he became a socialist and tried to convince the negotiators at the Paris Peace Conference to accept a plan for Vietnamese independence. In 1920 he joined the French Communist Party and became a student of Lenin's writings. In 1923 he went to the Soviet Union, and after a year of training was sent by the Communist International to Indochina. There he organized the Indochinese Communist Party in 1930. Forced to flee during the 1930s, he returned to Vietnam in 1943 and founded the communist-controlled League for the Independence of Vietnam, or Viet Minh, which led resistance campaigns against the occupying Japanese while building a base for a postwar independence movement. Only then did Nguyen adopt the name Ho Chi Minh, meaning "one who enlightens." With the defeat of the Japanese in 1945, he proclaimed the independent Democratic Republic of Vietnam and became its first president. Until his death in 1969, he led his country during eight years of warfare against the French and fifteen years of warfare against the anticommunist South Vietnamese regime established in 1954 at the Geneva Conference.

The following selection includes a brief excerpt from President Johnson's letter to Ho Chi Minh written in 1967 and the entire text of Ho's response. The exchange reveals the broad differences in the thinking of the two statesmen.

QUESTIONS FOR ANALYSIS

1. According to Johnson's letter, what had the Vietnamese proposed as conditions for beginning "direct bilateral talks"?
2. Why does Johnson reject the Vietnamese proposal, and what does he propose instead?

3. In the last paragraph of his letter, Ho Chi Minh states, "Our cause is absolutely just." What is the basis of his assertion?
4. Why does Ho reject President Johnson's proposal for negotiations? What counterproposal does he make?

His Excellency Ho Chi Minh
President, Democratic Republic of Vietnam

Dear Mr. President,

I am writing to you in the hope that the conflict in Vietnam can be brought to an end. The conflict has already taken a heavy toll — in lives lost, in wounds inflicted, in property destroyed, and in simple human misery. If we fail to find a just and peaceful solution, history will judge us harshly. . . .

In the past two weeks, I have noted public statements by representatives of your government suggesting that you would be prepared to enter into direct bilateral talks with representatives of the U.S. Government, provided that we ceased "unconditionally" and permanently our bombing operations against your country and all military actions against it. In the last days, serious and responsible parties have assured us indirectly that this is in fact your proposal.

Let me frankly state that I see two great difficulties with this proposal. In view of your public position, such action on our part would inevitably produce worldwide speculation that discussions were under way and would impair the privacy and secrecy of those discussions. Secondly, there would inevitably be grave concern on our part whether your government would make use of such action by us to improve its military position.

With these problems in mind, I am prepared to move even further toward an ending of the hostilities than your government has proposed in either public statements or through private diplomatic channels. I am prepared to order a cessation of bombing against your country and the stopping of further augmentation of U.S. forces in South Vietnam as soon as I am assured that infiltration into South Vietnam by land and by sea has stopped. These acts of restraint on both sides would, I believe, make it possible for us to conduct serious and private discussions leading toward an early peace. . . .

As to the site of the bilateral discussions I propose, there are several possibilities. We could, for example, have our representatives meet in Moscow where contacts have already occurred. They could meet in some other country such as Burma. You may have other arrangements or sites in mind, and I would try to meet your suggestions. . . .

Sincerely,

LYNDON B. JOHNSON

To His Excellency Mr. Lyndon B. Johnson
President
United States of America

Your Excellency,

On February 10, 1967, I received your message. This is my reply.

Vietnam is thousands of miles away from the United States. The Vietnamese people have never done any harm to the United States. But contrary to the pledges made by its representative at the 1954 Geneva Conference, the U.S. Government has ceaselessly intervened in Vietnam, it has unleashed and intensified the war of aggression in South Vietnam with a view to prolonging the partition of Vietnam and turning South Vietnam into a neo-colony and a military base of the United States. For over two years now, the U.S. Government has, with its air and naval forces, carried the war to the Democratic Republic of Vietnam, an independent and sovereign country.

The U.S. Government has committed war crimes, crimes against peace and against mankind. In South Vietnam, half a million U.S. and satellite troops have resorted to the most inhuman weapons and the most barbarous methods of warfare, such as napalm,[1] toxic chemicals and gases, to massacre our compatriots, destroy crops, and raze villages to the ground. In North Vietnam, thousands of U.S. aircraft have dropped hundreds of thousands of tons of bombs, destroying towns, villages, factories, roads, bridges, dikes, dams, and even churches, pagodas, hospitals, schools. In your message, you apparently deplored the sufferings and destructions in Vietnam. May I ask you: Who has perpetrated these monstrous crimes? It is the U.S. and satellite troops. The U.S. Government is entirely responsible for the extremely serious situation in Vietnam.

The U.S. war of aggression against the Vietnamese people constitutes a challenge to the countries of the socialist camp, a threat to the national independence movement, and a serious danger to peace in Asia and the world.

The Vietnamese people deeply love independence, freedom and peace. But in the face of the U.S. aggression, they have risen up, united as one man, fearless of sacrifices and hardships; they are determined to carry on their Resistance until they have won genuine independence and freedom and true peace. Our just cause enjoys strong sympathy and support from the peoples of the whole world including broad sections of the American people.

The U.S. Government has unleashed the war of aggression in Vietnam. It must cease this aggression. This is the only way to the restoration of peace. The U.S. Government must stop definitively and unconditionally its bombing raids and all other acts of war against the Democratic Republic of Vietnam, withdraw from South Vietnam all U.S. and satellite troops, recognize the South Vietnam National Front for Liberation,[2] and let the Vietnamese people settle [for] themselves their own affairs. Such is the basic content of the four-point stand of the Government of the Democratic Republic of Vietnam, which embodies the essential principles and provisions of the 1954 Geneva Agreements on Vietnam. It is the basis of a correct political solution to the Vietnam problem.

In your message, you suggested direct talks between the Democratic Republic of Vietnam and the United States. If the U.S. Government really wants these talks, it must first of all stop unconditionally its bombing raids and all other acts of war against the Democratic Republic of Vietnam. It is only after the unconditional cessation of the U.S. bombing raids and all other acts of war against the Democratic Republic of Vietnam that the Democratic Republic of Vietnam and the United States could enter into talks and discuss questions concerning the two sides.

The Vietnamese people will never submit to force; they will never accept talks under the threat of bombs.

Our cause is absolutely just. It is to be hoped that the U.S. Government will act in accordance with reason.

Sincerely,

HO CHI MINH

---

[1]Napalm is a military incendiary substance made up of gasoline, other fuels, and a gelling agent (made up of naphthenic and palmitic acids from which is derived the acronym *napalm*). A napalm-armed bomb or flamethrower broadcasts the substance over a wide area where it burns with intense heat. Its use to destroy villages and defoliate jungles to reveal enemy camps was bitterly protested by antiwar activists.

[2]The National Front for Liberation, or NLF, was founded in 1960 by supporters of Ho Chi Minh of South Vietnam. It became the umbrella organization under which guerrilla warfare was waged against the South Vietnamese government.

PART FOUR

Century's Close: From Cold War to Globalization

Writing contemporary history — the history of events that have just occurred — presents unique difficulties. The historian's most basic task — getting the facts right and determining "what happened" — is relatively easy. Historians of the recent past have lived through the events they are describing, can interview eyewitnesses and participants, and in the modern era have access not only to information contained in books, newspapers, and government documents, but also to visual evidence from films, video recordings, and photographs. Writing history, however, requires more than factual accuracy and telling "what happened." It also involves making interpretations, judging what's important and what's trivial, and determining how events and developments fit into long-term patterns and trends. To do these tasks well, historians need a perspective that includes knowledge of what preceded and what followed the events they are describing. Contemporary historians, with no knowledge of the future, will always lack this perspective, and can make only educated guesses about the meaning of events that have just taken place.

Consider, for example, the disintegration of the Soviet Union in the late 1980s and early 1990s. Soon after it occurred, politicians, journalists, and historians — indeed, everyone who had anything to say about it — characterized it as a historic turning point in human affairs. The demise of the Soviet Union, they argued, ended the Cold War, lifted the shadow of nuclear holocaust, revealed fatal flaws in communism, confirmed the superiority of capitalism, and opened up new possibilities for world peace and cooperation. U.S. political scientist Francis Fukuyama went even further; to him it meant the "end of history." Liberal democracy and capitalism had cleared the field of all competitors and would dominate human societies around the globe forever.

Events of the twenty-first century, however, may reveal that all of these assumptions about the breakup of the Soviet Union were incorrect. The Russians might abandon their not very successful experiment with capitalism and reinstate a communist dictatorship or something close to it. They might come under control of authoritarian nationalists who will, as the Nazis did in Germany, revive and remilitarize a weak and demoralized people and lead them on a path of military conquest and expansion. Such scenarios are unlikely, but if either were to occur, the "demise of Soviet communism" and "the humbling of Russia" that took place in the late 1980s and 1990s would no longer be viewed as a turning point, but rather as a temporary interruption of long-term patterns.

What is true about the fall of the Soviet Union also applies to any number of other events and trends of the late twentieth century. Is the recent intensification of Islamic fundamentalism a prelude to a "battle of civilizations" between the West and Islam or a passing phase in Islam's history? Are the recent gains made by Western women in education, job opportunities, and legal status the first stage of a movement toward greater gender equality worldwide or an early indication that feminism will remain a uniquely Western phenomenon? Will late-twentieth-century environmentalism be hailed as a triumph of human foresight or mourned as a movement that came too late and accomplished too little? Will China's recent economic growth be considered the first step in its emergence as a new superpower or the prelude to some unforeseen economic or political upheaval? Will recent population increases result in sustainability or catastrophe? No one will be able to answer these and countless other questions for another fifty years or more, and until then histories of the late twentieth century must remain tentative and provisional.

Perhaps the greatest challenge for contemporary historians is making sense of the combination of recent economic, political, technological, and cultural changes described by the word *globalization*. Variously defined, globalization refers to a world of free trade, open markets, and capitalist competition in which goods, services, and capital flow across seamless international borders. It also refers to a world in which a remarkable series of technological breakthroughs — computers, communications satellites, fiber-optic cable, jet aircraft, and the Internet — have destroyed the barriers of time and space. It refers, finally, to a world of cultural homogeneity in which tastes in music, art, architecture, personal dress, and countless other areas have becoming increasingly standardized and, for better or worse, Americanized.

Historians can agree that globalization represents an acceleration and intensification of a trend that has been a key feature of world history ever since the European overseas expansion of the 1500s and 1600s — greater interdependency and interaction among the world's peoples. Where globalization will take us, however, is impossible to predict. Its supporters see universal benefits from worldwide economic growth, strengthened democracies through better-informed citizenry, increased capacity to deal with global environmental problems, and even a heightened sense of human community. Its detractors, of which there are many, see a widening divide between haves and have-nots, dangerous political transitions, the triumph of an ethos of corporate greed, and a bland uniformity in world culture. Whichever side is correct, understanding the roots and meaning of globalization will be a primary challenge for future historians.

CHAPTER 12

The 1970s and 1980s: Years of Challenge and Change

After two decades of economic depression and war, the 1950s and 1960s were marked by optimism and high expectations in much of the world. By contrast, the 1970s and 1980s were years of self-doubt, lowered expectations, and disillusionment with once promising political formulas. Several factors contributed to this change, but the most important was the halt of postwar economic expansion. In the early 1970s the world entered an era in which inflation accompanied stagnation, periods of sluggish growth were interrupted by three major recessions, some areas of the world flourished while others languished, and an oil shortage in the 1970s was followed by an oil glut in the 1980s.

Why and how the world economy became so erratic is still unclear. Undoubtedly, a major factor was the steep increase in oil prices between October 1973, when a barrel of oil sold by members of the Organization of Petroleum Exporting Countries cost $2.59, and late 1980, when a barrel cost just over $30. Prices fell to under $20 a barrel by the mid 1980s, but by then higher energy costs had done their damage: inflation, shrunken corporate profits, trade deficits for oil-importing nations, and the erosion of consumer spending. Oil costs were not the only culprit, however. Currency fluctuations, inflationary wage settlements in the late 1960s and early 1970s, decreased state spending in the face of rising deficits, declining productivity and investments, and a failure of oil-producing states to recycle their immense profits through loans and investments all played a role.

The effects of the "Great Slowdown" varied enormously. Oil producers at first reaped huge profits, but they faced a crisis in the mid 1980s when oil prices plummeted by 30 to 40 percent. Japan, Hong Kong, South Korea, Taiwan, and Singapore, continued to find new markets for their cars, electronic goods, and textiles, and experienced only slight increases in unemployment and inflation. In the United States, however, the average unemployment rate between 1973 and 1989 was 7.1 percent, compared to 4.8 percent between 1960 and 1973; in Europe unemployment grew from less than 3 percent in 1970 to more than 10 percent in 1986. Inflation also was a severe problem. The inflation rate in Europe and the United States rose to 13 percent in 1974, fell back to 8 percent by 1976, and returned to 13 percent in 1979 before gradually falling in the 1980s.

For sub-Saharan Africa, Latin America, and much of Asia, the 1970s and 1980s were catastrophic. Rising energy costs and declining growth rates among the industrialized countries reduced demand and undercut prices for their agricultural and mineral exports, while their own energy bills went up like everyone else's. In these regions economic growth virtually stopped, and in a few cases ran into negative territory. Governments borrowed extravagantly, inflation soared, and poverty worsened.

Political change accompanied economic uncertainty. China, having survived the Great Leap Forward and the Cultural Revolution, abandoned Mao's effort to combine economic development and egalitarianism when new leaders after Mao's death made economic growth rather than ideological purity their priority. Events in Iran revealed the power of religious fundamentalism when Iranians overthrew the shah in 1979 and instituted a government led by clerics determined to rule according to Islamic law. Conservative governments in Great Britain under Margaret Thatcher and in the United States under Ronald Reagan cut taxes, fought union demands for higher wages, and sought to eliminate or at least slow the growth of entitlement programs established in the 1960s and 1970s. Throughout much of Latin America and Africa, dozens of democratic governments gave way to dictatorships.

Meanwhile the Cold War continued. Despite U.S. involvement in Vietnam, Soviet-U.S. relations improved during the 1970s. The two superpowers settled disputes over Berlin in 1971, agreed to limit the production of antiballistic missiles in 1972, and along with other European states accepted existing national boundaries in Europe and promised to protect human rights by signing the Helsinki Accords in 1975. By the early 1980s, however, détente, or accommodation, between the Soviet Union and the United States was in shambles, the victim of Soviet meddling in Africa and the Soviet invasion of Afghanistan in 1979. It was dealt a further blow by the policies of President Reagan, who, after taking office in 1981, boosted military spending, funded research on the "Star Wars" antimissile system, and denounced the Soviet Union with a vehemence not heard since the 1950s.

Then in 1985 the new premier of the Soviet Union, Mikhail Gorbachev, announced plans to rejuvenate Soviet communism by introducing policies based on glasnost, or openness, and perestroika, or restructuring. To the world's shock, this step led not to communism's revival but its demise. By 1991, communist regimes had disappeared throughout Eastern Europe, the Soviet Union had collapsed, and the Cold War, which had dominated international diplomacy for over four decades, had ended.

◆

New Forces in the International Economy

Two developments in the 1970s and 1980s provide evidence of fundamental changes in the world economy. The first was the emergence of the Organization of Petroleum Exporting Countries (OPEC) as a major economic force. During the 1970s, OPEC's twelve Asian, African, and Latin American members, whose economies had been largely controlled and manipulated by Western powers, shocked the world when they orchestrated a quadrupling of the price of oil in 1974 and then quadrupled it again in 1979. The second was the "economic miracle" that took place first in Japan and somewhat later in South Korea, Taiwan, Hong Kong, and Singapore. These "Asian Tigers" suddenly emerged as centers of international finance and leading exporters of steel, automobiles, electronic goods, and consumer items. The Pacific Rim took its place alongside the United States and Western Europe as a major force in the world economy.

The emergence of OPEC took place against a background of soaring demand for oil during the postwar boom. World oil consumption grew from approximately 3.9 billion barrels in 1953 to 20.4 billion barrels in 1973. Nonetheless, prices stayed low, mainly because they were set by huge oil companies, such as Texaco, Mobil, Standard Oil of California, British Petroleum, and the Royal Dutch/Shell Group, that were interested in keeping demand high and paying the oil producers as little as possible. Oil-producing nations sought higher prices, and in 1960 five of them, Iran, Iraq, Saudi Arabia, Venezuela, and Kuwait, founded OPEC to achieve this goal. Although membership in the 1960s and early 1970s expanded to include Qatar, Libya, Indonesia, Abu Dhabi, Ecuador, Gabon, and Nigeria, in 1973 the price of oil measured against inflation was still only half of what it had been in the early 1950s.

This changed dramatically in late 1973 and 1974 when a group of Arab oil producers — Saudi Arabia, Iraq, Kuwait, and the United Arab Emirates — decided to use oil as a political weapon after the outbreak in October 1973 of the fourth Arab-Israeli war, known as the Yom Kippur War in Israel and the Ramadan War in Muslim countries. To support Egypt and Syria, these Arab states voted to stop oil deliveries to the United States, which was sending the Israelis weapons, and the Netherlands, which had made available its airfields to Israel-bound U.S. supply planes. This step, combined with across-the-board cuts in production, drove up the price of oil to $10 a barrel, a level that OPEC nations were able to maintain throughout the 1970s and push even higher after the outbreak of the Iran-Iraq war in 1979.

As gasoline prices soared in the United States during the 1970s, many Americans traded in their gas-guzzling Detroit-made Fords, Chevrolets, and Chryslers for fuel-efficient Japanese Toyotas, Datsuns, and Hondas. The fact that twenty years earlier the Japanese auto industry had hardly existed underscores the rapid transformation of postwar Japan's economy. After their nation's defeat in World War II, Japanese business and government leaders perceived that Japan's economic recovery depended on producing manufactured goods not just for domestic and Asian markets, but for export throughout the world. With a probusiness government, an industrious and well-educated work force, high rates of savings, a talented entrepreneurial class, and an intense competitive spirit, the Japanese succeeded spectacularly. They moved from steel and shipbuilding in the 1950s to electronics, computers, consumer goods, and automobiles in the 1960s and 1970s. By the mid 1980s Japan had trade surpluses of more than $80 billion a year and one of the world's highest standards of living. By then South Korea, Taiwan, Singapore, and Hong Kong also had emerged as financial and industrial powers, and many commentators began to speak of the late twentieth century as the dawn of the Pacific Era in the world's economy.

Middle Eastern Politics and the Price of Oil

92 ◆ *Mana Saeed al-Otaiba,* THE ARAB OIL WEAPON

Abu Dhabi and Dabai, two small Arab sheikhdoms on the Persian Gulf that were for most of the nineteenth and twentieth centuries part of the British protectorate known as the Trucial States, joined five other sheikhdoms in 1971 to form the United Arab Emirates (UAE). Once the center of a thriving pearl industry, the sparsely populated sheikhdoms had fallen on hard times after cultured pearls were introduced into the world market in the 1920s. In the 1950s, however, British and French firms discovered oil in Abu Dhabi and Dabai, and within a decade annual exports totaled approximately seven hundred thousand barrels. By the late 1960s Abu Dhabi had joined OPEC, and its ruler, Sheikh Shakhbut ibn Sultan al Nahyan, whose annual income in the 1930s had amounted to $150,000, was receiving oil royalties in the range of $84 million per year. That was nothing compared to the $8 billion in annual royalties received by his successor, Sheikh Zaid, in the early 1980s.

With its founding in 1971, the United Arab Emirates assumed Abu Dhabi's place in OPEC and generally sided with Saudi Arabia in disputes over production and pricing. Along with Saudi Arabia's long-time oil minister, Ahmad Zaki Yamani, the UAE's director of petroleum affairs Mana Saeed al-Otaiba became a spokesperson for the Arab oil-producing states, especially during and after the oil crisis of 1973 to 1974. In the following comments from speeches in 1974 and early 1975, Mana Saeed al-Otaiba describes the Arabs' use of the "oil weapon" in the wake of the Arab-Israeli war of 1973.

QUESTIONS FOR ANALYSIS

1. How does Mana Saeed al-Otaiba interpret the strategy of the major oil companies in their dealings with OPEC after the outbreak of the fourth Arab-Israeli war?
2. According to Mana Saeed al-Otaiba, who actually made the decision to limit oil production and halt the sale of oil to the United States and the Netherlands?
3. What did the Arab oil producers hope to accomplish by the steps they took in late 1973 and 1974? According to Mana Saeed al-Otaiba, how successful were they?
4. What does Mana Saeed al-Otaiba see as the main deficiency of the international economy? How, in his view, will the steps taken by the oil-producing nations help eliminate it?

On 6 October 1973 the Holy Ramadan war broke out. . . .

By coincidence, on that day OPEC met in Vienna to consider the question of oil prices. . . . After a meeting between the Arabian Gulf oil ministers and the oil companies' delegation at which the ministers set out their countries' stand on the price issue, the oil company representatives asked for time to consult their principals and promised to return to the negotiations after two days. After this deadline elapsed and the companies had asked for another one-day delay, their negotiators finally came back late bringing with them a new request for a further adjournment of 15 days. When they were asked to meet the ministers to discuss the third request for postponement, they refused to attend and left Vienna suddenly without informing their fellow-negotiators. Faced with this improper conduct the Arabian Gulf oil ministers had no alternative but to settle their business themselves. They agreed to meet in Kuwait on 16 October to solve the oil price problem. . . .

All this happened in the blazing heat of the Ramadan war. What happened in Vienna was not far away from what was happening in Sinai and Golan. The oil companies grasped this organic link between what was happening in the two arenas, the arena of war in the Middle East and the arena of oil in Vienna. So the companies' trickery and repeated requests for delays

had something behind it — temporising and waiting until the result of the war going on in the Middle East would be clear. The oil companies were waiting for the war to end as wars had ended in the past, with an Arab defeat, so that the Arab negotiating position would be weak and they could be beaten in the oil arena as they were beaten in the arena of war. . . .

16 October arrived and the . . . Arabian Gulf oil ministers met in Kuwait and decided to fix oil prices themselves.

Since that day a new principle has been established in the oil industry: oil pricing must be decided upon by the legal owners of the oil.

On the following day 17 October, the Arab oil ministers met in Kuwait to employ the full weight of the oil weapon in the service of the battle. . . .

After a long debate lasting more than seven hours continuously, agreement was reached among the Arab oil producers — except for Iraq which withdrew from the meeting — on adopting . . . a comprehensive production cut by at least five per cent. The Abu Dhabi delegation had its own view of this decision but agreed to it so as to preserve an Arab consensus. Abu Dhabi felt that it was essential to take a more effective measure against those states which showed open hostility to the Arab nation, especially the USA which had opened its war arsenal to Israel and provided it with the most modern weapons, as well as with military experts and with volunteers. . . .

Shortly after the meeting broke up we called a press conference at which we announced Abu Dhabi's decision to cut off oil supplies to the US in line with special instructions from His Highness Shaikh Zayed bin Sultan Al Nahayan. . . . This initiative taken by Abu Dhabi elicited a big reaction both in the Arab world and on the international scene. In the event the rest of the Arab states followed Abu Dhabi's example three days later and cut off oil supplies to the US. . . .

In taking this decision Abu Dhabi was motivated by its belief that the Arabs must win this battle, and that if they were defeated this time they would have nothing left to count on for the future. All Abu Dhabi's actions sprang from its belief in Arab rights, and its belief that justice must prevail in the world. This step was truly a pioneering move, surprising enemies as much as it surprised friends. It was the embodiment of the fortitude of the right, however small, against the wrong, however great, in a world where the powerful rule. . . .

◆ ◆

. . . I shall try here to summarise the effects which followed from the Arab use of the oil weapon and which led to the revelation of reality to many in the world who had been blinded and deceived by lying Zionist propaganda.

(1) The Arabs discovered themselves through their use of the oil weapon and realised the extent of the power represented by this weapon in their possession if it is well used.

(2) The whole world understood the extent of the economic power which lies in the hands of the Arabs. If they act together, which they actually did in using the oil weapon, they can influence the world balance of power and oblige the world to understand their problems and respect their feelings. This led many states to seek to win the friendship of the Arabs.

(3) There is no doubt the consensus among the Arab states in using the oil weapon hastened

their advent as a major economic and political force in the world, because they are the major source of crude oil and gas, both as regards production and reserves, and an emerging repository of financial power.

(4) Through oil the Arabs were able to isolate Israel politically from the world, win more friends and influence a number of other states which used to side with Israel. This has revealed the falsehood of the lies with which Israel used to deceive a large number of small peace-loving states, lies which kept repeating that it was the Arabs who were calling for war and who were striving to exterminate the Israelis and throw them into the sea. These lies did not last long; it soon became clear that this artificial mini-state represented the cancer which was spreading and expanding at every opportunity at the expense of the neighbouring Arab states.

(5) More than 30 African states broke off diplomatic relations with Israel when it became clear to them that the Arab cause was the cause of right and justice. Here it was up to the Arab oil-exporting states to give freely in order to reward friendly African states collectively and individually. The sum of $150 million was allotted in 1974 for aid to African states which were affected by the rise in oil prices. . . .

(6) A number of oil-exporting countries have gained great material benefits as a result of the Arab use of the oil weapon. The output cutback and embargo measures have resulted in a world oil supply shortage and a feeling on the part of many consumer states that they must try to obtain sufficient crude oil to assure their needs for a reasonable period of time. . . . In these circumstances industrial states vied with each other to pay high prices for non-Arab oil. . . . We find it necessary to mention this, to point out the positive role of the Arab oil weapon in respect of non-Arab oil-exporting states, which we Arabs affect and are affected by. . . .

(8) As for the USA, they were exposed to the power of the Arab oil weapon from the first moment because of the unlimited support

they gave to Israel during the Ramadan war. After the embargo on Arab oil exports to the USA had been imposed, American public opinion, which had been deceived by Zionist propaganda, began to shift from an anti-Arab position to one of understanding for the Arab position. . . .

◆ ◆

The economic problems the world faces today, under whose weight the world economy is groaning and which are undermining the development of the Third World . . ., go far beyond the subject of oil. This is the contrary of what is alleged by some industrial states which lay the whole blame for the current economic crisis on oil and oil prices. . . .

The faulty structure of the world economy has rested for long centuries on a division of the world into two — a rich world and a poor world, a world which enjoys everything and a world deprived of everything, a world which plunders wealth to build civilisation, industry and progress, and another which is oppressed. . . . This is the situation that the OPEC states

have grasped and refused to accept, and are now endeavouring to correct. . . .

Some of the industrial countries, the main oil consumers, reacted by spreading much propaganda to the effect that the oil-exporting countries were undermining the world economies, forgetting that they had previously exploited these states and blocked their development, and also forgetting that we also are part of that world economy and belong to the international family. . . . The state of the world economy is like a man who has broken his leg, and the bone has been set in a crooked position; all the doctor can do is break the crooked bone again and set it true, despite the pain the new break caused, this being undoubtedly best for the patient. That is the story of the world economy. The industrial countries were alarmed in case another group of primary producers might also organise their ranks in a club like OPEC and call for fair prices for the resources and raw materials they produce. This state of affairs would not, of course, please some of the industrial countries which have grown used to getting these primary products cheap. . . .

Japan's Economic Miracle

◆

93 ◆ *Akio Morita,* MADE IN JAPAN

After World War II, a former Japanese naval lieutenant, Akio Morita, and a defense contractor, Masaru Ibuka, borrowed $500 to form the Tokyo Telecommunications Engineering Corporation. With plans to produce consumer goods for the domestic market, they built a small factory in Tokyo and began to manufacture electric rice cookers. In their first year they had sales of $7500 and a profit of $300. With an infusion of capital from Morita's father, the head of a family-owned sake brewery, the firm moved into consumer electronics with the marketing of a tape recorder in Japan in the early 1950s. Later in the decade the firm burst into the international market with a miniaturized radio that used transistors, tiny new capacitors developed by Bell Laboratories in the United States, rather than electronic tubes. Named Sony from the Latin word *sonus* for sound, the radios became so popular that Morita and Ibuka changed their company's name to the Sony Corporation in 1958. Beginning in the 1960s, the corporation branched out into chemicals, insurance, the recording industry, and real estate while introducing a stream of successful new products, including transistorized tape recorders, videotape cameras and recorders, and color televisions. Although growth slowed in the 1970s, Sony rebounded in the 1980s and 1990s with new products such as the Walkman, digital audiotape, and compact disks and with acquisitions such as the purchase of Columbia Films from Coca-Cola in 1989 for $3.4 billion.

During the 1980s Morita, having presided over one of Japan's most spectacular economic success stories, relinquished some of his duties to younger men. This gave him time to write his memoirs, which were published in English in 1986 with the title *Made in Japan.* In the book Morita discusses the unique features of Japanese business philosophy, underscoring the differences between Japanese and American attitudes and practices. It became required reading in many U.S. business schools before the Japanese economy entered a prolonged slump in the early 1990s. Morita died of pneumonia in 1999 at the age of seventy-eight.

QUESTIONS FOR ANALYSIS

1. According to Morita, what were some of the obstacles Japan had to overcome to build its economy in the postwar years?
2. Why does Morita believe that good employee-employer relations are the key to business success?
3. What are some of the steps taken by the Sony Corporation to ensure good employee relations?
4. According to Morita, what are some of the differences between business executives in Japan and in the United States?
5. Why does Morita believe that Japanese business methods and philosophy are superior to those of Americans?

SELLING TO THE WORLD

Although our company was still small and we saw Japan as quite a large and potentially active market, it was the consensus among Japanese industrialists that a Japanese company must export goods in order to survive. With no natural resources except our people's energy, Japan had no alternative. And so it was natural for us to look to foreign markets. Besides, as business prospered, it became obvious to me that if we did not set our sights on marketing abroad, we would not grow to be the kind of company Ibuka and I had envisioned. We wanted to change the image of Japanese goods as poor in quality, and, we reasoned, if you are going to sell a high-quality, expensive product, you need an affluent market, and that means a rich, sophisticated country. Today, over 99 percent of all Japanese homes have color TV; more than 98 percent have electric refrigerators and washing machines; and the penetration rate for tape recorders and stereo systems is between 60 and 70 percent. But in 1958, the year after we produced our "pocketable" transistorized radio, only 1 percent of Japanese homes had a TV set, only 5 percent had a washing machine, and only two-tenths of 1 percent had an electric refrigerator. Fortunately, the Japanese economy began to grow vigorously from the mid-fifties onward.

Double-digit increases in the gross national product and low inflation gave a great boost to consumer spending. Many people say Japan's true postwar era really began in 1955, the year we introduced the first transistorized radio in Japan. The country's GNP grew, amazingly, by 10.8 percent. Japanese households needed everything, and because of the high savings rate, which in those days was over 20 percent, the people could afford to buy. So with good and growing markets at home and potential markets abroad, the world was beginning to look bright to us. . . .

We were doing well, although we still had tough competition getting our name known in Japan, where brand consciousness and brand loyalty are very high. Overseas we were all on an even footing. And perhaps we were in a better position abroad than anybody. Quality Japanese consumer goods were virtually unknown before the war. The image of anything marked "Made in Japan" that had been shipped abroad before the war was very low. Most people in the United States and Europe, I learned, associated Japan with paper umbrellas, kimonos, toys, and cheap trinkets. In choosing our name we did not purposely try to hide our national identity — after all, international rules require you to state the country of origin on your product — but we certainly did not want to emphasize it and run the risk of being rejected before we could demonstrate the quality of our products. But I must confess that in the early days we printed the line "Made in Japan" as small as possible, once too small for U.S. Customs, which made us make it bigger on one product.

ON MANAGEMENT

There is no secret ingredient or hidden formula responsible for the success of the best Japanese companies. No theory or plan or government policy will make a business a success; that can only be done by people. The most important mission for a Japanese manager is to develop a healthy relationship with his employees, to create a familylike feeling within the corporation, a feeling that employees and managers share the same fate. Those companies that are most successful in Japan are those that have managed to create a shared sense of fate among all employees, what Americans call labor and management, and the shareholders.

I have not found this simple management system applied anywhere else in the world, and yet we have demonstrated convincingly, I believe, that it works. For others to adopt the Japanese system may not be possible because they may be too tradition-bound, or too timid. The emphasis on people must be genuine and sometimes very bold and daring, and it can even be quite risky. But in the long run — and I emphasize this — no matter how good or successful you are or how clever or crafty, your business and its future are in the hands of the people you hire. To put it a bit more dramatically, the fate of your business is actually in the hands of the youngest recruit on the staff.

That is why I make it a point personally to address all of our incoming college graduates each year. The Japanese school year ends in March, and companies recruit employees in their last semester, so that before the end of the school year they know where they are going. They take up their new jobs in April. I always gather these new recruits together at headquarters in Tokyo, where we have an introductory or orientation ceremony. This year I looked out at more than seven hundred young, eager faces and gave them a lecture, as I have been doing for almost forty years. . . .

The new employees are getting their first direct and sobering view of what it will be like in the business world. I tell them what I think is important for them to know about the company and about themselves. I put it this way to the last class of entering employees:

"We did not draft you. This is not the army, so that means you have voluntarily chosen Sony. This is your responsibility, and normally if you join this company we expect that you will stay for the next twenty or thirty years.

"Nobody can live twice, and the next twenty or thirty years is the brightest period of your life. You only get it once.

"When you leave the company thirty years from now or when your life is finished, I do not want you to regret that you spent all those years here. That would be a tragedy. I cannot stress the point too much that this is your responsibility to yourself. So I say to you, the most important thing in the next few months is for you to decide whether you will be happy or unhappy here. So even though we recruited you, we cannot, as management, or a third party, make other people happy; happiness must be created yourself." . . .

The concept of lifetime employment arose when Japanese managers and employees both realized that they had much in common and that they had to make some long-range plans. The laws made it difficult legally, and expensive, to fire anybody, but that didn't seem like such a bad idea, since workers were badly in need of work, and struggling businesses needed employees who would remain loyal. Without class disputes, despite the Communist and Socialist party propaganda, the Japanese, who are a homogeneous people, were able to cooperate to provide for their common welfare. I have often said that the Japanese company has become very much a social security organization.

In the postwar era, the tax laws make it useless for a company to pay an executive a lot of money, because the graduated tax rises sharply very quickly, and you are very soon in the highest bracket. Company-paid amenities such as worker dormitories and allowances for commuting, for example, help workers make up for the tax system. Tax shelters and tax avoidance are virtually unknown in Japan. Today, the salary for a top management official is rarely more than seven or eight times that of an entry-level junior executive trainee. This means Japan has no multimillion-dollar brass, and companies give no huge executive bonuses, no stock options, no deferred income, no golden parachutes, and therefore the psychological, as well as the

real, gap between employees is narrower than in other countries. There may be some exceptions to the general rule, but I am sure they are few.

What we in industry learned in dealing with people is that people do not work just for money and that if you are trying to motivate, money is not the most effective tool. To motivate people, you must bring them into the family and treat them like respected members of it. Granted, in our one-race nation this might be easier to do than elsewhere, but it is still possible if you have an educated population. . . .

AMERICAN AND JAPANESE STYLES

But the differences between U.S. and Japanese companies go beyond the cultural. If you ask a Japanese executive, "What is your most important responsibility?" he will invariably say that continued employment and improving the livelihood of the workers is at or near the top of the list. In order to do that, the company must make a profit. Making a profit will never be at the top of the list. Most of the American business executives I know put the highest priority on return to the investors or this year's profit. They have the responsibility because the investors gave it to them, and to stay in their jobs they have to continue to keep the investors happy. The board of directors represents the investors, and if top management fails to give the return the investors feel they need, he will be fired. For that reason he is entitled to use the factory and the machinery of the company, and also the workers, as tools to accomplish his aim. This can be detrimental.

Visiting an American television plant in the Midwest a few years ago, I commented to the manager that I thought he really needed to buy some more modern equipment in order to improve the company's productivity. He shocked me when he told me that his compensation was based on the company's financial performance and that he was not going to do anything, like making long-range investments, that might cut his compensation for the sake of the next manager who would be along in a year or so. . . .

Generally, in the United States, management's attitude toward the labor force and even the lower-level executives is very hierarchical, much more so than in Japan, an Oriental country where Westerners always expect to see such hierarchies. When I visited the Illinois television assembly plant of Motorola, one of the first things I noticed was that the offices were air-conditioned, but out on the shop floor it was stifling, people were dripping with sweat, and big noisy fans were blowing the hot air around. The workers were plainly uncomfortable, and I thought, "How can you get quality work from people laboring under such conditions? And what kind of loyalty can they be expected to show to the big bosses in their cool offices!" In Japan people often used to say that the shop floor where the goods were made was always more comfortable than the workers' homes. That has changed as the Japanese workers have become more affluent, and air-conditioning has become more common at home. By the middle of 1984, more than half of Japan's homes and apartments had it. But back in the late fifties, we air-conditioned our factories before the offices.

Amenities are not of great concern to management in Japan. The struggle for an office with a carpet, a water carafe, and an original oil painting on the wall is not common. Just recently a U.S. company, the maker of highly complex computerized graphics equipment, formed a joint venture with a Japanese company and the Japanese partner said to his foreign associate: "We would like you to design the showroom, but please allow us to design the office space upstairs." It seemed reasonable enough. The showroom was beautifully appointed, with soft lighting and comfortable chairs for visitors and clients. The equipment was highlighted using modern display techniques, and there were video demonstrations and elegant four-color brochures on the company and its equipment. Upstairs, the entire office staff was housed in one big open room without partitions, just a grid of desks with telephones, filing cabinets and other necessary furniture in a simple, very Spartan arrangement. The U.S. partner raised his eyebrows, and his Japanese colleague explained, "If Japanese clients come into the office of a new and struggling company and see plush carpet and private offices and too much comfort, they become suspicious that this company is not serious, that it is devoting too much thought and company resources to management's comfort, and perhaps not enough to the product or to potential customers. If we are successful after one year, we might put up low partitions. After two or three years, we might give the top executive a closed office. But for now we have to all be reminded that we are struggling together to make this company a success."

◆

Environmentalism, Economic Development, and Social Justice

By the early 1990s, it was estimated that five million British, five million Germans, and close to fourteen million Americans, about one in every seven adults, were members of some sort of environmental organization. Such statistics are one indicator of the broad support for environmental causes that emerged in Western industrialized nations during the 1970s and 1980s. Further evidence is provided by the emergence in the United States and Western Europe of proenvironment "green" political parties that in France, Sweden, Austria, and especially West Germany have had success in national elections. In the U.S. presidential election of 2000, Green Party candidate Ralph Nader received only 3 percent of the vote, but by attracting the support of voters who might otherwise have voted for Democrat Al Gore, may well have tipped the election in favor of the Republican candidate, George W. Bush.

The strongest indication of environmentalism's strength in the 1970s and 1980s was its impact on legislation and public policy. In the United States in the early 1970s, President Nixon signed laws on clean air and water, pesticides, hazardous chemicals, and endangered species, and created the Environmental Protection Agency to enforce them. Many European states in the 1970s also established agencies and passed laws that made environmental management and protection part of their governments' responsibilities. Despite internal divisions and organized opposition to many of its programs, the environmental movement became an important cultural and political force in the Western democracies during the 1970s and 1980s.

Nothing comparable happened outside the West. The environmental record of communist states, for example, was abysmal. With the Soviet Union providing a model, communist governments sought economic development at all costs, with an emphasis on huge public works projects, mammoth factories, and giant agricultural collectives. China experimented with small-scale rural factories during the Great Leap Forward, but the initiative failed disastrously, and in any case was inspired by political ideology, not environmental awareness. Year after year communist plant managers struggled to meet state-imposed production goals, oblivious to the environmental calamities they were causing. The explosion of the Soviet Union's Chernobyl nuclear reactor in 1986 was only the most notorious of literally thousands of environmental missteps that made the Soviet Union and Eastern Europe a land of dying forests, noxious air, polluted rivers, and high rates of cancer, lung disease, and infections.

Economic development also took precedence over the environment in the less developed regions of Africa, Latin America, and Asia. For countries desperately trying to modernize their economies, curbing development to preserve energy supplies, protect rain forests, or meet environmental standards set by experts from affluent societies had little appeal. At the environmental conference sponsored by the United Nations in Stockholm in 1972, the Indian prime minister Indira Gandhi told the delegates that if pollution was the price of progress, then India wanted pollution.

Despite the prodevelopment stance of most governments, environmentalism had some backing in developing countries during the 1970s and 1980s. These movements often found support among poor people whose livelihoods were threatened by polluting factories, commercial logging, oil drilling, or large dams. Examples include efforts in the mid 1980s by the Penan people of Malaysia to halt commercial logging in their homeland through blockades and demonstrations; peasant protests in Thailand in the late 1970s to put an end to the conversion of natural forest into plantations; numerous grassroots campaigns in India to stop large-scale dam projects, protect forests, and limit pollution from factories and mines; and efforts by Brazilian rubber tappers and indigenous peoples to block and reverse the destruction of the Amazon rain forest.

Such movements on behalf of environmental protection and social justice received worldwide publicity and support from European and U.S. environmental groups. But they also encountered resistance in their own countries from state officials, developers, and foreign corporations. It was an unequal struggle, in which proponents of "environmentalism of the poor" won occasional battles but had little success changing their leaders' convictions that economic development was more important than preserving the environment.

Saving the Rain Forest in Brazil
❖

94 ◆ Chico Mendes, *FIGHT FOR THE FOREST*

With its headwaters in the Peruvian Andes just one hundred miles from South America's Pacific coast, the Amazon River stretches four thousand miles across Brazil before it flows into the Atlantic Ocean. Along with its tributaries, it drains 1.2 billion acres of land and contains the world's largest tropical forest area. Beginning in the 1960s, when the Brazilian government began to construct thousands of miles of roads in the region, the Amazon territory became a magnet for landless peasants and, more importantly, for loggers, miners, land speculators, and cattle ranchers. As a result, deforestation occurred at a staggering rate. In thirty years almost 10 percent of the rain forest, approximately 150 million acres, was destroyed.

The devastation of the Amazon rain forest has become a major concern of environmentalists around the globe, who are convinced that it has grave implications for problems of global warming and species extinction, among others. At first, however, the struggle to limit development in the region was carried on by poor people who lived in the region itself and made their living by harvesting forest products such as rubber, Brazil nuts, jute, and various palm tree products. Although many of these people had been living in the region for generations, they lacked legal titles to their lands and were expelled when ranchers arrived and turned forest into pasture.

Resistance by rubber tappers (individuals who tap rubber trees to collect latex for sale) was organized by Chico Mendes (1944–1988), a rubber tapper himself from the westernmost Brazilian state of Acre. In 1975 he helped found the Federation of Rural Workers of Acre, whose members sought to block the destruction of the forest through *empates*, or "standoffs," in which they formed nonviolent human blockades around forest areas threatened with clearing. The movement spread to other parts of Brazil, and in 1985 rubber tappers from the entire Amazon region formed the National Council of Rubber Tappers. With the support of the region's indigenous peoples, they demanded the establishment of "extractive reserves," lands protected from development on which rural workers could continue to tap rubber trees and gather fruits, nuts, and fibers. Mendes's campaign also attracted international support. Between 1985 and 1988 he made several trips to the United States, where, with the backing of environmental and human rights organizations, he lobbied Congress and the World Bank to withhold funds for Amazon development projects and support his proposals for extractive reserves. He was now a figure of international prominence, and also a target of numerous death threats from ranchers. On December 22, 1988, he momentarily left the protection of his bodyguards to step out on his back porch, where he was assassinated by the son of a local rancher.

Just weeks before his murder, Mendes granted an extensive interview to an English friend and supporter Tony Gross, who published the interview as a book, *Fight for the Forest*, in mid 1989. In the following passages Mendes discusses the sources of support and opposition for his movement.

During the 1990s the Brazilian government, with support from the World Bank, established extractive reserves in part of the rain forest. But deforestation continues.

QUESTIONS FOR ANALYSIS

1. According to Mendes, who are the allies of the rubber tappers in their campaign to halt deforestation in the Amazon?
2. What are the main sources of opposition to the rubber tappers' campaign against deforestation?
3. How does Mendes view his opponents' arguments and tactics? How does Mendes respond to these arguments? How did he and supporters respond to their opponents' tactics?
4. What vision does Mendes have for the future of the Amazon region?
5. In your opinion, was the environment or social justice Mendes's major concern?

[EXTRACTIVE RESERVES]

We accepted that the Amazon could not be turned into some kind of sanctuary that nobody could touch. On the other hand, we knew it was important to stop the deforestation that is threatening the Amazon and all human life on the planet. We felt our alternative should involve preserving the forest, but it should also include a plan to develop the economy. So we came up with the idea of extractive reserves.

What do we mean by an extractive reserve? We mean the land is under public ownership but the rubber tappers and other workers that live on that land should have the right to live and work there. I say 'other workers' because there are not only rubber tappers in the forest. In our area, rubber tappers also harvest brazil nuts, but in other parts of the Amazon there are people who earn a living solely from harvesting nuts, while there are others who harvest babacu[1] and jute. . . .

. . . A sustainable fishing industry could be developed, exploiting the resource in a rational way. The enormous variety of plants with medicinal properties in this forest could prove very important to the country, if only some research was done. . . . I believe if this happened,

---

[1] A species of palm tree. Its nuts are a source of palm oil. The husks are used as fuel, its leaves are made into fiber for making hats and baskets, and the juice from its stalks is used to make a fermented drink.

and if the government took it all seriously, then in ten years the Amazon region could be very rich and have an important role in the national economy. . . .

[EMPATES — "STANDOFFS"]

. . . The *empates* are organised in the following way. When a community is threatened by deforestation it gets in touch with other communities in the area. They all get together in a mass meeting in the middle of the forest and organise teams of people to take the lead in confronting the workers cutting down the trees with their chainsaws and so on — all this in a peaceful but organised way. These teams try and convince the workers employed by the landowners to leave the area. The rubber tappers also dismantle the camps used by those workers to force them out. We are often attacked by the police because the landowners always apply to the courts for police protection. The judicial system has always done what the landowners wanted and sent in the police and there have been a lot of arrests.

One important point is that the whole community — men, women and children — takes part in the *empate*. The women stay at the front to prevent the police from shooting us. The police know if they open fire, they will kill women and children. . . .

[SUPPORTERS AND ENEMIES]

We . . . wanted to seek out the leaders of the Indian peoples in Acre and discuss how to unite our resistance movements, especially since Indians and rubber tappers have been at odds with each other for centuries. In Acre the leaders of the rubber tappers and Indian peoples met and concluded that neither of us was to blame for

this. The real culprits were the rubber estate owners, the bankers and all the other powerful interest groups that had exploited us both.

People understood this very quickly, and from the beginning of 1986 the alliance of the peoples of the forest got stronger and stronger. . . .

. . . Our biggest assets are the international environmental lobby and the international press. I'm afraid we have had more support from abroad than from people in Brazil, and the opposite should be the case. It was only after international recognition and pressure that we started to get support from the rest of Brazil. . . .

. . . We have had a lot to do with the Church but there have been clashes at times, because although the Church has an important role in our struggle, it is only prepared to go so far. For example it has been very difficult about our interest in linking up with political parties. . . . We have good links with the Prelacy[2] of Acre-Purus, but things are much worse in the Juruá Valley where the Church is very conservative. We have a good relationship with the Church at Carauari, another region in the state of the Amazonas. I think the links we've had with the Church have been positive and we've been able to build up a working relationship which benefits both the Church and the rubber tappers. . . .

. . . People in the cities have always ignored us. However, since the CNS[3] was set up we have begun to get some support, for example from Acre University, which is quite an important political institution. We know the great majority of professors in the university either support the UDR[4] or are very conservative, but we hope to get some support from the new Rector there. Student support has been a bit unsteady but it's increasing now the Greens[5] are getting organised in Acre.

We have found it very difficult to get proper legal assistance. . . .

---

[2]The bishop and other churchmen who administer a diocese.
[3]Conselho Nacional dos Seringueiros (National Rubber Tappers' Council), founded in 1985.
[4]Uniao Democratica Ruralistica (Democratic Rural Union), an organization of landowners founded in 1985, originally

to oppose land reform legislation being considered by the National Congress.
[5]Partido Verde (Green Party), a political party dedicated to progressive and environmental causes.

Our union doesn't have enough money to employ a lawyer, but in July 1988 the Institute of Amazon Studies helped us obtain the services of a lawyer from Paraná, Genésio Felipe. . . . He covers the whole of Acre, so he's got a big job on!

I'm afraid we don't get much help from the lawyers round here. There are dozens of lawyers in Acre but they are all the children of landowners and other sectors of society that are against the workers' movement.

. . . We know we face powerful opposition. As well as the landowners and businessmen who dominate the Amazon region, we are up against the power of those who voted against land reform in the Constituent Assembly.[6] The voting power of these people in Congress has been a problem for us and has encouraged the growth of the right-wing landowners' movement, the Rural Democratic Union. . . . The defeat of the land reform proposal was a big victory for the landowners and land speculators. Now, since the establishment of the UDR in Acre, we've got a real fight on our hands. . . .

. . . We know, through people who have been to UDR meetings here, that their aim is to destroy the Xapuri[7] union by striking at the grassroots organisations of the Xapuri rubber tappers. They think if they can defeat Xapuri they can impose their terms on the whole state and further afield in the Amazon region as well. . . . In this fight, our only defence is the pressure put on the authorities by Brazilian society and the international scientific community. . . . There was a time when the state government seemed to be paying a lot of attention to environmental problems and to the rubber tappers. But we soon realised it was just putting on a show of defending the environment so the international banks and other international organisations would approve its development projects.

We can't see how the authorities can say they defend the ecological system while at the same time deploying police to protect those who are destroying the forest. That happened, for example, in the case of the Ecuador rubber estate where there were many nut and rubber trees. . . .

. . . People have used all kind of arguments against us. The landowners say we're holding back progress and harming the country's economy. They say rubber is not important to the economy and the future lies with cattle raising. Others say the Amazon is a vast expanse of uninhabited territory and that it should be developed. . . .

The landowners use all the economic power at their disposal. They bribe the authorities; it's common knowledge that they've bought off the IBDF[8] staff in the Amazon region. They also use the law. They request police protection for the workers hired to cut down the trees, saying it is their land so they can do whatever they like with it. They accuse the rubber tappers of trespassing when we try and stop the deforestation. They turn to the courts for support and protection, claiming the land is private property. But the rubber tappers have been here for centuries! . . .

The other tactic the landowners use, and it's a very effective one, is to use hired guns to intimidate us. Our movement's leaders, not just myself but quite a few others as well, have been threatened a lot this year. We are all on the death list of the UDR's assassination squads. . . .

We are sure this will be the landowners' main tactic from now on. They are going to fight our movement with violence and intimidation. There's no doubt in our minds about that.

---

[6] A land reform program that would have redistributed approximately 170,000 square miles of land to small farmers was proposed in 1985; after intense lobbying by landowning and business interests, only a watered-down version was passed.

[7] Xapuri is a city in the Brazilian state of Acre, where Mendes helped found a local chapter of the Rural Workers' Union in the 1970s.

[8] Instituto Brasiliero de Desenvolvimento Florestal (Brazilian Forestry Development Institute), an agency of the federal government with responsibility for enforcing laws relating to forest use.

Yangzi! Yangzi!

◆

95 ◆ *Li Boning and Hou Xueyu,*
VIEWS OF CHINA'S THREE GORGES PROJECT

The Yangzi, which flows 3,700 miles from the mountains of Tibet to the East China Sea, is the longest river in Asia and the fourth longest river in the world. The source of 70 percent of China's rice crop, the site of five cities with populations of two million or more, and a key component of China's transportation system, the Yangzi Valley provides a home for more than three hundred million people. But the river also has been the cause of much devastation and suffering. Despite efforts to control its waters, the Yangzi regularly floods, frequently with catastrophic results. In the twentieth century alone, major floods occurred in 1910, 1911, 1931, 1935, 1949, and 1954. Though none equaled the devastation caused by the inundation of 1870, the flood of 1931 caused approximately thirty thousand deaths, created millions of refugees, and covered an area larger than the state of New York.

To end Yangzi flooding and produce hydroelectric power, Chinese politicians and engineers had eyed the scenic Three Gorges area, some 240 miles west of the city of Wuhan, as a potential dam site ever since Sun Yat-sen first mentioned it in his "Plan to Develop Industry" in 1919. Having been considered and dropped by the Nationalist government of Chiang Kai-shek, the idea was revived by the communists in 1953, just one year before a flood destroyed sections of the cities of Wuhan and Nanjing and killed thousands. For thirty years experts debated the feasibility of the project, the dam's size and placement, the desired depth of the water level above the dam, and plans to relocate displaced people. Many of these issues were still unresolved even as the government in the 1980s developed designs and arranged financing from the World Bank and investors from Sweden, Japan, Canada, and the United States. In 1988 the State Planning Commission approved building a milewide dam that would create a reservoir stretching 350 miles upstream and displacing 1.9 million people. All that was needed was approval from the National People's Congress, the rubber-stamp parliament scheduled to meet in March 1989.

Shockingly, when the congress met, more than two hundred delegates expressed opposition to the project, and once more it was put on hold. A major factor in these developments was the appearance in February 1989 of *Yangzi! Yangzi!*, a collection of letters, essays, and interviews by scientists, hydrologists, and engineers who opposed the dam. The publication of *Yangzi! Yangzi!*, edited by a female journalist, Dai Qing, was an extraordinary event in a society where dissent was rare and the government closely controlled the media. But it derailed the Three Gorges project only temporarily. Once the government had suppressed the prodemocracy movement that crested in the spring of 1989 but was abruptly halted by the Tiananmen Square Massacre in June, it silenced critics of the Three Gorges project. In October 1989, *Yangzi! Yangzi!* was officially banned, and its editor, Dai Qing, was jailed for close to a year. In 1991 the government decided to proceed with the project, which was proposed for approval by the People's National Congress in April 1992. Although 177 delegates voted against the project and 649 abstained, 1,767 delegates voted to approve it. Construction began in 1994.

Both of the following selections appeared in the 1989 edition of *Yangzi! Yangzi!* The first excerpt is from a 1988 speech of Li Boning, a government official who had served as deputy minister of the Ministry of Water Resources and Electric Power. The editor, Dai Qing, included his pro-dam speech to give balance to her book. The second excerpt is from an interview of a distinguished botanist, Hou Xueyu, who opposed the dam, by the journalist Zhu Jianhong.

QUESTIONS FOR ANALYSIS

1. According to Li Boning, what are the potential advantages of going forward with the Three Gorges Dam project?
2. According to Li, what are the weaknesses of the alternative proposals suggested by the opponents of Three Gorges?
3. According to Hou Xueyu, what are the potential environmental dangers of the project?
4. According to Hou, what are the weaknesses of the "solutions" proposed by the dam's advocates to alleviate environmental damage?
5. How does Hou explain the fact that only ten "experts" refused to approve the plan for the Three Gorges Dam project?
6. What are the grounds of the basic disagreement between Li and Hou on the subjects of economic development and the environment?

[LI BONING, "OPINIONS AND RECOMMENDATIONS"]

As a result of numerous experiments and comparisons along with the urgency of the realization of the four modernizations, it is clear that there is no alternative to the Three Gorges project for flood control, electricity, navigation, economic development in the reservoir area, and extensive economic benefits. . . . Thus, harnessing the Yangzi River floods for the economic development of the lower and middle reaches can ensure the security of hundreds of thousands of human lives and millions of *yuan*[1] worth of property. In addition, it can relieve acute electricity shortages and strains on the coal supply for the thermal power plants in central and eastern China. It can also realize the image of the Yangzi River as a golden waterway by permitting a fleet of 10,000-ton ships to sail directly from Wuhan to Chongqing.[2] . . .

Some comrades favor the idea of "tributaries first and the mainstream of the river second" with regard to the construction of reservoirs and hydro-electric power plants along the Yangzi River. They contend that the tributary reservoirs require less investment and offer quicker results than the Three Gorges project, which would

---

[1]The basic unit (Y) of Chinese currency.
[2]Chongqing is approximately six hundred miles from Wuhan.

therefore make the Three Gorges unnecessary. This assumption has no scientific basis at all. . . .

Even if every possible effort is made in this respect, it would not be possible to start construction within a few years' time. In comparison with thermal plants of the same scale, the Three Gorges project could save 40 million tons of coal per year. . . . Given the present overload on railway transportation, relying on thermal plants to meet the demands for electricity in central and eastern China would necessitate laying more than 1,000 kilometers of additional track and opening up of several large-scale coal mines to ensure the supply for the thermal plants. This is not an economical use of time or money. Furthermore, the thermal plants create considerable pollution and coal is a valuable but non-renewable source of energy. . . .

Although nuclear power is a very promising energy source, we need some time to accumulate our own experience in this field, because of its belated development in our country. . . . Besides, the nuclear plants cannot control flooding or improve navigation. . . .

. . . The safety of the Yangzi and Yellow rivers has an important bearing on the nation as a whole. Catastrophic floods could disrupt our overall national economic planning and delay implementation of the four modernizations. At the present time, when the whole nation is working heart and soul to overcome economic difficulties, we could not sustain such a devastating blow. . . .

. . . As for the debate on the Three Gorges project, is it democratic and scientific to listen to the opinions held by the minority alone — to reject the project — without any sound scientific evidence? . . . [Those who oppose the project] simply repeat old slogans of the 1950s, inventing more and more accusatory labels for the achievements made by the scientists and experts, and arbitrarily dismiss them with many irrelevant accusations. It does not conform with the values we have been promoting, that is, respect for knowledge, respect for science and respect for intellectuals.

[HOU XUEYU, "AN ENORMOUS ENVIRONMENTAL DISASTER"]

Zhu Jianhong: Once the Three Gorges dam is built, it will be the largest hydro-electric project in the world. . . . Could you tell us something more about its impact?

Hou Xueyu: The project will submerge 19 counties and more than 400,000 mu[3] of cultivated land, including some of the richest soil along the river basin. Along with the well-known mustard tuber, medicinal herbs and grain, 73,900 mu of orange groves, which produce a net profit of Y1,500 per mu, will be lost. The losses would be at least Y100 million per year, Y1 billion in a decade.

Zhu Jianhong: It has been suggested that, in order to make up for the losses caused by the project, new land for orange groves be opened up on terraced fields.

Hou Xueyu: This is an irresponsible suggestion. After the rich plains are gone, only rocky hills with thin layers of poor topsoil would be left. Those terraced fields could easily be washed away by heavy rainfall in the area. . . .

Zhu Jianhong: However, after the completion of the reservoir, the newly developed water resources could be used as fish ponds, even if the soil were destroyed. So the losses can still be made up. What do you think of this?

Hou Xueyu: I don't think it could be made up in this way. Water and soil are not interchangeable. The rich arable land destroyed by the reservoir could never be reclaimed. Of course, fish could be raised; but, as you know, reservoir construction will destroy some existing fish ponds. . . .

Apart from irreparable damage to the soil, the natural beauty and cultural heritage of the

---

[3]One *mu* equals approximately one eighth of an acre.

area would be permanently damaged as well. I think the Three Gorges is the most beautiful of all the world's gorges. The surrounding areas have many national treasures, some more than 5,000 years old. These include the famous ruins of the ancient Daxi culture,[4] and tombs from the Warring States period [475–221 B.C.], the Eastern Han [25 B.C.–200 A.D.], and the Ming [1368–1622] and Qing [1662–1912] dynasties, most of which are scattered below 180 meters. . . . All of this would be inundated if the reservoir were built, and tourism would suffer incalculable economic losses.

Zhu Jianhong: But some have suggested that these historical relics could always be moved to safer places.

Hou Xueyu: They have, and one even recommended building a museum to display these relics. Even if they could be moved, their authenticity would be destroyed, together with the unique value and cultural significance of the original context. For instance, how would it strike you to compare the on-site remains of a 5,000 year-old tombs with museum reconstructions? . . .

Zhu Jianhong: You mentioned that the construction of the project could destroy fish ponds. Can you elaborate on this point?

Hou Xueyu: The middle reaches of the Yangzi River . . . is one of the major breeding grounds for black, silver, grass and variegated carp. . . .

Breeding requires a water temperature of 18 degrees centigrade. However, with the discharge of reservoir water, that temperature cannot be retained, thereby reducing the breeding period by 20 days. Because of changes in the river-bed after the completion of the reservoir, the quantities of fish would be reduced, eventually resulting in decreased output. Some rare species would be affected too, including Lipotesvexillifer, Chinese paddlefish, and sturgeon. In danger of extinction, these species have been given priority protection by the state. . . .

Furthermore, reservoir construction would bring about changes in water quality and temperature at the mouth of the Yangzi River, and consequently reduce fish production. For instance, anchovies, white bait, hilsa herring, and prawns — all found in semi-salty water — will probably diminish in quantity. . . .

Zhu Jianhong: What other serious effects would the Three Gorges project cause?

Hou Xueyu: Tremendous losses would be inflicted on industry and mining. The plan to set the high-water level at 180 meters would submerge 624 factories, including six major factories in Chongqing. Some mineral resources would also be lost since the mining areas would be below water level after construction of the reservoir. . . .

Zhu Jianhong: Some have said that a new environmental balance can be reached if the programs for population relocation and development of new towns and cities are carefully formulated and properly carried out.

Hou Xueyu: I think the destruction would outweigh a new balance. The saying "man can conquer nature" is unrealistic. . . . Nature will not allow it. If one doesn't consider natural conditions, it is impossible to work out a program beneficial to the people. . . .

Zhu Jianhong: Some feel it inevitable that the environment pay some price for the economic benefits the project will produce. What do you think?

Hou Xueyu: Environmental interests and economic benefits go hand in hand. A better environment will enhance economic benefits. Otherwise, the economic benefits, no matter how high, will have to pay for the environmental damage. In the end, it is the common people who will suffer these losses. It is one-sided and unscientific to consider only the benefits, such as the production of electric power, without counting the cost to the environment and natural resources. . . .

---

[4]In 1959 excavations in Daxi, a village at the east entrance of Qutang Gorge, one of the Three Gorges, revealed ruins of villages estimated to be between 4000 and 6000 years old along with pottery and stone, jade, and bone wares.

Zhu Jianhong: Among the 412 experts who participated in the leading group's assessment, only 10 refused to sign the assessment report, and you are one of the 10.[5]

Hou Xueyu: I was invited only to show the public that people of different opinions were included. There were many others who possess valuable knowledge and insight with regard to this project who were not invited. . . . As far as I know, some experts who were not in agreement with the report, signed it, for various reasons.

Zhu Jianhong: What are the "various reasons"?

Hou Xueyu: That's very complicated. For example, some experts were persuaded by their leaders, who went to their houses to ask their approval. How could they refuse? Some were told that it was already finalized by the Party Central Committee. What was the use of opposing it? So on and so forth.

Zhu Jianhong: Will you still insist on your position?

Hou Xueyu: Certainly yes. . . . Our generation will have made an irrevocable mistake if navigation on the golden waterway is severed.

---

[5]Thirteen "experts' groups" on topics ranging from seismology to ecology to construction had been appointed to evaluate aspects of the project and report to the Leading Group for the Assessment of the Three Gorges Project. Hou had been a member of the Experts' Group on Ecology and Environment.

◆

Religion and Politics in the 1970s and 1980s

During much of the twentieth century, it would not have been unreasonable to conclude that religion was a dying force among the world's peoples. The Islamic Brotherhood's popularity in the Arab world during the 1930s and 1940s and the Hindu-Muslim strife accompanying Indian independence are examples of religion's continuing vigor, but in general organized religion was on the defensive. Avowedly atheist regimes in the Soviet Union and communist China sought to obliterate religious belief and practice altogether. In the West, mainline Protestant churches experienced declining membership and attendance, and the Roman Catholic Church found it increasingly difficult to attract young men to the priesthood. In Turkey, Iran, India, and Indonesia, governments embraced aggressively secularist policies as part of campaigns to modernize their economies, educational systems, and culture.

For all of these reasons, when the people of Iran in 1979 rose up against the Western-oriented, secularist government of Shah Muhammad Reza Pahlavi and instituted an Islamic republic guided by religious values and laws, many considered it an aberration or a sign of a defect within Islam. It is now clear, however, that Iran's revolution was neither. It was one of many examples of religion's continuing vitality and growing political importance in the 1970s and 1980s.

The most striking sign of religion's vigor in the late twentieth century was the phenomenon of religious fundamentalism. Fundamentalists, irrespective of their confessional allegiance, share two basic beliefs. First, they reject modernism, secularism, and all other intellectual and religious tendencies that challenge or belittle religious truths passed down by tradition or set forth in sacred texts. Second, they believe that these religious truths should regulate and inspire all aspects of public and private life.

In the late twentieth century, fundamentalist movements appeared in every major faith and in states at every level of economic development. The religious right in the United States flexed its political muscle at the local, state, and national levels during the 1980s and 1990s; conservative religious Jews in Israel increased their influence on foreign and domestic policy. Fundamentalism was strongest, however, in the Middle East, North Africa, India, and Southeast Asia, where affirmation of traditional religious values provided a way to strengthen cultural identity and limit the influence of foreign, Western-inspired values.

Most fundamentalists are conservative in that they oppose social, political, and cultural changes that threaten practices sanctioned by their religion. But deeply religious individuals also have promoted progressive social and political movements in many parts of the world. A Baptist minister, Martin Luther King, Jr., with broad support from the nation's clergy, led the civil rights movement in the United States. Religious people also played important roles in the struggle against apartheid in South Africa, in various movements on behalf of nuclear disarmament, and even in the events that led to the downfall of communism in Eastern Europe in the 1980s. In Latin America during the 1970s and 1980s, while poverty worsened and much of the region groaned under harsh authoritarian rule, Catholic clergy committed themselves to serving the poor, called for social justice and democracy, and denounced dictatorship. They did so at great risk. No fewer than 850 priests, nuns, and bishops were murdered by right-wing death squads or individual assassins in the 1970s and 1980s. Their martyrdom is convincing evidence of religion's enduring power in the late twentieth century.

Latin American Catholicism and the Theology of Liberation

❖

96 ◆ FINAL DOCUMENT OF THE THIRD GENERAL CONFERENCE OF THE LATIN AMERICAN EPISCOPATE

When some six hundred bishops gathered in Puebla, Mexico, in 1979 for the Third General Conference of the Latin American Episcopate, they sensed that the Latin American Church, with 35 percent of the world's Catholics, was at a crossroads. In the 1960s reformist and even revolutionary currents had emerged among the clergy. This was in part a response to the liberal atmosphere in the broader church after the Second Vatican Council of 1962 and in part an expression of the growing conviction that the Church's indifference to social injustice distorted Christ's teachings and threatened to lose the masses to Marxism or religious apathy. During the 1960s bishops spoke out in favor of land reform; young priests went into urban slums to establish clinics, schools, and self-help organizations; and Catholic intellectuals developed a new "theology of liberation," which centered the Church's mission on ministering to the poor. Their efforts culminated in decisions made at the second conference of Latin American bishops in Medellin, Columbia, in 1968, by which bishops committed the Church to the task of liberating Latin America's poor from economic and social injustice.

This leftward shift provoked a counterreaction in the 1970s. Conservative bishops denounced reformers as more Marxist than Christian, and many Catholics expressed reservations about the clergy's political activism. Conservatives hoped to regain control of the Church at the third Catholic bishops' conference in Puebla in 1979. Well-known liberation theologians were excluded, and conservative bishops drafted a policy statement that, if accepted, would have endorsed capitalism and rejected the clergy's involvement in politics. Remarks by Pope John Paul II, who addressed the opening of the conference, seemed to support the progressives, however, and after two weeks of discussion, the delegates approved a generally progressive statement from which the following excerpts are drawn.

After Puebla, the Latin American Church remained divided. Churchmen in Chile and Brazil continued to speak out against military regimes, and clergy in Central America were still in the forefront of the struggle for social change. Overall, however, conservatives made gains, especially in Argentina and Columbia. This trend was supported by an increasingly conservative Pope John Paul II, who named conservatives as bishops and approved the disciplining of Leonardo Boff, the popular Brazilian liberation theologian, in the mid 1980s. While the Catholic Church struggled to clarify its mission, more Latin Americans abandoned religion or joined one of the many Pentecostal Protestant sects spreading through the region.

QUESTIONS FOR ANALYSIS

1. What is the document's overall assessment of the economic and political state of Latin America?
2. What can be gleaned from the document about the bishops' views of the underlying causes of Latin American poverty?
3. Why, according to the Puebla statement, should Latin American poverty be especially intolerable to Catholics?
4. What statements in the document seem to confirm the view that it was a compromise between progressives and conservatives?
5. Critics of the Puebla statement contend that it was essentially worthless because it lacked concrete proposals to deal with Latin America's problems. Do you agree with such criticisms?

Viewing it in the light of faith, we see the growing gap between rich and poor as a scandal and a contradiction to Christian existence. . . . The luxury of a few becomes an insult to the wretched poverty of the vast masses. . . . This is contrary to the plan of the Creator and to the honor that is due him. In this anxiety and sorrow the Church sees a situation of social sinfulness, all the more serious because it exists in countries that call themselves Catholic and are capable of changing the situation. . . .

This situation of pervasive extreme poverty takes on very concrete faces in real life. In these faces we ought to recognize the suffering features of Christ the Lord, who questions and challenges us. They include:

- the faces of young children, struck down by poverty before they are born, their chance for self-development blocked by irreparable mental and physical deficiencies; and of the vagrant children in our cities who are so often exploited, products of poverty and the moral disorganization of the family;
- the faces of young people, who are disoriented because they cannot find their place in society, and who are frustrated, particularly in marginal rural and urban areas, by the lack of opportunity to obtain training and work;
- the faces of the indigenous peoples, and frequently of the Afro-Americans as well; living marginalized lives in inhuman situations, they can be considered the poorest of the poor;
- the faces of the peasants; as a social group, they live in exile almost everywhere on our continent, deprived of land, caught in a situation of internal and external dependence, and subjected to systems of commercialization that exploit them;
- the faces of laborers, who frequently are ill-paid and who have difficulty in organizing themselves and defending their rights;

- the faces of the underemployed and the unemployed, who are dismissed because of the harsh exigencies of economic crises, and often because of development-models that subject workers and their families to cold economic calculations;
- the faces of marginalized and overcrowded urban dwellers, whose lack of material goods is matched by the ostentatious display of wealth by other segments of society;
- the faces of old people, who are growing more numerous every day, and who are frequently marginalized in a progress-oriented society that totally disregards people not engaged in production.

We share other anxieties of our people that stem from a lack of respect for their dignity as human beings, made in the image and likeness of God, and for their inalienable rights as children of God.

. . . Our mission to bring God to human beings, and human beings to God, also entails the task of fashioning a more fraternal society here. And the unjust social situation has not failed to produce tensions within the Church itself. On the one hand they are provoked by groups that stress the "spiritual" side of the Church's mission and resent active efforts at societal improvement. On the other hand they are provoked by people who want to make the Church's mission nothing more than an effort at human betterment.

There are other novel and disturbing phenomena. We refer to the partisan political activity of priests — not as individuals, as some had acted in the past . . ., but as organized pressure groups. And we also refer to the fact that some of them are applying social analyses with strong political connotations to pastoral work.

The Church's awareness of its evangelizing mission[1] has led it in the past ten years to publish numerous pastoral documents about social

---

[1]*Evangelization* means "preaching Christianity with the view of bringing about conversion or rededication to the faith."

justice; to create [organizations] designed to express solidarity with the afflicted, to denounce outrages, and to defend human rights; . . . and to endure the persecution and at times death of its members in witness to its prophetic mission. Much remains to be done, of course, if the Church is to display greater oneness and solidarity. Fear of Marxism keeps many from facing up to the oppressive reality of liberal capitalism. One could say that some people, faced with the danger of one clearly sinful system, forgot to denounce and combat the established reality of another equally sinful system. . . . We must give full attention to the latter system, without overlooking the violent and atheistic historical forms of Marxism. . . .

To this are added other anxieties that stem from abuses of power, which are typical of regimes based on force. There are the anxieties based on systematic or selective repression; it is accompanied by accusations, violations of privacy, improper pressures, tortures, and exiles. There are the anxieties produced in many families by the disappearance of their loved ones, about whom they cannot get any news. There is the total insecurity bound up with arrest and detention without judicial consent. There are the anxieties felt in the face of a system of jus-

tice that has been suborned or cowed. As the Supreme Pontiffs point out, the Church . . . must raise its voice to denounce and condemn these situations, particularly when the responsible officials or rulers call themselves Christians.

Then there are the anxieties raised by guerrilla violence, by terrorism, and by the kidnappings carried out by various brands of extremists. They, too, pose a threat to life together in society. . . .

The free-market economy, in its most rigid expression, is still the prevailing system on our continent. Legitimated by liberal ideologies, it has increased the gap between the rich and the poor by giving priority to capital over labor, economics over the social realm. Small groups in our nations, who are often tied in with foreign interests, have taken advantage of the opportunities provided by these older forms of the free market to profit for themselves while the interests of the vast majority of the people suffer.

Marxist ideologies have also spread among workers, students, teachers, and others, promising greater social justice. In practice their strategies have sacrificed many Christian, and hence human, values; or else they have fallen prey to utopian forms of unrealism. Finding their inspiration in policies that use force as a basic tool, they have only intensified the spiral of violence.

A Platform for the Religious Right in the United States

❖

97 ◆ *Jerry Falwell, AN AGENDA FOR THE 1980s*

In the late 1970s proudly fundamentalist religious leaders and their followers, mainly Protestant, emerged as a powerful force in U.S. political life. Claiming to represent the views of the "moral majority," they rejected what they perceived as the disastrous legacy of the late 1960s and the 1970s: crime, drugs, illegitimacy, sexual permissiveness, pornography, failed schools, and soaring divorce rates. They sought to reverse America's moral decline by affirming the traditional values, religious and otherwise, they believed had made the United States great but now were threatened.

Among the stars of the religious right was the Virginia-based pastor and televangelist, Jerry Falwell. Born in 1933 into the family of a Lynchburg, Virginia, businessman, Falwell dreamed of becoming a professional baseball player or engineer before he experienced a religious conversion as a sophomore at

Lynchburg College and decided to become a minister. After graduating from the Baptist Bible College of Missouri, he founded the Thomas Road Baptist Church in Lynchburg in 1956. He gained a national following in the 1970s when his radio program, *The Old Time Gospel Hour,* began to be televised nationally. Having expanded his mission to include Liberty University in Lynchburg, a home for unwed mothers, and a treatment center for alcoholics, in 1979 he assumed leadership of the Moral Majority Incorporated, a religious special-interest group whose main tenets are described in his "An Agenda for the 1980s."

After registering (by its own count) four million new conservative voters in the early 1980s, the Moral Majority gradually began to lose support and was disbanded by Falwell in 1989. Falwell continues to be an important figure in contemporary American politics and religious life. His Liberty Baptist Church in Lynchburg has twenty-two thousand members, twelve thousand of whom can worship at one time in the church's giant sanctuary. In 2000 Falwell agreed to become director of People of Faith, an organization that sought to raise $15 million and register ten million new voters in support of conservative candidates.

QUESTIONS FOR ANALYSIS

1. According to Falwell, what are the manifestations of America's moral decline?
2. What has been the cause of this decline?
3. How does Falwell define morality? How does his definition differ from one that would likely have been offered by the authors of the Puebla Declaration? (See source 96.)
4. In what ways is the platform of the Moral Majority a specific repudiation of the legacy of the 1960s and 1970s?

The 1980s are certainly a decade of destiny for America. The rising tide of secularism threatens to obliterate the Judeo-Christian influence on American society. In the realm of religion, liberal clergy have seduced the average American away from the Bible and the kind of simple faith on which this country was built. We need to call America back to God, back to the Bible, and back to moral sanity. . . . During the 1960s and 1970s, people felt confused and began to turn away from the liberalized institutional church that was not meeting their spiritual needs. As attendance drastically declined in the mainline denominations, it dramatically increased in conservative denominations. Liberalism is obviously losing its influence on America. The time has come for Fundamentalists and Evangelicals to return our nation to its spiritual and moral roots. . . .

. . . Something had to be done. The federal government was encroaching upon the sovereignty of both the church and the family. The U.S. Supreme Court had legalized abortion-on-demand. The Equal Rights Amendment,[1] with its vague language, threatened to do further damage to the traditional family, as did the rising sentiment toward so-called homosexual rights. Most Americans were shocked, but kept

---

[1]The Equal Rights Amendment (ERA) was a proposed amendment to the Constitution approved by Congress and submitted to the states for approval in 1972. It provided that "Equality of Rights under the law shall be not denied or abridged . . . on account of sex." Having been ratified by only thirty-five states (three short of the necessary two-thirds), efforts to pass the amendment ended in 1982 when the time limit expired.

hoping someone would do something about all this moral chaos.

Facing the desperate need in the impending crisis of the hour, several concerned pastors urge me to put together a political organization that could provide a vehicle to address these crucial issues. . . . They urged that we formulate a nonpartisan political organization to promote morality in public life and combat legislation that favored the legalization of immorality. Together we formulated the Moral Majority, Inc. . . .

Here is how Moral Majority stands on today's vital issues:

1. *We believe in the separation of Church and State.* Moral Majority, Inc., is a political organization that provides a platform for religious and nonreligious Americans who share moral values to address their concerns. . . . We are Americans who are proud to be conservative in our approach to moral, social, and political concerns.

2. *We are pro-life.* We believe that life begins at fertilization. We strongly oppose the massive "biological holocaust" that is resulting in the abortion of one-and-a-half-million babies each year in America. We believe that unborn babies have the right to life as much as babies who have been born. . . .

3. *We are pro-traditional family.* We believe that the only acceptable family form begins with a legal marriage of a man and woman. We feel that homosexual relationships and common-law relationships should not be accepted as traditional families. We oppose legislation that favors these kinds of "diverse family form," thereby penalizing the traditional family. We do not oppose civil rights for homosexuals. We do oppose "special rights" for homosexuals who have chosen a perverted lifestyle rather than a traditional way-of-life.

4. *We oppose the illegal drug traffic in America.* The youth of America are in the midst of a drug epidemic. Through education, legislation, and other means, we want to do our part to save our young people from death on the installment plan through illegal drug addiction.

5. *We oppose pornography.* While we do not advocate censorship, we do believe that education and legislation can help stem the tide of pornography and obscenity that is poisoning the American spirit today. Economic boycotts are a proper way in America's free enterprise system to help persuade the media to move back to a sensible and reasonable moral stand. . . .

6. *We support the state of Israel and Jewish people everywhere.* It is impossible to separate the state of Israel from the Jewish family internationally. Many Moral Majority members, because of their theological convictions, are committed to the Jewish people. Others stand upon the human and civil rights of all persons as a premise for support of the state of Israel. Support of Israel is one of the essential commitments of Moral Majority. No anti-Semitic influence is allowed in Moral Majority, Inc.

7. *We believe that a strong national defense is the best deterrent to war.* . . . The only way America can remain free is to remain strong. Therefore we support Reagan administration efforts to regain our position of military preparedness — with a sincere hope that we will never need to use any of our weapons against any people anywhere.

8. *We support equal rights for women.* We agree with President Reagan's commitment to help every governor and every state legislature to move quickly to ensure that, during the 1980s, every American woman will earn as much money and enjoy the same opportunities for advancement as her male counterpart in the same vocation.

9. *We believe ERA is the wrong vehicle to obtain equal rights for women.* We feel that the ambiguous and simplistic language of the proposed amendment could lead to court interpretations that might put women in combat, sanction homosexual relationships, and financially penalize widows and deserted wives. . . .

This is how Moral Majority, Inc., is contributing to bringing America back to moral sanity:

1. *By educating millions of Americans concerning the vital moral issues of our day.* . . .

2. *By mobilizing millions of previously "inactive" Americans.* We have registered millions of voters and reactivated more millions of frustrated citizens into a special-interest group who are effectively making themselves heard in the halls of Congress, in the White House, and in every state legislature.

3. *By lobbying intensively in Congress to defeat any legislation that would further erode our constitutionally guaranteed freedom,* and by introducing and/or supporting legislation that promotes traditional family and moral values, followed by the goal of passage of a Human Life Amendment, which is a top priority of the Moral Majority agenda. . . .

4. *By informing all Americans about the voting records of their representatives so that every American,* with full information available, can vote intelligently following his or her own convictions. . . .

5. *By organizing and training millions of Americans who can become moral activists.* . . .

6. *By encouraging and promoting private schools in their attempt to excel in academics while simultaneously teaching traditional family and moral values.* . . .

Moral Majority, Inc., does not advocate the abolition of public schools. Public schools will always be needed in our pluralistic society. We are committed to helping public schools regain excellence. That is why we support the return of voluntary prayer to public schools and strongly oppose the teaching of the "religion" of secular humanism in the public classroom.

The Place of Hinduism in Modern India

98 ◆ *Girilal Jain, EDITORIALS*

Independent India has never been free of religious tensions. Even after Muslims were given their own state of Pakistan in 1947, religious pluralism characterized India's population: today it is composed of approximately 83 percent Hindus, 11 percent Muslims, 2.6 percent Christians, slightly over 1 percent Sikhs, and smaller numbers of Jains, Parsis, and Buddhists. None of these groups has been completely satisfied with India's constitution, which proclaims India to be a secular state with partiality toward no religious group. Many Hindus, however, believe that the government bends over backwards to protect Muslims and Sikhs; Muslims and Sikhs, conversely, are convinced that the government panders to Hindus. In the early 1980s religious tensions intensified as Muslims began to make converts among low-caste Hindus in the south, Sikhs agitated for an independent Punjab, and Hindus organized their own political party, the Bharatiya Janata (Indian People's Party), or BJP, whose goal was the "Hinduization" of India. Founded in 1982, BJP representation in parliament rose from two members in 1984 to 185 in 1996, fifty more than that of the Congress Party, which had enjoyed a parliamentary majority in all but four years since independence.

An important spokesman for Hindu nationalism and the BJP before his death in 1993 was the journalist Girilal Jain, who was editor-in-chief of the New Delhi *Times of India* between 1978 and 1988. Born into a poor rural family in 1922 and educated at Delhi University, Jain was jailed by the British during the 1942 Quit India campaign. As a journalist he was best known for his impassioned support of Indira Gandhi, prime minister between 1966 and 1970 and 1980 and 1984. During the 1980s he was drawn to Hindu nationalism and the BJP.

The following editorials were written in 1990, when Hindu-Muslim tensions were peaking over the Babri mosque in the city of Ayodhya built in the sixteenth century on the site of a Hindu temple believed to be the birthplace of the Hindu god-king Ram. Hindus demanded the destruction of the mosque, which was no longer used, so a temple in honor of Ram could be built. In December 1992, Hindus stormed the mosque and destroyed it, precipitating a government crisis and causing violence that took the lives of thousands. The government, with its commitment to religious pluralism and democracy, survived, but religious tensions remained high.

QUESTIONS FOR ANALYSIS

1. What are the reasons for Jain's disenchantment with India's government?
2. What does Jain mean when he says that the issues that concern the BJP have to do with "civilization," not religion?
3. How does Jain define "the West"? How does he view the West's role in Indian history?
4. Why, according to Jain, is the controversy over the Ayodhya mosque so significant for India's future?
5. In Jain's viewpoint, why have the Muslims been satisfied to go along with the secularist policies of the Indian state?
6. What is Jain's vision of India's future?

A specter haunts dominant sections of India's political and intellectual elites — the specter of a growing Hindu self-awareness and self-assertion. Till recently these elites had used the bogey of Hindu "communalism"[1] and revivalism as a convenient device to keep themselves in power and to "legitimize" their slavish imitation of the West. Unfortunately for them, the ghost has now materialized.

Millions of Hindus have stood up. It will not be easy to trick them back into acquiescing in an order which has been characterized not so much by its "appeasement of Muslims" as by its alienness, rootlessness and contempt for the land's unique cultural past. Secularism, a euphemism for irreligion and repudiation of the Hindu ethos, and socialism, a euphemism for denigration and humiliation of the business community to the benefit of ever expanding rapacious bureaucracy, . . . have been major planks of this order. Both have lost much of their old glitter and, therefore, capacity to dazzle and mislead. . . .

The Hindu fight is not at all with Muslims; the fight is between Hindus anxious to renew themselves in the spirit of their civilization, and the state, Indian in name and not in spirit and the political and intellectual class trapped in the debris the British managed to bury us under before they left. The proponents of the Western ideology are using Muslims as auxiliaries and it is a pity Muslim "leaders" are allowing themselves to be so used. . . .

Secularist-versus-Hindu-Rashtra[2] controversy is, of course, not new. In fact, it has been with us since the twenties when some of our forebears

---

[1]Communalism is a system in which rival minority groups are devoted to their own interests rather than those of the whole society; in the context of Indian politics the term refers to loyalties of religious communities.

[2]*Rashtra* is Hindi for state, or polity.

began to search for a definition of nationalism which could transcend at once the Hindu-Muslim divide and the aggregationist approach whereby India was regarded as a Hindu-Muslim-Sikh-Christian land. But it has acquired an intensity it has not had since partition. . . .

India, to put the matter brusquely, has been a battleground between two civilizations (Hindu and Islamic) for well over a thousand years, and three (Hindu, Muslim and Western) for over two hundred years. None of them has ever won a decisive enough and durable enough victory to oblige the other two to assimilate themselves fully into it. So the battle continues. This stalemate lies at the root of the crisis of identity the intelligentsia has faced since the beginning of the freedom movement in the last quarter of the nineteenth century. . . .

The more resilient and upwardly mobile section of the intelligentsia must, by definition, seek to come to terms with the ruling power and its mores, and the less successful part of it to look for its roots and seek comfort in its cultural past. This was so during the Muslim period; this was the case during the British Raj;[3] and this rule has not ceased to operate since independence.

Thus in the medieval period of our history there grew up a class of Hindus in and around centers of Muslim power who took to the Persian-Arabic culture and ways of the rulers; similarly under the more securely founded and far better organized and managed Raj there arose a vast number of Hindus who took to the English language, Western ideas, ideals, dress and eating habits; . . . they, their progeny and other recruits to their class have continued to dominate independent India.

They are the self-proclaimed secularists who have sought, and continue to seek, to remake India in the Western image. The image has, of course, been an eclectic one; if they have stuck to the institutional framework inherited from the British, they have been more than willing to take up not only the Soviet model of economic development,[4] but also the Soviet theories on a variety of issues such as the nationalities problem and the nature of imperialism and neo-colonialism.

Behind them has stood, and continues to stand, the awesome intellectual might of the West, which may or may not be anti-India, depending on the exigencies of its interests, but which has to be antipathetic to Hinduism. . . .

Some secularists may be genuinely pro-Muslim. . . . But, by and large, that is not the motivating force in their lives. They are driven, above all, by the fear of what they call regression into their own past which they hate and dread. Most of the exponents of this viewpoint have come and continue to come understandably from the Left, understandably because no other group of Indians can possibly be so alienated from the country's cultural past as the followers of Lenin, Stalin and Mao, who have spared little effort to turn their own countries into cultural wastelands. . . .

The state in independent India has, it is true, sought, broadly speaking, to be neutral in the matter of religion. But this is a surface view of the reality. The Indian state has been far from neutral in civilizational terms. It has been an agency, and a powerful agency, for the spread of Western values and mores. It has willfully sought to replicate Western institutions, the Soviet Union too being essentially part of Western civilization. It could not be otherwise in view of the orientation and aspirations of the dominant elite of which Nehru[5] remains the guiding spirit.

Muslims have found such a state acceptable principally on three counts. First, it has agreed to leave them alone in respect of their personal

---

[3]*Raj* is Hindi for reign, or rule; often used to refer to the British colonial administration.
[4]In 1951 the government adopted a series of five-year plans for the nation's economic development in imitation of the Five-Year Plans initiated by Stalin in 1928. The

plans featured central planning and state ownership of major enterprises.
[5]Jawaharlal Nehru (1899–1964), India's first prime minister, was a major target of Jain because of his commitment to socialism and secularism (see Chapter 11, source 90).

law. . . . Secondly, it has allowed them to expand their traditional . . . educational system in madrasahs[6] attached to mosques. Above all, it has helped them avoid the necessity to come to terms with Hindu civilization in a predominantly Hindu India. This last count is the crux of the matter. . . .

In the past up to the sixteenth century, great temples have been built in our country by rulers to mark the rise of a new dynasty or to mark a triumph. . . . In the present case, the proposal to build the Rama temple[7] has also to help produce an "army" which can in the first instance achieve the victory the construction can proclaim.

The raising of such an "army" in our democracy, however flawed, involves not only a body of disciplined cadres, which is available in the shape of the RSS,[8] a political oganization, which too is available in the Bharatiya Janata Party, but also an aroused citizenry. . . . The Vishwa Hindu Parishad[9] and its allies have fulfilled this need in a manner which is truly spectacular.

The BJP-VHP-RSS leaders have rendered the country another great service. They have brought Hindu interests, if not the Hindu ethos, into the public domain where they legitimately belong. . . .

The Nehru order is as much in the throes of death as its progenitor, the Marxist-Leninist-Stalinist order. A new order is waiting to be conceived and born. It needs a mother as well as a mid-wife.

---

[6]Madrasahs were advanced schools of learning, or colleges, devoted to Islamic studies.
[7]This refers to the controversy about the Babri mosque in Ayodhya; see source introduction.
[8]RSS stands for Rashtriya Swayamsevak Sangh, a militant

Hindu organization founded in 1925 and dedicated to the strengthening of Hindu culture.
[9]The Vishwa Hindu Parishad (VHP), or World Hindu Society, was founded in 1964. It is dedicated to demolishing mosques built on Hindu holy sites.

◆

Third World Women Between Tradition and Change

During the twentieth century, political leaders of industrialized nations, revolutionaries such as Lenin and Mao, and nationalist heroes as different as Ataturk and Gandhi all supported the ideal of women's equality with men. The United Nations Charter of 1945 commits the organization to the same ideal, and the UN Universal Declaration of Human Rights of 1948 reaffirms the goal of ending all forms of gender-based discrimination. Beginning in the 1960s powerful feminist movements with agendas ranging from equal educational access to legalized abortion took root in the Western industrialized nations and to a lesser degree in Asia, Latin America, and Africa.

Despite this broad support for gender equality, progress for women worldwide was uneven in the 1970s and 1980s. In developed industrial societies, women undoubtedly made great strides. Large numbers of women entered professions such as law, medicine, and university teaching; contraception and legal abortions were made available in most nations; laws forbidding gender-based discrimination were passed. Nonetheless, even in developed countries women still earned less than men for doing the same job, were underrepresented in managerial positions, and played a less significant role in politics than did men. Furthermore, movements for gender equality met strong opposition from individuals and groups who were convinced that women's liberation threatened the family, undermined morality, and would leave women unhappy and unfulfilled.

In less economically developed parts of the world, attainment of gender equality faced even more obstacles. Being small, the pool of educated women was less able to promote the development of feminist movements, and advocates for women's rights were few. Supporters of feminism were mainly middle-class, urban women whose concerns had little appeal or even meaning for millions of women in urban slums or rural villages whose lives were a daily struggle against poverty. Religious fundamentalists in the Islamic world and elsewhere also sought to keep women in traditional roles. Even in China and India, both of which adopted strong antidiscrimination laws, it proved difficult to modify, let alone eradicate, centuries-old educational patterns, work stereotypes, marriage customs, and attitudes. More so than in almost any other area of modern life, tradition has held its own against those movements and ideologies that have sought to liberate Third World women from the burdens of patriarchy and inequality.

Women and Iran's Islamic Revolution

❖

99 ◆ Zand Dokht,
THE REVOLUTION THAT FAILED WOMEN

Although the Pahlavi rulers of Iran, Reza Shah (1925–1941) and Muhammad Reza Shah (1941–1979), gave women political rights, allowed them to abandon the veil for Western-style dress, and encouraged female literacy and higher education, in the 1970s millions of Iranian women shared in the growing disgust with their government's autocracy, corruption, and secularism. Women played an important role in the massive demonstrations that preceded Muhammad Reza Shah's downfall in 1979 and led to his replacement by a government led by an Islamic fundamentalist, Ayatollah Ruhulla Khomeini (1902–1989). True to its Islamic principles, Khomeini's government revoked Pahlavi legislation on women and the family and reinstated traditional Islamic practices.

Iranian women who had taken advantage of educational opportunities and had benefited professionally during the Pahlavi years opposed the Islamic republic's effort to turn back the clock. In 1979 representatives from various women's organizations founded the Women's Solidarity Committee, an organization dedicated to the protection of women's rights in Iran. Although later banned in Iran itself, Iranian women living in England maintained a branch of the organization in London. Known as the Iranian Woman's Solidarity Group, in the 1980s it published pamphlets and newsletters on issues pertaining to women in Iran. The following selection, written by a Solidarity Committee member, Zand Dokht, appeared in one of its publications in 1981.

QUESTIONS FOR ANALYSIS

1. In what specific ways did the Islamic Revolution in Iran affect women?
2. According to the author, how do Iran's new leaders envision woman's role in society?
3. How does the author explain the fact that so many Iranian women supported the revolution that toppled the shah?
4. Why, in the author's view, did the shahs' reforms fail to satisfy large numbers of Iranian women?

When Khomeini created his Islamic Republic in 1979, he relied on the institution of the family, on support from the women, the merchants, and the private system of landownership. The new Islamic constitution declared women's primary position as mothers. The black veil, symbol of the position of women under Islam, was made compulsory. Guards were posted outside government offices to enforce it, and women were sacked from their jobs without compensation for refusing to wear the veil. The chairman of the Employment Office, in an interview with the government's women's magazine said, "We can account for 100,000 women government employees being sacked as they resisted the order of the revolutionary government when it was demanded of them to put the veil on."

Schools were segregated, which meant that women were barred from some technical schools, even some religious schools, and young girls' education in the villages was halted. Lowering the marriage age for girls to 13, reinstating polygamy and *Sighen* [temporary wives] . . . meant that women did not need education and jobs, they only needed to find husbands.

The Ayatollahs[1] in their numerous public prayers, which grew to be the only possible national activity, continuously gave sermons on the advantages of marriage, family, and children being brought up on their mother's lap. They preached that society would be pure, trouble free, criminal-less (look at the youth problem in the West) if everybody married young, and if men married as many times as possible (to save

the unprotected women who might otherwise become prostitutes). The government created a marriage bank at a time when half the working population was unemployed, whereby men were given huge sums — around £3,500 — to get married. Another *masterpiece* of the revolutionary Islamic government was to create a system of arranged marriages in prisons, between men and women prisoners, to "protect" women after they leave prison.

Because abortion and contraception are now unobtainable, marriage means frequent pregnancy. If you are 13 when you get married, it is likely that you will have six children by the time you are 20. This, in a country where half the total population are already under 16, is a tragedy for future generations.

Religious morality demands that all pleasures and entertainments be banned. Wine, music, dancing, chess, women's parts in theater, cinema and television — you name it, Khomeini banned it. He even segregated the mountains and the seas, for male and female climbers and swimmers.

But compulsory morality, compulsory marriage, and the compulsory wearing of the veil did not create the Holy Society that Khomeini was after; but public lashings, stonings, chopping of hands and daily group executions sank Iran into the age of Barbarism.

Perhaps nowhere else in the world have women been murdered for walking in the street open-faced. The question of the veil is the most important issue of women's liberation in Muslim

---

[1] *Ayatollah* is a title of respect for a high Shiite Muslim religious leader.

countries. The veil, a long engulfing black robe, is the extension of the four walls of the home, where women belong. The veil is the historical symbol of woman's oppression, seclusion, denial of her social participation and equal rights with men. It is a cover which defaces and objectifies women. To wear or not to wear the veil, for Muslim women is "the right to choose." . . .

Why do women, workers and unemployed, support this regime which has done everything in its power to attack their rights and interests? The power of Islam in our culture and tradition has been seriously underestimated . . . and it was through this ideology that Khomeini directed his revolutionary government. The clergy dealt with everyday problems and spoke out on human relationships, sexuality, security and protection of the family and the spiritual needs of human beings. It was easy for people to identify with these issues and support the clergy, although nobody knew what they were later to do. When Khomeini asked for sacrifices — "we haven't made the Revolution in order to eat chicken or dress better" — women (so great in the art of sacrifice) and workers accepted these anti-materialist ideas. . . .

Women's attraction to Khomeini's ideas was not based simply on his Islamic politics, but also on the way he criticized the treatment of women — as secretaries and media sex objects — under the Shah's regime. Women were genuinely unsatisfied and looking for change. Some educated Iranian women went back to Iran from America

and Europe to aid the clergy with the same messages, and became the government's spokeswomen. They put on the veil willingly, defended Islamic virtues and spiritual values while drawing from their own experiences in the West. They said it was cold and lonely, Western women were only in pursuit of careers and self-sufficiency, and that their polygamous sexual relationships had not brought them liberation, but confusion and exploitation. These women joined ranks with an already growing force of Muslim women, to retrieve the tradition of true/happy Muslim women — in defense of patriarchy.

The mosque is not just a place of prayer, it is also a social club for women. It provides a warm, safe room for women to meet, chat or listen to a sermon, and there are traditional women-only parties and picnics in gardens or holy places. Take away these traditional and religious customs from women which the Shah — with his capitalist and imperialist reforms, irrelevant to women's needs — tried to do and a huge vacuum is left. Khomeini stepped in to fill that vacuum. The reason why Khomeini won was that the Shah's social-economic program for women was dictatorial, bureaucratic, inadequate (especially in terms of health education) and therefore irrelevant to women's needs. What little the Shah's reform brought to women was just a token gesture. Women dissatisfied with the Shah's reform felt that they had benefited little from him and would not miss it if it was taken away.

An African Perspective on Female Circumcision

❖

100 ◆ Association of African Women for Research and Development, *A STATEMENT ON GENITAL MUTILATION*

Female circumcision is a general term describing a variety of ritual procedures ranging from the drawing of blood, to clitoridectomy (the removal of the clitoris), to infibulation (the removal of the clitoris, the labia minora, and most of the labia majora, the remaining sides of which are joined together to leave a small opening). The operation, which in different regions takes place anytime from shortly after birth to the onset of puberty, is usually performed by midwives or village women without benefit of anesthesia or antibiotics. No accurate statistics on the prevalence of the practice exists. It is most common in sub-Saharan Africa, especially in the Sudan region, but it is also practiced in New Guinea, Australia, Malaysia, Brazil, Mexico, Peru, India, Egypt, and the southern and eastern parts of the Arabian Peninsula. Presumably instituted to encourage chastity by dulling a woman's sexual desire, the practice has come under harsh criticism both from within the societies in which it exists and from outsiders, especially from the West. Efforts to suppress the practice have had, however, little effect among peoples who consider the custom part of their ethnic and religious heritage and a rite of passage into adulthood.

Denunciations of female circumcision by Westerners and Western-inspired campaigns to end the practice have frequently backfired, especially in Africa, where the custom is most deeply rooted. The following statement, issued in 1980 by the Association of African Women for Research and Development (AAWORD), which was founded in 1977 in Dakar, Senegal, reveals that even Africans who oppose the practice resent Western interference.

QUESTIONS FOR ANALYSIS

1. What is the basis of the authors' assertion that critics of female circumcision are guilty of "latent racism"?
2. How have Western criticisms of female circumcision hindered the efforts of African critics to limit the practice?
3. In the view of the authors, what would be an appropriate Western approach to the issue of female circumcision?
4. How might an ardent Western critic of African female circumcision counter the arguments contained in the AAWORD statement?

In the past few years, Western public opinion has been shocked to find out that in the middle of the 20th century thousands of women and children have been "savagely mutilated" because of "barbarous customs from another age." The good conscience of Western society has once again been shaken. Something must be done to help these people, to show public disapproval of such acts.

There have been press conferences, documentary files, headlines in the newspapers, information days, open letters, action groups — all this to mobilize public opinion and put pressure on governments of the countries where genital mutilation is still practiced. . . .

. . . In trying to reach their own public, the new crusaders have fallen back on sensational-ism, and have become insensitive to the dignity of the very women they want to "save." They are totally unconscious of the latent racism which such a campaign evokes in countries where ethnocentric prejudice is so deep-rooted. And in their conviction that this is a "just cause," they have forgotten that these women from a different race and different culture are also *human beings*, and that solidarity can only exist alongside self-affirmation and mutual respect.

This campaign has aroused three kinds of reaction in Africa:

1. the highly conservative, which stresses the right of cultural difference and the defence of traditional values and practices whose supposed aim is to protect and elevate

women; this view denies Westerners the right to interfere in problems related to culture;

2. which, while condemning genital mutilation for health reasons, considers it premature to open the issue to public debate;

3. which concentrates on the aggressive nature of the campaign and considers that the fanaticism of the new crusaders only serves to draw attention away from the fundamental problems of the economic exploitation and oppression of developing countries, which contribute to the continuation of such practices.

Although all these reactions rightly criticize the campaign against genital mutilation as imperialist and paternalist, they remain passive and defensive. As is the case with many other issues, we refuse here to confront our cultural heritage and to criticize it constructively. We seem to prefer to draw a veil of modesty over certain traditional practices, whatever the consequences may be. However, it is time that Africans realized they must take a position on all problems which concern their society, and to take steps to end any practice which debases human beings.

AAWORD, whose aim is to carry out research which leads to the liberation of African people and women in particular, *firmly condemns* genital mutilation and all other practices — traditional or modern — which oppress women and justify exploiting them economically or socially, as a serious violation of the fundamental rights of women. . . .

However, as far as AAWORD is concerned, the fight against genital mutilation, although necessary, should not take on such proportions that the wood cannot be seen for the trees. Young girls and women who are mutilated in Africa are usually among those who cannot even satisfy their basic needs and who have to struggle daily for survival. This is due to the exploitation of developing countries, manifested especially through the impoverishment of the poorest social classes. In the context of the present world economic crisis, tradition, with all of its constraints, becomes more than ever a form of security for the peoples of the Third World, and especially for the "wretched of the earth." For these people, the modern world, which is primarily Western and bourgeois, can only represent aggression at all levels — political, economic, social and cultural. It is unable to propose viable alternatives for them.

Moreover, to fight against genital mutilation without placing it in the context of ignorance, obscurantism, exploitation, poverty, etc., without questioning the structures and social relations which perpetuate this situation, is like "refusing to see the sun in the middle of the day." This, however, is precisely the approach taken by many Westerners, and is highly suspect, especially since Westerners necessarily profit from the exploitation of the peoples and women of Africa, whether directly or indirectly.

Feminists from developed countries — at least those who are sincerely concerned about this situation rather than those who use it only for their personal prestige — should understand this other aspect of the problem. They must accept that it is a problem for *African women*, and that no change is possible without the conscious participation of African women. They must avoid ill-timed interference, maternalism, ethnocentrism and misuse of power. These are attitudes which can only widen the gap between the Western feminist movement and that of the Third World. . . .

On the question of such traditional practices as genital mutilation, African women must no longer equivocate or react only to Western interference. They must speak out in favour of the total eradication of all these practices, and they must lead information and education campaigns to this end within their own countries and on a continental level.

The Impact of the Indian Dowry System

❖

101 ◆ EDITORIAL AGAINST DOWRY

Although some improvement in the status of Hindu women took place under British rule, major steps toward gender equality were taken only after Indian independence in 1947. Women received the right to vote, hold political office, own property, and divorce their husbands; in addition, the government outlawed child marriage and polygamy, and eased restrictions against intercaste marriages. In 1961, the government also outlawed dowries, the gifts of property a new bride's family was expected to make to the husband or the husband's family. It was hoped that such a step would lessen the financial burdens of families with daughters and encourage men from higher castes to marry women from lower castes.

As the following editorial shows, however, the practice of dowries continued, often with tragic results for young married women. This anonymous editorial was originally published in 1979 in *Manushi*, an Indian magazine for women.

QUESTIONS FOR ANALYSIS

1. According to the author of this editorial, is the giving and taking of dowries the result of recent developments or of long-standing Indian traditions?
2. According to the author, why have efforts to end the practice of dowries failed?
3. What does the author see as the solution to the problem?
4. According to the author, to what degree do dowry murders fit into a general pattern of mistreatment of women in Indian society?

Most people are not even aware that the giving and taking of dowry is a legal offense. Since the Prohibition of Dowry Act was passed in 1961, the custom has flowered and flourished, invading castes and communities among whom it was hitherto unknown — sprouting new forms and varieties. It is percolating downwards and becoming so widespread even among the working classes that it is no longer possible to consider it a problem of the middle class alone.

With the entire bourgeois mass media oriented towards viciously promoting the religion of mindless consumerism, demands for dowry are becoming more and more "modernized."

Marriages are made and broken for such items as cars, scooters, TVs, refrigerators and washing machines, wedding receptions in five-star hotels or an air ticket plus the promise of a job for the son-in-law in a foreign country.

In India, we have a glorious heritage of systematic violence on women in the family itself, sati[1] and female infanticide being the two better-known forms. Today, we do not kill girl-babies at birth. We let them die through systematic neglect — the mortality rate among female children is 30-60% higher than among male children. Today, we do not wait till a woman is widowed before we burn her to death.

---

[1]Sati is the custom in which a Hindu widow is willingly cremated on the funeral pyre of her dead husband as a sign of devotion to him.

We burn her in the lifetime of her husband so that he can get a new bride with a fatter dowry.

"Woman burnt to death. A case of suicide has been registered. The police are enquiring into the matter." For years, such three-line news items have appeared almost every day in the newspapers and gone unnoticed. It is only lately that dowry deaths are being given detailed coverage. It is not by accident that fuller reporting of such cases has coincided with a spurt of protest demonstrations.

We, as women, have too long been silent spectators, often willing participants in the degrading drama of matrimony — when girls are advertised, displayed, bargained over, and disposed of with the pious injunction: "Daughter, we are sending you to your husband's home. You are not to leave it till your corpse emerges from its doors." It is significant that in all the cases of dowry murders recently reported, the girls had on previous occasions left the in-laws' houses where they were being tortured and felt insecure. Their parents had insisted on their going back and "adjusting" there.

Death may be slow in coming — a long process of killing the girl's spirit by harassment, taunts, torture. It may be only too quick — fiery and sudden. Dousing the woman with kerosene and setting her on fire seems to have become the most popular way of murdering a daughter-in-law because with police connivance it is the easiest to make out as a case of suicide or accident.

And for every one reported murder, hundreds go unreported, especially in rural areas where it is almost impossible to get redress unless one is rich and influential. . . .

Why is it that gifts have to be given with the daughter? Hindu scriptures proclaim that the girl herself is the most precious of gifts "presented" by her father to her husband. Thus the money transaction between families is bound up with the marriage transaction whereby the girl becomes a piece of transferrable property. So little is a woman worth that a man has literally to be paid to take her off her father's hands.

The dramatic increase in dowry-giving in the post-independence period reflects the declining value of women in our society. Their only worth is as reproducers who provide "legitimate" heirs for their husbands' property.

Most people opposing dowry feel that the problem can be solved by giving girls an equal share in their fathers' property. This was one of the reasons why daughters were given near-equal rights in the Hindu Succession Act, 1956. And yet the law has been reduced to a farce because in most cases, daughters are pressured to, or even willingly sign away their rights in favor of their brothers. In any case, it is the woman's husband who usually controls any property she inherits. So the property transaction remains between men, women acting only as vehicles for this transaction.

This will continue to be so as long as the majority of women remain economically dependent on men and as long as this dependence is reinforced by our social values and institutions so that even those women who earn seldom have the right to control their own income. . . .

. . . We appeal, therefore, to all the women's organizations to undertake a broad-based united action on this issue and launch an intensive, concerted campaign instead of the isolated, sporadic protests which have so far been organized, and which can have only a short-term, limited impact.

Perhaps even more urgent is the need to begin the movement from our own homes. Are we sure that none of us who participated so vociferously in these demonstrations will take dowry from our parents or give it to our daughters in however veiled a form? That we will rather say "No" to marriage than live a life of humiliations and compromises? Do we have the courage to boycott marriages where dowry is given? Even the marriage of a brother or sister or of a dear friend? Will we socially ostracize such people, no matter how close they are to us? All the protest demonstrations will be only so much hot air unless we are prepared to create pressures against dowry beginning from our own homes.

Communism's Reform, Communism's Retreat

After World War II, global politics entered an era of moral and ideological absolutes. On one side was the communist world composed of the Soviet Union, its Eastern European satellites, and China. With authoritarian, one-party governments and centralized economic planning, these states proclaimed their commitment to Marxism and the worldwide demise of capitalism. On the other side was a bloc of states led by the United States that claimed it represented the "free world"; its goal was the defense of capitalism and the spread of liberal democracy. For more than forty years these two blocs organized themselves into military alliances, built up huge nuclear arsenals, supported giant intelligence establishments, and competed for support among the world's nonaligned nations. For both sides the dualisms of the Cold War — communism versus capitalism, the United States versus the Soviet Union, NATO versus the Warsaw Pact — gave clarity, direction, and meaning to international politics.

By the end of the twentieth century, however, communism was no longer a significant force in world affairs. Only four marginal states, Cuba, Laos, Vietnam, and North Korea, were still officially communist and maintained socioeconomic systems that for much of the twentieth century defined what it meant to be communist — one-party rule, tight censorship, collectivized agriculture, and state-controlled economies. China still called itself communist, but in practice had enthusiastically embraced the capitalist road that Mao had so passionately abhorred.

Although communism collapsed in Eastern Europe and the Soviet Union in a brief two-year period between 1989 and 1991, it had been losing ground for more than a decade. Despite the crushing of the Czech reform movement by Soviet troops in 1968, communist orthodoxy was weakening in Eastern Europe. Hungary developed a mixed socialist-capitalist economy that became the strongest in the region, and in 1980 and 1981 Poland was rocked by strikes and demonstrations for political and economic reform sponsored by Solidarity, a new, independent organization of labor unions that was forced to go underground in December 1981 after the communist regime outlawed it and declared martial law.

Chinese communism also underwent significant changes in the late 1970s and 1980s. After Mao Zedong's death in 1976, his successor, the pragmatic Deng Xiaoping, deemphasized ideology and egalitarianism in favor of rapid economic development. He approved the opening of small private businesses, fostered a market economy in agriculture, opened China to foreign investment, supported scientific and technological education, and encouraged Chinese exports of manufactured goods. The results were spectacular, with annual growth rates of 12 percent achieved by the early 1990s. China remained authoritarian and officially communist, but with its commitment to entrepreneurialism and the free market, it was worlds apart from the isolated, ideology-driven China of previous decades.

Within the Soviet Union the era of reform began in 1985 when General Secretary Mikhail Gorbachev introduced policies of glasnost (openness) and perestroika (restructuring) to rejuvenate the Soviet communist system. But his efforts to save communism by democratization and economic liberalization released forces he could not control, and by the end of 1991, communist rule had disappeared throughout Eastern Europe, the Soviet Union had broken apart, and the Cold War was over. No one doubted that a new era of world politics had dawned.

China's New Course

❖

102 ◆ Deng Xiaoping, SPEECHES AND WRITINGS

After emerging as a unified empire in the third century B.C.E., China had been the world's most successful state in terms of size, wealth, technological sophistication, and the continuity of its political institutions. This was easy to forget in the nineteenth and twentieth centuries when China became a pawn of the Western powers and a victim of political breakdown, military defeat, and economic decline. In the 1980s, however, China's leaders set a new course for their country, which, if successful, might restore China to preeminence in Asia, if not primacy among the world's powers.

The man responsible for China's change of direction was Deng Xiaoping, the victor in the struggle for power that followed Mao Zedong's death in 1976. Born into the family of a well-off landowner in 1904, Deng was sent to France after World War I to continue his education. Having spent all his money, he worked in a factory before returning to China by way of the Soviet Union, where he studied in 1925 and 1926. On his return to China he joined the Communist Party and became one of Mao's loyal followers in the long struggle against the Guomindang and the Japanese. After 1949 he became a member of the politburo, with responsibilities for overseeing economic development in south China. Following the Party line, he supported the Stalinist model for China's economic development through investment in heavy industry, agricultural collectivization, and central planning. This was scrapped in 1958 when Mao instituted the Great Leap Forward. In the wake of its failure, Deng and other moderates dismantled the communes and reintroduced centralized planning.

This made Deng a prime candidate for vilification during the Cultural Revolution. Having fallen from power, he was paraded through the streets in a dunce cap and put to work in a mess hall and a tractor repair shop. As the intensity of the Cultural Revolution diminished, Deng was reinstated as a Party official, and after Mao's death he led the moderates in their struggle with the radicals led by Mao's widow, Jiang Qing. Deng's faction won, and in December 1978, the Communist Party's Central Committee officially abandoned Mao's emphasis on ideology and class struggle in favor of a moderate, pragmatic policy designed to achieve the "four modernizations" in science and technology, agriculture, industry, and the military. To encourage economic growth, the government fostered free markets, competition, and private incentives. Although Deng claimed that China had entered its "second revolution," it was an economic revolution only. Reformers who demanded the "fifth modernization" — democracy — were arrested and silenced in 1979. A decade later when hundreds of thousands of Chinese demonstrated for democratic reform in 1989 in Beijing, the government crushed the demonstrators with soldiers and tanks, thus assuring the continuation of the Party dictatorship. Deng withdrew from public life in the 1990s, and died in early 1997.

The following excerpts are from speeches and interviews given by Deng between 1983 and 1986.

QUESTIONS FOR ANALYSIS

1. According to Deng, what had been the shortcomings of China's economic development planning under Mao Zedong?
2. According to Deng, how is China's new economic policy truly Marxist and truly socialist?
3. How does Deng view China's role in the world? What implications, in his view, will China's new economic priorities have for its foreign policy?
4. What is Deng's rationale for opposing democracy in China?
5. What similarities and differences do you see between Deng's economic program for China and Stalin's plans for the Soviet Union in the late 1920s and the 1930s (see Chapter 4, source 34)?

MAOISM'S FLAWS

After the founding of the People's Republic, in the rural areas we initiated agrarian reform and launched a movement for the co-operative transformation of agriculture,[1] while in the cities we conducted the socialist transformation of capitalist industry and commerce.[2] We were successful in both. However, from 1957 on, China was plagued by "Left" ideology, which gradually became dominant. During the Great Leap Forward in 1958, people rushed headlong into mass action to establish people's communes. They placed lopsided emphasis on making the communes large in size and collective in nature, urging everyone to "eat from the same big pot," and by so doing brought disaster upon the nation. We won't even mention the "cultural revolution." . . . During the 20 years from 1958 to 1978 the income of peasants and workers rose only a little, and consequently their standard of living remained very low. The development of the productive forces was sluggish during those years. In 1978 per capita GNP was less than $250. . . .

Comrade Mao Zedong was a great leader, and it was under his leadership that the Chinese revolution triumphed. But he made the grave mistake of neglecting the development of the productive forces. . . .

---

[1]Following the communist victory in 1949, large estates were confiscated from landlords and redistributed to the peasantry. But in the early 1950s agriculture became collectivized under state control, and peasants essentially became paid agricultural laborers who turned over their crops to the government in return for wages.

[2]During the 1950s private businesses involved in manufacturing and finance were phased out and became state enterprises subject to centralized state control.

The fundamental principle of Marxism is that the productive forces must be developed. The goal for Marxists is to realize communism, which must be built on the basis of highly developed productive forces. What is a communist society? It is a society in which there is vast material wealth and in which the principle of from each according to his ability, to each according to his needs is applied. . . .

Our experience in the 20 years from 1958 to 1978 teaches us that poverty is not socialism, that socialism means eliminating poverty. Unless you are developing the productive forces and raising people's living standards, you cannot say that you are building socialism.

After the Third Plenary Session[3] we proceeded to explore ways of building socialism in China. Finally we decided to develop the productive forces and gradually expand the economy. The first goal we set was to achieve comparative prosperity by the end of the century. . . . So taking population increase into consideration, we planned to quadruple our GNP, which meant that per capita GNP would grow from $250 to $800 or $1,000. We shall lead a much better life when we reach this level, although it is still much lower than that of the developed countries. That is why we call it comparative prosperity. When we attain that level, China's GNP will have reached $1,000 billion, representing increased national strength. And the most populous nation in the world will have shaken off poverty and be able to make a greater contribution to mankind. With a GNP of $1,000 billion as a springboard, within 30 or 50 more years — 50, to be more accurate — China may reach its second goal, to approach the level of the developed countries. . . . We began our reform in the countryside. The main point of the rural reform has been to bring the peasants' initiative into full play by introducing the responsibility system and discarding the

system whereby everybody ate from the same big pot. . . . After three years of practice the rural reform has proved successful. I can say with assurance it is a good policy. The countryside has assumed a new look. The living standards of 90 per cent of the rural population have been raised. . . .

. . . Urban reform is more complicated and risky. This is especially true in China, because we have no expertise in this regard. Also, China has traditionally been a very closed society, so that people lack information about what's going on elsewhere. . . .

It is our hope that businessmen and economists in other countries will appreciate that to help China develop will benefit the world. China's foreign trade volume makes up a very small portion of the world's total. If we succeed in quadrupling the GNP, the volume of our foreign trade will increase considerably, promoting China's economic relations with other countries and expanding its market. Therefore, judged from the perspective of world politics and economics, China's development will benefit world peace and the world economy. . . .

TRUE SOCIALISM

Our modernization programme is a socialist programme, not anything else. All our policies for carrying out reform, opening to the outside world and invigorating the domestic economy are designed to develop the socialist economy. We allow the development of individual economy, of joint ventures with both Chinese and foreign investment and of enterprises wholly owned by foreign businessmen, but socialist public ownership will always remain predominant. The aim of socialism is to make all our people prosperous, not to create polarization. If our policies led to polarization, it would mean that we had failed; if a new bourgoisie emerged,

---

[3]The Third Plenary Session of the Eleventh Central Committee of the Chinese Communist Party, held in December 1978, approved the "four modernizations" program favored by Deng.

it would mean that we had strayed from the right path. In encouraging some regions to become prosperous first, we intend that they should help the economically backward ones to develop. Similarly, in encouraging some people to become prosperous first, we intend that they should help others who are still in poverty to become better off, so that there will be common prosperity rather than polarization. A limit should be placed on the wealth of people who become prosperous first, through the income tax, for example. In addition, we should encourage them to contribute money to run schools and build roads, although we definitely shouldn't set quotas for them. . . .

In short, predominance of public ownership and common prosperity are the two fundamental socialist principles that we must adhere to. . . .

SPECIAL ECONOMIC ZONES

In establishing special economic zones[4] and implementing an open policy, we must make it clear that our guideline is just that — to open and not to close.

I was impressed by the prosperity of the Shenzhen[5] Special Economic Zone during my stay there. The pace of construction in Shenzhen is rapid. It is particularly fast in Shekou, because the authorities there are permitted to make their own spending decisions up to a limit of U.S. $5 million. Their slogan is "time is money, efficiency is life." In Shenzhen, it doesn't take long to erect a tall building; the workers complete a storey in a couple of days. The construction workers there are from inland cities. Their high efficiency is due to the "contracted responsibility system," under which they are paid according to their performance, and to a fair system of rewards and penalties.

A special economic zone is a medium for introducing technology, management and knowledge. It is also a window for our foreign policy. Through the special economic zone we can import foreign technology, obtain knowledge and learn management, which is also a kind of knowledge. . . . Public order in Shenzhen is reportedly better than before, and people who slipped off to Hong Kong have begun to return. One reason is that there are more job opportunities and people's incomes and living standards are rising, all of which proves that cultural and ideological progress is based on material progress.

CHINA'S FOREIGN RELATIONS

While invigorating the domestic economy, we have also formulated a policy of opening to the outside world. Reviewing our history, we have concluded that one of the most important reasons for China's long years of stagnation and backwardness was its policy of closing the country to outside contact. Our experience shows that China cannot rebuild itself with its doors closed to the outside and that it cannot develop in isolation from the rest of the world. It goes without saying that a large country like China . . . must depend mainly on itself, on its own efforts. Nevertheless, while holding to self-reliance, we should open our country to the outside world to obtain such aid as foreign investment capital and technology. . . .

CHINA'S POLITICAL FUTURE

The recent student unrest[6] is not going to lead to any major disturbances. But because of its nature it must be taken very seriously. Firm measures must be taken against any student who creates trouble at Tiananmen Square. . . .

---

[4]Special economic zones (SEZ) were restricted areas in which foreign firms could establish plants and house foreign personnel.
[5]A district next to Hong Kong.

[6]Deng made these remarks in December 1986, when student demonstrations and speechmaking on behalf of the prodemocracy movement had been going on in Tiananmen Square in Beijing for several years.

In the beginning, we mainly used persuasion, which is as it should be in dealing with student demonstrators. But if any of them disturb public order or violate the law, they must be dealt with unhesitatingly. Persuasion includes application of the law. . . . It is essential to adhere firmly to the Four Cardinal Principles;[7] otherwise bourgeois liberalization will spread unchecked — and that has been the root cause of the problem. . . .

Without leadership by the Communist Party and without socialism, there is no future for China. This truth has been demonstrated in the past, and it will be demonstrated again in future. When we succeed in raising China's per capita GNP to $4,000 and everyone is prosperous, that will better demonstrate the superiority of socialism over capitalism, it will point the

way for three quarters of the world's population and it will provide further proof of the correctness of Marxism. Therefore, we must confidently keep to the socialist road and uphold the Four Cardinal Principles.

We cannot do without dictatorship. We must not only affirm the need for it but exercise it when necessary. Of course, we must be cautious about resorting to dictatorial means and make as few arrests as possible. But if some people attempt to provoke bloodshed, what are we going to do about it? We should first expose their plot and then do our best to avoid shedding blood, even if that means some of our own people get hurt. However, ringleaders who have violated the law must be sentenced according to law. . . . If we take no action and back down, we shall only have more trouble down the road.

---

[7]Issued by Deng in 1979, the Four Cardinal Principles were (1) the socialist path, (2) the dictatorship of the proletariat, (3) party leadership, (4) Marxism–Leninism–Mao Zedong thought.

Visualizing China in the Modernization Era

❖

103 ◆ CHINESE POSTER ART FROM THE 1980s

Although China's leaders in the 1980s rejected much of Mao Zedong's legacy, they continued the practice of using posters to convey their political message. Not surprisingly, however, as is shown in the following posters, their message was dramatically different. The first poster, *Advance Bravely Along the Road of Socialism with Chinese Characteristics* (1989) shows a group of Chinese advancing toward the future against a dramatic background of construction projects, doves, and unfurled banners. The second poster, *The Age of Smiling* (1988), shows an attractive young woman, brimming with courtesy and polite behavior, who is selling two brands of cola that were popular in China in the 1980s but were swept away by Pepsi-Cola and Coca-Cola in the 1990s.

QUESTIONS FOR ANALYSIS

1. Consider the backgrounds to *Advance Bravely* and *The Age of Smiling*. What do they communicate about the government's vision of China's future?
2. What are the social backgrounds of the people depicted in *Advance Bravely*? How do their backgrounds differ from those of the individuals who are featured in the posters from Mao's era (see Chapter 10, source 83)?

3. Consider the outward appearance and demeanor of the individuals in
   Advance Bravely and *The Age of Smiling*. How do they differ from those of
   the individuals depicted in the posters from the 1960s and 1970s? What
   explains these differences?

Advance bravely along the road of socialism with Chinese characteristics (1989)

The Age of Smiling (1988)

A Plan to Save Communism in the Soviet Union

104 ◆ Mikhail Gorbachev, PERESTROIKA

The Soviet Union in the 1970s and 1980s was still one of the world's two super-powers. It had an enormous army, what was perceived as an impressive indus-trial establishment, a solid record of technological achievement, and a seemingly unshakable authoritarian government. No one saw any reason why it would not continue to be the United States's great rival in international affairs. In reality, industrial and agricultural production was stagnating, the people's morale was plummeting, and a fossilized bureaucracy — the nomenklatura — was mired in old policies and theories that no longer worked. Against this background Mikhail Gorbachev became general secretary of the Communist Party in March 1985 and began the task of reviving Soviet communism by introducing reforms based on glasnost, or openness, and perestroika, or restructuring.

Gorbachev, the son of peasants and with training in law and agricultural economics, joined the Communist Party and steadily advanced in the Party hierarchy. In 1979 he became a member of the politburo, the ultimate power in the Soviet state, and in 1985 was elevated to the position of general secretary at the age of fifty-four. After serving as the Soviet leader for two years, he published a book, *Perestroika*, from which the following excerpts are taken. In them Gorbachev outlines his goals for communism in the Soviet Union.

QUESTIONS FOR ANALYSIS

1. What conditions in the Soviet Union convinced Gorbachev that Soviet society and government were in need of reform?
2. In Gorbachev's analysis, what caused Soviet society to lose its momentum?
3. How, in Gorbachev's view, will the individual in Soviet society be affected by his reforms?
4. To what extent is Gorbachev's idea of perestroika democratic?
5. What similarities and differences do you see between Gorbachev's statements about perestroika and Deng Xiaoping's plans for China (see source 103)?
6. Compare and contrast Gorbachev's views of Soviet society with those of Soviet and Eastern European dissidents from the 1960s and early 1970s (see Chapter 10, sources 77 and 79).

Over the past seven decades — a short span in the history of human civilization — our country has traveled a path equal to centuries. One of the mightiest powers in the world rose up to replace the backward semi-colonial and semi-feudal Russian Empire. . . .

At some stage — this became particularly clear in the latter half of the seventies — something happened that was at first sight inexplicable. The country began to lose momentum. Economic failures became more frequent. . . . Elements of what we call stagnation and other phenomena alien to socialism began to appear in the life of society. A kind of "braking mechanism" affecting social and economic development formed. And all this happened at a time when scientific and technological revolution opened up new prospects for economic and social progress. . . .

. . . In the last fifteen years the national income growth rates had declined by more than a half and by the beginning of the eighties had fallen to a level close to economic stagnation. A country that was once quickly closing on the world's advanced nations began to lose one position after another. . . .

It became typical of many of our economic executives to think not of how to build up the national assets, but of how to put more material, labor, and working time into an item to sell it at a higher price. Consequently, for all our "gross output," there was a shortage of goods. We spent, in fact we are still spending, far more on raw materials, energy, and other resources per unit of output than other developed nations. Our country's wealth in terms of natural and manpower resources has spoilt, one may even say corrupted, us. . . .

The presentation of a "problem-free" reality backfired: a breach had formed between word and deed, which bred public passivity and disbelief in the slogans being proclaimed. It was only natural that this situation resulted in a credibility gap: everything that was proclaimed from the rostrums and printed in newspapers and textbooks was put in question. Decay began in public morals; the great feeling of solidarity with each other that was forged during the heroic times of the Revolution, the first five-year plans, the Great Patriotic War,[1] and postwar rehabilitation was weakening; alcoholism, drug addiction, and crime were growing; and the penetration of the stereotypes of mass culture alien to us, which bred vulgarity and low tastes and brought about ideological barrenness, increased.

Political flirtation and mass distribution of awards, titles, and bonuses often replaced genuine concern for the people, for their living and working conditions, for a favorable social atmosphere. An atmosphere emerged of "everything goes," and fewer and fewer demands were made on discipline and responsibility. Attempts were made to cover it all up with pompous campaigns and undertakings and celebrations. . . . The world of day-to-day realities and the world of feigned prosperity were diverging more and more. . . .

By saying all this I want to make the reader understand that the energy for revolutionary change has been accumulating amid our people and in the Party for some time. And the ideas of perestroika have been prompted not just by pragmatic interests and considerations but also by our troubled conscience, by the indomitable commitment to ideals which we inherited from the Revolution and as a result of a theoretical quest which gave us a better knowledge of society and reinforced our determination to go ahead. . . .

. . . Here I think it is appropriate to draw your attention to one specific feature of socialism. I have in mind the high degree of social protection in our society. On the one hand, it is, doubtless, a benefit and a major achievement of ours. On the other, it makes some people spongers.

There is virtually no unemployment. The state has assumed concern for ensuring employment. Even a person dismissed for laziness or a breach of labor discipline must be given another job. Also, wage-leveling has become a regular feature of our everyday life: even if a person is a bad worker, he gets enough to live fairly comfortably. The children of an outright parasite will not be left to the mercy of fate. We have enormous sums of money concentrated in the social funds from which people receive financial assistance. The same funds provide subsidies for the upkeep of kindergartens, orphanages, Young Pioneer[2] houses, and other institutions related to children's creativity and sport. Health care is free, and so is education. People are protected from the vicissitudes of life, and we are proud of this.

But we also see that dishonest people try to exploit these advantages of socialism; they know only their rights, but they do not want to know their duties: they work poorly, shirk, and drink hard. . . . They give little to society, but nevertheless managed to get from it all that is possible and what even seems impossible; they have lived on unearned incomes.

The policy of restructuring puts everything in its place. We are fully restoring the principle of socialism. "From each according to his ability, to each according to his work," and we seek to affirm social justice for all, equal rights for all, one law for all, one kind of discipline for all, and high responsibilities for each. Perestroika raises the level of social responsibility and expectation. . . .

It is essential to learn to adjust policy in keeping with the way it is received by the masses, and to ensure feedback, absorbing the ideas, opinions, and advice coming from the people. The masses suggest a lot of useful and interesting things which are not always clearly perceived "from the top." That is why we must prevent at all costs an arrogant attitude to what people are saying. In the final account the most important thing for the success of perestroika is the people's attitude to it.

---

[1]The name for World War II in the Soviet Union.

[2]A youth organization sponsored by the Soviet regime.

Thus, not only theory but the reality of the processes under way made us embark on the program for all-around democratic changes in public life which we presented at the January 1987 Plenary Meeting of the CPSU[3] Central Committee.

The Plenary Meeting encouraged extensive efforts to strengthen the democratic basis of Soviet society, to develop self-government and extend glasnost, that is openness, in the entire management network. We see now how stimulating that impulse was for the nation. Democratic changes have been taking place at every work collective, at every state and public organization, and within the Party. More glasnost, genuine control from "below," and greater initiative and enterprise at work are now part and parcel of our life. . . .

Perestroika means overcoming the stagnation process, breaking down the braking mechanism, creating a dependable and effective mechanism for the acceleration of social and economic progress and giving it greater dynamism.

Perestroika means mass initiative. It is the comprehensive development of democracy, socialist self-government, encouraging of initiative and creative endeavor, improved order and discipline, more glasnost, criticism, and self-criticism in all spheres of our society. It is utmost respect for the individual and consideration for personal dignity.

Perestroika is the all-around intensification of the Soviet economy, the revival and development of the principles of democratic centralism in running the national economy, the universal introduction of economic methods, the renunciation of management by injunction and by administrative methods, and the overall encouragement of innovation and socialist enterprise. . . .

Perestroika means priority development of the social sphere aimed at ever better satisfaction of the Soviet people's requirements for good living and working conditions, for good rest and recreation, education, and health care. It means unceasing concern for cultural and spiritual wealth, for the culture of every individual and society as a whole.

Perestroika means the elimination from society of the distortions of socialist ethics, the consistent implementation of the principles of social justice. It means the unity of words and deeds, rights and duties. It is the elevation of honest, highly-qualified labor, the overcoming of leveling tendencies in pay and consumerism. . . .

. . . The essence of perestroika lies in the fact that it *unites socialism with democracy* and revives the Leninist concept of socialist construction both in theory and in practice. Such is the essence of perestroika, which accounts for its genuine revolutionary spirit and its all-embracing scope.

The goal is worth the effort. And we are sure that our effort will be a worthy contribution to humanity's social progress.

---

[3]Communist Party of the Soviet Union.

CHAPTER 13

The Century's Last Decade

The twentieth century's last decade had a promising start. After forty years of international tension, ideological conflict, and the threat of nuclear holocaust, the Cold War was over, and according to the U.S. president George Bush a "new world order" had dawned. No one claimed to know exactly what the new order would be like. All but the most cynical, however, hoped that the end of Soviet totalitarianism marked the beginning of a more peaceful and promising era for humanity. Such dreams may yet be realized, but the 1990s were anything but peaceful and harmonious. By decade's end optimism was tempered by a realization that a world without a cold war did not mean a world without conflict and danger.

The 1990s did have their share of impressive, even inspiring, achievements. The inauguration of Nelson Mandela, a black man, as president of South Africa in 1994 definitively ended that nation's apartheid system, one of the century's cruelest expressions of racial bigotry, and inspired hope that human beings elsewhere could resolve conflicts and end injustices. In Eastern Europe new democracies took root, and in Africa, a continent of dictators in the 1970s and 1980s, thirty-six of its fifty-four countries held free elections. Human beings in the 1990s lived longer, and educated more of their children. Population growth slowed, with the mean number of births per woman in Asia, Africa, and Latin America declining to half of what it had been two decades earlier. Scientific and technological advances continued. The mapping of the human genetic code and advancements in computer technology and global communications reconfirmed the awesome power of the human mind.

Other developments in the 1990s were less encouraging. Long-festering conflicts between Protestants and Catholics in Northern Ireland and between Palestinian Arabs and Israelis in the Middle East seemed on the verge of resolution, only to have painstakingly achieved compromises blasted away by renewed violence. Wars — anywhere from twenty-five to thirty-five in each year of the decade — continued to be fought, and nuclear war and nuclear accidents were still possibilities. At decade's end, the five ac-knowledged nuclear powers, the United States, the Russian Fed-eration, France, Great Britain, and China, had thirty thousand nuclear weapons in their arsenals, and Israel, India, and Pakistan had an undetermined number. The United States continued to plan for a "Star Wars" defensive shield against nuclear attack, and Iraq, North Korea, and Libya all reputedly supported research programs for developing nuclear arms.

Environmental problems persisted. Nothing as traumatic as the Chernobyl nuclear disaster took place, but in 1998 land clearing efforts started fires in the Indonesian rain forest that caused a toxic haze to settle over much of Indonesia and Southeast Asia, closing schools and offices, sickening thousands, and causing the death of 234 passengers on an Indonesian airliner that crashed in the smoke.

The decade's most disturbing events took place in Bosnia, Rwanda, Kosovo, and East Timor, where ethnic and religious hatreds gave rise to unspeakable atrocities that raised troubling questions about our very nature as human beings.

Facing new and old problems, the international community showed little unanimity about how to respond. International conferences sponsored by the United Nations on the environ-ment (Rio de Janeiro, 1992), human rights (Vienna, 1993), popu-lation growth (Cairo, 1994), women's rights (Beijing, 1995), and global warming (Kyoto, 1997) revealed wide disagreements on fundamental issues, especially between developed and developing countries. In 1990 and 1991, when the flow of oil to the indus-trialized world was threatened by Iraq's invasion of Kuwait, the United States and its allies acted decisively to defeat the armies of Saddam Hussein in the Persian Gulf War. But when faced with other crises — ethnic cleansing in Bosnia, famine and AIDs in Africa, mass murder in Rwanda — the response was slow, tenta-tive, and, in the case of Rwanda, so slight as to be useless.

Optimism at the end of the 1990s was also tempered by an acknowledgment that none of the century's major ideologies was likely to make good its promises for humanity. At various points in the twentieth century, advocates of fascism, communism, na-tionalism, the welfare state, and free market capitalism all claimed to have discovered in their particular ideology a blueprint for a better, perhaps even utopian, future. By century's end, fascism and communism had been discarded, the survival of the nation-state was being called into question, social programs in welfare states were being scaled back, and free market capitalism had proved its ability to produce wealth but not the capacity to provide justice or security.

The twentieth century, so it seemed, destroyed or discredited every ideology that claimed to have a formula for a radically new society and a radically different future. It did not, however, destroy hope. True, it was a century of genocides, wars, and injustices. It was also a century in which many wrongs were righted, many illusions were dispelled, and many human beings proved themselves capable of great vision and courage.

◆

The Debate on Free Trade and Economic Globalization

In July 1944 economists and officials from forty-four nations met in the New Hampshire resort town of Bretton Woods to lay the foundations for the world economy after World War II. Their goal was to create an institutional framework for trade, investment, and finance that would foster economic expansion and strengthen global capitalism, and by doing so would contribute to political stability and peace. The institutions that grew out of the Bretton Woods meeting remained the core of the world economy for the rest of the twentieth century: the International Monetary Fund (IMF), which promotes monetary cooperation and exchange; the World Bank, which makes loans for economic development projects; and the General Agreement on Tariffs and Trade (GATT), which, until it was replaced by the World Trade Organization (WTO) in 1995, provided rules for settling trade disputes and negotiating reductions in trade barriers and tariffs.

All three Bretton Woods institutions, especially GATT, were dedicated to the principles of liberalizing international commerce and free market capitalism. Protectionism, universally practiced in the first half of the twentieth century, had, so the planners believed, hindered growth, inflated prices, sharpened national rivalries through trade wars, and contributed to the collapse of international trade during the Great Depression. Liberalizing world trade would unleash capitalism's full potential and bring about worldwide economic growth. Not incidentally, it also would open markets for the agricultural and manufactured goods of the United States, whose representatives played a preponderant role in framing the Bretton Woods agreements and in administering the organizations they created.

To encourage free trade, GATT sponsored seven sets of negotiations, or "rounds," in the 1960s and 1970s in which member nations negotiated reductions in tariffs and other trade barriers. After the seventh round, the Tokyo Round, in 1979, worldwide tariff levels had fallen from about 40 percent to 5 percent, with tariff duties eliminated completely for some commodities. Despite GATT's accomplishments, the world was still not a free trade utopia. In every country free trade had its critics among economists, consumers, union members, and politicians, and powerful economic interests — Japanese rice farmers, U.S. automakers, and French winemakers, among others — clamored for protection from foreign competitors. Even after having lowered tariffs, therefore, many governments found ways to limit imports through nontariff barriers (NTBs) such as quotas, special labeling and packaging requirements, and complex customs procedures and rules. By the late 1970s, with global recession setting in, more governments took steps to keep foreign products out of their domestic markets, and the prospects for free trade looked dim.

Beginning in the mid 1980s, however, with the backing of multinational corporations eager to tap into new markets and the support of newly elected European and U.S. politicians dedicated to free market principles, free trade made a comeback. By the mid 1980s the European Community, which had begun as the European Common Market in 1957 with six members, had expanded to twelve nations, creating a powerful free trade zone in Europe. In addition, in 1986 the eighth round of GATT-sponsored tariff discussions, the Uruguay Round, got under way. After eight years of bargaining, the final protocol, twenty-two thousand pages in length, was a breakthrough for international free trade. Agricultural products and services such as engineering, accounting, and advertising were included for the first time, and steps were taken to eliminate NTBs. Most importantly, the Uruguay Round established the World Trade Organization, a body that would replace GATT and, from its headquarters in Geneva, Switzerland, have authority to investigate grievances, settle trade disputes, and enforce rules. Finally, in 1990 the leaders of Mexico, Canada, and the United States announced their intention to establish a free trade zone in North America. Three years later in 1993, the North American Free Trade Agreement (NAFTA), with strong support from the Clinton administration, gained congressional approval, and in 1995 so did the provisions of the Uruguay Round.

Free trade was once more ascendant, and its supporters were confident that a new era of capitalist expansion was at hand. But free trade still had many opponents, and as the twentieth century closed, the debate about its benefits and liabilities continued.

The Dangers of NAFTA, GATT, and Free Trade

❖

105 ◆ Ralph Nader,
FREE TRADE AND THE DECLINE OF DEMOCRACY

During the nationwide debate preceding the congressional vote on the North American Free Trade Agreement in December 1993, opponents denounced the treaty's economic, political, and environmental implications. A leading critic was Ralph Nader, a lawyer from Connecticut who in the 1960s emerged as a prominent consumer advocate when he published a book, *Unsafe at Any Speed,* about ˋ˗ngers of flawed automobile design. In the 1970s and 1980s Nader rallied for a wide range of consumer and environmental causes, and helped found organizations such as the Center for the Study for Responsive Law, the Public Interest Research Group, Congress Watch, and the Tax Reform Group. In 2000 he ran for president on the Green Party ticket, receiving 3 percent of the popular vote. The following article was published in 1993 in an anthology, *The Case Against "Free Trade."*

QUESTIONS FOR ANALYSIS

1. According to Nader, why are multinational corporations so supportive of NAFTA and the new GATT proposals?
2. What will be the economic implications of NAFTA for the U.S. economy, according to Nader?
3. What, in Nader's view, are the potential political dangers of free trade?
4. Why is Nader convinced that there are "no winners" in free trade?
5. What is Nader's alternative to an international economy based on free trade?

Citizens beware. An unprecedented corporate power grab is underway in global negotiations over International trade.

Operating under the deceptive banner of "free" trade, multinational corporations are working hard to expand their control over the international economy and to undo vital health, safety, and environmental protections won by citizen movements across the globe in recent decades.

The megacorporations are not expecting these victories to be gained in town halls, state offices, the U.S. Capitol, or even at the United Nations. They are looking to circumvent the democratic process altogether, in a bold and brazen drive to achieve an autocratic far-reaching agenda through two trade agreements, the U.S.-Mexico-Canada free trade deal (formally known as NAFTA, the North American Free Trade Agreement) and an expansion of the General Agreement on Tariffs and Trade (GATT), called the Uruguay Round.

The Fortune 200's GATT and NAFTA agenda would make the air you breathe dirtier and the water you drink more polluted. It would cost jobs, depress wage levels, and make workplaces less safe. It would destroy family farms and undermine consumer protections such as those ensuring that the food you eat is

not compromised by unsanitary conditions or higher levels of pesticides and preservatives.

And that's only for the industrialized countries. The large global companies have an even more ambitious set of goals for the Third World. They hope to use GATT and NAFTA to capitalize on the poverty of Third World countries and exploit their generally low environmental, safety, and wage standards. At the same time, these corporations plan to displace locally owned businesses and solidify their control over developing countries' economies and natural resources. . . .

U.S. corporations long ago learned how to pit states against each other in "a race to the bottom" — to profit from the lower wages, pollution standards, and taxes. Now, through their NAFTA and GATT campaigns, multinational corporations are directing their efforts to the international arena, where desperately poor countries are willing and able to offer standards at 19th century American levels and below.

It's an old game: when fifty years ago the textile workers of Massachusetts demanded higher wages and safer working conditions, the industry moved its factories to the Carolinas and Georgia. If California considers enacting environmental standards in order to make it safe for people to breathe, business threatens to sᵗ down and move to another state.

The trade agreements are crafted to enable corporations to play this game at the global level, to pit country against country in a race to see who can set the lowest wage levels, the lowest environmental standards, the lowest consumer safety standards. . . .

Enactment of the free trade deals virtually ensures that any local, state, or even national effort in the United States to demand that corporations pay their fair share of taxes, provide a decent standard of living to their employees, or limit their pollution of the air, water, and land will be met with the refrain, "You can't burden us like that. If you do, we won't be able to compete. We'll have to close down and move to a country that offers us a more hospitable business climate." This sort of threat is extremely powerful — communities already devastated by plant closures and a declining manufacturing base are desperate not to lose more jobs, and they know all too well from experience that threats of this sort are often carried out.

Want a small-scale preview of the post-GATT and NAFTA free trade world? Check out the U.S.-Mexico border region, where hundreds of U.S. companies have opened up shop during the last two decades in a special free trade zone made up of factories known as *maquiladoras.* . . . Here are some examples of conditions that prevail in the U.S.-Mexico border region:

- In Brownsville, Texas, just across the border from Matamoros, a *maquiladora* town, babies are being born without brains in record numbers; public health officials in the area believe there is a link between anencephaly (the name of this horrendous birth defect) and exposure of pregnant women to certain toxic chemicals dumped in streams and on the ground in the *maquiladoras* across the border. Imagine the effect on fetal health in Matamoros itself.
- U.S. companies in Mexico dump xylene, an industrial solvent, at levels up to 50,000 times

what is allowed in the United States, and some companies dump methylene chloride at levels up to 215,000 times the U.S. standards, according to test results of a U.S. Environmental Protection Agency certified laboratory. . . .

- Working conditions inside the *maquiladora* plants are deplorable. The National Safe Workplace Institute reports that "most experts are in agreement that *maquila* workers suffer much higher levels of injuries than U.S. workers," and notes that "an alarming number of mentally retarded infants have been born to mothers who worked in *maquila* plants during pregnancies."

In many instances, large corporations are already forcing U.S. workers and communities to compete against this Dickensian[1] industrialization — but the situation will become much worse with NAFTA and Uruguay Round expansion of GATT. . . .

Worst of all, the corporate-induced race to the bottom is a game that no country or community can win. There is always some place in the world that is a little worse off, where the living conditions are a little bit more wretched. . . .

. . . "Non-tariff trade barriers," in fact, has become a code phrase to undermine all sorts of citizen-protection standards and regulations. Literally, the term means any measure that is not a tariff and that inhibits trade — for instance restrictions on trade in food containing too much pesticide residue or products that don't meet safety standards. Corporate interests focus on a safety, health, or environmental regulation that they don't like, develop an argument about how it violates the rules of a trade agreement, and then demand that the regulation be revoked. . . .

. . . Already, a Dutch and several U.S. states' recycling programs, the U.S. asbestos ban, the U.S. Delaney clause prohibiting carcinogenic additives to food, a Canadian reforestation program, U.S., Indonesian, and other countries'

꿈

ˉels of the famous English writer Charles
9) focused on the bleakness of early

restrictions on exports of unprocessed logs . . ., the gas guzzler tax, driftnet fishing and whaling restrictions, U.S. laws designed to protect dolphins, smoking and smokeless tobacco restrictions, and a European ban on beef tainted with growth hormones have either been attacked as non-tariff barriers under existing free trade agreements or threatened with future challenges under the Uruguay Round when it is completed. . . .

U.S. citizen groups already have enough problems dealing in Washington with corporate lobbyists and indentured politicians without being told that decisions are going to be made in other countries, by other officials, and by other lobbies that have no accountability or disclosure requirements in the country. . . .

To compound the autocracy, disputes about non-tariff trade barriers are decided not by elected officials or their appointees, but by secretive panels of foreign trade bureaucrats. Only national government representatives are allowed to participate in the trade agreement dispute resolution; citizen organizations are locked out.

. . . As the world prepares to enter the twenty-first century, GATT and NAFTA would lead the planet in exactly the wrong direction. . . . No one denies the usefulness of international trade and commerce. But societies need to focus their attention on fostering community-oriented production. Such smaller-scale operations are more flexible and adaptable to local needs and environmentally sustainable production methods, and more susceptible to democratic controls. They are less likely to threaten to migrate, and they may perceive their interests as more overlapping with general community interests.

Similarly, allocating power to lower level governmental bodies tends to increase citizen power. Concentrating power in international organizations, as the trade pacts do, tends to remove critical decisions from citizen influence — it's a lot easier to get ahold of your city council representative than international trade bureaucrats.

Formulas for Economic Success and Failure

◈

106 ◆ David R. Henderson, *ECONOMIC MIRACLES*

David R. Henderson, a Canadian by birth, received his B.A. from the University of Winnipeg and Ph.D. in economics from the University of California at Los Angeles. He has had academic appointments at the University of Rochester, the University of Santa Clara, and Washington University of St. Louis. During the Reagan administration he served as a senior economist on energy and health policy for the President's Council of Economic Advisers. Since the mid 1990s he has held appointments as a research fellow with the Hoover Institution in Palo Alto, California, and as an associate professor of economics at the Naval Postgraduate School in Monterey, California. In his numerous writings he has strongly criticized government spending while promoting the benefits of freedom and free markets. In his article, "Economic Miracles," published in the journal *Society* in 1995, he offers his views on the benefits of free trade and economic deregulation.

QUESTIONS FOR ANALYSIS

1. According to Henderson, what explains the contrasting economic experiences of South Korea and India in the post–World War II era? What economic lessons does he draw from the experiences of Chile?

2. How, according to Henderson, does government regulation hamper economic performance?
3. Why does Henderson believe that high marginal tax rates so negatively affect economic performance?
4. How would Nader have responded to Henderson's arguments for free trade and economic deregulation?

Our adventure in looking at economic "miracles" begins with a tale of two countries. Their names are withheld to increase the suspense. For now, they will be called country A and country B. In 1950, these two nations are similar in many ways. Measured in 1990 dollars, country A has a per capita income of $240; country B's is $550. Both countries are so far behind the industrialized world that most observers think neither can ever attain a comfortable standard of living, let alone narrow the gap.

Country A has a number of things going for it: ample natural resources, a huge domestic market, railways and other infrastructure that are good by Third-World standards, and competent judges and civil servants. Country B lacks all of these. Country A's savings rate is 12 percent of its gross national product . . ., while country B's in an anemic 8 percent.

In the early 1950s, country A's government begins a policy of heavy government intervention in both international trade and domestic business. Not only does the government impose tariffs in excess of a hundred percent, but it also requires all importers to get permission to import, often refusing to give that permission. Moreover, country A's government imposed detailed regulation on each industry. Let's say that you run a company in country A and you decide that you want to increase production. You cannot just do so without a license from the government. You want to enter an industry, but you cannot do so without a license. You cannot even diversify your product line without government-granted license. And often the ~ment refuses to grant these licenses.

~u might ask.
í the bureaucrats answers why.
ithout the industrial licensing

regime, this country would fritter away its resources producing lipstick. . . .

Country A's government also owns and runs entire industries: atomic energy, iron and steel, heavy machinery, coal, railways, airlines, telecommunications, and electricity generation and transmission.

What are the results of all this government intervention? By 1990, country A's income per capita is up from $240 to $350.

Country B's government, with fewer natural resources, less infrastructure, and a lower savings rate, pursues a different policy. It allows much freer trade. And, although it regulates industries, by comparison with country A, it is a model of laissez faire. The result? By 1990, country B's per capita GNP is $5,400, and country B did well in spite of a major war conducted there between 1950 and 1953.

Country A is India. Country B is South Korea. . . .

ECONOMIC POLICIES TO AVOID

. . . By the mid-1950s, Indian firms had to get permission to import components or capital goods, and the government imposed massive tariff rates on those imports that it did allow. These restrictions, combined with many others, caused massive inefficiency. The Indian Tariff Commission complained that everything made a noise in Indian-made cars except the horn. India's economy stagnated.

Then, in June 1991, in the midst of a foreign-debt crisis, newly elected Prime Minister Narasimha Rao and his finance minister, Dr. Manmohan Singh, an economist who had argued in favor of opening India's economy to the rest of the world, began to free the economy. Import controls, except for those on consumer goods, were dismantled, and in three years the highest tariff rates fell by almost half, to 65 percent. The government planned to lower tariffs to 25 percent within four years. . . .

The results of these and other reforms have already been dramatic. Per capita gross domestic product (GDP) is growing at 2.5 percent a year. Exports in 1993 rose by more than 20 percent, to over $22 billion, and are expected to increase another 20 percent in 1994. . . . India's middle class, now numbering 150 million, and with incomes of 30,000 rupees ($20,000 in U.S. purchasing power), is growing by 5 to 10 percent a year. . . .

In the 1950s and 1960s, Chile was highly protectionist, with tariffs averaging over 100 percent. By 1972, socialist president Salvador Allende damaged trade by having the government take it over. Between 1961 and 1972, real GDP grew moderately, averaging 4.2 percent. In 1973, the year of the coup that toppled Allende, economic growth was –5.6 percent.

In desperation, the Pinochet regime turned to the so-called "Chicago boys," native Chileans who had studied economics at the University of Chicago. . . . From 1974 to 1979, trade was liberalized, with average tariffs falling to 10 percent. After two years of adjustment, 1974 and 1975, in which real GDP grew by 1 percent and 12.9 percent respectively, economic growth took off, averaging 7.2 percent a year between 1976 and 1981. . . .

A new round of trade liberalization began in 1985, bringing average tariff levels down to 11 percent by 1991. Between 1986 and 1991, Chilean economic growth averaged 6.7 percent. Economists Rudiger Dornbusch of MIT and Sebastian Edwards of UCLA, both experts on Chile's economy, wrote, "For the second time in two decades, one speaks of a Chilean "miracle."

What India and Chile learned the hard way is that protectionism stunts growth. Its opposite, an open economy, allows each country to specialize in producing the goods and services in which it has a comparative advantage, and

protectionism removes some of the incentive to specialize. . . .

Avoid Price Controls

Virtually the whole economics profession rejects price controls. . . . The reason is simple: If governments keep prices well below their free-market competitive level, suppliers have much less incentive to supply; demanders have an artificial incentive to demand more. The result is a shortage that gets worse the bigger the gap between controlled prices and the price that would have existed in a free market.

A student of mine from Indonesia, when asked what were the major things he learned in my public policy course, focused on one. He said that he had always wondered why so many rice fields in his country were no longer being used to grow rice and why Indonesia had switched from rice exporter to importer. He now knew the answer: price controls on rice. Indonesia's case is familiar in Third World countries. Many of those countries governments, dominated by urban dweller, impose price controls on agricultural crops and cause huge shortages, and then subsidize imports.

Avoid High Marginal Tax Rates at All Income Levels

In 1979, newly elected Prime Minister Margaret Thatcher cut the United Kingdom's top tax rate on earned income from 83 percent to 60 percent and on so-called "unearned" income (income from interest and dividends) from 98 percent to 60 percent. President Ronald Reagan in 1981, along with Congress, cut marginal tax rates by 23 percent of three years and cut the top tax rate from 70 percent to 50 percent immediately. Following their example, many countries around the world cut marginal tax rates at all income levels. . . .

These tax cuts led to economic booms virtually everywhere they were tried. . . .

Why did such cuts in marginal tax rates lead to economic booms? The reason is that the marginal tax rate is the price people pay to the government for earning income. When the price falls, people will find ways of earning more — by working harder, working smarter, working longer, and moving from the underground economy to the above-ground economy. Similarly, a reduction in the marginal tax rate raises the cost of taking deductions, causing people to take fewer deductions. . . .

Deregulate

. . . One factor that is surprisingly unimportant for economic growth is natural resources. There is little relationship between a country's natural resource base and its degree of economic development. Two of the most resource-rich countries in the world are Russia and Brazil. Both countries, especially Russia, are in terrible economic shape. Hong Kong, on the other hand, which is nothing but a rock at the edge of the ocean — and not even a large rock — is doing quite well economically. . . .

The basic lesson to be learned from the postwar evidence on countries' economic growth is that growth's major enemy is heavy government intervention — whether through tariffs, price controls, high taxes, lavish government spending, or detailed regulation. Therefore, the way to increase economic well-being is to scale back government dramatically. This does not mean that government should do nothing. It has a crucial — role to protect its citizens from foreign invasion, to protect them from each other, to maintain and enforce property rights, and to enforce contracts. But most functions that it performs beyond those few hamper not only freedom but also economic well-being.

◆

The New Immigration and Its Critics

An Indian software designer working in Silicon Valley . . . a Korean shopkeeper in Los Angeles . . . a Haitian cutting sugar cane in the Dominican Republic . . . a Thai girl working as a prostitute in Berlin . . . a Bosnian Muslim forced to flee his homeland to escape ethnic cleansing . . . victims of drought in Mali . . . a Chinese man working fourteen-hour days in New York to pay off the "skinhead" who smuggled him into the United States . . . a Russian playing professional hockey in Detroit. All of these and millions of other human beings from every corner of the globe were part of the changing patterns of international migration at the close of the twentieth century.

Migration has always been a part of human history, but never has it played so prominent a role as in the last forty years of the twentieth century, a time when more human beings chose or were forced to migrate than ever before. In a report issued in 2000, the International Organization for Migration, a Geneva-based agency advocating immigrants' rights, estimated that the number of international migrants, legal and illegal, reached 90 million in 1990, grew to 150 million in 2000, and would continue to grow for at least two more decades. In the 1990s, approximately three in every one hundred human beings were international migrants, and, in contrast to earlier periods when two-thirds of all migrants were males, almost half of these migrants were women.

The geography of migration also changed. Europe, for example, was transformed from a land of emigrants to a land of immigrants. Between 1500 and the mid twentieth century, Europe provided most of the millions of immigrants who populated the Americas, Australia, New Zealand, and parts of Africa. In the late twentieth century, however, this outflow virtually stopped, and Europe became a destination for migrants from the Middle East, the Caribbean, Africa, and Eastern Europe. Migration also changed for the United States, Canada, and Australia, the world's major immigration destinations; during the late twentieth century, all three nations abandoned quota systems that had discriminated against non-Europeans. As a result, Asians in Australia, Asians and West Indians in Canada, and Asians, West Indians, and Latin Americans in the United States became the dominant immigrant groups.

Many factors contributed to these changes: growing economic disparities between rich and poor nations; changing demographic patterns, resulting in slow-growing, aging populations in industrialized states, and younger, fast-growing populations in Africa, Latin America, and Asia; the intensification of ethnic strife and political conflict in many parts of the world; cheaper and faster means of transportation; new technologies that make possible instant communication between immigrants and family and friends at home; the creation of free trade areas that encourage movements of labor; the liberalization of immigration laws in Canada, Australia, and the United States; and, in developing nations, the weakening of restraints on women's independence and freedom of movement. In other words, migration is one part of the transnational revolution that is reshaping societies around the globe.

Migration can be disruptive, even traumatic, for the migrants themselves, for the countries they are leaving, and for the countries of their destination. This certainly was the case in the late twentieth century, when the number of migrants swelled and most immigrants practiced religions, spoke languages, and came from racial stock different from the majority of those in their new country's population. Thus, as the number of immigrants rose, so too did the number of individuals and organizations demanding immigration restrictions. Opponents of immigration worried about immigration's economic effects, the difficulty of assimilating newcomers, pressures on government services, and, on a deeper level, the dilution and erosion of distinct national cultures in an era of globalization.

The Failure of Multiculturalism

◈

107 ◆ *Jörg Haider, THE FREEDOM I MEAN*

In the second half of the twentieth century Austria became a land of immigration. Between 1945 and 1990 approximately 2.6 million people came to Austria as immigrants or refugees. Most either returned home or moved on to some other country, but approximately 650,000, most of them non-German speakers, stayed and became Austrian citizens. Many of these immigrants were refugees from the Soviet bloc, who, for example, fled Hungary after the Soviet repression of the Hungarian Revolution of 1956 or Czechoslovakia after the crushing of the Prague Spring in 1968. Between 1992 and 1994 Austria also accepted many thousands of Bosnian Muslims fleeing persecution during the Yugoslavian civil war. In addition, beginning in the 1950s Austria became the home of numerous guest workers, mainly unskilled Yugoslavs or Turks who took menial jobs with low salaries. In 1991 there were 260,000 registered guest workers in Austria, and they and their families made up approximately 80 percent of the 550,000 legally registered foreigners in the country.

Unease over immigration to Austria played into the hands of right-wing politicians whose xenophobia and thinly veiled racism echoed discredited Nazi doctrines of the 1930s and 1940s. The leading critic of Austria's immigration policies in the 1980s and 1990s was Jörg Haider (b. 1952), a lawyer who took control of the Austrian Freedom Party in the mid 1980s. Under Haider's leadership, with a platform of nationalism and opposition to immigration, the Freedom Party regularly polled 20 percent in national elections, making it the third-largest party after the Social Democrats and the Austrian People's Party. Following a strong showing in parliamentary elections in late 1999, the Freedom Party joined a coalition government with the People's Party in early 2000. Haider remained on the sidelines, but six members of his party received ministerial posts. Appalled that a European state should empower a party whose doctrines evoked the racism of Nazism, the United States and Israel withdrew their ambassadors from Austria, and the European Union imposed economic and diplomatic sanctions. Haider resigned as head of the Freedom Party in February 2000, but he continued to serve as governor of the Austrian state of Carinthia. In September the European Union, despite protests from France and Germany, ended its sanctions against Austria. Public opinion polls showed continuing strong support for the Freedom Party, and Haider has affirmed his ambition to serve one day as Austrian chancellor.

In 1992 Haider published a collection of speeches and writings entitled *The Freedom I Mean.* In the essay "Multiculturalism and the Love of One's Country," he presents his views on immigration.

QUESTIONS FOR ANALYSIS

1. According to Haider, what has been the cause of the recent upsurge of immigration to Austria?
2. How would Haider define "nation"?
3. According to Haider, why is multiculturalism doomed to failure?
4. In Haider's view, how has the increase in immigration disrupted Austrian society?
5. According to Haider, why do political parties of the left oppose immigration restrictions?
6. What are Haider's short- and long-term solutions to Austria's immigration "problem"?

Of course no country alone can solve the global problem of migration. The discrepancies in wealth between East and West have triggered monumental migration movements, which challenge all the states in Europe. Mass poverty in the Third World, a population explosion and dramatic destruction of the environment, mean that in Africa alone more than 40 million people cannot live in their home countries, but are in search of some other place to survive. . . .

Our job is to tackle the reasons behind migration. Whoever in his own country has no hope for the future will naturally look to go somewhere else. Those who do this, however, should recognize that they come as guests and should behave as such, respecting their host country accordingly.

All the states in the West should try to help people in need so that it is possible for them to stay in their Home Lands and encourage them to rebuild their countries. Let us not forget the generation of our parents, who amidst the ruins and rubble of bombed Germany and Austria did not run away in search of the golden West. With guts, hard work and grit, they rebuilt their countries. They could serve as an example for the youth of Eastern Europe. Or should they all run away, leaving a generation behind whose lives have been ruined by Communism to face further misery?

. . . Since the Left failed to convert people to Marxist Socialism it has been in search of a new ideology, and new enemies. They found their new ideology in the idea of a multi-cultural society which to some has the same appeal as a classless society. But the experiment of a multi-cultural society has never worked anywhere in practice. Wherever and whenever it was tried, immense social problems, ghettos, slums, crime and social unrest ensued. The USA is the best example of this. In the American "melting pot" neither a social nor a cultural balance has been successful. The disturbances in Los Angeles[1] are just an example of many. . . .

Order in a state requires a minimal consensus on basic values. This is endangered when incompatible norms meet each other in an enclosed area. This is the crux of the problem of a multi-cultural society. . . . In many European cities this is best illustrated by immigrants of Islamic faith. In France there are over three million Muslims, in Britain about a million, in Germany roughly 1.7 million. The social

order of Islam is diametrically opposed to Western values. . . .

However one assesses the danger of Islamic fundamentalism, the problems posed by the encounter of two very different cultural spheres remain. This is not easy to overcome as we could see from the dispute in France over whether Islamic schoolgirls should wear headscarves. In Austria there was an outcry when Islamic parents demanded that the crucifix be removed from schoolrooms because it offended the religious feelings of their children!

This is the kernel of the problem of a would-be multi-cultural society. It is not the immigrants who integrate into the society and culture they find themselves in; instead they expect from the natives that they should accept their customs. Peaceful integration on these terms is not likely.

A society which does not rest on a shared value system leads inexorably into chaos and the breakup of law and order. This may be [all right] for the fans of leftist teaching with its anarchist tendencies. For citizens who want to live in peace in their country, such "utopian" dreams quickly turn into a nightmare. The arguments of the advocates of multi-cultural society are not only naive and divorced from the real world but for the most part are plain cynical. This is especially true for the argument that we need large immigration to offset the decline in the birth rate. The same people who are for abortion on demand and constantly devalue the family justify unrestricted immigration to compensate for the results. . . .

The question is, who should decide which path to take? In my opinion: the people. Whoever doubts the role of the people as the highest sovereign questions the very essence of democracy. People have the right not just to go to the polls every four years but are entitled to have a say in questions which are decisive for the future of

[1]In 1992 Los Angeles experienced widespread street-fighting and looting in which blacks clashed with Latinos and Koreans.

their country. For this reason I and my party introduced at the beginning of 1993 the popular initiative "Austria first", which included the following 12 points:

1. *A constitutional provision: "Austria is no country of immigration".*

On account of its size and density of population, Austria is no country of immigration. Whereas on average in Europe there are 100 inhabitants per square kilometer of settled land, this amounts to 230 inhabitants in Austria.

2. *An end to immigration until a satisfactory solution to the problem of illegal foreigners has been found, until the {housing} shortage has been resolved and until unemployment goes down to 5%.*

In Vienna about 100,000 foreigners live illegally. This puts extra pressure on the labor market and {housing}. Only through an end to immigration can further social conflicts between the indigenous population and foreigners be prevented.

3. *An ID requirement for foreign employees at the work place which should be presented for the work permit and for registration for health insurance.*

Only controls can put a stop to the illegal hiring of foreigners, which has meant not only tax evasion and the bypassing of compulsory social insurance contributions, but has also led to a decline in wage levels. . . .

4. *An expansion of the police-force (aliens and criminal branches) as well as better pay and resources to trace illegal foreigners and to effectively combat crime, especially organized crime.*

To be effective, it is necessary to increase manpower. This can only be achieved through making the profession more attractive. In the first instance this includes an increase in pay.

5. *Immediate creation of permanent border controls (customs-police) in place of the army.*

The auxiliary employment of the army on Austria's border has become a long-term feature. The creation of a separate border patrol from the police and customs officials is absolutely vital.

6. *A reduction of tension in schools by limiting the percentage of pupils with a foreign mother tongue in elementary and vocational schools to a maximum of 30%; in case of more than 30% of foreign speaking children, special classes for foreigners should be set up.*

The preservation of our cultural identity, the achievement of educational goals and the need for integration all make a limitation on the percentage of foreign-speaking children in classes indispensable.

7. *Reduction of tension in schools through participation in regular education by those with only adequate knowledge of German.*

In preparatory classes children of school age with a foreign mother tongue should be taught German in order to enable them to take part in education in the regular school classes.

8. *No right to vote for foreigners in general elections.*

The opposite demand of the government coalition and the Greens[2] is primarily aimed at new votes, gaining to compensate for recent losses.

9. *No premature granting of Austrian citizenship.*

We demand that the 10 year period laid down in the law should be kept and exceptions should be kept to a minimum.

---

[2]The Social Democrats and the Austrian People's Party had ruled Austria as coalition partners since the 1960s. The Green Party, founded in the early 1980s with a proenvironment, progressive agenda, was supported by approximately 5 percent of the electorate in national elections.

10. *Rigorous measures against illegal business activities of foreigners and the abuse of social benefits.*

Many associations of foreigners run restaurants and clubs which do not meet commercial, health or legal requirements. Some serve as centres for the black market.

11. *Immediate deportation and residence ban for foreign offenders of the law.*

The crime rate among foreigners, especially in Vienna, has soared, making it necessary to provide extra detention cells. In practice deportees cannot be detained because of the acute lack of cells.

12. *The establishment of an Eastern Europe Foundation to prevent migration.*

The lasting improvement of conditions of life in Eastern European countries should be provided by specially targeted economic help to prevent emigration for economic reasons.

Too Many Immigrants

❖

108 ◆ Roy H. Beck, *THE CASE AGAINST IMMIGRATION*

The United States is a nation of immigrants, but the number of immigrants diminished dramatically from the 1920s through the 1960s, largely due to restrictive legislation passed in the 1920s. Immigration averaged 185,000 persons a year between 1925 and 1965, and around 250,000 a year in the 1950s and early 1960s. This was a far cry from the average of 880,000 immigrants a year between 1901 and 1910. A major change took place in 1965 with the passage of the Immigration and Nationality Act. This law abolished the quota system adopted in 1924 that favored immigrants from western Europe, limited those from southern and eastern Europe, and totally excluded Asians. The new law made family reunification and the nation's need for skills more important determinants of who would be admitted than nationality. The provision for family reunification meant that if a single family member could gain legal immigrant status, it opened the door to his or her spouse, dependent children, adult children, parents, brothers and sisters. Thus a single immigrant could begin a chain reaction that enabled a large extended family to immigrate.

After the new legislation, legal immigration, mainly from Asia, Latin America, and the Caribbean, rose from an average of 450,000 immigrants per year in the 1970s, to 730,000 in the 1980s, and to over a million in the 1990s. These figures do not include illegal immigrants, who may have numbered as many as three million to five million by the mid 1980s. By the early 1990s more than twenty million Americans had been born in other countries, and legal immigration accounted for almost 40 percent of American population growth.

Against a backdrop of economic recession, a movement to curb legal and illegal immigration into the United States gathered strength in the early 1990s. A leading spokesperson for immigration reform was the journalist Roy H. Beck, who in 1996 published a widely read book, *The Case Against Immigration.* Though trained as a lawyer, Beck became a journalist with jobs at newspapers in Cincinnati; Grand Rapids, Michigan; and Dallas. An active member of the United Methodist Church, he edited the denomination's newsletter in the 1980s. Deeply concerned about environmental issues and poverty, he became convinced that population growth and high immigration were at the root of many social and economic problems in the United States. Since 1991 Beck has edited the quarterly journal *The Social Contract,* which publishes material on population, the environment, and immigration.

QUESTIONS FOR ANALYSIS

1. According to Beck, what have been the most damaging effects of high immigration on U.S. society?
2. In Beck's view, which groups have been most adversely affected by high immigration? Which groups have benefited?
3. Why, according to Beck, has Congress been slow to react to the "immigration crisis," despite widespread support among the general populace for immigration reform?
4. In what ways are Beck's and Haider's views of immigration similar? How are they different?
5. How do the views of Haider and Beck compare to the ideas expressed by the U.S. senator, Henry Cabot Lodge, at the end of the nineteenth century (see Chaper 1, source 9)?

Although we often hear that the United States is a nation of immigrants, we seldom ask just what that means. It can be difficult to ask tough questions about immigration when we see nostalgic images of Ellis Island, recall our own families' coming to America, or encounter a new immigrant who is striving admirably to achieve the American dream.

But tough questions about immigration can no longer be avoided as we enter a fourth decade of unprecedentedly high immigration and struggle with its impact on job markets, on the quality of life and social fabric of our communities, and on the state of the environment. . . .

Until recently, policymakers and politicians of every stripe had ignored what public opinion polls found to be the public's growing dissatisfaction with the abnormally high level of immigration. Majority public opinion can be shallow, fleeting, and wrong, but an honest look at major trends during the recent mass immigration shows that ordinary Americans'

concerns can hardly be dismissed as narrow and unenlightened:

- Whole industries in the 1970s and 1980s reorganized to exploit compliant foreign labor, with the result that conditions have deteriorated for all workers in those industries.
- Long trends of rising U.S. wages have been reversed.
- Poverty has increased.
- The middle-class way of life has come under siege; income disparities have widened disturbingly.
- Aggressive civil rights programs to benefit the descendants of slavery have been watered down, co-opted, and undermined because of the unanticipated volume of new immigration. A nearly half-century march of economic progress for black Americans has been halted and turned back.
- The culture — and even — language — of many local communities has been transformed

against the wishes of their native inhabitants. Instead of spawning healthy diversity, immigration has turned many cities into caldrons of increased ethnic tension and divisiveness.

- A stabilizing U.S. population with low birth rates (like other advanced nations) has become the most rapidly congesting industrialized nation in the world (resembling trends in Third World countries). Vast tracts of remaining farmland, natural habitat, and ecosystems have been destroyed to accommodate the growing population. . . .
- Numerous organized crime syndicates headquartered in the new immigrants' home countries have gained solid beachheads of operations. Law enforcement agencies have been confounded just as they thought they were near victory over the crime organizations that other ethnic groups had brought with them. . . .

. . . Some observers fear that the volume of non-European immigration threatens to swamp America's cultural heritage; others welcome an ever more multicultural society. Nonetheless, the chief difficulties that America faces because of current immigration are not triggered by *who* the immigrants are but by *how many* they are. . . . It is time to confront the true costs and benefits of immigration numbers, which have skyrocketed beyond our society's ability to handle them successfully. . . .

Who wins and who loses? A glance through the roster of immigration winners quickly finds business owners who have followed a low-wage labor strategy. Land developers, real estate agents, home mortgage officials, and others who tend to profit from population growth are winners. Owners of high-tech industries have lowered their costs by importing skilled immigrants who will work at lower wages than college-educated Americans. People who can afford nannies, gardeners, and housekeepers have benefitted from lower costs. . . . Others have won by having the security, prestige, or pay of

their jobs enhanced by the high immigrant flow. That would include immigration lawyers, refugee resettlement agency personnel, officials of immigrant-advocacy groups, and educators and other social services employees who work the immigrants.

Unfortunately, the roster of immigration losers is much larger and includes some of America's most vulnerable citizens: poor children, lower-skilled workers, residents of declining urban communities, large numbers of African Americans, the unskilled immigrants who already are here and face the most severe competition from new immigrants, and even some of America's brightest young people, who lose opportunities to pursue science-based careers because of some corporations' and universities' preferences for foreign scientists and engineers. . . .

. . . Finally, it is the local community as a whole that is forced to assume the costs of immigration. . . . Some of the subsidy is monetary: social services to foreign workers who do not earn enough money to rise above poverty; issuance of new school bonds to educate the foreign workers' children; additional infrastructure to handle an expanding population that cannot pay enough taxes to cover the costs; social services to American workers who lose jobs or drop into poverty wages because of the foreign job competition.

. . . We cannot deny that cutting immigration will hurt some citizens. Most immigration lawyers might lose their livelihood and have to enter other specialties. Not surprisingly, they and their organization, the American Immigration Lawyers Association, have been the most aggressive in fighting any reductions whatsoever. . . . Also suffering from the change — at least temporarily — would be the businesses which the lawyers represent and which have decided to rely heavily on foreign labor. . . . A number of national church bureaucracies and other private refugee organizations might have to cut their staffs. On the other hand, the charitable organizations should be able to find plenty of humanitarian work to do overseas — where nearly all refugees are, anyway — as well as among the black underclass and other impoverished citizens here in America. . . . Then there are the ethnic immigrant organizations that had counted on a continuing flow of their countrymen to boost the power of their budding political machines. . . .

Those few groups that stand to lose money, power, or prestige with a cut in immigration wield tremendous power on Capitol Hill. People representing the broad public interest will have to speak very loudly to be heard. The majority of members of Congress previously earned their living in self-employed occupations or as executives; they think like employers who love a labor surplus instead of like most Americans who depend on paychecks and benefit from tight-labor markets. . . .

Immigration is so high now that the cuts proposed in Congress reduce the numbers only back to the level of the Great Wave.[1] In fighting that slight reduction, the National Association of Manufacturers[2] proclaimed the great myth about immigration: "Legal immigration strengthens and energizes America. Throughout America's history, legally admitted immigrants have been a source of strength and vitality to our nation. Our current legal immigration policies are specifically designed to reflect American values and serve national interests."

Nothing could be further from the truth, if "national interest" is defined by what is good for the majority of the public. High immigration almost always has reflected the values and served the interest of a small elite at the *expense* of the national interest.

---

[1]The "Great Wave" of immigration to the United States from the 1890s to the 1910s.
[2]The National Association of Manufacturers, founded in 1895, is an organization of U.S. industrial and business firms joined together to further their trade, business, and financial interests, and to publicize the advantages of free enterprise. Its headquarters is in Washington, D.C., where it carries on extensive lobbying activity.

◆

Ethnic Hatreds and Racial Reconciliation

More so than at any other time in human history, racism was a source of oppression and suffering in the twentieth century. Modern racism in the West, with its belief in the superiority of white people of European descent and the inferiority of people of color, took shape in the nineteenth century out of a mix of misapplied Darwinian theory, nationalism, slavery in the Americas, and the growing disparity between "advanced" Europeans and "backward" Africans, Asians, native Australians, and native Americans. Twentieth-century racism gave comfort to imperialists; justified segregation in the United States and South Africa; inspired restrictive immigration laws directed against Asians, southern Europeans, blacks, and Latinos; provided the Nazis with their core beliefs; and was a source of injustice and inequality in many societies.

To the credit of millions of human beings who stood up against racial bigotry and fought to change the institutions it sustained, racism weakened in the second half of the twentieth century. The Nazis were defeated and Nazism totally discredited, colonialism came to an end, segregation laws were eliminated in the United States, and immigration quotas directed against Asians, African, and Latin Americans were discarded. Between 1990 and 1994, the world's last avowedly racist regime ended when the white leaders of South Africa bowed to pressures from their own people and the international community and dismantled the apartheid system. By century's end, racists still existed, and many societies, none more so than the United States, struggled to deal with the legacy of their racist pasts. But at least for the moment, racism was losing its hold.

The same cannot be said for ethnic conflict. Rivalries based on differences in language, religion, and culture have existed throughout history, but as long as most human beings lived in large empires or stateless societies, the destructive potential of such rivalries was limited. In empires ethnic conflicts could be adjudiated or forcefully suppressed by a higher government authority, and in stateless societies conflicts with a neighboring people could be avoided by migration. In the twentieth century — an era of nation-states — neither option was possible. With the end of colonialism in Africa and Asia and the breakup of the Soviet Empire at century's end, many newly created nations had populations consisting of different ethnic groups that became bitter rivals for political power, economic favors, and cultural ascendancy. In a few cases ethnic rivalries were resolved through compromise, and in many more instances they were restrained by authoritarian governments. As the 1990s amply revealed, however, they also led to civil wars, the disintegration of states, and cruelty of the worst kind.

Serbs, Bosnians, and Ethnic Cleansing

◈

109 ◆ *T. D. Allman, SERBIA'S BLOOD WAR*

Created after World War I, multiethnic, religiously divided Yugoslavia was held together tenuously by an authoritarian monarchy in the 1920s and 1930s, and more firmly by the communist government of Marshal Josip Tito from 1945 until Tito's death in 1980. Communist rule continued in the 1980s, with the presidency rotating among representatives of the nation's eight provinces, but it failed to contain destructive nationalist rivalries that between 1990 and 1995 led to the secession of four provinces, a brutal civil war, and the ultimate ruination of the state.

After festering in the 1980s, Yugoslavia's ethnic tensions burst into open conflict in 1991 when the largely Catholic provinces in Slovenia and Croatia declared their independence. Serbs living in Croatia, who were Orthodox, rather than Catholic, Christians, refused to accept Croatian independence, and the government of Serbia, Yugoslavia's most populous state, backed Croatian Serb militias and sent in regular Yugoslavian troops to aid their rebellion. Serbia's rabidly nationalist dictator, Slobodon Milošević, hoped to blocked Croatian independence, or, failing in that goal, sought to conquer as much Croatian territory as possible and include it in an expanded Greater Serbia. Within a few months the Serbs held almost 40 percent of Croatia, and had driven many thousands of Croats from their homes to create ethnically pure Serb enclaves.

In 1992 another Yugoslavian province, Bosnia-Herzegovina, which was mainly Muslim but had large Croat and Serb minorities, also voted for independence. Bosnian Serbs refused to accept the vote, and a complex civil war involving Bosnian Croats, Bosnian Muslims, Bosnian Serbs, Serbia, and newly independent Croatia soon erupted. While Croatia helped itself to Bosnian territory in the west, the Bosnian Serbs, with the aid of the Yugoslavian (essentially Serbian) army took control of most of the province and began a brutal campaign to kill or drive out Bosnia's Muslims through a policy that came to be known as "ethnic cleansing."

Ethnic cleansing was a euphemism for acts of cruelty not visited upon Europe since the Nazi era. Men gang-raped girls barely beyond puberty, slit the throats of neighbors, blew up Muslim homes and mosques, and sent thousands of Bosnian Muslims to concentration camps where they were starved, beaten, tortured, mutilated, taunted, humiliated, and murdered. The Bosnian city of Sarajevo, host of the Winter Olympics in 1984, was reduced to rubble after three years of sniping and artillery fire. The United Nations sent in peacekeepers to enforce cease-fires and protect Muslim enclaves, but the Serbs snubbed their noses at the UN and continued to "cleanse" Muslim villages and neighborhoods. The fighting and murdering ended only in 1995 after the United States arranged the Dayton Peace Agreement, by which Bosnia was to remain a single state that included a Bosnian-Croat federation and a Serb republic.

In 1993 the prominent American journalist T. D. Allman toured the Bosnian countryside, visited concentration camps, and interviewed Serb leaders, including President Milošovíc. He wrote about his visit in an article, "Serbia's Blood War," which was published in the American magazine *Vanity Fair.* In the following excerpts, Allman describes his experiences in Prijedor, a Muslim town taken over by the Serbs; at a concentration camp; and at a dinner hosted by the police chiefs of the cities of Prijedor and Banja Luka, which was also attended by an American writer for *Newsday,* Roy Gutman.

QUESTIONS FOR ANALYSIS

1. What, according to Allman's account, were the methods used by the Serbs to carry out ethnic cleansing?
2. How were the methods of ethnic cleansing related to its ultimate goals?
3. What evidence does Allman's account provide about Serbian attitudes toward the Bosnian Muslims?
4. On the basis of Allman's encounters and conversations with various Serbs, how would you characterize the Serbs' view of themselves, their role in history, and their future? Whom do they blame for the deaths of the Bosnian Muslims?
5. What do the Banja Luka police chief's comments about Jews reveal about his beliefs?

[DEATH IN PRIJEDOR]

The shiny glass teacups and spotless, ironed tea towels are still on their shelves in the kitchen, next to the downstairs bedroom, where the explosion crushed the couple to death. The TV sits in the living room, its vacant glass eye somehow intact, and the little red Lada station wagon waits in the garage, its finish still gleaming.

This town is called Prijedor. It's in northeastern Bosnia, a region paradigmatic of what the world has come to call "ethnic cleansing." . . .

"The Serbs came in the night," a neighbor whispers in German. "The explosion was at one." They put dynamite in the sanctuary of the mosque and around the minaret. When the minaret collapsed, the explosion blew out the back wall of their house. The mother and father were killed instantly. "The children were sleeping upstairs with their grandmother," he adds, "and survived. They fled. No one knows where." . . .

After inspecting the debris of the mosque, which was really just a neighborhood chapel, we drive over to see the Roman Catholic church the Serbs blew up. . . . The church is a tangle of cement and iron girders now, but the steeple stands — or rather it leans — twisted, pock-marked, scorched by the explosion. . . .

It's getting late now, and people scurry past us into their houses, refusing to answer questions. I knock on several doors. Finally, a Serb opens his door. His house faces the side of the church. Windows in his house were shattered. "Blowing up the church was a bad thing to do," he says. He explains why: "Serbs live around here. Serb property was damaged. Serb people were hurt." . . .

[LIFE IN A CONCENTRATION CAMP]

. . . Some 1,200 men are packed into this cattle shed, located on an unprotected mountainside. They are arranged in six long lines, and each man has only the space of a folded blanket where he can sit or lie down on the floor, which is not really a floor, only gravel. The gravel slopes downward, so when it rains or snows the thin blankets are soaked, chilling the emaciated men, none of whom have coats. There is no heating in this shed, or in any of the other sheds in this camp, where some 5,000 people face winter in the same conditions. . . .

Here, as in the intellectual salons of Belgrade, one encounters the lack of shame or guilt that normally characterizes pathological behavior. To the contrary, the Serbs are proud of this camp. They believe it proves they are treating their "prisoners of war" decently. But aside from the fact that conditions here do not comply with the Geneva Convention,[1] there's another note-worthy aspect to these "prisoners of war": none of them are soldiers. They are all still wearing the same light summer civilian clothing they had on when they were apprehended months ago. When I ask the Serb authorities about weapons captured from these "prisoners of war," they say there are none.

Another curiosity: there are no wounded here, or in the camp hospital, which is actually just a small dispensary. They do have men who are suffering, but from disease or malnutrition, not wounds. This raises the question of what the Serbs in Bosnia do with real POWs. "They kill them all," an international relief official who has investigated these matters explains later.

The camp hospital is manned by imprisoned Croat and Bosnian Muslim doctors. . . .

The doctors are terrified . . . and later I learn why. In Bosnia it is Serb practice when they "cleanse" a town like Prijedor to terrorize average people, especially women and children, into fleeing after signing over their houses and other property to what is called "the Serbian Republic of Bosnia and Hercegovina." Men capable — even though not culpable — or armed resist-ance are imprisoned, like the prisoners in this camp. Then they kill the non-Serb elite: the doctors, lawyers, engineers, rich businessmen, and elected officials, like the mayor of Prijedor, who, along with 48 other of the town's notables, was never seen alive again after being seized by Serb gunmen. . . .

I try to compose a purely technical line of inquiry: "Given the physical circumstances of this camp — the mountain exposure, lack of shelter from the cold, and limited sanitary

---

[1]The Geneva Convention is one of a series of international agreements to provide for humane treatment of the wounded, prisoners of war, and civilians in time of war. The first Convention was signed in 1864, the most recent in 1949.

facilities — what will be the public-health implications of the onset of winter?"

"Forty percent of the people here will die," the doctor answers. . . .

[SUPPING WITH THE DEVIL]

At Banja Luka's Bosna Hotel, which looks like a Ramada Inn, I sup with the Devil, and it occurs to me that I have neglected to bring a long spoon. Actually, the police chief of Prijedor, seated on my right, is amiable, though didactic. Over cocktails he delivers a long discourse on his specialty, which he describes as "ethnic warfare." By his own account he played a major role in "cleansing" Prijedor, and helped run the notorious Omarska camp.

As the first course arrives he opines that it's "very mean" of the media to say Serbs have committed war crimes. "You Americans do not understand ethnic warfare," he says, "because you fight only clean wars, like Kuwait and Vietnam. We do not have that luxury. We Serbs are fighting to save ourselves from genocide." He explains, almost pedantically: "In ethnic warfare the enemy doesn't wear a uniform or carry a gun. Everyone is the enemy." . . .

Our host, the Bania Luka police chief, plays good cop; the Prijedor police chief is the bad cop. . . .

. . . Like nearly all the Serbs I meet, [the Prijedor police chief] believes that Serbia is a great nation, chosen to play a special role in history, and that the world is destined to pay dearly for the folly of not recognizing this fact. "We Serbs forgive, but we don't forget," he says more in sorrow than anger. "We won't forget the West sided with the Muslims and Croats."

"Yes, the world will pay a big price for opposing us," another official agrees.

"What price?" I ask.

"World War I began here," he answers matter-of-factly. "World War III will begin here, too."

This prospect seems to alarm none of our Serb dinner companions. To the contrary, they see it as proof they are right and "the world" is wrong.

"You come from a decadent civilization," the Prijedor police chief elaborates. "You have forgotten who your real enemies are."

At this point the Banja Luka police chief, the good cop, breaks in. "Mr. Gutman," he says amiably, "I think you are Jewish."

"Yes," Roy answers.

"We like Jews!" he says, beaming. "Jews understand Muslims. They know how to deal with them."

Roy resumes his questioning without comment. Is it true, he asks, that Serbs killed all the male children in the village of Verbanći? Can our Serb dinner companions enlighten us on the reports that 167 people were crushed to death trying to escape through an air-conditioning duct because they were suffocating in the room where they were being held? And what about the ravine story: how, after a bus full of Muslims was stopped and the passengers killed, the bodies were thrown down a ravine?

There are three official responses to all such questions, punctuated by smiles and toasts to Serb-American understanding: "Muslim lies." "Croat lies." And: "We are investigating."

Still, even in the good cop's smile, there is puzzlement. Why should this Jew care about Muslim bodies thrown down a ravine? Can't he understand we are all fighting the same enemy — or at least should be? . . .

After a few hours, the debris of the meal lies around us. "A number of the prisoners we saw are starving," I say.

"Because they are Muslims," the official who predicted World War III interjects. "We do everything for them, but sometimes we have only pork grease for cooking, so they refuse to eat." . . .

I begin again. "What did you do to your mayor?" I ask the police chief of Prijedor. "He was freely elected. He was your boss, wasn't he?"

"He was elected by Muslims."

"They say you killed him."

"He escaped."

"Along with the 48 other officials and civic leaders?"

"Yes. Same night. We never saw them again."

"More slivovitz!"[2] the good cop says.

I take another sip and ask, "Do you want your children to be killers or computer salesmen?"

At this point the police chief of Prijedor stands up, looks at me, and says, "I am leaving." There's no anger or hatred in his look, only the realization he's been wasting his time. First he had to be polite to the Jew. . .: Now he's squandered the whole dinner trying to talk sense into the American.

Our dinner party goes on for another hour. The good cop wants his sons to be computer salesmen. "When the war is over," he assures us, "American investment will be welcome in Banja Luka."

---

[2]A plum brandy popular in Balkan countries.

Genocide in Rwanda: 1994

◆

110 ◆ *Fergal Keane, SEASON OF BLOOD*

Their weapons were primitive: Iron bars, nail-studded clubs, and machetes were all they had. Nonetheless, in less than three months government-trained terrorists, with the help of thousands of their countrymen, carried out the twentieth century's most intense and efficient genocide. The place was Rwanda, a landlocked country in east central Africa about the size of Maryland; the time was April, May, and June 1994. In less than ninety days Hutus killed between five hundred thousand and eight hundred thousand Tutsis, as much as 10 percent of their country's population, at a rate three times faster than the Nazi murder of Jews in World War II.

The Rwandan tragedy was grounded in long-standing ethnic rivalries, fears, and resentments, fanned to the point of mass murder by fanatics and desperate politicians. The region of modern Rwanda and Burundi was settled by Bantu-speaking Hutus around the eleventh century. After 1500 they gradually succumbed to the political authority of the Tutsis, pastoralists who moved into the region from the north and, despite making up only 15 percent of the population, reduced the Hutus to semiservile status. When the region became part of German East Africa in the late 1800s, the Germans relied on Tutsi chieftains to administer their colony, and the Belgians did the same after they took over the colony following World War I. Under Belgian rule, Tutsis monopolized administrative posts, army commissions, and places in Rwanda's schools. The Belgians also instituted a pass system in 1933, which classified every Rwandan as a Hutu, Tutsi, or Twa, a pygmoid people that made up only 1 percent of the population. "Race" had little to do with whether one was a Hutu or Tutsi. The Belgians decided that anyone with ten head of cattle or more was a Tutsi, anyone with less was a Hutu, and that a newborn's "ethnicity" would be inherited from his or her father.

In the late 1950s, with independence approaching, the Hutus, fearing future Tutsi domination, rebelled. With Belgian authorities doing little to halt the violence, the Hutus killed thousands of Tutsis and forced many thousands more into exile. The Belgians, believing Tutsi power had been destroyed, replaced Tutsi administrators with Hutus, and when independence came, Hutus dominated the new state. Under the dictatorial rule of Grégoire Habyarimana, Rwanda remained stable in the 1970s and 1980s despite widespread graft, poverty, AIDS, and population pressures. This changed in 1990 when Rwanda was invaded by the army of the Rwandan Patriotic Front (RPF), an organization of Tutsi refugees supported by Uganda, which proclaimed as its goal a multiethnic, democratic state to which Tutsi exiles could return. After three years of fighting, the RPF and Habyarimana signed an agreement that provided for power sharing and future free elections. The compromise enraged Hutu extremists, who launched a hate-filled propaganda campaign against the Tutsis and began to train killing squads (*interahamwe*) made up largely of unemployed young men who were promised the land of Tutsis they killed. Then on April 6, 1994, President Habyarimana was killed after his plane was shot down, probably by Hutu extremists. Claiming the crash had been the work of Tutsi "cockroaches," these same extremists launched their killing squads against Rwanda's Tutsis.

As the killings, rapes, and maimings continued, and the RPF army once more took the field, the world expressed shock but did little, until a small contingent of French troops arrived in late June. By then the RPF had conquered the country, declared a cease-fire, and instituted a coalition government that included Hutu moderates. With more than a million killed or forced into exile, the Rwandan genocide was over.

When the killing began, Fergal Keane, a young Irish-born television reporter for the British Broadcasting Company (BBC), was dispatched to Rwanda to cover the story. With a Ugandan driver, Moses, another BBC reporter, David, two South African cameramen, Glenn and Tony, and Frank, a soldier from the RPF, Keane made his way across Rwanda, preparing a series of award-winning news reports and recording the material for the book he published in 1995, *Season of Blood.*

In the first part of the following excerpt, Keane recounts his visits to an orphanage, to a Rwandan river where thousands drowned, and to a church in Nyarubuye where three thousand Tutsis were slaughtered. In the second part he describes his encounter with two Hutu academics, the rector of the National University of Rwanda at Butare and vice-rector, Dr. Birchmans.

QUESTIONS FOR ANALYSIS

1. What aspects of the Rwandan massacre particularly disturb Keane?
2. How do the actions he describes differ from those of the Serbs in Bosnia?
3. On the basis of Keane's account, what can you conclude about the ultimate goals of the Hutu extremists?
4. How does Dr. Birchmans view the events in Rwanda? How do his views resemble those of the Serbian police chiefs interviewed by Allman?
5. What is the meaning of the episode when Keane was invited to the rector's home to view the World Cup soccer match on television?

[CHILDREN'S STORIES]

A group of children gathered around us. Among them was another girl whose head and right arm were heavily bandaged. I cannot remember her name but her story left me wordless. 'The Interahamwe came to our house and they asked all who are *inyenzi* (cockroaches) to step outside. They knew that we were Tutsis, these people, because some of them are our neighbours. When we did not come out they broke down the door. We were inside and could hear them shouting. And then they came through the front door and I followed my parents and brothers and sisters out into the fields at the back and we ran. But they ran fast and caught us and they killed my family members and they thought they had killed me too. They hit me with the machetes and clubs and then threw all the bodies together so that I was lying under my mother who was dead. But I was not dead and at night I crawled away and hid in the fields where the grass was very high. Then after a time the soldiers of the RPF came and they helped me and brought me here.' . . .

. . . The militias were always on the alert for the exclamations of small frightened voices. Once caught, children were much easier to kill. The little body frames were clubbed and hacked down within minutes. Some, however, survived their appalling injuries. There were many accounts of children who hid under mounds of bodies until they felt it was safe to crawl out. Rose [the director of the orphanage] said that many of the children called out at night in their sleep. Some called for dead parents; others screamed out in the grip of some nightmare whose depth of terror even she, with her experience of war, could not begin to contemplate. For some children the destruction of their entire family groups had robbed them of the will to live. Frequently as we journeyed through Rwanda, we would hear of little boys and girls who had literally died of sorrow, withdrawing from everyone and refusing to eat or drink, until they finally wasted away. . . .

[DEATH AT THE RIVER]

The Kagera River flows from the highlands of Rwanda, down through the country until it crosses the border into Tanzania and then Uganda, finally filtering out into the vastness of Lake Victoria. The river therefore became an ideal carriageway for the dispersal of evidence of Rwanda's genocide. People were routinely lined up beside the river for execution and then pushed into the flood. An alternative method of killing was to force people to jump into the fast running water. Most drowned within a few minutes. The Interahamwe gangs noted that this was a particularly efficient way of killing small children, who were more easily carried off in the current. . . . There were so many bodies it seemed the earth could not hold them. When the dead finally reached Lake Victoria, Ugandan fishermen went out in their boats to recover them and give them a decent burial. Moses and Edward had heard of many men going out day after day without being paid, to gather in the corpses. Colleagues had seen the bodies of mothers and children who had been tied together and thrown into the water. There were thousands of corpses.

[THE SLAUGHTER AT NYARUBUYE]

. . . As I walk towards the gate, I must make a detour to avoid the bodies of several people. There is a child who has been decapitated and there are three other corpses splayed on the ground. . . . I must walk on, stepping over the corpse of a tall man who lies directly across the path, and, feeling the grass brush against my legs, I look down to my left and see a child who has been hacked almost into two pieces. . . .

. . . I begin to pray to myself. 'Our father who art in heaven . . .' These are prayers I have not said since my childhood but I need them now. . . .

. . . We pass a classroom and inside a mother is lying in the corner surrounded by four children.

The chalk marks from the last lesson in mathematics are still on the board. But the desks have been upturned by the killers. It looks as if the woman and her children had tried to hide underneath the desks. We pass around the corner and I step over the remains of a small boy. Again he has been decapitated. To my immediate left is a large room filled with bodies. There is blood, rust coloured now with the passing weeks, smeared on the walls. . . .

. . . While we are waiting for Glenn and Tony to pack the equipment away, we hear a noise coming from one of the rooms of the dead. . . . 'What is that? Did you hear that?' I ask. Edward notices the edge of fear in my voice and strains his ear to listen. But there is no more sound. 'It is only rats, only rats,' says Moses. As we turn to go I look back and in the darkness see the form of the marble Christ gazing down on the dead. The rats scuttle in the classrooms again.

[ENCOUNTERS IN BUTARE]

. . . It is a beautiful evening. The sun is dipping below the thick garden of trees that surrounds the university. Long, slanting rays of golden light come through the window, illuminating the round face of Mr Birchmans and the full glass of whisky he holds in his chubby fingers. Birchmans is a fat man. He has a moon face and big eyes that bulge when he makes one of his frequent denunciations of RPF. . . .

I fill the glasses again and ask Birchmans what has happened to the Tutsis who lived in Butare. They have all left, he says. But surely he must have know about the massacres? No, he has seen nothing like that. Yes, he knows that people have been killed, but in a war people are killed. . . .

'But did the Tutsis deserve to die?'. . .

He pauses. He exhales. 'Killing is a terrible thing, but in war people are killed. That is how it happens.' . . .

The following night the rector [of the university] comes again to our door. 'Come with me,' he says. 'You are Irish, are you not?'

'Yes, I am,' I reply.

'You will like this, then,' he says, opening the door to his sitting-room, where his wife and several children of all ages are sitting in front of a large television screen. The reception is hazy but I can easily make out the green of the Irish football jerseys. I had forgotten that on the other side of the world, in the middle of the American summer, men were playing in the World Cup. 'Rwanda has no team in this tournament so we will cheer for you,' says the rector.

I am given the most comfortable seat in the room. A deep leather armchair. I notice several family photographs on the wall. There is a portrait of the Pope. When Ireland scores the room explodes into wild cheering. I smile inanely and express my gratitude. While I am sitting watching the game, in a town that has become a citadel of killers, there are thousands of my fellow countrymen cheering and drinking the night away in New York. I wish I was there. I wish I was anywhere but here. 'Goodnight, Monsieur Rector, but you will understand. I have a headache. I am not well and must sleep.' He gives me a puzzled look. There is an element of hurt in his expression. The rector cannot understand why I would reject the friendship of his family. But he says nothing about it. He only shrugs and bids me goodnight.

◆ ◆

. . . I am not an especially religious person but I went to Rwanda believing in a spiritual world in which evil was kept at bay by a powerful force for good. Sometimes the battle was close but I felt there was enough decency and love around to nourish the gift of hope. There will be many who say that I was foolish, naïve to ever have had such faith in man. Maybe they are right. In any event after Rwanda I lost that optimism. I am not sure that it will ever return. For now I can only promise to remember the victims: the dead of Nyarubuye, the wounded and the traumatized, the orphans and the refugees, all of the lost ones whose hands reach out through the ever lengthening distance. At the very outset I asked what it was that dreams asked of us.[1] Perhaps they request something very ordinary: simply that we do not forget.

---

[1]Keane began the book by describing the nightmares he experienced in the months after leaving Rwanda. In these terrifying dreams, "the brothers and sisters, the mothers and fathers and children, all the great wailing families of the night are back, holding fast with their withering hands, demanding my attention."

Let There Be Justice and Peace for All

❖

111 ◆ Nelson Mandela, *PRESIDENTIAL INAUGURATION SPEECH, MAY 10, 1994*

During the 1980s, as the South African system of apartheid entered its fourth decade, the Nationalist government under P. W. Botha sought to diffuse black resentment by introducing what the government perceived as major social and political reforms. In 1979 it legalized black labor unions, and in the mid 1980s it granted blacks greater property rights in cities, established black town councils with limited control over local affairs, revoked the ban on multiracial political parties, ended the prohibition against interracial marriage, and repealed the hated pass laws that had prohibited the movement of blacks into cities. With most of the nation's apartheid laws unchanged, however, and with blacks still excluded from participation in national politics, blacks responded with rent strikes, school boycotts, demonstrations, and strikes. The government declared a state of emergency, arrested thousands of government opponents, deployed the army in the townships to maintain law and order, and looked the other way when vigilantes attacked black activists.

Faced with a deteriorating economy, almost universal condemnation from the international community, and imminent civil war, President Botha was forced to step down as prime minister in 1989 and was replaced by F. W. de Klerk. Convinced that South Africa's only hope lay in abandoning apartheid, de Klerk in February 1990 lifted the ban on the African National Congress (ANC) and released Nelson Mandela, the leader of the ANC, from a twenty-seven-year prison sentence (see Chapter 11, source 89). In 1991 major apartheid laws were repealed, and ANC leaders and de Klerk's government began negotiations on a new constitution. Overcoming opposition from white rightists, radical black organizations, and the Inkatha Freedom Party, which represented the interests of the Zulus, the two sides drew up a constitution that went into effect in 1994.

In the first election, Nelson Mandela, the heroic black leader who had spent half his adult life in prison for opposing South Africa's white supremacist government, was chosen as the nation's first democratically elected president. His inauguration on May 10, 1994, with representatives of 150 countries in attendance, was a joyful celebration of a new beginning for South Africa. Coming at the end of a century that often showed humanity at its worst, it was also a reminder of the human capacity to right wrongs and overcome even the most extreme forms of injustice.

QUESTIONS FOR ANALYSIS

1. According to Mandela, who should be credited for bringing about the series of events that led to his inauguration?
2. When Mandela uses the phrase "the people of South Africa," to whom is he referring?
3. According to Mandela, what is the significance of his inauguration as president of South Africa?

Today, all of us do, by our presence here, and by our celebrations in other parts of our country and the world, confer glory and hope to new-born liberty. Out of the experience of an extraordinary human disaster that lasted too long, must be born a society of which all humanity will be proud. Our daily deeds as ordinary South Africans must produce an actual South African reality that will reinforce humanity's belief in justice, strengthen its confidence in the nobility of the human soul and sustain all our hopes for a glorious life for all.

All this we owe both to ourselves and to the peoples of the world who are so well represented here today. To my compatriots, I have no hesitation in saying that each one of us is as intimately attached to the soil of this beautiful country as are the famous jacaranda trees of Pretoria and the mimosa trees of the bushveld.

Each time one of us touches the soil of this land, we feel a sense of personal renewal. The national mood changes as the seasons change. We are moved by a sense of joy and exhilaration when the grass turns green and the flowers bloom.

That spiritual and physical oneness we all share with this common homeland explains the depth of the pain we all carried in our hearts as we saw our country tear itself apart in a terrible conflict, and as we saw it spurned, outlawed and isolated by the peoples of the world, precisely because it has become the universal base of the pernicious ideology and practice of racism and racial oppression.

We, the people of South Africa, feel fulfilled that humanity has taken us back into its bosom, that we, who were outlaws not so long ago, have today been given the rare privilege to be host to the nations of the world on our own soil.

We thank all our distinguished international guests for having come to take possession with the people of our country of what is, after all, a common victory for justice, for peace, for human dignity. We trust that you will continue to stand by us as we tackle the challenges of building peace, prosperity, non-sexism, non-racialism and democracy.

We deeply appreciate the role that the masses of our people and their political mass democratic, religious, women, youth, business, traditional and other leaders have played to bring about this conclusion. Not least among them is my Second Deputy President, the Honorable F. W. de Klerk.

We would also like to pay tribute to our security forces, in all their ranks, for the distinguished role they have played in securing our first democratic elections and the transition to democracy, from blood-thirsty forces which still refuse to see the light.

The time for the healing of the wounds has come.

The moment to bridge the chasms that divide us has come.

The time to build is upon us.

We have, at last, achieved our political emancipation. We pledge ourselves to liberate all our people from the continuing bondage of poverty, deprivation, suffering, gender and other discrimination.

We succeeded to take our last steps to freedom in conditions of relative peace. We commit ourselves to the construction of a complete, just and lasting peace.

We have triumphed in the effort to implant hope in the breasts of the millions of our people. We enter into a covenant that we shall build the society in which all South Africans, both black and white, will be able to walk tall, without any fear in their hearts, assured of their inalienable right to human dignity — a rainbow nation at peace with itself and the world.

As a token of its commitment to the renewal of our country, the new Interim Government of National Unity will, as a matter of urgency, address the issue of amnesty for various categories of our people who are currently serving terms of imprisonment.

We dedicate this day to all the heroes and heroines in this country and the rest of the world, who sacrificed in many ways and surrendered their lives so that we could be free.

Their dreams have become reality. Freedom is their reward.

We are both humbled and elevated by the honor and privilege that you, the people of South Africa, have bestowed on us, as the first President of a united, democratic, non-racial and non-sexist South Africa, to lead our country out of the valley of darkness.

We understand it still that there is no easy road to freedom. We know it well that none of us acting alone can achieve success. We must therefore act together as a united people, for national reconciliation, for nation building, for the birth of a new world.

Let there be justice for all.

Let there be peace for all.

Let there be work, bread, water and salt for all.

Let each know that for each the body, the mind and the soul have been freed to fulfill themselves.

Never, never and never again shall it be that this beautiful land will again experience the oppression of one by another and suffer the indignity of being the skunk of the world.

Let freedom reign.

The sun shall never set on so glorious a human achievement!

God bless Africa!

Sources

PART ONE ◆ The World in an Era of Transformation and Western Dominance, 1880–1914

Chapter 1

Source 3: From C. G. K. Gwasa and John Iliffe, *Records of the Maji Maji Rising* (Nairobi: East African Publishing House, 1967), 4–8 (Historical Association of Tanzania, Paper Number 4).

Source 7: David J. Lu, *Japan: A Documentary History.* Copyright © 1997. Reprinted by permission from M. E. Sharpe, Inc., Armonk, NY 10504.

Source 8: Abdool Rehman, "Memorandum to Lord Selborne, High Commissioner of Transvaal, October 1905," from *Collected Works of Mahatma Gandhi,* Vol. V, pp. 96–98. Reprinted with permission.

Chapter 2

Source 10: From *Prescriptions for Saving China: Selected Writings of Sun Yat-sen,* edited by Julie Lee Wei, Ramon H. Myers, and Donald G. Gillin, with the permission of the publisher, Hoover Institution Press. Translation copyright © 1994 by the Board of Trustees of the Lelands Stanford Junior University.

Source 11: From Basil Dmytryshyn, *Imperial Russia: A Source Book, 1700–1917, Third Edition.* Copyright © Academic International Press (Gulf Breeze, Fla. 1999). Reprinted by permission.

Source 12: From *Zapata and the Mexican Revolution* by John Womack Jr. Copyright © 1968 by John Womack Jr. Used by permission of Alfred A. Knopf, a division of Random House, Inc.

Source 13: Bahithat al-Badiya, "A Lecture in the Club of the Umma Party, 1909," as appeared in Margot Badran and Miriam Cooke, *Opening the Gates.* Copyright © 1990. Reprinted by permission of the publisher, Indiana University Press.

Source 15: Reprinted with the permission of The Free Press, a Division of Simon & Schuster, Inc., from *Chinese Civilization: A Source Book* by Patricia Buckley Ebrey. Copyright © 1993 by Patricia Buckley Ebrey.

Source 17: From *Futurist Manifestos* by Umbro Apollonio, translated by F. T. Marinetti and R. W. Flint, copyright © 1970 by Verlag M. Dumont Schauberg and Gabriele Mazzotta editore. English translation © 1973 by Thames & Hudson Ltd. Used by permission of Viking Penguin, a division of Penguin Putnam, Inc.

PART TWO ◆ Decades of War, Economic Upheaval, and Revolution, 1914–1939

Chapter 3

Source 19: By Wilfred Owen, from *The Collected Poems of Wilfred Owen.* Copyright © 1963 by Chatto & Windus, Ltd. Reprinted by permission of New Directions Publishing Corp.

Source 23: V. I. Lenin, *Collected Works,* Vol. 24, pp. 21–25. Copyright © 1964 by Progress Publishers, Moscow, Russia. Reprinted by permission.

Source 24: V. I. Lenin, *Selected Works,* Vol. II, Book I, pp. 382–384. Copyright © 1964 by Progress Publishers, Moscow, Russia. Reprinted by permission.

Source 25: "Comments of the German Delegation to the Paris Peace Conference on the Conditions of Peace, October 1919," in *International Conciliation,* October 1919 (no. 143), pp. 1208, 1210–1213, 1215–1222.

Source 27: Reprinted and edited with the permission of The Free Press, a Division of Simon & Schuster, Inc., from *Chinese Civilization: A Source Book* by Patricia Buckley Ebrey. Copyright © 1993 by Patricia Buckley Ebrey.

Chapter 4

Source 28: From Frank Whitford, *Bauhaus,* Copyright © 1984, pp. 205–207.

Source 30: From H. Hessel Tiltman, *Slump! A Study of Stricken Europe Today,* © 1932, pp. 39–41.

Source 33: From Bell, Susan Groag and Karen M. Offen, eds., *Women, The Family, and Freedom: The Debate in Documents,* Vol. II, 1750–1880. Copyright © 1983 by the Board of Trustees of the Leland Stanford Junior University.

Source 35: From Rudolf Schlesinger, ed., *The Family in the U.S.S.R.* Copyright © 1949. Reprinted by permission of Taylor & Francis Books, Ltd.

Chapter 5

Source 36: Reprinted by permission of the editor from Benjamin Keen, ed., *Latin American Civilization.* Copyright © 1955, pp. 427–429.

Source 37: From *Seven Interpretive Essays on Peruvian Reality* by José Carlos Mariátegui, translated by Marjory Urquidi, Copyright © 1971. Reprinted by permission of the University of Texas Press.

Source 40: Jose Clemente Orozco, *An Autobiography,* trans. Robert Stephenson, © 1962, pp. 19–22. Published by the University of Texas Press.

Chapter 6

Source 42: J. C. Smuts, *Africa and Some World Problems,* © 1930, pp. 46–49, 59–60, 74–76, 90–93. Reprinted by permission of Oxford University Press.

Source 44: "Parable of the Eagle," from Edward W. Smith. From *Aggrey of Africa.* Copyright © 1929 by SCM Press.

Source 45: Donald Low, *The Mind of Buganda.* Copyright © 1971 D. A. Low. Reprinted by permission of the publisher, the University of California Press.

Source 46: Thomas Karis and Gwendolen M. Carter, eds., *From Protest to Challenge. A Documentary History of South Africa,* 1882–1964, vol. 1 (Stanford, Cal.: Hoover Institution Press, 1972), 344–346.

Source 49: Thomas Karis and Gwendolen M. Carter, eds., *From Protest to Challenge: A Documentary History of South Africa,* 1882–1964, vol. 1 (Stanford, Cal.: Hoover Institution Press, 1972), 16–18.

Chapter 7

Source 51: From *The Zionist Idea* by Arthur Hertzberg, copyright © 1959 by Arthur Hertzberg. Used by permission of Doubleday, a division of Random House, Inc.

Source 52: From *The Emergence of the Middle East* by Robert Langdon. © 1970. Reprinted with permission of Wadsworth, a division of Thomson Learning. Fax 800 730-2215.

Source 53: Mohandas Gandhi, *Indian Home Rule* (Madras, India: Ganesh & Co., 1922), pp. 30–35, 47–50, 63–64, 85–86, 90–91. Copyright © 1922. Used by permission of Ganesh & Co.

Source 55: Reprinted by permission of the author from Harry Benda and John Larkin, *The World of Southeast Asia.* Copyright © 1967.

Source 56: Reprinted with the permission of Scribner, a Division of Simon & Schuster from *Modern China from Mandarin to Commissar,* by Dun J. Li. Copyright © 1978 by Dun J. Li.

Source 57: From Mao Zedong, *Selected Works of Ma Tse-Tung.* Copyright © 1965. Reprinted by permission of International Publishers Co.

Source 58: From *Sources of Japanese Tradition, Vol. II,* by Tsunada, de Bary, and Keene. © 1964 Columbia University Press.

Source 59: David J. Lu, *Japan: A Documentary History* (Armonk, NY: M. E. Sharpe, 1997). Reprinted by permission of the author.

PART THREE ◆ From World War II to the Early 1970s: Decades of Conflict, Decolonization, and Economic Recovery

Chapter 8

Source 60: From Neville Chamberlain, *The Struggle for Peace.* Copyright © 1939 Hutchinson Publishing.

Source 62: From Rudolph Höss, edited by Steven Paskuly, *Death Dealer: The Memoirs of The SS Kommandant at Auschwitz,* pp. 141, 142, 156–159, 161–164 (Amherst, NY: Prometheus Books), copyright © 1992. Reprinted by permission of the publisher.

Source 63: Isaiah Trunk, *Jewish Responses to Nazi Persecution* (New York: Stein & Day, 1978), pp. 268–277, passim. Copyright © 1978 by Isaiah Trunk. Reprinted with permission of Scarborough House Publishers.

Source 65: Copyright © 1947 by *Harper's Magazine.* All rights reserved. Reproduced from the February issue by special permission.

Source 66: Arata Osada, *Children of Hiroshima* (London: Taylor and Francis, 1981), pp. 173–177, 265–269; original published in 1980 by Publishing Committee for "Children of Hiroshima."

Source 67: From *Origins of the Cold War: The Novikov, Kennan, and Roberts 'Long' Telegrams of 1946.* Copyright © by the Endowment of the United States Institute of Peace, 1993. Used with permission by the United States Institute of Peace, Washington, D.C.

Source 68: From *Origins of the Cold War: The Novikov, Kennan, and Roberts 'Long' Telegrams of 1946.* Copyright © by the Endowment of the United States Institute of Peace, 1993. Used with permission by the United States Institute of Peace, Washington, D.C.

Chapter 9

Source 70: "Fourth Press Conference Held by General Charles de Gaulle as President of the French Republic in Paris and the Elysee Palace on April 11, 1961," from *Major Addresses, Statements, and Press Conferences of General Charles de Gaulle, May 19, 1958–January 31, 1964* (New York: French Embassy Press and Information Division, 1964), pp. 113–118. Reprinted with permission of the French Embassy in the United States.

Source 71: From *The Feminine Mystique* by Betty Friedan. Copyright © 1983, 1974, 1973, 1963 by Betty Friedan. Used by permission of W. W. Norton & Company, Inc.

Source 72: "Letter from a Birmingham Jail," From Martin Luther King, Jr., *Why We Can't Wait* (New York: Harper and Row, 1963). Reprinted by arrangement with the Heirs to the Estate of Martin Luther King, Jr., c/o Writers House, Inc. as agent for the proprietor. Copyright 1963 by Martin Luther King, Jr., copyright renewed 1991 by Coretta Scott King.

Source 73: "The Obligation to Endure," from *Silent Spring.* Copyright © 1962 by Rachel L. Carson. Copyright © renewed 1990 by Roger Christie. Reprinted by permission of Houghton Mifflin Co. All rights reserved.

Source 74: From *The Times Were A Changin'* by Irwin Unger and Debi Unger. Copyright © 1998 by Irwin Unger. Used by permission of Three Rivers Press, a division of Random House, Inc.

Source 75: "No More Miss Amerca," by Robin Morgan from *Sisterhood is Powerful: An Anthology of Writings from the Women's Liberation Movement,* edited by Robin Morgan. Copyright © Robin Morgan, 1970. Reprinted by permission of Edite Kroll Literary Agency, Inc.

Source 75: From Anne Koedt, Ellen Levine, Anita Rapaone, *Radical Feminist,* Quadrangel Books. Copyright © 1973, pp. 385, 386.

Source 76: *The French Student Uprisings,* by Alain Schnapp and Pierre Vidal-Naquet. Translation by Maria Jolas, copyright © 1971 by Beacon Press. Originally published in French as *Journal de la Commune Etudiante: Textes et Documents Novembre 1967–Juin 1968,* copyright © 1969 by Editions du Seuil. Reprinted by permission of Georges Borchardt, Inc., Literary Agency.

Chapter 10

Source 77: From *An End to Silence: Uncensored Opinion in the Soviet Union* by Stephen F. Cohen, editor, translated by George Saunders. Copyright © 1982 by W. W. Norton & Company, Inc. Used by permission of W. W. Norton & Company, Inc.

Source 78: Richard Sakwa, *The Rise and Fall of the Soviet Union,* © 1999. Reprinted by permission of Routledge UK.

Source 79: Gale Stokes, ed., *From Stalinism to Pluralism* © 1996, pp. 126–127. Reprinted by permission of Oxford University Press.

Source 80: Translation copyright © 1968 by *The Current Digest of the Soviet Press,* published weekly at Columbus, Ohio. Reprinted by permission of the digest.

Source 82: Copyright © 1979 by Monthly Review Press. Reprinted by permission of Monthly Review Foundation.

Chapter 11

Source 84: From Yeyoshafat Herkabi, *The Palestine Convenant and Its Meaning.* Copyright © 1979. Reprinted with permission from Vallentine Mitchell Publishing.

Source 85: From *Who Stands Accused?* by Chaim Herzog. Copyright © 1978 by the State of Israel. Used by permission of Random House, Inc.

Source 86: Guerva, from "Message to the Tricontinental: Create Two, Three, Many Vietnams." Published in English by the Executive Secretariat of the Organization of the Solidarity of the Peoples of Africa, Asia, and Latin America, Havannah, Cuba, April 16, 1967.

Source 88: From General Idi Amin and the Ugandan Army, as found in Martin Mingue and Judith Molloy, *African Aims and Attitudes,* © 1974, pp. 361–365.

Source 89: Nelson Mandela, *No Easy Walk to Freedom,* ed. Ruth First (New York: Basic Books, 1965), pp. 163–168. Copyright © 1965. Used by permission of Heinemann Educational Books, Ltd.

Source 90: From Jawaharlal Nehru, *An Anthology,* Sarvepalli Gopal, ed., pp. 311, 312, 315, 327, 328, 330.

Source 91: From *President Ho Chi Minh Answers President L. B. Johnson.* Copyright © 1967, pp. 9–12, 27–29.

PART FOUR ◆ Century's Close: From Cold War to Globalization

Chapter 12

Source 92: Mana Saeed Al-Otaiba, *Essays on Petroleum.* Copyright © 1982 Croom Helm, pp. 46–47; 50–55; 75–76.

Source 93: From *Made in Japan* by Akio Morita and Edwin M. Reingold, and Mitsuko Shimomura, copyright © 1986 by E. P. Dutton. Used by permission of Dutton, a division of Penguin Putnam, Inc.

Source 94: "Fighting for the Forest," by Chico Mendes, from *Fight for the Forest,* © 1989 Latin America Bureau, London. Reprinted with permission.

Source 95: From Dai Qing, *Yangtze! Yangtze!* Copyright © 1994. Reprinted by permission of the publisher, Kogan Page Ltd.

Source 96: From the English translation of the final document of the Third General Conference of the Latin American Episcopate. Copyright © United States Catholic Conference, Inc., Washington D.C. Reprinted with permission. All rights reserved.

Source 97: Reprinted with permission from Ed Dobson, Jerry Falwell, and Ed Hindson, *The Fundamentalist Phenomenon: The Resurgence of Conservative Christianity.* Copyright © 1981.

Source 98: Girilal Jain, "On Hindu Rashtra," from Koenrad Elst, *Ayodya and After* (New Delhi: Crescent Printing Works, 1991). Reprinted by permission of the author.

Source 99: From Miranda Davies, *Third World, Second Sex.* Copyright © 1983. Reprinted by permission of Zed Books Ltd.

Source 100: From Miranda Davies, *Third World, Second Sex.* Copyright © 1983. Reprinted by permission of Zed Books Ltd.

Source 101: From Madhu Kishwar and Ruth Vanitar, *In Search of Answers: Indian Voices from Manusha.* Copyright © 1984. Reprinted by permission of Zed Books Ltd.

Source 102: Deng Xiaoping, *Fundamental Issues in Present-Day China* (Beijing: Foreign Languages Press, 1987), pp. 105–109; 42–44; 69–72; 101–102; 162–163. Pergamon Press.

Source 104: Pages 18, 19, 21–25, 30–36 from *Perestroika* by Mikhail Gorbachev. Copyright © 1987 by Mikhail Gorbachev. Reprinted by permission of HarperCollins Publishers, Inc.

Chapter 13

Source 105: Ralph Nader et al., *The Case Against Free Trade,* Earth Island Press, © 1993 North Atlantic Books.

Source 106: Reprinted by permission of Transaction Publishers, "Economic Miracles," by David R. Henderson, *Society,* Vol. 32, No. 59, September 1, 1995. Copyright © 1995 by Transaction Publishers; all rights reserved.

Source 107: Reprinted with permission by Swan Books, Pine Plains, New York.

Source 108: From *The Case Against Immigration* by Roy Beck. Copyright © 1996 by Roy Beck. Used by permission of W. W. Norton & Company, Inc.

Source 109: From T. D. Allman, *Why Bosnia?.* Copyright © 1993. Published by The Pamphleteer's Press. Reprinted by permission.

Source 110: Fergal Keene, *A Season of Blood,* (London: Penguin Books Ltd.), pp. 69–72, 74–75, 78–81, 171–174, 190–191. Copyright © 1995. Reproduced by permission of Penguin Books Ltd.

Source 111: Nelson Mandela, "Presidential Inauguration Speech, May 10, 1994," as appeared in *Historic Documents of 1994,* © 1995, pp. 249–251.

Photo Credits

SOURCES IN
THE HISTORY OF THE
MODERN MIDDLE EAST

Akram Fouad Khater

CONTENTS

PART II
Making Nations in the Middle East, 1900–1949

109

CHAPTER 9   Subaltern Groups   372

CHAPTER 10   The Future of the Middle East and North Africa   410

PREFACE

Students of Middle Eastern and North African history have been more separated from their subject matter than is the case with the study of American or European history because of unfamiliarity with the languages, customs, and culture of this part of the world. Consequently, they have had to struggle to glimpse and hear the voices of real human beings within the stories they read about this area. Without access to relatively unfiltered voices, most students have been hard-pressed to understand and explain the behavior and actions of individuals and groups. In other words, they have mostly been learning only a part of the history of the Middle East and North Africa. This text is meant to overcome that hurdle.

The idea behind the book emerged out of my own experiences as a professor of Middle Eastern history. Early on in my teaching career I relied mainly on secondary sources to teach. My goal, as is the goal of most who teach this subject, was to help students understand the way the modern Middle East—as a set of political, social, economic, and cultural spaces—came into existence. I strove to close the gap that separated the background of most of my students from this "alien" subject matter. But, most importantly, I wanted them to learn this history as the intermingled stories of a great variety of people full of weaknesses and strengths, who stumbled and rose many times in their collective and individual lives. I wanted students to see the peoples of the Middle East as historical actors like the rest of humanity, and not caricatures like the ones displayed far too often in Western popular media. Yet, despite my best attempts I found at the end of each semester that the students still clung to some of the stereotypes, and they still regarded the peoples who have lived in this region as the equivalent of historical stick figures.

Frustrated with this outcome, I began to experiment with the use of documents composed—orally or in a written format—by individuals or groups from the Middle East. It soon became evident that these experiments were producing positive results. Rather than speak of "Middle Easterners," students were compelled to speak, for example, of 'Adel Zua'ayter (a representative to the Syrian Congress of 1920 from the Palestinian town of Nablus) and his views about giving Syrian women the right to vote. In grappling with the debates surrounding these issues, the students came to understand the multiplicity of opinions that existed with regard to this issue. Furthermore, through a reading of the debate that rages for two hours, my students were exposed to the complex relationship between impending European colonial rule and the local social, political, cultural, and religious factors. Regardless of whether they agreed with one or the other positions proclaimed in this particular debate, the students came to appreciate that all the participants were human beings who were subject to larger forces of history, at the same time that they were trying to shape the course of history.

From this beginning, it occurred to me that it might be worthwhile to expand the scope of the primary sources to cover a longer time frame, as well as more geographical areas and subject matter. The result is this book.

While the pedagogical rationale for the book may be apparent by now, there remains the task of explaining the logic of its organization and the criteria for the selection of documents. There is no doubt that a book such as this one can be organized in a myriad of ways. However, in outlining its structure I was concerned with accomplishing two goals. First, I wanted this collection of documents to fit easily within the structure of most modern Middle Eastern history courses being taught in the United States today. Reflecting the outline of Middle Eastern history textbooks, most courses follow a roughly chronological order that begins with a treatment of the nineteenth century and the encounter with European imperialism. From there the narrative progresses to cover the construction of nations, the emergence of post-independence states, the Palestinian-Israeli conflict, the Iranian revolution and the rise of Islamic political movements, and ending with the Gulf War and its aftereffects. Similarly, this book is divided into four parts that roughly follow the same chronological order.

After a brief introductory chapter providing guidance on how to read a primary source, particularly in this subject area, Part I presents various documents from the nineteenth century that lay the groundwork for political reforms and responses to colonialism, as well as economic, social, and cultural changes. Part II presents documents on the making of nations in the aftermath of World War I, and the construction of nationalist ideas as well as the propagation of nationalist ideas at the popular level. Part III focuses on the emergence of the bureaucratic state in the Middle East and North Africa, and its impact upon political and social life in the region. The Palestinian-Israeli conflict contains within it many of these preceding themes, and so has been woven throughout the remaining chapters where it fits within the chronological framework.

Finally, the book concludes with a long section that examines the Middle East today. I have not included documents on the Gulf War because these abound and are easily accessible, and because from the perspective of the Middle East and North Africa the war was a symptom and catalyst of larger changes within the society, economy, and polity of these two areas. But this section does include articles on the aftermath of the terrorist attacks of September 11, 2001, and it concludes with assessments of globalization and its impact on Arab culture, and the effect of cultural pluralism in the Middle East and North Africa.

My concern in organizing the text was not simply to duplicate the timeline of a course in Middle Eastern history, however. I also wanted to introduce thematic approaches within the chronological organization. For example, in the first section of the book I have included—in addition to the traditional political and economic texts—documents that address the cultural changes that were taking place in the Middle East and North Africa toward the end of the nineteenth century. These documents seek to show students the process through which the Middle East and North Africa were changing (or not changing) along social and cultural lines, the causes of these changes, and their architects. I have tried to include such social and cultural documents throughout the collection in an attempt to present the student with more than the predominant political narrative. Thus, the discussion of homosexuality in Egypt brings marginal groups into the mainstream of history and compels us as readers to understand democratic change in a new context of sexual freedoms or lack thereof. In my estimation, this mixture of political and economic documents on the one hand and social and cultural texts on the other will provide a more complete and complementary collection.

This leads me to a second issue. No collection of primary sources will cover every conceivable subject in full. However, I would like to explain briefly another rationale for the selections that have been included. As mentioned previously, I tried to obtain a balance in the *type* of documents that were included. This balance was reached after subjecting the table of contents to several external revisions in which its strengths and weaknesses were noted by anonymous colleagues from various disciplines and with various geographical interests. As a result, I have attempted to include texts from Iran, North Africa, Turkey, and the Middle East. With this attempt at breadth, I tried to find and include documents that fit within the overall theme of the chapter and the chronology of the section. For example, within the topic of Islamic responses to nationalism, I included a selection by Hassan al-Banna from Egypt and another by Shaykh Ben Badis and the Association of Ulama of Algeria.

While by no means exhaustive in coverage, these two selections still provide students with a comparative basis. This is especially the case when these two documents are read in concert with the document entitled *The Proposed Enfranchisement of Muslims in Algeria.* In addition, some documents will allow students to read how one subject was treated in the early part of the nineteenth century, and how this same subject is seen at the end of the twentieth century. This comparative perspective adds another historical dimension to the collection by allowing students to observe changes over time. Moreover, I have sought to include documents that reach across various sectors of society—presenting in the process the point of view of some elites as well as the opinions of people from the lower classes.

I hope that through the use of these documents students will gain a greater appreciation for the humanity of Middle Eastern and North African history and will see them as less foreign than they might have otherwise.

In compiling and editing a book this diverse in coverage I quickly came to know the limitations of my knowledge and the need for a great deal of assistance from colleagues within the field of Middle Eastern Studies. These colleagues were most generous and responsive to my far too frequent requests for help, and this book is so much the richer because of their selfless contributions. They include Abbas Amanat, Julia Clancy-Smith, James Gelvin, Joshua Landis, Afsaneh Najmabadi, Donald Quataert, John Ruedy, Sarah Shields, and Elizabeth Thompson. The reviewers of the manuscript were most helpful in providing me with constructive criticism about the content, breadth, and organization of the manuscript. I thank them all for improving this book: Jere Bacharach, University of Washington; Carol L. Bargeron, Southwest Texas State University; Corinne Blake, Rowan University; John Calvert, Creighton University; Julia Clancy-Smith, University of Arizona; Hafez Farmayan, University of Texas; Cengiz Kirli, Purdue University; Stephen L. McFarland, Auburn University; Sarah Shields, University of North Carolina; and John VanderLippe, SUNY–New Paltz. I would also like to acknowledge the support I received from the History Department at North Carolina State University as well as the College of Humanities and Social Sciences while working on this project. I would be most remiss not to mention the amazing technical support personnel at CHASS who worked tirelessly for three days and two nights to bring back three-years worth of work by recovering the manuscript from the jaws of computer failure. The staff of the D.H. Hill library were equally generous in responding to my incessant demands for more and more arcane titles and articles.

My editors at Houghton Mifflin were a treasure trove of kindness, professionalism, competency, and empathy. They are Jean Woy, who first saw merit in my idea for this reader and who struggled with me through several iterations of its composition; Fran Gay, who had the responsibility of making the idea come to reality by gently prodding me to meet long overdue deadlines; and Lindsay Frost, who was the model of efficiency in turning the hundreds of disparate pages into this manuscript. I would also like to thank my copyeditor, Pat Herbst, who was most diligent in turning awkward phrases into flowing prose, and in catching contradictions and errors.

Finally, I would like to acknowledge the incredible support I received throughout this project from my wife, Jodi, and children, Lauren and Micah. Their love, humor, and joyful spirits shone through during the darkest moments when I thought all was lost and that I would need to recommence the project from the start.

A. K.

The Middle East During the Ottoman Empire, 1914

The Middle East Today

SOURCES IN THE HISTORY OF THE
Modern Middle East

INTRODUCTION:

How to Read a Primary Source

Primary sources offer fleeting glimpses into the past; they record the concerns, thoughts, and remarks of people from bygone eras. The relevance of these words or images to our own historical understanding—grounded as it is in our own time—is not always straightforward. In the following pages we consider how to approach such documents.

Every primary source presents a particular perspective. The author or authors of the source were trying to present their own point of view about a certain subject. Even when we think that a document has an objective tone, we must remind ourselves that the author was not objective, because he or she was working under the influence of strong, unavoidable cultural assumptions. Observing that all primary sources are tinged with bias, however, does not in any way call into question their value as ways to reconstruct the past. Actually, our awareness of their bias forces us to use them advisedly and carefully, rather than dismissing them or accepting them without comment. The biases of an author reveal quite a bit about some of the customs and ideas of the time period in which he or she was working. Thus, we not only can use the *explicit* content of a document to draw out a picture of a particular event, but we also can add our own *inferential* understanding of the mind-set of the author and, possibly, of persons around the author.

Another limitation to be aware of is that a primary source provides only a snapshot, at best, of a small part of a much larger historical tableau. Historians must guard against overestimating the implications of any single document by isolating it from its general context. In fact, the relevance of any document becomes apparent only when we clearly understand the context in which it was written.

With these caveats in mind, let us now examine a specific document.

1

United States Consulate,
Beirut, January 28th, 1885

Honorable Alvey A. Adee,
3rd Assistant Secretary of State
Washington D.C.

The year of 1884 will be remembered by the American communities in this Consular district with pain and distrust toward the Turkish Authorities. During the year, a number of complaints were made by Americans and American protégés (employés [sic]) in this Consular district against the arbitrary and illegal actions of the Turkish Authorities. Each complaint was carefully examined by me, and in all cases, proved well founded, before the matter was brought before the Turkish Authorities. In no instance, however, has a Turkish subject been punished, or the slightest satisfaction been given. From more than three years experience in Turkey, I am convinced that it is not the policy of the Turkish government to bring to justice a Turkish subject for any misdemeanor or unlawful act committed against an American citizen, residing in this part of the country. Letters addressed to the Governor General on important business wherein American interests were concerned have been left unanswered for months. I have complained on occasions to Constantinople of the discourtesy of the officials in not answering my letters, but little if any improvement has been made in this respect. When answers have been received relative to complaints against the illegal actions of the Authorities towards Americans, almost invariably the principal points have been ignored, and no Turkish subject has been punished, as stated above. On the other hand, the Authorities have been most energetic in making difficulties where American interests have been involved. Within the last few months schools and places of worship, which have been in existence for fifteen and twenty years, have been closed notwithstanding the petitions of the Turkish Protestant congregation and the protests of the Missionaries. One of the most flagrant acts recently has been the seizing and sealing (by the Governor's seal on the doors) of buildings which are the property of Dr. W. W. Coddy, American citizen, where schools have been taught; (no complaint has even been made against any one connected with these schools.) I have requested the Governor General to allow the schools to be reopened until such time as the Authorities may choose to grant a permission for continuing the same, and that the people be allowed to worship [as] heretofore. I have demanded that the seal be removed from the door of the building and the property be delivered up to the owner, Dr. Eddy or his agent; but as yet the Governor General of Syria Hamdi Pasha, has paid no attention to my letter on the subject, nor do I think that he will take any notice of the matter further than to say that the schools must have permits from the Authorities before they will be allowed to be opened; (these permits they are not likely to grant.) The matter has been referred by me to Constantinople for such action as our Minister may deem proper to take in the premises relative to the seizure of the property referred to. In conversation with the Political Director of Syria (a kind of Grand Advisor to the Governor General) about the unfriendly action of the Authorities towards American interests in Syria, I mentioned that as for the American Missionaries they give their lives and spend large sums of their countrymen's money in educating and civilizing the people without the least return in any sense; that we receive neither commercial nor any other benefit [from] the expenditure on the work done. His answer was: "If I close all your schools and colleges what can you do?" Such expressions from one in his position shows [sic] plainly that there is a deep feeling of unfriendliness towards American commercial and other interests. As you are aware the war in the Soudan [Sudan] is becoming a serious affair. No one seems to have any correct idea of what will be the end, but the feeling is that sooner or later England will fund and guarantee the interest on the Egyptian debt, and when the war [between Britain and Egypt] is over, quietly settle down there for good. After this, it is the general impression in the Levant that Europe will begin to divide up Turkey. Outside of the French Colony it is not thought that France is likely to get any territory in Turkey. Italy and Greece will accept whatever the Powers may choose to give them. All agree that the division will be a difficult matter, but repeat what has been said for years that Turkey can not go on much longer as she is bankrupt and great dissatisfaction is manifested in the Army as well as by the people all over the country. It is believed by many Turks that the unwise and illegal actions of this Government to all Foreigners will hasten the downfall of the Ottoman Empire. The foregoing is the feeling existing amongst the most enlightened clan of the Levant, and I submit the same for whatever it may be worth. The enclosed article, with translation will give you a pretty correct idea of the feeling of the Mussulmans [sic] in Turkey toward Christians in general and English in particular. The "Thamarat il-Finoon" is the official organ of the Moslem population in this part of the country, and the article was not published without the approval of the Governor General of Syria.

I am your most dedicated servant
John T. Robison

PS: The foregoing with enclosures are private but there is no objections [sic] to your making any use of them that you deem proper.

After reading any document, we should be able to answer four basic questions:

1. Who wrote the document?
2. Who was the document intended for?
3. When was the document written?
4. Why was the document written?

In this case, the first three questions are rather easy to answer. The author of the document is John T. Robison, the U.S. consul general—an official diplomatic representative of the government of the United States—in Beirut. Robison is writing to Alvey A. Adee, the third assistant secretary of state, in Washington, D.C. We can surmise that Adee is the State Department's officer in charge of the region that includes Beirut and possibly the Ottoman Empire as a whole. We also can surmise that Adee's rank, *third* assistant secretary, places him low within the hierarchy of the department. (The State Department assigned a *first* assistant secretary of state to oversee U.S. relations with England. Adee's rank indicates the relative importance of the Beirut post to the American foreign policy establishment. The Beirut district—if not the whole Ottoman Empire—ranked rather low in importance.) The document was penned on January 28, 1885.

After reaching those easy conclusions, we face the more difficult task of understanding the purpose and historical significance of the letter. Why did Robison bother to send a dispatch informing his superior in Washington about the closing of American schools and missions? On the one hand, a cynic might propose that Robison had nothing better to do, so he inflated a minor event into a diplomatic incident. On the other hand, the letter could have been motivated by the need to illustrate to the State Department the low regard of the Ottoman Empire for the United States. In fact, Robison clearly indicates the Ottoman position when he quotes the governor of Syria as saying: "If I close all your schools and colleges what can you do?" This comment seals and highlights the list of grievances Robison described earlier in the passage: namely, that American missions and schools in the district of Beirut were closed for no obvious reason—at least none disclosed to American personnel—and that all of his appeals for a resolution of this "injustice" were ignored. Robison gives the impression that the "Turkish" (Ottoman) officials were arbitrary and selective in their suppression of American missionary activities and did not interfere with French or British interests.

Of course, readers should not accept Robison's argument at face value. We do not need to believe that the Ottoman governor in Beirut had no rational reasons for his actions. In fact, Robison himself provides clues to the governor's reasons farther down in his letter (more on this later). What we can accept as a historical certainty is that Robison believed that the Americans in Beirut were subjected to unfair and arbitrary Ottoman actions.

Why did Robison bother establishing the fact that the Ottomans held American power in such low regard? He was probably incensed at the Ottoman dismissal of himself as a representative of the U.S. government—and at what he regarded as flagrant impoliteness. However, we should not be satisfied with this answer. We need to place the letter within a broader context. To understand Robison's distress about the closing of mission schools, we need to ask what purpose served by those institutions did he consider so important that he decided to write his report. Mission schools—the ones he mentions are American Presbyterian missions—were intended by their founders and financial backers to convert individuals to a particular type of Christianity. In most cases, missionaries found that education provided the easiest means to achieve that end. Rather than simply proselytizing in a predominantly Muslim land, the missionaries used education to attract local boys and girls to American culture and ideas in the hope that they would be converted to Christianity. The role of the schools in spreading American ideas is what made these schools so important to Robison; he viewed them as a tool to help establish the American presence and promote American interests in the Ottoman Empire. Young men and women who graduated from the mission schools would have acquired knowledge of American English, American history and geography, and American political ideas and culture. Later, this knowledge would predispose at least some of them to cultivate commercial and political relations with the United States. Furthermore, as educated individuals living in a place and time when illiteracy was widespread, they were likely to attain positions of importance in Ottoman society. Together, those two factors might promote American influence and interests in that region. Robison knew that mission schools were outposts of American influence that helped—deliberately or otherwise—develop and increase the reach of American industry and commerce. By closing the schools, the Ottoman governor of Syria was in essence limiting the ability of the United States to expand economically and politically into the Ottoman Empire.

Establishing this context helps us to understand the second part of Robison's letter. Right after quoting the governor's dismissive statement, Robison shifts to a discussion of the pending dissolution of the Ottoman Empire. At first glance this change of subject seems a non sequitur. What does the closing of mission schools have to do with the rumored European plans to subdivide the Ottoman Empire? Given the broad context just established, we see that Robison's comments make a great deal of sense. Robison, the representative of American interests in Beirut, was concerned about American influence in that region and would have viewed the pending breakup of the empire as posing a threat to that influence. If the europeans did succeed in their plans, American influence in the empire would decline. Notice that Robison does not say that, in the event of a breakup, any Ottoman provinces would be given to the United States, but he does say that Italy and Greece—both much smaller and less powerful than the United States—would be handed some slices of the empire. In other words, the letter as a whole was intended to present the U.S. State Department with an assessment of American influence in a potentially important area. In Robison's estimation, neither the Ottoman government nor the European powers (Britain, France, and Russia—in that order) were giving

American interests a great deal of attention, nor did they hold American influence and power in great esteem.

Furthermore, we can surmise that some Ottoman government officials considered mission schools detrimental to Ottoman interests. This opinion could have derived simply from xenophobia, as Robison suggests. Or it could be that some Ottoman officials saw all foreign mission schools as outposts undermining Ottoman power and authority but decided to close only the American schools because they lacked the power to enforce the decision on the French or British. These observations are speculations that should be verified. Nonetheless, Robison's allusion to the negative "feeling of the Mussulmans [*sic*] in Turkey [read: Ottoman Empire] toward Christians in general and English in particular" confirms our tentative analysis.

Thus, in addition to providing some information about one particular historical event, this document provides a glimpse into much larger issues. Analyzing its wording and placing it in a broader context provide some information about relations between the United States, and to a lesser extent the European powers, and the Ottoman government. We sense feelings common among some officials and part of the Muslim population in the Ottoman Empire toward foreign missionaries and their schools and toward the European powers. Also, this document makes us privy to some of the thoughts of one individual—John T. Robison. Most of this information becomes evident not from a literal understanding of Robison's words but from the posing and answering of a series of *why* questions that turn this isolated document into a glimpse of a wider and more relevant past. As you read the documents assembled in the remainder of this book, your task will be to use this strategy.

PART I

The Middle East and North Africa in the Nineteenth Century

The story of the nineteenth century in the Middle East and North Africa has generally been told as the history of an encounter between a dominant Europe and a slumbering Middle East. The date usually given for the beginning of this encounter is 1798—the year Napoleon invaded Egypt and the first time since the Crusades (1098–1242) that a European army occupied land in the Middle East. In this narrative, an imperialist Europe bent on worldwide expansion came to dominate the Middle East and North Africa over the course of the nineteenth century, either through physical occupation (the French in Algeria in 1832, the British in Egypt in 1887) or through control over the economic routes and markets in the two regions. This political and economic control led to cultural and social crises in practically every part of the Ottoman Empire, Iran, Egypt, and North Africa. First individuals and then social groups began to ask questions about the reasons for the ascendancy of Europe and the forced submission of the Middle East and North Africa. Different groups arrived at different answers.

Those who were educated in Europe or in European schools came to believe that the answer lay in the modernity of European political, social, economic, and cultural systems. A minority within this new *franji* (European) educated elite believed that the only way to defend themselves against European domination was to emulate the Europeans in schooling, social customs, political institutions, and economic approaches. A much larger number within this new elite believed that a combination of indigenous traditions and European ideas would best serve the purpose of "uplifting" their societies and nations. In fact, some religious reformers, like Jamal al-Din Al-Afghani and Muhammad 'Abduh, concluded that this process of selective modernization needed to be applied not only to the secular aspects of life but also to Islam—

7

the religion of the majority of the people residing in the Middle East and North Africa.

Opposing these views were a wide variety of individuals and groups who believed that any imitation of Europe was undesirable. For religious and secular reasons they argued that what worked for Europe would not work for the Middle East and North Africa. They vociferously argued that following in the footsteps of Europe would lead their societies down the road of permanent European domination. Muslims who believed that their society was ordained by Allah (*God,* in Arabic) warned that abandoning "authentic" tradition was anathema to God.

Although this traditional narrative is fairly accurate in depicting the history of the nineteenth century in the Middle East and North Africa, it tends to skew our image of the period in several important ways. The first and most obvious of these is the notion that the regions were made up of ossified societies and peoples that had not changed—or changed hardly at all—since medieval times. The familiar version of the story assumes that because Europe and the Ottoman Empire followed separate historical paths, and because Europe attained a technological edge in the nineteenth century, Europe was ahead (far ahead in some estimates) of the Middle East and North Africa in terms of morals and civilization. This assumption is very much the same as the assumption that European writers—and some Middle Eastern authors—espoused with little evidence to justify British and French attempts to dominate the region.

Second, the usual account assumes an omnipotent Europe able to impose its will on the peoples of the Middle East and North Africa in a uniformly transformative fashion. Any variations and subtleties in the history of the encounter between Europe and these two regions are lost amid such gross assumptions. More critically, this version of the story fails to acknowledge that the encounter was as transformative to England and France as it was to any of the regions where those European powers succeeded in attaining some semblance of influence. Finally, the familiar narrative fails to allow for the fact that even individuals who embraced European ways did so on their own terms, manipulating and changing those ways to fit the particular problems facing them in places such as Tehran, Cairo, and Algiers.

None of these critiques of the traditional narrative rejects the fact that European contact with the peoples of the Middle East and North Africa was a catalyst for historically important changes. Rather, they signal the need for a more balanced perspective on these changes, to place them in their proper context and thus evaluate them as one element of the history of these areas, not as the only element. The primary sources included in this part of the book are meant to provide exactly this type of nuanced image of Middle Eastern and North African history. They are meant to illustrate that peoples in this region sought and, to varying degrees, maintained control over their individual and collective lives in the face of larger forces—which they did not always understand.

This section is divided into three chapters. "Central Political Reforms and Local Responses" deals with political reforms and reactions to these reforms on the part of the Ottoman populace during the nineteenth century. It includes edicts of the Tanzimat period (Ottoman reforms), a satirical assessment of similar Iranian reforms, and a text from a major Muslim reformer who was concerned with modernizing Islam—Jamal al-Din Al-Afghani.

In the chapter titled "Economic Changes," the same theme of reform is carried over into the realm of economic changes that took place in the nineteenth century. It includes several economic treaties between various Middle Eastern political entities and European powers, as well as documents about local oppositions to some of these economic changes. Finally, "Social and Cultural Reformulations" focuses on the rise of a modern middle class through the construction of new concepts of woman, marriage, and family. The framers of these new ideas considered them essential for the creation of a modern nation and a healthy society that would be the equal of European societies in every respect, and yet remain Egyptian, Iranian, Algerian, Lebanese, and so on.

CHAPTER 1

Central Political Reforms
and Local Responses

The military defeats suffered by the Ottoman Empire in the eighteenth century and the invasion of Egypt by Napoleon in 1798 ushered in a new era in the Middle East and North Africa. It appeared to local observers that European forces suddenly were more powerful and certainly were more expansionist. By no means did this perception lead local inhabitants to assume the overall superiority of European culture, politics, or civilization. The defeats, however, did result in a certain amount of soul-searching by government officials and intellectuals. Many responses were proposed and sometimes adopted, though not always successfully. One of the lessons drawn out of the defeats by some Ottoman officials was the need to modernize the empire and its bureaucracy.

The Tanzimat was a period of reform that began in the 1830s and lasted through the dissolution of the Ottoman Empire after World War I (*tanzimat* is a Turkish word meaning "reorganization" or "restructuring"). In response to the decreasing military, political, and economic power of the empire, reformers (first the Young Ottomans, and later the Young Turks) embarked on a series of programs to modernize the imperial government and the way officials related to subject people across the various lands under imperial rule.

The notion of "modernity" was not easily or completely definable, but to government officials—especially those trained in Europe or European schools—modernity meant an increase in central government control and a shift from treating the population as "subjects" to treating them as "citizens."

Without assuming radical and rapid changes, we can still observe that such changes were attempted by studying the first three documents in this chapter. The first document, the *Hatt-I-Serif* decree, proposed a reform project to secularize the Ottoman courts and bring a greater degree of central control over the administration of the empire. The second was an attempt to transform the sociopolitical organization of the Ottoman Empire from the *millet* (sectarian communities) system to one of Ottoman citizens subject to the secular laws of the empire. The third document is an imperial decree presented to an Ottoman official in the province of Mosul (in modern-day northern Iraq) with regard to the nomadic tribes that predominated in the region. The opinion of the Bedouins expressed here provides valuable clues as to how some Ottoman officials understood the goals of the Tanzimat.

The fourth document, from the writings of the satirist Mirza Malkum Khan, provides glimpses of internal criticism of the Iranian government's and Islamic intellectuals' responses to European incursions. Malkum satirizes both groups and lampoons their efforts as half-hearted attempts to hold on to bygone days and waning powers. Although the great majority of the Iranian population probably disagreed—or at best partially agreed—with him, his satire is still important because it provides a critical perspective on the encounter between the Middle East and Europe.

Responding to Tanzimat reforms as well as to the growth of European cultural influence in the Middle East and North Africa, several Muslim intellectuals and religious reformers sought to influence the outcomes of these changes in ways that fit their own worldview. Two key Islamic voices responding to European imperialism are those of Jamal al-Din Al-Afghani (document 5) and his disciple Muhammad 'Abduh. Both men confronted an environment in which Islam and local cultures faced external pressure and criticism—direct and indirect. While some Muslim thinkers preferred to reject all attempts at reconciliation with European ways of life, these two sought some accommodation between the technological superiority of the West and their notion of Islamic society, traditions, and mores. Regardless of the degree of their success or failure, both thinkers were influential in shaping this cross-civilization dialogue and remain icons in the Muslim world.

The last document in this chapter indicates how after some seventy years of reform one minority—the Jewish community in Baghdad—evaluated the modernization of the Ottoman Empire.

1.   The Hatt-I-Serif Decree Initiates the Tanzimat, or Reform, Period in the Ottoman Empire, November 3, 1839

In the Tanzimat period of Ottoman history, attempts were made to modernize the empire and enable it to withstand European imperialist pressures. The aim of the Hatt-I-Serif decree—clothed as it was in the religious legitimacy of the Shari'a—was to allow the Ottomans to establish a stronger central government by means of reforms in the tax collection and military service systems. The purpose of these reforms was to weaken provincial governors' holds on their territories and simultaneously provide the central Ottoman government with more resources with which to face the European military and political might. The reforms were never fully implemented, but more important than any immediate changes was the fact that this decree initiated the period of Tanzimat, which lasted through the end of World War I, and whose impact went beyond military and political matters to touch social and cultural aspects of life in the Ottoman Empire.

All the world knows that since the first days of the Ottoman State, the lofty principles of the Kuran and the rules of the Şeriat were always perfectly observed. Our mighty Sultanate reached the highest degree of strength and power, and all its subjects [the highest degree] of ease and prosperity. But in the last one hundred and fifty years, because of a succession of difficulties and diverse causes, the sacred Şeriat was not obeyed nor were the beneficent regulations followed; consequently, the former strength and prosperity have changed into weakness and poverty. It is evident that countries not governed by the laws of the Şeriat cannot survive.

From the very first day of our accession to the throne, our thoughts have been devoted exclusively to the development of the empire and the promotion of the prosperity of the people. Therefore, if the geographical position of the Ottoman provinces, the fertility of the soil, and the aptitude and intelligence of the inhabitants are considered, it is manifest that, by striving to find appropriate means, the desired results will, with the aid of God, be realized within five or ten years. Thus, full of confidence in the help of the Most High and certain of the support of our Prophet, we deem it necessary and important from now on to introduce new legislation to achieve effective administration of the Ottoman Government and Provinces. Thus the principles of the requisite legislation are three:

1. The guarantees promising to our subjects perfect security for life, honor, and property.
2. A regular system of assessing taxes.
3. An equally regular system for the conscription of requisite troops and the duration of their service.

Indeed there is nothing more precious in this world than life and honor. What man, however much his character may be against violence, can prevent himself from having recourse to it, and thereby injure the government and the country, if his life and honor are endangered? If, on the contrary, he enjoys perfect security, it is clear that he will not depart from the ways of loyalty and all his actions will contribute to the welfare of the government and of the people.

If there is an absence of security for property, everyone remains indifferent to his state and his community; no one interests himself in the prosperity of the country, absorbed as he is in his own troubles and worries. If, on the contrary,

Translated by Halil Inalcik, from the Osmanli text in *Takvim-i Vekayi* as reproduced in *Tanzimat* (Istanbul, 1940) after p. 48; checked, against the text in Latin Turkish characters in A. Şerif Gözübüyük and Suna Kili, eds., *Türk Analyasa Metirleri* (Ankara, 1957), pp. 3–5, a text that appeared in *Düstür*, 1st ser. 1: 4–7. This document may also be found in J. C. Hurewitz, *The Middle East and North Africa in World Politics* (New Haven, Conn.: Yale University Press, 1975), pp. 269–271.

the individual feels complete security about his possessions, then he will become preoccupied with his own affairs, which he will seek to expand, and his devotion and love for his state and his community will steadily grow and will undoubtedly spur him into becoming a useful member of society.

Tax assessment is also one of the most important matters to regulate. A state, for the defense of its territory, manifestly needs to maintain an army and provide other services, the costs of which can be defrayed only by taxes levied on its subjects. Although, thank God, our Empire has already been relieved of the affliction of monopolies, the harmful practice of tax-farming [*iltizam*], which never yielded any fruitful results, still prevails. This amounts to handing over the financial and political affairs of a country to the whims of an ordinary man and perhaps to the grasp of force and oppression, for if the tax-farmer is not of good character he will be interested only in his own profit and will behave oppressively. It is therefore necessary that from now on every subject of the Empire should be taxed according to his fortune and his means, and that he should be saved from [any] further exaction. It is also necessary that special laws should fix and limit the expenses of our land and sea forces.

Military matters, as already pointed out, are among the most important affairs of state, and it is the inescapable duty of all the people to provide soldiers for the defense of the fatherland [*vatan*]. It is therefore necessary to frame regulations on the contingents that each locality should furnish according to the requirements of the time, and to reduce the term of military service to four or five years. Such legislation will put an end to the old practice, still in force, of recruiting soldiers without consideration of the size of the population in any locality, more conscripts being taken from some places and fewer from others. This practice has been throwing agriculture and trade into harmful disarray. Moreover, those who are recruited to lifetime military service suffer despair and contribute to the depopulation of the country.

In brief, unless such regulations are promulgated, power, prosperity, security, and peace may not be expected, and the basic principles [of the projected reforms] must be those enumerated above.

Thus, from now on, every defendant shall be entitled to a public hearing, according to the rules of the Şeriat, after inquiry and examination; and without the pronouncement of a regular sentence no one may secretly or publicly put another to death by poison or by any other means. No one shall be allowed to attack the honor of any other person whatsoever. Every one shall possess his property of every kind and may dispose of it freely, without let or hindrance from any person whatsoever; and the innocent heirs of a criminal shall not be deprived of their hereditary rights as a result of the confiscation of the property of such a criminal. The Muslim and non-Muslim subjects of our lofty Sultanate shall, without exception, enjoy our imperial concessions. Therefore we grant perfect security to all the populations of our Empire in their lives, their honor, and their properties, according to the sacred law.

As for the other points, decisions must be taken by majority vote. To this end, the members of the Council of Judicial Ordinances [Meclis-i Ahkam-i Adliyye], enlarged by new members as may be found necessary, to whom will be joined on certain days that we shall determine our Ministers and the high officials of the Empire, will assemble for the purpose of framing laws to regulate the security of life and property and the assessment of taxes. Every one participating in the Council will express his ideas and give his advice freely.

2. Sultan Abdul Majid's Islahat Fermani Decree Reaffirms the Privileges and Immunities of Non-Muslim Communities in the Ottoman Empire, February 18, 1856

On February 18, 1856, Sultan Abdul Majid issued a decree that aimed to make equal all of the citizens of the Ottoman Empire regardless of their religion. Although in part this reform was an attempt to please the British, it was also a serious attempt to transform the population of the empire from "subjects" to "citizens." By so doing, the reforming elites of the empire hoped to deter the rise of nationalist movements based on religion, such as the one that had separated Greece from the empire in 1829. Moreover, the decree was intended to limit the ability of the European powers (most notably France and Russia) to claim the right to protect their coreligionists in the empire from religious discrimination. Although this decree did not stop such interventions—in 1861, for example, French troops landed in Lebanon to protect the Catholics of the area—it marks a historical moment of transformation in the nature of the empire.

Let it be done as herein set forth.

To you, my Grand Vizier Mehemed Emin Aali Pasha, decorated with my imperial order of the medjidiye of the first class, and with the order of personal merit; may God grant to you greatness and increase your power.

It has always been my most earnest desire to insure the happiness of all classes of the subjects whom Divine Providence has placed under my imperial sceptre, and since my accession to the throne I have not ceased to direct all my efforts to the attainment of that end.

Thanks to the Almighty, these unceasing efforts have already been productive of numerous useful results. From day to day the happiness of the nation and the wealth of my dominions go on augmenting.

It being now my desire to renew and enlarge still more the new institutions ordained with a view of establishing a state of things conformable with the dignity of my empire and the position which it occupies among civilized nations, and the rights of my empire having, by the fidelity and praiseworthy efforts of all my subjects, and by the kind and friendly assistance of the great powers, my

United States, 46th Congress, special session (March 1881), Senate, Executive Documents, vol. 3, no. 3, *The Capitulations*, by E. A. Van Dyck, pt. 1, pp. 108–111. This document may also be found in J. C. Hurewitz, *The Middle East and North Africa in World Politics* (New Haven, Conn.: Yale University Press, 1975), pp. 315–318.

noble allies, received from abroad a confirmation which will be the commencement of a new era, it is my desire to augment its well being and prosperity, to effect the happiness of all my subjects, who in my sight are all equal, and equally dear to me, and who are united to each other by the cordial ties of patriotism, and to insure the means of daily increasing the prosperity of my empire.

I have therefore resolved upon, and I order the execution of the following measures:

The guarantees promised on our part by the Hatti-Humayoun of Gulhané, and in conformity with the Tanzimat, to all the subjects of my empire, without distinction of classes or of religion, for the security of their persons and property, and the preservation of their honor, are to-day confirmed and consolidated, and efficacious measures shall be taken in order that they may have their full entire effect.

All the privileges and spiritual immunities granted by my ancestors *ab antiquo,* and at subsequent dates, to all Christian communities or other non-Mussulman persuasions established in my empire, under my protection, shall be confirmed and maintained.

Every Christian or other non-Mussulman community shall be bound within a fixed period, and with the concurrence of a commission composed *ad hoc* of members of its own body, to proceed, with my high approbation and under the inspection of my Sublime Porte, to examine into its actual immunities and privileges, and to discuss and submit to my Sublime Porte the reforms required by the progress of civilization and of the age. The powers conceded to the Christian patriarchs and bishops by the Sultan Mahomet II and to his successors shall be made to harmonize with the new position which my generous and beneficent intentions insure to these communities.

The principle of nominating the patriarchs for life, after the revision of the rule of election now in force, shall be exactly carried out, conformably to the tenor of their firmans [Ottoman imperial decrees] of investiture.

The patriarchs, metropolitans, archbishops, bishops, and [rabbis] shall take an oath, on their entrance into office, according to a form agreed upon in common by my Sublime Porte and the spiritual heads of the different religious communities. The ecclesiastical dues, of whatever sort or nature they be, shall be abolished and replaced by fixed revenues of the patriarchs and heads of communities, and by the allocations of allowances and salaries equitably proportioned to the importance, the rank, and the dignity of the different members of the clergy.

The property, real or personal, of the different Christian ecclesiastics shall remain intact: the temporal administration of the Christian or other non-Mussulman communities shall, however, be placed under the safeguard of an assembly to be chosen from among the members, both ecclesiastics and laymen, of the said communities.

In the towns, small boroughs, and villages where the whole population is of the same religion, no obstacle shall be offered to the repair, according to their original plan, of buildings set apart for religious worship, for schools, for hospitals, and for cemeteries.

The plans of these different buildings, in case of their new erection, must, after having been approved by the patriarchs or heads of communities, be submitted to my Sublime Porte, which will approve of them by my imperial order, or make known its observations upon them within a certain time. Each sect, in localities where there are no other religious denominations, shall be free from every species of restraint as regards the public exercise of its religion.

In the towns, small boroughs, and villages where different sects are mingled together each community inhabiting a distinct quarter shall, by conforming to the above-mentioned ordinances, have equal power to repair and improve its churches, its hospitals, its schools, and its cemeteries. When there is question of their erection of new buildings, the necessary authority must be asked for, through the medium of the patriarchs and heads of communities, from my Sublime Porte, which will pronounce a sovereign decision according that authority, except in the case of administrative obstacles.

The intervention of the administrative authority in all measures of this nature will be entirely gratuitous. My Sublime Porte will take energetic measures to insure to each sect, whatever be the number of its adherents, entire freedom in the exercise of its religion. Every distinction or designation pending to make any class whatever of the subjects of my empire inferior to another class, on account of their religion, language, or race, shall be forever effaced from administrative protocol. The laws shall be put in force against the use of any injurious or offensive term, either among private individuals or on the part of the authorities.

As all forms of religion are and shall be freely professed in my dominions, no subject of my empire shall be hindered in the exercise of the religion that he professes, nor shall he be in any way annoyed on this account. No one shall be compelled to change their religion.

The nomination and choice of all functionaries and other employees of my empire being wholly dependent upon my sovereign will, all the subjects of my empire, without distinction of nationality, shall be admissible to public employments, and qualified to fill them according to their capacity and merit, and conformably with rules to be generally applied.

All the subjects of my empire, without distinction, shall be received into the civil and military schools of the government, if they otherwise satisfy the conditions as to age and examination which are specified in the organic regulations of the said schools. Moreover, every community is authorized to establish public schools of science, art, and industry. Only the method of instructions and the choice of professors in schools of this class shall be under the control of a mixed council of public instruction, the members of which shall be named by my sovereign command.

All commercial, correctional, and criminal suits between Mussulmans and Christians, or other non-Mussulman subjects, or between Christian or other non-Mussulmans of different sects, shall be referred to mixed tribunals.

The proceedings of these tribunals shall be public; the parties shall be confronted and shall produce their witnesses, whose testimony shall be received without distinction, upon an oath taken according to the religious law of each sect.

Suits relating to civil affairs shall continue to be publicly tried, according to the laws and regulations, before the mi[x]ed provincial councils, in the presence of the governor and judge of the place.

Special civil proceedings, such as those relating to successions or others of that kind, between subjects of the same Christian or other non-Mussulman faith, may, at the request of the parties, be sent before the councils of the patriarchs or of the communities.

Penal, correctional, and commercial laws, and rules of procedure for the mi[x]ed tribunals, shall be drawn up as soon as possible and formed into a code. Translations of them shall be published in all the languages current in the empire.

Proceedings shall be taken, with as little delay as possible, for the reform of the penitentiary system as applied to houses of detention, punishment, or correction, and other establishments of like nature, so as to reconcile the rights of humanity with those of justice. Corporal punishment shall not be administered, even in the prisons, except in conformity with the disciplinary regulations established by my Sublime Porte, and everything that resembles torture shall be entirely abolished.

Infractions of the law in this particular shall be severely repressed, and shall besides entail, as of right, the punishment, in conformity with the civil code, of the authorities who may order and of the agents who may commit them.

The organization of the police in the capital, in the provincial towns and in the rural districts, shall be revised in such a manner as to give to all the peaceable subjects of my empire the strongest guarantees for the safety both of their persons and property.

The equality of taxes entailing equality of burdens, as equality of duties entails that of rights, Christian subjects, and those of other non-Mussulman sects, as it has been already decided, shall, as well as Mussulmans, be subject to the obligations of the law of recruitment.

The principle of obtaining substitutes, or of purchasing exemption, shall be admitted. A complete law shall be published, with as little delay as possible, respecting the admission into and service in the army of Christian and other non-Mussulman subjects.

Proceedings shall be taken for a reform in the constitution of the provincial and communal councils in order to insure fairness in the choice of the deputies of the Mussulman, Christian, and other communities and freedom of voting in the councils. My Sublime Porte will take into consideration the adoption of the most effectual means for ascertaining exactly and for controlling the result of the deliberations and of the decisions arrived at.

As the laws regulating the purchase, sale, and disposal of real property are common to all the subjects of my empire, it shall be lawful for foreigners to possess landed property in my dominions, conforming themselves to the laws and police regulations, and bearing the same charges as the native inhabitants, and after arrangements have been come to with foreign powers.

The taxes are to be levied under the same denomination from all the subjects of my empire, without distinction of class or of religion. The most prompt and energetic means for remedying the abuses in collecting the taxes, and especially the tithes, shall be considered.

The system of direct collections shall gradually, and as soon as possible, be substituted for the plan of farming, in all the branches of the revenues of the state. As long as the present system remains in force all agents of the government and all members of the medjlis shall be forbidden under the severest penalties, to become lessees of any farming contracts which are announced for public competition, or to have any beneficial interest in carrying them out. The local taxes shall, as far as possible, be so imposed as not to affect the sources of production or to hinder the progress of internal commerce.

Works of public utility shall receive a suitable endowment, part of which shall be raised from private and special taxes levied in the provinces, which shall have the benefit of the advantages arising from the establishment of ways of communication by land and sea.

A special law having been already passed, which declares that the budget of the revenue and the expenditure of the state shall be drawn up and made known every year, the said law shall be most scrupulously observed. Proceedings shall be taken for revising the emoluments attached to each office.

The heads of each community and a delegate, designated by my Sublime Porte, shall be summoned to take part in the deliberations of the supreme council of justice on all occasions which might interest the generality of the subjects of my empire. They shall be summoned specially for this purpose by my grand vizier. The delegates shall hold office for one year; they shall be sworn on entering upon their duties. All the members of the council, at the ordinary and extraordinary meetings, shall freely give their opinions and their votes, and no one shall ever annoy them on this account.

The laws against corruption, extortion, or malversation shall apply, according to the legal forms, to all the subjects of my empire, whatever may be their class and the nature of their duties.

Steps shall be taken for the formation of banks and other similar institutions, so as to effect a reform in the monetary and financial system, as well as to create funds to be employed in augmenting the sources of the material wealth of my empire. Steps shall also be taken for the formation of roads and canals to increase the facilities of communication and increase the sources of the wealth of the country.

Everything that can impede commerce or agriculture shall be abolished. To accomplish these objects means shall be sought to profit by the science, the art, and the funds of Europe, and thus gradually to execute them.

Such being my wishes and my commands, you, who are my grand vizier, will, according to custom, cause this imperial firman to be published in my capital and in all parts of my empire; and you will watch attentively and take all the necessary measures that all the orders which it contains be henceforth carried out with the most rigorous punctuality.

3. An Ottoman Government Decree Defines the Official Notion of the "Modern" Citizen, June 19, 1870

Derived in part from knowledge about the way the French, British, and Austrian governments functioned, and in part from local needs and established customs, these Tanzimat reforms attempted to extend the reach of the Ottoman government internally while allowing it to face external threats. This document seeks to draw an irrevocable distinction between "primitive" nomadic tribes—Bedouins—and "urbane" people who live in cities and villages. It makes strong value judgments about each category and provides a clear-cut recommendation for dealing with the Bedouins. Pay particular attention to the language used to describe each group, and question the characterizations. Think about likely reasons behind the creation of the two categories. Do not assume that the author is describing reality in an objective manner. What ideological motivation do you think lies behind this depiction of the Bedouin way of life?

To the model of proverbs and peers, His Excellency Firhan Pasha Zayd 'Alwa. It is known that if one compares the tribes and people who live in the lifestyle of Bedouins [nomadic tribes] with those urbane people who live in the cities and villages, one will note the complexity in the customs of city-folk. In contrast, it will be noted that in comparison to the original creation of man and his internal self, the way of life of Bedouins is simple. In fact, the primitive and original state of man is most likely the same as that of the Bedouin. However, God has graced human beings with a characteristic that is absent from any other [species]. According to this characteristic, man cannot remain in his original state of creation but should prepare all that is needed for his food, drink, and clothing, and after this he must gather knowledge and develop commerce and other human necessities. He seeks to obtain other necessities as well, and every time he reaches a stage of acquisition, then he sees the need to advance and progress beyond what he had in the past. [. . .] Thus, it is apparent that even if the first state of man is to be a Bedouin, urbanity is a characteristic that cannot be separated from him. For the human being has become civilized [. . .] and the virtues of humanity cannot be attained except through the path of urbanization and civilization. Those who surpass their brethren and control all elements of this world, completely or partially, are those who live in the cities and who are civilized.

After proving that this is the case, we would like to explain and specify the reasons those people demand to remain in this state [of being Bedouins]. They remain in this state of deprivation of the virtues of humanity and the characteristics of civilization for several reasons. The first is that these people are ignorant of the state of the world and the nations. Because of their ignorance we have

Ottoman government decree issued to the Amir of Shamr, His Excellency Firhan Pasha, June 19, 1870. Ottoman archives of Directorate General of State Archives at the Prime Ministry (Tapu Tahrir: Mosul, 1869–1872). Translated by Akram Khater.

found our fathers desiring to stay unchanged in the state to which they were born. Secondly, the basis of the wealth of the tribes and clans is animals—in particular camels—and since it is difficult to manage and raise animals and camels in the cities—where they cannot find pasture—the people remain in their original state of being. [. . .] The third reason is that the mentioned peoples like wild animals who enjoy what they have gotten used to in terms of stealing and raiding the property of others of their own people and killing them. This has become a reason for their wildness and their insistence on staying in the state of Bedouinism. It should be obvious that the first reason—which is ignorance and illiteracy—is an ugly and unacceptable characteristic in all the creatures of this world. And the second reason is the subordination [to tradition] characteristic of animals, and it is contrary to the image according to which man was created, for God has created the human being to be the most honorable of all creatures, and He made all breathing creatures subservient to him. He who is a Bedouin has become accustomed to the opposite of this natural order, so that although he used to be over other creatures, he has become subservient.

The truth is that this fallen state is an insult to humanity, and accordingly if we investigate the immense harm these tribes cause to each other, we will find that it has no equivalence in magnitude. For the human being has been commanded to protect those of his kind and treat them well, and is not commanded to do the opposite. In fact, all the religions command this [good treatment of others], and in particular the Mohammedan Shari‘a. After proving that this is contrary to what has been commanded and is prohibited in all religions and in the Mohammedan Shari‘a, then anyone with intelligence will see that harming people and robbing them of their money and their cattle is contrary to humanity and Islam. He who dares to commit that which we have mentioned must be punished. In addition, we see that this implies that since living as a Bedouin [. . .] leads to these harmful results, then no one should stay in that state of being, especially since we have arrived at a time and epoch [. . .] where to stay in this fallen and immoral state of existence appears as an ugly habit in the eyes of the world. For these explained reasons, these people cannot stay even for a short period in this state, and these tribes and clans should be settled and gain good human characteristics. It is imperative upon the Sublime Government to facilitate the emergence of these moral characteristics. This is particularly the case since those tribes and clans that have been settled during the past two years have faced difficulties and material needs, and they have remained in their original state because they are deprived of access to agriculture and commerce. Thus, and in order to feed their children, they have dared to attack the fields belonging to the inhabitants of the cities and towns. And in that case the government will have to reimburse the farmers for their losses and to dispatch imperial troops to punish the perpetrators, all of which costs money. Thus, and before matters reach this state, we would advise to give the lands that extend from Tikrit [village in Iraq] to the borders of Mosul [main city in northern Iraq] and that are located east of the Tigris River to the Shamr clan. Furthermore, we recommend that these lands be designated as a Mutassarifiya [provincial government within the Ottoman Empire] and be named as Sandjak [province] of Shamr, and that they [the clan of Shamr] be settled in these lands until they dig the necessary canals to the Tigris and reclaim the lands and plant them like other people. Once it is apparent that they are settled, then this place should be designated as a Mutassarifiya, like the Mutassarifiya of al-Muntafak, and this Mutassarifiya should be placed under your authority, O, Pasha! [. . .] Because those [people] are used to being Bedouins, and because it will be difficult to sever those ties all at once, then we should grant some of them with animals a permit to pasture their animals on some of the lands, provided that they return to their places of residence. In order to encourage development of these lands, we should exempt those who reclaim the lands and dig the ditches and canals from all but the Miri tax. [. . .] Once this Sandjak is formed according to what has preceded, and a Mutassarifiya is subsequently established, then troops should be sent to keep the peace, and the Mutassarif should be assigned a deputy and a tax collector and all that he requires in terms of government officials. [. . .]

This official Ottoman decree has been issued by the ministry of the Vilayet of Baghdad, and let it be known to all.

4. Mirza Malkum Khan Satirizes Iran's Central Government and Religious Elites, 1880s

Like some of his contemporaries in Istanbul and Cairo, Mirza Malkum (1834–1898) was a political satirist who skewered existing political regimes and popular beliefs for their irrationality and corruption. Like writers such as Yaqub Sannu (in Egypt), Malkum was well traveled and well educated. Although he was born in Iran, he spent only ten years there. His father was a scion of the Armenian community in Iran, a community that during the nineteenth century was commercially powerful due to its connections to European mercantile interests. Malkum claimed descent from Jean-Jacques Rousseau through a distant grandmother. Malkum's father was originally Christian; he converted to Islam for personal and practical reasons. Throughout his life, Malkum proclaimed himself a Muslim. However, one scholar (Hamid Algar) argues that this profession was insincere at best and that Malkum used his proclamation of faith as a way to hide and justify his later criticisms and attacks on the Islamic faith.

Malkum's writings and lectures—some of which were delivered while he was living in England—seem to indicate his interest in an Islamic renaissance. Educated in France at the Armenian school from the age of ten, Malkum went on to study natural sciences and engineering, but his main focus of interest came to be political science. His studies, at least in his own opinion, made him an authority on the foundation of European civilization and on the reforms necessary for "civilizing" Iran. Usually writing from outside Iran, he was an effective critic of practices within the

Hamid Algar, *Mirza Malkum Khan* (Berkeley: University of California Press, 1973), pp. 300–308. Copyright © 1973 The Regents of The University of California. Reprinted by permission.

country and among the Iranian people, but living as an expatriate was also a dis-
advantage because it prevented him from fully grasping the intricacies of Iranian
society and culture and to a certain extent colored his judgments with Western con-
ceptions of his native land.

This selection from Malkum's writings provides a sampling of the political at-
tacks that Malkum launched in his newspaper, Qānūn, and the exaggerations in
which he was prone to indulge. The letters he quotes are fictitious and provide him
with stereotypical foils for his critiques of the religious and political establishments.

According to Hamid Algar, the following example of the journal Qānūn was
probably published in 1891. It represents Malkum's style of fabricating support for
his position and exaggerating the problems in Iran to the point of crisis. It is inter-
esting to note, as does Hamid Algar in his book on Malkum, that Malkum's critiques
of Shah Nasr ad-Din are always indirect.

We can convey to all supporters of the Law[1] the happy tidings that nowadays
all manner of thoughts are astir in Iran. Utterances are being made and courageous deeds performed that a few years ago none would have thought possible.

According to reliable information, a group of army officers and commanders has unanimously submitted the following declaration to the guardians of
the state:

O guardians of the state!

To what chaotic and miserable condition you have reduced Iran!
Why do you thus harass our wretched people? What law, what faith
can justify all this jailing, torturing, killing, and plundering? How
much longer are we soldiers to cause misery to our people at your be-
hest? What shame and humiliation we suffer at your hands as reward
for our obedience and endurance: see in what scandalous way you have
made of our military ranks and salaries a source of disgrace to the nation! You must think us entirely devoid of shame and honor to appoint
your lowliest domestic servants not only over us, the commanders of
the army, but over the minister of war, the offspring of the shah himself.[2] There are men among us whose ancestors, for fourteen generations, have sacrificed themselves in the service of the state, and now,
without the slightest qualm, you force them, for the sake of a few filthy
shāhīs'[3] salary, to go and kiss the shoes of some dirty youth in your

---

[1]Malkum's use of the words *qānūn* and *ādamīyat* in his journal is deliberately ambiguous:
they might convey either their general senses of "law" and "humanity" respectively, or,
more narrowly, designate his newspaper and the secret society that undertook its distribution, the League of Humanity. In order to retain some sense of ambiguity in English, I have
translated the words in question and spelled them with capital letters. [All footnotes in this
selection are Algar's.]

[2]The minister of war was Kāmrān Mīrzā Nā'ib us-Salṭana, third son of Nāṣir ud-Dīn Shāh
and governor of Tehran.

[3]*Shāhī:* a unit of currency equivalent, in the Qajar period, to one twentieth of a *qirān*.

ābdārkhāna[4] seventy times a day! Until today, we have been completely blind and unaware of our rights and duties. We imagined that the salaries we begged out of you with a thousand humiliations [literally, cuckoldries], you had somehow inherited from your fathers and that you bestowed them on us as an act of grace. But now we realize that our salaries are taken from the taxes which we, the people of Iran, pay for the protection of our rights and which you scandalously misuse to make prisoners of our nation. That time is past when we thought you to be our lords and masters and, deceived by your promises, subjected the property, life, and faith of the nation to your idiotic vagaries! The roaring flood of your oppressive deeds, the laments of the people, and the voice of Law have finally awakened us. Now we well understand that the Compassionate Lord did not create us for slavery to such as you! Now we are fully aware that, in accordance with the Law of God, we soldiers must be protectors of the people's rights, instead of ravening beasts unleashed by you to torture and trample underfoot our brothers in religion and fellow countrymen, at your whim and pleasure! Now we clearly realize that all this wretchedness of Iran is due to our apathy, neglect, and lack of union! We warn you that we have grasped the meaning and power of union, and we have become Men.[5] We are no longer alone, that you might continue to incite us against each other and make us the executioners of our people. Henceforth, instead of being your lowly slaves and the torturers of the nation, we shall be the proud servants of the people of Iran and protectors of the rights of all true Men. We shall still sacrifice our lives, but it will be for the sake of our human rights, not for the shameful rule of injustice which you regard as your eternal fief! Awake, o guardians of evil, for we soldiers have become Men!

One of the ministers of Iran, who has wasted his life in service to the state and the desire for its progress and advancement and who now in utter disgust eagerly awaits his death, has written a brief description of the present state of Iran. He says in conclusion:

"Do not imagine that the men who rule the state themselves gain any benefit from the ruinous situation created by their stupidity. It is true that they appear to enjoy many privileges, but in reality they, and all who follow in their

---

[4]*Ābdārkhāna:* the room or outhouse in which a servant prepares coffee, tea, sherbet, or a water pipe for his master and his guests. Amīn us-Sultān's father was, of course, Nāṣir ud-Dīn Shāh's *ābdār,* the servant entrusted with these tasks, and Malkum's repeated references to the *ābdārkhāna* are intended as a reminder to all of Amīn us-Sultāns lowly origin. It is implied that with his appointment to the premiership, the ministry has in effect been transformed into an *ābdārkhāna.*

[5]On the implications of the phrase "to become a man" (*ādam shudan*), see [Algar, 1973], p. 229.

wake, are the most wretched of us all. Which of our ministers can sleep tran-
quilly at night? What king other than our shah is imprisoned by servants and a
prey to [material] needs? Everyone knows that this monarch, whose doorman
is meant to be Darius and whose bodyguard reputedly consists of Khusrau and
Alexander,[6] trembles in fear by night and day, is surrounded by executioners
and has more difficulty supporting his family than his humblest servant! Were
ever the children of some black slave in America as poor and distraught as the
progeny of Fath 'Alī Shāh?[7] Is there anyone in the land who has suffered more
oppression than the children of 'Abbās Mīrzā?[8] Is there any humiliation and
degradation[9] that has not constantly been visited on the brothers of the present
shah?[10] As for his sons, ask them themselves: what hellish hovels they must go
to in order to pay with their liver's blood for a crust of bread graciously bestowed on them by the servants of the *ābdārkhāna!* And what should I say
concerning the sufferings endured by that noble being who has had the misfortune to see himself designated heir to the throne in this day and age? You
must surely be aware that there is not a peasant in the whole of Iran who is at
such a loss to secure his daily bread as this high-born prince! Where can one
openly declare that in this same province of Azerbayjan where the appointees
of the *ābdārkhāna* waste the salaries of twenty brigades on frivolous amusement, the future king of Iran does not even have a decent room in which to sit?
It is because of things such as this that I say all one can do is to spit and then go
and leave them all behind."

No, your Excellency. One must remain to become a Man, and by the propagation of Humanity to deliver one's progeny and nation from this ocean of
catastrophe.

Another minister writes:
"It was well said that one should fear a government that has no shame. See
the lengths to which their unprincipled shamelessness has gone! The guardians

---

[6]An allusion to the fulsome epithets bestowed on Nāṣir ud-Dīn Shāh in panegyric poetry, in
official documents and court chronicles.

[7]Fath 'Alī Shāh had a particularly numerous progeny. For a full account of his reproductive
achievements, see Aḥmad Mīrzā 'Aḍud ud-Daula, *Tārīkh-i 'Aḍudī, ed.* Ḥusayn Kūhī Kir-
mānī (Tehran, 1327 solar/1948), *passim.*

[8]That is, 'Abbās Mīrzā, the eldest son of Fath 'Alī Shāh who predeceased his father in 1833.

[9]Malkum uses the expression *pīsī vārid kardan,* a colloquialism meaning "to trouble, to vex,
to expose to disgrace" (see Muḥammad 'Alī Jamālzāda, *Farhang-i Lughāt-i 'Āmmīyāna*
[Tehran, 1341 solar/1962], p. 46). *Pīsī* literally signifies leprosy, and Malkum's use of the expression is intended to emphasize the helpless and undignified state in which the shah's
brothers find themselves. Much of the effectiveness of *Qānūn* resided in the unprecedented
literary use of vulgarisms such as this.

[10]Among the brothers of Nāṣir ud-Dīn Shāh, 'Abbās Mīrzā Mulkārā had a particularly disturbed career. He spent thirty years in exile in Baghdad under British protection, and, although later able to effect a reconciliation with his brother and return to Iran, he was
constantly regarded with distrust and suspicion. See his autobiography, *Sharḥ-i Ḥāl,* ed.
'Abd ul-Ḥusayn Navā'ī (Tehran, 1325 solar/1946).

of the realm now sit and forge blatant lies about well-tried servants of the state, lies which, as any child can see, prove only their stupidity and will end in their disgrace. Ask any of the celebrated European travelers whether he has ever encountered among some savage tribe a whore who would thus knowingly encompass her own disgrace by inventing transparent lies? A set of men who have made themselves the fountainhead of all the vices in the world, who continually surround themselves with mountainous heaps of scandal and disgrace— how dare they cause personal accusations to be printed in a newspaper![11] If the men of Law should wish to publish and reveal the deeds of these authors of Iran's misfortune, which one of them would ever dare, crouching in the corner of his stable, to show his head and face the stench of scandal and disgrace? But for such revelations there is no need: the pens of Humanity will pay no attention to the vices of these foremost scoundrels of the age. It is better to entrust their punish merit to the just verdict of the people of Iran."

A high-minded prince writes as follows:

"O men of Law! We members of the royal house are sincerely gratified at your efforts and intentions. The true meaning of service to the state and gratitude for favor received is precisely that which your eloquent pen sets forth. A thousand congratulations on your sense of honor and learning! The Qajar dynasty will be in your debt for all eternity! Even the blind can see that under present circumstances our monarchy is doomed. But none of us has dared to express the truth of the matter clearly, and it is you who has carried off the ball of manly courage. Continue to write, and write in harsh, straightforward terms, for our sleep of apathy is too deep to be dispelled by normal speech. Our monarch, as everyone is aware, is tired and imprisoned in his ābdārkhāna. It is as if he has abdicated and handed Iran over to these vicious rogues. If there is anything that can bring us to our senses, it is the whiplash of eloquent discourse. If today the monarch does not appreciate your manner of speaking the truth, be sure that the rush of events will soon prove, and his own imperial intuition confess, that the men of Law are the true well-wishers of the monarchy. So write on, noble servants of the state, write on! For our only hope lies in the popular enthusiasm that the spirit of Humanity has brought forth in the land of Iran."

O exalted prince!

We are performing our duty of service to the state; what are you doing? You can perform a thousand deeds for the salvation of the ship of state; why do you sit thus idly? You should have realized by now that although the foundation of the monarchy used to be the idiocy of the people, its preservation will henceforth be possible only through following the dictates of justice and the principles of Humanity. Who is better equipped than you to propagate those principles? Instead of waiting for the efforts of others to reform affairs, show some zeal yourself, and be the vanguard and protector of Humanity. You have

---

[11]Doubtless an angry allusion to the article published, by royal command, in the journal *Irān*. See [Algar, 1973], p. 180.

no excuse for delay in assuming this sacred task: all men of conscience are prepared [to help you], and the methods of propagation are inscribed in the breast of every self-respecting man. In accordance with these methods, and, using your intelligence and skill, gather together the Men you see around you, and attract them to your circle. Then appoint the more accomplished among them to be Trustees of Humanity[12] and encourage them in turn to found as many new circles as possible. Do not hesitate, for if you now grasp the grandeur of your destiny, you can without difficulty, by the spark of your words and the model of your example, kindle the light of Humanity in this realm, attain your highest goal and be a source of pride to Men until the end of time.

A respected merchant whose spirit soars high on account of Humanity writes from Tabriz:

"You can have little idea how the ministers of Tehran fear *Qānūn* and Humanity. They open everyone's letters, and anyone who has so much as glanced at *Qānūn* is arrested and asked why he has become a Man. The wise ones of Tehran seem to think they are extirpating the very names of *Qānūn* and Humanity from Iran, and they still imagine that *Qānūn* is a newspaper the contents of which become useless and outdated if it fails to arrive by post. They have not yet realized that if *Qānūn* comes by post or muleteer, today or next year, its contents will always be fresh. The more strictly it is prohibited, the more effective will be its ideas. Now the best present which can be brought from abroad is a page of *Qānūn*. Thanks to the measures of those wise men, the saddlebags of travelers and the pockets of pilgrims are stuffed to overflowing with copies of *Qānūn*. The day before yesterday, one of my partners found a thousand copies of *Qānūn* at the bottom of a crate of sugar that had just been brought from the customs. A trader in Salmās[13] found two hundred copies in a roll of broadcloth. What need, then, for new laws [to prevent the entry of *Qānūn*]? The copies which are already circulating among men of insight are enough to resurrect a graveyard. You can scarcely imagine how well some of our accomplished and learned men explain and expound on the principles of Humanity. Their commentary on each line of *Qānūn* is enough to fill a book. One of the great *mujtahids* openly says that the reading of *Qānūn* is the alchemy of union. The devil of disunity cannot penetrate the house where a page of *Qānūn* is to be found.[14]

"In short, men's thoughts are in a remarkable state of turmoil, and how, indeed, might it be otherwise? Did the people of Iran ever take an oath to lie abjectly beneath the kicks of a pitiless bunch of ruffians? The spirit of Iran everywhere bears witness that soon this edifice of tyranny shall collapse, and the banner of divine justice shall be hoisted throughout the realm."

---

[12]On the *Auṣiyā-yi Ādamīyat*, see [Algar, 1973], p. 233.

[13]A city in Azerbayjan, situated between Tabriz and Lake Riḍā'īya.

[14]This sentence is deliberately phrased to sound like a religious pronouncement, as if it were actually taken from the *fatvā* of a *mujtahid*.

Answers

H.A.   It has been sent. Always inform us of arrival.

M.ʻA.   The injustice committed against your own person you may naturally forgive. But as for the injustice inflicted by the wild beasts[15] of the state on your brothers in Humanity—to avenge it is incumbent on every Man.

A.T.   Send more to the *ʻatabāt.*

A.O.   The words of the vultures[16] are not worthy of attention.

Sh.M.   Consider these two brigades already prepared to sacrifice themselves for Humanity.

S.D.   God is greatest!

Declaration of the Guardians of the Victorious Ābdārkhāna

O people of Iran, what senseless words are these you now see fit to utter? Law, union, the protection of rights—what does all this mean? What law could be better than the sword of our executioners? What rights could be clearer than ours to enjoy your slavery? If you really wish, like other peoples, to reform and order your affairs anew and if—may God forbid—the people of Iran are to gain some honor and respect, then what is to become of our proprietary rights over you and your consecrated duties of servitude to us? Have not the vultures of our treasury explained to you a thousand times that whatever you have— life, property, religion, honor—all belongs to us? These shameless people who have started to speak of law are such unlettered idiots that we have been unable to find a particle of meaning in all the words they write, despite our learning and intelligence. It is for this very reason that in our tender concern for your welfare we anxiously seek to prevent your eyes from alighting on their writings. We do not doubt that with your sincere and slavish devotion to our angelic selves you will never look for unity, for unity is disbelief according to the norms by which we rule. If you wish to be sensible, you should exert your- selves to the utmost to be as far apart from and as hostile to each other as pos- sible. It is in particular necessary for some of you to be Babis so that we can rip open their stomachs as a warning to others and confiscate their property with a plausible excuse. It is also highly desirable for you to be divided into a num- ber of parties such as Shaykhī,[17] Mutasharriʻ,[18] Shiʻi, Sunni, and Dahrī,[19] which insult, curse, and torment each other. For then you become quite oblivious of

---

[15]*Jānvarān:* the counterpart in Malkum's terminology, of *ādamān* ("men"), designating Malkum's enemies, Amīn us-Sultān and those who carried out his instructions.

[16]*Lāshakhūrān:* another term denoting Malkum's adversaries.

[17]See p. 282, n. 5 [in Algar, 1973].

[18]Mutasharriʻ: one who binds himself to strict observance of the religious law (*sharīʻa*), in contradistinction to the Sufi who might exhibit antinomian tendencies.

[19]Dahrī: approximately, "materialist," "believer in eternal time." The word was originally applied to crypto-Manicheans, but its sense was later expanded to include any kind of heresy or disbelief.

your human rights, and without any trouble we can mount you like asses and load you with the burdens of disgrace to our heart's desire. Do not imagine that we will fail to appreciate your self-sacrificing services. Be sure that if ever you are as talented as Qā'im Maqām and serve the state as faithfully as he did, or if you are as skillful and devoted in restoring the fortunes of the monarchy as Mīrzā Taqī Khān,[20] without delay we shall ungrudgingly extend to you the same manful treatment we did to them. And if, God forbid, one of you should still persist in idle talk despite these oaths of ours, then know for certain that he shall immediately be marked as an ingrate, a traitor, and an infidel.

Of course, in your hearts you will in all justice agree that all the duties we assign you in your slavery correspond precisely to that Islam which we have produced especially for our own protection. Who observes the principles of our Islam better than we ourselves? See how firmly we have silenced your *mujtahids* and caused them humbly to submit to the raging beasts who are our servants! See how powerfully and thoroughly we have extirpated every trace of just practice and equitable behavior throughout the well-guarded land [of Iran]![21] Is there anyone who has ever sold the rights of the state and the means of livelihood of the people so cheaply to foreigners as we have done? The scandal and disgrace of bribes, the drunken arrogance of power, the invention of all kinds of foul sport, the squandering of the Muslims' treasury,[22] was ever there an age in which these evils were more flourishing? How is it possible that despite all these manifest bounties you are not night and day engaged in praying for the perpetuation of our wise and skillful rule? If, in accordance with the customs of this lofty institution, the beasts of state should plunder at their will your rights and all your possessions and reduce you to a state of abject beggary worse than that of any savage tribe, why should you grieve and sorrow? Do you not see how strictly we have forbidden the newspaper *Akhtar*[23] to say a word on matters such as these? And if we are able to expel you from your homeland whenever we choose, without interrogation, and to cut off your ear and nose and head without a trial, then what cause is there for surprise? Do you not know that our Bounteous Lord has created your entire being solely for our pleasure? So, o people of Iran, instead of following the path of error and seeking out the laws of God, try to appreciate our acts of compassion to our subjects, and ponder on your inherently slavish state. Be proud that we have made

---

[20]Here, as in his letter to *The Times* of March 16, 1891 (see [Algar, 1973,] p. 180). Malkum is again attempting to identify himself implicitly with two ministers who had given their lives for the sake of reform.

[21]*Mamālik-i Maḥrūsa:* the conventional designation for Iran in official documents and chronicles, here intended satirically.

[22]In order to arouse religious feeling, Malkum uses the expression *bayt ul-māl*, the term by which the treasury of the Islamic state was designated in the lifetime of the Prophet, instead of the usual *khazāna.*

[23]On the vicissitudes of *Akhtar,* see [Algar, 1973], pp. 186–187.

of the land over which Jamshīd[24] used to reign a blot on the history of the age and thus proven and recorded the extent of your dignity and honor. In gratitude for this bounty, fall upon the earth and kiss those *gīva's*[25] of the blessed *ābdārkhāna* which have trampled under their filthy heels such a nation as Iran and aroused the wonder of all mankind!

In reply to this proclamation of the present rulers of Tehran, the Spirit of Humanity cries out in tones that penetrate to every corner of the earth:

"O Iran of lofty fortune! It is not your allotted portion in this world to suffer the disgrace of slavery now imposed upon you! For centuries you were the throne on which the glory of Humanity reposed; why should you today lie buried in the graveyard of abjection? Where are those lions of heavenly lineage who bequeathed as a trust to your virtue and honor, glory and felicity in this world and the hereafter? Arise, o champion of wounded heart, for the days of darkness are at an end, and the sun of knowledge has illumined the world from East to West."

5. Jamal al-Din Al-Afghani Answers Ernest Renan's Criticism of Islam, May 18, 1883

Many scholars consider Jamal al-Din Al-Afghani to be one of the most prominent Islamic thinkers and political activists of the nineteenth century. In his lifetime many areas with large Muslim communities came under the direct or indirect control of the European imperial powers. This political, economic, and cultural subjugation prompted him to write various tracts that sought to explain the decline of the Islamic world historically, to defend Islam against its detractors (European and local), and to present a blueprint of sorts for a modernism that would fit within the boundaries of Islamic values.

Al-Afghani was born in 1838 in a town 180 miles from Kabul, Afghanistan, to a distinguished family. He was trained as a religious scholar and became fluent in various languages, including Arabic and Farsi. When he was eighteen, he began a series of travels that took him from India to Iran, the Ottoman Empire, Egypt, and France, where he lived long enough to become exposed to the philosophies and political ideas of the time. He died in 1897 in the Ottoman Empire under suspicious circumstances.

Al-Afghani believed that Islam was not incompatible with science and rationality, as some thinkers (including Ernest Renan, the French philosopher to whom he responds in this document) argued. Rather, Al-Afghani maintained, rigid interpretations of religion and the weight of local traditions made the Islamic world appear "backward," and, according to Al-Afghani and his disciple Muhammad 'Abduh, believers ought not abandon Islam but seek to interpret its scriptures from the

---

[24]A legendary king of pre-Islamic Iran, generally equated with Solomon.
[25]*Gīva:* A kind of canvas shoe, with a sole made of pieces of rag pressed together, commonly worn by peasants in Iran.

perspective of modern society. This ijtihad *(loosely translated as "rational interpretation") would free Islamic societies from outworn traditions and become an engine for social, economic, educational, and political change. At the same time, Islam
would provide the necessary moral guidelines to restrain science from transgressing
ethical boundaries.*

*In this selection, Al-Afghani responds to Ernest Renan's attacks on Islam. Try to
identify Al-Afghani's main ideas and to evaluate his arguments. What do you think
of his vision of Islam? What are the limitations of that vision? To what extent do you
think it would have been possible to apply Al-Afghani's ideas?*

Sir,

I have read in your estimable journal of last March 29 a talk on Islam and
Science, given in the Sorbonne before a distinguished audience by the great
thinker of our time, the illustrious M. Renan, whose renown has filled the West
and penetrated into the farthest countries of the East. Since this speech suggested to me some observations, I took the liberty of formulating them in this
letter, which I have the honor of addressing to you with a request that you accommodate it in your columns.

M. Renan wanted to clarify a point of the history of the Arabs which had
remained unclear until now and to throw a live light on their past, a light that
may be somewhat troubling for those who venerate these people, though one
cannot say that he has usurped the place and rank that they formerly occupied
in the world. M. Renan has not at all tried, we believe, to destroy the glory of
the Arabs which is indestructible; he has applied himself to discovering historical truth and making it known to those who do not know it, as well as to those
who study the influence of religions in the history of nations, and in particular
in that of civilization. I hasten to recognize that M. Renan has acquitted himself marvelously of this very difficult task, in citing certain facts that have
passed unnoticed until this time. I find in his talk remarkable observations, new
perceptions, and an indescribable charm. However, I have under my eyes only
a more or less faithful translation of this talk. If I had had the opportunity to
read it in the French text, I could have penetrated better the ideas of this great
thinker. He receives my humble salutation as an homage that is due him and as
the sincere expression of my admiration. I would say to him, finally, in these
circumstances, what al-Mutanabbi, a poet who loved philosophy wrote several
centuries ago to a high personage whose actions he celebrated: "Receive," he
said to him, "the praises that I can give you; do not force me to bestow on you
the praises that you merit."

M. Renan's talk covered two principal points. The eminent philosopher applied himself to proving that the Muslim religion was by its very essence opposed to the development of science, and that the Arab people, by their nature,
do not like either metaphysical sciences or philosophy. This precious plant,

Nikki R. Keddie, *An Islamic Response to Imperialism: Political and Religious Writings of Sayyid Jamāl
ad-Dīn "al-Afghānī"* (Berkeley: University of California Press, 1968), pp. 181–187. Reprinted by permission of the author.

M. Renan seems to say, dried up in their hands as if burnt up by the breath of the desert wind. But after reading this talk one cannot refrain from asking oneself if these obstacles come uniquely from the Muslim religion itself or from the manner in which it was propagated in the world; from the character, manners, and aptitudes of the peoples who adopted this religion, or of those on whose nations it was imposed by force. It is no doubt the lack of time that kept M. Renan from elucidating these points; but the harm is no less for that, and if it is difficult to determine its causes in a precise manner and by irrefutable proofs, it is even more difficult to indicate the remedy.

As to the first point, I will say that no nation at its origin is capable of letting itself be guided by pure reason. Haunted by terrors that it cannot escape, it is incapable of distinguishing good from evil, of distinguishing that which could make it happy from that which might be the unfailing source of its unhappiness and misfortune. It does not know, in a word, either how to trace back causes or to discern effects.

This lacuna means that it cannot be led either by force or persuasion to practice the actions that would perhaps be the most profitable for it, or to avoid what is harmful. It was therefore necessary that humanity look outside itself for a place of refuge, a peaceful corner where its tormented conscience could find repose. It was then that there arose some educator or other who, not having, as I said above, the necessary power to force humanity to follow the inspirations of reason, hurled it into the unknown and opened to it vast horizons where the imagination was pleased and where it found, if not the complete satisfaction of its desires, at least an unlimited field for its hopes. And, since humanity, at its origin, did not know the causes of the events that passed under its eyes and the secrets of things, it was perforce led to follow the advice of its teachers and the orders they gave. This obedience was imposed in the name of the supreme Being to whom the educators attributed all events, without permitting men to discuss its utility or its disadvantages. This is no doubt for man one of the heaviest and most humiliating yokes, as I recognize; but one cannot deny that it is by this religious education, whether it be Muslim, Christian, or pagan, that all nations have emerged from barbarism and marched toward a more advanced civilization.

If it is true that the Muslim religion is an obstacle to the development of sciences, can one affirm that this obstacle will not disappear someday? How does the Muslim religion differ on this point from other religions? All religions are intolerant, each one in its way. The Christian religion, I mean the society that follows its inspirations and its teachings and is formed in its image, has emerged from the first period to which I have just alluded; thenceforth free and independent, it seems to advance rapidly on the road of progress and science, whereas Muslim society has not yet freed itself from the tutelage of religion. Realizing, however, that the Christian religion preceded the Muslim religion in the world by many centuries, I cannot keep from hoping that Muhammadan society will succeed someday in breaking its bonds and marching resolutely in the path of civilization after the manner of Western society, for which the Christian faith, despite its rigors and intolerance, was not at all an invincible obstacle. No, I cannot admit that this hope be denied to Islam. I plead here with M. Renan not the cause of the Muslim religion, but that of several hundreds of millions of men, who would thus be condemned to live in barbarism and ignorance.

In truth, the Muslim religion has tried to stifle science and stop its progress. It has thus succeeded in halting the philosophical or intellectual movement and in turning minds from the search for scientific truth. A similar attempt, if I am not mistaken, was made by the Christian religion, and the venerated leaders of the Catholic church have not yet disarmed so far as I know. They continue to fight energetically against what they call the spirit of vertigo and error. I know all the difficulties that the Muslims will have to surmount to achieve the same degree of civilization, access to the truth with the help of philosophic and scientific methods being forbidden them. A true believer must, in fact, turn from the path of studies that have for their object scientific truth, studies on which all truth must depend, according to an opinion accepted at least by some people in Europe. Yoked, like an ox to the plow, to the dogma whose slave he is, he must walk eternally in the furrow that has been traced for him in advance by the interpreters of the law. Convinced, besides, that his religion contains in itself all morality and all sciences, he attaches himself resolutely to it and makes no effort to go beyond. Why should he exhaust himself in vain attempts? What would be the benefit of seeking truth when he believes he possesses it all? Will he be happier on the day when he has lost his faith, the day when he has stopped believing that all perfections are in the religion he practices and not in another? Wherefore he despises science. I know all this, but I know equally that this Muslim and Arab child whose portrait M. Renan traces in such vigorous terms and who, at a later age, becomes "a fanatic, full of foolish pride in possessing what he believes to be absolute truth," belongs to a race that has marked its passage in the world, not only by fire and blood, but by brilliant and fruitful achievements that prove its taste for science, for all the sciences, including philosophy (with which, I must recognize, it was unable to live happily for long).

I am led here to speak of the second point that M. Renan treated in his lecture with an incontestable authority. No one denies that the Arab people, while it was still in the state of barbarism, rushed into the road of intellectual and scientific progress with a rapidity only equaled by the speed of its conquests, since in the space of a century, it acquired and assimilated almost all the Greek and Persian sciences that had developed slowly during several centuries on their native soil, just as it extended its domination from the Arabian peninsula up to the mountains of the Himalaya and the summit of the Pyrenees.

One might say that in all this period the sciences made astonishing progress among the Arabs and in all the countries under their domination. Rome and Byzantium were then the seats of theological and philosophical sciences as well as the shining center and burning hearth of all human knowledge. Having followed for several centuries the path of civilization, the Greeks and Romans walked with assurance over the vast field of science and philosophy. There came, however, a time when their researches were abandoned and their studies interrupted.

The monuments they had built to science collapsed and their most precious books were relegated to oblivion. The Arabs, ignorant and barbaric as they were in origin, took up what had been abandoned by the civilized nations, rekindled the extinguished sciences, developed them and gave them a brilliance they had never had. Is not this the index and proof of their natural love for sciences? It is true that the Arabs took from the Greeks their philosophy as they stripped the Persians of what made their fame in antiquity; but these sciences, which they usurped by right of conquest, they developed, extended, clarified, perfected, completed, and coordinated with a perfect taste and a rare precision and exactitude. Besides, the French, the Germans, and the English were not so far from Rome and Byzantium as were the Arabs, whose capital was Baghdad. It was therefore easier for the former to exploit the scientific treasures that were buried in these two great cities. They made no effort in this direction until Arab civilization lit up with its reflections the summits of the Pyrenees and poured its light and riches on the Occident. The Europeans welcomed Aristotle, who had emigrated and become Arab; but they did not think of him at all when he was Greek and their neighbor. Is there not in this another proof, no less evident, of the intellectual superiority of the Arabs and of their natural attachment to philosophy? It is true that after the fall of the Arab kingdom in the Orient as in the Occident, the countries that had become the great centers of science, like Iraq and Andalusia, fell again into ignorance and became the center of religious fanaticism; but one cannot conclude from this sad spectacle that the scientific and philosophic progress of the Middle Ages was not due to the Arab people who ruled at that time.

M. Renan does do them this justice. He recognizes that the Arabs conserved and maintained for centuries the hearth of science. What nobler mission for a people! But while recognizing that from about A.D. 775 to near the middle of the thirteenth century, that is to say during about five hundred years, there were in Muslim countries very distinguished scholars and thinkers, and that during this period the Muslim world was superior in intellectual culture to the Christian world, M. Renan has said that the philosophers of the first centuries of Islam as well as the statesmen who became famous in this period were mostly from Harran, from Andalusia, and from Iran. There were also among them Transoxianan and Syrian priests. I do not wish to deny the great qualities of the Persian scholars nor the role that they played in the Arab world; but permit me to say that the Harranians were Arabs and that the Arabs in occupying Spain and Andalusia did not lose their nationality; they remained Arabs. Several centuries before Islam the Arabic language was that of the Harranians. The fact that they preserved their former religion, Sabaeanism, does not mean they should be considered foreign to the Arab nationality. The Syrian priests were also for the most part Ghassanian Arabs converted to Christianity.

As for Ibn-Bajja, Ibn-Rushd (Averroes), and Ibn-Tufail, one cannot say that they are not just as Arab as al-Kindi because they were not born in Arabia, especially if one is willing to consider that human races are only distinguished by their languages and that if this distinction should disappear, nations would not take long to forget their diverse origins. The Arabs who put their arms in the service of the Muslim religion, and who were simultaneously warriors and apostles, did not impose their language on the defeated, and wherever they established themselves, they preserved it for them with a jealous care. No doubt Islam, in penetrating the conquered countries with the violence that is known, transplanted there its language, its manners, and its doctrine, and these countries could not thenceforth avoid its influence. Iran is an example; but it is possible that in going back to the centuries preceding the appearance of Islam, one would find that the Arabic language was not then entirely unknown to Persian scholars. The expansion of Islam gave it, it is true, a new scope, and the Persian scholars converted to the Muhammadan faith thought it an honor to write their books in the language of the Koran. The Arabs cannot, no doubt, claim for themselves the glory that renders these writers illustrious, but we believe that they do not need this claim; they have among themselves enough celebrated scholars and writers. What would happen if, going back to the first period of Arab domination, we followed step by step the first group from which was formed this conquering people who spread their power over the world, and if, eliminating everything that is outside this group and its descendants, we did not take into account either the influence it exercised on minds or the impulse it gave to the sciences? Would we not be led, thus, no longer to recognize in conquering peoples other virtues or merits than those that flow from the material fact of conquest? All conquered peoples would then regain their moral autonomy and would attribute to themselves all glory, no part of which could be legitimately claimed by the power that fructified and developed these germs, Thus, Italy would come to say to France that neither Mazarin nor Bonaparte belonged to her; Germany or England would in turn claim the scholars who, having come to France, made its professorships illustrious and enhanced the brilliance of its scientific renown. The French, on their side, would claim for themselves the glory of the offspring of those illustrious families who, after [the revocation of] the edict of Nantes, emigrated to all Europe. And if all Europeans belong to the same stock, one can with justice claim that the Harranians and the Syrians, who are Semites, belong equally to the great Arab family.

It is permissible, however, to ask oneself why Arab civilization, after having thrown such a live light on the world, suddenly became extinguished; why this torch has not been relit since; and why the Arab world still remains buried in profound darkness.

Here the responsibility of the Muslim religion appears complete. It is clear that wherever it became established, this religion tried to stifle the sciences and it was marvelously served in its designs by despotism.

Al-Siuti tells that the Caliph al-Hadi put to death in Baghdad 5000 philosophers in order to destroy sciences in the Muslim countries down to their roots. Admitting that this historian exaggerated the number of victims, it remains nonetheless established that this persecution took place, and it is a bloody stain for the history of a religion as it is for the history of a people. I could find in the past of the Christian religion analogous facts. Religions, by whatever names they are called, all resemble each other. No agreement and no reconciliation are possible between these religions and philosophy. Religion imposes on man its faith and its belief, whereas philosophy frees him of it totally or in part. How could one therefore hope that they would agree with each other? When the Christian religion, under the most modest and seductive forms, entered Athens and Alexandria, which were, as everyone knows, the two principal centers of science and philosophy, after becoming solidly established in these two cities its first concern was to put aside real science and philosophy, trying to stifle both under the bushes of theological discussions, to explain the inexplicable mysteries of the Trinity, the Incarnation, and Transubstantiation. It will always be thus. Whenever religion will have the upper hand, it will eliminate philosophy; and the contrary happens when it is philosophy that reigns as sovereign mistress. So long as humanity exists, the struggle will not cease between dogma and free investigation, between religion and philosophy; a desperate struggle in which, I fear, the triumph will not be for free thought, because the masses dislike reason, and its teachings are only understood by some intelligences of the elite, and because, also, science, however beautiful it is, does not completely satisfy humanity, which thirsts for the ideal and which likes to exist in dark and distant regions that the philosophers and scholars can neither perceive nor explore.

6.   Baghdadi Jews React to the Modernization of the Ottoman Empire, May 28, 1908

In 1908 the Committee of Union and Progress (commonly known as the Young Turks) came to power in Istanbul and remained in control of the Ottoman Empire until its dissolution in 1918. Since its formation in exile in Paris in 1889, the CUP had presented itself as a liberal organization seeking to decentralize political power and championing political rights and a greater degree of equality among the ethnically and religiously varied citizenry of the empire. Although the CUP became increasingly oppressive— thus alienating many early supporters—at least at first it offered the promise of freedoms unparalleled in the history of the Ottoman Empire. This document is a report by a teacher from the Alliance Israélite Universelle, a French Jewish organization that aimed to modernize non-European Jews by establishing French-language schools amidst those communities. He describes the reaction of Jews in Baghdad, Iraq, to the arrival of the CUP to power. Highly contemptuous of the local Iraqi Muslims, his words give—perhaps—an exaggerated image of the glee of the local Jews, as well as the writer's take on Muslims' feelings about the CUP and the reasons behind them.

Baghdad, 28 May 1909
[. . .]

The Christians and the Jews both gave a very enthusiastic welcome to the new regime.[1] The Jews especially had anxiously followed every turn taken in the combat being waged between autocracy and freedom; they knew instinctively that their fate depended on the outcome of this battle. For them the triumph of liberty was not simply the fulfillment of a spiritual and intellectual

---

[1]A reference to the Young Turks, who came to power in 1908. [All footnotes in this document are Rodrigue's.]

aspiration; it was a question of life itself. This triumph represented a safeguard against an arbitrary government and protection against the fanaticism of the population, which, from that moment, lost all official sanctioning of its harassment of the Jews.

Although the non-Muslims joyously greeted the news of the constitution, the majority of the Muslims were cold and hostile. The reason for their discontent must be attributed to various causes:

The Muslims already sensed that the new regime would strike heavy blows against their fanaticism. The dream of a good Muslim would be to see Islam triumph throughout the world, and toward this dream he must eliminate the infidel, whatever the means. With the freedom granted by the constitution, the good Muslim finds himself obliged to hold his hatred in check, and he can no longer indulge in methodical persecutions. The Muslims cannot conceive that the infidels should benefit from the same rights as they. Jews, their equals, brothers of the Muslims: what an upheaval in their way of thinking! To their eyes it is quite audacious to consider treating Muslims on an equal footing with the infidels; the latter are for them *kefirs*, impure beings, execrated by God, and must disappear from the face of the earth.

By protecting the Jews from the ill-will and injustice of the Muslims, the constitution has exasperated them. They find their hands are tied and they are forced to maintain a certain respect, at least an apparent respect, for the infidels. [. . .]

During the long months which followed the promulgation of the constitution, and especially during the recent unrest in Constantinople after the coup d'état of Abdul Hamid, the non-Muslims were not always certain of what tomorrow would bring. They feared renewed aggressions and their fear contributed quite a bit to the spreading of alarming rumors. Among themselves they were saying the Muslims would certainly be moved by what was happening in Constantinople and that, reactionaries by nature, they would lend a hand to the reactionaries in the capital in striking a decisive blow to the liberal institutions. [. . .]

Since the definitive victory of the Committee for Union and Progress, there has been more light on the horizon and more sense of security in the city. As the reactionaries are no longer in a position to take advantage of an equivocal situation, they are forced to resign themselves. They did not receive the news of Abdul Hamid's ousting with great enthusiasm, but they could not manifest their discontent very openly. They no longer have the support of the government, which had no other choice but to take a liberal attitude.

Will the new regime have a profound effect on the conscience of the population? Is it an answer to the hopes of the people? Will they know how to put their new rights to good use? The Christians and the Jews, although they have

Archives of the Alliance Israélite Universelle, Irak I.C.4. This document may also be found in Aron Rodrigue, *Images of Sephardi and Eastern Jewries in Transition: The Teachers of the Alliance Israélite Universelle, 1860–1939* (Seattle: University of Washington Press, 1999), pp. 263–265.

not been well prepared for liberty, have fervently aspired to it. They have suffered tyranny too long not to embrace liberty fully. Their spirits are finally released: their lives and their possessions protected. It is only a question of time and education before they are able to profit from the changes which have taken place in the country.

[. . .]

In no other country are the laws more in advance of habits and customs than in Mesopotamia. The social condition of the Muslims is very backward, and as the Muslims are the majority, the backlash is felt among the Jews and the Christians. One example of this is the extreme scorn and disdain which the Muslim feels toward women; to him they are inferior beings who must be left to wallow in ignorance and in tedium. Women are made to take care of the home and to be slaves to the masters . . .

[. . .]

And so we see that the Muslims are the stumbling block to all progress; they are a dead weight which also drags down the rest of the population. Since they are enemies of all innovation, they look with a critical eye upon any effort on the part of the others to create a better life. Thus, they would like to stop the others from wearing European dress. This is considered a sign of civilization to them. They also want to put a stop to the habit of caring for one's personal appearance. They are capable of stoning a Turkish subject should he wear a hat. The others must model themselves after the Muslims, and even remain at a lower level than they.

To bring down this bastion of fanaticism and ignorance and to bring thousands of individuals back to life and to action, the new government must put all of its efforts in the instruction and education of the masses. The only way to purify the contaminated air which stifles the city is to allow new air to come in. Thus, they should organize a system of instruction which answers modern needs and is based on modern ideas. The government will no doubt meet with stubborn resistance on the part of the *ulemas* [Muslim clergy], who run the Islamic schools and who see to it that the Koran is not open to close examination. But the government is stronger than they are, and it must firmly impose its will.

[. . .]

The victory won by the Committee for Union and Progress will be a simple illusion if the Committee does not manage to institute an educational system throughout the empire. Liberty will be simply a word devoid of meaning, and even a source of danger, if the population is not prepared to deal with it wisely. This preparation will come only when the population becomes aware of its own rights and potentials.

[. . .]

A. Franco

CHAPTER 2

Economic Changes

The Industrial Revolution, which took off first in England in the early eighteenth century and later in continental Europe, had dramatic effects on the Middle East and North Africa. Based as it was on the rapid production and consumption of textiles, this revolution required two main ingredients to succeed: markets and raw materials. Factory owners in Birmingham and Lyons—among other places—needed ever expanding markets if they were to continue accumulating wealth and capital. At first, England and the rest of Europe provided adequate outlets for the yards of manufactured textiles, but by the nineteenth century this was no longer the case. Thus, many manufacturers cast glances at markets farther afield, including those located within the Ottoman Empire and Iran.

The fact that the Ottoman Empire and Iran entered the nineteenth century with a military considerably weaker than that of the European states made it easy for the latter to gain access to Ottoman markets. The first document, a treaty between Russia and Iran, exemplifies the direct relationship between European military power and their economic gains in the Middle East. Partly in exchange for expelling Muhammad 'Ali (governor of Egypt) from Ottoman lands he had occupied in the early 1830s, the British government extracted serious economic concessions from the Ottomans through the Treaty of Balta Liman (1838). The agreement (document 2) provided for the abolition of all monopolies within the Ottoman Empire—monopoly was a tool that Muhammad 'Ali used to develop the Egyptian economy—and granted all foreign goods entering the empire the very low tariff rate of 3 percent. Other Europeans states soon followed Britain's lead and wrested from the empire equally favorable trade agreements, all of which opened the empire more than ever to European goods.

The economic inequality resulting from such agreements was compounded by the financial strain of modernizing the imperial army and bureaucracy. The Tanzimat reforms were driven in part by the political and military losses that the empire suffered at the hands of various European powers. Some of the funding for modernization came from tax increases in the provinces, but provincial governors struggled—many times successfully—to retain local control over their resources. Thus, the imperial government found it necessary to borrow more and more money from European banks and governments, which were eager to provide short-term, high-interest loans. The onerous foreign debt and state mismanagement of the borrowed funds and of state budgets brought Egypt and the Ottoman Empire to the brink of bankruptcy. Fearing default on the various loans threatened by Khedive Isma'il in Egypt, England and France intervened militarily in Egypt and politically in the Ottoman Empire to force the establishment of a public debt administration in each. Dominated by European powers, these administrations took direct control of the state budgets, in Egypt (document 3) and the Ottoman Empire.

Iran, too, did not escape European advances. In the nineteenth century it became the scene of a political tug of war between Russia and England. In 1857 the British prevailed on Shah Nasir al-Din to grant them commercial concessions similar to those granted by Egypt and the Ottoman Empire. While Russia sought to gain greater political control over Iran—at least the northern parts of it—England sought to promote economic development that would strengthen the central government of Iran while at the same time providing the British with an economic advantage over the Russians. The shah of Iran attempted to manipulate this rivalry to his advantage by providing concessions to the British and the Russians alternately. For example, in 1872 Baron Julius de Reuter obtained exclusive rights to develop all railways, canals, and dams in Iran in addition to extensive privileges in mining and agriculture. In this way, Shah Nasir al-Din exchanged the long-term development of Iran for modest initial fees and royalties.

Documents 4 through 7 provide examples of economic agreements between the Ottoman and the Iranian governments, on the one hand, and various European interests, on the other. From central governments in the Middle East and North Africa, European governments and companies extracted potentially lucrative agreements. Among the outcomes of such agreements were European control of the Suez Canal (document 4) and the establishing of the Imperial Bank of Persia by Britain (document 5). However, the Europeans' ability to capitalize on such opportunities was not guaranteed. The Ottoman and Iranian central governments had little effective control over outlying regions of their territories. Moreover, although government officials in Istanbul and Tehran may have agreed to certain concessions, their provincial counterparts in Mosul or Tabriz were not always willing to cooperate. Whether seeking to protect their local power and sources of wealth or to defend the principle of sovereignty, local authorities often hindered the implementation of these agreements. Also, local populations both passively and actively resisted what they considered to be the unfair terms of the concessions, some of which posed threats to their economic well-being. Ordinary people resented the intrusion of foreigners and their local agents.

Documents 6 and 7, about the French tobacco monopoly and tobacco smuggling, provide clues to the relationship among European interests and Ottoman and Iranian imperial and local interests. The complexity of this relationship should keep us from accepting the notion that technological superiority guaranteed Europeans unfettered access to the economies of the Middle East and North Africa. Rather, it appears that negotiation, frustration, and failure were as much part of this history as Europeans' success in achieving their imperialist and capitalist goals. Also, it is important to note that the Europeans were able to win concessions not simply because of their industrial superiority. In subtle and blunt ways, France, England, and Russia parlayed their military might into political influence that led to economic benefits for European merchants and industrialists.

1. The Treaty of Peace and Commerce (Treaty of Turkmanchai) Between Iran and Russia, February 10–22, 1828

Throughout the nineteenth century, the Russian Empire sought to expand its influence south into the Middle East, toward warm-water ports, and to counter British and French interests encroaching into that area. More so than either Britain or France, the Russian Empire used military campaigns to conquer territory and to encourage the Ottomans and the Persians to sign treaties advantageous to Russian interests. From 1826–1828 the Russians conducted successful campaigns against the army of the shah of Iran and forced the shah to sign a peace treaty in the village of Turkmanchai, in the province of Azerbaijan, that permitted them to annex the provinces of Erivan and Nakhichevan. Moreover, the treaty allowed the Russians exclusive naval rights over the Caspian Sea. Annexed to these political elements of the treaty were commercial concessions giving the Russians greater access to local Iranian markets. This is an example of the deliberate and direct use of European military power to extract political and economic gains at the expense of indigenous governments.

1. The Treaty of Peace

ART. I. There will be, dating from this day, peace, friendship and perfect understanding between His Majesty the Emperor of all the Russias on one hand, and His Majesty the Shah of Persia on the other, their Heirs and Successors, their States and their respective Subjects, in perpetuity.

ART. II. Considering that the hostilities taken place between the High Contracting Parties, and happily terminated today, have brought to an end the obligations which the Treaty of Gulistan imposed upon them, His Majesty the

British and Foreign State Papers, 33-884. This document can also be found in J. C. Hurewitz, *The Middle East and North Africa in World Politics* (New Haven, Conn.: Yale University Press, 1975), pp. 232–237.

Emperor of all the Russias and His Majesty the Shah in Shan [King of Kings] of Persia have judged it appropriate to replace the said Treaty of Gulistan by the present Clauses and Stipulations, which are designed to regulate and to consolidate more and more the future relations of peace and friendship between Russia and Persia.

ART. III. His Majesty the Shah of Persia, both in his name as in that of his Heirs and Successors, cedes in entire ownership to the Russian Empire the Khanate of Erivan on both sides of the Araxe, and the Khanate of Nakhitchevan. In consequence of this cession, His Majesty the Shah undertakes to turn over to the Russian Authorities, within six months at the latest, from the date of signature of the present Treaty, all the archives and all public documents concerning the administration of the two Khanates above-mentioned.

ART. IV. The two High Contracting Parties agree to establish, as the frontier between the two States, the following line of demarcation: In parting from the point of the frontier of the Ottoman States, the nearest in a straight line from the summit of the little Ararat, this line will continue to the summit of this mountain from whence it will descend to the source of the river known as the Lower Karassou which flows from the southern side of the Little Ararat and it will follow its course until its discharge in the Araxe, opposite Cherour. Arrived at this point, this line will follow the bed of the Araxe to the Fortress of Abbas-Abad; around the exterior works of this place which are situated on the right bank of the Araxe, there will be traced a radius of a half agatch, or three versts and a half from Russia, which will extend in all directions; all the land which will be enclosed in this radius will belong exclusively to Russia and will be demarked with the greatest exactitude in the space of two months, dating from this day, From the locality where the eastern extremity of this radius will have rejoined the Araxe, the frontier line will continue to follow the bed of this river to the ford of Jediboulouk, from whence the Persian Territory will extend the length of the bed of the Araxe for a distance of three agatch or twenty-one versts from Russia; arrived at this point, the frontier line will traverse in a direct manner the plain of Moughan to the bed of the river known as Bolgarou, to the place situated at three agatch or twenty-one versts below the conjunction of the two small rivers known as Odinabazar and Sarakamyche. From there, this line will reascend from the left bank of the Bolgarou to the junction of the said rivers Odinabazar and Sarakamyche and will extend the length of the right bank of the river of Odinabazar to its source and from there to the summit of the heights of Djikoir so that all the waters which flow towards the Caspian Sea will belong to Russia, and all those [whose] watershed is of the Persian side will belong to Persia. The limit of the two States being marked here by the crest of the mountains, it is agreed that the declination from the side of the Caspian Sea will belong to Russia and that their opposite slope will belong to Persia. From the crest of the heights of Djikoir, the frontier will follow the summit of Kamarkouia, the mountains which separate the Talyche from the district of Archa. The crests of the mountains, separating on all sides the watershed, will determine here the frontier line in the same manner as stated above concerning the distance included between the source of the Odinabazar and the summits of Djikoir. The frontier line will follow thereafter, from the summit of Kamarkouia, the crests of the mountains which separate the district of Zouvante from that of Archa to the limit of that of Welkidji, always conforming to the principle enunciated in connection with the watershed. The district of Zouvante, with the exception of the part situated on the opposite side of the summit of the said mountains, will fall in this way in division to Russia. Beginning with the limit of the district of Welkidji, the frontier line between the two States will follow the summits of Klopouty and of the principal chain of mountains which traverse the district of Welkidji to the northern source of the river called Astara, always observing the principle relative to the watershed. From there the frontier will follow the bed of this river to its discharge in the Caspian Sea, and will complete the line of demarcation which will separate in future the respective possessions of Russia and Persia.

ART. V.   His Majesty the Shah of Persia in testimony of his sincere friendship for His Majesty the Emperor of all the Russias, solemnly recognizes by the present Article, both in his name as in that of his Heirs and Successors to the throne of Persia, as belonging forever to the Russian Empire, all the countries and all the islands situated between the line of demarcation designated by the preceding Article on the one side, and the crest of the mountains of the Caucasus, and the Caspian Sea on the other, as well as the peoples, nomads and others who inhabit these countries.

ART. VI.   With a view to recompensing the considerable sacrifices that the war, which occurred between the two States, has occasioned to the Russian Empire, as well as the losses and damages which have resulted therefrom for Russian subjects, His Majesty the Shah of Persia undertakes to make them good by means of a pecuniary indemnity. It is agreed between the two High Contracting Parties that the total of this indemnity is fixed at ten kupours of silver tomans or 20,000,000 silver roubles and that the method, the terms and the guarantees of payment of this sum will be regulated by a special arrangement which shall have the same force and value as if it were inserted word for word in the present Treaty.

ART. VII.   His Majesty the Shah of Persia having judged it fitting to appoint as his Successor and Heir Presumptive his August Son Prince Abbas Mirza, His Majesty the Emperor of all the Russias, with a view to giving to His Majesty the Shah public evidence of his friendly dispositions and of his desire to contribute to the consolidation of this order of succession, undertakes to recognize as from today, in the August Person of His Royal Highness Prince Abbas Mirza, the Successor and Heir Presumptive of the Crown of Persia and to consider Him as the Legitimate Sovereign of this Kingdom from his ascension to the throne.

ART. VIII.   Russian merchant vessels will enjoy, as in the past, the right to navigate freely on the Caspian Sea and along its coasts and to land there. They will find in Persia aid and assistance in case of shipwreck. The same right is accorded to Persian merchant vessels to navigate on the old footing in the Caspian Sea and to enter Russian Rivers where, in case of shipwreck, the Persians will receive reciprocally aid and assistance.[1]

As for war vessels, those which bear the Russian military flag being *ab antiquo* the only ones which have had the right to navigate on the Caspian Sea, this same exclusive privilege is, for this reason, equally reserved and assured today, so that, with the exception of Russia, no other Power shall be able to have war vessels on the Caspian Sea.

ART. IX. His Majesty the Emperor of all the Russias and His Majesty the Shah of Persia, having at heart to strengthen by all means the ties so happily reestablished between them, are agreed that the Ambassadors, Ministers, and Chargés d'Affaires, who may be reciprocally delegated near the respective High Courts, whether to discharge a temporary Mission or to reside there permanently, will be received with the honors and distinction befitting their rank and conformable with the dignity of the High Contracting Parties, as with the sincere friendship which unites them and conformable with the customs of the country. An understanding to this effect will be reached by means of a special Protocol regarding the ceremonial to be observed by both sides.

ART. X. His Majesty the Emperor of all the Russias and His Majesty the Shah of Persia, considering the reestablishment and the extension of commercial relations between the two States as one of the first benefactions which the return of peace should produce, have agreed to regulate in a perfect accord all provisions relative to the protection of commerce, and to the safety of the respective subjects, and to embody them in a separate Act annexed hereto, drawn up between the respective Plenipotentiaries and which is and will be considered as forming an integral part of the present Treaty of Peace.

His Majesty the Shah of Persia reserves to Russia, as in the past, the right of appointing consuls or commercial agents wherever the good of commerce will demand it, and he undertakes to endow these consuls and agents, none of which shall have a suite of more than ten persons, with the protection, the honors and the privileges belonging to their public character. His Majesty the Emperor of all the Russias promises on His side to observe a perfect reciprocity in respect of the consuls and commercial agents of His Majesty the Shah of Persia. In case of well-founded complaint on the part of the Persian Government against one of the Russian consuls or agents, the Minister or Chargé d'Affaires of Russia, residing at the Court of His Majesty the Shah, and under the immediate

---

[1] On 24 November 1869, a decision of the Council of the Empire of Russia was published, prohibiting the establishment of companies for the navigation of the Caspian Sea, except by Russian subjects, and the purchase by foreigners of shares in such companies (Sir Edward Hertslet, *Treaties, etc., concluded between Great Britain and Persia*. London: Butterworths, 1891). [All footnotes in this document are Hurewitz's.]

orders of whom they will be placed, will suspend him from his functions and will confer provisionally the office upon whom he will deem fitting.

ART. XI.   All the affairs and suits of the respective subjects, suspended by the intervention of the War, will be resumed and terminated in accordance with justice after the exclusion of Peace. The debts that the respective subjects may have the one in favor of the other, as well as to the treasury, will be promptly and entirely liquidated.

ART. XII.   The High Contracting Parties agree by common accord in the interest of their respective subjects to fix a term of three years in order that those among them who (own) immobile property on both sides of the Araxe may have the right to sell or exchange it freely. His Imperial Majesty of all the Russias excepts, however, from the benefit of this provision, so far as it concerns Him, the former Sardar of Erivan, Houssein Khan, his brother Hassen Khan and Kerim Khan, the former Governor of Nakhitchevan.

ART. XIII.   All prisoners of war made in one way or another, whether in the course of the last War, or before, as well as the subjects of the two Governments reciprocally fallen into captivity, at no matter what time, will be freed within a period of four months and, after having been provided with food and other necessary objects, they will be directed to Abbas Abad in order to be turned over there into the hands of Commissioners, respectively charged with receiving them and to decide upon their eventual return to their homes The High Contracting Parties will undertake the same in respect of all prisoners of War and all Russian and Persian subjects reciprocally fallen into captivity, who may not have been freed within the period above-mentioned, whether by reason of the isolated distance where they are to be found, or for any other cause or circumstance. The two Governments reserve expressly the unlimited right to reclaim them at no matter what time, and they obligate themselves to restore them mutually in the measure that they may present themselves for that purpose, or in the measure that they may reclaim them.

ART. XIV.   The High Contracting Parties will not demand the extradition of fugitives and deserters who shall have passed under their respective jurisdiction before or during the war. At the same time, in order to prevent the mutually prejudicial consequences which might be able to result from the correspondence which some of these deserters may seek to hold with their former compatriots, or vassals, the Persian Government undertakes not to tolerate in its Possessions, situated between the Araxe and the line formed by the River known as Tohara, by Lake Urumiah, by the River called Djakatou and by the River known as Kizil-Ozane, to its descent into the Caspian Sea, the presence of individuals who will be designated now by name or who may be nominated to it in the future. His Majesty the Emperor of All the Russias promises equally on His side not to permit Persian deserters to establish themselves or to remain fixed in the Khanats of Karbag or of Nakhitchevan or in the part of the Khanat of Erivan situated on the right bank of the Araxe. It is, however, understood, that this clause is and will only be obligatory in respect of individuals possessing a public character of a certain dignity, such as the Khans, the Begs and the spiritual leaders or mullahs, whose personal example, intrigues and clandestine correspondence may be able to exercise a pernicious influence on their former compatriots, those formerly under their administration or their vassals. In so far as concerns the mass of the population in the two countries, it is agreed between the High Contracting Parties that the respective subjects who shall have passed or who may pass in the future from one State into the other, will be free to establish themselves or to sojourn wherever the Government under whose domination they will be placed will find it proper.

ART. XV.   With the beneficent and salutary aim of restoring tranquility in his States and of removing from his subjects all that may aggravate the evils which have brought on them the war to which the present Treaty has put an end so happily, His Majesty the Shah accords a full and complete amnesty to all the inhabitants and functionaries of the province known as Azerbaijhan. No one of them, without exception of category, may be either pursued, nor molested for his opinions, for his acts or for the conduct which he may have pursued, either during the war or during the temporary occupation of the said province by Russian troops. There will be, moreover, accorded them a period of one year dating from this day in order to transport themselves freely with their families from Persian States into Russian States, to export and to sell their movable property, without the Governments or the local authorities being able to place the least obstacle in the way thereof, nor to deduct previously any tax or any recompense on the goods and objects sold or exported by them. As for their immovable property there will be accorded a term of five years to sell or to dispose thereof as may be desired. There are excepted from this amnesty those who may have rendered themselves culpable within the period of time abovementioned of one year of some crime, or misdemeanor liable to penalties punished by the Courts.

ART. XVI.   Immediately after the signature of the present Treaty of Peace, the respective plenipotentiaries will hasten to send the necessary notices and injunctions in all localities for the immediate cessation of hostilities.

2. The Commercial Treaty

ART. I.   The two High Contracting Parties desiring to make their respective subjects enjoy all the advantages which result from a reciprocal liberty of commerce, have agreed upon the following:

Russian subjects provided with passports in proper order shall be able to engage in commerce throughout the whole extent of the Persian Kingdom, and to proceed equally in the neighboring States of the said Kingdom.

In reciprocity thereof Persian subjects shall be able to import their merchandise into Russia, either by the Caspian Sea or by the land frontier which separates Russia from Persia, to exchange it or to make purchases for exportation, and they will enjoy all the rights and prerogatives accorded in the States of His Imperial Majesty to the subjects of the most favored friendly Powers.

In case of the decease of a Russian subject in Persia, his movable and immovable property, as belonging to the subject of a friendly Power, will be turned over intact to his relatives or associates, who will have the right to dispose of the said property as they may judge fitting. In the absence of relatives or associates the disposition of the said property will be confided to the Mission or to the Consuls of Russia without any difficulty on the part of the Russian authorities.

ART. II.   Contracts, bills of exchange, bonds and other written instruments between the respective subjects for their commercial affairs will be registered with the Russian Consul and with the Hakim (Civil Magistrate) and there, where there is no Consul, with the Hakim alone, so that in case of dispute between the two parties one can make the researches necessary in order to decide the difference in conformity with justice.

If one of the two parties without being provided with the documents drawn up and legalized as stated above, which will be valid before every court of justice, should desire to institute a suit against the other in producing only proofs of testimonials, such pretensions will not be admitted at all unless the defendant himself may recognize the legality thereof.

Every undertaking entered into between the respective subjects in the forms above prescribed will be religiously observed and the refusal to give satisfaction therein which may occasion losses to one of the parties will give place to a proportional indemnity of the part of the other. In case of bankruptcy of a Russian merchant in Persia, his creditors will be recompensed with the goods and effects of the bankrupt, but the Russian Minister, the Chargé d'Affaires or the Consul shall not refuse if demanded their good offices to assure themselves whether the bankrupt has not left in Russia available properties which may serve to satisfy the same creditors.

The provisions drawn up in the present Article will be reciprocally observed in respect of Persian subjects who engage in commerce in Russia under the protection of its laws.

ART. III.   With a view to assuring to the trade of the respective subjects the advantages which are the object of the previous stipulations, it is agreed that merchandise imported into Persia or exported from that Kingdom by Russian subjects and equally the products of Persia imported into Russia by Persian subjects, whether by the Caspian Sea or by the land frontier between the two States, as well as Russian merchandise which Persian subjects may export from the Empire by the same means, will be subject, as in the past, to a duty of five per cent, collected one time for all at entry or departure, and will not be subject thereafter to any other customs dues. If Russia may judge it necessary to draw up new customs regulations or new tariffs, it undertakes however not to increase even in this case the rate above-mentioned of five per cent.

Art. IV.   If Russia or Persia find themselves at war with another Power it will not be forbidden to the respective subjects to cross with their merchandise the territory of the High Contracting Parties to proceed into the confines of the said Power.

Art. V.   Seeing that after existing usages in Persia it is difficult for foreign subjects to find for rent houses, warehouses or premises suitable as deports for their merchandise, it is permitted to Russian subjects in Persia not only to rent but also to acquire in full ownership houses for habitation and shops as well as premises to store therein their merchandise.

The employees of the Persian Government shall not be able to enter by force in the said houses, shops or premises, at least without having recourse in case of necessity to the authorization of the Russian Minister, Chargé d'Affaires or Consul who will delegate an employee or dragoman to assist in the visit to the house or the merchandise.

Art. VI.   At the same time the Minister or the Chargé d'Affaires of His Imperial Majesty, the employees of the Russian Mission, Consuls and Dragomans, finding for sale in Persia neither the effects to serve for their clothing nor many objects of food which are necessary to them, shall be able to introduce free of tax and of dues, for their own account, all objects and effects which may be destined solely to their use.

The public servants of His Majesty the Shah residing in the States of the Russian Empire will enjoy perfect reciprocity in this regard.

Persian subjects forming part of the suite of the Minister or Chargé d'Affaires or Consuls, and necessary for their service, will enjoy, so long as they shall be attached to them, their protection on an equality with Russian subjects, but if it may happen that one amongst them renders himself culpable of some misdemeanor and that he makes himself liable thereby to punishment by the existing laws, in this case the Persian Minister or Hakim and, in his absence, the competent local authority, shall address himself immediately to the Russian Minister, Chargé d'Affaires or Consul, in the service of which the accused is to be found in order that he may be delivered to justice; and if this request is founded on proofs establishing the culpability of the accused, the Minister, Chargé d'Affaires or Consul will interpose no difficulty for the satisfaction thereof.

Art. VII.   All suits and litigations between Russian subjects will be subject exclusively to the examination and decision of the Russian Mission or Consuls in conformity with the laws and customs of the Russian Empire; as well as the differences and suits occurring between Russian subjects and those of another Power where the parties shall consent thereto.

When differences or suits shall arise between Russian subjects and Persian subjects, the said suits or differences will be brought before the Hakim or Governor and will be examined and judged only in the presence of the Dragoman of the Mission or the Consulate.

Once juridically terminated, such suits may not be instituted a second time. If, however, the circumstances were of a nature to demand a second examination, it may not take place without notification to the Russian Minister, Chargé d'Affaires or Consul and in this case the affair will only be considered and judged at the Defter, that is to say, in the Supreme Chancellery of the Shah at Tabriz or at Teheran, likewise in the presence of a Dragoman of the Russian Mission or Consulate.

ART. VIII.   In case of murder or other crime committed between Russian subjects the examination and the decision of the case will be the exclusive concern of the Russian Minister, Charge d'Affaires or Consul by virtue of the jurisdiction over their nationals conferred upon them.

If a Russian subject is found implicated with individuals of another nation in a criminal suit he cannot be pursued nor harried in any manner without proofs of his participation in the crime, and in this case even as in that where a Russian subject may be accused of direct culpability, the courts of the country may only proceed to take cognizance and give judgment concerning the crime in the presence of a delegate of the Russian Mission or Consulate, and if they are not to be found at the place where the crime has been committed, the local authorities will transport the delinquent there where there is a constituted Russian Consul or Agent.

Testimonies for the prosecution and for the defense of the accused will be faithfully collected by the Hakim and by the Judge of the locality, and invested with their signature; transmitted in this form there where the crime has to be judged, these testimonies will become authentic documents or parts of the suit unless the accused proves clearly their falsity.

When the accused shall have been duly convicted and sentence shall have been pronounced, the delinquent will be turned over to the Minister, Chargé d'Affaires or Consul of His Imperial Majesty who will return him to Russia to receive there the punishment prescribed by the laws.

ART. IX.   The High Contracting Parties will take care that the stipulations of the present Act may be strictly observed and fulfilled, and the Governors of their Provinces, Commandants and other respective authorities will not permit themselves in any case to violate them, under penalty of a grave responsibility and even of dismissal in case of complaint duly proven.

2.   The Treaty of Balta Liman Gives the British Economic Advantages Within the Ottoman Empire, August 16, 1838

Despite the economic prowess of English industrialists, their access to the vast markets of the Ottoman Empire was limited by the system of tariffs and monopolies in existence throughout most of the Middle East and North Africa. Although from the perspective of the English, these practices were prohibitive of "free trade," in fact they also protected local economies and workers from being overwhelmed by European goods. All of this changed in 1838 with the signing of the Treaty of Balta Liman. At the time the Ottoman Empire was feeling militarily threatened by the expansionist ambitions of Muhammad 'Ali, the governor of Egypt. By 1833, in large part because of his modernized army, Muhammad 'Ali had extended his control to all of Syria and appeared to be threatening Anatolia, the heartland of the Ottoman Empire. Britain considered Muhammad 'Ali a threat because of his attempts to foster a local industrial revolution at the expense of European imports. The Ottomans signed the Treaty of Balta Liman in exchange for British military support in ousting Muhammad 'Ali from Syria and severely curtailing his regional power. In exchange Britain, and subsequently France and the Netherlands, gained almost unfettered access to the markets of the empire—an outcome that had momentous repercussions on the economy of the Middle East and North Africa for years to come.

ART. I. All rights, privileges, and immunities which have been conferred on the subjects or ships of Great Britain by the existing Capitulations and Treaties, are confirmed now and for ever, except in as far as they may be specifically altered by the present Convention: and it is moreover expressly stipulated, that all rights, privileges, or immunities which the Sublime Porte now grants, or may hereafter grant, to the ships and subjects of any other foreign Power, or which may suffer the ships and subjects of any other foreign Power to enjoy, shall be equally granted to, and exercised and enjoyed by, the subjects and ships of Great Britain.

ART. II. The subjects of Her Britannic Majesty, or their agents, shall be permitted to purchase at all places in the Ottoman Dominions (whether for the purposes of internal trade or exportation) all articles, without any exception whatsoever, the produce, growth, or manufacture of the said Dominions; and the Sublime Porte formally engages to abolish all monopolies of agricultural produce, or of any other articles whatsoever, as well as all *Permits* from the local Governors, either for the purchase of any article, or for its removal from one place to another when purchased; and any attempt to compel the subjects of Her Britannic Majesty to receive such *Permits* from the local Governors, shall be considered as an infraction of Treaties, and the Sublime Porte shall immediately punish with severity any Vizirs and other officers who shall have been guilty of such misconduct, and render full justice to British subjects for all injuries or losses which they may duly prove themselves to have suffered.

ART. III. If any article of Turkish produce, growth, or manufacture, be purchased by the British merchant or his agent, for the purpose of selling the same for internal consumption in Turkey, the British merchant or his agent shall pay, at the purchase and sale of such articles, and in any manner of trade therein, the

Great Britain, *Parliamentary Papers, 1839,* vol. 50: pp. 291–295. This document may also be found in J. C. Hurewitz, *The Middle East and North Africa in World Politics* (New Haven, Conn.: Yale University Press, 1975), pp. 265–266.

same duties that are paid, in similar circumstances, by the most favoured class of Turkish subjects engaged in the internal trade of Turkey, whether Mussulmans or Rayahs.

ART. IV.   If any article of Turkish produce, growth, or manufacture, be purchased for exportation, the same shall be conveyed by the British merchant or his agent, free of any kind of charge or duty whatsoever, to a convenient place of shipment, on its entry into which it shall be liable to one fixed duty of nine per cent, *ad valorem,* in lieu of all other interior duties.

Subsequently, on exportation, the duty of three per cent., as established and existing at present, shall be paid. But all articles bought in the shipping ports for exportation, and which have already paid the interior duty at entering into the same, will only pay the three per cent. export duty.

ART. V.   The regulations under which Firmans are issued to British merchant vessels for passing the Dardanelles and the Bosphorus, shall be so framed as to occasion to such vessels the least possible delay.

ART. VI.   It is agreed by the Turkish Government, that the regulations established in the present Convention, shall be general throughout the Turkish Empire, whether in Turkey in Europe or Turkey in Asia, in Egypt, or other African possessions belonging to the Sublime Porte, and shall be applicable to all the subjects, whatever their description, of the Ottoman Dominions: and the Turkish Government also agrees not to object to other foreign Powers settling their trade upon the basis of this present Convention.

ART. VII.   It having been the custom of Great Britain and the Sublime Porte, with a view to prevent all difficulties and delay in estimating the value of articles imported into the Turkish Dominions, or exported therefrom, by British subjects, to appoint, at intervals of fourteen years, a Commission of men well acquainted with the traffic of both countries, who have fixed by a tariff the sum of money in the coin of the Grand Signior, which should be paid as duty on each article; and the term of fourteen years, during which the last adjustment of the said tariff was to remain in force, having expired, the High Contracting Parties have agreed to name conjointly fresh Commissioners to fix and determine the amount in money which is to be paid by British subjects, as the duty of three per cent upon the value of all commodities imported and exported by them; and the said Commissioners shall establish an equitable arrangement for estimating the interior duties which, by the present Treaty, are established on Turkish goods to be exported, and shall also determine on the places of shipment where it may be most convenient that such duties should be levied.

The new tariff thus established, to be in force for seven years after it has been fixed, at the end of which time it shall be in the power of either of the parties to demand a revision of that tariff; but if no such demand be made on either side, within the six months after the end of the first seven years, then the tariff shall remain in force for seven years more, reckoned from the end of the preceding seven years; and so it shall be at the end of each successive period of seven years.

3. An Egyptian Khedival Decree Establishes a European-Controlled Public Debt Administration, May 2, 1876

By the second half of the nineteenth century, France, Britain, and Russia had established their political and economic influence within the Ottoman Empire, Iran, Egypt, Algeria, and Tunisia. The growth of foreign influence reduced the power of governments vis-à-vis European consuls and the governments and commercial interests they represented. Some local governments—most notably in the Ottoman Empire and Egypt—attempted to reverse their fortunes by consolidating the power of their rule and at the same time seeking ways to modernize their bureaucracies, armies, and economies. These expensive projects, however, could not be solely supported by tax revenue collected from a primarily peasant population. Thus, some of these governments acquired loans from European banks. The loans were meant to fund the laying down of railroad track, the digging of irrigation canals, "modern" education, and the outfitting of new armies. Generally, the loans were of the high-interest, short-term type, because of the risk of default that the lending banks faced or claimed to face. With the influx of large amounts of money came the potential for, and the reality of, corruption and financial mismanagement, particularly in governments where independent oversight was nonexistent.

In Egypt, the thoughtful and thoughtless projects of Khedive Isma'il dragged the country into serious indebtedness. His initial attempt to service the outstanding and ballooning loans through selling the Egyptian shares in the Suez Canal Company and through new generous tax laws for the wealthy landowners of Egypt only postponed the seemingly inevitable bankruptcy of the government. Facing the prospect of Egyptian default on the loans, Italian and French advisers pressured Isma'il to issue the following edict establishing a European-controlled public debt administration that would manage Egypt's finances and the servicing of its debt at a rate of 7 percent. The British, however, balked at this arrangement and later forced the issuance of a decree (dated November 18, 1876) that placed all of Egypt's finances under French and British control.

We, the Khedive of Egypt, desiring to take definitive and opportune measures for obtaining the unification of the different debts of the State and those of the Daira Sanieh, and also desiring the reduction of the excessive charges resulting from these debts, and wishing to bear solemn testimony to our firm intention to secure every guarantee to all persons interested, have resolved to

---

Great Britain, *Parliamentary Papers, 1876*, vol. 83, pp. 71–72. This document may also be found in J. C. Hurewitz, *The Middle East and North Africa in World Politics* (New Haven, Conn.: Yale University Press, 1975), pp. 185–187.

establish a special Treasury charged with the regular service of the public debt, and to appoint to its management foreign Commissioners, who at our request will be indicated by the respective Governments as fit officials to fill the post to which they will be appointed by us in the quality of Egyptian officials, and under the following conditions. Having consulted our Privy Council, we have decreed, and do hereby decree, as follows:—

ART. 1.   A Treasury of the Public Debt is established, charged with receiving the funds necessary for the interest and the redemption of the debt, and with applying them to this object exclusively.

ART. 2.   The officials, the local Treasuries, or the special Administrations, after collecting, receiving, or accumulating the revenues specially devoted to the payment of the debt, are or shall be in future charged to pay them into the Central Treasury or to keep them at the disposal of the Intendants of Public Expenditure ("Ordonnateurs des Dépenses de l'Etat"). The Intendants of Public Expenditure are, by virtue of the present Decree, bound to pay these revenues on account of the State Treasury into the special Treasury of the Public Debt, which will be considered in this respect as a special Treasury. These officials, treasuries and administrations can only procure a valid discharge by means of the vouchers which will be delivered to them by the said Treasury of the Public Debt. Any other order or voucher will not be valid. These same officials, treasuries or administrations will every month send to the Minister of Finance a statement of the receipts or collections made by themselves directly or paid in by the receivers of the revenues specially devoted to the debt and the payments made into the special Treasury of the Public Debt. The Minister of Finance will communicate these statements to the Administration of the Treasury of the Public Debt.

The Treasury of the Public Debt shall receive from the Daira Sanieh the entire sum necessary for the interest and redemption of the amount of its unified debt, and it shall likewise receive the funds for the yearly payment due to the English Government, and representing the interest on the Suez Canal shares.

ART. 3.   If the payments of the revenue devoted to the debt be insufficient to meet the half-yearly charges, the special Public Debt Department will demand from the Treasury, through the intermediary of the Minister of Finance, the sum required to complete the half-yearly payments; the Treasury will have to deliver this sum a fortnight before the payments are due. If the funds in hand constitute a surplus over the amount necessary for the payment of the interest and the sinking fund, the special Treasury of the Public Debt will pay this surplus at the end of each year to the general Treasury of the Exchequer. The Treasury of the Pubic Debt will submit its accounts, which will be examined and reported upon according to law.

ART. 4.   The suits which the Treasury and its Directors, on its behalf, acting in the name and in the interests of the creditors, mostly of foreign nationality, may consider they have to bring against the financial administration represented by the Minister of Finance in so far as regards the guardianship of the guarantees of the debt which we have confided to the said Treasury, will be brought in the terms of their jurisdiction before the new tribunals which, in conformity with the agreement entered into with the Powers, have been instituted in Egypt.

ART. 5.   The Commissioners selected as stated above will have the direction of the special Treasury of the Public Debt. They will be appointed by us for five years, and will sit in Cairo. Their functions may be continued after the five years have expired, and in case of the death or resignation of one of them the vacancy will be filled by us in the manner of the original appointment. They may intrust one of themselves with the functions of President, and the latter will notify his nomination to the Minister of Finance.

ART. 6.   The cost of exchange, insurance, and conveyance of specie abroad, as well as the commission for the payment of the coupons, will be borne by the Government. The Directors of the Treasury will come to a previous arrangement with the Ministers of Finance with regard to all these operations, but the Minister will decide whether the despatch of these sums is to be effected in specie or by letters of exchange.

ART. 7.   The Treasury will not be allowed to employ any funds, disposable or not, in operations of credit, commerce, industry, &c.

ART. 8.   The Government will not be able, without an agreement with the majority of the Commissioners directing the Treasury of the Public Debt, to effect in any of the taxes specially devoted to the Debt any changes which might result in a diminution of the revenue from these taxes, At the same time, the Government may farm out one or several of these taxes, provided that the contract entered into insure a revenue at least equal to that already existing, and may also conclude Treaties of commerce introducing modifications in the Customs duties.

ART. 9.   The Government undertakes not to issue any Treasury Bonds or any other new bonds, and not to contract any other loan of any nature whatsoever. This same engagement is entered into in the name of the Daira Sanieh. Nevertheless, in case the Government, from urgent national reasons, should find itself placed under the necessity of having recourse to credit, it may do so within the limits of strict necessity, and without doing anything to affect the employment of the revenues set apart for the Treasury of the Public Debt, or to cause their diversion from their destination. These totally exceptional loans can only be contracted after an agreement on the subject with the Commissioners directing the Treasury.

ART. 10.   In order that the arrangements stated in the preceding article shall not place obstacles in the way of the Administration, the Government may open a running account with a bank to facilitate its payments by means of anticipations to be regulated in accordance with the year's receipts. The debit or credit balance will be settled at the end of each year. This current account must never be overdrawn during the year by more than 50,000,000 fr.

4.   Convention on Free Navigation of the Suez Canal Between the European Powers and the Ottoman Empire, October 29, 1888

The Suez Canal was a crucial part of European-dominated international trade. The British, in particular, were constantly and acutely concerned with maintaining links to the economically critical South Asian parts of their empire. In the wake of the 'Urabi revolt, which threatened to topple Khedive Tawfiq in Egypt, the British and the French became alarmed at the prospect of restricted access to the Suez Canal. Thus, in 1882 the British landed an expeditionary force, which defeated the 'Urabi forces opposing the khedive and restored calm to Egyptian politics. The intervention was meant to be a brief military operation, but the British remained in power in Egypt until 1956. The Convention on Free Navigation has to be read against this backdrop. The "Powers" mentioned in this document are Austria, Germany, Italy, the Netherlands, the Ottoman Empire, Russia, and Spain, in addition to Britain and France, all of whom signed the convention in 1888. However, the convention did not become fully operational until 1904, when French reservations about the power it gave the British, who were occupying Egypt, were allayed.

ART. I.   The Suez Maritime Canal shall always be free and open, in time of war as in time of peace, to every vessel of commerce or of war, without distinction of flag.

Consequently, the High Contracting Parties agree not in any way to interfere with the free use of the Canal, in time of war as in time of peace.

The Canal shall never be subjected to the exercise of the right of blockade.

ART. II.   The High Contracting Parties, recognizing that the Fresh-Water Canal is indispensable to the Maritime Canal, take note of the engagements of His Highness the Khedive towards the Universal Suez Canal Company as regards the Fresh-Water Canal; which engagements are stipulated in a Convention bearing date the 18th March, 1863, containing an *exposé* and four Articles.

They undertake not to interfere in any way with the security of that Canal and its branches, the working of which shall not be exposed to any attempt at obstruction.

ART. III.   The High Contracting Parties likewise undertake to respect the plant, establishments, buildings, and works of the Maritime Canal and of the Fresh-Water Canal.

Great Britain, *Parliamentary Papers, 1889,* Commercial no. 2, C. 5623. This document may also be found in J. C. Hurewitz, *The Middle East and North Africa in World Politics* (New Haven, Conn.: Yale University Press, 1975), pp. 455–456.

ART. IV.   The Maritime Canal remaining open in time of war as a free passage, even to the ships of war of belligerents, according to the terms of Article I of the present Treaty, the High Contracting Parties agree that no right of war, no act of hostility, nor any act having for its object to obstruct the free navigation of the Canal, shall be committed in the Canal and its ports of access, as well as within a radius of 3 marine miles from those ports, even though the Ottoman Empire should be one of the belligerent Powers.

Vessels of war of belligerents shall not revictual or take in stores in the Canal and its ports of access, except in so far as may be strictly necessary. The transit of the aforesaid vessels through the Canal shall be effected with the least possible delay, in accordance with the Regulations in force, and without any other intermission than that resulting from the necessities of the service.

Their stay at Port Saïd and in the roadstead of Suez shall not exceed twenty-four hours, except in case of distress. In such case they shall be bound to leave as soon as possible. An interval of twenty-four hours shall always elapse between the sailing of a belligerent ship from one of the ports of access and the departure of a ship belonging to the hostile Power.

ART. V.   In time of war belligerent Powers shall not disembark nor embark within the Canal and its ports of access either troops, munitions, or materials of war. But in case of an accidental hindrance in the Canal, men may be embarked or disembarked at the ports of access by detachments not exceeding 1,000 men, with a corresponding amount of war material.

ART. VI.   Prizes shall be subjected, in all respects, to the same rules as the vessels of war of belligerents.

ART. VII.   The Powers shall not keep any vessel of war in the waters of the Canal (including Lake Timsah and the Bitter Lakes).

Nevertheless, they may station vessels of war in the ports of access of Port Saïd and Suez, the number of which shall not exceed two for each Power.

This right shall not be exercised by belligerents.

ART. VIII.   The Agents in Egypt of the Signatory Powers of the present Treaty shall be charged to watch over its execution. In case of any event threatening the security or the free passage of the Canal, they shall meet on the summons of three of their number under the presidency of their Doyen, in order to proceed to the necessary verifications. They shall inform the Khedivial Government of the danger which they may have perceived, in order that that Government may take proper steps to insure the protection and the free use of the Canal. Under any circumstances, they shall meet once a year to take note of the due execution of the Treaty.

The last-mentioned meetings shall take place under the presidency of a Special Commissioner nominated for that purpose by the Imperial Ottoman Government. A Commissioner of the Khedive may also take part in the meeting, and may preside over it in case of the absence of the Ottoman Commissioner.

They shall especially demand the suppression of any work or the dispersion of any assemblage on either bank of the Canal, the object or effect of which might be to interfere with the liberty and the entire security of the navigation.

Art. IX.   The Egyptian Government shall, within the limits of its powers resulting from the Firmans, and under the conditions provided for in the present Treaty, take the necessary measures for insuring the execution of the said Treaty.

In case the Egyptian Government should not have sufficient means at its disposal, it shall call upon the Imperial Ottoman Government, which shall take the necessary measures to respond to such appeal; shall give notice thereof to the Signatory Powers of the Declaration of London of the 17th March, 1885; and shall, if necessary, concert with them on the subject.

The provisions of Articles IV, V, VII, and VIII shall not interfere with the measures which shall be taken in virtue of the present Article.

Art. X.   Similarly, the provisions of Articles IV, V, VII, and VIII shall not interfere with the measures which His Majesty the Sultan and His Highness the Khedive, in the name of His Imperial Majesty, and within the limits of the Firmans granted, might find it necessary to take for securing by their own forces the defence of Egypt and the maintenance of public order.

In case His Imperial Majesty the Sultan, or His Highness the Khedive, should find it necessary to avail themselves of the exceptions for which this Article provides, the Signatory Powers of the Declaration of London shall be notified thereof by the Imperial Ottoman Government.

It is likewise understood that the provisions of the four Articles aforesaid shall in no case occasion any obstacle to the measures which the Imperial Ottoman Government may think it necessary to take in order to insure by its own forces the defence of its other possessions situated on the eastern coast of the Red Sea.

Art. XI.   The measures which shall be taken in the cases provided for by Articles IX and X of the present Treaty shall not interfere with the free use of the Canal. In the same cases, the erection of permanent fortifications contrary to the provisions of Article VIII is prohibited.

Art. XII.   The High Contracting Parties, by application of the principle of equality as regards the free use of the Canal, a principle which forms one of the bases of the present Treaty, agree that none of them shall endeavour to obtain with respect to the Canal territorial or commercial advantages or privileges in any international arrangements which may be concluded. Moreover, the rights of Turkey as the territorial Power are reserved.

Art. XIII.   With the exception of the obligations expressly provided by the clauses of the present Treaty, the sovereign rights of His Imperial Majesty the Sultan, and the rights and immunities of His Highness the Khedive, resulting from the Firmans, are in no way affected.

ART. XIV. The High Contracting Parties agree that the engagements resulting from the present Treaty shall not be limited by the duration of the Acts of Concession of the Universal Suez Canal Company.

ART. XV. The stipulations of the present Treaty shall not interfere with the sanitary measures in force in Egypt.

ART. XVI. The High Contracting Parties undertake to bring the present Treaty to the knowledge of the States which have not signed it, inviting them to accede to it.

5. The Concession for the Imperial Bank in Iran, January 30, 1889

In order to establish modern economies able to compete in the European-dominated international market, many of the central governments in the Middle East and North Africa sought to create modern central banks, to issue bank notes and make loans to the state and private institutions. Many of these banks established their own industrial, mining, and commercial interests funded through the financial dealings of the bank. The concession for the Imperial Bank in Iran, signed on January 30, 1889, was one such attempt to establish a modern banking institution. The idea originated with Baron Julius de Reuter, who in 1872 had received from the Iranian government a general concession guaranteed by a £40,000 sterling note. As the Russian and British rivalry over Iran intensified, the English government mediated various disagreements between Reuter and the Iranian government. Out of these negotiations emerged the 1889 concession.

The difficulties pending for a long time between the Government of His Imperial Majesty the Shah of Persia and Baron Julius de Reuter having been definitely overcome and the concession granted to the said Baron Julius de Reuter on 25 July 1872 annulled, the following has been mutually agreed upon:

ART. 1. By the present concession the Government of His Imperial Majesty the Shah of Persia grants to Baron Julius de Reuter and his associates or representatives the right to found a state bank in the Persian Empire under the name of Imperial Bank of Persia. This right is granted for a period of sixty years from the date of signature of the present concession by His Imperial Majesty the Shah. The seat of the association and the residence of the Bank shall be established at Tehran, and the Bank may establish branches in other cities in Persia or abroad. In order to develop Persia's commerce and augment its wealth, the Imperial Bank, aside from the purposes that an institution of credit serves, may undertake on its own behalf or on behalf of a third [party], any kind of

---

Translated from the French text in Iran, Archives of the Ministry of Foreign Affairs, Tehran. This document may also be found in J. C. Hurewitz, *The Middle East and North Africa in World Politics* (New Haven, Conn.: Yale University Press, 1975), pp. 457–461.

financial, industrial, or commercial endeavor it believes favorable to this end, on condition that none of these enterprises shall be contrary to the treaties, laws, customs, or religion of the country and that the Persian Government shall be informed in advance. The Imperial Bank shall not have the right to accept a mortgage, or to buy immovable [property such as] lands, villages, etc., in the territory of the Empire, with the exception of land needed for the construction of a suitable establishment in Tehran and branches in the provinces. It is equally forbidden for the Bank to discount or to make advances on Government drafts that shall not have been drawn on the Bank.

ART. 2.   The capital of the Imperial Bank shall be 100 million francs, or £4 million sterling. Consequently, a certain number of securities may be created that the Bank shall issue in series. The Bank shall be considered established when the first series of 25 million francs, or £1 million sterling, has been subscribed. The subscription shall be opened in various capitals, such as Tehran, Berlin, London, Paris, Saint Petersburg, and Vienna, if the governments of the several Powers permit it. The securities shall be [payable] to the bearer and the Bank may also issue registered securities. The Bank, when it is judged advantageous, may augment its capital and the number of its securities on agreement with the Government.

ART. 3.   The Imperial Bank shall have the exclusive right as State Bank to issue notes payable to the bearer on demand. It shall never issue notes amounting to more than 20 million francs, or £800 thousand sterling, without informing the Persian Government. In order to further the development of public credit and place a limit on the circulation of silver money, while augmenting that of gold, the Imperial Bank accepts in principle the establishment of a single standard based on the *toman,* but within ten years after the Bank's establishment the Government of His Imperial Majesty and the Directors of the Bank shall agree on the most proper ways and means to attain this end. However, taking into consideration the demands of the actual monetary situation, the issuance of Imperial Bank notes shall be based primarily on the silver *kran.*

These notes shall be accepted by all agents and employees of the Imperial Government and shall be [considered] legal tender in all transactions in Persia. However, should the Bank not be able to redeem one of these notes, the circulation of Bank notes shall be forbidden throughout the Empire and the Bank shall be forced to redeem all its notes. To guarantee this reimbursement, the Bank expressly promises to maintain for two years from the time it begins its operations a cash balance equal to half [the value] of its notes in circulation, and after this period of two years, equal to at least one-third. The difference between the cash balance in specie and the amount of the notes issued shall be guaranteed by the titles to movable and immovable valuables belonging to the bank and deposited in its coffers in Persia.

The Imperial Bank shall be obligated to pay its notes on sight at the place of their issuance. Nevertheless, its branches' notes may be reimbursed in Tehran. The bank notes shall be in the Persian language. Paper money [of denominations] less than two tomans may not be issued without the authorization of the Government. The bank notes shall carry a sign or stamp indicating their inspection by the Persian Government and shall be signed by a Director or Administrator and by the principal cashier of the establishment where they were issued.

The Government of His Imperial Majesty the Shah pledges not to issue any sort of paper money for the duration of this concession nor to authorize the creation of any other bank or establishment having similar privileges.

ART. 4.   The Imperial Government does not guarantee the capital of the Bank. It may, if it wishes, subscribe to it or promote the subscription of Persian subjects to the amount of one-fifth of the capital called for, or [it may choose not to] participate in any way.

The division of the capital into securities, the number and value of bank notes conforming to the provisions of Article 3 of the present instrument, the organization and administration of the Bank, the nomination of managers and employees of the Bank in Persia or abroad, and the financial management of the Bank with the profits that it may make or the losses it may suffer shall be entirely in the hands of the concessionaire and his associates or representatives, at their risk and peril.

The Government of His Imperial Majesty the Shah shall exercise its high surveillance on the Bank by appointing an Imperial High Commissioner. This High Commissioner shall have the right to acquaint himself with the management of the Bank and to see that the affairs of the Bank are conducted in conformity with this instrument of concession. He shall officially attend General Meetings as well as gatherings of the Council of Administration at Tehran whenever invited. He shall control the issuance of bank notes with strict observance of the provisions of Article 3 of the present concession. He shall supervise relations between the Bank and the Imperial Treasury. He may not interfere with the administration and management of the Bank's affairs and his duties shall not impose any responsibility on the Imperial Government.

ART. 5.   The purpose of [establishing] this Bank as a national institution being the public welfare and the welfare of the State, the Government of His Imperial Majesty grants it the military protection indispensable to the security of its principal seat and branches.

The Government as protector of the enterprise shall facilitate, wherever possible, the acquisition of necessary lands and sites upon which the Bank shall establish its principal seat and branches, intervening equitably between [the Bank] and the landowners. The Bank, its premises and branches, shall be entirely exempt from any kind of tax or duty. The same shall be true for its securities, notes, receipts, and checks and for all documents emanating from it on its affairs and transactions. But if the Imperial Government should introduce a stamp tax the Bank shall not accept any bill of exchange or other instrument circulating in Persia without a State stamp.

ART. 6.   The Imperial Bank shall facilitate the payments of the Imperial Treasury in Persia or abroad. For each service the Government demands of [the

Bank] the Government and the Bank's Directors shall mutually determine the commission to be paid to the Bank. After its establishment and the payment of its capital, the Imperial Bank undertakes to lend the Government of His Imperial Majesty the Shah for a period of ten years the sum of 1 million francs, or £40 thousand sterling, at an [interest] rate of 6 percent. The interest and amortization, shall, according to His Imperial Majesty's wishes, be deducted from the 6 percent of the Bank's net profits assured to the Government by Article 7 of the present instrument. Moreover, the Bank, after its establishment, shall also place itself at the disposal of the Imperial Government for all loans or advances that [the Imperial Government] may need, against such collatoral as may be agreed upon in each case by the Imperial Government and the Bank. Otherwise, these advances or loans shall be considered an equivalent guarantee for the sum of the notes issued. The Government shall repay these loans or advances within a period specified by the respective conventions. The total interest shall be discharged regularly at the end of each Persian fiscal year, to wit, on 20 March. The first of these advances above the aforementioned sum of 1 million francs shall be 5 million francs, or £200,000 sterling, at the current rate of exchange, i.e., at the rate of 8 percent.

ART. 7.   At the end of each Persian fiscal year, on 20 March, the Imperial Bank must turn over to the Government of His Imperial Majesty the Shah, or transfer to his credit, 6 percent of the annual net profits. Should this share of the profits, fixed at 6 percent, not reach an annual sum of 100 thousand francs, or £4 thousand sterling, the Bank must furnish the balance, charging it [alone] or the total sum to its trade expenses without the right of any deduction whatsoever in the said share of profits resulting from the balance sheet of the following year.

ART. 8.   The guarantee of £40 thousand sterling that was deposited in 1872 in the Bank of England by Baron Julius de Reuter shall serve the Persian Government as a guarantee for the establishment of the Imperial Bank. The day after its establishment, the Persian Government shall return to the said Baron the aforementioned sum of £40 thousand sterling. If the Imperial Bank is not founded within a period of nine months from His Imperial Majesty's signature of the present instrument, the said guarantee shall fall to the Persian Government, and the present concession shall be considered null and void [*non avenues*] unless a war erupts in Europe between the Great Powers or Persia finds itself engaged [in war] or in any other situation [caused by] an act of God.

ART. 9.   At the moment of the establishment of the Imperial Bank, its principal Administrators shall publish the statutes by which the Bank is to be regulated. These statutes must conform strictly to the stipulations of the present concession. After the establishment of the Bank the said statutes may be modified only by the decision of a General Assembly of stockholders, who in any modifications must always respect the stipulations of the present instrument.

ART. 10.   The Imperial Bank shall be under the high protection of His Imperial Majesty the Shah and of his Government for the exercise and maintenance of the rights granted to it by the present concession, and [the Bank] pledges to respect the general laws of the country in their entirety. Should a dispute arise between the Persian Government and the Bank or between the Bank and individuals, the two parties shall each choose one or two arbitrators and the decision of these arbitrators shall be final. Should the votes be split, the said arbitrators shall name a referee to judge in the last instance.

ART. 11.   The Imperial Bank being ready immediately to undertake the sacrifices necessary to employ the resources of the country for the exploitation of its natural wealth, the Persian Government grants to the said Bank, for the entire duration of the present concession, the exclusive and definitive privilege to exploit throughout the Empire mines of iron, copper, lead, mercury, coal, petroleum, manganese, borax, [and] asbestos [that] belong to the State and [have] not previously [been] ceded to other [parties]. As an annex to the concession the Persian Government shall give Baron de Reuter an official list of the mines already granted, on the day the present [instrument] is signed. [Since] mines of gold, silver, and precious stones, etc., belong exclusively to the State, [any] Bank engineers who [should] discover them shall be obliged immediately to inform the Government of His Imperial Majesty the Shah. Except for indispensable engineers and foremen, all the minor laborers that the Bank may engage shall be chosen from among the subjects of His Imperial Majesty the Shah. The Persian Government shall, by all the means in its power, aid the Bank to procure labor at the price prevailing in the country. All mines that the Bank may not have begun to exploit ten years from its establishment shall be considered abandoned and the State may dispose of them without the concessionary Bank being able to [oppose its actions].

ART. 12.   The land necessary for the exploitation of these mines and the establishment of a means of communication with the nearest and most rapid lines of transport shall be given to the Imperial Bank from State lands. The Imperial Government shall aid the Bank by all the means in its power to deal with individual landowners in the most favorable conditions, should there be any along the said road of communications. The materials necessary for the exploitation shall enter Persia without any duty whatsoever. The lands and buildings of the said exploitations shall be free of all duties and taxes.

ART. 13.   The Persian Government shall levy an annual premium of 16 percent on the net profits of all mines exploited by the Imperial Bank. At the expiration of the term of the present concession the lands exploited by the mines, with their buildings, offices, and material, shall be returned to the Persian Government according to the general rules followed by the Powers who have stipulated the most favorable conditions in this matter.

ART. 14.   In return for the rights guaranteed to him by the present contract, Baron Julius de Reuter formally and completely renounces without reserve all other rights and privileges that had been granted him by the previous concession of 25 July 1872 [which is] annulled by the present [instrument]. . . .

6.   The Concession for the Tobacco Monopoly in Iran, March 8, 1890

A British company headed by Major G. F. Talbot sought and obtained a concession from the government of Shah Nasir al-Din to produce, locally sell, and export all to-bacco in Iran. This concession included tunbaku, *the tobacco, used widely by Irani-ans in their water pipes. Unhappiness with the monopolistic terms of the concession and the fact that it constrained one of the pleasures of Iranian daily life coalesced with rising frustration in Iran against European domination and intervention. The financially disadvantageous terms of the agreement fueled local anger against the "sale of the country" to foreigners. Many historians consider the revolt against the concession to be the beginning of the nationalist Iranian movement that culmi-nated fifteen years later in the constitutional revolution.*

The monopoly of buying, selling, and manufacturing all the tootoon and tobacco in the interior or exterior of the Kingdom of Persia is granted to Ma-jor Talbot by us for fifty years from the date of the signing of this Concession, in accordance with the following stipulations:—

1. The concessionnaires will have to pay 15,000*l.* per annum to the exalted Imperial Treasury whether they benefit or lose by this business, and this money shall be paid every year, five months after the beginning of the year.

2. In order merely to ascertain the quantities of tootoon and tobacco pro-duced in the protected provinces (of Persia) the concessionnaires will keep a register of the cultivators who wish to work under the conditions of this Con-cession, and the Persian Government will issue strict orders to the local Gov-ernors to compel the cultivators of tobacco and tootoon to furnish such a registration.

Permission for sale, &c., of tootoon, tobacco, cigars, cigarettes, snuff, &c., is the absolute right of the concessionnaires, and no one but the proprietors of this Concession shall have the right to issue the abovementioned permits.

The Guilds of the sellers of tobacco and tootoon who are engaged in this trade will remain permanent in their local trade and transactions, on condition of possessing permits which will be given to them by the concessionnaires.

3. After deducting all the expenses appertaining to this business and pay-ing a dividend of 5 percent. on their own capital to the proprietors of this Con-cession, one quarter of the remaining profit will yearly be paid to the exalted Imperial Treasury, and the Persian Government will have the right to inspect their (the concessionnaires') yearly books.

4. All the materials necessary for this work which the proprietors of this Concession import into the protected provinces (Persia) will be free of all cus-toms duties, taxes, &c.

Great Britain, *Parliamentary Papers, 1892*, Vol. 79, pp. 211–213. This document may also be found in J. C. Hurewitz, *The Middle East and North Africa in World Politics* (New Haven, Conn.: Yale Univer-sity Press, 1975), pp. 462–463.

5. Removal and transfer of tootoon and tobacco in the protected provinces (of Persia) without the permission of the proprietors of this Concession is prohibited, except as such quantities [as] travellers may have with them for their own daily use.

6. The proprietors of this Concession must purchase all the tootoon and tobacco that are produced in the protected provinces and pay cash for it. They must purchase all the tobacco, &c., fit for use that is now in hand, and the price that is to be given to the owner or the producer will be settled in a friendly manner between the producer or the owner and the proprietors of this Concession, but in case of disagreement between the parties the case will be referred to an Arbitrator accepted by both sides, and the decision of the Arbitrator will be final and will be carried out.

7. The Persian Government engages not to increase the revenues, taxes, and customs that are now levied on tootoon, tobacco, cigars, cigarettes, and snuff for fifty years from the date of the signing of the Concession, and the proprietors also undertake that all the customs that the Persian Government now obtain from tobacco shall be continued as they are.

8. Any person or persons who shall attempt to evade (the rules) of these Articles will be severely punished by the Government, and any person or persons found to be secretly in possession of tobacco, tootoon, &c., for sale or trade, will also be fined [and] severely punished by the Government. The Government will give its utmost help and support in all the business of the proprietors of this Concession, and the proprietors of this Concession undertake in no way to go beyond their own rights consistent with these Articles.

9. The proprietors of this Concession are permitted, should they wish, to transfer all their rights, Concessions, undertakings, &c., to any person or persons, but, prior to this, they must inform the Persian Government.

10. The producer or owner of tootoon and tobacco, whenever his crop of tobacco and tootoon is gathered, shall at once inform the nearest agent of the proprietors of this Concession of the quantity, in order that the proprietors of this Concession may be able to carry out the engagement in above-mentioned Article 6, and to purchase it quickly.

11. The proprietors of this Concession have no right to purchase lands, except to the necessary extent, for store-houses and abodes, and what may be necessary to carry out this Concession.

12. The cultivators, in accordance with certain conditions which will be made in conjunction with the Government, are entitled to be given an advance to a limit for their crop.

13. If, from the date of the signing of this Concession until one year, a Company to carry it out is not formed, and the work does not begin, this Concession will be null and void, except that war or such like may prevent the formation of a Company.

14. In case of misunderstanding arising between the Persian Government and the proprietors of this Concession, that misunderstanding shall be referred to an Arbitrator accepted by both sides, and in case of the impossibility of consent to the appointment of an Arbitrator, the matter will be referred to the

arbitration of one of the Representatives, resident at Tehran, of the Government of the United States, Germany, or Austria, to appoint an Arbitrator, whose decision shall be final.

15. This Concession is exchanged in duplicate with the signature of His Imperial Majesty, registered in the Foreign Ministry, between Major Talbot and the Persian Government, and the Persian text of it is to be recognized.

7. Tobacco Smuggling and the French Régie Monopoly in the Ottoman Empire, 1895

In 1881, under pressure from England and France, the Ottoman Empire relinquished control over its internal finances to a European-dominated public debt administration, and by the end of the century, several European companies were attempting to profit from Ottoman political weakness by negotiating monopolies or quasi-monopolies over various parts of the Empire's economy. These negotiations were hardly between equals, for the Empire was in serious financial trouble because of the cost of modernization, trade that favored European countries, Ottoman mismanagement of funds, European usurious loan practices, and so on. The French Régie Cointeresse des Tabacs de l'Émpire Ottoman acquired a monopoly over the purchase and sale of tobacco produced in the Empire. Much to the chagrin of the company, however, the monopoly was undermined by local government authorities and popular resentment. This document is a 1895 company report detailing some of the difficulties. Though highly subjective in tone (condemning Ottoman inaction and the brazenness of local smugglers), this report mentions real sources of opposition to the French monopoly.

We have already noted the inaction of the authorities with regard to our requests, especially in Nazareth, where the hostility of the local governor has paralyzed our operations:

In the same town we have been refused all assistance despite our incessant demands. Our Koldjis [inspectors] cannot—without risking imprisonment—carry out any seizure operation [of contraband] as long as the smugglers are constantly released by the authorities.

Our searches are constantly hindered, which keeps us from carrying out these operations. The greatest protection is afforded to cultivators with the effect of increasing the value of their tobacco. The [Ottoman] authorities refuse to name, according to the terms of Article 26 of the Réglement [the agreement between the Ottoman government and the private-public French tobacco company], a representative for the sale of tobacco at the commercial price.

Bestand des Politischen Archivs des Auswartigen/Aktengruppe: Turkei 110. Translated by Akram Khater.

Our warehouse in Derende was pillaged, and in the warehouses of Hafil, Beharenzen, Karkala, and Direiki considerable quantities of tobacco were completely destroyed.

One case of tobacco was pillaged between Deliktach and Sivas, and our office in Gurun was besieged in an attempt to pillage it. We have lost in Tokat 15,000 kilograms of tobacco.

The smugglers are very powerful in Nazareth.

In Tokat we have encountered everywhere armed resistance. The Koldjis and the police wanted to carry out a search operation in the village of Moubad, where 170 bales of contraband tobacco were discovered. However, the villagers repulsed them after attacking and injuring many of the agents who were part of that expedition.

A note sent by the general administration [of the French tobacco company] to the [Ottoman] Ministry of Interior has remained unanswered.

In Amassia, the governor has expressly acknowledged that search operations are impossible.[. . .]

This sentiment of hostility reveals itself in all contacts between the [Ottoman] authorities and our employees, and all measures are taken to make more difficult the exercise of our monopoly [over tobacco].

In Trebizonde a convoy of more than 160 loads was attacked in Platana by bands of 100 or 200 smugglers armed with rifles, and they confronted with impunity our Koldjis and fired upon them.

An imperial order decreeing the mobilization of imperial troops against these bands has not been executed, and the local authorities want an order for each particular case [of smuggling activity].[. . .]

The Régie [French tobacco company with monopoly over tobacco commerce in the Ottoman Empire] does not have sufficient means to interdict such expeditions. Moreover, when on more than one occasion we attempted to carry out such operations, the local authorities intervened and punished the Koldjis, even though the latter were serving the interests of the [Ottoman] state.

If our Koldjis have the misfortune of injuring a smuggler, then they are considered criminals and punished with hard labor.

At Cheiran a real battle took place between the smugglers and our inspectors, with one Koldji killed. The smugglers were able to continue their work of importing great quantities of tobacco, because Saadedin Pasha [the local Ottoman governor] disarmed our Koldjis and kept them from pursuing the smugglers.

CHAPTER 3

Social and Cultural Reformulations

The social and cultural manifestations of the economic and political interactions between Europe and the Middle East and North Africa during the nineteenth century had a profound impact on the latter two regions. This is not to imply that the cultures of those regions were previously isolated before their encounter with Europe. Nor is it to imply that those cultures were static replications of past traditions and customs. Rather, during the nineteenth century the extent and rate of interaction between the indigenous cultures of the Middle East and North Africa, on the one hand, and Europe, on the other, increased dramatically. Furthermore, the superior military, political, and economic power that Britain and France—the two main imperial powers—wielded made this interaction one of unequal proportions. In many important ways it was an interaction that was more conflictual than consensual.

This cultural encounter was brought about through the arrival of unprecedented numbers of European merchants, warships, diplomats, and missionaries in the Middle East and North Africa. It also was an outcome of the dispatch of students from Istanbul and Cairo to Paris and London, where they were to study French and English, among other subjects. Among many of the educated indigenous elites, these interactions, as well as the decisive military defeats of Ottoman and Egyptian troops, raised serious and critical questions about their societies and the reasons for their weakness in the face of superior European technologies. The answers to these questions were hardly uniform. A few intellectuals argued that only complete emulation of European ideas would ensure the future of the region. Others took the exact opposite position, contending that any turning away from existing norms would mean further surrender to European designs. Between these poles was a wide range of opinion. What is striking about this debate—it raged throughout the nineteenth century but was particularly intense in the last two decades—was its concentration on gender roles. Regardless of the ideological position taken, commentators

66

infused the definition of the roles of men and women with heightened importance for society and nation.

This debate sheds some light on the transformation of societies in the Middle East and North Africa. Having lived in Paris in the 1820s, the Egyptian author of the first document draws a vivid, implicit contrast between Parisian and Egyptian ways of life. The next six documents cover various topics in the ongoing discussion about social and cultural change: women's role in management of the home (document 2), advocacy of expanded rights for the "new woman" (document 3), the need to bring "enlighted" and "modern" notions about work, education, and family life to remote Jewish communities (document 4), advocacy of education for girls (documents 5 and 6), and the need to end the actual and metaphorical veiling of Muslim women (document 7). It is important to remember that advocates of change were not the only people expressing their views. Indeed there was a great deal of opposition to many of the proposed changes. The simple fact that article after article arguing for change continued to be written indicates that changes were not coming about very quickly.

1. Rifa'a Tahtawi Reflects on Paris, Its People, Their Ideas, and Lives in the 1820s

Shaykh Rifa'a Raf'i al-Tahtawi (1801–1873) was born into a wealthy landowning family in Tahta, Upper Egypt. After Muhammad 'Ali assumed power in Egypt in 1805, Tahtawi's family (like other elite families) was driven out of their home and into poverty. However, Rifa'a proved to be an outstanding student, and his intellectual ability gained him admission to Al-Azhar University, an old and distinguished Islamic university. After graduating in 1823, he spent two years teaching at Al-Azhar and reading European books at the house of his mentor Shaykh Hassan Muhammad al-Attar. Subsequently he was assigned to be the Imam (religious leader) of an educational mission that Muhammad 'Ali was sending to France— then the center of science and the arts. Determined to be more than an Imam, Tahtawi immersed himself in the study of French and in the translation of Western books into Arabic. He wrote about his experiences in France and his contact with Parisian society and intellectual circles in his book, Takhlis al-Ibriz fi Tafseel Bariz *(A Paris Profile), first published in 1839. This excerpt from that book reveals a bit about the cultural interaction between one Muslim from Egypt and elements of French culture.*

Shaykh Rifa'a Raf'i al-Tahtawi, *Takhlis al-Ibriz fi Tafseel Bariz* (A Paris Profile) (Cairo: Mustafá al-Bābī al-Halabī, 1958), pp. 30–34. Translated by Akram Khater.

Chapter Two: Speaking of the People of Paris

You should know that Parisians are Christians with intelligent minds and impressive understanding and depth of thought with regard to difficult issues. They are not like Coptic Christians [members of an Egyptian Christian sect], who are naturally inclined to ignorance and lack of wisdom. Neither are they prisoners of tradition. Rather, they always wish to know and understand the origins of things, to the point that even ordinary people know how to read and write and enter into deep discussions, according to their capacity. The common people in this country are not like those in most uncivilized countries. Knowledge about all the sciences, arts, and handicrafts is recorded in books. Even the lowliest of crafts requires of its practitioner the ability to read and write in order to master his trade. Every artist has to create in his art something never created before, and—in addition to seeking profit—artists are motivated in their innovative endeavors by the desire for good reputation and distinction.[. . .]

The inclination of French women is to seek after new things and to love change in all things, but especially in the manner of dress. They can never settle [on a single style of clothing], and styles are always changing among them. This does not mean that they completely change their clothes; instead they mix and match various elements. For example, they do not exchange a hat for a turban, but they sometimes wear a hat for a while, and then after a time they change to a hat of another style or color.

They [men and women] are characterized by their lightness of spirit and demeanor. Thus you may find a French notable running along the road like a child. They are also prone to shifts in mood—from happiness to sadness and back, and from seriousness to jocularity and back—to the point that an individual may do many contradictory things in a single moment. But this occurs only in trivial matters; on serious issues such as their political views, their opinions do not change. Everyone remains faithful to their beliefs and opinions, which they hold throughout their lives. Because they love France, they travel a great deal, even spending many years traveling between the East and the West, and they may even risk their lives to benefit their country.[. . .]

They also like foreigners and seek their company, particularly if the foreigner is wearing expensive clothes. This leads them to ask about the country [of foreigners] and the traditions of their people.[. . .] And it is common for souls to seek after that which they do not possess.

They offer solace with their words and deeds but not with their money. However, they do not refrain from lending—not giving—money to their friends, unless they are certain that they will not get their money back. They are more miserly than generous toward others, and we mention this in our chapter about their traditions, in the section about hospitality.[. . .] They generally fulfill all their obligations, and they never ignore their duties, for they are always working whether they are rich or poor. [. . .] They love a good reputation and shun self-aggrandizement and hatred, for they are—as they describe themselves—more pure in heart than sheep. When angry, they are fiercer than tigers, and if one of them becomes angry, then he may prefer death to life; hardly any time passes without someone killing himself because of poverty or love. One of their most outstanding characteristics is trustworthiness and absence of treachery. [. . .] They are spendthrifts, wasting their money on sinful pleasures and entertainment and gambling. Their men are slaves to their women and obey their orders. [. . .] Some say that women in the East are like the furniture of the house and French women are like spoiled children. [. . .]

French men do not think ill of their wives even though they may have many great faults, but if one of them (even a notable) found evidence that his wife had committed adultery, he would leave her. [. . .]

Among their good characteristics is their disinclination toward homosexuality and the love of young men, for this is something that is at odds with their nature and moral sense. In their speech and poetry they do not mention homosexual love. It is not proper in the French language to say that a man fell in love with a boy, for such a relationship is considered taboo. If a Frenchman translated one of our books, he would alter the text to say that "I fell in love with a girl," as opposed to a boy as in the original. The French consider homosexuality as a fallen state of being, and they are right, for each of the sexes is attracted to a trait that is found in the opposite sex, just as magnets attract iron and electricity attracts things. If two people of the same sex are attracted to each other, the natural state of being is upset, and for the French this behavior is so offensive that they rarely ever mention homosexuality in their books. [. . .]

Among their immoral traits is the lack of chastity among the women and the absence of male protection of the women's honor. [. . .] Generally, Paris is like other French and European cities in that it is full of sin, heresies, and immoral behavior, even though it may be the French Athens. [. . .] Parisians are the Athenians of this age; their minds are Roman and their ethics are Greek. [. . .] The French reject supernatural things and believe that [. . .] the purpose of religion is to help human beings do good deeds and avoid evil. They also believe that the development of a country and the advancement of its people in the literary arts and ethics make religions irrelevant and that in the advanced kingdoms peculiar laws are enacted. Among their ugly habits is their claiming that their scientists and learned men are greater and more intelligent than the prophets. They have many unseemly beliefs such as the denial by some of predestination, even though it is possible to believe in it [. . .] without abandoning the idea of free will. [. . .]

It is not acceptable among the French to employ a black slave in the kitchen and for housekeeping because they believe that blacks lack the necessary cleanliness. French women are extremely beautiful and gentle, and they excel at social interaction. They always use makeup, and they interact with men in the parks, and men and women may even get to know each other through outings in such places on Sundays or during the ballet or in ballrooms on Monday nights. [. . .]

It is said that Paris is paradise for women, fragrance for men, and hell for horses. This is because the women are endowed with either money or beauty, men are the slaves of women, and horses pull carriages day and night over the cobblestones of the streets of Paris. [. . .]

Chapter Five: Of the Foods of the People of Paris, and Their Manners in Eating and Drinking

[. . .] The slaughterhouses are located at the edge of the city and not within it, and this is for two reasons. One is to avoid the bad smells, and the second is to avoid damage by the cattle in case they escape. The French have different ways of butchering. [. . .] They hit the bulls on the head with iron mallets so that they become dizzy, and they repeatedly do so until the bull is dead, then slaughter it in the manner of sheep. I sent an Egyptian servant of mine as usual to the slaughterhouse to purchase some meat, but when he saw the horrible way in which the bulls were treated, he returned, thanking God for not making him a bull in the land of the French. [. . .] The number of their winehouses is far too large to count, and only the lowliest of people go to these places with women prostitutes, and they are loud. [. . .] One day I was passing one of these places in a street in Paris when a drunkard yelled at me: "Oh Turk! Oh Turk!" And he grabbed my clothes. I was close to a confectioner's shop, so I brought him in and seated him on a chair and jokingly asked the owner, "Would you please give me candy for this man?" The shop owner responded: "This is not like your country, where it is permissible to sell and buy people." I responded that in his present state the drunkard was not a human being!

2.   *Anis al-Jalis,* an Egyptian Magazine, Defines a Vision of Women and Their Role in Society, 1899

In the last three decades of the nineteenth century, many journals and magazines dedicated partially or completely to women and their issues came into existence in the Middle East and North Africa. These magazines were published mainly in Istanbul, Tehran, Beirut, Cairo, Algiers, Tunis, and other large cities. They varied in political outlook, in content and style, and in purpose. Some focused on fashion, home economics, and the etiquette of middle-class life. Others pronounced themselves to be platforms for educating women in political, social, and cultural matters. As a group, these journals were seeking to define a particular vision of women and women's role in society. Despite their many profound disagreements, they gave a voice to women within the newly articulated modern public sphere. Most of their disparate editorials and articles maintained that women—however they and their roles were defined—were essential for the construction of a modern society and nation. The subject of these two articles from Anis al-Jalis *is women's important role in the management of the home.*

"Management of the Home," *Anis al-Jalis,* 2, nos. 3 and 4 (1899): pp. 110–112. Translated by Akram Khater.

[1]

The woman is a "sultana" [queen] in her house where she disposes freely of her judgments in whatever manner she pleases. Through its reins [which] are in her hand, she guides the home to the depths of despair or to the fertile lands of happiness. For she is either the source of its light and the herald of its peace, or the harbinger of its misery and the cause of its darkness. Every woman, even if she is of little significance or lowly status, occupies that position of authority and dominion within her home. Hence, she either makes it tranquil and herself its owner, or a hell and herself its devil. Every house, however dark and poor it may be, can borrow light from the smiles of the woman, and bliss and joy from the goodness of her morals. Thus, [the home] thrives like the bloom of the flower from the rays that her love and compassion casts over it From her attention and good care of it [the home] has the best of that which enjoys the characteristic of [being] idle. Certainly the children of the virtuous woman and her husband are crowned with happiness and they live a long life in happiness and joy. And now that the woman has become aware of her importance and realized the full magnitude of that which she was assigned then she must be a source of contentment for her relatives so that she herself will be happy. And, indeed, for her not to be deceived by the ornaments of vain glory, nor by the attention that admirers bestow upon her fleeting beauty. Rather, she must capture the heart of her husband and children and to attract them to her with the fulfillment of her desire and her hard work.

Do not suppose that the duty of a woman is limited to love and to the attraction of her hearts, for she has another more important and lofty task. It is to help in carrying the burdens of life and sharing in dealing that which has been fated for her of joy and agony. Furthermore, she cannot be judged by words but by deeds, and therefore the subjects of her government must be happy and joyful. [However, their happiness should be] on the condition that she does not assign their affairs to those who are without experience or care so as not to expose the ship of her home to danger in the tumultuous sea of life. For she is the captain of the ship guiding it with her hand, nay she is the soul of this body that cannot survive without it [the soul].

And she must be energetic with courage and patience, and she must see all with her eyesight without missing the slightest of details. If she needs guidance in a matter that is too complicated for her to manage and too difficult to solve then let her ask for help from her life's partner, that is the man who will be her greatest ally in her mission. For, even if he is the possessor of power and the one delegated to gain a livelihood on the outside, he still has within the home the grand patronage and the high perception. Let the woman, then, depend on the hear[t] of her husband and let her be guided by the light of his knowledge and intelligence to complete the important work which she does and the various duties that the natural life forces upon her.

Let the woman not ignore the truth of the task that nature has readied for her and that her upbringing has prepared her for: that is that she must be before all a mother and wife. And let her not allow the rare intelligence and wide knowledge, that she sometimes may have, to be causes for ignoring her duties. For she has duties toward others which are no less important [than those that she has toward herself]. Also, she cannot live an isolated life away from people, nor can she come short in fulfilling her duties toward them, otherwise she will expose herself to the arrows of blame and criticism.

There are many conditions and guidelines for this work and duties which cannot be completely described in one article. Rather, it requires great detail to accomplish the required goal, and for that we have decided with the permission of Allah to provide a special section for it in every section of the issues of this magazine. We will dedicate this section to speaking about the management of the home and what comes under that from other related matters. And this we do to fulfill the duties of service which we have vowed to accomplish with sincere advice, and without withholding effort or energy, and on Allah we depend.

[2]

As we promised in the previous issue, today we will include a new section to talk about the management of the house. As the readers know this is a large topic which is not limited only—as the nature of its title may indicate—to what is related to the inside of the house from cleaning it to the upkeep of its furniture. Rather, and in truth, it concerns that which is more important than that; that is everything that relates to social and familial life in all of its stages and conditions. [It includes] the coexistence of a married couple in a manner that reinforces the ties of love and harmony and that seals that contract which connects them with the seal of joy and happiness so that no misery and unhappiness would enter into their lives. [It also includes] the raising of the children and taking care of them in a way that would refine their manners and straighten their crookedness in order to improve their fate and for them to be able to make themselves and others happy in life. Among the duties of the individual toward people and himself is to clearly see his limits so that he would not transgress them. Thus he would safeguard his honor and will live respected and in security. And many other things are included under this section which makes it one of the most important subjects and the most useful because it is directly important to the individual. For this section will look at his private state and affairs and will elucidate ways for his comfort and happiness and will teach him the means to repulse misery with happiness. Thus it would be correct to call this type of work the Science of Social Chemistry for what it attempts to do in creating harmony amongst the various constituents of society. Moreover, [it would be correct to call it thus] for establishing harmony between the alienated members of the same household and for merging them into a single body that is well organized in connection and affiliation and for what that bring[s] about in terms of change from misery and bitterness in life to happiness and sweetness, and for lightening the heavy load and making the difficult easy. Thus, it would be even more appropriate to call this section the Management of Life or the World, and not the Management of the Household, for the house is in reality the world scaled down. And if it [the household] is managed well according to well organized rules then half of life—if not all of it—would be improved.

We said in the previous issue that the woman is the goddess of the house, and i[n] her hands she holds its reins leading wherever she wishes. Here we again repeat those words and add to them that the woman has the first and more exacting role in managing the house, for she alone is capable of [bringing about] the happiness of the man or his misery. And if we insist upon the need to educate the woman and to improve her status, we only do so as she can fully comprehend the full magnitude of the task assigned to her and the secret of her position vis à vis the man, and thus she would work fully aware of the responsibility that has been placed upon her shoulders. And if the man—who is enmeshed in civilization—does not spare any effort in improving the tools and equipment which he uses for his material needs and to guarantee his comfort and happiness, then should he not be concerned about that status of the woman, and she is one who cannot be dispensed with? Should he not be concerned with her well-being in order to improve his own existence? The woman, then, is the source of everything and upon her depends the luck of the man in his world. For in every home where you find a moral, rational, working and knowledgeable woman [there you will find that] happiness is its companion and the nightingale of joy sings in its space, and for every home where you find an ignorant and immoral woman you should bewail it and shed your tears for it and you should know that the companion of that home is misery and wretchedness.

It has been said in the popular sayings that the "man harvests and the woman builds." This means that the work of the man is dependent upon gain and profit at the outside and that the woman is the one who receives from him what he earns through his labor and efforts and spends it [in] its proper places as she is directed by sound mind and careful consideration that is fully aware of the conditions of the home and that is an expert in its affairs. These words are the epitome of wisdom because many ruined homes have been rebuilt thanks to the woman and the goodness of her work, and because many poor houses have become rich with the expertise of the woman and the soundness of her policy. In addition, many flourishing homes have been ruined because of what befell them from destruction by the woman, and many women have lost the most precious things that they had and that is the love of their men because of their [the women's] affliction with laziness and dereliction of their domestic duties. The truth is that there is nothing more difficult for the active and hard-working man—who spends his day laboring to gain his living—than to see next to him a lazy and ignorant woman who does nothing but spend money and waste her time, who does not wake up until after her poor husband had spent many hours in toil and work. And what is strange is that we hear many women complaining about their husbands because they are not satisfied with their lives, when if they [the women] had bothered to examine their conscience they would find that they [the women] are the cause of that complaint. So, if they [the women] wish not to hear anything of that sort, then let them begin to complete their domestic duties without neglect or carelessness. Then, they will receive in place of complaints and blame thanks, gratitude, compliments and peace.

3. Qasim Amin Argues for the Emancipation of Women in Egypt, 1900

Qasim Amin (1863–1908), a French-educated Egyptian lawyer, belonged to the upper middle classes of Egyptian society. He achieved fame/notoriety at the turn of the twentieth century for his advocacy for Egyptian women in his books The Liberation of Women *(1898) and* The New Woman *(1900). Amin, however, was more concerned with modernizing patriarchy, and making it similar to patriarchy in western Europe, than he was in achieving true equality for women. He regarded gender as a dividing line around which clustered distinctly different roles for men and women, with the latter occupied primarily if not solely with maintaining a modern house for their husbands and children. Amin never intended to imply that women— as individuals—should have access to the same education and work as men, let alone the same political rights.*

Amin argued that the "liberation" of women was an essential prerequisite for the liberation of Egyptian society from foreign domination. He based some of his arguments in The Liberation of Women *on the Qur'an. Although a few other writers—most of them women, such as Zaynab Fawwaz, Hind Nawfal, and A'isha al-Taimuriya—had written and spoken on the same subject, none had access to as widespread or public an audience as Amin, mainly because they were women. In other words, Amin was neither the first nor the last to speak of giving women more rights; rather, he became a lightning rod for the early phase of the feminist movement in Egypt and around the Middle East (his books were translated into Turkish and Farsi). He promoted the debate on women in Egypt from a side issue to a major national concern. But for broaching such a sensitive issue, he himself came under severe attack. Ironically, much of the criticism that was heaped on him was the same that he had used in an earlier book* Les Egyptiens *(1894), in which he replied to a French document that cast the status of Egyptian women in a negative light.*

In response to criticism of The Liberation of Women, *Amim wrote* The New Woman, *in which he defended his position and extended his ideas. In this book, Amin relied less on arguments based on the Qur'an and Hadith (sayings of the Prophet); he more openly used the ideas and arguments of European intellectuals. This excerpt from* The New Woman, *allows us to understand not only Amin's arguments but also the premises of the opponents of those ideas.*

Qasim Amin, *The New Woman: A Document in the Early Debate on Egyptian Feminism*, trans. Samiha Sidhom Peterson (Cairo: American University in Cairo Press, 2000), pp. 1–4, 87–93. Copyright © 2000 The American University. Reprinted by permission of the American University in Cairo Press.

In the Name of God, the Merciful, the Compassionate:

The new woman is one of the fruits of modern civilization. Her appearance in the West was a consequence of the scientific discoveries that freed the human mind from the powers of delusion, suspicion, and superstition, providing all individuals with control over their lives and charting for them a path to follow. Such changes occurred because science explored all issues, examined every idea, and rejected any proposition not proved to be in the public interest. This search resulted in abolishing the power of the clergy, eliminating the privileges of nobility, establishing a constitution for monarchies and rulers, and freeing black people from the bondage of slavery. It finally challenged most of the privileges that men had defined as theirs, which in effect had implied that women were not equal to men in any sphere.

Europeans used to have the same opinion of women that we have today: that women are inferior due to their mental deficiencies, their low status in religion, and their primary role as temptresses and agents for the Devil. They used to say that woman, "long of hair, short of mind," was created for no other reason than to serve man. European scholars, philosophers, poets, and religious leaders considered it foolish to educate women. Moreover, they scoffed at the woman who abandoned her household for intellectual pursuits. They accused such women of intruding on what they called "men's domain."

When the veil of ignorance was finally lifted from European men, they admitted that they themselves were instrumental in the inferior position of women, and that they had not allowed them to change and develop. They also realized that a woman was a human being like them, that she had the right to enjoy her freedom and to use her capabilities, and that depriving a woman of beneficial experiences was unacceptable.

These changes initiated a new phase for the Western woman. She started cultivating her mind, refining her manners, and gradually gaining her rights. She participated with men in human affairs and was a partner in their search for knowledge, a listener in church, a contributor to literary debates, a participant in scientific meetings, and a traveler to various countries. In a short time, that female who had been animal-like—decorated with ornaments, garbed in fashion, and immersed in amusement—was replaced by a new woman who was a sister to man, a companion to her husband, a tutor to her children—a refined individual.

This transformation is all we intend. We hope the Egyptian woman achieves this high status through the appropriate avenues open to her, and that she will acquire her share of intellectual and moral development, happiness, and authority in her household. We are convinced that if this goal were achieved, it would prove to be the most significant development in Egypt's history.

Holding such a belief, would it be acceptable for us to refrain from the pursuit of our goal because the general public is unaware of it, or because writers have demonstrated discontent with it, differing in opinion, being skeptical, or giving it a low priority?

Our reasons for writing are not motivated by a desire to gain the applause of the ignorant and general public. These people do not understand the clearly stated word of God when it is presented to them. In fact the only way they understand it is when its original intentions are distorted to them through the opinion of a sheikh. Such religious leaders are quite ignorant of the meaning of their religion; they are unpatriotic, and are unable to consider their country except through an ugly image of outmoded manners and ridiculous traditions. We are, however, writing to the educated individuals, especially to the young who are our future hope. They will indeed be the generation to have benefited from the exposure to a proper education, enabling them to bring the question of women to the place of concern and consideration it deserves.

It is unnecessary to discuss again the topic of the veil, since we examined it closely in *The Liberation of Women*, where we quoted passages from the Quran that clearly permit women to uncover their face and hands in addition to explaining their relationship to men. [. . .] It therefore seems clear that our religion does not support the opinion of those scholars who uphold the more extensive use of the veil. If indeed this issue has two sides, it is acceptable for us to give more weight to the opinion that supports human freedom and the general welfare of our society.

In a recent issue of *al-Manar*, the owner of that magazine supported our viewpoint:

> This is the legal decision regarding the debate. It is well known that the law forbade being alone with a woman who is not related. Analysis of writings covering the early period of Islam indicates that there was indeed extensive public interaction among men and women. It is sufficient for you to be aware that the women of the Prophet, God bless him and grant him salvation, who indeed were commanded to go further in the use of the veil, used to interact with men. In fact 'Aisha was even a commander in the army, directing it in the well-known Battle of the Camel. I cannot therefore imagine how an obstinate individual can insist that a woman should not interact with men other than those within the legal degree of consanguinity that precludes marriage.

This is the opinion of a man whose religious standing is well known by all. If individuals at al-Azhar concerned themselves with understanding the intent of their religion instead of their preoccupation with the analysis of verbal expression, grammar, and linguistic construction, they would have opinions no different from ours.

The inferior and backward status of Islamic countries in comparison to other countries is daily attributed in various writings to the role of the Islamic scholars. Such writings in effect describe Islamic scholars as having an inadequate understanding of their religion and not observing the precepts of Islam. However, when a different opinion is presented, potentially beneficial to society, these same writers and intellectuals turn to the religious leaders for guidance. They request a legal opinion from the same Islamic scholars, forgetting that those who resist reform are unaware of the knowledge to be gained through an understanding of contemporary disciplines that may refine their thinking, improve their moral standards, or assist them in their evaluation of various activities. These religious leaders have refused, for example, to include in their teachings knowledge from the disciplines of history or geography, un-less forced. Their scope of knowledge or religious understanding means they are not in a position to provide an adequate opinion on any major concern, to say nothing of one of the most important issues in human history.

Anyone familiar with the Islamic legal system is aware that the Islamic per-spective on the status of women is one to be proud of, especially when it is compared with other religious traditions. This is because Islam, some twelve centuries ago, granted women rights that have only been achieved by Western women during the past couple of centuries. In fact, Western women are still de-prived of some of their rights and are presently concerned with claiming them.

Our legal system stipulates that women may manage their own resources. In addition it has urged the education and development of women and has not prohibited them from pursuing any profession or occupation. Islam has even gone so far in the equality between men and women as to permit women when necessary to be guardians over men, and to occupy the position of mufti or qadi, a position that entails the administering of justice. 'Umar ibn al-Khattab, may God be pleased with him, appointed women as supervisors in the markets of al-Medina, in spite of the availability of men, some of whom were the Com-panions of the Prophet. In contrast, until last year the French legal system did not grant women the right to enter the legal profession. Since our Islamic legal system, the Shari'a, protects women and grants her freedom, is it proper for us today to forget its intentions or to neglect the mechanisms that would help women to take advantage of these precious rights? Is it proper for us to waste our time in theoretical debates that only deter us from advancing toward re-forming our condition?

I do not believe that such a stand is appropriate, and I hope that many of my readers will share my opinion.
[. . .]

Conclusion: The Current State of Thought on Women in Egypt

During the past few years, Egyptians have begun to be aware of their poor so-cial condition, their faces show the pain of it, and they have recognized the ur-gent need for improvement. They have heard about how Westerners live, they have mixed and lived with many of them, and have learned of the extent of their progress. When they saw that Westerners enjoy a good life, broad independ-ence, self-determination, and other prerogatives that they themselves are not permitted and without which life has no value, there awoke in them a yearning to catch up and a desire to earn some of that happiness. Leaders have appeared among us, supporting ideas that they believe will guide our country toward the path of success. One calls for work and activity, another for harmony, unity, and the elimination of all sources of disagreement, a third for patriotism and self-sacrifice, while a fourth calls for adherence to religious teachings, and so on.

But these leaders have neglected a very important point, namely that with-out women's involvement it will be impossible to bring about any change in society. If women gain an understanding of the meaning of these causes, and if they identify with them or are committed to them, they will be able to bring up their children in the best way possible, in the mold of human perfection.

No social condition can be changed unless education and upbringing are directed toward that change. In bringing about any kind of reform, it is not enough to identify the need for change, to order its implementation through governmental decrees, to lecture about it, to invite people to address it, or to write about it in journals and books. None of these efforts can change a country, warn it of its predicament, or transform its life: any change in a country is a result of the totality of its virtues, characteristics, moral qualities, and customs, which are not inherent in people but are acquired through upbringing, that is to say, through women.

If Egyptians wish to improve their condition, they must start at its source. They must realize that unless their household and families provide a sound environment for preparing men with the necessary qualities for success, there will be no hope of acquiring any worthwhile status among the advanced countries of the world or in the realm of human civilization. Households and families, however, cannot provide a sound environment unless their women are educated, and unless they have shared the ideas, hopes, disappointments, and activities of men.

This simple and straightforward truth, which I publicly stated last year, was considered a kind of folly by many and labeled a violation of Islam by the jurisprudents. Many school graduates thought it an excessive imitation of Western life. Some even went so far as to say that it was a felony against the homeland and religion. Their writings moreover suggested that the emancipation of Eastern women was one of the goals of Christian countries, who intended by this to bring about the destruction of Islam, and that Muslims who supported this were not Muslims. These claims and other fantasies are not understood by simple souls who listen to them or by those who are ignorant and accept them.

We do not wish to respond to such criticism except to state that if the Europeans intended to harm us, they would leave us in our present condition, because there would be no better way to achieve their goals. This is without a doubt the truth, and it will inevitably reveal itself, as truth always does, no matter what people may do to conceal or ignore it.

Anyone who contemplates our present condition will find aspects that demonstrate that our women have broken through a phase of slavery, and that only a thin veil now separates them from freedom. Thus we can see that:

1. A new perception among Egyptians has developed regarding the importance of educating their daughters.

2. Seclusion of women is gradually decreasing, and will eventually disappear.

3. Young men are reluctant to marry according to traditional patterns and are attempting to change the process so that they can become better acquainted with the person they will marry.

4. The government and some private citizens, headed by Sheikh Muhammad ʿAbduh, the grand mufti of Egypt, are involved in reforming the Shariʿa

courts. An examination of the important report issued by the grand mufti on the role of these courts indicates that many aspects of these reforms will affect Egyptian families. His statement on polygamy is of particular significance:

> I will raise my voice to protest against polygamy among the poor. Many a poor man has four, three, or two wives, and is unable to support them. There is constant conflict over finances and marital rights. Yet he does not divorce any of them. Conflict continues among them and among their children. As a result, neither the husband nor his wives are able to live according to God's ordinances. No one knows the harm of this to our religion and our country.

Many women whose husbands have been sentenced to hard labor for life or other long prison terms have complained this year to the Ministry of Justice over their miserable condition. They have no formal avenue through which they can terminate their marriage, and they do not have a family provider who can support them and their children. The Ministry of Justice was therefore forced to request a formal legal opinion from the grand mufti of Egypt on the legal action that could be taken by the courts on this issue. The grand mufti investigated this and similar problems and was able to provide guidance to the Ministry of Justice through eleven articles based on the Malikite school of jurisprudence. The following is a list of the articles developed for the benefit of the poor:

I. If the husband refuses to support his wife, and if it is recognized that he has the means to do so, his estate will be used to support her. If he does not have the means to support her, and he continues not to support her, the judge will pronounce her divorced immediately. If the husband claims that he is unable to support her, and is unable to prove this, then the judge will rule that he provide support for her immediately. If the husband proves that he is unable to support his wife, the judge will give him a chance to do so within one month. If after that time the husband is unable to support his wife, the judge will pronounce her divorced from her husband.

II. If the husband is sick or imprisoned and is therefore unable to support his wife, the judge will concede the time required for his recovery or release. If the husband's recovery is delayed or his prison sentence is long, and if there is fear of harm or temptation, then the judge will pronounce the wife divorced from her husband.

III. If the husband is absent for a short while without leaving adequate support for his wife, the judge will declare a time limit. If the husband does not provide the necessary support, and if he is not present to provide that support after the identified time, the judge will pronounce the wife divorced from her husband. If the husband's location is unknown, or the absence is long, and if it is proven that he has no money that he can use to support his wife, the judge will pronounce her divorced from her husband.

IV. If the absent husband has property, credit, or a deposit with someone, then the wife has the right to adequate support from that money or credit. She must prove the existence of the credit or the deposit. Her request will be granted without the necessity of a legal guardian. She will be required, however, to state under oath that she is entitled to the support from the estate of her absent husband, and to state that he has left no resources for her support, nor authorized anyone to support her.

V. The judge's decree of divorce for non-support is revocable on appeal. The husband can petition the return of his wife if his resources are established and if he is ready to support her, as long as this takes place during the legally prescribed period. If proof of his resources is not established, and he is unable to support her, then he has no right to appeal.

VI. If a husband is missing in a Muslim country, and if his wife has no news of him, she can submit an appeal to the Ministry of Justice in which she identifies the area where she believes or knows her husband to be. The Ministry of Justice is responsible at that point for locating her husband through notifications sent to governors or the police. If the police fail to find any trace of him, there will be a postponement of four years, after which she must wait the prescribed period of widowhood of four months and ten days. Then it will be lawful for her to remarry without any special ruling.

VII. If the missing man returns, or if it is established that he is alive, before the second husband consummates the marriage, and the second husband does not know that the first husband is alive, then the wife belongs to the first husband. This is the case even after the official marriage contract, or after consummation if the second husband knows that the first is alive. If it appears that the husband died during the legally prescribed period of widowhood or after it, before the second marriage contract or after it, the woman will inherit from the first husband, as long as the second husband has not consummated the marriage without knowing that the first husband is alive. If the second husband dies after consummation of the marriage without knowing that the first husband is alive, the wife does not inherit from the second husband.

VIII. A wife of a man reported missing in a battle among Muslims, and who was reported to have been present at the battle, may submit the matter to the Minister of Justice. After a search is made and he is not found, the wife may marry after the legally prescribed period of widowhood. Her first husband's property can be transferred into inheritance if nothing is known of him. If the only evidence is that he left with the army, the ruling concerning him is the same as that in the two preceding paragraphs.

IX. The wife of a man missing in a war between Muslims and non-Muslims may present the matter to the Ministry of Justice. After searching for him, a delay of one year will be imposed on her. When that year is completed, she will observe the legally prescribed period of widowhood. It is then permissible for her to remarry, and his property is changed into inheritance after the year is completed. Whenever a delay is imposed on the wife of a missing man, she is supported from his property unless she fears temptation for herself, in which case she may submit an appeal to the judge to grant a divorce as soon as the accuracy of her claim is established to his satisfaction.

X. When a disagreement between a husband and wife becomes serious and when it cannot be resolved through any of the methods stipulated by the Quran, then an appeal is presented to the district judge. It is up to him at that point to appoint two arbitrators of good reputation, one from the relatives of the husband, the second from the relatives of the wife, preferably neighbors. If the relatives prefer to be excused, the judge will appoint arbitrators who are unrelated and send them to the couple. If the arbitrators are able to reconcile the couple according to the prescribed methods, their arbitration will be acceptable. Otherwise the arbitrators should recommend divorce or submit the matter to the judge. The judge will make a decision on the basis of their recommendations. The divorce is single and irrevocable and the role of the two arbitrators is over.

XI. The wife may appeal to the judge for divorce from the husband if he harms her, and if such harm is not legally permissible, such as desertion without legal reason, beating, and cursing without legal reason. The wife must prove these things by legal methods.

The rector of al-Azhar approved this plan, and sent the mufti the following letter:

We have examined Your Excellency's speech number nineteen, delivered on the fourth of the current month, and the accompanying draft of the law that includes eleven articles based on the Maliki school. Our opinion regarding the ideas presented in this material is the same as yours. We have therefore signed it as an indication of our approval. We would also like to thank you for your concern with this important matter. Enclosed please find the signed documents.

The Poor Salim al-Bishri, the Malikite
Servant of Knowledge and the Poor at al-Azhar
6 Rabi' II, 1318

These two issues, polygamy and a woman's divorce rights, are among the most important problems that we drew attention to in *The Liberation of Women,* and we are very pleased that such an important scholar and wise jurisprudent as Sheikh Muhammad 'Abduh found these issues worthy of his interest and that he supported our proposals with his resonant voice.

All these signs and others to be seen in our homes every day show that the condition of the Egyptian woman is improving and progressing. Furthermore, this movement does not spring from speculation or reflection, but is a result of dealing with Westerners and in accordance with the well-known law of natural history that stipulates that every animal adapts to its environment. The fact that our will is not central to this movement of change is reflected in the strong opposition that we encounter whenever the issue is raised, even from those who were experiencing these changes in themselves and in their homes. And this is not surprising, for it is our nature always to follow our prejudices.

We are already beyond the time when we must know what it is we want.

If our purpose in life is merely to survive for a few years, in whatever condition, noble or base, rich or poor, free or enslaved, educated or ignorant, good or bad, then I see that the freedom and education that has so far been granted to the Egyptian woman is unnecessary, and there is no reason to prevent a man from having any number of wives, or from marrying a woman every day and divorcing her the next, or from locking up his wives, daughters, sisters, mother, and grandmother if he wishes.

Women in some African and Asian countries live hidden away in their homes, seeing and seen by no one. A woman's life in some of these countries has reached such a low level that she must kill herself after her husband's death, because she must not enjoy life after he is gone. We need only look at these countries and ask them the secret of the advancement of their women in ignorance and isolation: perhaps what we find there will strengthen our pretext for tightening the seclusion and suppression of women!

But if our goal is indeed that which we read and hear about every day, namely that Egyptians wish to be a vital, advanced, and civilized nation, then we must say to them:

There is a way that will take you out of this predicament you complain of and elevate you to the highest stages of civilization, according to and beyond your wishes, and this is to free your women from the shackles of ignorance and seclusion. We are not the first to propose this idea, and we do not deserve credit for it. Other nations have used it before us and have tried it and benefited from it. Consider Western countries and you will find great differences among them. The training of the American woman, her manners, her customs, and ethical standards are different from those of the French woman, who differs again from the Russian woman. And the Italian woman has nothing in common with the Swedish or the German woman. But all these women, in spite of differences of climate, race, language, or religion, are all the same in one respect: they have their freedom and enjoy their independence.

Freedom has elevated the Western woman from her previous inferior status. When education was added, she was determined to participate alongside men in the progress of their society. This led her to take on active roles in society different to, but no less important than, those of men. The merchant who spends his day in a store selling his merchandise; the clerk who spends a few hours in a government office writing a memorandum to another department;

the engineer who builds a bridge to facilitate transportation between towns; the doctor who amputates a limb to save a life; the judge who mediates in disputes: not one of these men has the right to claim that his work is more beneficial to society than that of a woman who brings to society a man brought up to be of benefit to himself, his family, and his country.

We are not saying to you as others do: "Unite and cooperate with one another," or "Purify yourselves of the faults you know are in your character," or "Serve your family and your homeland," or any other such hot air. We know that change cannot be achieved through the advice of a leader, the orders of a sultan, the magic of a magician, or the miracles of a saint. Change, as we have noted, is brought about through the preparation of the minds of the rising generation.

This is the natural, long-term course, which is strewn with obstacles. The simplest difficulties, though, are those that end in victory and success, and the shortest routes are those that lead to the chosen destination.

4. Teachers of the Alliance Israélite Universelle Write About Child Marriages, Domestic Violence, and the Treatment of Children Among Jews in North Africa, 1902–1915

The Alliance Israélite Universelle was founded in Paris in 1860 to work "toward the emancipation and moral progress of the Jews." To advance this aim, the Alliance established schools in North Africa and the Middle East as vehicles to modernize Sephardic and Eastern Jews by transmitting Enlightenment ideas from the métropole *(Paris) to what they considered to be the peripheries of Jewish civilization. This aim, described in a special issue of the Alliance's magazine,* Cahier, *is worth quoting at length:*

> *Jews . . . lived like their Arab neighbors, far from the great currents of expansion in industry and science of the Western World, a primitive existence, made more difficult by their special legal status as Jews. . . . Always, since its beginnings more than a century ago, the Alliance sought to instill in the children not only love of culture and knowledge, but also the respect of the rights of man, and the meaning of the struggle for liberty and for the dignity of the individual. . . . The pure Jewish tradition on one hand, and the Western ideals brought over from France on the other, became the banner under which so many dedicated men and women carried out their task with such devotion.[1]*

Another aim of the organization was to support all Jews suffering from persecution because of their Judaism. The Alliance was deeply embroiled in the imperial politics of France, seeking to extend French Jewish influence to Jewish communities in any region. Moreover, it saw itself as the standard-bearer of progress and reform

---

[1]*Cahier* 16, no. 4 (1887): p. 23.

and as the savior of world Jewry from persecution. This self-image began to change only when the Zionist movement (the political movement to establish a Jewish homeland in Arab Palestine) became more powerful and effective after World War I (for documents on Zionism see the chapter "Contested Nationalisms").

The following Alliance reports from Marrakesh and Fez, in Morocco, indicate the attitudes of European Jews toward their local coreligionists (it is interesting to note that Christian missionaries and European diplomats were expressing very similar attitudes about local Christian and Muslim communities). Despite the inherently biased commentary, these documents provide valuable information about Jewish communities in North Africa. When reading these documents, keep in mind that many residents of those communities resented the Alliance's interference in their lives. Some communities succeeded in blocking the establishment of Alliance schools or prohibited their children from attending the schools. Instead of assuming that this outcome was a result of ignorance or fear, try to understand the dynamics that would have affected the relationship between the Alliance and the local Jewish communities.

A Sympathetic Account of the Condition of the Women of Marrakesh, 1902

Marrakesh, 13 August 1902

[. . .]

We have spoken on many occasions of the condition of women in the cities of the East and of Africa. Everywhere there is the same indifference to the wife on the part of the husband. Everywhere she remains in the background, happy enough if she is not being beaten or ill-treated. In Marrakesh one senses this unfortunate situation more so than anywhere else. Let us consider the case of an affluent family, in which the wife is not obliged to work to gain a living. Her existence is not for that devoid of worry. She must not—and, in any case, does not—dare raise her voice to her husband. Her opinion, good or bad, is considered worthless, and the husband, a veritable tyrant, will do whatever he pleases concerning either his wife or his children. A mother must not even think of defending her children against the authoritative hand of their father. When the father thinks it is necessary to beat his child, the mother must stand immobile in her corner, even when her maternal instincts rebel at the sight of the unjust treatment to which her son, or more often her daughter, is being subjected.

It goes without saying that even in the affluent families the wife must never be seated at the same table as her husband and male children. On Saturdays and holidays a high table, surrounded with chairs and properly arranged, is set up in the main room. The husband, the male children, and the guests take their places around it.

Archives of the Alliance Israélite Universelle, France XIV.F.25. These documents may also be found in Aron Rodrigue, *Images of Sephardi and Eastern Jewries in Transition: The Teachers of the Alliance Israelite Universelle, 1860–1939* (Seattle: University of Washington Press, 1999), pp. 85–91.

In another room, a low table with only a simple cloth for ornament is set up for the women, the girls, and the female servants. Here the female servants are treated like children of the family and eat at the same table with their mistress. Naturally, the choicest dishes are served first at the men's table. What is left, if there is anything left, is considered sufficient to feed the women.

I have had the opportunity, on several occasions, to attend family celebrations such as weddings, Bar Mitzvahs, engagements. In each of these cases, the celebration extends over a period of several days and never in any case does a woman have the right to sit at the table of honor. It is true that in my case there was an exception to the rule, and the poor ladies looked on with wide eyes when I received the honor of being served first. This was a sign of deference with which they had never been treated and they could not have been more astonished.

Even in the most respectable families polygamy is permitted and it is not surprising to see the two wives living in the same house. Each one has her own floor of the house. And what is more, they often get along quite well with each other. I currently have in class two little girls who are children of the same father but different mothers. The other day I was telling the older girl that she should be nicer to her little sister and help her with her homework once in a while. What was her response? "But she's not my sister; my mother is not her mother." I have to say that little girls only see their fathers at rare intervals here; as far as they know, their only parent is their mother! It was perfectly natural that the two girls did not see themselves as related at all.

So even though she is not obliged to work or struggle, the woman whose husband is well-off is still exposed to the ill-treatment, the indifference, and even the disdain of her husband.

How must it be for the woman who is obliged to work in order to feed her children? In this case, which is more or less the rule for the majority of women, her condition is worthy of compassion. All of the work and all of the worries of the home fall to her. The husband, for lack of any other occupation, can go out and get drunk. When he comes home, dinner must be ready and there must be food in the house. He has no thought to the manner in which his wife procures the necessary money or how hard she works for it . . . Most of them do sewing; some have struggled to save enough money to buy a sewing machine. They are paid between four and five centimes per meter of work done on the machine.

The less fortunate of them head to a square in the Arab district early in the morning and there they squat on the ground, rain or shine, and wait for the Arab women, who bring them some item to mend. In this way they try to earn some forty centimes per day.

Others embroider shoes; they are no less unfortunate. When the Sultan was in Marrakesh with his retinue, there was plenty of work and they made a good living. Since His Majesty has left our city, these poor workers have known the blackest misery and the most unhappy of lives.

The water carriers are another category of women to be pitied. They can be seen at the crack of dawn, going back and forth from the public fountain to the homes of their clients with their jars on their shoulders: this goes on until nightfall. As payment for their work they receive only a piece of bread or a bowl of soup.

On many occasions I have admired the dedication and the strength of will of the women in Marrakesh. How many times has some poor woman come to beg on behalf of her husband? The husband has borrowed money from an Arab; when the loan has come to term he does not have the money to pay. The husband is charged and brought before the *Pasha,* who of course puts the Jew in jail, and here is the miserable wife trying to move heaven and earth to have her husband freed.

No matter how she is treated or how many times she is refused, she does not become discouraged. She spends the day in the excessive heat running from place to place and from person to person, dragging her children along behind her; she has no time to earn the money to feed them. With enough begging and pleading she finally manages to gather enough money to pay off part of her husband's debt. This money serves to hold off the creditor for a month or so, when the loan will again come due and the whole process will begin again. Such scenes are repeated time and time again in the poor families, always because the husband has gotten into debt.

And do you think that the wife is rewarded for such devotion? When the husband feels so inclined he can go to the rabbi and, for one or two pesetas, divorce his wife; she is left with full responsibility for the children. Other times the husband will go off to another town and never be heard from again. Then it is up to the wife to work and struggle to make enough money to feed her children. In light of these conditions our task was perfectly clear: to make of our young girls women who are different from their mothers. We think it essential that the lessons learned in school serve to help these women. Once they have developed better judgment and a keener intelligence, they will no longer be at the mercy of their husbands' whims. Their wishes and their decisions must count for something in the running of the home. They too must be allowed to voice an opinion on questions concerning their children. Once a woman has received some instruction and has begun to develop her intellect, it will not take long for her husband to recognize that in his wife he has a companion whose advice and opinions are worthy of consideration. In this way the wife will no longer be an object of indifference or disdain to her husband but a sensible companion who can advise and assist him.

Obviously we can achieve such results only over a period of time. For now we can make sure that the girls who have spent two or three years in our school will have fewer hardships than any who have not been with us. The counsel they are given on a daily basis, as well as their lessons, will, I hope, prove to be of valuable assistance in creating their future happiness. This is our goal, and all of our efforts are aimed at the accomplishment of this task.

Because of their work, the number of matters to which they must attend, and the ever-present worries of the women of Marrakesh, they scarcely have the time to take good care of their children.

[. . .]

Education. What most surprises the parents of your girls is the cleanliness and the polite manners acquired by the children at the school.

All of our efforts in this direction have been crowned with success.

Prior to the foundation of our school the young girls one would see in the streets were dirty, unkempt, and barefoot; now they are unrecognizable, as they come to school every day perfectly presentable.

Even today, at the end of the school day, a good number of women stand in their doorways to watch the "girls from the school" pass by. There is whispering and chattering. "Look over there. So-and-so's daughter is wearing stockings and shoes; see that other one with the hat?" These little scenes are played out day after day.

At present our girls laugh about it and are amazed that, not long ago, they could have gone out of the house without stockings, sometimes even without shoes.

In my first letters to the Central Committee, I found many occasions to discuss the character of our girls: dishonest, sly, selfish. Those were the principal faults against which we had to fight. They would not hesitate an instant to accuse one of their friends, even their best friends, or to try and fool the teacher. Some progress has been made in this direction also. I am not saying that the girls are models of solidarity, cooperation, and kindness. But I have noted with satisfaction that there is no longer the same spirit of cunning and deceit among my students. Before, it was always a question of who could find the best ruse to get out of a difficult situation. There was joy on their faces when one of their classmates was being punished. Now they have stopped trying to trick their teacher, and when they have done something wrong, I am able to get at the truth of the matter, something that was impossible in the beginning.
[. . .]

Mrs. M. Coriat

The Population of Fez Resists the Work of the Alliance, 1903

Fez, 1 September 1903

[. . .]
. . . We are held in esteem because people know that above us is the Alliance, which for them is a charitable organization and nothing more. But to join us in running the school, to help us in overcoming the thousand problems we face here every day, to contribute with us in the work of the Alliance, to show enthusiasm for the presence of these schools, from which they are the first to benefit and which put them at an intellectual level equal to that of the other communities in the cities along the coast and in Turkey: these things they would never deign to do . . .
[. . .]

For these good people, schools are a superfluous luxury. Only the poor, and not all of them, and some families who have traveled or who benefit from European protection send us their children. The others, the vast majority of the

Jews, stubbornly continue to send their children to vile little *Talmudei-Torah* to learn the Talmud and the Torah.

So many times I have been stunned to hear people who are considered intelligent say that the schools are totally useless in Fez, that what children need to be taught first and foremost is Hebrew and nothing else, that these children will never need to know a European language. Several of our fellow Jews still consider our schools profane and impious places.

I was given manifest proof of this attitude on the part of the Jews of Fez, and manifest proof of their fanaticism, during the *maamad* [meeting of the community council] we held to discuss whether a new school or a new *Talmud-Torah* should be founded. All the important people of Fez attended the meeting. After I had read them the letter from the Alliance and stressed the advantages which would result for the community of Fez if a new, larger school were founded to replace the thousand filthy hovels where Hebrew is so poorly taught, they responded in one voice that they would have nothing to do with such an institution. Since I know that they do not like any interference from a foreigner in their affairs, I told them that the *Talmud-Torah* would be administered entirely by them and that our only responsibility would be to direct and guide the teachers. They replied that they considered it a great sin to bring 1,000 Jewish children together. To guard against the evil eye, they told me, it is better to have smaller, unattractive, and pitiful-looking *Talmudei-Torah* of 50 to 100 children, where the evil eye would be powerless, than a large *Talmud-Torah* with 1,000 children, which would inevitably bring the worst calamities upon the Jewish community. For these good people, hygiene and good education are not important, they are afraid of the evil eye . . .
[. . .]

This obstinacy on the part of our fellow Jews in refusing to send their children to school can be traced to several sources. Fez is a city inhabited only by Muslims and Jews, all equally fanatic, all animated by hostile feelings toward foreigners, and enemies of any innovation. The sanctity of this place and the fierce fanaticism of its inhabitants have until now kept away all Europeans, the only representatives of progress. Furthermore, the difficulty of communication with the outside and the dangerous conditions of the roads have prevented our fellow Jews from traveling. They have not seen much of the world and are therefore not very appreciative of the benefits of education. To this must be added the persecutions to which the Jews have always been subjected. This is why the customs and ways of our fellow Jews in Fez have changed so little until now, and why fanaticism is still so prevalent here. And it does not look like there will soon be a change in these customs, which are so faithfully handed down from generation to generation and with which the Jews here are so comfortable and content.
[. . .]

J. Valadji

5. Articles in Iranian Magazines Emphasize the Link Between the Education of Girls and the Advancement of Iranian Society, 1907, 1909

Like Cairo, Beirut, and Istanbul at the turn of the twentieth century, Tehran was a center for the publishing of journals, magazines, and newspapers—most of them focused on reforming society and reformulating the cultural practices of Iranians. Their names—The True Dawn, The New Woman, The New Egyptian, and so on—indicate their goals. Their impact varied with the extent of their distribution and readers' receptiveness to new ideas. Today, articles from these publications provide us with an idea of the debates going on at that time and help us understand how members of at least one group—the middle classes—were seeking to reshape their community, society, and nation.

The following articles address the issue of education for girls. The writers of both contend that it is a necessity for girls to be educated if the nation is to become "civilized" and "modern." Notice that the writers use nation *and* civilization *in a new way. This raises the question of how these terms emerge and how they are understood by the emerging middle classes. Do they denote absolute ideas that apply universally or locally specific ideas that are defined with reference to local conditions and ideas?*

1. Girls' Education Is the Basis of Civilization and Moral Refinement

The best path to civilization is the education, training of girls. The first necessity of moral refinement for girls is to be educated, trained, and cultured. Every nation that wants to become civilized has to begin educating and training girls from an early age. Each nation, according to their own religious laws and practices, should provide it [education] for them with any means possible.

Indeed, these girls will become mothers themselves, and their children will socialize with one another and their habits and disposition will spread among each other. But if they have all been educated in a good manner and with moral refinement, then there can be established in that nation a higher civilization. In this manner, the nation will develop and complete its march of progress by becoming civilized.

On the other hand, if the girls (children) are trained and raised by an uneducated mother, then the bad moods, habits, and disposition will have a bad affect on the children. Along with the growth and mental maturity, an indecent manner will be formed and become a habit; and it will also spread among the children. Therefore, barbarism will develop among the people and they will never become a civilized nation. One savant says: "Every behavior that comes to view, or any word that is said, whether good or bad, will have affect on the

---

"Girls' Education Is the Basis of Civilization and Moral Refinement," *True Dawn* (February 1907).

child either directly or indirectly. And if that word or behavior was proper, it will have a positive influence, and if it was improper, indeed it could have a negative result on the child. Truly, the child's mind and soul absorbs any word and behavior, good or bad, faster than the elders."

Every character and manner, good or bad, when experienced by a child will develop inside him and will be there. When Confucius, a Chinese savant, saw the moral refinement that resulted from educating girls, he understood that it is the greatest and most desired outcome from their education. He took advantage of this idea and instituted it as a law in the Chinese nation. Thus, each girl that is educated and trained in decent manner and has not committed a sin will receive a specific amount of money from government.

One day Napoleon arrived in one of the schools in France, and told the teachers: "I have provided the best necessities for education in France. I have made any resources available for learning by any means, so why is public instruction not improving, and why are the children not learning or advancing in their knowledge?" The teachers replied: "The home school teachers in France are not educated. The reason for retrogression and the lack of children's learning is because of the uneducated and untrained mothers."

Therefore, our nation [Iran] which has taken off the tattered garment of barbarism and savagery, and has put on the sash of honor and civilization, should not neglect the importance of girls' education and culture.

2. Girls' Schooling

It is essential to build a school for boys, but schools are more important for girls because boys do not go to school before the age of eight. Rather, [boys] are raised and learn their behavior from their mothers. Thus, if the mother gains her education through schools, her children will learn good behavior and virtue from her. In contrast, if the mother has not been to school, her child is compelled to ill-natured behavior, like her.

So it is obvious that good education for a mother has a direct effect on her child. In the past, any woman who had a good education left a good name in history. In addition, a girl who was well-educated was also well-respected by her father, husband, and relatives, and at any time in history, she was well-received by the public. Nor has Islam ever banned educational advancement in the family of the Prophet, or subsequent royal families. It has never been reported that Islam has said that a girl could not obtain education or should remain ignorant. According to Islam, women are equal to men with regard to human rights. For inheritance, Islam has given the son twice [the inheritance] as that of a daughter. The reason is simple, because the man has to provide food and shelter for the woman it would have been unjustified if both had equal inheritance. It is irrational to criticize Islamic principles for not giving man and woman equal inheritance. If you heard that man and woman have to be equal, it is not in the matter of inheritance, but rather in education, human qualities, and equality in thoughts and opinions. The first woman believers, Khadija, and Fatima Zahra, praise be to them, because of their good qualities, chastity, and worship of God, were superior to all women throughout the world.

Ghatr Al-Tazy, the mother of Al-Muqtadir bi-Allah of the Abbasids [a medieval Islamic ruling dynasty], presided over civil trials and entertained foreign ambassadors. She earned the confidence of the Abbasids' Caliph [ruler]. Zubayda, the wife of Haroun Al-Rashid, had an abundant knowledge in literature, and one of her public works is "Zubayda's Fountain" [built] on the Road to Mecca. Moreover, she financed the renovation of the city of Alexandria.

Buran, the daughter of Hassan ibn Sahl, and the secretary of Mamoun Al-Rashid's wife, was popular for her wisdom, politeness, and generosity. She built several hospitals at her own expense in Baghdad. Her Highness, Sakina Khatoon, the daughter of Husayn, son of Ali [the cousin of the Prophet], praise upon him, was outstanding in literature and the Arabic language. In royal families, during old times and new, there were always several women who became rulers. If they were not distinguished in wisdom and knowledge, they would not have reached those ranks.

His excellency, the editor of the newspaper, *Fareedeh ol 'Alam Al-Islami Fasli-Moshamma*, has written on this matter, which I do not want to repeat. But its conclusion and observations about this matter [are] that the Iranians, in every city, according to its population, should build schools for women. By doing so they would serve humanity. And there are indications that several individuals are taking steps to fulfill this. God willing, when this promise is fulfilled I will present it.

Prosperity for Iranians.

6.   Bahithat al-Badiya Advocates Greater Educational and Economic Rights for Egyptian Women, 1909

Far too often it is assumed that Muslim women are without voice or speak only to reiterate male conservative opinions. As this document and the next demonstrate, these impressions are mistaken. Bahithat al-Badiya (1886–1918) grappled with complex issues surrounding the role of women in a rapidly changing Egyptian society. Nationalists were demanding Egypt's independence from Britain, a constitutional government, and a more modern state. Socially and culturally, things were also in flux. Egyptian intellectuals and elites debated the merits of "modernity" (which some understood as "Western") and "tradition" (understood as "Eastern")

Bahithat al-Badiya, "A Lecture in the Club of the Umma Party, 1909," in *Opening the Gate*, trans. Ali Badran and Margot Badran (Bloomington: Indiana University Press, 1990), pp. 228–238. Reprinted by permission of Miriam Cooke.

*and their relationship in practical terms. To Bahithat al-Badiya, "modernity" meant
greater educational and economic rights for Egyptian women, which in turn would
strengthen the nation and support its march to independence. In this lecture, which
she gave to a group of elite Egyptian women, she not only addressed these issues
but proposed a program for change, which she spent her remaining years seeking
to implement.*

Ladies, I greet you as a sister who feels what you feel, suffers what you suffer
and rejoices in what you rejoice. I applaud your kindness in accepting the invitation to this talk where I seek reform. I hope to succeed but if I fail remember
I am one of you and that as human beings we both succeed and fail. Anyone
who differs with me or wishes to make a comment is welcome to express her
views at the end of my talk.

Our meeting today is not simply for getting acquainted or for displaying
our finery but it is a serious meeting. I wish to seek agreement on an approach
we can take and to examine our shortcomings in order to correct them. Complaints about both women and men are rife. Which side is right? Complaints
and grumbling are not reform. I don't believe a sick person is cured by continual moaning. An Arab proverb says there is no smoke without fire. The English
philosopher, Herbert Spencer, says that opinions that appear erroneous to us are
not totally wrong but there must be an element of truth in them. There is some
truth in our claims and in those of men. At the moment there is a semi-feud between us and men because of the low level of agreement between us. Men blame
the discord on our poor upbringing and haphazard education while we claim it
is due to men's arrogance and pride. This mutual blame which has deepened the
antagonism between the sexes is something to be regretted and feared. God did
not create man and woman to hate each other but to love each other and to live
together so the world would be populated. If men live alone in one part of the
world and women are isolated in another both will vanish in time.

Men say when we become educated we shall push them out of work and
abandon the role for which God has created us. But, isn't it rather men who
have pushed women out of work? Before, women used to spin and to weave
cloth for clothes for themselves and their children, but men invented machines
for spinning and weaving and put women out of work. In the past, women
sewed clothes for themselves and their households but men invented the
sewing machine. The iron for these machines is mined by men and the machines themselves are made by men. Then men took up the profession of tailoring and began to make clothes for our men and children. Before women
winnowed the wheat and ground flour on grinding stones for the bread they
used to make with their own hands, sifting flour and kneading dough. Then
men established bakeries employing men. They gave us rest but at the same
time pushed us out of work. We or our female servants, used to sweep our
houses with straw brooms and then men invented machines to clean that could
be operated by a young male servant. Poor women and servants used to fetch
water for their homes or the homes of employers but men invented pipes and
faucets to carry water into houses. Would reasonable women seeing water

pumped into a neighbour's house be content to fetch water from the river which might be far away? Is it reasonable for any civilised woman seeing bread from the bakery, clean and soft, costing her nothing more than a little money, go and winnow wheat and knead dough? She might be weak and unable to trouble herself to prepare the wheat and dough or she might be poor and unable to hire servants or to work alone without help. I think if men were in our place they would have done what we did. No woman can do all this work now except women in the villages where civilisation has not arrived. Even those women go to a mill instead of crushing wheat on the grinding stones. Instead of collecting water from the river they have pumps in their houses.

By what I have just said, I do not mean to denigrate these useful inventions which do a lot of our work. Nor do I mean to imply that they do not satisfy our needs. But, I simply wanted to show that men are the ones who started to push us out of work and that if we were to edge them out today we would only be doing what they have already done to us.

The question of monopolising the workplace comes down to individual freedom. One man wishes to become a doctor, another a merchant. Is it right to tell a doctor he must quit his profession and become a merchant or vice versa? No. Each has the freedom to do as he wishes. Since male inventors and workers have taken away a lot of our work should we waste our time in idleness or seek other work to occupy us? Of course, we should do the latter. Work at home now does not occupy more than half the day. We must pursue an education in order to occupy the other half of the day but that is what men wish to prevent us from doing under the pretext of taking their jobs away. Obviously, I am not urging women to neglect their home and children to go out and become lawyers or judges or railway engineers. But if any of us wish to work in such professions our personal freedom should not be infringed. It might be argued that pregnancy causes women to leave work, but there are unmarried women, others who are barren or have lost their husbands or are widowed or divorced or those whose husbands need their help in supporting the family. It is not right that they should be forced into lowly jobs. These women might like to become teachers or doctors with the same academic qualifications. Is it just to prevent women from doing what they believe is good for themselves and their support? If pregnancy impedes work outside the house it also impedes work inside the house. Furthermore, how many able-bodied men have not become sick from time to time and have had to stop work?

Men say to us categorically, "You women have been created for the house and we have been created to be breadwinners." Is this a God-given dictate? How are we to know this since no holy book has spelled it out? Political economy calls for a division of labour but if women enter the learned professions it does not upset the system. The division of labour is merely a human creation. We still witness people like the Nubians whose men sew clothes for themselves and the household while the women work in the fields. Some women even climb palm trees to harvest the dates. Women in villages in both Upper and Lower Egypt help their men till the land and plant crops. Some women do the fertilising, haul crops, lead animals, draw water for irrigation, and other chores.

You may have observed that women in the villages work as hard as the strongest men and we see that their children are strong and healthy.

Specialised work for each sex is a matter of convention. It is not mandatory. We women are now unable to do hard work because we have not been accustomed to it. If the city woman had not been prevented from doing hard work she would have been as strong as the man. Isn't the country woman like her city sister? Why then is the former in better health and stronger than the latter? Do you have any doubt that a woman from Minufiya (a town in the Delta) would be able to beat the strongest man from al-Ghuriya (a section of Cairo) in a wrestling match? If men say to us that we have been created weak we say to them, "No it is you who made us weak through the path you made us follow." After long centuries of enslavement by men, our minds rusted and our bodies weakened. Is it right that they accuse us of being created weaker than them in mind and body? Women may not have to their credit great inventions but women have excelled in learning and the arts and politics. Some have exceeded men in courage and valour, such as Hawla bint al-Azwar al-Kindi who impressed Umar ibn al-Khattab with her bravery and skill in fighting when she went to Syria to free her brother held captive by the Byzantines. Joan of Arc who led the French army after its defeat by the English encouraged the French to continue fighting and valiantly waged war against those who fought her nation. I am not giving examples of women who became queens and were adept in politics such as Catherine, Queen of Russia; Isabel, Queen of Spain; Elizabeth, Queen of England; Cleopatra; Shajarat al-Durr, the mother of Turan Shah, who governed Egypt. Our opponents may say that their rule was carried out by their ministers who are men but while that might be true under constitutional rule it is not true under absolute monarchies.

When someone says to us that's enough education it discourages us and pushes us backwards. We are still new at educating our daughters. While there is no fear now of our competing with men because we are still in the first stage of education and our oriental habits still do not allow us to pursue much study, men can rest assured in their jobs. As long as they see seats in the schools of law, engineering, medicine, and at university unoccupied by us, men can relax because what they fear is distant. If one of us shows eagerness to complete her education in one of these schools I am sure she will not be given a job. She is doing that to satisfy her desire for learning or for recognition. As long as we do not work in law or become employed by the government would our only distraction from raising children be reading a book or writing a letter? I think that is impossible. No matter how much a mother has been educated or in whatever profession she works this would not cause her to forget her children nor to lose her maternal instinct. On the contrary, the more enlightened she becomes the more aware she is of her responsibilities. Haven't you seen ignorant women and peasant women ignore their crying child for hours? Were these women also occupied in preparing legal cases or in reading and writing.

Nothing irritates me more than when men claim they do not wish us to work because they wish to spare us the burden. We do not want condescension, we want respect. They should replace the first with the second.

Men blame any shortcomings we may have on our education, but in fact our upbringing is to blame. Learning and upbringing are two separate things—only in religion are the two connected. This is demonstrated by the fact that many men and women who are well educated are lacking in morals. Some people think that good upbringing means kissing the hands of women and standing with arms properly crossed. Good upbringing means helping people respect themselves and others. Education has not spoiled the morals of our girls, but poor upbringing, which is the duty of the home not the school, has done this. We have to redouble our efforts to reform ourselves and the young. This cannot happen in a minute as some might think. It is unfair to put the blame on the schools. The problem lies with the family. We must improve this situation.

One of our shortcomings is our reluctance to take advice from each other. When someone says something, jealousy and scorn usually come into play. We also are too quick to ridicule and criticise each other over nothing, and we are vain and arrogant.

Men criticise the way we dress in the street. They have a point because we have exceeded the bounds of custom and propriety. We claim we are veiling but we are neither properly covered nor unveiled. I do not advocate a return to the veils of our grandmothers because it can rightly be called being buried alive, not *hijab*, correct covering. The woman used to spend her whole life within the walls of her house not going out into the street except when she was carried to her grave. I do not, on the other hand, advocate unveiling, like Europeans, and mixing with men, because they are harmful to us.

Nowadays the lower half of our attire is a skirt that does not conform to our standards of modesty (*hijab*) while the upper half like age, the more it advances the more it is shortened. Our former garment was one piece. When the woman wrapped herself in it her figure was totally hidden. The wrap shrunk little by little but it was still wide enough to conceal the whole body. Then we artfully began to shrink the waist and lower the neck and finally two sleeves were added and the garment clung to the back and was worn only with a corset. We tied back our headgear so that more than half the head including the ears were visible and the flowers and ribbons ornamenting the hair could be seen. Finally, the face veil became more transparent than an infant's heart. The purpose of the *izar* is to cover the body as well as our dress and jewellery underneath, which God has commanded us not to display. Does our present *izar*, which has virtually become "a dress" showing the bosom, waist, and derrière, conform with this precept? Moreover, some women have started wearing it in colours—blue, brown and red. In my opinion we should call it a dress with a clown's cap which in fact it is. I think going out without it is more modest because at least eyes are not attracted to it.

Imams have differed on the question of *hijab*. If the getups of some women are meant to be a way to leave the home without the *izar* it would be all right if they unveiled their faces but covered their hair and their bodies. I believe the best practice for outdoors is to cover the head with a scarf and the body with a dress of the kind Europeans call *cache poussière,* a dust coat, to cover the body right down to the heels, and with sleeves long enough to reach the wrist. This is being done now in Istanbul, as I am told, when Turkish women go out to neighbourhood shops. But who will guarantee that we will not shorten it and tighten it until we transform it into another dress? In that instance, the road to reform would narrow in front of us.

If we had been raised from childhood to go unveiled and if our men were ready for it I would approve of unveiling for those who want it. But the nation is not ready for it now. Some of our prudent women do not fear to mix with men, but we have to place limits on those who are less prudent because we are quick to imitate and seldom find our authenticity in the veil. Don't you see that diamond tiaras were originally meant for queens and princesses and now they are worn by singers and dancers.

If the change that some women have made in the *izar* is in order to shed it when they go out that would be all right if these women would only uncover their faces but keep their hair and figures concealed. I think the most appropriate way to dress outside is to cover the head and wear a coat with long sleeves which touches the ground the way the European women do. I am told this is the way women in Istanbul dress when they go out shopping. But who can guarantee that we are not going to shorten it and tighten it until we transform it into something else?

The way we wear the *izar* now imitates the dress of Europeans, but we have outdone them in display (*tabarruj*). The European woman wears the simplest dress she has when she is outside and wears whatever she wishes at home or when invited to soirées. But our women are just the opposite. In front of her husband she wears a simple tunic and when she goes out she wears her best clothes, loads herself down with jewellery and pours bottles of perfume on herself . . . Not only this, but she makes a wall out of her face—a wall that she paints various colours. She walks swaying like bamboo in a way that entices passersby or at least they pretend to be enticed. I am sure that most of these showy women (*mutabarrajat*) do this without bad intentions, but how can the onlooker understand good intentions when appearances do not indicate it?

Veiling should not prevent us from breathing fresh air or going out to buy what we need if no one can buy it for us. It must not prevent us from gaining an education nor cause our health to deteriorate. When we have finished our work and feel restless and if our house does not have a spacious garden why shouldn't we go to the outskirts of the city and take the fresh air that God has created for everyone and not just put in boxes exclusively for men. But, we should be prudent and not take promenades alone and we should avoid gossip. We should not saunter moving our heads right and left. If my father or husband will not choose clothes I like and bring them to the house, why can't he take me with him to select what I need or let me buy what I want?

If I cannot find anyone but a man to teach me should I opt for ignorance or for unveiling in front of that man along with my sisters who are being educated? Nothing would force me to unveil in the presence of the teacher. I can remain veiled and still benefit from the teacher. Are we better in Islam than

Sayyida Nafisa and Sayyida Sakina—God's blessings be upon them—who used to gather with *ulama* and poets. If illness causes me to consult a doctor and there is no woman doctor should I abandon myself to sickness, which might be light but could become complicated, through neglect or should I seek help from a doctor who could cure me?

The imprisonment in the home of the Egyptian woman of the past is detrimental while the current freedom of the Europeans is excessive. I cannot find a better model [than] today's Turkish woman. She falls between the two extremes and does not violate what Islam prescribes. She is a good example of decorum and modesty.

I have heard that some of our high officials are teaching their girls European dancing and acting. I consider both despicable—a detestable crossing of boundaries and a blind imitation of Europeans. Customs should not be abandoned except when they are harmful. European customs should not be taken up by Egyptians except when they are appropriate and practical. What good is there for us in women and men holding each other's waists dancing or daughters appearing on stage before audiences acting with bare bosoms in love scenes? This is contrary to Islam and a moral threat we must fight as much as we can. We must show our disdain for the few Muslim women who do these things, who otherwise would be encouraged by our silence to contaminate others.

On the subject of customs and veiling I would like to remind you of something that causes us great unhappiness—the question of engagement and marriage. Most sensible people in Egypt believe it is necessary for fiancés to meet and speak with each other before their marriage. It is wise and the Prophet himself, peace be upon him and his followers, did not do otherwise. It is a practice in all nations, including Egypt, except among city people. Some people advocate the European practice of allowing the engaged pair to get together for a period of time so that they can come to know each other, but I am opposed to this and am convinced this is rooted in fallacy. The result of this getting together is that they would come to love each other, but when someone loves another that person does not see the faults of that person and would not be able to evaluate that person's morals. The two get married on the basis of false love and without direction and soon they start to quarrel and the harmony evaporates. In my view, the two people should see each other and speak together after their engagement and before signing the marriage contract. The woman should be accompanied by her father, or an uncle or a brother and she should wear simple clothing. Some might protest that one or two or more meetings is not enough for the two persons to get to know each other's character, but it is enough to tell if they are attracted to each other. However, anyone with good intuition can detect a person's moral character in the eyes and in movements and repose and sense if a person is false, reckless and the like. As for a person's past and other things one should investigate by talking with acquaintances, neighbours, servants, and others. If we are afraid that immoral young men would use this opportunity to see young women without intending marriage her guardian should probe the behaviour of the man to ascertain how serious he is before allowing him to see his daughter or the young woman for whom he is responsible. What is the good of education if one cannot abandon a custom that is not rooted in religion and that is harmful. We have all seen family happiness destroyed because of this old betrothal practice.

By not allowing men to see their prospective wives following their engagement we cause Egyptian men to seek European women in marriage. They marry European servants and working class women thinking they would be happy with them rather than daughters of pashas and beys hidden away in 'a box of chance'. If we do not solve this problem we shall become subject to occupation by women of the West. We shall suffer double occupation, one by men and the other by women. The second will be worse than the first because the first occurred against our will but we shall have invited the second by our own actions. It is not improbable, as well, that these wives will bring their fathers, brothers, cousins and friends to live near them and they would close the doors of work in front of our men. Most Egyptian men who have married European women suffer from the foreign habits and extravagance of their wives. The European woman thinks she is of a superior race to the Egyptian and bosses her husband around after marriage. When the European woman marries an Egyptian she becomes a spendthrift while she would be thrifty if she were married to a westerner.

If the man thinks the upper class Egyptian wife is deficient and lacking in what her western sister has why doesn't the husband gently guide his wife? Husband and wife should do their utmost to please each other. When our young men go to Europe to study modern sciences it should be to the benefit, not the detriment, of Egypt. As these men get an education and profit themselves they should also bring benefit to their compatriots. They should bring to their country that which will profit it and dispense with whatever is foreign as much as possible. If a national manufacturer of silk visits the factories of Europe and admires their efficiency he should buy machinery that would do work rapidly rather than introduce the same European-made product because if he does he will endanger his own good product.

If we pursue everything western we shall destroy our own civilisation and a nation that has lost its civilisation grows weak and vanishes. Our youth claim that they bring European women home because they find them more sophisticated than Egyptian women. By the same token, they should bring European students and workers to Egypt because they are superior to our own. The reasoning is the same. What would be the result if this happens? If an Egyptian wife travels to Europe and sees the children there with better complexions and more beautiful than children in Egypt would it be right that she would leave her children and replace them with western children or would she do her best to make them beautiful and make them resemble as much as possible that which she admired in those other children? If the lowliest western woman marrying an Egyptian is disowned by her family shall we be content with her when she also takes the place of one of our best women and the husband becomes an example for other young men? I am the first to admire the activities of the western woman and her courage and I am the first to respect those among them who deserve respect, but respect for others should not make us overlook the good of the nation. Public interest is above admiration. In many of our ways we follow the views of our men. Let them show us what they want. We are ready to follow their views on condition that their views do not do injustice to us nor trespass on our rights.

Our beliefs and actions have been a great cause of the lesser respect that men accord us. How can a sensible man respect a woman who believes in magic, superstition, and the blessing of the dead and who allows women peddlars and washerwomen, or even devils, to have authority over her? Can he respect a woman who speaks only about the clothes of her neighbour and the jewellery of her friend and the furniture of a bride? This is added to the notion imprinted in a man's mind that woman is weaker and less intelligent than he is. If we fail to do something about this it means we think our condition is satisfactory. Is our condition satisfactory? If it is not, how can we better it in the eyes of men? Good upbringing and sound education would elevate us in the eyes of men. We should get a sound education, not merely acquire the trappings of a foreign language and rudiments of music. Our education should also include home management, healthcare, and childcare. If we eliminate immodest behaviour on the street and prove to our husbands through good behaviour and fulfillment of duties that we are human beings with feelings, no less human [than] they are, and we do not allow them under any condition to hurt our feelings or fail to respect us, if we do all this, how can a just man despise us? As for the unjust man, it would have been better for us not to accept marriage to him.

We shall advance when we give up idleness. The work of most of us at home is lounging on cushions all day or going out to visit other women. How does the woman who knows how to read occupy her leisure time? Only in reading novels. Has she read books about health or books through which she can profit herself and others? Being given over to idleness or luxury has given us weak constitutions and pale complexions. We have to find work to do at home. At a first glance one can see that the working classes have better health and more energy and more intelligent children. The children of the middle and lower classes are, almost all of them, in good health and have a strong constitution, while most of the children of the élite are sick or frail and prone to illness despite the care lavished on them by their parents. On the other hand, lower class children are greatly neglected by their parents. Work causes poisons to be eliminated from the blood and strengthens the muscles and gives energy.

Now I shall turn to the path we should follow. If I had the right to legislate I would decree:

1. Teaching girls the Quran and the correct Sunna.

2. Primary and secondary school education for girls, and compulsory preparatory school education for all.

3. Instruction for girls on the theory and practice of home economics, health, first aid, and childcare.

4. Setting a quota for females in medicine and education so they can serve the women of Egypt.

5. Allowing women to study any other advanced subjects they wish without restriction.

6. Upbringing for girls from infancy stressing patience, honesty, work and other virtues.

7. Adhering to the *Sharia* concerning betrothal and marriage, and not permitting any woman and man to marry without first meeting each other in the presence of the father or male relative of the bride.

8. Adopting the veil and outdoor dress of the Turkish women of Istanbul.

9. Maintaining the best interests of the country and dispensing with foreign goods and people as much as possible.

10. Make it encumbent upon our brothers, the men of Egypt, to implement this programme.

7. Nazira Zein el-Din, an Egyptian Feminist, Comments on the Unveiling and Veiling of Women, 1928

Seeking to reclaim Islam from strictly male interpretations, Nazira Zein el-Din (born ca. 1905) offers a liberal interpretation of the religion. The daughter of a Lebanese judge, early in her life Nazira began to question traditional religious and cultural assumptions about the role of women in Islamic societies. In particular, she focused on the hijab, the veiling that some Muslim women used to cover their heads and bodies. In Turkey, secular reforms allowed women greater access to public life and permitted them to remove the veiling. In contrast, Nazira noted, in Syria unveiled women were not even permitted to leave home. In 1928 she published a treatise—excerpted here—arguing, from her research and study of Islamic texts, that Islam regards women as completely equal to men and the Qur'an does not require the veiling of women. Her book, which sparked fiery discussions in Lebanon and throughout the Arab world, can be seen as part of the dialogue about culture, religion, society, and politics in the Middle East that emerged at the end of the nineteenth century and focused in many ways on gender roles.

Two Views: One View on the Unveiled World and the Other on the Veiled World

Ladies and gentlemen, in the beginning I compared opposites, the numbers of the veiled and the unveiled. I found that the veiled are not more than a few million

Nazira Zein al-Din, *Unveiling and Veiling: Lectures and Views on the Liberation of the Woman and Social Renewal in the Arab World* (Cairo, 1928), pp. 64–69. This document may also be found in Charles Kurzman, *Liberal Islam* (New York: Oxford University Press, 1998), pp. 101–106.

Muslims living in towns. Those in the villages of the Islamic world and more than 1700 million in other nations are not veiled. They have rejected the veil that they had previously worn. I have noticed that the nations that have given up the veil are the nations that have advanced in intellectual and material life. Such advancement is not equaled in the veiled nations. The unveiled nations are the ones that have discovered through research and study the secrets of nature and have brought the physical elements under their control, as you see and know. But the veiled nations have not unearthed any secret and have not put any of the physical elements under their control but only sing the songs of a glorious past and ancient tradition. With such singing they sleep in stagnation.

I have seen many intellectuals of the nations where women are still veiled advocating unveiling, but I haven't seen anyone in the unveiled nations advocating or preferring the veil. That is, I haven't seen anyone who has tried unveiling and then has preferred the veil. Even if some Westerner in his hypocritical words makes the veil appear in a favorable light, he is only pleased with the beauty of the Oriental veil while at the same time he would reject the veiling of his mother, wife, sisters, and daughters because of the harm in the veil he favors for others.

I cannot imagine that in the advanced nations which have discovered the secrets of nature and harnessed its powers, which have not let anything pass without examining it to the fullest, where the struggle between right and wrong is continuous until right becomes victorious, nations which have produced works on social subjects we view as masterpieces of literature and sociology, have neglected to study veiling and unveiling to understand the benefits and disadvantages. I cannot think that our own ignorance brings us any greater understanding of what honor is than the unveiled nations possess in learning nor that our conduct is superior to theirs, nor that their women going outside unveiled enjoying their freedom is evidence of their lower conduct and corrupt morals.

Yes, I looked into all that and I could not but consider it evidence of their superior education and elevated conduct. When our esteemed ladies who wear the veil go to a Western country, they take off the veil and the men accompanying them do not prevent them from doing this the way they do when they are at home or after they return. This is because we have more faith in the conduct of Westerners than in our own conduct. The conduct of Westerners has been influenced by mingling with women and thus Western men have based their habits and morals on logic and reason looking to benefits and positive results while our conduct and morals are based on our customs whatever they may be.

I shall never forget a conversation between an Eastern man advocating the veil and an unveiled Western woman who enjoyed her freedom and independence. The Easterner said to the Westerner, "Our nature cannot accept your customs. Our customs are more noble than yours and our men support our women. The man according to his right walks in front of his wife but in your country the woman walks in front of the man as if she were the provider."

The Western woman said, "If you really want to protect your wife please let her go in front of you so that you can watch out for her for the way our men do, rather than letting her walk behind you so that she would misuse her freedom and get hurt."

The Eastern man paused and said, "Truly, Westerners ground their customs in reason. Reason alone should dictate custom."

It is not fitting for us to say that we who are only a few million, most of whom are not advanced, are more honorable than the one and a half billion people (in the world), most of whom are more advanced than we are.

It is not honorable for us to deny our shortcomings and believe we are perfect and claim that our customs are the best customs for every time and place. This conceit and false presumption is a barrier to the reform we seek. When the nation feels its shortcomings, that is the first step in its advancement.

It is inconceivable that we claim to be defenders of honor while the veil is our strongest shield. We must understand as everyone else does that honor is rooted in the heart and chastity comes from within and not from a piece of transparent material lowered over the face.

We have to realize, as the advanced unveiled world does, that good behavior and honor come from sound upbringing grounded in noble principles and virtues. We are shortsighted if we think that the veil keeps evil away from women and that those in the rest of the world exceeding one and a half billion are all in the wrong while we are in the right.

He Who Bears Falsehood to the People
Has to Provide Evidence to Them

I have mentioned the above, ladies and gentlemen, fearful that I might be confronted by someone who does not use logic and reasoning to make his points, but relies on untruths concerning the advanced unveiled nations. He may look where vice is but he does not wish to rise up to see where virtue resides. He might have seen their baser women and generalizes from them, subsuming the noble and honorable in his generalization, and hurls accusing arrows of untruths at them even though human beings should not be like flies pouncing on tails (of animals) and ignoring their heads.

He does not dare to lord scientific and industrial knowledge over the unveiled nations because these are tangible matters. Therefore he accuses them of lack of morals and good conduct because these are not tangible. Thus he is overwhelming in this even though his accusation is false.

You know gentlemen, nations are like trees whose rotten fruits fall to the ground and vermin, humans and animals go after them. Those who are wise and advanced look only to the good and ripe fruits, by which the tree is identified.

My antagonist seems to be ignorant of that or is playing the role of the ignorant. He wants to know the tree by the fallen fruits he sees beneath it. Moreover, he does not want to recognize that in every nation, however advanced, there is a lower class overcome by corruption whose morals and conduct have deteriorated because they did not have the chance to be educated and to develop so that they could reach the higher level in the nation.

Gentlemen, we should do our best to see to it that the majority in our nation are able to have an education and the means to develop. Then it would be possible for us to be proud before our nations. . . .

We should not believe everything we hear and take our evidence from falsehood, especially evidence that brings great evil to the nation by obstructing reform and maintaining continual backwardness.

We should abstain from hurling lies and falsehoods at others, which is alien to morality and decent debate and only brings down those who lie. Instead we should subscribe to truth, sound reasoning, unbiased knowledge, and correct behavior. In accordance with the will of God Almighty and the will of His Prophet, may God bless him. . . .

How Men Should Support Women

Gentlemen, you have heard the response of the Western woman to the Eastern man who was proud to support his woman and to walk in front of her. Yes, let men support women in principle. Every man supports his own wife spending money on her, but he has no authority over any other woman. A verse from the Qur'an was sent by God about this in relation to Sa'd ibn al-Rabi from al-Naqba and his wife Habiba; the words are related specifically to husband and wife. Men should know that authority is limited by the benefit deriving from it. Therefore, men should attain high moral development as God wants and society requires. This would make women strong and self-dependent, for when people have virtue, dignity, and honor they turn away from evil, not out of fear of punishment, nor because of reward, nor because of an immovable obstacle, but because evil is ugly and such a person would not allow herself to engage in lowly acts.

The Prophet, God bless him, said, "I was sent to help you attain the highest morality." Does not the highest morality come from the soul? Pieces of cloth over faces shall never be a measure of morality.

The Veil (*Niqab*) Is an Insult to Men and Women

It is not beneficial to men and women that men should just support women physically and financially, nor is it beneficial that man rule over those whom the *shari'a* [Islamic law] did not give him the right. It greatly harms the two sexes that every man continues to insult his mother, daughter, wife, and sister, suspiciously accusing them of bad morals and keeping them confined to a cage, as the venerable Qasim Amin [Egypt, 1865–1908] said, "With their wings cut off, heads bent down, and eyes closed. For him (man) is freedom and for them (women) enslavement. For him is education and for them ignorance. For him is sound reasoning and for them inferior reasoning. For him is light and open space and for them darkness and imprisonment. For him are orders and for them obedience and patience. For him is everything in the universe and for them part of the whole he has captured."

May God be merciful to Qasim and bless his pen, about which "The Poet of the Two Countries" has said, "He tears down the ugly and builds the beautiful, returning to the *sunna* [the practices of the Prophet] of the Drawer. He sheds light even when he writes with the dark water of the night."

Unfortunately, if the veil (*hijab*) implies the inability of the woman to protect herself without it, it also reveals that man, however well brought up and in spite of supporting the woman, is a traitor and a thief of honor: his evil should be feared and it is better that the woman escapes from him.

You, Man, the Supporter

If some women, because of the ignorance into which you have cast them, have not recognized the insult to them and to men by the veil, is it easy for you, the man who has kept himself free seeking perfection and good conduct, to bear this insult that comes to you and to your mother, daughter, wife, and sister?

Does the woman who escapes from you, or approaches you lowering the veil over her face, or turns her back on you, confirm your high status, as she might think and say and you might think and say, or is it a great insult? Does this constitute the woman's decorum, chastity and modesty? If so, then men should not be without these precious attributes; let them wear veils and let them meet each other and meet women lowering veils over their faces the way women do. . . .

On Man's Superiority in His Rights to Inheritance, Legal Testimony, Polygamy, and Arbitrariness in Divorce as Evidence Not to His Advantage but Against Him

I noticed in some of the articles written against women and their liberation, as well as against their removal of the veil, that the authors boast of the fact that in his Holy Qur'an, God favored men over women—mind and soul—in three different matters:

First, God made a woman entitled to inherit only half of what a man inherits.

Second, God considers her testimony (legally) worth only half of his.

Third, He, the Almighty, allowed a man to marry up to four wives and divorce them at will, without their consent.

The authors of these articles conclude from this that the woman is mentally and spiritually inferior. Hence they think that God, the Almighty, decided to favor a man over a woman in these three areas. But as far as I am concerned, I conclude otherwise. I understand the argument to be against men rather than in their favor.

Indeed, I examine Islam through the greatest words of God and the sayings of His Prophet. I then see God enthroned in greatness, freedom, equality, justice, goodness, and perfection. I become so overwhelmed and so elated that I feel my soul about to leave my body. I only wish that those who pretend to protect Islam and raise its banners would look in the same way as I do and see what I see. I wish they did not look at Islam through the narrow vision of commentaries and interpretations which interpret Islam in ways they want to see it. Islam is far beyond that. It is much greater.

God's permissibility only showed man's cruel heart, his inability to submit to truth and justice, and his immoral character, acquired from the worst pre-Islamic customs. Such a character, as is well known, is in contradiction with the nature of noble human mentality.

Man subjected to slavery those he deemed weak among women as among men, treating them according to his whims like merchandise or cattle. Had it not been for the viciousness in his mind, his misguided soul and cruel heart, God would not have granted him then such allowances that He disliked and which were meant to vanish with time.

We have thus far seen [in earlier sections of the author's book] what the woman's condition was, under the yoke of man throughout the world in general and in pre-Islamic Arabia in particular, just before the Qur'an was revealed to our Prophet, God bless him and grant him salvation.

God dislikes slavery. He dislikes polygamy and any violation of women's rights. God loathes divorce. His divine throne shakes every time the word is uttered on earth, as I will explain in detail below in a discussion of divorce [not included in this excerpt].

God revealed His holy message all filled with the spirit of freedom, justice and equality among people. He does not differentiate between them for His esteem, except on the basis of their faith in Him. How would then the Almighty condone the enslavement of His human creation in whom He instilled life, and for whom He ordered angels to bow in honor and respect? Did God, we might ask, instill life in the strong who take others into slavery but not in the weak who are enslaved by others? Of course not! God gave life to all. Yet, since the days of Adam, peace be upon him, man has disobeyed God and gone astray.

If Adam himself, who was a prophet, "disobeyed God's order and went astray," what of his male offspring who have realized their strength and became misguided by it? In their arrogant ways, they took into slavery whoever they saw as weak.

God sent His Prophet, peace and salvation be upon him, to mankind in that corrupt land of ignorance. He warned him in these holy words: "If you were rude and arrogant, people would desert you." And as goes one of the Prophet's own sayings: "Teach others, be lenient not harsh, preach but do not alienate anyone."

In his book *Al-Islam ruh al-madaniyya* [*Islam, The Spirit of Civilization*], Shaykh [Mustafa] Al-Ghalayini [Ottoman Empire-Lebanon, 1886–1945] wrote: "It was considered wise in Islam not to totally abolish some of the reprehensible traditions such as polygamy, as there were so many difficulties involved." He also went on to say: "Slavery and harsh treatment of captives are odious acts by Islamic standards. Slavery was considered inherited from the era of savageness. Politically, however, it was not ruled absolutely forbidden in those days." In fact if all those customs had been entirely abolished by God, several problems would have ensued. The least of these is that men would have broken away from God's religion and deserted His Prophet. Moreover, not many of His commandments would have been obeyed.

In pre-Islamic Arabia, women as well as male slaves were under the domination of financially powerful men who owned them and enjoyed them at will. These materialistic men used to get as infatuated with their wealth as they were with themselves. A man in those days would own as many as one hundred women and a large number of male slaves. Like property or cattle they were inherited as a part of an estate. How can we then take it for granted that they could be set free from man's ownership and made equal to him in every way, at the same time, and not in a gradual fashion? God said in the Holy Qur'an, "And if We willed it for them to either kill themselves or leave their land, only a few of them would." [Sura 4, Verse 66] Thus it was out of God's wisdom to eliminate some of these reprehensible customs, while leaving traces of them to turn men's attention to Him so they would not give up His religion and abandon His Prophet.

As for a woman's legal testimony, should the fact that it is considered worth only half of that of a man's be grounds for women's mental inferiority? If so, a non-Muslim's legal testimony for or against a Muslim is not accepted; can that also be considered evidence for non-Muslims' mental inferiority? Or was it rather a decision resulting from some unusual circumstances in those days?

In the final analysis, it was no other than God's kindness to the woman to consider her testimony worth half that of a man's. The latter interpreted it as a privilege and became satisfied with it. In reality, legal testimony is no other than a bothersome obligation. It is as if God wanted to reassure men and relieve women from such an obligation at the same time. It seems as if testimony were expressly ruled outside a woman's competence, so that only men would be called upon to testify in courts. There is no reason to believe that God decided that because of a deficiency in the woman's faith or intelligence. Women possess a great deal of goodness and spiritual righteousness, and as the Prophet's saying goes, "One good woman is better than a thousand improper men."

Through God's wisdom, the persistence of a few traces of those bad customs is a way of soothing the minds of those who practice them. His wisdom is revealed in several ways and verses. In the tradition of His Prophet, God bless him and grant him salvation, there is proof that the dangers in the persistence of such traces of vile traditions are removed. Thus their impact is reduced and they become acceptable rather than offensive.

God knew that people with insight would erase all traces of reprehensible customs, following this way the wisdom implied by those Qur'anic verses and Prophet's teachings. God was indeed aware that such wisdom was not unknown to His people. Hence he allowed the taking of slaves but was eager for their freedom, in the same way that He was yearning to abolish polygamy and end discrimination between men and women in their rights. This is one of the interpretations suggested by the famous scholar Muhammad 'Abduh [Egypt, 1849–1905].

Below however is another quotation from [Muhammad] Jamil Bayhum [Lebanon, 1887–1978], the author of *Al-Mar' a fi al-tarikh wa al-shara'i'* [*Woman in History and Religious Legal Systems*]:

> Some commentators have interpreted these opinions as implying a ban on polygamy, because allowing it must depend on fairness in treatment while such indiscriminate justice is highly improbable. But this is in no way an uncommon interpretation as long as laws are subject to considerations of culture and civilization. Just as Christians were somehow able to discover that their religion prohibits polygamy, when it actually did not object to it, it would be easy for Muslims to enact legislation forbidding polygamy, in appreciation of the general world condition, progress and the advancement of women.

Indeed that would be easier for Muslims than making laws condoning all the vile sins such as drinking alcohol, prostitution, usury and idolatry, or disapproving of some of God's ordinances like stoning, requital or other legal punishments. Such laws are constantly being enacted.

Don't you see that slavery was discontinued in Islamic countries like everywhere else and that punishment is administered to whoever engages in it? Don't you see that polygamy has become considered evil by enlightened communities around us, and that the great independent Islamic nation of Turkey has banned it and reserves for it the harshest of punishments?

Don't you see that, through government laws, Islamic countries have made a woman's legal testimony equal to a man's both in witnessing legal punishment as well as in other cases? They gave her equal right for inheriting land, and in Turkey, a woman's right is equal to that of a man for testimony in all cases and transactions, and in inheritance for any kind of property.

By enacting laws to eliminate those vile traditions, the Islamic governments were not in contradiction with God's message and the teachings of His Prophet. Those governments understood the reasoning behind those teachings. They abolished slavery and ended any discrimination between man and woman. Not only did they interpret the surface meanings of those Qur'anic verses and Prophet's teaching; but also they interpreted their essence in depth in the manner of people with insight and reason.

This is indeed an important and broad subject. To cover it with a presentation of convincing evidence would require lengthy explications that are beyond the scope of my present lecture series. God willing, I shall deal with it in a special lecture.

Nevertheless, I think that we should realize right now the reason which led to the persistence of those reprehensible customs and why they had such an impact on the absolute equality of man and woman and amongst men (as slaves and free men). Perhaps that reason is man's cruelty, his error, arbitrariness, and the evil side in his character prevailing over the good side. That is what led God's wisdom, to permit something reprehensible that He never condoned as fair and just.

Right now, we must realize that this reason for that has nothing to do with a woman's faith or her intelligence. In no way was the inequality between a helpless slave and a powerful free man a result of mental or spiritual deficiency so that inequality between man and woman in the matters mentioned should result from her mental and spiritual deficiency.

If God had truly condoned slavery, polygamy and inequality between man and woman, He would not have made the man accountable for expenditures for the woman's dowry, her support and that of her children's which are equal or greater than what she misses in inheritance. If so, indeed, God would not have established laws leading to the disappearance of slavery and the avoidance of polygamy; and His Prophet would not have preferred females over males in several matters. In fact, here are some of his sayings:

> When you give to your children, be fair in your giving and give equally. If I personally had a preference to make (in giving to my own), I would prefer giving to my daughters.

> Whoever goes to market and buys something to bring back home, especially for the females in his family, will enjoy God's care, and whoever is in God's care will be protected from all suffering.

> Purchasing a choice gift for members of your family is like giving charity. Priority should go to the females, because bringing joy to a female is like crying humbly in fear and respect of God and whoever cries in fear of God will be spared from the fires of Hell.

Therefore if females were deficient in mind and in faith, they would not be worthy of such preferential thoughts by the Prophet of God. He is much beyond preferring stupidity over intelligence, and a lack of faith over an abundance of it. He once also said, "Fear God in your treatment of the weak, slaves and women."

As for this last piece of advice given by the Prophet of God, we must stand facing Mecca, humbly and in reverence, in order to hear it. He uttered it from his death bed, at a time he was in distress, because he had not completely removed all of the differences between the slaves and the free, and between men and women. He uttered the following final words, his voice stammering, until his very last word:

> Prayer . . . Prayer . . . If any slaves are in your possession, do not burden them with what they are unable to do. God. God . . . of Women. They are in your hands. . . . You took them with God's trust.

He uttered these words and passed away. Peace be upon you, o Prophet of God, peace be upon you, o beloved of God. Peace be upon you, Lord of the first and last prophets. Peace be upon you the day you were born, the day you died, and the day you will be resurrected.

PART II

Making Nations in the Middle East, 1900–1949

A common misconception about the Middle East and North Africa is that the nations that now exist in the two regions have always been in conflict. However, conflicts there, as everywhere else, have taken place at specific points in time and for specific reasons. Recent conflicts that appear eternal—Arab-Israeli, Iraq-Iran, Iraq-Kuwait—actually derive from a twentieth-century phenomenon: nationalism.

Before World War I, the Middle East and North Africa were fluid geopolitical spaces in which peoples with various languages, cultures, and ethnicities intermingled in the cities and larger towns and many others lived in rural isolation. This description is not intended to imply the absence of territorial or communal conflicts or a static political environment. However, despite tensions that varied greatly in intensity and consequences, most people were able to live within their limited world, either coexisting with or oblivious to others. World War I and the subsequent French and British occupation of much of the Middle East helped bring fundamental changes to this geopolitical system. The basic shift was from a multicultural political community to a number of political entities *supposedly* ethnically unified (though in reality still quite varied). The expectation of ethnic unity—the most common indicator of nationalism at that time—was affirmed by the remapping of the region into "nations" with fixed borders drawn to separate, for example, the newly formed Iraq from the equally novel Syria.

For the people living in the Middle East and North Africa, this political (and cultural) remapping was disorienting and oppressive, even as it opened new possibilities. The basic premise of the mandate system was that the British and the French would remain in control until the peoples of the regions were "capable of ruling themselves." In other words, the litmus test for ending colonial domination was the ability of the newly formed entities to govern themselves as nations. Thus, for example, for the people living in Syria to free themselves from colonial rule and the arbitrary divisions imposed on them, they would need to accept the idea of the "nation of Syria" and prove to the Europeans that the new "nation" was capable of administering itself amid attempts by colonial forces to disrupt any political action or programs that could threaten their mandates.

The task of constructing a nation was perplexing to people long accustomed to being members of an empire and of small communities. None of their political experiences prepared them to conceive of a political entity that was smaller than an empire and larger than a city or village. Moreover, the continuing realities of a multiethnic and multilingual society posed immediate and obstinate obstacles to achieving the "ideal" of ethnically unified nations. In fact, the existence of different ethnic, religious, and linguistic groups in each of the new nations guaranteed from the outset a struggle over who would organize each nation and how power would be distributed. This dizzying set of puzzles was compounded by technological problems (how to reach the multitudes of people living in villages, who still formed the majority of each "national" population), economic problems (the new borders not only sundered trading links that had long sustained the local economies but also subjected the "national" economies to the whims and needs of the colonizers), political problems (what type of government and constitution to establish), and cultural problems (which sources of "tradition" to draw from to lay the foundation for the idea and "history" of the nation).

Out of these questions emerged a host of ideas about the meaning and definition of the "nation." Local groups proclaimed a culturally or religiously distinct nationalism. Thus, nationalists in Lebanon, Egypt, and Turkey insisted, respectively, that the "Lebanese," "Egyptians," and "Turks" constituted the national population, and they rejected any notion of subcultures, be they Kurdish, Armenian, Coptic, and so on. This definition of the "nation" drew strict distinctions along the borders separating each nationality. Thus, for instance in the minds and words of some Lebanese nationalists, Lebanon and Syria became essentially, incontrovertibly, and eternally separate "nations"; any similarities between them were dismissed as coincidental rather than deriving from any historical connection.

Political organizations articulating broader, geographical notions of the "nation" also emerged. The "nation" of "Greater Syria" (encompassing modern-day Iraq, Syria, Lebanon, and Israel/Palestine) was advocated by Antun Sa'adeh, founder of the Syrian Social Nationalist Party (SSNP). An appeal to a distant and unchanging past provided the underpinning for this approach. In the ideology of the SSNP, ancient Mesopotamia became directly linked to modern Syria, bypassing in the process Arab and Muslim history, not to mention the countless other peoples and cultures that had populated the region at one time or another. Imagining a still larger "nation," Pan-Arabists postulated that all "Arabs"—defined by a common language and culture—belonged together in a single nation that would re-create the glories of the past. In this formulation of the "nation," religion—specifically Islam but also Christianity and Judaism—become incidental effects of the main cause: Arabness. There also emerged a religious form of nationalism, which proposed that Islam offered the only viable and acceptable foundation for the Muslims of the Middle East. Moreover, Pan-Islamists argued that the emerging forms of secular nationalism were European imperial ploys meant to weaken the "Islamic world" (although such a unified "world" had never existed).

In addition to debating competing ideas about the characteristics of a "nation," many individuals and groups bent on imagining a singular new political entity had to deal with issues such as gender, class, and ethnicity—however obliquely. As alternative and potentially controversial political focal points, these issues had to be examined within every particular nationalist discourse. Thus, we find texts from Turkey, Iran, Egypt, Algeria, and elsewhere describing the nation as a "woman" and linking liberation of the nation to liberation of the women of the nation. The purpose of such liberation, however, was to advance the nation rather than to improve the lot of individual women. Women's status was to be improved for the sake of society and the nation, not for women's own sake. In this manner, liberation—in its gendered manifestation—was presented as a nationalist project and not as a humanistic and universal ideal. A similar process took place with regard to class and ethnicity.

Nationalist stirrings in the Middle East, then, led to rupture and discontinuity with the past. The documents in this section show the attempts by various individuals and groups to make sense of this change, to control its direction, and to build nations where there were none before. In their variety, these documents represent the myriad ideological sources of nationalism, the arguments about the form and substance of the "nation" and about the relationship between society and state, and the tension between ideas of the "nation" set forth by the intellectual and political elites and those of the popular classes. In reading these documents against each other, we can begin to appreciate the daunting complexity of the project of nation-making. As we learn about external pressures, internal dissensions, and practical difficulties, we are able to look beyond accounts that imbue these political entities with a "naturalness" that tends to flatten the political and cultural terrain and downplay conflict. In other words, the documents in the next two chapters shed light on the human drama behind the creation of Middle Eastern nations.

CHAPTER 4

Ideas of Nationalism

In the creation of nations in the Middle East and North Africa, ideas played a formative role. Some ideas reflected the political aims of the Western imperial powers. Other, indigenous ideas originated within the Middle East and North Africa and reflected the thinking and hopes of an array of intellectuals and activists. In this chapter we examine both types of ideas.

Documents 3 and 4 show the British planning and negotiating to advance their imperial interests when World War I ends. The Husayn-McMahon correspondence, an exchange of letters between the amir of Mecca and the British High Commissioner in Egypt (document 3), indicates differing visions of the future of the region. While the British were making promises—however ambiguous—to Husayn, European Zionists were seeking and obtaining support for their project of establishing a Jewish homeland in Palestine—an area that Husayn and most other Arabs understood to be included within the promised Arab kingdom. Document 4 pertains to Britain's Balfour Declaration. Document 5, from the Treaty of Sèvres (1920), details the postwar division of the Ottoman Empire and provides us with a map of European interests and goals in the region. Atatürk's speech in 1927 (document 6) provides an example of opposition toward European designs in favor of indigenous concepts of the nation.

Indigenous intellectuals and activists had their own ideas about nationhood. Most ambitious was the idea of Arabism. Proponents said that all Arabs—defined by a common linguistic, cultural, and historical heritage—belonged together in one nation. The specifics of this vision were the subject of many disagreements and much debate. The ideas of Michel 'Aflaq, however, are considered to be the founding principles of this brand of nationalism (document 11). Antun Sa'adeh (document 9) proposed a more modest physical and cultural definition of the "nation." He suggested that the "fertile crescent" (an area that includes modern-day Lebanon, Jordan, Israel, Palestine, Syria, and Iraq) was the "natural" homeland of a culture that, at least in Sa'adeh's opinion, predated Arabs and Islam. Even among those who agreed about the geographical definition of the "nation" there remained the complex task of explaining the founding principles of the nation and its constituency. Ahad Ha-Am explored these issues as they pertained to the creation of a Jewish state (document 2).

An even more delimited vision of the "nation" was proposed for Egypt, Lebanon, and Algeria. Proponents of local nationalism argued that history or natural boundaries made for "eternal" nations with "essential" qualities that distinguished them from all other surrounding areas. For example, in Egypt some intellectuals like Taha Husayn (document 10) contended that their country was uniquely Egyptian as it combined European, Pharaonic, and Arab-Muslim cultural influences. To such thinkers, this implied a distinctiveness from all their Arab neighbors that constrains nationalism in Egypt to the borders of that country. Similarly, Leo Pinsker—a Jewish intellectual from Russia—articulated the idea that Jews would never be accepted within European societies except as pariahs, so Jewish political and cultural salvation could come about only from the creation of a Jewish state that excluded all other ethnicities (document 1). This limited ethnic nationalism was born out of the persecution of Jews in Europe and out of acceptance of the basis of that persecution—the belief that ethnicities are essential and eternal and one must be dominant.

In conjunction with all these ideas, there emerged a strand of thought that engaged nationalist projects from an Islamic perspective. For people with these beliefs, like Hassan al-Banna (document 12), Islam was the primary point of political reference and identity. Thus, for them secular nationalism was a departure from accepted norms and posed a political threat. Their responses ranged from complete rejection of nationalism to an attempt to infuse various nationalist ideologies with strong Islamic content. At the same time there existed those thinkers such as 'Ali 'Abd al-Raziq (document 7) who rejected any political role for Islam and insisted on the separation between the state/nation and religion. Going one step further, Messali Hadj (document 8) proposes a Communist vision of the nation that not only sidelines religion in politics but also seeks to restructure the class hierarchy of society.

Regardless of their ideological bent, the authors of the documents in this chapter shared the common goal of bringing about a physical manifestation of their various visions of the "nation." Embedded in each definition were altruistic ideals and mundane goals deriving from self-interest. In reading these documents, try to identify each of these elements and to differentiate between them. Also, try to dissociate rhetoric from reality. In other words, read the documents as proposed ideals and not necessarily as the accepted vision of the totality of the "people."

1.   Leo Pinsker, a Jewish Intellectual, Proposes a "Jewish Homeland," 1882

Leo Pinsker (1821–1891) was a leading figure in the eastern European haskalah *(Jewish enlightenment). Along with Moshe Leib Lilienblum, Eliezer Ben Yehudah, and other Jewish intellectuals, Pinsker for many years believed that Jewish secular and liberal tradition would permit the assimilation of Jews into non-Jewish societies. He himself had studied medicine at Moscow University and had been decorated by the tsar for his medical work on behalf of the Russian army during the Crimean War. However, his outlook on the future of Jews in Russia and in other nations was radically altered by the terrible anti-Jewish pogroms that broke out in 1881.*

After the assassination of Tsar Alexander II in 1881 by revolutionaries, his successor—Alexander III—suspended the program of reforms that had been in place and attempted to isolate Russia from liberal influences. Some of the new tsar's aides argued that the revolutionary mood in Russia was the fault of Jews, who were "the primary bearers of revolutionary infection, the source of all that was vicious in modern capitalism."[1] This anti-Semitic mood and the government's desire to divert the attention of the Russian peasantry away from the real sources of their woes combined to give rise to anti-Jewish riots that were, if not state sponsored, at least unopposed by the agents of the government. The horrendous scenes of murder, rape, and pillage were made even worse by the infamous Russian laws of 1882, which restricted the livelihood of Jews as well as the places where they were permitted to reside.

Those blatantly discriminatory laws and the pogroms transformed the views of leading Jewish intellectuals. Pinsker, among others, could not sustain his belief in integration into the mainstream of European society in the face of such anti-Jewish violence and sentiment. He embraced the cause of Jewish nationalism and wrote his influential Auto-Emancipation *(1882)—a precursor to Theodore Herzl's* The Jewish State *(1896).*

"If I am not for myself, who will be for me?
And if not now, when?"
—HILLEL

That hoary problem, subsumed under the Jewish question, today, as ever in the past, provokes discussion. Like the squaring of the circle it remains unsolved, but unlike it, continues to be the ever-burning question of the day. That is

---

[1]David Vital, *The Origins of Zionism* (Oxford: Oxford University Press, 1975), p. 51.

Leon Pinsker, *Auto-Emancipation: An Appeal to His People,* By a Russian Jew, trans. Dr. D. S. Blondheim, Federation of American Zionists, 1916 (Masada, Youth Zionist Organization of America, 1939).

because the problem is not one of mere theoretical interest: it renews and re-vives in every-day life and presses ever more urgently for solution.

This is the kernel of the problem, as we see it: *the Jews comprise a distinctive element among the nations under which they dwell, and as such can neither assimilate nor be readily digested by any nation.*

Hence the solution lies in finding a means of so readadjusting this exclusive element to the family of nations, that the basis of the Jewish question it will be permanently removed.

This does not mean, of course, that we must think of waiting for the age of universal harmony.

No previous civilization has been able to achieve it, nor can we see even in the remote distance, that day of the Messiah, when national barriers will no longer exist and all mankind will live in brotherhood and concord. Until then, the nations must narrow their aspirations to achieve a tolerable *modus vivendi.*

The world has yet long to wait for eternal peace. Meanwhile nations live side by side in a state of relative peace, secured by treaties and international law, but based chiefly on the fundamental equality between them.

But it is different with the people of Israel. There is no such equality in the nations' dealings with the Jews. The basis is absent upon which treaties and international law may be applied mutual respect. Only when this basis is established when the equality of Jews with other nations becomes a fact, can the Jewish problem be considered solved.

An equality of this kind did exist in the now long forgotten past, but unfortunately, under present conditions, the prospect that will readmit the Jewish people to the status of nationhood is so remote as to seem illusory. It lacks most of the essential attributes by which a nation is recognized. It lacks that autochthonous life which is inconceivable without a common language and customs and without cohesion in space. The Jewish people has no fatherland of its own, though many motherlands; no center of focus or gravity, no government of its own, no official representation. They home everywhere, but are nowhere at home. The nations have *never* to deal with a Jewish nation but always with mere *Jews.* The Jews are not a nation because they lack a certain distinctive national character, inherent in all other nations, which is formed by common residence in a single state. It was clearly impossible for this national character to be developed in the Diaspora; the Jews seem rather to have lost all remembrance of their former home. Thanks to their ready adaptability, they have all the more easily acquired characteristics, not inborn, of the people among whom fate has thrown them. Often to please their protectors, they recommend their traditional individuality entirely. They acquired or persuaded themselves into certain cosmopolitan tendencies which could no more appeal to others than bring satisfaction to themselves.

In seeking to fuse with other peoples they deliberately renounced to some extent their own nationality. *Yet nowhere did they succeed in obtaining from their fellow-citizens recognition as natives of equal status.*

But the greatest impediment in the path of the Jews to an independent national existence is that they do not feel its need. Not only that, but they go so far as to deny its authenticity. . . .

In the seemingly irrelevant circumstances, that the Jews are not regarded as an independent nation by other nations, rests in part the secret of their abnormal position and of their endless misery. Merely to belong to this people is to be indelibly stigmatized a mark repellent to non-Jews and painful to the Jews themselves. However, this phenomenon is rooted deeply in human nature.

Among the living nations of the earth the Jews are as a nation long since dead.

With the loss of their country, the Jewish people lost their independence, and fell into a decay which is not compatible with existence as a whole vital organism. The state was crushed before the eyes of the nations. But after the Jewish people had ceased to exist as an actual state, as a political entity, they could nevertheless not submit to total annihilation—they lived on spiritually as a nation. . . .

A fear of the Jewish ghost has passed down the generations and the centuries. First a breeder of prejudice, later in conjunction with other forces we are about to discuss, it culminated in Judeophobia.

Judeophobia, together with other symbols, superstitions and idiosyncrasies, has acquired legitimacy phobia among all the peoples of the earth with whom the Jews had intercourse. Judeophobia is a variety of demonopathy with the distinction that it is not peculiar to particular races but is common to the whole of mankind, and that this ghost is not disembodied like other ghosts but partakes of flesh and blood, must endure pain inflicted by the fearful mob that imagines itself endangered.

Judeophobia is a psychic aberration. As a psychic aberration it is hereditary, and as a disease transmitted for two thousand years it is incurable.

It is this fear of ghosts, the mother of Judeophobia that has evoked this abstract—I might say Platonic hatred—thanks to which the whole Jewish nation is wont to be held responsible for the real or supposed misdeeds of its individual members, and to be libeled in so many ways, to be buffeted about so shamefully.

Friend and foe alike have tried to explain or to justify this hatred of the Jews by bringing all sorts of charges against them. They are said to have crucified Jesus, to have drunk the blood of Christians, to have poisoned wells, to have taken usury, to have exploited the peasant, and so on. These and a thousand and one other charges against an entire people have been proved groundless. They showed their own weakness in that they had to be trumped up wholesale in order to quiet the evil conscience of the Jew-baiters, to justify the condemnation of an entire nation, to demonstrate the necessity of burning the Jew, or rather the Jewish ghost, at the stake. He who tries to prove too much proves nothing at all. Though the Jews may justly be charged with many shortcomings, those shortcomings are, at all events, not such great vices, not such capital crimes, as to justify the condemnation of the entire people. In individual cases, indeed, these accusations are contradicted by the fact that the Jews get along fairly well with their Gentile neighbors. This is the reason that the charges preferred are usually of the most general character, made up out of whole cloth, based to a certain extent on a priori reasoning, and true at best in individual cases, but not admitting of proof as regards the whole people.

In this way have Judaism and Anti-Semitism passed for centuries through history as inseparable companions. Like the Jewish people, the real wandering Jew, Anti-Semitism, too, seems as if it would never die. He must be blind indeed who will assert that the Jews are not *the chosen people,* the people chosen for universal hatred. No matter how much the nations are at variance in their relations with one another, however diverse their instincts and aims, they join hands in their hatred of the Jews; on this one matter all are agreed. The extent and the manner in which this antipathy is shown depend of course upon the cultural status of each people. The antipathy as such, however, exists in all places and at all times, whether it appears in the form of deeds of violence, as envious jealousy, or under the guise of tolerance and protection. To be robbed as a Jew or to be protected as a Jew is equally humiliating, equally destructive to the self-respect of the Jews

Having analyzed Judeophobia as an hereditary form of demonopathy, peculiar to the human race, and having represented Anti-Semitism as proceeding from an inherited aberration of the human mind, we must draw the important conclusion that we must give up contending against these hostile impulses as we must against every other inherited predisposition.

No people, generally speaking, likes foreigners. Ethnologically, this cannot be brought as a charge against any people. Now, is the Jew subject to *this* general law to the same extent as the other nationalities? Not at all! The aversion which meets the foreigner in a strange land can be repaid in equal coin in his home country. The non-Jew pursues his own interest in a foreign country openly and without giving offense. It is everywhere considered natural that he should fight for these interests, alone or in conjunction with others. The foreigner has no need to *be,* or to *seem* to *be,* a patriot. But as for the Jew, not only is he not a native in his own home country, but he is also not a foreigner; he is, in very truth, the stranger *par excellence.* He is regarded as neither friend nor foe but an alien, of whom the only thing known is that he has no home.

One *distrusts* the foreigner but does not *trust* the Jew. The foreigner has a claim to hospitality, which he can repay in the same coin. The Jew can make no such return, consequently he can make no claim to hospitality. He is not a guest, much less a welcome guest. He is more like a beggar, and what beggar is welcome! He is rather a refugee; and where is the refugee to whom a refuge may not be refused?

The Jews are aliens who can have no representatives, because they have no country. Because they have none, because their home has no boundaries within which they can be entrenched, their misery too is boundless. The *general law* does not apply to the Jews as true aliens, but there are everywhere *laws for the Jews,* and if the general law is to apply to them, a special and explicit by-law is required to confirm it. Like the Negroes, like women, and unlike all free peoples, they must be *emancipated.* If, unlike the Negroes, they belong to an advanced race, and if, unlike women, they can produce not only women of distinction, but also distinguished men, even men of greatness, then it is very much the worse for them.

Since the Jew is nowhere at home, nowhere regarded as a native, he remains an alien everywhere. That he himself and his ancestors as well are born in the country does not alter this fact in the least.

In the great majority of cases, he is treated as a stepchild, as a Cinderella; in the most favorable cases he is regarded as an adopted child whose rights may be questioned; *never* is he considered a legitimate child of the fatherland.

The German proud of his Teutonism, the Slav, the Celt, not one of them admits that the Semitic Jew is his equal by birth; and even if he be ready, as a man of culture, to admit him to all civil rights, he will never quite forget that his fellow-citizen is a Jew The *legal emancipation* of the Jews is the culminating achievement of our century. But *legal* emancipation is not *social* emancipation, and with the proclamation of the former the Jews are still far from being emancipated from their exceptional *social position.*

[. . .]

This degrading dependence of the ever alien Jew upon the non-Jew is reinforced by another factor, which makes amalgamation of the Jews with the original inhabitants of a land absolutely impossible. In the great struggle for existence, civilized peoples readily submit to laws which help to transform their struggle into a peaceful competition, a noble emulation. In this respect a distinction is usually made between the native and the foreigner, the first, of course, always receiving the preference. Now, if this distinction is drawn even against the foreigner of equal birth, how harshly is it applied to the ever alien Jew! The beggar who dares to cast longing eyes upon a country not his own is in the position of a young virgin's suitor, guarded against him by jealous relatives! And if he nevertheless prosper and succeed in plucking a flower here and there from its soil, woe to the ill-fated man! He must expect the fate of the Jews of Spain and Russia.

The Jews, moreover, do not suffer only when they meet with notable success. Wherever they are congregated in large numbers, they must, by their very preponderance, hold an advantage in competition with the non-Jewish population. Thus, in the western provinces [of Russia] we see the Jews squeezed together, leading a wretched existence in dreadful poverty, while charges of Jewish exploitation are continually pressed.

To sum up then, to the living the Jew is a corpse, to the native a foreigner, to the homesteader a vagrant, to the proprietary a beggar, to the poor an exploiter and a millionaire, to the patriot a man without a country, for all a hated rival.

[. . .]

If we already knew where to direct our steps, were we compelled to emigrate again, we could surely make a vast step forward. We must set vigorously to work to complete the great task of *self-liberation.* We must use all the resources which human intellect and human experience have devised, instead of leaving our national regeneration to blind chance. The territory to be acquired must be fertile, well-situated and sufficiently extensive to allow the settlement of several millions. The land, as national property, must be inalienable. Its selection is, of course, of the first and highest importance, and must not be left to off-hand decision or to certain preconceived sympathies of individuals, as has alas, happened lately. This land must be *uniform* and continuous in extent, for it lies in the very nature of our problem that we must possess as a counterpoise to our disposition *one single refuge,* since a *number* of refuges would again be equivalent to our old dispersion. Therefore, the selection of a permanent, national land, meeting all requirements, must be made with every precaution and confided to one single body, through a committee of experts selected from our directorate. Only such a supreme tribunal will be able, after thorough and comprehensive investigation, to give an opinion and decide upon *which of* the two continents and upon *which* territory in them our final choice should fall. Only then, and not before, should the directorate, together with an associated body of capitalists, as founders of a stock company later to be organized, acquire a tract of land sufficient for the settlement, in the course of time, of several million Jews. This tract might form a small territory in North America, or a sovereign Pashalik in Asiatic Turkey recognized by the [Ottoman] Porte and the other Powers as neutral. It would certainly be an important duty of the directorate to secure the assent of the Porte, and probably of the other European cabinets to this plan. Under the supervision of the directorate, the land purchased would have to be divided by surveyors into small parcels, which could be assigned according to the local conditions to agricultural, building, or manufacturing purposes. Every parcel laid off thus (for agricultural, house and garden, town-hall, factory, etc.) would form a lot which would be transferred to the purchaser in accordance with his wishes.

After a complete survey and the publication of detailed maps and a comprehensive description of the land, a part of the lots would be sold to Jews for an adequate payment at a price, exactly fixed in proportion to the original purchase price, perhaps a little above it. Part of the proceeds of the sale, together with the profits, would belong to the stock company, and part would flow into a fund to be administered by the directorate, for the maintenance of destitute immigrants. For the establishment of this fund the directorate could also open a national subscription. It is definitely to be expected that our brethren everywhere would hail with joy such an appeal for subscriptions and that the most liberal donations would be made for so sacred a purpose.

Each title-deed delivered to the purchaser, with his name entered and signed by the directorate and the company, must bear the exact number of the lot upon the general map so that each purchaser would know exactly the location of the piece of ground—field, or building lot—which he purchases as his individual property.

Assuredly, many a Jew, who is still bound to his old home by an unenviable occupation, would gladly grasp the opportunity to throw out an anchor to windward by such a deed and to escape those sad experiences so numerous in the immediate past

That part of the territory which would be assigned to the directorate for free distribution, against the national subscription mentioned and the expected profits, would be given to destitute but able-bodied immigrants, recommended by local committees.

Since the donations to the national subscription would not come in at once, but say in annual contributions, the colonization, also, would be carried out gradually and in a fixed order.

If the experts find in favor of Palestine or Syria, this decision would not be based on the assumption that the country could be transformed in time by labor and industry into a quite productive one. In this event the price of land would rise in proportion. But should they prefer North America, however, we must hasten. If one considers that in the last thirty-eight years the population of the United States of America has risen from seventeen millions to fifty millions, and that the increase in population for the next forty years will probably continue in the same proportion, it is evident that immediate action is necessary, if we do not desire to eliminate for all time the possibility of establishing in the New World a secure refuge for our unhappy brethren.

Every one who has the slightest judgment can see at first glance that the purchase of lands in America would, because of the swift rise of that country, not be a risky, but a lucrative enterprise.

Whether this act of national self-help on our part might turn out profitably or otherwise, however, is of little consequence as compared with the great significance which such an undertaking would have for the future of our unsettled people; for our future will remain insecure and precarious unless a radical change in our position is made. This change cannot be brought about by the civil emancipation of the Jews in this or that state, but only by the auto-emancipation of the Jewish people as a nation, the foundation of a colonial community belonging to the Jews, which is some day to become our inalienable home, our country.

There will certainly be plenty of counter-arguments. We will be charged with reckoning without our host. What land will grant us permission to settle a nation within its borders? At first glance, our building would appear from this standpoint to be a house of cards to divert children and wits. We think, however, that only thoughtless childhood could be diverted by the sight of shipwrecked voyagers who desire to build a little boat in order to leave inhospitable shores. We even go as far as to say that we expect, strangely enough, that those inhospitable people will aid us in our departure. Our "friends" will see us leave with the same pleasure with which we turn our back upon them.

Of course, the establishment of a Jewish refuge cannot come about without the support of the governments. In order to obtain the latter and to insure the perpetual existence of a refuge, the molders of our national regeneration must proceed with caution and perseverance. What we seek is at bottom neither new nor dangerous to anyone. Instead of the many *refuges* which we have always been accustomed to seek, we would fain have *one single refuge*, the existence of which, however, would have to be politically assured.

Let "Now or never" be our watchword. Woe to our descendants, woe to the memory of our Jewish contemporaries, if we let this moment pass by!

The Jews are not a living nation: they are everywhere aliens; therefore they are despised.

The civil and political emancipation of the Jews is not sufficient to raise them in the estimation of the peoples.

The proper, the only solution, is in the creation of a Jewish nationality, of a people living upon its own soil, the auto-emancipation of the Jews; their return to the ranks of the nations by the acquisition of a Jewish homeland.

We must not persuade ourselves that humanity and enlightenment alone can cure the malady of our people.

The lack of national self-respect and self-confidence of political initiative and of unity, are the enemies of our national renaissance.

That we may not be compelled to wander from one exile to another, we must have an extensive, productive land of refuge, a *center* which is our own. The present moment is the most favorable for this plan.

The international Jewish question must have a national solution. Of course, our national regeneration can only proceed slowly. We must take the first step. Our *descendants* must follow us at a measured and not over-precipitant speed.

The national regeneration of the Jews must be initiated by a congress of Jewish notables. No sacrifice should be too great for this enterprise which will assure our people's future, everywhere endangered.

The financial execution of the undertaking does not present insurmountable difficulties.

Help yourselves, and God will help you!

2.   Ahad Ha-Am's "The Jewish State and the Jewish Problem," a Counterargument to the Idea of a Jewish State, 1897

Not all Jewish thinkers agreed with the Zionists that a Jewish state would solve the "Jewish problem" of the persecution of Jewish minorities in various European countries. Asher Zvi Ginzberg (his pen name Ahad Ha-Am is a Hebrew phrase meaning "one of the people") was one of those thinkers. Ha-Am (1856–1927) was born in the Ukraine. In 1868 he began a process of self-education that first led him through the works of Maimonides and other thinkers of the medieval Jewish enlightenment.

From there he progressed to the works of modern Jewish thinkers and finally to the wider world of Russian and German literature and philosophy. Because of a series of personal problems and disappointments, Ha-Am was very pessimistic and prone to self-doubt and was unwilling to assume a position of leadership within the emerging Zionist nationalist movement—even though he was offered the opportunity on at least two occasions. Nevertheless, he was an influential thinker whose writings and advice were sought by leaders such as Chaim Weizmann. More important, his critical essays provided a counterweight to the overly positivist ideas and programs of mainstream Zionism. In the essay reprinted here, he challenges the optimistic vision of the Zionists.

Some months have passed since the Zionist Congress, but its echoes are still reverberating in daily life and in the press. All kinds of gatherings—small and large, local and regional—are taking place. Since the delegates returned home, they have been calling public meetings and repeatedly regaling us with tales of the wonders that were enacted before their very eyes. The wretched, hungry public is listening, becoming ecstatic, and hoping for salvation. It is inconceivable to them that "they"—the Jews of the West—can fail to succeed in what they propose. Heads grow hot and hearts beat fast, and many "leaders" who had for years—until last August—lived only for Palestinian settlement, and for whom a penny donation in aid of Jewish labor in Palestine or the Jaffa School was worth the world, have now lost their bearings and ask one another: "What's the good of this sort of work? The days of the Messiah are near at hand, and we busy ourselves with trifles! The time has come for great deeds, for great men, men of the West, have enlisted in the cause and march before us."

There has been a revolution in their world, and, to emphasize it, they have given the cause itself a new name: It is no longer "Love of Zion" (Hibbat Zion), but "Zionism" (Zioniyuth). Indeed, there are even "precisionists" who, being determined to leave no loophole for error, use only the European form of the name ("Zionismus")—thus announcing to all and sundry that they are not talking about anything so antiquated as Hibbat Zion, but about a new, up-to-date movement, which comes, like its name, from the West, where people are innocent of the Hebrew language.

Nordau's address on the general condition of the Jews was a sort of introduction to the business of the Congress. It described in incisive language the sore troubles, whether material or spiritual, which beset the Jews the world over. In eastern countries their trouble is material: they must struggle without letup to satisfy the most elementary physical needs—for the crust of bread and the breath of air which are denied them because they are Jews. In the West, in lands where the Jews are legally emancipated, their material condition is not particularly bad, but their spiritual state is serious: they want to take full advantage of their legal rights, and cannot; they long to be accepted by the gentile majority and to become part of the national society, but they are kept at arm's

Arthur Hertzberg, ed., *The Zionist Idea: A Historical Analysis and Reader* (Garden City, N.Y.: Doubleday, 1959), pp. 262–269.

length; they hope for love and brotherhood, but they encounter looks of hatred and contempt on all sides; they know that they are in no way inferior to their neighbors in ability or virtue, but they have it continually thrown in their faces that they are of an inferior type and that they are unfit to rise to the level of the Aryans. And more to the same effect.

Well—what then?

Nordau himself did not touch on this question, which was outside the scope of his address. But the whole Congress was the answer. Beginning as it did with Nordau's address, the Congress meant this: that in order to escape from all these troubles it is necessary to establish a Jewish State.

There is no doubt that, even when the Jewish State is established, Jewish settlement will be able to advance only by small degrees, as permitted by the resources of the people themselves and by the progress of the economic development of the country. Meanwhile the natural increase of Jewish population both within the Palestinian settlement and in the Diaspora, will continue, with the inevitable result that, on the one hand, Palestine will have less and less room for the new immigrants, and, on the other hand, despite continual emigration, the number of those remaining outside Palestine will not be appreciably diminished. In his opening speech at the Congress, Dr. Herzl, wishing to demonstrate the superiority of his State idea to the previous form of Palestinian colonization, calculated that by the latter method it would take nine hundred years before all the Jews could be settled in their land. The members of the Congress applauded this as a conclusive argument. But it was a cheap victory. The Jewish State itself, do what it will, will find no way to make a more favorable calculation.

The truth is bitter, but with all its bitterness it is better than illusion. We must admit to ourselves that the "ingathering of the exiles" is unattainable by natural means. We may, by natural means, someday establish a Jewish State; it is possible that the Jews may increase and multiply within it until the "land is filled with them"—but even then the greater part of our people will remain scattered on foreign soils. "To gather our scattered ones from the four corners of the earth" (in the words of the Prayer Book) is impossible. Only religion, with its belief in a miraculous redemption, can promise such a consummation.

But if this is so, if the Jewish State, too, means not an "ingathering of the exiles" but the settlement of a small part of our people in Palestine, then how will this solve the material problem of the Jewish masses in the lands of the Diaspora?

The material problem will not be ended by the establishment of a Jewish State, and it is, indeed, beyond our power to solve it once and for all. (Even now there are various means at our disposal to alleviate this problem to a greater or lesser degree, e.g., by increasing the proportion of farmers and artisans among our people *in all lands,* etc.) Whether or not we create a Jewish State, the material situation of the Jews will always basically depend on the economic condition and the cultural level of the various nations among which we are dispersed.

Thus we are driven to the conclusion that the real and only basis of Zionism is to be found in another problem, the spiritual one.

But the spiritual problem appears in two differing forms, one in the West and one in the East, which explains the fundamental difference between western "Zionism" and eastern "Hibbat Zion." Nordau dealt only with the western form of the problem, apparently knowing nothing about the eastern; and the Congress as a whole concentrated on the first, and paid little attention to the second.

The western Jew, having left the ghetto and having sought acceptance by the gentile majority, is unhappy because his hope of an open-armed welcome has been disappointed. Perforce he returns to his own people and tries to find within the Jewish community that life for which he yearns—but in vain. The life and horizon of the Jewish community no longer satisfy him. He has already grown accustomed to a broader social and political life, and on the intellectual side the work to be done for our Jewish national culture does not attract him, because that culture has played no part in his earliest education and is a closed book to him. In this dilemma he therefore turns to the land of his ancestors and imagines how good it would be if a Jewish State were re-established there—a State and society organized exactly after the pattern of other States. Then he could live a full, complete life within his own people, and he could find at home all that he now sees outside, dangled before his eyes but out of reach. Of course, not all the Jews will be able to take wing and go to their State; but the very existence of the Jewish State will also raise the prestige of those who remain in exile, and their fellow citizens will no longer despise them and keep them at arm's length, as though they were base slaves, dependent entirely on the hospitality of others. As he further contemplates this fascinating vision, it suddenly dawns on his inner consciousness that even now, before the Jewish State is established, the mere idea of it gives him almost complete relief. It provides an opportunity for communal work and political excitement; his emotions find an outlet in a field of activity which is not subservient to non-Jews; and he feels that, thanks to this ideal, he stands once more spiritually erect and has regained his personal dignity, without overmuch trouble and purely by his own efforts. So he devotes himself to the ideal with all the ardor of which he is capable; he gives rein to his fancy and lets it soar as it will, beyond reality and the limitations of human power. For it is not the attainment of the ideal that he needs; its pursuit alone is sufficient to cure him of his spiritual disease, which is that of an inferiority complex, and the loftier and more distant the ideal, the greater its power to exalt.

This is the basis of western Zionism and the secret of its attraction. But eastern Hibbat Zion originated and developed in a different setting. It, too, began as a political movement; but, being a result of material evils, it could not be content with an "activity" consisting only of outbursts of feeling and fine phrases, which may satisfy the heart but not the stomach. Hibbat Zion began at once to express itself in concrete activities—in the establishment of colonies in Palestine. This practical work soon clipped the wings of fancy and demonstrated conclusively that Hibbat Zion could not lessen the material woe of the

Jews by one iota. One might, therefore, have thought that, when this fact became patent, the Hovevei Zion would give up their effort and cease wasting time and energy on work which brought them no nearer their goal. But, no: they remained true to their flag and went on working with the old enthusiasm, though most of them did not understand, even in their own minds, why they did so. They felt instinctively that they must go on; but, as they did not clearly appreciate the nature of this feeling, the things that they did were not always effectively directed toward the true goal, to which they were unconsciously dedicated.

For at the very time when the material tragedy in the East was at its height, the heart of the eastern Jews was sensitive to another tragedy as well—a spiritual one; and when the Hovevei Zion began to work for the solution of the material problem, the national instinct of the people felt that in this work it would find the remedy for its spiritual trouble. Hence the people rallied to this effort and did not abandon it even after it had become obvious that it was an ineffective instrument for curing the material trouble of the Jews.

The eastern form of the spiritual problem is absolutely different from the western. In the West it is the problem of the Jews; in the East, the *problem of Judaism.* The first weighs on the individual; the second, on the nation. The one is felt by Jews who have had a European education; the other, by Jews whose education has been Jewish. The one is a product of anti-Semitism, and is dependent on anti-Semitism for its existence; the other is a natural product of a real link with a millennial culture, and it will remain unsolved and unaffected even if the troubled of the Jews all over the world attain comfortable economic positions, are on the best possible terms with their neighbors, and are admitted to the fullest social and political equality.

It is not only the Jews who have come out of the ghetto; Judaism has come out, too. For the Jews the exodus from the ghetto is confined to certain countries and is due to toleration; but Judaism has come out (or is coming out) of its own accord, wherever it has come into contact with modern culture. This contact with modern culture overturns the inner defences of Judaism, so that it can no longer remain isolated and live a life apart. The spirit of our people desires further development; it wants to absorb the basic elements of general culture which are reaching it from the outside world, to digest them and to make them a part of itself, as it has done before at various periods of its history. But the conditions of its life in exile are not suitable for such a task. In our time culture expresses itself everywhere through the form of the national spirit, and the stranger who would become part of culture must sink his individuality and become absorbed in the dominant environment. In exile, Judaism cannot, therefore, develop its individuality in its own way. When it leaves the ghetto walls, it is in danger of losing its essential being or—at very least—its national unity; it is in danger of being split up into as many kinds of Judaism, each with a different character and life, as there are countries of the dispersion.

Judaism is, therefore, in a quandry: It can no longer tolerate the *Galut* form which it had to take on, in obedience to its will-to-live, when it was exiled from its own country; but, without that form, its life is in danger. So it seeks to return to its historic center, where it will be able to live a life developing in a natural way, to bring its powers into play in every department of human culture, to broaden and perfect those national possessions which it has acquired up to now, and thus to contribute to the common stock of humanity, in the future as it has in the past, a great national culture, the fruit of the unhampered activity of a people living by the light of its own spirit. For this purpose Judaism can, for the present, content itself with little. It does not need an independent State, but only the creation in its native land of conditions favorable to its development; a good-sized settlement of Jews working without hindrance in every branch of civilization, from agriculture and handicrafts to science and literature. This Jewish settlement, which will be a gradual growth, will become in course of time the center of the nation, wherein its spirit will find pure expression and develop in all its aspects to the highest degree of perfection of which it is capable. Then, from this center, the spirit of Judaism will radiate to the great circumference, to all the communities of the Diaspora, to inspire them with new life and to preserve the over-all unity of our people. When our national culture in Palestine has attained that level, we may be confident that it will produce men in the Land of Israel itself who will be able, at a favorable moment, to establish a State there—one which will be not merely a State of Jews but a really Jewish State.

This Hibbat Zion, which concerns itself with the preservation of Judaism at a time when Jewry is suffering so much, is something odd and unintelligible to the "political" Zionists of the West, just as the demand of R. Johanan ben Zakkai for "Yavneh" was strange and unintelligible to the comparable party of his time. And so political Zionism cannot satisfy those Jews who care for Judaism; its growth seems to them to be fraught with danger to the object of their own aspiration.

The secret of our people's persistence is—as I have tried to show elsewhere—that at a very early period the Prophets taught it to respect only the power of the spirit and not to worship material power. Therefore, unlike the other nations of antiquity, the Jewish people never reached the point of losing its self-respect in the face of more powerful enemies. As long as we remain faithful to this principle, our existence has a secure basis, and we shall not lose our self-respect, for we are not spiritually inferior to any nation. But a political ideal which is not grounded in our national culture is apt to seduce us from loyalty to our own inner spirit and to beget in us a tendency to find the path of glory in the attainment of material power and political dominion, thus breaking the thread that unites us with the past and undermining our historical foundation. Needless to say, if the political ideal is not attained, it will have disastrous consequences, because we shall have lost the old basis without finding a new one. But even if it is attained under present conditions, when we are a scattered people not only in the physical but also in the spiritual sense—even then, Judaism will be in great danger. Almost all our great men—those, that is, whose education and social position have prepared them to be at the head of a Jewish State—are spiritually far removed from Judaism and have no true conception of its nature and its value. Such men, however loyal to their State and devoted to its interests, will necessarily envisage those interests by the standards of the foreign culture which they themselves have imbibed; and they will endeavor, by moral persuasion or even by force, to implant that culture in the Jewish State, so that in the end the Jewish State will be a State of Germans or Frenchmen of the Jewish race. We have even now a small example of this process in Palestine.

History teaches us that in the days of the Herodian house Palestine was indeed a Jewish State, but the national culture was despised and persecuted. The ruling house did everything in its power to implant Roman culture in the country and frittered away the resources of the nation in the building of heathen temples, amphitheaters, and so forth. Such a Jewish State would spell death and utter degradation for our people. Such a State would never achieve sufficient political power to deserve respect, while it would be estranged from the living inner spiritual force of Judaism. The puny State, being "tossed about like a ball between its powerful neighbors, and maintaining its existence only by diplomatic shifts and continual truckling to the favored of fortune," would not be able to give us a feeling of national glory; the national culture, in which we might have sought and found our glory, would not have been implanted in our State and would not be the principle of its life. So we should really be then— much more than we are now—"a small and insignificant nation," enslaved in spirit to "the favored of fortune," turning an envious and covetous eye on the armed force of our "powerful neighbors"; our existence in such terms, as a sovereign State would not add a glorious chapter to our national history.

Would it not be better for "an ancient people which was once a beacon to the world" to disappear than to end by reaching such a goal as this? Mr. Lilienblum reminds me that there exist today small States, like Switzerland, which are safeguarded against interference by the other nations and are not forced to "continual truckling." But a comparison between Palestine and small countries like Switzerland overlooks the geographical position of Palestine and its religious importance for all the world. These two facts will make it quite impossible for its "powerful neighbors" (by which expression, of course, I did not mean, as Mr. Lilienblum interprets, "the Druses and the Persians") to leave it alone. Even after it has become a Jewish State, they will all still keep an eye on it, and each power will try to influence its policy in a direction favorable to itself, after the pattern of events in other weak states (like Turkey) in which the great European nations have "interests."

In sum: Hibbat Zion, no less than "Zionism," wants a Jewish State and believes in the possibility of the establishment of a Jewish State in the future. But while "Zionism" looks to the Jewish State to furnish a remedy for poverty and to provide complete tranquillity and national glory, Hibbat Zion knows that our State will not give us all these things until "universal Righteousness is enthroned and holds sway over nations and States"—it looks to a Jewish State to provide only a "secure refuge" for Judaism and a cultural bond to unite our nation. "Zionism," therefore, begins its work with political propaganda; Hibbat

Zion begins with national culture, because only *through* the national culture and *for its sake* can a Jewish State be established in such a way as to correspond with the will and the needs of the Jewish people.

3. The Husayn-McMahon Correspondence, Negotiating the Establishment of an "Arab Kingdom" in the Middle East, 1915–1916

The ambiguity of the Husayn-McMahon correspondence has left a trail of misunderstandings and conflict with regard to the geopolitics of the modern Middle East. Husayn ibn-Ali (1855–1931) was the amir of Mecca around the time World War I broke out. His distrust of the Ottoman Committee of Union and Progress (Young Turks) and his own political ambition led him in 1915 to open negotiations with the British. Sharif Husayn (sharif is an honorary title indicating a claim to descent from the Prophet Muhammad) offered the British the possibility of his support through an "Arab" revolt against the Ottoman authorities. The term Arab *as he used it referred to the Arab tribes within the Arabian Peninsula. In return, Husayn expected British support for the establishment of an Arab kingdom under his leadership.*

Britain was very receptive to the idea, and the ensuing negotiations (July 1915–March 1916) between Sir Henry McMahon (the British High Commissioner in Egypt) and Sharif Husayn focused on the extent of the borders of the proposed Arab kingdom. A disagreement—whose resolution was postponed until after the war—arose about the Syrian coastal lands. Husayn insisted that they should be included in his kingdom. The British demurred, because they wanted to protect their own interests in those areas as well as the interests of their ally France.

1. From Sharif Husayn, 14 July 1915

Whereas the whole of the Arab nation without any exception have decided in these last years to accomplish their freedom, and grasp the reins of their administration both in theory and practice; and whereas they have found and felt that it is in the interest of the Government of Great Britain to support them and aid them in the attainment of their firm and lawful intentions (which are based upon the maintenance of the honour and dignity of their life) without any ulterior motives whatsoever unconnected with this object;

And whereas it is to their (the Arabs') interest also to prefer the assistance of the Government of Great Britain in consideration of their geographic position and economic interests, and also of the attitude of the above-mentioned Government, which is known to both nations and therefore need not be emphasized;

Great Britain, *Parliamentary Papers, 1939, Misc. No. 3,* Cmd. 5957.

For these reasons the Arab nation sees fit to limit themselves, as time is short, to asking the Government of Great Britain, if it should think fit, for the approval, through her deputy or representative, of the following fundamental propositions, leaving out all things considered secondary in comparison with these, so that it may prepare all means necessary for attaining this noble purpose, until such time as it finds occasion for making the actual negotiations:—

Firstly.—England will acknowledge the independence of the Arab countries, bounded on the north by Mersina and Adana up to the 37th degree of latitude, on which degree fall Birijik, Urfa, Mardin, Midiat, Jezirat (Ibn 'Umar), Amadia, up to the border of Persia; on the east by the borders of Persia up to the Gulf of Basra; on the south by the Indian Ocean, with the exception of the position of Aden to remain as it is; on the west by the Red Sea, the Mediterranean Sea up to Mersina. England to approve the proclamation of an Arab Khalifate of Islam.

Secondly.—The Arab Government of the Sharif will acknowledge that England shall have the preference in all economic enterprises in the Arab countries whenever conditions of enterprises are otherwise equal.

Thirdly.—For the security of this Arab independence and the certainty of such preference of economic enterprises, both high contracting parties will offer mutual assistance, to the best ability of their military and naval forces, to face any foreign Power which may attack either party. Peace not to be decided without agreement of both parties.

Fourthly.—If one of the parties enters into an aggressive conflict, the other party will assume a neutral attitude, and in case of such party wishing the other to join forces, both to meet and discuss the conditions.

Fifthly.—England will acknowledge the abolition of foreign privileges in the Arab countries, and will assist the Government of the Sharif in an International Convention for confirming such abolition.

Sixthly.—Articles 3 and 4 of this treaty will remain in vigour for fifteen years, and, if either wishes it to be renewed, one year's notice before lapse of treaty is to be given.

Consequently, and as the whole of the Arab nation have (praise be to God) agreed and united for the attainment, at all costs and finally, of this noble object, they beg the Government of Great Britain to answer them positively or negatively in a period of thirty days after receiving this intimation; and if this period should lapse before they receive an answer, they reserve to themselves complete freedom of action. Moreover, we (the Sharif's family) will consider ourselves free in work and deed from the bonds of our previous declaration which we made through Ali Effendi.

2. From Sir Henry McMahon, 24 October 1915

I have received your letter of the 29th Shawal, 1333, with much pleasure and your expressions of friendliness and sincerity have given me the greatest satisfaction.

I regret that you should have received from my last letter the impression that I regarded the question of the limits and boundaries with coldness and hesitation; such was not the case, but it appeared to me that the time had not yet come when that question could be discussed in a conclusive manner.

I have realised, however, from your last letter that you regard this question as one of vital and urgent importance. I have, therefore, lost no time in informing the Government of Great Britain of the contents of your letter, and it is with great pleasure that I communicate to you on their behalf the following statement, which I am confident you will receive with satisfaction:—

The two districts of Mersina and Alexandretta and portions of Syria lying to the west of the districts of Damascus, Homs, Hama and Aleppo cannot be said to be purely Arab, and should be excluded from the limits demanded.

With the above modification, and without prejudice of our existing treaties with Arab chiefs, we accept those limits.

As for those regions lying within those frontiers wherein Great Britain is free to act without detriment to the interest of her ally, France, I am empowered in the name of the Government of Great Britain to give the following assurances and make the following reply to your letter:—

1. Subject to the above modifications, Great Britain is prepared to recognize and support the independence of the Arabs in all the regions within the limits demanded by the Sharif of Mecca.

2. Great Britain will guarantee the Holy Places against all external aggression and will recognise their inviolability.

3. When the situation admits, Great Britain will give to the Arabs her advice and will assist them to establish what may appear to be the most suitable forms of government in those various territories.

4. On the other hand, it is understood that the Arabs have decided to seek the advice and guidance of Great Britain only, and that such European advisers and officials as may be required for the formation of a sound form of administration will be British.

5. With regard to the vilayets of Bagdad and Basra, the Arabs will recognise that the established position and interests of Great Britain necessitate special administrative arrangements in order to secure these territories from foreign aggression, to promote the welfare of the local populations and to safeguard our mutual economic interests.

I am convinced that this declaration will assure you beyond all possible doubt of the sympathy of Great Britain towards the aspirations of her friends the Arabs and will result in a firm and lasting alliance, the immediate results of which will be the expulsion of the Turks from the Arab countries and the freeing of the Arab peoples from the Turkish yoke, which for so many years has pressed heavily upon them.

I have confined myself in this letter to the more vital and important questions, and if there are any other matters dealt with in your letter which I have omitted to mention, we may discuss them at some convenient date in the future.

It was with very great relief and satisfaction that I heard of the safe arrival of the Holy Carpet and the accompanying offerings which, thanks to the clearness of your directions and the excellence of your arrangements, were landed without trouble or mishap in spite of the dangers and difficulties occasioned by the present sad war. May God soon bring a lasting peace and freedom to all peoples!

I am sending this letter by the hand of your trusted and excellent messenger, Sheikh Mohammed Ibn Arif Ibn Uraifan, and he will inform you of the various matters of interest, but of less vital importance, which I have not mentioned in this letter.

4. The Balfour Declaration, Stating the British Government's Support for a Jewish Homeland in Palestine, and Discussions Leading to Issuing It in 1917

In November 1917 the British government issued the Balfour Declaration promising the Zionists help in establishing a Jewish homeland in overwhelmingly Arab Palestine. Many historians see this promise as one of the main causes of the subsequent Palestinian-Israeli conflict. The documents presented here detail some of the discussion that took place before the final version of the Balfour Declaration was approved by the War Cabinet—a ministerial executive committee that was a much-reduced version of the government of Prime Minister David Lloyd George.

The British Federation of Zionists (represented by Chaim Weizmann and Nahum Sokolow) lobbied the British government for support of their project. The British, however, faced the difficulty that under the secret terms of the Sykes-Picot Agreement (1916) between Britain and France, Palestine was to be governed by an international mandate and not simply by the British in the postwar era. Furthermore, the British knew from the Husayn-McMahon correspondence that many Arabs expected Palestine to be part of a postwar Arab kingdom led by Sharif Husayn himself. However, several factors tipped the balance in favor of the Zionists. First, the British wanted to ascertain that American Zionists would encourage the U.S. Congress to join the British war effort against the Germans. The War Cabinet suspected that the Germans were preparing to offer the Zionists some support. Thus, after asking the Zionists to obtain French support for a British mandate over Palestine, the War Cabinet authorized Foreign Secretary Lord Balfour to issue his declaration of support.

The following documents summarize discussions within the War Cabinet about the ramifications of supporting the Zionists. Observe that throughout these discussions no mention was made of the wishes of the Arab inhabitants of Palestine or their right to self-determination.

"The Balfour Declaration," *Times* (London), 9 November 1917, p. 1.

Foreign Office
November 2nd, 1917

Dear Lord Rothschild [a French Zionist],

I have much pleasure in conveying to you, on behalf of His Majesty's Government, the following declaration of sympathy with Jewish Zionist aspirations which has been submitted to, and approved by, the Cabinet.

"His Majesty's Government view with favour the establishment in Palestine of a national home for the Jewish people, and will use their best endeavours to facilitate the achievement of this object, it being clearly understood that nothing shall be done which may prejudice the civil and religious rights of existing non-Jewish communities in Palestine, or the rights and political status enjoyed by Jews in any other country."

I should be grateful if you would bring this declaration to the knowledge of the Zionist Federation.

Yours sincerely,
Arthur James Balfour

1. Cambon Letter to Sokolow, 4 June 1917

You were good enough to present the project to which you are devoting your efforts, which has for its object the development of Jewish colonization in Palestine. You consider that, circumstances permitting, and the independence of the Holy Places being safeguarded on the other hand, it would be a deed of justice and of reparation to assist, by the protection of the Allied Powers, in the renaissance of the Jewish nationality in that Land from which the people of *Israel* were exiled so many centuries ago.

The French Government, which entered this present war to defend a people wrongfully attacked, and which continues the struggle to assure the victory of right over might, can but feel sympathy for your cause, the triumph of which is bound up with that of the Allies.

I am happy to give you herewith such assurance.

2. Official Zionist Formula, 18 July 1917

H. M. Government, after considering the aims of the Zionist Organisation, accepts the principle of recognising Palestine as the National Home of the Jewish people and the right of the Jewish people to build up its National life in Palestine under a protection to be established at the conclusion of Peace, following upon the successful issue of the war.

H. M. Government regards as essential for the realisation of this principle the grant of internal autonomy to the Jewish nationality in Palestine, freedom of immigration for Jews, and the establishment of a Jewish National Colonising Corporation for the re-settlement and economic development of the country.

The conditions and forms of the internal autonomy and a charter for the Jewish National Colonising Corporation should, in the view of H. M.

Government, be elaborated in detail and determined with the representatives of the Zionist Organisation.

3. Minutes of War Cabinet Meeting No. 227, Minute No. 2, 3 September 1917

The War Cabinet had under consideration correspondence which had passed between the Secretary of State for Foreign Affairs and Lord Rothschild on the question of the policy to be adopted towards the Zionist movement. In addition to the draft declaration of policy included in the above correspondence, they had before them an alternative draft prepared by Lord Milner. They had also before them a Memorandum by Mr. Montagu entitled "The Anti-Semitism of the present Government."

It was suggested that a question raising such important issues as to the future of Palestine ought, in the first instance, to be discussed with our Allies, and more particularly with the United States.

On the question of submitting Lord Milner's draft for the consideration of the United States Government, Mr. Montagu urged that the use of the phrase "the home of the Jewish people" would vitally prejudice the position of every Jew elsewhere and expand the argument contained in his Memorandum. Against this it was urged that the existence of a Jewish State or autonomous community in Palestine would strengthen rather than weaken the situation of Jews in countries where they were not yet in possession of equal rights, and that in countries like England, where they possessed such rights and were identified with the nation of which they were citizens, their position would be unaffected by the existence of a national Jewish community elsewhere. The view was expressed that, while a small influential section of English Jews were opposed to the idea, large numbers were sympathetic to it, but in the interests of Jews who wished to go from countries where they were less favourably situated, rather than from any idea of wishing to go to Palestine themselves.

With reference to a suggestion that the matter might be postponed, the Acting Secretary of State for Foreign Affairs pointed out that this was a question on which the Foreign Office had been very strongly pressed for a long time past. There was a very strong and enthusiastic organisation, more particularly in the United States, who were zealous in this matter, and his belief was that it would be of most substantial assistance to the Allies to have the earnestness and enthusiasm of these people enlisted on our side. To do nothing was to risk a direct breach with them, and it was necessary to face this situation.

The War Cabinet decided that—

The views of President Wilson should be obtained before any declaration was made, and requested the Acting Secretary of State for Foreign Affairs to inform the Government of the United States that His Majesty's Government were being pressed to make a declaration in sympathy with the Zionist movement, and to ascertain their views as to the advisability of such a declaration being made.

4. Minutes of War Cabinet Meeting No. 245, Minute No. 18, 4 October 1917

With reference to War Cabinet 227, Minute 2, the Secretary of State for Foreign Affairs stated that the German Government were making great efforts to capture the sympathy of the Zionist Movement. This Movement, though opposed by a number of wealthy Jews in this country, had behind it the support of a majority of Jews, at all events in Russia and America, and possibly in other countries. He saw nothing inconsistent between the establishment of a Jewish national focus in Palestine and the complete assimilation and absorption of Jews into the nationality of other countries. Just as English emigrants to the United States became, either in the first or subsequent generations, American nationals, so, in future, should a Jewish citizenship be established in Palestine, would Jews become either Englishmen, Americans, Germans, or Palestinians. What was at the back of the Zionist Movement was the intense national consciousness held by certain members of the Jewish race. They regarded themselves as one of the great historic races of the world, whose original home was Palestine, and these Jews had a passionate longing to regain once more this ancient national home, Other Jews had become absorbed into the nations among whom they and their forefathers had dwelt for many generations. Mr. Balfour then read a very sympathetic declaration by the French Government which had been conveyed to the Zionists, and he stated that he knew that President Wilson was extremely favourable to the Movement.

Attention was drawn to the contradictory telegrams received from Colonel House and Justice Brandeis.

The Secretary was instructed to take the necessary action.

The War Cabinet further decided that the opinions received upon this draft declaration should be collated and submitted to them for decision.

5. Minutes of War Cabinet Meeting No. 259, Minute No. 12, 25 October 1917

With reference to War Cabinet 245, Minute 18, the Secretary mentioned that he was being pressed by the Foreign Office to bring forward the question of Zionism, an early settlement of which was regarded as of great importance.

Lord Curzon stated that he had a Memorandum on the subject in course of preparation.

The question was adjourned until Monday, 29th October, or some other day early next week.

6. Minutes of War Cabinet Meeting No. 261, Minute No. 12, 31 October 1917

With reference to War Cabinet 245, Minute 18, the War Cabinet had before them a note by the Secretary, and also a memorandum by Lord Curzon on the subject of the Zionist movement.

The Secretary of State for Foreign Affairs stated that he gathered that everyone was now agreed that, from a purely diplomatic and political point of view, it was desirable that some declaration favourable to the aspirations of the Jewish nationalists should now be made. The vast majority of Jews in Russia and America, as, indeed, all over the world, now appeared to be favourable to Zionism. If we could make a declaration favourable to such an ideal, we should be able to carry on extremely useful propaganda both in Russia and America. He gathered that the main arguments still put forward against Zionism were twofold:—

(*a.*) That Palestine was inadequate to form a home for either the Jewish or any other people.

(*b.*) The difficulty felt with regard to the future position of Jews in Western countries.

With regard to the first, he understood that there were considerable differences of opinion among experts regarding the possibility of the settlement of any large population in Palestine, but he was informed that, if Palestine were scientifically developed, a very much larger population could be sustained than had existed during the period of Turkish misrule. As to the meaning of the words "national home," to which the Zionists attach so much importance, he understood it to mean some form of British, American, or other protectorate, under which full facilities would be given to the Jews to work out their own salvation and to build up, by means of education, agriculture, and industry, a real centre of national culture and focus of national life. It did not necessarily involve the early establishment of an independent Jewish State, which was a matter for gradual development in accordance with the ordinary laws of political evolution.

With regard to the second point, he felt that, so far from Zionism hindering the process of assimilation in Western countries, the truer parallel was to be found in the position of an Englishman who leaves his country to establish a permanent home in the United States. In the latter case there was no difficulty in the Englishman or his children becoming full nationals of the United States, whereas, in the present position of Jewry, the assimilation was often felt to be incomplete, and any danger of a double allegiance or non-national outlook would be eliminated.

Lord Curzon stated that he admitted the force of the diplomatic arguments in favour of expressing sympathy, and agreed that the bulk of the Jews held Zionist rather than anti-Zionist opinions. He added that he did not agree with the attitude taken up by Mr. Montagu. On the other hand, he could not share the optimistic views held regarding the future of Palestine. These views were not merely the result of his own personal experiences of travel in that country, but of careful investigations from persons who had lived for many years in the country. He feared that by the suggested declaration we should be raising false expectations which could never be realised. He attached great importance to the necessity of retaining the Christian and Moslem Holy Places in Jerusalem and Bethlehem, and, if this were to be effectively done, he did not see how the

Jewish people could have a political capital in Palestine. However, he recognised that some expression of sympathy with Jewish aspirations would be a valuable adjunct to our propaganda, though he thought that we should be guarded in the language used in giving expression to such sympathy. . . .

5.   Division of the Ottoman Empire: The Treaty of Sèvres, August 10, 1920

Even before World War I ended, the British and the French (along with other Allies) had determined that the Ottoman Empire would not survive in its prewar form. In 1916, in secret negotiations (the Sykes-Picot Agreement), France and Britain agreed to divide the Arab Middle East among themselves. In 1920, diplomats at the Peace Conference of Versailles incorporated some of the ideas of Sykes-Picot into the peace settlement; the final division of the Ottoman lands was spelled out in the Treaty of Sèvres, concluded on August 10, 1920. The treaty harshly reduced the area of Ottoman control to a small portion of Anatolia (most of modern-day Turkey). The Arab lands of the Ottoman Empire were divided between the French and the British. This dismembering proved critical in shaping the nations of the modern Middle East and set the stage for later conflicts borne out of contrary expectations and aspirations among the populations of the region.

Part III: Political Clauses

Section I. Constantinople

ART. 36.   Subject to the provisions of the present Treaty, the High Contracting Parties agree that the rights and title of the Turkish Government over Constantinople shall not be affected, and that the said Government and His Majesty the Sultan shall be entitled to reside there and to maintain there the capital of the Turkish State.

Nevertheless, in the event of Turkey failing to observe faithfully the provisions of the present Treaty, or of any treaties or conventions supplementary thereto, particularly as regards the protection of the rights of racial, religious or linguistic minorities, the Allied Powers expressly reserve the right to modify the above provisions, and Turkey hereby agrees to accept any dispositions which may be taken in this connection.

Great Britain, *Treaty Series* (1920), no. 11, Cmd. 966, pp. 16–32. This document may also be found in J. C. Hurewitz, *The Middle East and North Africa in World Politics* (New Haven, Conn.: Yale University Press, 1975), pp. 220–225.

Section II. Straits

ART. 37.   The navigation of the Straits, including the Dardanelles, the Sea of Marmora and the Bosphorus, shall in future be open, both in peace and war, to every vessel of commerce or of war and to military and commercial aircraft, without distinction of flag.

These waters shall not be subject to blockade, nor shall any belligerent right be exercised nor any act of hostility be committed within them, unless in pursuance of a decision of the Council of the League of Nations.

ART. 38.   The Turkish Government recognizes that it is necessary to take further measures to ensure the freedom of navigation provided for in Article 37, and accordingly delegates, so far as it is concerned, to a Commission to be called the "Commission of the Straits," and hereinafter referred to as "the Commission," the control of the waters specified in Article 39.

The Greek Government, so far as it is concerned, delegates to the Commission the same powers and undertakes to give it in all respects the same facilities.

Such control shall be exercised in the name of the Turkish and Greek Governments respectively, and in the manner provided in this Section.

ART. 39.   The authority of the Commission will extend to all the waters between the Mediterranean mouth of the Dardanelles and the Black Sea mouth of the Bosphorus, and to the waters within three miles of each of these mouths.

This authority may be exercised on shore to such extent as may be necessary for the execution of the provisions of this Section.

ART. 40.   The Commission shall be composed of representatives appointed respectively by the United States of America (if and when that Government is willing to participate), the British Empire, France, Italy, Japan, Russia (if and when Russia becomes a member of the League of Nations), Greece, Roumania, and Bulgaria and Turkey (if and when the two latter States become members of the League of Nations). Each Power shall appoint one representative. The representatives of the United States of America, the British Empire, France, Italy, Japan and Russia shall each have two votes. The representatives of Greece, Roumania, and Bulgaria and Turkey shall each have one vote. Each Commissioner shall be removable only by the Government which appointed him. . . .

Section III. Kurdistan

ART. 62.   A Commission sitting at Constantinople and composed of three members appointed by the British, French and Italian Governments respectively shall draft within six months from the coming into force of the present Treaty a scheme of local autonomy for the predominantly Kurdish areas lying east of the Euphrates, south of the southern boundary of Armenia as it may be hereafter determined, and north of the frontier of Turkey with Syria and Mesopotamia, as defined in Article 27, II. (2) and (3). If unanimity cannot be secured on any question, it will be referred by the members of the Commission to their respective Governments. The scheme shall contain full safeguards for the protection of the Assyro-Chaldeans and other racial or religious minorities within these areas, and with this object a Commission composed of British, French, Italian, Persian and Kurdish representatives shall visit the spot to examine and decide what rectifications, if any, should be made in the Turkish frontier, where, under the provisions of the present Treaty, that frontier coincides with that of Persia.

ART. 63.   The Turkish Government hereby agrees to accept and execute the decisions of both the Commissions mentioned in Article 62 within three months from their communication to the said Government.

ART. 64.   If within one year from the coming into force of the present Treaty the Kurdish peoples within the areas defined in Article 62 shall address themselves to the Council of the League of Nations in such a manner as to show that a majority of the population of these areas desires independence from Turkey, and if the Council then considers that these peoples are capable of such independence and recommends that it should be granted to them, Turkey hereby agrees to execute such a recommendation, and to renounce all rights and title over these areas.

The detailed provisions for such renunciation will form the subject of a separate agreement between the Principal Allied Powers and Turkey.

If and when such renunciation takes place, no objection will be raised by the Principal Allied Powers to the voluntary adhesion to such an independent Kurdish State of the Kurds inhabiting that part of Kurdistan which has hitherto been included in the Mosul Vilayet.

Section IV. Smyrna

ART. 65.   The provisions of this Section will apply to the city of Smyrna and the adjacent territory defined in Article 66, until the determination of their final status in accordance with Article 83. . . .

ART. 67.   A Commission shall be constituted within fifteen days from the coming into force of the present Treaty to trace on the spot the boundaries of the territories described in Article 66. This Commission shall be composed of three members nominated by the British, French and Italian Governments respectively, one member nominated by the Greek Government, and one nominated by the Turkish Government.

ART. 68.   Subject to the provisions of this Section, the city of Smyrna and the territory defined in Article 66 will be assimilated, in the application of the present Treaty, to territory detached from Turkey.

ART. 69.   The city of Smyrna and the territory defined in Article 66 remain under Turkish sovereignty. Turkey however transfers to the Greek Government the exercise of her rights of sovereignty over the city of Smyrna and the said territory. In witness of such sovereignty the Turkish flag shall remain permanently hoisted over an outer fort in the town of Smyrna. The fort will be designated by the Principal Allied Powers.

ART. 70.   The Greek Government will be responsible for the administration of the city of Smyrna and the territory defined in Article 66, and will effect this administration by means of a body of officials which it will appoint specially for the purpose.

ART. 71.   The Greek Government shall be entitled to maintain in the city of Smyrna and the territory defined in Article 66 the military forces required for the maintenance of order and public security.

ART. 72.   A local parliament shall be set up with an electoral system calculated to ensure proportional representation of all sections of the population, including racial, linguistic and religious minorities. Within six months from the coming into force of the present Treaty the Greek Government shall submit to the Council of the League of Nations a scheme for an electoral system complying with the above requirements; this scheme shall not come into force until approved by a majority of the Council.

The Greek Government shall be entitled to postpone the elections for so long as may be required for the return of the inhabitants who have been banished or deported by the Turkish authorities, but such postponement shall not exceed a period of one year from the coming into force of the present Treaty.

ART. 73.   The relations between the Greek administration and the local parliament shall be determined by the said administration in accordance with the principles of the Greek Constitution. . . .

ART 83.   When a period of five years shall have elapsed after the coming into force of the present Treaty the local parliament referred to in Article 72 may, by a majority of votes, ask the Council of the League of Nations for the definitive incorporation in the Kingdom of Greece of the city of Smyrna and the territory defined in Article 66. The Council may require, as a preliminary, a plebiscite under conditions which it will lay down.

In the event of such incorporation as a result of the application of the foregoing paragraph, the Turkish sovereignty referred to in Article 69 shall cease. Turkey hereby renounces in that event in favour of Greece all rights and title over the city of Smyrna and the territory defined in Article 66. . . .

Section VI. Armenia

ART. 88.   Turkey, in accordance with the action already taken by the Allied Powers, hereby recognises Armenia as a free and independent State.

ART. 89.   Turkey and Armenia as well as the other High Contracting Parties agree to submit to the arbitration of the President of the United States of America the question of the frontier to be fixed between Turkey and Armenia in the Vilayets of Erzerum, Trebizond, Van and Bitlis, and to accept his decision thereupon, as well as any stipulations he may prescribe as to access for Armenia to the sea, and as to the demilitarisation of any portion of Turkish territory adjacent to the said frontier.

ART. 90.   In the event of the determination of the frontier under Article 89 involving the transfer of the whole or any part of the territory of the said Vilayets to Armenia, Turkey hereby renounces as from the date of such decision all rights and title over the territory so transferred. The provisions of the present Treaty applicable to territory detached from Turkey shall thereupon become applicable to the said territory.

The proportion and nature of the financial obligations of Turkey which Armenia will have to assume, or of the rights which will pass to her, on account of the transfer of the said territory will be determined in accordance with Articles 241 to 244, Part VIII (Financial Clauses) of the present Treaty.

Subsequent agreements will, if necessary, decide all questions which are not decided by the present Treaty and which may arise in consequence of the transfer of the said territory.

ART. 91.   In the event of any portion of the territory referred to in Article 89 being transferred to Armenia, a Boundary Commission, whose composition will be determined subsequently, will be constituted within three months from the delivery of the decision referred to in the said Article to trace on the spot the frontier between Armenia and Turkey as established by such decision.

ART. 92.   The frontiers between Armenia and Azerbaijan and Georgia respectively will be determined by direct agreement between the States concerned.

If in either case the States concerned have failed to determine the frontier by agreement at the date of the decision referred to in Article 89, the frontier line in question will be determined by the Principal Allied Powers, who will also provide for its being traced on the spot.

ART. 93.   Armenia accepts and agrees to embody in a Treaty with the Principal Allied Powers such provisions as may be deemed necessary by these Powers to protect the interests of inhabitants of that State who differ from the majority of the population in race, language, or religion.

Armenia further accepts and agrees to embody in a Treaty with the Principal Allied Powers such provisions as these Powers may deem necessary to protect freedom of transit and equitable treatment for the commerce of other nations.

Section VII. Syria, Mesopotamia, Palestine

ART. 94.   The High Contracting Parties agree that Syria and Mesopotamia shall, in accordance with the fourth paragraph of Article 22, Part I (Covenant of the League of Nations), be provisionally recognised as independent States subject to the rendering of administrative advice and assistance by a Mandatory until such time as they are able to stand alone.

A Commission shall be constituted within fifteen days from the coming into force of the present Treaty to trace on the spot the frontier line described in Article 27, II (2) and (3). This Commission will be composed of three members nominated by France, Great Britain and Italy respectively, and one member nominated by Turkey; it will be assisted by a representative of Syria for the Syrian frontier, and by a representative of Mesopotamia for the Mesopotamian frontier.

The determination of the other frontiers of the said States, and the selection of the Mandatories, will be made by the Principal Allied Powers.

ART. 95.   The High Contracting Parties agree to entrust, by application of the provisions of Article 22, the administration of Palestine, within such boundaries as may be determined by the Principal Allied Powers, to a Mandatory to be selected by the said Powers. The Mandatory will be responsible for putting into effect the declaration originally made on November 2, 1917, by the British Government, and adopted by the other Allied Powers, in favour of the establishment in Palestine of a national home for the Jewish people, it being clearly understood that nothing shall be done which may prejudice the civil and religious rights of existing non-Jewish communities in Palestine, or the rights and political status enjoyed by Jews in any other country.

The Mandatory undertakes to appoint as soon as possible a special Commission to study and regulate all questions and claims relating to the different religious communities. In the composition of this Commission the religious interests concerned will be taken into account. The Chairman of the Commission will be appointed by the Council of the League of Nations.

ART. 96.   The terms of the mandates in respect of the above territories will be formulated by the Principal Allied Powers and submitted to the Council of the League of Nations for approval.

ART. 97.   Turkey hereby undertakes, in accordance with the provisions of Article 132, to accept any decisions which may be taken in relation to the questions dealt with in this Section.

Section VIII. Hedjaz

ART. 98.   Turkey, in accordance with the action already taken by the Allied Powers, hereby recognises the Hedjaz as a free and independent State, and renounces in favour of the Hedjaz all rights and titles over the territories of the former Turkish Empire situated outside the frontiers of Turkey as laid down by the present Treaty, and comprised within the boundaries which may ultimately be fixed.

ART. 99.   In view of the sacred character attributed by Moslems of all countries to the cities and the Holy Places of Mecca and Medina, His Majesty the King of Hedjaz undertakes to assure free and easy access thereto to Moslems of every country who desire to go there on pilgrimage or for any other religious object, and to respect and ensure respect for the pious foundations which are or may be established there by Moslems of any countries in accordance with the precepts of the law of the Koran.

ART. 100.   His Majesty the King of the Hedjaz undertakes that in commercial matters the most complete equality of treatment shall be assured in the territory of the Hedjaz to the persons, ships and goods of nationals of any of the Allied Powers, or of any of the new States set up in the territories of the former Turkish Empire, as well as to the persons, ships and goods of nationals of States, Members of the League of Nations.

Section IX. Egypt, Soudan, Cyprus

1. Egypt

ART. 101.   Turkey renounces all rights and title in or over Egypt. This renunciation shall take effect as from November 5, 1914. Turkey declares that in conformity with the action taken by the Allied Powers she recognizes the Protectorate proclaimed over Egypt by Great Britain on December 18, 1914.

ART. 102.   Turkish subjects habitually resident in Egypt on December 18, 1914, will acquire Egyptian nationality *ipso facto* and will lose their Turkish nationality, except that if at that date such persons were temporarily absent from, and have not since returned to, Egypt they will not acquire Egyptian nationality without a special authorisation from the Egyptian Government.

ART. 103.   Turkish subjects who became resident in Egypt after December 18, 1914, and are habitually resident there at the date of the coming into force of the present Treaty may, subject to the conditions prescribed in Article 105 for the right of option, claim Egyptian nationality, but such claim may in individual cases be refused by the competent Egyptian authority.

ART. 104.   For all purposes connected with the present Treaty, Egypt and Egyptian nationals, their goods and vessels, shall be treated on the same footing, as from August 1, 1914, as the Allied Powers, their nationals, goods and vessels, and provisions in respect of territory under Turkish sovereignty, or of territory detached from Turkey in accordance with the present Treaty, shall not apply to Egypt.

ART. 105.   Within a period of one year after the coming into force of the present Treaty persons over eighteen years of age acquiring Egyptian nationality under the provisions of Article 102 will be entitled to opt for Turkish nationality. In case such persons, or those who under Article 103 are entitled to claim Egyptian nationality, differ in race from the majority of the population of Egypt, they will within the same period be entitled to opt for the nationality of any State in favour of which territory is detached from Turkey, if the majority of the population of that State is of the same race as the person exercising the right to opt.

Option by a husband covers a wife and option by parents covers their children under eighteen years of age.

Persons who have exercised the above right to opt must, except where authorised to continue to reside in Egypt, transfer within the ensuing twelve months their place of residence to the State for which they have opted. They will be entitled to retain their immovable property in Egypt, and may carry with them their movable property of every description. No export or import duties or charges may be imposed upon them in connection with the removal or such property.

ART. 106.   The Egyptian Government shall have complete liberty of action in regulating the status of Turkish subjects in Egypt and the conditions under which they may establish themselves in the territory.

ART. 107.   Egyptian nationals shall be entitled, when abroad, to British diplomatic and consular protection.

ART. 108.   Egyptian goods entering Turkey shall enjoy the treatment accorded to British goods.

ART. 109.   Turkey renounces in favour of Great Britain the powers conferred upon His Imperial Majesty the Sultan by the Convention signed at Constantinople on October 29, 1888, relating to the free navigation of the Suez Canal.

ART. 110.   All property and possessions in Egypt belonging to the Turkish Government pass to the Egyptian Government without payment.

ART. 111.   All movable and immovable property in Egypt belonging to Turkish nationals (who do not acquire Egyptian nationality) shall be dealt with in accordance with the provisions of Part IX (Economic Clauses) of the present Treaty.

ART. 112.   Turkey renounces all claim to the tribute formerly paid by Egypt.

Great Britain undertakes to relieve Turkey of all liability in respect of the Turkish loans secured on the Egyptian tribute.

These loans are:

The guaranteed loan of 1855;

The loan of 1894 representing the converted loans of 1854 and 1871;

The loan of 1891 representing the converted loan of 1877.

The sums which the Khedives of Egypt have from time to time undertaken to pay over to the houses by which these loans were issued will be applied as heretofore to the interest and the sinking funds of the loans of 1894 and 1891 until the final extinction of those loans. The Government of Egypt will also continue to apply the sum hitherto paid towards the interest on the guaranteed loan of 1855.

Upon the extinction of these loans of 1894, 1891 and 1855, all liability on the part of the Egyptian Government arising out of the tribute formerly paid by Egypt to Turkey will cease.

2. *Soudan*

ART. 113.   The High Contracting Parties declare and place on record that they have taken note of the Convention between the British Government and the Egyptian Government defining the status and regulating the administration of the Soudan, signed on January 19, 1899, as amended by the supplementary Convention relating to the town of Suakin signed on July 10, 1899.

ART. 114.   Soudanese shall be entitled when in foreign countries to British diplomatic and consular protection.

3. *Cyprus*

ART. 115.   The High Contracting Parties recognise the annexation of Cyprus proclaimed by the British Government on November 5, 1914.

ART. 116.   Turkey renounces all rights and title over or relating to Cyprus, including the right to the tribute formerly paid by that island to the Sultan.

ART. 117.   Turkish nationals born or habitually resident in Cyprus will acquire British nationality and lose their Turkish nationality, subject to the conditions laid down in the local law.

Section X. *Morocco, Tunis*

ART. 118.   Turkey recognises the French Protectorate in Morocco, and accepts all the consequences thereof. This recognition shall take effect as from March 30, 1912.

ART. 119.   Moroccan goods entering Turkey shall be subject to the same treatment as French goods.

ART. 120.   Turkey recognises the French Protectorate over Tunis and accepts all the consequences thereof. This recognition shall take effect as from May 12, 1881.

Tunisian goods entering Turkey shall be subject to the same treatment as French goods.

Section XI. *Libya, Aegean Islands*

ART. 121.   Turkey definitely renounces all rights and privileges which under the Treaty of Lausanne of October 18, 1912, were left to the Sultan in Libya.

ART. 122.   Turkey renounces in favour of Italy all rights and title over the following islands of the Aegean Sea; Stampalia (Astropalia), Rhodes (Rhodos), Calki (Kharki), Scarpanto, Casos (Casso), Pscopis (Tilos), Misiros (Nisyros), Calymnos (Kalymnos), Leros, Patmos, Lipsos (Lipso), Sini (Symi), and Cos (Kos), which are now occupied by Italy, and the islets dependent thereon, and also over the island of Castellorizzo. . . .

Section XIII. General Provisions

ART. 132.   Outside her frontiers as fixed by the present Treaty Turkey hereby renounces in favour of the Principal Allied Powers all rights and title which she could claim on any ground over or concerning any territories outside Europe which are not otherwise disposed of by the present Treaty.

Turkey undertakes to recognize and conform to the measures which may be taken now or in the future by the Principal Allied Powers, in agreement where necessary with third Powers, in order to carry the above stipulation into effect. . . .

ART. 139.   Turkey renounces formally all rights of suzerainty or jurisdiction of any kind over Moslems who are subject to the sovereignty or protectorate of any other State.

No power shall be exercised directly or indirectly by any Turkish authority whatever in any territory detached from Turkey or of which the existing status under the present Treaty is recognised by Turkey.

---

6.   Mustafa Kemal ("Atatürk") Outlines His Vision of the Recent Nationalist Past of Turkey and the Future of the Country, 1927

At the close of World War I, the Allies were intent on dismembering the Ottoman Empire, partly to punish the Ottomans for siding with the Central Powers and partly to extend British and French imperialist influence and presence into the eastern Mediterranean. According to the Treaty of Sèvres (1920), Italy and France would subdivide the southeastern region of Anatolia, an independent Armenian state centered around Erzurum would be established in the northeastern part, and Greece laid claim to extensive parts of southwestern Anatolia. The Turkish population of Anatolia was humiliated and left with an absurdly small territory to call its own. In addition, the Ottoman government was deprived of any real decision-making power; the Allies were in effect the real rulers at Istanbul, the capital.

In response to Allied occupation, various resistance groups emerged throughout Anatolia. By 1919 these disparate guerrilla groups were organized and led by army officers who were disillusioned with the armistice that the Allies forced the Ottoman sultan to sign. From the ranks of these officers emerged Mustafa Kemal (1881–1938), who slowly but surely gained absolute control of the national independence movement and later of independent Turkey.

Mustafa Kemal (known as Atatürk, which means "father of the Turks") delivered the following speech at the national convention of the People's Party of the Republic held in Ankara between October 15 and 20, 1927. He presented his version of the struggle for national independence. It is important to notice how he came to define the idea of "Turkey" and "Turk." Of equal importance is the purpose behind

---

Internet Atatürk Library, "The Speech." http://ataturk.turkiye.org/soylev/txwrdpdf/speech/pdf/spchdizi.htm (24 January 2003).

telling such a tale. In reading the text, keep in mind that he was presenting a uni-fying nationalistic account of the birth of Turkey. Whether "true" or not, the story remains one of the key elements of Turkish nationalism.

Gentlemen,

I landed at Samsun on the nineteenth day of May of year 1919. This was the general state of affairs:

The group of Powers which included the Ottoman Government had been defeated in the Great War. The Ottoman Army had been crushed on every front. An armistice had been signed under severe conditions. The prolongation of the Great War had left the people exhausted and impoverished. Those who had driven the people and the country into the World War had fled and now cared for nothing but their own safety. Vahdettin, the degenerate occupant of the [Ottoman] throne and the Caliphate, was seeking for some despicable way to save his person and his throne, the only objects of his anxiety. The Cabinet, of which Damat Ferit Pasha was the head, was weak and lacked dignity and courage. It was subservient to the will of the Sultan alone and agreed to every proposal that could protect its members and their sovereign.

The Army had been deprived of their arms and ammunition, and this state of affairs continued. The Entente Powers did not consider it necessary to respect the terms of the armistice. On various pretexts, their men-of-war and troops remained at Istanbul. The Vilayet of Adana was occupied by the French; Urfa, Maras, Antep by the English. In Antalya and Konya were the Italians, whilst at Merzifon and Samsun were English troops. Foreign officers and officials and their special agents were very active everywhere. At last, on the 15th May, that is to say, four days before the following account of events begins, the Greek Army, with the consent of the Entente Powers, had landed at Izmir.

Christian elements were also at work all over the country, either openly or in secret, trying to realize their own particular ambitions and thereby hasten the breakdown of the State. Certain information and authentic documents that fell into our hands later on prove that the Greek organization "Mavri Mira," established by the patriarchate in Istanbul, was forming bands, organizing meetings and making propaganda in the Vilayets. The Greek Red Cross and the Official Emigrants Commission supported the work of the "Mavri Mira." The formation of Boy Scouts in the Greek schools directed by the "Mavri Mira" were [sic] reinforced by the admission even of young men over twenty years of age. The Armenian Patriarch, Zaven Efendi, also worked in connection with the "Mavri Mira." The preparations made by the Armenians progressed side by side with those made by the Greeks. A society called the "Pontus" at Trabzon, Samsun, and other places along the entire Black Sea coast, having their headquarters in Istanbul, worked openly and successfully.

Considered Means for Salvation

On account of the appalling seriousness of the situation which was apparent everywhere, particularly in all the Vilayets, certain prominent personalities had begun to develop countermeasures to improve the situation. This resulted in new organizations being started. Thus, for instance, there were unions or societies at Edirne and surrounding districts called "Trakya-Pasaeli." In the east, at Erzurum and Elazig, the "Union of Defense of the National Rights of the Eastern Provinces" had been formed, also with their headquarters in Istanbul. Again, in Trabzon there was a society called the "Defense of Rights" and in Istanbul a "League for the Separation of Trabzon and its District." Through the exertions of the members of this league, sub-committees had been established at Of and in the district of Lazistan.

Some of the young patriots at Izmir, who since the 13th May had noticed distinct indications of the approaching occupation of the town, had held meetings about the distressing condition of affairs during the night of the 14th, and in principle had agreed to oppose the occupation by the Greeks, which at that time was considered to be practically an accomplished fact, designed to end in annexation, and resisted it on the principle of "No Annexation." During the same night, those of the inhabitants who were able to meet at the Jewish cemetery at Izmir drew up a protest and spread it broadcast. But as the Greek troops actually landed on the following morning this attempt failed to achieve the desired result.

National Organizations and Their Political Aims

I would like to give you a short account of the object and political aims of these organizations.

I had already had a conversation in Istanbul with some of the leaders of the "Trakya-Pasaeli" Society. They considered that the breakdown of the Ottoman Empire was extremely probable. In face of the threatened danger of the dismemberment of their country, their first thought was to save Eastern Trakya and later on if possible, to form a Turco-Islamic community that would include Western Trakya. The only way by which they thought they could realize this aim was to put their trust in England or, if this was not possible, in France. With this object they tried to get in touch with certain political personalities belonging to foreign countries. It was believed that their intention was to establish a Trakya Republic.

The object of the "Defense of the National Rights of the Eastern Provinces Union," on the other hand (Art. 2 of their regulations), was to use all lawful means to ensure the free exercise and development of their religious and political rights for all elements inhabiting these provinces; to defend, if it should become necessary, the historical and national rights of the Muslim population of these provinces; to institute an impartial inquiry for the purpose of discovering the motives, the instigators and agitators implicated in the extortions and cruelties committed in the Eastern Provinces, so that the guilty ones might be punished without delay; to do their utmost to remove the misunderstandings that existed between the different elements in the country, and to restore the good relations that had formerly existed between them; and, finally, to appeal to the Government to alleviate as far as it lay in their power the misery resulting from the war.

Acting on these principles that emanated from the Central Committee in Istanbul, the Erzurum Branch decided to undertake, in defense of the rights of the Turks, to inform the civilized world by means of convincing documents that since the deportation the people had been taking no part whatever in the excesses. Further, that the property of the Armenians had been protected up to the time when the country was invaded by the Russians. On the other hand that the Muslims had been compelled to suffer from the cruelest acts of violence and that some Armenians who had been saved from deportation had, in disobedience of orders, attacked their own protectors. The Branch were doing their very best to resist any attempt to annex the Eastern Provinces.

The members of the Erzurum Branch of the "Defense of the National Rights of the Eastern Provinces" resolved, as stated in their printed report, after having studied the propaganda circulated in these provinces as well the Turkish, Kurdish and Armenian questions, from the scientific and historical point of view, to concentrate their further efforts on the following points:

1. On no account to emigrate;
2. Forthwith to form scientific, economic and religious organizations;
3. To unite in the defense of even the smallest part of the Eastern Provinces that might be attacked.

It can be seen that the headquarters of the "Defense of the National Rights of the Eastern Provinces" were far too optimistic in their expectation to succeed through civil and scientific means. They continued to exert themselves indefatigably in this direction. For the purpose of defending the rights of Muslims dwelling in the Eastern Provinces they published a French journal, which they called *Le Pays*. They acquired the right to publish a magazine called *Hadisat*. They also presented memorials to the representatives of the Entente Powers in Istanbul and tried to send a delegation to Europe.

From the foregoing statements, it appears to me to be clearly evident that the possible cession of the Eastern Provinces to Armenia was the most important reason for this Society having been formed. They anticipated that this possibility might become a reality if those who tried to prove that the Armenians were in the majority in these provinces, claiming the oldest historical rights, were to succeed in misleading the public opinion of the world by alleged scientific and historic documents and by perpetuating the calumny that the Muslim population was composed of savages whose chief occupation was to massacre the Armenians. Consequently, the Society aimed at the defense of the national and historic rights by corresponding methods and arguments.

The fear also existed that a Greek Pontic State might be founded on the shores of the Black Sea. At Trabzon several persons had formed another society with the object of protecting the rights of the Muslim population, to safeguard their existence and prevent them from falling under the yoke of the Greeks.

Their political aim and program is already sufficiently obvious from its name: "The Society for the Cession of the Territory of Trabzon," whose head office was in Istanbul. In any case, they set out with the idea of separating this district from the Central Government.

Organizations, in the Country and in Istanbul, Hostile to the National Existence

Besides these organizations, which were being formed in the manner I have described, other societies and enterprises began to make their appearance. In the provinces of Diyarbakir, Bitlis and Elazig, among others, there was a "League for the Resuscitation of the Kurds" with its head offices also in Istanbul. Their aim was to erect a Kurdish State under foreign protection.

Work was going on at Konya and the surrounding district for the formation of a league having for its object the revival of Islam—also with its offices in Istanbul. There were organizations named "Unity and Freedom" and "Peace and Salvation" throughout almost the whole country.
[. . .]

Closer Examination of the State of Affairs

Let us return to a closer examination of the facts, so that we may rapidly review them as a whole.

Morally and materially, the enemy Powers were openly attacking the Ottoman Empire and the country itself. They were determined to disintegrate and annihilate both. The Padisah-Caliph had one sole anxiety—namely, to save his own life and comfort. The members of the government had the same feeling. Without being aware of it, the nation had no longer anyone to lead it, but lived in darkness and uncertainty, waiting to see what would happen. Those who began to understand clearly the terrors and the extent of the catastrophe were seeking some means whereby to save the country, each guided by the circumstances that surrounded him and the sentiments that inspired him. The Army existed merely in name. The commanders and other officers were still suffering from the exhaustion resulting from the war. Their hearts were bleeding on account of the threatened dismemberment of their country. Standing on the brink of the dark abyss which yawned before their eyes, they racked their brains to discover a way out of the danger. . . .

Here I must add and explain a very important point. The Nation and the Army had no suspicion at all of the Padisah-Caliph's treachery. On the contrary, on account of religious and traditional ties handed down for centuries, they remained loyal to the throne and its occupant. Seeking for means of salvation under the influence of this tradition, the security of the Caliphate and the Sultanate concerned them far more than their own safety. That the country could possibly be saved without a Caliph and without a Padisah was an idea too impossible for them to comprehend. And woe to those who ventured to think otherwise! They would immediately have been looked down upon as men without faith and without patriotism and as such would have been scorned.

I must mention another point here. In seeking ways to save the situation, it was considered to be especially important to avoid irritating the Great Powers—England, France and Italy. The idea that it was impossible to fight even one of these Powers had taken root in the mind of nearly everybody. Consequently, to think of doing so and thus bring on another war after the Ottoman Empire, all-powerful Germany and Austria-Hungary together had been defeated and crushed would have been looked upon as sheer madness. . . .

Considered Means for Salvation

Now, Gentlemen, I will ask you what decision could have been arrived at under such circumstances for salvation?

As I have already explained, there were three propositions that had been put forward:

1. To demand protection from England;
2. To accept the United States of America as a mandatory Power.

The originators of these two proposals had as their aim the preservation of the Ottoman Empire in its complete integrity and preferred to place it as a whole under the protection of a single Power, rather than allow it to be divided among several States.

3. The third proposal was to deliver the country by allowing each district to act in its own way and according to its own capability. Thus, for instance, certain districts, in opposition to the theory of separation, endeavored to remain an integral part of the Empire. Others holding a different opinion already appeared to regard the dismemberment of the Empire as an accomplished fact and sought only their own safety.

My above explanations are inclusive of the leading motives of these three kinds of propositions.

My Decision

I did not think any of these three proposals could be accepted as sagacious, because the arguments and considerations on which they were based were groundless. In reality, the foundations of the Ottoman Empire were themselves shattered at that time. Its existence was threatened with extermination. All the Ottoman districts were practically dismembered. Only the fatherland, affording protection to a mere handful of Turks, still remained, and it was now suggested also to divide this. Such expressions as: the Ottoman Empire, Independence, Padisah-Caliph, Government—all of them were mere meaningless words.

Whose existence was it essential to save? And with whose help? And how?

Therefore, what could be a serious and correct resolution?

In these circumstances, one resolution alone was possible, namely, to create a New Turkish State, the sovereignty and independence of which would be unreservedly recognized.

This was the resolution we adopted before we left Istanbul and which we began to put into execution immediately after we set foot on Anadolu soil at Samsun.

Independence or Death

These were the most logical and most powerful arguments in support of this resolution:

The foundational principle is that the Turkish nation should live in honor and dignity. Such a condition can only be attained by complete independence. No matter how wealthy and prosperous a nation is, if it is deprived of its independence it no longer deserves to be regarded otherwise than as a slave in the eyes of civilized world.

To accept the protectorate of a foreign Power is to admit lack of all human qualities, weakness and incapacity. It is not at all thinkable that those who have never been in such a humiliating state will appoint a foreign master out of their own desire.

But the Turk is both dignified and proud; he is also capable and talented. Such a nation will prefer to perish rather than subject itself to the life of a slave.

Therefore, Independence or Death!

[...]

As for the Caliphate, it would only have been the laughing-stock in the eyes of the civilized world, enjoying the blessings of science and technology. As you see, in order to carry out our resolution, questions had to be dealt with about which the nation had hitherto known practically nothing. It was imperative that questions which were considered dangerous to discuss publicly be discussed openly. We were compelled to rebel against the Ottoman Government, against the Padishah, against the Caliph of all Muslims, and we had to bring the whole nation and the army into a state of rebellion.

Dividing the Implementation into Stages and Reaching the Aim by Degrees

It was essential that the entire nation take up arms against whoever would venture to attack the fatherland of Turks and Turkish independence. It would undoubtedly have been of little advantage if we had made clear to the public at the very beginning all the implications of a resolution of such far-reaching importance. On the contrary, it was necessary to proceed by stages, utilizing all opportunities to prepare the feeling and the spirit of the nation and to try to reach our aim by degrees. This is actually what happened. If our attitude and our actions during nine years are examined in their logical sequence, however, it becomes evident that our general behavior has never deviated from the lines laid down in our original resolution, nor from the purpose we had set out to achieve.

In order to dispel any doubts which might be entertained, one fact is urged upon us for mutual examination.

As the national struggle, carried on for the sole purpose of delivering the country from foreign invasion, developed and was crowned with success, it was natural and inevitable that it would gradually, step by step to the present day, have established all the principles and forms essential in government founded on national sovereignty. The sovereign of the dynasty who, thanks to his traditional instincts, foresaw this fatal course of historical events, declared himself from the very beginning the most embittered enemy of the national struggle. I, also from the first moment on, anticipated this historical progress. But I did not disclose all of my views although I have maintained them all the time. If I had spoken too much about future prospects our realistic endeavors would have been looked upon as dreams; and consequently from the outset it would have caused the alienation of those who—discouraged by the closeness of dangers that threatened from without—were fearful of possible changes which would be contrary to their tradition, their way of thinking and their psychology. The only practical and safe road to success lay in dealing with each problem at the right time. This was the way to ensure the development and restoration of the nation. This was how I acted.

7. 'Ali 'Abd al-Raziq, an Egyptian Religious Scholar, Argues for the Separation of State and Religion, 1928

In the 1960s the conservative Islamic thinker Sayyid Qutb argued that the only true form of government in a predominantly Islamic society is the khilafat, *or Islamic state that is distinct from a secular constitutional government. Forty years earlier, 'Ali 'Abd al-Raziq (1888–1966), a professor at Al-Azhar University in Cairo, argued the exact opposite. In a short book he contended that Islam does not prescribe a particular form of government because it is a faith and not a political ideology. This argument—which went against the general view of Islam as* deen wa-dunya *(religion and politics)—unleashed a torrent of controversy and led to the removal of 'Abd al-Raziq from his post at the university. Even Islamic modernists like Rashid Rida considered this argument to be incorrect and a threat to Islamic society.*

1

I saw then that there exist obstacles that are not easily overcome by those who are of the opinion that the Prophet, peace be upon him, in addition to the Message [which he carried], was also a political king and a founder of a political state. I saw that every time these people attempted to avoid a trap, they would

---

'Ali 'Abd al-Raziq, *al-Islam wa-usul al-hukm, bahth fi al-Khilafah wa-al-hukumah fi al-Islam* (Bayrut: Dar Maktabat al-Hayah, 1966). This document may also be found in Charles Kurzman, *Liberal Islam* (New York: Oxford University Press, 1998), pp. 29–35. Copyright © 1998 by Oxford University Press, Inc. Used by permission of Oxford University Press, Inc.

fall into the next, and each time they attempted to rid themselves of a problem, the problem would confront them again more intensely than before.

There remains before the reader just one school of thought, and I hope that the reader will find that it offers a convenient starting point. . . . This is that Muhammad, peace be upon him, was a Messenger of a religious call, full of religiosity, untainted by a tendency to kingship or a call for government, and that he did not have a government, nor did he rule, and that he, peace be upon him, did not establish a kingdom, in the political sense of the term or anything synonymous with it. For he was but a messenger like his brethren, the preceding messengers. He was not a king nor the founder of a state, nor did he seek to rule. The above may not be a well-known view, and may in fact be resented by many Muslims, although it has great vision and is based on strong evidence.

2

Before we proceed to prove this, we must warn readers about an error that they may fall into unless they observe [the following] accurately and carefully— namely that the Message in itself obliges the Messenger to have some kind of leadership and authority over his people, but this is nothing like the leadership of kings and the authority they have over their subjects. Therefore, one should not confuse the leadership of the Message with that of kings, since they are so different that they could be opposites. Readers have seen that the leadership of Moses and Jesus with regards to their followers was not a kingly leadership, rather it was similar to the leadership of most messengers.

3

The nature of the honest religious call obliges its carrier to have primarily a perfection of the senses, whereby he will lack nothing in his body, sentiments, or feelings, and have nothing that would repulse. And, he must have—because he is a leader—a strong presence to awe those around him, and an attraction that would make him sympathetic enough that men and women would love him. He must also have spiritual perfection, which is necessary for his communication with the other world.

The Message requires its carrier to enjoy considerable social distinction among his people: and as it has been said: "God does not raise a prophet unless he is loved by his people, and unless he commands authority over his clan."[1] The Message also requires its carrier to have the kind of strength which will prepare him to influence the minds of people so that they will in heed his call.

---

[1]As the two Shaykhs [Muslim ibn al-Hajjaj, circa 821–875, and Muhammad ibn Isma'il Bukhari, 810–870] have narrated: "Thus prophets are sent from the best families of their clans . . ." which is part of a long *hadith* [tradition of the Prophet]. See *Taysir al-wusul ila al-jami' al-usul* [*The Facilitation of Arriving at the Compendium of Fundamentals*, by 'Abd al-Rahman Ibn al-Dayba' (1461–1537)], part 3, p. 320.

For God, may He be elevated, does not take the Message lightly and does not raise a messenger of righteousness unless He wants his call to be heeded, and that its teachings be engraved on the tables of the world, eternally preserved and intermixed with the realities of this world: "We have sent no apostle but that he should be obeyed by the will of God." (Qur'an, Sura 4, Verse 64)[2] "Surely messengers have been mocked before you; but what they had mocked rebounded on the mockers themselves. Say: 'Travel in the land and see what happened to those who disbelieved.'" (Sura 6, Verse 10) "But God wished to confirm the truth by His words, and wipe the unbelievers out to the last, so that Truth may be affirmed and falsehood negated, even though the sinners be averse." (Sura 8, Verses 7–8) "Our word had already been given before to Our servants, the apostles, that they would be helped. And that certainly, Our armies will be victorious [over them]." (Sura 37, Verses 171–173) "We will certainly help Our messengers and those who believe, in this world and on the day the witnesses take the stand, the day when their excuses will not benefit the evil-doers, and the condemnation and evil abode will be theirs." (Sura 40, Verses 51–52) The status of the Message grants its carrier a wider authority than that which exists between ruler and ruled, and ever) wider than that of a father over his children.

The Messenger may tackle the politics of his people as a king would, but the Prophet has a unique duty which he shares with no one, namely to communicate with the souls embedded in bodies, and to remove visual obstacles in order to look in upon the hearts embedded in chests. He has the right, nay, he must open up the hearts of his followers in order to reach the sources of love and hate, of good and evil, the passages of thought, the places of obsessions, the origins of intentions, the repository of morality. His is open work in general politics and concealed work in managing the relationship between partners, allies, master and slave, parents and children, and those relationships that only husband and wife are privy to. He has patronage over that which is manifest and that which is latent in life, as well as the management of the affairs of body and soul, and our worldly and heavenly relationships. He directs the politics of worldly living and that of the next world. The Message gives its carrier—as it is seen and beyond the way it is being seen—the right to communicate with each soul, care for it and manage its affairs, as well as the right to unlimited free conduct for every heart.

4

Readers should note that, in addition to the above, the Message of the Prophet, peace be upon him, specialized in a myriad of things that other messengers did not deal with. For he, peace be upon him, came with a call that God chose for

---

[2][Translations of Qur'anic verses are taken, with modifications, from *Al-Qur'an: A Contemporary Translation*, translated by Ahmed Ali, revised definitive edition (Princeton, N.J.: Princeton University Press. 1988).—Editor]

him to rally the people to. And God ordained that he deliver it in its entirety, and that he preside over it in order to complete the call to religion, so that grace be established and conflict not arise, and so that all religion be to God. This Message grants its carrier the kind of extreme perfection that human nature seeks to achieve, the kind of psychological strength that is the end-limit of what God had fated for His chosen messengers, and enough of God's support that would be compatible with this great and general call. In this vein, God has said: "Great have been the blessings of God on you." (Sura 4, Verse 113) "For you are always before Our eyes." (Sura 52, Verse 48). And in the *hadith* [tradition of the Prophet]: "By God, God will never humiliate you."[3] "For—without boasting of it—of all of Adam's children, I am my Lord's favorite."[4]

For this purpose, the authority of the Prophet, peace be upon him, was, because of his Message, a general authority; his orders to Muslims were obeyed; and his government was comprehensive. For nothing that the arm of government can reach is beyond the authority of the Prophet, peace be upon him, and any imaginable kind of leadership or authority is included in the Prophet's, peace be upon him, reign over the believers.

If it is reasoned that it is possible for a messenger's authority over his people to have gradations, then I would say that Muhammad, peace be upon him, should have the right to exercise the highest possible authority of all messengers, peace be upon them, command the highest possible obedience, have the strength of the prophecy, the authority of the Message, and the influence of the honest call, which God had fated to be raised over the call to wrongdoing and to remain on earth. The authority is sent by Heaven, from God, to him whose divine revelation is delivered by Heaven's angels. This sacred power, special to those worshipers of God whom He had raised as messengers, does not hold within it the meaning of kingship, nor does it resemble the power of kings, nor can the [authority of the] sultan of all sultans approximate it. This is the true leadership of the call to God and of the delivery of His Message, not kingly leadership. It is a message and a religion; it is a prophetic government not a government of sultans.

Once again we warn the reader not to confuse the two kinds of governments, and not to conflate the two kinds of trusteeships—the trusteeship of the Messenger, on account of his being a messenger, and the trusteeship of powerful kings. The Messenger's trusteeship over his people is a spiritual trusteeship whose origin is faith from the heart, and the heart's true submission followed by the submission of the body. On the other hand, the trusteeship of the ruler is a material one. It depends on subduing bodies without any connection to the heart. While the former is a trusteeship leading to God, the latter is one for managing life's concerns and populating the earth. While the former is religion,

---

[3]Reported by 'A'isha [wife of the Prophet, circa 614–678] at the beginning of the Revelation. Recorded by the two Shaykhs.

[4]Reported by Anas [ibn Malik, a companion of the Prophet, 710–796], recorded by [Abu 'Isa Muhammad] al-Tirmidhi [collector of *hadith*, died 892].

the latter is the world. The former is divine, the latter is human. The former is a religious leadership, the latter a political one—and there is much distance between politics and religion.

5

Having said this, we would like to draw readers' attention to something else. There exist a number of words [dealing with our subject matter] that are used as synonyms, and others as antonyms. A disagreement or a difference in point of view arises as a result of such usage. In addition, this creates a confusion in judgement. Such words are "king," "sultan," "ruler," "commander" "caliph," "state," "kingdom," "government," "caliphate," and so on. If we were to ask if the Prophet, peace be upon him, was a king or not, we would be asking if he, peace be upon him, had attributes other than being a messenger. Would it be correct to state that he indeed founded, or began to found, a political unity or not? Kingship in our use of it here—and there is no embarrassment faced by the reader who may wish to call him caliph, sultan, commander, or whatever pleases him—means a ruler over a people who have political unity and who have civilization. As for "government," "state," "sultanate," or "kingdom," we mean that which political scientists mean by the English words "kingship," "state," or "government" and the like.

We do not doubt that Islam constitutes religious unity or that Muslims form a unified group: or that the Prophet called for that political unity and had in fact achieved it before his death; and that he, peace be upon him, headed this religious unity as its only prayer leader (*imam*), its strong manager, its master whose orders are never questioned. And that in the interest of this Islamic unity, he, peace be upon him, struggled with all his might, and with the victorious support of God, conquered. He, peace be upon him, received the support of God's angels until he delivered his Message and completed his trusteeship. For he, peace be upon him, had the kind of authority over his people that no king before him or after him ever had. "The Prophet is closer to the faithful than they are themselves." (Sura 33, Verse 6) "No believing men and women have any choice in a matter after God and His Messenger have decided it. Whoever disobeys God and His Messenger has clearly lost the way and gone astray." (Sura 33, Verse 36)

And he who wants to term this religious unity a state and this authority of the Prophet, peace be upon him—which was an absolute authority—a kingship or caliphate, and the Prophet himself, peace be upon him, a king, caliph, or sultan, and so on, he is free to do so. For this is a matter of semantics which should not stop us here. What is important in what we have said is the meaning, and that we have specified to the reader with precision.

The crucial thing is to find out whether the leadership of the Prophet, peace be upon him, over his people was the leadership of the Message, or a kingly leadership. And whether the different aspects of his trusteeship that we observe at times in the biography [of the Prophet], peace be upon him, were aspects of a political state, or of a religious leadership. And whether this unity over which the Prophet, peace be upon him, presided was a unity of a state and a government or a religious unity proper, not a political one. And, finally, whether he, peace be upon him, as only a messenger or a king and a messenger.

6

The Glorious Qur'an supports the view that the Prophet, peace be upon him, had nothing to do with political kingship. Qur'anic verses are in agreement that his heavenly work did not go beyond delivering the Message, which is free of all meanings of authority. "He who obeys the Messenger obeys God; and if some turn away (remember) we have not sent you as a warden over them." (Sura 4, Verse 80) "This (Book) has been called by your people a falsehood, though it is the truth. Say: 'I am not a warden over you. A time is fixed in every prophecy: you will come to know in time.'" (Sura 6, Verse[s] 66–[67]) "So follow what is revealed to you by your Lord, for homage is due to no one but God, and turn away from idolators. Had He willed it, they would not have been idolators. We have not appointed you their guardian, nor are you their pleader." (Sura 6, Verses 106–1 07) "If your Lord had willed it, all the people on the earth would have come to believe, one and all." (Sura 10, Verse 99) "Say: 'O people, the truth has come to you from your Lord, so he who follows the right path does so for himself, and he who goes astray errs against himself, and I am not a guardian over you.'" (Sura 10, Verse 108) "We have not sent you as warden over them." (Sura [17], Verse 54) "Have you considered he take his own lust as his god? Can you act as a trustee for him?" (Sura 25, Verse 43) "We have sent down this Book to you with the truth for all mankind. So, he who comes to guidance does so for himself, and he who goes astray does so for his own loss; on you does not lie their guardianship." (Sura 39, Verse 41) "If they turn away (you are not responsible); we have not appointed you a warden over them. Your duty is to deliver the message." (Sura 42, Verse 48) "We are cognisant of what they say; but it is not for you to compel them. So keep on reminding through the Qur'an whoever fears my warning." (Sura 50, Verse 45) "Remind them: you are surely a reminder. You are not a warden over them, other than him who turns his back and denies, in which case he will be punished by God with the severest punishment." (Sura 88, Verses 21–24)

As the reader can see, the Qur'an clearly prohibits the Prophet, peace be upon him, from serving as a guardian of people, or their trustee, or a subduer . . . or a dominator. Moreover, he did not have the right to force people to become believers. In addition, he who is not a guardian or a dominator is not a king; for the prerequisite to kingship is absolute domination and which constitute an authority without limits. And he who was not a trustee over his people is also not a king. For God has said: "Muhammad is not the father of any of man among you, but messenger of God, and the seal of the prophets. God has knowledge of every thing." (Sura 33, Verse 40)

[. . .]

7

If we were to go beyond God's Book to the *sunna* [practice] of the Prophet, peace be upon him, we would find the matter even clearer, and the argument more insistent:

One of the Prophet's biographers[5] narrates the story of a man who came upon the Prophet, peace be upon him, to take care of a matter. As he stood before him, an intense shiver and fear overtook him. The Prophet, peace be upon him, said: " Be calm, for I am no king nor a subduer, for I am the son of a woman of Quraysh who used to eat dried meat in Mecca." And it has been said in the *hadith* that when the Prophet was given the choice by the angel Israfil of being a king-prophet or a worshipping prophet, the Prophet, peace be upon him, looked up to [the angel] Gabriel, peace be upon him, as his consultant. Gabriel looked down to the ground, indicating humility. And as the story goes, Gabriel indicated for him to be humble. So the Prophet said: "A worshipping prophet." As is evident, this makes it very clear that the Prophet, peace be upon him, was not a king, and did not seek kingship, nor did he, peace be upon him, desire it.

Look between the two covers of the Qur'an for open or latent evidence supporting those who think that the Islamic religion has a political character, and then look for evidence, as hard as you can, among the *hadiths* of the Prophet, peace be upon him—these pure sources of religion which are within your hands, close to you. If you were to look in them for evidence or anything resembling it, you will find no proof, only guesses, and guessing does not replace Truth.

8

Islam is a religious call to God and is a school of thought, from among many such schools, which seeks to reform a certain type of people, guiding them to what will render them closer to God, may He be elevated, and opening up the path to everlasting happiness, which God had prepared for His righteous worshipers. [Islam] is a religious unity that God sought as a bond linking all people, and with which he wanted to surround all the regions of the earth. [. . .]

It is reasonable to say that the world could adopt one religion and that all human beings could be organized into one religious union. However, for the entire world to adopt one government and to be grouped in a shared political union would be foreign to human nature and have nothing to do with God's will. For this is a worldly aim, and God, may He be elevated, has rendered it a matter to be resolved by our minds, and has left people free to manage it in the

---

[5]*The Biography of the Prophet*, by Ahmad bin Zayni Dahlan, who died in the year 1304 of the *hijra* [1923 A.D.]. From the book entitled *Iktifa' al-qanu' bima huwa matbu'* [*The Contentment of the Satisfied with What Is Printed*].

manner that their minds, knowledge, interests, desires, and tendencies would guide them. God's wisdom in this aims at maintaining differences among people. "But if your Lord had pleased, He could have made all human beings into one community (*umma*). But they would still have differed from one another, except those on whom your Lord had mercy." (Sura 11, Verses 118–119) In addition, in order that competition continue among people so that [the] population [of the earth] would be achieved. "If God did not make people deter one another, this earth would indeed be depraved. But gracious is God to the people of the world." (Sura 2, Verse 251) And, so that the Book's purpose be achieved and God's will be done.

This is one of the worldly concerns on which the Prophet, peace be upon him, had denied himself the right to pass judgment or arbitration. For he, peace be upon him, stated that "you are more knowledgeable of your worldly concerns." This is a worldly concern; and the world from beginning to end, and all that it encompasses of concerns and goals, is too trivial for God to have it managed by anything beside the minds He endowed us with, and what He had placed within us of sentiments and desires, and what He had taught us of names and of what things are called; all this is too trivial for God to raise a Messenger to deal with, and it is too trivial for God's Messengers to be concerned with and occupy themselves in managing it.

[. . .]

8. The Program of L'Étoile Nord-Africaine: Full Independence for Algeria, May 28, 1933

L'Étoile Nord-Africaine (North African Star) was an organization established in France in 1924 by the French Communist Party for the purpose of attracting North African migrant factory workers. Although the specific aim of L'Étoile was to uphold the rights of "North African Muslims," this goal was couched within the rubric of universal Marxism. L'Étoile quickly became a mass party with over 100,000 members. Within about ten years of its establishment, the majority of the members were Algerian, and its goal shifted to attaining Algerian independence from France. Accordingly the party's platform and aims were tailored to fit that redefined goal, and the party abandoned the Marxist label—while holding on to some Marxist ideas of social and economic justice—in favor of a more "authentic" Islamic nationalist approach. This change occurred under the leadership of Messali Hadj, one of Algeria's foremost preindependence politicians. L'Étoile was banned several times in France and in Algeria, and party leaders alternated between exile and hiding, on the one hand, and public activism, on the other.

Translated from the French text in *L'Afrique Française* (1934), vol. 44, pp. 575–576. This document may also be found in J. C. Hurewitz, *The Middle East and North Africa in World Politics* (New Haven, Conn.: Yale University Press, 1975), pp. 441, 443–444. Reprinted by permission of the author.

This document consists of the party program announced in 1933; it is a manifesto making known the party's new political aims. To understand its ideology, pay particular attention to the language and to what is not said, as well as to what is said.

Our Program

The political program of our Etoile Nord-Africaine, maturely studied and profoundly analysed by the former provisional Executive Committee, was presented, read and approved by all the members the Association summoned in National Assembly at 4 o'clock on 28 May 1933 to 49 rue de Bretagne, Paris (3e).

The content of these articles is simple, very comprehensible, and above all wholly responsive to the aspirations of the Algerian people.

It is expressly recommended that the Algerian people read it attentively, understand it, and apply it. We should consider it as a National Pact, knitting together the whole of the Muslim Algerian population, working with devotion and sacrifice for the defense of our interests, our immediate claims, and the independence of our country.

For our salvation, for our future, for occupying a place in the world worthy of our race, let us all swear on the Quran and by Islam to work without interruption for its realization and final triumph.

This political program for Algeria is almost the same as that of Morocco and Tunisia, obviously taking into account the general position of these two countries and their political constitutions.

Political Program Adopted by the General Assembly of 28 May 1933

1. The immediate abolition of the odious *Code de l'indigénat* [stipulating the rights of natives] and all discriminatory measures;

2. Amnesty for all those imprisoned under special surveillance or exiled for an infraction of the Indigénat or a political offense;

3. Absolute freedom to travel in France and abroad;

4. Freedom of the press, association, assembly, and political and syndical rights;

5. Replacement of the Financial Delegations elected with restricted suffrage by a national Algerian parliament elected with universal suffrage;

6. Abolition of mixed communes and military territories and replacement of these institutions by municipal assemblies elected with universal suffrage;

7. Access of all Algerians to the civil service without discrimination. Equal employment [and] equal salary for all;

8. Compulsory instruction in the Arabic language. Opportunity for education at every level. Creation of new Arab schools. Simultaneous publication of all official acts in the Arabic and French languages;

9. With regard to military service, unquestioned respect for the verse of the Quranic surah that says "He who deliberately kills a Muslim is condemned to misery for eternity and deserves divine anger and damnation";

10. The application of the social and work laws. The right to unemployment aid and family allowances for Algerian families in Algeria. Immediate abolition of the Social Insurance [program];

11. Enlargement of agricultural credit to the small fallahin. More rational organization of irrigation. Development of the means of communication. Nonrefundable aid from the government for victims of periodic famines.

Second Part

1. Full independence for Algeria;
2. Full withdrawal of occupation forces;
3. Establishment of a national army.

National Revolutionary Government

1. A Constituent Assembly elected with universal suffrage;
2. Universal suffrage at every level and eligibility for all inhabitants of Algeria in every assembly;
3. The Arabic language considered as the official language;
4. The return to the Algerian state of ownership of banks, mines, railroads, ports, and public services that were taken over by the conquerors;
5. The confiscation of large estates taken over by the feudal allies of the conquerors, the colons, and the financial societies, and the return of confiscated land to the peasants. Respect for medium and small properties. The return to the Algerian state of lands and forests monopolized by the French state;
6. Compulsory free education at all levels in the Arabic language;
7. Recognition by the Algerian state of the right to form syndicates [and] coalitions, [the right] to strike, and its [obligation to] frame social laws;
8. Immediate aid to fallahin in the form or non-interest agricultural loans, for the purchase of machinery, seed, and fodder, the organization of irrigation, and the improvement of the means of communication, etc.

North African Musulmans

The paper *El-Ouma* is your paper. It defends you, instructs you, educates you, unmasks all the traitors, all the betrayers, all the enemies of our fatherland, of our cause; it will lead you on the right path without fear or failure.

By its news, it will put you in touch with the entire Islamic world. Make it live, help it, protect it, make it read, advertise it everywhere in order that it may become the flag and the rallying point for all the vibrant strength of the North African Musulmans.

9. Antun Sa'adeh Declares His Vision of "Greater Syria" or Regional Nationalism, June 1, 1935

Antun Sa'adeh (1904–1949) was born in Lebanon to a Christian family. In 1921 he left Lebanon with his siblings to join his father in Brazil. During his stay in Brazil (about nine years), he became involved with politics within the Lebanese emigrant community and published many articles in the emigrant press. He established the Free Syrians Party, which agitated against French occupation of Syria and Lebanon, and he called on the pope, the League of Nations, and the press in South America to support an independent Syria. After returning to Lebanon, he taught German at the American University in Beirut and lectured about his concept of "Greater Syria."

According to Sa'adeh, Syria—which he defined geographically as Palestine, Lebanon, Syria, and parts of Iraq—always had been a national entity with a distinct culture and civilization, separate from the Arab world. His interpretation of the history of this area—a viewpoint actively rejected by many contemporaneous intellectuals and nationalists—led him to argue that "Greater Syria" transcended Arab, Islamic, and Christian history and was the product of unique geographical features that determined its "eternal national" character.

To implement his idea of a "greater Syria," Sa'adeh established the Syrian Social Nationalist Party (SSNP) in 1934, with himself at its head as al-Za'im (leader). His ideas about nationalism were influenced by the fascist tendencies then emerging in Europe. He was executed in 1949, along with six members of the SSNP, by the Lebanese government because of an attempted coup d'état. In the speech included here, Sa'adeh announces the establishment of the SSNP, its ideology, and its goals.

Ever since the hour in which our social national ideology began to bring together thoughts and feelings, to unite the forces of youth threatened with dispersion by the political and national chaos that blanket our country, and to transform this union into a new system (*nizam*) with new methods, deriving its life from the new nationalism, namely the system of the Syrian Social Nationalist Party—ever since that hour, dawn has followed darkness and movement has come out of lethargy and the force of organization has burst out of confusion. We have become a nation after having been mere human herd, and a state resting on four fundamental pillars—freedom, duty, organization, power—which are symbolized by the four pointers on the flag of the Syrian Social Nationalist Party.

Ever since that hour we have repudiated by our actions the judgment of history and begun our true history—the history of freedom, duty, organization, and power, the history of the Syrian Social Nationalist Party, the true history of the Syrian nation.

Ever since the hour in which we united our hearts and our hands to stand or fall together for the sake of the realization of the highest ideal proclaimed in the principles of the Syrian Social Nationalist Party and in its aim—ever since

Antun Sa'adeh, "Speech of June 1, 1935 of the Leader of the Syrian Social Nationalist Party." http://www.ssnp.com (12 February 2003).

that hour we have put our hands on the plow and directed our eyes forward toward the ideal. We have become one community, one living nation seeking the beautiful free life, a nation loving life because it loves liberty and loving death when death is a path to life.

Before the Syrian Social Nationalist Party was constituted, the Syrians were not a nation in the true sense of the word. All that existed was a certain dissatisfaction with an unnatural situation which the Syrian people could not accept and in which they could not find satisfaction for their vital needs. Some people took up the leadership of this popular dissatisfaction and exploited it in order to obtain the positions they sought, and they bolstered up this leadership by the remains of family power derived from the principles of a bygone age—principles which consider the people as herds to be disposed of by certain families, dissipating the interests of the people for the sake of their personal power. And when these so-called leaders found that the family and the home were not sufficient in this age to uphold leadership, they resorted to certain words beloved by the people—the words of liberty, independence, and principles—and they played upon these words, words which are sacred when they indicate an ideal for a living nation, but which are corrupt when they fire a means for assuming leadership and a screen behind which lurk ambition and private aims.

The word "principles" should be noted in particular, for it should represent the living power and the basic needs of the nation. . . .

Thus it came to pass that in this age, which is the age of the struggle of nations for survival, and in this difficult time when the factors of corruption and division and national nullification are rampant amidst our people, the Syrian Social Nationalist Party rose, as dawn rises from the darkest hours of the night, to proclaim a new principle. This is the principle of will—the will of a people that wants sovereignty over itself and over its country (*watan*) in order to realize its lofty ideal; the will of life for a truly enduring nation. . . .

The Syrian Social Nationalist Party therefore is not a mere society or group, as may still appear to some members whom time has not yet permitted to understand the fundamental principle which the Syrian Social Nationalist Party embodies, or the need of the Syrian nation in this age. The Syrian Social Nationalist Party is indeed much more than a society which brings together a number of members, or a club which was established for a particular set of people or youth. The Party is an idea and a movement which embraces the life of a nation in its entirety. It is the renovation of a nation which some imagine to have collapsed forever because the various factors which have conspired against its national spirit have been so great that an ordinary nation could have hardly borne their impact and still preserve its existence or the hope of surviving. It is the rise of an extraordinary nation—a nation unique in its capacities, surpassing in its powers, rich in its characteristics—a nation which does not accept the grave as its place in the sun. . . .

From now on, our will guides the rudder. Every member of the Syrian Social Nationalist Party feels that he is being liberated from foreign hegemony and from external dominating factors because he feels that the Party is like his own independent state, which does not derive its power from a mandate or rely upon external authority. The truth, fellow comrades, is that we have bound ourselves together in this Party for the sake of a very important task, which is the establishment of our state, so that every one of us will become a subject of his independent state. This task is no doubt difficult. Will we be capable of it? The answer to this question stirs in our souls and resounds in our breasts, and may issue from our mouths. To inscribe it on the pages of history will depend upon our struggle, for history does not record hopes or intentions, but actions and facts. And I do not doubt, with these faces displaying the manifestations of power and resolution before me, that our actions and our facts confirm the judgment of our will, which does not know incapacity.

Within the Party, we have liberated ourselves from foreign authority and from external factors, but we still have to deliver our nation and liberate our whole country. In this important work we shall meet many difficulties, internal and external, which we must overcome, beginning with the first, namely, the internal, because we cannot overcome the external difficulties completely except after having conquered the internal ones. The first internal difficulty which confronts us is the lack in our community of deep national traditions to be reared on and to hold to. Our personal selves are always in conflict with our general self in all that has to do with our national causes and the way we meet them. Add to this the conflicting traditions derived from our sectarian organizations, and the effect of these traditions in resisting the national unity of the people.

I must declare here that the Syrian Social Nationalist Party has found a means of overcoming these difficulties by its system (*nizam*) which breaks down both the traditions that oppose the unity of the nation and individual psychologies which opposes the psychological individuality of the nation. Our final success depends, in fact, upon our understanding of this truth and upon the application of the four pillars of the Party which bind us indissolubly, namely freedom, duty, organization, and power. . . .

Likewise, I have on this occasion to declare that the system (*nizam*) of the Syrian Social Nationalist Party is not a Hitlerite or a Fascist system, but that it is purely a Syrian system which does not stand on unprofitable imitation, but on basic originality which is one of the characteristics of our people. It is the system which is indispensable for the molding of our national life, and for the preservation of this remarkable renaissance (*nahda*) which will change the face of history in the Near East and liberate it from the influence of the reactionary forces which cannot be trusted and which may constitute a serious danger, threatening every renovating movement with corruption under the auspices of the traditional parliamentary system that is powerless to reform itself.

Embodied in the principles of the Syrian Social Nationalist Party is the way of liberating our thoughts from decadent beliefs and fancies which have prevented us from seeking what we ought to seek. Such is the fancy, cultivated by a group of spiritually weak and mentally sterile people, that we are a weak nation incapable of doing anything and with no hope of achieving a purpose or a desire and that the best that we can do is to recognize our incapacity and let our national self disappear from among the nations and be content with any state which we attain. The members of the Syrian Social Nationalist Party have liberated themselves from such false fancies and have taken upon themselves to liberate the rest of the nation from them. This is a responsibility incumbent upon every member of the Syrian Social Nationalist Party, a responsibility which is greater than all other responsibilities, a responsibility in comparison with which every other responsibility is small indeed. As the sense of this responsibility develops and grows, there grows with it the living force of every member of our group.

The rising Syria [which] is built on the new national forces represented by the Syrian National Party will be different from the old Syria laid down by tradition, given over to the fancies of those who have lost their national spirit and their self-confidence. The Syria of the Syrian Social Nationalist Party is the Syria of national unity organized in such a way as to make the abilities stored up in it a general force capable of achieving what it wants. We have full faith that the spirit created by our principles will achieve a final victory and overcome all the internal difficulties. If this needs time, it is because time is a necessary condition for every important achievement.

As for the external difficulties, these become small once we overcome the internal ones and once the will of our nation is crystallized in our system (*nizam*) which guarantees its unity and prevents the divisive forces prevalent outside the Party from infiltrating into our solid unity for which we are ready to sacrifice everything. At this juncture, I do not wish to deal with our external problem as a whole. This I shall do on another occasion which I hope will be soon. Now, I shall merely mention a general principle which applies to the whole of our history, namely, that the destiny of Syria has been decided by external bargaining without the actual participation of the Syrian nation itself. It is on this principle that the big powers rely on in their rivalry to spread their influence upon us. I wish to declare now that the establishment of the Syrian Social Nationalist Party and its continuous growth will take it upon themselves from now on to dispel such fancies from the heads of ambitious politicians.

We feel now the existence of a strong Italian propaganda in this country in particular, and in the Near East in general. We feel a similar propaganda from Germany and similar ones from other countries. The Leadership of the Syrian Social Nationalist Party warns all its members against failing prey to foreign propaganda. We recognize that there are considerations which call for the establishment of friendly relations between Syria and foreign nations, in particular the European states, but we do not believe in the principle of propaganda. Syrian thought must remain free and independent. When it comes to foreign relations, we are always ready to clasp the hands that are extended to us with a frank, good intention and in a situation of common understanding and agreement.

The foreign states which desire to establish solid, free relations with us should recognize in the first place our right to live and should be ready to respect this right. Otherwise, the new Syria will not remain silent in the face of political maneuvers intended to lead our nation to make the political mistakes which were committed in the past and which have done her so much harm.

The task of preserving our national revival is among the most important tasks of the Syrian Social Nationalist Party and we shall not fail to undertake it in the best possible way. Foreign propaganda may spread in the chaos of parties, but when it reaches the Syrian Social Nationalist Party i[t] finds a solid barrier through which it cannot pass because the Syrian Social Nationalists form a Party which is not built on anarchy and because they follow only the policy decided upon by their party. They are not a disordered group but an organized force.

I repeat once more this organized force will change the face of history in the Near East. Our forefathers witnessed the conquerors of the past and trod on their remains. But we, we shall put an end to conquests.

Amidst the confusion of irresponsible talk and shouting spread all over this nation, the Syrian Social Nationalists undertake their work with calmness and confidence; and the spirit of the Syrian Social Nationalist Party is growing in the body of the nation and it is organizing its groups. The day shall come, and that day is near, when the world will see a new sight and an event: the sight of men clad in black sashes on gray suit[s], with sharpened spears shining above their heads; men walking behind the banners of the Red Tempest carried by giants of the army. The forests of spears will advance in well-organized ranks and the Syrian nation shall have a will which cannot be checked. For this is destiny.

10. Taha Husayn Writes of Egypt as a Mixture of Pharaonic, Arab, and Western Cultures, 1938

In seeking to create nations, Arab intellectuals engaged in a process of imagining historical unity within their respective geographical areas. This exercise entailed the construction of a national identity that was as much cultural as it was political. For some this culture was "purely" Arab; for some it was grounded in a particular religion. A few others looked toward European cultures in their search for a coherent cultural model. A number of intellectuals did not see culture as "pure" in any real sense but believed that it consisted of cross-currents of various subcultures and ideas. Among this last group was the Egyptian write Taha Husayn (1889–1973).

Born into modest circumstances and blinded by illness at the age of two, in 1902 Taha Husayn enrolled in Al-Azhar University, the leading orthodox center for Islamic learning. Feeling stifled by the conservative intellectual atmosphere that predominated there, in 1908 he transferred to the newly established and secular Cairo University. After finishing his doctoral work, he traveled to France and studied

Taha Husayn, *The Future of Culture in Egypt,* trans. Sidney Glazer, American Council of Learned Societies, Near Eastern Translation Program, no. 9 (New York: Octagon Books, Farrar, Straus and Giroux, 1975), pp. 1–4, 7, 15, 21–22. Reprinted by permission of Hippocrene Books, Inc.

at the Sorbonne. From these experiences he forged a very independent and analytical mind. His intellectual work embroiled him in several controversies about religion and its role in society and politics. One of his most impressive works is Mustaqbal al-thaqafah fi Misr *(The Future of Culture in Egypt), from which the following selection is excerpted.*

1

The subject to be treated in this discourse is the future of culture in Egypt, now that our country has regained her freedom through the revival of the constitution and her honor through the realization of independence. We are living in an age characterized by the fact that freedom and independence do not constitute ends in themselves, but are merely means of attaining exalted, enduring, and generally practical goals.
[. . .]

Like every patriotic educated Egyptian who is zealous for his country's good reputation, I want our new life to harmonize with our ancient glory and our new energy to justify both the opinion we entertained of ourselves while we were seeking independence and the opinion held by civilized nations when they recognized our independence and cordially welcomed us to Geneva.
[. . .]

2

I do not like illusions. I am persuaded that it is only God who can create something from nothing. I therefore believe that the new Egypt will not come into being except from the ancient, eternal Egypt. I believe further that the new Egypt will have to be built on the great old one, and that the future of culture in Egypt will be an extension, a superior version, of the humble, exhausted, and feeble present. For this reason we should think of the future of culture in Egypt in the light of its remote past and near present. We do not wish, nor are we able, to break the link between ourselves and our forefathers. To the degree that we establish our future life upon our past and present we shall avoid most of the dangers caused by excesses and miscalculations deriving from illusions and dreams.

At the outset we must answer this fundamental question: Is Egypt of the East or of the West? Naturally, I mean East or West in the cultural, not the geographical sense. It seems to me that there are two distinctly different and bitterly antagonistic cultures on the earth. Both have existed since time immemorial, the one in Europe, the other in the Far East.

We may paraphrase the question as follows: Is the Egyptian mind Eastern or Western in its imagination, perception, comprehension, and judgment? More succinctly put—which is easier for the Egyptian mind: to understand a Chinese or Japanese, or to understand an Englishman or a Frenchman? This is the question that we must answer before we begin to think of the foundations on which we shall have to base our culture and education. It seems to me that the simplest way to do this is by tracing the complicated development of the Egyptian mind from earliest times to the present.

The first thing to note is that, so far as is known, we had no regular, sustained contacts with the Far East that could have affected our thinking and political or economic institutions. The available archaeological remains and documents reveal little more than that Egyptians at the end of the Pharaonic period evinced some desire to explore the Red Sea coasts, which they left only with great caution, chiefly for the sake of goods from India and South Arabia. Their attempts were tentative, unorganized, and ephemeral.

The contacts between ancient Egypt and the lands of the East scarcely went beyond Palestine, Syria, and Mesopotamia, that is, the East that falls in the Mediterranean basin, but there is no doubt that they were strong and continuous and that they exerted an influence on the intellectual, political, and economic life of all the countries involved. Our mythology relates that Egyptian gods crossed the Egyptian frontiers in order to civilize the people in these regions. Historians tell us that the kings of Egypt at times extended their sway over them. Ancient Egypt was a major power politically and economically not only in comparison with her neighbors, but with the countries that cradled the European civilization with which we are examining our kingship.

It would be a waste of time and effort to set forth in detail the ties binding Egypt to the ancient Greco-Aegean civilization. School children know that Greek colonies were established in Egypt by the Pharaohs before the first millennium B.C. They also know that an Eastern nation, Persia, successfully invaded our country at the end of the sixth century B.C. But we resisted fiercely until the Alexandrian era, having recourse at one time to Greek volunteers, and at another time allying ourselves with the Greek cities.

The meaning of all this is very clear: the Egyptian mind had no serious contact with the Far Eastern mind; nor did it live harmoniously with the Persian mind. The Egyptian mind has had regular, peaceful, and mutually beneficial relations only with the Near East and Greece. In short, it has been influenced from earliest times by the Mediterranean Sea and the various peoples living around it.

[. . .]

5

Islam arose and spread over the world. Egypt was receptive and hastened at top speed to adopt it as her religion and to make the Arabic of Islam her language. Did that obliterate her original mentality? Did that make her an Eastern nation in the present meaning of the term? Not at all! Europe did not become Eastern nor did the nature of the European mind change because Christianity, which originated in the East, flooded Europe and absorbed the other religions. If modern European philosophers and thinkers deem Christianity to be an element of the European mind, they must explain what distinguishes Christianity from Islam; for both were born in the geographical East, both issued from one noble source and were inspired by the one God in whom Easterners and Westerners alike believe.

[...]

9

In order to become equal partners in civilization with the Europeans, we must literally and forthrightly do everything that they do; we must share with them the present civilization, with all its pleasant and unpleasant sides, and not content ourselves with words or mere gestures. Whoever advises any other course of action is either a deceiver or is himself deceived. Strangely enough we imitate the West in our everyday lives, yet hypocritically deny the fact in our words. If we really detest European life, what is to hinder us from rejecting it completely? And if we genuinely respect the Europeans, as we certainly seem to do by our wholesale adoption of their practices, why do we not reconcile our words with our actions? Hypocrisy ill becomes those who are proud and anxious to overcome their defects.

[...]

12

Other objectors to Western civilization use two lines of argument, one dangerous, the other ridiculous. Sometimes they assert that it is ultra-materialistic and a source of misery both to Europe and to the rest of the world. At other times they insist that Europe is tired of her own civilization, as evidenced by the number of writers, scholars, and philosophers who are turning away from it and seeking nourishment in the spirituality of the East. Why then, they ask, should we abandon the good that the Europeans themselves desire for the evil that they are rejecting?

Certainly, there is a good deal of materialism in European civilization, but it is absurd to deny that it possesses spiritual content. The brilliant successes of modern science and the inventions that have changed the face of the earth spring from imaginative and creative minds. European history is replete with men like Descartes and Pasteur, who cheerfully devoted their time and effort to ideas alone. Besides scientists and scholars, there are such men as airplane test-pilots who expose themselves to horrible injury and even death in order to extend man's mastery over nature

Yes, we know of writers, poets, and philosophers who are tired of European civilization; yet they will sacrifice their lives for it. Some of them look toward the East, or appear to do so, but you can be sure that they would flatly refuse to live like Easterners. Dissatisfaction with modern life is a characteristic of men who are alive and progressing. Submissive contentment is a characteristic of lazy, decadent people. When Europeans tell us that their civilization is materialistic and hateful, they are either truthful—in which case we know that they seek its improvement—or lying, their purpose being to induce us to shun this civilization so that they may retain all its benefits for themselves, while we remain stationary, clinging to our spiritual civilization which makes us their slaves.

Moreover, what is this spiritual East? It is assuredly not our Near East which, as previously noted, is the cradle of the mind that I have been lauding. This area was also the source of divine religions adopted both by Europeans and Easterners—Christians, Jews, and Muslims alike. Can these religions be spirit in the East and matter in the West?

No, the spiritual East by which some Europeans are fascinated is clearly not the Near East but the Far East. It is the East of India, China, and Japan with religions and philosophies that scarcely resemble our own. In all seriousness, do we want to embrace the religion, philosophy, and motive-forces of the Chinese just when they are rapidly Westernizing themselves? Years ago, for example, China applied to the League of Nations for experts to organize its educational system on the European pattern. The country, as is well known, is being pulled in two directions, one toward the democratic Western League, the other toward Russia and communism.

This talk of a spiritual East is sheer nonsense. Egyptians who deride European civilization and praise the spirituality of the East are joking, and they realize it. They would be the last to choose to live like the Chinese or Hindus. Nevertheless, their arguments are dangerous and demoralizing, particularly to the youth, who are thereby led away from the European civilization which they know toward the Eastern civilization they do not know. Stories about the East and West are told only by those with a superficial understanding of both. The younger generation must be protected from such false knowledge, and the best, if not only, method is to provide them with a sound education.
[. . .]

11.   Syrian Michel ʿAflaq Addresses the Relationship Between Arabism and Islam, 1943

Michel ʿAflaq (b. 1912) was a Christian and a member of the emerging urban middle class in Damascus, Syria. He received a "modern" education in secular schools and colleges in Syria and continued his university education in Europe. His experience with French colonialism, the corruption and inefficacy of many of the traditional political elites, and his exposure to socialism in Paris, where he attended university during the early 1930s, prompted him to articulate a new political vision for Syria and for the Arab world as a whole.

Michel ʿAflaq, *Choice of Texts from the Baʿth Party's Founder's Thought* (Florence: Cooperativa Lavoratori, 1977), pp. 71–83. Translated by Akram Khater.

'Aflaq and fellow student Salah al-Bitar argued for nationalist independence from colonialism, for a united and singular Arab nation, and for justice and equality among all social classes. After they returned to Syria, both men began to attract a following among students at the high school where they taught. After Syria's independence in 1946, 'Aflaq formed a political party, known as Ba'ath (Renaissance), based on the aforementioned principles and dedicated to the resurgence of Arab civilization. In the speech quoted here, he addresses the complex relationship between Arabism and Islam, seeking to harmonize seemingly opposing ideas. Despite his Christian background—and in opposition to many other Christians who were if not antagonistic then at least suspicious of a state dominated by Islam—'Aflaq believed that Arabism and Islam could not be separated, but at the same time he maintained that Arabism as an ideology preceded and was superordinate to Islam and thus should be the basis for the modern Arab nation.

[. . .] Today, we are facing the contradiction between our glorious past and the shameful present. The Arab personality used to be a complete whole, with no difference between its soul and mind, between its words and actions, between its private and public morals, and Arab life was complete. [. . .] But today we know only the schizophrenic psyche, and we know only a partial and impoverished life; if the mind enters it then the spirit leaves it, and if emotion exists in it then reason departs from it. [. . .] It [current Arab life] is always deprived of some fundamental power, and it is time for us to remove this contradiction so that we can regain the unity of the Arab character. [. . .]

Our relationship to our heroic ancestors is nothing more than a formality, and the connection between our modern history and our glorious past is not organic but parasitic. Today we must revive within us the traits and perform the tasks that [. . .] make our relationship a legitimate reality. We must remove whatever we can of the stumbling blocks of inertia and decadence until the original glorious blood flows in us once again. [. . .]

Islam Is a Permanent Experience and Readiness

Sirs: The Islamic movement embodied in the life of the Prophet is not simply a historical event for Arabs that can be explained in time and place and through reasons and results. Rather, and because of its depth, power, and reach, it is directly linked with the absolute life of Arabs. In other words, it is a truthful image and an eternal symbol of the nature of the Arab spirit and its rich potential and original direction. [. . .] Islam is the vital jolt that moves the internal forces of the Arab nation [. . .] removing out of its path the dams of tradition and the shackles of norms. Thus, it reestablishes the connection of that nation with the deeper meanings of the universe [. . .] and it begins to express its excitement and wonder with new words and glorious works, and it cannot remain bounded within and so it overflows with thought and action onto other nations. [. . .]

This experience [early Islamic history] is not a historical event that is to be mentioned simply out of pride and to tell a story; it is a constant readiness within the Arab nation—if Islam is correctly understood—to rise every time matter controls the soul and appearances overcome substance. It divides within in order to achieve higher unity and proper harmony, and it is an experience meant to strengthen its morals every time they softened. [. . .] Within this experience is repeated the heroic epic story of Islam with all of its chapters of preaching, persecution, emigration, war, victory, and failure, until the final victory of Truth and Faith [this is the sequence of events of the life of Prophet Muhammad].

The life of the Prophet—which embodies the Arab spirit in its absolute truth—cannot be known in the mind but through living and experiencing it. Therefore, this knowledge cannot be a beginning but a result. The Arabs, ever since they lost their vitality—that is, hundreds of years ago—have been reading the story of the life [of the Prophet] [. . .] without understanding it, because to comprehend its meaning requires an extreme level of passion and of depth and honesty of feeling that they do not yet have. [. . .]

The spirits of our heroes have left and deserted us a long time, because heroism is no longer an Arab trait. One fears that this blind aggrandizement of the Prophet is an expression of inability and impotence more than it is an appreciation of greatness. Our era is so far from heroism that we have come to regard it [heroism] with fear and wonder, as if it is from a world different from ours. In reality, the true appreciation of heroism can emanate only from sharing and [. . .] experiencing it. No one who has not achieved at least a meager level of heroism in life can truly appreciate the Hero.

Until now we have looked upon the life of the Prophet from the outside, as a wonderful picture made for us to appreciate and to sanctify. We must begin to look at it from the inside, to live it. Every Arab at the present time can live the life of the Arab Prophet, even if with the ratio of a pebble to a mountain, or a drop of water to the sea. It is natural that any man—no matter how great—will not be able to accomplish what Muhammad did. But it is also natural that any man—no matter how limited his ability—can be a miniature version of Muhammad, as long as he belongs to the nation that gathered its forces to produce Muhammad or, more to the point, as long as this man is a member of the nation that Muhammad gathered all of his forces to produce. [. . .]

Islam Is the Renewal and Completion of Arabism

An Arab man received a heavenly message, so he began to call people to it. The only people around him were Arabs, and few heeded his call. But many fought against it, so he emigrated with the Believers. The polytheists fought him until Truth vanquished and all believed in him. The epic of Islam cannot be separated from its natural stage, which is the land of the Arabs, and from its heroes, and they are all Arabs. The idolaters of the Quraish [a powerful tribe in Mecca that opposed the Prophet] were as necessary for Islam as the Believers, and those who fought the Prophet contributed to the victory of Islam as much as those who aided and supported him. God is capable of revealing the Qur'an to his

Prophet in one day, but that required more than twenty years. He is capable of making his religion victorious and to lead all of humanity to it in one day, but that did not happen in less than twenty years. He is capable of revealing Islam centuries before it appeared and to any nation of his creation, but he revealed it at a particular time and he chose for that the Arab nation and its Arab Prophet-Hero. The glaring truth, then, is that the choice of the Arabs to deliver the message of Islam was because of their fundamental character and virtues. The choice of the epoch in which Islam was revealed was because the Arabs had matured enough to accept this message and to carry it to the world. Postponing the victory of Islam for those many years was meant to allow Arabs to arrive at the truth by themselves and through their personal experiences within the world, and after trials and pains, despair and hope, failure and victory. In other words, faith had to emanate from within the depths of their souls so that it would be the True Faith mixed with experience and connected to the essence of life. Islam, then, was an Arab movement and its meaning was the renewal and completion of Arabism. The language of Islam was Arabic, the Islamic perspective was that of the Arab mind, the virtues that Islam advocated were apparent or inherent Arab virtues, and the vices that it struggled against were Arab vices on their way to extinction. The Muslim at that time [seventh century A.D.] was none other than the Arab, but the new, complete, and advanced Arab. [. . .]

The Humanity of Islam

Does this mean that Islam was founded only for Arabs? If we say that, then we depart from the truth and go against reality. For every great nation that has deep connections with the eternal truths strives toward universal eternal values. Islam [. . .] is in its reality Arab and in its ideal humanistic.

Arabs are unique among all other nations in the following characteristic: their national awakening was intimately connected to a religious message, or put another way, this message revealed the national awakening. Arabs did not expand for the sake of expansion, and they did not conquer lands simply for economic reasons or racial motivation or from a desire to control and enslave. Rather, they did so to fulfill a religious duty full of truth, guidance, compassion, justice, and charity. They spilled their own blood for its cause. [. . .] Since the connection between Arabism and Islam is intimate, and since we see in Arabism a body whose spirit is Islam, then there is no fear that the Arabs will be extremists in their nationalism. It will not become the fanaticism of colonialism and imperialism. [. . .]

It is only natural that Arabs will not be able to perform this duty unless they are a rising strong nation, because Islam can be embodied only in the Arab nation and its virtues, morals, and talents. The first duty that the humanity of Islam demands is that Arabs should be strong and sovereign.
[. . .]

Arabs and the West

A century and a half ago the West and Arabs encountered each once again through Bonaparte's campaign in Egypt. That genius symbolized this contact by hanging placards on which were written Qur'anic verses next to the Rights of Man. Since that time Arabs (or their foreign leaders) have pushed their modern renaissance in that dubious direction. They stretch themselves, the texts of their history, and the Qur'an beyond the breaking point in order to demonstrate that the principles of their civilization and ideology are not different from the principles of Western civilization, and that they preceded Westerners in announcing and applying these principles. This can only mean one thing: They stand as the defendant vis-à-vis the West, admitting the validity of Western values and their superiority. The fact is that the Western invasion of the Arab mind—coming as it did at a time when that mind had dried up to such an extent that it was an empty mold—allowed that civilization to fill this mold with its ideas and meanings. [. . .] We do not disagree with Europeans about the principle of liberty, but we disagree with their understanding of the meaning of liberty.

Europe, today as in the past, is afraid of Islam. But it knows now that the power of Islam (which in the past expressed the power of the Arabs) is reborn in a new guise, which is Arab nationalism. Therefore it has directed all of its weapons against this new power, while we see it [Europe] befriending and supporting the traditional form of Islam. Illiterate Islam, which is limited to superficial worship and banal and meaningless symbols, is becoming Europeanized, today in thought and tomorrow in thought and name as well. The day will come when the nationalists will find themselves to be the only defenders of Islam. [. . .]

The Honor of Arabism

Among the European concepts that have invaded the modern Arab mind are two ideas about nationalism and humanism that entail great error and danger. The idea of absolute nationalism in the West is logical in its attempt to separate nationalism from religion because religion entered Europe from the outside— it is foreign to its nature and history. [. . .] Islam is not a foreign ideology for the Arabs, nor is it a moral abstraction; it reveals more than anything else their existential feelings and their outlook on life, and it is the strongest expression of the unity of their personality, in which language merges with feeling and thought, and reflection with work. [. . .] Our nationalism is a living complex organism, and any separation of its parts can threaten it with death. [. . .] Arab Christians will know, when their nationalism is fully awakened and they reclaim their authentic heritage, that for them Islam is a national culture in which they must immerse themselves until they understand and love it. [. . .] If reality is still far from this wish, then the new generation of Arab Christians must undertake the task of accomplishing this with courage [. . .] sacrificing their pride and private interests, since nothing is equal to Arabism and the honor of belonging to it.

Abstract Humanism

The second danger is that of the European idea of abstract humanism, which considers all of humanity to be similar without any roots in the land and not subject to time, whereby the reforms and changes that derive out of the needs of one people can be applied to another.

[. . .] Some believe today that simply applying some reforms to the conditions of the Arabs is sufficient to rejuvenate the nation. We find in this a sign of decadence because it is a reversal of perspective when the [. . .] result takes the place of the reason. The fact is that reforms must derive from specific roots, as flowers emerge from a tree. This root is spiritual before anything else: it is the belief of the nation in its message. [. . .]

The New Arab Generation

Sirs: Today we celebrate the memory of the Hero of Arabism and Islam. Islam is nothing more than the outcome of agonies, the pains of Arabism, and these agonies have come back to the land of the Arabs with a vengeance that the Arabs of pre-Islamic times did not know. May it bring forth in us today a cleansing and reforming revolution such as the one whose banner was carried by Islam. [. . .]

We, the new Arab generation, are carrying a message, not policy, belief, and ideology, not theories and discourses. We are not afraid of the local nationalist factions that are supported by foreign weapons, driven by racial hatred against Arabs, because God, nature, and history are with us. They do not understand us because they are strangers to us, strangers to truth and heroism; they are fake, artificial, and contemptible. The only people who understand us are those who have experienced and understood Muhammad's life from within, as an ethical experiment and historical event. [. . .]

12.   Hasan al-Banna Proclaims Egyptian Nationalism and the Religious Basis for an Islamic State, 1949

Hasan al-Banna (1906–1949) grew up in an Egypt that was in many ways a British colony. He came of age at a time when it appeared that the European "West" was directly or indirectly dominating Muslim societies. This hegemony was accompanied by attacks on Islam from colonial quarters, as well as from indigenous and secular groups and individuals. In 1928, amid the political chaos and cultural confusion in Egypt— and in the larger Islamic world—al-Banna established the Muslim Brotherhood.

This political party was dedicated to restoring Egyptian independence from the British and—perhaps more important—to the social and political regeneration of Egypt through the establishment of a "truly" Islamic polity and society.

By this al-Banna meant the reconstruction and reestablishment of the type of polity that existed briefly after the death of the Prophet Muhammad, when religious leadership and political leadership were ostensibly one and the same. Furthermore, and in addition to having a believing Muslim lead the umma, al-Banna believed that such a polity could come into existence only when Islamic laws—and only Islamic laws—govern society. The Brotherhood, however, did not look to the past for the specifics of its program. Rather, it was a thoroughly "modern" phenomenon that sought to reinterpret the Shari'a within the technological, economic, political, and social contexts of the twentieth century. Like his Pakistani counterpart Mawdudi, al-Banna argued that the fact that the loudspeaker, was invented in the West should not deter a Muslim from using it—after making it an "Islamic loudspeaker." Al-Banna remained the Supreme Guide of the Muslim Brotherhood until his assassination by the Egyptian government in 1949. In this document he spells out some of his ideas for creating an Islamic nation in Egypt.

A Bold Step but a Successful One

Excellency,

. . . [I]t would be inexcusable for us to turn aside from the path of truth—the path of Islam—and to follow the path of fleshly desires and vanities—the path of Europe. Along the path of Europe are to be found outer show and cheap tinsel, pleasures and luxuries, laxity and license, and comforts that captivate the soul, for all of these things are loved by the soul, as the Almighty says: "Made beautiful for mankind is the love of fleshly desires for women, and children, and heaped-up mounds of gold and silver, and branded horses, and cattle, and tilled land. That is the comfort of this world" [Q.3:14].

But the path of Islam is glory, impregnability, truth, strength, blessedness, rectitude, stability, virtue, and nobility. Follow it along with the *umma,* may God grant you success! "Say: 'Shall I inform you of something better than that? For those who are godfearing in the presence of their Lord, there are Gardens beneath which rivers flow, they being in them forever, and purified spouses, and the approbation of God. God is aware of His worshippers'" [Q.3:15].

Luxuries only annihilate nations, and her comforts and coveted possessions have only convulsed Europe: "And when We wish to destroy a city, We command its men of wealth, and they commit transgression in it, and the sentence against it is justified, and We destroy it utterly" [Q.3:16].

God (Blessed and Almighty is He!) sent His Apostle as a mercy to the worlds until the Day of Resurrection, and sent His Book with him as a light and a guidance until the Day of Resurrection. The leadership of the Apostle

Five Tracts of Hasan al-Banna (1906–1949): A Selection from the Majmu 'at Rasa'il al-Imam al-Shahid Hasan al-Banna, trans. Charles Wendell, *Near Eastern Studies,* vol. 20 (Berkeley: University of California Press, 1978), pp. 75–77. Reprinted by permission.

(May God bless and save him!) survives in his Sunna, and the authority of the Qur'ān is secure through his proof. Humanity is marching inevitably toward them both, with the might of the mighty and the humility of the humble, from near and from afar, so that God's Word should be realized: "that He may make it triumphant over every religion" [Q.9:33].

Be the first to come forward in the name of God's Apostle (May God bless and save him!) bearing the vial of Qur'ānic healing, to save the tormented, sick world! It is a bold step, but one crowned with success, God willing (Blessed and Almighty is He!), for God is victorious in His affairs: "Then the believers will rejoice in God's succor. He succors whom He will, for He is the Mighty, the Merciful" [Q.30:4–5].

Some Steps Toward Practical Reform

Excellency,

Having given a clear presentation of the spiritual mood that should prevail within the nation in its modern renaissance, we would like to point out, by way of conclusion, some of the practical manifestations and results which this mood should dictate. We are going to mention here only the broadest topics, since we are well aware that each one of these questions demands extensive and intensive study, taxing the energies and capacities of specialists. We know too that we have not yet plumbed all the puzzling problems and demands of the nation, nor all the manifestations of the renaissance. We do not believe that the fulfillment of these demands is a mere trifle which can be accomplished overnight, and we know that before many of them there are manifold obstacles which will require vast patience, great wisdom, and keen determination. We know all this and can take it in our stride. And besides this, we know that where there is genuine resolve, the way will be made plain, and that if a strong-willed nation chooses the path of goodness, it shall, by God Almighty's will, attain what it desires. Stride forward, and God will be with you! Following are the principal goals of reform grounded on the spirit of genuine Islam:

First: Political, judicial, and administrative:

(1) An end to party rivalry, and a channeling of the political forces of the nation into a common front and a single phalanx.

(2) A reform of the law, so that it will conform to Islamic legislation in every branch.

(3) A strengthening of the armed forces, and an increase in the number of youth groups; the inspiration of the latter with zeal on the bases of Islamic *jihād.*

(4) A strengthening of the bonds between all Islamic countries, especially the Arab countries, to pave the way for practical and serious consideration of the matter of the departed Caliphate.

(5) The diffusion of the Islamic spirit throughout all departments of the government, so that all its employees will feel responsible for adhering to Islamic teachings.

(6) The surveillance of the personal conduct of all its employees, and an end to the dichotomy between the private and professional spheres.

(7) Setting the hours of work in summer and winter ahead, so that it will be easy to fulfill religious duties, and so that keeping late hours will come to an end.

(8) An end to bribery and favoritism, with consideration to be given only to capability and legitimate reasons [for advancement].

(9) Weighing all acts of the government in the scales of Islamic wisdom and doctrine; the organization of all celebrations, receptions, official conferences, prisons and hospitals so as not to be incompatible with Islamic teaching; the arranging of work-schedules so that they will not conflict with hours of prayer.

(10) The employment of graduates of Al-Azhar in military and administrative positions, and their training.

Second: Social and educational:

(1) Conditioning the people to respect public morality, and the issuance of directives fortified by the aegis of the law on this subject; the imposition of severe penalties for moral offenses.

(2) Treatment of the problem of women in a way which combines the progressive and the protective, in accordance with Islamic teaching, so that this problem—one of the most important social problems—will not be abandoned to the biased pens and deviant notions of those who err in the directions of deficiency or excess.

(3) An end to prostitution, both clandestine and overt: the recognition of fornication, whatever the circumstances, as a detestable crime whose perpetrator must be flogged.

(4) An end to gambling in all its forms—games, lotteries, racing, and gambling-clubs.

(5) A campaign against drinking, as there is one against drugs: its prohibition, and the salvation of the nation from its effects.

(6) A campaign against ostentation in dress and loose behavior; the instruction of women in what is proper, with particular strictness as regards female instructors, pupils, physicians, and students, and all those in similar categories.

(7) A review of the curricula offered to girls and the necessity of making them distinct from the boys' curricula in many of the stages of education.

(8) Segregation of male and female students; private meetings between men and women, unless within the permitted degrees [of relationship], to be counted as a crime for which both will be censured.

(9) The encouragement of marriage and procreation, by all possible means; promulgation of legislation to protect and give moral support to the family, and to solve the problems of marriage.

(10) The closure of morally undesirable ballrooms and dance-halls, and the prohibition of dancing and other such pastimes.

(11) The surveillance of theatres and cinemas, and a rigorous selection of plays and films.

(12) The expurgation of songs, and a rigorous selection and censorship of them.

(13) The careful selection of lectures, songs, and subjects to be broadcast to the nation; the use of radio broadcasting for the education of the nation in a virtuous and moral way.

(14) The confiscation of provocative stories and books that implant the seeds of skepticism in an insidious manner, and newspapers which strive to disseminate immorality and capitalize indecently on lustful desires.

(15) The supervision of summer vacation areas so as to do away with the wholesale confusion and license that nullify the basic aims of vacationing.

(16) The regulation of business hours for cafés; surveillance of the activities of their regular clients; instructing these as to what is in their best interest; withdrawal of permission from cafés to keep such long hours.

(17) The utilization of these cafes for teaching illiterates reading and writing; toward this end, the assistance of the rising generation of elementary schoolteachers and students.

(18) A campaign against harmful customs, whether economic, moral, or anything else; turning the masses away from these and orienting them in the direction of ways beneficial to them, or educating them in a way consonant with their best interests. These involve such customs as those to do with weddings, funerals, births, the *zār*, civil and religious holidays, etc. Let the government set a good example in this respect.

(19) Due consideration for the claims of the moral censorship, and punishment of all who are proved to have infringed any Islamic doctrine or attacked it, such as breaking the fast of Ramadān, willful neglect of prayers, insulting the faith, or any such act.

(20) The annexation of the elementary village schools to the mosques, and a thoroughgoing reform of both, as regards employees, cleanliness, and overall custodial care, so that the young may be trained in prayer and the older students in learning.

(21) The designation of religious instruction as a basic subject in all schools, in each according to its type, as well as in the universities.

(22) Active instigation to memorize the Qur'ān in all the free elementary schools; making this memorization mandatory for obtaining diplomas in the areas of religion and [Arabic] language; the stipulation that a portion of it be memorized in every school.

(23) The promulgation of a firm educational policy which will advance and raise the level of education, and will supply it, in all its varieties, with common goals and purposes; which will bring the different cultures represented in the nation closer together, and will make the first stage of its process one dedicated to inculcating a virtuous, patriotic spirit and an unwavering moral code.

(24) The cultivation of the Arabic language at every stage of instruction; the use of Arabic alone, as opposed to any foreign language, in the primary stages.

(25) The cultivation of Islamic history, and of the national history and national culture, and the history of Islamic civilization.

(26) Consideration of ways to arrive gradually at a uniform mode of dress for the nation.

(27) An end to the foreign spirit in our homes with regard to language, manners, dress, governesses, nurses, etc.; all these to be Egyptianized, especially in upper-class homes.

(28) To give journalism a proper orientation, and to encourage authors and writers to undertake Islamic, Eastern subjects,

(29) Attention to be given to matters of public health by disseminating health information through all media; increasing the number of hospitals, physicians, and mobile clinics; facilitating the means of obtaining medical treatment.

(30) Attention to be given to village problems as regards their organization, their cleanliness, the purification of their water supply, and the means to provide them with culture, recreation, and training.

Third: the economic:

(1) The organization of *zakāt* in terms of income and expenditure, according to the teachings of the magnanimous Sacred Law; invoking its assistance in carrying out necessary benevolent projects, such as homes for the aged, the poor, and orphans, and strengthening the armed forces.

(2) The prohibition of usury, and the organization of banks with this end in view. Let the government provide a good example in this domain by relinquishing all interest due on its own particular undertakings, for instance in the loan-granting banks, industrial loans, etc.

(3) The encouragement of economic projects and an increase in their number; giving work to unemployed citizens in them; the transfer of such of these as are in the hands of foreigners to the purely national sector.

(4) The protection of the masses from the oppression of monopolistic companies; keeping these within strict limits, and obtaining every possible benefit for the masses.

(5) An improvement in the lot of junior civil servants by raising their salaries, by granting them steady increases and compensations, and by lowering the salaries of senior civil servants.

(6) A reduction in the number of government posts, retaining only the indispensable ones; an equitable and scrupulous distribution of the work among civil servants.

(7) The encouragement of agricultural and industrial counseling; attention to be paid to raising the production level of the peasant and industrial worker.

(8) A concern for the technical and social problems of the worker; raising his standard of living in numerous respects.

(9) The exploitation of natural resources, such as uncultivated land, neglected mines, etc.

(10) Priority over luxury items to be given to necessary projects in terms of organization and execution.

This is the message of the Muslim Brotherhood. We submit it, and place ourselves, our talents, and all we possess in the hands of any committee or government desirous of taking a step forward, hand in hand with an Islamic nation, toward progress and advancement. We will answer the call, and we are prepared to sacrifice ourselves. We hope that by so doing we will have fulfilled our trust and said our piece, for religion means sincerity toward God, His Apostle, His Book, the Imāms of the Muslims, and their community at large. God is our sufficiency; He is enough; and peace to His chosen worshippers!

CHAPTER 5

Contested Nationalisms

Every nation emerges from the interplay of ideas, but the implementation of those ideas depends on the goodwill and willingness to compromise of a sizable number of people. Dealing with the political, economic, and social implications of the new nationalist labels—"Turkish," "Syrian," "Iranian," "Algerian," and so on—was hardly a straightforward process. Nationalism brought with it the *ideal* of increased and in some cases equal political participation by the citizenry. Thus, the shift from being a subject in an empire or monarchy to a citizen of a republic—however imperfect—was momentous and required a great deal of intellectual adjustment and political imagination from the elites and general public alike. Moreover, this shift had to be accomplished amid ideological conflicts, in which political and religious leaders sought to attract individuals and groups to their various causes and conceptions of the "nation." Unfortunately, we have very little historical documentation that chronicles these changes and their impact. The documents in this chapter provide a few examples of the public discourse that accompanied the emergence of nations in the Middle East and North Africa.

We read (document 11) about the violent confrontation between two groups in Alexandretta—a region contested between Syria and Turkey, two post–World War I nations. One group advocated annexing the region to Turkey; the other proclaimed its allegiance to Arab Syria. What is ironic about this incident is that both groups of individuals were ethnically Kurds, not Arabs or Turks. This profusion of identities belies simplistic notions of either Turkish nationalism or Arab nationalism even as the various protagonists adhered to one or the other of those causes. An article from a Syrian newspaper published in the capital city of Damascus (document 5) also sheds light on the discrepancy between ideals and reality by charging that some "Syrians" were not ardent enough in their nationalism. While the writer argues that this lack of patriotism borders on treason, for us it is evidence of a difference of opinion among "Syrians." The article exposes the possibility of resistance to the construction of a specific definition of "Syrian" identity—very much in the same manner that the notion of being "American" has undergone many historical changes.

Perhaps no place embodies the conflict over the definition of the "nation" more than Palestine. There, the aspirations of two different peoples—Jews and Arabs—came clashing together in a most painful manner that still generates repercussions. Each community presented its claim to the land as the only valid claim. Zionist Jews submitted to the postwar Peace Conference at Versailles a memorandum detailing Jewish rights to the land on the basis of a historical title (document 2). The Resolution of the General Syrian Congress in July 1919 attested to and championed the Arab claim for the benefit of the European powers meeting in Versailles (document 3). The Arabs based their claim to Palestine on the fact that they have been inhabiting the land for centuries. Departing from either of these narrowly focused definitions of Palestine was a third view that envisioned the land as capable of housing Arabs and Jews under the rubric of a bi-national state. Document 12 provides examples of this latter idea as well as of the Arab aspirations for Palestine. In this contest over nations, as in many others, the desire of the local populations was not always the only consideration. External influences were at times paramount in shaping nations, as is illustrated by U.S. support for Israel (document 13). Similar tensions were at work between Turkey and Syria over the ownership of Alexandretta (document 11).

Conflict over national identity was not always limited to exchanges of words or a few blows. In attempting to create the mythology of a singular ethnicity within the "nation," nationalists sought to ignore the existence of multiethnic communities. For some nationalists, any proclamation of a separate identity other than the proposed national one was considered a threat to the essense and existence of the "nation." At times this led to terrible events such as the killing of Armenians in Turkey between 1915 and 1917, described by Henry Morgenthau, the American ambassador to Turkey (document 1). The accusation that genocide occurred in Turkey is hotly contested by most Turks, who reject that notion as pure propaganda—as did Atatürk (see document 6 in the chapter "Ideas of Nationalism"). Regardless of this denial, historical evidence does prove that some form of ethnic cleansing took place.

Summarizing some of the conflicting visions of the "nation" is a report compiled by the King-Crane Commission, dispatched by President Woodrow Wilson to poll inhabitants of the Middle East about their views of their political future (document 4). This American commission gathered myriad opinions indicating the range of people's ideas about nationalism shortly after World War I.

A document from Tunisia provides an even more detailed map of the complexity and contradictions inherent in nationalist movements and projects (document 10). The Jewish community in Tunisia—which had lived within the larger Arab milieu and spoke Arabic for many centuries—came in contact with the Zionist project around the turn of the twentieth century. Zionism—Jewish political nationalism—presented this community of Jews with the opportunity to support the idea of a Jewish nation based on ethnicity/religion. At the same time, the Alliance Israélite Universelle—a French Jewish philanthropic organization—was actively seeking to attract these Jews toward political identi-fication with France. Last but not least, the historical relationship of this Jew-ish community to Tunisia itself created a third political identity in competition with the other two. Some members of the Jewish community in Tunisia at-tempted to strike a compromise among these ideas; others simply adhered to one ideology.

Similarly, in Algeria and the "Greater Syria," the definition of the citizen within the nation was a subject of great controversy. In Algeria (documents 7, 8, and 9), there was a tug of war between French colonial authorities that sought to naturalize Algerians as French citizens and Algerian intellectuals who re-jected French naturalization on the premise that it would deny Algerian inde-pendence. At the constitutional conference in "Greater Syria" the debate was centered on the relationship between gender and citizenship (document 6). What quickly emerges as a central issue is the conflict of affording women equal political rights within a socially conservative "nation."

The documents in this chapter clearly show the difficulty of defining na-tionalism at the popular level. They help us assess simplistic nationalist narra-tives that seek to erase all competing ideologies in favor of one dominant idea of the "nation." Furthermore, they highlight some of the tools necessary to ar-ticulate political consciousness and the vision of a newly proposed collective political entity. In other words, some of these documents clearly show the modernity of nationalism, which, paradoxically, its proponents claimed was an "eternal" presence in history.

1. Henry Morgenthau Recounts Aspects of Nationalist-Driven Ethnic Cleansing of Armenians in Turkey, 1915

The massacre of large numbers of Armenians (up to one million according to some estimates) is a very dark period in the history of the Ottoman Empire. It also is a hotly contested subject between the Armenian community and the Turkish govern-ment, producing lawsuits and a great deal of rhetoric.

The Turkish government and its supporters argue that the number of Armeni-ans said to have been killed is inflated, and they deny that there was any system-atic attempt to eradicate that ethnic community. They also contend that those Armenians actually killed were not innocent civilians but traitorous combatants re-cruited by Armenian political organizations collaborating with Russia for the pur-pose of establishing an Armenian homeland in parts of the Ottoman Empire. Armenians and their supporters completely and vociferously disagree with this char-acterization. They contend the Committee of Union and Progress (the Young Turks) began a campaign of ethnic cleansing against Armenians in 1915. A major part of

Henry Morgenthau, *The Murder of a Nation* (New York: Armenian General Benevolent Union of America, 1915), pp. 30–43, 50–54, 64–67.

this campaign was the expulsion of Armenians from their homes in Anatolia and into the Syrian desert. Along the way they were attacked, robbed, and killed, and countless numbers of people starved on what was in effect a death march.

Aside from the differing accounts of what transpired, these events offer a clear example of the fault lines present in nationalist projects centered on a pure and singular ethnic definition of the "nation." Reprinted here is an excerpt from a book authored by Henry Morgenthau, the U.S. ambassador to Turkey between 1913 and 1916. Morgenthau describes some of the atrocities and explains the nationalist logic behind the Armenian genocide.

The destruction of the Armenian race in 1915 involved certain difficulties that had not impeded the operations of the Turks in the massacres of 1895 and other years. In these earlier periods the Armenian men had possessed little power or means of resistance. In those days Armenians had not been permitted to have military training, to serve in the Turkish army, or to possess arms. As I have already said, these discriminations were withdrawn when the revolutionists obtained the upper hand in 1908. Not only were the Christians now permitted to bear arms, but the authorities, in the full flush of their enthusiasm for freedom and equality, encouraged them to do so. In the early part of 1915, therefore, every Turkish city contained thousands of Armenians who had been trained as soldiers and who were supplied with rifles, pistols, and other weapons of defense. The operations at Van once more disclosed that these men could use their weapons to good advantage. It was thus apparent that an Armenian massacre this time would generally assume more the character of warfare than those wholesale butcheries of defenseless men and women which the Turks had always found so congenial. If this plan of murdering a race were to succeed, two preliminary steps would therefore have to be taken: it would be necessary to render all Armenian soldiers powerless and to deprive of their arms the Armenians in every city and town. Before Armenia could be slaughtered, Armenia must be made defenseless.

In the early part of 1915, the Armenian soldiers in the Turkish army were reduced to a new status. Up to that time most of them had been combatants, but now they were all stripped of their arms and transformed into workmen. Instead of serving their country as artillerymen and cavalrymen, these former soldiers now discovered that they had been transformed into road labourers and pack animals. Army supplies of all kinds were loaded on their backs, and, stumbling under the burdens and driven by the whips and bayonets of the Turks, they were forced to drag their weary bodies into the mountains of the Caucasus. Sometimes they would have to plough their way, burdened in this fashion, almost waist high through snow. They had to spend practically all their time in the open, sleeping on the bare ground—whenever the ceaseless prodding of their taskmasters gave them an occasional opportunity to sleep. They were given only scraps of food; if they fell sick they were left where they had dropped, their Turkish oppressors perhaps stopping long enough to rob them of all their possessions—even of their clothes. If any stragglers succeeded in reaching their destinations, they were not infrequently massacred. In many instances Armenian soldiers were disposed of in even more summary fashion, for it now became almost the general practice to shoot them in cold blood. In almost all cases the procedure was the same. Here and there squads of 50 or 100 men would be taken, bound together in groups of four, and then marched out to a secluded spot a short distance from the village. Suddenly the sound of rifle shots would fill the air, and the Turkish soldiers who had acted as the escort would sullenly return to camp. Those sent to bury the bodies would find them almost invariably stark naked, for, as usual, the Turks had stolen all their clothes. In cases that came to my attention, the murderers had added a refinement to their victims' sufferings by compelling them to dig their graves before being shot.

[. . .] The Young Turks displayed greater ingenuity than their predecessor, Abdul Hamid. The injunction of the deposed Sultan was merely "to kill, kill," whereas the Turkish democracy hit upon an entirely new plan. Instead of massacring outright the Armenian race, they now decided to deport it. In the south and southeastern section of the Ottoman Empire lie the Syrian desert and the Mesopotamian valley. Though part of this area was once the scene of a flourishing civilization, for the last five centuries it has suffered the blight that becomes the lot of any country that is subjected to Turkish rule; and it is now a dreary, desolate waste, without cities and towns or life of any kind, populated only by a few wild and fanatical Bedouin tribes. Only the most industrious labour, expended through many years, could transform this desert into the abiding place of any considerable population. The Central Government now announced its intention of gathering the two million or more Armenians living in the several sections of the empire and transporting them to this desolate and inhospitable region. Had they undertaken such a deportation in good faith it would have represented the height of cruelty and injustice. As a matter of fact, the Turks never had the slightest idea of reëstablishing the Armenians in this new country. They knew that the great majority would never reach their destination and that those who did would either die of thirst and starvation, or be murdered by the wild Mohammedan desert tribes. The real purpose of the deportation was robbery and destruction; it really represented a new method of massacre. When the Turkish authorities gave the orders for these deportations, they were merely giving the death warrant to a whole race; they understood this well, and, in their conversations with me, they made no particular attempt to conceal the fact.

All through the spring and summer of 1915 the deportations took place. Of the larger cities, Constantinople, Smyrna, and Aleppo were spared; practically all other places where a single Armenian family lived now became the scenes of these unspeakable tragedies. Scarcely a single Armenian, whatever his education or wealth, or whatever the social class to which he belonged, was exempted from the order. In some villages placards were posted ordering the whole Armenian population to present itself in a public place at an appointed time—usually a day or two ahead, and in other places the town crier would go through the streets delivering the order vocally. In still others not the slightest warning was given. The gendarmes would appear before an Armenian house and order all the inmates to follow them. They would take women engaged in their domestic tasks without giving them the chance to change their clothes. The police fell upon them just as the eruption of Vesuvius fell upon Pompeii; women were taken from the washtubs, children were snatched out of bed, the bread was left half baked in the oven, the family meal was abandoned partly eaten, the children were taken from the schoolroom, leaving their books open at the daily task, and the men were forced to abandon their ploughs in the fields and their cattle on the mountain side. Even women who had just given birth to children would be forced to leave their beds and join the panic-stricken throng, their sleeping babies in their arms. Such things as they hurriedly snatched up— a shawl, a blanket, perhaps a few scraps of food—were all that they could take of their household belongings. To their frantic questions "Where are we going?" the gendarmes would vouchsafe only one reply: "To the interior."

In some cases the refugees were given a few hours, in exceptional instances a few days, to dispose of their property and household effects. But the proceeding, of course, amounted simply to robbery. They could sell only to Turks, and since both buyers and sellers knew that they had only a day or two to market the accumulations of a lifetime, the prices obtained represented a small fraction of their value. Sewing machines would bring one or two dollars—a cow would go for a dollar, a houseful of furniture would be sold for a pittance. In many cases Armenians were prohibited from selling or Turks from buying even at these ridiculous prices; under pretense that the Government intended to sell their effects to pay the creditors whom they would inevitably leave behind, their household furniture would be placed in stores or heaped up in public places, where it was usually pillaged by Turkish men and women. The government officials would also inform the Armenians that, since their deportation was only temporary, the intention being to bring them back after the war was over, they would not be permitted to sell their houses. Scarcely had the former possessors left the village, when Mohammedan *mohadjirs*—immigrants from other parts of Turkey—would be moved into the Armenian quarters. Similarly all their valuables—money, rings, watches, and jewellery—would be taken to the police stations for "safe keeping," pending their return, and then parcelled out among the Turks. Yet these robberies gave the refugees little anguish, for far more terrible and agonizing scenes were taking place under their eyes. The systematic extermination of the men continued; such males as the persecutions which I have already described had left were now violently dealt with. Before the caravans were started, it became the regular practice to separate the young men from the families, tie them together in groups of four, lead them to the outskirts, and shoot them. Public hangings without trial—the only offense being that the victims were Armenians—were taking place constantly. The gendarmes showed a particular desire to annihilate the educated and the influential. From American consuls and missionaries I was constantly receiving reports of such executions, and many of the events which they described will never fade from my memory. At Angora all Armenian men from fifteen to seventy were arrested, bound together in groups of four, and sent on the road in the direction of Caesarea. When they had travelled five or six hours and had reached a secluded valley, a mob of Turkish peasants fell upon them with clubs, hammers, axes, scythes, spades, and saws. Such instruments not only caused more agonizing deaths than guns and pistols, but, as the Turks themselves boasted, they were more economical, since they did not involve the waste of powder and shell. In this way they exterminated the whole male population of Angora, including all its men of wealth and breeding, and their bodies, horribly mutilated, were left in the valley, where they were devoured by wild beasts. After completing this destruction, the peasants and gendarmes gathered in the local tavern, comparing notes and boasting of the number of "giaours" that each had slain. In Trebizond the men were placed in boats and sent out on the Black Sea; gendarmes would follow them in boats, shoot them down, and throw their bodies into the water.

When the signal was given for the caravans to move, therefore, they almost invariably consisted of women, children, and old men. Any one who could possibly have protected them from the fate that awaited them had been destroyed. Not infrequently the prefect of the city, as the mass started on its way, would wish them a derisive "pleasant journey." Before the caravan moved the women were sometimes offered the alternative of becoming Mohammedans. Even though they accepted the new faith, which few of them did, their earthly troubles did not end. The converts were compelled to surrender their children to a so-called "Moslem Orphanage," with the agreement that they should be trained as devout followers of the Prophet. They themselves must then show the sincerity of their conversion by abandoning their Christian husbands and marrying Moslems. If no good Mohammedan offered himself as a husband, then the new convert was deported, however strongly she might protest her devotion to Islam.

At first the Government showed some inclination to protect these departing throngs. The officers usually divided them into convoys, in some cases numbering several hundred, in others several thousand. The civil authorities occasionally furnished ox-carts which carried such household furniture as the exiles had succeeded in scrambling together. A guard of gendarmerie accompanied each convoy, ostensibly to guide and protect it. Women, scantily clad, carrying babies in their arms or on their backs, marched side by side with old men hobbling along with canes. Children would run along, evidently regarding the procedure, in the early stages, as some new lark. A more prosperous member would perhaps have a horse or a donkey, occasionally a farmer had rescued a cow or a sheep, which would trudge along at his side, and the usual assortment of family pets—dogs, cats, and birds—became parts of the variegated procession. From thousands of Armenian cities and villages these despairing caravans now set forth; they filled all the roads leading southward; everywhere, as they moved on, they raised a huge dust, and abandoned débris, chairs, blankets, bedclothes, household utensils, and other impedimenta, marked the course of the processions. When the caravans first started, the individuals bore some resemblance to human beings; in a few hours, however, the dust of the road plastered their faces and clothes, the mud caked their lower members, and the slowly advancing mobs, frequently bent with fatigue and crazed by the brutality of their "protectors," resembled some new and strange animal species. Yet for the better part of six months, from April to October, 1915, practically all the highways in Asia Minor were crowded with these unearthly bands of exiles. They could be seen winding in and out of every valley and climbing up the sides of nearly every mountain—moving on and on, they scarcely knew whither, except that every road led to death. Village after village and town after town was evacuated of its Armenian population, under the distressing circumstances already detailed. In these six months, as far as can be ascertained, about 1,200,000 people started on this journey to the Syrian desert.

"Pray for us," they would say as they left their homes—the homes in which their ancestors had lived for 2,500 years. "We shall not see you in this world again, but sometime we shall meet. Pray for us!"

[. . .]

On the seventieth day a few creatures reached Aleppo. Out of the combined convoy of 18,000 souls just 150 women and children reached their destination. A few of the rest, the most attractive, were still living as captives of the Kurds and Turks; all the rest were dead.

My only reason for relating such dreadful things as this is that, without the details, the English-speaking public cannot understand precisely what this nation is which we call Turkey. I have by no means told the most terrible details, for a complete narration of the sadistic orgies of which these Armenian men and women were the victims can never be printed in an American publication. Whatever crimes the most perverted instincts of the human mind can devise, and whatever refinements of persecution and injustice the most debased imagination can conceive, became the daily misfortunes of this devoted people. I am confident that the whole history of the human race contains no such horrible episode as this. The great massacres and persecutions of the past seem almost insignificant when compared with the sufferings of the Armenian race in 1915. The slaughter of the Albigenses in the early part of the thirteenth century has always been regarded as one of the most pitiful events in history. In these outbursts of fanaticism about 60,000 people were killed. In the massacre of St. Bartholomew about 30,000 human beings lost their lives. The Sicilian Vespers, which has always figured as one of the most fiendish outbursts of this kind, caused the destruction of 8,000. Volumes have been written about the Spanish Inquisition under Torquemada, yet in the eighteen years of his administration only a little more than 8,000 heretics were done to death. Perhaps the one event in history that most resembles the Armenian deportations was the expulsion of the Jews from Spain by Ferdinand and Isabella. According to Prescott 160,000 were uprooted from their homes and scattered broadcast over Africa and Europe. Yet all these previous persecutions seem almost trivial when we compare them with the sufferings of the Armenians, in which at least 600,000 people were destroyed and perhaps as many as 1,000,000. And these earlier massacres, when we compare them with the spirit that directed the Armenian atrocities, have one feature that we can almost describe as an excuse: they were the product of religious fanaticism and most of the men and women who instigated them sincerely believed that they were devoutly serving their Maker. Undoubtedly religious fanaticism was an impelling motive with the Turkish and Kurdish rabble who slew Armenians as a service to Allah, but the men who really conceived the crime had no such motive. Practically all of them were atheists, with no more respect for Mohammedanism than for Christianity, and with them the one motive was cold-blooded, calculating state policy.

The Armenians are not the only subject people in Turkey which have suffered from this policy of making Turkey exclusively the country of the Turks. The story which I have told about the Armenians I could also tell with certain modifications about the Greeks and the Syrians. Indeed the Greeks were the first victims of this nationalizing idea. I have already described how, in the few months preceding the European War, the Ottoman Government began deporting its Greek subjects along the coast of Asia Minor. These outrages aroused little interest in Europe or the United States, yet in the space of three or four months more than 100,000 Greeks were taken from their age-long homes in the Mediterranean littoral and removed to the Greek Islands and the interior. For the larger part these were bona-fide deportations; that is, the Greek inhabitants were actually removed to new places and were not subjected to wholesale massacre. It was probably for the reason that the civilized world did not protest against these deportations that the Turks afterward decided to apply the same methods on a larger scale not only to the Greeks but to the Armenians, Syrians, Nestorians, and others of its subject peoples. In fact, Bedri Bey, the Prefect of Police at Constantinople, himself told one of my secretaries that the Turks had expelled the Greeks so successfully that they had decided to apply the same method to all the other races in the empire.

The martyrdom of the Greeks, therefore, comprised two periods: that antedating the war, and that which began in the early part of 1915. The first affected chiefly the Greeks on the seacoast of Asia Minor. The second affected those living in Thrace and in the territories surrounding the Sea of Marmora, the Dardanelles, the Bosphorus, and the coast of the Black Sea. These latter, to the extent of several hundred thousand, were sent to the interior of Asia Minor. The Turks adopted almost identically the same procedure against the Greeks as that which they had adopted against the Armenians. They began by incorporating the Greeks into the Ottoman army and then transforming them into labour battalions, using them to build roads in the Caucasus and other scenes of action. These Greek soldiers, just like the Armenians, died by thousands from cold, hunger, and other privations. The same house-to-house searches for hidden weapons took place in the Greek villages, and Greek men and women were beaten and tortured just as were their fellow Armenians. The Greeks had to submit to the same forced requisitions, which amounted in their case, as in the case of the Armenians, merely to plundering on a wholesale scale. The Turks attempted to force the Greek subjects to become Mohammedans; Greek girls, just like Armenian girls, were stolen and taken to Turkish harems and

Greek boys were kidnapped and placed in Moslem households. The Greeks, just like the Armenians, were accused of disloyalty to the Ottoman Government; the Turks accused them of furnishing supplies to the English submarines in the Marmora and also of acting as spies. The Turks also declared that the Greeks were not loyal to the Ottoman Government, and that they also looked forward to the day when the Greeks inside of Turkey would become part of Greece. These latter charges were unquestionably true; that the Greeks, after suffering for five centuries the most unspeakable outrages at the hands of the Turks, should look longingly to the day when their territory should be part of the fatherland, was to be expected. The Turks, as in the case of the Armenians, seized upon this as an excuse for a violent onslaught on the whole race. Everywhere the Greeks were gathered in groups and, under the so-called protection of Turkish gendarmes, they were transported, the larger part on foot, into the interior. Just how many were scattered in this fashion is not definitely known, the estimates varying anywhere from 200,000 up to 1,000,000. These caravans suffered great privations, but they were not submitted to general massacre as were the Armenians, and this is probably the reason why the outside world has not heard so much about them. The Turks showed them this greater consideration not from any motive of pity. The Greeks, unlike the Armenians, had a government which was vitally interested in their welfare. At this time there was a general apprehension among the Teutonic Allies that Greece would enter the war on the side of the Entente, and a wholesale massacre of Greeks in Asia Minor would unquestionably have produced such a state of mind in Greece that its pro-German king would have been unable longer to keep his country out of the war. It was only a matter of state policy, therefore, that saved these Greek subjects of Turkey from all the horrors that befell the Armenians. But their sufferings are still terrible, and constitute another chapter in the long story of crimes for which civilization will hold the Turk responsible.

[...]

"Suppose a few Armenians did betray you," I said. "Is that a reason for destroying a whole race? Is that an excuse for making innocent women and children suffer?"

"Those things are inevitable," he [Talaat Pasha (1874–1921), part of the CUP triumvirate who became the Prime Minister of the Ottoman Empire in 1917] replied.

This remark to me was not quite so illuminating as one which Talaat made subsequently to a reporter of the *Berliner Tageblatt,* who asked him the same question. "We have been reproached," he said, according to this interviewer, "for making no distinction between the innocent Armenians and the guilty; but that was utterly impossible, in view of the fact that those who were innocent to-day might be guilty to-morrow"!

One reason why Talaat could not discuss this matter with me freely, was because the member of the embassy staff who did the interpreting was himself an Armenian. In the early part of August, therefore, he sent a personal messenger to me, asking if I could not see him alone—he said that he himself would provide the interpreter. This was the first time that Talaat had admitted that his treatment of the Armenians was a matter with which I had any concern. The interview took place two days afterward. It so happened that since the last time I had visited Talaat I had shaved my beard. As soon as I came in the burly Minister began talking in his customary bantering fashion.

"You have become a young man again," he said; "you are so young now that I cannot go to you for advice any more."

"I have shaved my beard," I replied, "because it had become very gray—made gray by your treatment of the Armenians."

After this exchange of compliments we settled down to the business in hand. "I have asked you to come to-day," began Talaat, "so that I can explain our position on the whole Armenian subject. We base our objections to the Armenians on three distinct grounds. In the first place, they have enriched themselves at the expense of the Turks. In the second place, they are determined to domineer over us and to establish a separate state. In the third place, they have openly encouraged our enemies. They have assisted the Russians in the Caucasus and our failure there is largely explained by their actions. We have therefore come to the irrevocable decision that we shall make them powerless before this war is ended."

On every one of these points I had plenty of arguments in rebuttal. Talaat's first objection was merely an admission that the Armenians were more industrious and more able than the dull-witted and lazy Turks. Massacre as a means of destroying business competition was certainly an original conception! His general charge that the Armenians were "conspiring" against Turkey and that they openly sympathized with Turkey's enemies merely meant, when reduced to its original elements, that the Armenians were constantly appealing to the European Powers to protect them against robbery, murder, and outrage. The Armenian problem, like most race problems, was the result of centuries of ill-treatment and injustice. There could be only one solution for it, the creation of an orderly system of government, in which all citizens were to be treated upon an equality, and in which all offenses were to be punished as the acts of individuals and not as of peoples. I argued for a long time along these and similar lines.

"It is no use for you to argue," Talaat answered, "we have already disposed of three quarters of the Armenians; there are none at all left in Bitlis, Van, and Erzeroum. The hatred between the Turks and the Armenians is now so intense that we have got to finish with them. If we don't, they will plan their revenge."

"If you are not influenced by humane considerations," I replied, "think of the material loss. These people are your business men. They control many of your industries. They are very large tax-payers. What would become of you commercially without them?"

"We care nothing about the commercial loss," replied Talaat. "We have figured all that out and we know that it will not exceed five million pounds. We don't worry about that. I have asked you to come here so as to let you know that our Armenian policy is absolutely fixed and that nothing can change it. We will not have the Armenians anywhere in Anatolia. They can live in the desert but nowhere else."

I still attempted to persuade Talaat that the treatment of the Armenians was destroying Turkey in the eyes of the world, and that his country would never be able to recover from this infamy.

"You are making a terrible mistake," I said, and I repeated the statement three times.

"Yes, we may make mistakes," he replied, "but"—and he firmly closed his lips and shook his head—"we never regret."

[. . .]

2. The Zionist Organization's Memorandum to the Peace Conference in Versailles Asks for Support for the Establishment of a Jewish State in Palestine, February 3, 1919

After obtaining British support for establishing a Jewish homeland in Palestine (see document 4, the Balfour Declaration, in the chapter "Ideas of Nationalism"), Zionist organizations sought to articulate and consolidate that idea into a more concrete project and brought their vision to the victorious Allies meeting in Versailles at the Peace Conference. One goal of the conference was to map the geopolitics of the postwar Middle East and Africa, so its decision about who would receive colonial control over Palestine was of momentous importance to Zionists and Arabs alike.

The Zionist project was a secular political program, but the language used in parts of this memorandum had religious connotations that the writers knew would resonate with a Western Christian audience. Of particular interest is the idea of "redemption" of a "lost" land, which implicitly dismisses centuries of Arab occupation of the region and brings to mind the logic used by nineteenth-century European imperialists to justify their occupation and colonization of the African continent. This concept of "manifest destiny" is textually linked to the idea of scientific and rational reclamation of the land, thus linking the ancient history of the Jews in Palestine (before the Diaspora of 70 C.E.) and the modernity of their European descendants.

The Zionist Organisation respectfully submits the following draft resolutions for the consideration of the Peace Conference:

1. The High Contracting Parties recognise the historic title of the Jewish people to Palestine and the right of the Jews to reconstitute in Palestine their National Home.

2. The boundaries of Palestine shall be as declared in the Schedule annexed hereto.

3. The sovereign possession of Palestine shall be vested in the League of Nations and the Government entrusted to Great Britain as mandatary of the League.

David Hunter Miller, *My Diary at the Conference of Paris* (New York, 1924), vol. 5, pp. 15–29.

4. (Provision to be inserted relating to the application in Palestine of such of the general conditions attached to mandates as are suitable to the case.)

5. The mandate shall be subject also to the following special conditions:

I. Palestine shall be placed under such political, administrative and economic conditions as will secure the establishment there of the Jewish National Home and ultimately render possible the creation of an autonomous Commonwealth, it being clearly understood that nothing shall be done which may prejudice the civil and religious rights of existing non-Jewish communities in Palestine or the rights and political status enjoyed by Jews in any other country.

II. To this end the Mandatary Power shall *inter alia*

a. Promote Jewish immigration and close settlement on the land, the established rights of the present non-Jewish population being equitably safeguarded.

b. Accept the co-operation in such measures of a Council representative of the Jews of Palestine and of the world that may be established for the development of the Jewish National Home in Palestine and entrust the organisation of Jewish education to such Council.

c. On being satisfied that the constitution of such Council precludes the making of private profit, offer to the Council in priority any concession for public works or for the development of natural resources which may be found desirable to grant.

III. The Mandatary Power shall encourage the widest measure of self-government for localities practicable in the conditions of the country.

IV. There shall be for ever the fullest freedom of religious worship for all creeds in Palestine. There shall be no discrimination among the inhabitants with regard to citizenship and civil rights, on the grounds of religion or of race.

V. (Provision to be inserted relating to the control of the Holy Places).

The Boundaries of Palestine Schedule

The boundaries of Palestine shall follow the general lines set out below:

Starting on the North at a point on the Mediterranean Sea in the vicinity of Sidon and following the watersheds of the foothills of the Lebanon as far as Jisr El Karaon, thence to El Bire, following the dividing line between the two basins of the Wadi El Korn and the Wadi Et Teim thence in a southerly direction following the dividing line between the Eastern and Western slopes of the Hermon, to the vicinity West of Beit Jenn, thence Eastward following the northern watersheds of the Nahr Mughaniye close to and west of the Hedjaz Railway.

In the East a line close to and West of the Hedjaz Railway terminating in the Gulf of Akaba.

In the South a frontier to be agreed upon with the Egyptian Government. In the West the Mediterranean Sea.

The details of the delimitations, or any necessary adjustments of detail, shall be settled by a Special Commission on which there shall be Jewish representation.

Statement

The Historic Title

The claims of the Jews with regard to Palestine rest upon the following main considerations:

(1) The land is the historic home of the Jews; there they achieved their greatest development, from that centre, through their agency, there emanated spiritual and moral influences of supreme value to mankind. By violence they were driven from Palestine, and through the ages they have never ceased to cherish the longing and the hope of a return.

(2) In some parts of the world, and particularly in Eastern Europe, the conditions of life of millions of Jews are deplorable. Forming often a congested population, denied the opportunities which would make a healthy development possible, the need of fresh outlets is urgent, both for their own sake and in the interest of the population of other races, among whom they dwell. Palestine would offer one such outlet. To the Jewish masses it is the country above all others in which they would most wish to cast their lot. By the methods of economic development to which we shall refer later, Palestine can be made now as it was in ancient times, the home of a prosperous population many times as numerous as that which now inhabits it.

(3) But Palestine is not large enough to contain more than a proportion of the Jews of the world. The greater part of the fourteen millions or more scattered through all countries must remain in their present localities, and it will doubtless be one of the cares of the Peace Conference to ensure for them, wherever they have been oppressed, as for all peoples, equal rights and humane conditions. A Jewish National Home in Palestine will, however, be of high value to them also. Its influence will permeate the Jewries of the world: it will inspire these millions, hitherto often despairing, with a new hope; it will hold out before their eyes a higher standard; it will help to make them even more useful citizens in the lands in which they dwell.

(4) Such a Palestine would be of value also to the world at large, whose real wealth consists in the healthy diversities of its civilisations.

(5) Lastly the land itself needs redemption. Much of it is left desolate. Its present condition is a standing reproach. Two things are necessary for that redemption—a stable and enlightened Government, and an addition to the present population which shall be energetic, intelligent, devoted to the country, and backed by the large financial resources that are indispensable for development. Such a population the Jews alone can supply.

Inspired by these ideas, Jewish activities particularly during the last thirty years have been directed to Palestine within the measure that the Turkish administrative system allowed. Some millions of pounds sterling have been spent in the country particularly in the foundation of Jewish agricultural settlements. Those settlements have been for the most part highly successful.

With enterprise and skill the Jews have adopted modern scientific methods and have shown themselves to be capable agriculturalists. Hebrew has been revived as a living language, it is the medium of instruction in the schools and the tongue is in daily use among the rising generation. The foundations of a Jewish University have been laid at Jerusalem and considerable funds have been contributed for the creation of its building and for its endowment. Since the British occupation, the Zionist Organisation has expended in Palestine approximately £50,000 a month upon relief, education and sanitation. To promote the future development of the country great sums will be needed for drainage, irrigation, roads, railways, harbours and public works of all kinds, as well as for land settlement and house building. Assuming a political settlement under which the establishment of a Jewish National Home in Palestine is assured the Jews of the world will make every effort to provide the vast sums of money that will be needed. . . .

[Here follow a recital of the Balfour Declaration and of its endorsement by the French Foreign Minister and reference to support of Zionism and the Balfour Declaration by other allied governments.]

Great Britain as Mandatary of the League of Nations

We ask that Great Britain shall act as Mandatary of the League of Nations for Palestine. The selection of Great Britain as Mandatary is urged on the ground that this is the wish of the Jews of the world and the League of Nations in selecting a Mandatary will follow as far as possible, the popular wish of the people concerned.

The preference on the part of the Jews for a British Trusteeship is unquestionably the result of the peculiar relationship of England to the Jewish Palestinian problem. The return of the Jews to Zion has not only been a remarkable feature in English literature, but in the domain of statecraft it has played its part, beginning with the readmission of the Jews under Cromwell. It manifested itself particularly in the 19th century in the instructions given to British Consular representatives in the Orient after the Damascus Incident; in the various Jewish Palestinian projects suggested by English non-Jews prior to 1881; in the letters of endorsement and support given by members of the Royal Family and Officers of the Government to Lawrence Oliphant and finally, in the three consecutive acts which definitely associated Great Britain with Zionism in the minds of the Jews viz.—the El Arish offer in 1901; the East African offer in 1903, and lastly the British Declaration in favour of a Jewish National Home in Palestine in 1917. Moreover, the Jews who have gained political experience in many lands under a great variety of governmental systems, whole-heartedly appreciate the advanced and liberal policies adopted by Great Britain in her modern colonial administration. . . .

[Here follows a recital of the selection of Great Britain as mandatory power by the American Jewish Congress and a conference of Palestine Jews at Jaffa.]

Boundaries

The boundaries above outlined are what we consider essential for the necessary economic foundation of the country. Palestine must have its natural outlets to the seas and the control of its rivers and their headwaters. The boundaries are sketched with the general economic needs and historic traditions of the country in mind, factors which necessarily must also be considered by the Special Commission in fixing the definite boundary lines. This Commission will bear in mind that it is highly desirable, in the interests of economical administration that the geographical area of Palestine should be as large as possible so that it may eventually contain a large and thriving population which could more easily bear the burdens of modern civilised government than a small country with a necessary limitation of inhabitants.

The economic life of Palestine, like that of every other semi-arid country depends on the available water supply. It is, therefore, of vital importance not only to secure all water resources already feeding the country, but also to be able to conserve and control them at their sources.

The Hermon is Palestine's real "Father of Waters" and cannot be severed from it without striking at the very root of its economic life. The Hermon not only needs reafforestation but also other works before it can again adequately serve as the water reservoir of the country. It must therefore be wholly under the control of those who will most willingly as well as most adequately restore it to its maximum utility. Some international arrangement must be made whereby the riparian rights of the people dwelling south of the Litani River may be fully protected. Properly cared for these head waters can be made to serve in the development of the Lebanon as well as of Palestine.

The fertile plains east of the Jordan, since the earliest Biblical times, have been linked economically and politically with the land west of the Jordan. The country which is now very sparsely populated, in Roman times supported a great population. It could now serve admirably for colonisation on a large scale. A just regard for the economic needs of Palestine and Arabia demands that free access to the Hedjaz Railway throughout its length be accorded both Governments.

An intensive development of the agriculture and other opportunities of Transjordania make it imperative that Palestine shall have access to the Red Sea and an opportunity of developing good harbours on the Gulf of Akaba. Akaba, it will be recalled, was the terminus of an important trade route of Palestine from the days of Solomon onwards. The ports developed in the Gulf of Akaba should be free ports through which the commerce of the Hinterland may pass on the same principle which guides us in suggesting that free access be given to the Hedjaz Railway.

Proposals to the Mandatary Power

In connection with the Government to be set up by the Mandatary of the League of Nations until such time as the people of Palestine shall be prepared to undertake the establishment of representative and responsible Government proposals will be made in due course to the Mandatary Power to the following effect:

1. In any instrument establishing the constitution of Palestine the Declarations of the Peace Conference shall be recited as forming an integral part of that constitution.
2. The Jewish people shall be entitled to fair representation in the executive and legislative bodies and in the selection of public and civil servants. In giving such representation the Mandatary Power shall consult the Jewish Council hereinafter mentioned.

   Neither law nor custom shall preclude the appointment of a citizen of Palestine as chief of the executive.
3. That in encouraging the self government of localities the Mandatary Power shall secure the maintenance by local communities of proper standards of administration in matters of education, communal, or regional activities. In granting or enlarging local autonomy regard shall be had to the readiness and ability of the community to attain such standards. Local autonomous communities shall be empowered and encouraged to combine and cooperate for common purposes.
4. Education without distinction of race shall be assisted from public funds.
5. Hebrew shall be one of the official languages of Palestine and shall be employed in all documents, decrees and announcements and on all stamps, coins, and notes issued by the Government.
6. The Jewish Sabbath and Holy Days shall be recognised as legal days of rest.
7. All inhabitants continuing to reside in Palestine who on the   day of   , 19   , have their domicile in Palestine, except those who elect in writing within six months from such date to retain their foreign citizenship, shall become citizens of Palestine, and they and all persons in Palestine or naturalised under the laws of Palestine after the   day of   , 19   , shall be citizens thereof and entitled to the protection of the Mandatary Power on behalf of the Government of Palestine.

Land Commission

Recognising that the general progress of Palestine must begin with the reform of the conditions governing land tenure and settlement, the Mandatary Power shall appoint a Commission (upon which the Jewish Council shall have representation) with power:

a. To make survey of the land and to schedule all lands that may be made available for close settlement, intensive cultivation and public use.

b. To propose measures for determining and registering titles of ownership of land.

c. To propose measures for supervising transactions in land with a view of preventing land speculation.

d. To propose measures for the close settlement, intensive cultivation and public use of land, where necessary by compulsory purchase at a fair pre-war price and further by making available all waste lands unoccupied and inadequately cultivated lands or lands without legal owners, and state lands.

e. To propose measures for the taxation and the tenure of land and in general any progressive measures in harmony with the policy of making the land available for close settlement and intensive cultivation.

f. To propose measures whereby the Jewish Council may take over all lands available for close settlement and intensive cultivation.

g. In all such measures the established rights of the present population shall be equitably safeguarded.

The Jewish Council for Palestine

1. A Jewish Council for Palestine shall be elected by a Jewish Congress representative of the Jews of Palestine and of the entire world, which shall be convoked in Jerusalem on or before the First day of January, 1920, or as soon thereafter as possible, by the Provisional Jewish Council hereinafter mentioned.

The Jewish Congress shall determine its functions as well as the constitution and functions of the Jewish Council in conformity with the purpose and spirit of the Declarations of the Peace Conference and of the powers conferred by the mandatary power upon the Jewish Council.

2. The Jewish Council shall be recognised as a legal entity and shall have power:

a. To co-operate and consult with and to assist the Government of Palestine in any and all matters affecting the Jewish people in Palestine and in all such cases to be and to act as the representative of the Jewish people.

b. To participate in the development and administration of immigration, close land settlement, credit facilities, public works, services, and enterprises, and every other form of activity conducive to the development of the country. The organisation of Jewish education to be entrusted to such Council.

c. To acquire and hold Real Estate.

d. To acquire and exercise concessions for public works and the development of natural resources.

e. With the consent of the Jewish inhabitants concerned or their accredited representatives, to assess such inhabitants for the purpose of stimulating and maintaining education, communal, charitable and other public institutions (including the Jewish Council) and other activities primarily concerned with the welfare of the Jewish people in Palestine.

f. With the approval of the Mandatary Power and upon such terms and conditions as the Mandatary Power may prescribe, to administer the immigration laws of Palestine in so far as they affect Jewish immigration.

g. With the approval of the Mandatary Power, to issue bonds, debentures, or other obligations, the proceeds of any or all of which to be expended by the Jewish Council for the benefit of the Jewish people or for the development of Palestine.

h. The Jewish Council shall hold all of its property and income in trust for the benefit of the Jewish people.

3. A provisional Jewish Council of representatives of the Zionist Organisation, of the Jewish population in Palestine, and of such other approved Jewish organisations as are willing to cooperate in the development of a Jewish Palestine shall be formed forthwith by the Zionist Organisation. Such Provisional Jewish Council shall exercise all of the powers and perform all of the duties of the Jewish Council until such time as the Jewish Council shall be formally constituted by the Jewish Congress

4. Finally when in the opinion of the Mandatary Power, the inhabitants of Palestine shall be able to undertake the establishment of Representative and Responsible Government, such steps shall be taken as will permit the establishment of such government through the exercise of a democratic franchise, without regard to race or faith; and the inhabitants of Palestine under such government, shall continue to enjoy equal civil and political rights as citizens irrespective of race or faith. . . .

[Here follows a description of the Zionist Organization.]

3. The Resolution of the General Syrian Congress at Damascus Proclaims Arab Sovereignty over Greater Syria, July 2, 1919

In 1919, during the Peace Conference at Versailles, President Woodrow Wilson appointed an American commission headed by Henry King (president of Oberlin College in Ohio) and Chicago businessman Charles R. Crane. The purpose of the King-Crane Commission was to solicit the opinions of the local inhabitants of Syria and Palestine about their political future in light of the dissolution of the Ottoman Empire. This resolution of the General Syrian Congress formulated to provide the

King-Crane Commission with a specific and unified notion of what the "Arabs" of Greater Syria desired. The document leaves no doubt about their rejection of the Zionist project for a Jewish homeland in what the U.S. Congress—and most Arabs—regarded as Arab Palestine.

We the undersigned members of the General Syrian Congress, meeting in Damascus on Wednesday, July 2nd, 1919, made up of representatives from the three Zones, viz., the Southern, Eastern, and Western, provided with credentials and authorizations by the inhabitants of our various districts, Moslems, Christians, and Jews, have agreed upon the following statement of the desires of the people of the country who have elected us to present them to the American Section of the International Commission; the fifth article was passed by a very large majority; all the other articles were accepted unanimously.

1. We ask absolutely complete political independence for Syria within these boundaries. The Taurus System on the North; Rafah and a line running from Al Jauf to the south of the Syrian and the Hejazian line to Akaba on the south; the Euphrates and Khabur Rivers and a line extending east of Abu Kamal to the east of Al Jauf on the east; and the Mediterranean on the West.

2. We ask that the Government of this Syrian country should be a democratic civil constitutional Monarchy on broad decentralization principles, safeguarding the rights of minorities, and that the King be the Emir Feisal, who carried on a glorious struggle in the cause of our liberation and merited our full confidence and entire reliance.

3. Considering the fact that the Arabs inhabiting the Syrian area are not naturally less gifted than other more advanced races and that they are by no means less developed than the Bulgarians, Serbians, Greeks, and Roumanians at the beginning of their independence, we protest against Article 22 of the Covenant of the League of Nations placing us among the nations in their middle stage of development which stand in need of a mandatory power.

4. In the event of the rejection by the Peace Conference of this just protest for certain considerations that we may not understand, we, relying on the declarations of President Wilson that his object in waging war was to put an end to the ambition of conquest and colonization, can only regard the mandate mentioned in the Covenant of the League of Nations as equivalent to the rendering of economical and technical assistance that does not prejudice our complete independence. And desiring that our country should not fall a prey to colonization and believing that the American Nation is farthest from any thought of colonization and has no political ambition in our country, we will seek the technical and economical assistance from the United States of America, provided that such assistance does not exceed 20 years.

From the King-Crane Commission Report in *Foreign Relations of the United States: Paris Peace Conference, 1919*, vol. 12: pp. 780–781. This document may also be found in J. C. Hurewitz, *The Middle East and North Africa in World Politics* (New Haven, Conn.: Yale University Press, 1975), pp. 180–182.

5. In the event of America not finding herself in a position to accept our desire for assistance, we will seek this assistance from Great Britain, also provided that such assistance does not infringe the complete independence and unity of our country and that the duration of such assistance does not exceed that mentioned in the previous article.

6. We do not acknowledge any right claimed by the French Government in any part whatever of our Syrian country and refuse that she should assist us or have a hand in our country under any circumstances and in any place.

7. We oppose the pretentions of the Zionists to create a Jewish commonwealth in the southern part of Syria, known as Palestine, and oppose Zionist migration to any part of our country; for we do not acknowledge their title but consider them a grave peril to our people from the national, economical, and political points of view. Our Jewish compatriots shall enjoy our common rights and assume the common responsibilities.

8. We ask that there should be no separation of the southern part of Syria. known as Palestine, nor of the littoral western zone, which includes Lebanon, from the Syrian country. We desire that the unity of the country should be guaranteed against partition under whatever circumstances.

9. We ask complete independence for emancipated Mesopotamia and that there should be no economical barriers between the two countries.

10. The fundamental principles laid down by President Wilson in condemnation of secret treaties impel us to protest most emphatically against any treaty that stipulates the partition of our Syria country and against any private engagement aiming at the establishment of Zionism in the southern part of Syria; therefore we ask the complete annulment of these conventions and agreements.

The noble principles enunciated by President Wilson strengthen our confidence that our desires emanating from the depths of our hearts, shall be the decisive factor in determining our future; and that President Wilson and the free American people will be our supporters for the realization of our hopes, thereby proving their sincerity and noble sympathy with the aspiration of the weaker nations in general and our Arab people in particular.

We also have the fullest confidence that the Peace Conference will realize that we would not have risen against the Turks, with whom we had participated in all civil, political, and representative privileges, but for their violation of our national rights, and so will grant us our desires in full in order that our political rights may not be less after the war than they were before, since we have shed so much blood in the cause of our liberty and independence.

We request to be allowed to send a delegation to represent us at the Peace Conference to defend our rights and secure the realization of our aspirations.

4. The American King-Crane Commission Report Summarizes the Popular Ideas of Nationalism in the Middle East, 1919

The report of the King-Crane Commission is probably one of the most objective documents indicating the moods, uncertainties, and opinions that prevailed in the region after the war. The contradictory demands are as interesting as the agreements, because they indicate the state of flux that predominated in the Levant and Mesopotamia.

The Story of the Tour

The whole area visited by the commission during the 42 days from June 10 to July 21 is Occupied Enemy Territory under the supreme authority of General Allenby. The administration is conducted under the Turkish laws, with small local modifications, in many cases continuing in office part or all of the officials left behind by the Turks. A system of military governors and officers assigned to special duties, such as financial and medical advice, liaison work, etc., parallels the civil administration. The whole area is in four portions, known respectively as O. E. T. A. (Occupied Enemy Territory Administration) South, West, East, and North, and administered under the guidance respectively of English, French, Arab, and French officers. The order of description followed below is by these areas, and is nearly coincident with the itinerary of the commission, the only exception being that much of O. E. T. A. East was visited before O. E. T. A West. Fifteen days were spent in the South, ten in the West, fifteen in the East, and two in the North.

The Geography of the Claims

[. . .]

III. Specific Requests as Given in the Table

[. . .]

A. *Territorial Limits*

1. The largest percentage for any one request is that of 1,500 petitions (80.4 per cent) for United Syria, including Cilicia, the Syrian Desert, and Palestine. The boundaries of this area are usually defined as "The Taurus Mountains on the north; the Euphrates and Khabur Rivers and the line extending east of Abu

"King-Crane Report on the Near East," *Editor & Publisher* (New York: Editor & Publisher Co., 1922).

Kamal to the east of Al Juf on the east; Rafa and the line running from Al Juf to the south of Akaba on the south; and the Mediterranean Sea on the West." In addition to being the first plank of the Damascus program [see document 3 in this chapter] a United Syria received strong support from many Christians in all the O. E. T. As., as the number of petitions indicates.

2. In opposition to Syrian Unity, six of the nineteen pro-Zionist petitions ask for a separate Palestine, and presumably it is implied in the others.

3. In addition, two Christian groups in Palestine asked for a separate Palestine under the British, in preference to a United Syria under the French.

4. Twenty-four petitions, chiefly from Christian sources in O. E. T. A. South, asked for an autonomous Palestine within the Syrian State. For many other delegations this was doubtless implied in the general request for independence and a non-centralized government.

5. In opposition also to a United Syria are the 203 petitions (16.9 per cent) asking for an independent Greater Lebanon. One hundred and ninety-six of these came from Lebanon and 139 are copies of the French-Lebanon program.

6. The request for a United Syria is made even more emphatic by the 1,062 protests against an Independent Greater Lebanon. These include the Damascus program petitions and some from Protestant and other Christian sources in Lebanon.

7. Thirty-three Lebanese delegations representing both Moslems and Christians, fearing the economic future of a separate Lebanon, asked for autonomy within a Syrian State. Others also regarded autonomy as implied in the request for independence and a non-centralized government.

8–9. The Valley of Bekaa is usually regarded as an integral part of Greater Lebanon. Eleven petitions, however, make especial reference to its inclusion, while eight ask that the Valley remain in the Damascus area.

10–11. Similarly, while Cilicia is definitely included in the demand for a United Syria made by 1,500 petitions, two petitions asked specifically for it, while three requested that it be given to the Armenian State.

B. Independence

1. The second largest percentage of all, 1,370 (73.5 per cent), is for "Absolute Independence," the second cardinal point of the Damascus program, supported generally by all Moslem delegations. It is certain from the oral statements that accompanied the petitions that the term "Absolute Independence" was seldom used in the sense of an entire freedom from any foreign guidance, such as that of a mandatory under the League of Nations, inasmuch as the request was frequently combined with a choice of mandate, and in all but a few cases with either a choice of mandate or a request for foreign "assistance." While a few of the Young Arab clubs certainly desired freedom from all foreign control, the great majority asked for independence and defined a mandate to

mean only economic and technical assistance, because of a widespread fear that the mandatory arrangement would be used to cloak colonial annexation.

2–3. Only a slightly smaller number, 1,278 (68.5 per cent), asked for the independence of Iraq, or Mesopotamia. To these should be added 93 of the 97 petitions for the independence of all Arab countries as in only four petitions do both requests appear, and the second includes the first. The phrasing "for all Arab countries" was first used in Palestine, and dropped for the special mention of Iraq in the Damascus program. A total of 1,371 petitions, therefore, asked for the independence and economic freedom of the Iraq regions.

C. Form of Government

1–2. The establishment of a "democratic, non-centralized, constitutional" kingdom is one of the points of the Damascus program, as the number of petitions for it, 1,107 (59.3 per cent), indicate. All but five of these petitions, also, ask that Emir Feisal be made the king. These petitions were especially numerous in O. E. T. A. East, where 1,005 of 1,157 request both a kingdom and the Emir as king. This part of the program had apparently not been developed when the commission was in Palestine, as only five of 260 O. E. T. A. South petitions referred to a kingdom, and only two mentioned Emir Feisal.

3. A request for a democratic representative government, presumably of a republican character, came to the commission from 26 Christian groups in O. E. T. A. West, and eight groups in O. E. T. A. East, a total of 34 (1.8 per cent). This request was usually made in opposition to the Moslem idea of a Syrian kingdom under Feisal.

4. The request for proper safe-guarding of the rights of minorities included in the Damascus program was also made by many of the Christian groups in Lebanon. The total is 1,023 (54.9 per cent). This request received a more united support from both Moslems and Christians than any other, except anti-Zionism.

5–6. Five requests for the retention of Arabic as the official language (rather than Hebrew) and ten requests for the abolition of foreign capitulations (officially annulled by the Turks, but without sanction of the Powers) came from scattered points in O. E. T. A. South.

7. Nineteen (1.02 per cent) petitions were received for the autonomy of all the provinces of Syria. This is in addition to the separate requests for autonomy of Lebanon and Palestine. Once more it should be said that many regarded a large measure of local autonomy as implicit in the general idea of a democratic, non-centralized government, but these nineteen groups made special reference to it.

D. Choice of Mandate

With regard to choice of mandate, five classes of requests had to be distinguished, as shown in the tables [not included]. In addition to definite requests for a given nation as the mandatory power, a few groups gave their preference, "if a mandatory is obligatory," i.e., rather under protest, while the great majority asked for "assistance" rather than a mandatory, because of a misunderstanding, and the fear referred to above that a "mandate" is a convenient cloak for colonial aggression. Petitions of these three classes have therefore been grouped in the summary as "Total first choice." In addition preferences for second choice of mandate and "assistance" have been tabulated.

1. The total of the petitions asking for Great Britain as first choice is 66 (3.5 per cent). Forty-eight came from Palestine; 13 are from Greek Orthodox delegations, and four from the Druses. The second choice total is 1,073 (57.5 per cent), due to the 1,032 requests for British "assistance" if America declined, in accordance with the Damascus program.

2. The French total for first choice is 274 (14.68 per cent), all but 59 of them from the Lebanon district. The second choice total is three.

3. The 1,064 requests for American "assistance" according to the Damascus program, with 57 selections of America as mandatory power, and eight more if a mandate is obligatory, make up the first choice total of 1,129 (60.5 per cent). The second choice total is 11.

4. Twenty-three petitions received at Jenin, Haifa, and Nazareth just before the Damascus program was adopted, left the choice of mandate to the Syrian Congress. This means, therefore, an additional 23 for American first choice and British second choice total.

E. Zionism

1–2–3. The petitions favoring the Zionist program have been analyzed above in the discussion of programs. In opposition to these are the 1,350 (72.3 per cent) petitions protesting against Zionist claims and purposes. This is the third largest number for any one point and represents a more widespread general opinion among both Moslems and Christians than any other. The anti-Zionist note was especially strong in Palestine, where 222 (85.3 per cent) of the 260 petitions declared against the Zionist program. This is the largest percentage in the district for any one point.
[…]

I. The Area Under British Occupation (O. E. T. A. SOUTH)

1. NARRATIVE.   Owing to changes of plan at a late date, the commission arrived in Jaffa at a time when the British authorities were not expecting it, and the program followed there was arranged mainly without their help. The endeavor was made to ascertain the opinions and desires of every important group, sect, and organization, of a few well-informed representative individuals, and of significant minorities of sub-divisions, especially in cases where

there seemed to be disposition, for any reason, to suppress these. Because of the numerous sub-divisions of the Christians and particularly of the Roman Catholics, it was inevitable that from the beginning the commission would give a disproportionate number of interviews and amount of time to them. The commissioners had prepared a statement of their purposes, to be found elsewhere in this report, which was read to important groups, and given to the press in lieu of interviews. Care was taken to make it clear, in response to frequent questioning, that the policy of the United States in regard to accepting a mandate anywhere was unformed and unpredictable, and that the commission had no power of decision. Automobiles were secured from the American Committee for Relief in the Near East, in order to be as little as possible dependent upon others than Americans. Word was given out that the commission would not accept general social invitations or consent to demonstrations. [. . .]

Zionism

[. . .]

E. We recommend, in the fifth place, serious modification of the extreme Zionist program for Palestine of unlimited immigration of Jews, looking finally to making Palestine distinctly a Jewish State.

(1) The Commissioners began their study of Zionism with minds predisposed in its favor, but the actual facts in Palestine, coupled with the force of the general principles proclaimed by the Allies and accepted by the Syrians, have driven them to the recommendation here made.

(2) The commission was abundantly supplied with literature on the Zionist program by the Zionist Commission to Palestine [see document 4 in this chapter]; heard in conferences much concerning the Zionist colonies and their claims; and personally saw something of what had been accomplished. They found much to approve in the aspirations and plans of the Zionists, and had warm appreciation for the devotion of many of the colonists and for their success, by modern methods, in overcoming natural obstacles.

(3) The commission recognized also that definite encouragement had been given to the Zionists by the Allies in Mr. Balfour's often quoted statement [and] in its approval by other representatives of the Allies. If, however, the strict terms of the Balfour Statement [see document 4 in the chapter "Ideas of Nationalism"] are adhered to—favoring "the establishment in Palestine of a national home for the Jewish people," "it being clearly understood that nothing shall be done which may prejudice the civil and religious rights existing in non-Jewish communities in Palestine"—it can hardly be doubted that the extreme Zionist Program must be greatly modified.

For "a national home for the Jewish people" is not equivalent to making Palestine into a Jewish State; nor can the erection of such a Jewish State be accomplished without the gravest trespass upon the "civil and religious rights of existing non-Jewish communities in Palestine." The fact came out repeatedly in the Commission's conference with Jewish representatives, that the Zionists looked forward to a practically complete dispossession of the present non-Jewish inhabitants of Palestine, by various forms of purchase.

In his address of July 4, 1918, President Wilson laid down the following principle as one of the four great "ends for which the associated peoples of the world were fighting": "The settlement of every question, whether of territory, of sovereignty, of economic arrangement, or of political relationship upon the basis of the free acceptance of that settlement by the people immediately concerned and not upon the basis of the material interest or advantage of any other nation or people which may desire a different settlement for the sake of its own exterior influence or mastery." If that principle is to rule, and so the wishes of Palestine's population are to be decisive as to what is to be done with Palestine, then it is to be remembered that the non-Jewish population of Palestine—nearly nine-tenths of the whole—are emphatically against the entire Zionist program. The tables show that there was no one thing upon which the population of Palestine were more agreed than upon this. To subject a people so minded to unlimited Jewish immigration, and to steady financial and social pressure to surrender the land, would be a gross violation of the principle just quoted, and of the people's rights, though it kept within the forms of law.

It is to be noted also that the feeling against the Zionist program is not confined to Palestine, but shared very generally by the people throughout Syria as our conferences clearly showed. More than 72 per cent—1,350 in all—of all the petitions in the whole of Syria were directed against the Zionist program. Only two requests—those for a united Syria and for independence—had a larger support. This general feeling was only voiced by the "General Syrian Congress," in the seventh, eighth, and tenth resolutions of the statement. (Already quoted in the report.)

The Peace Conference should not shut its eyes to the fact that the anti-Zionist feeling in Palestine and Syria is intense and not lightly to be flouted. No British officer, consulted by the commissioners, believed that the Zionist program could be carried out except by force of arms. The officers generally thought that a force of not less than 50,000 soldiers would be required even to initiate the program. That of itself is evidence of a strong sense of the injustice of the Zionist program, on the part of the non-Jewish populations of Palestine and Syria. Decisions, requiring armies to carry out, are sometimes necessary, but they are surely not gratuitously to be taken in the interests of a serious injustice. For the initial claim, often submitted by Zionist representatives, that they have a "right" to Palestine, based on an occupation of 2,000 years ago, can hardly be seriously considered.

There is a further consideration that cannot justly be ignored, if the world is to look forward to Palestine becoming a definitely Jewish state, however gradually that may take place. That consideration grows out of the fact that Palestine is "the Holy Land" for Jews, Christians, and Moslems alike. Millions of Christians and Moslems all over the world are quite as much concerned as the Jews with conditions in Palestine, especially with those conditions which touch upon religious feeling and rights. The relations in these matters in Palestine are most delicate and difficult. With the best possible intentions, it may be doubted whether the Jews could possibly seem to either Christians or Moslems proper guardians of the holy places, or custodians of the Holy Land as a whole.

The reason is this: The places which are most sacred to Christians—those having to do with Jesus—and which are also sacred to Moslems, are not only not sacred to Jews, but abhorrent to them. It is simply impossible, under those circumstances, for Moslems and Christians to feel satisfied to have these places in Jewish hands, or under the custody of Jews. There are still other places about which Moslems must have the same feeling. In fact, from this point of view, the Moslems, just because the sacred places of all three religions are sacred to them, have made very naturally much more satisfactory custodians of the holy places than the Jews could be. It must be believed that the precise meaning, in this respect, of the complete Jewish occupation of Palestine has not been fully sensed by those who urge the extreme Zionist program. For it would intensify, with a certainty like fate, the anti-Jewish feeling both in Palestine and in all other portions of the world which look to Palestine as "the Holy Land."

In view of all these considerations, and with a deep sense of sympathy for the Jewish cause, the commissioners feel bound to recommend that only a greatly reduced Zionist program be attempted by the Peace Conference, and even that, only very gradually initiated. This would have to mean that Jewish immigration should be definitely limited, and that the project for making Palestine distinctly a Jewish commonwealth should be given up.

There would then be no reason why Palestine could not be included in a united Syrian State, just as other portions of the country, the holy places being cared for by an International and Inter-religious Commission, somewhat as at present under the oversight and approval of the Mandatary and of the League of Nations. The Jews, of course, would have representation upon this commission.

The recommendations now made lead naturally to the necessity of recommending what power shall undertake the single Mandate for all Syria.

[. . .]

5. A Writer for *al-Asima*, the Syrian Government Newspaper, Seeks to Establish the Popular Idea of the "Nation," October 23, 1919

At a time when Syria was plunged into political chaos in the wake of World War I, many writers attempted to create a sense of certainty about the future of the nation. Some Syrian elites had thrown their political support behind the concept of an Arab kingdom to be led by Amir Faisal, the son of Sharif Husayn (see document 3 in

Muhib al-Din al-Khatib, "Public Opinion," *al-Asima*, 23 October 1919, vol. 1, no. 69. Translated by Akram Khater.

*the chapter "Ideas of Nationalism"). Other elites saw in the arrival of French man-
date forces the possibility of maintaining their power. And still others were indecisive
about which path to take and whom to support. The Syrian public held equally
mixed feelings.*

*Writing in the midst of this confusion, Muhib al-Din al-Khatib, the author of
this article, tries to strike a note of certainty. Notice the language he uses to describe
the "nation," the juxtaposition of individual and communal interests, and the way
in which he tries to resolve the tension between "old" and "new." Throughout, he
is seeking to establish a popular idea of the "nation." What audience was he addressing, and why did he find it necessary to strongly juxtapose the individual and
the "nation"?*

Public Opinion

It would be a grave mistake to measure the general public by the actions of
some individuals, and to assume those to represent the average citizen. Those
who deeply explore these matters will note that the general population has a
communal spirit that overcomes individual interests and erases their narrowly-
focused designs and desires. The nation has an independent collective personality that is stronger than partial personalities, and the latter will and should
dissolve into the first in the case of contradiction of interests.

The public spirit and that of the nation are derived from history and are led
by the hands of the past. As long as history is filled with glorious events, and as
long as the past contains beneficial models for the present and future then you
can be certain that the masses will move forward. One need not doubt those
who presently appeal to the true glory and who demand the right renaissance,
and who preach eternal future happiness. Whoever opposes this—because of
illegitimate designs and purpose or self-interest—will be swept away by the
public spirit just like garbage is swept away by raging torrents of water.

In many of my previous articles I have criticized the shortcomings of some
individuals in their duty toward this nation, and complained about their lack of
initiative in many matters that they should have exerted more effort in accomplishing. This would have been particularly the case had they risked few existing privileges for greater and desired benefits, and had they sacrificed unworthy
and temporary comforts in order to arrive at eternal happiness and peace. However, regardless of how much I may have complained and criticized, I do not
mean to imply that the shortcomings of those individuals will keep the nation
from achieving ambitions, or will keep it from progressing to the social level
worthy of a nation with an honorable past and glorious history. It will achieve
its ambitions in any case, and it will occupy its deserved place whether we
wished it or not. This is ordained by the spirit of the nation and the needs of its
people that derive from its past and history. However, the agreement of its individuals to perform their duties, and the cooperation of all of its people in
these tasks will hasten the process of arriving at the results and will make the
nation more respectable in the eyes of outsiders.

I have said that the spirit of the people and their personality are independent from those of the individuals. This is easily apparent to anyone who

contemplates these issues, because the individual derives his decision from his selfish interests, and he expends his effort toward that end. But the people derive their decisions from their past, extracting from it a general purpose, then the masses exert themselves in achieving this ancient goal. There are individuals with enough foresight to see an intersection between their personal interests and the general good, and thus [they] would work toward that goal in conjunction with the masses. But there are others who are short-sighted and cannot see the point of intersection, and thus they work for a purpose other than the general good. Those are the ones of whom I have complained, even though I believe they are too weak to counter the tide of public opinion.

I heard someone yesterday faulting the Syrian public opinion because it is ever changing. I see these changes as evidence of the sensitivity of public opinion to the various stages that public policy has gone through. Whoever knows the Syrian people intimately, and who listens to them intently, will know with certainty that the public opinion in these lands is composed of two main elements: the first is its historical traditions to which the Syrian public adheres to faithfully, and these traditions are firmly established regardless of the shape it may take, and it will never dissipate or disappear. The illiterate old woman, the religious scholar and the enlightened youth are all equal in respecting the historical traditions and to safeguard the public good. No one can even contemplate that the people will lose faith in this central tenet of our society, or that these traditions will be influenced by the changes in our environment and world. The second element is subjective and of limited duration and is formed of the total of internal and external influences, and will evolve according to various stages and according to the changes in these influences. Many people are mystified by its evolution because they do not know that the people will filter all external influences through the sieve of its traditions. . . .

Thus, the Syrian public opinion combines the two characteristics of change and continuity. It adopts continuity from its belief in past traditions and loyalty to its eternal goal. At the same time it leans toward change because of its flexibility with regard to the demands of our time, trying throughout to balance the new requirements with the old traditions. . . . This is the secret behind the optimism of the Syrian people. . . . The Syrian people contains [sic] all the characteristics of change and forward movement because these characteristics are decreed by God in His creation, and that which God decrees cannot be changed.

6. Women and the Vote in Syria: A Parliamentary Debate About the Relationship Between Gender and Citizenship in the Proposed State, April 25, 1920

This document is a transcription of the proceedings of a Syrian parliamentary session during which delegates to the Greater Syria Conference were attempting to compile a constitution. Their purpose for doing so was to thwart European (French and British) efforts to claim political control over the region. In the course of the

discussions, delegates posed questions about the meaning of the Syrian "nation"
and its implications. Notice that a multitude of opinions were being presented from
various parts of "Greater Syria"— Palestine, Lebanon, and Syria.

On the 25th of April, 1920, Article 79—which specifies the characteristics of
the voter—of the Basic Constitution was to be discussed. Lebanon's delegate
(District of al-Kharoub-Sheheem), Mr. Ibrahim Al-Khatib, stood up and suggested giving the right to vote to women who had come of age and who had
finished their secondary education. Subsequently, a clamor and uproar went
through the hall which was interrupted by an impromptu and eloquent speech
by the legal scholar Shaykh Sa'id Murad al-Ghazi (delegate of Gaza). [He
spoke] about the right of the woman to vote, and the fact that the Islamic
Shari'a has specified that the woman should govern, work, be knowledgeable
and eloquent. [He concluded] by asking, then how could she not be a voter? At
this point, the Secretary of the Conference invited Mr. Izzat Druza (Nablus) to
debate Ibrahim al-Khatib's suggestion.

Shaykh 'Abd al-Qadir al-Kilani (Hama) spoke to the young men of the
Conference saying, "The Europeans have walked the path of modernization
for 300 years, and their traditions do not prohibit the woman from participating in any activity, yet show me one country of the countries of Europe which
has given women that right [voting right]?"

VOICE: (*from the floor of the Conference*) England, Sweden.

So he responded to them, "If you want the uplifting of women then open
schools for them. Giving the woman the right to vote means her right to be a
delegate, so do you want amongst you female delegates?"

SA'ADALLAH AL-JABIRI: Why not? She already goes to the market and buys . . .

AL-KILANI: The presence of the woman as voter or delegate with this igno-
    rance and immorality is harmful, but when the good morals are developed
    then we can look into the matter [of voting rights for women].

SA'ADALLAH AL-JABIRI: I note the words of the gentleman, that he sees no rea-
    son in the end that should keep her from voting.

AL-KILANI: Yes, yes then we will look Into the matter positively, the *hijab* is
    indeed an innovation, but when some demanded that it be removed the ig-
    norant rabble began to follow the [unveiled] women mocking them. We are
    afraid that this decision [about voting?] will cause social and political un-
    rest. This idea [women's right to vote] is too premature, and I request that
    we reject it.

DA'AS AL-JURJIS (HOSN AL-AKRAD): We do not want to remain in the state of
    a man who has suffered from a stroke that left one half of him healthy and
    the other paralyzed. The nation is made up of the man and the woman.

al-Hawadith, 25 April 1975, pp. 47–53. Translated by Akram Khater.

Therefore, we must reflect on this suggestion [women's right to vote] with honesty and sincerity. I would like to thank Mr. Al-Kilani because I understood from him that he supports the suggestion even though he does not think it appropriate for this moment in time! It is true that 98% of our women are ignorant, which is why he [al-Kilani] made education a requirement and that is correct! Therefore, if we give only the educated woman the right to vote then he would approve of that. Turkey has given the woman the right to vote and the author Khalida Adib is about to enter the parliament. What you observed during the war (WWI) of the service of women in the army is evidence of the importance of the help of the gentler sex. And the presence of the lady in the armed services is far more important than the process of voting. And the danger that some of the present brothers see [in giving such a right to women] can be removed because a woman has the right not to give an opinion, and the lady who is careful to avoid having the pen touch her fingertips has the right to not vote.

Aʜᴍᴀᴅ ᴀʟ-Qᴀᴅᴀᴍᴀɴɪ (Dᴀᴍᴀꜱᴄᴜꜱ): Allah has made her with half a brain.

Dᴀ'ᴀꜱ ᴀʟ-Jᴜʀᴊɪꜱ: It is very important to place this principle [woman's right to vote] in our Basic Law, especially given our current political situation, therefore I demand the acceptance of the suggestion and to move it to committee (*applause from the right and the middle*).

'Aᴅᴇʟ Zᴜ'ᴀʏᴛᴇʀ (Nᴀʙʟᴜꜱ): There is no doubt that each and every one of us want[s], desires, and must work to make the woman arrive at a level of advancement where she can take her right. And despite what has been said about the benefit of giving women the right to vote, I still see its approval at this moment does not coincide with the welfare of the nation. Some of the European nations have not taken this step except after it had undergone developments that lasted hundreds of years, while we are now only at the beginning of our societal life. Every nation has traditions and wise mores, and if the laws are not based upon these then it is to be feared that revolutions and unrest will break out (*applause from the middle*). Yes, it is true that the *Shari'a* [Islamic jurisprudence] may give the woman the right to vote, but it does not say that the nation is obliged to pass legislation that give the woman the right to participate in it [the electoral process]. Permission is one thing, and obligation is another. We are now in a difficult situation. We came to this place to express the opinion of the nation, and if we pass legislation that it [the nation] does not accept, and we are in our current situation, then will we have kept that trust?

Vᴏɪᴄᴇꜱ: No, No . . .

'Aʙᴅ ᴀʟ-Qᴀᴅɪʀ ᴀʟ-Kʜᴀᴛɪʙ (Dᴀᴍᴀꜱᴄᴜꜱ): I request that we table this article for discussion, until the nation can look at it, and if it supported it then it [the nation] has the final say, and if it did not support it then it has the final say as well. Educated women are far and few in between, and we cannot take the exceptions to be the basis of the law, and I beg of you not to undertake a matter that will do greater harm than good.

SUBHI AL-TAWIL (LATAKIA): The matter is purely societal and does not effect the *hijab*. And the woman if she is selected is not required to unveil herself (*applause*). Even if this election [of a woman into the Parliament] does nothing but prove a woman's right [to be elected] then it is sufficient.

AHMAD AL-QADAMANI (DAMASCUS): And from where did you get this right and from which *Shari'a*?

SUBHI AL-TAWIL (LATAKIA): An educated woman is better than a thousand ignorant men, so why would we give men the right to vote and yet deprive educated women from that same right?

AHMAD AL-QADAMANI (DAMASCUS): How many men like you are there in Latakia?

SUBHI AL-TAWIL (LATAKIA): If you have something to say then please come to the podium, and do not speak from the floor. Yes, there are very few educated girls, but it is not obligatory for them to vote. Some of the speakers have said that Europe is now trying to give women the right to vote. What is meant by that is to give them the right to sit in the seats of the Parliament But the right to vote had been given to them hundreds of years ago.

AHMAD AL-QADAMANI (DAMASCUS): We in Damascus do not want that [women voting] to be the case, so just make it so in Latakia!

SUBHI AL-TAWIL (LATAKIA): I request that an open-ballot vote be taken on the suggestion of brother Ibrahim al-Khatib.

At this point Shaykh Sa'id Murad (Gaza), the champion of women's rights, stood up, and he was received with applause. And a commotion arose that was interrupted by Riyad al-Sulh (Beirut) saying: "Before Shaykh Sa'id speaks, [let me say that] it is possible that a group of the members [of parliament] may be of different views than his, but honoring knowledge is a must therefore, gentlemen, I ask you to applaud" (*loud applause*).

SHAYKH SA'ID MURAD (GAZA): This is a very important subject that I do not deny disagreement over it. Disagreement is the *sunna* [law] of the universe. But what I would like for this matter is for you to consider to look [at it] rationally rather than with emotions. I request that we do not mix up the matter of the *hijab* with this subject at hand. What prompts me to speak about this subject is what I have read in the writings of the Westerners and their newspapers, for they have said: The East needs the West to be its guardian, because it [the East] has decreed upon itself the ignorance of its half (*uproar*). I am speaking in colloquial Arabic that everyone can understand; the Westerners say: We must be the guardians over the East, whose one half of society has been decreed to be ignorant. Therefore, I say that there is no ... (*at this point the following members withdrew from the session: 'Abd al-Qadir al-Khatib, Muhammad al-Mujtahid, Ahmed al-Qadamani, Ibrahim al-Shaykh Hussein, Ahmad al-'Ayash, Khalil al-Talhuni*).

THE PRESIDENT: We have lost the quorum.

SA'ADALLAH AL-JABIRI: Even though the quorum is lost we particularly want to hear the words of the gentleman.

IZZAT DRUZA (SECRETARY): There is a quorum.

SHAYKH SA'ID MURAD, *continued:* We say to the Westerners from this podium words that will reach their parliaments. There are no traditions in the East that decree the ignorance of half of its people. We are also ready at every opportunity to remove this ignorance from men and women alike. Islamic jurisprudence had decided to accept the testimony of a woman, and to accept references of *hadiths* to her, and to accept her as teacher and judge in legal matters except the criminal cases. I am not speaking here of the *hijab* for it is a secondary matter. And it is as if my brothers would have me confuse the issue of voting with that of the *hijab* when the subject is clearly about a woman's right. And those who gave us the right to legislate in this parliament have given her also the right to vote. Yes, I do not deny that all laws should be in step with the spirit of the nation, and a legislation cannot be enforced unless it is distilled from the spirit of the nation. [However,] what makes this subject a problem for some of the brothers—despite my belief in their honesty, sincerity and patriotism—is that they are confusing the matter of the *hijab* with the matter of education which is the means for election. So, if you want to discuss the *hijab* then discuss it without me being a member in this session. However, the subject of women's education was discussed half a century ago and the proponents have won. And now you can see the capitals and the countries full of girls' schools. And since we are in agreement about the education of the woman, then I wanted at this point to advance the subject of election after the matter of education hoping that it will as successful as the latter. And this we progress till we arrive at the desired goal. First, we must acknowledge the right of the woman to elect a member of the parliament. And this is similar to a woman testifying, for the judge accepts the testimony of women according to their class and traditions. Similarly, we can allow women to vote in a manner that does not force her to remove the *hijab*. And all I want for Europe to understand is that—while it maybe more advanced than us in manufacture and material things—we are more civilized than it in our civil code. And if Europe wants to progress and complete its civil code, then it must turn to the East and adopt from it. And just as we do not want to deny its [Europe's] unique characteristics, it must not deny ours. I want for every citizen to be proud of his "Syrianness," in the same manner that the greatest minister in the West is proud of his patriotism. The only link of the woman's subject [with regard to the vote] is to the matter of education, and we must acknowledge that Allah has given her the same rights as he has given you. So be kind to those on earth and He who is in the heavens will be merciful to you. This is one of the pure social issues that benefits greatly from the Qur'anic text.

RAFIQ AL-TAMIMI (AL-KHALIL-HEBRON): Mr. Sa'id Murad has spoken eloquently about this subject, but despite that [I must insist] that this matter is not a religious one, but a civil one relating to social relations more than spiritual issues. In the past the woman in the West did not have a separate individuality, rather right after marriage her person was mixed with that of her husband. Thus, she had no right to buy or sell. But the West has progressed, and the civilized nations have given the woman control over of her legal rights. Europe that has been late in giving this right [voting right] must not be better than us, especially since Islam has given the woman this right 1,200 years ago. However, we can harmonize between the old and new ideologies. The right to vote is a duty that covers all the citizens. But it is deaf, for every citizen should vote, but he is not penalized if he does not cast his vote. In other words, the woman has the liberty to use or refuse this right. And we say unto the men who do not accept to give women the right to vote, that you can influence your women. However, if there exists even the smallest group of people in the country who demand the granting of such a right then we must pave the way for it. If we give women this right then this does not mean that they must go to the city hall to vote, but rather they can meet in a designated place and vote. And for this reason I agree with the suggestion of Shaykh Ibrahim al-Khatib. I congratulate this conference which has defended the woman in the previous session, and has uplifted her status, when the rabble and the insolent fools in the capital had taken a stand against the gentler sex. I congratulate this conference because it knows that a nation whose half is ignorant cannot guarantee personal liberty. If the conference, which represents the nation, cannot put a stop to the attacks of the insolent against veiled women in the streets then we can kiss freedom goodbye.

IBRAHIM AL-KHATIB: If I had known that the minds [here] were ready to accept my suggestion to this degree then I would have suggested giving the woman more than this right (*murmurs from the seats of the Free Party, to which this member belongs*) . . . Mr. President, I declare that I have withdrawn from the Free Party because of what it contains of ignoramuses.

TAWFIQ MUFARIJ (KOURA): Withdraw your comment, Withdraw your comment!!

IBRAHIM AL-KHATIB: I withdraw it. If voting was a job then we would have obliged the woman to do it, but it is right that she has a choice in using it. We have limited this right to those women who are educated, who hold secondary degrees, and we have said that they have the right to give their opinion in writing!! I insist upon my suggestion, and I request that it should be accepted . . .

MR. RASHID RIDA (PRESIDENT OF THE CONFERENCE, LEBANON): (*Long storm of applause*): This matter has been discussed from a religious and social angle. But there are more than these two perspectives, and that is the feelings and sentiments of the nation. Had we been deciding upon a lesson then it would have been necessary for every person to give their opinion. However, he who wants to pass a practical legislation in the name of the nation must pay attention to its sentiments. Many speakers have spoken about this subject [women's right to vote] from the perspective of the Shari'a, but they did not give its due. The Shari'a is a very wide topic, and while pure religious matters are based on the text, matters relating to the world are based on consideration of public interests that change according to time and place. For, if we suppose that the leaders decide that it is in the interest of the nation to give women the right to vote, then we can find a precedent for it in the Shari'a, but until now this has not occurred. . . . Then there is another matter that is worthy of consideration. For voting pre-supposes individual freedom, and here I wonder: can a woman, living under the guardianship of her husband, use the right to vote if her husband forbids her from that?

SA'ADALLAH AL-JABIRI (ALEPPO): And does he have the right to forbid her from giving testimony in the courts?

RASHID RIDA: Yes. But I am not saying that I have decided on this matter, because I have not examined it very carefully. Do you suppose that that which the woman has learned in secondary school is sufficient to allow her to gain the right to vote? The Shari'a is quite open, so that if it can be proven that giving this right will be of benefit to the nation then the Shari'a allows it. However, the nation has sent for a particular reason . . . but we must maintain our status with the nation in whose name we speak, and to know the extent of the influence of our laws on her. The ratio of educat[ed] women amongst us is less than two percent, that is less than the percentage mentioned by Mr. Al-Kilani!! I have read in many magazines that when they, in Europe, have used women in many different tasks they have discovered that she has half the strength of the man. I submit that we must fight those reactionaries who desire for the woman to remain ignorant, however no benefit can come at this time from the issue of voting. . . . You know that the general public or public opinion will not accept the establishment of that [voting rights for women]. One shout at this critical time is sufficient to cause a public uprising. Despite my respect for the opinion of the "suggester" and my belief in his patriotism and sincerity, I request that we table the issue of the woman's right to vote and not include it within the law.

MOUNAH HAROUN (LATAKIA): I reply to the gentleman, and support the opinion of Shaykh Sa'id Murad saying: I have read in the religious interpretation that Mr. Rashid Rida himself publishes the following Qur'anic verse: "And they [the women] have the same [rights] as responsibilities." This means that the rights of the woman are the same as those of the man. And in the same interpretation [we read]: "Men are the guardians of the women," and that is by one degree. Beyond that then equality is an obligation. Therefore, I say that giving the right to vote to the woman is not contrary to the Shari'a.

RASHID RIDA: It appears that I have opened for you doors to matters that have not been clarified. Mr. Mounah Haroun has taken parts of my statement so that it appears as proof for his point, when it [my statement] is proof against him. For the degree which separates men from women is the degree of guardianship. But we do not want to enter here into interpretation. Rather we say, there is not benefit in this matter, and that we do not have the time to open the door of the people for the fanatics. Ten years ago I came to Damascus [from Egypt] and gave a lecture on the issue of *Tawhid* [monotheism] and the world was turned upside down against me. Now you oblige me to say quite frankly that in taking this decision [you will cause for] speeches to be made in the mosques and in societies against the Conference, and you will open matters that are of no practical benefit to us.

TAWFIQ MUFARIJ (KOURA): If the matter was related to the Shari'a then I would not speak of it, but this matter has nothing to do with religion, and I find it strange that the debate has arrived to this stage.

'ADEI ZU'AYTER (NABLUS): You did not understand the words of Mr. Rashid. He has dealt with this issue from the perspective of public welfare and the circumstances of the country.

TAWFIQ MUFARIJ (KOURA): All religions do not oppose this matter, and if Allah has given the woman a right then how can we forbid her from using it?

DOCTOR SAYID TALI' (LEBANON): How sad the woman is ... you are discussing her rights in the Parliament while she is being insulted on the streets!! It is nice to be talking about the rights of the woman, and we all support that but I would like to remind you of a historical incident. When Japan wanted to craft a constitution for itself it called upon specialists from all the countries, and amongst those was an expert that was applauded by the attendees [of the constitutional session]. So he went to the Prime Minister and said to him: "My legal opinions have garnered the trust of all, so I hope that you will use as basis for your constitution. So he [the Prime Minister] replied to him: "We will take that which suits our country and leave aside that which does not." If I was in Europe I would have agreed to give this right to the woman all the while supporting my opinion with proofs and evidence, but since we are in Syria then I cannot do so. Here we are enacting legislation for the whole Syrian nation, and every law that does not correspond to the spirit of the nation is useless. . . . Syria cannot bear this law [woman's right to vote] now!

RIYAD AL-SULH: When I stand at this podium I do not ask about coffeehouses and homes, and whether it is with me or against me. Principally, I submit that we should give this right to the woman, and if the cafés of Damascus do not accept this, then the other districts will accept it with pleasure. And for me the greatest thing that this Conference has done is to leave the podium free [of interference]. . . . Please know, gentlemen, that the departure of six or seven members from this hall is of no consequent to me. Rather it proves their inability to defeat the truth. Still, I see that what the brothers have propose[d] is a compromise for the two ideas . . . it is a suggestion that we temporarily table this matter for now. . . .

GEORGE HARFOUSH (BEIRUT): I would like to say to you that the misbehavior which occurred amidst the general public in Damascus because of this debate had also occurred in Europe. . . . But this Conference has proven through its work that it walks in step with the free city. . . . Tomorrow Europe will read in its newspapers that the members of the Syrian Conference have suggested giving the woman the right to vote. . . . And rest assured that with that we will have had greater impact than twenty delegations, and accordingly I support the opinion of those demanding the need to give the woman her right.

THE PRESIDENT: Do you not find that we have had enough debate?

VOICES: Enough.

THE PRESIDENT: We have the following suggestion from Uthman Sultan and Theodore Antaki and fifteen members: "We suggest not dealing with the subject of giving the woman the right to vote, and recording the suggestion in the minutes of the Conference, and leaving the legal paragraph as it currently is." Whomsoever accepts this let him raise his hand (*and here many hands were raised in support of this suggestion . . . and the session was concluded*).

7. Ferhat Abbas Appeals for the Equality of Muslim Algerians and French Algerians, February 23, 1936

Ferhat Abbas (1899–1985) was born at Taher, Algeria, and he obtained his training as a pharmacist at the University of Algiers. By 1931 he was heavily involved in politics. He was elected to the general council of Constantine in 1933, the municipal council of Setif in 1935, and the Délégations Financières [Financial Delegations] in 1936; all of these were administrative and financial assemblies to which an Algerian Muslim could be elected according to French colonial law.

Early in his political career Abbas believed that Algeria should eschew the path of Arab nationalism and instead should become a semi-independent province of France—a relationship somewhat like the current relationship between Puerto Rico and the United States. This belief stood him in contrast to other Algerian politicians—Marxist or religious—who believed that Algeria should be completely independent from France. In the letter reprinted here, which was published in one of Algeria's French colonial newspapers, Abbas appeals for equality between Algeria's indigenous peoples and the colons—French colonists—who practically controlled the economy and government of Algeria. Abbas hoped to find some common ground between French and local Algerian culture. Other nationalists (such as the Syrian Michel 'Aflaq—see document 11 in the chapter "Ideas of Nationalism") and the great majority of colonists rejected this goal.

After 1936, severely disappointed by the failure of the reforms instituted by the leftist French Popular Front government, Abbas gradually shifted toward an autonomist position and in 1938 founded the Union Populaire Algérienne *(Algerian Popular Union). After World War II, after serving briefly in the French army, where he experienced anti-Arab racism, he formulated a new plan for an autonomous Algeria, but the plan came to naught because France was not willing to end its control of Algeria. In 1944 Abbas founded the organization* Amis du Manifeste de Liberation *(Friends of the Liberation Manifesto) re-formed in April 1946 as the*

Ferhat Abbas, "On the Margins of Nationalism. I am France!" *Liberté*, 27 February 1936, p. 3. Translated by Akram Khater.

Union Democratique du Manifeste Algérien *(Democratic Union of the Algerian Manifesto), which called for an autonomous Algeria in federation with France and was seen as a rival and an alternative to* L'Étoile Nord-Africaine, *Messali Hadj's more radical organization (see document 8 in the chapter "Ideas of Nationalism").*

By this time the French colonial regime considered Abbas anti-French and imprisoned him on several occasions. His years in jail convinced him finally that there was no way for Algerians to attain equality within a French-controlled Algeria. Thus, in 1956, when the Algerian armed revolt against the French was in full swing, he escaped to Cairo and joined the Front de Libération Nationale *(FLN) (Front for National Liberation). However, he could not play a large role—he disagreed with the approach of the FLN leaders—and he left Cairo in 1961. Later he served in the National Assembly of independent Algeria, but his political career was circumscribed by his opposition to the ruling FLN party and several of its leaders.*

With the lightness of thought characteristic of misinformed individuals, the newspaper *Le Temps*—without doubt inspired by colonial capital or the demented notions of some politicians—has resumed the attacks against Muslim Algeria by throwing in its face all the old accusations that the colonial arsenal has been using periodically for the past fifty years: nationalism, religious fanaticism, Wahabism [Islamic fundamentalism originating in the Arabian Peninsula in the late eighteenth century].

We recall the campaign carried out against us in 1935 and the subsequent arrival of the minister of the interior here. With the intelligence of a knowledgeable man, Mr. Régnier observed the character of our action and observed the spirit of the people whom we represent. He listened carefully and observed, then returned to Paris to announce with conviction and solemnity, from the podium of the Senate tribunal: "I trust the indigenous peoples [Arabs and Berbers]."

We thought that these wonderful words would be heard by the whole world and, placing our trust in the government of the [French] Republic [which had colonized Algeria in 1836] and even in our past adversaries, we awaited reforms and real changes. We hoped for the end of the Algerian malaise. We naively confused sentiment with action, and honor with politics. By believing the beautiful promises that were made to us, we entered a game controlled by our enemies. [. . .]

These forces exerted a great effort in opposing the decision of the arbitration. [. . .] We defended ourselves in 1935. We will defend ourselves today. [. . .] The truth, once more, will overcome lies. Most of all the land: we are ready with the help of God and men, we will be victorious in recapturing the land.

It is not within my ability to defend Shaykh Ben Badis and Shaykh al-Okbi and with them all of the 'ulama' [Muslim religious and legal scholars]. The question that interests me, and that was posed by *Le Temps*, is about teaching Arabic. That language is to the Islamic religion what the church is to the Catholic religion. It [Islam] cannot survive without it. The belief of an ignorant Muslim is nothing more than a tissue of superstitions. It [the language] constitutes the cement of faith. Is it then necessary under these circumstances to affirm our attachment to the teaching of the Arabic language, the basis of our belief?

This education is closely connected to freedom of thought. The suppression or even hindering of that education is a declaration of war against the Muslim religion. It is above all a declaration of war against teaching. We must see things as they are: Wahabism and Pan-Arabism are fragile facades behind which hide the real designs of our colonial educators. The majority of people to whom they deny French education must be deprived of Arabic education. Neither French culture nor Arab culture [will benefit Algerians]. Rather, [these policies will produce] an army of [Algerian] domestic servants and nonbelievers who would be easy to exploit, or at least fill the prisons and camps with them.

That is not what we desire.

In a country where more than 800,000 children are deprived of schooling, all of our attention is focused on education. This concern is translated into incessant demands to the public authorities for the creation of schools. It is equally translated into the thanks that we owe to private initiatives, and in particular to the 'ulama', for the considerable number of children whom they rescued from a terrible life on the streets. [. . .]

If the 'ulama' are "racists" or "Pan-Islamist" [as the French colonial press labeled them], then we the political friends of Dr. Ben-Djelloul would be nationalists. The accusation is not new. I have discussed this question with many different individuals. My opinion is known. Nationalism is a sentiment that drives a people to live within its territorial frontiers, a sentiment that has created this network of nations. If I discovered the "Algerian Nation," then I would be a nationalist but I would not have committed a crime. Men who have died for the national ideal are honored daily and respected. My life is not more valuable than theirs, yet I will not make this sacrifice. As a nation, Algeria is a myth, and I have not discovered it. I have interrogated history; I have interrogated the dead and the living; I have visited cemeteries: no one spoke to me about it. Of course I have found the "Arab Empire," and the "Muslim Empire," which honor Islam and our race, but these empires are gone. They are the equivalent of the Roman Empire and of the medieval Holy Roman Empire. They were born for an epoch and for a humanity that no longer exist.

Can an Algerian Muslim seriously dream of building the future with the dust of the past? Don Quixotes do not belong to our century. We are not building sand castles. Therefore, once and for all, we have put aside daydreams and chimeras to link our future with that of the French project in this country [Algeria]. [. . .] The protection of this work is the primary goal of our political action. And if I am in need of a single fact to support our doctrine, I will cite one that was revealed to me in my own research. In 1918 the amount of life insurance taken out by local Algerians was barely a few hundred thousand [French] francs. Today the amount is more than 20 million francs. It seems to me that if we were anti-French nationalists, the last thing we would do is place our resources in French banks. How could I be against France when for the past twenty to thirty years I have been investing in the French economy my meager resources on which I count for my existence in my old age and to educate my children?

Enough pleasantries! Our actions and ideas are the same. No one before has seriously believed in our nationalism. What they struggled for in the name of this word is our economic and political emancipation. And we desire this double emancipation with all of our will and our social ideals.

Six million Muslims live in this land, which became French one hundred years ago. They live in slums, barefoot, without clothes or bread. From this multitude of the starving we want to create a modern society through education, by defending the peasant, and through social welfare. We want to elevate the dignity of these men and women until it is equal to that of the French.

Would any other colonial policy be more fruitful? Do not forget that without the emancipation of the indigenous population, French Algeria will not long endure. France is me, because I have the numbers [native-born Muslim Algerians outnumbered French immigrants by 6 to 1]: I am the soldier, I am the worker, I am the craftsman, and I am the consumer. To dismiss my collaboration, my well-being, and my reward for work is a terrible heresy. The interests of France are my interests from the moment that our interests become those of France.

Rational action and ideas are the obstacles [facing] feudal Algeria [a small percentage of French Algerians owned most of the land]. The provocations of the latter [French colonists] are increasing. They cause us grief because we have taken our schoolbooks seriously. Perhaps they want us to go backward, but it is too late. We are the children of the modern world, created by French spirit and effort. Our motto is "Forward!"

8.   The *Projet* Blum-Violette: The Proposed Enfranchisement of Muslims in Algeria, 1936

French colonial policy was predicated on the notion of a mission civilisatrice, *a civilizing mission that would uplift supposedly inferior indigenous peoples to the heights of French culture and civilization. By the beginning of the twentieth century, assimilation was an integral part of that overall goal. The indigenous* évolués *(evolved peoples) were expected to be "like" the French in language, habits, and values. The exact means of attaining this goal were not necessarily uniform across the great variety of French colonial possessions, and it was left to the local colonial administrators to implement the goal in a manner compatible with local politics.*

In Algeria, where there was a significant and politically powerful community of

Paul-Émile Viard, *Les Droits Politiques des Indigenes d'Algerie* (Paris: Librairie du Recueil Sirey, 1937), pp. 78–82. This document may also be found in J. C. Hurewitz, *The Middle East and North Africa in World Politics* (New Haven, Conn.: Yale University Press, 1975), pp. 505, 507, 508. Reprinted by permission of the author.

French colonists, the local administration stipulated the abandonment of Islamic law—Shari'a—as a prerequisite for the political enfranchisement of Muslim Algerians, who were being subjected to French colonial rule without being able to participate in the political process of ruling the country. The following document is a bill coauthored by Maurice Violette, speaker of the French parliament, and Léon Blum, the prime minister of the Popular Front government in France. It was intended to remove the stipulation that Muslim Algerians must renounce the Shari'a before they would be enfranchised. The bill was widely denounced by the French colons of Algeria, who feared it would dilute their political, economic, and social control over that country and their influence in the French parliament. Many demonstrations were held in support of the bill by Algerian Muslims and Berbers in large towns and cities in Algeria. Ultimately, the bill never came to a vote, and the project was abandoned.

Within this document are expressions of nationalism different from the notions of the emerging nationalist movement in Algeria, which was demanding independence from French colonial rule. The bill appealed to a particular group of well-educated Algerian Muslims who were well integrated into the French economy and culture and who saw themselves as intermediaries between France and the majority of Algerians. Thus, it sheds some light on the relationship between nationalist projects and interest groups within society.

1. Explanatory Statement

The *sénatus-consulte* of 14 July 1865 and the imperial decrees of 21 April and 12 May 1866 following this *sénatus-consulte* have organized a procedure for the naturalization of native Muslims that gives them, once naturalized, the benefit of all the legislation applicable to French citizens and for the most part, according to common law, covers children yet to be born of the naturalized person.

The law of 4 February 1919 is also concerned with facilitating the naturalization of French Muslims of Algeria, introducing for this purpose in our legislature a simplified procedure, whose effectiveness the government tries to assure and with which it is determined in accordance with the lawmaker's wish to bring about all the effects the Civil Code has on naturalization.

But experience has shown that it was impossible to continue treating as subjects without essential political rights French natives of Algeria who have fully assimilated French thought but who for family or religious reasons cannot give up their personal status. Algerian natives are French. It would be unjust to refuse henceforth the exercise of political rights to those among them who are the most cultured and who have furnished important guarantees of loyalty.

It is therefore fitting to resolve the problem posed by their situation without touching their personal status. Indeed, it must not be forgotten that all rules determining personal status are set forth in the Muslims' holy book. What remains of this solemn promise made by so many governments, notably at the time of the centenary (1930), that we should not realize the urgency of this necessary task of assimilation that affects in the highest degree the moral health of Algeria.

2. The Proposed Bill

ART. 1.   The French Algerian natives of the three departments of Algeria who fulfill the conditions enumerated in the following paragraphs shall be allowed to exercise the political rights of French citizens without modification of their status or civil rights, and this shall be definitive except for the application of French legislation on the forfeiture of political rights:

1. The French Algerian natives who have left the army with an officer's rank;
2. The French Algerian native noncommissioned officers who have left the army with the rank of master-sergeant or higher after serving for fifteen years or separating with a certificate of good conduct;
3. The French Algerian natives having completed military service and obtained both the Military Medal and the *croix de guerre;*
4. The French Algerian native holders of one of the following diplomas: diploma of higher education, *baccalauréat* of secondary education, higher certificate, elementary certificate, diploma of completion of secondary studies, diploma of *médersa,* graduating diploma of a large national school or of a national school of professional, industrial, agricultural, or commercial education, as well as civil servants recruited in a competitive examination;
5. The French Algerian natives elected to the Chambers of Commerce and Agriculture or designated by the Administrative Council of the economic region and by the Chambers of Agriculture of Algeria, under the conditions stipulated in Article 2;
6. The French Algerian native financial delegates, general councillors, municipal councillors of autonomous communes, and president of *jama'al* or local councils who have held office for the duration of a mandate;
7. The French native Algerian *bashaghas, aghas,* and *qaids* who have held office for at least four years;
8. The French Algerian native commanders of the National Order of the Legion of Honor or members of this order for military reasons; [and]
9. The native workers, holders of the Labor Medal (*médaille du travail*) and the secretaries of regularly constituted workers' unions who have held office for at least ten years.

ART. 2.   The Administrative Council of the economic region of Algeria at its sessions following the entry into force of the present law shall designate by decree of the Governor General two hundred businessmen, industrialists, or artisans for each Algerian department, who shall henceforth be invested with the political rights granted by Article 1 of the present law. The three Algerian Chambers of Agriculture at their first sessions each year following the entry into force of the present law shall each designate two hundred farmers, under the same conditions and with the same aim. The Administrative Council of the economic region of Algeria, under the same conditions as above, shall designate fifty businessmen, industrialists, or artisans for each Algerian department, and the three Algerian Chambers of Commerce shall each designate fifty farmers under the same conditions and with the same aim.

ART. 3.   The convictions stipulated in Articles 15 and 16 of the law of 2 February 1852, as well as any intervening repeal [of rights] of functionaries enumerated in Article 1, paragraphs 6 and 7, and removal from the ranks of the Legion of Honor and the Military Medal shall entail automatic removal from the electoral lists.

ART. 4.   Every French Algerian native benefiting from the provisions of the present law may lose the benefit of the preceding provisions by the application of the provisions of Article 9, paragraph 5, of the law of 10 August 1927.

ART. 5.   The provisions of the present law have no retroactive effect and apply only to French Algerian natives who at present or may in the future fulfill the conditions that it enumerates. The representation of Algeria in the Chamber of Deputies is assured in the proportion of one deputy per 20,000 registered electors or fraction of 20,000.

ART. 6.   The Minister of the Interior is charged with the application of the present law.

9.   Shaykh Ben Badis Pronounces a Fatwa (Religious Edict) Against the French "Naturalization" of Algerians, August 10, 1937

The Association of the 'Ulama' of Algeria was established in 1931 by a group of Muslim 'ulama' (religious and legal scholars) under the leadership of Shaykh Ben Badis. The purpose of the organization was to rejuvenate Islam by reforming and "purifying" it of popular religious practices common in North Africa. The reformers believed that Islam could survive and indeed thrive in the modern world only if it returned to its roots —the Qur'an and Hadith—and if Islamic scholarship became infused with the modern scientific method and rationality (for similar views from the nineteenth century, see document 5 by Al-Afghani in the chapter "Central Political Reforms and Local Responses"). This belief placed the reformers on a collision course with the conservative Marabouts ("Saints") and Brotherhoods popular in the countryside.

The reformers used the mosques to attack the obscurantism, heterodoxy, superstitions, and subservience of their coreligionists. Moreover, they began to articulate through Islam a nationalist ideology that undermined French colonial power. A

Al-Basha'ir, Journal of the Association of the 'Ulama' of Algeria, 14 January 1938. Translated by Akram Khater.

book published by a member of the association—Ahmad Tawfiq al-Madani—sum-marized their nationalist doctrine in the motto "Islam is my religion; Arabic is my language; Algeria is my country." This slogan eventually became the official motto of the independent Algerian state.

Because of this political activity, the French colonial administration issued an order in 1933 denying reformist 'ulama' access to any of the official mosques. In re-sponse, a wave of agitation and unrest ensued during the next few years. French authorities closed Al-Hadith, a madrassa (religious school) opened in Tlemcen by Shaykh Ibrahimi, a reformist 'ulama.' In response, the journal of the association—Al-Basha'ir—published this fatwa (religious edict) by Shaykh Ben Badis against the French "naturalization" of Algerians.

In the name of God, the Most Merciful and Compassionate,

So that our Muslim brothers will know:

1. The action of acquiring a non-Muslim nationality implies the abandon-ment of Islamic law. Even the renunciation of a single precept of the Qur'an leads, according to the doctrine accepted by all of the 'ulama' of Islam, to apos-tasy. A naturalized person is thus an apostate.

According to French civil laws, the children of a naturalized French person are fully French. Therefore, neither they nor their descendants will know the privileges granted to the followers of Islam, because of actions taken by their parents, actions that we find reprehensible. The naturalized person cannot pu-rify himself of this mistake, of this sin, except by sincerely repenting and by penitence accompanied by a complete return to Islamic law.

But after becoming subject to French civil laws through naturalization, how can someone return to an environment that he voluntarily abandoned? In our opinion, there is one way for this to happen: the person must leave the country where he is subject to French laws and move to a country where he would be subject to Islamic legislation. If he does not want to leave but affirms the sincerity of his contrition, we cannot believe him. It is our duty to refuse him the benefits of our rituals.

2. A person who is condemned by a Muslim *qadi* [judge] conforming to the precepts of Islam, and who seeks to overturn the judgment by appealing to a foreign jurisdiction [. . .] is also an apostate. If he desires to merit the graces of God again, he must desist from his appeals and submit completely to the sentence of the Muslim judge.

3. Whoever provides testimony according to clauses contrary to the teach-ings of Islam is also an apostate.

4. He who marries a non-Muslim woman risks the lives of his offspring. He deprives them of all the advantages and privileges reserved by Islam for its fol-lowers. If the marriage is concluded with complete knowledge of the conse-quences that may follow, then the spouse should be considered an apostate. If the marriage is consummated under duress [. . .] then the sin is less but is still con-demnable because the naturalized placed his children in a dangerous situation.

May God forgive us our sins, and may we always walk along the straight path.

10.   Nationalism and the Jewish Community in Tunisia, March 5, 1938

The Alliance Israélite Universelle *and the Zionist movement had a rather complex relationship. Although both were intent on improving the lot of Jews throughout the world, they followed quite different—and at times contradictory—paths. The Alliance approached its task from a European perspective, seeking to "modernize" the Jews of the Middle East and North Africa by inculcating them with an "enlightened" French education.* Alliance *members believed that this education and the resulting closer relations with France would allow the Jews of these two regions to attain greater rights* within *their respective nations or countries. The Zionists, in contrast, believed that the only solution for the "Jewish problem" was the creation of a* separate *nation for Jews (in the "Ideas of Nationalism" chapter, see document 1, Leo Pinsker's 1882 appeal). The Alliance report reprinted here provides an example of the clash of these two views in the Jewish community of Tunisia.*

Tunis, 5 March 1938

Antisemitism and Zionism in Tunisia: How They Affect the School

. . . Yes, antisemitism exists in the Regency. The relations between Jews and Arabs are certainly satisfactory, but there are certain indications which do not escape the notice of those who are aware and which suggest that there are currents of discontent on the part of the Arabs toward the Jews. This discontent is especially caused by the jealousy of the Arabs when they see too many Jews succeeding in commerce and in the liberal professions (most of the businessmen, lawyers, and doctors in Tunis are Jewish) and little by little taking over the life of the nation. The Destourian movement[1] serves only to increase and spread this discontent. They resent not only the French but also the Jews. Obviously, antisemitism does not figure directly in the program of the *Destour,* but it is implied. A violent spirit of chauvinistic nationalism and a call for "National Awakening" animate the Tunisian youth of today and dictate to them quite unfavorable sentiments toward the Jews.

[. . .]

At the same time, it is no less certain that Zionism, too, exists and is rapidly developing. The Jewish daily newspapers, *La Nouvelle Aurore, Tel-Aviv,* and *La Semaine Juive,* regularly devote long articles to this topic. They comment at length on the activities of the Zionist movement, its efforts, its successes, the obstacles it faces in Palestine; they keep the public informed of the situation of

---

[1]The Tunisian nationalist movement.

Archives of the Alliance Israélite Universelle, Tunisie I.G.3. This document may also be found in Aron Rodrigue, *Images of Sephardi and Eastern Jewries in Transition: The Teachers of the Alliance Israélite Universelle, 1860–1939* (Seattle: University of Washington Press, 1993), pp. 252–256. Copyright © 1993. Reprinted by permission of University of Washington Press.

the Jews in the various countries and show how that situation is daily growing worse. What is most distressing is that this movement is not simply a Zionist movement but rather a party with clearly Revisionist tendencies: often it is only a question of Mr. Jabotinsky and his projects. And this movement has grown even among the Boy Scouts. It is saddening to observe that these troops of Jewish Scouts are becoming involved in politics. This is damaging not only to the Scouts themselves but to the entire population.

Thus the two movements growing stronger and stronger in Tunisia are Zionism and antisemitism. Are these two movements opposed? Should we believe that the former encourages the latter or that it is a remedy to it? Is it because of Zionism that antisemitism is developing? Is Zionism the solution to antisemitism? Are the Jews here justified in lending themselves to such a degree to political preoccupations of this nature?

Without trying to give a direct answer to such delicate questions, I will limit myself to applying these questions to what can be seen in the school. [. . .]

In general terms, all of our students, like most young people today—this is the *"mal du siècle"*—are taken with politics, and this is regrettable. Under the pretext of keeping informed, they scour the newspapers and become passionately involved in public and international issues. In this way, they waste a good portion of their time, often to the detriment of their studies and sound thinking. Indeed, through this kind of reading they acquire a mass of misguided opinions, which they take for Gospel and of which it is very difficult to rid them.

This is also true for my pupils, who are older adolescents preparing for the *brevet élémantaire*. Among them are several Muslims affiliated with the Destourian party . . . When I am giving my course on civics (in the second year of preparation for the diploma), there are always a few of them who point out certain so-called inequities or injustices which make them indignant. I cannot help but notice that the same idea is always behind these remarks: "make room for the Tunisians who are living in the streets and dying of hunger while scores of Frenchmen and Jews occupy all the respected positions."

Although I never allow myself to become involved in politics in the classroom and I do not tolerate the slightest allusion to this subject, I make it my duty to reply to these remarks, to analyze them, and to refute them. I believe that if these young people have been led astray in their circle of family and friends, it is up to us to show them the truth. Most often I succeed in convincing them and in disposing them toward higher sentiments and more just ideas.

The Jews live side by side with the Muslims, and on excellent terms. The Jews too, in their way, take an interest in politics. Obviously in their circle of family and friends, the sole topic of conversation is Zionism. How could they keep from talking about it, from discussing it at length, from considering all the possibilities and all the theories, and from enumerating all the solutions? Their minds are so steeped in these ideas that they cannot help but expose their personal sentiments, sometimes even in their compositions. Allow me to tell you about one case:

I had assigned the following topic (again it is a question of the students in the second year of preparation for the diploma), which is, as it happens, a regular topic in the program: "What emotions, what dreams does the word *partir!* [to leave] suggest to you?" A few spoke about Palestine and discussed the ideal of every Jew, to leave one day for the Holy Land. Thus far there could be nothing more legitimate and natural. But they did not stop there. "Why should I work for this ungrateful land?" I am quoting word for word from one composition, "Why pour out my efforts here while my country awaits me? I do not want to live in exile and sacrifice myself for foreigners . . ."

Such ideas denote a special mentality. If the students speak about this even in their school compositions, that means that they certainly talk about this among themselves and with their Muslim friends. What might happen when these Muslims, strongly influenced by Destourian ideas (therefore nationalistic and antisemitic ideas), revolt and challenge their Jewish friends so full of misunderstood Zionist ideas? This is what will happen: the relations between them, which have been excellent up until now, will become more and more strained and will contribute to profound dissension between the two sections of the Tunisian population. On the one side, the Arabs will spread the word that the Jews are foreigners, who have only to leave, that this is not their home, and that they are living as parasites. On the other side, the Jews, continuing along these lines, will neglect even their most basic civic duties.

Such is, then, the precise state of mind of our students today, and such are the serious consequences in which it may result.

[. . .]

How can we struggle effectively against such a situation? Should we systematically speak out against both the Destourian movement and Zionism? Is it wise to tell our students, even in an indirect and discreet manner: "You are both wrong; give up these ideas." In so doing, would we not risk shocking them and deeply wounding the sentiments they hold most dear?

It would appear that the solution lies elsewhere; this solution is twofold: 1. It is our duty to strengthen the civic and moral education of our students. They should understand that the first duty of the Jew is to the country in which he lives. Because they have the privileges accorded all citizens, it is right that they also accept the duties of citizens and carry them out fully. Even more than this: the Jews must always regulate their behavior and their lives in such a manner that they not become targets for those malicious minds who are always looking for faults and who never fail to generalize them. I would like to quote here a few of the noble words spoken by the Chief Rabbi of Geneva, Mr. Poliakoff, who visited our school when he was in Tunis and left an elevated moral teaching in the minds of our older students: "My dear children! Never forget that the Jews are closely bound together. The slightest fault, the slightest questionable affair on the part of one, is quickly generalized and attributed to all . . . We have a heavy burden to bear: for centuries the name Jew has been a synonym for coward, thief, usurer; this name represented all moral baseness. It is through our actions and our conduct that we can show the world the injustice that has been done to us and that we suffer still today. You must lead lives that are dignified, irreproachable, and exemplary from a moral, civic, and religious point of view. Then those who seek only to denigrate and belittle us, to deny us our very existence, will be able to find no fault in you . . ."

And so the first duty of any Jew is to be a "good citizen," worthy of the country in which he lives and worthy of his glorious heritage.

2. But it is not enough to give the students a solid civic and moral base. They must also be turned away from politics, which is the source of contention, disorder, and so many fruitless, if not tragic, discussions. The mind of the adolescent, just beginning to awaken, has need of nourishment. He seeks it out, and because most often he is surrounded by discussions of politics, he turns to politics himself. But could not this active mind and this hunger for learning, which are typical of the adolescent, be put to other, more profitable use?

Since he has this passion for all that is new to him and for all that is capable of awakening, strengthening, and developing his most pure and noble sentiments, why not warn him against the wrong road and show him the right path, the path rich in positive results?

And what path could this be?

This path has just been discovered by the students at the *Lycée Carnot* in Tunis: they founded a paper, which they write, edit, and publish entirely on their own. All questions of politics are excluded; the paper treats topics in literature, the arts, the sciences, sports, and anything that has to do with daily life. The first issue has already come out, and to judge by the favorable opinion of the public and the encouragement offered by the authorities concerned, this paper promises to prosper for a long time to come.

Does not an initiative such as this deserve to be imitated? Could we not do something along those lines, obviously on a more modest scale, with some of our students? We could encourage the students in their French (a subject in which they are generally quite weak), lead them toward sound and instructive reading, introduce them to literary masterpieces rather than insipid serial novels, develop in them artistic taste and sensibility (some of them are gifted in this area; they have shown me their sonnets and their sketches, and they are quite good), talk with them about sports, which so fascinate them, and speak to them of friendship and brotherhood between Arab and Jewish classmates. And as we do all this, we would be stimulating a spirit of healthy competition, which could bring only good results. Is not this the most effective way to turn them away from politics completely and to channel their growing energy in a manner that is both instructive and enjoyable? . . .

These are the solutions resulting from my reflections on antisemitism and Zionism and their effects on the school.

[. . .]

M. Cohen

11.   The Contest for Alexandretta Between Syria and Turkey, May 1938

For much of its premodern history, Alexandretta, with its capital city Antioch, was considered as part of Bilad al-Sham, *the area known today as Syria. In 1920 the sanjak (province) of Alexandretta was awarded to Syria by the League of Nations in the guise of a French mandate. In 1936 Alexandretta became the subject of a complaint to the League of Nations by Turkey, which claimed that the privileges of the Turkish minority in the sanjak were being infringed. (In 1921 there were only 87,000 Turks amid a population of 220,000 that was primarily Arab). In 1937 the sanjak was given autonomous status by an agreement, arranged by the League, between France (the mandatory power in Syria) and Turkey. Riots broke out between the various "national" and "ethnic" groups (primarily Arabs and Turks but also Kurds and Armenians). The result, in 1938, was the establishment of joint French and Turkish military control. In 1939, France transferred the sanjak to Turkey, and it became Hatay province. The transfer was the outcome of a highly contested and suspect referendum. Turkish peasants had been trucked into Antioch to vote, and Arabs had boycotted the election because they said it was fraudulent. After the votes were counted, close to fourteen thousand Armenians, who had fled Turkey because of the anti-Armenian genocide of 1914, left Hatay province and moved to Lebanon. Most historians agree that France's motivation for ceding the province to Turkey, despite Hatay's Arab majority, was to persuade Turkey to side with the Allies against Germany in the event of war.*

The letter and deposition included here refer to the 1938 rioting and indicate the complexity of the subject of national identity.

[1]

Request No. 912
Received: 16 May 1938   Kirik-Han May, 15, 1938
Responded: 17 May 1938

To the President of the Commission
League of Nations, Antioch
Sir,
     We undersigned, in the name of Arab in habitants of the villages of Kefer-kale and Ak Kouyou, in the district of Mourad Pasha, most humbly request your energetic protection against an armed Turkish band which has been raiding these two villages during the nights of the 13th and 14th Inst. The band is composed of the following Turkish proprietors of the district: Reshid Agha of Yeni Keuy, Abdullah Agha of Ak Pounar, Ahmed Agha of Jingil Aghlou and

League of Nations Archives, Geneva, Switzerland. Translated by Akram Khater.

Mohamed Riza of Keferkale. These people having with them about another six of their men and being armed to teeth are menacing us to be murdered in case we vote for Arabs which is our nationality. Since five days the villages of Keferkale and Ak Kouyou have been called to report to your Bureau at Mourad Pasha for inscription. Turks have reported, but we Arabs are being prevented to proceed there by this armed band.

In the name of justice we request your high protection against these aggressors and your energetic intervention to give safety to proceed to Mourad Pasha to vote there to our Arab nationality.

We remain Sirs, Your most obedient servants.

Hussein Bin Mohamed of Keferkale
Matar Edelli of Ak Kouyou
Ahmed el Gedro of Ak Kouyou

[2]

Alexandretta Police
Rayhaniyye Station

Deposition of Plaintiff Sido bin Dawuud
a Taxi driver stationed at Rayhaniyye

Half an hour after I began working in front of the Karim's Coffeehouse, when I saw Haydar Hassan Misto, and his brothers Uthman and Abdu and a fourth person whose name I do not know, going to the Arabs' club in Rayhaniyye. They were followed by more than 20 of their friends. They all shouted, "We are looking for the boss (Agha)." When they did not see him, the four individuals I mentioned first said, "here is one of the children of the one we are looking for," and they pulled out their revolvers that they were carrying and pointed them at me. Mr. Halafi Shaykh Mustafa Ramadan, Abu Omar Kassir and many other individuals whose names I cannot recall intervened on my behalf.

My witnesses are: Abdo from the neighborhood, . . . The aggressors and I are all from a Kurdish tribe. They asked why I was wearing a hat, and why I do not join the Arabs' club. I responded by saying that I am simply a taxi driver. Amongst those of them who carried weapons was a certain Khalil who I recognized . . . and he has three gold-crowned teeth.

5/10/1938

12.   The Arab Case for Palestine and the Case for a Binational
State, March 1946

Zionists believed overwhelmingly that the only way to ensure a secure future for Jews was to establish a Jewish homeland in Palestine. Arabs in Palestine were thoroughly opposed to that idea. They considered Palestine to be their ancestral home. They constituted a clear majority there and fervently believed that the establishment of a Jewish state would deprive them of their sovereign rights and dispossess them of their land and livelihood. Moreover, they considered Palestine to be part of the larger Arab culture and civilization and believed that the creation of a Jewish state would undermine that relationship. Any proposal to divide the land between Jews and Arabs was seen by the Arabs as a gross injustice, taking what was rightfully Arab and giving it to foreigners who only recently immigrated into Palestine.

A small minority among Zionists within and outside Palestine worried that the establishment of a Jewish homeland in Palestine would indeed be unjust. From the perspective of this small group, the moral authority of Zionism and Judaism would—at least in the long run—be undermined if an unacceptable state were forcibly imposed on the Arabs. Concern for the future relations between Arabs and Jews led a few Jews and Arabs to propose a binational state in which the two communities could coexist.

The Arab case and the case for a binational state are made in the following documents.

The Arab Case for Palestine: Evidence Submitted by the Arab Office, Jerusalem, to the Anglo-American Committee of Inquiry, March 1946

The Problem of Palestine

1. The whole Arab People is unalterably opposed to the attempt to impose Jewish immigration and settlement upon it, and ultimately to establish a Jewish State in Palestine. Its opposition is based primarily upon right. The Arabs of Palestine are descendants of the indigenous inhabitants of the country, who have been in occupation of it since the beginning of history; they cannot agree that it is right to subject an indigenous population against its will to alien immigrants, whose claim is based upon a historical connection which ceased effectively many centuries ago. Moreover they form the majority of the population; as such they cannot submit to a policy of immigration which if pursued for long will turn them from a majority into a minority in an alien state; and they claim the democratic right of a majority to make its own decisions in matters of urgent national concern. . . .

2. In addition to the question of right, the Arabs oppose the claims of political Zionism because of the effects which Zionist settlement has already had

Evidence Submitted by the Arab Office, Jerusalem, to the Anglo-American Committee of Inquiry, March 1946.

upon their situation and is likely to have to an even greater extent in the future. Negatively, it has diverted the whole course of their national development. Geographically Palestine is part of Syria; its indigenous inhabitants belong to the Syrian branch of the Arab family of nations; all their culture and tradition link them to the other Arab peoples; and until 1917 Palestine formed part or the Ottoman Empire which included also several of the other Arab countries. The presence and claims of the Zionists, and the support given them by certain Western Powers have resulted in Palestine being cut off from the other Arab countries and subjected to a regime, administrative, legal, fiscal and educational, different from that of the sister-countries. Quite apart from the inconvenience to individuals and the dislocation of trade which this separation has caused, it has prevented Palestine participating fully in the general development of the Arab world.

First, while the other Arab countries have attained or are near to the attainment of self-government and full membership of the U.N.O., Palestine is still under Mandate and has taken no step towards self-government; not only are there no representative institutions, but no Palestinian can rise to the higher ranks of the administration. This is unacceptable on grounds of principle, and also because of its evil consequence. It is a hardship to individual Palestinians whose opportunities of responsibility are thus curtailed; and it is demoralizing to the population to live under a government which has no basis in their consent and to which they can feel no attachment or loyalty.

Secondly, while the other Arab countries are working through the Arab League to strengthen their ties and coordinate their policies, Palestine (although her Arab inhabitants are formally represented in the League's Council) cannot participate fully in this movement so long as she has no indigenous government; thus the chasm between the administrative system and the institutions of Palestine and those of the neighbouring countries is growing, and her traditional Arab character is being weakened.

Thirdly, while the other Arab countries have succeeded in or are on the way to achieving a satisfactory definition of their relations with the Western Powers and with the world-community, expressed in their treaties with Great Britain and other Powers and their membership of the United Nations Organization, Palestine has not yet been able to establish any definite status for herself in the world, and her international destiny is still obscure.

3. All these evils are due entirely to the presence of the Zionists and the support given to them by certain of the Powers; there is no doubt that had it not been for that, Arab Palestine would by now be a self-governing member of the U.N.O. and the Arab League. Moreover, in addition to the obstacles which Zionism has thus placed in the way of Palestine's development, the presence of the Zionists gives rise to various positive evils which will increase if Zionist immigration continues.

The entry of incessant waves of immigrants prevents normal economic and social development and causes constant dislocation of the country's life; in so far as it reacts upon prices and values and makes the whole economy dependent upon the constant inflow of capital from abroad it may even in certain circumstances lead to economic disaster. It is bound moreover to arouse continuous political unrest and prevent the establishment of that political stability on which the prosperity and health of the country depend. This unrest is likely to increase in frequency and violence as the Jews come nearer to being the majority and the Arabs a minority.

Even if economic and social equilibrium is re-established, it will be to the detriment of the Arabs. The superior capital resources at the disposal of the Jews, their greater experience of modern economic technique and the existence of a deliberate policy of expansion and domination have already gone far toward giving them the economic mastery of Palestine. The biggest concessionary companies are in their hands; they possess a large proportion of the total cultivable land, and an even larger one of the land in the highest category of fertility; and the land they possess is mostly inalienable to non-Jews. The continuance of land-purchase and immigration, taken together with the refusal of Jews to employ Arabs on their lands or in their enterprises and the great increase in the Arab population, will create a situation in which the Arab population is pushed to the margin of cultivation and a landless proletariat, rural and urban, comes into existence. This evil can be palliated but not cured by attempts at increasing the absorptive capacity or the industrial production of Palestine; the possibility of such improvements is limited, they would take a long time to carry out, and would scarcely do more than keep pace with the rapid growth of the Arab population; moreover in present circumstances they would be used primarily for the benefit of the Jews and thus might increase the disparity between the two communities.

Nor is the evil economic only. Zionism is essentially a political movement, aiming at the creation of a state: immigration, land-purchase and economic expansion are only aspects of a general political strategy. If Zionism succeeds in its aim, the Arabs will become a minority in their own country; a minority which can hope for no more than a minor share in the government, for the state is to be a Jewish state, and which will find itself not only deprived of that international status which the other Arab countries possess but cut off from living contact with the Arab world of which it is an integral part.

It should not be forgotten too that Palestine contains places holy to Moslems and Christians, and neither Arab Moslems nor Arab Christians would willingly see such places subjected to the ultimate control of a Jewish Government.

4. These dangers would be serious enough at any time, but are particularly so in this age, when the first task of the awakening Arab nation is to come to terms with the West; to define its relationship with the Western Powers, and with the westernized world community on a basis of equality and mutual respect, and to adapt what is best in Western civilization the needs of its own genius. Zionist policy is one of the greatest obstacles to the achievement of this task: both because Zionism represents to the Arabs one side of the Western spirit and because of the support given to it by some of the Western Powers. In fact Zionism has become in Arab eyes a test of Western intentions towards them. So long as the attempt of the Zionists to impose a Jewish state upon the

inhabitants of Palestine is supported by some or all of the Western Governments, so long will it be difficult if not impossible for the Arabs to establish a satisfactory relationship with the Western world and its civilization, and they will tend to turn away from the West in political hostility and spiritual isolation; this will be disastrous both for the Arabs themselves and for those Western nations which have dealings with them.

5. There are no benefits obtained or to be expected from Zionism commensurate with its evils and its dangers. The alleged social and economic benefits are much less than is claimed. The increase in the Arab population is not primarily due to Zionist immigration, and in any case would not necessarily be a sign of prosperity. The rise in money wages and earnings is largely illusory, being offset by the rise in the cost of living. In so far as real wages and the standard of living have risen, this is primarily an expression of a general trend common to all Middle Eastern countries. The inflow of capital has gone largely to raising money prices and real estate values. The whole economy is dangerously dependent upon the citrus industry. The benefits derived from the establishment of industries and the exploitation of the country's few natural resources have been largely neutralized by the failure of Jewish enterprises to employ Arabs.

The Zionist contention that their social organizations provide health and social services for the Arab population is exaggerated; only a minute proportion of the Arabs, for example, are looked after by Jewish health organizations. Even if true it would prove nothing except that the Government was neglecting its responsibilities in regard to the welfare of the population. Arab voluntary social organizations have grown up independently of Jewish bodies and without help from them. Even in so far as social and economic benefits have come to the Arabs from Zionist settlement, it remains true on the one hand that they are more than counterbalanced by the dangers of that settlement, and on the other that they are only incidental and are in no way necessary for the progress of the Arab people. The main stimulus to Arab economic and social progress does not come from the example or assistance of the Zionists but from the natural tendency of the whole Middle Eastern areas, from the work of the Government and above all from the newly awakened will to progress of the Arabs themselves. The Arabs may have started later than the Jews on the road of modern social and economic organization, but they are now fully awake and are progressing fast. This is shown in the economic sphere for example by the continued development of the Arab citrus industry and financial organizations, in the social sphere by the growth of the labour movement and the new Land Development Scheme.

If any proof were needed of this, it could be found in the progress made during the last three decades by the neighbouring countries. None of the Arab countries is stagnant today: even without the example and capital of the Zionists, they are building up industries, improving methods and extending the scope of agriculture, establishing systems of public education and increasing the amenities of life. In some countries and spheres the progress has been greater than among the Arabs of Palestine, and in all of them it is healthier and more normal.

The Zionists claim further that they are acting as mediators of Western civilization to the Middle East. Even if their claim were true, the services they were rendering would be incidental only: the Arab world has been in direct touch with the West for a hundred years, and has its own reawakened cultural movement, and thus it has no need of a mediator. Moreover the claim is untrue: so long as Jewish cultural life in Palestine expresses itself through the medium of the Hebrew language, its influence on the surrounding world is bound to be negligible; in fact, Arab culture today is almost wholly uninfluenced by the Jews, and practically no Arabs take part in the work of Jewish cultural or educational institutions. In a deeper sense the presence of the Zionists is even an obstacle to the understanding of Western civilization, in so far as it more than any other factor is tending to induce in the Arabs an unsympathetic attitude towards the West and all its works.

6. Opposition to the policy of the Zionists is shared by all sections of the Palestinian Arab people. It is not confined to the townspeople but is universal among the rural population, who stand to suffer most from the gradual alienation of the most fertile land to the Jewish National Fund. It is felt not only by the landowners and middle class but by the working population, both for national reasons and for reasons of their own. It is not an invention of the educated class; if that class have seen the danger more clearly and sooner than others, and if they have assumed the leadership of the opposition, that is no more than their duty and function.

Moreover not only the Arab Moslem majority are opposed to Zionism but also and equally the Arab Christian minority who reject Zionism both because they share to the full in the national sentiments of other Arabs and because as Christians they cannot accept that their Holy Places should be subject to Jewish control, and cannot understand how any Christian nation could accept it.

7. The sentiments of the Palestinian Arabs are fully shared by the other Arab countries, both by their Government and their peoples. Their support has shown itself in many ways: in Pan-Arab Conferences, in the moral and material support given by the whole Arab world to the revolt of 1936–39, in the diplomatic activities of Arab Governments, and most recently in the formation of the Arab League, which has taken the defense of Palestine as one of its main objectives. The members of the Arab League are now taking active measures to prevent the alienation of Arab lands to the Zionists and Jewish domination of the economic life of the Middle East. . . .

8. In the Arab view, any solution of the problem created by Zionist aspirations must satisfy certain conditions:

i. It must recognize the right of the indigenous inhabitants of Palestine to continue in occupation of the country and to preserve its traditional character.

ii. It must recognize that questions like immigration which affect the whole nature and destiny of the country, should be decided in accordance with democratic principles by the will of the population.

iii. It must accept the principle that the only way by which the will of the population can be expressed is through the establishment of responsible representative government. (The Arabs find something inconsistent in the attitude of Zionists who demand the establishment of a free democratic commonwealth in Palestine and then hasten to add that this should not take place until the Jews are in a majority.)

iv. This representative Government should be based upon the principle of absolute equality of all citizens irrespective of race and religion.

v. The form of Government should be such as to make possible the development of a spirit of loyalty and cohesion among all elements of the community, which will override all sectional attachments. In other words it should be a Government which the whole community could regard as their own, which should be rooted in their consent and have a moral claim upon their obedience.

vi. The settlement should recognize the fact that by geography and history Palestine is inescapably part of the Arab world; that the only alternative to its being part of the Arab world and accepting the implications of its position is complete isolation, which would be disastrous from every point of view; and that whether they like it or not the Jews in Palestine are dependent upon the goodwill of the Arabs.

vii. The settlement should be such as to make possible a satisfactory definition within the framework of U.N.O. of the relations between Palestine and the Western Powers who possess interests in the country.

viii. The settlement should take into account that Zionism is essentially a political movement aiming at the creation of a Jewish state and should therefore avoid making any concession which might encourage Zionists in the hope that this aim can be achieved in any circumstances.

9. In accordance with these principles, the Arabs urge the establishment in Palestine of a democratic government representative of all sections of the population on a level of absolute equality; the termination of the Mandate once the Government has been established; and the entry of Palestine into the United Nations Organization as a full member of the working community.

Pending the establishment of a representative Government, all further Jewish immigration should be stopped, in pursuance of the principle that a decision on so important a matter should only be taken with the consent of the inhabitants of the country and that until representative institutions are established there is no way of determining consent. Strict measures should also continue to be taken to check illegal immigration. Once a Palestinian state has come into existence, if any section of the population favours a policy of further immigration it will be able to press its case in accordance with normal democratic procedure; but in this as in other matters the minority must abide by the decision of the majority.

Similarly, all further transfer of land from Arabs to Jews should be prohibited prior to the creation of self-governing institutions. The Land Transfer

Regulations should be made more stringent and extended to the whole area of the country, and severer measures be taken to prevent infringement of them. Here again once self-government exists matters concerning land will be decided in the normal democratic manner.

10. The Arabs are irrevocably opposed to political Zionism, but in no way hostile to the Jews as such nor to their Jewish fellow-citizens of Palestine. Those Jews who have already entered Palestine, and who have obtained or shall obtain Palestinian citizenship by due legal process will be full citizens of the Palestinian state, enjoying full civil and political rights and a fair share in government and administration. There is no question of their being thrust into the position of a "minority" in the bad sense of a closed community, which dwells apart from the main stream of the State's life and which exists by sufferance of the majority. They will be given the opportunity of belonging to and helping to mould the full community of the Palestinian slate, joined to the Arabs by links of interest and goodwill, not the goodwill of the strong to the powerless, but of one citizen to another.

It is to be hoped that in course of time the exclusiveness of the Jews will be neutralized by the development of loyalty to the state and the emergence of new groupings which cut across communal divisions. This however will take time; and during the transitional period the Arabs recognize the need for giving special consideration to the peculiar position and the needs of the Jews. No attempt would be made to interfere with their communal organization, their personal status or their religious observances. Their schools and cultural institutions would be left to operate unchecked except for that general control which all governments exercise over education. In the districts in which they are most closely settled they would possess municipal autonomy and Hebrew would be an official language of administration, justice and education.

11. The Palestinian State would be an Arab state not (as should be clear from the preceding paragraph) in any narrow racial sense, nor in the sense that non-Arabs should be placed in a position of inferiority, but because the form and policy of its government would be based on a recognition of two facts: first that the majority of the citizens are Arabs, and secondly that Palestine is part of the Arab world and has no future except through close co-operation with the other Arab states. Thus among the main objects of the Government would be to preserve and enrich the country's Arab heritage, and to draw closer the relations between Palestine and the other Arab countries. The Cairo Pact of March, 1945, provided for the representation of Palestine on the Council of the Arab League even before its independence should be a reality; once it was really self-governing, it would participate fully in all the work of the League, in the cultural and economic no less than the political sphere. This would be of benefit to the Jewish no less than the Arab citizens of Palestine, since it would ensure those good relations with the Arab world without which their economic development would be impossible.

12. The state would apply as soon as possible for admission into U.N.O., and would of course be prepared to bear its full share of the burdens of establishing a world security-system. It would willingly place at the disposal of the

Security Council whatever bases or other facilities were required, provided those bases were really used for the purpose for which they were intended and not in older to interfere in the internal affairs of the country, and provided also Palestine and the other Arab states were adequately represented on the controlling body.

The state would recognize also the world's interest in the maintenance of a satisfactory regime for the Moslem, Christian and Jewish Holy Places. In the Arab view however the need for such a regime does not involve foreign interference in or control of Palestine: no opportunity should be given to Great Powers to use the Holy Places as instruments of policy. The Holy Places can be most satisfactorily and appropriately guarded by a Government representative of the inhabitants, who include adherents of all three faiths and have every interest in preserving the holy character of their country.

Nor in the Arab view would any sort of foreign interference or control be justified by the need to protect the Christian minorities. The Christians are Arabs, who belong fully to the national community and share fully in its struggle. They would have all the rights and duties of citizens of a Palestinian state, and would continue to have their own communal organizations and institutions. They themselves would ask for no more, having learnt from the example of other Middle Eastern countries the dangers of an illusory foreign "protection" of minorities.

13. In economic and social matters the Government of Palestine would follow a progressive policy with the aim of raising the standard of living and increasing the welfare of all sections of the population, and using the country's natural resources in the way most beneficial to all. Its first task naturally would be to improve the condition of the Arab peasants and thus to bridge the economic and social gulf which at present divides the two communities. Industry would be encouraged, but only in so far as its economic basis was sound and as part of a general policy of economic development for the whole Arab world; commercial and financial ties with the other Arab countries would so far as possible be strengthened, and tariffs decreased or abolished.

14. The Arabs believe that no other proposals would satisfy the conditions of a just and lasting settlement. In their view there are insuperable objections of principle or of practice to all other suggested solutions of the problem.

1. The idea of partition and the establishment of a Jewish state in a part of Palestine is inadmissible for the same reasons of principle as the idea of establishing a Jewish state in the whole country. If it is unjust to the Arabs to impose a Jewish state on the whole of Palestine, it is equally unjust to impose it in any part of the country. Moreover, as the Woodhead Commission showed, there are grave practical difficulties in the way of partition; commerce would be strangled, communications dislocated and the public finances upset. It would also be impossible to devise frontiers which did not leave a large Arab minority in the Jewish state. This minority would not willingly accept its subjection to the Zionists, and it would not allow itself to be transferred to the Arab state. Moreover, partition would not satisfy the Zionists. It cannot be too often

repeated that Zionism is a political movement aiming at the domination at least of the whole of Palestine; to give it a foothold in part of Palestine would be to encourage it to press for more and to provide it with a base for its activities. Because of this, because of the pressure of population and in order to escape from its isolation it would inevitably be thrown into enmity with the surrounding Arab states and this enmity would disturb the stability of the whole Middle East.

2. Another proposal is for the establishment of a bi-national state, based upon political parity, in Palestine and its incorporation into a Syrian or Arab Federation. The Arabs would reject this as denying the majority its normal position and rights. There are also serious practical objections to the idea of a bi-national state, which cannot exist unless there is a strong sense of unity and common interest overriding the differences between the two parties. Moreover, the point made in regard to the previous suggestion may be repeated here: this scheme would in no way satisfy the Zionists, it would simply encourage them to hope for more and improve their chances of obtaining it. . . .

The Case for a Bi-national State*

The Arab Contention

The Arabs say that "the existence of the Jewish National Home, whatever its size, bars the way to the attainment by the Arabs of Palestine of the same national status as that attained, or soon to be attained, by all the other Arabs of Asia" (Royal Commission, p. 307). That is so. And they ask if they are not as fit for self-government as the Arabs of other countries. They are.

Arab Concessions

But the whole history of Palestine shows that it just has not been made for uni-national sovereign independence. This is an inescapable fact which no one can disregard. Although the Arabs cannot have a uni-national independent Arab Palestine, they can enjoy independence in a bi-national Palestine together with their Jewish fellow-citizens. This will afford them a maximum of national freedom. What the bi-national State will take away from them is sovereign independence in Palestine. There are other Arab States with sovereign independence. But we contend that the sovereign independence of tiny Palestine, whether it be Jewish sovereignty or Arab sovereignty, is a questionable good in this post-war period, when even great States must relinquish something of their sovereignty and seek union, if the world is not to perish. We contend that for this Holy Land the idea of a bi-national Palestine is at least as inspiring as that of an Arab sovereign Palestine or a Jewish Sovereign Palestine.

---

*Reprinted from M. Buber and J. L. Magnes, *Arab-Jewish Unity* (London: Victor Gollancz Ltd., 1947).

Jewish Concessions

On the other hand, the bi-national Palestine would deprive the Jews of their one chance of a Jewish State. But this bi-national Palestine would be the one State in the world where they would be a constituent nation, i.e. an equal nationality within the body politic, and not a minority as everywhere else. The absence of a Jewish State would make more difficult direct access by the Jewish people to U.N.O. To compensate for this, some form should be devised for giving the Jewish people a recognised place within the structure of the United Nations Organisation.

Nevertheless, the concessions the Jews would have to make on these matters are, we think, more far-reaching than the concessions the Arabs of Palestine would have to make. But the hard facts of the situation are that this is not a Jewish land and it is not an Arab land—it is the Holy Land, a bi-national country— and it is in the light of such hard facts that the problem must be approached.

The Advantages of a Bi-National Palestine

Before proceeding to outline our suggestions as to the political structure of the bi-national Palestine, we should like finally to point out some of the advantages of bi-nationalism based on parity in a country which has two nationalities.

FAILURE OF MINORITY GUARANTEES
1. The breakdown of the minority guarantees provided for in the Versailles Peace treaties is proof that in a bi-national country the only safeguard for a minority is equality with the majority. There is no prospect of peace in a country where there is a dominant people and a subordinate people. The single nation-State is a proper form for a country where there is but one legally recognised nationality, as, for example, the United States. But in countries with more than one recognised nationality—and they are numerous in Europe and in Asia— bitterness is engendered among the minority because the civil service, the military, the economic key positions, foreign affairs, are in the hands of the ruling class of the majority nation. Parity in a multi-national country is the only just relationship between the peoples.

SWITZERLAND
2. The multi-national state is an effective method of affording full protection for the national languages, cultures and institutions of each nationality. That there can be full cultural autonomy combined with full allegiance to the multi-national political state is proven in Switzerland's history for more than 100 years. The Swiss are divided by language, religion and culture; nor do the linguistic and religious groupings coincide in the various cantons. Yet all of these divergencies have not been obstacles to political unity. This is a newer form of democracy which is as important for multi-national states as the more familiar form of democracy is for uni-national states. The Swiss example is most relevant to Palestine, although there are, of course, many points of difference.

OTHER MULTI-NATIONAL COUNTRIES

The Soviet Union is a newer example of a multi-national State. The new Yugoslav State is an attempt at multi-national federalism. Professor Seton Watson outlines a bi-national solution of the age-long problem of Transylvania. Roumanian domination, Hungarian domination, partition had all been tried without success.

BI-NATIONALISM A HIGH IDEAL

3. In many senses the multi-national state represents a higher, more modern and more hopeful ideal than the uni-national sovereign independent State. The old way of having a major people and a minor people in a State of various nationalities is reactionary. The progressive conception is parity among the peoples of the multi-national State. The way of peace in the world to-day and to-morrow is through federation, union. Dividing up the world into tiny nationalistic sovereign units has not been the success the advocates of self-determination had hoped for at the end of the First World War. (Cobban, *National Self-Determination.*) The peoples who have been placed by fate or by history in the same country have warred with one another for domination throughout the centuries. The majority have tried to make the State homogeneous through keeping down the minority nationalities. The federal multi-national State, based on the parity of the nationalities, is a most hopeful way of enabling them to retain their national identity, and yet of coalescing in a larger political framework. It results in separate nationalities, yet a single citizenship. This is a noble goal to which the youth of multi-national countries can be taught to give their enthusiasm and their energies. It is a modern challenge to the intelligence and the moral qualities of the peoples constituting multi-national lands.

13.   President Harry Truman's Statement Supporting Jewish Immigration into Palestine, October 4, 1946

In August 1945 U.S. President Truman wrote Clement Atlee, the British prime minister, asking him to lift the British government's restrictions on Jewish immigration into Palestine, and to issue admission permits for 100,000 Jews. Truman wrote this letter—which was leaked to the press—partly because of his and most Americans' sympathy for the plight of the Jews of Europe in the wake of the Holocaust. Also, his move was calculated to help New York City Democrats attract the Jewish vote in the upcoming mayoral election. Ernest Bevin, the British foreign secretary, was disturbed by what he regarded as unilateral American statements not helpful to the situation in the Middle East. Yet, given Britain's need for American financial aid for post–World War II reconstruction, Bevin was reluctant to criticize American foreign policy publicly.

Michael Cohen, *Palestine and the Great Powers, 1945–1948* (Princeton, N.J.: Princeton University Press, 1982), pp. 58–59.

Thus, in an attempt to contain American policy, he proposed the formation of the Anglo-American Committee of Inquiry to explore "the possibility of relieving the position [of Jews] in Europe by immigration to other countries outside of Europe." The final version of the group's mandate, however, amended under American pressure, said that the committee's aim was "to make estimates of those who wish or will be impelled by their conditions to migrate to Palestine or other countries outside of Europe."[1] Despite that change, Bevin made it clear—in private and public—that the British government did not regard Palestine as the solution to the Jewish refugee problem and that he envisaged a Palestinian and not a Jewish state in Palestine. This position convinced David Ben-Gurion and other Zionist leaders that military operations against the British were necessary. Violent attacks by the Zionist paramilitary organizations Irgun and Lehi soon began to take their toll on the British, who responded increasingly in kind. At the same time, the Arab population of Palestine, which still amounted to double the number of Jews, rejected any proposal that would deny the Arab character of the country. Some Zionist leaders were willing to accept partition plans, but the Arab leadership considered such proposals unjust.

As the conflict intensified, the Anglo-American Committee of Inquiry tried to strike a compromise. On the one hand, members called for the admission of 100,000 Jewish immigrants into Palestine and the removal of land sale restrictions that had been in place since the 1939 White Paper (a British policy statement issued on May 17, 1939, that questioned the creation of a Jewish homeland in Palestine in the face of Arab opposition). On the other hand, members stated that any attempt to establish an independent state or states in Palestine would lead to civil strife. Instead, the committee envisioned a binational state in which Arabs and Jews would share power equally. On the day the committee made its recommendation (April 30, 1946), Truman announced U.S. support for the part of the report that recommended allowing 100,000 Jews to emigrate to Palestine, as well as allowing the Zionists to purchase land there more freely. In some ways, Truman timed his unilateral and abridged announcement to lead up to the 1946 U.S. congressional elections.

I have learned with deep regret that the meetings of the Palestine Conference in London have been adjourned and are not to be resumed until December 16, 1946. In the light of this situation it is appropriate to examine the record of the administration's efforts in this field, efforts which have been supported in and [out] of Congress by members of both political parties, and to state my views on the situation as it now exists.

It will be recalled that, when Mr. Earl Harrison reported on September 29, 1945, concerning the condition of displaced persons in Europe, I immediately urged that steps be taken to relieve the situation of these persons to the extent at least of admitting 100,000 Jews into Palestine. In response to this suggestion the British Government invited the Government of the United States to cooperate in setting up a joint Anglo-American Committee of Inquiry, an invitation which this Government was happy to accept in the hope that its participation would help to alleviate the situation of the displaced Jews in Europe and would assist

---

[1]Michael Cohen, *Palestine and the Great Powers, 1945–1948* (Princeton, N.J.: Princeton University Press, 1982), pp. 58–59.

in finding a solution for the difficult and complex problem of Palestine itself. The urgency with which this Government regarded the matter is reflected in the fact that a 120-day limit was set for the completion of the Committee's task.

The unanimous report of the Anglo-American Committee of Inquiry was made on April 20, 1946, and I was gratified to note that among the recommendations contained in the Report was an endorsement of my previous suggestion that 100,000 Jews be admitted into Palestine. The administration immediately concerned itself with devising ways and means for transporting the 100,000 and caring for them upon their arrival. With this in mind, experts were sent to London in June 1946 to work out provisionally the actual travel arrangements. The British Government cooperated with this group but made it clear that in its view the Report must be considered as a whole and that the issue of the 100,000 could not be considered separately.

On June 11, I announced the establishment of a Cabinet Committee on Palestine and Related Problems, composed of the Secretaries of State, War, and Treasury, to assist, me in considering the recommendations of the Anglo-American Committee of Inquiry. The alternates of this Cabinet Committee, headed by Ambassador Henry F. Grady, departed for London on July 10, 1946, to discuss with British Government representatives how the Report might best be implemented. The alternates submitted on July 24, 1946 a report, commonly referred to as the "Morrison plan," advocating a scheme of provincial autonomy which might lead ultimately to a bi-national state or to partition. However, opposition to this plan developed among members of the major political parties in the United States—both in the Congress and throughout the country. In accordance with the principle which I have consistently tried to follow, of having a maximum degree of unity within the country and between the parties on major elements of American foreign policy, I could not give my support to this plan.

I have, nevertheless, maintained my deep interest in the matter and have repeatedly made known and have urged that steps be taken at the earliest possible moment to admit 100,000 Jewish refugees to Palestine.

In the meantime, this Government was informed of the efforts of the British Government to bring to London representatives of the Arabs and Jews, with a view to finding a solution to this distressing problem. I expressed the hope that as a result of these conversations a fair solution of the Palestine problem could be found. While all the parties invited had not found themselves able to attend, I had hoped that there was still a possibility that representatives of the Jewish Agency might take part. If so, the prospect for an agreed and constructive settlement would have been enhanced.

The British Government presented to the Conference the so-called "Morrison plan" for provincial autonomy and stated that the Conference was open to other proposals. Meanwhile, the Jewish Agency proposed a solution of the Palestine problem by means of the creation of a viable Jewish state in control of its own immigration and economic policies in an adequate area of Palestine instead of in the whole of Palestine. It proposed furthermore the immediate issuance of certificates for 100,000 Jewish immigrants. This proposal received wide-spread attention in the United States, both in the press and in public forums. From the discussion which has ensued it is my belief that a solution along these lines would command the support of public opinion in the United States. I cannot believe that the gap between the proposals which have been put forward is too great to be bridged by men of reason and good-will. To such a solution our Government could give its support.

In the light of the situation which has now developed I wish to state my views as succinctly as possible:

1. In view of the fact that winter will come on before the Conference can be resumed I believe and urge that substantial immigration into Palestine cannot await a solution to the Palestine problem and that it should begin at once. Preparations for this movement have already been made by this Government and it is ready to lend its immediate assistance.

2. I state again, as I have on previous occasions, that the immigration laws of other countries, including the United States, should be liberalized with a view to the admission of displaced persons. I am prepared to make such a recommendation to the Congress and to continue as energetically as possible collaboration with other countries on the whole problem of displaced persons.

3. Furthermore, should a workable solution for Palestine be devised, I would be willing to recommend to the Congress a plan for economic assistance for the development of that country.

In the light of the terrible ordeal which the Jewish people of Europe endured during the recent war and the crisis now existing, I cannot believe that a program of immediate action along the lines suggested above could not be worked out with the cooperation of all people concerned. The administration will continue to do everything it can to this end.

PART III

The Rise of Postindependence States, 1950–2000

European colonialism, which tore at the fabric of society, nationalist projects that sought forcibly to create new "authentic" nations, and the economically debilitating effects of World War II left most countries in the Middle East and North Africa in a state of chaos. The old political landowning elites, leftovers from the Ottoman era, and the new middle-class elites, formed in the second half of the nineteenth century, proved incapable of providing the majority of the people with a unifying goal or with solutions to very real economic and social problems. For example, in the 1930s and 1940s King Farouk and his coterie in Egypt appeared completely incapable—and at times unwilling—to eject the British from Egypt. Furthermore, their conspicuous consumption stood in stark contrast to the poverty that predominated among peasants and the urban poor. Nor were most middle-class political parties much more effective. The Wafd Party—which presented itself as the party of the "people"—emerged from World War II with very little credibility. After twenty years at the helm of Egyptian political life, the Wafd appeared no closer to achieving complete and true independence for Egypt. Furthermore, the entanglement of its leadership in a series of political corruption scandals, and the unwillingness of these leaders to enact any laws that would ameliorate the lives of the peasants, bankrupted the political fortunes of the party.

The confusion was compounded by the dearth of national institutions that could bring some semblance of unity and order to most of the new nations in the Middle East and North Africa. In large part, this situation stemmed from the goals of the mandate powers. France, for instance, refrained from investing in a civil service infrastructure capable of independently administering Syria and Lebanon. French colonial fiscal policies were crafted primarily to benefit the economy of France, not to encourage the economies of Lebanon and Syria

247

to grow independently. Such policies—meant to prolong the presence of the colonial powers—kept most countries from establishing visible national institutions that would cut across the various dividing lines in society (class, gender, ethnicity, religion, etc.). The one institutional exception was security organizations—the military or the police.

Security organizations were national institutions in which individuals from all walks of life could participate on equal terms. An 'Alawi Muslim from the environs of Latakia, a Sunni Muslim from Damascus, a Greek Orthodox Christian from Aleppo, and a Druze from the Golan could join the same Syrian army, wear the same uniform, march side by side in parades, and salute the same flag. Membership in the army did not eliminate divisiveness or overcome communal loyalties. But the army became one of the most visible symbols of Syria's status as a "nation." From outside Syria and from within, the army presented an image of unity and order that contrasted sharply with the political chaos that reigned in civil society during the 1930s and later. The army appeared "clean" in the face of rampant political corruption; it seemed strong while the civilian politicians seemed ineffective; it was national when the political leadership was sectarian; and it was composed of ordinary people, not the ruling elites.

Those contrasts were heightened by the loss of Palestine to the Zionists in 1948. Although the soldiers and officers of the various Arab regiments that fought in that war performed fairly well, the war was perceived to have been lost because of the ineptitude of Arab general commands, the lack of real support from Arab capitals, and the outdated weapons with which Arab regimes had armed their troops. This humiliation convinced many officers in various Arab armies that the time had come to overthrow the old political regimes and provide a new direction for the "nation."

During the 1950s and early 1960s this conclusion inspired action in various parts of the Middle East. In Egypt in 1952, for example, Gamal Abdel Nasser and the Free Officers overthrew King Farouk and established a "revolutionary" government whose self-avowed goal was to rescue the nation from colonialism and restore its national dignity. Over the following years, this goal also motivated military leaders who rose to power in Iraq, Libya, Syria, Algeria, and Yemen. The widespread desire to bring an end to years of humiliating and oppressive colonialism is understandable. The appeal of such a goal is especially apparent when we take into consideration the European "Orientalist" traditions, which throughout the nineteenth century and later characterized the Middle East and North Africa as backward. Also for people in Egypt and elsewhere, a strong, unified, and coherent government offered a welcome reprieve from the pervading chaos. Thus, despite some strong opposition to the idea of military rule, Nasser in Egypt, Hafez al-Assad in Syria, and other leaders elsewhere were seen as potential saviors of the beleaguered "nation"—an impression that these leaders strongly encouraged.

In the case of Nasser, this impression became more powerful after he successfully nationalized the Suez Canal in 1956 and refused to back down in the face of British, French, and Israeli military aggression. (The importance of this moment in Arab history can be gauged by the incredible success of the movie *Nasser '56,* produced in 1993 in the wake of the Gulf War, which retold the story of Nasser and his victory in very positive terms.) This success legitimized for a while the emergence of single-party rule centered on the cult of the *za'im* (leader). In the new state, the leader and the nation began to become indistinguishable. The belief was widespread that only the za'im could possibly know what was good for the people, and anyone who opposed him or his ideas was considered a traitor to the "nation."

One of the leader's goals was indeed to improve the lives of the people of the nation (if for no other reason than to keep them from revolting). Nevertheless, a state defined in this manner had little legitimacy. This paternalistic approach was sustainable only as long as the benefits of authoritarianism seemed to outweigh its detriments. While opportunities for a better life were available to large numbers of people, the state could justify and people would tolerate political authoritarianism and the rejection of any opposition—legitimate or otherwise. However, this situation could not be sustained for long. Economically, states all across the Middle East and North Africa soon proved incapable of properly managing the economy. From conservative regimes such as Iran and Saudi Arabia to "revolutionary" states such as Egypt and Algeria, ruling elites faltered in their handling of the economy. Corruption, graft, overly ambitious projects, lack of economic diversity, overpopulation, and a residue of economic dependence on the West combined to create serious economic crises at various times for various states. Politically, many of these states also faltered—albeit at different times and for different reasons. For instance, in 1967 Egypt, Syria, and Jordan suffered a humiliating defeat at the hands of the Israeli army. This defeat of conservative (Jordan) and "revolutionary" (Egypt and Syria) regimes alike destroyed the credibility of leaders who had based their claims to legitimacy on the premise that they were advancing their countries. Within forty-eight hours, superior Israeli military technology emptied years of military parades and bombastic speeches of any meaning. The facades that had provided flimsy excuses for the suppression of various freedoms and for sordid human rights records came crashing down, leaving the ruling elites exposed to criticism from all angles.

The chapters in this section attempt to document in a variety of ways the emergence and initial success of these states, as well as the challenges they faced. Included here are documents that highlight attempts to create dominant state ideologies leaving little room for any opposing ideas. Also presented are critiques of these types of states—of their failures to fulfill their promises and to improve the lives of their peoples.

CHAPTER 6

Restricting Authority

The struggle to create modern nations between the two world wars was a politically exhausting and debilitating struggle between competing ideologies and groups that sometimes presented radically different visions of the "nation" to the population at large. In Egypt, this period of experimentation with democratic processes is known as the "Liberal Experiment." Between 1926 and 1939, Egypt experienced widespread freedom of the press, a plethora of political parties ranging from communists on the left to Muslim Brothers on the right, and a series of public elections. Unfortunately, for most Egyptians this experiment was ultimately a failure. Consecutively elected parliaments failed to provide relief for the economic woes of either the peasants—still the majority of the population—or the workers. Most remained impoverished and subject to exploitation by landowners, bankers, and industrialists. Politically, the electoral process was severely undermined and tarnished, because King Farouk dissolved the Egyptian parliament whenever he deemed its goals to be at odds with his desires, and the occupying British forces constantly interfered in the selection of the Egyptian cabinet. Also, the corrupt practices of the once-popular Wafd Party convinced most Egyptians that the democratic process was a farce.

If this experiment in Egypt—where a "modern" bureaucratic state had been in existence since the beginning of the nineteenth century—failed to fulfill people's aspirations for a politically independent and economically healthy nation, the situation was even worse elsewhere in the Middle East and North Africa. In countries such as Syria and Iraq, the population was far more ethnically, religiously, and linguistically diverse than in Egypt, and modern governing institutions were much less numerous than in Egypt. In places such as Syria and Algeria, the colonial powers (France in these cases) prevented most of the indigenous population from participating in the administration of the country. These factors, in addition to economic hardship resulting from years of colonial rule and economic mismanagement, increased the complexity of nation building and intensified the political chaos.

World War II worsened this situation, leaving most countries in the Middle East and North Africa greatly impoverished. Without a Marshall Plan but with ongoing and intensified European extraction of local resources, the peoples of these countries were pushed farther down the economic ladder. Most of the indigenous ruling elites—whose hallmark was conspicuous consumption—were increasingly viewed as illegitimate rulers. For many in the Middle East, the crisis of political legitimacy came to a head with the loss of Palestine to the Zionists in 1948. When the creation of Israel was announced in May of that year, the armies of Transjordan, Syria, and Egypt (with some volunteers from Iraq and Saudi Arabia) announced that they would soon retake the land for the Arabs. Unfortunately for them, the first Arab-Israeli war led to an even greater loss, as Israel claimed 73 percent of Palestine, as opposed to the 50 percent allocated by the United Nations' 1948 partition plan. This devastating loss highlighted the gap between the bombastic rhetoric of the Arab ruling elites and their actual ability to create modern nations capable of safeguarding the interests of their peoples.

In the wake of this defeat, political opposition to the ruling elites intensified and discontent grew on the streets of Cairo, Amman, Damascus, and Baghdad. Most of these nascent nations appeared to teeter on the brink of disintegration. Against this chaotic background, the military in these countries seemed islands of strength, stability, and unity. From the armed forces emerged a new group of political activists. Generally, they were officers—such as Gamal Abdel Nasser of Egypt—who had risen into the middle ranks of the military from a humble socioeconomic background. Their allegiance was to the "nation" and not primarily to a political party. They were still untarnished by the political and financial corruption sullying the ruling elites, and they had the military wherewithal to at least overthrow the existing government. And this is what transpired throughout the 1950s in Egypt, Syria, and Iraq, and later in the 1960s in Libya, Algeria, and Yemen.

Elsewhere in countries such as Iran, Jordan, and Morocco, the state was controlled by a monarchy that based its rule in large part on its army and on support from Western powers. Saudi Arabia, however, offered a still different model. The power of the Saudi monarchy derived from the alliance between the tribe of Bin Saud, originally from the eastern region of modern-day Saudi Arabia, and the Wahabis, members of an ultraconservative religious reformist movement that emerged in the eighteenth century in the same region of the country. Their symbiotic relationship was based on the religious legitimacy that the Wahabis gave to the Saudi monarchy and the willingness of the Saudis to allow the Wahabis to instill their retrograde vision of Islam within the kingdom.

Thus, by the 1960s, the great majority of the countries in the Middle East and North Africa were authoritarian states. Even Israel, which proclaimed itself a democratic state, limited the privilege of full political participation by definition and in practice to its Jewish citizens—some would argue to Jews of European descent—thus politically marginalizing its Arab citizens.

Included in this chapter are documents that examine the rise of authoritarianism in various countries. Excerpts of the confidential diary of Asadollah Alam, Iran's court minister between 1969 and 1977, provide invaluable glimpses into the ambitions and follies of the shah of Iran, Muhammad Reza Pahlavi (document 1). In document 2, Saddam Hussein, the authoritarian president of Iraq, proclaims his notion of history as a tool for "educating" the masses and particularly children about the revolution. This document illustrates the power of rhetoric in authoritarian discourse; such power is in many ways far more effective than military weapons and oppression. The constitution of Saudi Arabia (document 3) explains the claim of the ruling House of Saud to a religious source of legitimacy and highlights the nature of Saudi rule. Document 4 is an interview with a human rights activist in Turkey who discusses the army's role in shaping the political process in that country.

In most of these documents we find that behind the rise of the authoritarian state in the Middle East is the personification of the nation. Many rulers came to see themselves as the embodiment of the "nation" and their wishes and desires as the wishes and desires of the "people." The greater their illegitimacy, the more oblivious they became to what their people really hoped for, and the more they came to believe in their own fiction or in some fiction constructed by their sycophantic entourages.

1.   Asadollah Alam's Diary Details Some Elements of the Shah of Iran's Rule in 1976 and 1977

Asadollah Alam descended from the non-Qajar aristocracy that ruled the eastern provinces of Iran before the rise of the Pahlavi dynasty to the monarchy. After the fall of Muhammad Mosaddeq—the nationalist prime minister of Iran—in August 1953 as a result of an American-concocted coup d'état, Shah Muhammad Reza Pahlavi (1919–1980) was reinstated to power, and he was finally able to implement his vision of unlimited personal power within Iran. Alam shared and even encouraged the shah's view of government. Alam's first task—which he carried out successfully—was to promote the social reforms known as the White Revolution, to be implemented under the sole leadership of the shah. This move was an attempt to remove any constitutional blocks to the absolutism that the shah so desired and that Alam supported wholeheartedly. Alam was responsible for violently putting down several revolts against the regime of the shah, first by tribal leaders in the Fars region and then by religious clergy led by Ayatollah Ruhollah Khomeini (document 3 in the chapter "Crisis of the State" is a 1975 denunciation of the shah by Khomeini). These successes, however, only set the stage for the weakening and down-

Asadollah Alam, *The Shah and I: The Confidential Diary of Iran's Royal Court, 1966–1977*, ed. Alinaghi Alikhani, trans. Alinaghi Alikhani and Nicolas Vincent (London: I. B. Tauris & Co., 1991), pp. 508–510, 515–516, 523–527, 540, 542–543, 545–546, 547, 549, 550. Reprinted by permission of I. B. Tauris & Co Ltd, London.

fall of the shah. The quite successful social reforms opened a host of educational op-portunities to a greater number of Iranians than ever before, and a generation of educated young people grew up expecting and then demanding more political rights and a greater say in the governing of the country. These demands ran in the face of the autocratic tendencies of the shah, which were encouraged by Alam. By the end of his regime—in the late 1970s, about which Alam writes here—the shah had become politically isolated and insulated from the mounting opposition to his rule, and the violence of his police machine—the Savak—barely kept in him power.

Friday, 10 September [1976]

. . . Met the Israeli representative this evening. Discussed joint action to per-suade the US Senate to accept arms sales to Iran. He suggested that HIM [His Imperial Majesty] raise the issue with Shimon Perez, the Israeli Defence minis-ter, who is due to be received tomorrow. He also told me that Senator Hubert Humphrey is considering making a tour of the Middle East; Iran, Israel and Saudi Arabia in particular . . . It would be a good idea if our Washington am-bassador could extend an invitation along these lines, since it would help our position in regard to arms. He stressed that we must act quickly if we're to forestall Saudi Arabia and so be the first to attract the senator's attention . . .

Tuesday, 14 September

Audience. Discussed the race for the US presidency, where Carter seems still to be leading. We then turned to the underlying reasons for the hostility shown us by the American media. I remarked that the Americans are fools and that their opposition to our arms purchases shows them bowing to Soviet propaganda. If they had any sense they would be crying out for us to buy more not less weapons, since it would increase our dependence on the USA to an even greater extent. "Quite so," HIM replied. "Soviet propaganda is remarkably ef-fective and the Americans are even more remarkably stupid. Combine these two factors and you arrive at the present débâcle; every single congressman and pundit acting directly contrary to their own best interests." . . .

Princess Ashraf has again asked the government to pay the expenses of her trip to England, greatly to HIM's annoyance. He instructed me to notify every member of the Imperial family that such impertinent requests to the govern-ment will be severely dealt with in future.

This afternoon I received a prominent American journalist named Helen Copley; a supporter of ours. We spent an hour discussing the Information Plan. She suggested we set up a special news agency in the USA, the better to influence public opinion . . .

Saturday, 18 September

Audience . . . HIM asked me to write to Ardeshir Zahedi, urging him to liaise closely with Israel's embassy in Washington . . .

Last Wednesday on HIM's instructions, I cabled General Nassiri in Washington following his prostate operation, notifying him that the Shahanshah had most graciously agreed to pay his medical and travel expenses. Ardeshir Zahedi telephoned yesterday to say that the general had also received money from the PM and that he's now bewildered whether he has HIM to thank for this second payment. "The PM said nothing about it to me," HIM remarked with a smile.

It seems our PM takes a keen interest in the well-being of the men from Savak! . . .

Sunday, 19 September

Audience. HIM declared he felt better today than he's felt for many years . . .

Shahriar Shafiq,[1] HIM's nephew by his sister Princess Ashraf, presently an officer in the navy, was at last night's dinner. He and HMQ [Her Majesty the Queen] spent the entire time moaning on about Tehran's chaotic traffic congestion, the incompetence of municipal bureaucracy in Bandar Abbas, and so forth. I told HIM I strongly disapprove of such talk; fair enough if they raised these problems during the day, but they're not appropriate topics for the dinner table and do nothing but damage to HIM's health. Even Hitler spent his evenings listening to music, even at the height of the war. HIM gave a wry smile as if to say such things are beyond his power to change . . .

Reported that Danny Chamoun, the son of the former Lebanese President, has asked for an audience in order to pass on a message from his father. "I'd be ill-advised to receive him in present circumstances," HIM remarked. "His father has grown old and more than a little mad." I pointed out that the old man put up a brave resistance to the left-wingers . . . "Quite so," HIM replied, "but the determination with which he acted merely proves the degree of his madness." . . .

Met the Israeli representative after lunch. He predicts the US-presidential elections will be a very close-run affair . . .

[. . .]

Sunday, 17 October

. . . Discussing our image abroad, HIM referred to an interview he gave recently to Mike Wallace of NBC.[2] "The bloody man's questions were incredibly hostile. He more or less forced me into declaring that the USA is controlled by the Jews and that it's this same influence which has persuaded Carter to oppose

---

[1]The son of Ahmad Shafiq, an Egyptian, who was the second husband of Princess Ashraf. A graduate of the British Royal Naval College, Dartmouth, Shahriar was regarded as a competent and straight-forward military officer, unaffected by and uninterested in Court life. He was assassinated in Paris in December 1979 amid speculation that the revolutionary regime in Tehran regarded him as a threat. [All footnotes in this document are Alikhani's.]

[2]See Mike Wallace, *Close Encounters* (New York, 1985), pp. 334–335.

our purchasing arms." . . . "Tell the Israelis," HIM said, "that the bastard was so malicious I had no choice but to speak my mind. He more or less dragged it out of me." I reminded him that everyone, the Court press department, our Jewish advisers and myself, had pleaded with him not to receive this man Wallace. Yet he insisted on going ahead and just look where it's led us. "There's no use wringing our hands," he replied. "What's done is done. But tell Ardeshir Zahedi that he's not to arrange interviews with such vultures ever again." Here too, I pointed out that it's a standing order of our new campaign that no one is to arrange foreign press interviews for HIM. It was for precisely this reason we asked for the Foreign Minister to be admitted to our steering committee. HIM finally approved this last suggestion . . .

Monday, 18 October

Audience . . . Some time ago HIM's sister, Princess Fatemeh, asked for a 707 army plane to fly her, Mrs Diba and seventy other ladies on pilgrimage to Mashad. Knowing what HIM's reaction would be I avoided reporting the matter whilst we were in Birjand. However last night the Princess telephoned to press her claim and I was forced to raise it at today's audience. HIM was furious. "Do they suppose the military have nothing better to do," he said, "than to act as courier to a bunch of redundant old bags in search of God's mercy?" He was so angry that we both kept a tense silence for quite some time. I bitterly regretted having raised the matter.

I asked whether his skin rash was any better. He now believes it was due to the calcium tablets he was taking and has noted a marked improvement since he gave them up. His doctors are due to give him a blood test next week, but he rejected my suggestion that they bring along a dermatologist, saying that the rash is due to some sort of internal reaction not to any problem with his skin.

Reported that Princess Shahnaz has asked for a three-fold increase in salary. "Has she gone mad?," HIM replied. "I said raise her salary, not treble it! I'd never be able to justify it to the others. They'd all be clamouring to follow suit." . . . He added that he intends making a tour of inspection of the Tehran barracks next Thursday afternoon. I pointed out that since next Wednesday is a religious holiday, everything will be shut down until the Saturday after.[3] In any case military offices are always closed on Thursday afternoons. He did nothing more than smile by way of reply; in other words warning me to mind my own business . . .

There have been municipal elections across the country. Despite being allowed greater licence than normal, people in Tehran seemed utterly indifferent to the whole thing. Of the city's 5 million inhabitants, only about 70,000 bothered to vote. Since the Rastakhiz Party made no attempt to drum up attendance at the polling stations, it only goes to show that nobody's particularly interested in these elections. A worrying sign . . .

---

[3]Thursday and Friday constitute the weekend in Iran.

Monday, 22 November

... Met Yankelovich together with the deputy head of the information and press department of Israel's Foreign Ministry. Between them they have drawn up a lengthy report on Iran's image in the western media. Most interesting and yet alarming to discover how little we really knew of the situation. I am pleased that it is I who should have the responsibility of passing the real facts on to HIM.

Thursday, 25 November

Audience. Amongst other things, reported that Princess Shahnaz was expecting to lunch with the Egyptian Vice-President during her trip to Cairo, but at the last moment Sadat himself telephoned to invite both her and the Vice-President to be his guests ...

Remarked that when I bid farewell to HMQ yesterday on her departure for Egypt, I found her surrounded by the usual bunch of ill-mannered dimwits. It's only to be expected they should turn up in Kish, Nowshahr, Birjand, even in Amman, but really Cairo is another matter altogether. Their Majesties enjoy a special relationship with Egypt which these people can only jeopardize ... "But what's to be done?" HIM replied. "HMQ is genuinely attached to them. Even her mother has warned her, several times, yet she was told to mind her own business so harshly she daren't raise the subject ever again." ...

"Incidentally," he said, "I don't suppose you've heard about President Tito's latest statement? He's announced that Yugoslavia needs a strong military defence and can no longer rely on the promises of outsiders." I remarked this seemed very much in line with what HIM has been saying about Iran. "Precisely," he said. "We have to alert the Iranian public to this issue. My political testament consists of little else; above all it emphasizes that the army is the very cornerstone of this country's future. The testament needs to be made public." I replied that it would be better to wait until the Crown Prince's twentieth birthday.

"The other day," HIM continued, "I was asked by the US ambassador why Amouzegar had been appointed Secretary-General of the Party. I explained that Amouzegar is an excellent administrator; he's not a freemason, and I can trust him. No one is perfect, of course. Amouzegar also happens to be extremely mean. He's envious of other people's success and over keen to be generous towards his brothers and his family. But then, as I say, nobody is perfect." ...

[...]

Friday, 26 November

... Talked for an hour this afternoon with Joseph Kraft, an American journalist who has been a good friend to Iran. He told me the Carter administration is bound to turn against us, as our policies are mutually incompatible. During his election campaign Carter declared it undesirable that there should be any further military build-up in the Middle East; he blamed Iran for the rise in oil prices, and attacked our record on human rights . . . I asked Kraft what we might do to overcome this problem. In his opinion, HIM should visit Carter at the White House as soon as possible. In addition we should dismiss our ambassador in Washington; he's too obviously a supporter of the former regime and has turned our embassy into something not far short of the Playboy Club.

I expressed surprise that Carter should be so taken in by the propaganda of our enemies. Our political prisoners are communists, and in this country communist activity is illegal. To say that we deny political liberty is merely to parrot the slogans of our enemies . . . As for our re-armament, I presume Carter has sufficient intelligence not to rush to hasty judgments. We're spending so much money on US military supplies that no US government, let alone the arms manufacturers, could afford to deny us . . . I added that even if Carter is foolish enough to opt for confrontation, we are not lacking in the means to retaliate. The USA has no monopoly over arms manufacture, and we can always turn to France or Germany, or exchange our gas for Soviet hardware . . .

I didn't bother pointing out the extent to which HIM has the support of his nation. The internal situation is sound. The workers and the farmers are content and the middle classes grow richer day by day. Set against this, what does it matter if a few so-called intellectuals express opinions at odds with our own. In any case what do these blasted dissidents hope to gain? Education and the health service are already free. People are allowed a large degree of control over their own affairs. "Mr Joseph Kraft," I said, "you are a friend of Iran. But if you have been sent here to bully us, I must tell you bluntly that we give not a damn for other peoples' opinions. You can rest assured HIM has no intention of visiting the USA either in the immediate future or for some time to come."

Kraft remarked that, though he'd already met the PM and most of the cabinet, no one had spoken to him as harshly as me. I replied I had done no more than express an honest opinion to someone I assumed to be a friend. It was up to him to interpret my words in whatever way he chose. "Sure," he said, "but the opinions you express are really those of the Shah." I replied that having been granted an audience himself he was already in a position to judge how closely my views accord with those of my Shahanshah. I told him, however, that I had been given no prior briefing and that in any case HIM accounts the entire subject as of very little significance. Kraft was amazed at this, remarking that what I had said about HIM visiting the USA was more or less word for word what the Shah himself had told him.

Saturday, 27 November

Audience . . . Reported my conversation with Kraft. HIM was pleased with the way I'd handled it. "How can they ignore the prestige of my country?," he said. "How can they think of throwing up business worth $4 billion a year; likely to top $50 billion over the coming decade? I only wish the PM and the cabinet had spoken as you did." He went on to say that we are in the midst of negotiations with the Soviet Minister of Foreign Trade for the supply of Russian long-range artillery. "And we can turn to Western Europe for tanks and aircraft. Then we shall set how these American gentlemen react."

Met the Israeli representative after lunch. He told me that Yankelovich is seriously concerned that his report has offended HIM.

Again met Kraft. He claims that the US embassy here is misleading our government in claiming that Carter has no alternative but to fall into line with previous American policy towards Iran. Apparently the senators who were here recently disbelieved the US ambassador's stories about close relations between Iran and Israel. They asked Kraft to check up on the matter. "And," he said, "I had to tell them that everything was just as the ambassador told them. Even so it gives you a good idea how much faith our senators put in the word of their own officials." ...

Sunday, 28 November

Audience ... Described the findings by our press department on Yankelovich's report of American public opinion.[4] HIM almost exploded with rage, saying, "How can the bastard have dared be so impertinent? His report was based on wholly negative assumptions. It was not his business to question whether the country enjoys political liberty, nor whether torture is employed against political prisoners. He should not concern himself with whether we are contributing to peace in the Middle East." I replied that the question of peace was entirely valid, and that Yankelovich's other points were all the subject of intense interest in the USA and therefore of relevance to a report on US opinion. He and his associates must be allowed to diagnose the problem if they're to prescribe a remedy "We shall see," said HIM, "but in my opinion he and his colleagues are being manipulated by the oil companies. They're out to frighten us." I replied that as far as I can tell there is no evidence to support such an allegation. "Very well," HIM said more angrily than ever, "if you're too blind to see what's been going on, then it's pointless my trying to explain it to you." Again I did my best to point out that it was we ourselves who asked Yankelovich and his firm to study our image in the West, to show us where we were going wrong and to suggest improvements ... But HIM remained silent and I thought it best to change the subject. Even then his sullen mood persisted and he did no more than snap out brief comments on the matters I had to report ...

---

[4]"A Study of the Attitudes of the American Public and Leadership Towards Iran," based on interviews with leading figures in American business, politics, the media, etc. The Court's press department worked closely with the American public relations consultants, agreeing with their methods and findings.

Wednesday, 1 December

Audience . . . Reported that Amnesty International's survey of Iran is extremely hostile. "Quite so," HIM remarked. "But Parviz Radji, our ambassador in London, has answered their criticisms very well." I pointed out that Amnesty's report has received considerable publicity world-wide, but that Radji's remarks merited no more than a brief reference from the BBC. "Fair enough," he replied, "you must cable Radji immediately. Tell him if his statement isn't published, then he must bring it out himself via advertising space in the newspapers." I also had to report that West German radio has broadcast criticisms of Savak. This put HIM in a worse mood still . . .

Tuesday, 14 December

Audience . . . Cautiously and with a great deal of apprehension I submitted Yankelovich's latest report, setting out proposals for the internal structure of our Information Plan. HIM read it through carefully and without any sign of annoyance. He then instructed me to ensure it's implemented. I was not unduly surprised by this. HIM is a complex individual. He knows very well that Yankelovich can be of service in improving our foreign propaganda, particularly given his influence with Carter and the American Jewish community . . . [. . .]

Tuesday, 10 May 1977

Audience . . . Kermit Roosevelt, a CIA agent involved in the downfall of Dr. Mosaddeq in August 1953, plans to publish an account of the coup. I reported that I've now examined the book and found it most undesirable. It portrays HIM as a waverer, forced into various crucial decisions, for example the appointment of General Zahedi as Prime Minister, by pressure from Roosevelt. The man is . . . hoping to present himself as a hero. HIM said he had no idea the book contained so much nonsense. He agreed I must try to prevent publication . . .

Thursday, 12 May

Audience . . . The telephone rang in the midst of our conversation. Clearly it was to report an enormous fire at an oil field somewhere. I was alarmed and, contrary to my usual discretion, asked HIM for details. "Oh, it's nothing disastrous," he said. "It's in Saudi Arabia. Why else do you suppose I sat here so relaxed?" I told him he's enjoying an extraordinary spell of luck. First, the cold winter in the USA, then the storms in the Gulf, and now this fire; the Americans are having little success in sabotaging our oil policy . . . "Quite so," he

agreed. "What's more, Carter is beginning to see sense. He's no longer preaching the same old nonsense he did during the election."
[. . .]

Saturday, 21 May

Audience . . . Much to HIM's disgust the new US ambassador, William Sullivan, has issued a statement to Congress, referring to the existence of religious opposition groups here in Iran . . . "Doesn't he realize these people are Islamic Marxists, mere Soviet puppets," HIM said. I replied that, whilst various of them may well be manipulated by the Soviets, or for that matter by Washington, there are others who act solely out of ignorant fanaticism . . . HIM remarked that he had no objection to girls wearing scarves at school or university; "But veils are out of the question . . . Tell my private secretariat to inform the government accordingly." . . .

Monday, 23 May

Audience . . . Reported a meeting I held yesterday with the British ambassador Sir Anthony Parsons. He is favourably impressed with the new British Foreign Secretary, David Owen, a man in his early thirties. The ambassador has explained to him that it's pointless to accuse Iran of violating human rights. We've granted substantial social improvements to our people over the past few years; a move unprecedented elsewhere in the world. The foreign media judge us from too narrow an angle . . .

Referring to Carter's speech of last night, HIM said, "He's announced he's willing to supply weapons to NATO, Israel, the Philippines, South Korea, Australia and New Zealand without any conditions attached; he didn't so much as mention Iran. Does he suppose that, strategically speaking, Iran is less significant than a country like New Zealand? Perhaps the Americans and the Soviets have devised some scheme to divide the world between themselves." I replied that this was quite out of the question. The Americans will never abandon us. As for Carter's pronouncements, they're intended merely to impress American public opinion. Like it or not, these idiot Americans are convinced we're violating human rights . . .

Sunday, 29 May

Audience . . . Discussing the USA, I remarked I'd been impressed by the latest letter HIM received from Carter. It indicates he's slowly starting to see sense. "He had no choice," HIM said . . .

[Writing on 24 May 1977 President Carter, in the warmest terms, thanked the Shah for accepting an invitation to visit Washington the following November.]

HIM remarked that, when he was in the southern suburbs a couple of days ago, he saw thousands of women wearing the veil . . . "These bloody mullahs don't dare admit that Islam and Marxism are at opposite ends of the spectrum," he said. "Why did Ayatollah Khonsari beat about the bush for such a long time and then, in the end, decide against speaking out?" I replied that they all go in fear of their lives. "Have they nothing better to think of than saving their own skins?" HIM asked. "Of course not," I said . . .

[. . .]

Wednesday, 8 June

Audience . . . Reported that Carter has given an interview to an American magazine, stating he is delighted by the excellent relationship between the USA and Saudi Arabia. "Quite so," HIM remarked. "People are always pleased to have a lackey." I suggested Carter really is doing his best to get on with us. "I have no cause for complaint," HIM said.

He then told me he had good news. "I've decided to give up attending my sisters' dinner parties, and to cease inviting that bunch of creeps to the palace. They had begun to get on my nerves. Every time we played bridge or *belote,* and someone laid down a card, some other bloody fool would interrupt to ask a personal favour . . . I told HMQ my decision last night. She was not at all pleased." . . . I congratulated him, pointing out that I've been begging him to do this for the past ten years.

Sunday, 11 June

A reception this morning in the gardens of the Niavaran Palace, attended by 500 members of the Association of Scholars and Intellectuals. In theory they're supposed to examine policy problems and submit their findings to the government . . . The Association was established at a time when HIM was anxious to provide some sort of balance, other than the Mardom party, to the power of Iran Novin. Its members seem oblivious to the fact they've been made redundant by the introduction of single party politics . . .

Audience . . . Referring to this morning's reception HIM said, "I have to cater to the vanity of these people. Not that I don't appreciate their hard work. Their organization should be kept going for the rest of this year." I said I had no objection to this, although the poor devils clearly don't realize how superfluous they have become. "What do you mean?," HIM snapped back. I explained my reasoning. He was disconcerted to find that I'd guessed his motives from the very start . . .

Sunday, 12 June

Audience . . . The Imperial Air Force is at daggers drawn with Iranair over which one of them is responsible for servicing HIM's private jet. I have looked into the matter, and the air force have sent in a report justifying their claim. "Then they probably deserve to be in charge," HIM said. "Form a committee and get things sorted out. Maybe the plane ought to be a joint responsibility." [...]

Friday, 17 June

... Ayatollah Khonsari telephoned to complain that the city of Qom is without water or electricity. I contacted HIM who told me to inform the PM who duly promised to send someone to investigate. I told him that this simply isn't good enough; hunger and thirst are serious matters, not to be glossed over in his usual way ... He grew a little abashed at this and promised to take action. [...]

Sunday, 26 June

Audience ... Asked about the report by the International Red Cross; their President was granted an audience yesterday. "It's still confidential and for our eyes only," HIM said. "But even so it claims that out of 3,000 political prisoners, 900 bear signs of torture. Precisely the same figure was given by the Commission I myself appointed. The report goes on to say that signs of torture have vanished altogether over the past few months." ... I told him that in my view this is serious news indeed, and only goes to show that the dissidents had real cause for protest. We can only hope no word of it gets out. "It's for our eyes only," HIM repeated. "No one can leak it, save we ourselves." I pointed out that, nowadays, nothing can be considered secret, and that it's a pity we did nothing to improve prison conditions on our own initiative. He made no attempt to reply ...
[...]

Tuesday, 28 June

Audience. Reported meeting the US ambassador yesterday. He suggested we inform the American public about recent improvements in the way political prisoners are handled. "Why can't they do it themselves?," HIM asked. "Their media should pass on news of what we've been doing." I replied they have no reason to help us. Indeed, their media claims the improvements are due solely to pressure from Carter.

We then turned to Yankelovich and the Information Plan which HIM rejected ... "MG craved a role as part-time ambassador in Washington and part-time Foreign Minister," HIM said. "He wanted Yankelovich made our secret political representative in the USA." I've long known HIM harboured such ideas, hence my decision in Paris a few months ago to drop the entire affair. Who knows, even I might have fallen under his suspicions ...

As we were talking news came through of an attempt to assassinate Saddam Hussein of Iraq. Apparently he escaped with only a slight scratch to the eye . . . I remarked that his death would have been a grave disappointment to us. "Quite so," HIM replied. "But for him, there'd have been no compromise over the Shatt al-Arab." . . .

Wednesday, 29 June

. . . Escorted HMQ to the airport, ostensibly on her way to attend the summer seminar at Aspen, Colorado, though her real reason for going is to establish personal contact with Rosalind Carter, the President's wife . . .

2. Iraq's Saddam Hussein Proclaims History as a Tool for Educating the Masses About the Revolution and Comments on the Role of Women in the Revolution, 1975, 1978

One of the most striking aspects of authoritarian government is not the use of physical violence to achieve its goals and to minimize opposition but rather the attempt to shape citizens' views about a broad range of subjects. This hegemonic approach to the hearts and minds of the populace, coupled with the technical ability to interfere on such an intimate and daily basis, distinguishes the post–World War II governments in the Middle East and North Africa from their prewar counterparts. The Ottomans and the Egyptian government under Muhammad 'Ali and his descendants sought to centralize power and to extend their bureaucratic influence more effectively throughout their lands. However, their ability and interest in shaping people's daily lives and thoughts was minimal at best, mainly because they regarded people simply as subjects, not citizens.

After World War II, however, ideas of citizenship and nationhood became political realities not easily ignored. Many regimes—such as the Ba'ath in Syria and Iraq, Nasser in Egypt, the shah in Iran, Israel vis-à-vis its Arab inhabitants, and the Christian ruling elite of Lebanon—attempted to shape the meaning of these ideas in a way that would bolster their power to rule. Mass media offered the most effective means of spreading their interpretations of "citizen" and "political participation" while excluding opposing ideas. Although these regimes were never completely successful in squelching opposition and contrarian ideas, they enjoyed a large measure of success.

In the following selections, ideas of the "citizen" and the "nation" are set forth in speeches by Saddam Hussein (b. 1937), perhaps the most notorious of the authoritarian rulers in the Middle East and North Africa. Hussein's childhood and upbringing and exposure to colonial rule seem to have convinced him that maintaining absolute control upheld by violence was the best strategy for governing a fractious nation like Iraq. He applied this logic ruthlessly as an operative in the Ba'ath Party, as vice president of that party, and as president of Iraq. Upon attaining power in 1979, Hussein immediately purged the party of any opponents through execution and exile. On one chilling occasion, he convened the Ba'ath leadership in a hall and called the names of individuals whom he considered to be "traitors" to the cause. Those individuals were immediately taken outside and they "disappeared" before the eyes of the remaining delegates. Scenes of men pleading for their lives and Hussein dabbing away crocodile tears were recorded on film and shown to all party members. Hussein's attempt to strike fear in the hearts of his opponents resembled Stalinist methods of controlling access to information and shaping ideas to fit state propaganda. The speeches included here indicate the worldview that Hussein projected to Iraq in the years before he became president.

1. On Writing History

"We must not speak about the writing of history in isolation from current times and circumstances" *Saddam Hussein's Pronouncement in discussing the Report of the National Educational Committee for the Correction of School Curriculum, 1975*

It is only that several things should be taken into consideration in modern curriculums: age, the educational and scientific capabilities of the students and pupils; thus one does not say the same things—in terms of content and approach—to high school students as one would to elementary school students.

When we speak to young children, who have limited scientific understanding, we must speak about some political or historical issues that we wish for them to internalize, in the absolute without any qualifications. For example, when we speak of Arab unity we must not occupy the little student with details and to engage him in a discussion of whether we are indeed a single nation or not. It is enough to speak of the Arab as one nation assuming that to be an absolute reality, with a brief summary about the role that colonialism played in dividing the [Arab] countries and nation in order to weaken it and maintain control over it. We should also portray the path to unity through struggle in a simplified form as well. Thus, when we speak about the Ba'ath Arab Socialist Party [the party that brought Hussein to power and that he leads] as a leading party, we should speak about it to the children as if it is an absolute reality. As to the details of why and how it became a leading party then we can show that through a discussion about the accomplishments of the party, the role of the party in saving the Iraqi people, and through a discussion of the Revolution without fatiguing the students at this stage with complicated theoretical, philosophical or political analyses. This is especially the case with the generation that did not live through the period preceding the Revolution of 17–30 June, 1968 [which brought the Ba'ath to power] . . . Discussing the Revolution, and the Arab Ba'ath Socialist Party without speaking of the dark era that preceded the revolution—in social, political, economic, cultural and military terms—will not provide [a] historical and objective context for understanding the Revolution. The June revolution is great because of the accomplishments it attained from 18–30 June 1968 until now; but its greatness appears greater when we understand what preceded the revolution. It is important to speak of the dark period which preceded the revolution in detail so that coming generations will

---

Saddam Hussein, *On Writing History* (Beirut: Dar al-Tal'ia, 1979). Translated by Akram Khater. Reprinted by permission of the American Committee on Jerusalem.

understand the greatness of their revolution. We must avoid speaking in detail about matters that are constantly and rapidly changing because they will appear small in later stages. . . .

Here I find it necessary to speak, educate and concentrate on the fact that Iraq is part of the Arab nation more than speaking about the Iraqi people being part of the Arab nation. In this manner we can achieve our goal without upsetting opposing nationalist tendencies amongst the other part of our people.

In our national education we must speak about self-rule [for the minorities]. And when we address the subject of self-rule we must not get lost in too many details so as not to make the administrative structure of self a "Chinese Wall" that separates the Arab from the Kurd in Iraq. For instance, when we speak about Iraqi folklore we do not see it necessary to speak about Kurdish folklore, and another that is Arab and a third that is Turkish . . . etc. Rather, it should be presented simply as Iraqi folklore. So we would say for example: this is a dance from the South of Iraq from al-Nassiriya [an Iraqi town], and this is a dance from al-Sulaymaniya [another city]. . . . Exaggerated actions to show that we care about local nationalisms [within Iraq] will cause immense harm in our short- and long-term plans. . . . To take for example our starting point, by way of imagining equality between the Arab and others, as saying that the Arab wears the *'iqaal* (one type of headdress) and the Kurd wears *laffat* [another type of headdress] around the head . . . is a big mistake because this image will have negative psychological effects and will lead to dangerous ideological and political results. Perhaps there is someone who is purposely plotting to maintain a Chinese wall that separates our people psychologically and mentally. . . .

When we speak about our people's nationalist sacrifices we must not limit our discourse to talking about political and military actions. Rather we need to point to the big sacrifices that the citizens have done, and continue to perform, in the field of production and other activities in order to build up the nation. He who endangers himself to save a machine is worthy of mentioning with pride in order to strengthen the tendency to consider work a basic tenet in the honor and progress of the nation . . . and to strengthen the tendency among the sons of our people to safeguard the socialist property.

2. The Revolution and the Woman

. . . When we want to speak about the liberation of the woman and her historical role in building society, and about the equality in rights between her and the man, how should we approach this subject?

There are certain known givens with regard to the starting position in this subject. When we discuss the practical aspects of this subject, it is assumed that we are in agreement about the basic premises which make equality between the man and the woman, for the purpose of building the society with a combined effort, a given since it is one of our basic principles. . . .

Saddam Hussein, *The Revolution and the Woman* (Beirut: Dar al-Tal'ia, 1979). Reprinted by permission of the American Committee on Jerusalem.

But should we continually immerse ourselves in the details of daily work, by talking about the ability of the woman ... in order to prove that the woman, like the man can grasp every opportunity and can do anything? Is this correct? I think this approach is wrong. . . . Rather than approach this matter within such a context, we should approach from a different perspective, not to escape the basic premise but to use objective premises to support our argument. . . . In this manner we concentrate on equality in rights, balance of rights; we concentrate on rejecting the idea that places the woman in a secondary position [to the man]; we reject the feudal and tribal mentality and perspective; we reject the idea which makes the woman subservient to the man. . . . This approach is better than saying that a woman can equally do anything that a man can, because then you will find someone who says: therefore, we must apply military service on women, because that is one of the conditions of equality, and it is one way to prove that men and women are equal in capabilities. . . .

Thus, at the same time that women cannot permanently serve in the Armed Forces in a widespread manner, and particularly in the active units, men cannot take over the role of raising and nurturing children as the women do. In the same manner that the man is distinguished from the woman by serving in the army, the woman [is] distinguished from him in nurturing children, and both are central roles in our society.

My advice to all the women of Iraq is to concentrate on the proper manner of dealing with this subject, and which . . . makes the man support the woman in this direction rather than oppose her. . . . Our discourse on the woman and her role in society should be balanced, and that our perspective on this subject should be balanced as well. There has been talk here, in this place, and in other places whereby some of you have asked to lift the guardianship off women since they have become mature enough to take care of themselves. And others have asked for this guardianship to continue using the excuse that we should take into consideration the particular circumstances of the woman. . . . One time we speak of her as a weak creature . . . and at other times we speak of her as the leader of society. One time we speak of the lack of the special circumstances, as we call them, for the woman to perform her duties in the countryside and the factory, and in building roads and bridges, and at another time we reject the mentality which distinguishes in a hierarchical fashion between man and woman with regard to job and educational opportunities. Our discourse about the woman and her role in our society should be balanced!

Why, for example, did we in 1976 approve the training of women in the popular army when it was not approved in 1970? We have not ceased, and have not ignored our initial and revolutionary position about changing society, but we postponed the application of these ideas until we could prepare the groundwork to accomplish our goals without great losses. . . .

We must not offer colonialism a technical opportunity, since it no longer has a strategic opportunity to oppose the Revolution. Therefore, it and its agents have been seeking technical opportunities through the mistakes that we commit, either in hurrying matters too much or in postponing too long. . . .

It is vital that you concentrate on self-criticism [of women]. For when we concentrate on the shortfall of women with regard to their duties, and this is initiated by the General Union of Iraqi Women [an arm of the Ba'ath Party] as was done in this report, then we are not belittling the historic role of women in building society.

3. The Constitution of Saudi Arabia Bases the Legitimacy of the Ruling House of Saud on Religion, 1992

Many of the more conservative regimes in the Middle East and North Africa, such as Saudi Arabia and Morocco, are monarchies. In the twenty-first century, this political system appears to outsiders as well as to citizens of these countries as an anomaly—a fact not lost on the ruling families. In an era of democratic reforms sweeping the globe, their political legitimacy is questioned in muted and loud tones. In the case of Saudi Arabia, the ruling family—the Sauds—deflects some of the criticism through the "carrot" of a welfare state that provides services to Saudi citizens. The "stick" part of this formula is strict control over information, political expression, and access to power. Both the "carrot" and the "stick" are made possible by oil wealth, which allows the state to provide free education and health care and to guarantee employment, while it uses a secret police force to maintain control over dissidents.

In many ways such an arrangement is made possible by the help of an outside power. Many people in the Middle East and North Africa consider Saudi Arabia and other monarchies as little more than puppets of the United States. Whether because of direct involvement in the oil industry, or because of military support, the United States is seen as the mainstay of the Saudi regime. The authoritarian control exercised by the Saudis is justified in this excerpt from the Saudi constitution—a constitution that is the regime's most "liberal" compromise.

(Adopted on: March 1992)
(Adopted by Royal decree of King Fahd) (ICL Document Status: Oct 1993)

Chapter 1 General Principles

Article 1

The Kingdom of Saudi Arabia is a sovereign Arab Islamic state with Islam as its religion; God's Book and the Sunnah of His Prophet, God's prayers and peace be upon him, are its constitution, Arabic is its language and Riyadh is its capital.
[...]

Constitution of Saudi Arabia, http://www.the-saudi.net/saudi-arabia/saudi-constitution.htm (27 January 2003).

Chapter 2 [Monarchy]

Article 5

(a) The system of government in the Kingdom of Saudi Arabia is that of a monarchy.

(b) Rule passes to the sons of the founding King, Abd al-Aziz Bin Abd al-Rahman al-Faysal Al Sa'ud, and to their children's children. The most upright among them is to receive allegiance in accordance with the principles of the Holy Koran and the Tradition of the Venerable Prophet.

(c) The King chooses the Heir Apparent and relieves him of his duties by Royal order.

(d) The Heir Apparent is to devote his time to his duties as an Heir Apparent and to whatever missions the King entrusts him with.

(e) The Heir Apparent takes over the powers of the King on the latter's death until the act of allegiance has been carried out.

Article 6

Citizens are to pay allegiance to the King in accordance with the holy Koran and the tradition of the Prophet, in submission and obedience, in times of ease and difficulty, fortune and adversity.

Article 7

Government in Saudi Arabia derives power from the Holy Koran and the Prophet's tradition.

Article 8 [Government Principles]

Government in the Kingdom of Saudi Arabia is based on the premise of justice, consultation, and equality in accordance with the Islamic Shari'ah.

Chapter 3 Features of the Saudi Family

Article 9

The family is the kernel of Saudi society, and its members shall be brought up on the basis of the Islamic faith, and loyalty and obedience to God, His Messenger, and to guardians, respect for and implementation of the law, and love of and pride in the homeland and its glorious history as the Islamic faith stipulates.

[. . .]

Article 13

Education will aim at instilling the Islamic faith in the younger generation, providing its members with knowledge and skills and preparing them to become useful members in the building of their society, members who love their homeland and are proud of its history.

Chapter 4 Economic Principles

Article 14

All God's bestowed wealth, be it under the ground, on the surface or in national territorial waters, in the land or maritime domains under the state's control, are the property of the state as defined by law. The law defines means of exploiting, protecting, and developing such wealth in the interests of the state, Its security and economy.
[. . .]

Article 17

Property, capital, and labor are essential elements in the Kingdom's economic and social being. They are personal rights which perform a social function in accordance with Islamic Shari'ah.

Article 18

The state protects freedom of private property and its sanctity. No one is to be stripped of his property except when it serves the public interest, in which case fair compensation is due.

Article 19

Public confiscation of money is prohibited and the penalty of private confiscation is to be imposed only by a legal order.
[. . .]

Article 39 [Expression]

Information, publication, and all other media shall employ courteous language and the state's regulations, and they shall contribute to the education of the nation and the bolstering of its unity. All acts that foster sedition or division or harm the state's security and its public relations or detract from man's dignity and rights shall be prohibited. The statutes shall define all that.
[. . .]

Article 43 [Royal Courts]

The King's Court and that of the Crown Prince shall be open to all citizens and to anyone who has a complaint or a plea against an injustice. Every individual shall have a right to address the public authorities in all matters affecting him.

Chapter 6 The Authorities of the State

Article 44

The authorities of the state consist of the following: the judicial authority, the executive authority, the regulatory authority. These authorities cooperate with each other in the performance of their duties, in accordance with this and other laws. The King shall be the point of reference for all these authorities.

Article 45

The sources of the deliverance of fatwa in the Kingdom of Saudi Arabia are God's Book and the Sunnah of His Messenger. The law will define the composition of the senior ulema body, the administration of scientific research, deliverance of fatwa and its (the body of senior ulemas) functions.

Article 46

The judiciary is an independent authority. There is no control over judges in the dispensation of their judgements [*sic*] except in the case of the Islamic Shari'ah.
[. . .]

Article 57

   (a) The King appoints and relieves deputies of the prime minister and ministers and members of the Council of Ministers by Royal decree.

   (b) The deputies of the prime minister and ministers of the Council of Ministers are responsible, by expressing solidarity before the King, for implementing the Islamic Shari'ah and the state's general policy.

   (c) The King has the right to dissolve and reorganize the Council of Ministers.

Article 58

The King appoints those who enjoy the rank of ministers, deputy ministers and those of higher rank, and relieves them of their posts by Royal decree in accordance with the explanations included in the law. Ministers and heads of independent departments are responsible before the prime minister for the ministries and departments which they supervise.

Article 59

The law defines the rules of the civil service, including salaries, awards, compensations, favors and pensions.

Article 60

The King is the commander-in-chief of all the armed forces. He appoints officers and puts an end to their duties in accordance with the law.

Article 61

The King declares a state of emergency, general mobilization and war, and the law defines the rules for this.
[. . .]

Article 68 [Consultative Council]

A Consultative Council is to be created. Its statute will specify how it is formed, how it exercises its powers and how its members are selected.

Article 69

The King has the right to convene the Consultative Council and the Council of Ministers for a joint meeting and to invite whoever he wishes to attend that meeting to discuss whatever matters he wishes.

4.   Human Rights Activist Yilmaz Ensaroglu Discusses the Role of the Army in Turkey, 1997

Modern Turkey was established as a constitutional republic by an authoritarian army led by Mustafa Kemal (Atatürk) (see document 6 in the chapter "Ideas of Nationalism"). The legacy of Kemalism can be summarized as popular secular nationalism overseen and "protected" by statist economic and military policies. Kemalism sought to create a "modern" society whose characteristics are strictly "defended" by the military. This paradox has led to several periods of army intervention in civilian

Turkish Daily News, 17 November 1997.

politics, and even periods of army rule. In the 1960s and 1970s, Turkey was em-
broiled in what many consider its worst constitutional and civil rights crisis. The doc-
ument included here implicates the army in the use of death squads in the earlier
period and in the more recent army "coups." It is an interview with Yilmaz En-
saroglu, president of Mazlum Der, a Turkish human rights organization. Yilmaz
Ensaroglu also acted as deputy president of the same organization between 1992
and 1996. Originally from the eastern province of Agri, Ensaroglu is an imam hatip
graduate who was active in labor union movements before becoming a human
rights activist. He served a prison term for charges of having violated former consti-
tutional Article 163 banning fundamentalist activities.

Rights Were Curbed More with Each New Constitution in Turkey

President of Mazlum Der, the Organization for Human Rights and Solidarity
with the Oppressed, Yilmaz Ensaroglu, stated that human rights violations in
Turkey have a legal basis and that more limitations were brought on freedoms
and rights with each new constitution.

The following interview is the third of its kind on human rights and covers
the views of the conservative-religious section's approach to human rights violations, which isn't actually much different from those speaking for "secular"
human rights associations. Ensaroglu said the word *Mazlum* (the suffering,
the oppressed) was often confused with *Muslim* and wanted to stress that it
wasn't so.

Malzum Der however was established in 1991, at the time of the foundation of the Human Rights Association (IHD), to defend the rights of the believers and the religious sectors of society. These sectors felt the other human
rights associations were pro-leftist and didn't care much for the defense of the
rights of others. Today Mazlum Der has close cooperation with the IHD. Ensaroglu said: "Mazlum Der was established not as a human rights association to
compete with the others but on the contrary as one which will cooperate by
filling up the gaps left by the others."

- Let's start with the general question as to how you assess developments regarding human rights in Turkey, whether there has been any improvement?

I personally don't think that there have been improvements because in our
country the individual's rights and liberties can be limited, for the sake of the
state, according to constitutional provisions. This is our system. Whereas, constitutions in other countries, are social agreements guaranteeing the rights and
liberties of the individual. In our case, human rights and liberties are curbed
with the Constitution. It is a great pity that there is a legal basis for a large section of human rights violations. And we see that certain verdicts are given with
very subjective assessments of our judges, and most recently, decisions go even
beyond subjective assessments, and decisions against the existing laws are being given—laws are altogether suspended.

- Since when has this been happening?

I would say in the past one-and-a-half or two years. And in the past six months there has been a renewed escalation especially against the freedom of thought and expression.

- Why? Is it because of a certain fear that there may be threats against the state?

Well the fear has always been there and our problem is actually this fear—the state's fear, not of the individuals. From the beginning there is a structure which takes the state as the ultimate and sacred being. This structure has also chosen an official race, language and official religion. Such a system was formed and it was called democracy. But when you look at it, this democracy isn't really functioning either in Parliament, nor in political parties. . . .

- Also in the Welfare Party [Refah]?

Of course, I am not making any discrimination. I am talking of all the parties represented in Parliament. But we don't know the exact structure of some other parties which aren't represented in Parliament, so I am talking about those that we know. A so-called oligarchic structure exists in all the parties in Parliament. Deputies aren't elected there because they have the support of the people but because their party nominated them. They are appointed there by their chairmen and these deputies in Parliament therefore cannot voice the problems of the people. They simply obey the chairman.

- Is democracy interrupted at that point?

Yes, and what happens then? I think, for years, the country has been run with the policies defined by a couple of bureaucrats through a couple of feudal leaders.

- Who are these feudal leaders?

They are the party chairmen. I mean the bureaucrats decide on the policies and define these policies, and the party leaders put these policies into application. When a Refah deputy was attacked by police forces nobody reacted because he was from Refah, then after some time another deputy was attacked in the May 1 demonstrations, and because this deputy was from the Republican People's Party, everyone said he was a leftist anyway, so nobody defended him. Then a day came when a whole group of deputies were kicked out of Parliament. . . . This is actually the credibility, the honour of Parliament that we should seriously be concerned about.

- Then there isn't any meaning in asking whether this government is any better than the other or vice versa?

Exactly, there is no meaning in asking whether there has been any improvements in human rights with this government or the previous one. I suggested to the EU term president when speaking with us, that it was useless for them to go and speak with government officials. I said they should go and speak with the National Security Council instead. I am terribly ashamed when I say this but there is such a problem in my country . . . the most typical example is the practice of the Emergency Rule. All parties when in opposition say the Emergency Rule should end, then the same party which has said this in opposition comes to power and in power it defends its continuance.

- Well this government at least ended the practice in many provinces. . . . However shouldn't we then have no political parties?

Maybe it is much better, because we will then know that is the problem in the Turkish system. But this isn't the case and we have a Parliament, we call our system democratic, we have deputies but all the policies are framed at the National Security Council—by the military bureaucracy. I mean even a party which remained determined to oppose those policies for years when in opposition—you know that the Refah had always voted against the extension of the Emergency Rule Region in the Southeast—when in power started saying that the Emergency Rule was needed.

- This is a universal trend. We are trying to find the answer to the question as to how we can overcome this. As to how shall we achieve a free society not a chaotic one.

That is true. I think we can achieve a free society when such a consciousness is spread all over the society. In Turkey, people aren't fully aware of their rights and the state is seen as sacred. Even if individuals are against this state, still at the back of their mind they feel it is not correct to be against it. The state should be brought down to act as a tool which serves the happiness and comfort of the citizens.

Also, the state shouldn't just respect but should be based on human rights; its reason of existence should be human rights. When we look at our constitutional history we see that with each new constitution, rights have been more and more curbed. And the 1982 Constitution defines human rights as being "within the limits brought by this Constitution."

- Do you have an explanation for that?

I think the main factor behind this notion is that in Turkey the majority of the elite and the bureaucracy do not know the people. The elite and the people are strangers to each other and this isn't something new but a trend that has been continuing since the Ottoman period. And at this point there are serious differences in the values of the elite and the people. The state has always wanted to shape people instead of serving them. And within such an understanding, in our case "limitation" becomes the rule and "freedom" an exception.

- Isn't it up to the political parties to change this situation? And you as an association defending the human rights of the believers of society, why haven't you pressed the Welfare Party to do certain things to change the situation while they were in office? For example Refah violated the right of women to be elected to Parliament; didn't you do anything against this?

To tell the truth we haven't conducted any specific work on Refah. But whenever we have certain statements or bulletins, we send it to all parties in Parliament, and naturally to Refah. I personally do not know to what degree the women in Refah wanted to become candidates in the elections. I haven't looked into that.

But I want to say that our association somehow has always had good relations with opposition parties but when they have come to power, disagreements have started. It has been the same case with Refah. We had many disagreements when that party came to power. Double standards hold true for all.

- Generally speaking, can you make your voice heard?

As I said double standards are everywhere, and it doesn't make any difference whether it is the leftists, rightists or religious groups. . . . All have this double standard unfortunately. Therefore whenever we brought up human rights violations when Refah was in power, pro-Refah newspapers wouldn't even print that news.

We voiced a very strong reaction against the Metin Goktepe incident and said that we felt ashamed because of the attitude of the press towards a colleague. But none of the newspapers, including the one Goktepe was working for, gave any place to our association's reaction. Only the daily *Cumhuriyet* covered our reaction, and how, we don't still know. Our biggest problem is that the public doesn't know us very well.

- What are other ways of making yourself known?

Of course the best way is through the media. But we try with extra effort to attend conferences and debates and make use of various platforms. However, I see with regret that the outside world—of course this may be due to other reasons—follows our activities more. Whenever we issue a report and—if by chance the *Turkish Daily News* also publishes it—the next day at least five embassies call us and ask for the full text of that report.

We all know that the outside world is closely following human rights in Turkey. And now for the first time our own officials are contacting us, calling us and trying to learn our views. This is a very important development, an important progress. And we want this approach to continue.

- Can we say that Europe's close interest to human rights in Turkey is also alerting our officials on the subject, that this is a positive development?

Yes of course, and also human rights shouldn't be made an issue of national pride. I say this to foreigners and I tell them that it is our right to also show the same sensitivity vis-à-vis human rights violations in their countries.

I tell them that if I am talking very openly about human rights violations in my country then you should also be as open with me about, for example, the situation of Turks in German prisons.

[. . .]

CHAPTER 7

Crisis of the State

Authoritarian regimes in the Middle East and North Africa have tried to consolidate their power through repression, populist economic and social policies, and propaganda. But the voices of opposition—religious and secular—as well as shifting political circumstances around the world have kept these regimes from completely attaining their goals.

Perhaps one of the most effective voices of opposition throughout the Middle East and North Africa has been that of Islamic political movements. In part their effectiveness is due to the fact that most states in those areas have succeeded in suppressing leftist secular opposition. The relative ease of this repression is due to the secular nature of those opposition movements, which leaves members open to the false but damaging charge of being atheists or unbelievers. Such labels limit the basis of popular support for leftist ideas and programs among populations that tend to be overwhelmingly religious—even if only at the cultural level. Furthermore, the socialist and intellectual language of leftist organizations makes their ideas and programs inaccessible and— perhaps more important—irrelevant to the majority of the peoples of the region.

By contrast, none of these states ever has been fully able to silence the religious right. Most of them instituted governmental restrictions on places of worship, required licenses for clerics, and jailed, tortured, and killed religious dissidents. Nevertheless, the ubiquity of religious institutions and the lack of any acceptable formal religious hierarchy provided those on the religious right with a good deal of maneuvering space and staying power. Furthermore, the states—even the most self-avowedly secular ones—sought "moderate" religious support at various critical moments in order to shore up their disintegrating legitimacy. Thus, as the Syrian philosopher Sadiq al-'Azm notes in document 2, the government of Nasser appealed to religion as a way to distract attention away from the humiliating defeat Egypt suffered in 1967—a defeat for which he initially accepted responsibility (document 1). Nasser's successor—

Anwar el-Sadat—employed the religious opposition as a bulwark against the leftist elements in the country that opposed him.

It is this cynical employment of religion that accounts for the preponderance of religious criticism of the state and its abuse of power. Among the best known of these opposition figures is Ayatollah Ruhollah Khomeini, who was a teacher of Islamic theology in Qom, the religious capital of Iran. There was a consistent stream of criticism of the rule of the shah in Iran, but Khomeini denounced the regime as un-Islamic (document 3). This charge resonated far more strongly among religious students, peasants, and the urban poor than attacks on the shah by a leftist party like the Tudeh. The language that Khomeini used contained references to Islamic history and traditions with which even the uneducated were familiar and comfortable. Thus, it appeared that Khomeini and other religious opposition figures were providing an indigenous call for justice and were presenting an Islamic alternative to a shah supported by the "West." The report from the American embassy in Iran (document 5) highlights further how this message resonated with the majority of Iranians, and the platform of the Islamic Salvation Front (document 7) incorporates the same type of religious language into the definition of Algeria and by extension into the definition of the legitimate ruler of that nation. Also included in this chapter is the introduction to an Islamist book about an attack by the Syrian regime against its own people in Hama (document 6). Although this is a highly biased and charged essay, it is a very important source for understanding how Islamists viewed the ruling regimes in the Middle East. The language found in this document is used almost universally by Islamic opposition movements.

Of course, not all opposition was or is religion based. In the documents about the Lebanese civil war (document 4), we find two disparate views about the definition of the "nation" and the distribution of state power. The definitions serve as road maps to the distribution of political, economic, and cultural power. In Lebanon, criticism of the state was based on the belief that in its pre-1975 incarnation it provided power for Christians at the expense of Muslims. The near demographic parity of these two communities as well as the radicalization of politics in the region (a consequence of the Arab-Israeli conflict) brought about calls for change in state institutions and in both domestic and foreign policy. However, as with any demand for change, the reluctance of the dominant group to abandon its hold on authority was as strong as the desire of the opposing side to change the balance of power.

Challenges to the distribution of power within the state also have emerged in the past thirty years in Israel. From its beginning in 1948, Israel has been defined as a "Jewish state." However, from its inception, Israel also has been home to a growing minority of Arab citizens. From the perspective of this Arab community, the Jewish-state definition of Israel is insulting: it ignores the presence of the Arabs and relegates them to the position of second-class citizens. By the end of the 1970s the Arab community not only had grown numerically—in relation to the larger Jewish community—but also had become more educated and articulate in its rejection of its alienated status. The growing demand for meaningful recognition as equals is apparent in shifts in voting, as Arabs withdraw support for Jewish-Israeli parties and vote instead for Arab-Israeli parties. Not only in electoral politics but in every avenue of social, cultural, and economic affairs have Arabs found their voice. Thus, more and more Arab-Israeli writers write in Hebrew about their experiences, in direct or oblique criticism of what they perceive as racism against them. The last document in this chapter is one example of this cultural manifestation of opposition to the definition of Israel as a Jewish state.

1. Egyptian President Gamal Abdel Nasser Resigns from Office Following the 1967 Arab-Israeli War, June 9, 1967

In 1967, in six days, Israeli armed forces were able to defeat Egyptian, Syrian, and Jordanian forces in a decisive manner and to conquer more Arab land—including Egypt's Sinai Peninsula. This outcome was profoundly shocking to the psyches of ordinary people and leaders alike—at least before excuses began to be fabricated to explain away the humiliation of so swift a loss. The shock was all the worse because the preceding decade had seemed full of promise—for "modernization" of society and the state, for an Arab renaissance with Nasser at the helm, and even for the possibility that at least part of Palestine would be recaptured. The war of 1967 crushed these dreams and exposed the emptiness of promises made (read Halim Barakat's novel Days of Dust *[1974] for a painfully eloquent description of the mood that prevailed on the "Arab street" during this war). Nasser's resignation speech was an acknowledgment—albeit fleeting—of his personal failure and by extension the failure of the state that he led. Many historians argue that this speech marks the start of the dissolution of the postindependence army-ruled states.*

Brothers, at times of triumph and tribulation, in the sweet hours and bitter hours, we have become accustomed to sit together to discuss things, to speak frankly of facts, believing that only in this way can we always find the right path however difficult circumstances may be.

We cannot hide from ourselves the fact that we have met with a grave setback in the last few days, but I am confident that we all can and, in a short time, will overcome our difficult situation, although this calls for much patience and wisdom as well as moral courage and ability to work on our part. Before that, brothers, we need to cast a glance back over past events so that we shall be able to follow developments and the line of our march leading to the present conditions.

"Nasser's Resignation Broadcast," BBC Radio Monitoring Service, Cyprus. From Voice of the Arabs Radio, Cairo, 9 June 1967.

All of us know how the crisis started in the Middle East. At the beginning of last May there was an enemy plan for the invasion of Syria and the statements by his politicians and all his military leaders openly said so. There was plenty of evidence concerning the plan. Sources of our Syrian brothers were categorical on this and our own reliable information confirmed it. Add to this the fact that our friends in the Soviet Union warned the parliamentary delegation, which was on a visit to Moscow, at the beginning of last month, that there was a premeditated plan against Syria. We considered it our duty not to accept this silently. This was the duty of Arab brotherhood, it was also the duty of national security. Whoever starts with Syria will finish with Egypt.

Our armed forces moved to our frontiers with a competence which the enemy acknowledged even before our friends. Several steps followed. There was the withdrawal of the United Nations Emergency Force and the return of our forces to the Sharm al Shaykh post, the controlling point in the Straits of Tiran, which had been used by the Israeli enemy as one of the after-effects of the tripartite aggression against us in 1956. The enemy's flag passing in front of our forces was intolerable, apart from other reasons connected with the dearest aspirations of the Arab nation.

Accurate calculations were made of the enemy's strength and showed us that our armed forces, at the level of equipment and training which they had reached, were capable of repelling the enemy and deterring him. We realised that the possibility of an armed clash existed and accepted the risk.

Before us were several factors—national, Arab and international. A message from the US President Lyndon Johnson was handed to our Ambassador in Washington 26th May asking us to show self-restraint and not to be the first to fire, or else we should have to face grave consequences. On the very same night, the Soviet Ambassador asked to have an urgent meeting with me at 05.30 [as broadcast] after midnight. He informed me of an urgent request from the Soviet Government not to be the first to open fire.

In the morning of last Monday, 5th June, the enemy struck. If we say now it was a stronger blow than we had expected, we must say at the same time, and with complete certainty that it was bigger than the potential at his disposal. It became very clear from the first moment that there were other powers behind the enemy—they came to settle their accounts with the Arab national movement. Indeed, there were surprises worthy of note:

1. The enemy, whom we were expecting from the east and north, came from the west—a fact which clearly showed that facilities exceeding his own capacity and his calculated strength had been made available to him.

2. The enemy covered at one go all military and civilian airfields in the UAR. This means that he was relying on some force other than his own normal strength to protect his skies against any retaliatory action from our side. The enemy was also leaving other Arab fronts to be tackled with outside assistance which he had been able to obtain.

3. There is clear evidence of imperialist collusion with the enemy—an imperialist collusion, trying to benefit from the lesson of the open collusion of

1956, by resorting this time to abject and wicked concealment. Nevertheless, what is now established is that American and British aircraft carriers were off the shores of the enemy helping his war effort. Also, British aircraft raided, in broad daylight, positions on the Syrian and Egyptian fronts, in addition to operations by a number of American aircraft reconnoitering some of our positions. The inevitable result of this was that our land forces, fighting most violent and brave battles in the open desert, found themselves at the difficult time without adequate air cover in face of the decisive superiority of the enemy air forces. Indeed it can be said without emotion or exaggeration, that the enemy was operating with an air force three times stronger than his normal force.

The same conditions were faced by the forces of the Jordanian Army, fighting a brave battle under the leadership of King Husayn who—let me say for the sake of truth and honesty—adopted an excellent stand; and I admit that my heart was bleeding while I was following the battles of his heroic Arab Army in Jerusalem and other parts of the West Bank on the night when the enemy and his plotting forces massed no less than 400 aircraft over the Jordanian front.

There were other honourable and marvellous efforts. The Algerian people, under their great leader Hawwari Bumedien, gave without reservation and without stinting for the battle. The people of Iraq and their faithful leader Abd ar-Rahman Arif gave without reservation or stinting for the battle. The Syrian Army fought heroically, consolidated by the forces of the great Syrian people and under the leadership of their national Government. The peoples and governments of Sudan, Kuwait, Yemen, Lebanon, Tunisia and Morocco adopted honourable stands. All the peoples of the Arab nation, without exception, adopted a stand of manhood and dignity all along the Arab homeland; a stand of resolution and determination that Arab right shall not be lost, shall not be humiliated, and that the war in its defence is advancing, regardless of sacrifice and setbacks, on the road of the sure and inevitable victory. There were also great nations outside the Arab homeland who gave us invaluable moral support.

But the plot, and we must say this with the courage of men, was bigger and fiercer. The enemy's main concentration was on the Egyptian front which he attacked with all his main force of armoured vehicles and infantry, supported by air supremacy the dimensions of which I have outlined for you. The nature of the desert did not permit a full defence especially, in face of the enemy's air supremacy. I realised that the armed battle might not go in our favour. I, with others, tried to use all sources of Arab strength. Arab oil came in to play its part. The Suez Canal came in to play its part. A great role is still reserved for general Arab action. I am fully confident that it will measure up to its task. Our Armed Forces in Sinai were obliged to evacuate the first line of defence. They fought fearful tank and air battles on the second line of defence.

We then responded to the cease-fire resolution, in view of assurances contained in the latest Soviet draft resolution, to the Security Council, as well as French statements to the effect that no one must reap any territorial expansion from the recent aggression, and in view of world public opinion, especially in Asia and Africa, which appreciates our position and feels the ugliness of the forces of international domination which pounced on us.

We now have several urgent tasks before us. The first is to remove the traces of this aggression against us and to stand by the Arab nation resolutely and firmly; despite the setback, the Arab nation, with all its potential and resources, is in a position to insist on the removal of the traces of the aggression.

The second task is to learn the lesson of the setback. In this connection there are three vital facts: (1) The elimination of imperialism in the Arab world will leave Israel with its own intrinsic power; yet, whatever the circumstances, however long it may take, the Arab intrinsic power is greater and more effective. (2) Redirecting Arab interests in the service of Arab rights is an essential safeguard: the American Sixth Fleet moved with Arab oil, and there are Arab bases, placed forcibly and against the will of the peoples, in that service of aggression. (3) The situation now demands a united word from the entire Arab nation; this, in the present circumstances, is irreplaceable guarantee.

Now we arrive at an important point in this heartsearching by asking ourselves: does this mean that we do not bear responsibility for the consequences of the setback? I tell you truthfully and despite any factors on which I might have based my attitude during the crisis, that I am ready to bear the whole responsibility. I have taken a decision in which I want you all to help me. I have decided to give up completely and finally every official post and every political role and return to the ranks of the masses and do my duty with them like every other citizen.

The forces of imperialism imagine that Jamal Abd al-Nasser is their enemy. I want it to be clear to them that their enemy is the entire Arab nation, not just Jamal Abd al-Nasser. The forces hostile to the Arab national movement try to portray this movement as an empire of Abd al-Nasser. This is not true, because the aspiration for Arab unity began before Abd al-Nasser and will remain after Abd al-Nasser. I always used to tell you that the nation remains, and that the individual—whatever his role and however great his contribution to the causes of his homeland—is only a tool of the popular will, and not its creator.

In accordance with Article 110 of the Provisional Constitution promulgated in March 1964 I have entrusted my colleague, friend and brother Zakariya Muhiedin with taking over the [post] of President and carrying out the constitutional provisions on this point. After this decision, I place all I have at his disposal in dealing with the grave situation through which our people are passing.

In doing this I am not liquidating the revolution—indeed the revolution is not the monopoly of any one generation of revolutionaries. I take pride in the brothers of this generation of revolutionaries. It has brought to pass the evacuation of British imperialism, has won the independence of Egypt and defined its Arab personality, and has combated the policy of spheres of influence in the Arab world; it has led the social revolution and created a deep transformation in the Egyptian reality by establishing the people's control over the sources of their wealth and the result of Arab action; it recovered the Suez Canal and laid down the foundation of industrial upsurge in Egypt; it built the High Dam to bring fertile greenness to the barren desert; it laid down a power network over the whole of the north of the Nile Valley; it made oil resources gush out after a long wait. More important still, it gave the leadership of political action to the alliance of the people's working forces, the constant source of renewed leaderships carrying the banners of Egyptian and Arab struggle through its successive stages, building socialism, succeeding and triumphing.

I have unlimited faith in this alliance as the leader of national action: the peasants, the workers, the soldiers, the intellectuals and national capital. Its unity and cohesion and creative response within the framework of this unity are capable of creating—through work, serious work, difficult work, as I have said more than once—colossal miracles for this country in order to be a strength for itself, for its Arab nation, for the movement of national revolution and for world peace based on justice.

The sacrifices made by our people and their burning spirit during the crisis and the glorious pages of heroism written by the officers and soldiers of our armed forces with their blood will remain an unquenchable torch in our history and a great inspiration for the future and its great hopes. The people were splendid as usual, noble as their nature, believing, sincere and loyal. The members of our armed forces were an honourable example of Arab man in every age and every place. They defended the grains of sand in the desert to the last drop of their blood. In the air, they were, despite enemy supremacy, legends of dedication and sacrifice, of courage and willingness to perform the duty in the best way.

This is an hour for action; not an hour for sorrow. It is a situation calling for ideals and not for selfishness or personal feelings. All my heart is with you, and I want all your hearts to be with me. May God be with us all, a hope in our hearts, a light and guidance. Peace and the blessing of God be with you.

2. Sadiq al-'Azm, an Arab Intellectual, Critiques the Arab State and Clergy for Their Use of Religion, 1968

In 1967 Sadiq al-'Azm was a professor of philosophy at American University in Beirut when the Arab armies of Egypt, Syria, and Jordan suffered a humiliating defeat at the hands of the Israelis. Like many Arabs, al-'Azm was shocked by the swift and disastrous course of the war (which lasted a mere six days), especially after years of propaganda about progress and modernization in Egypt, the self-declared standard-bearer of the "progressive" Arab states. Like other Arabs, al-'Azm sought explanations for this abysmal turn of events.

Some Arabs presented a religious justification for the failure—namely, that Muslims had strayed from the path of God and God punished them by abandoning them at their time of great need. However, as a secular intellectual, Sadiq al-'Azm rejected this explanation and posited that the problem lay in exactly that type of thinking. He—and others such as the Syrian poet Adonis—argued that religion in the Middle East hinders rationality and produces fatalism and a culture that is shackled to the past. Moreover, the disillusioned al-'Azm argued, although some Arab states had constructed facades of modernism based on equality, progress, and democracy, they remained hamstrung by backward-looking religious thought. He

*criticized these states for manipulating religious ideas to gain legitimacy and re-
main in power while maintaining their authoritarian rule. Al-'Azm wrote the following criticism of the state, religion, and their relationship in 1968 for the Arab journal*
Arab Studies.

Those who know the editorials of Muhammad Hasanayn Haykal about the
state of the Arab world after the defeat of June 1967 may remember that the famous [Egyptian] editorialist has said on more than one occasion that undoing
the effects of [Israeli] aggression without resorting to war and military power
will require nothing short of a miracle. Then he added that our age is not an age
of miracles. . . . However, circumstances seem to belie Haykal with regard to
his comments about miracles since on June 5, 1968 *Al-Ahram* [Egypt's leading
and semi-official daily newspaper] carried the press release of Pope Kyrallis the
Sixth [the Coptic Christian pope] in which he declared and affirmed the truth
of the apparition of the Virgin Mary at al-Zaytoun Church. Furthermore, *Al-
Ahram* carried a photo on its front page that it declared to be a photographic
recording of the Virgin or her shadow that had appeared. . . .

Soon after, the whole Egyptian press became immersed in a sudden religious hallucination and it adopted "this great national issue" and began to publicize it and to exert itself in "finding scientific evidence" for the existence of
miracles. The Egyptian press searched for scientists and university professors
who would testify that the appearance of the Virgin is a scientific fact that cannot be doubted. . . . Furthermore, the press made quite clear that the apparition
of the Virgin has long term political, social, and touristic implications for the
Arab masses in Egypt and with regard to reclaiming the land occupied after
June 5 [1967]. . . .

Naturally, this religious hysteria has been reflected in Lebanon, and *Al-
Anwar* [a Lebanese daily] has begun publicizing the phenomenon. So it was
that it [the newspaper] appeared with news of a serious scientific study that
proves "that the apparition of the Virgin in Cairo is a factual truth." . . .

The dangerous aspect of this sudden religious phenomenon within Arab
media is not the traditional belief in miracles that is prevalent amongst the
people, and the belief in the appearance of the Virgin and in her ability to do so
at will. The stories and tales of supernatural and healing miracles are as old as
humanity, and it is not limited to one religion. . . . However, the dangerous aspect in the subject of the apparition of the Virgin is that this popular movement . . . did not follow a spontaneous course whereby the believers would go
on pilgrimage to the said church and some would be healed, others would die,
and still others would believe and that would be the end of the story; as all such
stories should end. The course of events was exactly the opposite of that in
Egypt where the government's agencies—its press, media and ministries—

Sadiq Jalal al-'Azm, "The Miracle of the Appearance of the Virgin Mary and Removing the Evidence of
[Israeli] Aggression," *Critique of Religious Thought* (Beirut: Dar al-Tal'ia for Publication, 1968), pp. 151–
179. Translated by Akram Khater. Reprinted by permission of the American Committee on Jerusalem.

adopted the story of the apparition of the Virgin and publicized it and concluded from it what it wished in terms of political and touristic implications.
Thus it transformed it into a religious hysteria that has swept the great majority of citizens. . . . It would have been easy [to dismiss this event] if the media
that publicized this religious fever was that of a reactionary Arab country seeking to cover its material and intellectual deficits . . . under the cloak of religiosity and by linking defeat and victory to supernatural powers beyond human
control. But what is really tragic is that this task was carried out by a press
overseen and directed by the Arab Socialist Union [of Egypt]. . . . All that we
heard in the aftermath of the [Arab] defeat [of June 1967] about modern science
and technology and the scientific method in thinking, planning and preparing
ourselves, and about rationality in our words, declarations and behaviors, has
gone up in smoke in a single moment as a result of the effect of this religious
hysteria. . . . Let it be known that the preoccupation of the Arab masses with
supernatural events and miracles and their stories in the second half of the
twentieth century, and particularly in these difficult times, will never help us in
successfully resolving our pressing worldly problems, and will not help us attain our vital national rights regardless of whether the Virgin was angry or not
about the loss of Jerusalem [to the Israelis].

In this essay I would like to present some basic comments and reflections
about what have been called the miracle of the appearance of the Virgin. I will
base my research on the press releases and commentaries that [have] been published about it either officially or semi-officially for the purpose of uncovering
several important facts included in those releases and for the purpose of supporting what I said at the beginning of this article. . . . In other words, I want
to make evident the fabrications . . . that are part of what has been said and
published about the apparition of the Virgin in Cairo in the hope of presenting
a humble effort toward inviting the Arab mind to return once again to measured, rational and objective thought . . . and to move away from the waves of
religious hysteria and . . . demagoguery that [have] wasted enough of Arab
time and efforts. . . .

We can find the political implications of this large religious phenomenon in
various sections written about the apparition of the Virgin and its relationship
to the removal of the effects of the [Israeli] aggression and liberating occupied
Arab lands. *Al-Ahram* printed the following headline on its second page: "The
apparition of the Virgin indicates that God will help us be victorious and that
Heaven has not abandoned us." In other words, after all that has happened it is
still asked of Arabs to beseech Heaven for victory and to beg the Almighty for
it instead of asking Arabs to depend on themselves. . . . It was declared during
the packed press conference that followed the appearance of the Virgin at this
time and specifically in Egypt that:

> "We have said that the saints and martyrs appear to the believers at the
> greatest time of need to support and encourage them. It [is] for that
> reason that the Virgin has come to strengthen the will of the blessed
> and believing Egyptian people . . . to call upon them to cling to its

beliefs in this particular time when atheist calls are ringing. . . ." (*Al-Ahram*, p. 3)

It is clear from this . . . that the Virgin did not appear to call upon the Arab people of Egypt to uphold its revolution and to deepen its commitment to its socialism . . . to respond to the Israeli challenge. Rather she came to ask this people to hold on to worn-out and inherited traditions and supernatural ideology that dominate the mind; that is to face the future by returning to the past instead of surging forward. . . .

Does the Virgin have to descend from Heaven for the Arabs to realize that the liberation of Palestine is a matter of the greatest importance? . . . Do the Arabs today need comfort and soothing talk or criticism, rejection and concern that would fuel them in facing occupation and the serious challenges surrounding them? . . .

In the face of such talk it should be clear to every Arab that the crisis generated by the defeat is not an immediate crisis at all. It is [a] vital and existentialist crisis that threatens the Arab being in its entirety, and that Arabs should prepare themselves to face this crisis not as a passing moment but as a continuous problem that will become worse. . . . Any other interpretation of this crisis which seeks to make light of its dangers and intensity is nothing more than trickery and gratuitous flattery. Contrary to what Father Gregorius said, neither miracles nor the appearance of the Virgin . . . will truly uplift the morale of the Arab people and will regain its confidence in its current leadership. . . .

(4) Frankly, it seems to me that the intellectual, cultural and scientific standards of the clerical system within the Egyptian Coptic church are very low. . . . This has become clear to me after looking into announcements by clerics . . . about the miracle of the apparition of the Virgin. Following are some examples about what I mean:

(a) During a meetings at the Ma'alaqa Church . . . Father Samuel gave a speech in which he emphasized "a historical and scientific truth" which is that during the time of the Fatimids [11–12th centuries] al-Muqattam mountain was in a location [other] than its current one. However, the Caliph [Fatimid ruler] asked one of the patriarchs of the Coptic church to move the mountain from its old location to where it is now. . . ."

We would propose to the respected Patriarchs, on this occasion, to carry al-Muqattam mountain as soon as possible and to place it directly over Israeli military central command during the meeting of their general staff, and this would be of great benefit for the Arab cause. . . .

(d) One of the Bishops participating in the press conference said the following about the scientific explanation for the appearance of the Virgin:

"Scientifically, it has been proven that every person has his own 'ethereasness' that cannot be erased and that can be embodied at any moment in the shape of ethereal atoms that takes the full appearance of the individual. . . . For example, science has been able to photograph tens of men or women that died hundreds of years ago. If all of this requires sophisticated electronic equipment . . . then I think that

saints and martyrs do not need any of this. . . . belief will suffice."
(*Al-Ahram*, p. 3)

One does not need to be an accomplished scientist or an expert in electronics and "ethereals" to realize that this [is] nothing more than nonsense. It is more pathetic and dangerous than myths because it claims to speak in the name of science and in a language that appears reasoned. . . . It is shameful for the Arab mind in the second half of the twentieth century to repeat such nonsense. . . . Is this the cultural guidance that the Arab masses need after the Defeat [of June 1967]?

3.   Ayatollah Ruhollah Khomeini Denounces the Rule of the Shah of Iran, 1975

Ayatollah Ruhollah Khomeini (1900–1989) was one of the architects and leaders of the revolution that overthrew Shah Muhammad Reza Pahlavi of Iran in 1979. After settling in the city of Qom (the main center for Shi'ite Islamic learning in Iran) in 1923, Khomeini began to lecture and write on Islamic ethics and law. In the early 1960s he quickly gained prominence among seminary students and then attracted a larger audience in Iran when he began to criticize the shah and his government. In speeches and essays Khomeini contended that the shah's government was illegitimate because it did not follow the precepts of Islam, and because it allowed Western influences to dilute what he regarded as Iran's authentically Islamic heritage. His opposition to the shah and his growing popularity soon attracted the attention of the shah's secret police—the Savak. His persistent and strident denunciations of the shah's corruption, oppression of the masses, and compromising of Iran's sovereignty led to his arrest in 1963 by the Savak and his exile to Turkey in 1964. A year later, he was allowed to reside in the city of Najaf in southern Iraq.

From exile, Khomeini continued to exhort his followers to oppose the shah and to critique the Iranian state. In 1975, the shah planned a celebration of the twenty-five hundredth anniversary of the Persian Empire. He intended the festival to legitimate his weak regime by linking it to a long heritage of kings who predated Islam. Khomeini condemned the upcoming celebration. The staging of this event and Khomeini's critique were critical steps toward revolution. In reading this document, try to understand Khomeini's points within the context of the shah's government, which many Iranians considered illegitimate, and to decipher the alternative view of government that Khomeini was presenting. (For an insider's view of the shah in 1976 and 1977 see document 1 in the chapter "Restricting Authority.")

Now, according to numerous letters and reports I have received, one of the unfortunate aspects of the present situation in Iran is that a large number of

Ayatollah Ruhollah Khomeini, "The Incompatibility of Monarchy with Islam," in Hamid Algar, *Islam and Revolution* (Berkeley, Calif.: Mizan Press, 1981), pp. 201–208. Reprinted by permission.

people have died of hunger. While these tragic circumstances and conditions prevail, millions of tumans are to be spent celebrating in honor of the monarchy. According to reports, 80 million tumans are to be spent on decorating and lighting up Tehran alone. Experts have been invited from Israel to take care of the arrangements—from Israel, that stubborn enemy of Islam and the Qur'an, which a few years ago attempted to corrupt the text of the Qur'an, and now imputes to the Qur'an unworthy statements, which our students abroad vigorously refute and deny (may God strengthen them). Israel, which is at war with the Muslims and plans to occupy all the lands of Islam up to Iraq and (God forbid) to destroy the noble shrines of Islam! Israel, which set fire to the Masjid al-Aqsa, a crime that the Iranian regime tried to cover up with all sorts of propagandistic proposals to rebuild the mosque! Israel, which has turned more than a million Muslims into refugees and occupied the lands of the Muslims! That state is now to arrange the celebrations for the Iranian monarchy, and that state is supplied with Iranian oil by tankers. Ought the people of Iran to celebrate the rule of a traitor to Islam and the interests of the Muslims who gives oil to Israel? Who was responsible for the events of Khurdad 15; who killed, according to one of the *ulama*, four hundred people in Qum alone; who had fifteen thousand people massacred throughout Iran; who sent his agents to Fayziya Madrasa to insult the Qur'an and Imam Ja'far (upon whom be peace)? They set fire to the students' turbans, threw some of them off the roof of the building, and behaved scandalously, filling the prisons with our patriots. Many of these best sons of our people were tortured to death in prison by his agents. Are we now to honor the rule of such a monarch with a celebration?

What benefit have our people ever derived from such rulers that we should now celebrate and light up our cities? Are we to commemorate Agha Muhammad Qajar, that bloodthirsty savage? Or the monarch who massacred people in the mosque of Gauhar Shad in such numbers that the walls were stained with blood and the gates of the mosque had to be closed so that none might see the spectacle?

[...]

Only recently, because of a slogan uttered in the university that ran counter to his lowly inclinations, he sent his bandits to the university and had them beat the students atrociously. According to reports that reached here, some female students needed surgery as a result of the blows and wounds they received. Their only crime was opposing the twenty-five hundredth anniversary celebrations and saying, "We have no need of this festival. Put an end to the hunger of our people; do not celebrate over the corpses of our people."

[...]

Are we not to protest that the oil belonging to Iran and Islam is sold to a state at war with the Muslims? Why is Israel able to gain influence in the affairs of a Muslim country? Of course, the answer will be, "We are given orders, and we have no choice but to obey. These are our orders, and we have to carry them out." The Shah himself in one of his speeches, which was later reproduced in a book, stated, "The allies, after occupying Iran, thought it fitting that I should be in control of affairs, and they agreed to my accession to the throne." May God curse them for thinking it fitting and casting us into disaster! Naturally, someone who is a puppet has to serve his masters; he cannot do otherwise. And they follow their desires and appetites ("They eat as the beasts eat"); they care not where their nourishment comes from nor how it is obtained. As long as their needs and requirements are met, the world may drown in blood and fire, and entire peoples may be destroyed.

Are we not to speak out about these chronic ailments that afflict us? Not to say a single word about all these disasters? Is it incompatible with our position as religious scholars to speak out? Were not the Prophet and the Commander of the Faithful, 'Ali (peace be upon both of them) religious scholars, and did they not preach long sermons? In the Shaqshaqiya sermon about a certain person who made illicit use of the money belonging to the community, far harsher and more uncompromising expressions occur than those we have used. How is it that now, when it is the turn of the present generation of religious scholars to speak out, we invent excuses and say that it is "incompatible" with our status to speak out?

[...]

If the *'ulama* of Qum, Mashhad, Tabriz, Isfahan, Shiraz, and the other cities in Iran were to protest collectively today against this scandalous festival, to condemn these extravagances that are destroying the people and the nation, be assured that results would be forthcoming. There are more than 150,000 students and scholars of the religious sciences in Iran. If all these scholars, authorities, proofs of Islam, and ayatullahs were to break the seal of silence and make a collective protest to remove the endorsements of their silence from the list of crimes committed by the regime, would they not achieve their aims? Would the authorities arrest them all, imprison and banish them, destroy them? If they were able to, they would destroy me before anyone else, but their interests do not permit them to do so.

Would that they did destroy me, so that I might no longer be tormented by the tragic state of our country. The tyrannical regime imagines that I am very happy and satisfied with my life, and so they think they can threaten me. But what life is this that I lead? Death as soon as possible would be better than this life; then I might join the presence of the Most Noble One in the hereafter and be delivered from this life of misfortune. What life is it that I lead, constantly hearing the cries and moans of our oppressed and tyrannized people? The crimes committed by this tyrannical regime and the acts of treachery against Islam and the Muslims have robbed me of all peace. News constantly arrives to the effect that the prisons are full of patriots, that innocent people are dying from the effects of pitiless torture, that bandits and ruffians are attacking the university to kill and wound the students, and that girls are being tortured by having boiling water poured on their heads. It is just like the time of Ibn Ziyad and Hajjaj, when if it was thought that someone might be a follower of the Shi'a, he was seized and destroyed. So, too, they attack and arrest and torture now on the strength of mere suspicion. Nobody's life is safe. If someone offers religious advice or utters a word from the pulpit, he is immediately carried off to prison. If someone distributes a few copies of a critical pamphlet, they arrest him and take him off to some unknown destination.

[...]

Come to your senses; awaken Najaf! Let the voice of the oppressed people of Iran be heard throughout the world. Protest to the government of Iran by letter and telegraph. It costs nothing to write a letter; for God's sake, write to the Iranian government. Tell them to abandon this abominable festival, these scandalous extravagances. If these latest excesses are not prevented, still worse misfortunes will descend upon us and we will be confronted with even more distasteful events. Every day new events are created, new disasters for the wretched people of Iran. They even have a special expert for dreaming up these events, these idiotic spectacles. If matters continue on their present course, we will be faced with events in the near future that none of us can even imagine.

[...]

It is the duty of the Muslim people of Iran to refrain from participation in this illegitimate festival, to engage in passive struggle against it, to remain indoors during the days of the festival, and to express by any means possible their disgust and aversion for anyone who contributes to the organization or celebration of the festival. Let the festival organizers know that they are despised by the Islamic community and by all alert peoples throughout the world, that they are hated by all lovers of freedom, and that Islam and the Muslims are repelled by the very notion of monarchy.

It is also your duty to make your opposition to this festival known by any means at your disposal and to pray for your fellow Muslims—those wretched, starved, and hungry people in Iran—for those who suffer imprisonment, torture, and banishment; for those innocent girls who have severe wounds inflicted on them. Pray for them and for all victims of the Iranian regime, and ask God Almighty to grant them His aid.

And peace be upon you.

4. Documents About One of the Major Political Arguments Underlying the Lebanese Civil War, 1975

In April 1975 civil war broke out in Lebanon. It lasted until 1989, although some observers contend it continues today albeit in a nonmilitary manner. On the surface, the war appeared to be an internal conflict, but it was far more than that.

The war was a manifestation of regional conflicts. These antagonisms—some of them between Arabs, others between Arabs and Israelis—played out in Lebanon because the absence of a strong central government there facilitated external interference and the flow of weapons, both of which fed a bloodbath lasting nearly two decades.

The war in Lebanon threatened the whole region because it was caused by a deeply flawed political system. One group in Lebanon—Maronite Christians—dominated the political, economic, and social sectors of the whole country. This type of imbalance was not unique to Lebanon; it was the norm throughout a region where democracy was a fleeting dream for most. Thus, the outbreak of civil war in Lebanon caused serious alarm in other countries in the region that suffered from similar imbalances. Many countries began to warn of possible "Lebanonization" of their own internal politics.

On a fundamental level, the war in Lebanon represented a crisis in the national identity of a country born—like most other Middle Eastern and North African countries—in the wake of independence from European colonial rule. In Lebanon, the implications of the national mythologies constructed in the first half of the twentieth century were coming home to roost. Lebanon's identity as a "nation" was precariously maintained for some twenty years by means of the "National Charter," which established the power-sharing formula that permitted Christians to maintain a slim margin of control over the government. However, in the early 1970s, the changing demographics of the country (Muslims began to outnumber Christians), the intensification of the Palestinian-Israeli conflict (over 300,000 Palestinians living in refugee camps in Lebanon were demanding the right to fight Israel across Lebanese borders), and economic crises, which polarized the country's population more than ever between haves and have-nots, coalesced to severely test the formula. Ultimately, the pressure became so great that civil war broke out.

The following documents present Muslim and Christian visions of Lebanon. Muslim views are presented by the prime minister, Rashid al-Sulh, and by Muhsin Salim. Pierre Gemayel, the head of the main right-wing Christian party, and one of his advisers, N.T., respond. Besides shedding light on a critical issue in Lebanon, this exchange of opinions conveys tensions unsettling all nations of the region—tensions resulting from differing visions of the "nation" and from unequal access to state power and benefits.

Statement of the Prime Minister of Lebanon, Mr. Rashid al-Sulh, in the Resignation Session in the Parliament, May 15, 1975

[...]

Dear Members of the Parliament,

[...]

I wish today to present you with a statement to clarify my position with regard to the current events, because of its critical importance. . . .

At noon on the 13th of April a horrendous crime was committed in Ayn al-Rumaneh [a suburb of Beirut] against a bus carrying Lebanese and Palestinian citizens. . . .

It is clear that the Phalangist party [right-wing Christian party led by Pierre Gemayel] is fully responsible for the massacre, and for the subsequent complications, and for the material and moral damages that befell the country as a result. And this was clear from the first moment of the ugly crime, and

---

Harb al-sanatayn, 1975–1976/al-Nahār (Bayrūt: Dār al-Nahār, 1976). Translated by Akram Khater.

because the party refused to condemn the crime, and refused to turn over those responsible for it for three days, then its subsequent and clear declaration of responsibility through handing over two of those who committed the massacre and its promise to hand over others.

The real dimension of the Phalangist responsibility for the event becomes clear when we tie it to its precedents, and to the attempts that followed it to expand the resulting conflict and to turn it into a widespread confrontation between the Lebanese and the Palestinians, and even among the Lebanese themselves.

For a long time the Phalangist party has been politically and materially and practically preparing in all of its measures for such actions.

The memoranda that were issued with or without occasion, have dealt with the issue of the Palestinian presence on Lebanese soil, and openly call for opposing it and agitate against this presence with a consistent and constant call to go outside the official government policy regulating the Lebanese-Palestinian and Lebanese-Arab relations. . . .

All this intense political preparation which sought to inflame sectarian hatred, was accompanied by feverish military preparations with the establishment of an armed militia which obtained its weapons from known quarters, as affirmed by the Chief Muslim Mufti of the Lebanese Republic. . . . This was premised on the notion that the Palestinian fighters had weapons, when everyone knows that it is directed against the Israeli enemy, while the other weaponry has no other purpose but to prepare to strike against the Palestinian resistance movement, and to create internal conflicts that will drive the country toward chaos in order to protect sectarian and isolationist privileges that most of the Lebanese have come to reject.

[. . .]

Dear Members of the Parliament,

I must in conclusion frankly and clearly present to your esteemed parliament what I deem to be important conclusions that my tenure as prime minister has only confirmed. These are conclusions that derive from the convictions of the great majority of the Lebanese. The sectarian privileges which form the basis of the Lebanese political system have become, in light of the developments in Lebanon and its relationship to its Arab milieu, a stumbling block which prohibits any progress and threatens to . . . undermine that which the builders of independence had constructed [a united nation].

It is this reality which prohibits the real sharing of power and the proper distribution of authority within the various parts of government . . . and it prohibits the establishment of a proper democratic parliamentary representation, and keeps us from strengthening the army and enabling it to perform its natural role as the defender of the nation. . . . this is what prohibits the establishment of real equality between the citizens in a manner that will eradicate abject poverty and will improve those neglected areas [mostly in the predominantly Muslim areas].

. . . We are confronted with only two options for escaping this deteriorating situation: establish a new formula within the context of the current political system and in light of the present demographic and social status of the Lebanese religious sects. Or, establish a new democratic formula within the context of the requirement for a national renaissance at the social, political and economic levels; a formula that will lead eventually toward the secularism of the state institutions and to social justice and total development at the same time. . . .

I and the nationalist groups choose without any hesitation the second option which derives from the logic of history, and the reality of our nation and the spirit of the times and the outlook of the new generation.

Thus, it is imperative to deal with the country's situation in a radical manner that will come into effect in stages according to the following principles:

First, implement real democratic reform that guarantees correct distribution of power among the various elements of government, and that affords the possibility of establishing political representation that reflects the true popular will through democratic reforms of the election legislation.

Second, commit to the common Arab requirements for facing the Zionist enemy . . . by supporting the Palestinian people and its struggle with all possible means, regardless of the sacrifices. . . .

Third, reform the law organizing the army and subject it to political authority and maintain sectarian balance in its ranks and provide it with all the necessary human and material requirements so that it will be able to perform its basic national duty, and avoid dragging it into internal matters. . . .

Message of Pierre Gemayel, Leader of the Christian Right-Wing Phalangist Party, to the Muslims of Lebanon, June 24, 1976

My Muslim Brothers,

This voice, the voice of a human being who persists in proclaiming—amidst the wave of despair, and despite the state of disintegration that has overwhelmed the people and all institutions—the civilized character that has defined the facade and core of Lebanon.

It is a voice from the heart and soul, indeed it is an act of faith that I had decided to undertake without being appointed by anyone to do so, and without any formalities. It appears to me that the proclamation of this faith, in all sincerity, is better than all the arbitrations and resolutions meant to resolve the conflict that outnumber the days of this crisis, and that has until now succeeded only in widening and deepening the feeling of despair.

In any case, Lebanon is now in need of something like a miracle in order to survive the evils of division and to be re-born again . . . and is there anything other than faith that can bring about miracles?!

. . . [The faith I speak of is] faith in Lebanon of course, and faith on the part of his children in the first place. If they lack this burning faith then it is certainly dead. If it burns in their bosoms then it is alive and will not die. The miracle of which I speak is not of divine provenance, but it derives from the labor of man. In any case, the borders of countries have not been recorded in the Bible or the Qur'an, and neither the Qur'an nor the Bible has stated that Lebanon is for the Christians or Muslims, or for both parties. And God, all glory to him, has not taken sides with these people or those.

According to these basic facts, the Muslims and Christians of Lebanon do not have the right to disagree because of God. Rather it is their duty to unite in him, because He is the God of all of humanity, and because He is—before people began to interject Him in their earthly conflicts—the absolute good, beauty and love. In addition, Christians and Muslims do not have the right to bring religion into their conflicts about Lebanon. Neither Islam nor Christianity can dictate consecrating this land for themselves. It goes without saying that monopolizing Lebanon by this or that group is not one God's commands. . . . Rather the spirit of monopoly is one of the earthly sins. . . .

The role of the Lebanese, Christians and Muslims, in this circumstance is one of the most important roles. The message has not been given to anyone else. . . . And if each people are assigned a role or task in this world through which to perform a service to all of humanity, then the Lebanese have no better role than this one through which they can serve themselves, their religions, man, liberty and all the other human values. Islam does not need another Islamic country, nor does Christianity need another Christian addition. . . .

[He goes on to discuss the Palestinian armed presence in Lebanon and argues that it is the cause of the civil war raging in the country.]

[. . .]

While the Christians have demanded that the Palestinians' ability to interfere in Lebanon's internal politics should be stopped, you [the Muslims] have insisted upon allowing to proceed along the same path. . . . There is no alternative at this [juncture] from the return to real sovereignty [for Lebanon] and there is no alternative to demarcating these boundaries [between Palestinian refugee camps and the rest of Lebanon]. So, is this possible if your cooperation is not more forceful than your acquiescence with chaos [PLO fighters carrying out military operations against Israel from Lebanese soil]? And is this possible if you do not declare in some form this solidarity [with the demands of the Christians] and if you do not affirm it?

It is for this purpose that I address you today, appealing to your conscience, pleading with you to save this nation that is threatened with division and dissolution. I hope that you will be today as you were in the forties when you decided to build with your Christian brothers a nation that is not like all the other countries, and nation that is not like all the other nations. I cannot imagine your ambition today to be for anything less than an ideal nation that Islam, Christianity, Arabism and all of humanity so desperately need. The matter rests with your decision. Indeed the salvation of this nation has never depended upon this decision as it does today. So declare [your allegiance to an independent Lebanon] as you declare your faith in God daily, and you will receive from the Christians all the gratitude, love, and loyalty.

Response of Muhsin Salim to the Call of Pierre Gemayel

To the Honorable Lebanese Shaykh [honorific title]:

Your latest appeal, which was broadcast through "The Voice of Lebanon" [radio station] on the 24 of June, 1976, calls for rejuvenating the unique Lebanese formula [sectarian division of political power with Christians maintaining a slight margin over Muslims] upon [a] new basis and for the return of the brotherly cooperation between the Muslims and Christians in the nation, and to work to remove from Christians their fear about the subject of Arabism which they have been advocating lately. It appears that this appeal, which emanates from the bottom of your heart and from the purity of your Lebanese feeling, has received positive reactions among the Muslims who care ever so much about the unity of the land and people of Lebanon, and about proclaiming its true Arab cultural identity, and that Lebanon should remain the land of liberty and humanity as you demanded in your appeal.

What I would like to say to you on this occasion, in response and as a comment on your aforementioned appeal, is the natural response for every Lebanese Muslim who lives in the land of Lebanon and who loves his country and wishes to safeguard its free and independent existence. Your appeal, O honorable Shaykh, penetrated to the depth of our essence [the Lebanese Muslims], it has occupied our thoughts and reflections, and has received a good response. This is so not only because it was issued by you but also because it expresses the essence of our thoughts, worries and fears about the unknown future and destiny of this nation if we—as Muslims and Christians—do not agree upon a common factor to save our nation from destruction and extinction.

But how we do we put the appeal into effect? This is the question that we posed to ourselves when we heard the appeal, since you did not tell us—the Muslims in Lebanon—what we should do and from whence we must begin to revive the Lebanese formula around which the Lebanese were united in the past.

You did not tell us what practical steps the Muslims in Lebanon must take so that Lebanon will return to its sovereignty and authenticity, in a manner that would be acceptable to their Christian brothers.

The Lebanese Muslims, whom you addressed in your last appeal and in the wake of the disaster that befell them and all their Lebanese brothers recently, wish you had specified in a later statement how you see the process for reviving the Lebanese formula. What are the foundations upon which it should be based, and what methods must be adopted to practically and clearly designate the Arab identity of Lebanon in a manner that would be acceptable to all the Lebanese equally, Muslims and Christians? I believe that the subject of Lebanon's identity and specifying its Arabness in a responsible and practical manner is one of the most important subjects that occupy the Lebanese at the present time. It may be that this subject lies at the center of all the other numerous problems and issues that concern the Lebanese.

If the Arab identity of Lebanon can be specified in a clear and frank manner . . . which is acceptable to all the Lebanese groups and particularly the

Muslim ones, then we can find a solution to all the other issues since it will become secondary in relation to this fundamental problem.

The Lebanese have been satisfied to use the expression coined by the past Riyad al-Sulh, the prime minister of the first independent government in Lebanon, in his first governmental statement, which states that "Lebanon has an Arab facet." This extremely brief expression has been considered to be the basis and formula through which the Lebanese deal with Arabism.

Since the establishment of the Arab League in 1945, and the entrance of this country as a permanent member, and throughout the 30 years that Lebanon have participated in the work and decisions of the Arab League, we have not heard once that Lebanon stood in opposition to any of the League's decisions. This confirms Lebanon's attachment to its Arabness, and to [its] commitment to really and effectively share with all Arabs in their national stances. As for Palestine, which is the biggest Arab cause, Lebanon was and remains the one carrying its banner in all venues to the point that Lebanon was the voice of all the Arabs in defending it at the podium of the United Nations. . . . How can Lebanon turn away from its Arabness when its language and heritage are Arabic, when it is completely [linked] to the Arab world, when it exists in an Arab milieu and its destiny is an Arab destiny, and its economy an Arab economy, and its outlooks are Arab, and everything about it definitely states that it is an inseparable part of the Arab world.

However, and in addition to all of this, Lebanon has a particular characteristic that sets it apart from any other Arab country . . . and unique features that Lebanon cannot and must not ignore because they are intimately linked to its unique personality and glorious and great history. . . .

Isn't it strange that no one objects when Arab Egypt takes pride in its ancient and Pharaonic history, and objects when Lebanon takes pride in its ancient history and heritage, and accuses it of denying its Arabness. . . .

So, O Venerable Lebanese Shaykh,

We are with you in your appeal, and are ready to revive the unique Lebanese formula which unites the Lebanese in a unified Lebanon upon new foundations that are just and equal and that are nurtured by love and mutual trust.

But before we discuss any other subject we must begin from the beginning, and the beginning here is the agreement to specify the identity of Lebanon and its Arabness in a scientific and national fashion, without any confusion. . . . This can only be achieved by establishing a committee of Lebanese scholars, intellectuals and politicians from all sects to agree upon drawing a document that provides a scientific and political definition for the identity of Lebanon.

Response by N.T. to Muhsin Salim's Letter to Pierre Gemayel

1. We applaud your desire—presented in your letter to Shaykh Pierre Gemayel—to find the "practical steps that the Lebanese Muslims must take in order for Lebanon to return to its unity in a manner acceptable to their Christian brothers." However, we wish this was the desire of all Muslims, leaders

and followers, knowing all the while that if it were thus then they [the Muslims] would have exhausted every means to achieve it.

2. You say in your letter: "Before anything else we need to specify clearly and frankly the identity of Lebanon and its Arabness . . . for the Arabness of Lebanon is the thorniest of issues and the basis of disagreement among the Lebanese." We have two comments on your statement:

FIRST OBSERVATION.   Presenting the problem in this manner assumes that Lebanon is an orphan with no identity, and that it needs an identity other than [t]his. My dear sir, this assumption needs correction. At least half of the Lebanese—and perhaps you are among them—believe that Lebanon is an independent political entity that exists on its own and that does not require description or definition because it is in their eyes a complete nation and their aspirations and dreams stop at its borders. They are only loyal to it, they do not contemplate any cause or problem in the far or near world but from the perspective of its interests, and every time the interests of Lebanon conflict with any others they will unhesitantly champion the cause of Lebanon. . . . They believe in Lebanon the way they believe in God who is only known as "He is He."

Those see that the identity of Lebanon cannot be the subject of debate, argument or disagreement. The question about the identity of Lebanon cannot be posed any more than a question can be posed about the identity of France or Germany or the Soviet Union or others. . . .

The fact is that there is in Lebanon a second group of citizens who consider Lebanon to be a part of a larger whole, and that it is a temporary stage that must be transcended at the earliest opportunity. This group also believes that any conflict between the interests of Lebanon and those of the "larger whole" or even those of another part of this whole, must be resolved by sacrificing the interests of Lebanon.

Here is the real problem: the issue of loyalty to Lebanon; is it an absolute loyalty that Lebanon deserves or a conditional and temporary one which ranks lower than loyalty to Syrian or Arab nationalism?

SECOND OBSERVATION.   You demand, on one hand, commissioning a committee of scholars, intellectuals and politicians "to agree upon drawing a document that provides a scientific and political definition for the identity of Lebanon." Then, on the other hand, you link this identity with Arabism when you ask about "the method that should be adopted to define the Arab identity of Lebanon in a clear and scientific manner. . . ."

It seems to me that you have already pre-determined the decision which you ask the committee to make. Thus, you cannot imagine but an Arab identity for Lebanon. Will you then permit us to ask you: why do you ignore all the multitudes of those Lebanese who reject any other name for their Lebanon, not out of arrogance or animosity to anyone but for fear that the appellation will lead into the unknown. They are afraid that [such adjectives] will empty Lebanon of its contents and fill it with another unknown entity, a content that can be described as explosive in the tragic manner we have witnessed for the past sixteen months. . . .

"The unique character" and "unique characteristics which are linked to Lebanon's unique personality, history and civilization," are due—as you know, my dear sir—to the multi-ethnic nature of this country. Its varied cultural groups did not meet accidentally, but were gathered across a long history by one unifying factor which is their desire for liberty and their revolt against the oppressive rule of the majority and their intent to hold on to their unique identities. . . .

This pluralism, that is concomitant with the creation of Lebanon, has a progressive and civilizational value that supersedes Arabism, and all other one-faceted values. Thus, it would be unjust and wrong not to benefit from its wealth by finding political and cultural frameworks to guard and protect it and to highlight its great civilizational wealth.

To take as a point of departure the imposition of an Arab identity, and it is the cultural identity of but one group, on all of Lebanon is a rejection of this pluralism and an attempt by the few to control the whole and to absorb it. It is an act of oppression and hegemony that is rejected and fought by all sects who see in it a threat to its liberty, and therefore to its existence.

In addition, we do not understand this insistence on forcing Arabism on Lebanon. What is the use of it, when you know that the concept of Arabism is unclear, and it is difficult to make the concept of all? . . .

If Arabism is a common language, then there is no disagreement that Lebanon was given the language of the Arabs. . . .

If Arabism is a matter of geographical belonging from which are derived common regional interests, such as the European nature of France, Italy, Germany . . . then geography and the natural relations between countries and people are realistic matters that are not objects of disagreements. . . .

If Arabism is free commitment to common causes, then your letter clearly indicates that Lebanon has rendered special service to the causes of the Arabs, at times beyond its capacity . . . and despite all of this commitment the Arabists of Lebanon are still not satisfied. . . .

Will Arabism be something other than all of this, other than language, geography and free commitment to common causes? Are there any concepts left other than race and religion that can be attached to it? The first is not reasonable, and the second is not acceptable to non-Muslims. So, are you going to force the unity of race and religion?

You say: "I believe that the subject of Lebanon's identity, and specifying its Arabness . . . is one of the most important subjects that occupy the Lebanese at the present time. . . ."

No my dear sir! It is not the identity of Lebanon—or the gender of angels—that today tops the concerns of the Lebanese! Lebanon is burning; it is being torn apart, and raped. The most important matter is that Lebanon should continue to exist as a nation for a free people.

The role of the Muslims, quite simply, is to prove at least once that their loyalty to Lebanon is above and beyond their loyalty to any other cause, nationalism or ideology. . . .

5.   American Consular Documents Reveal U.S. Diplomats' Assessment of the Revolution in Iran, 1978

Who knew what was happening in the months leading up to and following the 1979 revolution in Iran? Secret American documents published after the takeover of the United States embassy in Tehran in November 1979 contain a wealth of first-hand day-to-day accounts and analyses. These documents, which normally would have been declassified decades from now, were obtained by the New York Public Library and are available for all to see. The document reprinted here gives an indication of what was going through the minds of American diplomats and analysts. It is an analysis of Iranians' feelings toward the shah of Iran written by a political officer at the U.S. consulate in Shiraz on September 23, 1978. It is striking to read the political officer's astute remarks about the political situation, yet his conclusions appear in retrospect to be far off the mark. This document and the excerpts from the diary of the shah's court minister (document 1 in the chapter "Restricting Authority") let us glimpse the complexity of the U.S.-Iranian relationship and its consequences for the people and government of Iran.

Department of State
AIRGRAM
Classification: Confidential
Message reference No.: A-23
To: Department of State
Info: AMCONSULS Isfahan and Tabriz (via internal pouch)
From: AMCONSUL Shiraz   Date: 9/23/78
Drafted by: Political officer Victor L. Tomseth
Subject: Political attitudes in southern Iran

SUMMARY AND INTRODUCTION.   Recent conversations with a variety of people in southern Iran have revealed considerable unanimity as regards [to] dislike for the regime headed by the Shah but little unity on other issues including the place of Islam.

The discontent is undoubtedly profound, but aside from students of the radical left who advocate overthrow of the Shah and establishment of a republic, few people can agree on a constructive alternative to the government as it has been practiced for the last 15 years.

Calls for early elections free from manipulation are heard fairly frequently. However, thoughtful Iranians, even those whose dislike for the present regime is intense, concede that in the absence of constraints on who can run and under what conditions, elections are likely to produce a Majles whose members will be incapable of uniting on any issue other than their grievances with the past government.

Under such circumstances, it seems inevitable that despite lack of enthusiasm for his leadership, the Shah will continue as Iran's ultimate political arbitrator. END SUMMARY AND INTRODUCTION.

It has been extremely difficult to find anyone in southern Iran with a good word for the Shah in recent days. Iran's population profile gives some indication why.

Almost half of all Iranians have been born since 1963, the last time the country faced an economic or political crisis of significance. Almost two thirds have been born since 1953, the last time an alternative to the Shah's rule was a serious possibility.

Few people among this group are impressed with comparisons of then and now, comparisons that have profound meaning for someone who has seen Iran transformed from a poverty-stricken country whose sovereignty was ignored by the great powers to one of the world's wealthier and more influential nations and who played a key role in that transformation. The post-1953 generation has been promised the millennium and its comparisons are made by that standard.

Even those old enough to remember the old days of 1953 and earlier have their grievances with the regime. These range from the secularization of the state to the arrogance of high government officials to the collapse of the real estate market to corruption to continuing (and often growing) inequities in Iranian society.

The Shah and his advisors have not been unaware of sources of discontent such as those enumerated above, and have usually reacted to them.

However, sometimes actions taken to alleviate pressures building in one area (e.g., controls on real estate speculation designed to curtail the number of overnight millionaires and close the gap between rich and poor) have created new pockets of unhappiness (i.e., among land owners, not all of whom by any means count their holdings in numbers of villages, who hoped to sell their properties for enough money to send their children off to college or for a retirement nest egg).

Other times, the determination to modernize Iran has led to decisions (e.g., giving women the vote) which were known would be opposed (i.e., by religious conservatives).

Change always poses a threat to vested interests, but it does not follow that the changes the Shah has wrought in Iran were foreordained to produce a degree of opposition to his rule which is now so manifest among the Iranian populace.

Rather it would appear that the manner in which these changes were effected has often been a more fundamental factor in the reaction to them than the changes themselves. Iranians seem overwhelmingly to resent having been excluded from virtually all political decisions of the last 15 years.

As one middle-aged Iranian, who says he remembers what it was like during Mossadeq's time, put it, "It bothered me less that the government decided to impose [an] exit tax on Iranians leaving the country than it did to have (former Minister of Information Darioush) Homayoun announce the decision without going to the trouble of consulting the Majles whose members in accordance with the constitutions are supposed to represent the interests in government."

Another, a businessman, referring to government interference in the hours shops can be open, said: "We Persians for the most part retain a 'hand-to-mouth mentality,' the heritage of the time when Iran was still a poor country. Small shopkeepers are thus inclined to maintain hours convenient to housewives whose habits are conditioned by the memory of a former day when they might not have known at noon when buying bread for lunch where the money would come from to buy the ingredients for dinner.

"In practice, we may not work more than the forty-hour week common in the West, but we do not like to be told by Harvard-educated bureaucrats who think they know better than we what is best for us [and] how and when to work it."

Aside from their commonly shared unhappiness with their government, however, Iranians in southern Iran are deeply divided on most other issues. Rural people, for example, while they may be deeply religious, are generally uninterested in the agitation for the return of Ayatollah Khomeini which has taken place in many urban areas.

They are inclined to view the issue as irrelevant to their major concerns—the weather, the availability of water, the price of wheat, etc. Recent arrivals from the countryside in cities where religious agitation has taken place, on the other hand and notwithstanding the attitudes of their rural relatives, have often figured prominently in such activities.

The explanation for this seeming contradiction appears to lie in the trauma they experience in trying to adjust to urban life. Frequently, their religion is the only institution familiar to them in their new surroundings, and they are thus highly susceptible to the religious emotionalism that surrounds a cause such as Khomeini's.

The business community, too, is divided on the religious issue. The more fervent among its members have willingly closed their shops in protest against the government and in mourning for fallen martyrs, often at great financial loss.

Others have usually closed as well, but often more in fear of retaliation for not closing than in sympathy for the causes espoused by the ulema. They may take their religion seriously and dislike the regime every bit as much as the fanatics, but they are also concerned about their businesses and they resent the disruptions frequent closures bring.

Contempt for the Islamic fundamentalists is perhaps even more profound than opposition to the regime among many members of the modernist element of society in southern Iran.

An Ahvaz banker characterized those who had participated in religious demonstrations (and numerous bank trashings) in that city as "illiterate Arabs who had taken leave of their senses under the influence of religious leaders hardly less ignorant than themselves."

A senior military officer in Shiraz described the clergy in general as the worst of Iranian society, lazy louts who entered religious schools for no more noble reason than to avoid conscription.

An American-trained engineer at Shiraz's Iran Electronics Industries in comparing Reza Shah (whom he admires) to Ataturk concluded that the latter was a greater leader because he had gotten rid of all of Turkey's ulema whereas Reza Shah had made the mistake of leaving some alive. His mastery of historical fact might have been shaky, but he left no doubt where he stood on the religious issue.

Lack of unanimity on the place of Islam is paralleled on secular political issues as well. Aside from those who have demanded the Shah's ouster and the establishment of a republic (a view which still seems to be confined to relatively small minorities on the extreme left and right in southern Iran), few Iranians seem to have considered alternatives to the kind of leadership he has provided.

Critiques are usually limited to where he has failed with little consideration given to how past deficiencies might be rectified. There does seem to be a consensus that the present Majles and all those who have served in governments during the past 15 years are discredited. Accordingly, early elections free from government manipulation are frequently advocated.

Thoughtful Iranians, however, recognize that there is as yet little of the discipline required for orderly elections present in their country. Most of the parties and political groupings which have emerged in recent weeks are held together by no more reliable glue than the personalities of their leaders.

Under the circumstances, these Iranians concede that elections without limitations on who can run and the size of parties which can field candidates are likely to produce a Majles whose membership would be an assemblage of mini-parites incapable of uniting on any issue other than the inadequacy of past governments, hardly a viable alternative to the Shah.

In sum, Iran is confronted with a difficult dilemma. Many Iranians, if southern Iran can be taken as representative of the rest of the country, are dissatisfied with the character of the leadership they want in its place.

Further, short of violent revolution and the imposition of a regime which in all likelihood would be every bit as autocratic as the Shah's, the Iranian people do not appear at this time to possess the self-discipline to find a way out of their predicament.

Thus, it seems that by default, the Shah will continue as the ultimate arbitrator of Iran's political future.

6.   The Massacre of the Muslim Brothers of Syria in Hama, 1982

In February 1982, for twenty-seven consecutive days, elements of the Syrian army surrounded the city of Hama and unleashed their full power on the inhabitants. Tens of thousands were killed; many more were injured. This harsh attack on civilians and militias alike came as an immediate response to an attack by the Muslim Brotherhood on a military college in which approximately fifty-four cadets had been killed. From a wider perspective, the massacre was one of numerous attempts by the regime of Hafez al-Assad to quell mounting opposition to its authoritarian rule.

The Muslim Brotherhood was a Sunni political group whose members were dedicated to establishing an "Islamic state" according to their definition of that concept. Their animosity to the regime in Syria derived from the fact that it was dominated by 'Alawi Muslims—a Shi'ite Islamic sect that most Sunnis considered heretical. (For information about the ideology of the Muslim Brotherhood by Hasan al-Banna, see document 12 in the chapter "Ideas of Nationalism.")

The following document is the introduction to one of the very few books written about the Hama massacre. The writer clearly opposes the Assad regime and sympathizes with the Muslim Brotherhood, so his representation of the regime must be seen as not necessarily objective. The book describes in as much detail as possible the attack on Hama, but its purpose is to present propaganda against the Assad regime. This does not mean that the details are necessarily inaccurate but that the presentation cannot be taken as absolutely true. The writer presents his position in stark terms, allowing readers to understand the Muslim Brotherhood's point of view.

[. . .] People have read and heard many things about tragic events in modern times, but they have not encountered a tragedy of such significance or depth. . . . They have not heard or known of a tragedy like the tragedy at Hama.

We must not forget that Hama faced the Crusaders and other invaders; that is why the Ayyubid kings adopted Hama as their first capital. Although the hordes of Crusaders approached the other principal cities of Syria, these hordes could not approach Hama.

During the French mandate, Hama remained a thorn in the side of the French and continued—for a quarter of a century—to fight and struggle against them. France punished Hama by depriving it of the means of development and left it a backward rural city. It was prevented from establishing institutions and from entering the industrial age; yet despite all of this, the people of Hama increased in strength.

Thus, it is not surprising that the current regime [of Hafez al-Assad] found Hama to be a stumbling block on the path of the conspiracy that the Syrian regime planned to carry out in order to neutralize Syria's central role in the Middle East. As [Miles] Copeland stated [in *The Game of Nations: The Amorality of Power Politics* (1969)], and as others like him have said, Syria

---

Hama: The Tragedy of This Era That Has Surpassed the Massacres of Sabra and Santilla (Cairo: Dar al-'Itsam Publishing House). Translated by Akram Khater.

represents a source of trouble for the American Empire. . . . It is for this reason that Copeland and other intellectuals and ideologues in the Western intelligence services have tried to neutralize this role, trying all means in the process: military coups, depending upon agents who were sometimes leaders and at other times on secret agents; but they did not succeed. Then finally they established this regime [Assad] to put an end to Syria's traditional role.

Because Hama was an obstacle to this terrible plot, reports leaked from the institutions of the Syrian regime that said that Hafez al-Assad and his band were planning evil things for this city appear logical. They wanted to erase it from the face of the map, to reconstitute its demographic makeup and thus rid themselves of opposition from this city, and to make Hama an example for other Syrian regions—or so they thought!

In this book the reader will read about the executive decree issued by the High Security Council—two months before the tragedy—giving Rifa'at, the brother of Hafez al-Assad and his partner, a free hand in enforcing martial law and providing him with 12,000 members of the Defense Companies to attack the northern cities and "purify" them of opposition. Hama was to be the first area of operations. Members of the High Security Council said to Rifa'at: You may kill up to 5,000 without requesting anyone's approval. They identified 100 families that he could wipe out, and they permitted him to commit mayhem—which is nothing new for him, but this time it was to be done under the guise of governmental decree.

Two years before the tragedy of February, the reader will note, the authorities allowed their agents and men to commit crimes in this city . . . to the point of attacking and killing children.

The intelligent reader will certainly be aware of the meaning of the changes that Hafez al-Assad has made in the Syrian penal code, which used to require no more than one month in prison for someone carrying a rifle without a permit. Hafez al-Assad increased the penalty from one month to five years; then in a new decree he increased the penalty to twenty years or even execution—all this in attempt to deprive people of the means to resist.

The reader will also be aware of the media blackout that Hafez al-Assad imposed on the events in Hama in order to isolate the city from the rest of the provincial governments and public opinion. The full scope of this conspiracy will be apparent when the reader learns the size of the repressive security force that camped within the city at that time (Military Intelligence, National Security Intelligence, Politburo) in addition to the encampment of the 47th Armored Division in the suburbs of the city and the introduction of the 21st Mechanized Division on the third day of the events in order to continuously and rapidly support and augment the regime's forces and militias. [. . .]

Two months before the events, the people of Hama were saying: We die every day, or a part of the city dies[. . . .] How long will this continue?

Each house was searched more than ten times. Soldiers of Hulegu [a thirteenth-century Mongol invader] would barely have left a house before others reentered. But what most offended the city were attacks on the honor and dignity of the people. Women were not safe from the soldiers' shameful and dishonorable behavior. Children often were killed in front of their parents. If an informer told the soldiers, "I saw a man enter this building, and he did not leave," they would force their way into the apartments within the building, and if they searched and did not find any fighters, they would destroy the building on top of those living in it. Many innocent families were killed in this manner, and all the while Hafez al-Assad was claiming that all was quiet in Syria and that he had eradicated a gang of Muslim Brothers. [. . .]

The reader will realize that the people of Hama faced a plot to exterminate them and believed that they had reached the end of the road. So residents of the city of all sects and groups, young and old, children and women alike, rose against the regime to defend their land, their lives, and their honor. Christians stood shoulder to shoulder with Muslims. The Christians of Syria distinguished themselves in a way that will have a great impact on the future of Syria and the region. [. . .]

The Syrian army suffers from the same problems as the civilians. It has been diverted from its primary mission, safeguarding the nation and its borders, to become a tool of oppression. Moreover, assassinations within its ranks have not ceased, because internal opposition [to al-Assad's regime] has not stopped and will not stop.

Hafez al-Assad wanted to give supporters of his sectarian regime control over various parts of the army. [. . .] In January 1982—shortly before the events in Hama—he executed fifty officers, and the regime covered up the executions by inventing a story about an attempted coup. In reality, the operation was simply a mop-up of officers whose loyalty was in doubt.

The suffering of the Syrian army is compounded because members of the military suffer from the same sectarian discrimination that afflicts the civilian population: discrimination on the basis of religion, persecution of anyone with an independent voice, demeaning behavior with no reason or cause, and repression that reaches a criminal level. At the same time, the army is used to kill its own members or to kill the people of neighboring countries, such as the Lebanese and Palestinians.

The Syrian army will remain, from the point of view of the Syrian people, a positive nationalist element that will participate in turning the tide [against al-Assad] in the final determining hours. Despite all the executions and all the wounds, it will remain a national army that will erase its dishonor [. . .] and will join with the people in solidarity. [. . .]

As for the Syrian cities—specifically at the time of the massacre in Hama—they stood in solidarity with each other through the unity of the people, but they were in no position to rise in support of Hama because the people were not armed and because of the intense media blackout. Nevertheless, the city of Aleppo attempted to go on strike as an expression of protest [against the attacks on Hama], but the regime threatened it with bombardment and destruction. Nuhad al-Qadi, the mayor of Aleppo, announced to the merchants: "Whosoever goes on strike will be hung in front of his store." Damascus also attempted to go on strike, but Hafez al-Assad summoned all members of the chambers of commerce to his palace and threatened whoever dared to strike with the same fate. It is important to note that the [French] foreign occupiers did not dare to say such things.

Perhaps the explosion of a car in the Ministry of Information building and at the center for the distribution of the regime's newspaper *al-Ba'ath* on February 18, 1982, in the capital Damascus is the best evidence of the solidarity of other Syrian cities with Hama. Michael Frenchman, former editor of *The* [London] *Times* newspaper, recounted that he was in the office of Zuhayr Kana'an, the deputy minister of information, when the explosion took place. Frenchman said that he was talking with the deputy about "how calm Damascus was that day" when the loud explosion occurred!

But that was not all. Other things happened that were comic and disgusting at the same time. After Hama was destroyed, the regime—using its usual, well-known police-state methods—organized the population of the villages of Jabal al-Alawi in a supportive demonstration, and a representative of Hafez al-Assad asserted: "Those are the people of Hama celebrating its destruction! They are dancing on the bodies of their children!"

Did this creature, who stood before a city that was destroyed on top of its people, know anything about decency [. . .]?

People speak of Nero, who burned his capital, Rome, two thousand years ago in order to enjoy the sight of fire, and we do not know whether this is a true or fictional story. However, a thousand years from now, people will say that Syria—during a bizarre period—was ruled by a deviant sect that lacked ethical values, standards, and beliefs and had no loyalty for the people or the nation, and that its traitorous leader declared, without a hint of hesitation, that the people of Hama were demonstrating in support of him after he destroyed their city around them.

In fact, the tragedy of Hama is one indicator of the corruption of the whole regime. Today in Syria it is impossible for an honest citizen—someone who fears and knows God—to achieve any position of note within the power structure. Rather, a person can obtain a position of power in Syria only through immorality, corruption, or apostasy, or by placing oneself above the values and heritage of the nation. There are some high-ranking party members in Syria, who know this truth and who secretly cooperate and dialogue with the opposition. They are pathetic, for not one of them dares to pray, and some of them even refrain from fasting during Ramadan in order to stay in power and to show that they are worthy of their responsibilities within the regime of Hafez al-Assad.

O Arabs and Muslims, people and governments.

O rulers of this world and O people of this earth.

O Man in every place [. . .] remember your responsibility toward the Syrian people.

O rulers of the Arab world, do not forget to take into consideration the future of your relationship to the Syrian people.

It is a dangerous thing for you to adopt silence and this acquiescent position.

The people of Syria know with certainty that the regime in Syria is temporary and does not represent the wishes of any individual in the nation. The
regime itself acknowledges this point. Otherwise, what is the meaning of its attempt to safeguard its rule by destroying a whole city?

7. The Platform of the Islamic Salvation Front in Algiers Bases Its Ideology on Respect for Islamic Values, June 18, 1995

*The Islamic Salvation Front (FIS) was founded in Algiers on February 18, 1989, and
was legalized by the Interior Ministry on September 16, 1989. It centers its ideology on strict respect for Islamic values. This means legislators in parliament have to
defer to the imperatives of the Shari'a in all fields. Before the first round of the December 1991 parliamentary elections, some FIS leaders spoke of banning secular
and socialist parties if the FIS won a majority of the seats. Far from being homogeneous, however, the FIS is marked by philosophical dissension between the
Djazaara clan (the "Djazarists," supporters of dialogue and gradual Islamization,
close to the Egyptian Muslim Brothers) and the Salaafiya clan (the "Salafists," "supporters of the radical Islamization of Algerian society and more internationalist).*

*The FIS is Algeria's leading political party. It rapidly attracted young unem-
ployed and marginalized Algerians, an important segment of the population. In the
June 12, 1990, local elections, it won 54.3 percent of the vote, demonstrating its
strength in a large number of regions. The FIS subsequently won 47.3 percent of the
vote (there was an abstention rate of 41 percent) during the first round of the parliamentary elections of December 26, 1991. The FIS party benefited from a single-
member voting system in two rounds, based on an arbitrary division of constituencies
to favor large voting blocs (the government designed this system to weaken the position of the democratic parties).*

*Two months after the army's show of strength interrupted the electoral process
on January 11, 1992, the FIS was outlawed. The local governments it controlled were
dissolved, the mosques it controlled were depoliticized, and FIS activists were jailed.
Party members reorganized in exile (in Europe and the United States) and illegally in
Algeria.*

*The Army of Islamic Salvation (AIS), the FIS's armed branch, became active in
July 1992, attacking the army and public targets. The AIS is also responsible for
murdering intellectuals. Links between the FIS and the most violent armed Islamic
groups remain tenuous. Some Islamist leaders condemn in increasingly strong
terms the bloody acts committed by the GIA (French acronym for Armed Islamic
Group) against the civilian population. In this document, the FIS outlines its vision
for ending the bloody crisis that was tearing apart Algeria. It presents a framework
for allowing the FIS leadership to reenter the political mainstream and to distance
itself from the GIA and its terrorist acts.*

The Islamic Salvation Front Platform. http://www.medea.be/en/index058.html (February 2002). Translated by Akram Khater. Reprinted by permission of Medea Institute.

In the Name of Allah, the Most Merciful and Compassionate, Algeria, June 18, 1995.

The Necessary Principles and Procedures to Exit the Crisis

The Algerian people is adherent to its noble religion, and its Arab and Amazaghit [Amazight] heritage, and continues to follow the civilizational and cultural path of its nation with all their Islamic, Arab, North African and national dimensions, and is loyal to his glorious history and his immortal revolutions for independence, and to the sacrifices of past generations, The unity of the nation has been built, and has lasted across generations, upon these unchanging givens and solid foundations.

Algerians have reclaimed their sovereignty and independence from French colonialism after great sacrifices through which they sought to "establish the sovereign social democratic republic of Algeria within the boundaries of Islamic principles," as was specified in the communiqué of November 1, 1954. Thus, they became worthy of reclaiming their legitimate right to be led by choice not through force, through agreement not oppression, and through the good not the evil.

Then, political pluralism and public rights became a public right after the events of October 5, 1988. When the current crisis led to neglect of the people's wishes, and to depriving Algerians of the sources of their liberty, and the increase in the bloody confrontation between Algerians, then there is no hope for exiting this crisis except through a return to legitimacy, in the shadow of unity, security liberty, and justice in all their political, economic, social and cultural dimensions.

Since the previous attempts have not succeeded in arriving at the pursued legitimate and just political solution, then it has become necessary to establish as follows the necessary principles and procedures for exiting the crisis:

1. Principles

a. Islam is the religion of the Algerian nation and state, and is the source of its ideology, [morality] and legislations. It must remain above all other considerations because of its position among the foundations of the nation.

b. It is necessary to maintain the Algerian identity in its Islamic, Arab and Amazight dimensions, and to reject any conflict between these three fundamental principles upon which the unity and legitimacy of the nation is built.

c. It is necessary to work according to the Constitution of 23 February, 1988, until it is changed or amended through popular will expressed by legitimate methods.

d. Respect political pluralism within the context of national values.

e. Respect human rights, and guarantee individual and communal freedoms in the political, social and religious spheres, as well as the freedom of expression; all within the context of the nation's values and its founding principles.

f. The right of the people to choose its leaders, representatives, and its goals through free elections.

g. Guarantee the respect of political succession through the method of free selection by the Algerian people, through plural elections.

h. Refrain from using violence as a means to stay in power or to gain access to it, and the right of the people to defend his selection through legal means.

i. Isolate the institutions of the National Popular Army from political issues and struggles, to hold them to their constitutional duties.

2. Procedures

a. Remove the Prohibition of the Islamic Salvation Front.

b. Remove the state of emergency and all extra-legal measures, and allow the police to resume its normal security operations, and to free the work in the arenas of politics, media, social and missionary from any fetters.

c. Stop the confrontations between the two sides, after expanding the process of consultation to include all whose participation will be necessary in reaching decisions, and to postpone dealing with all unresolved issues relating to the conflict until legitimate rule has been established.

d. Compensate all victims of the crisis.

e. Release all prisoners, and stop legal and extra-legal executions, and cease all pursuits of individuals and groups, with returning civil and political rights to all.

f. Appoint a neutral government that would be given the task to organize elections and [manage] civil matter[s], and to establish a committee to oversee the implementation of the agreement, and that would regulate all the procedures of return to legitimate rule [...]

g. Work to re-establish normal life, and lift all emergency rules, particularly in the field of the media, and to encourage all political and social forces to [safeguard civil liberties.]

h. Announce the agreement in total transparency according to the manner agreed upon by the two parties.

3. Initial Procedures (The Authorities will commit to implement these immediately after implementing the initial agreement.)

a. Release the older prisoners and the active leadership, and remove all restraints in order to allow them to seriously pursue a solution.

b. Close all prisons in the desert, and release all women prisoners.

c. Improve the situation of the prisoners.

d. Cease from escalating the official media campaign.

e. The way the media handles these procedures will be regulated by the two parties.

4. Basic Observation

This document is the result of discussions of the *shuyukh* of the Islamic Salvation Front, who are part of the permanent leadership of that organization. It is the end result of an arduous series of contacts and discussions with representatives of the interim government. It represents preliminary suggestions, and includes necessary principles and procedures for ending the crisis. After discussions with the government, the latter must allow the *shuyukh* to expand the consultation about the preliminary agreement—that is the result of these discussions—to anyone whose participation they [the *shuyukh*] deem necessary for making the decision or implementing it, so that the agreement will be finalized.

The *Shuyukh* [Imprisoned]: Madani Abbasi, Ali Ben Hadjm Abd al-Qadir Hashani; [Free]: Abd al-Qadir Khamkham, Ali Jaddi, Kamal Qammazi, Umar Abd al-Qadir.

8.   Report on Arab Israelis: Breaking the Stranglehold of Alienation, October 27, 2000

In June 1948 Israel was founded as a "Jewish state." However, this narrowly focused designation was immediately undermined by the presence of a steadily growing Arab minority. As the percentage of Arabs within the Israeli population has grown, Arabs' visibility in society and politics has increased. After remaining politically quiet and rather invisible through the 1970s, the Arab community has begun to assert its political weight by voting for Jewish Knesset (Israeli parliament) members sympathetic to the causes of Arabs in Israel or for Arab-Israeli candidates.

Culturally, the moment when many Israeli Jews came to acknowledge the presence of Arabs in their midst was the publication of Anton Shammas's novel Arabesques in 1986. Shammas, an Arab Israeli, wrote in Hebrew. Arabesques is a fictionalized memoir and account of his childhood and life in the so-called Jewish state, whose definition erases his memories of his Palestinian roots and denies his right to exist as a full citizen. The maelstrom that erupted around the publication of the book and the accolades it received brought to Israeli national consciousness questions about the nature of the state and its definition. Since that time, the discussion has increased in intensity with the numerical growth of the Arab community and the increase in Arabs' social, economic, and cultural influence.

At the beginning of the confrontation between Palestinians in the Occupied Territories and the Israeli army that started in September 2000, many Arab Israelis *took to the streets to protest Israeli policies in the Territories and, at the same time, to protest their own status as second-class citizens. These demonstrations and the heavy-handedness of Israeli police efforts to put them down ignited once more the discussions about the definition of the "state" of Israel and its relationship to the Arab citizens. The following document, which appeared in Ha'aretz, a center-leftist Israeli newspaper, is an example of these discussions about an ongoing crisis.*

From the heights of the Katzir settlement, standing on the ridge that overlooks Wadi Ara from the southwest, the picture is clear. From here, looking down onto the Arab villages in the valley, "it isn't difficult to understand why the Arabs feel strangled, and why they are bursting with rage," says Shuli (Shalom) Dichter, co-director of Sikkuy, an association involved in the struggle for equal rights for the Arab citizens of Israel. Dichter, a resident of Wadi Ara, explains that government strategy regarding the Arab communities in the region is one of enclosure, i.e., of restricting the potential for Arab growth by means of a belt of Jewish settlements on the south side of the valley, and a wide stretch of land, the disputed al-Roha lands that the Israel Defense Forces commandeered more than two years ago for public purposes, to the north. "That's the whole story," Dichter says, "both from a physical and from a consciousness-symbolic point of view."

For Dichter, the story dates back to his childhood. He grew up on Kibbutz Ma'anit, at the entrance to Wadi Ara, with the slogan that Ma'anit "plowed the first furrow of Jewish settlements" on the western slopes of the hills of Samaria. Founded in 1942 by the Hashomer Hatzair movement, the kibbutz, according to Dichter, was intended to drive a wedge between the settlements of Wadi Ara and those of the Triangle region and to upset the closely-knit, rural Arab web that existed there.

In 1948, the Arab settlements of Wadi Ara absorbed numerous refugees from the Jezreel Valley and expanded significantly. The population of these settlements continued to increase as a result of natural growth. Since the establishment of the state, the Arab population has increased sixfold; the land it occupies, on the other hand, has shrunk by some 40 percent. There has not been a single new Arab settlement established in Israel since 1948.

Wadi Ara is still licking its wounds from the outburst of violence in the area at the beginning of the month [October 2000]. Vandalized by the demonstrators, the traffic lights at some of the crossroads along Road 65 are still not functioning. Electricity and telephone services in the villages are not yet fully operational because the Israel Electric Corporation and Bezeq technicians are afraid to enter them. Jewish suppliers are not sending goods to the stores. Some of the towns are still flying black flags in memory of residents killed in the riots.

Dichter's car passes by the peace-and-coexistence sukka (a hut traditionally constructed for the Jewish festival of Tabernacles). The sukka was set up by the Menashe local council, most residents of which are Jewish, at the southern entrance to the valley. "Together, we will halt the destruction," boasts a large banner above the sukka. Dichter laughs: "We'll love you, but don't run riot any more," he spits out mockingly. The old format of coexistence has been destroyed, he says, and it's a good thing. Dichter proposes building on the ruins with an alternative relationship between Jews and Arabs in Israel.

In June of this year, the association headed by Dichter—together with his Arab co-director, Dr. Assad Ganem, a political science lecturer at The University of Haifa—published its annual report on equality and the integration of Arab citizens within the state. The report systematically reviews one government ministry after another, revealing the Jewish majority's discrimination against the Arab minority, which makes up 18.6 percent of the population of the country. The so-called coexistence between Jews and Arabs in Israel has been based on the very discrimination that cries out from the pages of the report.

This basis—the "fragile texture of the relationship" between Jews and Arabs and between Arab citizens and the establishment—is "an exhausted structure that cannot be relied on," writes Dichter in the preface to the report. Preserving this fragile texture, he writes, is tantamount to maintaining a status quo of inequality, which "certainly does not ensure stability in the relations between the citizens."

Dichter was not surprised by the outburst of rage among Arab citizens of the country. The "delicate tissue" of the relations between the two nationalities in Israel has been stretched, like a membrane, across a reality of inequality, injustice and oppression, he says. Now, "the coexistence has turned out to be a bluff that has blown up in our faces"; it has existed in the framework of a controlling relationship—an uneven relationship between a ruling majority and a ruled minority.

These same sentiments were expressed among Arab Israelis years ago, filtering through into the public consciousness. Jews who are involved in contacts and dialogue with Arabs are also beginning to internalize this awareness now. One of them is Ronen Dori, a resident of Katzir and principal of the Mevo'ot Iron comprehensive high school that serves the Jewish settlements in the area.

Some three years ago, Dori's school joined a project known as YAMI (the Hebrew acronym for "children teaching children"), which was designed to promote understanding between Arab and Jewish children. The Arab children were to teach Arabic to the Jewish children, while the Jewish children were to teach Hebrew to their Arab compatriots.

The equation soon proved to be flawed: The Arab children already knew Hebrew; the Jewish children found it difficult to communicate with their Arab counterparts, believing them to be conservative and too patriotic; the Arab children couldn't free themselves of nationalist and political rhetoric.

The Jewish children, Dori says, felt they were making a huge sacrifice just by agreeing to visit Umm al Fahm. After the customary cordialities, their Arab hosts told them exactly how they felt about the Jewish public. Among other things, one of the Arab students said that if they could, the Palestinian citizens of Israel would wipe out the Jews. The Jewish students, most of whom live on the kibbutzim of the Hashomer Hatzair movement, were shocked. "Concerned parents called after the meetings and said: 'What's going on here? You have turned our children into fascists,'" Dori recalls.

"Rather than bringing people closer together," Dori says, "the project erected walls of alienation." He and his colleagues decided, therefore, that before trying to bring the two populations closer together, it would be best to first focus on laying the groundwork for such a process by dedicating two school hours a week to discussions on civics, tolerance, differences and identity. The other teachers and school principals involved in the YAMI project adopted a similar approach.

"I realized that the perception of coexistence that formed the basis of the project was wrong; coexistence hadn't proved itself. It hadn't got us anywhere because we hadn't touched on the nerve center of the Arab society," Dori says. He adds that the next stage in the relationship between the two nations "must be full participation of the Arab Israelis, with affirmative action and complete equality. Our quality of life as Jews in this country will be influenced by the living conditions of our friends no less than by our own living conditions—not just from an economic point of view, but from all aspects. Participation will bring responsibility, and responsibility is the basis for good citizenship."

A village of some 36,000 residents, which was declared a city but looks like a refugee camp bursting at the seams, Umm al Fahm is sorely lacking in land and adequate infrastructure. The municipality has an overall deficit of some NIS 25 million, with a current deficit of around NIS 3.5 million. The municipal tax collection rate is a mere 11 percent.

Based on the figures accompanying a four-year development program for the Arab sector, approved this week by the government, this is the typical profile of an Arab local council, providing public services accordingly. The buildings in Umm at Fahm are so "tightly packed" that some of the alleyways between them aren't wide enough for four-wheel vehicular transport.

Umm at Fahm's distress is particularly stark in relation to the conditions at the nearby cooperative settlement, Mei Ami. The Jewish settlement is spacious and green. Each of the 50 families lives in a handsome, single-storey house. In the afternoons, the moshav is empty and quiet.

Mei Ami and Umm al Fahm are separated by the access road to the Jewish settlement, along which the residents of Mei Ami are making every effort to preserve a distance from the houses of the Arabs—something like a demilitarized zone. One of the houses of Umm al Fahm that is located near the road is that of Khaled Mahamid. For the past three years, the owner's son, attorney Ra'id Mahamid, has been fighting against a petition that was submitted to the High Court of Justice by members of the Jewish settlement. The petitioners want the court to order the authorities to carry out a demolition order that was issued against a portion of Mahamid's house; the reason for the demolition order: renovation work that the Mahamid family did inside the house itself. Mahamid consulted with the local planning and building committee, which told him that renovations inside a house do not require a permit. The regional committee thought otherwise.

Mahamid's house was built in the late 1950s. The road to Mei Ami was paved in the early 1970s. After the road was paved, a number of residents of

Umm al Fahm, Mahamid's neighbors, renovated and enlarged their houses, while others built new ones; the residents of Mei Ami complained. The legal authorities approved demolition orders, but did not implement them.

In 1995, the management committee of Mei Ami petitioned the High Court of Justice, demanding that the houses be demolished. A separate petition was filed with regard to the Mahamid family home, which was renovated in 1997. The petition was upheld and the court granted the authorities a number of extensions for the implementation of the order; the last of which comes to an end in December. The Mahamid family is living in fear: Any day now, a demolition team could come and tear down their house.

The Mahamid family home is just one of the 20,000 houses in the Arab sector over which a demolition order hangs. The authorities issue such orders, but in most cases, they are not carried out. There's no need to; a "marked" house, with the demolition axe at its neck, conveys a message to others to refrain from any building in the vicinity.

The most popular medical clinic in Umm al Fahm is the al-Nur clinic of the Islamic Movement. It is located on the ground floor of a large mosque in the "city" and is equipped with one of the three mammography instruments that exist in Arab settlements (the other two are in Nazareth). There are 62 such machines in Jewish towns and cities in Israel, despite the fact that the incidence of breast cancer among Arab women is higher than that among Jewish women. The clinic is so proud of its mammography unit that it still boasts the celebratory banners that were posted to mark the opening of the unit more than 18 months ago.

The willingness of Arab women to undergo checkups has increased significantly over the past two years, but for most of them, access to mammography is problematic. Three machines are simply not sufficient for a population of almost two million people.

At the entrance to Umm al Fahm—across from the petrol station that was torched and is yet to be renovated, and opposite the junction at which youths confronted police for more than a week—lies the al-Babur restaurant. Prior to the recent violent incidents, most of its patrons were Jewish Israelis. Today, for the most part, the restaurant is empty. Brothers Nassat and Hussam Abbas, dejected in the face of the losses they have suffered since Rosh Hashanah, wonder whether relations between Jews and Arabs in Israel have reached a point of no return. Nassat is convinced that the past situation will soon be restored and that Jews will return to dine in their restaurant. Hussam is not so sure. "This time, it was different," he says. "This time, people were killed—many people."

Shuli Dichter believes there is a chance, but that it does not lie in returning to the status quo of the past. On the contrary, he says, "despite all the pain, now is the time for goodwill," now is the time in which coexistence can be based on a profound recognition of the fact that living together also includes an element of conflict between two communities with different national identities. In fact, he says, the state now has the power to channel the national conflict between the two communities toward a democratic, parliamentary, civic struggle, with full participation for all.

It's possible, Dichter says, "if only the state would recognize the collective rights of the Arabs, just as it recognizes those of the Jews." And this includes everything—from signposts and the names of junctions and streets, to the equal distribution of resources.

PART IV

The Middle East Today

The 1991 Gulf War ushered in a new phase in the history of the Middle East. The war was the culmination of a series of crises that thoroughly discredited and delegitimized most of the authoritarian states in the Middle East. After 1967 the military or military-supported states in the Middle East came under mounting criticism for their mismanagement of national economies, their brutal political oppression, their suppression of freedom, and their political and military ineptitude. Alternative ideas previously considered by only a few groups or intellectuals gained popularity during the last three decades of the twentieth century. These ideas can be loosely grouped into three categories: political Islam, secular minority-group ideas, and economic reform.

Political Islam first appeared in the living rooms of America in 1979, in news reports of blindfolded Americans being held hostage by a group of bearded and jubilant students in Tehran. Since that time, Islam has acquired the reputation of being a religion of fanaticism, irrationality, and hatred of the "West." In popular media the word *jihad*—mistranslated as "holy war"—has been used repeatedly to connote those tendencies and to position "Islam" as the new threat—after the collapse of the Soviet Union—to Western civilization. [In reality, *jihad* means "struggle" and can manifest itself in three different ways. The most important of these manifestations is the act of cleansing oneself from sin. The least important of these is "jihad of the sword" or war, which is to be conducted only in the defense of Muslims and strictly prohibits killing noncombants.]

Widespread acceptance of these notions is unfortunate, because they are not correct. This is not to deny that some Muslims carry out acts of violence and justify them in the name of their religion. Such groups of extremists have always existed across the spectrum of secular and religious ideologies, but the existence of such groups among Muslims, for example, should not be interpreted to mean that all Muslims are prone to violence. A moment of reflection reveals that such a generalization is as absurd as the idea that all Christians, Jews, or Buddhists are of one nature and one nature only. The notion that Islamic groups are anti-Western, medieval, or traditional is equally unfortunate. Indeed, many members of Islamic political movements are fully immersed in the modern world. Rather than seeking to retreat from it to a premodern existence, their intent is to shape modernity according to their understanding of religion and its precepts.

Apart from these considerations is the complicated task of understanding why Islamic political movements have acquired prominence and attracted a greater following since the 1970s. Instead of dismissing such movements, we must try to understand—even if we happen to disagree with and disapprove of their goals and tactics—who they are, what they seek, and how they came about.

One of the first clues to the rise of vibrant Islamic political movements is to be found in the crisis of the state—the theme of the chapter "Crisis of the State." The emergence of military dictatorships, and of regimes dependent on military support, such as Iran or Turkey, in many countries of the Middle East and North Africa considerably limited the opportunity for political expression and opposition. For example, during the 1960s and 1970s, the shah's government established single-party rule in Iran, and the rubberstamp Iranian parliament made a mockery of constitutional government. Moreover, the shah's secret police—the notorious Savak—established an extensive spy network whose sole purpose was to monitor, arrest, torture, and sometimes kill opponents of the regime. This trend, common throughout the Middle East and North Africa, left only a few public spaces where people could voice their discontent. Among the most prominent were mosques or religious institutions, which could be controlled or co-opted to some extent but, unlike secular political parties and their offices, not closed or suppressed.

In addition, at various times, many countries in these regions underwent severe economic crises. Part of the blame can be placed at the feet of ruling elites who mismanaged state funds through incompetence and corruption. However, other structural problems also contributed to these downturns. Rapid population growth, especially among the young in the second half of the twentieth century, meant that a diminishing percentage of the population had to produce enough to feed and satisfy the needs of an increasingly larger segment of society. More to the point, as young men and women finished their education, they expected jobs that would allow them to live independent lives (their own apartments, marriage, children, and so on). Unfortunately, even the strongest economies could not have accommodated this surge in the labor force, and the economies of Egypt, Algeria, and Syria were hardly strong. For example, Algeria's main source of hard currency was (and still is) the export of petroleum. As oil prices took a downturn in the 1980s, state revenues also plummeted. This meant that services, which the state had been providing (such as subsidies of food, transport, and fuel), had to be cut severely, and it was the Algerian lower classes who bore the brunt of the cuts. Simultaneously, the one safety valve—emigration to France—that in the 1960s and 1970s had allowed hundreds of thousands of young Algerians to escape poverty was being shut. Economic hard times in France and an intolerant mood of racism against Arabs meant that few Algerians were allowed to immigrate into France during the latter part of the 1980s. Together the decrease in oil prices and the closing off of French borders to Algerians left hundreds of thousands of young Algerian men and women jobless and penniless. The unemployment rate in Algeria in 1989 was 36 percent, and it was double that among the eighteen-to-twenty-five age group. This situation left many frustrated and angry, and as they searched for reasons for their dilemma, they focused on their government as the culprit.

The globalization of Western—particularly American—culture also had some detrimental effects on many societies in the Middle East and North Africa (for documents pertaining to this issue, see the chapter "The Future of the Middle East and North Africa"). The spread of American pop music, fashion, food chains, and movies and television brought a set of values at times jarring to many local sensibilities. For example, the 1970s television show *Dallas* was one of the most popular shows in Egypt. On Thursday evenings the streets of Cairo were nearly empty as people followed the unfolding soap opera of immense wealth, unbridled greed, barely concealed sex, and betrayal. Although all these themes were, of course, familiar to the elites of Egypt, they remained private matters, not public displays as on *Dallas.* The show contradicted the premises of public morals in Egyptian society and created tension between local values inculcated through upbringing and foreign values projected from television sets. Some Egyptians found this tension threatening because it represented a loss of "authenticity" and morality. Without necessarily agreeing with such dire and one-sided assessments, we can still understand the reasons for and costs of such tension on society. What complicated this cultural clash—whether perceived or real—was the imbalance in power behind the cultural representations. *Dallas,* Coca-Cola, and McDonald's arrived in these societies with far more polished images (even if the content left much to be desired) than the images of any local products; foreign companies sometimes dwarfed their local counterparts. Only those few Egyptians who had disposable income could afford to drink Coke, eat at McDonald's, and wear Nike shoes. Thus, Western products became expensive icons of cultural superiority and symbols of class divisions and gave rise to further tension.

Islamic political movements became popular after 1967 because—for many of the lower classes—they held the promise of resolving these tensions. Various Islamic political movements applied the vague notion that "Islam is the Solution" to political, economic, and cultural problems. Modern Islamic thinkers such as Sayyid Qutb, Ayatollah Khomeini, and Abbas Madani gave a political voice to people who had been deprived of one. Their ideology promised a more equitable distribution of income without resorting to communism, and it provided the framework for an "authentic" and strong culture. Beyond these vague promises, there existed (and still exists) a very wide spectrum of

Islamically based programs. In fact, the very meaning of Islam as a way of life continues to be debated throughout the Islamic world. Thus, we cannot speak of a singular Islamic political movement or aim.

The forces that help explain the rise of Islamic political movements also produced secular movements that were suspicious of the Islamists and rejected the imposition of religious solutions and ideas on society. Since the 1970s, feminists, environmentalists, homosexuals, and ethnic minorities have sought to deal with the same issue as the Islamists, but from a secular perspective. The fact that they have not been as successful, organized, or well financed as the Islamists does not detract from their critical role in shaping the regions today. Their voices, ideas, and arguments indicate the diversity of opinion in the Middle East and North Africa. The existence of these various viewpoints is evidence of the expansion of the call for democracy. There have always been such voices, but now they are more vocal and determined. They are achieving gains not thought possible only twenty years ago. For example, in Iran (which is seen by the United States as a theocratic and medieval state) democracy is flourishing in astonishing ways—from an overwhelming 96 percent turnout for elections to an astounding number of magazines and newspapers that insistently (despite frequent closures) demand reforms and greater freedoms. Even in Syria, where the Assad state has long been able to dominate public discourse, new public intellectual "salons" were held in 2000 to demand a loosening of government control over freedom of speech and political opposition.

Running somewhat in tandem with these new movements is the attempt to construct new types of economies throughout the two regions. This movement—labeled *khaskhasa,* or privatization—is made up of private and public initiatives (with a great deal of encouragement from the United States, the European Union, and the World Bank) that seek to turn state-owned institutions and factories into privately and semi-privately held interests. The privatization movement extends from public utilities to banks and factories. Several factors are propelling it. Most notable is the fact that in the rush toward globalization of trade and commerce, with few exceptions (Tunisia and Israel) the states of the Middle East and North Africa lag far behind the economies of the so-called Asian Tigers, the United States, and Europe. This economic trend has political ramifications that threaten the hold of the ruling elites, so the concern for creating a more open economy has been growing steadily among them. Less cynically, most governments do express some level of concern for the welfare of the population and consider the lack of economic opportunities to be detrimental to the nation as a whole.

Yet the trend toward privatization has also raised some serious concerns. Critics argue that it is nothing more than a process that is opening their countries further to American and European economic dominance. They concede that privatization may help a small segment of society, but they contend that its overall cost for the less fortunate majority is too high. Globalization too seems to be nothing more than a continuation and intensification of "Western" domination, which is generating a sense of alienation among young men and women.

Thus, the shift toward a more privatized economy appears to have contradictory and controversial impacts on the societies of the Middle East.

The documents in this part of the book highlight the historical forces and ideas explored in this introduction. These documents cover the spectrum from a sampling of the writing of one of the most influential and revolutionary Islamic political thinkers of the twentieth-century—Sayyid Qutb—to a feminist interpretation of the rights of women in Islam; from the comments of homosexuals in Egypt to the complaints of Arab soccer players in Israel; and from the declaration of the Iranian Communist party to a discussion of the impact of globalization on the Middle East.

CHAPTER 8

Islamic Political Movements
Since 1964

Until 1979 most Americans were ignorant of Islam in its multiple manifestations. The Iranian revolution of that year and later events brought this ignorance to an abrupt end. Unfortunately, this new encounter resulted from violence. Islam acquired a reputation for violence in the American media because of a series of attacks by "Muslims" on American interests culminating in the atrocities of September 11, 2001. Subsequently, many pundits, academics, and foreign policy experts told American audiences that the only interaction with "Islam" was through violence. Hollywood released one film after another depicting dark-skinned, supposedly Arabic-speaking terrorists attacking the United States. Mutual distrust created a chasm that was widened by ignorance. "Why do they hate us?" asked people on both sides of the divide.

This chapter presents some documents intended to achieve three goals. The first is to explain the rise of Islamic political movements (the "Islamists") in the Middle East and North Africa as a phenomenon of the late twentieth century. The second is to present liberal views of Islam that are at odds with the more extreme interpretations of that religion. The third is to present the most extreme Islamist vision—that of Usama Bin Laden and the World Islamic Front (document 6). All of these documents together show the breadth of interpretation within modern Islamic movements.

A variety of Islamic political movements emerged in the late 1960s and became viable and credible political movements after the 1980s. Scholars do not agree on a single reason that led to the rise of Islamist movements, but most agree that common historical political, economic, and cultural factors are behind the emergence of most of them. In the postindependence period, most state regimes ruling over a majority of Muslims tended to be authoritarian. This was most definitely the case in the Middle East, as we saw in the preceding part of this book. The political repression practiced to varying degrees by these regimes minimized legitimate political opposition and almost completely crushed secular liberal and leftist opposition. In some cases, such as in Egypt, the state achieved this outcome through an alliance with "moderate" Islamists, who provided the state with legitimacy and support in its repressive campaigns. In other places, such as Iran, repression extended to religious as well as secular opposition. This repression, carried out by pro-Western and pro-Soviet regimes alike, discredited not only the regimes themselves in the eyes of the majority of the population, but also the regimes' supporters: the United States and the Soviet Union. Thus, there emerged a movement seeking an "authentic" form of political expression that would not fall into either camp. Islam—or, more accurately, politicized Islam—provided this new ideology.

The concept of political Islam is not new. Throughout Islamic history there have been self-consciously Islamic movements whose purpose was to renew and reform Islam in a manner that would recapture the presumed utopia of Medina at the time of the Prophet. While most of these movements did not intend to re-create the time of the Prophet, they did seek to rediscover the "purity" of original Islam as they assumed it was when Muhammad was the leader of the umma, the community of believers. This idealized past gave impetus over the course of Islamic history to a variety of movements that can be labeled reformist. In the eighteenth century one such movement—the Wahabis— swept through the Arabian Peninsula seeking to eradicate popular forms of Islam and unify Muslims under its strict interpretation of the religion. Other such movements coursed through West Africa, Libya, and Sudan during the nineteenth century. The Muslim Brotherhood was yet another such movement in Egypt during the first half of the twentieth century.

This genealogy of political movements contains the common thread of attempts to renew the religion (a tendency found in every religion). Yet despite the universalist claims of these movements, each was solidly grounded in its own local historical circumstances. Moreover, the articulation of a new Islamist ideology—presented most clearly and radically by Sayyid Qutb (document 1)— did not mean that every Muslim joined one of these organizations. Membership began to swell only as the economic well-being of the region took a sharp downturn in the 1980s because of the fall of oil prices and a general worldwide recession. These economic hard times meant that many university-educated men were hard-pressed to find employment and start families. Frustration over their economic misery—accentuated by the conspicuous consumption of the ruling elites—drove some *but not all* of these young men to seek meaning for their lives in different venues. The most extreme tended to join extremist Islamic movements that promised justice and equality in the wake of an anticipated Islamic revolution. The Iranian revolution of 1979 stood as proof that such a revolution was possible even against the most powerful of Westernized and Western-supported regimes.

The rise of globalization with its overwhelmingly Westernized culture threatened to rob people in the Middle East and North Africa of their identity and to replace it with a consumption-driven one. This threat was real to people on the receiving end of American products ranging from lurid TV shows such as *Dallas* and *Baywatch* to Nike shoes and Levi's jeans. This cultural onslaught was another factor that propelled some to seek refuge and certainty in their Islamic faith.

Yet all of these factors did not produce a common notion of what "Islam" is and how it pertains to daily life. Conservative Muslim thinkers argued that Islam contains a blueprint for a state and society that is culturally authentic, politically just, and economically equitable. This vision, however, was difficult to implement to the satisfaction of all, and many ideas emerged about the meaning of an "Islamic state." Conservatives insisted that the process leading to the attaining of an Islamic state had to be legal and peaceful. A small minority disagreed. They argued that there could be no negotiations with non-Muslims or with heretical Muslims (the extremists themselves decided what constituted "heresy"). Nor could there be any accommodation of multiple points of view about the nature of the state in a predominantly Islamic country. Instead, they contended, a fundamentalist re-creation of the early Islamic society and state offered the only possible solution to the woes mentioned previously. Also there emerged at this time a group of Muslims who sought to interpret Islam as a liberal religion quite compatible with modern politics, society, and economy. They still saw in it a means to create a distinct and strong identity in the face of external threats. And they insisted that this identity would allow Muslims to engage the world in a dignified dialogue rather than turn inward into an isolated and xenophobic space.

The documents presented in this chapter cover this vast expanse of interpretation and help us to understand that Islam, like Christianity or the elusive "West," is far from monolithic. Sayyid Qutb (document 1) and his successor Usama Bin Laden (document 6) articulate a new and militant vision of jihad that exhorts Muslims to understand and use their religion as an activist political ideology facing a hostile world composed of heretics and unbelievers. Confronting this particular interpretation are the more humanistic and liberal views of the Iranian thinkers Ali Shari'ati (document 2) and Mehdi Bazargan (document 3), who see Islam as a religion that promotes social justice and allows for liberal thought. Fatima Mernissi (document 4) goes one step further and argues that Islam has been misinterpreted from a conservative male perspective, thus rendering its application oppressive to women. She argues that a proper understanding of the teachings of the Qur'an and of the Prophet would in fact provide Muslim women with greater freedoms and rights than they currently enjoy in most Muslim societies. According to Farag Foda (document 5), an Egyptian journalist who was assassinated for his secular views, Islam should remain an issue of personal faith with little if any role in public life. His caustic editorials about Islamic conservatives and extremists sought to highlight the absurdities of modern religious politics and thought in Egypt. Finally, Ehsan Ahrari and Muna Shuqair (document 7) reflect from differing perspectives on the events of September 11, 2001. While acknowledging that the perpetrators of these terrorist attacks were religious extremists who are the products of secular events, the two authors differ in their explanation for the reasons behind the emergence of such groups. Ehsan Ahrari argues that these aberrant individuals and groups are signs—and products—of the internal flaws of un-democratic Arab societies that have been saddled by authoritarian, corrupt, and incompetent regimes. Muna Shuqair, on the other hand, argues that U.S. policies in the Middle East and North Africa are at least in part responsible for engendering the anger and hostility that led to the events of September 11.

1. Egyptian Writer Sayyid Qutb Articulates a New, Influential Vision of Jihad, 1964

Sayyid Qutb (1906–1966) is arguably the most influential writer on political Islam to have emerged in the last fifty years. Qutb seems to have provided many modern Islamic political groups with their ideological justification for opposing—sometimes violently—the state and for rejecting its authority as "un-Islamic." In the early part of his life (before the 1950s) Qutb was a moralist who wrote essays exhorting Muslims to adhere to the ethical values of Islam in their daily existence. However, after spending two years in the United States (1948–1950), and after being introduced to the writings of another Islamic political writer, Sayyid Mawdudi, he became convinced that only the establishment of an Islamic state would allow for the existence of a just and moral society. In other words, he came to the conclusion that individual morality could not survive or even be perfectly attained as long as the society and the state remained in a state of immorality. Thus, upon his return to Egypt, he joined the Muslim Brotherhood (see document 12, about Hasan al-Banna, in the chapter "Ideas of Nationalism") and became chief editor of the Brotherhood newspaper. In 1954—when the Brotherhood was outlawed on the pretext that it was trying to overthrow the Egyptian government—Qutb was sentenced to fifteen years in jail, of which he served ten. During this period his ideas about the Islamic state and society fully matured, and when he was released in 1964 (because of the intercession of many Muslim figures), he wrote his most famous work, Milestones. Because of this book he was arrested a second time and sentenced to death for inciting Muslims to revolt against the secular government of Gamal Abdel Nasser.

When writers with defeatist and apologetic mentalities write about "Jihaad in Islam," and try to remove this 'blot' from Islam, they mix up two things: first, that this religion forbids the imposition of its belief by force, as is clear from the verse: "There is no compulsion in religion" (2:256), while on the other hand it tries to annihilate all those political and material powers which stand between people and Islam, which force one people to bow before another people and prevent them from accepting the sovereignty of God. These two principles

Sayyid Qutb, *Milestones* (Lahore: International Islamic Federation of Student Organizations, 1977), pp. 102–114, 131–140.

have no relation with each other nor is there room to mix them. In spite of this, these defeatist-type people try to mix the two aspects and want to confine Jihaad to what today is called "defensive war." The Islamic Jihaad has no relationship to modern warfare, either in its causes or in the way in which it is conducted. The causes of Islamic Jihaad should be sought in the very nature of Islam and its role in the world, in its high principles, which have been given to it by God and for the implementation of which God appointed the Prophet— peace be on him—as His Messenger and declared him to be the last of all prophets and messengers.

This religion is really a universal declaration of the freedom of man from servitude to other men and from servitude to his own desires, which is also a form of human servitude; it is a declaration that the sovereignty belongs to God alone and that He is the Lord of all the worlds. It means a challenge to all kinds and forms of systems which are based on the concept of the sovereignty of man; in other words, where man has usurped the Divine attribute. Any system in which the final decisions are referred to human beings, and in which the sources of all authority are human, deifies human beings by designating others than God as lords over men. This declaration means that the usurped authority of Allah be returned to Him and the usurpers be thrown out—those who by themselves devise laws for others to follow, thus elevating themselves to the status of lords and reducing others to the status of slaves. In short, to proclaim the authority and sovereignty of God means to eliminate all human kingship and to announce the rule of the Sustainer of the universe over the entire earth. In the words of the Qur'an,

> "He alone is God in the heavens and in the earth." (43:84)

> "The command belongs to God alone. He commands you not to worship anyone except Him. This is the right way of life." (12:40)

> "Say: O People of the Book, come to what is common between us: that we will not worship anyone except God, and will not associate anything with Him, and will not take lords from among ourselves besides God; and if they turn away, then tell them to bear witness that we are those who have submitted to God." (2:64)

The way to establish God's rule on earth is not that some consecrated people—the priests—be given the authority to rule, as was the case with the rule of the Church, nor that some spokesmen of God become rulers, as is the case in a "theocracy." To establish God's rule means that His laws be enforced and that the final decision in all affairs be according to these laws.

The establishing of the dominion of God on earth, the abolishing of the dominion of man, the taking away of sovereignty from the usurper to revert it to God, and the bringing about of the enforcement of the Divine Shari'ah and the abolition of man-made laws cannot be achieved only through preaching. Those who have usurped the authority of God and are oppressing God's creatures are not going to give up their power merely through preaching; if it had been so, the task of establishing God's religion in the world would have been very easy for the Prophets of Allah! This is contrary to the evidence from the history of the Prophets and the story of the struggle of the true religion, spread over generations.

This universal declaration of the freedom of man on the earth from every authority except that of God, and the declaration that sovereignty is God's alone and that He is the Lord of the universe, is not merely a theoretical, philosophical and passive proclamation. It is a positive, practical and dynamic message with a view to bringing about the implementation of the Shari'ah of God and actually freeing people from their servitude to other men to bring them into the service of God, the One without associates. This cannot be attained unless both "preaching" and "the movement" are used. This is so because appropriate means are needed to meet any and every practical situation.

Because this religion proclaims the freedom of man on the earth from all authority except that of God, it is confronted in every period of human history—yesterday, today or tomorrow—with obstacles of beliefs and concepts, physical power, and the obstacles of political, social, economic, racial and class structures. In addition, corrupted beliefs and superstitions become mixed with this religion, working side by side with it and taking root in peoples' hearts.

If through "preaching" beliefs and ideas are confronted, through "the movement" material obstacles are tackled. Foremost among these is that political power which rests on a complex yet interrelated ideological, racial, class, social and economic support. Thus these two—preaching and the movement—united, confront "the human situation" with all the necessary methods. For the achievement of the freedom of man on earth—of all mankind throughout the earth—it is necessary that these two methods should work side by side. This is a very important point and cannot be over-emphasized.

This religion is not merely a declaration of the freedom of the Arabs, nor is its message confined to the Arabs. It addresses itself to the whole of mankind, and its sphere of work is the whole earth. Allah is the Sustainer not merely of the Arabs, nor is His providence limited to those who believe in the faith of Islam. Allah is the Sustainer of the whole world. This religion wants to bring back the whole world to its Sustainer and free it from servitude to anyone other than God. In the sight of Islam, the real servitude is following laws devised by someone, and this is that servitude which in Islam is reserved for God alone. Anyone who serves someone other than God in this sense is outside God's religion, although he may claim to profess this religion. The Prophet—peace be on him—clearly stated that, according to the Shari'ah, "to obey" is "to worship." Taking this meaning of worship, when the Jews and Christians "disobeyed" God, they became like those who "associate others with God."

Tirmidhi has reported on the authority of 'Adi bin Hatim that when the Prophet's message reached him, he ran away to Syria (he had accepted Christianity before the Prophet's time), but his sister and some of the people of his tribe became prisoners of war. The Prophet—peace be on him—treated his sister kindly and gave her some gifts. She went back to her brother and invited him to Islam, and advised him to visit the Prophet—peace be on him. 'Adi agreed to this. The people were very anxious to see him come to Medina. When he came into the presence of the Prophet, he was wearing a silver cross. The Prophet—peace be on him—was reciting the verse, "They (the People of the Book) have taken their rabbis and priests as lords other than God." 'Adi reports: "I said, 'They do not worship their priests.'" God's Messenger replied, "Whatever their priests and rabbis call permissible, they accept as permissible, whatever they declare as forbidden, they consider as forbidden, and thus they worship them."

This explanation of the above verse by the Prophet—peace be on him—makes it clear that obedience to laws and judgments is a sort of worship, and anyone who does this is considered out of this religion. It is taking some men as lords over others, while this religion has come to annihilate such practices, and it declares that all the people of the earth should become free of servitude to anyone other than God.

If the actual life of human beings is found to be different from this declaration of freedom, then it becomes incumbent upon Islam to enter the field with preaching as well as the movement, and to strike hard at all those political powers which force people to bow before them and which rule over them, unmindful of the commandments of God, and which prevent people from listening to the preaching and accepting the belief if they wish to do so. After annihilating the tyrannical force, whether it be in a political or a racial form, or in the form of class distinctions within the same race, Islam establishes a new social, economic and political system, in which the concept of the freedom of man is applied in practice.

It is not the intention of Islam to force its beliefs on people, but Islam is not merely "belief." As we have pointed out, Islam is a declaration of the freedom of man from servitude to other men. Thus it strives from the beginning to abolish all those systems and governments which are based on the rule of man over men and the servitude of one human being to another. When Islam releases people from this political pressure and presents to them its spiritual message, appealing to their reason, it gives them complete freedom to accept or not to accept its beliefs. However, this freedom does not mean that they can make their desires their gods, or that they can choose to remain in the servitude of other human beings, making some men lords over others. Whatever system is to be established in the world ought to be on the authority of God, deriving its laws from Him alone. Then every individual is free, under the protection of this universal system, to adopt any belief he wishes to adopt. This is the only way in which "the religion" can be purified for God alone. The word "religion" includes more than belief; "religion" actually means a way of life, and in Islam this is based on belief. But in an Islamic system there is room for all kinds of people to follow their own beliefs, while obeying the laws of the country which are themselves based on the Divine authority.

Anyone who understands this particular character of this religion will also understand the place of Jihaad bis saif (striving through sword), which is to clear the way for striving through preaching in the application of the Islamic movement. He will understand that Islam is not a "defensive movement" in the narrow sense which today is technically called a "defensive war." This narrow meaning is ascribed to it by those who are under the pressure of circumstances and are defeated by the wily attacks of the orientalists, who distort the concept of Islamic Jihaad. It was a movement to wipe out tyranny and to introduce true freedom to mankind, using resources according to the actual human situation, and it had definite stages, for each of which it utilised new methods.

It we insist on calling Islamic Jihaad a defensive movement, then we must change the meaning of the word "defense" and mean by it "the defense of man" against all those elements which limit his freedom. These elements take the form of beliefs and concepts, as well of political systems, based on economic, racial or class distinctions. When Islam first came into existence, the world was full of such systems, and the present-day Jahiliyyah also has various kinds of such systems.

When we take this broad meaning of the word "defense," we understand the true character of Islam, and that it is a universal proclamation of the freedom of man from servitude to other men, the establishment of the sovereignty of God and His Lordship throughout the world, the end of man's arrogance and selfishness, and the implementation of the rule of the Divine Shari'ah in human affairs.

As to persons who attempt to defend the concept of Islamic Jihaad by interpreting it in the narrow sense of the current concept of defensive war, and who do research to prove that the battles fought in Islamic Jihaad were all for the defense of the homeland of Islam—some of them considering the homeland of Islam to be just the Arabian peninsula—against the aggression of neighboring powers, they lack understanding of the nature of Islam and its primary aim. Such an attempt is nothing but a product of a mind defeated by the present difficult conditions and by the attacks of the treacherous orientalists on the Islamic Jihaad.

Can anyone say that if Abu Bakr, 'Umar or 'Othman had been satisfied that the Roman and Persian powers were not going to attack the Arabian peninsula, they would not have striven to spread the message of Islam throughout the world? How could the message of Islam have spread when it faced such material obstacles as the political system of the state, the socioeconomic system based on races and classes, and behind all these, the military power of the government?

It would be naive to assume that a call is raised to free the whole of humankind throughout the earth, and it is confined to preaching and exposition. Indeed, it strives through preaching and exposition when there is freedom of communication and when people are free from all these influences, as "There is no compulsion in religion"; but when the above-mentioned obstacles and practical difficulties are put in its way, it has no recourse but to remove them by force so that when it is addressed to peoples' hearts and minds, they are free to accept or reject it with an open mind.

Since the objective of the message of Islam is a decisive declaration of man's freedom, not merely on the philosophical plane but also in the actual conditions of life, it must employ Jihaad. It is immaterial whether the homeland of Islam—in the true Islamic sense, Dar ul-Islam—is in a condition of peace of whether it is threatened by its neighbours. When Islam strives for peace, its objective is not that superficial peace which requires that only that part of the earth where the followers of Islam are residing, remain secure. The peace which Islam desires is that the religion (i.e., the law of the society) be purified for God, that the obedience of all people be for God alone, and that some people should not be lords over others. After the period of the Prophet—peace be on him—only the final stages of the movement of Jihaad are to be followed; the initial or middle stages are not applicable. They have ended, and as Ibn Qayyim states: "Thus, after the revelation of the chapter 'Bra't,' the unbelievers were of three kinds: adversaries in war, people with treaties, and Dhimmies. The people with treaties eventually became Muslims, so there were only two kinds left: people at war and Dhimmies. The people at war were always afraid of him. Now the people of the whole world were of three kinds: one, the Muslims who believed in him: two, those with whom he had peace (and from the previous sentence we understand that they were Dhimmies): and three, the opponents who kept fighting with him."

These are the logical positions consonant with the character and purposes of this religion, and not what is understood by the people who are defeated by present conditions and by the attacks of the treacherous orientalists.
[...]

As we have described earlier, there are many practical obstacles in establishing God's rule on earth, such as the power of the state, the social system and traditions and, in general, the whole human environment. Islam uses force only to remove these obstacles so that there may not remain any wall between Islam and individual human beings, and so that it may address their hearts and minds after releasing them from these material obstacles, and then leave them free to choose to accept or reject it.

We ought not to be deceived or embarrassed by the attacks of the orientalists on the origin of Jihaad, nor lose self-confidence under the pressure of present conditions and the weight of the great powers of the world to such an extent that we try to find reasons for Islamic Jihaad outside the nature of this religion, and try to show that it was a defensive measure under temporary conditions. The need for Jihaad remains, and will continue to remain, whether these conditions exist or not!

In pondering over historical events, we should not neglect the aspects inherent in the nature of this religion, its declaration of universal freedom, and its practical method. We ought not to confuse these with temporary needs of defense.

No doubt this religion must defend itself against aggressors. Its very existence in the form of a general declaration of the universal Lordship of God and of the freedom of man from servitude to any being other than God, and its organising a movement under a new leadership other than the existing jahili leadership, and its creating a distinct and permanent society based on the Divine authority and submission to One God, is sufficient cause for the surrounding jahili society, which is based on human authority in some form or another, to rise against it for its own preservation and for the suppression of Islam. Clearly, under these conditions, the newly-organised Islamic community will have to prepare itself for defense. These conditions inevitably occur and come into existence simultaneously with the advent of Islam in any society. There is no question of Islam's liking or disliking such a situation, as the struggle is imposed upon Islam; this is a natural struggle between two systems which cannot co-exist for long. This is a fact which cannot be denied, and hence Islam has no choice but to defend itself against aggression.

But there is another fact which is much more important than this fact. It is in the very nature of Islam to take initiative for freeing the human beings throughout the earth from servitude to anyone other than God; and so it cannot be restricted within any geographic or racial limits, leaving all mankind on the whole earth in evil, in chaos and in servitude to lords other than God.

It may happen that the enemies of Islam may consider it expedient not to take any action against Islam, if Islam leaves them alone in their geographical boundaries to continue the lordship of some men over others and does not extend its message and its declaration of universal freedom within their domain. But Islam cannot agree to this unless they submit to its authority by paying Jizyah, which will be a guarantee that they have opened their doors for the preaching of Islam and will not put any obstacle in its way through the power of the state.

This is the character of this religion and this is its function, as it is a declaration of the Lordship of God and the freedom of man from servitude to anyone other than God, for all people.

There is a great difference between this concept of Islam and the other, which considers it confined to geographical and racial limits, and does not take any action except out of fear of aggression. In the latter case, all its inherent dynamism is lost.

To understand the dynamism of Islam with clarity and depth, it is necessary to remember that Islam is a way of life for man prescribed by God. It is not a man-made system, nor an ideology of a group of people, nor a way of life peculiar to a given race. We cannot talk about external reasons for Jihaad unless we overlook this great truth and unless we forget that the fundamental question here is the sovereignty of God and the obedience of His creatures, it is impossible for a person to remember this great truth and still search for other reasons for Islamic Jihaad.

The true estimate of the difference between the concept that war was forced upon Islam by Jahiliyyah because its very nature demanded that jahili societies would attack it, and the concept that Islam takes the initiative and enters into this struggle, cannot be made in the early stages of its movement.

In the early stages of the Islamic movement it is difficult to discriminate between these two concepts, because in either case Islam will have to do battle. However, in the final stages, when the initial battles are won, the two concepts make a great difference—a great difference in understanding the purposes and the significance of the Islamic message. And herein lies the danger.

There is also a great difference in the idea that Islam is a Divinely-ordained way of life and in the idea that it is a geographically-bounded system. According to the first idea, Islam came into this world to establish God's rule on God's earth, to invite all people toward the worship of God, and to make a concrete reality of its message in the form of a Muslim community in which individuals are free from servitude to men and have gathered together under servitude to God and follow only the Shari'ah of God. This Islam has a right to remove all those obstacles which are in its path so that it may address human reason and intuition with no interference and opposition from political systems. According to the second idea, Islam is merely a national system which has a right to take up arms only when its homeland is attacked.

In the case of either concept, Islam has to strive and to struggle; but its purposes and its results are entirely different, both conceptually and practically.

Indeed, Islam has the right to take the initiative. Islam is not a heritage of any particular race or country; this is God's religion and it is for the whole world. It has the right to destroy all obstacles in the form of institutions and traditions which limit man's freedom of choice. It does not attack individuals nor does it force them to accept its beliefs; it attacks institutions and traditions to release human beings from their poisonous influences, which distort human nature and which curtail human freedom.

It is the right of Islam to release mankind from servitude to human beings so that they may serve God alone, to give practical meaning to its declaration that God is the true Lord of all and that all men are free under Him. According to the Islamic concept and in actuality, God's rule on earth can be established only through the Islamic system, as it is the only system ordained by God for all human beings, whether they be rulers or ruled, black or white, poor or rich, ignorant or learned. Its law is uniform for all, and all human beings are equally responsible within it. In all other systems, human beings obey other human beings and follow man-made laws. Legislation is a Divine attribute; any person who concedes this right to such a claimant, whether he considers him Divine or not, has accepted him as Divine.

Islam is not merely a belief, so that it is enough merely to preach it. Islam, which is a way of life, takes practical steps to organise a movement for freeing man. Other societies do not give it any opportunity to organise its followers according to its own method, and hence it is the duty of Islam to annihilate all such systems, as they are obstacles in the way of universal freedom. Only in this manner can the way of life be wholly dedicated to God, so that neither any human authority nor the question of servitude remains, as is the case in all other systems which are based on man's servitude to man.

Those of our contemporary Muslim scholars who have been defeated by the pressure of current conditions and the attacks of treacherous orientalists, do not subscribe to this characteristic of Islam. The orientalists have painted a picture of Islam as a violent movement which imposed its belief upon people by the sword. These vicious orientalists know very well that this is not true, but by this method they try to distort the true motives of Islamic Jihaad. But our Muslim scholars—these defeated people—search for reasons of defense with which to negate this accusation. They are ignorant of the nature of Islam and of its function, and that it has a right to take the initiative for human freedom.

These research scholars, with their defeated mentality, have adopted the Western concept of "religion," which is merely a name for "belief" in the heart, having no relation to the practical affairs of life, and therefore they conceive of religious war as a war to impose belief on peoples' hearts.

But this is not the case with Islam, as Islam is the way of life ordained by God for all mankind, and this way establishes the Lordship of God alone—that is, the sovereignty of God—and orders practical life in all its daily details. Jihaad in Islam is simply a name for striving to make this system of life dominant in the world. As far as belief is concerned, it clearly depends upon personal opinion, under the protection of a general system in which all obstacles to freedom of personal belief have been removed. Clearly this is an entirely different matter and throws a completely new light on the Islamic Jihaad.

Thus, wherever an Islamic community exists which is a concrete example of the Divinely-ordained system of life, it has a God-given right to step forward and take control of the political authority, so that it may establish the Divine system on earth, while it leaves the matter of belief to individual conscience. When God restrained Muslims from Jihaad for a certain period, it was a question of strategy rather than of principle; this was a matter pertaining to the requirements of the movement and not to belief. Only in the light of this explanation can we understand those verses of the Holy Qur'an which are concerned with the various stages of this movement. In reading these verses, we should always keep in mind that one of their meanings is related to the particular stages of the development of Islam, while there is another general meaning which is related to the unchangeable and eternal message of Islam. We should not confuse these two aspects.

2. Iranian Intellectual Ali Shari'ati Examines Man from the Viewpoint of Islam, 1968

Like many secular and religious Iranian thinkers, Ali Shari'ati (1933–1977) grew up in the middle of the twentieth century aware of the economic, political, and social problems that embroiled Iran. He experienced the abject poverty of the lower classes during his years at the Teacher's Training College. He was well aware of the

Ali Shari'ati, "Man and Islam," *On the Sociology of Islam*, trans. Hamid Algar (Berkeley, Calif.: Mizan Press, 1968), pp. 70–81, a translation of *Insan va Islam*, a lecture given at the Petroleum College of Abadan. The introductory paragraph has been omitted. Reprinted by permission.

political dissatisfaction with the shah of Iran and the criticism of the shah's author-itarian rule (see Khomeini's denunciation of the shah—document 3 in the chapter "Crisis of the State"). However, one of the elements that distinguished Shari'ati was the eclectic nature of his education. After receiving his degree from the Teacher's College, he received a scholarship to complete his graduate studies at the Sorbonne, from which he received a doctorate in sociology in 1965. Upon his return to Iran he was immediately arrested on the charges that he had participated in anti-shah po-litical activities in Paris. After being released, he taught sociology at Mashhad Uni-versity and attracted a large following. After he was expelled from the university, he continued to lecture at Hussein-e-Ershad Religious Institute. While there, he became extremely popular: literally thousands of students attended his lectures, and his first book sold over sixty thousand copies in its first edition despite government attempts to limit its availability.

This popularity was due to the fact that Shari'ati was an intellectual who sought to understand the problems of Muslim societies and to find solutions deriv-ing as much from that context as from his understanding of Western ideas. He be-lieved and argued that Islam and Islamic history contain within them the means to modernize Islamic societies. Indeed, he did not regard "Western" humanitarian val-ues to be at odds with Islamic religious ideas and practices—as some other secular intellectuals postulated. Rather, he contended that the two could and should inter-mingle as long as this interaction takes place in a manner that does not dilute or dismiss Islamic values. The popularity of these ideas and his implied and open criti-cism of the shah's regime led to his expulsion from Iran in 1977 to London, where he was assassinated by the Savak, the shah's secret police.

The question of man is the most important of all questions. The civilization of today is based upon humanism, the nobility of man and the worship of man. It is believed that the religions of the past crushed the personality of man and compelled him to sacrifice himself to the gods. They forced him to regard his own will as totally powerless when confronted by the will of God. They com-pelled him always to be seeking something from God by way of prayer, sup-plication and entreaty. The philosophy of humanism is, then, a philosophy that, since the Renaissance, has opposed religious philosophies—philosophies founded on belief in the unseen and supranatural realm—and its aim has al-legedly been to restore nobility to man. The roots of humanism lie in Athens, but as a universal philosophy, it has become the basis of the modern civilization of the West. In reality, it arose as a reaction to scholastic philosophy and me-dieval Christianity.

My purpose tonight is to examine—within the limits of my capability and the present occasion—the question of man from the viewpoint of our religion, Islam, and to seek an answer to the question: what kind of a phenomenon does Islam see in man? Does it see in man a powerless creature whose ultimate aim and ideal is to stand helpless before God? Does Islam deny man all notion of nobility? Or, on the contrary, does belief in Islam itself impart a form of no-bility to man, and make an acknowledgement of his virtues? This is the topic I wish to discuss.

In order to understand the place of "humanism" in different religions, and the concept of man that each of them holds, it is best to study the philosophy of the creation of man that each has set forth. However, I do not have the opportunity now to examine all the religions of East and West from this point of view. I will speak only of the philosophy of creation that exists in Islam and those pre-Islamic religions of which Islam is the continuation—the religions of Moses, Jesus and Abraham.

How is the creation of man explained in Islam or the Abrahamic scriptures, of which Islam is the culmination and perfection? Can we deduce the status and nature of man from the manner in which the creation of man is described in the Qur'an, the Word of God, or in the words of the Prophet of Islam? From examining the story of Adam—the symbol of man—in the Qur'an, we can understand what kind of a creature man is in the view of God and therefore in the view of our religion. By way of introduction, let me point out that the language of religion, and particularly the language of the semitic religions, in whose prophets we believe, is a symbolical language. By this we mean a language that expresses meaning through images and symbols—the most excellent and exalted of all the languages that men have ever evolved. Its value is more profound and eternal than that of expository language, i.e., the clear and explicit language that expresses meaning directly. A simple and straightforward language, one deprived of all symbol and image, may be easier for purposes of instruction, but it has no permanence. For, as the celebrated Egyptian philosopher Abd ar-Rahman Badawi has pointed out, a religion or philosophy that expounds all of its ideas and teachings in simple, one-dimensional and straightforward language will not be able to survive. Those addressed by religion or philosophy represent different types and classes—both the common folk and the educated. The audience of a religion is, moreover, not a single generation or age, but different and successive generations which follow upon each other throughout history. They inevitably differ with each other with respect to way of thought, level of thought, and angle of vision. The language that a religion chooses in order to convey its concepts must, then, be a versatile and multi-faceted language, each aspect and facet of which addresses itself to a particular generation and class of men. If the language be monofaceted, it will be comprehensible only to a single class, and totally without value for all other classes; accessible to one generation, but beyond the reach of the next. It will be impossible to extract any new meaning from it. It is for this reason that all literary works written in symbolic language are immortal. For example, the poems of Hafiz are immortal, and whenever we read them we deduce a new meaning from them, in proportion to the depth of our thought and taste and outlook. But the history of Bayhaqi is something different, as is, too, the *Gulistan* of Sa'di. When we read the *Gulistan*, its meaning is quite apparent to us, and we enjoy its verbal beauty and structure. But many of the ideas it contains are outmoded, precisely because it is clear what Sa'di had to say, and what he had to say is false! But the style of Hafiz is multi-faceted and symbolical; depending on his taste and manner of thought, everyone can interpret its symbols in a certain sense, thus deducing new meanings from the text.

It is for this reason that religions must employ a symbolic language; they are addressed to different human types and different generations of men. There are numerous concepts in religion that were not clearly understood at the time of their appearance. If religion had *not,* on the one hand, expressed its ideas in common, familiar language, it would have been incomprehensible to the people of that age; but if it *had* expressed its ideas in common language, religion would have had no meaning in later times. It was therefore necessary that religion should speak in images and symbols that would become comprehensible with the development of human thought and science. Symbolism represents the highest of styles in European literature—symbolism, which is the art of speaking in symbols and images and concealing profound ideas in images that apparently mean something else but have an inner significance that man can discover in accordance with his own degree of profundity.

It was necessary, then, that the story of the creation of Adam, of man, be told in symbolic fashion, so that today, after fourteen centuries of progress in the human and natural sciences, it should still be readable and comprehensible.

How was man created, in the view of Islam?

First God addresses the angels, saying, "I wish to create a viceregent for Myself upon earth." See how great is the value of man according to Islam! Even the post-Renaissance humanism of Europe has never been able to conceive of such exalted sanctity for man. God, Who in the view of Islam and all believers, is the greatest and most exalted of all entities, the creator of Adam and the master of the cosmos, addresses the angels and presents man to them as His viceregent. The whole mission of man according to Islam becomes evident from this divine address. The same mission that God has in the cosmos, man must perform on earth as God's viceregent. The first excellence that man possesses is, then, being God's representative on earth.

The angels cry out saying, "You wish to create one who will engage in bloodshed, crime, hatred and vengeance." (Since before Adam, there had been other men who, like the man of today, busied themselves in bloodshed, crime, corruption and sin, and the angels wished to remind God that if He were to create man again and grant him a second opportunity on earth, man would again engage in bloodshed and sin.) But God replies, "I know something that you do not know," and then sets about the task of creating man.

It is at this point that the symbolic aspect of the narrative begins. See what profound truths concerning man are hidden beneath these symbols! God desires to create a viceregent for Himself out of earth, the face of the globe. One might expect that the most sacred and valuable of materials would have been selected, but God chose, on the contrary, the lowest of substances. The Qur'an mentions on three occasions the substance from which man was fashioned. First it uses the expression "like potter's clay" (55:14); that is, dry, sedimentary clay. Then the Qur'an says, "I created man from putrid clay" (15:26), foul and evil-smelling earth; and finally it uses the term *tin,* also meaning clay (6:2,

23:12). So God set to work, and willed to create a viceregent for Himself; this precious viceregent He created out of dry clay, and then He inhaled some of his own spirit into the clay, and man was created.

In human language, the lowest symbol of wretchedness and baseness is mud. No creature exists in nature lowlier than mud. Again in human language, the most exalted and sacred of beings is God, and the most exalted, sacred and noble part of every being is its spirit. Man, the representative of God, was created from mud, from sedimentary clay, from the lowliest substance in the world, and then God inhaled into him not His blood or His body— so to speak—but His spirit, the most exalted entity for which human languages possess a name. God is the most exalted of beings, and His spirit is the most exalted entity conceivable, the most exalted concept that could ever arise in the human mind.

Thus man is a compound of mud and divine spirit, a bi-dimensional being, a creature with a dual nature, as opposed to all other beings which are one-dimensional. One dimension inclines to mud and lowliness, to stagnation and immobility. When a river overflows, it leaves behind a certain muddy sediment that lacks all motion and life, and the nature of man, in one of its dimensions, aspires to precisely this state of sedimentary tranquility. But the other dimension, that of the divine spirit, as it is called in the Qur'an, aspires to ascend and to mount up to the highest summit conceivable—to God and the spirit of God.

Man is composed, then, of two contradictory elements, mud and the spirit of God; and his splendor and importance derive precisely from the fact that he is a two-dimensional creature. The distance between his two dimensions is the distance between clay and the spirit of God. Every man is endowed with these two dimensions, and it is his will that enables him to decide either to descend toward the pole of sedimentary mud that exists in his being, or to ascend toward the pole of exaltation, of God and the spirit of God. This constant striving and struggle takes place in man's inner being, until finally he chooses one of the poles as the determinant for his destiny.

After thus creating man, God taught him the names. (As will be apparent to you, I am paraphrasing the verses of the Qur'an as I proceed.) What does this teaching of the names mean? It is not yet certain. Everyone has expressed a certain opinion, and every commentator has suggested his own interpretation. Everyone has interpreted it according to his own outlook and way of thought. But whatever be the correct explanation, there can be no doubt that the verse centers on the notion of teaching and instruction. When the creation of man was completed, God taught His viceregent the names so that man became a possessor of the names. Then the angels cried out in protest, "We were created of smokeless fire and man was created of clay; why do you prefer him to us?" And God replies, "I know something you do not know; fall down at the feet of this two-dimensional creature of mine." All the angels of God, great and small, are commanded to fall down in prostration before this creature.

This is true humanism. See how great is the dignity and stature of man; so great, indeed, that all the angels, despite their inherent superiority to man and the fact that they are created of light while he is created of mud and clay, are commanded to fall down before him. God tests them because of their protest, and asks the angels concerning the names; they do not know the names, but Adam does know them. The angels are defeated in this test, and the excellence of Adam—which lies in his knowledge of the names—becomes apparent. This prostration of the angels before Adam serves to clarify the Islamic concept of man. Man knows certain things that the angels do not know, and this knowledge endows man with superiority to the angels despite the superiority of the angels to man with respect to race and origin. In other words, the nobility and dignity of man derive from knowledge and not from lineage.

Another point to be considered is the creation of woman from the rib of man, at least according to the translations usually made from the Arabic.[1] But the translation "rib" is incorrect, and the word so translated has the real meaning, in both Arabic and Hebrew, of "nature, disposition or constitution." Eve—that is, woman—was created, then, out of the same nature or disposition as man. Since the word has been mistranslated as "rib," the legend arose that woman was created from the left rib of Adam, and therefore all women are lacking one rib!

A great man like Nietzsche said that man and woman were created as totally separate creatures, and only came to resemble each other because of their constant association through history. The ancestries of man and woman he held to be totally different. Almost all scholars and philosophers have conceded that man and woman are of the same stock, yet they have always tried to belittle the nature of woman and present the nature of man as superior. But the Qur'an says, "We have created Eve from the same nature or disposition as Adam; man and woman proceed from the same substance."

Another remarkable matter concerning the creation of man is that God summons all of His creation, all the phenomena of nature such as inanimate objects, plants, animals, and tells them, "I have a trust that I wish to offer to all of you—earth, heavens, mountains, oceans and beasts." They all refuse to accept it, and instead, man accepts it. It is thus clear that man has another virtue and excellence, deriving from his courageous acceptance of the Trust that God offered to all beings and they rejected. Man is not only the viceregent of God in this world and on this earth, but also—as the Qur'an makes clear—the keeper of His Trust. Now what is the meaning of the Trust? Everyone says something different. Maulana Jalal ad-Din Rumi says that the Trust means man's will, his free will, and this is also my opinion.

It is by means of his will that man attains superiority over all other creatures in the world. He is the only being able to act counter to his own instinctual nature, something no animal or plant can do. For example, you will never

---

[1]The creation of Eve is not directly mentioned in the Qur'an, so the author is presumably referring to accounts such as that given in Kisa'i's *Qisas al-Anbiya*, Cairo, 1312, pp. 18 ff. (TR.) [All footnotes in this document are Algar's.]

encounter an animal voluntarily engaging in a two-day fast, or a plant committing suicide out of grief. Plants and animals can neither render great services nor commit treachery. It is not possible for them to act in a way different from that in which they have been created. It is only man who can rebel against the way in which he was created, who can defy even his spiritual or bodily needs, and act against the dictates of goodness and virtue. He can act either in accordance with his intelligence or in opposition to it. He is free to be good or to be evil, to resemble mud or to resemble God. Will is, then, the greatest property of man, and the affinity between God and man is apparent from this fact.

For it is God Who inhales into man some of His own spirit and makes of him the bearer of His Trust, and man is not merely the viceregent of God upon earth but also His relative—if the expression be permitted. The spirits of God and man both possess an excellence deriving from the possession of will. God, the only entity and being possessing an absolute will and capable of doing whatever it wishes, even in contradiction to the laws of the universe, inhales some of His spirit in man. Man can act like God, but only to a certain degree; he can act against the laws of his physiological constitution only to the extent permitted by his similarity to God. This is the aspect held in common by men and God, the cause of their affinity—free will, the freedom for man to be good or evil, to obey or rebel.

The following conclusions can be drawn with regard to the philosophy of the creation of man in Islam:

All men are not simply equal; they are brothers. The difference between equality and brotherhood is quite clear. Equality is a legal concept, while brotherhood proclaims the uniform nature and disposition of all men; all men originate from a single source, whatever their color.

Secondly, man and woman are equal. Contrary to all the philosophies of the ancient world, man and woman were created out of the same substance and material at the same time and by the same Creator. They share the same lineage, and are brothers and sisters to each other, descended from the same mother and father.

Thirdly, the superiority of man to the angels and the whole of creation derives from knowledge, since man learned the names and the angels fell in prostration before him; despite the superiority of their descent to that of man, they were compelled to humble themselves before him.

More important than all this, man's being stretches out over the distance between mud and God, and since he possesses will, he can choose either of the two opposing poles these represent. Again since he possesses will, a certain responsibility comes into being. From the point of view of Islam, man is the only being responsible not only for his own destiny but also for the fulfillment of a divinely entrusted mission in this world; he is the bearer of God's Trust in the world and in nature. It is he who has learned the names—and, in my opinion, the proper meaning of "names" is the truths of science, since the name of a thing is its symbol, its defined, conceptual form. The teaching of the names by God means, therefore, the bestowal of the ability to perceive and comprehend the scientific truths inherent in the world. Through this primordial instruction by God, man gained access to all the truths existing in the world, and this constitutes a second great responsibility for man. Man must fashion his destiny with his own hands. Human society is responsible for its own fate, and the human individual is responsible for his own fate: "Yours is what you acquire and theirs is what they acquire" (Qur'an, 2:134). The fate of past civilizations is no more and no less than what they brought down on themselves, and your fate will consist exactly of what you are now fashioning with your own hands. Man thus has a great responsibility toward God, since he possesses free will.

Here we must add this observation, that history has witnessed a great tragedy; namely, man has not been recognized as a two-dimensional being. In contrast with other religions that posit God and the Devil to exist within nature in mutual combat, Islam teaches that only one force exists in nature—the force of God. But within man, Satan wages war against God, and man is their battlefield. The dualism of Islam, unlike religions of the past, posits the existence of two "deities," two hypostases, in the inner being and disposition of man, not in nature. Nature knows only of a single hypostasis; it belongs to the realm, and is subject to the will, of a single power, the power of God. In Islam, Satan is not a contestant with God; he is a contestant against man, or rather against the divine half of man. And since man is a two-dimensional creature composed of God and of clay, he has need of both elements. The religion and ideology that he needs to believe in and to found his life upon must fulfill both kinds of need and pay both of them due attention. The tragedy is that history tells a different tale. History tells us that all societies and civilizations were oriented exclusively either to the hereafter and renunciation of this world, or to this world of dust. The civilization of China began by being oriented to this world, by giving primacy to pleasure and beauty and striving to enjoy the gifts of nature to the full, as the life of the Chinese aristocracy testifies. Then came Lao Tse, bringing a religion exclusively oriented to the hereafter, and emphasizing the spiritual and other-worldly dimension of man. Indeed, he led the Chinese so far in that direction, that a people who had lived purely for the sake of pleasure became monks, gnostics and mystics. He was succeeded by Confucius, who reoriented society toward this world and summoned the Chinese to the pleasures of worldly life, causing them to revert to their former preoccupations.

India, the land of rajas and legends, was oriented to the other world by the teachings of the Vedas and the Buddha, devoting itself to abstemiousness, monasticism and mysticism. It is for this reason that India is now famous for men sleeping on beds of nails, or subsisting for forty days on a single date or almond, for remaining behind the progress of civilization.

In Europe, ancient Rome devoted itself to murder and bloodshed, to establishing political mastery of the world, to accumulating all the wealth of Europe and Asia; it immersed itself in enjoyment and pleasure, in gladiator fights and the like. Then came Jesus, who directed society to concentrate on the hereafter, so that Rome changed its orientation from pleasure and worldliness to asceticism and contemplation of the hereafter, the ultimate result of this being the Middle Ages. The medieval world was one of war and bloodshed and military ascendance on the one hand; and one of monasteries, nunneries and retreats, on the other. Europe was delivered from this orientation only by the Renaissance, which caused the pendulum to swing in the other direction. Today we see that European civilization is so worldly in its orientation, and so exclusively defines the purpose of man's life as pleasure and enjoyment, that, as Professor Chandel has put it, the life of contemporary man consists only of making the tools of life. This is the idiocy of the contemporary philosophy of man, the result of a purpose-free technology. The whole meaning of civilization has been robbed of any ideal, and the world has gone so far in the direction of worldliness that it almost seems as if another Jesus were needed.

As is apparent from the philosophy of man in Islam, he is a two-dimensional being and needs, therefore, a religion which will also be two-dimensional and exert its force in the two different and opposing directions that exist in man's spirit and human society. Only then will man be able to maintain his equilibrium. The religion needed is Islam.

Why Islam?

In order to understand any religion, one must study its God, its Book, its Prophet, and the best individuals whom it has nurtured and raised.

First, the God of Islam is a two-dimensional God. He has the aspect of Yahwa, the god of the Jews, who interests himself in human society, in the affairs of this world, who is stern, severe in punishment, and tyrannical, and also the aspect of the god of Jesus, who is compassionate, merciful and forgiving. All of these divine attributes can be found in the Qur'an.

As for the book of Islam, the Qur'an, it is a book that like the Torah contains social, political and military provisions, even instructions for the conflict of warfare, the taking and setting free of prisoners; that is interested in life, in building, in prosperity, in struggling against enemies and negative elements; but it is also a book that concerns itself with the refinement of the soul, the piety of the spirit, and the ethical improvement of the individual.

The Prophet of Islam also possesses two contrasting aspects, aspects which would be contradictory in other men, but in him have been joined in a single spirit. For he was a man constantly engaged in political struggle against his enemies and the disruptive forces in society, concerned with building a new society and a new civilization in this world; and also a guide leading men to a particular goal; that is, also a man of prayer, piety and devotion.

And then three men trained by him—Ali, Abu Dharr and Salman—were supreme examples of two-dimensional men. They were both men of politics and battle, struggling for a better life and constantly present in circles of discussion and learning, and also men of piety and purity, not less than the great monks and mystics of the East. Abu Dharr was a man of politics and piety; the reflections of Abu Dharr concerning the nature of God can serve as a key to the understanding of the Qur'an. Look at all the Companions of the Prophet; they were all men of the sword, concerned with improving their society, men of justice, and at the same time, great men of thought and feeling.

The conclusion I wish to draw is this: in Islam man is not humbled before God, for he is the partner of God, His friend, the bearer of His trust upon earth. He enjoys affinity with God, has been instructed by Him, and seen all of God's angels fall prostrate before him. Two-dimensional man, bearing the burden of such responsibility, needs a religion that transcends exclusive orientation to this world or the next, and permits him to maintain a state of equilibrium. It is only such a religion that enables man to fulfill his great responsibility.

3. Iranian Liberal Mehdi Bazargan Advocates Freedom as a Vital Necessity for Government and Religion, 1974

Mehdi Bazargan (1907–1995) was one of the leading liberal Islamic thinkers in Iran. Throughout his life, he attempted to achieve democracy within Iranian politics, as well as within the conservative Shi'a clerical establishment. While Shah Muhammad Reza Pahlavi was in power through the 1960s and 1970s, Bazargan maintained his opposition to that regime through organizations like the Iranian Human Rights Association, which he cofounded in 1977. After the 1979 revolution, Khomeini appointed Bazargan to the position of prime minister, only to work constantly against his policies. This led Bazargan to leave the government in frustration and to spend the twilight of his political life in opposition to the radical Islamic government and the attempts by the conservative clerics to maintain a stranglehold on power in Iran.

Freedom as a Vital Necessity for Government and Religion

Let me reiterate: freedom means freedom to oppose, criticize, and object—even if the criticism is untrue and unjust. Where there is freedom there are opponents and currents that disturb routine stability and normalcy. Otherwise, freedom would be meaningless and useless.

This notion of freedom is hard for many zealous—if sincere—people to digest, as they consider such a freedom unwise and deleterious to the survival of the nascent Islamic Republic [of Iran]. They may even consider it a blunder on their part to have allowed this notion of freedom to prevail in the constitution of the Islamic Republic of Iran.

Mehdi Bazargan, *Din va Azad: Bazyayi-ye arzesh'ha* (Religion and Liberty) (Tehran: Netzahe Azadi-ye Iran, 1983), pp. 59–88. This document, translated by Mohammad Sadri, can also be found in Charles Kurzman, *Liberal Islam* (New York: Oxford University Press, 1996), pp. 81–84. Reprinted by permission.

However, omniscient, compassionate God has not only sanctioned freedom in many affairs, he has made it the very foundation of survival and revival in the world. Let me elaborate on this point.

Opposition, the Cause of Movement and Life

In general, an object in a given force field will, of necessity, behave in a calculable and predictable way. For any object, whether a stone, a plant, or a human society, force means movement. For example, a piece of metal that is released within earth's gravitational field will fall in a straight line. Its position and velocity are calculable at every moment. Similarly, the behavior of a human being who is motivated only by the demands of his or her appetite is predictable. However, if in the place of one force, two or more forces are introduced—for example if a powerful magnet is placed in the path of the falling piece of metal—its trajectory and velocity will change. It will, to use a poetic expression, be freed from the slavery of a single cause of motion. The scenario is most intriguing when the affected object has the power to choose its level of susceptibility to the external influences. That is, when it has "free will." In this case, the person whose choice is not readily predicable and calculable for others—or even for oneself—could be said to possess "free will."

Therefore, freedom requires, as the case of Satan's temptations teach us, the existence of an oppositional force, along with a power of choice on behalf of the individual or the society. Opposition promulgates movement and change, which may, in turn, lead to decline or progress, depending on the choice of the agent involved.

Motion and change in the case of inanimate objects, even constructed objects such as machines, lead to erosion and deterioration (in the jargon of thermodynamic theory, the increase of entropy). In other words, inanimate objects aim at final rest and quiet. However, objects endowed with life, particularly human beings, thrive on movement and opposition. They acquire new capabilities and aptitudes and accumulate experience and virtue because of opposition and change. Movement, a result of need, agitation, and love, is a blessing and a source of survival and evolution, while rigidity is a cause of stasis, decline, and death. Animals and human beings, once they feel need, danger, or attraction, tend to move, willy-nilly, either toward the object of their desire or away from the source of danger. Therefore, without opposition, as a source of motivation or agitation there would be no progress.[1] The oppositional motivator can lead to reform and revival.[2]

---

[1] See my *'Eshq va parastesh, ya termodinamik-e ensan* [*Love and Worship, or the Thermodynamics of Humanity*].

[2] It is obvious that opposition in this context is an external force, different from materialist-dialectical opposition, involving an internal antithesis that is said to be inevitable, global, and social.

Our Islamic Revolution, our nationalist struggles, revivalist Islamic associations and movements, the earlier Constitutional Revolution of Iran—the awakening and activism of the Eastern countries in general after several hundred years of slumber and humiliation—were all the result of the encounter with Western civilization. The wondrous European Renaissance too was a result of conflicts, dissatisfactions, and objections to medieval Christian hegemony.

Similarly, the missions of the prophets were in the past the source of conflicts that revolutionized towns and tribes that were wallowing in the darkness of idolatry and the cesspool of corruption and inequity.

Conflict, one of whose quintessential representations for human beings is Satan, is the cause of a plethora of blessed events, from the natural cycle of life here on earth to the higher cycle of resurrection in the hereafter. The Qur'an frequently compares the colossal events of Judgment Day with seasonal rain and the revival of life on earth. Rain itself is the result of atmospheric disturbances and opposing forces of cold and warm weather systems. The science of meteorology has established, through hourly reports from weather stations, that rain-bearing continental weather fronts are comprised of successive fronts of dense clouds. These clouds are the result of expanding, rising, and condensing warm tropical weather and its collision with the cold and heavy weather systems that flow from the northern regions. The heavy winds occupy the lower areas and push the warm humid weather up.[3]

The Opponents of Freedom

The opponents of freedom resort to the adage: "A head that does not ache does not need to be wrapped." Their argument goes like this: We know we are on the true path. We believe in Islam and possess good will and proper judgment. What need is there for further inquiry and learning? We can simply devote ourselves, body and soul, to the realization of the true doctrine. The entire nation and its leadership support this endeavor, Why should we let the enemies of God and the republic, the supporters of America, or those who do not follow our line—in short, people of suspicious intent or judgment—to muddy the waters, confuse minds, disturb society, and weaken the government? Such freedom and criticism will provide fodder for foreign radio propaganda which will, in turn, cause our youth to hesitate or deviate from the straight path. It is thus better to remove all the impediments from the path of the revolution and to conduct our affairs quickly and effectively—that is, without the nagging distractions of free expression and opposition.

These gentlemen, even if they are sincere, are deluded and naive about their own monopoly of the truth and about the notion of freedom. Freedom is

---

[3]See [my] book *Bad va baran dar Qur'an* [*Wind and Rain in the Qur'an*] where many verses (more than 115 passages) are quoted that bear witness to this argument. [A series of citations follows.—Editor]

not a luxury; it is a necessity. When freedom is banished, tyranny will take its place.

In the first place, those whose belief system is based on reason and truth are not afraid of opponents' criticism and propaganda. In the words of Sa'di [Persian poet, 1184–1292], "He who has clear accounts, has no fear of accountants."

Secondly, freedom of expression, opposition, and criticism awakens the negligent and holds back treason, monopoly, and tyranny. If the objections are unjustified, let the accused respond and thus dispel the clouds of suspicion and slander. This will strengthen the national resolve. The Qur'an considers such examinations as the means of separating the good from the bad.[4] Conversely, suppression of freedom is an indication of a fundamental weakness or flaw in the government's intentions or actions. Consider the following Qur'anic debate: a believer in the pharaoh's family reasons with his affluent and powerful kin to listen to the message of Moses: "If he is a liar, his lie will be his own loss; but in case he speaks the truth, some of what he predicts will befall you." (Sura 40, Verse 28) In response, the pharaoh reiterates the argument of all dictators, tyrants, and zealots: "I show you only what I see (is right); and guide you but to the right path." [Sura 40, Verse 29] How can people exercise their religious obligation to call others to virtue and to warn them against vice in an Islamic society, without the freedom of conscience and expression, and in the absence of political and legal security? These are duties that Muslims are recommended to fulfill lest evil-doers dominate them and their prayers remain unanswered.

Thus the survival of a just system and its progress on the path of virtue and excellence is guaranteed by the freedom of expression and legal opposition. The protection of religion against abuse, ignorance, superstition, and deviance, too, requires that the mace of excommunication and compulsion be removed from society and the media. It is necessary to avoid painting a varnish of religiosity and godliness on human affairs, save that which necessarily and authentically belongs to religion. It is also necessary that some room is left for reflection and maneuver in all debates.

We have established, under the rubric of "Religion and Nation," that God addresses people themselves immediately and directly, without intermediaries. Everyone is directly responsible, and people's reason, knowledge, thought, perception, reflection, and will are the ultimate arbiter. We have the Qur'anic injunction, "If you do not know, then ask the keepers of (knowledge and) remembrance," (Sura 21, Verse 7) which indicates that it is proper to inquire, and to augment one's knowledge. In the meantime, the Qur'an has envisioned, without censure, the existence and expression of disagreements and differences of opinion among the faithful. It recommends the disagreements with the

---

[4]Sura 3, Verse [141]: "This is so that God may try the faithful and destroy the unbelievers."
Sura 3, Verse [154]: "God had to try them to bring out what they concealed in their breasts, and to bring out the secrets of their hearts, for God knows your innermost thoughts."

rulers to be referred to the Prophet and to God; which in our days, would mean the body of religious knowledge.[5]

Disagreement becomes unacceptable and disruptive only when it takes place at the executive level and when the responsible managers, instead of harmony and disciplined cooperation, engage in discord and in-fighting, each playing their own tune and doing their own thing. The principle of division of powers and their mutual non-interference and orderly checks and balances pervades Iran's old and new constitutions, and those of other parliamentary democratic systems. People and their representatives have a right to discuss, investigate, supervise, and decide public affairs within certain limits and without interfering in the progress, rigor, and effective management of the executive affairs as determined by the legislature. And now let me address the questions that were posed earlier:

The First Question

Has Islam abandoned people to do whatever they please? Is there no responsibility and restraint in this world?

Being free and autonomous is one thing, and being responsible for one's beliefs and actions quite another. God has given us freedom of opinion and action within certain parameters, but He has given us plenty of warning through His messengers and holy books, that rebellion, disbelief, and injustice will have dire results that will follow from our actions both in this life and in the hereafter. The consequences may be heeded and avoided beforehand, or they may be understood only after they have materialized, as stated in Sura 30, Verse [41]: "Corruption has spread over land and sea from what men have done (and do) themselves that (God may let) them taste a little bit of what they have done: They may come back [to the right path]."

God bestows both freedom and guidance concerning the consequences of actions. His mercy is infinite and His vengeance great. Thus freedom exists; so do responsibility and restraint. The choice is ours.

The Second Question

Should the Islamic government and the religious scholars in the leadership not check crime and treason? Should chaos and license rule?

---

[5]The text of Sura 4, Verse [59], is as follows: "O you who believe, obey God, and obey the Prophet and those in authority among you; and if (mutual opposition occurs and) you are at variance over something, refer this (matter and disagreement) to God and the Messenger [...]" It is noteworthy that on five or six other occasions the faithful are told to obey God and the Prophet; only in this occasion is the phrase "those in authority" added, and that is qualified by the phrase "among you" (which could mean elected rulers). It is further stipulated that in case there appears a disagreement between the people and the rulers it should be referred to the other two authorities [God and the Prophet].

First, the issue of individual liberty in violation of others' rights has been addressed in the first question. Absolute freedom of choice, as we understand it in the Qur'an, prevails in the relationship of God and man—not in that of society and the individual, where mutual rights and responsibilities are at stake. God may forgive transgression against His laws but, as we know, God cannot forgive people for transgressing against the rights of people. We do not enjoy the same level of freedom in our dealings with other people as we do in our personal relationship with God.

Second, religious scholars, as religious scholars, have no rights or responsibilities save those delegated to them within the democratic system of the Islamic government.

Third, self-defense and the prevention of injustice and corruption in an Islamic society are not only warranted but required. The principle of "neither inflicting nor suffering harm" is paramount in Islam, both on the individual and the societal level. Since everyone is entitled to enjoy a measure of freedom and honor, the freedom of all is necessarily limited. Furthermore, being a beneficiary of social privileges creates mutual responsibilities that the Islamic government, derived from people's will, is duty-bound to supervise.

The details of this issue and the form of intervention of the state and participation of the people, which should be exercised with utmost justice and mercy, are a separate discussion that should be analyzed under the rubric of Islamic government.

4. Moroccan Feminist Fatima Mernissi Argues That Islam Has Been Misinterpreted on the Subject of the Position of Women, 1988

Fatima Mernissi, born in Morocco in 1940, is widely recognized—by supporters and detractors—as a leading Muslim feminist. Trained as a psychologist, she became famous because of her radio show, on which she dealt openly and critically with the position of women in Moroccan society. Later, she proceeded to critically analyze the sources of women's oppression in Arab and Islamic societies. While painting at times with a far too broad scholarly brush, she nonetheless presented one of the first systematic critiques of Islamic practices from within the religion. Other feminists, such as the Egyptian Nawal al-Saadawi, had come to the conclusion that religion is at the root of Arab patriarchy. Mernissi, in contrast, contended from the beginning that misunderstanding or misapplication of the true meaning and intent of Islam and its Prophet had led to the rise of patriarchy. Thus, she argued, there is no inherent conflict between Islam and modernity, but rather between modernity and conservative interpreters of the religion.

Fatima Mernissi, The Veil and the Male Elite: *A Feminist Interpretation of Women's Rights in Islam*, ed. Mary Jo Lakeland (Reading, Mass.: Perseus Books, 1991). This document may also be found in Charles Kurzman, *Liberal Islam* (New York: Oxford University Press, 1996), pp. 112–114, 119–121, 126. Reprinted by permission of Perseus Books Publishers, a member of Perseus Books, L.L.C.

"Can a woman be a leader of Muslims?" I asked my grocer, who, like most grocers in Morocco, is a true "barometer" of public opinion.

"I take refuge in God!" he exclaimed, shocked, despite the friendly relations between us. Aghast at the idea, he almost dropped the half-dozen eggs I had come to buy.

"May God protect us from the catastrophes of the times!" mumbled a customer who was buying olives, as he made as if to spit. My grocer is a fanatic about cleanliness, and not even denouncing a heresy justifies dirtying the floor in his view.

A second customer, a schoolteacher whom I vaguely knew from the newsstand, stood slowly caressing his wet mint leaves, and then hit me with a *hadith* [tradition of the Prophet] that he knew would be fatal: "Those who entrust their affairs to a woman will never know prosperity!" Silence fell on the scene. There was nothing I could say. In a Muslim theocracy, a *hadith* is no small matter. The *hadith* collections are works that record in minute detail what the Prophet said and did. They constitute, along with the Qur'an (the book revealed by God), both the source of law and the standard for distinguishing the true from the false, the permitted from the forbidden—they have shaped Muslim ethics and values.

I discreetly left the grocery store without another word. What could I have said to counterbalance the force of that political aphorism, which is as implacable as it is popular?

Silenced, defeated, and furious, I suddenly felt the urgent need to inform myself about this *hadith* and to search out the texts where it is mentioned, to understand better its extraordinary power over the ordinary citizens of a modern state.

A glance at the latest Moroccan election statistics supports the "prediction" uttered in the grocery store. Although the constitution gives women the right to vote and be elected, political reality grants them only the former. In the legislative elections of 1977, the eight women who stood for election found no favor with the six and a half million voters, of whom three million were women. At the opening of Parliament, there was not one woman present, and the men were settled among their male peers as usual, just as in the cafes. Six years later, in the municipal elections of 1983, 307 women were bold enough to stand as candidates, and almost three and a half million women voters went to the polls. Only 36 women won election, as against 65,502 men![1]

To interpret the relationship between the massive participation of women voters and the small number of women elected as a sign of stagnation and backwardness would be in accordance with the usual stereotypes applied to the Arab world. However, it would be more insightful to see it as a reflection of changing times and the intensity of the conflicts between the aspirations of women, who take the constitution of their country seriously, and the

---

[1]Morocco, Ministère de l'Artisanat et des Affaires Sociales, *Les Femmes marocaines dans le développement économique et social, décennie 1975–1985* [*Moroccan Women in Social and Economic Development, the Decade 1975–1985*].

resistance of men, who imagine, despite the laws in force, that power is necessarily male. This makes me want to shed light on those obscure zones of resistance, those entrenched attitudes, in order to understand the symbolic— even explosive—significance of that act which elsewhere in the world is an ordinary event: a woman's vote. For this reason, my misadventure in a neighborhood grocery store had more than symbolic importance for me. Revealing the misogynistic attitude of my neighbors, it indicated to me the path I should follow to better understand it—a study of the religious texts that everybody knows but no one really probes, with the exception of the authorities on the subject: the *mullas* [religious scholars] and *imams* [prayer leaders].

Going through the religious literature is no small task. First of all, one is overwhelmed by the number of volumes, and one immediately understands why the average Muslim can never know as much as an *imam*. [Muhammad ibn Isma'il] Al-Bukhari's [810–870] prestigious collection of traditions, *Al-Sahih* (*The Authentic*), is in four volumes with an abstruse commentary by one [Muhammad ibn 'Abd al-Hadi] al-Sindi [died 1726], who is extremely sparing with his comments.[2] Now, without a very good commentary a non-expert will have difficulty reading a religious text of the ninth century.... This is because, for each *hadith*, it is necessary to check the identity of the Companion of the Prophet who uttered it, and in what circumstances and with what objective in mind, as well as the chain of people who passed it along—and there are more fraudulent traditions than authentic ones. For each *hadith*, al-Bukhari gives the results of his investigation. If he speaks of X or Y, you have to check which Companion is being referred to, what battle is being discussed, in order to make sense of the dialogue or scene that is being transcribed. In addition, al-Bukhari doesn't use just one informant; there are dozens of them in the dozens of volumes. You must be careful not to go astray. The smallest mistake about the informant can cost you months of work.

What is the best way of making this check? First of all, you should make contact with the experts in religious science (*faqihs*) in your city. According to moral teaching and the traditional conventions, if you contact a *faqih* for information about the sources of a *hadith* or a Qur'anic verse, he must assist you. Knowledge is to be shared, according to the promise of the Prophet himself. *Fath al-bari* by [Ibn Hajar] al-'Asqalani (he died in year 852 of the *hejira* [1372–1449 A.D.]) was recommended to me by several people I consulted. It consists of 17 volumes that one can consult in libraries during their opening hours. But the vastness of the task and the rather limited reading time is enough to discourage most researchers.

The schoolteacher in the grocery store was right: the *hadith* "those who entrust their affairs to a woman will never know prosperity" was there in al-'Asqalani's 13th volume, where he quotes al-Bukhari's *Sahih*, that is, those

---

[2]Al-Bukhari. *Al-Sahih* (*Collection of Authentic Hadiths*), with commentary by al-Sindi (Beirut, Lebanon: Dar al-Ma'rifa, 1978). The *hadith* quoted by the schoolteacher is in volume 4, p. 226.

traditions that al-Bukhari classified as authentic after a rigorous process of selection, verifications, and counter-verifications.[3] Al-Bukhari's work has been one of the most highly respected references for 12 centuries. This *hadith* is the sledgehammer argument used by those who want to exclude women from politics. One also finds it in the work of other authorities known for their scholarly rigor, such as Ahmad ibn Hanbal [780–855], the author of the *Musnad* and founder of the Hanbali school, one of the four great schools of jurisprudence of the Sunni Muslim world.[4]

This *hadith* is so important that it is practically impossible to discuss the question of women's political rights without referring to it, debating it, and taking a position on it. . . .

According to al-Bukhari, it is supposed to have been Abu Bakra [died circa 671] who heard the Prophet say: "Those who entrust their affairs to a woman will never know prosperity." Since this *hadith* is included in the *Sahih*—those thousands of authentic *hadith* accepted by the meticulous al-Bukhari—it is a priori considered true and therefore unassailable without proof to the contrary, since we are here in scientific terrain. So nothing bars me, as a Muslim woman, from making a double investigation—historical and methodological—of this *hadith* and its author, and especially of the conditions in which it was first put to use. Who uttered this *hadith*, where, when, why, and to whom?

[. . .]

If one follows the principles of Malik for *fiqh* [Islamic jurisprudence]. Abu Bakra must be rejected as a source of *hadith* by every good, well-informed Malikite Muslim.

To close this investigation, let us take a brief look at the attitude of the religious scholars of the first centuries toward that misogynistic *hadith* that is presented to us today as sacred, unassailable truth. Even though it was collected as *sahih* (authentic) by al-Bukhari and others, that *hadith* was hotly contested and debated by many. The scholars did not agree on the weight to give that *hadith* on women and politics. Assuredly there were some who used it as an argument for excluding women from decision making. But there were others who found that argument unfounded and unconvincing. Al-Tabari was one

---

[3]Ibn Hajar al-'Asqalani, *Huda al-sari, muqaddimat Fath al-bari* [*The Traveller's Guide, Introduction to "The Creator's Conquest"*], commonly known as *Fath al-bari* [*The Creator's Conquest*]. It comprises al-Bukhari's text with a commentary by al-'Asqalani. The *hadith* that concerns us here, on the necessity of excluding women from power, is found on p. 46 of volume 13 of the edition of Al-Matba'a al-Bahiya al-Misriya (1928) and on p. 166 of volume 16 of the edition of Maktaba Mustafa al-Babi al-Halabi fi Misr (1963). (Future page references are to the 1928 edition.)

[4]The Muslim world is divided into two parts: the Sunnis (orthodox) and the Shi'ites (literally, schismatics). Each group has its own specific texts of *fiqh* (religious knowledge), especially as regards sources of the *shari'a* (legislation and laws). The Sunnis are split between four *madhahib* (schools). . . . The differences between them most frequently relate to details of juridical procedures.

of those religious authorities who took a position against it, not finding it a sufficient basis for depriving women of their power of decision making and for justifying their exclusion from politics.[5]

After having tried to set straight the historical record—the line of transmitters and witnesses who gave their account of a troubled historical epoch—I can only advise redoubled vigilance when, taking the sacred as an argument, someone hurls at the believer as basic truth a political axiom so terrible and with such grave historical consequences as the one we have been investigating. Nevertheless, we will see that this "misogynistic" *hadith*, although it is exemplary, is not a unique case.

Throughout my childhood I had a very ambivalent relationship with the Qur'an. It was taught to us in a Qur'anic school in a particularly ferocious manner. But to my childish mind only the highly fanciful Islam of my illiterate grandmother, Lalla Yasmina, opened the door for me to a poetic religion. . . . This dual attitude that I had toward the sacred text was going to remain with me. Depending on how it is used, the sacred text can be a threshold for escape or an insurmountable barrier. It can be that rare music that leads to dreaming or simply a dispiriting routine. It all depends on the person who invokes it. However, for me, the older I grew, the fainter the music became. In secondary school the history of religion course was studded with traditions. Many of them from appropriate pages of al-Bukhari, which the teacher recited to us, made me feel extremely ill at ease: "The Prophet said that the dog, the ass, and woman interrupt prayer if they pass in front of the believer, interposing themselves between him and the *qibla* [the direction of Mecca]."[6] . . .

By lumping [woman] in with two familiar animals, the author of the *hadith* inevitably makes her a being who belongs to the animal kingdom. It is enough for a woman to appear in the field of vision for contact with the *qibla*—that is, the divine—to be disturbed. Like the dog and the ass, she destroys the symbolic relation with the divine by her presence. One has to interrupt one's prayer and begin again.

Arab civilization being a civilization of the written word, the only point of view we have on this question is that of Abu Hurayra [died 678]. According to [Shams al-Din] Ibn Marzuq [1311–1379], when someone invoked in front of 'A'isha the *hadith* that said that the three causes of interruption of prayer were dogs, asses, and women, she answered them: "You compare us now to asses and dogs. In the name of God, I have seen the Prophet saying his prayers while I was there, lying on the bed between him and the *qibla*. And in order not to disturb him, I didn't move."[7] The believers used to come to 'A'isha for verification of what they had heard, confident of her judgment, not only because of her closeness to the Prophet, but because of her own abilities:

---

[5]'Asqalani, *Fath al-bari*, volume 13, p. 47.
[6]Bukhari, *Sahih*, volume 1, p. 99.
[7]Bukhari, *Sahih*, volume 1, p. 199.

I have seen groups of the most eminent companions of the Prophet ask her questions concerning the *fara'id* [the daily duties of the Muslim, the rituals, etc.], and Ibn 'Ata' said: "'A'isha was, among all the people, the one who had the most knowledge of *fiqh,* the one who was the most educated and, compared to those who surrounded her, the one whose judgment was the best."[8]

Despite her words of caution, the influence of Abu Hurayra has nevertheless infiltrated the most prestigious religious texts, among them the *Sahih* of al-Bukhari, who apparently did not always feel obliged to insert the corrections provided by 'A'isha. The subject of many of these *hadith* is the "polluting" essence of femaleness.

To understand the importance for Islam of that aspect of femaleness, evoking disturbance and sullying, we would do well to look at the personality of Abu Hurayra, who, as it were, gave it legal force. Without wanting to play the role of psychoanalytical detective, I can say that the fate of Abu Hurayra and his ambivalence toward women are wrapped up in the story of his name. Abu Hurayra, meaning literally "Father of the Little Female Cat," had previously been called "Servant of the Sun" ('Abd al-Shams).[9] The Prophet decided to change that name, which had a very strong sense of idolatry about it. "Servant of the Sun" was originally from Yemen, that part of Arabia where not only the sun, a female star in Arabic, was worshipped, but where women also ruled in public and private life. Yemen was the land of the Queen of Sheba, Bilqis [tenth century B.C.], that queen who fascinated King Solomon [reigned 962–922 B.C.], who ruled over a happy kingdom, and who put her mark on Arab memory, since she appears in the Qur'an:

[Hud-hud] said: "I have found (a thing) that thou apprehendest not, and I come unto thee from Sheba with sure tidings."

Lo! I found a woman ruling over them, and she hath been given (abundance) of all things, and hers is a mighty throne.

I found her and her people worshipping the sun instead of God. . . . (Sura 27, Verses 22–24)

Abu Hurayra came from the Yemeni tribe of the Daws.[10] At the age of 30 the man named "Servant of the Sun" was converted to Islam. The Prophet gave him the name 'Abdallah (Servant of God) and nicknamed him Abu Hurayra (Father of the Little Female Cat) because he used to walk around with a little

---

[8]Ibn Hajar al-'Asqalani, *Al-Isaba fi tamyiz al-sahaba* [*A Biographical Dictionary of the Companions of the Prophet*] (Cairo: Maktaba al-Dirasa al-Islamiya Dar al-Nahda, no date), volume 8, p. 18.

[9]'Asqalani, *Al-Isaba,* volume 7, p. 427.

[10]'Abd al-Mun'im Salih al-'Ali al-'Uzzi, *Difa' 'an Abi Hurayra* [*In Defense of Abu Hurayra*], second edition (Beirut, Lebanon: Dar al-Qalam; Baghdad: Maktaba al-Nahda, 1981), p. 13.

female cat that he adored.[11] But Abu Hurayra was not happy with this nick-name, for he did not like the trace of femininity in it: "Abu Hurayra said: 'Don't call me Abu Hurayra. The Prophet nicknamed me Abu Hirr [Father of the Male Cat], and the male is better than the female.'"[12] He had another reason to feet sensitive about this subject of femininity—he did not have a very masculine job. In a Medina that was in a state of full-blown economic development, where the Medinese, especially the Jews, made an art of agriculture, and the immigrant Meccans continued their commercial activities and managed to combine them with military expeditions, Abu Hurayra preferred, according to his own comments, to be in the company of the Prophet. He served him and sometimes "helped out in the women's apartments."[13] This fact might clear up the mystery about his hatred of women, and also of female cats, the two seeming to be strangely linked in his mind.

He had such a fixation about female cats and women that he recalled that the Prophet had pronounced a *hadith* concerning the two creatures—and in which the female cat comes off much better than the woman. But 'A'isha contradicted him, a Companion recounted:

> We were with 'A'isha, and Abu Hurayra was with us. 'A'isha said to him: "Father of the Little Cat, is it you who said that you heard the Prophet declare that a woman went to hell because she starved a little female cat and didn't give it anything to drink?"
>
> "I did hear the Prophet say that," responded Father of the Little Cat.
>
> "A believer is too valuable in the eyes of God," retorted 'A'isha, "for Him to torture that person because of a cat. . . . Father of the Little Cat, the next time you undertake to repeat the words of the Prophet, watch out what you recount."[14]

It is not surprising that Abu Hurayra attacked 'A'isha in return for that. She might be "The Mother of the Believers" and "The Lover of the Lover of God," but she contradicted him too often. One day he lost patience and defended himself against an attack by 'A'isha. When she said to him, "Abu Hurayra, you relate *hadith* that you never heard," he replied sharply, "O Mother, all I did was collect *hadith*, while you were too busy with make-up and your mirror."[15]

[. . .]

---

[11]'Asqalani, *Al-Isaba*, volume 7, p. 426.

[12]'Asqalani, *Al-Isaba*, volume 7, p. 434.

[13]'Asqalani, *Al-Isaba*, volume 7, p. 441.

[14]Imam [Muhammad ibn Bahadur al-] Zarkashi [circa 1344–1392]. *Al-Ijaha li-irad ma is-tadrakathu* 'A'isha 'ala alsahaba [*Collection of 'A'isha's Corrections to the Statements of the Companions*], second edition (Beirut, Lebanon: Al-Maktab al-Islami, 1980), p. 118.

[15]'Asqalani, *Al-Isaba*, volume 7, p. 440.

With this anecdote we come back to our point of departure, the relationship of "Father of the Little Female Cat" to femaleness and to the very mysterious and dangerous link between the sacred and women. All the monotheistic religions are shot through by the conflict between the divine and the feminine, but none more so than Islam, which has opted for the occultation of the feminine, at least symbolically, by trying to veil it, to hide it, to mask it. Islam as sexual practice unfolds with a very special theatricality since it is acted out in a scene where the *hijab* [veil] occupies a central position. This almost phobic attitude toward women is all the more surprising since we have seen that the Prophet has encouraged his adherents to renounce it as representative of the *jahiliya* and its superstitions. This leads me to ask: Is it possible that Islam's message had only a limited and superficial effect on deeply superstitious seventh-century Arabs who failed to integrate its novel approaches to the world and to women? Is it possible that the *hijab*, the attempt to veil women, that is claimed today to be basic to Muslim identity, is nothing but the expression of the persistence of the preIslamic mentality, the *jahiliya* mentality that Islam was supposed to annihilate?

5.   Egyptian Editorialist Farag Foda Critiques Islamic Movements in Egypt, 1989 and 1992

The documents in this chapter deal mainly with Islamic political movements. It is also important to note at least one example of secular criticism of such movements and their aims. Reprinted here are two essays by Farag Foda, (1947–1992), an Egyptian commentator who was assassinated by a group of extremist Islamists—al-Jihad—for his "attacks on Islam." His assassination—along with attacks on other secularists in Egypt—was meant to silence criticism of the religious right in Egypt and to limit public debate about "Islamic values" to parameters narrowly defined by the most reactionary Islamists.

1. God Forbid!

God forbid that anyone should think I would defend Egypt's Copts! Dividing Egyptians into Muslims and Copts is detestable to me. To me, Egyptians are just Egyptians and they will continue to be Egyptians until God inherits this earth and everything on it. And yet there are these aberrations in history when history deviates from its proper course here and there, but it soon comes back to its proper course because ultimately it is only what is proper that holds true.

Farag Foda, *Before the Fall*, trans. Legal Research and Resource Center for Human Rights (Cairo: Legal Research and Resource Center for Human Rights, 1992). http://www.geocities.com/lrrc.geo/Foda/fodacopt.htm (10 January 2003). Reprinted by permission.

When I speak in defense of something, I speak in defense of Egypt. I will not condone injustice for any Egyptian. I refuse to accept the proposition that one citizen has the right to testify because he is an Egyptian Muslim and another be denied that right because he is not a Muslim. (This is what Mr. Al Hamzah Di'bis stated in *Al-Nour* newspaper, citing the testimony of Mr. Ibrahim Faraj in his book about Mustafa al-Nahhas.) I also refuse to have the right to govern, to legislate, to serve in the courts or to defend the country given to one group of Egyptians and denied to another. Let me repeat: this is a country; it does not belong to one group and not another. Now that we are on the verge of the 21st century, I cannot accept the notion that someone would call upon a group of Egyptians to refrain from taking the initiative to greet another group of Egyptians. I cannot accept the notion that someone would call upon one group of Egyptians to harass the other group if they should meet. I cannot accept such an admonition on the grounds that it is based on a prophetic tradition when the authenticity of that tradition is doubtful and its lines of attribution are weaker than the threads of a spider web. I cannot accept the claim that the October War was a religious war between Muslims and Jews. The only thing I will accept is that it was a war between Egyptians and Israelis. It was in that war that the blood of Muslim Egyptians was mixed with the blood of Coptic Egyptians. The only reason both Muslims and Copts were fighting was to defend Egypt. Muslim Egyptians lost their lives, and their families laid them to rest as martyrs; and Coptic Egyptians lost their lives, and their Coptic families laid them to rest as martyrs too.

It is a most splendid thing when the two religions unite to acknowledge the ultimate sacrifice of those who were defending our dear country. But what we have here is a sickness of the heart; what we have is narrow-mindedness and stupidity that could lead the entire country to ruin. Is there anything more ruinous than for fellow countrymen to become divided because they resent each other? Is there anything more ruinous than for countrymen to become involved in civil strife, as some of them see themselves as oppressed while some see others as oppressors? And yet if one were to look at matters closely, and examine the situation with scrutiny, one would find that nothing in this situation has to do with religion or faith. Instead, one would find that this is a matter of politics. It is a rugged and difficult course built by politicians who do not care at all about the country's future as long as they can get one vote here or there. It is a rugged course built by political clergymen who do nothing but proclaim slogans and do not concern themselves with setting forth programs or particulars; the only thing they care about is toying with people's emotions in the absence of the voice of reason.

Ye who cry and moan for Islam: cry and moan no more! Islam is alive and well. The only danger to Islam comes from you when you compel the young and inexperienced to drop out of the university because its modern sciences are secular. The danger to Islam comes from your efforts to fill young people's heads with superstition, the least of which is that thunder is the fart of a great devil! You tell them that women lead us into evil and that all society is ignorant and foolish. And God only knows that you are the most ignorant and most foolish among all Muslims. Islam has been and will always be the religion of knowledge and reason. It would be better for Islam and for Muslims if people were to study biology, physics, and chemistry and spend no time studying what religion has to say [about] [. . .] someone who frees a slave who has money, or [. . .] of someone who sets an illegitimate child free. It would be better if people were to study the modern sciences rather than the case of someone who has been dyed yellow, or the matter of women wearing capes. It would be better for Islam and Muslims if young people were to study the sciences rather than interdictions against stirring up unrest in Ethiopia [or treatises about] putting out fires at night, cauterization, snuff, magical incantations, antidotes and leeches.

The fact that members of al-Jihad organization find no other way to raise funds for their organization but rob jewelry stores owned by Copts, killing the owners and seizing their property, has nothing to do with Islam. I do not want to go on at length in this vein so as not to inflame a healing wound. But this was the independent opinion issued by someone who deserves to have us scream in his face and exclaim: What Islam is this? Islam has never been a religion of terrorism. There was nothing Islamic about killing a citizen who was sitting peacefully in his store. There was nothing Islamic about killing a man and depriving his children of their father; there is nothing Islamic about destroying homes for no other reason than that those people subscribe to a religion different from your own. Homes were destroyed and an Egyptian citizen lost his life because the leader of a religious group made an erroneous independent judgment and a mistake.

Someone like me has to be saddened and distressed when he reads this strange statement by Dr. Ahmed Umar Hashim [published in *al-Liwa al-Islami* newspaper issue no. 153]: "Islam does not prohibit Muslims from doing business with non-Muslims, but it prohibits them from having close friendships with non-Muslims because close friendships can exist only between Muslims." No sir, not at all: close friendships can exist between Egyptians whether they are Muslims or Copts. It makes no difference. To say otherwise is to create disunity and division among Egyptians.

Someone like me has to be saddened and distressed when it is proclaimed that an Indian Muslim would be closer to an Egyptian Muslim than an Egyptian Copt. That is not true at all, and it will never be true. Egyptians, I mean all Egyptians, are distinguished by the love they have for their country and the loyalty they feel for their land. To say otherwise is to have an ulterior motive, a sickness in the heart, evil intentions, a grim view, and no patriotism. To say otherwise is a major offense against the country.

God only knows who is behind this vicious attack which is creating disunity among the ranks, dividing groups, frustrating our people and breaking up our solidarity.

2. Egyptian Laws, Women, and Religion

Today's speech revolves around three main issues: first, the Egyptian legislation between religious and civil laws, and second, a discussion on the *hijab,* and third, what I would call the *"fikh* of vexing."

The first issue is obviously broad and requires more than one lecture, but I shall try and be brief in presenting a case study. In today's editorial of the newspaper entitled *Al Gareeda,* an Islamic newspaper published by the Ahrar Party, there was a paragraph saying that Dr. Rifaat al-Mahgoub [then speaker of parliament] insists on ignoring Islamic Shari'a laws without showing them to the People's Assembly which would then approve them to replace local laws that permit adultery and other sins. In truth, this paragraph gives us the "case study" that we want to address today. Please note that as long as "they" lift their hands to us with a closed Book, the issue becomes complex and difficult. If we open the Book, they will find themselves in a difficult and complicated position. The problem is that in all of Egypt, no one has the courage to discuss the position of saying "No," because Islamists have succeeded in portraying those who discuss issues as apostates, and that anyone who opposes them is an atheist. People fear for no reason. I will speak today, because time is limited, about the *hodood* of adultery in Islamic Shari'a when compared to local laws. We would like to ask ourselves: is it true that local laws, meaning the ones made by people for the benefit of people, allow adultery and promiscuity? I would like to point out one fact before I proceed, and that is that if the *hodood* [sins] of adultery are applied as they exist in the *fikh* [theology] books, all vice crimes over the past 25 years will receive a "not guilty" verdict without exception. Every officer in the vice police squad should also be lashed 80 times in each of those cases, because the case is not legally valid according to Shari'a.

Second, if the proposed adultery laws are passed in the people's assembly, all rape crimes will receive a "not guilty" verdict, and those who catch the rapist will have to receive 80 lashes as well. Third, there is no shame in religion, as the saying goes, and according to religious law, there should be four witnesses who have seen the "incident" and who have seen the male organ inside the female pelvis. This would have been possible a long time ago, when there were tents that hovered with the breeze, and when people were able to see such an event happening. Today, there are houses, the doors are locked and the windows are shut. Today, four witnesses have no means of witnessing anything except through two means: one is peeping through the hole of the door, and then the second comes in and peeks, and then the third and then the fourth person, and this is, according to the *fikh* another crime. Another solution would be for him to sit with them and watch. This obviously means he is a pimp, and is yet another crime!

Excerpts from a speech given by Farag Foda on October 21, 1989, at the Arab Women Solidarity Association. Trans. Legal Research and Resource Center, http://www.geocities.com/lrrc.geo/Foda/foda.htm (10 January 2003). Reprinted by permission.

There is another point in the issue of adultery. Say a man is working in Libya, and has been there for three or two years, and his wife suddenly sends him a letter saying that she is pregnant. This is of course a classic case of adultery. But no no. Ibn Hanbal [one of the schools of thought] [said] that there is a theory of "stagnant pregnancy," where a sperm could remain in a mother's womb for three years. Medicine says this is impossible, but it is not important, because Ibn Hanbal said three years, and the woman is scot free, because her husband most probably has divine powers! This is all about the laws ignored by the People's Assembly with which Islamists claim they want to save society from the adultery that is rampant on the streets. Listen to the following cases that the proposed laws discuss (incidentally there is no stoning in Islam because the Qur'an only specified 100 lashes for adulterers, and the verse that discussed stoning preceded the verse that discussed lashing):

- What is not on the agenda of the proposed laws are kisses, hugs and harassment of women, and those are not part of the articles specifying adultery. That means that kisses in films do not fall into the boundaries of adultery. So kisses on the streets and in cinemas do not count.
- What Westerners call "Oral sex" is not in the realm of adultery either because the male organ was not in the female.
- Perverse relations between men and women also do not fall under this category, because the male organ "missed" the female's by an inch!
- A man and woman spending time in a closed place, regardless of the sounds they make, does not constitute adultery. So if they stayed three days in a furnished flat or in an hotel, it is still not adultery.
- If a man caught his wife with her lover committing adultery, this cannot be established proof, although the man is with her in bed. The story comes from a *hadith* where a man called Saad bin Adab went to the Prophet and asked him: does this mean if I find a man in bed with my wife I should go and get four witnesses? And the Prophet answered yes, so he left him in anger. This is when the verses came to the Prophet saying that in such a case a man should repeat four times as a witness that he had seen his wife, and she is brought and asked to testify also.
- Also, this brings us to the issue of marriage of pleasure, where a man and woman may marry for a certain period of time for pleasure, even for an hour, and then divorce immediately.

According to the proposed Islamic law, therefore, if people are caught committing adultery, they bring forth four witnesses to say they are married for pleasure, and there is no legal punishment for this.

It should also be remembered that when God gives an order with limitations and boundaries, he gives first certain licenses in His mercy and then if people still persist in sinning, he punishes them fiercely. Some people claim that they want us to go back to the first century after *higra* when life was pure and loyal and beautiful and good. Fine, but in that time, when the boundaries of adultery were specified, there were licenses with unlimited slaves and several wives, after which there could be a severe punishment if the man still committed adultery. You want to apply the boundaries of adultery, no, first you must open a slave market on the Pyramids street, in Al-Ataba and in Roxi, and one near Al Higaz St. Isn't that the logic behind it? One should marry one or two or three and even four women. What prevents people today from doing that is the economic crisis where one could hardly manage to marry and support even one woman, so if those people are serious about applying the Shari'a, let them first solve our problems and give us this license, and give us financial support to marry the second and the third, and unlimited finances to he who marries a fourth. There would then be four wives and unlimited slaves in Al Higaz St., so why should anyone want to commit adultery? Before talking to us about limits and boundaries, give us licenses.

By this talk I only mean one thing: as long as words are just being said without thinking, it frightens some people who will say let us just stone the offenders. But people who have real faith will think oh God, stoning people in public is a crime! They hide things in their stories and if you discuss it with them, they themselves will withdraw from it and you will discover how ignorant they were.

This is a message for those who avoid constructive discussions and those who control our media. They believe one should run away instead of confronting these issues. Although you have the answers, you will only be attempting to close a dirty wound, for it is bound to open later and the issue will never be finished. Compare this with fourth-century laws, where such laws now punish rapists with hanging! Local laws prove adultery by the mere presence in a room together or any "likelihood" of adultery. A journalist walking by the river Nile saw two people kissing and was very upset that the Shari'a is not applied in this country. We tell him all right, please apply it, and he will find that they shall not be guilty of anything.

I merely want to show here that we, the supporters of civil law, want only the benefit of our society, where human beings make their own laws and then may change them as time goes by. We reject anyone who tells us he has been inspired by God to monitor our society and its people.

Second: the issue of the *hijab*.

The truth is that I have always viewed the issue of the *hijab* as one of personal choice, where one may choose the *hijab*, the *nikab*, or at the other end of the spectrum, shorts. These are all choices that are truly private. I have always known, according to my humble knowledge, that what was mentioned in the Qur'an concerning the *hijab* was something general, and does not mention *hijab* in particular, but mentions being appropriately covered. According to my knowledge also, what discussed the particulars of the *hijab* was the *sunna*. But they start getting more and more extremist, and they tell us for instance that a woman must not even show except one eye, which is the left eye! This makes me wonder, why did God really create women's right eyes? Is it to see darkness or dreams? This is truly funny. Why didn't He create them with one eye only to avoid the earthquakes and volcanoes they create when we see both their eyes?

I have always asked myself and continue to do so to this very day: is there something wrong perhaps with my manhood? I see women all the time whose hairs are loose and who are smiling, but they do not excite in me any bad feelings. Rather, I have every respect for them. They do not make me have sexual urges or wet dreams, but make me think. I have never felt there was a devil standing there between us, but that between us there was all respectfulness and dignity and appreciation. The problem is therefore not me, and I think I am all right. It is quite the contrary: the problem is in them. It is their excessive "manhood," and we therefore advise them to take some tranquilizers or see some doctor to suppress their urges. Perhaps they should fast.

They attack women hostesses on television. Listen to this paragraph in one of their newspapers about one such hostess: "Her eyes! Oh her eyes! It explodes with pleasure. And her lips, oh her lips!"

I obviously thought when I read it, "well this man is truly sick!" The *Al Nour* newspaper made an investigative report on girls from the Girl's College. Note that this is a segregated college, and yet listen to this: a girl said that the problem is that they have to change their clothes sometimes in front of other girls, and of course among those girls are Christian girls, and the latter obviously see them, especially the ones wearing the *hijab*. This, to them, is a problem, and this is based on Ibn Katheer's interpretations where he said that Muslim women should not undress before non-Muslim women because the latter will go and describe them to their husbands! This reminds me of those who claim that in an Islamic fundamentalist state there will be paradise of freedom of belief!!

The third point I shall discuss is what I call the *fikh* of "vexation." This basically means that some people simply seek to vex us every time they see us happy. For instance, there was this song by Abdel Wahab [a famous singer] called "Don't ask why?" where he said "we do not know why we are born nor where we are going." But then this was considered heresy of course. We don't know why we were born? Why, to praise Him, why else? The singer was therefore considered an apostate and heretic and was asked to repent. Do they have anything personal against Abdel Wahab? No. They merely want to vex us because we were pleased with the song and because we enjoyed it.

Or for instance, as we all know that there is an epidemic of kidney problems, and some people need kidney transplants. But ah, they tell us that transplants are *haram* and that the patient should be left to die. Who cares? As you realize, news of the one-eyed *hijab* and news of kidney transplants might bring a heart attack to any sane person. This means going into intensive care. But one famous sheikh comes along and tells us that this will hinder God's will. Let the guy go and meet his Creator. That is to say, my father today gets a heart attack and people come from the hospital for him, but I don't allow them because our Lordship said we must leave him to meet his God. Why don't I throw him out the window then to meet his God even faster? My goodness, this is crazy.

Or for instance about AIDS patients who got it from blood transfusion. . . . Instead of being compassionate and trying to help them, a *fatwa* says we should kill them! Of course this *fatwa* was broadcast throughout the world and Muslims looked like barbarian monsters, and our scandal became a "scandal international."

Today, in the absence of real enlightened thinkers, they have succeeded in calling for the Islamic state, claiming that Islam is "state and religion." But let us see who said that: it is none other than Hassan al Banna and his followers. Today, we are governed by the law and the constitution, and they want us governed by Islam. But let us ask them, which Islam are they talking about? And which interpretation of it?

6.   Islamic Fundamentalist Usama Bin Laden Calls on Muslims to Take Up Arms Against America, 1998

Usama Bin Laden became a household name in the United States after the terrorist attack of September 11, 2001. As a young man who came from a very privileged background in Saudi Arabia—his family owned a multi-million-dollar construction company—he seemed an unlikely candidate to lead an organization—al-Qa'eda—that visited horror on the United States. However, he had been involved in a struggle to oust the Soviet Union from Afghanistan in the 1980s. He, as well as thousands of Arab Muslims who volunteered for that war, helped to defeat the Soviet army—with a great deal of help from the United States, Pakistan, and Saudi Arabia. That victory—couched in terms of a "holy war"—as well as the Iranian revolution of 1979 convinced Bin Laden and other Islamic fundamentalists that they could and should attempt a similar task in the remainder of the Islamic world. Their aim was to re-create an Islamic state that would unite the Islamic world and replace secular or quasi-Islamic governments. The fact that the majority of Muslims did not agree with their vision and certainly not with their violent tactics was not a consideration.

Intellectually isolated and xenophobic, these mujahideen *(Muslim guerrillas fighting a jihad) convinced themselves that they were fighting for Allah. Throughout the 1990s they failed to achieve their goals because many of the authoritarian governments in the Middle East and North Africa succeeded in crushing the various attempts of these activists and in exiling a majority of them. These extremists then contended that the United States was responsible for their failure because it supported un-Islamic regimes in the region. Many Arabs had grown frustrated with American foreign policy in the region during the 1990s, so it was a natural step for Bin Laden to argue that he was fighting against "America" because of its "iniquity" toward Arabs. He hoped that this transparent excuse—one that he did not care about before 1998—would ignite the frustration of the Arab world into a massive revolution in his support. The two documents presented here are an "interview" by some of his followers and an announcement of the creation of a new World Islamic Front. They reveal the worldview of Usama Bin Laden and his organization.*

"Interview with Usama Bin Laden by His Followers," *Nida'ul Islam* 15 (October–November 1996). Translated by Akram Khater.

1. Interview with Usama Bin Laden by His Followers, 1998

- What is the meaning of your call for Muslims to take up arms against America in particular, and what is the message that you wish to send to the West in general?

The call to wage war against America was made because America has spearheaded the crusade against the Islamic nation, sending tens of thousands of its troops to the land of the two Holy Mosques, over and above its meddling in its affairs and its politics and its support of the oppressive, corrupt, and tyrannical regime that is in control. These are the reasons behind the singling out of America as a target. And not exempt from responsibility are those Western regimes whose presence in the region offers support to the American troops there. We know at least one reason behind the symbolic participation of the Western forces and that is to support the Jewish and Zionist plans for expansion of what is called the Great Israel. Surely, their presence is not out of concern over their interests in the region. [. . .] Their presence has no meaning save one and that is to offer support to the Jews in Palestine who are in need of their Christian brothers to achieve full control over the Arab Peninsula, which they intend to make an important part of the so called Greater Israel. [. . .]

- Many of the Arabic as well as the Western mass media accuse you of terrorism and of supporting terrorism. What do you have to say to that?

There is an Arabic proverb that says "She accused me of having her malady, then snuck away." Besides, terrorism can be commendable and it can be reprehensible. Terrifying an innocent person and terrorizing him is objectionable and unjust, also unjustly terrorizing people is not right.

Whereas, terrorizing oppressors and criminals and thieves and robbers is necessary for the safety of people and for the protection of their property. There is no doubt in this. Every state and every civilization and culture has to resort to terrorism under certain circumstances for the purpose of abolishing tyranny and corruption. Every country in the world has its own security system and its own security forces, its own police, and its own army. They are all designed to terrorize whoever even contemplates an attack on that country or its citizens. The terrorism we practice is of the commendable kind, for it is directed at the tyrants and the aggressors and the enemies of Allah, the tyrants, the traitors who commit acts of treason against their own countries and their own faith and their own prophet and their own nation. Terrorizing those and punishing them are necessary measures to straighten things and to make them right. Tyrants and oppressors who subject the Arab nation to aggression ought to be punished. The wrongs and the crimes committed against the Muslim nation are far greater than can be covered by this interview. America heads the list of aggressors against Muslims. The recurrence of aggression against Muslims everywhere is proof enough. For over half a century, Muslims in Palestine have been slaughtered and assaulted and robbed of their honor and of their property. Their houses have been blasted, their crops destroyed. And the strange thing is that any act by them to avenge themselves or to lift the injustice befalling them causes great agitation in the United Nations, which hastens to call for an emergency meeting only to convict the victim and to censure the wronged and the tyrannized whose children have been killed and whose crops have been destroyed and whose farms have been pulverized. [. . .]

In today's wars, there are no morals, and it is clear that mankind has descended to the lowest degrees of decadence and oppression. They rip us of our wealth and of our resources and of our oil. Our religion is under attack. They kill and murder our brothers. They compromise our honor and our dignity and if we dare to utter a single word of protest against the injustice, we are called terrorists. This is compounded injustice. And the United Nations insistence to convict the victims and support the aggressors constitutes a serious precedent that shows the extent of injustice that has been allowed to take root in this land. [. . .]

- What is your relationship with the Islamic movements in various regions of the world, such as Chechnya and Kashmir and other Arab countries?

Cooperation for the sake of truth and righteousness is demanded from Muslims. A Muslim should do his utmost to cooperate with his fellow Muslims. But Allah says of cooperation that it is not absolute, for there is cooperation to do good, and there is cooperation to commit aggression and act unjustly. A Muslim is supposed to give his fellow Muslim guidance and support. He [Allah] said "Stand by your brother be he oppressor or oppressed." When asked how were they to stand by him if he were the oppressor, he answered them, saying, "by giving him guidance and counsel." It all goes to say that Muslims should cooperate with one another and should be supportive of one another, and they should promote righteousness and mercy. They should all unite in the fight against polytheism, and they should pool all their resources and their energy to fight the Americans and the Zionists and those with them. They should, however, avoid side issues and rise over the small problems, for these are less detrimental. Their fight should be directed against unbelief and unbelievers. [. . .]

- We heard your message to the American government and later your message to the European governments who participated in the occupation of the Gulf. Is it possible for you to address the people of these countries?

As we have already said, our call is the call of Islam that was revealed to Muhammad. It is a call to all mankind. We have been entrusted with good cause to follow in the footsteps of the Messenger and to communicate his message to all nations. It is an invitation that we extend to all the nations to embrace Islam, the religion that calls for justice, mercy, and fraternity among all nations, not differentiating between black and white or between red and yellow except with respect to their devotedness. All people who worship Allah, not each other, are equal before him. We are entrusted to spread this message and to extend that call to all the people. We nonetheless fight against their governments and all those who approve of the injustice they practice against us. We fight the governments that are bent on attacking our religion and on stealing our wealth and on hurting our feelings. And as I have mentioned before, we fight them, and those who are part of their rule are judged in the same manner. [. . .]

- In your last statement, there was a strong message to the American government in particular. What message do you have for the European governments and the West in general?

Praise be to Allah and prayers and peace upon Muhammad. With respect to the Western governments that participated in the attack on the land of the two Holy Mosques regarding it as ownerless, and in the siege against the Muslim people of Iraq, we have nothing new to add to the previous message. What prompted us to address the American government in particular is the fact that it is on the head of the Western and the crusading forces in their fight against Islam and against Muslims. The two explosions that took place in Riyadh and in Khobar recently were but a clear and powerful signal to the governments of the countries that willingly participated in the aggression against our countries and our lives and our sacrosanct symbols. It might be beneficial to mention that some of those countries have begun to move toward independence from the American government with respect to the enmity that it continues to show toward the Muslim people. We only hope that they will continue to move in that direction, away from the oppressive forces that are fighting against our countries. We, however, differentiate between the Western government and the people of the West. If the people have elected those governments in the latest elections, it is because they have fallen prey to the Western media, which portray things contrary to what they really are. And while the slogans raised by those regimes call for humanity, justice, and peace, the behavior of their governments is completely the opposite. It is not enough for their people to show pain when they see our children being killed in Israeli raids launched by American planes, nor does this serve the purpose. What they ought to do is change their governments that attack our countries. The hostility that America continues to express against the Muslim people has given rise to feelings of animosity on the part of Muslims against America and against the West in general. Those feelings of animosity have produced a change in the behavior of some crushed and subdued groups, who, instead of fighting the Americans inside the Muslim countries, went on to fight them inside the United States of America itself

The Western regimes and the government of the United States of America bear the blame for what might happen. If their people do not wish to be harmed inside their very own countries, they should seek to elect governments that are truly representative of them and that can protect their interests. [. . .]

The enmity between us and the Jews goes far back in time and is deep-rooted. There is no question that war between the two of us is inevitable. For this reason it is not in the interest of Western governments to expose the interests of their people to all kinds of retaliation for almost nothing. It is hoped that people of those countries will initiate a positive move and force their governments not to act on behalf of other states and other sects. This is what we have to say, and we pray to Allah to preserve the nation of Islam and to help them drive their enemies out of their land.

- American politicians have painted a distorted picture of Islam, of Muslims, and of Islamic fighters. We would like you to give us the true picture that clarifies your viewpoint. [. . .]

The leaders in America and in other countries as well have fallen victim to Jewish Zionist blackmail. They have mobilized their people against Islam and against Muslims. These are portrayed in such a manner as to drive people to rally against them. The truth is that the whole Muslim world is the victim of international terrorism, engineered by America at the United Nations. We are a nation whose sacred symbols have been looted and whose wealth and resources have been plundered. It is normal for us to react against the forces that invade our land and occupy it. [. . .]

- Quite a number of Muslim countries have seen the rise of militant movements whose purpose is to stand up in the face of the pressure exerted on the people by their own governments and other governments. Such is the case in Egypt and Libya and North Africa and Algiers, and such was the case in Syria and in Yemen. There are also other militant groups currently engaged in the fight against the unbelievers and the crusaders, as is the case in Kashmir and Chechnya and Bosnia and the African horn. Is there any message you wish to convey to our brothers who are fighting in various parts of the Islamic World?

[. . .] Tell the Muslims everywhere that the vanguards of the warriors who are fighting the enemies of Islam belong to them and the young fighters are their sons. Tell them that the nation is bent on fighting the enemies of Islam. Once again, I have to stress the necessity of focusing on the Americans and the Jews, for they represent the spearhead with which the members of our religion have been slaughtered. Any effort directed against America and the Jews yields positive and direct results, Allah willing. It is far better for anyone to kill a single American soldier than to squander his efforts on other activities.

2. Jihad Against Jews and Crusaders: World Islamic Front Statement

23 February 1998

Shaykh Usamah Bin-Muhammad Bin-Ladin

Ayman al-Zawahiri, amir of the Jihad Group in Egypt

Abu-Yasir Rifa'i Ahmad Taha, Egyptian Islamic Group

Shaykh Mir Hamzah, secretary of the Jamiat-ul-Ulema-e-Pakistan

Fazlur Rahman, amir of the Jihad Movement in Bangladesh

Praise be to God, who revealed the Book, controls the clouds, defeats factionalism, and says in His Book: "But when the forbidden months are past, then

Usama Bin Laden, "Jihad Against Jews and Crusaders," *Nida'ul Islam* 15 (October–November 1996). Translated by Akram Khater.

fight and slay the pagans wherever ye find them, seize them, beleaguer them, and lie in wait for them in every stratagem (of war)"; and peace be upon our Prophet, Muhammad Bin-'Abdallah, who said: I have been sent with the sword between my hands to ensure that no one but God is worshiped, God who put my livelihood under the shadow of my spear and who inflicts humiliation and scorn on those who disobey my orders.

The Arabian Peninsula has never—since God made it flat, created its desert, and encircled it with seas—been stormed by any forces like the crusader armies spreading in it like locusts, eating its riches, and wiping out its plantations. All this is happening at a time in which nations are attacking Muslims like people fighting over a plate of food. In the light of the grave situation and the lack of support, we and you are obliged to discuss current events, and we should all agree on how to settle the matter.

No one argues today about three facts that are known to everyone; we will list them, in order to remind everyone:

First, for over seven years the United States has been occupying the lands of Islam in the holiest of places, the Arabian Peninsula, plundering its riches, dictating to its rulers, humiliating its people, terrorizing its neighbors, and turning its bases in the peninsula into a spearhead through which to fight the neighboring Muslim peoples.

If some people have in the past argued about the fact of the occupation, all the people of the peninsula have now acknowledged it. The best proof of this is the Americans' continuing aggression against the Iraqi people using the peninsula as a staging post, even though all its rulers are against their territories being used to that end, but they are helpless.

Second, despite the great devastation inflicted on the Iraqi people by the crusader-Zionist alliance, and despite the huge number of those killed, which has exceeded 1 million. [. . .] despite all this, the Americans are once again trying to repeat the horrific massacres, as though they are not content with the protracted blockade imposed after the ferocious war or the fragmentation and devastation.

So here they come to annihilate what is left of this people and to humiliate their Muslim neighbors.

Third, if the Americans' aims behind these wars are religious and economic, the aim is also to serve the Jews' petty state and divert attention from its occupation of Jerusalem and murder of Muslims there. The best proof of this is their eagerness to destroy Iraq, the strongest neighboring Arab state, and their endeavor to fragment all the states of the region—such as Iraq, Saudi Arabia, Egypt, and Sudan—into paper statelets and through their disunion and weakness to guarantee Israel's survival and the continuation of the brutal crusade occupation of the peninsula.

All these crimes and sins committed by the Americans are a clear declaration of war on God, his messenger, and Muslims. And 'ulama' have throughout Islamic history unanimously agreed that the jihad is an individual duty if the enemy destroys the Muslim countries. This was revealed by Imam Bin-Qadamah in "Al-Mughni," Imam al-Kisa'i in "Al-Bada'i," al-Qurtubi in his interpretation, and the shaykh of al-Islam in his books, where he said: "As for the fighting to repulse [an enemy], it is aimed at defending sanctity and religion, and it is a duty as agreed [by the 'ulama']. Nothing is more sacred than belief except repulsing an enemy who is attacking religion and life."

On that basis, and in compliance with God's order, we issue the following fatwa to all Muslims:

The ruling to kill the Americans and their allies—civilians and military—is an individual duty for every Muslim who can do it in any country in which it is possible to do it, in order to liberate the al-Aqsa Mosque and the holy mosque [Mecca] from their grip, and in order for their armies to move out of all the lands of Islam, defeated and unable to threaten any Muslim. This is in accordance with the words of Almighty God, "and fight the pagans all together as they fight you all together," and "fight them until there is no more tumult or oppression, and there prevail justice and faith in God."

This is in addition to the words of Almighty God: "And why should ye not fight in the cause of God and of those who, being weak, are ill treated (and oppressed)?—women and children, whose cry is: 'Our Lord, rescue us from this town, whose people are oppressors; and raise for us from thee one who will help!'"

We—with God's help—call on every Muslim who believes in God and wishes to be rewarded to comply with God's order to kill the Americans and plunder their money wherever and whenever they find it. We also call on Muslim 'ulama', leaders, youths, and soldiers to launch the raid on Satan's U.S. troops and the devil's supporters allying with them, and to displace those who are behind them so that they may learn a lesson.

Almighty God said: "O ye who believe, give your response to God and His Apostle, when He calleth you to that which will give you life. And know that God cometh between a man and his heart, and that it is He to whom ye shall all be gathered."

Almighty God also says: "O ye who believe, what is the matter with you, that when ye are asked to go forth in the cause of God, ye cling so heavily to the earth! Do ye prefer the life of this world to the hereafter? But little is the comfort of this life, as compared with the hereafter. Unless ye go forth, He will punish you with a grievous penalty, and put others in your place; but Him ye would not harm in the least. For God hath power over all things."

Almighty God also says: "So lose no heart, nor fall into despair. For ye must gain mastery if ye are true in faith."

7.   Reflections on the Terrorist Attacks of September 11, 2001

The attacks on the World Trade Center and the Pentagon of September 11, 2001, were a cataclysmic event on many different levels. One such level is reflected in the tensions that emerged within the relationship between the Arab world and the United States. These tensions were focused on the questions—asked on both sides of this relationship—"Why do they hate us?" It was a question that was meant to explain what most—Americans and Arabs alike—agreed to be a horrendous crime and a dangerous precedent that could lead the world into more dire circumstances. The answers however were certainly not the same. Most Arabs tended to focus on the foreign policy of the United States in the Middle East and what they perceived to be its detrimental impact on the stability of the region and biases toward Israel and conservative—or in American foreign policy parlance, "moderate"—regimes. Many Arab observers, including Muna Shuqair who authored one of the two articles presented here, argued that the United States created its own worst enemy through its "arrogant" approach toward the Middle East that was centered on safeguarding its access to oil and blind support for Israel. On the other hand, many American observers, including Ehsan Ahrari who authored the first article, have argued that the terrorist attacks on the United States are clear indications of deep flaws that reside within the societies and polities of the Arab world. According to these observers, it is the authoritarian nature of these countries that creates an oppressive political environment, a deeply flawed educational system that discourages liberal thought, and economies that are grossly unjust in their distribution of wealth—and it is that un-democratic environment that produces extremists. There are certainly merits to both arguments, and it remains for you to contemplate their veracity and ability to explain the events of September 11.

1. Facing the "Real" Enemy in the Arab Middle East

The September [11, 2001,] terrorist attacks on the United States triggered a debate over "why they hate us," involving the Arab Middle East as well as the entire Muslim world. On the Arab side, the same question was asked at the popular level. However, since free debates are not allowed in authoritarian systems, the international community did not get the real flavor of that debate.

The United Nation's Human Development Program (UNDP) has done the world a great service by commissioning a report on the state of Arab societies prepared by a group of Arab intellectuals. It does not answer the "why they hate us" question for the region. However, it does underscore what is wrong with their polities, and who the real enemy is. It is not the West. It is the authoritarian rule and its perpetrators. Here are some of the highlights of that report, which can be viewed in full in PDF format at: http://www.undp.org/rbas/ahdr/:

Ehsan Ahrari, "Facing the 'Real' Enemy in the Arab Middle East," *Asia Times* (online edition), 13 July 2002. Copyright © 2002 Asia Times Online. Reprinted by permission.

- The 22-nation Arab League (280 million people) produced a combined gross domestic product of US$531.2 billion in 1999, less than the single Western nation Spain.
- The real income of the average Arab citizen was just 13.9 percent that of the average citizen of Organization for Economic Cooperation and Development (OECD) countries.
- Only 0.6 percent of the population uses the internet, and the personal computer penetration rate is only 1.2 percent.
- Arab governments' overall investment in research and development does not exceed 0.5 percent of the GNP.
- The unemployment rate across Arab countries is about 15 percent, which is "among the highest rate in the developing world."
- Manufacturing exports have remained stagnant and private capital flows have lagged those of other regions.
- Even in oil and oil-related products, which accounts for over 70 percent of export from the region, the rate of growth was only 1.5 percent per year.
- No generation of young Arabs has been as large as today's.
- Despite recent progress made on the status of women, more than half of Arab women are still illiterate. They also suffer from inequality of opportunity in employment-status, wages, and gender-based occupational segregation.

The authoritarian rulers know only too well that their very survival depends on the continued backwardness and acute economic underdevelopment of their societies. Thus, as the rest of the world becomes enlightened with the spread of the information revolution and reaps the benefits stemming from enhanced globalization and industrialization, Arab countries remain at the very bottom of those phenomena. Policies of authoritarian regimes are directly responsible for their plight.

Authoritarian rule, more often than not, is also notoriously inept, corrupt and unresponsive to popular needs. The UNDP's report makes these points in sedate bureaucratic language. Consider its following observations: "There is a substantial lag between Arab countries and other regions in terms of participatory governance." And "freedoms of expression and association are frequently curtailed. Obsolete norms of legitimacy prevail." Finally, government spending and policy changes "are evident in lack of accountability, transparency and integrity, along with ineffectiveness, inefficiency and unresponsiveness to the demands of peoples and of development." The temperate language of this report notwithstanding, it is still a scathing criticism of the state of affairs in the Arab countries, and was released at a time when the search for "what went wrong?" and "who did it to us?" is on.

Once such a biting criticism of the state of affairs of Arab polities is circulated worldwide, it is reasonable to expect that sweeping reforms will be introduced and "qualitative changes," to quote Karl Marx, will be brought about. Marx was not right about the feasibility of a classless society; however, he was definitely right about the fact that qualitative change may only be brought about as a result of a cataclysmic change and through an implosion from within, especially when the "enemy" is the regime (or, in this instance, regimes) in power. Needless to say, Marx was referring to nondemocratic societies, since democratic societies are procedurally equipped to bring about such changes through periodic elections.

However, the trouble with all societal implosions is that no one can predict the outcome. Mikhail Gorbachev's *glasnost* and *perestroika* were examples of the fact that although he only meant to reform the archaic political system, he ended up with an entirely unintended outcome—the implosion of the Soviet Union. Implosion in a country may not mean the emergence of a representative system of government. Even if some semblance of democracy emerges, still no one can be certain whether a less democratic system will become more or even less democratic, and when. Iran is a good example of this particular point. In the absence of such a certainty, an alternative would be "managed" democratic change. But which regime would be willing to bring about managed change? More to the point, who is going to persuade any government in the Arab world to bring about managed democratic change?

The continuation of the status quo in the Arab world is not acceptable, for it only postpones cataclysmic changes in most, if not all, Arab polities. It is not possible for people to suffer endlessly, especially when they see on their televisions the uplifting outcomes of globalization and industrialization in the standards of living of their European and Asian counterparts. Managed democratic change from within emerges as the only realistic option. The United States, the only declared global proselytizer for democracy, may be able to play a limited and a low-key role in this direction.

In the past, the United States has been pussyfooting around this issue in that region. President George W. Bush's insistence in his June 24 speech on the interim Palestinian state was an important development in the sense that it called for the establishment of a democratic government in the Palestinian-administered territories. However, given the highly controversial nature of that speech, there is a fear that other Arab states, wittingly or otherwise, missed that point entirely.

But if introduction of democracy in the Palestinian-administered territories becomes a successful reality, Jordan might be the next candidate. Lebanon also stands a high probability of becoming a democracy, since it does not have a strongman like Saddam Hussein of Iraq. Syria under Bishara Assad is not yet the repressive dictatorship that it was under his father, Hafiz Assad. However, given the fact that the old guard and the security apparatus created by senior Assad is still very much intact, Syria is not likely to become less authoritarian, or more democratic, any time soon. Iraq is a hopeless case of a continued tyranny. Even if Saddam is toppled, there is no certainty that Iraq will start its march toward democracy soon thereafter.

In North Africa, Morocco may be a leading candidate for managed democratic change. But the remaining states of that region are likely to remain under authoritarian repression for the foreseeable future. In fact, both Hosni Mubarak and Muammar Gaddafi are grooming their sons to be their heirs apparent. Sadly, hereditary dictatorship is also a long-standing phenomenon of the Arab Middle East.

That leaves the Gulf monarchies as the next region of challenge. However, the Persian Gulf monarchies are not uniform in their practice of authoritarian rule. Qatar, Bahrain, Oman and Kuwait are already experimenting with limited democracy, and a discreet American encouragement for enhancing the scope of that experimentation might not be a bad idea.

Saudi Arabia, the largest state of the Arabian Peninsula, remains an archetype of authoritarian rule. It is also a country where Islamic orthodoxy is extremely well entrenched. So opening up the Saudi polity will be a great challenge, and only the ruling elite of that country may be able to bring that about. The current generation of Saudi rulers, sons of King Abdel Aziz, may not be the ones to play a crucial role in that direction. A general expectation is that the grandsons of Abdel Aziz might become the harbingers of political change, However, those who support this view provide no hard evidence to prove this point.

As the stoutest obstacle to change, authoritarian rule is the real enemy, but also has great potential for becoming an equally powerful force for change. Given the magnitude of development-related changes for the Arab countries, the extant regimes had better become its initiators and managers, especially if they do not wish to be swept aside. Political change in the Arab world is coming. There is nothing uncertain about that proposition. What is questionable is whether the real enemy of change will become its promoter and manager.

2. America's Inability to Understand Sept. 11 Rests with Warped Self-Image and Perception of Values and Power

One year after September 11, 2001, America appears unable to get over the shock and the resultant feeling of general rage and need for revenge. Sections of the American people have been able to do so. But the US administration seems incapable of the rational thought needed to analyze the crisis, consider its causes and thus deal with it in a manner that prevents its repetition. The shock blinded America, wounded its pride and made it vengeful. It was deluded by its own power and will continue to be so as long as it believes that it can deal with the challenges it faces by force.

Rage and vengeance prompted America to seek to dry up the wellsprings of terrorism by war, first in Afghanistan. One year on it is preparing to attack Iraq, while signaling that Iran, Syria and Lebanon could follow. Its fury has

---

Muna Shuqair, "America's inability to understand Sept. 11 rests with warped self-image and perception of values and power," *The Daily Star*, 30 September 2002. Reprinted by permission.

even turned it against traditional friends like Saudi Arabia, on grounds that the terrorists were natural products of its education system.

The reasons for America's failure to move on from rage to reflection, and thus to a measured and wise approach to dealing with Sept. 11, have to do with its self-image and the rationale that governs its behavior as the sole superpower. America refuses, consciously and deliberately at times, unconsciously at others, to bear responsibility for its actions. It views itself in terms approaching perfection and infallibility, as though it never wronged or committed or condoned crimes against Third World peoples. It thus assumes that feelings of hatred and hostility toward it are directed at fundamental aspects of that perfection at American values of democracy, human rights, modernity, science and progress. Thus it divides the world into two: a free and democratic world at whose pinnacle it sits, and a backward and undemocratic world that necessarily opposes and hates it. In other words, the conflict is between America as it sees itself and the others as it sees them, a conflict of identities, cultures and civilizations that is totally decoupled from the historical experience of encounters between the superpower and the peoples who have suffered from its power and tyranny.

America does not understand, or does not want to understand, that it does not necessarily represent the promised model to the "Other"—including the Arab- and Islamic-"Other"—because its values of freedom and democracy have not made it into a moral force in the world. Refusal to take responsibility for one's actions conflicts with those values, as does denying others rights one reserves for oneself. So does backing repressive and oppressive regimes, turning a blind eye to crimes committed by allies, intervening in criminal ways in countries whose regimes it opposes, and assassinating leaders merely because one disagrees with their policies. Through these and other actions and biases prompted by a narrow perception of self-interest, the model America has managed to project to many peoples is a loathsome one.

The assumption that the American dream must be a universal dream disregards the fact that some peoples, groups, and individuals see only the nightmarish side of that dream and associate it with aggression, injustice and hypocrisy. Freedom cannot be a supreme value when it applies to oneself but not to others, or is decoupled from the values of equality and justice—which mandate that all peoples be viewed as being worthy of life, liberty, independence and the right to self-determination. The scientific reasoning America cherishes—and whose technological output has oppressed peoples worldwide—is also totally at odds with its division of the world into good and evil. Without attempting to define either, it appropriated good for itself and proceeded to address the world with the arrogant and reductionist logic of "with us or against us."

A sole superpower cannot be a great power without a moral message, both to earn the respect of other peoples by showing them respect, and to enable it to play a credible role as a fair arbiter in world affairs. America failed to make the transition to that role, but emerged from the Cold War still captive to its prejudice—the Arab-Israeli conflict being a case in point—to take on minor regional players that do not even begin to constitute a match for the military might it developed to confront a rival superpower.

America's new wars are not defensive. No other country could or would dare threaten it. They are to protect its interests. But treating oneself and one's interests as the same thing is wrong even from a pragmatic standpoint. A threat to some of one's interests is not a threat to oneself But that is the rationale for attacking Iraq, despite the lack of evidence that Baghdad has anything to do with Sept. 11.

The US believes Iraq's policies threaten American oil interests and Israel's security. The claim that it wants to rid the Iraqi people of a dictator who attacks them with weapons of mass destruction is merely a pretext to conceal its self-interested motives. This is tantamount to imperial days when colonial powers would start wars and redraw maps to advance their interests.

America has not managed to understand the phenomenon of Islamic terrorism. To link Islam, or even an Islamic group, to terrorism is to misconceive both. The linkage should be between a certain understanding of Islam and the behavior it inspires, which may or may not be terrorism. It is not terrorism for an Islamic group to resist an occupier, or a people to resist their occupiers or oppressors. The values of freedom and independence cannot be selectively applied or monopolized by a single people, country or religion.

Nor has America understood the relationship between terrorist activity and the religious ideological motives that may inspire it. Although nothing could justify or legitimize the horrific slaughter of innocents on Sept. 11, understanding a phenomenon does not mean condoning or judging it. It is not a matter of zealous young Muslims killing themselves to become martyrs or enter paradise. In their perception, that only happens if they strike at an aggressor who has humiliated them or their peoples and denied them their humanity. Martyrdom is only achieved against an enemy hostile to Islam and Muslims and who has attacked them and violated their sanctities.

When the phenomenon of terrorism stemming from a religious ideological world view is looked at from a cultural and political perspective, it can be understood for what it is: an expected consequence of peoples being sentenced to injustice, humiliation, despair and despondency, as perceived consequences of the direct or proxy application of the superpower's might. Such an understanding leads to the conclusion that the phenomenon needs to be tackled by a combination of political and cultural means, in addition to any security measures.

But merely using military muscle against the kind of religious-inspired terrorism that prompts groups of young men to kill themselves to wreak vengeance against America, will not eradicate the phenomenon. It will ultimately strengthen it, forcing it to retreat and conceal itself at first, before it is reconstituted in new guises and re-emerges in even more resentful and ruthless forms.

CHAPTER 9

Subaltern Groups

Although Islamic political movements have played an important role in the Middle East and North Africa, it would be a serious mistake to assume that they completely define the range of political and social movements in the regions. In fact, as a result of some of the challenges that have led to the rise of political Islam, nonreligious social movements have emerged. By their very existence or through their activism, these secular movements and groups undermine the image of state and society as monolithic. Their members, through their lifestyles and actions, try to claim and define a social space in opposition to the moral conservatism of the Islamists and the oppression of the state. In this chapter we present some of these subaltern groups.

Leftist politics has been integral to the rise of the modern Middle East and North Africa. Socialist and communist ideas have spawned political movements and have played a role in shaping the organizational structure and approaches of mainstream and right-wing politics. For example, the dedication of the Tudeh (Masses) Party of Iran to Marxist ideology has helped to shape modern Iran and its politics. Even though the party is today outlawed in Iran by the conservative government, it continues to play a subversive political role. Thus, the statement of the party's central committee—self-aggrandizing without doubt—provides a glimpse into the ideas and history of one communist organization in the Middle East and North Africa (document 8).

Stereotypes of women in the Middle East and North Africa portray them as members of a veiled community, powerless in the face of male domination. However, despite a great deal of discrimination against women in these regions, the situation for women is far more complex than the stereotypes imply. In Iran, the law requires women to wear the chador (a loose robe covering the body from head to foot and leaving only the face exposed), yet many women run for political office, vote for liberal candidates, and actively participate in every aspect of life. Women in Tunisia have far more rights than women in Algeria or Libya. In Israel, the law guarantees women many rights, but the

Jewish religious right is constantly seeking to deprive women of those very rights. What even this cursory look at the variety and complexity of women's lives reveals is that women are not passive victims of history; they challenge the status quo in small and large ways on a daily basis. Document 1, an article detailing Arab feminist action against violence targeting women, is one example of such a challenge.

Gender politics is another facet of social movements in the Middle East and North Africa. Document 2 presents an Internet discussion about education for women in Saudi Arabia and the role they ought to play after marriage. As families attempt to deal with pressing economic needs, individual desires, and collective challenges, answers to the question of whether a woman should pursue education or marriage vary considerably. The discussion about Saudi women allows us to go beyond the stereotype of these women as silent, veiled nonentities. Their voices—never silent—are ever more present with the rise of new technologies that allow them access to public spaces previously denied.

More challenging to the social structure and mores of any society is homosexuality. This is a subject that remains taboo in Egypt, although 150 years ago Rifa'a Tahtawi wrote of its ubiquity and social acceptance in Egypt (see document 1 in the chapter "Social and Cultural Reformulations"). Today the subculture of homosexuals in Egypt is seen as a challenge to heterosexuality and religious "morality" simply by its existence. A reading of document 6 allows us to appreciate the diversity of social life in places we normally view through an extremely reductionist lens.

Every country in the Middle East and North Africa has a nationalist myth of creation that projects the image of a unified people living in a unified land. Israel declared itself a "Jewish state," practically every Arab nation declared itself to be "Arab," and Turkey projects itself as singularly "Turkish." These broad ethnic designations, however, are called into question by the ethnic diversity evident in every part of the regions. If during most of the twentieth century, ethnic minorities remained silent out of fear or necessity, this is no longer the case in the twenty-first century. Minority rights have become a critical political issue in these countries, even if the ruling majority chooses to ignore the topic and its ramification for the nationalist myth.

This chapter contains three documents dealing with that issue. Document 4 is a proclamation by the Imazighen (Berbers) of Algeria decrying the designation of that country as an "Arab" nation despite the presence of a sizable non-Arab minority. This issue is especially frustrating for the Imazighen because they are descendants of the original inhabitants of the area, who predate the Arab conquest in the seventh century. Document 7 focuses our attention on Israel, where the Arab-Israeli minority actively challenges the notion that the state is simply Jewish. Their very existence stands as testimony against this exclusionary definition. In addition to voting and becoming more politically outspoken, the Arab Israelis challenge the Zionist mythology by their presence in every walk of life. Document 7 spotlights the interaction of Jewish and Arab soccer players and coaches in Israel. Document 5 describes the attempts by

Kurds in Turkey to break through the official silence about their existence as a minority group and to challenge the contention that Turkey is only for Turks.

Finally, environmental issues and politics represent a new axis of grass-roots challenges to state authority. This is demonstrated in document 3, which explores environmental activism in Egypt and Turkey.

Collectively, the documents in this chapter demonstrate that the nations of the Middle East and North Africa are not simply "Muslim" or "Jewish" or "Arab." A host of additional categories—ethnic and linguistic among others—and interests define the myriad lives there.

1. The Arab Women's Court Vows to Resist Violence Against Women, 1995 and 1998

At the beginning of the twenty-first century, Arab women, like women elsewhere, are still struggling for full equality with their male counterparts. Despite some similarities, however, the issues have changed since the early days of the Arab feminist movement, which began one hundred years ago. Today, Arab, Iranian, Turkish, and Israeli women have the right to work in the public sphere, although they still experience discrimination. Now, women in most Middle Eastern and North African nations enter the universities as a matter of course; a century ago they were fighting to gain access to secondary education. The change in women's status and power is especially apparent in the shift in feminist language over the past one hundred years. If you compare the early pronouncements in the documents in the chapter "Social and Cultural Reformulations" with the wording of this document, you will find here some new ideas and concepts that are indicators of real change.

This document derives from a website listing the accomplishments of "The Women's Court." The organization is described as follows: "the Women's Court—the Permanent Arab Court to Resist Violence Against Women—is a . . . popular court that aims at fighting all forms of violence practiced against women in Arab societies." Among its objectives are to publicize violence against women and to change laws that condone if not encourage such actions. At public hearings women lawyers from across North Africa and the Middle East convene to address particular cases with symbolic importance and to render judgments that serve as metaphors for larger issues. Much of the language of the court is symbolic; this organization does not have the legal power to enforce its decisions. Yet public pressure demands responses even from people who reject the court's claims. This document provides a glimpse of feminist activity in the Middle East and North Africa. A cursory Internet search will allow you to explore the greater scope of feminist activism there.

The Women's Court: The Permanent Arab Court to Resist Violence Against Women, "Accomplishments." http://www.arabwomencourt.org/womenscourt/accomplishments/accomplishments.htm (10 January 2003). Reprinted by permission.

Public Hearings 1995 and 1998

Prior to the establishment of the Court, and upon the initiative of the El-Taller organization, a group of Arab NGOs referred to as the Arab Women Court held a public hearing on June 29th and 30th 1995. At this hearing, 33 live testimonies of women coming from 14 different Arab countries were heard. The testimonies reported great pain and suffering and focused on the various types of social and legal crimes as well as the erroneously so-called "honor crimes."

During its first year of existence and building on the field experience of its members, the Women's Court: the Permanent Arab Court To Resist Violence Against Women realized the necessity of raising awareness on the personal status codes existing in the Arab counties in order to reveal to the public the injustice that these codes are inflicting on women. In fact, the personal status observed at both the legislative and applied levels in most Arab countries is one of the most important mechanisms for subjugating and oppressing women within the framework of gender social relations within the family. The Court decided to dedicate its second public hearing (held in Beirut, Lebanon on March 15th to 17th 1998) on these laws and to focus on four major issues: Marriage, Divorce, Custody and Alimony, and Inheritance.

Testimonies 1995

". . . I do not recall the day of my excision, said Fatima from Mauritania, "but what has remained engraved in my memory is the agony and affliction I began to feel when I grew up and became aware of the horror inflicted on my body. At the age of ten, I was taken to where a group of us, 8 to 10 years old, were awakened every day at 5 A.M. and placed before jugs containing one liter of milk each. The exercise was to have each one of us drink, under tight control, between 30 and 40 liters of milk daily. If anyone of us threw up . . . she would be forced to drink the amount she had vomited. I shall never forget the case of a friend of mine who drank herself to death. Frightened by her death, I became more obedient and soon, grew into one of the fattest girls of the group. By the following winter the second phase of the fattening process began . . . In our society, fat means beautiful and the purpose is to turn the young girl into a docile creature ready for the marriage imposed upon her.

"The third and more damaging kind of violence was forced marriage; I was given to marriage to a man much older than me, a marriage which led to divorce leaving me with children that I love."

"My name is Souad, a survivor of Sabra and Shatila massacre in Palestinian camps, in 1982, when Israel invaded Beirut.

"On Thursday, 17 September 1982 at 5 A.M., 13 soldiers backed by Israel, broke into our home. I was then sixteen. My youngest sister (hardly a year and a half old) was the first to die from a shot in her head, crying mamma . . . I was raped by three of them, one after the other . . .

"They returned again the day after and sneered at me. As they heard words of depreciation I could not withhold, they shot me, point [blank] in the breast and head.

"I did not die but fell unconscious and lost the ability to move until the third day, when I was shaken into consciousness by a voice from outside . . . My condition has not changed since the massacre. I became a cripple condemned to a wheelchair. I fear nothing and desire nothing than ultimate victory and the end of this painful drama."

Statement of Justice 1995

After listening to the live testimonies and careful review and deliberation, the panel of judges at the public hearing issued the following verdict:

> The Tribunal condemns the cultural concepts, values and regimes which deny the humanity and rights of women.

> The Tribunal believes that the unconditional joining by the Arab states to the international treaty to eliminate all kinds of discrimination against women, will strengthen the standing of the Arab women, preserve their rights, ensure equality, and help to eliminate the phenomena of violence.

> The Tribunal notices that the majority of laws implemented in the Arab states fall short in achieving equality and justice for women and fail to conform with the principles of a democratic society.

> The Tribunal believes that achieving justice requires wide rang[ing] legal and procedural reforms including among others the personal status code, the laws organizing employment, citizenship, criminal law and social security.

> The Tribunal considers killing and harming individuals under the pretext of defending honor a crime punishable by law and no special clause should be included to ease the punishment.

> The Tribunal condemns all forms of traditional practices containing discrimination or violence against women, especially excision, and considers these practices a crime.

> The Tribunal believes that Israeli occupation of the Arab land is a continuous violation of international law, human rights, and UN Security Council resolutions. The Israeli occupation is a major cause for the continuation of political violence against the peoples of the region, in particular women. Furthermore and in accordance with the Geneva accords, the Tribunal calls on releasing the illegally held prisoners in Israeli jails.

> The Tribunal calls for joint efforts to be undertaken by all those who believe in human rights in order to stop violence against women.

Statement of Rights 1995

We, the women participating in the Arab Woman Court, held in Beirut, between June 28th and 30th 1995, as testifiers and audience to these live testimonies commit ourselves and raise our voices pledging the rejection of all forms of violence practiced against women.

We reject violence because it is an abuse of women's rights, because it violates women's human dignity and because it is the worst of all forms of discrimination against them;

We pledge to cut the strings of silence which covers such violence and to put a hand of solidarity into the hands of all those who help us in our fight throughout the world, especially in the third world.

We reject all forms of violence and will fight them at the local and international levels, no matter how well it may be disguised and how justified others might claim.

We reject violence regardless of how it is categorized—political, economical, or social.

We reject violence whomever the entity carrying it out against us may be—father, brother, husband, son, governor, foreign elements, or any entity of the new world order; whether it is signed by states, religious institutions, local, regional or international bodies.

We reject all forms of violence in circumstances of war or peace.

We reject all forms of violence no matter what it is called or how it is justified.

We reject all forms of violence whether it is directed at individuals, women or organized groups, whether the act itself be legal or illegal, individual or affecting groups.

Testimonies 1998

Rania, a 23 old Jordanian woman university graduate, was forced by her parents to marry her cousin. She had no option but to flee from her parental home two weeks before the wedding day. She did so only after all methods used to express her rejection—persuasion and even resorting to [attempted] suicide—failed to bear fruit.

The result was the murder of Rania in a primitive, brutal manner just because she sought her right to free choice as guaranteed by all religious laws.

The lovely brunette was an educated young woman who spoke in a convincing manner. When she contacted the people in charge in the "People's Talk" program on Jordan's television, they gave her the pseudonym of Haneen to help her broadcast her messages to her parents. In those letters, Rania/Haneen expressed her deep love for her parents. Her maternal aunt—who appeared later to have planned to get rid of her niece—started to send messages to the TV program, claiming that Rania had been forgiven and begging her on air to come back home. In one of these messages, the father talked beseechingly to his own daughter: "come back, come back, my dear daughter."

Two weeks later, Rania was shot dead, murdered because she decided to escape, and refused to marry her cousin. The executioner of the crime—planned by the father and his kinsmen—was Rania's younger brother who is no older than fifteen years (being a minor protects him from severe sentencing).

Yet another victim of outdated tribal customs!

"I got married at the age of eighteen," said Z.B. from Syria. "My husband deprived me of the opportunity to continue my university studies, and forced me to serve his mother . . . He started to beat me to severe bleeding . . . He then drove me out of my house with no clothes and no money . . . My husband started to drink heavily and womanizing to the extent that he started to get some women into our own apartment.

"He kept insisting on the need to give birth to a son. As soon as I had given birth to our son, his attitude worsened. He prohibited me from going out of the house . . . Beating and abuse were no longer confined to our home. He began to torture me while starving my kids and myself. He began to threaten me of throwing me out of the house. One night, he severely beat me, I tried to commit suicide but was saved by my parents.

"The Court did not rule that I get an alimony, because my husband claimed to be poor . . . When my eldest daughter reached the end of her nurture age, my husband took her and started setting her against me. She now considers me repulsive and refuses to see me. Lately my husband took my other children, but two days later, he sent our young son home and said: 'I will take him back when he grows up.'

"He denies me any chance to see my daughters. I'm raising my son without any alimony and without being divorced, while expecting his father to take him away from me."

Statement of Justice 1998

After listening to numerous live testimonies, the judges at the public hearing recommended the following:

> Drafting a uniform domestic civil law dealing with the personal status codes that is based on the respect of the human rights whereby all citizens would be treated in a nondiscriminatory manner.

> Prompting each Arab country to join and abide by the international human rights conventions including the international convention for the elimination of all forms of discrimination against women (especially article 16 bearing on prejudices within families).

> Working for the amendment of the codes enforced in the respective Arab countries to suit the provisions of the international conventions already agreed on and signed by the respective Arab nations.

Setting up institutions specialized with the purpose of looking after the victims of domestic violence, counseling, guidance and essential services tending for legal and judicial help.

Reforming judicial procedures related to domestic issues such as shortening the interval of the trials and speeding up the implementation of the judicial verdicts, reducing the court expenses, and calling on social experts aid.

Establishing a governmental fund that would disburse the divorce allowance to separated and divorced women.

Emphasizing the necessity of the independence and immunity of the jurisdiction, eliminating the exclusive and private courts. Courts must be equipped with capable personnel and staffed with women lawyers and judges. Besides, a special department for appeal must be established in quest for an amicable settlement.

Educating the public over basic human rights and relevant legal knowledge only to be included in the school civic education curriculum.

The Court also perceives that the elimination of violence and discrimination in all its forms requires the unity of the efforts of the non-governmental organizations (NGOs) with the various sections and forces concerned with the progression of society. This could take place in the frame of a broad and efficient Arab movement to exercise pressure in different directions to effect the indispensable change towards reinforcing the rights of the Arab citizen, whether man or woman, and enabling him to be his own decision maker to achieve his objectives.

Statement of Rights 1998

We, the Arab women participating in the Arab Women's Court held in Beirut from the 15th to the 17th of March 1998, have taken upon ourselves since 1995 to struggle for complete equity before the law. Our struggle is part and parcel of the international conventions, especially the international declaration of human rights and the convention of eliminating all forms of violence against women. We end our 2nd Arab public hearing with the following Statement of Rights:

We request that Arab governments fully abide by the Convention of Eliminating all forms of Discrimination Against Women (CEDAW).

We call for an equitable civil status law that would guarantee the freedom of getting married and the right to end the marriage.

We demand the prohibition of polygamy as it is a form of violence against women.

We demand that physical, psychological, and sexual violence, undeclared divorce (separation), and arbitrary divorce be categorized as crimes punishable by law.

In case of divorce, we call for an equal distribution of wealth and property and for sharing the cost of child support (when woman is employed), otherwise the father ought to bear the total cost.

We demand equal access to the children, allowing the child to choose his or her guardian.

Despite their major role in the economy, women are not equally treated when it comes to inheritance and still impeded by the prevailing norms and mentality. Therefore, we request that all obstacles, be it [*sic*] legal or traditional, be removed immediately.

2. Internet Discussion of Marriage and Education for Saudi Women, 1996

The Internet—extremely popular among Saudi Arabians in general and Saudi women in particular—offers a new venue for discussion of social issues, beyond the circle of immediate friends or family. The anonymity of the Internet permits some discussions to be far more forthright and honest than earlier discussions in the Middle East. The two sections of this document—an article and readers' comments from wide-ranging locations—exemplify this new development. Such articles are bringing to public attention new subjects or at least are providing a wider range of opinion. In either case, their impact is real.

Marriage or Education, a Dilemma for Saudi Women

If you had to choose between getting married or studying, which would you choose? As female education moves further and further every year, more and more Saudi women are faced with just this decision. The problem is particularly acute among those who are educated in highly-specialized fields. Medicine, for example, requires a minimum of six years university attendance and further degrees can take up to another five years. Most female medical students marry and have children while they are studying, but there are a few who remain single for a variety of reasons.

Many Saudi women work in their selected professions and acquire higher degrees within the framework of marriage. A laboratory technologist says, "I made it clear to my husband that I wanted to finish my education. I even put it as a clause in the marriage contract. For me, ambition is the most important element. I don't see a clear-cut choice between either marriage or education. If you really want to make them both work, you can, but it does take a lot of perseverance. Right now, I'm pushing my husband to let me go to Riyadh to get a

Dina Ibrahim, "Marriage or Education, a Dilemma for Saudi Women," *Arab News,* 29 November 1996. http://www.arab.net/arabview/articles/ibrahim2.html. Reprinted by permission.

higher degree. This means moving and changing the children's schools, but it looks like he's going to agree."

For some parents of female medical students, education is one thing but employment is another. Students tell of a colleague whose father did not object to her finishing medical school but when she finished and it was time for her to work in a hospital, he refused permission.

Fatma remains unmarried at the age of 37. She is a doctor specializing in internal medicine and has been working for the past nine years. "I was engaged once when I was 18, but I didn't want to get married so early. I wanted to finish my education and if my family had found a man who would have accepted that, I would have married him. But they didn't," she says.

Another medical student says, "The average age for marriage ranges from 20–25. After the age of 25, the quality of men looking to get married declines, so it is better to get married while a student than to wait and in the end stay unmarried or marry an older man such as a widower or even become someone's second, third or fourth wife."

Some educated women are treasured assets to younger men who are just starting out. By the time she had finished her doctoral studies, Nura was 32 and unmarried. Her mother arranged a marriage for her to a younger man whose mother was happy to marry him off to an older woman, because she had a job and could support both of them until he got on his feet.

There may be a shortage of men who are willing to support their wives until they complete their education, but they do exist. Talal Abu Jaffar considers himself a supporter of women's education. "But," as he puts it, "there are limits." He wants each of his four daughters to finish secondary school since he feels it is important for them to read and write, to learn about Islam and the Qur'an and to be knowledgeable in the sciences. This knowledge, in his opinion, is for them to pass on to their children. Once they have finished school, marriage becomes a priority. As for a college education, he says, "I will not allow my daughters to go to a college while they are still unmarried. When they marry, it is up to their husbands whether they get a college education or not."

Other men are selective about which degree their wives study for. "When we were first married, I advised my wife to stay away from medicine and sciences because they would take up too much of her time and there are no colleges or jobs for women with degrees in engineering and such. I convinced her to go to the literary side. That way, she can get a job as a teacher, but if she had gone into the sciences, she would have ended up frustrated because those are traditionally male occupations," said Abu Khalid, a legal consultant.

A woman who has a Master's Degree in English Literature and teaches at the Women's College in Dammam said, "My husband at first tried to dissuade me from getting a college degree. We were married quite young and he thought it best if I stayed at home and had children. Well, I did have three children but I certainly didn't stay at home." She managed to convince her husband to let her study and he agreed as long as it did not interfere with her domestic duties. "When I had my first son, I was in my second year as an undergraduate. It took me six years instead of four to finish my degree, but I did it and after I got it, my husband was the one who encouraged me to get a Master's Degree."

So far, the two main branches of college education with the most employment opportunities for women are either medicine or teaching. Female medical students, doctors and teachers are calling for augmentation and diversification of these opportunities. One student said, "My sister is a very talented artist, but there is no college she can attend here. If we want to send her to a fine arts program, the only alternative is to send her abroad and even if we do that, she won't find a job. Employment opportunities are very few. I chose medicine simply because I didn't want to be a teacher, not because of any real desire to be a doctor. If I could have studied computer science or business or economics, I would have been much happier because medicine is extremely stressful."

Education and employment continue to pose formidable challenges to these women. The married ones struggle to perform their duties as wives, students, mothers and career women. The unmarried ones face social and emotional friction. Nevertheless, both groups share the immense satisfaction of being able to work and study within their own unique conservative framework, thereby proving beyond any doubt that they are valuable assets in their quest to serve and complement today's Saudi society.

Feedback [from the Internet]

Selected comments we have received about this article are shown below. If you want to add your own comments, please fill in our feedback form.

ABDALLAH S. GAMAR, U.S.A. I haven't finished the topic yet but if its all about getting married and continuing work or education I would agree if both parties agree. However I would love to get married right now or as soon as possible, if you know someone who is interested please let her e-mail me. I am working and trying to finish my college education, inshallah, in psychology. I am a male 35 light skinned.

MS. NARGIS NAQVI, MINNEAPOLIS, U.S.A. This is an interesting subject and one that has caused a lot of confusion. My personal experience and opinion is that, Islamically, we are all supposed to obtain as much of an education as we can, men and women alike, but if it causes hurdles and problems for married women then, if their marriage is worth it, they should put that first. If husbands are unnecessarily strict then they should read some rights in Islam granted to women. In any case, women are not supposed to work unnecessarily if their husbands can provide for them (or their fathers can provide for them if they are not married), but in a place like Saudi Arabia where men and women don't mix at work, working just enhances the mind and makes one wiser to the ways of the world. They become better companions to their husbands who should be more understanding and supportive. For women with children, if education is going to cause problems like travelling to another place, etc., I feel that instead of being selfish, we can work out ways that help us be good mothers, wives and also continue with our needs in life. If education is one such need, then there are ways to acquire it without causing disturbance. Always remember the clue to a happy life: If you keep what Allah has said about our duties and responsibilities, men and women alike, then you will always make the best decision.

DR. SOMIAH ALNEMRI, VANCOUVER, CANADA   This is very complicated subject, especially to our conservative culture and society. We need to address everything with regard to Islamic teaching. In the Holy Qur'an, women are ordered to stay at home and not expose themselves like the time before Islam (*Algaheliah Alola*). On the other hand, there are other Hadiths from the Prophet Mohamed (SAW) encouraging continuous learning from early childhood to old age for mankind (male and female). That is why we need to ask our Olama—what is the extend [*sic*] of this education for women? And what is the application of that order to stay at home? Then we can get a balance between married life and education, especially for us as medical doctors.

H. S. FAISAL, RIYADH, SAUDI ARABIA   This is just a minor point with regards to the girl that studied medicine because she did not want to become a teacher. There is a computer science department for girls in King Saud University. I would like to further add that it seems to me that the problem of educating women should not exist in Saudi Arabia. First of all it is absolutely irrational to claim that educated women do not benefit their families. And second, it is the duty of every female to insist on her education and to enlighten the men in her life as to the benefits of her obtaining an education. Every woman should advocate and implement the benefits of any education from an Islamic, social and familial angle. As we are in the 20th century and heading towards the 21st century, the debate about whether or not women should be educated seems to be highly retrogressive.

ABDULLAH ALHMEED, LAWRENCE, KANSAS, U.S.A.   The question of whether a woman should sacrifice her education to get married or the other way around is a ridiculous question! As we are proceeding to the 21st century, our sisters and daughters should not be faced by this question when they want, or when the time comes, to get married. As women compose almost half of our society and have a very important role in raising our future generation, in line with men, and participating in the job market, women's education should not be a question but rather a necessity in order to improve our methods of raising our children, improving our productivity and eventually improving our society. It seems to me that educating a women [*sic*] is just as important as educating a man. I think that the doors should be open to every woman willing to complete her education without any questions. The woman's family and husband should understand that education is the corner stone for societies to progress and compete with other societies. Furthermore, working after pursuing a college degree is also as important as education Not only does work improve the economic situation of the family, but it adds another dimension of thinking for both the wife and husband. It might be true that the work of the wife causes some "organizational" problems within the family, but definitely the advantages of it would outweigh these problems. In summary, society in general and the woman's family and husband should find and establish some methods so that our girls are not faced with this tough question!

HELAL SAMARGANDY, KHOBAR, SAUDI ARABIA   Education is necessary for women as well as men. However, there are some things which MUST be taken into consideration. For example, Islamic orders and commands must be respected and followed and this is a very big subject. Also, good and bad "Al-Masalih wa Al-Mafasid" for the family, children, husband, etc. must be considered. This would bring many, many different situations. Each situation has its own sentence. However, we have to be careful about any subject related to women because our enemies (Kuffar or Munafqoon) want to damage the Islamic culture and Islam itself using any tool and one of these tools is SEX. Anything you want to do in your life requires effort and you face some resistance. Why do we raise women's problems in education or any kind of problem when this problem is a human problem. For example, many men stop their wives' education after marriage because of the feeling that it conflicts with their family's needs. Why do some women want to get everything without giving up anything. I am talking to the Muslim women: Do you want to go to Jannah? The way to that is by following Allah and his Prophet and then your husband. You can do anything as long as it does not conflict with Islamic orders.

ISHAAK EBRAHIM, JOHANNESBURG, SOUTH AFRICA   Why is this question posed? What are the sharia rulings regarding women in the workplace? Is it necessary for women to work, or can their husbands, fathers or family not support them? Does the western world dominate the way they live and think? Is Allah not the provider and sustainer? Does he not promise to provide in the holy Qur'an? It is a noted fact that career women's marriages do not last due to having affairs with colleagues. Remember, between every man and woman is the devil.

UBEDULLAH PATEL, LOS ANGELES, CALIFORNIA, U.S.A.   Bismillah Walhamdu-lillah Was Salaatu Was Salaam 'ala Rasulillah As-Salaam Alaikum Wa-Rahmatul-lahi Wa-Barakatuhu Sahabah—19th Rabi-ath-Thani 1419 (13 August 1998) I like to marry in Madina. Can you suggest me; is there any WEB site for matrimonial? Jazakallah Khair As-Salaam Alaikum Wa-Rahmatullahi Wa-Barakatuhu

3.   Grassroots Environmental Movements in Egypt and Turkey, 1997 and 2000

Although people—regardless of where they live—have always shown some level of concern about their immediate natural surroundings, not until the last quarter of the twentieth century did environmental politics emerge at the local or state level. In the Middle East and North Africa, environmental activism and concerns became publicly prominent only in the last ten years, as many "Green" parties began to influence the state environmental policies. Such pressure groups are not welcomed by states and private industries that are keen on keeping their environmental mistakes away from public scrutiny. But the immediacy and relevance of environmental issues such as air pollution and the novelty of environmental politics have allowed many nongovernmental organizations (NGOs) to use environmental issues as a way to challenge the authority of the state to make public policy. Though not always (if ever) successful, these organizations are still able to shape the public discourse; their activities force the state to acknowledge, even if only through some symbolic gesture, that it not the only arbiter of public issues. Environmental politics seems to have allowed some degree of democratization of public life in the Middle East and North Africa. The first of the two articles that follow describes the efforts of a low-income, Egyptian community to establish a "green" area in their midst, while the second article recounts the attempts of Turkish Greenpeace activists to stop industrial pollution.

1. Mobilization in a Cairo Neighborhood: Community Participation and Environmental Change

Cairo—a city upwards of 14 million inhabitants—is known to be one of the most polluted cities in the world. Although measures of pollutants in some places in Cairo exceed internationally recognized standards, popular collective action organized around environmental issues is rare. The case of Ezbet Mekawy, an industrial area in northern Cairo, and the successful struggle of the residents there to close local lead smelting factories is a reference point regarding possible forms of popular organizing in response to environmental pollution and sheds light on the limits and merits of community participation as experienced within the wider political context in Egypt.

A low-income urban industrial area, Ezbet Mekawy was originally an agricultural village in the outskirts of the Qalyubia governorate. In the 1920s, it witnessed an influx of people seeking low-income informal housing. During the 1950s and 1960s, small industrial workshops began to appear in the area. Today, remnants of the village—its maze-like, narrow unpaved alleyways, food vendors peddling from their donkey carts, garbage heaps and animals—merge with large industrial factories that have sprung up in the area. Air pollution has been but one of the negative impacts of this misguided and unplanned development process.

As early as 1968, inhabitants filed individual complaints against one of the lead smelters in the area. After the smelter was closed for two months, the owner reached an agreement with the authorities to raise the smoke stack so that emitted smoke would be carried further away from nearby houses. By the mid 1970s, the smelter extended its operation to three shifts a day, almost nonstop, using four stacks. The factory smelted up 24 tons of lead daily, 16 tons of which

Inas Tewfik, "Mobilization in a Cairo Neighborhood: Community Participation and Environmental Change," *MERIP Reports,* Winter 1997. Reprinted by permission.

were emitted into the surrounding environment in the form of black smoke laden with lead oxides and other pollutants. The problem was intensified by Ezbet Mekawy's downwind location. As one community member remembers, "If you spat, your saliva would be mixed with lead." Environmental pollution in the area caused severe health problems, including respiratory tract problems, cancer, stunted physical and mental growth, and in some cases even death.

In reaction to this situation, a group of volunteers from the neighborhood was formed in 1989 to close down the lead smelters in the area. The organizer of this community protest movement and its unofficial leader was imprisoned in 1971 for two years due to his involvement in a left, underground movement against the regime of the late President Sadat. The core organizers of the community protest identified with Nasserite beliefs. Many were members of the old socialist party or, as young men, were enlisted into Nasserite youth organizations. The political history of the community members provided a unifying frame of reference for organizing protests against the lead smelters.

Collective action was facilitated by the fact that, as one leader of the movement describes, "In times of need or crisis, we all become one. Having witnessed several deaths in their community, people were already aware of the dangers of the lead smelters. All they needed was for someone to pull these efforts together; someone to lead them forward."

Living in the same neighborhood enabled them to meet informally in the mosque after prayers, in coffee shops or on special occasions where possible actions and the latest developments could be discussed. It was decided from the start to adopt a peaceful strategy to communicate their complaints to the officials by filing official protests and enlisting the media to propagate their case to the general public and officials alike.

Throughout the struggle, various actors appeared on the scene. Both members of the People's Assembly for the area—one representing the ruling National Democratic Party and the other representing the leftist Tagammu' party—became involved in the struggle. They wrote a report on the hazardous effects the smelters posed to the community which was presented at the parliamentary discussions of the then new environmental law. Their involvement, however, was regarded by many in the protest movement as a ploy aimed at winning more votes for the coming elections.

A newly established health center (that began operating in 1992)—aimed at establishing an alternative health care system based on preventive as well as on curative services—found Ezbet Mekawy to be fertile ground for achieving these goals. Doctors at the center concentrated on providing the community members with "scientific" evidence of the negative health effects of the lead smelters through a series of soil, blood and air quality tests. In addition to this, popular perceptions and awareness of the environmental hazards of lead smelters were formed by the everyday experience of the residents. Such awareness, at its peak, was crystallized by the death of several members of the community.

The initial idea of filing a lawsuit against the governorate for granting permits for these smelters to operate in a residential area—neglecting industrial safety measures and codes for health standards which regulate the operation of these industrial outlets—was seen as tedious and without the possibility of obtaining any results in the immediate future. To justify their demands, the community members made use of an existing law that prohibits the operation of industrial outlets which prove to be affecting the public health or safety of those living in residential areas.

As knowledge of environmental issues expanded, the phrase "environmental pollution" became part of their language of protest for the first time. As a result, the problem was no longer confined to the local level—an owner who is not complying with industrial safety measures—but became regarded as an issue of public interest.

Stressing the point that these smelters were the source of environmental pollution and ill health in the area, protest letters were signed by community members and then sent to officials such as the prime minister, the president, the minister of interior, the minister of environment, the governor of Cairo, the head of the people's assembly, the minister of justice, and the minister of local administration.

After government officials failed to respond seriously to these protests, community members decided to take the battle onto the pages of newspapers and broadcast media. Stories focusing on the plight of Ezbet Mekawy quickly became an issue of interest to the broader public in Cairo especially because it fed into the public debate on a new environment law that was being prepared and discussed at that time. In addition to one television program and two radio programs, a series of articles written by and interviews with community members appeared in both government and opposition publications.

Several ideas for possible actions were debated during the course of the protests. One suggestion was to stand in front of the entrance to one of the smelters to get the attention of the police who would be forced to investigate this action. Community members refrained from doing this for fear that the police might resort to the emergency law and interpret their peaceful act as jeopardizing public safety and retaliate by jailing the participants.

Movement members decided to appeal to foreign governments with the hope that they would put pressure on their Egyptian counterpart to take more serious measures in stopping environmental pollution. When it became known that the German government had a specialized aid program directed towards environmental protection in Egypt, newspaper articles, pictures of sick children, medical reports and copies of the closure orders were prepared to be sent to Germany—an action to be taken only as a last resort. The documents were never sent.

The collective protests to close down the smelters were met with more than six closure orders from the government. None of them, however, were effectively implemented. The executive body justified its non-implementation of the orders on the grounds that 200 workers would lose their source of income and the governorate would be unable to provide an alternative location for these factories. Documents from the ministry of insurance and social affairs subsequently prove that only seven workers were legally registered in one of the factories. Moreover, the government's closure order did not oblige the governorate to provide the smelters with an area of land upon which to relocate their operations. In March 1994, work at the smelters was finally terminated when a third memo to cut off the electricity and water supplies to the smelters was issued from the governorate.

The collective action of the community had overcome several obstacles. At the local level, bureaucracy was the first impediment. While smoke poisoning from the lead smelters continued on a daily basis, protest letters took months to circulate from one government department to the other. At the same time, the owners of one of the lead smelters tried, in vain, to bribe the leader of the movement and thereby co-opt any further collective protest. Likewise, local officials were bribed to obstruct and delay the implementation of closure orders. Nevertheless, efforts to close down the smelter were successful largely because the demands did not constitute a threat to the formal power or interests of the state.

By choosing to follow legal and peaceful means in communicating their demands to officials, collective participation acted as a buffer against other possible acts of destruction and violence. While authentic collective action and participation must take place on the grassroots level, its success is largely dependent upon the responsiveness and tolerance of the state. In the case of Ezbet Mekawy, through community mobilization, residents effectively shifted the existing power structures on the micro-level of the community in order to reclaim control over their public space and mobilize around attempts to terminate the work of the lead smelting factories.

2. Environmental Protest Turns Ugly

Yarimca, Turkey, August 15, 2000 (ENS)—Fourteen people were arrested today amid a violent confrontation between Turkish police, factory security and environmental activists protesting pollution from the Petkim Chemical Complex in Izmit Bay.

Members of the environmental group Greenpeace hung a 25 meter long banner on the quayside reading "Earthquakes Strike Once, the Chemical Industry Strikes Everyday."

On August 17 last year, an earthquake hit the region. As part of its latest Mediterranean Toxic Tour, Greenpeace said it wants to highlight both the pollution caused by chemical plants in the region and the dangers of building them near seismic fault lines.

Other protesters climbed onto cranes and factory premises opening flags voicing opposition to the use of toxic substances.

According to Greenpeace, Petkim's security staff were violent towards the activists and pushed two into the water. Fourteen of the 16 Greenpeace activists dispatched from the *MV Greenpeace* are now in police custody.

Environment News Service, "Environmental Protest in Turkey Turns Ugly." http://ens-news.com/ens/aug2000/2000-08-15-12.asp (10 January 2003). Copyright Environment News Service (ENS) 2000. Republished with permission from ENS online.

"The devastation caused by the Marmara earthquake last year brought to the fore the hazards posed behind chemical plants' closed doors," said Tolga Temuge, a toxics campaigner in Turkey. "Yet, the Bay of Izmit did not die on the 17th of August of last year. It was murdered by the industry a long time ago. We are demanding zero toxic discharges and the phase-in of alternative clean technologies."

Samples taken by Greenpeace of the toxic waste pumped into the environment by Petkim repeatedly revealed substances that are included as priority contaminants for elimination from discharges into the sea under Annex I of the Barcelona Convention for the Protection of the Marine Environment and Coastal Region of the Mediterranean.

In 1975, all nations bordering the Med, except Albania, Algeria and Syria, met in Barcelona and promised to "take all appropriate measures to prevent, abate and combat pollution in the Mediterranean Sea area and to protect and improve the marine environment in the area."

This led to the Mediterranean Action Plan, launched by the United Nations, and was the beginning of what is now known as the Barcelona Convention. Today, all Mediterranean states, including the EU, are members of the Barcelona Convention.

But the convention's six protocols have yet to be ratified by all members. So far, Tunisia has ratified all protocols while Monaco, Italy and Spain have ratified all protocols except the Hazardous Waste and Offshore Protocols.

The focus of the *MV Greenpeace* Mediterranean tour is to pressure all governments in the region to ratify the Barcelona Convention.

Greenpeace's requests to the Turkish government for reliable data on the hazardous waste generated by industrial plants have proved fruitless. The group says the Turkish Ministry for Environment replied to a Greenpeace letter last month admitting that it could not provide the data.

"We urge the public to stand up and fight for their right to know," said Temuge. "We demand a Toxics Use Inventory and a Toxics Use Reduction Act to replace the poisons produced by the chemical industry which are dispersed in our food and in the tissues of our children."

The *MV Greenpeace* Mediterranean tour is the latest in a series of tours in the region that began in 1986.

4. The Imazighen (Berbers) of Algeria Decry the Pronouncement of the Country as "Arab," 1998

Before the Arabs arrived in North Africa in the seventh century, the population of the region was overwhelmingly Amazigh (Berber). Except for the coastal cities and towns, most of the land was occupied by these tribal and settled peoples. Although nearly all the Imazighen (the plural of Amazigh) converted to Islam and many of them joined Arab armies in pushing the Muslim conquests as far as the Iberian

Peninsula and France, they constituted a distinct ethnic group with its own culture and language (Tamazight). Berbers suffered from discrimination at the hand of Arab rulers, and in response they protested and at times revolted in opposition. In the twentieth century, this situation did not improve. As nationalist struggles for independence intensified in North Africa around the middle of the past century, the ideology of that struggle became more monocultural (see the chapter "Contested Nationalisms"). In Algeria, where the indigenous population fought against a century of French occupation and exploitation, the ruling FLN (National Liberation Front) defined Algeria as an Arab-Muslim state and nation. Hidden beneath that label is the reality of Berber (Amazigh) existence. Despite some symbolic gestures acknowledging the existence of other-than-Arab cultures in Algeria, many Berbers in Algeria (and elsewhere) consider themselves to be an oppressed minority.

For an Immediate Abrogation of the Law Pertaining to the Generalization of the Arabic Language in Algeria

Call

We, the cultural, social, women's associations . . . ; women and men gathered together this day, 21 May 1998, at the headquarters of the Tamazgha Association (Paris), having discussed the contents and consequences of the law pertaining to the generalization of the Arabic language in Algeria, and which will become effective on 5 July 1998.

In the course of the debates, the following arguments clearly emerged to justify our action against this law which must be abrogated.

This law aims at excluding Tamazight (the Berber language)—which is already marginalized by the fact that it is not recognized constitutionally—in a way that it was never excluded before. A law which prohibits individuals to express themselves in meetings, judiciary audiences, and the parliament . . . is a villainous law because it denies the human being the right to legitimately use his language.

Tamazight, which has only a small development space circumscribed in time, is being suppressed on purpose. The law pertaining to the generalization of the Arabic language is encoded in straight lines of judicial texts with an eye toward bringing about the linguistic assimilation of the Imazighen (Berbers), an objective that has been the goal of those who for decades have sought to deny the Amazigh [Berber] identity.

The Jacobinism[1] which is the ideological foundation of this law aims to efface the cultural and linguistic wealth that have been the nourishing sap for the civilization of the region [North Africa].

---

[1]Jacobins, the radical wing of the French Revolution, instituted a series of extreme social and economic reforms. They achieved historical notoriety for instituting, through local Jacobin clubs, the Reign of Terror. Jacobinism thus became synonymous with dictatorship.

Collective for the Abrogation of the Law Regarding the Arabization of Algeria. http://www.kabyle.com (May 2001). Translated by Akram Khater.

This law aims to exclude the use and employ of French at the level of public administrations, universities, hospitals, socio-economic sectors, etc. It also aims to exclude the Francophone elite, [who] are [educated] . . . in Algerian schools [and who] represent the technical and scientific cadres in all sectors.

It condemns the emigration—which is the source of financial contributions, scientific, technical and economic knowledge—to a non-return [to Algeria]; because that inhumane law aims to expel out of Algeria close to two million emigrants and their children.

That law aims then at the destruction of the socio-economic apparatus and making it "archaic" because the French language is in reality the third language in use in Algeria.

The application of the law of Arabization within the educational system has already caused irreparable damage to the level of education whose consequences are visible in Algeria in all sectors.

This law is aimed as much at both the Francophone elite and cadres as at the Amazigh. For all these reasons, we reject this unjust and irresponsible law because:

- It marginalizes an important part of Algerian men and women;
- It is an attempt to isolate Algeria from the rest of the world;
- It stops the modernization of Algeria and the attainment of democracy.

We appeal to associations, women and men, celebrities, artists, intellectuals, academics . . . who reject this law, to join the Collective created for the purpose of focusing our action around a specific point which is the abrogation of this law.

The Collective remains OPEN to all those who sympathize with this struggle.

C.A.L.A.A.

Paris, 21 May 1998.

5.   A Kurdish Activist's Letter Appealing to Berna Yilmaz, the Spouse of the Turkish Prime Minister, September 27, 1998

The Kurds are an ethnic community whose ancestral homeland is divided among the modern nations of Iran, Iraq, and Turkey. Thus, the desire of Kurdish nationalists for a separate nation of their own has come into continuous and often violent conflict with the nationalist claims of those three countries. For a brief moment after World War I, with the support of President Woodrow Wilson, it appeared that the dream of

Leyla Zana, "An Open Letter to the First Lady of Turkey," 27 September 1998, American Kurdish Information Network (AKIN), trans. staff of the American Kurdish Information Network. http://kurdistan.org/Leyla/firstlady.html (27 January 2003). Reprinted by permission.

a Kurdish nation would come true, and such a state was included in the Treaty of Sèvres (see document 5 in the chapter "Ideas of Nationalism"). However, the maps drawn up after the war made no allowance for any such territory, and from the early days of the Turkish republic, the Kurds suffered persecution that resulted in— among others things—the banning of Kurdish names, language, and culture. Subsequently several Kurdish liberation movements, like the Kurdistan Workers Party (PKK), emerged for the purpose of making independent Kurdistan a reality. However, internal Kurdish conflicts, entanglement in regional politics (such as the Gulf War), and Kurdish acts of terrorism against civilians have made this dream unattainable so far. Yet there is no doubt that the plight of the Kurds and the persecution of their political leaders have captured the imagination of many foreigners.

One of those Kurdish political leaders is Leyla Zana, a Kurd elected to the Turkish parliament. In March 1994 the Turkish parliament voted to lift the parliamentary immunity of Leyla Zana and five other Kurdish MPs because they made public announcements supporting Kurdish rights and independence. The State Security Court prosecutor Nusret Demirel successfully prosecuted the accused for seeking to "separate the . . . Turkish Republic through legal ways," and they received jail sentences for their activism on behalf of the Kurds. From her jail cell, Leyla Zana wrote the following letter appealing to the wife of the Turkish prime minister.

Dear Berna Yilmaz,

Because you are the wife of Prime Minister, you probably receive hundreds if not thousands of letters from people all over the country.

Some ask for peace,

Some for work.

Other[s] share with you a problem with the hope that you will be part of its solution.

Some want to reach goals that may not be attainable.

There are still others who write you and tell you that they can not [*sic*] pay the cost of an operation for their loved ones and those who can not pay for the prescribed medication.

Some may be the relatives of deceased ones in the hospitals who may ask you to write to a hospital to let it release the body of the deceased person since they can not pay for the hospital costs. And of course, there are other letters, the ones that congratulate you for your work or recognize you for your achievements.

I thought I too would add a letter, be another one in your mail list. You don't know me or you may know me through the media or shall I say the way media has projected me.

For example, a "Bandit!," a "Terrorist!," a "Separatist!," a "Traitor!" or a convicted member of PKK. The list goes on.

I am not the least concerned to be associated with these descriptions. They, in a way, point to the alleged players on the stage whose roots go back to history. I want to refer to a bleeding geography and also to the concerted efforts of the ruling circles to deny the very existence of a people. I am referring to the struggle of those who are standing up to oppression for peace, freedom, brotherhood, democracy and labor rights. I have in mind their principled stands and how they were seen fit to assume those names. In other words, I am referring to the reality of my country, of its peoples and the state of affairs that are unfolding in it.

If it needs to be stated again, I belong to those who seek peace.

I know you through the media. Your warm disposition, friendly face, interested and humble ways that come across in numerous places. So I am writing this letter to you as a woman and also as a mother. Because I think we have at least those two things in common. But then I may be mistaken.

You may ask what prompted this letter?

A few years back, I read in an interview your views about the ongoing conflict. You were asked to comment on the war between the Turkish army and the PKK. While you did the usual, calling the question a problem of the southeast, but you also uttered the taboo words, the need for peace and a humane approach to resolve the conflict. I may not be quoting you verbatim, but I remember you saying that you did not want the mothers to cry and that you were very worried about the state of things.

These words were moving, not the usual remarks of the wife of Prime Minister. There was no disguised form of chauvinism, racism, and the talk about blood in your remarks.

Then I remember the accident/incident in which your son hurting himself in a sporting event was sent to Austria with a private plane to get proper medical care. The televised images of your sadness were real. You were distraught. You wanted to be with your son and the anxiety was showing all over your face.

It was the anxiety of a mother. Watching you, I did not want to think that you were the wife of Prime Minister, I wanted to understand you as a mother. A part of you had been hurt and you wanted to be with your son as soon as possible. And you finally got to see him.

And yet, there are mothers in Turkey, forget about being able to be with their children, do not even know where they are. They can not reach them, embrace them, smell them or touch them.

They do not even have a grave site for them, a place these mothers could shed their tears.

These mothers, for years now, every Saturday, meet in front of Galatasaray High School at noon, with pictures of their loved ones in their hands. They want to share their pain by means of peaceful sit-ins.

They do not loiter, they do not block the traffic, and they do not attack the spectators.

They want to sit there in front of that high school to voice their deadening silence about their losses.

The names of their loved ones were Mehmet, Hasan, Yavuz, Aysel and Savas at one time. But they all have one name now: disappeared ones.

The names of the mothers are Emine, Esma, Yildiz, and Pervin. Now, they have one name as well: the mothers of disappeared ones or Saturday Mothers.

Do you know what is happening to them for weeks now?

Elite police forces with their batons, shields, and guns accompanied with the sounds of siren attack these mothers, pull their hairs, haul their bodies, beat their torsos, subject them to pressurized water and force them to board the waiting busses [*sic*] for police stations. They are then kept for a few days and then released. These mothers gather in front of that high school for what they feel in their hearts. Will they ever stop coming? Dauntlessly, they come back. Their crime is to be the Saturday Mothers. Their crime is to love their sons and daughters.

You are a mother and they are mothers.

You have a son named Hasan and another named Yavuz. They had sons at one time.

You love your children. These mothers are even denied a [*sic*] opportunity to express their love for their children.

Moreover, these mothers don't want other mothers to face their predicament. In other words, they love the children of others as well. They don't want any disappearances. They love peace so that war will not consume their loved ones. And because of that, they keep coming back to the same spot for weeks and sit for hours without getting tired. In other words, their love is boundless, deep and universal.

One Saturday, I urge you, please, to go to Galatasaray High School. Go see those mothers. Take them a flower, a carnation, or a September rose, and be part of their pain. If only for a few minutes, be a Saturday Mother, be a mother of the disappeared. Don't be afraid of elite police forces. Don't be afraid of the sounds of siren that have legitimized lawlessness, injustice, and oppression. The police won't touch you. No, they will not be able to touch you. Then, believe me, you will love yourself more and your children too.

You can be one of the "first" ones to do so. You can set aside the so-called traditions of hundreds of years.

Remember that Princess Diana broke the tradition of remaining aloof, and became one of the people, and was mourned by millions when her untimely death arrived. And she lives today in the hearts of additional millions because of her principled stand against the threat of mines.

Back to our country, the cease-fire that PKK declared goes on despite the provocation, despite the silence of many in the positions of authority. You said, mothers should not cry. But mothers are still crying even as one side to this war is willing to take the road of peace.

Here is a golden opportunity for you. You can bring the crying Turkish and Kurdish mothers together. And the mothers of disappeared as well.

Or you could choose to be the mother of only Yavuz and Hasan. . . .

6. Journalist Lilian Liang Discusses Homosexuality in Egypt, 1999

One of the taboo subjects in the Middle East and North Africa is homosexuality. This unwillingness to acknowledge the existence of homosexuals—and AIDS—within society is a modern phenomenon that developed toward the end of the nineteenth century. Before that time, poetry celebrating homosexuality was common, and homosexual activities were tolerated, though not approved by everyone (see Rifa'a Tahtawi's reflections—document 1 in the chapter "Social and Cultural Reformulations"). One outcome of the "modernization" of the region was the shunning of alternative sexual lifestyles in favor of a heterosexual model based on the idea of the nuclear family. Today, the strength of the taboo is slowly diminishing. The climate of democracy that is straining to exist in the Middle East and North Africa allows a modicum of space for homosexual and other subcultures to emerge publicly. The document included here—about homosexuality in Egypt—provides a glimpse into such subcultures. Furthermore, it allows you to understand marginal democratic movements that are mostly quietly—but sometimes loudly—demanding a place in the civil societies of the regions.

Many girls at Alexandria University have fallen for the charms of 22-year-old Michael, an Egyptian art student with delicate features and green almond-shaped eyes. But he has lost count of the number of times he has refused to go out on dates—and not because he likes playing hard to get. He is just more interested in spending time with his French boyfriend. "I tell the girls straight away that it's not personal and that I am gay," he explains with a shy smile. "They are shocked in the beginning, but then we become friends."

Michael started having homosexual intercourse when he was 12 but his first steady relationship happened when he was 16. After it was over, he got depressed and had to be medicated for a year—which was when he told his family about his sexual orientation.

"Homosexuality is becoming more apparent in the Egyptian society," says Dr. Josette Abdalla, assistant professor of Psychology at the American University in Cairo (AUC). "This is in part the result of more exposure to mass media, western influences and more access to papers, satellite dishes and TV."

According to her, these factors are making Egyptians more aware of their own sexuality. The changes are happening slowly, however. Numbers and visibility are increasing, but homosexuality is still a taboo in the country. Even though everybody knows it has always existed—in literature and real life—nobody talks about it. Crossing the safe line between the familiar world of heterosexuality and venturing into the unknown of open homosexuality is still a risk most don't take.

"It is a contradictory phenomenon," explains Ted Swedenburg, assistant professor of Anthropology at University of Arkansas and a Middle East expert. "In the past, it was not very much talked about, but it was more accepted. Now, homosexuality is more visible and causing more reaction." The reaction is more of a backlash, however. Instead of becoming more liberal, society is becoming more conservative. According to Swedenburg, it could be because it is easier to deal with things when they remain out of sight.

Michael complains about the attitude towards what he thinks are the millions of homosexuals present in Egypt, including gays and lesbians. "Even if

Lilian Liang, "Hiding Themselves in the Crowd," *Middle East Times,* 12 November 1999.

the government accepts [homosexuality] and makes it official, the people will still refuse it," he says. "They think that being gay is shameful and brings Egypt a bad reputation."

He is probably right. The reaction of society, especially the family, is still the main factor hindering homosexuals in admitting their orientation according to health care experts.

"It's a big shame to the family because it's not only about the homosexual himself," says Dr. Sanaa Nassif, HIV/AIDS program officer at Caritas Egypt. "His sister is going to be known as the sister of a homosexual and his father will be known for having a homosexual son."

Ashraf (like most quoted in this article, not his real name), a 30-year-old doctor in Cairo, preferred to spare his family from such comments. Gay for more than half of his life now, his parents still don't know about his sexual choice. Instead, they keep asking him when he will get married. "I will never tell them that I'm gay," he says. "I don't want to hurt them." Intolerance to homosexuality is not only found inside the family. Societal norms still hold a very strict position regarding sexuality and even people who have daily contact with the gay scene have a hard time accepting them. Mohammed, manager of a famous gay hangout in a Cairo five-star hotel, doesn't sympathize with his customers, despite the business they generate. "Money with a bad reputation, how good is that?" he asks. "Even prostitutes are more respectable than gays."

Hassan, a 26-year-old actor in Cairo, remembers the days when homosexuals had more freedom and less restrictions.

"Five years ago, I gave a birthday party and invited around 30 people," he recalls. "About 200 people showed up, some complete strangers. I didn't even know there were that many gays in Egypt." But despite the increasing numbers, the situation is getting worse.

In addition to prejudice, homosexuals also have to deal with police abuse—they are sometimes arrested when leaving pubs and beaten up for no apparent reason.

Ahmed, who owns a restaurant in Alexandria, has never been arrested, but prefers to play it safe. "A friend of mine was taken and forced to sign a document admitting that he was making out in the street, which was not true," he recalls. "Now every time police are out there, I call everyone to warn them."

Episodes like these usually happen only to the more affluent gays, especially because they are the ones who have money to spend in pubs and restaurants. Homosexuals from poorer segments of society meet at public places, such as Ataba Square or Ramsis Station, where the crowds make the meetings harder to spot.

"Some lower-class men become homosexuals just because they don't have enough money to afford a prostitute," says Dr. Nassif. "If they have money, they usually go for a woman."

According to her, lower-class homosexuals differ from their richer counterparts not only in the way they dress and places they go, but also in the way they behave.

"Most lower-class homosexuals don't look or behave in a feminine way," says Dr. Nassif. Unlike the high-class gay scene, they don't have feminine gestures or voices—many don't even see themselves as gays, especially if they play the more active role in sexual relations.

"If they are active, they are considered even more masculine because they are not sleeping with a woman, but with a man, who is stronger," explains Nassif.

Sometimes leading a dual life, like most homosexuals in Egypt, might cause more problems than just prejudice and rejection. In the face of these pressures, some homosexuals can't maintain the facade—and end up with serious psychological problems such as paranoia and depression. "One of my clients was so obsessed with the idea that someone would find out about him being gay that every time somebody spat near him, he thought that the person knew about it," says Dr. Nassif. "He would take it as a sign of disdain."

According to the psychiatrist, most of her clients are from poor backgrounds because they are less afraid of exposing themselves. "Because of their economic situation, many of them think they are not worthy of respect," she explains. "That sometimes makes it easier for them to seek help."

By help she means counseling, not treatment. It is common to see homosexuals denying their own identity and seeking out a "cure." One of Dr. Nassif's clients was so busy trying not to be gay he quit his job and stayed at home to avoid risky situations.

According to her, problems like these could be avoided if more information about the issue were available, especially for young people. "Because nobody talks about it, these people spend a lot of time thinking about sex and creating wrong ideas," says Dr. Nassif.

With homosexuality becoming more visible in Egypt, some believe that the solution to their dilemma lies in reversing the conservative trend in society.

"There must be more freedom," says Swedenburg. "It all comes with more freedom of expression and education." He feels homosexuals need to play a major role in the process, but steps have to be taken slowly, starting with the individual.

"I hope I'm setting the example for other people like me," says Michael. "If you accept and respect yourself, everybody will accept and respect you."

7. Arab and Israeli Soccer Players Discuss Ethnic Relations in Israel, 2000

In September 2000, Israeli-Palestinian relations rapidly deteriorated into violent conflict. The immediate cause was the visit of Ariel Sharon (at that time an Israeli ex-minister of defense considered by Palestinians to be a war criminal) to al-Haram al-Sharif—the third holiest Islamic site and a place that most Jews consider to be the site of the Temple. Sharon's visit was the spark that lit pent-up Palestinian frustrations with the Oslo peace process. Earlier attempts at peace appeared bankrupt, and the gap between Arab and Jew yawned wider. In the West Bank and Gaza, Israeli occupation forces came under attack by stone-throwing civilians and armed Palestinian police, and Israelis sought to maintain their hold through increasingly violent measures against the Palestinian population.

These tensions spilled over quickly into Israel itself, where the Arab-Israeli population arose in protest for two reasons: (1) to demonstrate in sympathy with Palestinian Arabs in the Occupied Territories and demand an end to Israeli occupation and (2) to express frustration at their own status as second-class citizens within the state of Israel. Although academicians had been discussing the discriminatory nature of the Israeli state and society, only a few liberal intellectuals were interested in the topic. The majority of Israeli Jews were unaware of, or uninterested in, the plight of the Arab Israelis.

The emotional intensity of the demonstrations caught most Israeli Jews by surprise, and ultimately they were angered by what they saw as Arab-Israeli betrayal of the state. During bitter protest demonstrations, some Arab Israelis were shot and killed by Israeli police, and others were attacked by Jewish mobs. These events exacerbated the situation, despite attempts by politicians and intellectuals to contain the potentially explosive issue by calling for committees of inquiry into the plight of the Arab Israelis and into the use of excessive violence by Israeli police against Arab-Israeli demonstrators.

Arab Israelis were posing fundamental questions about the nature of the state of Israel. Is it a Jewish state, and if it is, then where does that leave the Arab Israelis? Furthermore, if Israel is a democracy, then how should it deal with ethnic discrimination against citizens of Arab descent, who are growing in numbers at a faster rate than Jewish citizens of the state? This document explores the ways in which Arab and Jewish soccer players handle these tensions and questions in order to come up with a winning team.

Two weeks ago, having suffered three losses and four ties, Maccabi Ahi Nazareth found itself last in the National League. The team's lackluster performance did little to improve the atmosphere in Nazareth, its mood already dampened by the recent rioting and its harsh economic consequences. In an effort to keep from sinking to a lower league, the team's management fired coach Samir Issa and appointed Eli Mahpoud in his place. Surprisingly, the replacement of an Arab coach with a Jewish one, even in these tense times, was accepted in Nazareth without protest. The Ahi Nazareth fans, it seems, just want their team to stay in the National League, the second of the six divisions in Israeli soccer, under the Premier League. If nothing else, at least that. This is Mahpoud's second stint in Nazareth. Last season, when Maccabi Ahi Nazareth found itself in similar straits, Mahpoud came on as its coach and succeeded in keeping it in the National League. When the season ended, he accepted the better contract offered by Maccabi Kiryat Gat. But the relationship with Kiryat Gat proved short-lived, and Mahpoud found himself out of a job—a common

Uriya Shavit, "Playing for Keeps," *Ha'aretz*, 3 November 2000. Copyright © 2000. Reprinted by permission.

enough occurrence in the dizzying game of musical chairs that is Israeli soccer. When the offer from Nazareth came, Mahpoud agreed almost immediately.

The recent outbreak of violence, he says, had little influence on his deliberations on whether or not to accept the job. "I was worried only that the roads might be closed, and I would not be able to make it to practice. Those around me were more concerned than I was. I did not give much thought to what happened in Nazareth. I like to think positive. There are radical minorities everywhere. I don't know the city, but I do know the team and its fans, and they're wonderful people. They welcomed me warmly when I signed back on."

The first game under Mahpoud's renewed reign, played against Hapoel Jerusalem, ended in a sweet 2–1 victory. The night before, shots had been fired on the Jewish neighborhood of Gilo in Jerusalem. Only a handful of fans accompanied the Nazareth team to the game. Mahpoud says he did not know how his players would be received at Teddy Stadium. "Naturally, we were a little anxious, but in the end it was wonderful: When I sent out one of our players, the Jerusalem fans applauded. It was heartwarming."

Driving to practice from his home in Petah Tikva last week, Mahpoud was unwilling to talk politics. His radio was tuned to the all-music station Galgalatz throughout the two-hour trip to Nazareth and to local sports news on the 90-minute drive back. The fact that he coaches an Arab team is mere coincidence, as far as he is concerned. People who work in sports, he believes, should worry only about sports.

Mahpoud claims that the team's four Jewish players—Sagi Strauss, Shlomi Ben-Hamu, Arik Hangali and Emil Castiel—were similarly unaffected by the current crisis. "The rioting in Nazareth had no effect on anyone in the team, Jewish or Arab," he says. "None of the Jewish players came and said they wanted to leave. Soccer players are soccer players: they want to play."

The National League is the perennial "not quite" league. Its players earn their living playing soccer, but most of them never make it to the big money. Ahi Nazareth's Jewish players were all in the Premier League once, and they all hope to be back there someday. Some of the Arab players have also played in top "Jewish" teams. Under the great mantra of "professionalism," they can play together without stopping to worry about their identity or relationship with their communities. They all share the same dream: to go as far as they can. There are, however, some significant differences. For the Arab players, their own ethnic origin is one major obstacle on the way to making the dream come true.

Issam Issami, the team's striker, is a Druze who served in the Israeli army. He spent last season playing for Maccabi Netanya and had hoped to move to Betar Jerusalem for the current season. "I was at the Betar tryouts this summer. By the end of the first week, I felt I was not welcome there. Fans yelled curses at me during the first practice. The players didn't say anything to my face, but I knew that behind my back they were asking, 'Why did they have to bring the Arab player?' I knew what would happen if I made a mistake during the first game, that the crowd would call me a dirty Arab. Jerusalem has Jews and goys. I'm a goy to them. I spent three years in the army, and I'm a goy to them."

Is it possible that you simply weren't good enough for Betar?

"Of course that's what they'd say. But that's not what I feel. Look, it's my country. I feel that it's my country. But you won't give me the space to feel that. You act like it's not my country, not in soccer, and not in other areas."

Life as an Arab player

Mahpoud, once a star player in Hapoel Petah Tikva, was first recommended for the job by his friend Azmi Nassar, who two years ago led the Palestinian national team to third place in the Pan Arab Games. Nassar says he thought Mahpoud would work well with an Arab team. "He's an honest person, understands a lot about soccer. He has this restaurant in Petah Tikva where he works with Arab employees, and he gets along with them. I was sure he would not be patronizing or dismissive toward the Arab players."

Nassar is now coach of Bnei Sakhnin, the National League's other Arab team. Bnei Sakhnin now faces a double challenge. It is struggling not only to remain in the league, but also to maintain its status as "Israel's leading Arab team." Maccabi Ahi Nazareth is its arch-enemy. Last week the two teams played each other; Bnei Sakhnin won 2–1.

In the days preceding this much-awaited match, Mahpoud and Nassar's friendship helped take some of the sting out of the fierce rivalry. There was, however, another reason why passions did not quite rise to their expected frenzy: up until the last minute, it was not clear whether the game would even take place.

The police refused to allow the match to be held in Nazareth. When Kiryat Eliezer was suggested as an alternative site, the insurance company demanded an exorbitant security deposit. "It's hard to prepare a team for a match this way," Mahpoud said last Tuesday, during the break between morning and afternoon practice. "You have to divide up the practice load, follow a plan, and you can't do that under these conditions. The Arab teams are harmed through no fault of their own."

Do you support the Arab players' claims that they suffer from discrimination?

"People in Ahi Nazareth say that the referees are prejudiced against them. In some games I feel that it's true. I think it's mostly because we're a small team, even for the second league. But it's also true that the life of an Arab player is much harder.

"They tell me that players on rival teams curse them, calling them 'dirty Arab' and names like that. That infuriates me. I always tell them that you can't allow yourself to be affected by these provocations. This is their job, their livelihood, and they have to keep it. I also get sworn at by the fans of rival teams. When I was coaching a Jewish team, the curses were much softer. Here people yell, 'You son of a bitch, why are you coaching Arabs?'"

What about your friend Azmi Nassar?

"Azmi did not get a single offer from a Jewish team, despite his many successes. I don't know why that is. He's an excellent coach. Speaking in purely professional terms, he has what it takes to coach a Premier League team. Maybe it's because soccer is such an emotional business. If his team failed, well, you know the kind of position the administration would then be in, having hired an Arab coach."

[. . .]

Carpools and Music

Having finished their lunch, four of the Ahi Nazareth players sit around a table in a downtown restaurant and talk. Shlomi Ben Hamu lives in Herzliya, is married and has a child, and once played for Hakoah Ramat Gan and Hapoel Petah Tikva. Arik Hangali lives in Bat Yam. Last season he played for Ironi Rishon Letzion. Ashraf Suliman, the chairman's nephew, lives in Nazareth and grew up on the local team. Abed Titi, who lives in Tira, is the National League's leading goal-maker after nine rounds of playing, even though Ahi Nazareth is still a game short.

The four are friends, and not only on the soccer field. Titi, Ben Hamu and Hangali carpool to practice, meeting each day at the Netanya junction. Whoever is driving gets to choose the music, so that Ben Hamu and Hangali are constantly exposed to the latest Arab hits.

SULIMAN: We in Nazareth want good players. We don't care if they're Jewish, Arab or foreign, as long as they play well.

HANGALI: I never thought I'd end up playing for an Arab team, but from the moment I got here, I felt at home. I was treated very warmly, and I knew I was staying. You have to know how to keep sports and politics apart. We're in sports, we all have the same goal. I feel that I represent the city of Nazareth. I have no problem with that. But I also represent myself—if I don't play well, I'll disgrace myself, too. We're not repressing reality. Titi and Suliman are really our friends. If a few extremists raised some hell, is that any reason to be mad at them?

TITI: We only want peace and quiet. What does anyone, Jewish or Arab, have to gain from people being killed? Why can't we all have fun together?

SULIMAN: Iad Lawabneh, the first casualty from Nazareth, was a big fan of ours. He was killed 15 minutes before our game against Kiryat Gat began. Our management asked to have the game postponed, but it wasn't. We lost.

BEN HAMU: I had no problem playing when the riots started. I never thought of leaving the team. All in all, I know both the people here and the administration. People in my family were worried about me, said I should look into other options. But eventually, when things calmed down, those fears disappeared, too.

HANGALI: When we came to practice on the days of the rioting, we found fans waiting. They said they'd look out for us. Today, when people in Tel Aviv ask me whether I'm afraid to go to Nazareth, I laugh. What's there to be afraid of?

BEN HAMU: Joining Nazareth changed something for me. I didn't know any Arabs before, had no Arab friends. I knew nothing about their mentality. Today I get together with friends from the Arab team even after practice. We go out to eat or go bowling. Today all I want is for there to be peace. [. . .]

8. Self-Reflection by the Communist Party of Iran, 2001

Most recent articles and reports about Iran—and about the Middle East and North Africa in general—concentrate on Islamic politics, thus giving the impression that secularism and leftist politics are completely absent from the political spectrum and that all thought and action are firmly contained within the rubric of Islam. This approach to understanding these areas obscures the range of ideas that exist in practically every part of the Middle East and North Africa. Even if secular and leftist movements remain limited in their membership and overall role in public life, their voices create a counterpoint to the rightist politics of most Islamic movements and to the authoritarianism of the state.

The following document is a statement by one of the oldest leftist political parties in the Middle East—the Tudeh (Masses) Party of Iran. Founded in 1941 by a group of young Iranian Marxists, the party sought a broad variety of social and economic reforms to better the lot of workers and peasants. Partly because of its political platform, and partly because of its organizational success, Tudeh became the largest and most efficient political party in Iran. Many people in Iran believed that it would dominate the government shortly after World War II. In part, Tudeh failed to come to power because the United States and Britain were strongly opposed to the party since they believed that it would allow the Soviet Union too much influence in that oil-rich region. Reprinted here is a statement issued by the party on its sixtieth anniversary. It offers a glimpse of Tudeh's view of the history of Iran and its vision of the country's future.

Six decades of historic and heroic struggle by the party of workers, women, youth, students and intellectuals to emancipate the country from the chain of imperialism, reactions, dictatorship and to achieve democracy, freedom, independence and social justice.

Central Committee of the Tudeh Party of Iran, "Statement of the Central Committee of the Tudeh Party of Iran on the Sixtieth Anniversary of the Party," from "Nameh Mardom," Central Organ of the Tudeh Party of Iran, no. 618, 23 September 2001, reprinted in *Tudeh News*, no. 207, October 2001.

✳   ✳   ✳

October 2, 2001, marks the sixtieth anniversary of Tudeh Party of Iran (TPI), the party of the working class of our country. Sixty years ago, political prisoners just released from Reza Shah's prisons, along with other freedom seeking persons in our country, founded the party. The founders of TPI were comrades of the great revolutionary and thinker, Dr. Taghi Erani. They strove to continue the path of the Social Democratic Movement and the Communist Party of Iran before them.

The appearance of TPI in the political arena of Iran was an important historical event, creating an undeniable impact on the political, cultural and social life of our country. In those days, political parties survived on the good grace of the regime and so played the role of defending internal reaction and imperialism. In contrast, TPI raised the banner for the rights of the toiling masses. From the very onset, the party faced the wrath and attacks from all those who benefited entirely from internal reaction, dictatorship and imperialism.

The Tudeh Party of Iran: Impact on the Political and Cultural Life of Our Society

The party's impact on the society can be investigated in many ways. TPI was the only political organisation in the country that [was] based on realizing the aspirations and the will of the working class. It played a unique role in organising and educating the working class. In the short period that the party enjoyed freedom of activity, it influenced the progress of our country.

When TPI stepped into the political-class struggle, Iran was a semi-feudal and semi-capitalist society, deeply influenced by a reactionary and imperialistic culture. In those days, women had no right to vote. Foreign imperialist countries imposed their policies on the government and political figures. Peasants were sold along with the land they worked on. Political and cultural backwardness, and superstition dominated Iranian society.

Within a few years of activity, our party made deep inroads into the political-cultural life of the country. The first programme of TPI, delivered to its first congress in 1944, is a historic document showing the revolutionary essence, far sightedness, intellectual clarity and progressive thinking of our party. It was the first programme of a political party in the Iranian contemporary history offering the means of achieving trade union rights, reduction of working hours to eight per day, creating a social security system, establishing land reform, right of women to elect and to be elected and gain equal rights and the right of religious and ethnic minorities.

More importantly, our party was able to organise a large social force from among the workers, women, youth and students aimed at realising these progressive aspirations. Members of our party played an outstanding role in creating organisations: the "United Central Council of the Workers and Toilers" in 1944, the first peasant unions in 1943, the "Democratic Organisation of Iranian

Women" (broadly based women's organisation dedicated to the struggle for women's rights), the "Organisation of the Tudeh Youth" in 1943 (a progressive organisation of youth and students). All these reflected clearly the effect our party had in organising a vast social struggle for fundamental change[s] in the social life of our society.

Our party has also played a major role in introducing new thoughts, particularly in introducing Marxism and Leninism to Iranians in the last six decades. The publication of hundreds of books, journals and scientific articles created a qualitative change in the familiarity of different generations in our country in differen[t] scientific fields especially in the fields of politics, economics and social sciences. Today, even after sixty years, those seeking to study the classics on Marxism in Farsi (Persian language), their main source of reference will be the publications of TPI. The reactionary and imperialist forces do not fear our party for its material strength, but because of its immense intellectual influence and its ability to influence events in the country.

The Role and Effect of the Tudeh Party of Iran in the Most Important Events of Contemporary Iranian History

A scientific study of contemporary Iranian history cannot, in all fairness ignore the key role TPI has played in the most important events of the last six decades. The degree of creativity and far sightedness displayed by our party had been enormous. Our party has utilised the experiences of democratic movements both in Iran and internationally to direct the process of events towards creating a democratic, just, free and independent Iran. Revolutionary thinking, boldness and search for new solutions to continue the process, proposing solutions and showing the way forward during extremely complex times of the democratic movement are among the unique characteristics of TPI.

The first battlefield for our party was the struggle against fascism and its destructive effect on the political life of the country. The 1940s coincided with the aggression of the united front of fascist Germany, Italy and Japan who had dreams of domination and absolute slavery around the world. In Iran, the ruling reactionaries of the time were preparing themselves to welcome the frontrunners of Nazi Germany. Poisonous and reactionary thinking of the Nazis had been disseminated amongst the Iranian people tainted with lies and anti-communist propaganda and had successfully poisoned important segments of the society.

Under these circumstances, our newly formed working class party, embarked on creating the party structures, educating its cadres in the scientific ideology of Marxism-Leninism. It also exposed the true nature of fascism and the danger threatening the sovereignty and freedom of the nations. The party also strove to unite the national forces against this danger and to organise and lead the democratic movement to push forward and consolidate the gains made in the democratic rights and freedoms. The publications of the daily "Mardom" [the people] also known as the "antifascist Mardom" and the wide ranging activities of the members of the TPI were able to transform the poisonous political climate of the country and unite the broad based population of the country against the fascism and its dangers.

Another arena of struggle for the party in those years was to unite and organise all democratic forces for the nationalisation of the oil industry and to struggle against the corrupt Pahlavi dynasty, under Moha[mm]ed Reza Shah, propped up by the imperialists. Many historical documents, some of which were recently released by imperialist countries like [the] United States and Britain's document centres, bear witness to the fact that reaction and the imperialism had viewed and targeted the party as its main enemy. Even the political opponents of TPI believed that the party had been attacked by the forces of reaction and imperialism because of its unflinching persistence in promoting the people's interests and aspirations.

Dr. Shayegan, a prominent leader of Iran's "National Front," one of Dr. Mosadegh's comrades, and also the defence lawyer of the imprisoned Tudeh Party leaders, said: "Today, I can also prove that they should not be on trial. . . . They have been contributing to this country. To understand the reality, it is necessary to understand their ideas. . . . They did not think of themselves or the interest of their families. They work for the public good. . . . They have made a wonderful class of thought, a class of educating the people. The attack against the Tudeh Party starts from this point that they were educating the people. They taught the workers and peasants the cause of their unfortunate existence, the root causes of their living conditions and what had to be done for liberation. This was the biggest crime of the Tudeh Party."

During this highly dynamic period of history, until the coup d'etat of August 18, 1953, the Tudeh Party of Iran succeeded in deepening the anti-imperialist aspect of the movement for the nationalisation of the oil industry, despite ongoing attacks by the security forces and its struggle in semi-clandestine conditions. Despite its initial opposition to Dr. Mosadegh's initial policies at the beginning of his premiership, TPI remained his sole ally. When important segments of the religious forces, under the leadership of Kashani and important members of the leadership of the "National Front," turned their back on Dr. Mosadegh and his government, the Tudeh Party stood by him to the end. It was the members of the Tudeh Party who to the last moment stood by the democratic movement and it was the Tudeh officers who sacrificed their lives and with their blood guaranteed the continuation of the democratic movement.

The coup of August 18, 1953 succeeded in bringing an absolute domination of the monarchical dictatorship entirely dependent on imperialism. TPI endured heavy losses but survived. Despite the fact that thousands of its members across the country were attacked, detained and tortured, our party, due to its deep roots among the masses, powered by the antagonistic contradictions of Iranian society, could not be brought it its knees.

Creating the underground organisation, the heroic struggles of our comrades like Comrade Tizabi, the historic trials in court of Comrade Hekmatjoo and Khavari, the struggles of comrades (like Touraj Haidari Bigvand) and later in 1970s, the founding of "Navid" underground organisation by Comrade Rahman Hatefi (Haider Mehregan) broke the fear created by the dictatorship. Thus the party was able to play its [part] in the 1979 Revolution.

The influence of "Navid" in the anti-dictatorial movement can be gauged by the fact circulation had reached hundreds of thousands on the verge of the revolution. TPI, realising the people's readiness for the final battle against the monarchy, anticipated the possibility of victory. At this point the party invited all the patriotic, nationalist and freedom fighters to unite in a united front to launch the final assault against the dictatorial regime of the Shah.

The party incessantly and without flinching for a moment, tried to unite the forces which were struggling in the same front. TPI, in its public address on July 21, 1978 offered its practical programme for a broad based front of forces which should begin overthrowing the monarchy and establish a republic that would embrace far-reaching changes in all aspects of social life.

Our party deployed all its political and organizational force behind the revolutionary struggle. Tudeh partisans fought side-by-side other progressive forces and freedom fighters in the barricades. During the first few days following the victory at the political phase of the revolution, and the total collapse of the monarchy, our party put forward the "United Front of the People" as the only way to guarantee the success, continuation and deepening of the revolution onwards to subsequent stages.

The documents of the 16th plenary session of the central committee stated: "The working class and its party, the Tudeh Party of Iran, will engage all its resources to protect the united front arising practically from all patriotic and freedom seeking sections of the society. Our party will counter all efforts of the enemy attempting to undermine this unity." Not getting a positive response to this clear invitation gave the enemies of the revolution an opportunity to attack the disjointed revolutionary forces.

Some leaders, particularly Khomeini, left the revolutionary path and along with it, the genuine and democratic aspirations of the revolution. Instead, they choose to impose on the people a backward minded, anti-democratic structure, thus stalling the revolutionary process that was underway. The influence of our party on the revolution was to such a degree that Ali Khamenei, the current supreme leader, admitted several years later (in 1993): "During a period of time and at the beginning of the revolution, everything was being manipulated by the Tudeh Party. . . . I and everyone else could feel that, just after the revolution, the Tudeh and the left, especially the Tudeh, were dominating everything and were trying to divert the path of the revolution."

But what was this diversion the supreme religious leader is referring to? Historic documents on the period just after the February 1979 revolution clearly indicates [sic] that our party was persistent in its struggle to realize the aspirations of the revolution. It transformed the political climate of the society by popularising progressive slogans: the necessity for land reform, a struggle for an affirmative employment law, opposing reactionary employment bills, mobilising the country's defences when Iraq invades Iranian territory, firmly opposing the continuation of the war after the enemy was driven back to the internationally recognised borders, standing against the bigoted attempts by the reactionaries [to] confuse their backward views with the true aims of the revolutions.

All these factors brought fear to the hearts of reaction. For these very reasons, the reactionaries mounted their assault on the gains of the revolution and our party, helping them to consolidate their despotic grip over the people. They had the complete backing of the intelligence services of the United States, Britain, Israel, Turkey and Pakistan. Thus their well-engineered and broad attack ended in the arrests and detention of thousands of our members and followers. The assault of 1983 against our party was an attack against the revolution and turning point in the fate of the revolution.

Tudeh Party of Iran in the Critical Events of Recent Years

The role and impact of the Tudeh Party of Iran on the events of the recent years in our country is another valid evidence of the creative approach of our party in relation to the events and f[i]nding solutions that have been proven right in the historical test of events.

While several political forces, influence[d] by western media, were hoping that a "pragmatic man" from within the regime will lead Iran towards "renovation" and even freedom, TPI in its Central Committee meeting in March of 1990, analysed the country's situation and the rulers maneouvers to save the regime. It concluded that: "our country has a medieval totalitarian religious regime in power. In the name of "Feghahat-e-Islam" (the absolute rule of the supreme religious leader), this regime has committed atrocious crimes and has no regard for human rights whatsoever. . . . If we accept the fact that the very concept of "Velayat-e-Faquih" . . . puts the destiny of millions of people in the hands of despots who consider themselves above any law, then we have to turn the edge of our struggle towards this fundamental obstacle.

The purpose of "freedom and peace" slogans selected in the plenary meeting of December 1981 was to broaden the spectrum of forces participating in the front to fight against the despotic rule of "Velayat-e-Faquih." Currently, both inside and outside Iran, forces and individuals opposing the principle of Velayat-e-Faquih are [many]. . . . At the same time, there are individuals and forces that presently play a certain role in the ruling regime. They have religious beliefs but there is evidence of their willingness to cooperate with other forces to dispose of Velayat-e-Faquih. [. . .] The principle of the supremacy of the rule of the spiritual leader that forms the core of the ruling regime's ideology will need to be replaced with a democratic principle, and therefore requires a fundamental change in the constitution.

Thus, the slogan "Dispose of Velayat-e-Faquih" is a tactical slogan aimed at achieving a strategic goal. The same is true of the struggle for freedom and democracy, which ultimately serves to reach that final goal. . . .

Today, eleven years after adopting this analysis, its legitimacy is evident for the vast section of political forces. It was based on such an understanding of the events in Iran, that our party, during the presidential elections of June 1997 and then June 2001, proclaimed that [it] is impossible to realise the slogans of the reform movement, achieve a civil society and freedom, while circumstances that allow the "Velayat-e-Faquih" regime to exist [prevail].

Four years after the presidential elections of June 9th 1997, and trying times, including the state-sponsored assassinations of prominent opponents of the regime, the vicious attack on the pro-reform 2nd Khordad movement (named after the date of the presidential elections of June 7th), in May, the increasing pressure on this movement to undermine its role as an organised pro-reform social force, along with the suppressing of critical press and finally the arrests of religious-national critics, have proven wrong all those theories purporting that all kinds of freedom can be had within the framework of [the] "Velayat-e-Faquih" regime.

Today, as in the past, TPI, drawing on its scientific ideology and its 60-year historic experience, believes that the future destiny of our people and achieving freedom and establishing a popular and democratic regime will be impossible unless all freedom-loving forces struggling for people's rights unite. Creating an anti-dictatorship front, relying on pro-reform social forces, i.e. the working class and other working people, the youth, students and brave women of our country, is the historical necessity of the current phase of struggle in our nation. We believe that without organising these forces, and within the framework of [the] "Velayat-e-Faquih" regime, achieving fundamental, democratic reforms and stability in our country is not possible.

Members, Supporters, and Friends of the Party!

The history of TPI is an indivisible part of the history of our people's struggle for freedom, against reaction and despotism. The history of TPI is an extension of the history of the Iranian Communist Party and the struggle that Iran's social democrats initiated a century ago. In the past sixty years, the Tudeh Party of Iran, through its class struggle and its intellectual influence and inspirational guidance, has proved to be a potent organising force and had left a remarkable legacy.

Exceptional dedication and selflessness of Tudeh partisans in the last 60 years fills the proud pages of our people's history. In spite of successive onslaughts by despotic regimes and reactionary forces in the past 60 years, the Tudeh partisans have continued to uphold the banner of struggle of the workers, resolutely. This history and struggle is not only our party's achievement, but also belongs to the history of the progressive and freedom-loving movement in our country.

However, this in no way means that the Tudeh Party of Iran has made no mistakes in its long years, while confronting enormous difficulties. The important task is to analyse and realistically rectify these mistakes in order to learn the necessary lessons from them.

The reactionary ruling regime, along with other professional anti-communists and enemies of our party continue to disseminate a massive amount of propaganda and malicious accusations against our party, as they have done in the past 60 years. But, our people can see through the dirty lies against our party. Our people are well aware of the heroic history of our party, which in more than six decades, has never rested from the struggle for their rights.

The party has endured vicious attacks by ruling regimes and imperialism, a total of tens of thousands years of imprisonment, brutal tortures, and thousands of martyrs. Not only have these failed to destroy our party, but as history testifies, the party of people's silenced heroes, the party of Ruzbeh's, Siamak's, Kayvan's and Vartan's, the party of patriotic army officers, the party of working class, and the party of martyrs of 16 Azar, the party of Tizabi's, Hekmatjoo's, Fatemeh Modaressi's, Rahman Hatefi (Mehregan)'s, and Keymanesh's, as always firmly and proudly lifts the glorious and bloodstained banner inherited from Heydar-Amughlu's and Erani's, and will not rest a moment until the victory of humanitarian ideals of the working class and working people of our country [is] achieved.

The future belongs to the oppressed people and popular movement, and Tudeh members and supporters, just as in the past six decades, will fight side-by-side [with] the people, and will persevere to establish an independent, democratic and free Iran.

*Warmest greetings to all Tudeh martyrs and all martyrs
of freedom, independence and social justice of our nation!*
*Warmest salutation to all political prisoners in Iran, who are resisting
in the dungeons of [the] "Velayat-e-Faquih" regime!*
*Long live international solidarity of all workers
and toiling people of the world!*
*Forward to the establishment of an anti-dictatorship united front
for freedom, independence and social justice,
and to dispose of the "Velayat-e-Faquih" regime!*
*Greetings on the 60th anniversary of the Tudeh Party of Iran,
the party of workers and toiling people of our people!*

CHAPTER 10

The Future of the Middle East and North Africa

Previous chapters focus on the past and present of the Middle East and North Africa. In this chapter, we look to the future. The two documents presented here touch on many of the questions facing the peoples of this area.

The first document is an essay about the relationship between the Middle East and North Africa, on the one hand, and globalization, on the other. The writer summarizes feelings of distrust and ambiguity about globalization, then criticizes these misgivings as shortsighted and argues that if the region is to play a role in shaping globalization, then its peoples will have to engage with this movement actively and effectively. He contends that the future importance of the region generally, and of the Arab world in particular, depends on this engagement and its outcome.

The writer of the second document heralds the emergence of a third era in modern Arab history. He argues that democracy, demilitarization, and cultural pluralism offer the only means for the region to become an effective participant in the world and a contributor to the formation of a global civilization. While maintaining that the United States and Israel have played a detrimental role in the modern history of the Middle East and North Africa, he contends that the time has come to deal seriously and honestly with internal problems previously pushed aside because of the specter of external threats. The authoritarian nature of the states, intolerance for cultural, social, and political deviations from the mainstream, and the miserable condition of most of the local and regional economies are the most pressing issues for the future. Only by addressing these problems, practically and through the construction of a new culture, can the region advance.

1. Selection from a Roundtable Discussion of Globalization and Its Impact on Arab Culture, October 26, 2000

Globalization has raised many troubling questions in the Middle East and North Africa. Some observers wonder whether globalization means the erasing of local cultures in favor of a hegemonic Western (mostly American) culture. Others search for clues as to whether globalization will improve the lot of humanity or simply create more misery for the majority while further enriching the Northern Hemisphere. Also, globalization raises questions about national boundaries: will they be swept aside in the pursuit of global markets? To answer some of these questions, the journal of the Ministry of Culture in Bahrain convened a roundtable of Arab intellectuals, including the author of this document: George Tarabishi, an author who resides in Paris and writes extensively on the Arab world for the French and Arab press. Tarabishi's point of view on this subject is a minority opinion in intellectual circles but not in business ones. His essay highlights various aspects of the argument about globalization in the Arab world.

When Muslim theological scholars used to determine that an issue is conflictual, they meant that it is permissible to disagree about it, that *ijtihad* [the application of reason] is necessary, and that this conflict and this *ijtihad* cannot be considered heretical. It is within this specific context that I declare that globalization is a conflictual matter. [. . .]

Globalizing the World

There is no doubt that the ability to read globalization as a conflictual matter derives from its seriousness as a phenomenon, from the looseness of its meaning, and from its capacity to be loaded with conflicting meanings and values. In addition, the vastness of this phenomenon and its multiple facets allows it to take as its basis an existential duality and thus a Manichaean reading that depends on feelings and value judgments more than on knowledge. Thus, these approaches to globalization deal with it on the level of the singularities of good and evil, or love and hate, or right and left. Therefore, anyone who speaks of globalization must define first what he means. For me, globalization [. . .] means nothing more than the world becoming one. Before economy, before media, and before cultural production, the world itself is becoming globalized. We must not forget that the world, in its largest meaning, is a modern concept. Before overcoming the law of distances with modern means of transportation and communication, the world was made of worlds. The borders within these worlds were not merely geographical but also linguistic, religious, and ethnic. It was rare to imagine that each of these partial worlds was the world in its totality.

George Tarabishi, "Globalization and Its Impact on Arab Culture: Globalization as a Matter of Conflict," *al-Bahrain al-Thaqafia,* no. 26, 26 October 2000. Translated by Akram Khater.

However, this world, which is being united by globalization—and herein lies the problem—cannot be unified except on the basis of its division into two dualities of a developed world and an underdeveloped world, a world of the rich and a world of the poor, a world that produces information and knowledge and a world where there is not even the means to consume these. According to a famous United Nations description [of the world], 20 percent of the world's population owns 80 percent of its riches, and 80 percent of its people own less than 20 percent of its resources. This places four-fifths of humanity on one side and one-fifth on the other side. According to another report, 20 percent of the world's rich own 85 percent of the global production, while 20 percent of the world's poor own no more than 1.1 percent.

Contrary to a strongly held belief, the globalization of the world—on the basis of this problematic dual division—is not limited to the economic sector alone. [. . .] In addition to economic globalization—which is without doubt the most obvious and most predisposed to quantification—there is technological globalization, environmental globalization, food globalization, legal globalization, media globalization, and finally cultural globalization.

Globalizing the Arab World

If the Arab countries do not have sufficient cultural capacity to absorb globalization, then the concept of counter-globalization, as it is being propounded in the Arab cultural arena today, appears as if it is being activated under an attractive theoretical name—what we have called the mechanism of hegemony [. . .] by a sizable number of intellectuals. It is true that the person who shaped this concept—the Tunisian linguist 'Abd al-Salam al-Masdi, has himself warned against dealing in a utopian fashion with the concept. [. . .] He clearly stated: "The concept of globalization that we have constructed in our cultural discussion in the book *Globalization and Counter-Globalization* does not mean that we deny the phenomenon of globalization. Nor do we object fundamentally to its existence. Nor are we in any way calling to completely oppose it. Had we done or claimed any of these, then we would be utopian in the absolute sense of the word. What we are calling for is the introduction of a new idea where counter-globalization would be a mentality that eschews negative criticism and embraces positive criticism."

Despite this [warning], it appears that this concept [counter-globalization] [. . .] has escaped like the genie from the bottle and has acquired an ideological independence that is not related to the rational purpose that produced it. It has imposed itself with incredible speed in the Arab world as a slogan for opposition and resistance, and as an alternative or contrary globalization, which some have defined as "the true globalization as opposed to the fake globalization," others as "the humane versus the monstrous globalization," or, as Mahmud Amin al-'Alam has said, "the globalization of truth not falsehood, the globalization of liberty not enslavement and hegemony, the globalization of science, knowledge and creativity not ignorance, alienation, underdevelopment and dependency."

To draw ourselves away from the intellectually crippling gravitational pull between *globalization* and *counter-globalization,* I believe that we must be armed with both a realistic and critical awareness. This is not meant to confront and counter but to improve our chances of benefiting from its [globalization's] advantages and avoiding its negative aspects. In the large global village that the world is on the verge of becoming, the Arab world—which is more divided than ever—is in need of becoming first a regional singular village. This, I believe, is the shortest path to enter the village of globalization—or its jungle, as its opponents claim—safely.

Since one of the possible definitions of globalization is the erasure of borders, and we are dealing specifically here with cultural globalization, let us then add quickly that the borders that we think we ought to remove in the Arab world are cultural borders. We are realistic enough to realize that the political borders in the Arab world—despite our previous ideological illusions about these borders being artificial—are currently and for the foreseeable future not subject to removal. However, the Arab world is capable, despite the consecration of its divisions and its regional and national characteristics with borders, of representing a singular cultural group. If it was not for this ability, then the Arab world would not have been able to distinguish itself—and be distinguished by others—as an Arab world.

So as not to float in the ethereal world of abstraction, let us say right away that it is new communication technologies that allow for the relatively safe and effective circumvention of Arab cultural borders. The first indication of this penetration is embodied in the Arab satellite television channels, which—regardless of what has been said about their performance or funding and purpose—have succeeded, however partially, in shrinking the Arab world despite its vastness and the invincibility of its political topography.

Another example is presented to us by the capability—which has become a reality in some cases—provided by new communication technologies to publish multiple editions of the same Arabic newspaper or magazine in various Arab capitals and at the same time. If, in the near future, we can develop the spread of the Internet in the Arab world, then another aspect of internal Arab borders—and we mean regional censorship of thought and the means of exchanging it through books, journals, and newspapers—will fall or at least be circumvented. On the Internet the scissors of the censor cannot intrude.

We do not need to view the circumventing or the removal of the cultural borders as solely negative. We can envision a type of positive Arab globalization in which the Arab League—after revising its purpose toward elevating its cultural role—can play an effective role. We can envision, within this context, the establishment of an Arab network that links Arab scientific and university institutions to limit the chaos of Arab research, to lessen duplication and the waste of effort and money, and to allow for a real possibility for coordination of university research and for disseminating that research so that it benefits the Arab world and does not remain locked away collecting dust. Within this context also, we can envision a network to link Arab museums and another network to "revive" Arabic manuscripts in Arab and foreign universities and libraries and thus allow all researchers access without having to travel and waste money and time.

Proponents of the theory of Arab cultural security may object that circumvention of the borders will not be accomplished solely by Arabs but by necessity will be carried out also by "foreign" forces. [. . .] As is sometimes said in the world of strategy, the best defense is offense. Therefore, we say that the best way to confront globalization is to be present, not absent. In any case, globalization is already here, whether we like it or not. So let us learn how to participate in it. [. . .] Just as globalization has made possible the emergence of a new economic pole in the world, the Asian pole, and just as it has made possible the crystallization of a European media pole (Euro News in opposition to CNN, for example), there is nothing to keep us from anticipating the emergence of an Arab cultural pole one day. Although light-years separate us from the realization of this dream—whose accomplishment is linked to a chain of democratic, modernizing, and radical changes in the Arab world—we see no reason not to look forward to it. Why? Simply because we refuse to limit ourselves between the jaws of the Fukuyama and Huntington pincers: neither the "end of history" nor the "clash of civilizations" is preordained. We reject the thesis that history is dominated by a singular universal civilization that crushes all else, and we reject the thesis of a history that, through global conflict, reshapes the world along lines of isolated and clashing civilizational islands. We believe that the world is heading toward becoming for the first time in history a single civilization with multiple cultures. Globalization may be the tool for this dialogue between world civilization and national cultures. But this dialogue should take place on the condition—which some may say is utopian—that globalization ceases to be a tool for *hegemony* and instead becomes a tool for *participation.*

To avoid appearing as if I am simply making a play on words, allow me to say that adjusting the equation of globalization from hegemony to participation does not presume absolute equality in the shares of the partners. Globalization is closer to an incorporated company, and our position within the corporation is decided by the size of our stock portfolio. According to our demographic size, our share cannot exceed 3.4 percent; otherwise, we would become hegemonic like others. But even this level is higher than what we can arrive at in the foreseeable future. [This is so] first, because the Arab world does not enter into the company of globalization as a singular stockholder. Its portfolio is distributed among many partners, who in many instances are fighting among themselves. Moreover, the Arab world, most of which belongs to the Third World—some parts even belong to the Fourth World—is not equal to the other stockholders in the globalization company in terms of its capacity for material and intellectual production. This disparity is particularly evident vis-à-vis the large partners who—despite being numerically small—own 80 percent of humanity's material production and 95 percent of its intellectual production. We will be realistic if we dream of increasing our share, in stages, from 0.001 to 1 percent within a time frame that is no less than a quarter of a century. This 1 percent is the minimum requirement for "takeoff," as the experiences of East and Southeast Asian nations indicate. If we, some or all of us, fail to "take off" in the next quarter of a century, we must not attribute our failure in adjusting the equation of globalization to a failure of globalization itself. The formula for globalization is open and multifaceted and ever changing in its values, and if there is an unknown that is difficult to determine, it is the Arab unknown, because we are living in a period of high tension between those who support and those who oppose modernity.

[. . .] The impact of globalization on us and our participation in globalization, specifically from a cultural perspective, is a matter of *how* in addition to *how much.* If we do not take this into consideration, then we risk our role by falling into the error of separating the tool and the spirit [of globalization]. Although such a division is possible economically and technologically, and even in the media, it is not possible culturally. From a cultural point of view, globalization is not a neutral phenomenon, for it occurs within a particular culture. At a time when Arab culture, like the other cultures of the world, has no option but to engage with it [globalization], then it would appear that this engagement, in the Arab case, will be conflictual rather than cooperative. This is so because the cultural values contained within globalization appear, to a large extent, at odds with predominant Arab values.

We can describe the culture of globalization as being of this world—we do not say secular—while Arab culture is still counted within the religious segment [of cultures] and is still preoccupied with matters of the spiritual world. The culture of globalization, because it is the culture of wealthy society, has a hedonistic tendency to squeeze all pleasure from the present moment and to engage in hyper-consumption. In contrast, Arab culture [. . .] is dominated by the logic of contentment, abstention, and thrift, and spiritual saving for future dark days.

The culture of globalization—by definition a visual culture—depends on the presence of the human body and does not hesitate to uncover and denude it, particularly the female body. Arab culture, in contrast, is a culture of modesty—manifested by covering the body, particularly the female body. The two cultures also diverge greatly on the issue of sexual abstinence and permissiveness. The culture of globalism goes to extremes in allowing for sexual love, while Arab culture goes to extremes in limiting it.

These differences, among others, make the intersection of Arab culture and the culture of globalism a point of painful ruptures. But a certain measure of rupture and pain may be necessary to provide the impetus for what we will call [. . .] cultural mobility. In our estimation, cultural mobility provides the ideal escape from the dual dangers that threaten the intersection of Arab culture and the culture of globalism. These are (1) the danger of isolationism and cocooning in a suffocating parochial or fundamentalist culture and (2) the danger of being torn away from the self and being swept away by a hegemonic globalizing cultural.

Cultural mobility, which combines the restraint of authenticity and the impetus of globalizing modernity, appears more capable than any other mechanism to control the speed and direction of Arab development and to avoid the pit-falls on either side of its path. [. . .] As we all know, the discourse about roots is today considered of great value in all of the world's cultures, which feel an undeniable need to hold on to their roots for fear of being uprooted by the winds of globalization, which can also undeniably take the form of a storm. However, holding on to cultural roots does not seem to us to be sufficient or a guarantee of the minimum level—let alone the ideal level—of cultural dynamism. [. . .] National cultures, including the Arab one, in their march toward integration with the culture of globalization, need wings as much as they need roots.

Nobody can predict what will happen to the Arab world in the next twenty-five years, and how the struggle over the mother of conflicts—which is globalization in our time—will be resolved. However, the study of reality, which does not allow for miraculous transformations—[. . .] forces us to be more pessimistic about the start of this new era, without being overly pessimistic about its end.

2. Lebanese Author Elias Khoury Argues for Democracy, Demilitarization, and Cultural Pluralism in the Middle East and North Africa, 2000

Elias Khoury has written several novels and short stories, some of which (such as his novel The Small Mountain, *1989) have been translated into English. Currently, he is the editor of the culture section in one of Lebanon's—and the Arab world's—leading daily newspapers,* Al-Nahar. *This essay is part of a collection of articles commissioned by his newspaper to celebrate the beginning of the new millennium. As an Arab-Lebanese intellectual, Khoury voices many of the feelings shared by other Arabs, elites and nonelites alike. His manifesto can be read not as the opinion of all Arabs but as the expression of a fairly powerful and common point of view.*

After the first defeat in Maysaloun [the battle where the French defeated the army of Prince Faisal and proclaimed the establishment of the French mandate over Syria] then in Palestine, and a second renaissance that became bankrupt after the defeat of the June war [1967], how do we establish an Arab culture that does not succumb to another retreat into history?

When I listen to Fairuz [a popular Lebanese singer] sing, "And we have memories in Maysaloun," I feel that Arab East there, I see it at the turn of

---

Elias Khoury, "Leaving Behind the Nightmare of the Arab Military Establishment: The Third Renaissance: The End of the Coup," *Al-Nahar*, 13 December 2000. Translated by Akram Khater.

the twentieth century, when the world took it from the Ottoman state to the defeat of the Arab nation project, when the minister of defense in the Faisal government died defending a kingdom [the proposed Arab kingdom] that was not born.

The memories of Maysaloun are not limited to the voice of Fairuz, but rather they merge with our consciousness of the second defeat that the Arabs were dealt in 1967, when dreams and words collapsed in six days of napalm [an incendiary explosive used by the Israelis], of loss and the crowds of new refugees. After the defeat of June, the Palestinian resistance established training camps, where a man—injured all over his body—by the name of Abu Ali Iyad led the volunteers to dream about a new beginning, before he died in the woods of Jarash and Ajloun. Between the two Maysalouns and after them, the Arabs lived a linguistic century whose main characteristic was to exchange reality with words. Perhaps the first correct word invented by modern Arab culture was *Al-Nakba* [The Disaster], which was used to describe the great defeat of 1948; and this can be attributed to our professor Constantin Zurayq [an Arab intellectual who coined the term]. Arab culture had to wait another half-century in order to give birth to another correct word that was created by the collective imagination, and it is *Intifada* [Palestinian rebellion against Israeli occupation in 1987], which was born through the rocks of children in Palestine. Perhaps these are the only two words in Arabic that are impossible to translate, not because they have no equivalent in other languages, but because translation deprives them of their uniqueness, and that is why they appeared transliterated in all the languages of the world.

The linguistic century that the Arabs have lived was a century in which language sought to trick reality. That is why the two renaissance movements at the beginning and the middle of the century were incomplete; and this lack of completion expresses in and of itself the frightening divorce between reality and language.

The first renaissance, which began in the nineteenth century and lasted through the 1930s, contained within it two symbols. The first was the rejection of Ottoman oppression and the call for the establishment of constitutional governments. The second symbol was the call for the independence and unity [of Arabs].

Between the two symbols, the first renaissance period failed the test of naming the historical moment in which it was born. It did not see in the defeat of the East by an ascending European power a point of departure for the establishment of the new and different. Rather it saw itself as an extension of the past. After the grand linguistic renaissance—which was started by al-Shidyaq, the two Yazijis, and the Burstanis [nineteenth-century intellectuals from Lebanon]—and after the literary modernization period founded by [Arab] emigrant authors, Arab culture found itself prisoner to the past in both its linguistic and religious dimensions. Ideas and thought thus remained bounded by borders drawn by Al-Afghani and Muhammad 'Abduh [see document 5 in the chapter "Central Political Reforms and Local Responses"]. Moreover, politics remained in the realm of dreaming about the rebirth of a golden era that had been trampled by the hooves of the Mongols [in the thirteenth century] long ago, before it was completely destroyed by the Mamluks.

This intellectual, linguistic, and political prevarication produced an incomplete first renaissance. Soon after the end of World War I this renaissance found itself incapable of building independence and unity. Faisal's experiment in independence was defeated in Syria, so it moved to Iraq to become its own contradiction. The Egyptian experiment, which was embodied in the 1919 revolution, fell because it could not achieve the dream of national independence [from the British], leaving to a young army officer by the name of Gamal Abdel Nasser the task of leading Egypt into independence, before he himself fell in the wake of the second defeat by Israel.

The first renaissance was born incomplete because it embodied a new consciousness that could not find social forces to support it. Despite its ability to reconcile various ideas and interests, this renaissance was far ahead of the social groups that carried it. Thus, consciousness was defeated by reality, and no new historical forces emerged to lead the Arab East toward unity and independence. [. . .]

Perhaps this impotence was represented in the suppression of two books: *Islam and the Principles of Government* by Ali 'Abd al-Raziq, and Taha Hussein's *Jahili* [pre-Islamic] *Poetry*. With these two there emerged confusion about the relationship between renaissance, on the one hand, and society and political elites, on the other. Moreover, it made clear how the wasted revolutions that colored the beginning of the Arab century with the blood of defeat led the Arabs toward their Grand Defeat of 1948.

The first renaissance was created by a mixture of intellectuals from different ideologies: nationalists, Islamists, enlightened secularists, liberals, and socialists. However, the second renaissance was principally built by armies, and it depended on nationalist ideology after adding to it a socialist flavor.

The idea of rebirth that was preached by the pioneers of the first renaissance was embodied in young officers from rural backgrounds, who—in turn—produced the markers of the Nasserite experiment: rural reform, nationalization of the Suez Canal, Syrian-Egyptian unity. [. . .]

However, the distinction of the second renaissance was its relationship to culture and intellectuals. In the beginning it was established by marginalizing the liberals; then it placed the communists in prisons, and finally it destroyed the Islamic trend. Thus, it destroyed the political and cultural elites in order to establish a direct relationship between the Leader and the masses—a relationship whose only conduits were government secret police and intelligence services.

The Officers could only avail themselves of the culture currently available to them, so they mixed [Sati] al-Husi and [Michel] 'Aflaq [see document 11 in the chapter "Ideas of Nationalism"] with an Arabized Marxism, and they depended on a Mamluk tradition [of authoritarian rule and patron-client politics] that Muhammad 'Ali could not destroy despite his famous feast at the Citadel [when he assassinated most of the Mamluk elites in 1805].

The effects of this mixing did not appear until the defeat of June 1967.

Before the defeat, the popularity of Nasser and his historical stature and charm were able to fill the gap between polity and society. However, when the weakness of the government of the Officers was uncovered, and their failure at war became evident, the charm turned into merciless repression. Nasser faced the demonstrations of students and their songs with impotence. Then Sadat came to establish a new era that quickly led to complete collapse. The Egyptian army needed only half a victory in the October [1973] war in order to declare its absolute rule and bring about the destruction of the political and intellectual structures that had created the first two periods of renaissance. Thus, the Islamic fundamentalist movement and thought, which swept the Arab world, emerged as a maker of the end of the stage.

This separation between culture and authority produced in Arab culture a special case called Beirut. It is a case that requires special study because it was characterized by a rich literary and intellectual milieu, and by an ability to continue the first renaissance through a cultural extension into the second renaissance that was expressed in thought, poetry, novels, theater, and art. This case existed in a margin whose weakness only became apparent during the Lebanese civil war, when it was completely destroyed by the final confrontation between the culture of the second renaissance—represented by the Lebanese left—and Arab regimes—embodied in the entrance of the Syrian forces into Lebanon in 1976. [. . .]

The second renaissance was a sharp separation between its language and its reality. It is true that it succeeded in establishing political independence (in Algeria in particular), and it is true that it dared to create a single Arab state, and it is true that it discussed the matters of development and social justice. However, it declared its impotence at three levels:

1. The first is the absence of democracy, which led—particularly after the defeat of June 1967—to destroying civil society.

2. The second is the inability to build Arab unity, and the marginalization of all kinds of common Arab efforts, until the Arab League became a Wailing Wall.

3. The third and most important level is military impotence. The second renaissance failed to build fighting armies, and this became most evident in the defeat of the military institutions in the war of 1967. The war of 1973 was arrested by the impossibility of achieving military victory [over the Israeli army], and thus it was satisfied by establishing a balance of power that was soon discarded by unilateral agreements (Camp David) and civil wars (Lebanon). The Palestinian resistance was established at the margins of defeat, with its two bloody experiments in Jordan and Lebanon. But it was as if it carried within it the elements of both resistance and collapse at the same time. The Palestinian experiment only escaped the abyss because of the Intifada, which was the first fruit of the steadfastness of Beirut [in the face of the Israeli invasion of 1982]. Despite the Oslo Agreements and the Bantustans

that were established in the West Bank and Gaza, the Intifada succeeded in declaring that the Palestinian Cause would remain the open Arab wound for a long forthcoming century.

The first renaissance was defeated in Maysaloun, but its defeat was not complete until the Palestinian Disaster, which led to the dispossession of a whole people of its land and its country.

The second renaissance was defeated in June 1967 but was only completely destroyed by the Lebanese tragedy and Iraqi horror, in which a whole people was made homeless within its own country. [. . .]

Can we now speak of a third renaissance, while we live in the darkness of decay, under the humiliation of siege and the death of dreams?

Can the Arabs emerge from their second defeat, when their country is either occupied or practically occupied and they are being led to a peace with Israel that is neither just nor balanced?

The third renaissance will not be established simply by an optimistic will, as Antonio Gramsci suggested during his long prison stay; it will be established through the optimism of the mind. That is, it will be established through an ability to look at reality, to name it, and to admit its facts in order to change that reality.

The third renaissance is not an intellectual need like the first one, and it is not a military need like the second one. It is a life necessity. Today the Arab World is under the threat of becoming outside of history, and this is not an exaggeration. It is poised to drown in ignorance and poverty, disease and hunger.

Leaving the nightmare of the twentieth century behind rests on three basic premises:

First, democracy. We learned during the two aborted renaissance movements that change cannot occur from above, nor can it be left to kings and officers. Revolution is not an authoritarian decision carried out by intellectuals or quasi-intellectuals. Revolution is a social act that is built by the institutions of civil society, through daily work that is, in turn, premised on marrying reality with dream.

Democracy is the prerequisite for Arab thought. Arabism is not like European nationalist movements in singularity. It does not belong to the nation-state and cannot be built on race and ethnicity. It is a plural Arabism that meets in language and culture, admitting the multiple sources that have formed the civilization of the Arabic-speaking peoples. Arabism is not a dream based on a memory of a bygone past; it is many horizons that crystallize the interests of Arab societies. [. . .]

Secondly, we must abandon the old language. Language is not a substitute for reality; rather it is a means to express experience and to approach reality. The condition of the third renaissance is to name things with their proper names. The Arab world cannot enter the twenty-first century without being aware of its defeat. Yes, the renaissance begins with naming our defeat. The Arabs have been defeated by the Israeli-American project, and they must admit it if they want to resist defeat. However, if they wish to stay in the waters of stagnation, then they need only to continue calling defeat victory, humiliation pride, and kneeling standing. The old lying language was the tool that dictatorial governments used to repress their people, to humiliate them, and to lead them to poverty, hunger, and submission.

The renaissance begins by returning language to language: by starting out from the reality of the historical defeat that the Arab world suffered at the hands of the Zionist-American power, and preparing from the starting point for a long resistance whose condition is to build plural, modern, and democratic Arab societies. The battle with Israel begins after the imposed empty "Peace," and it bases itself on the notion of justice, because it is the one human value that the god of the American market cannot destroy.

Thirdly, we must bring down the Arab military establishment. The game begun by the Arab officers of the Ottoman army is over. [. . .] Armies do not fight wars but as extensions of dynamic societies. But when the armies kill and destroy society, then they are fighting a retreating war and can only fight through surrender.

The condition of the third renaissance is to abandon the mirage of revolution through coups, and of liberty through chains. The twentieth century has witnessed the greatest cultural tragedy in history, when the humanity of the socialist idea was destroyed by Marxist revolutionaries, who established the society-prison in the name of freedom.

The Arab military establishment "crowned" the defeats of the Arabs with the two disasters of Iraq [the Iran-Iraq war and the Gulf War], the massacres of Algeria [between the government and the Islamic Salvation Front—see document 7 in the chapter "Crisis of the State"], and the hunger in Sudan, among other tragedies at the end of the twentieth century.

The Arab dictatorial regimes have succeeded not only in depriving people of bread and dignity, but also in depriving them of air! Arab decay has overflowed with blood, and if Arab societies are to escape extinction, they must break the chains and declare the end of the coups.

The Arabs must begin their third democratic renaissance at the beginning of the third millennium. Arab culture has not died under the boots of soldiers, as one would suspect from the silent and depressing image of Arab cities. Culture has not succumbed to the oil, which is polluted with blood, as it would appear from the perspective of the kings [in the Gulf region] who believe that the defeats of the end of the twentieth century will return the Arabs to the defeats of its beginning. Arab culture has not ceased to produce new ideas, poetry, novels, art, cinema, and theater. These are produced in jails, in exile, and in the besieged nations.

Today, at the end of the century of defeats crowned by the surrendering "Peace" [referring to Palestinian-Israeli Oslo agreement], the Third Arab Renaissance must establish a resisting, democratic, and pluralistic peace that will build the dream of independence and freedom, thus liberating the Arabs from slavery to the idols of authority and idols of the dead language.